1001 BOOKS

YOU MUST READ BEFORE YOU DIE

Chris –
Merry Christmas !!!
keep reading ...!!!
Grandpa and Suzanne

1001 BOOKS
YOU MUST READ BEFORE YOU DIE

GENERAL EDITOR PETER BOXALL

PREFACE BY PETER ACKROYD

UNIVERSE

A Quintet Book

First published in the United States of America in 2006 by
UNIVERSE PUBLISHING
A Division of Rizzoli International Publications, Inc.
300 Park Avenue South
New York, NY 10010
www.rizzoliusa.com

2007 2008 / 10 9 8 7 6 5 4
Fourth printing, January 2007

ISBN 10: 0-7893-1370-7
ISBN 13: 978-0-7893-1370-6
Library of Congress Control Number 2005929999
QUIN.KBOO

This book was designed and produced by
Quintet Publishing Limited
6 Blundell Street
London N7 9BH

Project Editor	Jenny Doubt
Design & Art Direction	Tristan de Lancey
Assistant Editors	Marianne Canty, Catherine Osborne, Ruth Patrick, Frank Ritter, Tara Woolnough
Managing Editor	Jane Laing
Publisher	Judith More

Manufactured in Singapore by Pica Digital Pte Ltd.
Printed in China by SNP Leefung Printers Ltd.

Contents

Preface

By Peter Ackroyd

"The life so short, the craft so long to learn." Chaucer's musings can be applied to the reading, as well as to the writing, of books. For many people, reading fiction remains the supreme pleasure. Many recall it as a first milestone reached and the great joy of childhood, only eventually partially obscured by the forced education of school and university, when reading all too often becomes a painful duty rather than a delight. But, somehow, the joy of the novel remains. It is the silent pleasure, the offspring of loneliness or absorption, the nurse of daydreams and reflections, the mistress of the passions, the instigator of adventure and change. And it can literally change lives.

Reading can also shape lives: There are remarkable instances of young people who became writers when they were charged by the experience of fiction—Charles Dickens was one of the most eminent examples of someone who was inspired to write his own novels (of which no fewer than ten are included here) by the reading of fairy tales and adventures. The tales of chivalry inspired many medieval knights. *Aesop's Fables*, one of the earliest books mentioned here, is the source and fountain of a thousand different narratives. Books create other books in an endless process of cross-pollination and it is sometimes hard to know where the inspiration of one volume ends and the source of another volume begins.

The patron saint of reading undoubtedly must be Saint Isidore of Seville, who remarked that all spiritual growth derives from reading. Reading is also the agent of imaginative development. In the age of the DVD and the computer screen, the merits of the word have become all the more apparent. It was fashionable, at the end of the last century, to proclaim that the book was dead and that literature per se had no future. Such expressions of sorrow (if indeed they were) have proved to be entirely premature. Bookshops are flourishing as never before, and the worldwide success of online book retailers tells its own story of increased and increasing literacy.

That is why this list (organized by publication date, with the exception of the very early titles, which are organized according to composition date) includes novels both well known and relatively unknown, from the universally celebrated works of Jane Austen and George Orwell to the relatively neglected fictions of Wyndham Lewis and Edith Wharton. There are trends in reading as there are in everything, but there are certain novels that stand outside the currents of ordinary change and represent something close to enduring human value. Among such novels we undoubtedly find Balzac's *Lost Illusions*, Emily Brontë's *Wuthering Heights,* and Toni Morrison's *Beloved*.

Other novels act as the symbol of an age or a period, such as William Beckford's *Vathek* and John Berger's *G.*, Zora Neale Hurston's *Their Eyes Were Watching God* and Alan Paton's *Cry the Beloved Country*. There are experimental novels, such as those of William Burroughs, and what could be called mainstream novels by writers such as Anthony Trollope and E. M. Forster, Isabel Allende, and J. D. Salinger. And then, of course, there are the novels that represent some kind of supreme achievement; among these, included here, must be placed Marcel Proust's *In Search of Lost Time* and John Bunyan's *Pilgrim's Progress*. But all of the novels listed here are worthy of notice. From Chinua Achebe to Stefan Zweig, all of them invite the pleasure of reading.

For my own part, the writing of fiction is a perpetual surprise. When I am writing history or biography, I am of course writing with the material already to hand; with fiction, however, the words come as a revelation of a theme or meaning that I had not previously contemplated. The words become the source rather than the product. That is perhaps why the reading of fiction is also a source of renewal and strength.

London, 2006

Introduction

By Peter Boxall, General Editor

There is an ancient connection between death, storytelling, and the number 1001. Since *The Thousand and One Nights*, the number has had a mythical, deathly resonance. Sheherezade, the storyteller of the *Nights*, recounts her tales, over a thousand and one long Arabian evenings, to her king and would-be executioner, as a means of staving off the moment of her own death. Each night the king intends to kill her, but Scheherezade conjures such succulent fragments of prose that he is compelled to let her live another day, so that he can steal from her another, subsequent night, and another instalment in her endless, freewheeling fiction. The infinitely open, unresolvable quality of Scheherezade's storytelling continues to lend the number 1001 something of the mathematical sublime, of the countless or the unlimited. But at the same time, the number also maintains the mortal urgency of Scheherezade's plight. As much as it suggests endless expanse, the number speaks also of precision, and of a cramped, urgent brevity. Scheherezade's stories are still often translated as *The Thousand Nights and One Night*, emphasizing this uneasy proximity, in the number itself, between the expansive and the contracted, the many and the one. Over the great stretch of the thousand and one nights, Scheherezade always has only one night to live; as the evenings glide smoothly away, death is a constant companion, lending to each passing night the peculiar vividness of the final moment, lending the whole, living, proliferating work the unmistakable savor of last things.

In compiling the following list of 1001 books you must read before you die, I have found myself very much in the grip of this Scheherezadian paradox. The story of the novel, as it is told here, is a long and rambling affair, full of surprising turns, and unlikely subplots. Weaving this multi-layered tale through reference to 1001 titles has seemed, from the beginning, to be a gargantuan task, and a task that could never end. The final list, including all the novels that one must read and excluding all the ones that it is safe to leave unread, could of course never be drawn up, just as Scheherezade's stories still have not ended, and will never end, this side of the knowable. But at the same time, the limits that the number has pressed upon me are cruel and narrow. One thousand and one is after all such a small number, given the extent of the subject matter. Each title here has to fight for its slender berth, and each entry is fueled by a certain concentrated energy, a struggle to make room for itself as desperate as if life depended upon it. Each novel is a work that you must read before you die, and while death is always a distant prospect, it is also always imminent, lurking in the shadows of every instant. Something you must do before you die might feel like a lazy aspiration, but it is also something you have to do in a hurry, or even now.

This contradiction between the roomy and the constricted can be felt moving throughout this book. The novel is represented here in all its variety, its inventiveness, its wit, as it stretches from the ancients—from Aesop, Ovid, Chariton—to the contemporary fiction of Amis, DeLillo, or Houellebecq. But at the same time the novel as a complete entity is forever beyond our grasp, refusing to be fully systematized, always something more than the sum of its parts. Indeed, it might be argued that the novel, as a stable, recognizable object, does not really exist. There is no consensus among readers and critics about when the novel as a form came into being; there is no definite boundary that separates a novel from a short story, from a novella, from a prose poem, from autobiography, witness testimony, or journalism, from a fable, or a myth, or a legend. And there is certainly no consensus concerning how one distinguishes between the trashy novel and the literary masterpiece. Rather, the novel as a form, and as a body of work, is an inspired idea that we can only grasp fleetingly, fragmentarily; an idea that makes prose fiction possible, but that is also itself something of a fiction.

The list that is offered here, then, does not seek to be a new canon, and does not claim to define or exhaust the novel. Rather, it is a list that lives in the midst of the contradiction between the comprehensive and the partial. It is a list that is animated by the spirit of the novel, by a love for what the novel is and does, but which nevertheless does not hope or aim to capture it, to sum it up, or put it to bed. Prose fiction lives in so many guises and different languages, across so many nations and centuries, that a list like this will always, and should always, be marked, formed, and deformed by what it leaves out. Rather than defending its borders against that which it excludes, this book offers itself as a snapshot of the novel, one story among others that one can tell about its history. The book is made up of entries from over 100 contributors—a cross-section of the international reading community, including critics, academics, novelists, poets, literary journalists—and the list is generated to a large degree from what this diverse group of readers tells us about what the novel looks like today. As such, this book reflects a set of priorities that are shared by today's readers, a certain understanding of where the novel comes from, a particular kind of passion for reading. But it does so in a spirit of love for the diversity and endlessness of the possibilities of fiction, rather than in any desire to separate the quality from the rabble, the wheat from the chaff. It speaks of a thousand and one things, but with a breathless urgency that derives partly from the haunting knowledge of how many other things there are to be said, how many other novels there are to be read, how short even the longest story can feel when faced with the endlessness of storytelling.

This combination of the long and the short, the exhaustive and the partial, is perhaps nowhere more evident in this book than at the level of each individual entry. There is clearly something insane about writing 300 words—the approximate length of each of these entries—on something as many-mansioned and multi-textured as a novel. Even a thin slip of prose, such as Charlotte Perkins Gilman's *The Yellow Wallpaper*, surely cannot be condensed into 300 words, so what of Dorothy Richardson's *Pilgrimage*, or Samuel Richardson's *Clarissa*, or Proust's *À la recherche*—novels that run into thousands of pages? What can 300 words hope to do in the face of such monsters? This is a question that vexed me, somewhat, at the start of this project. But as the book goes to press, it strikes me that the brevity of each of these entries is this book's greatest strength. What these entries seek to do is neither to offer a full critique of each title, nor to give us a flavor of the prose, nor even simply to provide a canned plot synopsis. What each entry does is to respond, with the cramped urgency of a deathbed confession, to what makes each novel compelling, to what it is about each novel that makes one absolutely need to read it. There is no other format that I can think of that could deliver this kind of entreaty more effectively, or with a more thrilling intensity. One contributor, in discussing with me what these entries might hope to achieve, hit upon a phrase that for me has come to define what this book does. He said that each entry might be thought of as a "micro-event," a miniaturized but complete reading experience that contains within it something of the boundlessness of the novel.

I have many people to thank for their help over the last months. Working on this project has been an extraordinary pleasure, mostly because of the incredible enthusiasm and goodwill shown by everybody who has been a part of it. My first debt of gratitude is to all of the contributors. I have been moved by how promptly and willingly all of the contributors have responded to the demands of this book, and I have been staggered by the sheer quality and imaginative exuberance of the work that has been produced. This really has been a labor of love and friendship, so thank you. There are also many, many people who contributed to the production of this book, but who are not listed as contributors. Maria Lauret was unable to be in the book, but I thank her for her help, and remember Paul Roth with love and sorrow. I have had countless discussions, over unnumbered kitchen tables, about what titles should be in this list, and I thank everybody who has made suggestions to me. I would particularly like to thank Alistair Davies, Norman Vance, Rose Gaynor, members of my family in Cardiff and London, in the U.S. and Turkey, and the entirety of the Jordan family. I am deeply grateful to Liz Wyse, whose clear intelligence and calm good humor made even the difficult moments a pleasure. Jenny Doubt saw this book through to publication with an extraordinary, unflappable professionalism, and with imaginative flair. Witnessing her ability to deal with the manifold pressures that a project like this produces in its final stages has left me gasping with admiration. The Art Director Tristan de Lancey and Picture Researcher Maria Gibbs have done an incredible job, and I am grateful to everybody at Quintet, in particular Jane Laing and Judith More. As always, my love and thanks go to the Boxall Jordans; to Hannah, who has been a central part of this project from the beginning, and to Ava and Laurie, for whom reading is a transformative pleasure that is only now beginning.

Working on this book has taught me a great deal about the novel. It has also taught me something about how contagious the love of books is, how much excitement, friendship, and pleasure they produce. I hope that some of the excitement, and some of the love and friendship, that went into making this book will be communicated in the reading of it.

Contributors

Vance Adair (VA) is a Teaching Fellow in the Department of English Studies at the University of Stirling. He has written on critical theory and early modern drama.

Susanna Araujo (SA)

Derek Attridge (DA) is the author of several books on the works of James Joyce. He is a Professor in the Department of English and Related Literature at University of York, England.

Sally Bayley (SB)

Alvin Birdi (ABi) is completing a DPhil on Beckett and Coetzee at the University of Sussex. He has taught at the Universities of Manchester, Middlesex, and Oxford.

Andrew Blades (ABl) was educated at Balliol College, Oxford and is undertaking a D.Phil on masculine identity in Aids literature. He is also the theater reviewer for *Stage* newspaper.

Anna Bogen (AB) is a DPhil candidate at the University of Sussex. Her thesis is about early twentieth-century fiction and women's education. She has published on children's literature, modernism, and women's writing.

Dr. Peter Boxall (PB) is a senior lecturer in English literature at the University of Sussex. He has published widely on twentieth-century fiction and drama.

Dr. Kate Briggs (KB) is a Research Fellow in Modern Languages and Literatures at Trinity College, Dublin.

Monika Class (MC) is a doctorial student at Balliol College, Oxford, working on a thesis on Wordsworth, Coleridge, De Quincey, and Carlyle.

Josh Cohen (JoC)

Liam Connell (LC) teaches literature at the University of Hertfordshire. His research interests are in postcolonial writing, modernism, and popular literature.

Jennifer Cooke (JC) is completing an English literature thesis on the plague in texts and culture. She tutors in the English Department at the University of Sussex and in the Media and Cultural Studies Department at the University of Middlesex. She also writes and publishes short fiction.

Clare Connors (CC) is Lecturer in English at the Queen's College, Oxford, where she teaches and writes about Victorian and modern literature and literary theory. She has published on Freud, George Eliot, Jean Rhys, and Alan Hollinghurst.

Abi Curtis (AC) was born in Rochford, educated at the universities of Sussex and Exeter, and is completing a PhD at the University of Sussex in Creative and Critical Writing. She has published fiction and poetry and was awarded an Eric Gregory Award for poetry in 2004.

Ulf Dantanus (UD) is Director of Studies for the Gothenburg Program at the University of Sussex. He has postgraduate degrees from Trinity College Dublin and Göteborg University. His main area of interest is Irish literature. He has published *Brian Friel: A Study* (1988) and contributed reviews and articles on the subject to many books and journals.

Jean Demerliac (JD) is a writer and freelance editor, who has written and translated Herman Melville. He has contributed to numerous publications and multimedia projects produced by the Electronic Publishing section at the Bibliothèque nationale de France. He also produced a series of video-animations based on Hetzel's engraved illustrations of Verne's novels.

Sarah Dillon (SJD)

Matthew Dimmock (MatD) is a Lecturer in English at the University of Sussex. He is the author of *New Turkes: Dramatizing Islam and the Ottomans in Early Modern England*, and the co-editor of *Cultural Encounters Between East and West, 1453–1699*.

Margaret Anne Doody (MD) is John and Barbara Glynn Family Professor of Literature at the University of Notre Dame, where she also serves as Director of the PhD Literature Program. She has written many critical works, including *True Story of the Novel* (1996), as well as six novels. Her latest book is *Mysteries of Eleusis* (2005).

Jenny Doubt (JSD) completed her MA at the University of Sussex in postcolonial literature. She works as a Project Editor in London, and is one of the Founding Editors of *Transgressions*, a twentieth century inter-disciplinary humanities journal. She has also published with the *African Review of Books*.

Lizzie Enfield (LE)

Lisa Fishman (LF)

Anna Foca (AF)

Seb Franklin (SF)

Andrzej Gasiorek (AG) is a Reader in twentieth-century English literature at the University of Birmingham, where he has been teaching for the last twelve years. He is the author of *Postwar British Fiction: Realism and After* (1995), *Wyndham Lewis and Modernism* (2004), and *J. G. Ballard* (2005).

Dr. Diana Gobel (DG) studied philosophy with literature at the University of Sussex and Modern History at Oxford. Since getting her DPhil she has worked as a freelance translator, copy editor, and researcher.

Richard Godden (RG) teaches American Literature in the Department of American Studies at the University of Sussex. He has published *Fictions of Capital: The American Novel from James to Mailer* (1990), and *Fictions of Labor: William Faulkner and the South's Long Revolution* (1997).

Reg Grant (RegG) is a freelance writer. He has an extensive knowledge of modern European literature, especially post-Second World War French fiction.

Christopher C. Gregory-Guider (CG-G) teaches twentieth-century literature and culture at the University of Sussex. He has published articles on W. G. Sebald, Iain Sinclair, photography, trauma, and memory. Other interests include narrative and filmic representation of mental illness and the cultural history of walking.

Eleanor Gregory-Guider (EG-G) currently lives in Sussex. She received a BA (Hons) in English and History from the University of Texas at Austin and a MA in eighteenth-century studies, focusing on literature and art history from the University of York.

Andrew Hadfield (AH) is Professor of English at the University of Sussex where he teaches Renaissance literature and contemporary literature and theory. His most recent book is *Shakespeare and Republicanism* (2005). He has written essays on Saul Bellow, T. H. White, and is a reviewer for the *Times Literary Supplement*.

Esme Floyd Hall (EH) is a writer who lives and works in Brighton. She has published three nonfiction titles with Carlton Books and has contributed to various newspapers and magazines, including *Sunday Times Style*, *Observer*, *She*, and *Zest*.

Doug Haynes (DH) is a lecturer in American Literature at Sussex University. He specializes in late twentieth-century American writing. He has published work on the novelists Thomas Pynchon and William Burroughs and has written on Surrealist black humor.

Thomas Healy (TH) is Professor of Renaissance Studies at Birkbeck College, University of London. He is the author of three critical studies, editor of two collections of essays, and co-editor of *The Arnold Anthology of British and Irish Literature in English*.

Margaret Healy (MH) teaches English at the University of Sussex. Her interests are Renaissance literature, medicine, and cultural theory of the body. She is writing a book on Shakespeare's Sonnets.

Jon Hughes (JH) is a lecturer in German at Royal Holloway, University of London. He is the author of a monograph on the work of Joseph Roth, and has published on various aspects of twentieth-century German and Austrian literature and film.

Rowland Hughes (RH) is a Lecturer in English literature at the University of Hertfordshire, where he teaches literature from the Renaissance to the present day. His research interests lie in eighteenth and nineteenth-century American literature and Anglo-American cinema.

Bianca Jackson (BJ) is a doctoral candidate writing on the sexually dissident subject in contemporary Indian Anglophone literature at the University of Oxford. She is also one of the founding editors of *Transgressions*, an inter-disciplinary arts and humanities journal.

David James (DJ) is associate tutor in the Department of English at the University of Sussex, where he wrote a DPhil on the evolution of a poetics of place and perception in British fiction from 1970 to the present.

Dr. Meg Jensen (MJ) is Head of the Department of Creative Writing at Kingston University, where she also lectures on nineteenth and twentieth-century English and American literature. Her work on the writing of Woolf, Mansfield, and Hardy includes *The Open Book* (2002).

Iva Jevtic (IJ)

Carole Jones (CJ) lives in Dublin and London, and teaches in the School of English, Trinity College. She has published articles on contemporary Scottish fiction and the representation of men and masculinity in recent writing.

Thomas Jones (TEJ) is an editor at the *London Review of Books*.

Hannah Jordan (HJ) is a freelance writer and critic. She is working on a children's novel, entitled *A Bohemian Christmas*.

Jinan Joudeh (JLSJ) has studied English and American Literature at Duke, Sussex, and Yale universities. She is currently working on modernist American fiction in the context of friendship, marriage, and theory.

Christine Kerr (CK) was born in London, England and received her PhD from the University of Sussex. She has taught English literature in Europe, Africa, and Asia and currently is a faculty member at Champlain College in Montréal.

Kumiko Kiuchi (KK) is a DPhil student in the English Literature Department at the University of Sussex. She was awarded her BA and one of her MAs in Japan. Her research interests include the problem of translation, modernism, the philosophy of language, and the work of Samuel Beckett.

Karl Lampl (KL) was born in Lilienfeld, Austria and studied at the University of Vienna. After moving to Canada he settled in Montreal, where he graduated from Concordia University and went on to teach languages and literature.

Anthony Leaker (AL) is doing a DPhil on twentieth-century America and European literature. He has taught at the University of Paris.

Vicky Lebeau (VL) is Reader in English at the University of Sussex. She is the author of *Lost Angels: psychoanalysis and cinema* (1995), *Psychoanalysis and cinema: the play of shadows* (2001).

Hoyul Lee (Hoy)

Graeme Macdonald (GM) is Lecturer in nineteenth and twentieth-century literature in the Department of English and Comparative Literary Studies at The University of Warwick, England.

Heidi Slettedahl Macpherson (HM) is Reader in North American literature at the University of Central Lancashire. She is the author of *Women's Movement* (2000) and the co-editor of *Transatlantic Studies* (2000), and *Britain and the Americas* (2005).

Peter Manson (PM)

Laura Marcus (LM) is Professor of English at the University of Sussex. She has published on nineteenth and twentieth-century literature. She has co-edited *The Cambridge History of Twentieth-Century English Literature*.

Victoria Margree (VM) received her DPhil in English Literature from the University of Sussex. She lectures at Sussex and the University of Brighton.

Nicky Marsh (NM) works at the University of Southampton, where she is director of the Center for Cultural Poetics. Her published work has appeared in journals including *New Formations, Postmodern Culture, Feminist Review,* and *Wasafari*.

Louise Marshall (LMar) is a lecturer in Restoration and eighteenth-century literature at the University of Wales. Her research focuses on drama. Louise's passion for eighteenth-century literature developed as an undergrad as a result of her first encounter with Smollet's *Humphrey Clinker*.

Andrew Maunder (AM)

Maren Meinhardt (MM) is Science and Psychology Editor at the *Times Literary Supplement*. She is writing a biography of Alexander von Humboldt.

Dr. Ronan McDonald (RM) is Director of the Samuel Beckett International Foundation and Lecturer in the School of English at the University of Reading. His publications include *Tragedy and Irish Literature* (2002) and the *Cambridge Introduction to Samuel Beckett* (2005), as well as articles and reviews on modern British and Irish literature.

Dr. Patricia McManus (PM) teaches courses on English literary and cultural history at the University of Sussex. She is currently writing a book on the English novel in the 1920s and 1930s.

Drew Milne (DM) is the Judith E. Wilson Lecturer in Drama and Poetry, Faculty of English, University of Cambridge. He has edited *Marxist Literary Theory* and *Modern Critical Thought*; and published several books of poetry. His novel is entitled *The Prada Meinhof Gang*.

Pauline Morgan (PM) completed a doctoral thesis on Elizabeth Bowen at the University of Sussex. Her literary research incorporates an exploration of psychoanalysis, ghosts, and music.

Jonathan Morton (JM) is a History teacher living in Oxford. He writes poetry, plays music, and makes short films and documentaries. He studied History and English literature and creative writing at U.E.A in Norwich and did an MA in Modern European History.

Alan Munton (AMu) is Archivist at the University of Plymouth, and a Lecturer in English. His Cambridge doctorate on Wyndham Lewis featured the first full discussion of Lewis' *The Childermass*, summarized here.

Paul Myerscough (PMy) is an editor at the *London Review of Books*.

Stephanie Newell (SN) lectures in postcolonial literature at the University of Sussex. She specializes in West African literature and African popular culture, and her publications include *Literary Culture in Colonial Ghana: "How to Play the Game of Life", West African Literatures: Ways of Reading,* and *The Forger's Tale: The Search for "Odeziaku."*

Deborah Parsons (DPa) is a Senior Lecturer in nineteenth and twentieth-century English Literature at the University of Birmingham. She is the author of *Streetwalking the Metropolis* (2000), *A Cultural History of Madrid* (2003), and *Djuna Barnes* (2003).

Julian Patrick (JP) is a professor of English and Comparative Literature at the University of Toronto where he teaches early modern literature, literary theory, and psychoanalysis in the Department of English and the Literary Studies Program. He is also working on the overlap between traditional mimesis and new-style representation in early modern literature.

Ruth Patrick (RLP) completed her degree in English Language and Literature at the University of Manchester and has since been working as an editor in a London. She is a member of the editorial panel for prose submissions on a London-Oxford based Interdisciplinary arts journal.

Andrew Pepper (AP) is a lecturer in English and American literature at Queen's University Belfast. He is the author of *The Contemporary American Crime Novel* (2000) and the co-author of *American History and Contemporary Hollywood Film* (2005). His first novel is *The Last Days of Newgate*.

Roberta Piazza (RPi) is a Lecturer in Modern Languages at the University of Sussex, where she has taught translation and modern Italian and European literatures. After an American doctorate and an MPhil in Linguistics, she is completing a DPhil on the dialogue of Italian cinema.

David Punter (DP) is Professor of English at the University of Bristol, where he is also Research Director for the Faculty of Arts. He has published extensively on Gothic and Romantic literature; on contemporary writing; and on literary theory, psychoanalysis, and the postcolonial, as well as four small volumes of poetry.

Robin Purves (RP) is a Lecturer in English literature at the University of Central Lancashire. He has published articles on nineteenth-century French writing, contemporary poetry and philosophy, and co-edited a special issue of the *Edinburgh Review*. Along with Peter Manson, he runs a press, *Object Permanence*.

Vincent Quinn (VQ)

Vybarr Cregan-Reid (VC-R)

Dr. Ben Roberts (BR) teaches at the University of Bradford. His main areas of interest are cultural theories of technology and counterfeit money in literature.

Dr. Anne Rowe (AR) is a Senior Lecturer at Kingston University. She is author of *Salvation by Art: The Visual Arts and the Novels of Iris Murdoch* and is the Director of the Center for Iris Murdoch Studies at Kingston University. She is also the European Director of the Iris Murdoch Society and European Editor of the *Iris Murdoch News Letter*.

Nicholas Royle (NWOR) is Professor of English at the University of Sussex. His major works include *E. M. Forster* (1999) and *The Uncanny* (2003). He is joint editor of the *Oxford Literary Review*.

David Rush (DR)

Martin Ryle (MR) teaches English and Cultural Studies at the University of Sussex, and has special interests in Irish writing and contemporary fiction. His critical writing includes work on George Gissing and Michel Houellebecq.

Darrow Schecter (DS) did a doctorate on Antonio Gramsci at the University of Oxford. He was a British Academy Post-Doctoral Fellow, and was granted a lectureship in Italian Studies at the University of Sussex. He is a Reader in Intellectual History in the School of Humanities at the University of Sussex. He has written books on various topics in European intellectual history and political theory.

Elaine Shatenstein (ES) has been a freelance book reviewer, newspaper columnist, and feature writer, as well as a guest speaker for literary groups, a writing instructor, and an editor. She has worked in broadcasting and film as a writer and producer, and was published in an anthology of social satire.

John Shire (JS) is a writer and photographer. His short fiction has appeared in many UK and U.S. publications. He has a virtual hand in two websites; www.libraryofthesphinx.co.uk and Invocations Press. A degree in Literature and Philosophy has done him no good whatsoever.

Tom Smith (TS) is a lecturer at the Faculty of International Business, University of Applied Sciences Furtwangen. His short stories have appeared in magazines and anthologies and he has also won an Ian St. James Award. He has an MA in Creative Writing and is working toward a DPhil at Sussex University.

Daniel Soar (DSor) is an editor at the *London Review of Books*.

Matthew Sperling (MS)

David Steuer (DS)

Simon Stevenson (SS) is Assistant Professor of English at National Dong Hwa University, Taiwan where he teaches literature and theory.

Esther MacCallum Stewart (EMcCS)

Céline Surprenant (CS) is a Senior Lecturer in French in the English Department at the University of Sussex. She is the author of *Freud's Mass Psychology: Questions of Scale* (2003). She has also translated Jean-Luc Nancy's *The Speculative Remark* (2001).

Julie Sutherland (JuS) received her PhD in English studies and seventeenth-century studies at the University of Durham. Canadian by birth, she returned to Canada to become Professor of Early Modern Drama at Atlantic Baptist University.

Keston Sutherland (KS) is a lecturer in English at the University of Sussex. He is the author of *Antifreeze*, *The Rictus Flag*, *Neutrality* and other books of poetry. He edits the occult leftist journal *Quid*, the *Q?* series of noise, and rant CD-Rs, and co-edits Barque Press.

Bharat Tandon (BT) is College Lector and Director of Studies in English at Jesus College, Cambridge, and teaches British and American literature. He writes regularly on contemporary British and American fiction and cinema for the *Times Literary Supplement* and the *Daily Telegraph*.

Jenny Bourne Taylor (JBT) is a Reader in English at the University of Sussex. She has written extensively on nineteenth-century literature and culture. Recent publications include, ed. with Martin Ryle, *George Gissing: Voices of the Unclassed* (2005) and ed. *The Cambridge Companion to Wilkie Collins* (2006).

Philip Terry (PT)

Samuel Thomas (SamT) completed his DPhil in English Literature at the University of Sussex. His research interests include Thomas Pynchon, Frankfurt School Critical Theory, and Eastern European writing.

Sophie Thomas (ST) is Lecturer in English at the University of Sussex, where she teaches eighteenth and nineteenth-century literature, and on MA programs in Critical Theory, and Literature and Visual Culture. She has published on a wide range of subjects, from Mary Shelley's novel *The Last Man*, to Coleridge's play *Remorse*.

Dale Townshend (DaleT) is Thesia Stuftung Research Fellow in the Department of English Studies, University of Stirling. He has published essays and chapters on the Gothic, Romanticism, critical theory, and late eighteenth and early nineteenth-century fiction, and has co-edited, four volumes in the *Gothic: Critical Concepts in Literary and Cultural Studies* series (2004). His monograph, *The Orders of Gothic*, is published by AMS Press.

David Towsey (DT) is a Lecturer in English at Hertford College, Oxford, and also teaches for the Oxford University Department of Continuing Education. He has published on literary theory and Romantic literature, and is currently working on late Victorian and Edwardian writing as part of a study of Walter de la Mare's short stories.

Garth Twa (GT) is the author of a short story collection called *Durable Beauty*, an award winning filmmaker, and is currently at work on his second book, *My Ice Age*, which explores his youth in an Eskimo settlement on the Arctic Circle and his years struggling on the outer fringes of Hollywood.

Cedric Watts (CW) is Research Professor of English at the University of Sussex. His many publications include books on Shakespeare, Keats, Cunninghame Graham, Conrad, and Graham Greene. He is co-author (with John Sutherland) of *Henry V, War Criminal? and Other Shakespeare Puzzles*.

Juliet Wightman (JW) has taught English Studies at the University of Stirling for several years. Her research focuses on the relationship between language and violence, with particular reference to Renaissance literature and drama.

Tara Woolnough (TW) lives and, given the opportunity, works in London. She eventually fulfilled her childhood ambition of becoming a college dropout, albeit at the rather late stage of doctoral studies; before that she obtained a degree in Classics, and an MA. She now works in publishing.

Marcus Wood (MW)

Title Index

cƿæt ƿæſ ſtan fah ſtıȝ

æ ȝædeɲe ȝuð by ƿue

nond locen hɲınȝ ıɲen ſ

um þa hıe tofele fuɲð

ne ȝeat ƿım ȝanȝan e

æme þe ſıde ſcyldaſ pc

oð þæſ ƿeceðeſ ƿæl · buȝ

yɲnan hɲınȝ don ȝuð

ȝaɲaſ ſtodon ſæ man na

1700

PRE

THE·PEACOCK'S·COMPLAINT·

THE Peacock con=
-sidered it wrong
That he had not the nightingale's
song;
So to Juno he went,
She replied, "Be content
With thy having, & hold thy
fool's tongue!"

·DO·NOT·QUARREL·WITH·NATURE·

Aesop's Fables

Aesopus

Aesop, according to legend, was a tongue-tied slave living on the Greek island of Samos, who miraculously received the power of speech, and subsequently won his freedom, only to be thrown to his death by the citizens of Delphi for insulting their oracle. But what we know as *Aesop's Fables*, is in reality a body of work from a huge variety of sources. Among the earliest recorded narratives, these stories have become embedded in the Western psyche, like the stories of Oedipus and Narcissus. Who isn't familiar, for example, with the story of "The Hare and the Tortoise," where the lazy hare is outrun, despite his speed, by the diligent tortoise? As well as stories about animals, *Aesop's Fables* contains tales about everyday people, as in the story of the boy who cried "wolf," and it also gathers together jokes, paradoxes, parables, and "just so" stories; whatever the actual characters, the tone is always didactic. "Zeus and the Camel" tells how, when the camel saw another animal's horns, she begged Zeus to give her horns as well, but Zeus was so angry at the camel's greediness, that instead he cropped her ears. In the story "Jupiter and the Frogs," a famous parable about power, the frogs ask Jupiter for a king. Not content with the king he sends them at first, an easy-going log, they ask for a more powerful ruler, only to be sent a water-snake, who kills them off one by one.

The *Fables* remain very popular today, having been translated into languages all around the world, and a great many subsequent works of literature develop ideas first explored in them. Without the example of Aesop, the world would never have had *The Romance of Reynard the Fox*, and Kafka's *The Metamorphosis* would be inconceivable. There would be no *Just So Stories* by Kipling, and Orwell would never have written *Nineteen Eighty-Four*. **PT**

Lifespan | *b. c.*620 BCE (Greece), *d.* 560 BCE
First Edition | 4 BCE, compiled by rhetorician
First Published | *c.*1475 (L. Symoneli & others, Paris)
Original Title | *Fabulae Aesopi*

Fabule Efopi cum commento.

◉ The title page of the edition of the *Fables* printed by Wynykn de Worde in London in 1503 shows a schoolmaster with his pupils.

◉ This illustration is from artist Walter Crane's 1887 *Baby's Own Aesop*—subtitled *Portable Morals Pictorially Pointed*.

Metamorphoses
Ovid

Lifespan | *b.*43 BCE (Italy), *d.*17 CE
First Published | 1488, by Antonius Nebrissensis
First Composed | Between *c.* 2–8
Original Language | Latin

Ovid's *Metamorphoses*, which assembles some two hundred and fifty stories from classical antiquity into one continuous narrative, is a mythological history of the world, beginning with the Creation and ending with the foundation of Rome and the apotheosis of Julius Caesar. The constant questioning of tradition and power is something encountered in many of Ovid's narratives: Arachne challenges the goddess Athene to a tapestry-making contest; Phaethon insists on taking the reins of the sun chariot from his father; Daphne escapes from Apollo's clutches by praying to a river god, who changes her into a tree. When Ovid retells stories of heroism, it is in a comic, deflating way, reminiscent of mock-epic. Whenever Perseus kills his enemies by turning them to stone with the head of the Medusa which he carries in a bag, it is not the heroic that we see, but the use of a disproportionate force not unlike employing nuclear weapons in a pub brawl.

The *Metamorphoses'* incorporation of dialogue within a narrative, along with its wit, playfulness, and sheer sense of fun, exemplifies much of what we now associate with the novel. Today Ovid's work continues to be metamorphosed, and has had an impact on a dazzling array of contemporary novelists, from Salman Rushdie and A.S. Byatt, to Cees Nooteboom and Marina Warner. **PT**

⬤ Cygnus is transformed into a swan and Phaeton's sisters turn into poplar trees in an engraved illustration of the *Metamorphoses*.

Chaireas and Kallirhoe
Chariton

Lifespan | *b. c.*1st century BCE (Greece), *d. c.*1st century
First Published | 1750
Language of First Publication | Latin
Original Title | *Peri Chairean kai Kallirhoen*

Dates suggested for this classical "novel" vary from 50 BCE to 200 CE, though this story of the lives of two young lovers from Syracuse is set during the time of the Persian Empire. The author, Chariton, tells us that he is secretary to a rhetor of Aphrodisias; the identity may be real or concocted. Chaireas and Kallirhoe have fallen in love at first sight, and are eventually allowed to marry, but jealous former suitors of the girl destroy Chaireas' trust in his wife. He kicks her in the stomach and she falls lifeless. Buried in the elaborate family tomb, Kallirhoe awakens and cries for help. Tomb robbers, who have been attracted by the valuables buried with the girl, take her away and sell her to a respectable and conscientious landowner, Dionysos, who lives on the coast of Ionia. He soon falls in love with the slave girl, who looks like Aphrodite. On finding she is pregnant by Chaireas, Kallirhoe agrees to marry Dionysos, giving her unborn child an unsuspecting father. Chaireas, who has discovered from the tomb-robbers that his wife is alive, goes in search of her. The two meet again in Persia, at a complicated trial over who has the right to be Kallirhoe's husband, but they are not truly reunited until Chaireas has proven his heroism in warfare, and the Great King of Persia has been partially defeated. The child is left in the care of Dionysos while Kallirhoe joins Chaireas and sails for home. Kallirhoe's fate at the hand of her two lovers inspires readers to root for a woman to commit adultery, and find her own voice. **MD**

Aithiopika

Heliodorus

Lifespan | c.3rd century (Syria)
First Published | 1534 (written c.250)
Original Language | Ancient Greek
Alternate Title | *Theagenes and Charicleia*

This influential early "novel" begins with a puzzling scene of carnage not explained until mid-story. The divinely beautiful heroine, Charikleia, and her lover, Theagenes, are captured by bandits, and the chief bandit insists that the heroine must marry him. The hero and heroine escape and once again fall in with their guide, the Egyptian priest Kalasiris. Kalasiris' mission is to restore the lovely Charikleia to her native royal house in Ethiopia. The girl's mother, the Queen of Ethiopia, had looked at a picture of white Andromeda at the moment of conception, causing the girl to be born the wrong color. Her mother was forced to give her up at birth, and Charikleia was adopted by a man of Delphi, where Kalasiris found her; Theagenes was already in love with her. They all journey to Ethiopia, as the Egyptian priest is confident that he will be able to explain the girl's identity; but when he suddenly dies, the young pair are left at the mercy of a Persian satrap's court and the jealousy of a noblewoman. The couple endure many ordeals before the young princess, white except for a ring of black flesh about her arm, arrives home and is ultimately accepted by her parents.

Riddles, wordplay, and ambiguous prophecies abound in this story which may have influenced Mozart's *The Magic Flute*. Heliodorus' elaborate and playful Greek is difficult, but early European translations have had an impact on modern literature, influencing writers as diverse as Shakespeare, Cervantes, and Henry Fielding. **MD**

The Golden Ass

Lucius Apuleius

Lifespan | b.c.123 (Madauros, modern Algeria), d.170
First Published | 1469 (written c.260)
First Published by | C. Sweynheim & A. Pannartz
Original Title | *Metamorphoses*

The Golden Ass is the only Latin novel to survive in its entirety. Its style is racy, boisterous, and irreverent, as was the mode of professional storytellers of the time, but ultimately the story is a moral one.

Lucius, a young Roman aristocrat who is obsessed with magic, is accidentally turned into an ass by his lover. In this guise, he is led on a series of adventures which cause him to witness and share the misery of the slaves and destitute freemen who, like Lucius, are reduced to little more than animals by the treatment of their wealthy owners. The book is the only work of literature from the ancient Greco-Roman world that examines first hand the conditions of the lower classes. Despite its serious subject matter, the tone is bawdy and sexually explicit, as Lucius spends time in licentious company. It is also significant for its portrayal of contemporary religions; in the final chapters of the book, Lucius is eventually turned back into a man by the goddess Isis. Lucius is subsequently initiated into her mystery cult, and dedicates his life to her. At this point the rowdy humor of the earlier novel is exchanged for equally powerful and beautiful prose. *The Golden Ass* is a precursor to the episodic picaresque novel, and its entertaining mixture of magic, farce, and mythology make for a read as compelling today as it must have been originally. **LE**

> ◗ This illustration by Jean de Bosschere, from a 1923 edition of *The Golden Ass*, shows a woman being attacked with a firebrand.

The Thousand and One Nights
Anonymous

Original Title | *Alf laylah wa laylah*
Original Language | Arabic
First Published | *c.*850
Source | from *Hazar Afsanah (A Thousand Tales)*

The tales that make up the collection known to us as *The Thousand and One Nights* are some of the most powerful, resonant works of fiction in the history of storytelling. The tales, told over a thousand and one nights by Sheherazade to King Shahryar, include foundational narratives such as "Sinbad", "Aladdin," and "Ali Baba and the Forty Thieves." These stories have an uncanny capacity to endure. But while the tales of *The Thousand and One Nights* are remarkable for their familiarity and their currency, perhaps their most important legacy is the concept of narrative itself that emerges from them.

It is in the *Nights* that an underlying, generative connection is fashioned between narrative, sex, and death—a connection which has remained at the wellspring of prose fiction ever since. King Shahryar is in the unseemly habit of deflowering and killing a virgin on a nightly basis, and the *Nights* opens with Sheherazade lining up to be the king's next victim. Determined not to meet with such a fate, Sheherazade contrives to tell the king stories; in accordance with her plan, they prove so compelling, so erotic, so luscious and provocative, that at the end of the night, he cannot bring himself to kill her. Each night ends with a tale unfinished, and each night the King grants her a stay of execution, so that he might hear the conclusion. But the storytelling that Sheherazade invents, in order to stay alive, is a kind of storytelling that is not able to end, that never reaches a climax. Rather, the stories are inhabited by a kind of insatiable desire, an open unfinishedness that keeps us reading and panting, eager for more, just as King Shahryar listens and pants. The eroticism of the tales, their exotic, charged texture, derives from this desirousness, this endless trembling on the point both of climax, and of death. **PB**

◉ The binding from a 1908 edition of the *Arabian Nights* stylishly captures the exoticism that attracted Westerners to tales of the East.

◑ Leon Bakst designed the costumes for the Ballet Russes version of Rimsky-Korsakov's *Sheherazade*, performed in Paris in 1910.

Gargantua and Pantagruel

François Rabelais

Lifespan | *b.c.*1494 (France), *d.*1553
First Published | 1532–1564, by F. Juste (Lyon)
Full Title | *Grands annales tresueritables des gestes merveilleux du grand Gargantua et Pantagruel*

"The appetite grows by eating."

The history of the modern novel begins with Rabelais. Allowing for some of the minor precedents which he subjected to pastiche, Rabelais' *Pantagruel*, published under his anagrammatic pseudonym Alcofribas Nasier, established a whole new genre of writing with a riotous mix of rhetorical energy, linguistic humor, and learned wit. In creating a comedy of sensory excesses, playing off various licentious, boozy, and lusty appetites, Rabelais also prefigures much in the history of the novel from *Don Quixote* to *Ulysses*. Perhaps his greatest achievement is his free-spiritedness, which combines high-jinking vulgar materialism with a profound, skeptical mode of humanist wit.

The novel itself tells the story of the gigantic Gargantua and his son Pantagruel. The first book details fantastic incidents in the early years of Pantagruel and his roguish companion Panurge. The second book, *Gargantua*, tracks back in time to the genealogy of Pantagruel's father, while making scholasticism and old-fashioned educational methods the object of satire. The third book develops as a satire of intellectual learning mainly through the heroic deeds and sayings of Pantagruel. In the fourth book, Pantagruel and Panurge head off on a voyage to the Oracle of the Holy Bottle in Cathay, which provides scenes for satire on religious excess. The fifth and most bitter book, takes them to the temple of the Holy Bottle where they follow the oracle's advice to "Drink!" The inconsequential plot hardly rises to the level of picaresque, but there is a feast of mirth in the telling. Thomas Urquhart's seventeenth-century translation of the first three books is a marvel in its own right, and preferable in many ways to twentieth-century attempts to translate the spirit of Rabelaisian rhetoric. **DM**

Euphues: The Anatomy of Wit

John Lyly

Lyly's *Euphues: The Anatomy of Wit* was published during the reign of Elizabeth I, for the consumption of a legendarily cultured and leisured audience of courtiers and nobility. While it is not exactly a novel, it has the general outline, as well as some of the features of what would later become the novel form. Though hardly read today, the text was significant enough to conjure an addition to the English lexicon in the word "euphuism," which means an affected elegance or overwroughtness in language.

Euphues is relentless in its display of verbal affectation, comprising a sort of ludicrous handbook of grand expressions and apothegms. The plot is negligible in its moralizing twists and countertwists, more or less just a frame over which the multitude of polite phrases is draped. What makes *Euphues* fascinating for the non-specialist reader is its great dexterity in handling and varying the conventional exempla of courtly speech. This dexterity smothers the impulse for any type of genuine literary originality—a quality which would later be prized as the single most important criterion of great literature. This is the sort of verbal ostentation and intricacy that would come to be most detested both by the pious authors of the Protestant Reformation and by Romantics such as Samuel Coleridge, for whom skill in the manipulation of conceits stood as evidence of either a corrupted intelligence or a heart cynically detached from its pen. Lyly himself was quite aware of these objections, and unruffled enough by them to acknowledge them in advance: "honnie taken excessiuelye cloyeth the stomacke though it be honnie," he once wrote. What he was canny enough to perceive is that the ruling class enjoys nothing so much as excessive consumption. **KS**

Lifespan | *b.* 1553 (England), *d.* 1606
First Published | 1578
First Printed by | T. East for G. Cawood (London)
Orginal Language | English

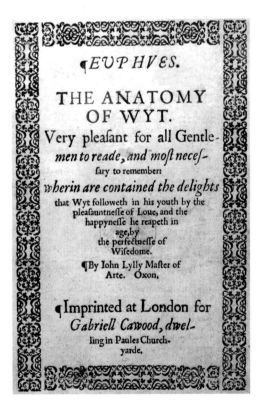

"It is a world to see."

In the first fifty years after publication, *The Anatomy of Wit* and its sequel, *Euphues and His England*, went through twenty-six editions.

The Unfortunate Traveller

Thomas Nashe

Lifespan | *b.* 1567 (England), *d.* 1601
First Printed | 1594, by T. Scarlet for C. Burby
Full Title | *The Unfortunate Traveller; or,
The Life of Jacke Wilton*

"My master beat the bush."

⬥ A contemporary woodcut shows Nashe in leg-irons, a likely
fate for a social satirist and outspoken enemy of puritanism.

The Unfortunate Traveller is perhaps the most brilliant Elizabethan novella. Nashe tells the complex and disturbing story of Jack Wilton, an amoral young recruit in Henry VIII's army in France. Wilton has a series of dangerous adventures, starting when he worms his way into the good offices of the army's Lord of Misrule, a cider seller. He convinces the man that the king regards him as an enemy spy, and receives a great deal of free drink. Eventually the king is confronted and the plot is exposed, resulting in a whipping for Wilton (although we are aware that in the real world a harsher punishment would have befallen him). Wilton then travels throughout Europe, witnessing the destruction of the Anabaptist Utopia established in Münster (a more dangerous form of misrule), before reaching Italy where he witnesses even more spectacular vice and cruelty, specifically the executions of two criminals, Zadoch and Cutwolfe. He encounters a banished English earl who tries to persuade him that travel is a cursed activity best avoided, concluding that we can learn nothing from travel that we could not have acquired in a "warm study." Eventually Wilton returns to England, horrified at what he has witnessed, and vows to remain at home in the future.

The Unfortunate Traveller is disturbing and funny by turns, with every description undercut by a powerful irony, so that we are not sure at the end whether we are being told that travel is an enlightening or a pointless process. Nashe's descriptions, especially those of violence, are a brilliant and unsettling combination of the ordinary and the extraordinary, notably when the dying Zadoch has his fingernails "half raised up, and then underpropped . . . with sharp pricks, like a tailor's shop window half-open on a holiday." **AH**

Don Quixote

Miguel de Cervantes Saavedra

Don Quixote stands at the head of a long line of fictions of which fictionality itself is the principal substance. Don Quixote has read himself into madness by reading too many books of chivalry, and so sets out to emulate the knights of old, first by getting himself some armour (out of pasteboard) and a steed (a broken down nag), and then by getting himself knighted. He goes to an inn, which he thinks a castle, meets prostitutes whom he thinks high-born ladies, addresses them and the innkeeper, who is a thief, in language so literary that they cannot understand it, and then seeks to get himself knighted by standing vigil all night over his armour. Apart from the burlesque parody of romances of chivalry, the ludicrous transformation of the sacred rituals and spaces of knighthood into their ad hoc material equivalents parallels a similar desacralizing going on Europe at the time.

In all this it is the knowing reader rather than the characters or the action that is the implied subject of address. Indeed, Cervantes here invents the novel form itself, by inventing the reader.

Reading begins with the Prologue's address to the "idle" reader, and by implication extends throughout the first book, as Quixote's friends attempt to cure his madness by burning his books to stop him reading. In the process we meet readers, and occasions for reading, of all kinds. In 1615, Cervantes published a second book in which Don Quixote becomes not the character reading but the character read as many of the people he meets have read Book I and know all about him and his non-reading sidekick Sancho Panza. Indeed this combination of the always already read and the force of perpetual reinvention is what continues to draw the reader in. **JP**

Lifespan | *b.*1547 (Spain), *d.*1616
First Published | 1605–1615, by Juan de la Cuesta
Full Original Title | *El ingenioso hidalgo Don Quixote de la Mancha*

"Hunger is the best sauce."

⬤ The first part of *Don Quixote* was originally published in Madrid in 1605; fewer than twenty copies of the first edition survived.

The Pilgrim's Progress

John Bunyan

Lifespan | b. 1547 (England), d. 1688
First Published | 1678–1684, by N. Ponder
Alternate Title | The Pilgrim's Progress from This
World to That Which Is to Come

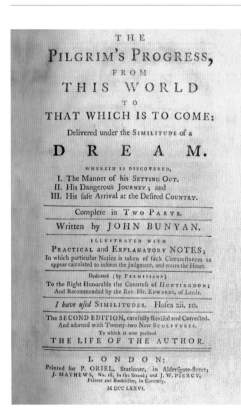

The 1776 edition displays the work's verbose full title, emphasizing the intended oneiric quality of the narrative.

In an engraving from the 1776 edition, Bunyan's heroes escape from Giant Despair and the mortal temptation of doubt.

One of the most popular works ever written in the English language, John Bunyan's *Pilgrim's Progress* continues to be published in new editions, remain on bestseller lists, and retain an enduring relevance today. Much of this appeal lies in its combination of unadorned piety with narrative simplicity, a combination that meant for centuries it was read in conjunction with the Bible as the primary work of Christian devotion and reflection. Bunyan was, however, a more controversial figure than the conservative reputation of *The Pilgrim's Progress* suggests. His own spiritual struggles are documented in his *Grace Abounding to the Chief of Sinners* (1666) and he probably wrote part of *The Pilgrim's Progress* in prison for religious dissent. If one avoids the anodyne modern spelling versions, one can still find in the protagonist Christian's journey a powerful sense of seventeenth-century religious conviction (the first part of modern editions was published in 1678, the second part followed in 1684).

The first part follows Christian as he journeys to the Celestial City, on the way encountering memorable characters such as Talkative, Faithful, Evangelist, and Hopeful, and passing through temptation and torment in the City of Destruction, Castle Doubt, and Vanity Fair. The second part traces the same journey undertaken by Christian's wife Christiana and his children, and takes on quite a different character. Regardless of a reader's personal religious convictions, these allegorical journeys become emblematic of the spiritual and moral struggle of the individual in the world. The Vanity Fair episode, in which the protagonists are assailed by temptation, apathy, self-love, and consumerist excess, seems as relevant to twenty-first century life as it was to seventeenth-century England. **MD**

Chriſtian and Hopeful Eſcape from Doubting Caſtle.

The Princess of Clèves

Marie-Madelaine Pioche de Lavergne, Comtesse de La Fayette

Dates | *b.* 1634 (France), *d.* 1693
First Published | 1678
First Published by | C. Barbin (Paris)
Original Title | *La Princesse de Clèves*

Mᵐᵉ Mˡᵉⁱⁿᵉ PIOCHE DE LA VERGNE.
Comtesse de la Fayette

"The Duc de Nemours was a masterpiece of Nature."

● The Comtesse de La Fayette helped found the modern
French literary tradition of the refined analysis of sentiments.

This profound story of forbidden love enflamed and then resisted until it dies an unnatural death takes place in the court of Henry II of France during the last years of his reign (*c.* 1558). The young heroine of the title enters a society in which the adulterous love affairs of the powerful and beautiful make up the only important action. Determined to protect the Princess from this world at the same time as introducing her to it, her mother agrees to an early marriage with the Prince of Clèves whom the Princess respects but cannot love passionately. She then falls utterly in love with the Duc de Nemours, the most sought after man at court, and he with her. Their love is never consummated, nor is it determined by accident or fate; it is both encouraged and resisted in the course of a series of scandalous scenes of intimacy and betrayal that were themselves received as a literary scandal by La Fayette's own society not merely because they were regarded as implausible, but because of their evident singularity of purpose.

In one scene, Nemours, aware that the Princess is watching, steals a portrait of her belonging to her husband. Nemours watches the Princess' reaction, noting that she does nothing to intervene. In a second, the Princess confesses to her husband that she is in love with another man while Nemours, that man, looks on unobserved and listens to her confession. In a third, Nemours, spied on by a servant of her husband, follows the Princess to her country house where he sees her contemplating a picture in which he is represented. All of these scenes provoke overwhelming and unresolvable turmoil in the Princess but offer the modern reader an experience of compelling narrative and emotional complexity. **JP**

Oroonoko

Aphra Behn

The order of the original title indicates the direction of the narrative: from fictional romantic beginnings in the west African country of Coramantien, to the hero's enslavement, to the subsequent events in Surinam that Behn herself may very well have witnessed during the 1660s. The movement chronicled by the title chronicles also suggests the importance of Behn's text to the history of the novel, as well as its interest for modern readers.

Oroonoko is a noble warrior-prince, the grandson of the king, with whom he clashes over the beautiful Imoinda, Oroonoko's lover and the object of the king's jealous and impotent affections. In revenge for the lovers' persistence, the king sells Imoinda as a slave while Oroonoko is betrayed into slavery. The two lovers meet again in Surinam where they are renamed Clemene and Caesar. Anxious to be free, Caesar persuades the slaves to revolt against their tormentors; the slaves are caught and Caesar is whipped almost to death. Clemene is now pregnant and, fearing that their child will also become a slave, they make a murder-suicide pact which concludes in tragedy, though not quite as Caesar had envisaged.

Behn's extended short story gives a uniquely participatory role to the narrator, who is not only an "eye-witness" to many of the events she recounts as "true history," but refers to herself as an actor in the story. As a female, however, she is unable to save Oroonoko from the "obscure world" he has fallen into. The result is an oddly skewed general uncertainty that is still profoundly affecting: exotic romance mixes with an acute account of the slave trade and, in Surinam, the relations between the local Carib Indians, the English plantation owners, the slaves, and the Dutch. Historical, readerly, and authorial consciousness are here joined. **JP**

Lifespan | *b.* 1640 (England), *d.* 1689
First Published | 1688
First Published by | W. Canning (London)
Full Title | *Oroonoko; or, The Royal Slave*

"He had nothing of barbarity in his nature . . ."

⊙ Probably Britain's first female professional author, Aphra Behn was also by turns a merchant's wife and inmate of a debtors' prison.

Il faut vous fuir, Ma[dame]
[je] sens bien. J'aurois dû b[ien]
[a]ttendre ; ou plustôt, il f[aut]
[v]oir jamais. Mais que j[e]
[m]'y prendre aujourdui [le]
[p]romis de l'amitié : Voy[ez]
[et] conseillez-moi.

Vous savez que je n[e]
[d]ans vôtre maison que [je]
[qu]e Madame vôtre mér[e]
[j]'avois cultivé quelques [plantes]
[el]le a cru qu'ils ne ser[ont]

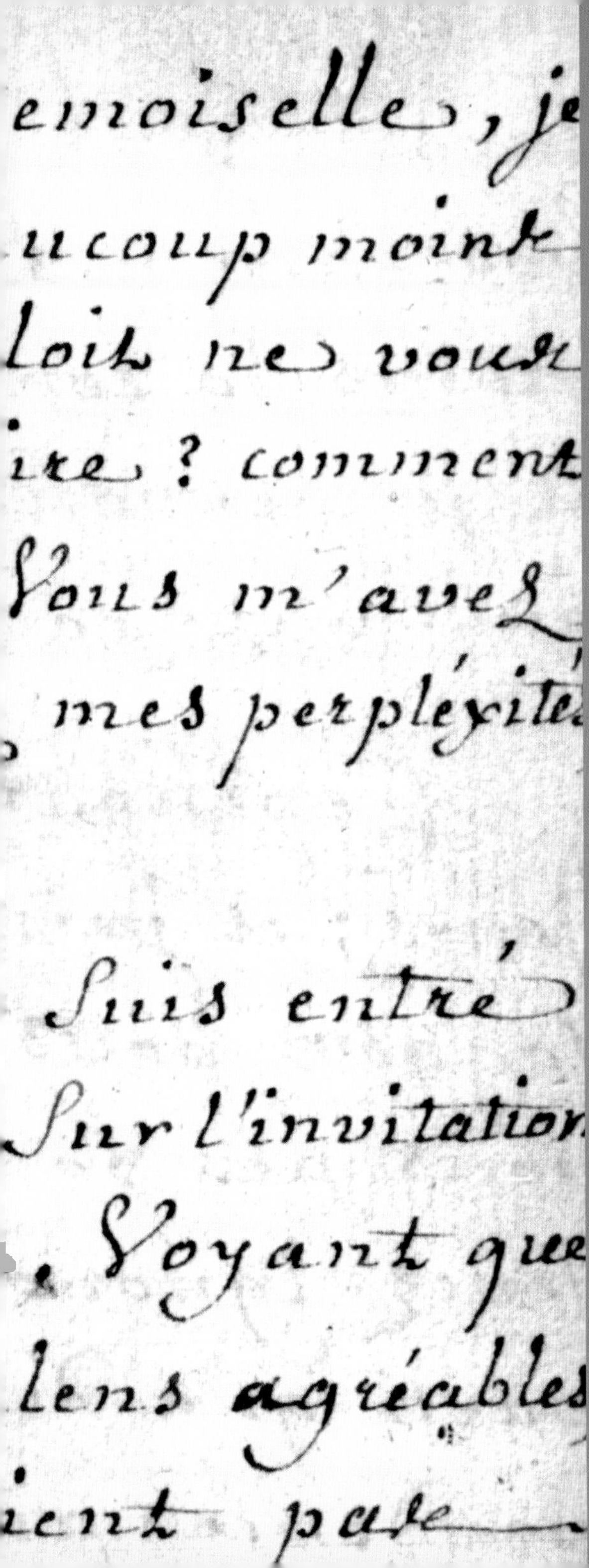
emoiselle, je
ucoup moins
loit ne vous
ire ? comment
Vous m'avez
mes perpléxités
Suis entré
Sur l'invitation
. Voyant que
Sens agréables
ient pas

1700s

Jean-Jacques Rousseau, *Julie; or, the New Eloise*, 1760

A Tale of a Tub

Jonathan Swift

Lifespan | *b.* 1667 (Ireland), *d.* 1745
First Published | 1704
First Published by | J. Nutt (London)
Pseudonym | Isaac Bickerstaff

In *A Tale of a Tub*, Swift adopts the persona of a hapless, pontificating satirist in order to savage a number of contemporary pieties and practices. Once the reader has battled through a welter of Apologies, Addresses, Dedications, and a Preface, the "author" of the piece introduces a religious allegory which is supposed to depict the decadence of the Catholic Church and the necessity of its Reformation. The tale concerns three brothers who abuse their father's legacy of coats—which they are forbidden to embellish by the terms of his will. They proceed to wilfully misinterpret the will in order to follow the dictates of fashion. One brother, Peter, swindles his way into a position of great authority and wealth, while the other brothers rebel and strip their coats of the fripperies they had once coveted. The tale is complicated by the teller's incompetence: he finds the allegory impossible to sustain and cannot resist embarking on absurd tangents, including "A Digression in Praise of Digressions."

Swift's main targets are witless propagandists for Calvinism, but the flexibility of the genre, pushed to its limits by the invention of an insane "author," sanctions free-wheeling assaults which threaten the viability of Swift's own perspective—even satire itself is satirized. The force of *A Tale of a Tub* is attributable to this almost autonomous ironic energy, capable of undermining anything with a power that even Swift's subsequent and more famous masterpieces rarely equalled. **RP**

Robinson Crusoe

Daniel Defoe

Lifespan | *b.* 1660 (England), *d.* 1731
First Published | 1719, by W. Taylor (London)
Full Title | *The Life and Strange Surprising Adventures of Robinson Crusoe of York, Mariner, Written by Himself*

Robinson Crusoe is thought by many to be the first English novel. It has haunted the literary and critical imagination since its publication, returning in guise after guise: in *The Swiss Family Robinson*; in Robert Zemeckis's movie *Castaway*; in J.M. Coetzee's novel *Foe*. The novel presents us with a fundamental scenario. The prolonged and intense solitude of Robinson, shipwrecked on a desert island, strips him of the tools that have allowed him to live, and confronts him with the essential problems of his existence. In the vast silence even words begin to desert him. He tries to keep a diary in order to stay in touch with his civilized self, but the small supply of watered-down ink that he salvages from the shipwreck gradually starts to fail and the words that he writes eventually disappear, leaving Robinson's diary as blank as his horizon.

This encounter with total solitude does not lead Robinson to madness, to silence, or to despair. Rather, Robinson finds in solitude the basis for a new kind of writing, and a new kind of self-consciousness. Just as he fashions new tools for himself from the materials that he has to hand, so he invents a new way of telling himself the story of his life and of his world. It is this narrative form that Robinson bequeaths to a world on the brink of Enlightenment, the narrative form in which we continue, even now, to tell ourselves the stories of our lives. **PB**

❯ John Hassall produced this cover image for a 1908 edition of *Robinson Crusoe*, designed primarily to appeal to children.

Love in Excess

Eliza Haywood

Lifespan | *b.* 1693 (England), *d.* 1756
First Published | 1719
First Published by | W. Chetwood (London)
Full Title | *Love in Excess; Or, The Fatal Enquiry*

Eliza Haywood's three-volume tale recounts the experiences of one Count D'elmont as he finds— and loses—his way along the often treacherous path to romantic and sexual fulfilment. Part the dashing hero and part the profligate rake, through the fault of others as well as his own, D'elmont becomes enmeshed in a series of compromising relationships. D'elmont's devotion to the lovely Melliora is the object of dispute throughout, and when this relationship is not directly under threat from such ambitious women as Alovisa, D'elmont himself indirectly threatens it through his participation in a range of complex ménages à trois. Letters intended to circulate privately between lovers are continuously intercepted, and lovers are farcically substituted to comic and tragic effect. However, as the title of the piece suggests, it is not long before D'elmont and others learn the importance of romantic moderation in a world otherwise characterized by passionate excess. When he replaces the mercenary marital ambitions of his early years with the mature embracing of conjugal affection, the hero eventually chooses his spouse based upon moderation, fidelity, and reserve.

Along with *Robinson Crusoe*, *Love in Excess* was one of the most popular early eighteenth-century novels. Haywood's frank treatment of desire and sexual passion renders her a key figure in the feminine tradition of amatory fiction that runs from Aphra Behn to Delarivier Manley and beyond. **DT**

Moll Flanders

Daniel Defoe

Lifespan | *b.* 1660 (England), *d.* 1731
First Published | 1722, by W. Chetwood (London)
Full Title | *The Fortunes and Misfortunes of the Famous Moll Flanders, &c.*

A master of plain prose, powerful narrative, and realistic detail, Daniel Defoe is regarded by many as the first true novelist. Appearing three years after his most famous work, *Robinson Crusoe*, *Moll Flanders* stands as one of the important precursors to the modern novel. Narrated in the first person, the novel relates the autobiography of Moll Flanders. Moll leads an eventful life which includes travel with gypsies, five marriages, incest, prostitution, and twelve years as one of London's most notorious and successful thieves. When she is finally caught, she escapes the death sentence with the help of a minister who encourages her to repent her evil ways. Transported to Virginia with one of her husbands, she buys her freedom, sets up as a planter, and increases her amassed wealth with the income from a plantation. In her old age, she returns to England where she resolves to spend the rest of her years in penitence for the life she has led.

Defoe paints an unforgettable picture of the seamy underside of England. A masterful gold digger, conniver, and survivor, Moll exploits her formidable talents to evade poverty. The novel's power lies in the force and attraction of Moll's character which catches the reader's imagination and sympathy. But it also lies in the delightfully subversive moral of the tale which seems not to be that wickedness will be punished, but rather that one can live a profligate life and not only get away with it, but in fact prosper from it too. **SJD**

Roxana

Daniel Defoe

Lifespan | *b.* 1660 (England), *d.* 1731
First Published | 1724
First Published by | T. Warner (London)
Original Title | *The Fortunate Mistress*

While *Roxana*, Defoe's last and most complex novel, is less familiar among general readers than *Robinson Crusoe*, it has been well known to those interested in the development of the novel, because of its frank portrayal of its heroine's fate—her early destitution and the exchanging of her body for food and shelter, her many children and their abandonment, her lovers, her failed reformations, and her enormous wealth.

Perhaps more important, however, than this list of sexual, social, and financial adventures is the voice that Defoe lends Roxana. In a notorious scene, Roxana puts her maidservant Amy into bed with her landlord-lover, saying to herself, and to us in effect, "I'm not a wife, but a whore, and I want my maid to be a whore too, and yet I am a wife and Amy is not a whore but a victim, and yet we'll do it all again". Such a voice, both self-estranging and self-engaging, becomes the string on which the events of the novel are strung, including relations with a French Prince, with the King of England, with a leading financial adviser, with an honest Dutch merchant. Scandalously, Roxana gets her children out of the way almost as soon as she has them, but towards the end, her daughter Susan, who has found employment as a servant girl in Roxana's own house, comes back to haunt her mother with a child's cry for recognition. Significantly Roxana's name is also Susan, and in this climax of self-confrontation the novel descends inconclusively towards a final abandonment. **JP**

Tookey sculp. from an Engraving by Gucht.

DANIEL DE FOE.

"I retain'd nothing of France, but the language: My Father and Mother being people of better Fashion, than ordinarily the people call'd Refugees."

◉ Engraved by James Tookey, this image shows Defoe in around 1715, when he was on the verge of writing his great fictional works.

Gulliver's Travels

Jonathan Swift

Everyone knows at least something about *Gulliver's Travels*. Variously read and re-written as a children's story, a political satire, a travel text, an animated film, and a BBC television series, Swift's perennial classic has been bowdlerized, added to, argued over, and adapted, but remains a constant presence in any widely accepted canon of English Literature.

The narrative follows the adventures of innocent abroad, Lemuel Gulliver, from misguided youth, through the distorting mirrors of Lilliput and Brobdignag, onto the more enigmatic islands of Laputa, Balnibarbi, Glubbdubdrib, Luggnagg, and Japan, followed by the crucially important land of the Houyhnhms and the Yahoos. Swift masterfully inserts such locations into the blank spaces of eighteenth-century maps (actually included in the first edition) and follows the conventions of the contemporary travel narrative with such precision that the real and the fantastical coalesce. Our only guide is Gulliver, whose unwavering confidence in the superiority of the Englishman and of English culture is slowly and inevitably picked apart by the assorted characters he encounters on his travels, some minute, some huge, some misguided, some savage, others guided entirely by reason. All offer comments to, and perspectives upon Gulliver, that force readers to question their own assumptions. It is a satire that may have lost some of its immediate political force, but one that still has a sting in its tail for us today, made all the more effective as Swift stages the climax of the tales within the bounds of the English nation-state. The vehemence with which Gulliver eschews the company of his fellows for his horses is an image that will remain with readers forever—for it is here that it becomes clear that he is not the main target of the satire. We are. **MD**

Lifespan | *b.* 1667 (Ireland), *d.* 1745
First Published | 1726, by B. Motte (London)
Full Title | *Travels Into Several Remote Nations of the World, by Lemuel Gulliver*

A page from Swift's manuscript of *Gulliver's Travels* displays a clear and disciplined hand at the service of a lucid brain.

Self-consciously superior, Gulliver enjoys terrifying the Lilliputians with a demonstration of English firepower.

A Modest Proposal

Jonathan Swift

Lifespan | *b.*1667 (Ireland), *d.*1745
First Published | 1729
First Published by | S.Harding (Dublin)
Pseudonym | Isaac Bickerstaff

Or, more properly, *A Modest Proposal for Preventing the Children of Poor People from Being a Burden to Their Parents, Or the Country, and for Making Them Beneficial to the Public*. The title is long but Swift's propagandizing pamphlet is as succinct and excoriating a work of satire as is possible to conceive. Penned after its author returned to Dublin to become Dean of St. Patrick's, the work expresses in equal measure contempt for English policy in Ireland and for Irish docility in taking it. A prolific writer, political journalist, and wit, Swift was skilled at transforming outrage to glacial irony.

The proposal here is anything but modest: Irish children can become less burdensome to their families and the state by being eaten by the rich. Children might become quality livestock for poor farmers. Young children, Swift suggests, are "nourishing and wholesome" whether they are "stewed, roasted, baked, or broiled", while older, less obviously tasty offspring might be spared for breeding purposes. The abundant advantages include reducing the numbers of "Papists", providing much-needed funds for the peasantry, boosting national income, and stimulating the catering trade. Swift also satirizes the callousness of the English protestant absentee landowners whose economics value mercantilism ahead of labor power. While, across his oeuvre, Swift is notoriously complicated in his politics, in this pungent pamphlet, we find him at his savage best. **DH**

Joseph Andrews

Henry Fielding

Lifespan | *b.*1707 (England), *d.*1754
First Published | 1742, by A.Millar (London)
Full Title | *The History of the Adventures of Joseph Andrews, and of His Friend Mr.Abraham Adam*

Joseph Andews actually begins as a "sequel" to *Shamela*, Fielding's short burlesque of Richardson's sensationally popular *Pamela*. However, it quickly surpasses the original, displaying Fielding's progress toward an original fictional voice and technique, and revealing his moral preoccupation with the question of "good nature" as the basis for real virtue.

In a comic inversion of typical gender roles, Joseph (Pamela's brother and a servant in the Booby household) virtuously resists the lustful advances of Mrs. Booby, not because he lacks masculine vigor (unthinkable for a Fielding hero), but because he faithfully loves the beautiful Fanny Goodwill. When he is dismissed by his irate mistress, Joseph embarks on a picaresque series of adventures with Parson Abraham Adams, who overshadows Joseph as the most vigorous presence in the novel. Adams' virtue is matched by his naïveté, continually entangling him and his companions in difficulties that test his good nature. Nabokov, among others, noted the cruelty of *Joseph Andrews*; Fielding seems to relish placing his virtuous heroes and heroines in compromising positions. The foolishness and eccentricity of both the Parson and Joseph, however, are vindicated by their physical and moral courage, their loyalty, and their benevolence—the comic morality of *Don Quixote* is an obvious model. Fielding manipulates the conventions of romance to bring about a happy ending, with a wink to his readers to acknowledge its artificiality. **RH**

Memoirs of Martinus Scriblerus

J. Arbuthnot, J. Gay, T. Parnell, A. Pope, J. Swift

Lifespan | births from 1667, deaths from 1745
Born | Ireland, Scotland, England
Full Title | *Memoirs of the Extraordinary Life, Works, and Discoveries of Martin Scriblerus*

The seventeen short chapters of the *Memoirs of Scriblerus*, finalized by Pope, offer a series of narratives that originated in a project begun in 1713, and continued at informal meetings of the Scriblerus Club, which met in the lodgings Dr. Arbuthnot occupied in St. James's Palace. The Club began to break up with the departure of Swift from London, and completely with the Queen's death in 1714. The project was, however, continued by correspondence, making early use of the recently established postal service.

The *Memoirs* draw on the rich store of satirical writing in Europe: from classical sources such as Horace and Lucian to later writers such as Rabelais, Erasmus, and Cervantes. The "learned phantome" Martinus Scriblerus has with "capacity enough, dipped into every art and science, but injudiciously." The Scriblerians target the modern age as the site of vaunting, false taste, corruption, and bad faith. In their critique of modern writing in the expanding print culture, they contrast ancient grandeur, passion, dignity, reason, and common sense with modern excess and venal behavior.

Here many strategies are employed: direct narrative, comic analysis, and exposition. Some of the works of the Scriblerians are themselves related to the *Memoirs*: for instance, Pope's *Dunciad*, Swift's *Gulliver's Travels*, Gay's *The Beggar's Opera*. Nor are the *Memoirs* without modern descendants, such as J. K. Toole's *A Confederacy of Dunces* (1980). **AR**

"Ye gods! annihilate but space and time, And make two lovers happy."

🔵 An anonymous 1729 print represents Pope as a monkey in a papal tiara, and below cites his own satirical verses against him.

Pamela

Samuel Richardson

Lifespan | *b.* 1689 (England), *d.* 1761
First Published | 1742
First Published by | C. Rivington (London)
Full Title | *Pamela: or, Virtue Rewarded*

"*O that I had never left my Rags nor my Poverty, to be thus expos'd to Temptations on one hand, or Disgusts on the other! How happy was I a-while ago!*"

◉ Pamela pictured at her writing desk, which she occupies at length to create the epistolary material of the novel.

Pamela sparked an unprecedented degree of public debate. The novel consists of letters written by fifteen-year old Pamela Andrews, the beautiful servant of wealthy Mr. B—. Pamela resists Mr. B—'s increasingly forceful efforts to seduce her, until, chastened by her virtue, he marries her. *Pamela* does not end with the heroine's marriage however, but follows her struggle to establish herself in her new role, and to gain acceptance from Mr. B.—'s peers.

Pamela is a novel about the abuse of power and the correct way to resist. For all Pamela's insistence that "virtue" is her only defense, she is really empowered by language—something that makes her resistance to her social superior a political as well as a moral act. Despite plotting a provincial servant girl as his heroine, Richardson's critique of the upper classes is limited; Pamela's "reward," after all, is to ascend into their ranks. Pamela herself suggests that Mr. B.—'s crime is not merely his sexual incontinence, but his failure to fulfil his pastoral role as her "Master."

Pamela was praised by some as a handbook of virtuous behavior, while others denounced it as thinly disguised pornography. A slew of parodies appeared in *Pamela*'s wake (most notably Fielding's *Shamela*) arguing that Pamela manipulates her sexuality for personal gain; that Richardson's moral intentions for the novel had been corrupted by the titillating subject matter. These ambiguities are what make *Pamela* so fascinating, for the modern reader no less than Richardson's contemporaries. **RH**

Clarissa

Samuel Richardson

Lifespan | *b.*1689 (England), *d.*1761
First Published | 1749
First Published by | Samuel Richardson (London)
Full Title | *Clarissa: or, The History of a Young Lady*

Richardson's ambitious narrative of tragic seduction is traced through the hundreds of letters written between Clarissa Harlowe, her confidante Anna Howe, the charming, but also cruel and duplicitous seducer Lovelace, and a supporting cast of family and acquaintances. In reading them, we find ourselves slowly absorbed into their individual personalities. Meaning is thus accumulated in each successive letter, but their sequence has its own dramatic structure and tension, maintained for the novel's length. Through this we are made to confront not only Lovelace's terrible manipulations, but also his power of allusive evocation, which flow from the same source. In a similar manner, Clarissa triumphantly claims her constant self, virtuous through and beyond death, but is reliant upon a complementary capacity for self-deception that uses the measure of her pen to calculate the distance between thought and action in those she observes. Henry James counted himself among *Clarissa*'s later admirers, perhaps because Richardson's achievement offered him a model for his own: the prose of suspicion, uncovering a similarly disconcerting awareness between its lines.

Like Marcel Proust's *Remembrance of Things Past* (1913–27), the sheer scale of *Clarissa* means that it can seem a novel that is more talked about than read. Yet for those readers who are prepared to spend time with it, *Clarissa* offers a proportionate amount of satisfaction. **DT**

Roderick Random

Tobias George Smollett

Lifespan | *b.*1721 (Scotland), *d.*1771
First Published | 1749
First Published by | J. Osborn (London)
Full Title | *The Adventures of Roderick Random*

Smollett's first novel is an account of the varied adventures of the quixotic Roderick Random. Praised for Smollett's depiction of the harsh realities of British naval life, *Roderick Random* is more than just a vivid account of life aboard a man-of-war. The novel follows Roderick as he travels the world attempting to find his own path both financially and morally. Despite his overriding roguish and crude behaviour, Roderick's education and eloquence help establish him as impoverished but gentlemanly. For Roderick, adversity provides moral education and improvement. However, it is only when he regains his true social standing and reclaims his paternal estate that Roderick is truly reformed.

Despite declaring his love for Narcissa, Roderick repeatedly engages in aimless and indiscriminate sexual relations with other women. His double standards are not consistently punished and he is ultimately rewarded in gaining Narcissa as a wife. However, Smollett's interpolated narrative, "The History of Miss Williams" provides a critical backdrop for Roderick's own sexual activity. This account of a woman who succumbs to her own sexual desire and descends into prostitution provides a sympathetic, although not condoning, portrayal. *Roderick Random* is a novel full of unexpected and peculiar twists and turns, and by the conclusion alert readers cannot entirely forgive Roderick for his debauchery. **LMar**

Tom Jones

Henry Fielding

Lifespan | *b.* 1707 (England), *d.* 1754
First Published | 1749
First Published by | A. Millar (London)
Full Title | *Tom Jones; or, the History of a Foundling*

THE

HISTORY

OF

TOM JONES,

A

FOUNDLING.

In SIX VOLUMES.

By HENRY FIELDING, Efq;

Mores hominum multorum vidit.

LONDON:

Printed for A. MILLAR, over-againſt
Catharine-ſtreet in the *Strand.*
MDCCXLIX.

The title page of the first edition of *Tom Jones*, published in
1749, bears the Latin tag, "He saw the customs of many men."

Michael Angelo Rooker's illustration of 1780 captures
the essentially benign comic verve of Fielding's satire.

Tom Jones is a picaresque comic novel in which
we follow the wanderings and vicissitudes of the
engaging hero as he, born illegitimate, grows up,
falls in love, is unjustly expelled from his foster-
father's home, and roams England. Warmhearted
but impetuous, Tom is repeatedly involved in
fights, misunderstandings, and bawdy adventures.
However, he is eventually narrowly saved from the
gallows and happily united with his true love, Sophia,
while his enemies are variously humiliated.

This is not only a long and complicated novel
but also a great one. Anticipating Dickens at his
best (Dickens reportedly said, "I have been Tom
Jones"), Fielding describes, with gusto, glee, mock-
heroic wit, and sometimes satiric scorn, the rich
variety of life in eighteenth-century England, from
the rural poor to the affluent aristocrats. Like his
friend Hogarth's paintings, Fielding's descriptions
imply the sharp observation of a moralist who is well
aware of the conflict between Christian standards,
which should officially govern social conduct, and
the power of selfishness, folly, and vice in the
world. In the society he depicts, Good Samaritans
are few and far between, and snares await the
innocent at every turn. Nevertheless, like an ironic
yet benevolent Providence, Fielding guides the
deserving lovers through the world's corruption to
their happiness.

Maintaining the spirit of Chaucer, Fielding relished
farcical entanglements and sexual comedy: his hero
is no virgin. Fielding was a brilliant experimentalist
(influencing Sterne), and *Tom Jones* is delightfully
postmodernistic: the narrator repeatedly teasingly
interrupts the action to discuss with the reader the
work's progress—critics are urged to "mind their
own business." **CW**

Fanny Hill

John Cleland

Lifespan | *b.* 1709 (England), *d.* 1789
First Published | 1749
First Published by | G. Fenton (London)
Original Title | *Memoirs of a Woman of Pleasure*

"Truth! Stark naked truth . . ."

◉ Like Cleland himself, the illustrator of *Fanny Hill* presents
erotic acts in a style calculated both to stimulate and amuse.

This book is undoubtedly the most famous erotic novel in English. Published in 1749 (though possibly written, in part, some time earlier), it is rooted in a realistically depicted eighteenth-century London, firmly connecting Cleland's work with that of his contemporaries, Richardson, Fielding, and Smollet.

At the beginning, Fanny is a beautiful fifteen-year-old country girl. Having lost her "innocence," she learns to exploit her sexuality to survive and advance herself in the world. In fashioning this controversial and illicitly popular work, Cleland drew on the largely French fashion for erotic fiction, and the existing genre of "whore's autobiography," which tended to present the whore's life as a warning against the miseries attendant on sexual indulgence. Strikingly, Cleland feels no compulsion to punish Fanny for her promiscuity, and she ends the novel happily married.

Aware that much pornography suffered from repetitiveness, Cleland eschews "crude" or slang terminology for sexual acts or organs, instead producing a dazzling array of metaphors and similes from a seemingly endless supply. Although he unflinchingly depicts the physiological pleasure of sex, for both men and women, Fanny's sexual appetites are surprisingly conservative—while relishing various heterosexual acts, she is conflicted about her own lesbian encounter, and repeatedly speaks with disgust about male homosexuality.

After surviving more than two centuries' worth of moral opprobrium, Cleland's masterpiece has now emerged as an important work in the development of the novel. It still, however, divides readers, between those who find its vibrant depiction of sexuality liberating, and those who see it as a transparent vehicle for male gratification. **RH**

Peregrine Pickle
Tobias George Smollett

The exploits of the egotistical Peregrine Pickle are the subject of Smollett's second novel. While the episodic construction and interpolated narratives are reminiscent of *Roderick Random*, *Peregrine Pickle* is more than a repetition of an earlier narrative. Peregrine is a fallible hero and this is emphasiszed by the frequently critical tone of the third-person omniscient narrator. The son of a short line of moderately successful merchants, Peregrine is despised by his own mother and adopted by his eccentric uncle, whose exploits provide much of the humor in the early part of the novel. Peregrine enjoys a privileged education that compounds his own misguided sense of self-importance. He undertakes the Grand Tour, traveling through Europe amid a profusion of excess, sexual intrigue, and rakish conduct and, on his return to London, attempts to ingratiate himself into fashionable society and political circles. He aspires to marriage with an heiress as a way of rising to the ranks of the nobility. However, Peregrine's ambitions are thwarted by his own destructive and corrupt behavior, demonstrating his inability to conduct himself in a manner appropriate to his financial standing. Eventually, during his incarceration in the Fleet prison, Pickle reforms. He marries Emilia and adopts the life of a country gentleman removed from the evils of fashionable society.

Despite its scatological humor, Smollett's satire engages with serious concerns such as the arbitrariness of French justice and the threat posed to social order by contemporary commercialization. Peregrine has to learn the responsibilities and privileges of social position before he can truly value his ultimate reward: a quiet life of felicity with his beloved Emilia. **LMar**

Lifespan | *b.*1721 (Scotland), *d.*1771
First Published | 1751 (revised 1758)
First Published by | T. Smollett (London)
Full Title | *The Adventures of Peregrine Pickle*

"... a pert jackanapes."

◉ Peregrine rescues the scantily-clad Emilia from a burning inn, a typical picaresque episode from Smollett's satire.

Amelia

Henry Fielding

Lifespan | *b.* 1707 (England), *d.* 1754
First Published | 1751
First Published by | A. Millar (London)
Original Language | English

Amelia, Fielding's final novel, is quite unlike his exuberant earlier fictions. With a sober, even documentary narrative technique, Fielding focuses unblinkingly upon the squalor, misery, and variety of the city of London, which he approaches with an uncompromising moral tone. For its first readers, this production of Fielding's combined the indecorous exposure of London life with a soft, unfocused sentimentality, failing to satisfy in any of its aspects.

It is precisely in these topics of condemnation, however, that the strength of *Amelia* lies. Within a few pages of its beginning, the novel's hero, Captain Booth, is thrown into the depths of Newgate Prison. There he encounters a gallery of grotesques whose unflinching physical descriptions are matched by a precise moral commentary, elucidating the systematic failures and hypocrisies responsible for their creation. Booth is himself lured back to the gaming table despite his admiration for the good. His wife, Amelia, provides us with a paradigm of that restoring virtue, set brilliantly against the temptresses of the world she inhabits.

In tracing her warmth and loyalty, Fielding does not fall prey to credulous sentimentality. Rather, he produces an encomium for the redeeming power of married life. Not only does Amelia's patient loyalty bring her husband economic security and social status, their achievement of domestic contentment displays the moral sense that will be required to reform the country they inhabit. **DT**

The Female Quixote

Charlotte Lennox

Lifespan | *b.* 1727 (U.S.), *d.* 1804
First Published | 1752
First Published by | A. Millar (London)
Alternate Title | *The Adventures of Arabella*

Charlotte Lennox's second novel, *The Female Quixote*, is a forerunner of Jane Austen's *Northanger Abbey*. In the absence of any broader education, Lennox's heroine Arabella's understanding of the world has been drawn entirely from seventeenth-century French Romances. Lennox comically displays the pitfalls of Arabella's failure to distinguish between fiction and reality. She expects lovers to fall at her feet, sees danger and disguise in commonplace situations, and breaks social strictures regarding appropriate female behavior. Arabella's illusion that the world conforms to the conventions of the romance novel gives her a confidence in herself and her position that is overturned by her eventual re-education. By showing the absurdity of Arabella's fantasy, Lennox subtly exposes how little power women in eighteenth-century society actually had. Rationalism finally triumphs over fantasy in the novel, and Arabella learns about her real position in society.

Although modern readers may find Lennox's comedy repetitious at times, the novel is still saved by the likeability of its main character—readers are disappointed when she finally succumbs to social convention, and touched by the genuine hilarity of the situations she creates for herself. Yet while readers may laugh at Arabella's naïveté, Lennox's exposure of the dangers of letting the imagination run wild does bring into question the eighteenth-century practice of limiting women's education. **EG-G**

Candide

Voltaire

Lifespan | *b.* 1694 (France), *d.* 1778
First Published | 1759, by G. & P. Cramer (Geneva)
Original Title | *Candide, ou l'Optimisme*
Given Name | François-Marie Arouet

Voltaire's *Candide* was influenced by various atrocities of the mid-eighteenth century, most notably an earthquake in Lisbon, the outbreak of the horrific Seven Years' War in the German states, and the unjust execution of the English Admiral John Byng. This philosophical tale is often hailed as a paradigmatic text of the Enlightenment, but it is also an ironic attack on the optimistic beliefs of the Enlightenment. Voltaire's critique is directed at Leibniz' principle of sufficient reason, which maintains that nothing can be so without there being a reason why it is so. The necessary consequence of this principle is the belief that the actual world must be the best of all possible worlds, since anything else would be inconsistent with the creative power of God.

At the opening of the novel, its eponymous hero, the young Candide, schooled in this optimistic philosophy by his tutor Pangloss, is ejected from the magnificent castle in which he is raised. The rest of the novel details the multiple hardships and disasters which Candide and his various companions meet in their travels. These include war, rape, theft, hanging, shipwreck, earthquake, cannibalism, and slavery. As these experiences gradually erode Candide's optimistic belief, the novel mercilessly lampoons science, philosophy, religion, government, and literature. A caustic and comic satire of the social ills of its day, Candide's reflections on human injustice, disaster, suffering, and hope remain as pertinent now as ever. **SD**

Mon capitaine.... tuait tout ce qui s'opposait à sa rage .

Candide , Ch. XI.

J. Moreau le S.ᵗ del.   Villeroy Sculp.ᵗ

"In this country [England] it is thought well to kill an admiral from time to time to encourage the others."

◉ A romantic illustration from an 1809 edition of *Candide* is captioned: "My captain … killed all that stood in the path of his fury."

Rasselas

Samuel Johnson

Lifespan | *b.*1709 (England), *d.*1784
First Published | 1759
First Published by | R. & J. Dodsley (London)
Full Title | *The Full History of Rasselas, Prince of Abissinia*

Dr. Johnson undoubtedly achieved greatest renown, and earned his place in history, with his seminal *Dictionary of the English Language*. But less well known is his first and only novel, *Rasselas*, published four years later, which tells the story of its eponymous hero, the Prince of Abissinia. Rasselas lives in the happy valley in which he and the other royal sons and daughters are kept secluded from the vagaries of human life, with their every want and desire provided for, until they succeed to the throne. By the age of twenty-six, however, Rasselas is dissatisfied and restless with this life in which he wants for nothing. Guided by a learned man, Imlac, he escapes from the valley in the company of his sister Nakayah and sets out to explore the world and discover the source of true happiness.

A parable in the literary tradition of Bunyan's *Pilgrim's Progress*, Rasselas' adventures and lengthy conversations provide a vehicle for Johnson's moral reflections on an astonishingly broad range of topics. These include poetry, learning, solitude, reason and passion, youth and age, parents and children, marriage, power, grief, madness, and desire.

Although Samuel Johnson's abilities as a novelist are overshadowed by his strengths as a moralist in this book, *Rasselas* remains of interest today both as a testament to the predominant concerns of the Enlightenment, and for the humor and universality of Johnson's reflections on these topics. **SD**

Julie; or, the New Eloise

Jean-Jacques Rousseau

Lifespan | *b.*1712 (Switzerland), *d.*1778 (France)
First Published | 1760
First Published by | Duchesne (Paris)
Original Title | *Julie; ou, la nouvelle Héloïse*

Julie, Rousseau's first novel, is modeled on the medieval story of *Eloise*, and the forbidden love between herself and her tutor, Abelard. Yet in *Julie*, Rousseau transforms secrecy and sinfulness into renunciation and redemption, in which it is the pupil and not the master who makes the central claim on our attention. Julie's relationship with her teacher, Saint-Preux, reformulates the twelfth-century conflict between bodily desire and religious purpose into a characteristically eighteenth-century study of right behavior. In this epistolary novel, Rousseau links the classical tradition of civic virtue with its Enlightenment counterpart of domestic order and the new birth of individual feeling which was to eventually culminate in the Romantic movement.

As befits this apparently paradoxical transition, the thematic structure of *Julie* is both rigorous and odd. In the first half, Julie alternately resists and is consumed by Saint-Preux's passion, which leads to his banishment from her father's house. By the second, he has returned to the new estate formed by Julie and her husband, Wolmar, where all three happily co-exist in the cultivation of both mind and landscape. In this static Elysium, the dangerous desires of the novel's first part are ethically recapitulated. For readers, this allegorical mirroring of virtue and desire makes Julie's triumph somewhat suspect. However, the irreducibility of the problem makes the difficulty of Rousseau's novel a persistently contemporary one. **DT**

Rameau's Nephew

Denis Diderot

Lifespan | b. 1713 (France), d. 1784
First Published | 1805 (composed 1761–1784)
First Published by | Goeschen (Leipzig)
Original French Title | Le Neveu de Rameau

Diderot is one of the most important figures of the French Enlightenment, a contemporary and equal of Rousseau and Voltaire. As well as editing the world's first Encyclopedia, he managed to create a body of work that includes novels, philosophical dialogues, scientific essays, art, and drama criticism. Diderot was a polymath of verve and originality, and nowhere is this more visible than in Rameau's Nephew. Part novel, part essay, part Socratic dialogue, it expanded the boundaries of what is possible in fiction.

The action is straightforward. While taking a stroll in the Palais-Royal gardens the narrator, a philosopher, bumps into the nephew of the great composer Rameau, and they become engaged in conversation. Underlying their discussion is the question of morality and the pursuit of happiness, which they approach from opposite poles. The prudish philosopher argues for the Greek ideal of virtue being equal to happiness. The nephew, witty cynic and lovable scoundrel, shows that conventional morality is nothing other than vanity, that the pursuit of wealth is society's guiding principle, and that what matters is how you are perceived, not how you actually are. The book is not a simple morality tale, however. Like its tragicomic hero, it is a complex challenge to all forms of reactionary thought and behavior. Too controversial to be published in Diderot's lifetime, it is also a savage indictment of the moral hypocrisy, intellectual pretensions, and spiritual vacuity of eighteenth-century Parisian society. **AL**

Émile; or, On Education

Jean-Jacques Rousseau

Lifespan | b. 1712 (Switzerland), d. 1778 (France)
First Published | 1762
First Published by | Duchesne (Paris)
Original Title | Émile; ou, De l'éducation

Rousseau's philosophical novel charts the ideal education of an imaginary pupil, Émile, from birth to adulthood. Émile is not taught to read until he himself thirsts for the knowledge, and his experience of literature is deliberately limited. According to Rousseau, Robinson Crusoe supplies the best treatise on an education according to nature, and it is the first book Émile will read.

Rousseau's educational philosophy regarding religion was also radical. He advocates delaying a child's religious education to prevent indoctrination or ill-conceived notions about divinity. Émile is thus not taught according to one doctrine but is equipped with the knowledge and reason to choose for himself. Early adolescence is a time which demands learning by experience rather than academic study. Émile is seen to pose and answer his own questions based on his observations of nature. During the transition between adolescence and adulthood Rousseau begins to focus on Émile's socialization and his sexuality.

In the final book, "Sophie: or Woman," Rousseau turns his attention toward the education of girls and young women. In this book, he disapproves of serious learning for girls on the basis that men and women have different virtues. Men should study truth; women should aim for flattery and tact. Rousseau's novel concludes with the marriage of Émile and Sophie, who intend to live a secluded but fruitful life together in the country. **LMar**

The Castle of Otranto

Horace Walpole

Lifespan | *b.* 1717 (England), *d.* 1797
First Published | 1765
First Published by | W. Bathoe & T. Lowndes (London)
Pseudonym | Onuphrio Muralto

The Castle of Otranto, Walpole's only novel, enjoys pride of place as the founding text of the gothic genre. The central narrative revolves around the prince of Otranto (the tyrannous Manfred) and his family, and develops from a mysterious incident at the inception of the story: the death of Conrad, Manfred's son and heir, crushed under the weight of a gigantic plumed helmet. This supernatural occurrence unleashes a train of events that leads to the restoration of the rightful heir to the title of Otranto. These events take place principally in the family castle, well appointed with vaults and secret passageways, which becomes the scene, as well as the embodiment, of mysterious deaths and hauntings. Largely a fantasy set in the chivalric Middle Ages, the novel nevertheless deals in violent emotions, and places its characters in psychological extremis. Cruelty, tyranny, eroticism, usurpation—all have become, along with the setting, the common currency of gothic narratives.

Walpole claimed that the story first came to him in a dream, and that he had been "choked by visions and passions" during its composition. Concerned for the reception his work might receive, he not only first published it under a pseudonym, but went so far as to pretend that it was the translation of a sixteenth-century Italian manuscript. The whimsy of Walpole's literary experiment is mirrored in the construction of his own gothic revival mansion, Strawberry Hill, which can still be visited today. **ST**

The Vicar of Wakefield

Oliver Goldsmith

Lifespan | *b.* 1730 (Ireland), *d.* 1774 (England)
First Published | 1766
First Printed by | B. Collins for F. Newbury (London)
Composed | 1761–1762

The Vicar of Wakefield, as the title suggests, tells the story of Dr. Primrose and his large family, who on the surface live an idyllic life in a rural parish. This tranquillity is disrupted by sudden impoverishment, which sets the plot in motion. The plot, though thin, includes thwarted marriages, unscrupulous behavior, lost children, fire, imprisonment, various disguises, and mistaken identity. Vulnerability attenuates the situation of all the characters who, like the vicar himself, are generally virtuous, but also susceptible to foolish and naïve behavior. The vicar is the novel's main narrator, which in itself produces a number of comic ironies; to fill in gaps, however, there are numerous stories within stories. The novel contains sentimental set-pieces, but its overall register is richly comic. Both the disasters that befall the characters and the equally dramatic reversals of fortune, are amusing.

One of the most striking aspects of Goldsmith's minor classic, clearly, is its heterogeneity. Not only is the plot untidy and digressive, but the text itself includes non-fictional elements, such as poems, sermons, and various disquisitions on politics, legal punishment, and poetics. All this reflects the diversity of Goldsmith's output as a writer: he was a poet, a playwright, and a novelist, but also took on a great deal of hack-work to make a living. **ST**

❯ Among the book illustrators of the time, Thomas Rowlandson made twenty-four illustrations for Goldsmith's masterpiece.

TRISTRAM SHANDY. VOL. II. Ch. 6. P. 17
Corporal Trim reading the Sermon to
Shandy's Father, Dr. Slop & Uncle Toby.

W. Hogarth delin.   Printed for C. Cooke

Tristram Shandy

Laurence Sterne

The book's full title, *The Life and Opinions of Tristam Shandy, Gentleman*, suggests a loosely biographical form, but the eponymous author-narrator scarcely gets so far as his third year, and remains studiously circumspect about his own opinions. While little of Tristram's life is divulged, the book generates an intimate relationship between the processes of reading and writing. Through digressions and interruptions, narrative expectations are dismantled with a freedom and vivacity that eliminates the very notion of plot. With its inventive conversation between spoken idiom and written circumspection, it is mischievously friendly, and as lewdly suggestive as anything that had ever been written. This book is the archetypal "experimental" novel, prefiguring modern and postmodern fiction. From Rabelais, Sterne develops comic fantasy, bawdy grotesque, and learned wit. From Cervantes, Sterne takes the picaresque combustion of narrative form, modulating into a more quixotic, but nevertheless realistic dissection of human folly. Portraits of Tristram's father, his mother, Uncle Toby, Yorick, Corporal Trim, and Widow Wadman, build up an oblique but intimate representation of family life. The comic brilliance of the literary surface obscures Sterne's deeper psychological realism, his almost Proustian analysis of sentimentality, notably the well-meant but ridiculous erudition of Tristram's father. The modulation of Toby's interest in warfare into his love-affair offers a fine comic characterization of the links between speech, personality, and the groin.

For all its garrulous intimacy, Sterne leaves much to the imagination. The book's diplomatic irony provides a subtle critique of the English gentleman, from class and sexuality to all the unacknowledged delicacies of property and propriety. **DM**

Lifespan | *b.* 1713 (Ireland), *d.* 1768 (England)
First Published | 1759–1767
First Published by| J. Dodsley (London)
Serialized | Nine volumes

⬆ Laurence Sterne's complex imagination found expression through wit, lewdness, sentiment, and garrulous rhetoric.

◀ William Hogarth produced prints of scenes from *Tristram Shandy* in the 1760s that have defined visualization of the book ever since.

A Sentimental Journey

Laurence Sterne

Lifespan | *b.*1713 (Ireland), *d.*1768 (England)
First Published | 1768, by G. Faulkner (Dublin)
Full Title | *A Sentimental Journey Through France and Italy by Mr. Yorick*

Overshadowed by *Tristram Shandy*, Sterne's shorter novel is nevertheless a comic gem. Combining autobiographical anecdote, incidental fiction, and pastiche of travel writing, the book chronicles the journey of Yorick and his servant La Fleur through France. The Grand Tour, that education in continental manners and art so important to the English gentleman, figures as an implied object of satire. However, there is not much grand about this journey, rather, we are confronted with a belittling and microscopic investigation of sensibility.

More than a mere story, the principle pleasure of this novel is its playful manipulation of conversational intimacy. The manner of the telling takes priority, while the author-narrator leaves different incidents suspended between sentimental interpretations and a more knowing realism. One notable example is a man lamenting his dead ass, related as an allegory from nature of how feeling toward an animal might provide an edifying example of humane fellow-feeling. The mourner has nevertheless overworked and starved the ass he mourns. Swiftly juxtaposing this with the unfeeling lash given to the animals on which the author's transport depends, the allegory is shot through with double entendres. Such gulfs between sentiment, material conditions, and narrative point of view are always close to the surface, even if financial considerations, earthly passions, and a continuously implied eroticism are politely deflected. **DM**

The Man of Feeling

Henry Mackenzie

Lifespan | *b.*1745 (Scotland), *d.*1831
First Published | 1771
First Published by | T. Cadell (London)
First Published | Anonymously

The first anonymously published edition of *The Man of Feeling* sold out in little more than six weeks, likening its cataclysmic effects to the stir caused by the publication of Rousseau's *The New Eloise* a decade earlier. Marking a crucial cultural moment in the history of literature, the "editor" of *The Man of Feeling* purports to offer his readers an historical account of the experiences of young Harley, the eponymous man of feeling himself. Each fictional episode that follows is designed with the express intention of exploring a particular emotive reaction, be it an emphatically non-erotic identification of a London prostitute, or the circulation of affection between a father and his estranged offspring. The represented emotions range broadly from pity, sympathy, and empathy to charity and benevolence.

The turns of plot in *The Man of Feeling* seem secondary to the careful cultivation of emotional response. Each tableau is linked to the next without much discernible concern for the generation of narrative suspense, while other sections, the editor informs his reader, are either missing or incomplete. Even so, the emphasis which this fiction brought to bear upon the emotional responses of both character and reader alike would prove crucial to a range of eighteenth-century writers, but would also provide much of the aesthetic foundation that later novelists could safely take for granted. As Dickens so well understood, the reader of fiction was there primarily to be moved. **DT**

Humphry Clinker

Tobias George Smollett

Lifespan | *b.* 1721 (Scotland), *d.* 1771
First Published | 1771
First Published by | W. Johnston & B. Collins (London)
Full Title | *The Expedition of Humphry Clinker*

Smollett's last novel is an epistolary narrative detailing the travels through Britain of Matt Bramble and his company including the servant hero, the impoverished Humphry Clinker. The letters reveal the characters of their very different authors. Matt Bramble is a hypochondriac misanthrope, his sister Tabitha, an aging husband-hunter, Jery Melford their nephew, an exuberant Oxford student, his sister Lydia a naïve sentimental romantic, and Tabitha's maid, Wyn Jenkins, a virtually illiterate social climber. These varied points of view provide a lively and wide-ranging narrative that engages the reader directly in deciphering not only the progress and adventures of the party but also the targets of Smollett's satire. The narrative allows for multiple interpretations of the events that unfold, and there is no one authoritative version. However, Clinker's moral integrity and religious zeal are constant throughout the accounts.

The party continually encounters mishap, with Clinker invariably at the center. Such mishaps include duels, romantic intrigues, jealous encounters, a false imprisonment, and innumerable disputes both large and small. Finally the love matches are made, and the plot tied up. Unlike Smollett's other titular heroes, Clinker reaps a reward that is unquestionably deserved. His naivety regarding the ways of the world and his morality are admirable traits, against which the flaws of his companions and his society are clearly exposed. **LMar**

"The capital is become an overgrown monster; which like a dropsical head, will in time leave the body and extremities without nourishment and support."

⊙ A suitably caricatural representation of the hypochondriac Matt Bramble engaged in a close encounter with a young widow.

The Sorrows of Young Werther

Johann Wolfgang von Goethe

Lifespan | *b.* 1749 (Germany), *d.* 1832
First Published | 1774
First Published by | Weygandsche Buchhandlung
Original Title | *Die Leiden des jungen Werthers*

"I shall perish under the splendor of these visions!"

🔵 German artist Johan Tischbein's famous portrait of his friend Goethe in the Roman Campagna was painted in 1786.

🔵 French composer Jules Massenet's late nineteenth-century operatic version of Werther is tender and romantic.

The Sorrows of Young Werther, the novel which first made Goethe internationally famous, tells a story of a young man afflicted by a rather extreme dose of eighteenth-century sensibility: Werther is a case study of over-reliance on emotion, imagination, and close introspection. Our hero is sent to the fictional village of Walheim on family business where he meets and promptly falls in love with Lotte. This attractive young woman, meanwhile, is engaged to another, the rational and rather dull local official Albert. Once established, this triangle places Werther at a complete impasse, and the impossibility of a happy resolution drives him to take his own life. Part of the novel's intrigue has always been its loose relation to actual events: Goethe's relationship with Charlotte Buff, who was engaged to his close friend Kestner, and the love-related suicide of another friend, Karl Jerusalem (who borrowed pistols from an unsuspecting Kestner for the deed). Another element of the novel's success was its effective use of the epistolary form. The narrative unfolds initially through Werther's letters to a single correspondent. When Werther's psychological state deteriorates, a fictive editor steps in, and the last part of the novel is his arrangement of Werther's final scraps and notes.

The novel struck a powerful chord in its own time, and its appearance was followed by what can only be called Werther mania: would-be Werthers wore his trademark blue jacket and yellow waistcoat, there was even Werther eau-de-cologne and china depicting scenes from the novel. Legend also has it that there were copy-cat suicides, which alarmed Goethe, since his depiction of Werther was more critical than laudatory. The novel was extensively revised in 1787 for a second version, which has become the basis for most modern editions. **ST**

THÉÂTRE NATIONAL DE L'OPÉRA COMIQUE

Drame lyrique
d'après
GOETHE
par M.M.
Edouard Blau
Paul Milliet
et Georges Hartmann

WERTHER

Musique
de
J. MASSENET

En vente au MENESTREL 2bis Rue Vivienne
HEUGEL & Cie Editeurs pour tous Pays. PARIS

Ste DES IMPres LEMERCIER. PARIS

Evelina

Fanny Burney

Lifespan | *b.* 1752 (England), *d.* 1840
First Published | 1778, anonymously
Full Title | *Evelina; or The History of a Young Lady's Entrance Into the World*

🔵 Fanny Burney was a diarist as well as a novelist, recording memorable experiences of life at the court of George III.

Samuel Johnson remarked of the twenty-six year-old Burney's debut novel *Evelina* that it "seems a work that should result from long experience and deep and intimate knowledge of the world." Her sense for character psychology and awkward social comedy are amply on show in *Evelina*. Adapting the form of the epistolary novel from predecessors such as Samuel Richardson, Burney traces the fortunes of her young heroine as she travels up from the country to negotiate the social world of London for the first time. Here she encounters a stream of suitors and some long-lost relatives whose grotesque lack of breeding drives her to the brink of physical collapse. She is eventually acknowledged as her absent father's true daughter. One of the novel's great strengths is the way in which Burney filters the bustle of London society through the shy consciousness of Evelina. In addition, the growth of her feelings toward the righteous Lord Orville is subtly and ironically rendered. Love-struck teenagers often enjoy writing down the names of their crushes, and there is a charming naturalism in the way Burney has Evelina mention Lord Orville slightly more often than necessary.

Evelina's comedy of manners may itself feel a little "mannered" at times, especially when set next to the novels of the writer she influenced most directly, Jane Austen. Burney is vulnerable to the same accusations about the limits of her social scene as are sometimes leveled at Austen—there is no urban squalor here. But for its depiction of psychological interactions in a solidly imagined social setting, *Evelina* marks a high point in late eighteenth-century fiction, one which proves that this kind of wit didn't just begin in 1811 with Austen's *Sense and Sensibility*. **BT**

Reveries of a Solitary Walker

Jean-Jacques Rousseau

Rousseau—philosopher, social and political theorist, novelist, and proto-Romantic—was one of the eighteenth century's leading intellectuals. *Reveries of the Solitary Walker*, the last book he wrote, is a wonderfully lyrical, heartfelt, and somewhat obsessive account of an aging man's reckoning with his past. Rousseau achieved a great deal of notoriety during his lifetime from a succession of popular and hugely important works. By attacking the state religion and denouncing contemporary society as morally corrupt, he not only challenged the establishment but also the Enlightenment thought that prevailed in the Parisian salons. Rousseau became the subject of a long-lasting campaign of derision and humiliation, and eventually went into exile.

The Reveries of the Solitary Walker finds Rousseau, "alone and neglected," torn between his love of solitude and his yearning for company, trying to assuage his crippling self-doubt and irrepressible need to address his persecutors. The novel's lasting appeal stems from this compelling tension between his sober, meditative philosophizing and his impassioned rage against the ills of society. Rousseau wants to show that he is at peace with himself, blissfully disengaged from society, and yet he is also constantly betrayed by his sense of injustice and pride. The combination of his circumstances and his inner turmoil make him one of the first—and most fascinating—modern examples of the prototype of the literary outsider.

Reveries is therefore a vital precursor to the great novels of isolation and despair by writers such as Dostoevsky, Beckett, and Salinger that have had such an enormous impact on the development of the novel. **AL**

Lifespan | *b.* 1712 (Switzerland), *d.* 1778 (France)
First Published | 1782
First Published in | *Oeuvres Complètes* (Poinçot)
Original Title | *Les Rêveries du promeneur solitaire*

CHOCOLAT POULAIN
GOUTEZ ET COMPAREZ! QUALITÉ SANS RIVALE

98. JEAN-JACQUES ROUSSEAU

⊙ Rousseau is depicted as the "solitary walker" on this card, one of a series on French writers given away with Poulain chocolate.

Dangerous Liaisons

Pierre Choderlos de Laclos

Lifespan | *b.* 1741 (France), *d.* 1803 (Italy)
First Published | 1782
First Published by | Durand (Paris)
Original Title | *Les Liaisons Dangereuses*

A recent series of successful film, theater, and ballet adaptations suggest that this gripping tale of love, deceit, and the art of seduction still holds a powerful grip on our collective imagination. Written by a lieutenant in the French army, *Les Liaisons Dangereuses* manages to shock and delight in equal measure. The action takes place among the aristocratic circles of pre-revolutionary France and centers on the ruthless, charming libertine Valmont and his rival, one-time lover, and partner in crime, Merteuil. Valmont is gifted with wealth, wit, and intelligence, and leads an idle life guided by a self-imposed code of conduct: to seek ever-greater glory in his seduction of unsuspecting society women. Merteuil is a sexually liberated young widow, of equal intelligence and malice, but unlike Valmont has to play the role expected of her by society, and so appears deeply serious and virtuous. Together, they create a complex web of relationships based on betrayal, lies, and sexual misconduct. Although all they truly seek is one another's admiration, their constant attempts to outdo the other has disastrous consequences as jealousy and hubris combine to undermine their own deeply flawed principles.

The use Laclos makes of the popular epistolary form is exemplary. For it is precisely in the delicious recounting of the events that his two leading characters derive their pleasure—a pleasure shared by the reader as we indulge in the eloquence and exquisite cruelty of this captivating masterpiece. **AL**

Confessions

Jean-Jacques Rousseau

Lifespan | *b.* 1712 (Switzerland), *d.* 1778 (France)
First Published | 1782, in *Oeuvres Complètes*
First Published by | Poinçot (Paris)
Part 2 Published | 1788, by P. Du Peyrou

Unpublished until after his death, Rousseau's *Confessions* are a landmark of European literature, and perhaps the most influential autobiography ever written. This is a work that had a defining impact not only on the novel, but on the development of the autobiography as a literary genre. Although Rousseau predicts having no imitators in this vein, he was seriously mistaken. Goethe, Tolstoy, and Proust all acknowledged their debt to Rousseau's pioneering attempt to represent his life truthfully—warts and all.

Rousseau famously argued that man's innate good nature was corrupted by society. Yet in the *Confessions* Rousseau acknowledges that he often behaved appallingly. One incident in particular stands out. When working as a young servant in the household of a wealthy Geneva aristocrat, Rousseau describes how he stole valuable old ribbon and then blamed the theft on a servant girl, Marion. Rousseau comments that he was "the victim of that malicious play of intrigue that has thwarted me all my life," simultaneously accepting responsibility for his actions and denying it.

Rousseau freely admits the contradictory nature of his character, one he felt was forced on him by circumstances beyond his control. Indeed, in line with his desire not to mislead the reader, he undoubtedly exaggerates his own sins and misdemeanors just to prove his point, which serves as yet another paradox of this compelling, frustrating, and vitally important work. **AH**

Cecilia

Fanny Burney

Lifespan | *b.* 1752 (England), *d.* 1840
First Published | 1782
First Published by | T. Payne and T. Cadell (London)
Full Title | *Cecilia, or Memoirs of an Heiress*

Cecilia Beverley is beautiful, intelligent, and an heiress to a large fortune. However, her wealth comes with a price: any man she marries must take her surname if she is to inherit. When Cecilia falls in love with a son from the proud Delvile family, her chance for future happiness seems bleak. Like another famous eighteenth-century novel by Jane Austen, a great admirer of Burney, this is a novel about pride and prejudice, and how both must be overcome in order for love and happiness to be achieved.

Fanny Burney's characters are brilliantly drawn, and the novel combines comedy, drama, and sharp social critique effortlessly. As with Burney's other novels *Evelina* and *Camilla*, *Cecilia* also offers a tour of eighteenth-century public social spaces—the opera house, the ballroom, the masquerade—each of which is used as a fitting stage for the characters to act out their various intrigues, follies, and dramas. While the novel begins relatively lightly, as the reader is drawn into the narrative, Burney introduces much darker, more gothic themes. Cecilia's integrity and independence in a world that seems dedicated to forcing her to compromise makes her an admirable as well as a likeable, character.

Readers should not be deterred by the length of Burney's novels—they are long because of the surprising twists and turns of the action-packed plots. In fact, all her novels are extremely well-paced, offering a thoroughly entertaining and highly enjoyable read throughout. **EJG**

The 120 Days of Sodom

Marquis de Sade

Lifespan | *b.* 1740 (France), *d.* 1814
First Composed | 1785
Original Title | *Les 120 Journées de Sodome, ou l'école du libertinage*

De Sade composed *The 120 Days of Sodom* while confined in the Bastille, and his only manuscript was lost to him forever when the revolutionary mob stormed the prison on July 14, 1789. Without his knowledge, it passed into the hands of an aristocratic French family and remained there until a corrupt German edition appeared in 1904. The first accurate publication was printed in several volumes between 1931 and 1935.

The book's stated intention is to appall propriety, morality, and the law. It is set at the end of the reign of Louis XIV, a time when war profiteers accumulated vast fortunes quickly and covertly. A group of wealthy libertines decides to pool the female members of their families as sexual resources to be held in common, and they minutely plan an immense and prolonged debauchery. Cycles of suppers devoted to a particular sexual vice are inaugurated before the participants formalize their perversions in a festival of absolute criminal licence in a remote, impregnable, and luxurious château. A complex set of statutes are formulated to preserve order in the midst of myriad acts of rape and murder and it is the arithmetical and permutational aspect of the sexual violence that is perhaps the novel's key. Alone in his cell, de Sade worked out a meticulous, purely imaginative, masturbatory economy of gradual gratification, fixated on images of debasement and cruelty which have been studied as much by clinicians as by gourmands of extremity. **RP**

Vathek

William Beckford

Lifespan | *b.* 1760 (England), *d.* 1844
First Published | 1786, by J. Johnson (London)
Original Language | French
Original Title | *Vathek, Conte Arabe*

Originally written in French when its author was only twenty-one, *Vathek* was inspired in part by William Beckford's sumptuous coming of age celebrations at his magnificent country estate of Fonthill in 1781.

Vathek is at once a comic farce and a tragic parable, drawing upon a prodigious body of learning in order to both revel in and parody the "oriental tale" popular in England since the translation of the *Arabian Nights*. The tale follows the exploits of the Caliph Vathek and his variously grotesque associates on an inexorable journey to damnation—a gloriously inevitable fate given the excesses of his court and his complete disregard for conventional morality. Beckford consciously fabricates a fantastical "eastern" setting to explore individual freedoms in a way that parallels his own controversial predilections—his sexual intemperance culminated in European exile soon after completing the text following a scandal with a young aristocrat.

Described on its publication in England as a combination of "the sombrous grotesque of Dante" with "the terrific greatness of Milton," *Vathek* influenced numerous literary figures including Hawthorne, Poe, Swinburne, and Byron. While it offers a remarkable insight into early orientalist fantasies of the "east," it is this quality, perhaps, that ensures its longevity; the potent combination of sexual and sensory inquiry with a prevailing sense of childlike wonder offers potentially instructive parallels with our own contemporary obsessions. **MD**

Justine

Marquis de Sade

Lifespan | *b.* 1740 (France), *d.* 1814
First Published | 1791
First Published by | Nicolas Massé (Paris)
Original Title | *Justine, ou les malheurs de la vertu*

It is in this novel's full title, *Justine, ou les malheurs de la vertu*, that we can perhaps find the most cogent definition of its continuing power to shock and absorb. De Sade's heroine is good, and because she is good, she suffers without redemption. Like Rochester's earlier poetry in England, de Sade's novels take human bodies and transform them into components within a copulating machine. In the case of *Justine*, it is a device that mathematically converts virtue into suffering with a remainder of readerly pleasure. Justine declares her scruples, flees, pleads for the lives of others, and professes her faith. In return, she is stripped, bitten, slapped, whipped, and penetrated, orally, anally, and vaginally.

In this way, de Sade brutally makes explicit what remains implicit in Richardson's eighteenth-century novel of sentiment, *Clarissa*. The woman's capacity to feel purely and empathetically makes her an object of utter fascination and degradation, perpetually brought down and renewed. This violent eroticism in the relationship between reader and heroine is properly named "sadistic"; de Sade draws us into a desirous complicity with Justine's tormentors and with himself as writer. Though he was committed to an asylum and his texts destroyed, the continuing challenge *Justine* offers to the comforts of our authority are not so easily erased. **DT**

> ❯ De Sade's unfortunate and virtuous heroine prepares to submit to one of a series of acts of violent abuse and sexual degradation.

The Adventures of Caleb Williams

William Godwin

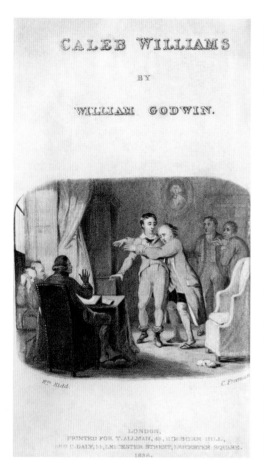

Lifespan | *b.* 1756 (England), *d.* 1836
First Published | 1794, by B. Crosby (London)
Alternate Title | *Things as They Are, or The Adventures of Caleb Williams*

Godwin's *Caleb Williams*, one of the most important and widely read novels of the turbulent 1790s, offers readers a potent mixture of personal history and political commentary. As a young man, self-educated and orphaned, Caleb finds himself in the employ of an enigmatic but apparently honorable local aristocrat, Falkland. Caleb's curiosity, however, leads him to uncover an unsavory fact about Falkland, namely that he had been the murderer of a tyrannous neighboring noble, a crime for which he allowed two innocent members of the local peasantry to be tried and executed. The stories of all these men illustrate the novel's central critique of an ossified class system that sanctions oppression and makes a mockery of the law. Falkland's response to Caleb's discovery of his secret is to follow, frame, and thoroughly persecute him. This had its historical analogue in the suspension of civil liberties when England declared war on Revolutionary France, including particularly those of writers suspected of holding seditious views. Indeed, Godwin's narrative was read, contentiously, as a parable of its times.

Readers have sometimes felt that the novel suffers to the extent that it is a fictional vehicle for Godwin's radical political philosophy, articulated in his *Enquiry Concerning Political Justice* (1793). Yet because of the psychological drama at the center of the plot, it has also been received as a gothic novel. For modern readers, the extreme nature of Caleb's persecution has distinctly Kafkaesque overtones. **ST**

> *"They told me what a fine thing it was to be an Englishman . . ."*

◉ The frontispiece of an 1838 edition of *Caleb Williams* underlines the gothic and sentimental elements in this radical fiction.

The Interesting Narrative

Olaudah Equiano

Lifespan | *b.* 1745 (Nigeria), *d.* 1797 (England)
First Published | 1794, by T. Wilkins (London)
Full Title | *The Interesting Narrative of the Life of Equiano, Or Gustavus Vassa, the African*

Olaudah Equiano's *Interesting Narrative* is a landmark text and a crucial read for anyone seeking to understand the complex issue of race in Britain and the lineage of Afro-British writing. This is the first first-hand account in English of the trans-Atlantic slave trade, presenting the full horror of the experience in order to justify and promote the abolitionist agenda. In a hostile political and literary climate, the success and popularity of Equiano's text (it passed through nine editions in his lifetime) succeeded in furthering this agenda.

The text follows Equiano's journey from his kidnapping in Africa, and incorporates slavery in the British navy; work on slave ships; the purchase of his own freedom; work on plantations; and finally a return to England. It is an explicitly religious meditation that simultaneously forges an identity for the author that is self-consciously both British and African. This is highlighted in his choice of names. While on abolitionist tours, in publications and in public he referred to himself as Gustavus Vassa; in this text his African identity is brought to the foreground, while the narrator is acutely conscious of his existence as both, of the duality of the migrant experience. The recent revelation that Vassa/Equiano may have been born in South Carolina, and that consequently he constructed his African identity, only enhances the remarkable insights the text offers into the ambiguities of such experience. As a result, it is as relevant now as it has ever been. **MD**

"I offer here the history of neither a saint, a hero, nor a tyrant."

◉ This portrait of the ex-slave author as an impeccable eighteenth-century gentleman appeared in the first edition of the book.

The Mysteries of Udolpho

Ann Radcliffe

Lifespan | *b.*1764 (England), *d.*1823
First Published | 1794
First Published by | P. Wogan (Dublin)
Original Language | English

An essential gothic novel, *The Mysteries of Udolpho* remains a classic today. It tells the story of Emily St. Aubert, who is imprisoned by her evil guardian, Montoni, in his grand gothic castle, Udolpho. Terror and suspense dominate Emily's life within Udolpho, as she struggles to withstand Montoni's perfidious schemes and her own psychological breakdown. The narration has a dream-like quality, which reflects Emily's confusion and horror and lends emphasis to the psychological battle she must engage in to survive her nightmares. Radcliffe's spectacular descriptions of landscapes are used partly to reflect emotion in the novel, particularly melancholia and dread—but also tranquillity and happiness. Radcliffe's characters are varied and well-drawn, but where she really succeeds is in the creation of a likeable and strong heroine.

Although rarely considered a feminist, Radcliffe conveys a significant underlying message about the importance of female independence. Despite her apparent weakness and the extremity of her fears, Emily ultimately defeats Montoni through the strength of her own free will and her moral integrity. *The Mysteries of Udolpho* offers not just the supernatural horrors created by the imagination; the true horror that Emily must face is the dark side of human nature, a more potent terror than anything conjured by the mind. **EJG**

Wilhelm Meister's Apprenticeship

Johann Wolfgang von Goethe

Lifespan | *b.*1749 (Germany), *d.*1832
First Published | 1795–1796
First Published by | Unger (Berlin)
Original Title | *Wilhelm Meisters Lehrjahre*

Despite Goethe's forbidding stature, this is a delightful novel. Goethe is engagingly worldly and wry, telling a story of intellectual development and education with warmth, in what is often considered the classic example of the bildungsroman.

Initially disillusioned by unrequited love, Wilhelm Meister travels forth on various adventures, and joins a group of itinerant players which affords him apprenticeship in life. Offering a group portrait of the life of theater, much imbued with Shakespeare, the novel celebrates and then undermines the theatrical vocation. The humane realism of the early parts of the novel deepens and modulates into something altogether more unusual once the surfaces of theatricality and social performance are penetrated, and mysterious characters hint at a different kind of literary symbolism and intellectual purpose. Goethe builds a richly ironic account of human self-development across its knowingly flimsy plot structure, somehow combining the ironizing good humor of Fielding's *Tom Jones* with something more philosophical. Not to be confused with *Wilhelm Meister's Travels*, this novel is especially recommended reading for deluded thespians and wannabe aesthetes. **DM**

❿ Mignon, the heroine of Goethe's *Wilhelm Meister*, represented by early twentieth-century Czech artist Franz Doubek.

The Monk

M. G. Lewis

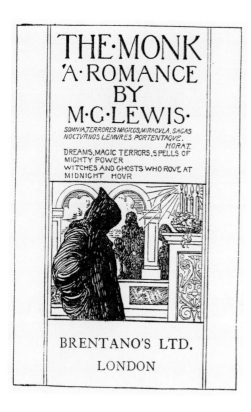

"Who but myself has passed the ordeal of youth, yet sees no single stain upon his conscience? . . . I seek for such a man in vain."

⊙ A 1913 edition updates Lewis' eighteenth-century horror story to appeal to the taste of early twentieth-century decadents.

Lifespan | b. 1775 (England), d. 1818 (at sea)
First Published | 1796
First Published by | J. Bell (London)
Full Title | The Monk: A Romance

An extravagantly, possibly gratuitously, dark gothic novel, M. G. Lewis' *The Monk* caused controversy when it was first published, and remains shocking and chilling today. Unlike Ann Radcliffe, whose gothic fiction always comes with rational explanations, Lewis embraces the supernatural alongside the most extreme and gruesome acts of human depravity and cruelty. The "monk" of the title is Ambrosio, who is admired for his piety. As we discover, however, Ambrosio is truly the most hypocritical and evil representative of the Catholic church imaginable. His crimes begin relatively modestly but quickly escalate into the darkest and most blasphemous acts possible. Nor is he the only character so perfidious—the prioress of a nearby convent shows that she too is capable of barbaric excesses of cruelty. The novel offers an extreme picture of how power, perhaps especially the power held by spiritual figures, can corrupt absolutely.

Despite a convoluted plot, the novel moves at a good pace and the story flows easily. Although Lewis does not employ extravagant descriptions of landscape, *The Monk* is nonetheless a highly visual novel, conjuring vivid and thus memorable images of horror and destruction. This is ultimately a story of the complete crushing of innocence, with no softening redemptive message to lighten the horror. *The Monk* continues both to fascinate and shock today, and few modern novelists could compete with the sheer grotesqueness of Lewis' vision. **EJG**

Camilla

Fanny Burney

Lifespan | *b.* 1752 (England), *d.* 1840
First Published | 1796
First Published by | T. Payne and T. Cadell (London)
Original Language | English

The full title of this novel is *Camilla or A Picture of Youth* and this is precisely what Burney gives us in this, her third novel. *Camilla* tells the story of a lively and spirited young girl's entry into the world, of her eventual coming of age. Camilla's story and those of her sisters—the beautiful Lavinia and the angelic, though disfigured and scarred, Eugenia—display the ideals, temptations, loves, doubts, and jealousies that both inform and trouble the passage from youth to adulthood. Burney's characters, especially the women, are realistic enabling the reader to easily be drawn in to their joys, sorrows, and concerns.

Burney's novel also gives a wonderful depiction of public entertainment and pleasure in late eighteenth-century England as well as the manners and fashions that made up the social theater—in particular the social restrictions and even dangers that confronted young women. Burney uses the emotional extremes of popular gothic fiction to show that danger can be found close to home.

In *Northanger Abbey*, Jane Austen's narrator alludes to Burney's novels *Camilla* and *Cecilia,* saying they are "work in which the greatest powers of the mind are displayed, in which the most thorough knowledge of human nature, the happiest delineation of its varieties, the liveliest effusions of wit and humour, are conveyed to the world in the best-chosen language." Austen's high praise is well-deserved, and makes the strongest case yet for reading this novel. **EJG**

Jacques the Fatalist

Denis Diderot

Lifespan | *b.* 1713 (France), *d.* 1784
First Published | 1796 (written 1773)
First Published by | Buisson (Paris)
Original Title | *Jacques le Fataliste et son maître*

Diderot's *Jacques the Fatalist* is among those very few extraordinary novels that seem to anticipate the distant future of the genre, leaping ahead of itself by one hundred and fifty years, into the company of Samuel Beckett's anti-fictional transgressions of the novel form. It is an exceptionally interesting novel with an exceptionally uninteresting plot. Like metafiction of the twentieth century, it comments continually on its own procedures of composition and guesses continually at the reasons why its story might have turned out as it did, satirizing the reader's appetite for romantic tales or the thrills of an improbable adventure. Diderot sprinkles a few such thrills into the narrative recounted by Jacques to his characterless Master as they roam about, but he is always sure to announce their arrival.

Diderot was a polymath—philosopher, critic, and political essayist; hence perhaps his distrust and comedic handling of the novel form. His most famous literary labor, taking him almost twenty-five years, was on the *Encyclopédie ou Dictionnaire raisonné des Sciences, des Arts et des Métiers,* the great expression of French Enlightenment rationality co-authored, among others, by the mathematician D'Alembert. *Jacques the Fatalist,* which Diderot wrote around 1770 but never published during his lifetime, was a curious departure into a parallel zone of philosophical thinking, in which the so-called "problems of existence" can be staged as farces of self-expression and storytelling. **KS**

J'étais à terre et l'on me traînait

The Nun

Denis Diderot

Lifespan | *b* 1713 (France), *d*. 1784
First Published | 1796 (written 1760)
First Published by | Buisson (Paris)
Original Title | *La Religieuse*

The playful origins of this epistolary novel, published posthumously, are intriguing. In 1760, Denis Diderot and his friends wrote a series of letters to the Marquis de Croismare. The letters purported to come from Suzanne Simonin, an illegitimate child who had been forced to take religious vows to expiate her mother's guilt. Having escaped from the convent, she apparently wanted the Marquis to help her annul her binding vows. In her letters, the nun recounts the details of her confinement against her will and describes its effect on her understanding of religion and her faith. The novel's reputation as a *succès de scandale* is due in great part to its unashamed and explicit depiction of the narrator's encounter with the cruelty prevalent in monastic institutions, and her attendant discovery of eroticism and spirituality.

The Nun has been considered an attack on Catholicism, typifying the French Enlightenment's attitude toward religion. It stirred public opinion anew when, in 1966, the Jacques Rivette movies version was banned for two years. More recently, *The Nun* has been much discussed for its emphatic portrayal of lesbianism and sexuality. Aimed at exposing the oppressive and unnatural structure of life in religious institutions, the narrator's fate at the hands of monastic power provides a striking model for narrative, and indeed, life reversals. **CS**

🔄 Nuns take the offensive in an illustration to Diderot's novel, captioned: "I was on the ground and they were dragging me."

Hyperion

Friedrich Hölderlin

Lifespan | *b*. 1779 (Germany), *d*. 1843
First Published | 1797 (vol. 1), 1799 (vol. 2)
First Published by | J. Cotta (Tübingen)
Full Title | *Hyperion, oder der Eremit in Griechenland*

Friedrich Hölderlin's novel—a kind of autobiography written in letters from Hyperion mostly to his friend Bellarmin, but with some to Diotima—appeared in two volumes between 1797 and 1799. The text is set in ancient Greece, yet some two hundred years after it was written, the words that describe invisible forces, conflicts, beauty and hope are still relevant.

There are explicable and inexplicable reasons for the text's ability to produce nearness out of distance, and vice versa. The explicable reasons have to do with the novel as a philosophical reflection on the Enlightenment and the French Revolution. On the philosophical level, it is an investigation into the separation between subject and object, between individual and individual, man and nature, as a condition of their unity. On the political level it expresses the ambivalence toward reason and revolutionary force as possible instruments of social and historical progress—elements which still exist in various twentieth-century forms.

Hölderlin's critical description of the German society of his day still pretty much fits bourgeois Western European existence in the third millennium. And those who have never felt Hyperion's Utopian longing for harmony with nature and God, free of all alienation, should ask the divine cashier for their money back. The inexplicable reasons have to do with love, language, and Diotima. But for this one has to delve into the experience of reading the novel oneself. **DS**

1. Рибо ―

2. инъ. "Эти говор. 1½

Рыксами облдивен /Х

duis видеть,

Сего у оны предведений

"Ребена Света ―

чаб? Что, что дет. Ка

Как было оно исто

приходит В ч.

самов оны сь центральны. Черев с

мъ васильни

пова ему

Странникъ, (по у дет

― Сестра ― Энеецыпу

ея, камергера А

дъбы далото зоо тот

слово на сторонъ

1800s

Castle Rackrent

Maria Edgeworth

Lifespan | *b.* 1767 (England), *d.* 1849 (Ireland)
First Published | 1800
First Published by | J. Johnson (London)
Full Title | *Castle Rackrent: an Hibernian Tale*

Though little known and read, Maria Edgeworth's first novel is a small gem—several gems, perhaps, since it tells four stories, of successive generations of the Rackrent family and their estate, linked by their narrator, Thady Quirk, loyal steward to the last three. The novel's subtitle indicates the nature of its humor: "an Hibernian tale taken from facts, and from the manners of the Irish Squires, before the year 1782." Sir Patrick is devoted to wild living, while the debt-ridden Sir Murtagh lives for the law. Sir Kit is an inveterate gambler, while the last, Sir Condy Rackrent, is a spendthrift politician and philanderer. Through varying degrees of neglect and profligacy, the estate is finally run into the ground; or rather, it ends up in the hands of a canny young lawyer, Jason Quirk, none other than old Thady's son. Once the reader's ear is tuned to the vernacular idiom of Thady Quirk (because he is illiterate, the novel affects to be the transcription of an oral narrative), the ironic comedy of the old butler's tale is easy to appreciate. Nevertheless, Edgeworth thought it necessary to include a glossary for her English readers.

Castle Rackrent has been long regarded as the first regional novel—it capitalizes on Edgeworth's firsthand knowledge of Anglo-Irish relations in the late eighteenth century—as well as the first historical novel. **ST**

❸ Maria Edgeworth was a member of an Anglo-Irish family, a background she exploited to advantage in her writing.

Elective Affinities

Johann Wolfgang von Goethe

Lifespan | *b.* 1749 (Germany), *d.* 1832
First Published | 1809
First Published by | J. F. Cotta (Tübingen)
Original Title | *Die Wahlverwandtschaften*

The phrase "elective affinities" is both precise and rich with ambiguity. It evokes a condition ripe with emotional and romantic possibilities. When Goethe chose *Wahlverwandtschaften* as his title, however, it was a technical term used solely in chemistry. That it subsequently came to have the connotations it does—both in German and in English—is in large part due to the power of Goethe's elegantly rigorous novel.

Using both a scientific configuration of desire and the symbolism of nature, Goethe's novel is a complex, yet measured and smoothly impersonal exploration of love. The marriage of Charlotte and Eduard is used to examine the perceptions of morality, fidelity, and self-development inscribed deeply within the concept of love. When this marriage is interrupted and challenged by the advent of the Captain and Ottilie, the state of marriage takes on a pastoral hue, at once idyllic and unreal. Through the reserved courtship between Charlotte and the Captain and the consuming passion forged between Eduard and Ottilie, the novel lingers on the irresistible chaos of desire.

The novel was condemned at first for its immoral thesis that love had a chemical origin. But it is rather a sustained reflection on the complications arising out of human intercourse and demonstrates the ways in which our experience of other people makes our experience of love and desire fluid and unreliable. Just as love cannot be caught and immobilized in marriage, desire cannot rest with one person. **PMcM**

"The enjoyment of Elinor's company"

Chapter XLIX

Sense and Sensibility

Jane Austen

Lifespan | *b*. 1775 (England), *d*. 1817
First Published | 1811 (anon.)
First Published by | T. Eggerton (London)
Original Language | English

Like her other novels, this is a marriage plot: its principal protagonists are all, eventually, united with the partners they deserve. Important as this resolution is, however, it is not where the principal satisfaction of Austen's narrative lies. Elinor and Marianne, the two sisters at its center, may well correspond to the sense and sensibility of the novel's title, but a simple identification of reason and passion as their enduring qualities would be unwise.

The creation of perspective, the transition between apparent extremes, is achieved primarily through language, in the precise placement and patterning of phrase, clause, and sentence to create character. As a result, her prose charts exactly the movement between the distortions and blindness of passion, and the reasonable good sense that always seems to succeed it. *Sense and Sensibility* was developed from an earlier novel in letters called *Elinor and Marianne*, but it was only by abandoning the epistolary form of her eighteenth-century precursors that Austen was able to achieve such analytical precision. Her shift in titles is instructive: we no longer move from one viewpoint to another, but remain within a common syntax that propagates the implications created by patterns of ideas. The novelist now writes with one voice, but in doing so she speaks for all the voices she creates. **DT**

Charles Brock's illustration of *Sense and Sensibility* sentimentalizes Austen's work to match the patronizing image of her as "gentle Jane."

The Absentee

Maria Edgeworth

Lifespan | *b*. 1767 (England), *d*. 1849 (Ireland)
First Published | 1812
First Published by | J. Johnson (London)
Original Language | English

Although Edgeworth had originally intended its plot to form the basis of a play, *The Absentee* was eventually published as a short novel in her *Tales From Fashionable Life*. The fiction is a daring political commentary on contemporary Anglo-Irish and tenant-landlord relations, exploring notions of absence and absenteeism among the fashionable set of Irish émigrés to England at the beginning of the nineteenth century. Landowners Lord and Lady Clonbrony have fled their rural Irish estates and taken up residence among the wealthy but morally bankrupt members of London society. Their desertion of Ireland, though, has left their impoverished tenants vulnerable to the abuse and corruption of the agents who oversee their property.

In part a satirical treatment of the foibles of life in the city, Edgeworth's fiction, in sympathy with the Irish national cause, also strikes at the heart of the emigrant's sad rejection and disavowal of native roots. Seeking to escape the follies of fashionable society and the threat of a loveless marriage, Lord Colambre, the son of Lord and Lady Clonbrony and the undisputed hero of the piece, returns incognito to his father's Irish estates. Having experienced there the dire consequences of absenteeism, Lord Colambre eventually manages to reverse the process. His romantic marriage for love takes precedence over property, and by the end of the narrative, the fickle ways of absenteeism have been replaced by the embrace of Irish roots. **DaleT**

Pride and Prejudice

Jane Austen

Lifespan | *b.* 1775 (England), *d.* 1817
First Published | 1813
First Published by | T. Eggerton (London)
Original Language | English

This unflattering sketch by her sister Cassandra is the only existing image of Jane Austen taken from real life.

In the 1940 film version, Laurence Olivier opposes Mr. Darcy's pride to the prejudice of Greer Garson's Elizabeth Bennett.

Pride and Prejudice is the second of four novels that Jane Austen published during her lifetime. As widely read now as it was then, Austen's romance is indisputably one of the most enduringly popular classics of English literature. Written with incisive wit and superb character delineation, *Pride and Prejudice* tells the story of the Bennett family, its ignorant mother, negligent father, and five very different daughters, all of whom Mrs. Bennett is anxious to see married off. Set in rural England in the early nineteenth century, its major plot line focuses on the second eldest daughter, Elizabeth, and her turbulent relationship with the handsome, rich, but abominably proud Mr. Darcy. Slighted by him when they first meet, Elizabeth develops an instant dislike of Darcy, who, however, proceeds to fall in love with her, despite his own better judgement. Subsequent to a disastrous and rejected marriage proposal, both Elizabeth and Darcy eventually learn to overcome their respective pride and prejudice.

Although the novel has been criticized for its lack of historical context, the existence of its characters in a social bubble that is rarely penetrated by events beyond it is an accurate portrayal of the enclosed social world in which Austen lived. Austen depicts that world, in all its own narrow pride and prejudice, with unswerving accuracy and satire. At the same time, she places at its center, as both its prime actor and most perceptive critic, a character so well conceived and rendered that the reader cannot but be gripped by her story and wish for its happy dénouement. In the end, Austen's novel remains so popular because of Elizabeth, and because of the enduring appeal to men and women alike of a well-told and potentially happily-ending love story. **SJD**

Mansfield Park

Jane Austen

Lifespan | *b.*1775 (England), *d.*1817
First Published | 1814
First Published by | T. Eggerton (London)
Original Language | English

One of Austen's more sober novels, *Mansfield Park* deals with her trademark themes—marriage, money, and manners. It tells the familiar story of a young woman, Fanny Price, and her pursuit of the right husband. Fanny is the archetypal poor relative, who is "rescued" from her large and impoverished family to be raised in her aunt's household, the seat of Sir Thomas Bertram, Mansfield Park. Effectively orphaned and an outsider, Fanny is variously tolerated and exploited, and suffers excruciating humiliations at the hands of her other aunt, the mean-spirited Mrs Norris. Her cousins, with the exception of the warm and principled Edmund, are shallow characters who court the attentions of any visiting gentry, such as the rakish Crawfords, with disastrous consequences. Fanny, by contrast, is stronger on virtue than vice, and her sterling qualities are steadily revealed, although readers sometimes find her conventional femininity off-putting.

Typically, Austen mocks the pretensions of the rich and idle—their double standards, their condescension, and indeed their claims to moral legitimacy. Also typical are Austen's allusions to the darker side of the Mansfield Park idyll, made through a few strategically placed details. The Bertram family fortune, it turns out, comes—on the backs of slaves—from plantations in Antigua. Intriguingly, how much attention we must give Jane Austen's attention to these details has recently placed the novel at the center of bitter critical dispute. **ST**

Emma

Jane Austen

Lifespan | *b.*1775 (England), *d.*1817
First Published | 1816
First Published by | T. Eggerton (London)
Original Language | English

Austen said of her fourth published novel that it would contain a heroine no one would like but herself—and as if to prove her wrong, generations of readers have warmed to the flawed protagonist of *Emma*, a young woman used to ruling over the small social world of the village of Highbury. The comedy as well as the psychological interest of the novel lies in seeing what happens when people fail to act as she hopes and ordains. She attempts to pair her protégée Harriet Smith with two unsuitable candidates, and completely fails to read the true direction of the men's affections. She also fails to decipher, until it is almost too late, the nature of her own feelings for Mr Knightley. Some recent readers view the novel as dangerously paternalistic for its moral education, but it should be said that *Emma* is less concerned to teach a lesson than to explore the mortifying effects of learning one.

Austen's trademark blending of an omniscient and ironic third-person narrative voice with a more indirect style that renders individual points of view here comes into its own. A form suited both to the novel's concerns with individual, solipsistic desires and to its overarching moral commitment to the importance of frankness and mutual intelligibility, it points the way toward later nineteenth-century works of novelistic realism. **CC**

🔊 A contemporary engraving represents the presumptuous vicar Mr. Elton, prematurely praising Emma's portrait of Harriet Smith.

Pickering.   Greatbatch.

EMMA.

*There was no being displeased with such
an encourager, for his admiration made
him discern a likeness before it was possible.*

Rob Roy
Sir Walter Scott

Lifespan | *b.* 1771 (Scotland), *d.* 1832
First Published | 1817
First Published by | A. Constable & Co. (Edinburgh)
Original Language | English

Despite its title, this fiction recounts more the experiences of one Frank Osbaldistone than any sustained history of the life of its eponymous outlaw, the legendary "Scottish Robin Hood." And yet, this distinctly Scottish romance was influential not only in consolidating the disparate accounts of the life of Rob Roy MacGregor, but also in mythologizing the Scottish highlands as the place of sublime but barbaric attraction for many English tourists. The novel is set against the backdrop of the Jacobite Rebellion of 1715. Scott's narrative tracks Frank's experiences as he journeys from his family home in London, to his uncle's residence in Northumbria, and on to Glasgow and the highlands of Scotland. Frank crosses the Scottish border in order to retrieve the assets of his father. This general movement northward brings with it exposure to a range of colorful personalities, not least the legendary Rob Roy, who assists Frank in the recovery of the assets.

Much of the narrative impetus derives from the conflicts and divisions that had plagued Great Britain ever since the Act of Union of 1707. But the vision that Scott ultimately offers up in *Rob Roy* is one in which the tensions between commerce and poetry, English and Scottish, Jacobite and Hanoverian, highland and lowland, Catholic and Protestant have been successfully reconciled. **DaleT**

Sir Edwin Landseer's portrait of Scott hints at romantic wildness behind the exterior of a nineteenth-century gentleman.

Ormond
Maria Edgeworth

Lifespan | *b.* 1767 (England), *d.* 1849 (Ireland)
First Published | 1817
First Published by | J. Johnson (London)
Original Title | *Ormond, A Tale*

Ormond maps the experiences of its hero, the dashing Harry Ormond, from his native Ireland to the Black Islands, England and Paris, and back again. Orphaned early, Ormand's destiny has been entrusted to the hands of Sir Ulick O'Shane, his rather irresponsible guardian who, in favoring the advancement of his natural son Marcus over his ward, compromises the hero's education at every turn. Utterly undaunted, Ormond takes up residence in the home of Cornelius O'Shane, the eccentric but endearing king of a small archipelago of islands situated off the Irish coast. Here, he self-consciously attempts to fashion himself as a "hero" in all the possible fictional implications of that term, and embarks upon an ambitious program of reading. Ormond resolves unequivocally "to shine forth an Irish Tom Jones."

Indeed, *Ormond* is as much about what it means to be a fictional hero as it is about anything else. Seeking out a heroine as the necessary complement to this role, Ormond does eventually find romantic fulfilment. By carefully juxtaposing the figure of Ormond with the churlish Marcus O'Shane, Edgeworth's novel graphically stages the tensions between two competing world views. Perhaps inevitably, *Ormond* comes to argue for the importance of personal agency over privilege, self-advancement over natural lineage. This novel also proved crucial in the efflorescence of the nineteenth-century bildungsroman. **DaleT**

Persuasion

Jane Austen

Lifespan | *b.* 1775 (England), *d.* 1817
First Published | 1818
First Published by | J. Murray (London)
Original Language | English

Looking on her with a face as pallid as her own.

"How quick come the reasons for approving what we like!"

🔊 Illustrating an 1897 edition of *Persuasion*, Hugh Thomson represents the aftermath of Louisa's fall on the Cobb at Lyme Regis.

The last book Austen was to complete, *Persuasion* is about second chances, and the triumph of true love over social obstacles, snobbishness, and other people's selfish concerns. If her earlier novels tended to champion the claims of the social over the individual, her last work redresses the balance a little. Its twenty-seven-year-old heroine, Anne Elliot, seems to have missed out on her opportunity for romantic fulfilment, having at the age of nineteen been persuaded by her mentor, Lady Russell, against marrying Captain Wentworth, on the grounds of his impecunity and poor prospects. Now older and capable of judging for herself, she is thrown once more into his company; and the novel conveys, with great intensity, her heightened consciousness in his presence, and her alert charting of the signs of his reawakening love for her. The course of this love does not run smooth. The now-wealthy and socially-acceptable Wentworth finds himself unwillingly committed to Louisa Musgrove, whose failure to listen even to sensible "persuasions" has cataclysmic consequences, manifested in the novel's best-known scene, in which she jumps and falls from the Cobb at Lyme Regis.

The political sensibility of *Persuasion* is perhaps more liberal than that of Austen's earlier works, the meritocracy of the Navy and the simple good sense of the maritime characters being championed over the effete indulgences of a delinquent and self-regarding aristocracy. In literary terms, too, the novel charts a liberal middle-way: while Anne sensibly recommends that the melancholy Captain Benwick read more of the work of prose moralists, the novel's own frequent references to the poetry of Scott and Byron declare also its allegiance to the Romantic literary tradition. **CC**

Northanger Abbey

Jane Austen

Catherine Morland, the heroine of *Northanger Abbey*, is a plucky tomboy longing for the kind of adventures that she fervently consumes in the popular gothic novels of the day. She is whisked off to Bath with her friends, the Allens, for her first foray into society. It is a time and place of rigid social decorum, where an ambiguously phrased salutation or a damp afternoon can cause as much seismic anxiety and dread as a blood-stained dagger or an imprisoned governess in one of her favorite books. In Bath she meets Henry Tilney and promptly falls forever in love as, she believes, a proper heroine should. Henry's appeal is immediate: he is an iconoclast, mocking conventions of mannerly conversation and conduct and is therefore a perfect match (though perhaps less for Catherine than for the equally ironic narrator of the book). Catherine is continually thwarted in her desires for dark adventures—by Austen's playful authorial intrusions as much as by a decided lack of dungeons and evil squires. "Remember the country and age in which we live," Tilney cautions her, " does our education prepare us for such atrocities?" Catherine learns some hard lessons. She leaves a world created by her fancy, whose parameters are drawn by romance novels. She must take her place in a world where she learns that real evil is not ill-treated wives locked away in cloisters, or drops of blood in dark secret chambers but rather in the rigid strictures of class and in the small-mindedness of society.

Written first and published last, *Northanger Abbey* is often likened to Austen's juvenilia. Certainly the wit is less subtle, less honed, than in her later works: here her blade is exposed and gleefully wielded. *Northanger Abbey* is not just a curiosity for the Austen scholar: it is a delight in itself. **GT**

Lifespan | *b.* 1775 (England), *d.* 1817
First Published | 1818
First Published by | J. Murray (London)
Original Language | English

The three villains in horsemen's greatcoats.

> *"Our pleasures in this world are always to be paid for . . . "*

⊚ Gothic fantasies of abduction are mercilessly deconstructed as Austen's Catherine Morland learns to tell romance from reality.

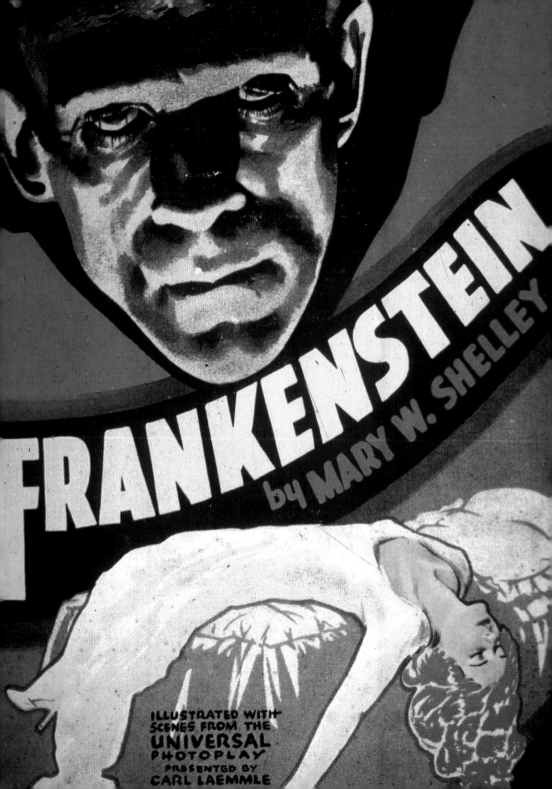

FRANKENSTEIN

by MARY W. SHELLEY

ILLUSTRATED WITH
SCENES FROM THE
UNIVERSAL
PHOTOPLAY
PRESENTED BY
CARL LAEMMLE

Frankenstein

Mary Wollstonecraft Shelley

Frankenstein has far more in common with *Dracula* than with any of the novels of generic late-gothicism. Both are commonly cited as early examples of the horror genre, and both have introduced a character to popular culture that has become distorted beyond all recognition, mainly through their representations in the Hammer, and earlier Universal, movie franchises. *Frankenstein,* and *Dracula* also, seems now more akin to the ultra-modern strain of science-fiction technohorror than any classical version of the genre. At the center of the story is the idea that our understanding of science can be developed and controlled, to the point that the tendency of Nature toward dissolution can be arrested; the impossibility of this desire is at the center of its "horror."

The subtitle of the novel, *The Modern Prometheus*, makes clear the connection with Greek mythology, but it is evident that *Frankenstein* is a novel that looks forward as well as back. The Swiss scientist and philosopher, Frankenstein, is inspired by occult philosophy to create a human-like figure, and give it life. The idea of reanimation is at the heart of much modern horror—the attempted violation of chaotic natural order in favor of linear certainty is something that modern society takes for granted, from the construction of unnatural environments to the continual attempts to postpone death and decline. *Frankenstein* is a novel that addresses such concerns from a point in history where the developments could only be imagined. Yet it remains in all sorts of ways an inescapable part of the culture it examines and foresees, and for these reasons alone it must continue to be read and reassessed. Effortless prose, grotesque imagery, and surreal imagination will ensure that it continues to be enjoyed. **SF**

Lifespan | *b.* 1797 (England), *d.* 1851
First Published | 1818
First Published by | Lackington et al. (London)
Full Title | *Frankenstein; or, the Modern Prometheus*

"The fallen angel becomes a malignant devil."

◉ Daughter of the radical feminist Mary Wollstonecraft, the author of *Frankenstein* married poet Percy Bysshe Shelley in 1816.

◉ The dominant images of Frankenstein in the popular imagination are supplied by James Whale's 1931 movie version.

Ivanhoe

Sir Walter Scott

Lifespan | *b.* 1771 (Scotland), *d.* 1832
First Published | 1820
First Published by | A. Constable & Co. (Edinburgh)
Full Title | *Ivanhoe; or, the Jew and his Daughter*

Ivanhoe details the political and cultural enmity between the subjugated Saxons and their Norman-French overlords during the reign of Richard the Lionheart in the twelfth century. Wilfred of Ivanhoe, a brave Saxon knight, returns from the Crusades to assist King Richard in recovering his throne from his usurping brother Prince John. To this endeavor, the assistance of a range of other personages, both historical and imaginary, is central. The narrative is urged forward by three confrontations of epic proportions: the tournament at Ashby-de-la-Zouche, the siege of Torquilstone Castle, and the rescuing of the heroine Rebecca from Templestowe, the seat of the Knights Templar. In each instance, conflict and bloody warfare ensue; at other moments, elements gleaned from gothic romance take precedence. Yet for all the delight that he takes in the sheer vitality of chivalry, Scott also subtly critiques warfare.

With its focus on medieval England, *Ivanhoe* signalled a change from the Scottish subject-matter of Scott's earlier *Waverley* novels. As a sustained examination of the political, chivalric, and romantic practices of old, this fiction not only galvanized for a number of later writers and readers not only their impression of the medieval past, but also pioneered the genre of the historical novel, the literary form most often used to express it. **DaleT**

❸ Scott's work inspired romantic artists such as Delacroix, whose *Abduction of Rebecca* (1858) is based on a scene from *Ivanhoe*.

The Monastery

Sir Walter Scott

Lifespan | *b.* 1771 (Scotland), *d.* 1832
First Published | 1820
First Published by | A. Constable & Co. (Edinburgh)
Original Language | English

Set in the lawless terrain of the Scottish Borders between the years 1550 and 1575, *The Monastery* records the fate of the isolated Catholic monastery of Kennaquhair as it comes into conflict with the competing doctrines of radical Protestant Reform. Scott's imagination for this historical romance seems to have been fueled by the ruins of Melrose Abbey close to his home at Abbotsford, themselves a testament to the religious and political struggles of Scotland's past. These broader ideological conflicts, though, are played out in the narrative through a range of intense relationships: between the Catholic Sub-Prior Eustace and his one-time school friend the Protestant preacher Henry Warden, between a lover and his beloved, between one brother and the next.

The sympathies ultimately offered up by the narrative are firmly Protestant in orientation. However, Scott's decidedly gothic penchant in *The Monastery* for terror, supernatural suspense, and muted forms of anti-Catholicism is carefully counterbalanced by the comic elements generated through the linguistic idiosyncrasies of Sir Piercie Shafton. Culminating in the arrival of the Reformers, the final procession of the monks of Kennaquhair, and the eventual dissolution of the monastery, Scott's romance is at once an account of his native Scottish past, and an anticipation of a national, political, and religious future. Both these themes are more thoroughly explored in the sequel to *The Monastery*, *The Abbot* (1820). **DaleT**

Melmoth the Wanderer

Charles Robert Maturin

Lifespan | *b.* 1782 (Ireland), *d.* 1824
First Published | 1820
First Published by | A. Constable & Co. (London)
Original Language | English

Melmoth occupies a curiously transitional position in literary history. As the final, belated representative of the gothic tradition in literature, it contains many of the key features of the genre: wild and remote, or otherwise exotic locations, a succession of strange stories, labyrinthine entrapments, and the dangerous lure, for the Protestant, of Catholic Europe. The question of identity is in the foreground from the outset, as we are introduced to John Melmoth, a young student who inherits his uncle's legacy. The estate includes a manuscript which tells the story of an ancestor, also called John Melmoth, who becomes the guiding thread for the novel. We discover that he has attained satanic immortality in exchange for his soul, yet he now uses this duration in order to seek his release from eternity by trying to drive another to take on his burden.

Melmoth's appeal to modernity resides not so much in the surprise and tension of the action that keeps us engaged but in its reflection on the nature of temptation and torment. The human mind is portrayed as both vanquisher and vanquished, and it is for this reason that, although quickly forgotten by his own generation, Maturin became a model for the twilight explorations of Poe, Wilde, and Baudelaire, among others. It is only in realizing this that we have begun to acknowledge Maturin's fundamental contribution to literary history. **DT**

The Albigenses

Charles Robert Maturin

Lifespan | *b.* 1782 (Ireland), *d.* 1824
First Published | 1824
First Published by | Hurst, Robinson & Co. (London)
Original Language | English

The narrative of Maturin's final novel, *The Albigenses*, is based on an episode in the religious wars of thirteenth-century Europe, when the Catholic Church struggled to crush the Albigensian heresy in southern France. In telling this story, however, Maturin largely draws upon Walter Scott's version of medieval Europe, and as a result, *The Albigenses* is susceptible to many of Scott's perceived failings.

Yet this is a book of compelling interest. Maturin transports us to a version of the Languedoc in which the sun never shines, and where nearly all significant events take place at night. The historical event-driven perspective thus shifts, imperceptibly, to the interior of the troubled mind. We are shown not only the cynical political calculation of Bishop Folquet, the papal emissary, but the corrupting lure of his oriental sensibility as his intoxicating rhetoric identifies the latent eroticism of the Albegeois maiden he attempts to seduce. In this way, Maturin manages to create a literary style that is simultaneously expressive of historical anxiety and interior exploration, both arising from the same needs and desires. *The Albigenses* was never reprinted following its original publication, and can now only be found in a very few research libraries. Yet despite its critics, it is continuous with Maturin's earlier achievements and like them may yet return to unsettle our assumptions. **DT**

The Private Memoirs and Confessions of a Justified Sinner

James Hogg

Lifespan | *b.* 1770 (Scotland), *d.* 1835
First Published | 1824
First Published by | Longman et al. (London)
Original Language | English

Hogg framed this metaphysical thriller so that it could be mistaken for a true story, including himself as a minor character in the narrative box of tricks. Purporting to be a historical reconstruction of the life of two brothers, George and Robert, narrated by the book's editor, along with the confessional manuscript of Robert, the novel offers a series of doubles and doublings. The editor's account, some hundred years after the actual events, is contrasted with the confessional religiosity of the sinner's account. These different stylistic perspectives give the book its bifocal structure, revealing the outside and intimate inside of a psychopathic killer who styles himself as a justified sinner. Abusing Calvinist doctrines of predestination—if you are born one of God's elect then you can do no wrong—the sinner's confession reveals an insane orgy of confused fanaticism, through which Hogg suggests a searing satire on religious fanaticism. Throughout the book, extremism is contrasted with healthier, more honorable and humane good sense, particularly in the resistance shown by the lower classes to their "betters." Robert is haunted by a shape-shifting stranger who can be read as a manifestation of the devil incarnate or as a symptom of psychological trauma. At once gothic comedy, religious horror story, mystery thriller, and psychological study, the novel is both terrifying and terrific. **DM**

"With regard to the work itself, I dare not venture a judgment, for I do not understand it."

⬆ This illustration from a late nineteenth-century edition of *Memoirs* is entitled: "Escape homewards and save your soul!"

Last of the Mohicans

James Fenimore Cooper

Lifespan | *b.* 1789 (U.S.), *d.* 1851
First Published | 1826
First Published by | J. Miller (London)
Full Title | *Last of the Mohicans, a Narrative of 1757*

The pivotal set-piece of *The Last of the Mohicans* is the massacre at Fort William Henry during the French and Indian War. This is the "factual" event around which Cooper, the first internationally renowned American novelist, builds a compelling tale of wilderness adventure. Drawing heavily on the American genre of the Native American captivity narrative, he creates a template for much American popular fiction, particularly the Western.

Frontiersman Natty Bompo had already been introduced as an old man in *The Pioneers* (1823); here he appears in middle age, as Hawkeye, a scout working for the British, with two Delaware Native American companions, Chingachgook and his son Uncas. Having crossed paths with Cora and Alice Munro, the daughters of a British colonel, they spend the rest of the novel rescuing them from captivity, escorting them to safety, or pursuing them through the wilderness.

Cooper's racial politics are conservative; though the novel raises the possibility of interracial romance between Uncas and the genteel Cora (who has a black mother), the prospect is quashed. Cooper laments the destruction of the wilderness, and of the Native Americans who inhabit it, but all are shown to succumb inevitably to progress, typical of the ideology of nineteenth-century America. **RH**

⬤ American landscape artist Thomas Cole painted this scene from
The Last of the Mohicans: Cora Kneeling at the Feet of Tamenund.

The Betrothed

Alessandro Manzoni

Lifespan | *b.* 1785 (Italy), *d.* 1873
First Published | 1827
First Published by | Pomba; Trameter; Manini
Original Title | *I Promessi Sposi*

Written in the Florentine dialect, *The Betrothed* was Manzoni's attempt to put forward an authoritative model for a standardized Italian language as a condition for the cultural and political unification of the country. The novel is set during the seventeenth-century Spanish occupation of the Italian peninsula, and based on an allegedly authentic manuscript that the author reproduces in perfectly baroque style. Manzoni is able to draw on parallels from history to depict his own era, when Italy was under Austrian domination.

From a peaceful little village in Lombardy, where two humble peasants are preparing for their wedding, the story introduces a circus of characters, who scheme to prevent or expedite that union. There is an impressive variety of actors, powerless and powerful, modest and aristocratic, religious and secular. Inspired by the new Romantic culture, *The Betrothed* examines the abuse of power in all its many forms. Priests use their knowledge of Latin to outwit their parishioners, fathers abuse their paternal authority to force their daughters into a nunnery, crooks kidnap a simple girl who has found refuge in a convent. But above all, obtuse foreign governments oppress and prevaricate without sympathy for the local population. Nevertheless, the novel's message is positive: people's faith in overcoming difficulties and their determination to pursue their goals facilitates a favorable resolution of the story with the union of the betrothed. **RPi**

The Red and the Black

Stendhal

Lifespan | *b.*1783 (France), *d.*1842
First Published | 1831
First Published by | Hilsum (Paris)
Original Title | *Le Rouge et le Noir*

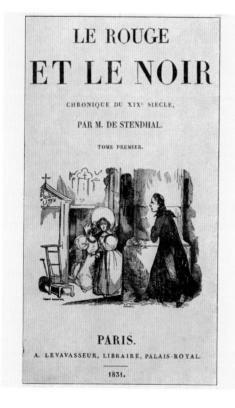

LE ROUGE
ET LE NOIR

CHRONIQUE DU XIXᵉ SIÈCLE,

PAR M. DE STENDHAL.

TOME PREMIER.

PARIS.
A. LEVAVASSEUR, LIBRAIRE, PALAIS-ROYAL.

1831.

⊙ The front cover of the first edition of Stendhal's *The Red and the Black* carries the subtitle "Chronicle of the 19th Century."

⊙ Fellow author Alfred de Musset produced this striking drawing of Stendhal dancing at an inn at Pont Saint-Esprit.

Set in France in the 1830s, *Le Rouge et le Noir* chronicles Julien Sorel's duplicitous rise to power and his subsequent fall. The son of a carpenter, Julien seeks initially to realize his Napoleonic ambitions by joining the priesthood. Despite some torrid liaisons during his training, Julien succeeds in becoming a priest and eagerly accepts the invitation of the Marquis de la Mole to become his personal secretary. Even Julien's affair with the Marquis' daughter, Mathilde, is the occasion of his ennoblement so that he can marry her without scandal. Before Julien has an opportunity to enjoy his aristocratic life, however, the Marquis receives from Mme de Renal (another of Julien's conquests when he was training for the priesthood) a letter that exposes him as a fraud. Prevented from marrying Mathilde, Julien exacts revenge.

Sometimes perceived as a bit too melodramatic to appeal to modern literary taste, *The Red and the Black* is immensely important in terms of the development of the novel as an art form. On the one hand it is a tale very much in the Romantic tradition. Sorel may be unscrupulous and roguish in the pursuit of his ambitions, yet set against a petty and constraining bourgeois French society, his energy and sheer gumption often lure the reader into a reluctant rapport. It is in Stendhal's narrative style, however, that this novel has proved to be most influential. In largely being told from the vantage point of each character's state of mind, the novel's convincing psychological realism prompted Emile Zola to proclaim it the first truly "modern" novel. It is for this reason, apart from the fact that it is a rollicking good yarn, that *The Red and the Black* should be reserved a place on every serious reader's bookshelf. **VA**

The Hunchback of Notre Dame
Victor Hugo

Lifespan | *b*. 1802 (France), *d*. 1885
First Published | 1831
First Published by | Flammarion (Paris)
Original Title | *Notre Dame de Paris*

VKToA HVGo

"The owl goes not into the nest of the lark."

◉ Victor Hugo was by far the most prolific and versatile author of the French Romantic school, both in poetry and prose.

◐ Nicolas Maurin's contemporary illustration shows a disgusted Esmerelda feeding the grotesque hunchback Quasimodo.

Victor Hugo's *Notre-Dame de Paris* is a historical novel in the tradition of Sir Walter Scott's *Ivanhoe*. It presents a vivid tableau of life in fifteenth century Paris, a city teeming with noble festivities, grotesque revelries, mob uprisings, and public executions, all of which take place around Notre-Dame de Paris. Hugo devotes two chapters to the description of the gothic church, bringing the reader into the very soul of Notre-Dame. From the dizzying heights of its stony gaze, he offers the reader a subjective view of Paris. The word *anankhe* ("fate"), etched on one of the walls, reveals the driving force of the gothic plot.

Quasimodo's fate is sealed when he is abandoned at birth by his mother on the steps of Notre-Dame. Adopted by the Archdeacon Claude Frollo, Quasimodo becomes bellringer of the tower, hiding his grotesque, hunchbacked figure away from prying Parisian eyes. Frollo is consumed by forbidden lust for the beautiful gypsy Esmeralda, who dances on the square below the cathedral. He convinces Quasimodo to kidnap her, but his attempts are foiled by the captain of the King's Archers, Phoebus, who also falls for Esmeralda. Quasimodo is imprisoned for the crime, and is abused and humiliated by his captors. After a particularly brutal flogging, he is tended to by Esmeralda who gives him water. From this point on, Quasimodo is hopelessly devoted to her. With all three characters under her spell, a dramatic tale of love and deceit ensues. The love obsessed Frollo spies on Phoebus and Esmeralda, stabbing the former in a jealous rage. Esmeralda is arrested and condemned to death for his murder, and despite a brave rescue attempt by Quasimodo is later hanged. Quasimodo, seeing Esmeralda hanging lifeless from the gallows, cries out, "There is all I loved." The theme of redemption through love struck a universal chord. **KL**

Eugénie Grandet

Honoré de Balzac

"Narrow minds can develop as well through persecution as through benevolence; they can assure themselves of their power by tyrannizing cruelly or beneficently over others."

⊙ This Jules Leroux illustration, taken from a 1911 edition of the novel, depicts Nanon and a Manservant carrying a keg.

Lifespan | *b.* 1799 (France), *d.* 1850
First Published | 1834
First Published by | Charles-Béchet (Paris)
Original Language | French

Like Walter Scott, Balzac wrote novels in part to clear debts and the pains of debt—capital accumulation and attendant moral corruption run right through *Eugénie Grandet*, which later became part of Balzac's larger grouping of novels *La Comédie Humaine*. Amid robust, moral critique of greed and the poverty of provincial experience, this novel combines convincingly drawn human characters with a sociological grasp of deeper changes in French society. The realist representation of Eugénie's father as a tyrannical miser shows the workings of avarice not just as an individual "sin," but as a reflection of the secular nihilism of financial calculation in nineteenth-century capitalism.

The plot has a classical simplicity and causal circularity, unfolding a bourgeois tragedy which the narrator declares more cruel than any endured by the house of Atreus. Eugénie's father's fixation on monetary gain limits her experience, and ultimately destroys the family. The novel unveils the full damage done to Eugénie, though she asserts some moral dignity through acts of precise generosity. With a grasp of temporal cycles that prefigures Proust, Balzac dramatizes both the critical framework of individual actions and the wheels of generational change. Comic bathos tempers the stark social realism; the entertainment Balzac wrings from the judgments of his more or less omniscient narrator is surprising. An ideal introduction to one of the great realist novelists. **DM**

Le Père Goriot

Honoré de Balzac

Lifespan | *b.* 1799 (France), *d.* 1850
First Published | 1834–1835
First Published by | Werdet (Paris)
Original Language | French

This is the story of a wealthy businessman who bequeaths a fortune to his two ungrateful daughters. Living alone in a shabby boarding house so that he can continue to give what little he has to his avaricious offspring, he also befriends an ambitious young man named Rastignac who exploits their association to further his own social aspirations. As intrigue, betrayal, and even murder become implicated in the daughters' rise into high society, various villains ensure that the narrative is enlivened by some sensational plot twists. Essentially, though, it is Goriot's unreciprocated love for his daughters that is the central tragedy around which Balzac chronicles the broader social malaise.

Constituting one of the works in Balzac's epic series, *La Comédie Humaine*, *Le Père Goriot* essentially transposes Shakespeare's *King Lear* to 1820s Paris. Against Goriot's selfless devotion to his family the novel explores in myriad ways how it is no longer filial bonds or ideals of community that sustains the social edifice, but a corrupt pseudo-aristocracy that is based on aggressive individualism and greed.

Although some may become impatient with the overly sinuous plot structure, it is Balzac's eye for detail and his gift for psychological realism that continue to inspire admiration. The sheer breadth of his artistic vision locates him firmly within the nineteenth-century tradition, but his narrative technique and attention to character still make Balzac a hugely important figure in modern fiction. **VA**

The Nose

Nikolay Gogol

Lifespan | *b.* 1809 (Ukraine), *d.* 1852
First Published | 1836 (Russia)
Original Title | *Nos*
Original Language | Russian

One of Gogol's best known stories, *The Nose* is quite possibly also one of the most absurd, and as such is a forerunner of a tradition that almost a century later would become very strong, not only in Russia, but all over Europe. It has also served as the basis for a wonderfully inventive and funny opera of the same name by Shostakovich.

Kovalev is a junior civil servant with a consciousness of his own importance and an equally acute sense of his place in the bureaucratic hierarchy. Alarmingly, he wakes up one morning to find his nose gone. While on his way to the relevant authorities to signal this loss, he is astonished to meet his nose dressed in the uniform of a civil servant several ranks above him. He attempts to address the errant nose, but is rebuffed on the grounds of rank. He tries to place a notice in the newspaper to ask for help in catching his nose, but fails. When his nose is later brought back to him by the police, the doctor says it cannot be put back on. Some time later, and for no apparent reason, Kovalev wakes up to find his nose mysteriously back in its place. The whole story is related in considerable detail, only to end with a list of all the implausibilities in this literally incredible story. Gogol even goes so far as to make the indignant statement that the greatest of these implausibilities is "how authors can choose such subjects" at all. Readers may well wonder why Gogol did choose to write *The Nose*, but they are unlikely to regret that he did. **DG**

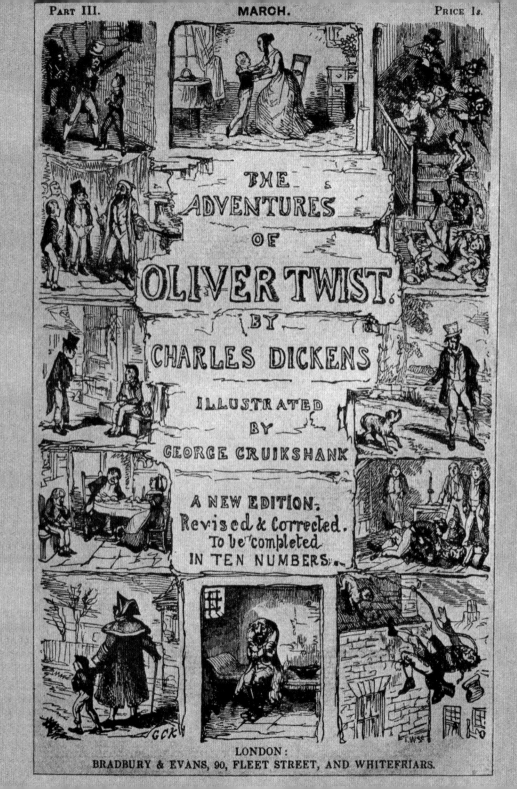

THE
ADVENTURES
OF
OLIVER TWIST.
BY
CHARLES DICKENS

ILLUSTRATED
BY
GEORGE CRUIKSHANK

A NEW EDITION,
Revised & Corrected.
To be completed
IN TEN NUMBERS.

LONDON:
BRADBURY & EVANS, 90, FLEET STREET, AND WHITEFRIARS.

Oliver Twist

Charles Dickens

Oliver Twist started life as one of Dickens' "Mudfog" sketches, a series of papers written for the early numbers of *Bentley's Miscellany*. The first two monthly parts, depicting Oliver's birth and upbringing in the workhouse, formed part of a series of radical melodramatic attacks on the 1834 New Poor Law. *Oliver Twist* is at once a picaresque story, a melodrama, and a fairy tale romance in which the foundling is revealed to have noble origins. It is also one of the first novels to feature a child as the central character; though in contrast with Dickens' later children Oliver both stays a pre-pubescent and remains untouched by the traumas he experiences. Oliver's curious blankness is central to Dickens's multiple purposes. It enables him to remain the passive victim of institutionalized violence in the workhouse—even the famous scene where he asks for more gruel is not an act of self-assertion, but the result of drawing lots. It allows him to remain free of corruption when he falls in with Fagin's criminal gang (in contrast with the "Artful Dodger") so that he can be recast as a middle-class child by his rescuer Mr. Brownlow. The conspiracy between the wicked master of the den of underage thieves, Fagin, and Oliver's half-brother Monks to turn Oliver into a criminal produces the tension between imprisonment and escape that drives and unites the novel. Oliver escapes from the workhouse and from Fagin's underworld den, only to be recaptured until he is finally united with his aunt Rose Maylie and adopted by Brownlow. The fact that this dismal pattern is eventually broken is entirely due to the intervention of the prostitute Nancy, who brings the two worlds together—but at the price of her violent murder by her lover Bill Sykes, in one of Dickens's most bloodthirsty scenes. **JBT**

Lifespan | *b.* 1812 (England), *d.* 1870
First Published | 1838 by R. Bentley (London)
Full Title | *The Adventures of Oliver Twist, or the Parish Boy's Progress*

⊙ George Cruikshank, the illustrator of *Oliver Twist*, created unforgettable images of Fagin and the Artful Dodger.

◒ The cover of the 1846 edition: by then *Oliver Twist* had already taken up an immovable place at the heart of Victorian culture.

The Life and Adventures of Nicholas Nickleby

Charles Dickens

> "Gold conjures up a mist about a man, more destructive of all his old senses and lulling to his feelings than the fumes of charcoal."

● Black-clad Master Wackford Squeers, headmaster of Dotheboys Hall, is depicted in the full color of his characterization.

Lifespan | *b.* 1812 (England), *d.* 1870
First Published | 1839
First Published by | Chapman & Hall (London)
Original Language | English

Dickens comes closest to the eighteenth-century picaresque novel in *Nicholas Nickleby*, which follows the fortunes of the hero and his sister Kate when they are pushed into the world after their father's disastrous financial speculation. The novel is an extended exploration of how families work as economic as much as domestic units, and of how peoples' identities are shaped by the roles they play.

Nicholas and Kate are both forced into exploitative labor by their wicked uncle Ralph. Kate becomes a milliner at Madame Mantolini's, where she falls prey to the sexual advances of the decadent roué Sir Mulberry Hawk. Nicholas becomes an usher at the truly grotesque and brutal Dotheboys Hall, the private school in which unwanted children are dumped by uncaring parents. The depiction of Dotheboys Hall combines grim comedy, in the figures of proprietors Mr. and Mrs. Squeers, with pathos, in the form of Smike, the mentally stunted youth abandoned as a child in the school. After fleeing the school, Nicholas wanders the country with Smike in search of employment, including work in Crummles's Theatre, a carnival world in which even Smike can play a useful part. In a final series of stark oppositions Nicholas and Kate once again find a home together, restored to them by the Cheeryble brothers, benevolent figures that magically reverse the family's misfortune. **JBT**

The Fall of the House of Usher

Edgar Allan Poe

Lifespan | *b.* 1809 (U.S.), *d.* 1849
First Published | 1839 by W. Burton (Philadelphia)
First Serialized | *Burton's Gentleman's Magazine*
Original Language | English

It seems to be stretching the definition of the word to its very limits to describe *The Fall of the House of Usher* as a "novel." However, despite the characteristic brevity of the narrative, the work deserves inclusion here, because it is simply impossible to imagine the modern novel without considering Poe's masterful writing, and this seminal tale in particular. The story is imbued with an atmosphere of foreboding and terror, underpinned by an equally strong exploration of the human psyche.

Roderick and Madeline Usher are the last of their distinguished line. They are, therefore, the "House of Usher," as is the strange, dark mansion in which they live. The narrator of Poe's tale is a childhood friend of Roderick's, summoned to the decaying country pile by a letter pleading for his help. He arrives to find his friend gravely altered, and through his eyes, we see strange and terrible events unfold. The reader is placed in the position of the narrator, and as such we identify strongly throughout with the "madman" watching incredulous as around him reality and fantasy merge to become indistinguishable. The unity of tone and the effortlessly engaging prose are mesmerizing, enveloping both subject matter and reader. For one who died so young, Poe left an incredible legacy, and it adds a resonance to this tale that his own house was to fall so soon. **DR**

The Charterhouse of Parma

Stendhal

Lifespan | *b.* 1783 (France), *d.* 1842
First Published | 1839
First Published by | Ambroise Dupont (Paris)
Original Title | *Le Chartreuse de Parme*

Movement is the operative principle of this story, which shifts quickly between several countries and decades. Many readers have remarked upon the disconcerting rapidity of these transitions, bringing narrative enjoyment to the foreground, but also perplexing us as to the overall shape of the story.

The novel's sense of movement is achieved not by progression, but by a constantly managed undercutting, which extends to character, theme, and judgement. We are told at the outset that this is the story of the Duchess Sanseverina, but, at least initially, its hero appears to be her idealistic nephew, Fabrice. Yet his principled bravery is not allowed to stand either; arriving at Waterloo his expectation of the camaraderie of war is undermined when his compatriots steal his horse. In the parts of the novel where summaries of a period of years alternate with passages spanning only hours, limpidity of duration is matched by an elevation of perspective—these range from the bell tower of Fabrice's childhood church, to the Farnese Tower in which he is incarcerated at the heart of the story. With imprisonment as its central theme, Stendhal's extreme freedom with the narrative seems resonantly undermining. As theme defeats theme, and one aspect of narrative technique shows up the limitations of another, the novel operates according to its own exhilarating logic. **DT**

Dead Souls

Nikolay Gogol

Lifespan | *b.* 1809 (Ukraine), *d.* 1852
First Published | 1842 (Russia)
Original Title | *Myertvye dushi*
Original Language | Russian

The writing of *Dead Souls* drove Gogol mad. It started off as a humorous idea for a story, the conceit being that Chichikov, a scheming opportunist, would travel through Russia buying up the rights to dead serfs (souls), who had not yet been purged from the census and could therefore—like all chattels—still be mortgaged. As the novel grew, so did Gogol's aspirations; his goal became no less than to rekindle the noble yet dormant core of the Russian people, to transform the troubled social and economic landscape of Russia into the gleaming great Empire that was its destiny. He no longer wanted to write about Russia: he wanted to save it. He was driven into messianic obsession and, having burnt Part Two—twice—after ten years of labor, he committed suicide by starvation.

Chichikov's travels across the expanse of Russia in a troika provided the opportunity for Gogol to shine as a satiric portrait artist, a caricaturist of the panoply of Russian types. He makes Russian literature funny—tragically funny. In Chichikov he created a timeless character, a huckster not unrecognizable in today's dotcom billionaires, able to exploit the stupidity and greed of landowners eager to get even richer themselves. Although Gogol was unable to deliver the key to Russian salvation he had envisaged, with what remains he has inarguably succeeded in writing his "great epic poem" which, hauntingly, did finally "solve the riddle of my existence." **GT**

A Christmas Carol

Charles Dickens

Lifespan | *b.* 1812 (England), *d.* 1870
First Published | 1843, by Chapman & Hall
Full Title | *A Christmas Carol, in Prose:*
Being a Ghost Story of Christmas

Over the course of a single Christmas Eve a miserly misanthrope, Ebeneezer Scrooge, relives five incidents from his past, visits scenes from the present Christmas to Twelfth Night, and is presented with a vision of a future that connects his own death to that of the child of Bob Cratchit, his long suffering clerk. Accompanied upon these journeys by a trio of supernatural guides, Scrooge finally repents and makes amends to those he has ill treated.

The story is darkly comic and tinged with pathos, making the customary Dickensian appeal to the transforming power of sentiment. While Dickens's novels became increasingly pessimistic about there ever being a society that would honor its obligations to the poor and the dispossessed, this issue is neatly sidestepped here. The prevailing fantasy of the story is that a softening of character rather than a more radical transformation of socio-economic structures is sufficient to bring about social harmony. It is perhaps because of, rather than in spite of, this collective wish fulfilment at the heart of the narrative that the novel has consolidated its reputation, not least through numerous film and stage adaptations. Ultimately, though, it is the masterful storytelling that will ensure *A Christmas Carol's* popularity—it would be a stony heart indeed that did not warm to its charms. **VA**

● The ghost of Marley appears to Scrooge in one of John Leech's hand-colored engravings that illustrated the first edition.

Marley's Ghost.

113

Lost Illusions

Honoré de Balzac

Lifespan | *b.* 1799 (France), *d.* 1850
First Published | 1843
First Published by | G. Charpentier (Paris)
Original Title | *Illusions Perdues*

"He had every kind of luck . . ."

◔ A man of monumental mental energy, Balzac regularly worked fifteen hours a day, writing eighty-five novels in two decades.

◑ This title page of *Les Illusions Perdues*—*Lost Illusions*—bears the author's own comments and annotations scrawled in ink.

A kind of westernised *Arabian Nights*, *Lost Illusions* is one of the central works of Balzac's 17-volume *Human Comedy* (1842–46). This series of studies of contemporary life, set during the period of restored monarchy in France, aimed to show how social, economic, and political factors mold individual and collective destinies. In the famous "Avant-propos" (Foreword), dated 1842, which unifies the 90 or so novels, populated by 3,000 characters (many of them recurring), that comprise the series, Balzac provocatively described his work as that of a naturalist, comparing men and women of different social and financial stations to zoological species.

As self-appointed record-keeper of his epoch, Balzac was interested in "all of society," but most significantly, the upheavals related to money. Balzac's fictions draw our attention to the many contrasts that define different cultural domains: between the royalists and the liberals in political life, the aristocracy and the bourgeoisie, the hoarders and the squanderers, the virtuous and the depraved, Paris and the provinces. Steeped in the imagery of the theater, the three parts of *Lost Illusions* tell the story of the provincial poet Lucien de Rubempré who languishes in provincial Angoulême in the company of his alter ego David Séchard, nurturing his ambitions. He is initiated into the Parisian literary, journalistic, and political world, and suffers successive disillusions. Marcel Proust praised the way in which Balzac's style aims "to explain," and is marked by its beautiful "naiveties and vulgarities." Some critics, on the other hand, while they celebrate Balzac's powers of observation, denigrate his "clumsy and inelegant style." From the first pages to the last, *Lost Illusions* provides ample opportunity to share Proust's admiration for the writer. **CS**

Illusions perdues

The Pit and the Pendulum

Edgar Allan Poe

> "I felt that my senses were leaving me. The sentence, the dread sentence of death, was the last of distinct accentuation which reached my ears."

⊙ An illustration of Poe's *Pit and the Pendulum* represents the victim's hallucinations as well as his horrific predicament.

Lifespan | *b.* 1809 (U.S.), *d.* 1849
First Published | 1843
First Serialized | *The Gift for 1843* (Philadelphia)
Original Language | English

This claustrophobic tale of horror and suspense has ensured Edgar Allan Poe a place at the forefront of the Romantic tradition. As one of America's first serious literary critics, he was dismissive of art and literature that was preoccupied with the mundane, himself preferring to deal with the unexpected and the puzzling—specifically, the supernatural.

Poe was highly regarded as a writer of poetry and prose, but his life was plagued by ill-health, money problems, and bouts of depression and mental illness that were aggravated by alcohol. Two years after the death of his wife, at the age of forty, he died after drinking himself into a coma.

It is therefore not surprising to find that so many of his stories feature the plight of desperate protagonists brought by terror to the brink of insanity. However, much of the criticism of Poe and his work, including attempts to seek out symbols for psychoanalytical interpretation, has confused the writer's own torment with that of his narrators. In *The Pit and the Pendulum* there is an overpowering atmosphere of dread—the dark chamber reeking of putrefaction and death, the frenzied rats, the immobilized victim's horror of the descending razor-edged pendulum—that has prompted much discussion about the writer's mental state. But this masterpiece, which draws on so many of the recurring motifs spawned by horror writers, should be read as the finely-wrought and compelling work of a gifted imagination. **TS**

Martin Chuzzlewit
Charles Dickens

Lifespan | *b.* 1812 (England), *d.* 1870
First Published | 1844, by Chapman & Hall
Full Title | *The Life and Adventures of Martin Chuzzlewit, his Relatives, Friends, and Enemies*

Dickens had recently returned from a lecture tour to the U.S., and *Martin Chuzzlewit* contains his most caustic response to this experience. He lampoons various aspects of the American character, from widespread boastfulness and aggressive nationalism, to poor manners at the dinner table. His satirical targets are not limited to America, however. From the large-scale, public fraud of the Anglo-Bengalee Assurance Company to the arch-hypocrisy of Mr. Pecksniff, the novel consistently attacks notions of self and selfishness, emphasizing the importance of a developing social consciousness.

The complex, coincidence-laden plot develops Dickens's sense of the way in which human lives interconnect by chance, the underlying order that can emerge from apparent randomness. Martin himself is overshadowed by the cast of eccentrics with whom he is surrounded. Young Martin's travels have elements of the picaresque, while the decline into villainy of the grasping, violent Jonas Chuzzlewit anticipates the more fully developed treatment of crime and detection in *Bleak House*. The novel also contains a typical strain of sentimentality, particularly in the characterization of the trusting, simplehearted Tom Pinch. Much of the most distinctive writing in *Martin Chuzzlewit* is character driven, however, and in Mr. Pecksniff and Mrs. Gamp, Dickens created two of his most memorable grotesques, both developed with an attention to detail that transcends simple caricature. **RH**

The Purloined Letter
Edgar Allan Poe

Lifespan | *b.* 1809 (U.S.), *d.* 1849
First Published | 1844
First Serialized | *The Gift for 1845* (Philadelphia)
Original Language | English

At a mere twenty pages, *The Purloined Letter* may barely rank even as a novella, but its significance is indisputable as artworks so diverse as Borges's tales, *The Name of the Rose*, and *The Usual Suspects* are difficult to conceive of without it.

Set in Paris, the third of Poe's pioneering detective tales sees sleuth C. Auguste Dupin tackle a blackmail plot that threatens to compromise the entire Royal Family. His task is to recover a certain compromising letter which has been stolen by the Minister D—. Despite the fact that the police know who has it, they cannot find it in any search of the man's property. Thus it falls to Dupin to solve the puzzle. Poe's masterstroke is to make the solution depend on our very definition of what a puzzle is. As Dupin notes, the police "never once thought it probable, or possible, that the Minister had deposited the letter immediately beneath the nose of the whole world." In replacing the letter with an exact copy, Dupin not only reveals to the police how they were fooled, but also foils the thief himself with his own trick. Poe was fascinated by all kinds of tricks, codes, and cryptograms, and the startling thoughts that people might only find what they expect to find, that secrets might be hidden in plain sight, are *The Purloined Letter's* enduring literary legacies. Radically self-contradictory, Poe's enigmatic exploration at once invents a type of modern detective story, and strikes at the heart of the logical assumptions on which that genre is founded. **BT**

LES TROIS MOUSQUETAIRES. — *Un mousquetaire, placé sur le degré supérieur, l'épée nue à la main, empêchait, ou, du moins, s'efforçait d'empêcher les trois autres de monter. Ces trois autres s'escrimaient contre lui de leurs épées fort agiles.* (Page 34.)

The Three Musketeers

Alexandre Dumas

Lifespan | *b*. 1802 (France), *d*. 1870
First Published | 1844
First Published by | Baudry (Paris)
Original Title | *Les Trois Mousquetaires*

The Three Musketeers is the most famous of around two hundred and fifty books to come from the pen of this prolific author and his seventy-three assistants. Dumas worked with the history professor Auguste Maquet, who is often credited with the premise for, and even the first draft of *Les Trois Mousquetaires*, although the text, like all his others, plays very fast and loose with the historical narrative.

D'Artagnan, the hero, is a Gascon, a young man who embodies in every aspect the hotheaded stereotype of the Béarnais people. Armed only with a letter of recommendation to M. de Tréville, head of King Louis XIV's musketeers, and his prodigious skill with a sword, this incomparable youth cuts a swathe through seventeenth-century Paris and beyond, seeking his fortune. The enduring quality of Dumas's texts lies in the vitality he breathes into his characters, and his mastery of the *roman feuilleton*, replete as it is with teasers and cliffhangers. *The Three Musketeers* is a romance par excellence, and the pace of the narrative carries the reader on a delirious journey. The strength of the characters, from the "Three Musketeers" themselves, to Cardinal Richelieu and the venomous "Milady," need scarcely be highlighted, so entrenched have they all become in Western culture. The charisma of Dumas's swaggering young Gascon certainly remains undimmed. **DR**

❸ The Musketeers display their skill with the sword in an early twentieth-century illustration of Dumas' swashbuckling romance.

La Reine Margot

Alexandre Dumas

Lifespan | *b*. 1802 (France), *d*. 1870
First Published | 1845
First Published by | Garnier Frères (Paris)
Original Language | French

Published shortly after *The Three Musketeers*, *La Reine Margot* confirmed Alexandre Dumas as the master of historical romance. History professor Auguste Maquet wrote the first draft, Dumas then elaborating the book with dialogue and descriptive passages. The violent action, vivid characters, and potential for lavish Renaissance period décor have attracted several filmmakers, most recently Patrice Chéreau in 1994.

The novel is set in one of the most dramatic periods of French history: the Religious Wars of the sixteenth century. The country's nobility are split into warring factions, with Catholics fighting the Protestant Huguenots. Proud, cultured, and beautiful, Marguerite de Valois—the "Reine Margot"—is sister of the Catholic King Charles IX. The novel opens in 1572 with her arranged marriage to Huguenot leader Henri of Navarre. This loveless wedding is the occasion for the St. Bartholomew's Day massacre, in which Huguenots are slaughtered in their thousands. The plot follows Margot's doomed romance with her Catholic lover, amid the murderous intrigues of the French court. Torture, execution, and poisoning ensure an ending littered with corpses.

La Reine Margot is the first volume of a loosely connected trilogy known as the *Valois Romances*. The other two volumes are rarely read today, but *La Reine Margot* has held its own through the strength of its characterization and the vivacity of its storytelling. Irresistibly readable, it also offers a painless lesson in French history. **RegG**

The Count of Monte-Cristo

Alexandre Dumas

Lifespan | *b.* 1802 (France), *d.* 1870
First Published | 1845–1846
First Published by | Pétion (Paris)
Original Title | *Le Comte de Monte-Cristo*

Dumas Alex.

"Only a man who has felt ultimate despair is capable of feeling ultimate bliss."

⌾ Alexandre Dumas earned a fortune from his popular novels, but his profligate spending ensured that he died in poverty.

Alexandre Dumas' very well-known serialized novel begins with the incarceration of the hero, Edmond Dantès, in the Château d'If, as a result of the denunciation by his rivals of his purported Napoleonic allegiance, just before Napoléon's return from Elba in 1815. During his fourteen-year imprisonment, the hero fortuitously meets the Abbé Faria, who educates him and reveals to him the secret of the great wealth hidden in the Island of Monte-Cristo. Edmond is able to make a dramatic escape, substituting himself for the Abbé's dead body, which—enclosed in a bag—is thrown into the sea. The transformation of Edmond into the Count of Monte-Cristo begins.

Now wealthy, the Count is able to make his denouncers suffer for their evil slander. Each of them will be subjected to a series of imaginative punishments, as the setting of the novel moves from Rome and the Mediterranean to Paris and its surroundings. The ingenious plots involve concealment and revelation, sign language, use of poisonous herbs, and all manner of other things. But beyond the exciting narrative, Dumas focuses on the corrupt financial, political, and judicial world of France at the time of the royal restoration, and the marginal figures, such as convicts, that infiltrate it.

Finally, the Count wonders if his program of retribution has not led him to usurp God's power in order to see justice done. This apparently fantastic and passionate tale of revenge, is a historical narrative in the manner of Walter Scott; that is, one that is not wholly accurate. Unfolding gradually, *The Count of Monte-Cristo* offers an unusual reflection on happiness and justice, omnipotence, and the sometimes fatal haunting return of the past. **CS**

Vanity Fair

William Makepeace Thackeray

For many, the defining moment of *Vanity Fair* occurs in its opening chapter. Becky Sharp, prospective governess, emerges from Miss Pinkerton's academy and flings her parting gift of Doctor Johnson's Dictionary back through the gates. This "heroical act" is our first indication of Becky's irreverent power to shape her own destiny, but in dispensing with that monument of eighteenth-century control and classification, Thackeray also symbolically, if not literally, inaugurates Victorian fiction.

Thackeray's novel is historical: set in the Regency period, it explores the limits of that world, as well as the constitutive conditions laid down for its own. Becky is central to this achievement, as her literary creation draws on the dualistic possibilities of that transitional moment. A constantly calculating adventuress who, devoid of all sentimentality, is thus the perfect mistress of a society in which everything is for sale and nothing possesses lasting value. Yet our perception of the way in which she operates sets her quite apart from any of the satirical heroines of contemporary literature. She is seductive because of her constant power to surprise, balancing often conflicting emotions such as ambition, greed, and selfishness, with poise, warmth, and admiration. Becky makes her way through a hollow world with the battle of Waterloo at its center, diagnosing the hypocrisies she exploits as well as acting as a foil to illuminate the few moments of generosity that are in evidence, her own included. As a result, she not only makes possible Tolstoy's Anna Karenina, formed directly under Thackeray's influence, but also Eliot's Gwendolen Harleth and Hardy's Sue Bridehead. Placed at the shifting heart of *Vanity Fair*, she causes its universe to be glitteringly compelling, and uncomfortably familiar. **DT**

Lifespan | *b.* 1811 (India), *d.* 1863 (England)
First Published | 1847
First Published by | Bradbury & Evans
Full Title | *Vanity Fair, a novel without a hero*

"I knew all along that the prize I had set my life on was not worth the winning."

◉ Becky Sharp, Thackeray's self-willed anti-heroine, is visualized in period dress by *Vanity Fair*'s original illustrator, Frederick Barnard.

Jane Eyre

Charlotte Brontë

Lifespan | *b.* 1816 (England), *d.* 1855
First Published | 1847
First Published by | Smith, Elder & Co. (London)
Pseudonym | Currer Bell

"Reader, I married him."

● George Richmond's 1850 chalk sketch of Charlotte Brontë captures her intelligence and unflinching personal integrity.

❿ This is the first page of the original manuscript of *Jane Eyre*, which was published under the pseudonym Currer Bell.

Charlotte Brontë's first published novel tells a story common to her later novel, *Villette*, of a young woman who must struggle for survival, and subsequently fulfilment, without the support of money, family, or obvious class privilege. The orphaned Jane is caught between two often conflicting sets of impulses. On the one hand, she is stoical, self-effacing, and self-sacrificial. On the other, she is a passionate, independent minded, and dissenting character, rebellious in the face of injustice, which seems to confront her everywhere. As a child, Jane Eyre suffers first as the ward of her aunt, the wealthy Mrs. Reed, and her abusive family, then under the cruelly oppressive regime at Lowood School, where Mrs. Reed finally sends her. As a young governess at Thornfield Hall, questions of class thwart her course toward true love with the Byronic Mr. Rochester, with whom she has forged a profound connection while caring for his illegitimate daughter.

Class, however, is less of a barrier to their union—and both characters are in any case contemptuous of its dictates—than the fact that he already has a wife. She is the infamous madwoman imprisoned in the attic (the Creole Bertha Mason from Spanish Town, Jamaica, whose story is imaginatively reconstructed by Jean Rhys in *Wide Sargasso Sea)*. Bertha's plight has been seen to offer a counterpoint to Jane's, as well as raising questions about the representation of women in nineteenth-century fiction. Strong elements of coincidence and wish fulfilment lead ultimately to the resolution of the central romantic plot, but *Jane Eyre* still speaks powerfully for the plight of intelligent and aspiring women in the stiflingly patriarchal context of Victorian Britain. **ST**

Jane Eyre

by Currer Bell

Vol. 1.st

Chap. 1.st

re was no possibility of taking a walk that day.
had been wandering indeed in the leafless shrubb
hour in the morning, but since dinner (Mrs
en there was no company, dined early) the cold w
nd had brought with it clouds so sombre, a rain
ting that further out-door exercise was now out
stion.

I was glad of it; I never liked long walks — espe
chilly afternoons; dreadful to me was the coming
the raw twilight with nipped fingers and toes and
dened by the chidings of Bessie, the nurse, and hum
the consciousness of my physical inferiority to Eliza,
d Georgiana Reed.

Agnes Grey

Anne Brontë

Lifespan | *b.* 1820 (England), *d.* 1849
First Published | 1847
First Published by | T. C. Newby (London)
Pseudonym | Acton Bell

Anne Brontë is frequently overshadowed by her elder sisters, and yet this early novel shows how much she deserves more recognition of her talents than she often receives. Drawn from her own experiences, Brontë offers a deeply personal and insightful account of the loneliness and painful ambiguities of a governess's role, which is such that she is at the complete mercy of her charges. The narrator of this novel, Agnes Grey, is a young woman who becomes a governess in order to alleviate her family's financial difficulties. The novel follows her woes and frustrations during her work for two very different families, the Bloomfields and the Murrays, who are equally unreasonable in their treatment of Agnes. Anne Brontë offers a sharp and insightful picture of middle-class social behavior and the hypocrisy and affectation that can accompany it.

Brontë's own personal investment in this story lends the novel a depth of emotion that makes Agnes a particularly sympathetic character. Despite her troubles Agnes retains an uncompromising sense of self-respect, stemming partly from her religious faith, which is given great expression in her simple and direct narrative. Fundamentally about morality and the propensity for cruelty and egotism in human nature, the novel demonstrates the importance of individual integrity. **EJG**

❸ A close-up of Anne and Emily Brontë, taken from Branwell's original portrait of all three Brontë sisters.

Wuthering Heights

Emily Brontë

Lifespan | *b.* 1818 (England), *d.* 1848
First Published | 1847
First Published by | T. C. Newby (London)
Pseudonym | Ellis Bell

There has been a great obsession with solitude in modern writing, and Emily Brontë's *Wuthering Heights* must stand as the most violent expression of the products of extreme austerity and isolation ever written. It is an utterly psychotic love story as far removed both from the novels of her two sisters and William Wyler's 1939 film adaptation as imaginable.

Emily Brontë was brought up with great simplicity, encountering only her father, an Irish pastor, and her sisters, with whom she traded stories to pass the time on their remote Yorkshire wasteland. Given her situation she could not possibly have acquired any true experience of love, so how could she possibly have distilled such unaffected beauty and crazed, passionate fury into a novel? There is a kind of awful modernity in the story of Catherine and Heathcliff, a model of society at its most efficient, squeezing out the elemental and the innocent freedom of childhood in favor of a calculated reason, and it is this process that plunges the two lovers into disaster. Catherine is able to deny the freedom of her youth for a place in adult society, Heathcliff is driven to a furious retribution that will stop at nothing. Here lies the fascination of *Wuthering Heights*, in a model of catastrophe as envisaged by a wholly innocent woman, somehow equipped with the ability to express such pure desperation. Doubtless this is the reason that compelled Georges Bataille to judge it "one of the greatest books ever written." **SF**

The Tenant of Wildfell Hall

Anne Brontë

Lifespan | *b.* 1820 (England), *d.* 1849
First Published | 1848
First Published by | T. C. Newby (London)
Pseudonym | Acton Bell

A sensational story of alchoholism and domestic abuse, *The Tenant of Wildfell Hall* scandalized reviewers on its publicaton. As *The American Review* put it, the book takes the reader "into the closest proximity with naked vice, and there are conversations such as we had hoped never to see printed in English." Nevertheless, the book sold remarkably well, and in a Preface to a second edition of the book, Anne Brontë (writing as Acton Bell) defended herself against her critics, by citing the novelist's moral duty to depict "vice and vicious characters . . . as they really are." Brontë also deplored the speculation about her gender, dismissing the judgement that, should the author be a woman, both she and the book were all the more to be condemned.

The Tenant of Wildfell Hall, with its feminist themes, is a powerful portrayal of a young woman's marriage to a Regency rake, her pious struggle to reform him, and, finally, her flight in order to protect their son against his father's corruption. Told largely from Helen Huntingdon's point of view, through letters and journals, the novel recounts an abusive relationship at a time in English history when married women had few legal rights. As the novelist May Sinclair wrote in 1913: "The slamming of Helen's bedroom door against her husband reverberated throughout Victorian England"—a reverberation that continues to resound for readers of this controversial, and rebellious, novel. **VL**

> *"She was trusted and valued by her father, loved and courted by all dogs, cats, children, and poor people, and slighted and neglected by everybody else."*

▲ Anne Bronte's unfortunate experiences as a governess provided material for her critique of women's position in society.

Mary Barton

Elizabeth Gaskell

Lifespan | *b.* 1810 (England), *d.* 1865
First Published | 1848
First Published by | Chapman & Hall (London)
Full Title | *Mary Barton, a Tale of Manchester*

Set in the industrial districts of Manchester, Gaskell's first novel offers a bleak, graphic depiction of urban poverty and its causes. The beautiful, virtuous Mary lives with her father, John Barton, an impoverished power loom weaver, who becomes active in the Chartism movement following the death of his son from starvation. The romance element of the plot focuses on Mary's choice between an upstanding young engineer, Jem Wilson, and Harry Carson, the pampered son of a rich industrialist. The political and romantic strands of the plot collide when, at the behest of his frustrated trade union, John Barton murders Carson.

The year 1848 was one of revolution throughout Europe, and *Mary Barton's* depiction of simmering class conflict caused a sensation. No novel had previously treated the working class so seriously; particularly innovative was Gaskell's unapologetic use of northern dialect throughout the novel. In writing such a politically engaged novel, Gaskell challenged the entrenched Victorian notion that female experience, and hence literary production, was limited to the domestic sphere. There are scenes of excessive sentimentality and didacticism, but Gaskell also develops fully rounded characters. Ultimately, she shows Christian faith to offer more consolation than radicalism, while stressing that the causes of class conflict need to be addressed. The bleakness of the novel, however, is not entirely alleviated by the tentatively happy ending. **RH**

Shirley

Charlotte Brontë

Lifespan | *b.* 1816 (England), *d.* 1855
First Published | 1849
First Published by | Smith, Elder & Co. (London)
Pseudonym | Currer Bell

Shirley, published two years after the successful *Jane Eyre*, is set during the Napoleonic wars, a time punctuated by domestic social conflict, surveying and discussing the failing harvests, the economic hardship, Luddite riots, and growing tension in early nineteenth-century Yorkshire. At the broken center of this analysis is not one woman but two; Shirley Keeldar is a property owner; financially and socially secure, she is passionate, fiercely unconventional, impetuous and unafraid of love. Known as Captain Shirley, she cannot freely be an independent woman but gladly accepts the role of usurper of masculine privilege. Shirley cannot be the heroine however. Brontë creates in Caroline Helstone a figure who occupies the same narrative space as Shirley, Caroline is demure, not willingly passive, yet beside Shirley she is a model of subservient femininity. These two women mediate the narrative; they are its focus yet they also act as the mediators of the explosive social context they inhabit.

Shirley has suffered from comparison with Brontë's *Jane Eyre*; where the latter is a focused, powerful study of the erotic relations generated by attraction and need, *Shirley* is clumsily general, a study of social relations penned by someone of firm convictions but inadequate knowledge. The narrative structure is often hesitant; the anger that is undeniably there is dispersed and uncontained. Yet the attraction of *Shirley* lies precisely in its flaws, and in its failure to resolve the dilemmas it generates. **PMcM**

David Copperfield

Charles Dickens

Lifespan | *b.* 1812 (England), *d.* 1870
First Published | 1850, by Collins (London)
Full Title | *The Personal History, Experience, and Observation of David Copperfield*

Often regarded as Dickens' most autobiographical work, David's account of his childhood ordeal working in his stepfather's warehouse, and his training as a journalist and parliamentary reporter certainly echo Charles Dickens' own experience. A complex exploration of psychological development, *David Copperfield*—a favorite of Sigmund Freud—succeeds in combining elements of fairy tale with the open-ended form of the bildungsroman. The fatherless child's idyllic infancy is abruptly shattered by the patriarchal "firmness" of his stepfather Mr. Murdstone. David's suffering is traced through early years, his marriage to his "child-wife" Dora, and his assumption of a mature middle-class identity as he finally learns to tame his "undisciplined heart."

The narrative evokes the act of recollection whilst investigating the nature of memory itself. David's development is set beside other fatherless sons, while the punitive Mr. Murdstone is counterposed to the carnivalesque Mr. Micawber. Dickens also probed the anxieties that surround the relationships between class and gender. This is particularly evident in the seduction of working-class Emily by Steerforth, and the designs on the saintly Agnes by Uriah, as well as David's move from the infantilized sexuality of Dora to the domesticated rationality of Agnes in his own quest for a family. **JBT**

◀ Dickens was photographed by Herbert Watkins in this confident pose at around the time *David Copperfield* was written.

The Scarlet Letter

Nathaniel Hawthorne

Lifespan | *b.* 1804 (U.S.), *d.* 1864
First Published | 1850
First Published by | Ticknor, Reed & Fields (Boston)
Original Language | English

The scarlet letter of the title is a gold-bordered, embroidered "A" that the puritanical community of seventeenth-century Boston forces adulteress Hester Prynne to wear. It is both a badge of shame and a beautifully wrought human artifact.

This novel, rich in a symbolism that contradicts its puritanical subject matter, demonstrates a community's failure to permanently fix signs and meanings. This waywardness is at the heart of a series of oppositions in the novel between order and transgression, civilization and wilderness, the town and the surrounding forest, adulthood and childhood. The more society strives to keep out wayward passion, the more it reinforces the split between appearance and reality. The members of this community who are ostensibly the most respectable are often the most depraved, the apparent sinners are often the most virtuous. The novel crafts intriguing symmetries between social oppression and psychological repression. Dimmesdale's sense of torment at his guilty secret, and the physical and mental manifestations of his malaise, reflects the pathology of a society that needs to scapegoat and alienate its so-called sinners. Eventually, individual virtue and personal integrity is able to break free from social control. Perhaps more so than any other novel, *The Scarlet Letter* effectively encapsulates the emergence of individualism and self-reliance from America's puritan and conformist roots. **RMcD**

Moby-Dick

Herman Melville

Lifespan | *b.* 1819 (U.S.), *d.* 1891
First Published | 1851
First Published by | Harper (New York)
Full Title | *Moby-Dick; or, The Whale*

"A whaleship was my Yale College and my Harvard."

🔹 Pictured here is the astute Herman Melville, age thirty-one, captured in paint by Asa W. Twitchell.

🔹 Rockwell Kent's illustration for a 1937 edition shows the great white whale upending a boatful of whalers into the ocean.

Moby-Dick is often cited as the Great American Novel, the high watermark of the nineteenth-century imagination. A huge, monstrous, and yet exquisitely refined creation, it continues to confound, enthrall (and often defeat) generations of readers around the world. Narrated by Ishmael, a Massachusetts schoolteacher who has forsaken his old life for the romance of the high seas, the novel chronicles the long sea voyage of the Pequod, a whaling ship led by the demonic Captain Ahab. Ahab is in search of the white whale that has robbed him of one of his legs. All other considerations (including the safety of his crew) become secondary to his monomaniacal quest. However, no summary can do justice to the breadth and complexity of Melville's novel. One can almost feel the book fighting with itself—balancing the urge to propel the narrative forward with the urge to linger, explore, and philosophize. *Moby-Dick* is a turbulent ocean of ideas, one of the great meditations on the shape and status of America— on democracy, leadership, power, industrialism, labor, expansion, and nature. The Pequod and its diverse crew become a microcosm of American society. This revolutionary novel borrowed from a myriad of literary styles and traditions, switching with astonishing ease between different bodies of knowledge. No one in American literature had written with such intensity and such ambition before. In *Moby-Dick*, one can find abstruse metaphysics, notes on the technicalities of dissecting a whale's foreskin, and searing passages of brine-soaked drama. *Moby-Dick* is an elegy, a political critique, an encyclopedia, and a ripping yarn. Just reading the novel constitutes an experience every bit as wondrous and exhausting as the journey it recounts. **SamT**

The House of the Seven Gables

Nathaniel Hawthorne

Lifespan | *b.* 1804 (U.S.), *d.* 1864
First Published | 1851
First Published by | Ticknor, Reed & Fields (Boston)
Original Language | English

Hawthorne draws heavily on his New England roots in this novel, which is marked by an extreme determinism, punctuated by withering observations of contemporary materialism, as the residual effects of familial guilt are traced through several generations. Nearly two centuries ago, Colonel Pyncheon constructed the eponymous house on land he had illegally confiscated from the Maule family, incurring a dreadful curse. As a result, the spring that had made the land valuable became stagnant, and the house was never a place of happiness. In the mid-nineteenth century the Colonel's descendant, Judge Jaffrey Pyncheon, has inherited the Colonel's power, greed, and hypocrisy. His lodger, the daguerreotypist Holgrave, is the novel's crucial unifying figure; the revelation of his true identity offers hope that the sins of the past need not endlessly pollute the future.

The surprising sentimentality of the conclusion palliates the bleak notion of inherited sin, but cannot efface it entirely. Hawthorne's acute historical consciousness meant that, for him, the past was always near at hand, shaping the physical, moral, and spiritual texture of the present; he felt out of step with nineteenth-century America's forward-looking faith in "progress," measured largely in economic terms. *The House of the Seven Gables* acknowledges this tension and explores the possibility of escaping from the burden of the past. **RH**

The Blithedale Romance

Nathaniel Hawthorne

Lifespan | *b.* 1804 (U.S.), *d.* 1864
First Published | 1852
First Published by | Ticknor, Reed & Fields (Boston)
Original Language | English

Hawthorne's third major novel in as many years is also his most consistently modern, focusing on a more contemporary context. In 1841, Hawthorne had joined the Brook Farm Associationist commune, where he remained for seven months until he became disillusioned with its failure to achieve its socialist ideals. The novel focuses on three major characters inhabiting Blithedale (based on Brook Farm): Zenobia, a voluptuous, strong-willed advocate of women's rights; Hollingsworth, a philanthropic blacksmith, with whom she falls in love; and the fragile, victimized seamstress Priscilla. Their passionate, peculiar power struggles are relayed through the perception of Miles Coverdale, Hawthorne's only first-person narrator. Coverdale's obsessive, voyeuristic personality, his constant observation and interpretation of other characters, give the novel its distinctive tone.

Although Hawthorne glances at a variety of contemporary issues—for example, Hollingsworth's idealistic commitment to prison reform—his main subject is the weakness of human nature, and the ease with which individual character flaws can overpower the most ardently held communal ideals. *The Blithedale Romance* offers the surprising spectacle of an author, conventionally burdened by the past, deliberately looking to the present and future of his nation, but finding little in the prospect to allay his cynicism about human relations. **RH**

Uncle Tom's Cabin; or, Life Among the Lowly

Harriet Beecher Stowe

Lifespan | *b.* 1811 (U.S.), *d.* 1896
First Published | 1852
First Published by | J. P. Jewett (Boston)
Original Language | English

The first American novel to sell more than a million copies, *Uncle Tom's Cabin* has a claim to be the most influential piece of fiction ever written. Stowe was galvanized by the passing of the Fugitive Slave Act in 1850 into writing what the poet Langston Hughes has called "America's first protest novel." It is an unashamed piece of propaganda; its primary aims are not artistic but political.

The saintly slave Uncle Tom, having lived most of his life with kindly owners, is sold for financial reasons at the novel's outset. Refusing to escape, Uncle Tom responds with Christian tolerance and forgiveness, maintaining his faith consistently until his brutal death. Although "Uncle Tom" has become a byword for black complicity in white oppression, for Stowe, Tom displays Christian virtues, and his Christ-like death positions him as the chief moral exemplar of the novel. Besides the overt emotional and physical suffering of slaves, Stowe emphasizes how slavery damages the morality and humanity of white slave owners themselves. The diverse cast of strong females, black and white, displayed how women too could help to achieve abolition.

Despite what we may now perceive as its obvious flaws, Stowe surely achieved her political aims with this phenomenally successful novel that was to play a significant role in the forthcoming American Civil War, inspiring anti-slavery activism, and deeply antagonizing slave-holding. **RH**

"'We don't own your laws; we don't own your country; we stand here as free, under God's sky, as you are; and, by the great God that made us, we'll fight for our liberty till we die."

⬥ Like any bestseller, *Uncle Tom's Cabin* fed off its own success, attracting new readers on the basis of numbers already sold.

CRANFORD

by
Mrs
Gaskell

George G. Harrap & Co. Ltd. London.

Cranford

Elizabeth Gaskell

Lifespan | *b.* 1810 (England), *d.* 1865
First Published | 1853
First Published by | Chapman & Hall (London)
Original Language | English

In *Cranford* Gaskell depicts, with a delicacy fully worthy of Jane Austen, a set of wholly credible lives which engross the reader even as the characters go about their mundane daily business. *Cranford* is a remarkable insight into social change in the early nineteenth century.

Cranford is essentially a town ruled by women, mostly single or widowed. The narrator, Mary, who no longer lives in Cranford and can thus see it from the outside, describes the occasional arrivals, departures, and deaths as seen through their impact on the women. There is a strong sense that life in Cranford is in genteel decline; that the men who should be here have defected to the nearby industrial town of Drumble, which exerts a powerful influence on life in Cranford. What is exceptional about the book is that, although the main characters often seem involved in events and squabbles of the most petty variety, we never lose our sympathy either for their struggles to make ends meet, or for their unceasing attempts to conceal the fragility of their circumstances; indeed, there is an astonishing bravery half-hidden within this tale of domestic incident. The reader is made to see that, as this way of life passes away, something valuable beyond the more obvious social facades is being lost. **DP**

◐ A 1940 edition of Gaskell's *Cranford* uses a portrait of the author herself as the centerpiece of its elaborate title page.

Villette

Charlotte Brontë

Lifespan | *b.* 1816 (England), *d.* 1855
First Published | 1853
First Published by | Smith, Elder & Co. (London)
Pseudonym | Currer Bell

Charlotte Brontë's final novel is her most disturbing work; *Villette* is a first-person story of a woman's quest for independence and emotional fulfilment. Like *Jane Eyre,* the central protagonist is an orphan forced to earn her own living as a teacher, who after various obstacles finds love with an unconventional older man. But in *Villette* the satisfying resolutions of the earlier novel are devastatingly undermined, as the reader is caught up within the claustrophobic and unstable consciousness of the narrator, Lucy Snowe. Lucy is secretive and duplicitous. She tells us little about her history and origins: we only know that her family are lost through some unnamed catastrophe. Moving through domestic roles—from houseguest, to female companion, to a teacher in a school in the Belgian town of Villette—she withholds crucial information. Lucy at times hovers on the brink of breakdown, and the novel plays on the instability of rationality—the gothic image of the ghostly nun, apparently her hallucination, turns out to be a shallow trick. *Villette* is thus a study of isolation and its effects; but Lucy is also a social being who craves company and is an acute observer, particularly of the examples of female power that populate the novel, such as Madame Beck, the controlling headmistress of the school. It is her very loneliness that makes Lucy's position representative, and the novel so compelling: as she notes, "a great many men, and more women, hold their span of life on conditions of denial and deprivation." **JBT**

Bleak House

Charles Dickens

Lifespan | *b.* 1812 (England), *d.* 1870
First Published | 1853
First Published by | Bradbury & Evans (London)
Original Language | English

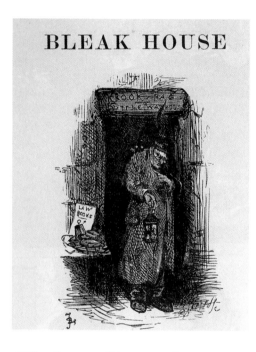

"The butterflies are free. Mankind will surely not deny to Harold Skimpole what it concedes to the butterflies."

H. K. Browne ("Phiz") produced suitably somber illustrations for Dickens' dark portrayal of fog-bound London in *Bleak House.*

Bleak House begins with fog: "Fog everywhere. Fog up the river, where it flows among green aits and meadows; fog down the river, where it rolls defiled among the tiers of shipping, and the waterside pollutions of a great (and dirty) city." And at the center of the fog, but murkier still, is the High Court. Legal corruption permeates this novel like a disease, issuing in particular from the Byzantine lawsuit of Jarndyce and Jarndyce, with which all the book's characters have a connection. This suit, the narrator tells us, has become so complicated and of such longevity "that no man alive knows what it means." People live and die as plaintiffs in the case. Structured around Chancery's machinations, Dickens' narrative is less picaresque than other of his works but nevertheless provides his customary, witty dissection of the layers of Victorian society. Whether in the sunny aristocratic milieu of the Dedlocks in Lincolnshire or the slums of Tom-All-Alone's in London, there is always someone with a stake in the Jarndyce case.

Really, it is the public sphere in general that *Bleak House* satirizes. Everything resembles Chancery: Parliament, the provincial aristocracy, and even Christian philanthropy is caricatured as moribund and self-serving. At some subterranean level, all public life is tainted with complicity between class, power, money, and law. Private and inner life is affected too. The narrative, which is split between the third person and the novel's heroine, Esther Summerson, concerns moral disposition as much as social criticism. Characters—from the wearyingly earnest to the brilliantly shallow, from the foolish and foppish to the vampiristic and dangerous—are all illuminated in the darkness of Dickens' outraged, urbane opus. **DH**

Walden

Henry David Thoreau

Walden is not exactly a novel, but it is indisputably a cornerstone of American literature, and deserves its place in this book. Between July 1845 and September 1847, Thoreau lived a solitary, austere, self-sufficient life in a simple cabin on the shore of Walden Pond, near Concord, Massachusetts, where he developed and practiced his personal and political philosophy. In a series of eighteen essays, distilled from his voluminous journal entries, *Walden* records Thoreau's thoughts and experiences of this time.

Convinced that "the mass of men lead lives of quiet desperation," Thoreau sought to "simplify" his life in every way, eating only what he found in the wild, or could cultivate himself. Apart from physical exercise such as walking, fishing, and swimming, the remainder of his time was devoted to observing the natural world around him, writing, reading, and thinking. His greatest luxury was the leisure to pursue these ends; he notes that "a man is rich in proportion to the number of things he can afford to let alone." Deeply influenced by the transcendental philosophy of Emerson, Thoreau rejected religious orthodoxy, seeking instead a personal bond with God, discovered through Nature. For Thoreau, however, Nature is not only spiritual; he describes with equal reverence his occasional approach toward primal savagery. He also refuses to feel hidebound by tradition, encapsulating the untapped potential of youth in the image of the West. This ethos underpins the appeal of *Walden* to generations of Americans, despite its rejection of aggressive capitalism. Thoreau's experiment was neither misanthropic nor revolutionary. Practical, honest, and beautiful, it is the record of one man's efforts to live "a life of simplicity, independence, magnanimity, and trust." **RH**

Lifespan | *b*. 1817 (U.S.), *d*. 1862
First Published | 1854
First Published by | Ticknor & Fields (Boston)
Full Title | *Walden; or, Life in the Woods*

"I went to the woods because I wished to live deliberately, to front only the essential facts of life . . . "

This frontispiece from the first edition of Thoreau's *Walden* emphasizes the return to a simplified lifestyle.

Hard Times

Charles Dickens

Lifespan | b. 1812 (England), d. 1870
First Published | 1854
First Published by | Bradbury & Evans (London)
Original Language | English

Mr. Gradgrind, the MP for Coketown, a fictional northern industrial town, runs a school according to strict utilitarian principles: the pupils (including his own children, Tom and Louisa) are drilled with facts and taught to mistrust their emotions. Into their household comes Sissy Jupe, brought up in the circus and abandoned by her father; though she struggles academically, she is warm and sympathetic. The deeply repressed Louisa marries the blustering industrialist Mr. Bounderby. One of Bounderby's employees is the luckless Stephen Blackpool, a weaver tormented by a loveless marriage to a drunken wife. Blackpool loses his job, is framed for a bank robbery by Tom, and ultimately dies a wincingly pathetic death. Chastened by Tom's crimes, Louisa's misery, Stephen's simple faith, and Sissy's compassion, Gradgrind sees the error of his ways, and retires from public life.

Unlike his contemporary Elizabeth Gaskell, Charles Dickens had little personal experience of the industrial North of England, nor was he particularly well-informed about the labor movement. *Hard Times* impressionistically conveys the dehumanizing nature of factory work, while providing few concrete details. Dickens merely balances the oppressive values of Gradgrind and Bounderby with escapism and love—a moral encapsulated by the lisping circus-owner, Sleary: "People mutht be amuthed. They can't be alwayth a learning, nor yet they can't be alwayth a working, they an't made for it." **RH**

North and South

Elizabeth Gaskell

Lifespan | b. 1810 (England), d. 1865
First Published | 1855, by Harper (New York)
First UK Edition | Chapman & Hall
First Serialized | 1854–55, by Household Words

North and South is, as its title suggests, a study in contrasts. Its heroine, the daughter of a clergyman who resigns because of his religious doubts, is displaced from the southern village of Helstone (a picturesque, pastoral, and traditional backwater) to the bustling manufacturing city of Milton Northern, a fictionalized Manchester. The city teems with the new energy of urban industrialization, its rising capitalist class, and all that comes with it: pollution, deprivation, worker unrest, illness, atheism, and a host of other apparent evils. In this environment, the Hale family are truly foreigners, with their country-gentry habits and values. It is a "condition of England" novel that looks unflinchingly at the plight of factory workers, and at worker-"master" relations.

To this end we find our heroine, Margaret Hale, befriending struggling families such as the Higginses, and speaking out for reconciliation between mill-hands and mill-owners. Interwoven in opposition to this story is the narrative of Margaret's coming of age, worked out in the romance plot between Margaret and her ideological antithesis, Mr. Thornton, a prominent factory owner and self-made man. Margaret loses her parents and the apparent certainty of her youthful rural values, but gains a more nuanced understanding of change, political as well as personal, and its possibilities. **ST**

❯ Gaskell was deeply concerned with social issues in Victorian society, such as the exploitation of child labor in cotton mills.

Madame Bovary

Gustave Flaubert

Madame Bovary is a revelation; almost one-hundred-and-fifty years old, it feels as fresh as if it were tomorrow's novel. Readers who are accustomed to think of nineteenth-century novels as rambling, digressive, plot-driven stories, will have a shock when they encounter a novel from that long century that is digressive and has a compelling plot but which wraps all these up in a prose style so exquisite the book feels fragile and sturdy all at once.

Flaubert takes the story of adultery and presents it as banal, an unheroic element of the unheroic provincial petit bourgeois world he is immersed in. But he also makes it beautiful, sordid, melancholy, and joyous, revels in emotions run amok and the mess of feelings that clichés can neither hide nor contain. Emma Bovary, a beauty confined to a marriage which bores her, yearns for the gigantic and gorgeous emotions she finds in the romance novels she devours. Her life, her husband, her imagination is not enough; she takes a lover and then another, but they too fail to sate her appetites. She shops, using an array of material objects as a means of fulfilment; when these also give way before the depths of her yearning, she finally kills herself, in debt and in despair.

Flaubert does not mock Emma Bovary; neither does he sentimentalize, moralize, or treat her joy or desperation as heroic. The impersonal, prosaic narrator, a monster of precision and detachment yet endearing, almost charming, mocks all with his aloofness, and cherishes all with his lavish and meticulous attention to detail. The result is a rich context—not just for Emma Bovary but for the novel, for writing itself. For so much scrupulous care to be given to something, that something must be precious. Flaubert makes this novel precious. **PMcM**

Lifespan | *b.* 1821 (France), *d.* 1880
First Published | 1857
First Published by | Charpentier (Paris)
Original Language | French

For writing *Madame Bovary*, Flaubert was prosecuted for offences against public morality—ensuring the book's notoriety.

The follies of the novel's eponymous heroine are presented mercilessly, yet without alienating the reader's sympathy.

Adam Bede

George Eliot

'There's Adam Bede a-carrying the little un.'

"Our deeds determine us, as much as we determine our deeds."

◉ The high-minded village carpenter Adam Bede has less impact on the reader than Eliot's more rounded female characters.

Lifespan | b. 1819 (England), d. 1880
First Published | 1859
First Published by | W. Blackwood & Sons (London)
Given Name | Mary Ann Evans

Set in the English Midlands, in the early nineteenth-century, the eponymous character, a carpenter, is in love with the flighty, shallow, and vain Hetty Sorel. She, in turn, is seduced by the likeable but irresponsible local squire, Arthur Donnithorne, who leaves town shortly after getting her pregnant. The main drama lies in the gripping rendition of Hetty's lonely and unsuccessful journey to find her lover, her eventual infanticide, and her moving confession to her cousin, Dinah Morris. The confession, in its charged moment of interpersonal communication and sympathy, provides the symbolic and moral climax of the book. Eliot's agnostic humanism enables her to retain—without any spiritual belief—the Christian ethical schema of confession, forgiveness, and redemption. At this moment Eliot's writing moves away from documentary fidelity to a heightened diction which conjures with the unknown and the sublime. Indeed, while the novel is peopled with lovingly sketched rural characters, it is almost more compelling at times such as this, when the language of realism modulates into something stranger. Despite its suggestion of a "beyond" to the everyday life of human affairs, the novel's "realist" impulse is to suggest that one should subdue one's own desires to an acceptance of duty and the here-and-now. Contemporary readers might find the conclusion somewhat hard to swallow, but there remains much to relish in this vividly narrated and emotionally convincing novel. **CC**

Oblomov

Ivan Goncharov

Lifespan | *b.* 1812 (Russia), *d.* 1891
First Published | 1859
Movie Adaptation | 1981
Original Language | Russian

One of the world's great novels, *Oblomov*, came to be seen as the definitive representation of the lethargic and myopic Russian aristocracy of the nineteenth century. A principal target of the novel is the institution of serfdom; like many Russian intellectuals, Goncharov felt that Russia could not modernize and compete with the rest of the developed world unless it abolished the institutions and social practices that hampered it so severely.

But *Oblomov* would not be a remarkable novel if it were only a critique of an important, but now long gone, problem. A bittersweet tragi-comedy, it centers on one of the most charming but ineffectual protagonists in literature. Oblomov is good-natured but lacks the willpower to put his ideas into practice. He relies on his much more able servant, Zakhar, to organize his pointless existence, in an updated version of the relationship between Don Quixote and Sancho Panza. Falling in love with the beautiful Olga, he simply cannot take the necessary actions to secure her affections, and he loses her to his practical but rather less appealing friend, Stolz. After this predictable failure Oblomov sinks further into lethargy, rarely leaving his bedroom, despite the good offices of his well-intentioned landlady. *Oblomov* is a brilliant and unusual novel about wasted opportunity: how many works of literature tell the story of a hero who fails to secure the object of his affections through inactivity? And how many can convince most readers that he is still a good man? **AH**

A Tale of Two Cities

Charles Dickens

Lifespan | *b.* 1812 (England), *d.* 1870
First Published | 1859
First Published by | Chapman & Hall (London)
Original Language | English

London and Paris, at the time of the French Revolution and the subsequent Terror, are the "two cities" of the title. Savage in its attack on the excesses of a decadent French aristocracy, this novel is equally severe in its censure of revolutionary violence and mob hysteria. Yet Dickens seems unconsciously fascinated by the violence he overtly condemns: the scenes of revolutionary upheaval are written with a verve never achieved in his descriptions of domestic happiness.

Structured according to a series of oppositions, the novel is interested in the relationship between good and evil, "the best" and "the worst." Much of the attraction of this book lies in the uncanny effects that its plethora of doubles generates. Charles Darnay, the novel's somewhat passive hero, renounces his noble origins, and comes to England where he falls in love with the equally virtuous Lucie Manette, daughter of a physician, who has languished in a French prison for eighteen years. A long period of domestic bliss ensues for all, which comes to an end when Darnay nobly returns to France to save a servant, but is himself imprisoned and condemned to death. His salvation comes from his double and alter ego, Sidney Carton, a self-confessed dissolute wastrel whose only good quality is a tender, unrequited passion for Lucie. With an act far superior to anything he has ever done before, Carton uses his physical similarity to Darnay to bring the book to a memorable conclusion. **CC**

Max Havelaar

Multatuli

Lifespan | *b.* 1820 (Netherlands), *d.* 1887
First Published | 1860
First Published by | De Ruyter (Amsterdam)
Original Language | Dutch

When it first appeared in print, *Max Havelaar* caused a stir that saw its author challenging the Dutch government to refute its essential truth: that, in fact, colonial policy as practiced in Java at the time was a series of extortions and cruel tyrannies that oppressed the peoples of the Dutch Indies by, among other abuses, forcing them to forego planting rice crops in order to supply their overseas masters with coffee and tea. There were no takers then, although much later, the substance of the book was found to be accurate.

This notoriety, and the book's success in provoking some positive changes in the region, much as *Uncle Tom's Cabin* helped to focus attention on the plight of, and consequently improve the situation for, American slaves, does not relegate it to the status of a worthy tract that has attained its purpose. Beyond the missionary service accomplished, *Max Havelaar* remains a work to be read and enjoyed for its satirical humor. Recounting the adventures of a colonial administrator at odds with the government he serves, it takes on and renders laughable the bourgeois businessman and colonial administrator alike.

Multatuli, which means "I have suffered greatly" is now the name of a literary prize in the Netherlands and a museum, and the Max Havelaar Foundation is a fair-trade labeling organization. While these homages are fitting, they remain only facets of a more complex novel. **ES**

The Marble Faun

Nathaniel Hawthorne

Lifespan | *b.* 1804 (U.S.), *d.* 1864
First Published | 1860, by Ticknor, Reed & Fields
Alternate Title | *Transformation, or, the Romance of Monte Beni*

Hawthorne warns us in his Preface that the Italian setting of *The Marble Faun* will function as "a sort of poetic or fairy precinct, where actualities would not be so terribly insisted upon, as they are … in America." The minimal plot focuses on four friends who have met in Rome: the sculptor, Kenyon, and the angelic painter, Hilda, both from New England; the beautiful, enigmatic Miriam, with a hint of scandal in her mysterious past; and Donatello, the young Italian count with an uncanny resemblance to the faun of the title, and an innocent, sensual approach to life. Their carefree existence is suddenly interrupted when Donatello, at Miriam's impulsive instigation, commits a murder, witnessed by Hilda.

At the demand of his publishers, Hawthorne included long passages from his travel notebooks; the result is an odd mixture of dreamlike fantasy and travelogue, which became highly popular with nineteenth-century tourists to Rome.

The encounter of Kenyon and Hilda's austere New England beliefs with the rich iconography and seductive consolation of Rome enacts a subtle drama of aesthetic and religious anxiety. Hawthorne's attitude to Italy is profoundly ambivalent: the oppressive depth of history confronts each of the characters with a sense of decay and redundancy. Marked by a complete absence of naturalism, rich symbolic patterning is far more important to Hawthorne than realism or plot resolution in this elusive moral fable. **RH**

The Woman in White

Wilkie Collins

Lifespan | *b.* 1824 (England), *d.* 1889
First Published | 1860
First Published by | S. Low, Son & Co. (London)
Original Language | English

Opening with the hero Walter Hartright's thrilling midnight encounter with the mysterious fugitive from a lunatic asylum, *The Woman in White* was an instant hit when it first appeared as a weekly serial.

Different narrators present their accounts like witnesses in a trial, and the contest for power within the story is acted out through the struggle over who controls the narrative itself. The plot investigates how a "legitimate" identity is built up and broken down through a set of doublings and contrasts. The rich, vapid heiress Laura, married to the villain Sir Percival Glyde, is substituted by her uncanny double, the woman in white, Anne Catherick. While Laura is drugged and placed in a lunatic asylum, Anne dies of a heart condition and is buried in Laura's place. The plot, mastermined by the engaging rogue Count Fosco, is narrated by Laura's feisty half-sister Marian, a character that many believe was based on Collins' friend, George Eliot. From the sensational moment when Walter Hartright sees his beloved Laura standing by her own grave, the story turns into a quest to reconstruct her. Walter's increasingly obsessive drive to prove Laura's identity leads to two disclosures of illegitimacy.

This book defined the sensation novel of the 1860s. Wild and uncanny elements of gothic fiction are transposed into the everyday world of the upper-middle-class family, appealing directly to the nerves of the reader and exploiting modern anxieties about the instability of identity. **JBT**

"Thus, the story here presented will be told by more than one pen, as the story of an offence against the laws is told in Court by more than one witness . . ."

◉ *The Woman in White* generates an atmosphere of disquiet and anxiety that is never dissipated by the unraveling of the plot.

The Mill on the Floss

George Eliot

"*If I got places, sir, it was because I made myself fit for 'em. If you want to slip into a round hole, you must make a ball of yourself; that's where it is.*"

⬤ Tom and Maggie Tulliver are about to be overwhelmed by the flood in a late-Victorian visualization of the novel's climax.

Lifespan | *b.* 1819 (England), *d.* 1880
First Published | 1860
First Published by | W. Blackwood & Sons (London)
Given Name | Mary Ann Evans

The Mill on the Floss reworks elements of Eliot's own history into a powerful study of childhood and of how a woman's identity is shaped and constrained by circumstance. Following the development of Maggie and Tom Tulliver, the two children of the miller of Dovecote Mill, it stresses the unpredictability of family inheritance. Stolid Tom takes after his mother, while his sister Maggie, dark, impulsive, and imaginative, favors her father. Unlike Tom, Maggie is intellectually sharp, and is a tomboy in contrast to her cousin Lucy Deane. The story is set in the 1840s within the wider provincial middle-class community of St. Oggs, and explores the competing forces of continuity and change. Tulliver is financially ruined by the modernizing lawyer Wakem; and while Tom labors to reclaim the family property, Maggie strives to overcome past feuds through her friendship with Philip, Wakem's disabled son. However it is the brother-sister bond and the conflict between the claims of family ties which drive the novel, embodied and underpinned by the relentless force of the river, the Floss. In a moment of impulse, Maggie gives way to her suppressed desire for Lucy's fiancé Stephen, drifting with him down the stream, before returning, disgraced, to her family with words that haunt the novel: "If the past is not to bind us, where does duty lie?" In a tragic denouement Maggie is ultimately reconciled with Tom; however, as the narrator comments on the aftermath of the flood, "Nature repairs her ravages—but not all." **JBT**

Castle Richmond

Anthony Trollope

Lifespan | *b.* 1815 (England), *d.* 1882
First Published | 1860
First Published by | Chapman & Hall (London)
Original Language | English

To read *Castle Richmond* is to experience a novel that ultimately fails. Centering on the lives and loves of the Anglo-Irish gentry, it is a tale of love and identity, enmeshed with those anxieties about inheritance rights and legitimacy which seem an indelible part of nineteenth-century realism. Trollope's eager humanist intimacy invites all and sundry to participate in the ambition and warmth of Victorian liberalism at its best.

What distinguishes *Castle Richmond* is its setting, in Cork in the mid-1840s, a time when the "Great Hunger" is, as the text puts it, "in full swing." Trollope knew Ireland as well as a traveling bureaucrat is able to know anywhere. He first went to Ireland as a surveyor's clerk for the Post Office in 1841, staying for ten years, and returned between 1853 and 1859. He would have witnessed the long years of disease and starvation, the government's mismanagement of the crisis, and the subsequent imposition of martial law, when fifteen thousand troops were dispatched to Ireland. In *Castle Richmond*, Trollope struggles to make sense of the famine and fails. The delicacy of his characters' philanthropy is damaged, crudely and violently, by their encounter with angry starvation. Conversations around mannered dinner-tables become macabre rather than civilized in the context of a fatal scarcity. The story's juxtapositions generate multiple ironies, albeit unintentionally, and the text's incapacity to smooth its parts into a whole, accumulate until the story itself unravels. **PMcM**

On the Eve

Ivan Turgenev

Lifespan | *b.* 1818 (Russia), *d.* 1883 (France)
First Published | 1860 (Russia)
Original Title | *Nakanune*
Original Language | Russian

Set in 1853, *On the Eve* deals with the problems facing the younger intelligentsia on the eve of the Crimean War, and speculates on the outcome of the emancipation of the serfs in 1861. The novel deals with the love affairs and friendships of a provincial Russian woman named Elena and a number of men—the intellectual Berzeniev, the artist Shubin, and Berzeniev's friend, the Bulgarian revolutionary Insarov. Berzeniev introduces Elena to Insarov and the two fall in love and secretly marry. Elena's parents, who have found her a suitable Russian fiancé, do not like Insarov, and she is forced to choose between staying with her parents and joining Insarov in Bulgaria. This is first and foremost a love story, set at a time of war and social change, but it is also an innovative novel. Although the central character is Elena, Insarov is a genuinely strong male character, a departure from the ineffectual heroes that had dominated Russian literature in the first half of the nineteenth century; perhaps it is because of this that the freedom fighter is Bulgarian rather than Russian. Turgenev manages to retain the romance of an old-fashioned Russia while giving the Bulgarian hero a political cause that is more profound than anything being pursued by his Russian contemporaries, personified by Elena's other companions. As well as a story of love and belief, *On the Eve* offers profound political and sociological comment on Russia, at a time when it was poised for revolutionary change. **EF**

Great Expectations

Charles Dickens

Lifespan | *b.* 1812 (England), *d.* 1870
First Published | 1861
First Published by | Chapman & Hall (London)
Original Language | English

Great Expectations works on numerous levels: as a political fairy-tale about "dirty money," an exploration of memory and writing, and a disturbing portrayal of the instability of identity.

Looking back from some undistinguished and unspecified future, Pip recalls his childhood, living with his fierce sister and her gentle, blacksmith husband in the Thames marshland, and the fateful effects of his encounter with the escaped convict Magwitch by his parents' graveside. When Pip later comes into a mysterious financial inheritance, he assumes that it can only come from the mummified Miss Havisham, preserved eternally at the moment of her own jilting. But Dickens' great stylistic coup is to make ceiling and floor change places—as in an Escher picture.

Shorter and more quickly composed than Dickens's giant social panoramas of the 1850s, *Great Expectations* gains from this pacing, as it unfolds like a fever-dream. Victorian writers were fond of "fictional autobiographies," but Dickens' novel has another layer of unsettling irony, in that it tells of someone who has been constructing himself as a fictional character. And as Pip shamefully reviews his past life on paper, it often seems that the act of writing is the only thing holding his fractured identities together. Perhaps autobiography should ideally be an act of recovery, but *Great Expectations* dramatizes instead the impossibility of Pip's lending his life coherence, or atoning for the past. **BT**

"I never had one hour's happiness in her society, and yet my mind all round the four-and-twenty hours was harping on the happiness of having her with me unto death."

⦿ Miss Havisham in her bridal gown intimidates the young
Pip in Marcus Stone's illustration of *Great Expectations*.

Silas Marner

George Eliot

Lifespan | *b.*1819 (England), *d.*1880
First Published | 1861
First Published by | W. Blackwood & Sons (London)
Full Title | *Silas Marner: the Weaver of Raveloe*

Silas Marner weaves elements of fairy tale and traditional ballad into an exploration of the meaning of the family and the nature of belonging. Set in a "far-off time" when "superstition clung easily around every person or thing that was at all unwonted," it charts the moral, psychological, and social transformation of Silas, the weaver. He is cast out of his northern primitive Methodist community, and arrives as a stranger in the rural Midlands village of Raveloe. Isolated and feared, the weaver is reduced to miserly obsession and mechanical repetition. His fractured identity is recreated when he adopts Eppie the abandoned child of an opium-addict. The story of Silas's social assimilation into the community, and of Eppie's upbringing contains some of Eliot's most powerful writing. Set within this redemptive tale is the disclosure of Eppie's origins as the child of a disastrous secret marriage: that of the son of the local squire, Godfrey Cass, who finally acknowledges Eppie as his own. Eppie, however decides to stay with her adoptive father and her working-class community, and the novel profoundly reworks the "family romance" that underpins so much English fiction, in which the child discovers noble origins and a "true self." Here, the family is seen primarily as a set of emotional and social bonds, rather than a genetic inheritance. Community takes the place of individual aspiration, and for all its static, pastoral quality *Silas Marner* is a moving exploration of how social selves are made. **JBT**

Fathers and Sons

Ivan Turgenev

Lifespan | *b.*1818 (Russia), *d.*1883 (France)
First Published | 1862
Original Title | *Otti I deti*
Original Language | Russian

Published only a year after the emancipation of the Russian serfs, and during a period when Russia's young intellectuals were increasingly agitating for revolution, *Fathers and Sons* was very much a novel of the time in its depiction of two generations with widely differing political and social values.

The central and most memorable character is the self-proclaimed nihilist, Bazarov, who claims to accept no form of authority, and is only interested in ideas that can be verified by scientific materialism. The narrative follows Bazarov and his acolyte Arkady as they visit their parental homes: what results is a confrontation between the old order of the traditional fathers and its new challengers, their idealistic sons. As well as the contemporary political resonances, this antagonism demonstrates the timeless conflict between youth and its elders. Tensions are also explored within the relationship of the charismatic, domineering Bazarov and his initially star-struck disciple, with their differences becoming manifest when they fall in love with the same woman.

Turnegev's skill lies at the level of characterization: the profound (mis)communication which operates between the main protagonists ensures that even when their actions and rhetoric may appear misguided, they are ultimately understandable and extremely human. *Fathers and Sons* remains a classic and beautifully drawn examination of the necessity and power of youthful idealism, and its pitfalls. **JC**

Les Misérables

Victor Hugo

Lifespan | *b.* 1802 (France), *d.* 1885
First Published | 1862
First Published by | A. Lacroix & Verboeckhoven
Original Language | French

The image of Cosette created by Hugo's illustrator Emile Bayard is now famous as the logo for the musical based on the novel.

An illustration shows the costumes designed for a French theatrical version of *Les Misérables*, performed in 1878.

Les Misérables is one of only a few novels that have taken on a vivid afterlife long after their initial publication. There have been (horribly) abridged versions, rewritings, movies, and, of course, the world-famous musical, yet in order to understand the true scale of Victor Hugo's achievement, one must return to the text itself.

Like Tolstoy's *War and Peace*, this novel is concerned with the way in which individual lives are played out in the context of epoch-defining historical events. What is "History"? Hugo asks us. Who creates "History"? To whom does it happen? What role does the individual play in such events? The character of Jean Valjean is thus the key to *Les Misérables*, an escaped convict whose desperate need to redeem himself through his adopted daughter, Cosette, lies at the heart of the novel. Valjean is pursued throughout by the extraordinary Inspector Javert, with whose life his becomes irrevocably entwined, and who is relentless in his determination to uphold the law and to apprehend him. This personal drama of hunter and prey is then cast into the cauldron of revolutionary Paris as Cosette falls in love with the radical idealist Marius and Valjean grapples with the possibility of losing all that he has ever loved. The novel draws the reader into the politics and geography of Paris with a vividness that is unparalleled, and then leads on, incorporating Hugo's characteristic meditations upon the universe, to the battle of Waterloo, and the final, astonishing denouement. There are not many texts that can be termed national classics, but *Les Misérables* is one, and is a landmark in the development of the historical novel that stands alongside the greatest works of Dickens and Tolstoy. It is also a deeply compelling read. **MD**

Acte I. Jean Valjean.   Jacquin.   Une Femme. (2.T) Mᵐᵉ Magloire.   Mˡˡᵉ Baptistine.   Un Brigadier.   Mʳ Miriel

(5ᵉ T) _ Javert.   Fantine.   (4ᵉ T). _ La Tenardier.   Fantine.   Tenardier.   (3ᵉ T) _ Petit Gervais.

(5ᵉ T) Fauchelevent.   Un Ouvrier.   (6ᵉ T) Jean Valjean.   (8ᵉ T) Sœur Simplice.   Fantine.   (9ᵉ T.) _ Cosette.

(10ᵉ T) Claquesous.   Tenardier.   Montparnasse   Eponine   (11ᵉ T) _ Cosette.   (12ᵉ T) Fauchelevent.

The Water-Babies

Charles Kingsley

Lifespan | *b.* 1819 (England), *d.* 1875
First Published | 1863
First Published by | Macmillan & Co. (Cambridge)
Full Title | *The Water-Babies: A Fairy Tale for a Land-Baby*

Often mistakenly thought of as a children's book, Charles Kingsley's masterpiece *The Water-Babies* was first published in *Macmillan's Magazine* just four years after Darwin's *The Origin of Species*. A ten-year-old chimneysweep named Tom, cruelly exploited by his master, Grimes, falls down the wrong chimney at Sir John Harthover's country estate into little Ellie's bedroom. There is a great hue and cry, and Tom, supposed to be a burglar, is chased through the grounds and drowns in a pond, but does not die. His memory of his land-dwelling life has gone and he is transmogrified into a water-dweller. He begins a voyage of physical and psychological exploration in this new world, rediscovering his own identity as he interacts with, and learns from, the other various sea creatures. In this watery realm Tom learns the teachings of Mrs Doasyouwouldbedoneby, and evolves from a dirt-encrusted chimneysweep into a clean, Victorian gentleman.

The Water-Babies touches upon most of Kingsley's favorite themes: the impact of poverty, education, sanitation, pollution, evolution. In Tom's spiritual regeneration, Kingsley presents a vision of nature as the tool of divine reality. It is this aspect of the novel, where he shows that he is able to present Darwin's theory of evolutionary development as a series of parables, that we see Charles Kingsley at his best. More interestingly though, Kingsley is also able to articulate and interact with notions of the degeneration of the species that would not become a common currency in the novel for another quarter of a century. In 1887, a special edition of the novel was published to commemorate Kingsley's death. The marvelous illustrations by Linley Sambourne are as violent, shocking, and completely unexpected as Kingsley's prose. **VC-R**

◉ Charles Kingsley's concern with the fate of the poor—he was a Christian Socialist—permeated many of his fictional writings.

◗ Tom the chimneysweep becomes an object of curiosity to his fellow water-dwellers in J. W. Smith's 1920s illustration.

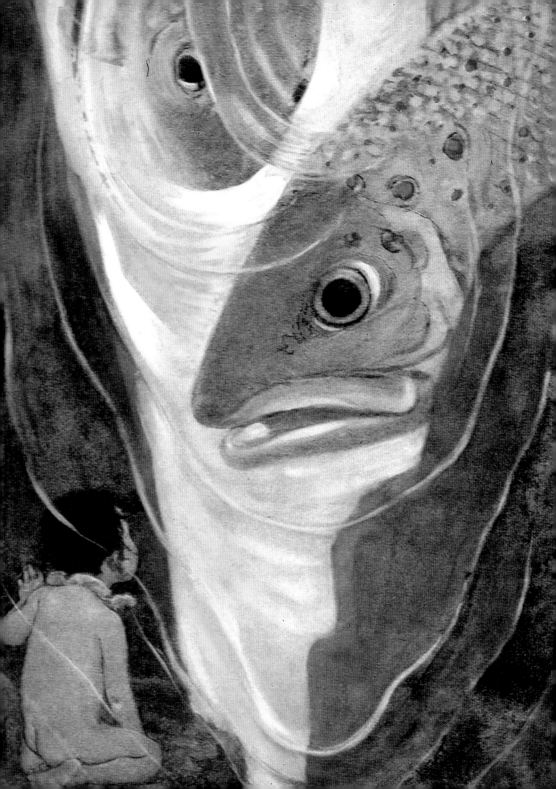

Notes from the Underground
Fyodor Dostoevsky

Lifespan | *b.*1821 (Russia), *d.*1881
First Published | 1864
First Published by | *Epokha* magazine
Original Title | *Zapiski iz podpolya*

As the title suggests, the anonymous narrator of Dostoevsky's *Notes from the Underground* is a voice from beneath the daylight world—a troubled consciousness leaking out from a crack in the floorboards of Russian society. The novel is both the apology and the confession of a bitter, misanthropic civic official living alone in St. Petersburg. Divided into two sections, it reflects two key stages in Russian intellectual life during the nineteenth century: the rationalist utilitarianism of the 1860s and the sentimental, literary romanticism of the 1840s. Across these two parts, the narrator launches a series of dazzling, provocative attacks on the many changing orders of his lifetime—aesthetic, religious, philosophical, and political. He is a highly educated but deeply disillusioned soul, savaging both the "beautiful and lofty" romanticism of his youth and the new socialist principles that correspond with his middle age. No target is immune from scorn.

On the one hand, this dark, strange work is a kind of "case study"—an analysis of alienation and self-loathing, a novel that situates itself on the faultline between society and the individual. On the other, it is a tragicomic theater of ideas. It offers a powerful rebuttal to both enlightenment idealism and the promises of socialist utopianism. *Notes from the Underground* is a shadowy, difficult, and compelling novel, which deserves to be recognized as far more than a critical prelude to Dostoevsky's later, more celebrated works. **SamT**

"The more conscious I was of goodness and of all that was 'sublime and beautiful,' the more deeply I sank into my mire and the more ready I was to sink in it altogether."

◉ Dostoevsky's life—political prisoner, compulsive gambler, religious idealist—was as full of contradictions as his novels.

Uncle Silas

Sheridan Le Fanu

Lifespan | *b.* 1814 (Ireland), *d.* 1873
First Published | 1864
First Published by | R. Bentley (London)
Full Title | *Uncle Silas: a Tale of Bartram-Haugh*

Uncle Silas arises principally from the genre of Victorian sensationalism, and, like the works of Wilkie Collins, combines the interest of a mystery with the compulsion of a determined investigation. Yet this story about the inheritance of a Derbyshire country house has also been shown to be a political allegory for the dissolution of Anglo-Irish society, and a meta-physical version of Emanuel Swedenborg's speculations about death and the afterlife.

The compelling heroine, Maud Ruthyn, is both investigator and victim, enquiring into her father's secrets, and then suffering the consequences in her uncle's house. His estate, Bartram-Haugh, represents one aspect of a poisonous paralysis of Protestant culture, but is also "a dream of romance," populated by the fantastic and the grotesque. There is nothing supernatural in *Uncle Silas*: all of its events can be accounted for by purely human malignity. We are led to suspect characters because of their excessive appetites, "fat-faced" appearance, and dull, cunning expressions. A lexicon of corporeality takes us from the merely unconventional or malicious, to those "lean," white-faced figures who, like Silas himself, are deathly visitants in the world of the living. As such, these creations lie behind the unsettling ghost stories of the Edwardian age, while Le Fanu's diagnosis of the Anglo-Irish tradition meant that he was also powerfully resonant for Yeats and Joyce, making *Uncle Silas* one of the less acknowledged antecedents of twentieth-century modernism. **DT**

Our Mutual Friend

Charles Dickens

Lifespan | *b.* 1812 (England), *d.* 1870
First Published | 1865
First Published by | Chapman & Hall (London)
Original Language | English

Charles Dickens' last completed novel consists of interwoven stories, forming a dense, multi-layered dissection of a corrupt social structure. Beginning with the striking image of the discovery of a body in the Thames, themes of death and rebirth, wealth and waste, link the two primary plots.

John Harmon fakes his own death by drowning to escape his dead father's behest: in order to inherit his father's considerable estate he must marry the socially ambitious Bella Wilfer. Under the name John Rokesmith, he takes a position as the secretary to Mr. Boffin, Old Harmon's former servant, who has inherited his wealth and adopted Bella. This strand follows Bella's moral regeneration, as she comes to see the corrupting influence of wealth, personified by the nouveau riche Veneerings and the Lammles.

Lizzie Hexham—perhaps Dickens' most idealized heroine—supports her brother Charley's education, but through him falls victim to the obsessive love of his schoolteacher, the repressed Bradley Headstone. Headstone's pursuit of Lizzie and mental breakdown is counterpoised to the moral reform of his rival, the upper-class dilettante Eugene Wrayburn. Mutability and recycling pervade the text: from the dust heaps where society's detritus is transformed into wealth; to the flotsam and jetsam in the Thames, home of corpses and the locus of rebirth; to the work of the doll's dressmaker, the uncanny Jenny Wren, and (in one of Dickens' weirdest scenes) the shop of Mr. Venus, dealer in prosthetic limbs and body parts. **JBT**

Alice's Adventures in Wonderland
Lewis Carroll

Lifespan | *b.* 1832 (England), *d.* 1898
First Published | 1865
First Published by | Macmillan & Co. (London)
Given Name | Charles Lutwidge Dodgson

🔵 Sir John Tenniel's original illustrations for *Alice in Wonderland* are an integral part of the book's imaginative universe.

🔵 Preceded by the white rabbit, Alice falls into the underworld in this illustration by W. H. Walker for a 1907 edition of the book.

Wholly familiar as an integral part of our culture, Carroll's trip down the rabbit hole is a children's book containing enough bizarre satire, wordplay, and comedy to satisfy any adult reader. Indeed, the Surrealist André Breton wrote of *Alice* that here, "accommodation to the absurd readmits adults to the mysterious realm inhabited by children." Far from patronizing children, the book is positively educative for jaded adults. Published in 1865, the same year as Lautréamont's infernal *The Songs of Maldoror* and Rimbaud's *A Season in Hell*, *Alice* may be a radically English, genteel journey into a dream landscape, yet it is not without its dark side.

Dozing on the bank of the River Isis, seven-year-old Alice spies the waistcoated White Rabbit anxiously checking his watch and decides, precipitously, to follow him underground. In her pursuit of the punctilious bunny, she stumbles into an assortment of odd predicaments. As she tipples potions and nibbles fungi she grows and shrinks from the size of a mouse to the size of a house, or sprouts a neck as long as a snake's. She encounters characters now inscribed on all our consciousnesses: the Mouse, bobbing in the "Pool of Tears," whose tale is typographically rendered as a tail; the hookah-puffing Caterpillar; the horrifying Duchess, nursing a pig; the disappearing grin of the Cheshire Cat; the tea-drinking Mad Hatter and March Hare squeezing Dormouse into a teapot; the murderous Queen of Hearts who plays croquet with flamingo-mallets; and the dolorous Mock Turtle, who teaches her the Lobster Quadrille. Ever the prim ingénue, Alice tries to confront madness with logic, in a story that digs gently at the unsympathetic puritanism of Victorian bourgeois child-rearing practice. This is a book that must be read with Tenniel's original illustrations. **DH**

PETER LORRE

EDWARD ARNOLD

DOSTOJEVSKIJ'S

RASKOLNIKOV

REGI: JOSEPH V STERNBERG

Crime and Punishment

Fyodor Dostoevsky

Crime and Punishment is a masterpiece of Russian and world fiction, as captivating as it is, in the end, mysterious. Quite near the novel's beginning, the protagonist Raskolnikov commits, for reasons opaque to himself and to the reader, a double murder. For the rest of the book he walks, rambles, or staggers through the streets of St. Petersburg. He is constantly in doubt as to whether his crime—which he barely regards as a crime at all—will be discovered. The concrete world he sees around him is constantly dissolving into the stuff of dreams.

It is often said that *Crime and Punishment* is a study of guilt, but this is not strictly accurate: Raskolnikov does not feel guilt, but he does feel terror and an extraordinary depth of alienation from the rest of humanity. Even though friends make their best efforts to help him, he is unable to accept their help. He is even unable to understand their feelings of love and sympathy, because he regards himself as an outcast—his ability to kill is the embodiment of that alienation rather than its cause or effect.

The other characters in the novel, because they are seen through the distorted lens of Raskolnikov's perception, are largely ciphers. As readers we are plunged into one man's delirium, a symbol for the incomprehension which might overtake us all if we looked closely enough at our fellow human beings. The novel is full of half-conversations; we are never certain whether Raskolnikov fully understands anything that is said to him, and certainly the other characters, because they are kept away from his secret, rarely understand anything he says to them. Although written in 1866, *Crime and Punishment* stands as the great antecedent to the twentieth-century literature of alienation represented in figures such as Camus and Beckett. **DP**

Lifespan | *b.* 1821 (Russia), *d.* 1881
First Published | 1866
First Serialized in | *Russkii Vestnik* periodical
Original Title | *Prestupleniye i nakazaniye*

"I wanted to murder . . . "

◉ This powerful photograph of Dostoevsky presents the image of a deeply serious individual haunted by inner demons.

◉ A Swedish poster for Josef von Sternberg's 1935 movie version of Dostoevsky's novel, with Peter Lorre as murderer Raskolnikov.

Journey to the Center of the Earth

Jules Verne

Lifespan | *b*. 1828 (France), *d*. 1905
First Published | 1866
First Published by | P-J. Hetzel (Paris)
Original Title | *Le Voyage au Centre de la Terre*

🔺 E. Riou's illustration for *Journey to the Center of the Earth* is captioned: "We descended a kind of winding stairs."

🔵 Jules Verne wrote other imaginary tales, a selection of which were published in this elaborately bound edition.

Journey to the Center of the Earth revives the literary tradition of the descent into hell, completely renewed in the form of science fiction. One of the great scientific questions of the mid-nineteenth century, which the novel explores, concerned the geothermic temperature deep within the earth's core, and the question of whether hot or cold temperatures prevail under the earth's crust. In the character of Axel, a kind of intellectual alter-ego, the novelist creates a defender of the theory of a central fire, who is opposed to his uncle, the woolly-minded professor Lindenbrock, defender of Humphrey Davy's theory of a cool center. With extraordinary imaginativeness, the novel adopts the latter hypothesis and takes place in a Gruyère-like Cold Earth, where the volcanoes and the sea are linked by a series of channels.

Having managed to enter the earth through an extinguished volcano in Iceland, named the Sneffels, the characters find themselves in a huge cavity, sheltering an "inner Mediterranean sea," which they explore until they are ejected by the volcanic lava flow of the erupting Stromboli chimney. Their journey can be divided into two main parts. The first takes the heroes back through time, through successive geological layers, until they reach the "primitive granite." The second is the discovery of the inner sea, that is, of a paleontological space populated with "living fossils," where all periods of biological classification are mixed. The discovery of a human jaw in Abbeville in 1863 prompted the writer to introduce into his narrative an "antediluvian shepherd," recalling the great anthropoids, who were—for the Darwinians who were debating the issue of evolution at the time—the ancestors of modern man. **JD**

Jules Verne

Voyages

Extraordinaires

LES

INDES-NOIRES

LE CHANCELLOR

MARTIN PAZ

Collection J. Hetzel

A. SOUZE

The Last Chronicle of Barset

Anthony Trollope

Lifespan | *b.* 1815 (England), *d.* 1882
First Published | 1867
First Published by | Smith, Elder & Co. (London)
Original Language | English

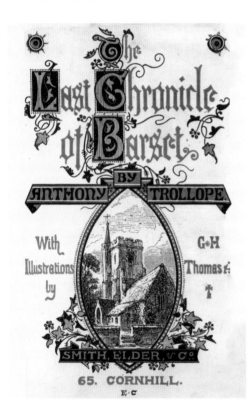

"It's dogged as does it."

⬆ The style of the title page stresses the novel's archaic rural charm rather than engagement with issues of power and gender.

Written between 1855 and 1867, the six novels that form the so-called *Barsetshire Chronicles* are a reflection of Trollope's fascination with everyday provincial life, together building up a panoramic view of the Church, marriage, politics, and country life in mid-Victorian England. *The Last Chronicle of Barset* has always held a special place among Trollope's novels. Its scope and scale, together with Trollope's masterly evocation of his famous mythical county, has meant that it is regarded as one of the most ambitious Victorian novels, and seems to sum up Trollope's work as a whole. It revisits the lives of some of Trollope's much-loved characters who appear in earlier Barsetshire novels. These include the poverty-stricken clergyman, Josiah Crawley, whose humiliation after being charged with stealing a check (wrongly as it turns out) forms the central crisis. Crawley, a proud, exasperatingly unsociable man suffering from career envy, revels in his status as victim-martyr. Here is a hero who is not at all likeable and who if not mad, is at least masochistic and selfish.

Parallel to the Crawley plotline, heroine Lily Dale clings onto the memory of the man who, some years before, had jilted her. Lily, a younger and prettier version of Dickens' Miss Havisham, now refuses to consider marrying anyone else, and at only twenty-four she determines to remain an "Old-Maid." Lily's obstinacy exasperated contemporary readers, but some recent critics have read Lily as a kind of protofeminist, whose strong sense of selfhood allows her to refuse to marry merely to conform to the expectations of her day. As the two central plots suggest, Trollope is concerned with lives as they are lived in society. His characters can only find true fulfillment by engaging as far as they are able with social life. **AM**

Thérèse Raquin

Émile Zola

Thérèse Raquin is not the best of Émile Zola's novels; it has the hesitancy of a beginning and the dogmatism of a defense, rather than the assured scope of his later masterpiece *Germinal* (1885). Yet it is precisely the properties of uncertainty and of extravagance that make *Thérèse Raquin* a significant novel. In it we see one of the most important novelists of the nineteenth century struggling with his form, seeking, not without desperation, to transform the novel into the social scalpel he so devoutly believed it could be.

In keeping with the developing creed of Naturalism, Zola chose two "specimens" to enact his theories about sexual desire and remorse. But Raquin and Laurent, her lover, are so heavily invested with the responsibility of embodying Zola's mechanical determinism, that they become strange tortured creatures; individuals rocked by chance and bewildered by the obscurity and intensity of their feelings, rather than being exemplars of physiology and material circumstance. The result is a novel divided against itself, a wonderful amalgam of wild eroticism and meticulous detachment. The impersonality of the third-person narrator is pushed to outrageous extremes as the would-be "scientific" narrator is forced to provide ever more elaborate, mystified and mystifying explanations of the conduct of the two lovers. Thérèse Raquin herself is a magnificent creation; she enters the text as a site of mute desires and fears, as the "human animal" without free will, subject to the inexorable laws of her physiology. Gradually, however, and then volcanically, her history cumulates to give her voice and movement, and a superb consciousness of herself as a woman and of the bodily pleasures of being a woman. **PMcM**

Lifespan | *b.* 1840 (France), *d.* 1902
First Published | 1867
First Published by | A. Lacroix (Paris)
Serialized Title | *Un Mariage d'Amour* (1867)

"Hatred was bound to come."

⊙ Parodying a scene from *Thérèse Raquin*, caricaturist Lebourgeois shows Zola confronting a French officer over the Dreyfus affair.

Little Women
Louisa May Alcott

Lifespan | b. 1832 (U.S.), d. 1888
First Published | 1868
First Published by | Roberts Bros. (Boston)
Full Title | Little Women, or, Meg, Jo, Beth, and Amy

A timeless evocation of idealized family life, *Little Women* was an instant success, and became one of America's best-loved classic novels. Originally written as a story for young "girls," its appeal has since transcended the boundaries of time and age, making it as popular with adults as it is with young readers, and as much loved now as when it first appeared.

Little Women chronicles the lives of the four March sisters, growing up in New England against the backdrop of the American Civil War. The story details their struggles with poverty and hardship, their moral failings and personal disappointments. While their father is away with the Union armies, the sisters, Meg, Jo, Amy, Beth, and their mother are left to fend for themselves, under the watchful eyes of their wealthy neighbors. The routine of their daily lives is punctuated by their letters and plays, misdemeanors and acts of kindness, as well as their dreams and aspirations. The girls' progress into womanhood is marked by Meg's departure to be married, Jo's struggles to become a writer, Beth's untimely death, and Amy's unexpected romance. Partially autobiographical, *Little Women* offers a representation of Alcott and her own sisters. Perhaps it is this immediacy which gives this evocative portrait of nineteenth-century family life a lasting vitality, endearing it to generations of readers and inspiring new women writers from Simone de Beauvoir to Joyce Carol Oates and Cynthia Ozick. **LE**

"Talent isn't genius, and no amount of energy can make it so. I want to be great, or nothing."

⊙ The publication of *Little Women* brought Louisa Alcott fame, but also led her to be stereotyped as a children's author.

The Moonstone

Wilkie Collins

Lifespan | *b.* 1824 (England), *d.* 1889
First Published | 1868
First Published by | Tinsley Brothers (London)
Original Language | English

The Moonstone is often regarded as the first—and, by some, the greatest—English detective novel. It concerns the theft of an invaluable diamond, but from this starting point it ranges across the whole history of the gem, from its original position adorning a Hindu god, through a succession of lootings, until it reappears in the nineteenth century as a wedding gift, and is immediately stolen. At this point Sergeant Cuff is brought in and, with a little help, he eventually unfolds the mystery.

One of the remarkable features of the novel is that it is told in the first person from a variety of viewpoints, which compounds the mystery since it is not always clear whose account the reader should trust. Collins' style—much of the novel is composed of dialogue between characters—enables the reader to move surprisingly rapidly through the intricacies of the plot. Over the course of this long novel, Collins displays a remarkable ability to unpack the workings of people's minds; unusually, perhaps, for a nineteenth-century male writer, the minds of women as much as of men. There is a remarkable vividness to the scenes in which the novel is set, and a force of action that holds the reader spellbound from start to finish. Considered a landmark in English literature, *The Moonstone* is a mystery to be unravelled, but it is also a presentation of the essentials of nineteenth-century society, related with the lightest of touches and with the utmost realism of dialogue and characterization. **DP**

The Idiot

Fyodor Dostoevsky

Lifespan | *b.* 1821 (Russia), *d.* 1881
First Published | 1868–1869
First Serialized in | *Russkii Vestnik* periodical
Original Title | *Idiot*

Dostoevsky's second long novel reworks the "holy fool" motif: the apparently naïve person who may secretly be wise. The "idiot" in this case is the saintly Prince Myshkin, an epileptic (like the author himself), whom we encounter returning to Russia from a Swiss sanatorium to stay with his distant relative, Mrs. Yepanchin, the wife of a wealthy general. Set in the rapidly developing St. Petersburg of the 1860s, the narrative follows Myshkin's impact upon the Yepanchins and the social milieu they inhabit. The prince serves as a catalyst for conflict between social hypocrisy and the emotions it masks, dealing with money, status, sex, and marriage. Like any good Russian novel, *The Idiot* includes a long list of characters with difficult names, and roils with intrigue and passion against the backdrop of an emergent bourgeois modernity.

At the outset, Myshkin befriends rich, wilful young buck Rogozhin, his opposite in every way. But the two men subsequently become rivals for the affections of Nastasya Filippovna. She is an orphan adopted by a General Totsky, who, it is strongly hinted, raped her in her adolescence. Her status is thus dubious, a fallen woman, but Myshkin, who can eerily divine inner characters, perceives in her a suffering soul; a spiritual bond forms between them, in sharp contrast to Rogozhin's fierce desire for her. How, Dostoevsky asks, does the ethereal, frequently insufferable spirituality of a Myshkin sit in relation to the more primitive drives of a Rogozhin? **DH**

Maldoror

Comte de Lautréamont

Lifespan | *b.* 1846 (Uruguay), *d.* 1870 (France)
First Published | 1868–1969
First Published by | Albert Lacroix (Paris)
Original Title | *Les Chants de Maldoror*

Although Lautréamont was unknown during his lifetime, his narrative prose poem *Les Chants de Maldoror* is now recognized as one of the earliest and most unsettling works of surrealist fiction. The first canto of *Maldoror* was published anonymously in Paris just two years before the author's early death aged twenty-four. However, it was not until a Belgian literary journal took the bold step of republishing Lautréamont's work in 1885 that he began to find an audience among the European avant-garde.

Maldoror tells the tale of the eponymous "hero" who rebels against God by committing an extraordinary succession of depraved and immoral acts. This is a wild, hallucinatory, poetic, and disturbing work—radical not only for its stylistic innovation (which the Surrealists so admired) but also for its blasphemous content. The tale encompasses murder, sadomasochism, putrefaction, and violence. It is a celebration of evil, a work that depicts Christ as a rapist and includes a protracted fantasy about intercourse with sea creatures. Each new act of inhumanity fails to bring Maldoror any kind of respite or satisfaction, and his fury increases as the book progresses. *Maldoror* retains its power to shock and bewilder, but perhaps its most interesting feature is the lyrical power of Lautréamont's prose, which succeeds in making the utterly repellent appear beautiful and enchanting—a disorienting effect that challenges both conventional morality and our assumptions about language itself. **SamT**

Phineas Finn

Anthony Trollope

Lifespan | *b.* 1815 (England), *d.* 1882
First Published | 1869
First Published by | Virtue & Co. (London)
Full Title | *Phineas Finn, the Irish Member*

Like the eponymous Irish hero of this novel, Anthony Trollope also had political ambitions, standing (unsuccessfully) as the Liberal candidate for Beverly in 1868. Chastened by his experiences, he channeled them into a series of six novels (the *Palliser* series) which analyze the lives and loves of government ministers and their families, set against the backdrop of parliamentary intrigue and real-life politicians. Phineas Finn MP is a familiar Trollopian hero: handsome, well mannered, impressionable, but weak and easily flattered. As he rises up the political greasy pole, attracting the notice of powerful government men, his private life grows more complicated. Although already engaged, Phineas becomes entangled with three different but equally alluring women—the brilliant Lady Laura Standish, the heiress Violet Effingham, and the mysterious Madame Max Goesler—all outstanding matches for the ambitious politician. Phineas' tendency to dither is typical of Trollope's young men and much of the novel is about how he reconciles his conscience with his ambitions and love of the bright lights. The capital of a great, self-confident empire, London is also a place where principled behavior is always threatened by political expediency, and good connections are much more important than mere ability. Trollope's interest lies not in political philsophy but rather in psychology, and in what makes mid-Victorian people "tick." His penetrating insights are much on display here. **AM**

Sentimental Education

Gustave Flaubert

Lifespan | *b.* 1821 (France), *d.* 1880
First Published | 1869, by M. Lévy Frères (Paris)
Original Title | *L'Education sentimentale—Histoire d'un jeune homme*

Sentimental Education is surely one of the greatest novels yet written, possibly even the greatest triumph in literary realism ever accomplished. It is a novelist's novel: though at first condemned as immoral by the Parisian reviewers on its publication in 1869, it was greatly admired by younger aspiring novelists. In the early twentieth century it stood as the measure to be matched by James Joyce and Ezra Pound. Flaubert was a tremendous laborer in his craft, obsessively preoccupied with the exactitude of every detail of social observation, as well as with literary style. He was the mythical master novelist, devoted beyond comprehension—the modern novelist, writing to a commercially imposed deadline, is the complete antithesis.

Sentimental Education follows Frédéric Moreau, an idle young man living on a grand inheritance. His ambitions and principles are discarded and dimmed in a thrillingly observed satire on the mentality of affluent consumers in a mid-nineteenth-century Paris defined by its ubiquitous exhibition of luxury goods and attitudes. But this is also the Paris of the July revolution of 1848. Frédéric drifts through the uprising, scintillated by death on the barricades as much as he is by a proprietorial relationship with a courtesan chosen to help him forget his true passion for another man's wife. The novel is at once gigantic in its historical perception, and minutely attentive to the slow suffocation of emotional and political idealism in a single heart. **KS**

> *"The artist must be in his work as God is in creation, invisible and all-powerful; one must sense him everywhere but never see him."*
>
> *Flaubert, 1857*

⬆ Eugène Giraud's caricature of Flaubert catches the air of misanthropic superiority with which he viewed the world.

War and Peace

Leo Tolstoy

Lifespan | *b.* 1828 (Russia), *d.* 1910
First Serialized | 1865–1869, in *Russkii Vestnik*
First Published | 1869, by M. N. Katkov (Moscow)
Original Title | *Voyna I Mir*

Л. Н. Толстой среди яснополянских детей.

"Our body is a machine for living. It is organized for that, it is its nature. Let life go on in it unhindered and let it defend itself, it will do more than if you paralyse it by encumbering it with remedies."

◔ Tolstoy achieved enormous prestige among the Russian people, revered as a spiritual leader and as a friend of the poor.

◑ In his later years Tolstoy gave away his fortune and lived like a peasant, condemning his great novels as worthless.

Leo Tolstoy's *War and Peace* is one of those few texts —James Joyce's *Ulysses* is another—that are too often read as some kind of endurance test or rite of passage, only to be either abandoned half way or displayed as a shelf-bound trophy, never to be touched again. It is indeed very long, but it is a novel that abundantly repays close attention and re-reading. Like the movies of Andrei Tarkovsky, who was greatly influenced by Tolstoy, once you enter into his Russia, you will not want to leave: and in this sense, the length of the text becomes a virtue, since there is simply more of it to read.

Based primarily upon the members of two prominent families, the Bolkonskys and the Rostovs, *War and Peace* uses their individual stories to portray Russia on the brink of an apocalyptic conflict with Napoléon Bonaparte's France. Events swiftly move the central characters toward this inevitable confrontation. No other writer surpasses Tolstoy in the scale of his epic vision, which encompasses the mood of whole cities, the movement of armies, the sense of foreboding afflicting an entire society. The skirmishes and battles are represented with astonishing immediacy, all crafted from interlinked individual perspectives. The interconnected nature of the personal and the political, and of the intimate and the epic, are masterfully explored. As Tolstoy examines his characters' emotional reactions to the rapidly changing circumstances in which they find themselves, he uses them to represent Russian society's responses to the demands of both war and peace. One final note: if you are going to read *War and Peace*, then don't opt for an abridged version. Tolstoy may be unjustly famed for his ability to digress, but to compromise the unity of the full version is to undermine the reading experience. **MD**

He Knew He Was Right

Anthony Trollope

Lifespan | *b.* 1815 (England), *d.* 1882
First Published | 1869
First Published by | Strahan (London)
Original Language | English

He Knew He Was Right is generally recognized as one of Trollope's darkest (and longest) works, which marks his transition into increasingly pessimistic writing. The central crisis of *He Knew He Was Right* arises from Louis Trevelyan's all-consuming belief that his wife, Emily, is being unfaithful (she is not). Louis, the focal point as regards marriage, sexuality, and the ensuing power relations, is a self-destructive obsessive, eaten up by jealousy, and set on the path to madness. But he is also a sensitive man and a devoted father, who provokes pity, exasperation, and fear in more-or-less equal parts. The harrowing depiction of Louis' decline, from oversensitivity to the attentions bestowed on his wife by other men, through the hiring of a private detective (Bozzle) to spy on her, to the kidnapping of his own son and flight to Italy, eventually culminates in tragedy.

As with his other novels, Trollope is interested in the compromises men and women have to make in order to live a secure, fulfilled existence. Trollope's own ambiguous attitude to women's roles emerges through the conflict between Louis, desperate to uphold old-fashioned cultural values centered on family, home, and wifely obedience, and his wife Emily, a strong-minded woman used to having her own way. Though often socially enlightened and forward-looking, Trollope is nonetheless an adherent to older codes of English behavior. **AM**

King Lear of the Steppes

Ivan Turgenev

Lifespan | *b.* 1818 (Russia), *d.* 1883 (France)
First Published | 1870 (Russia)
Original Title | *Stepnoy korol Lir*
Original Language | Russian

King Lear of the Steppes, a little-known novella, is Ivan Turgenev's literary appropriation of Shakespeare. It begins, in a narrative framing device, with a group of old friends discussing types of people they have known: everyone has met a Hamlet; someone once knew a potential Macbeth. But one speaker grabs their attention by saying that he once knew a King Lear—as though this were the ultimate impossibility and the ultimate storytelling challenge.

Turgenev's Lear, Martin Petrovich Harlov, is a plain-speaking, aristocratic country landowner who commands fear and respect from his peasants. He is mythically enormous, with a back that is "two yards long," and "as Russian as Russian could be." Among the symptoms of his Russianness are his bouts of superstitious gloom; he spends hours in his study pondering his mortality. This belief that death is imminent is his motive for dividing his estate between his two daughters; his only requirement for himself being that they look after him in his dotage. He is, of course, betrayed by both daughters and their scheming husbands, first manipulated and cowed, then driven out into the night.

The story is an ideal mythic vehicle for Turgenev's visual imagination, and it enables him to experiment with a narrative that fluently combines onstage set pieces with the sense of Russian history progressing behind the scenes. **DSoa**

Through the Looking Glass, and What Alice Found There

Lewis Carroll

Lifespan | *b.* 1832 (England), *d.* 1898
First Published | 1871
First Published by | Macmillan & Co. (London)
Given Name | Charles Lutwidge Dodgson

In 1871, six years after *Alice in Wonderland*, Carroll returned to the Alice character with a new idea: to follow her into the world behind the mirror. Having recently taught the real Alice (Liddell) how to play chess, he used the game as a narrative device. The Looking Glass world is set out like a chessboard; Alice begins as a pawn and becomes a queen, with each chapter of the story dedicated to a move toward this end. As events progress, a chess problem, shown in a diagram at the start of the book, is solved correctly.

More schematic than *Wonderland*, this novel is nevertheless equally full of memorable characters and ideas, many of which involve contradiction and inversion. In order to get anywhere in this topsy-turvy place, Alice must walk in the opposite direction; the Red Queen tells her that "here . . . it takes all the running you can do, to keep in the same place." Memory does not only go "backward"; the White Queen remembers things "that happened the week after next." We meet the "Contrariwise" twins Tweedledum and Tweedledee. Language also seems slippery, and meaning is elusive. Most famously, in the poem "Jabberwocky," we find Carroll's "portmanteau words," running together associations and meanings: "frumious," "mimsy," "slithy," and "brillig," among many others. Oysters, however, should avoid reading it. **DH**

"Why, sometimes I've believed as many as six impossible things before breakfast."

● Tenniel's visualization of the fearsome Jabberwocky in "the tulgey wood", confronted by the hero with "vorpal sword in hand".

Middlemarch

George Eliot

Lifespan | *b.* 1819 (England), *d.* 1880
First Published | 1871–1872, by Blackwood & Sons
Full Title | *Middlemarch, a Study of Provincial Life*
Given Name | Mary Ann Evans

"People glorify all sorts of bravery except the bravery they might show on behalf of their nearest neighbours."

In an early photograph, George Eliot is posed with an awkward expression that gives little idea of her high seriousness.

In *Middlemarch,* George Eliot focuses on the minutiae of ordinary lives led in a provincial English town, mapping in intricate detail the interior worlds of her many characters as a scientist might examine the tiny, interconnecting veins of a leaf through the lens of a microscope. It is through such insight and precision that Eliot achieves the measured realism for which *Middlemarch* is acclaimed, considered at the time of its publication as it is today to be one of the greatest English novels.

Middlemarch's impassioned heroine, Dorothea, is, like Lydgate—the young doctor whose story connects in vital ways with her own—an idealist. Convinced that there can be heroism in even the smallest of gestures, she mistakes her first husband's intellectual pursuits for a work of such proportions. But Mr. Causabon's deathly project aspires to reduce to a single, simplified principle the Darwinian diversity that represents the very life-force of the novel.

One of *Middlemarch*'s central concerns is the question of how women adapt to the roles that they have been allotted by society. We feel for Dorothea, painfully aware of her lack of education and financial dependency, as she strives bravely for heroism while her sister tinkles away contentedly on the piano. Struggling with their failings and wrong choices, trying to live well and to love well, the stories of Dorothea and Lydgate, interwoven with so many others, are at once intensely moving and acutely real. Eliot deftly spins her web of densely plotted suspense, and manages to lay bare the motivations of her characters with such compassion and understanding that we are soon caught up in the narrative, as their overlapping lives become entwined with ours. **KB**

Spring Torrents

Ivan Turgenev

The tone of *Spring Torrents* is perfectly poised between bitter regret for youth's lost passions and ironic awareness of their largely illusory quality. Dreading the approach of old age and the end of his rather aimless life, Dimitry Sanin finds "a tiny garnet cross" packed away in a drawer of his desk. The discovery evokes the wonderful, shameful story of his double love affair thirty years ago, when he was in Frankfurt, on his way back from the Grand Tour.

His intimate memories return in a series of vivid tableaux. First he recalls falling in love with Gemma, the daughter of an Italian pastry-cook, who has a devoted brother and protective widowed mother, an operatically loyal family servant, Pantaleone, and a dull German fiancé. Sanin fights a ridiculous duel with an officer who has spoken insultingly about Gemma, displaces the dull fiancé, and even overcomes the mother's doubts. All seems set for a happy ending. But then, seeking a buyer for his estate to raise money for the wedding, Sanin falls into the company of decadent Russians: an old school friend, Polozov, and his magical, dominant wife, Maria Nikolaevna. Soon Maria, riding some way ahead of Sanin, is leading him deep into the woods: "She moved forward imperiously, and he followed, obedient and submissive, drained of every spark of will and with his heart in his mouth."

Sanin is a commonplace man, and his romance, with its ingenuous virgin and experienced femme fatale, replays a familiar tale. Turgenev's theatrical treatment brings to the foreground the affair's predictable and almost absurd aspect. But his precise, lucid, and sympathetic observation makes us aware at the same time that to Sanin, who is young, this is intolerably real, and that nothing in his later life will count for anything in comparison. **MR**

Lifespan | *b*. 1818 (Russia), *d*. 1883 (France)
First Published | 1872 (Russia)
Original Title | *Veshniye vody*
Original Language | Russian

"To desire and expect nothing for oneself ... is genuine holiness."

Turgenev, 1862

⊙ A friend of writers such as Flaubert and Zola, Turgenev was better appreciated in western Europe than in his native Russia.

Erewhon

Samuel Butler

Lifespan | *b.* 1835 (England), *d.* 1902
First Published | 1872
First Published by | Trübner & Co. (London)
Full Title | *Erewhon; or, Over the Range*

"When I die at any rate I shall do so in the full and certain hope that there will be no resurrection, but that death will give me quittance in full."

Butler, Notebooks, 1912

⬢ Photographed here in 1898, Samuel Butler was a competent composer, painter, and translator as well as a satirical novelist.

As with many good science fiction texts, particularly utopian ones, *Erewhon* is more a comment on its own time which goes on to reflect prophetically on events of the future, than a genuinely futuristic text. Like More's "no place" of *Utopia*, *Erewhon's* reversed "nowhere" is a reflection on social unease and political development in the Victorian era, and its meditations on extreme and often contradictory social practices have as much currency today as they did then. As an allegory, *Erewhon* is at once reflective and disturbing, more so perhaps, as its dominant fears still lie at the heart of contemporary unease.

Butler's traveler Higgs finds himself in the world of Erewhon where everything is turned on its head. No machines are allowed—it is feared they will take over the world, a common science fiction theme. Criminals are sent to hospitals to recover from their misdeeds, education consists of studying anything as long as it has no relevance, and the sick are incarcerated.

Erewhon is a book that reflects directly on the implications of Darwinism, registering the shock that followed the publication of *The Origin of Species* (1859) among the reading public. *Erewhon* transposes these evolutionary ideas into a social context, once again identifying them with fear and distrust. Butler himself was profoundly influenced by Darwin's text, but like many science fiction writers, also saw the potential for development of such themes along unsettling lines. **EMcCS**

The Devils

Fyodor Dostoevsky

Lifespan | *b.* 1821 (Russia), *d.* 1881
First Published | 1872 (Russia)
Original Title | *Besy*
Original Language | Russian

Though *The Devils* is quite possibly the most violent of Dostoevsky's novels, it also brims with buffoonery and trenchant social satire. Set in the late 1860s, the story concerns the fortunes of a group of insurgents committed to unleashing anarchy in Russia. As a series of betrayals inevitably consumes the group, the novel portrays the catastrophic consequences that can ensue from abstract political theorizing.

The orgy of destruction depicted in the closing pages has often been cited as an example of the author's proneness to sensationalism. As its title suggests, however, this is a novel about purgation, and in the Dostoevskian universe the recuperation of society often comes at a heavy price. For example, the life is spared of the most dangerous character of the story, Peter Verhovensky (a psychopath who was loosely based on the ringleader of the so-called Nechaevists brought to trial in Russia). The fact that the innocent sometimes have to be sacrificed in order to regenerate society is only one of a series of provocative moral positions taken up by the novel.

The Dionysian frenzy that grips the action not only erases any easy understanding of the relationship between good and evil, it also points to the essential fragility of a society increasingly estranged from the moral certainties of the church. Within a generation Russia would surrender to convulsive social change; the novel offers a prescient and terrifying glimpse into the future of a society that has collectively lost its soul. **VA**

In a Glass Darkly

Sheridan Le Fanu

Lifespan | *b.* 1814 (Ireland), *d.* 1873
First Published | 1872
First Published by | R. Bentley (London)
Original Language | English

These five short stories of malign and supernatural forces were originally brought out in periodicals, but were later published together, united by the guiding narrative of the "German physician" Martin Hesselius, from whose casebooks the tales are drawn. His function, and hence that of the collection as a novel, could be regarded as regulative, bringing coherence and clarity—"the work of analysis, diagnosis and illustration"—to the darkness he observes.

If this is Le Fanu's intention, we must regard the book as a failure. Nobody is cured, no theory identified, no line of meaning uncovered. The stories are united instead by the lurid and persistent, figures of the preying imagination. These range from the avenging victims of a cruel judge to a small, black monkey of "unfathomable malignity," maddeningly singing through the head of the clergyman he tracks and corrupts. Whatever their origin, they all follow their targets with inexplicable determination. Yet they also have the power exemplified by the vampiric lesbian seductress Carmilla, perhaps the book's most memorable visitant. A specter of the body, not the soul, she absorbs the tale's narrator with "gloating eyes" that combine pleasure and hatred, physical excitement and disgust in equal measure. In confronting us with our own hitherto unapprehended fears and desires, Le Fanu shows these apparitions of ourselves to be the most modern, and enduring, of ghosts. **DT**

ONE SHILLING

JULES·VERNE'S·WORKS

LOW'S AUTHORISED & ILLUSTRATED EDITION

AROUND THE WORLD
IN
EIGHTY DAYS

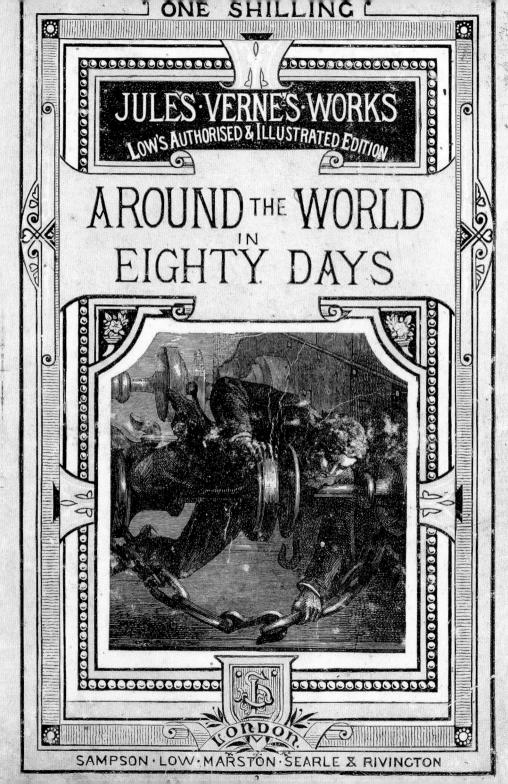

LONDON.

SAMPSON·LOW·MARSTON·SEARLE & RIVINGTON

Around the World in Eighty Days

Jules Verne

Lifespan | *b.* 1828 (France), *d.* 1905
First Published | 1873
First Published by | P. J. Hetzel (Paris)
Original Title | *Le Tour du monde en quatre-vingt jours*

Around the World in Eighty Days won Jules Verne worldwide renown, and was a fantastic success for the times, selling one hundred and eight thousand copies, with translations into English, Russian, Italian, and Spanish as soon as it was published. The book's new subject was bound to cause a great sensation: making a bet with the members of the Reform Club, Phileas Fogg, a rich British eccentric who lives as a recluse, lays his entire wealth as a wager that he can go around the world in eighty days.

Accompanied by his valet Passepartout, he sets out on a journey that first takes him to Suez, and on to meet a series of characters—cruel Hindus, a company of Japanese acrobats, Sioux Indians, and so on. Much of the richness and poetry of the novel depends on the antagonism between the characters Fogg and Passepartout. The geometric and impassive Phileas Fogg, a man of the "fog," who does everything as regularly as clockwork, and for whom the world is reduced to twenty-four time zones, contrasts with the emotive and lively Passepartout, who is forever in sympathy with places and people whom he meets. Yet numerous accidents and unpredictable events will finally get the better of the bachelor's little quirks. **JD**

◐ This dramatic cover image for Verne's novel was created by illustrator Louis Dumont for the first English edition in 1876.

The Enchanted Wanderer

Nicolai Leskov

Lifespan | *b.* 1831 (Russia), *d.* 1895
First Published | 1873 (Russia)
Original Title | *Ocharovanny strannik*
Original Language | Russian

Leskov is the least well-known of the giants of the Russian novel. In the English-speaking world he has been eclipsed by others such as Tolstoy and Gogol, possibly because his are the most purely Russian stories of them all, defying incorporation into the western European realist or psychological novel traditions. English translations of his stories are liable to be read as parodies of some stereotyped fable, or even as comedies, in places approaching the manner of Beckett. This is a great part of his appeal: to read him requires that we abandon all anticipation of plot and reader-style empathy with "real" characters. We must submit to the logic of the storyteller who knows by heart but not, apparently, by head, what he wants to tell us.

The Enchanted Wanderer is a vast reel of improbable misfortunes and adventures narrated by the hero to an audience on board a ship. The wanderer is enchanted, since at every step of his life some new adventure befalls him, from the most exotic and magical to the most ludicrously mundane. The great German literary critic Walter Benjamin wrote that the now almost lost craft of storytelling always depended on stories excluding psychological explanations for the actions of their characters: the lack of explanation sets the imagination free. Leskov is the great practitioner of that wonderful and beguiling craft. **KS**

Far from the Madding Crowd

Thomas Hardy

Lifespan | *b.* 1840 (England), *d.* 1928
First Published | 1874
First Published by | Smith, Elder & Co. (London)
Original Language | English

The pressures of late Victorian modernity, felt acutely in Hardy's later work, barely touch the world of *Far From the Madding Crowd*. The minor rustic characters seem to come from an earlier age, and Hardy here first applies the name "Wessex" to the topographical and imaginative landscape where his greatest novels are set.

However, Hardy's vision already encompasses injustice and tragedy. Fleeing from her husband, Bathsheba Everdene spends a foggy night beside a swamp, and shivers to see at sunrise its "rotting tree stumps" and the "oozing gills" of the fungi growing there. Nature has its poisons, as humanity has its ills. Of the five main characters, two are pathologically destructive: Sergeant Troy is dashing, but selfish and heartless, and Farmer Boldwood is in love only with his own obsessional desire. Fanny Robin, an innocent betrayed, prefigures Hardy's vindication of the "fallen woman" in *Tess*, but where Tess becomes defiant, Fanny remains passive. Even Bathsheba, independently minded, kind-hearted, and inconstant, causes more sorrow than joy. Only Gabriel Oak is thoroughly good, and he must wait until the last chapter for his reward. Plot and characters are strongly rather than subtly drawn, but the vivid presence of the natural and cultural background is striking. **MR**

"But a resolution to avoid an evil is seldom framed till the evil is so far advanced as to make avoidance impossible."

◉ Photographer Frederick Hollyer made this portrait of Thomas Hardy in 1884, a novelist then at the height of his powers.

The Temptation of Saint Anthony

Gustave Flaubert

Lifespan | b. 1821 (France), d. 1880
First Published | 1874
First Published by | Charpentier (Paris)
Original Title | La Tentation de Saint Antoine

Flaubert sought to write an epic of spiritual torment that might provide for French literature something of the centrality and quality that Goethe's *Faust* has for German literature. The work's dramatic form influenced the development of modernist play-texts in the novel, notably the "Circe" section of Joyce's *Ulysses*, while its catalog of borderline states and delirious imagery prefigured Lautréamont and Surrealism. It is perhaps the most successful novel that might also be called a prose poem. Its critical contrast between early Christianity and the poetics of modern fiction exemplifies the modernist dialogue between ancient and modern worlds.

The work portrays the reflected, inner life of a fictionalized Saint Anthony, based on the fourth-century Christian anchorite who lived in the Egyptian desert. Anthony undergoes trials of the mind, the temptations of sexuality and sensuality, and the torments of dialogue with Hilarion, the voice of scientific reason. Hilarion is followed by a cast of biblical proportions, from the Queen of Sheba to the Sphinx. With Flaubert's encyclopedia of biblical and profane imagery, the novel explores the language and meaning of religious, philosophical, and literary skepticism. Engaging with the delusions brought on by hunger and feelings of sin, the novel is a must for anyone interested in religion, hallucinations of the flesh, or modernist poetics. **DM**

The Hand of Ethelberta

Thomas Hardy

Lifespan | b. 1840 (England), d. 1928
First Published | 1876
First Published by | Smith, Elder & Co. (London)
Original Language | English

The artificial, indoor world of "society" lies at the foreground of this intriguing novel, although open air, daylight, and the plain wit of Ethelberta's native Dorset are always in the background. Comedy, adventure, and romance are pleasingly intertwined, in an ingenious if implausible plot that turns on the widowed heroine's stratagems for advancing her large working-class family, while concealing their existence. Ethelberta assumes that her entire London circle, including her fatuous male admirers Neigh and Ladywell, would disown her if they knew her father was a butler. But while Sue Bridehead (in *Jude*) will find that her education and emancipation set her at odds with the world, Ethelberta makes the most of similar advantages. First she secretly marries the son of the family she works for as a governess and then, on his death, sets up as a romance writer and storyteller. Ethelberta seems quite ready to sell herself to an aristocratic scoundrel, and give up romance and romance writing, for the right price. There are autobiographical parallels, too: Hardy as a Dorset-born outsider wondered, like Ethelberta, whether he would sink or swim in literary London, and was reticent about his family background. The plot's dry-eyed conclusion reflects its heroine's pragmatism, in a novel that celebrates compromise and steers clear of the intense emotions and tragic endings of Hardy's best-known work. **MR**

Daniel Deronda

George Eliot

Lifespan | *b.* 1819 (England), *d.* 1880
First Published | 1876
First Published by | W. Blackwood & Sons (London)
Given Name | Mary Ann Evans

Described as the most experimental of George Eliot's works, this is a novel deeply embedded in the turmoil of Victorian culture and politics. Eliot's aim was, as she writes to Harriet Beecher Stowe, to "rouse the imagination of men and women to a vision of human claims in those races of their fellow men who differ from them in customs and beliefs." She explored that vision through a man and a woman whose lives are entangled from the very first lines. Gwendolen Harleth is at the center of what has been described as the "English" half of the novel, a story of economic crisis and a brutal marriage, of the restrictive horror of "a woman's life" that continues to surprise readers for its refusal to conclude in conventional romance. At the same time, Eliot broke with literary and political expectation by putting Jewishness—orphaned Deronda's discovery of his Jewish identity—at the heart of the novel. The Victorian project of social regeneration and the literary project of making the self intelligible at a moment of massive social change are mapped onto the quest for a Jewish homeland.

The mixed reception from contemporary critics reflected Eliot's entanglement of themes. Yet it is precisely that duality of themes which sustains her portrayal of the burden of history—of family, of state—on both individual and national identity, and Gwendolen's struggle for moral survival and Deronda's struggle toward a nation are both vital to Eliot's representation of the future as uncertain. **VL**

Virgin Soil

Ivan Turgenev

Lifespan | *b.* 1818 (Russia), *d.* 1883 (France)
First Published | 1877 (Russia)
Original Title | *Nov*
Original Language | Russian

The predecessor of Tolstoy and Dostoevsky, by the 1870s Turgenev was the leading Russian novelist. With *Virgin Soil*, he became famous across Europe and the U.S. The novel depicts a group of young idealists influenced by the Populist movement at the dawn of the Revolution. When fifty-two people were arrested on charges of revolutionary conspiracy a month after the book's publication, a worldwide reading public sought explanations in the novel. *Virgin Soil* is not purely a work of social commentary. The main character, Nezhdanov, is a complex, intensely self-conscious student whose innermost desire is to be a poet. He is prevailed upon by his friends to be more active in the Populist cause he supports, and throughout the novel his genuine desire to help others competes with his yearning for solitude and intimacy. This tension is deftly played out as Nezhdanov leaves his garret to go among peasants and workmen, urging them to rebel. Quitting his aristocratic uncle's home with a young woman eager to pledge herself both to him and the Populist cause, Nezhdanov must live in hiding and literally disguise himself as "one of the people." The numerous characters are strikingly life-like, even as they evoke stereotypes of the culture that shaped them—from the alternately brooding and zealous Nezhdanov to the well-meaning buffoon Palkin, whose incompetence and egoistic foolishness raise questions about the complicity of innocence in the ravages of history. **LKF**

Drunkard

Émile Zola

Lifespan | *b.* 1840 (France), *d.* 1902
First Published | 1877
First Published by | A. Lacroix (Paris)
Original Title | *L'Assommoir*

In Zola's own words, this is "a work of truth, the first novel about the common people that does not lie and that smells of the common people." The narrative details the fluctuating fortunes of Parisian laundrywoman Gervaise Macquart, whose determination to transcend the slum milieu through hard work is ultimately thwarted by circumstance. Gervaise's roofer husband suffers a fall and stops working. His ensuing alcoholism drains Gervaise's assets and seduces her into the fatal *assommoir* (bar), affecting her moral and physical dissolution. Urban vicissitude is linked with moral improbity; individual misfortune linked with environmental disintegration. Gervaise's tragic, pathetic decline is inexorable, as her alcoholism leads to infidelity, inertia, squalor, alienation, and prostitution.

Zola's insistence on his novel's ethnographic credentials deflected accusations that it actually caricatured working-class life. Its authentic and innovative use of street language; its lewd, sexual frankness; anti-clericalism; anti-officialdom; its general filth, deprivation, and bad manners, were deemed immoral, unpalatable, and potentially inflammatory by conservative critics. *L'Assommoir* stakes a serious claim for working-class experience and popular culture as aesthetically worthy, formally challenging material for the artist. And in overthrowing artistic conventions and inciting debate on the appropriate form and material for modern art, it earns its place as one of the first truly modern novels. **GM**

"She was a mattress for the soldiers to lie on before she was twelve—and she's left one leg down there . . . "

⚫ André Gill's caricature suggests mutual respect between Balzac, old master of realism, and Zola, new master of naturalism.

METRO-GOLDWYN-MAYER PRÆSENTERER:
Metro Goldwyn Mayer
NY KOPI
GRETA
GARBO
FREDRIC
MARCH
ANNA KARENINA
ISCENESÆTTELSE: CLARENCE BROWN
PRODUCENT: DAVID O. SELZNICK

Anna Karenina

Leo Tolstoy

Lifespan | b. 1828 (Russia), d. 1910
First Serialized | 1873–1877, in *Russkii Vestnik*
First Published | 1877, by M. N. Katkov (Moscow)
Original Language | Russian

Anna Karenina is claimed by many to be the world's greatest novel. Whether or not that is the case, it is one of the finest examples of the nineteenth-century psychological novel. Tolstoy analyzes the motivation behind the actions of the characters, though without any moral judgement. Alongside the omniscient narration, Tolstoy frequently employs interior monologue, a stylistic innovation for the novel form which enables him to present his characters' thoughts and feelings in intimate detail.

Rebellious Anna Karenina succumbs to her attraction to a dashing officer, Count Vronsky, and leaves her loveless marriage to embark on a fervent and ultimately doomed love affair. In doing so, she sacrifices her child and subjects herself to the condemnation of Russian high-society. Anna's tragic story is interwoven with the contrasting tale of the courtship and marriage of Konstantin Levin and Kitty Shcherbatskaya, which closely resembles that of Tolstoy and his own wife. In his search for the truth, Levin expresses views about contemporary society, politics, and religion that are often taken to be those of the author himself.

The novel is valuable for its historical as well as its psychological aspects. Despite its length, *Anna Karenina* draws readers into a breathtaking world that is vital and all consuming in its realism. **SJD**

⬤ The success of her 1935 movie portrayal of Tolstoy's heroine made Greta Garbo the face of Anna Karenina around the world.

Return of the Native

Thomas Hardy

Lifespan | b. 1840 (England), d. 1928
First Published | 1878
First Published by | Smith, Elder & Co. (London)
Original Language | English

With his verbose, ornate style and sensitivity to class issues, Hardy seems a typical Victorian novelist. But the depth of his writing revealed a sensibility at odds with the strict Victorian social and sexual mores, tending towards atheism and subjective morality rather than an absolutist Christianity. This philosophy was out of place in Victorian England, predating the social and cultural upheaval of modernism. The novel is deeply rooted in the attitude, speech, and folk customs of the residents of the tract of windswept upland in Hardy's Wessex known as Egdon Heath. It is the return to the heath of the educated Clym Yeobright that supplies the title of the novel, which is a tragic story of relationships and differences in perception. The plot centers on Yeobright and Eustacia Vye, who determines to leave her true love, Damon Wildeve, to seek a new life with Yeobright, away from the heath. But escalating tragedy ultimately results in Yeobright becoming an itinerant moral preacher. In contrast, Diggory Venn, whose job it is to sell red sheep-dye to farmers, represents the embodiment of the heath, the omnipresent observer who mysteriously appears from time to time. Hardy's characters are all disturbingly unreliable—nothing is certain, nothing is objective. His depiction of the people, as well as of the heath, transcends the bounds of traditional Victorian certainty and produces a work where everything—even the ending—is ambiguous. **EF**

The Red Room

August Strindberg

Lifespan | b. 1849 (Sweden), d. 1912
First Published |1880
First Published by | A. Bonniers Förlag
Original Title | Röda rummet

The Red Room is often described as the first modern Swedish novel. Using Zola's naturalism and Dickens' social criticism Strindberg revitalized a stale, conventional tradition. Because its social and political satire was a little too close to the bone, its initial reception was controversial, but the novel is now recognized as a watershed in Swedish literature. In the opening chapter, with its famous bird's-eye view of Stockholm, Strindberg's vivid prose sparkles with energy and invention. The hero of the novel, the young and idealistic Arvid Falk, resigns from the Civil Service in disgust at the corruption he sees everywhere in the Establishment. He wants to become a writer and joins a group of bohemian artists, but struggles to free himself from his own prim and puritan inclinations. Falk's radical and reforming spirit is gradually softened, and he is tempted to adopt the selfish view of life advocated by the conservative journalist Struve. As so often in Strindberg, it is the tension between irreconcilable opposites that provides the narrative energy.

The subtitle, *Scenes of Literary and Artistic Life*, reveals a series of satirical excursions into the worlds of the arts, religion, government, and finance. The focus is on man in society, sometimes at the expense of in-depth characterization. But many of the minor characters, like the carpenter who threatens to reclaim the lost beds of the working classes from affluent middle-class ladies who offer him charity, are memorable in an eccentric Dickensian way. **UD**

The Brothers Karamazov

Fyodor Dostoevsky

Lifespan | b. 1821 (Russia), d. 1881
First Serialized | 1879–1880, in *Russkii Vestnik*
First Published | 1880, by M. N. Katkov (Moscow)
Original Title | *Bratya Karamazovy*

Dostoevsky's profound, gripping, and frequently nightmarish novel deals with four very different brothers: Alyosha the mystic, Dmitry the sensualist, Ivan the intellectual, and the twisted, cunning bastard child, Smerdyakov. This is the compelling story of what happens to them when their morally corrupting father is murdered by one of them. While there is an element of "whodunnit" and of courtroom drama, as well as a sordid love story, this is primarily a philosophical novel. It is both self-conscious and naïve, ironical, and serious in its philosophizing, connecting the fate and future of Russian man with no lesser questions than those of the nature of good and evil and the existence and justifiability of God. Notable is the "Grand Inquisitor" sequence, interpreted by some as a prescient criticism of totalitarianism, in which the self-confessed atheist Ivan tries to explain his rejection of God to his saintly brother Alyosha.

The tension between the complexity of Ivan's questioning and the undeveloped simplicity of the answers given by Alyosha, makes the novel intriguing and difficult to pin down. There is evidence that Dostoevsky intended his last and most important work to be a resounding exposition and defense of Christianity against the ungodly doctrines gaining ground in Russia at the time. It is a better novel for falling short of that aim. **DG**

❯ Dostoevsky's characters inhabit a distorted, nightmarish world that is a reimagined version of nineteenth-century Russia.

Nana

Émile Zola

Lifespan | *b.* 1840 (France), *d.* 1902
First Published | 1880
First Published by | A. Lacroix (Paris)
Original Language | French

Nana exposes a licentious Parisian sexual economy, hooked on prostitution and promiscuity. The respectable classes indulge in drunken orgies, homosexuality, sadomasochism, voyeurism, and more. An influential aristocrat, Count Muffat, is the epitome of this degradation and chastisement. His familial, political, and religious status is compromised by his infatuated devotion to Nana. She is an ostensibly luminous yet inherently tainted figure: debt, misogynistic violence, a dysfunctional family, class background, and an ultimately fatal sexual disease temper her success. Her eventual physical corrosion is horrific, reflecting the total corruption and disfigurement of both state and society. It is no coincidence that Nana's death throes take place against the backdrop of a screaming mob galvanized by the Franco-Prussian War, where the ultimate violent ruin, collapse, and purification of this stage of French history is completed.

Today's readers will find extraordinary prescience in the correlation of society's obsession with sex, celebrity, and power portrayed in *Nana*. A conscious emphasis on exploitation and disgraceful revelation is paramount in a novel that opens with a theatrical striptease, before going on to revisit connected themes of sexual and economic exhibitionism. Determinedly realist and deliberately explicit, *Nana* is a spectacular novel, which indicts a public appetite for voyeurism and sensationalism that to this day has never really abated. **GM**

Ben-Hur

Lew Wallace

Lifespan | *b.* 1827 (U.S.), *d.* 1905
First Published | 1880
First Published by | Harper & Bros. (New York)
Original Language | English

Prompted by a casual discussion about the life of Jesus, Lew Wallace began writing his epic tale of revenge and adventure with religious themes in mind, and this was the result; a parable that counterpoises Judah Ben-Hur, a Jew from Jerusalem, with the concurrent life of Jesus Christ.

When he accidentally dislodges a roof tile and it hits a Roman official, Ben-Hur is wrongly accused of murder and sent to the galleys by his former friend Messala, a Roman noble. The seeds of epic struggle and redemption are sown when a stranger offers Ben-Hur a glass of water, and from this point his struggle to attain citizenship and Christ's mission are inextricably linked. The popularity of the 1959 Hollywood epic, with its spectacular chariot race, perhaps overrides the blend of religious parable and adventure that obviously adapted itself so well to the stage (it was adapted for the theater in 1899, and proved enduringly popular) and then the screen. However, the film is that unusual breed, a strong adaptation of the text that takes on its key motifs without losing the religious intensity. *Ben-Hur* is characteristically remembered for elements that comprise only a tiny part of the text itself: an event rather than a narrative, and a set piece rather than a gradually unfolding epic. However, the text has lost none of its forceful message, while simultaneously representing the author's desire to appraise some of the central tenets of Christian belief through the figure of an apparently ordinary man. **EMcCS**

Bouvard and Pécuchet

Gustave Flaubert

Lifespan | *b.* 1821 (France), *d.* 1880
First Published | 1881
First Published by | A. Lemerre (Paris)
Original Title | *Bouvard et Pécuchet*

On a hot summer's day, two clerks named Bouvard and Pécuchet meet on the Boulevard Bourdon in Paris, and discover that they have not only written their names on exactly the same spot on their hats, but they have the same liberal political opinions, and most importantly, the same yearning for knowledge. Thanks to an inheritance, they retire to the countryside, where they propose to test all existing theories in all areas of knowledge. As they challenge the received ideas, the protagonists become more and more aware of inconsistencies that are spread everywhere in their manuals. From their first experiments in agronomy, Bouvard and Pécuchet enter into a repetitive cycle of events: they consult numerous encyclopedias and monographs, apply their knowledge, fail catastrophically in their experiments, regret the falsity and defects of their chosen field, and move on to a new one. They investigate all topics, from archaeology to theology, before giving up their quests and deciding to become copyists again.

This "grotesque epic," unfinished and published posthumously, stands out in the history of the novel. It encapsulates a dramatic passion for knowledge, embodied by the heroes' enthusiasm for the most practical or philosophical problems. Conveyed in Flaubert's economical style, Bouvard and Pécuchet's episodic enthusiasms, earnest endeavors, and recurring disillusions are an exceptionally disquieting and comical affair. **CS**

The Portrait of a Lady

Henry James

Lifespan | *b.* 1843 (U.S.), *d.* 1916 (England)
First Published | 1881
First Published by | Macmillan & Co. (London)
Original Language | English

Portrait of a Lady epitomizes James' favorite "international" theme; the relationship of naïve America and cultured Europe, and the contrast between their moral and aesthetic values. Isabel Archer is a beautiful and spirited young American woman, seeking aesthetic enrichment in Europe. She is not wealthy, but refuses two financially advantageous proposals of marriage, fearing they would curtail her imaginative and intellectual freedom. Yet ironically, when she receives a large inheritance, she realizes she has no actual aims or purpose with which to fill her future. Moreover it brings with it the sinister attentions of the charismatic, urbane aesthete Gilbert Osmond. When Isabel marries him, she discovers that she has been manipulated for her fortune. Escaping from the captivity of enforced domestic convention, she finds herself embroiled in a scene of complex sexual and moral emotions, which even Isabel herself struggles to understand. But she chooses instead to accept the responsibility of her own free choice, even when that means knowingly renouncing the greater liberty she so cherished. Despite her vanity and self-delusion, Isabel is steadfast in her effort to lead a noble life. Beneath the melodrama of the novel's plot, James masterfully reveals the more subtle tragedy of lost innocence and curtailed dreams. "The world's all before us—and the world's very big," Goodward entreats at the end of the novel. "The world's very small," Isabel now replies. **DP**

The House by the Medlar Tree

Giovanni Verga

Lifespan | *b.* 1840 (Sicily), *d.* 1922
First Published | 1881
First Published by | Treves (Milan)
Original Title | *I Malavoglia*

The novel constitutes the first part of a grand enterprise intended to portray the fight for life at all levels of social reality, from the dispossessed to the powerful. Verga surpassed the French naturalists' commitment to depicting reality faithfully, and created a narrative in which the author disappears to leave space for the characters, who speak in a new style that directly reflects their sentiments and inner thoughts. The story is that of a tightly-knit family of fishermen in a small Sicilian village, held together by their obedience to old traditions and patriarchal customs. The Toscanos represent the losers, who, like clams, hold on tightly to the sea-beaten rocks in a desperate attempt to resist the cruel waves of life, but in the end are swept away by the rough waters. Owners of a fishing boat, Padron 'Ntoni and his family are not utterly poor. Therefore, the catastrophe that hits them is a pitiless punishment for attempting to improve their life by engaging in an unfortunate entrepreneurial effort. The author's message is absolutely clear: change and progress in Sicily are simply not conceivable.

It was believed that the unification of the Kingdom of the Two Sicilies in 1861 would solve the problems of the south, but while the north thrived, the south was more destitute than ever. This crude and passionless eye-opening representation of southern life expresses this disillusionment. **RPi**

Treasure Island

Robert Louis Stevenson

Lifespan | *b.* 1850 (Scotland), *d.* 1894 (Samoa)
First Published | 1883
First Published by | Cassell & Co. (London)
Original Language | English

"If this don't fetch the kids, why, they have gone rotten since my day," Stevenson proclaimed on publication of his children's classic. With its evocative atmosphere, peopled with fantastic characters and set pieces, *Treasure Island* has spawned countless imitations. Films such as *Pirates of the Caribbean* still encourage the romanticism of piracy, and Stevenson's classic remains true to form despite various literary attempts to dispute his role in the popular canon.

However, Stevenson's text contains few of the elements commonly associated with it. The rip-roaring tale of pirates and parrots is there, but perhaps some of the romanticism is due not to the nominal hero, Jack Hawkins, who staidly adheres to law and order, but to the turncoat ship's cook, Long John Silver. Silver is a wonderful villain: erratic, bombastic, and deadly, and his obvious intelligence and relationship with Hawkins are both gripping and unpredictable. All the elements of a classic adventure are exaggerated by buried treasure, curses, strange meetings, storms, mutiny, and subterfuge. However, this tale of quest, siege, and recovery has one final trick in its rather unformed ending. Even though the villain escapes and the hero returns rich and prosperous, there is a feeling that all has only just begun. **EMcCS**

❯ A map drawn by author Robert Louis Stevenson depicts his fictional but impeccably realized *Treasure Island*.

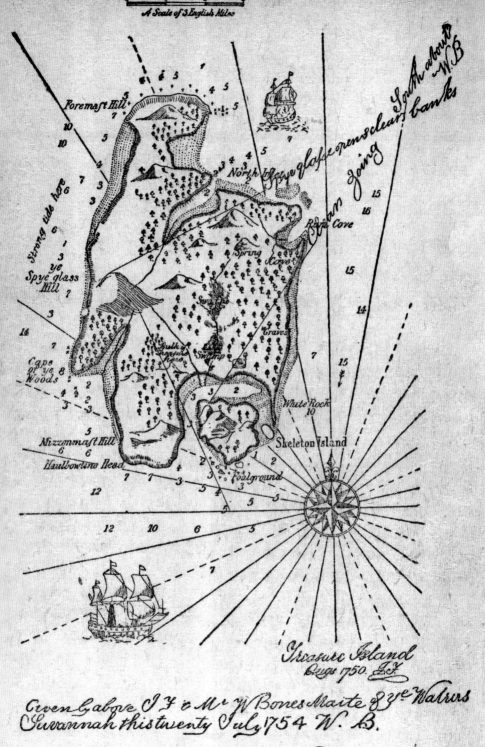

A Scale of 3 English Miles

Foremast Hill

North Inlet

Strong tide here

ye Spye glass Hill

Cape of ye Woods

Mizzenmast Hill

Haulbowline Head

Spy glasse pensclears banks going South about W.B

Rjat Cove

Spring Cove

Swamps

Graves

Bulk Timber House

Swamp

White Rock

Skeleton Island

Foalground

Treasure Island
Augt 1750. J.F.

Given above J.F. & Mr W. Bones Maite of ye Walrus
Savannah this twenty July 1754 W. B.

Facsimile of Chart: latitude and
longitude struck out by J. Hawkins

A Woman's Life

Guy de Maupassant

Lifespan | *b.* 1850 (France), *d.* 1893
First Published | 1883
First Published by | Corbeil (Paris)
Original Title | *Une Vie: l'humble vérité*

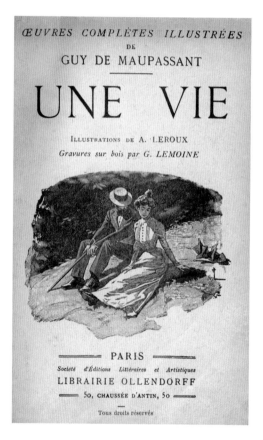

⬀ Despite its pessimistic depiction of *A Woman's Life*, Maupassant's novel also incorporates lyrical evocations of nature.

Guy de Maupassant wrote *A Woman's Life* over more than six years. Even though the story is set in the period that goes from the Restoration of the French monarchy to the 1848 Revolution, it shows a complete disregard for political history. Instead, it focuses exclusively on the life of a provincial aristocrat, Jeanne Le Perthuis des Vauds, from the moment when she leaves the convent to her death in the Caux country. Maupassant was strongly encouraged by Flaubert, who found the subject "excellent," and this story is the inverse of Flaubert's *Madame Bovary*. It recounts the story of a pious woman who suffers from a series of disillusions in her life, beginning with the unfaithfulness of a miserly, and ruthlessly ambitious husband. Jeanne's progressive descent into resignation, if not her actual sense of masochism toward the series of misfortunes that she must suffer (miscarriage, the mothering of a premature child who becomes a swindler, the death of her parents, solitude, poverty, and so on), recalls Flaubert's *Un Coeur Simple*.

A seminal work of naturalism, *A Woman's Life* is also the cruel story of life's traps and pitfalls, and the natural and animal "force" of its indifferent perpetuation. Maupassant's criticism of marriage, which restrains natural sexual instincts, of emotive women, and the outright pessimistic outlook of the story, show Schopenhauer's decisive influence on the so-called naturalist or determinist ideas of the time. Even though the distribution of the book was provisionally blocked by the publisher Hachette, who deemed that its content was "pornographic," *A Woman's Life* was well received by the critics, including by the opponents of naturalism, who were swayed by the emotion and the lyricism of certain of its descriptions. **JD**

The Death of Ivan Ilyich

Leo Tolstoy

The Death of Ivan Ilyich is a short novel but not a modest one. As the spiritual crisis of Levin, Tolstoy's self-portrait, had been left unresolved in Anna Karenina, here he describes the agony of ambivalence that led to that resolution, albeit through the story of a less complicated man, a man less liable to crises of self-understanding than Levin.

Ivan Ilyich is an ambitious bureaucrat jostling his way up the ladder of advantages in a corrupt Russia still harnessed by the czar's bureaucratic apparatus. He slides gracefully into the roles offered to him, adjusting the attitudes and ethics of his youth to fit with the exigencies of his career, and accepting gladly the circus of perks and consolations offered by fashionable society and its luxuries. He particularly enjoys playing cards, a pastime evidently despised by Tolstoy as much as by the German philosopher Schopenhauer, who thought it the most degraded, senseless and "automatic" behavior imaginable. Following what seems like an unremarkable injury, Ivan becomes gradually more incapacitated until finally he is unable to rise from the couch in his drawing room. Tolstoy describes with ferocious zeal the intensity of Ivan's physical suffering, which so exhausts him that eventually he gives up speaking and simply screams without remission, horrifying his attendant family. In the end, death proves not to be the destination of Ivan's tormented and ignorant spiritual journey. It is simply the wasted province of all that he leaves behind by relinquishing his life, all the possessions and affectations, and even the human intimacies that he permitted in order to pass off his life as a reality worth settling for. This is Tolstoy's most concentrated statement of renunciation of a pre-revolutionary corrupted social existence. **KS**

Lifespan | b. 1828 (Russia), d. 1910
First Published | 1884 (Russia)
Original Title | Smert Ivana Ilyitsha
Original Language | Russian

A signed portrait of Tolstoy depicts as a stern moralist who has renounced the frivolities of existence in conventional society.

Against the Grain

Joris-Karl Huysmans

Lifespan | *b.* 1848 (France), *d.* 1907
First Published | 1884
First Published by | Charpentier (Paris)
Original Title | *À rebours*

Joris-Karl Huysmans' *Against the Grain* is a sensuous joy of a novel. It guts the aesthetic, spiritual, and physical desires of the late nineteenth-century high bourgeoisie and feasts on the remains. Luxuriating in self-disgust and self-love, *Against the Grain* has been called "the breviary of Decadence," the mirror in which writers of the fin-de-siècle could recognize their own elegant longings for a world other than the coarsely materialistic one they inhabited.

Politically, "Decadence" incorporated sexual dissidence and stressed the sacredness of the body as a sensual matrix, but it was locked into a chronic antagonism with bourgeois materialism. Huysmans, Wilde, and Valéry all needed the bourgeoisie as much as they scorned them; without the utilitarian materialism and sentimentality of "respectable society," their love affair with debauchery and excess had nothing against which to define itself.

Against the Grain embodies and exploits this political slipperiness. The Duc Jean des Esseintes is a frail aesthete, a lover of ecstasies both debauched and spritual, and the lone descendent of his once forbiddingly manly family, founded by medieval warriors and patriarchs. He is a "degenerate," his lonely vices the consequence of the physical degeneration of the aristocracy. But the narrative lingers delicately over his experiments and despairs. The result is a lush, stylized study in intensity, a fascinating portrayal of an age through the eyes of one who abandoned it. **PMcM**

Marius the Epicurean

Walter Pater

Lifespan | *b.* 1839 (England), *d.* 1894
First Published | 1885, by Macmillan & Co. (London)
Full Title | *Marius the Epicurean: His Sensations and Ideas*

Walter Pater is perhaps best known as the author of *The Renaissance* (1873), ostensibly an overview of art and culture from that period, but in effect a manifesto for aesthetic existence that was to profoundly influence the artistic temperament of the fin-de-siècle. His contemporary, Oscar Wilde, enthusiastically adopted "the love of art for its own sake," as the principle that art never expresses anything but itself. Pater wrote *Marius the Epicurean* not only to imply the inadequacy of this Wildean reading, but also to provide a general model for the experience of art within the form of a life.

The subject matter of *Marius* is less important than the ideas with which it is concerned. It describes the education of the young Roman of its title, through several varieties of pagan philosophy, culminating in Christian faith and martyrdom. Marius develops, however, not through the events of his life, but as a reader, and the form of the novel sets out to reproduce that readerly experience. Reading, in this case, meaningfully connects past, present, and future, becoming itself a process of redemptive moral growth. The carefully constructed temporal simultaneity of Pater's novel makes us feel this as readers, as well as observing its effects in his hero. *Marius'* relative neglect is demonstrated by the fact that no modern edition of the work exists. But if we are to see literature as a process of spiritual as well as sensual formation, respecting both sides of Pater's equation, then reading it remains crucial. **DT**

Bel-Ami

Guy de Maupassant

Lifespan | *b.* 1850 (France), *d.* 1893
First Published | 1885
First Published by | V. Harvard (Paris)
Original Language | French

Maupassant is perhaps best known as a writer of short fiction, and he utilizes the shorter form as a structuring principle for his longer productions. The hero of *Bel-Ami*, Georges Duroy, arrives in Paris as an innocent from the provinces, but in realizing the ascendant power of journalism, rapidly apprehends (and cheerfully exploits) the amorality and decadence at its heart. This discovery occurs impressionistically, giving us lasting images of the cafés, boulevards, and newspaper offices of Maupassant's city. But everything has a price and a limitation, so that the attempt to inscribe it with authenticity or infinite worth only shows up its absence of value, and devalues its possessor.

In *Bel-Ami*, individual stories are women to be seduced, whose bodily presence is described with phenomenological exactitude. However, each woman also represents a calculation, where sexual desire is measured against practical benefit. The "bright silky kimono" of Clotilde de Marelle thus translates into a need that is "brutal" and "direct," a woman to be quickly discarded. But her successor's "loose white gown," represents the longer rhythm of his desire for social worth: she will be ravaged equally, but in a process that exploits her political as well as erotic value. Love, or authentic emotion, moves in inverse proportion to the cynical force of ambition. Maupassant encourages us to enjoy the latter for what it is, as long as we are not tempted to draw any more lasting lessons from his work. **DT**

"Tall, well-built, fair, with blue eyes, a curled mustache, hair naturally wavy and parted in the middle, he recalled the hero of the popular romances."

⊙ An illustration to Maupassant's novel represents the caddishness of the calculating seducer, driven by lust or ambition.

Adventures of
HUCKLEBERRY FINN.

(Tom Sawyer's Comrade.)

BY

MARK TWAIN.

ILLUSTRATED.

The Adventures of Huckleberry Finn

Mark Twain

Like many of the titles found in the "Children's Classics" section of bookshops, *The Adventures of Huckleberry Finn* is not a children's book as we understand the term these days, and it is not surprising that adaptations of Twain's work aimed at children are usually quite heavily edited. Sharing with *Tom Sawyer* (1876) a vivid portrayal of Mississippi small town life, replete with colorful characters, superstitions, slang, and river lore, these adventures are of a different kind. The contrast becomes clear quite early on, when the bloodthirsty boys' game of "highwaymen" and ransom organized by Tom is echoed in Huck's escape from his drunken, violent father. In order to avoid being followed, Huck fakes his own murder. Early on in his flight, he links up with the escaped slave Jim, and together they travel down the Mississippi. Along the way they meet an assortment of locals, river folk, good and bad people, and get mixed up with a pair of con men. Many of their adventures are comic, and Huck's naïveté in describing them is frequently used to humorous effect. However, the straightforwardness with which Huck relates his experiences allows the narrative to shift unexpectedly from absurdity into much darker terrain, as when he witnesses a young boy of his own age die in a pointless and ridiculous feud with another family.

It is these sudden shifts and the contrasts they produce which make this more than an adventure novel. Huck is not necessarily an innocent, but in telling his story he tends to take conventional morals and social relations at face value. By doing so, he brings a moral earnestness to bear on them which exposes hypocrisy, injustice, falsehood, and cruelty more subtly and more scathingly than any direct satire could. **DG**

Lifespan | *b.* 1835 (U.S.), *d.* 1910
First Published | 1885
First Published by | Dawson (Montreal)
Given Name | Samuel Langhorne Clemens

⌃ Mark Twain excelled at the ironic criticism of hypocrisy and injustice seen through the innocent eyes of childhood.

⌕ The first edition of *Huckleberry Finn* was illustrated by Edward Kemble, who created an unforgettable image of the young hero.

Germinal

Émile Zola

Anyone interested in the intersection between literature and politics should know this famous, explosive novel of class conflict and industrial unrest, set in the coalfields of northern France in the 1860s. Zola's uncompromising presentation of an impoverished, subterranean, and vulnerable working existence, paralleled by bourgeois luxury, leisure, and security, provoked controversy.

The title recalls the seventh month of the French revolutionary calendar, associated with mass insurrection, rioting, violence, poverty, and starvation. All feature in *Germinal*'s central story: the eruption and failure of a general strike and its universally negative outcome. The main narrative charts Étienne Lantier's emotional and political assimilation into a mining community, illuminating a dark disenfranchised world, ripe for revolt. His progression from neutral outsider to committed strike leader mobilizes a collective struggle subtly presented in tandem with the contradictions and compromises of individual belief and aspiration. The narrative is permeated with significant oppositions, but capitalism is the fundamental determinant, subjugating all of the protagonists. It is powerfully symbolized by the predominance of The Mine, animated throughout as a mythical, sacrificial beast. That no absolute victor emerges from the novel's concluding calamity is significant. Mining survives, the system prevails, more labor is required.

Germinal's much debated ending resonates with a challenging question: what is the potential for social change and transition? The final images of destruction and renewal suggest possible political evolution through the germination of individual and collective working-class endeavor. It is significant though, that this remains inconclusive. **GM**

Lifespan | *b*. 1840 (France), *d*. 1902
First Published | 1885
First Published by | Charpentier (Paris)
Original Language | French

⊙ A surprisingly weary image of Émile Zola, an author noted for the phenomenal energy he put into his research and writing.

◔ Émile Levy's poster for a stage version of *Germinal* expresses the melodramatic quality of Zola's apocalyptic vision of class war.

King Solomon's Mines

H. Rider Haggard

Lifespan | *b.* 1856 (England), *d.* 1925
First Published | 1885
First Published by | Cassell & Co. (London)
Original Language | English

Haggard's phenomenal bestseller was intended to rival *Treasure Island*, and its hero Allan Quartermain has proved an enduring figure in popular literature, being memorably recreated as an opium-raddled wreck in Alan Moore's *The League of Extraordinary Gentlemen* (2002). The tale itself is classic fantasy; Quartermain and his aides venture into uncharted reaches of Central Africa to discover the infamous King Solomon's Mines, repository of a legendarily huge treasure. Of course, the journey is fraught with peril and excitement. Quartermain encounters the Kukuanas, ruled by King Twala and the witch Gagool, who become increasingly more villainous as tension between the tribe and those intending to purloin the diamond mines intensifies.

Haggard's writing displays a deep knowledge of African, especially Zulu, cultures, which he had observed, and often admired, firsthand. Quartermain is an imperialist, but he is more tolerant and open to change than other contemporary characters, and it is notable that several of his adventures, including this one, involve attempts to save tribes from disappearing. This is possibly why his texts have survived—they identify a more generic threat to mankind through the destruction of an entire race. Haggard's central characters are bombastic and brash, yet Haggard makes the reader aware of this, and it is Quartermain who emerges as the culturally resourceful hero rather than his less observant, and more stereotypically belligerent colleagues. **EMcCS**

Kidnapped

Robert Louis Stevenson

Lifespan | *b.* 1850 (Scotland), *d.* 1894 (Samoa)
First Published | 1886, by Cassell & Co. (London)
Full Title | *Kidnapped: being Memoirs of the Adventures of David Balfour in the Year 1751, etc.*

Kidnapped, the book that brought Stevenson his first serious acclaim as a writer, is a highly effective example of popular adventure fiction expressing a series of complex political and historical ideas. The novel is set in Scotland against the background of the Battle of Culloden (1746), at which British forces brutally repressed the Jacobite rebellion. David Balfour and Alan Breck Stewart exemplify the social and political developments in Scotland post-Culloden. Their combined strengths demonstrate the effective potential of a unified Scotland, with Stevenson's traditionalist figures of the pragmatic Lowlander Whig (Balfour) and flamboyant Highland Jacobite (Stewart) together thwarting various plots and frequently acting as a counterpoise to the other.

Despite this inherent historicism it is certainly a mistake to regard Stevenson's vision as historically or culturally accurate; *Kidnapped*'s fundamental mission is as a tale of adventure and heroism. Balfour is not only kidnapped and sold into slavery, but wrecked upon the shores of Mull. He and Stewart are subsequently forced into hiding after Balfour witnesses a murder, and they escape over the Scottish Highlands. A series of dramatic obstacles serve to demonstrate how the two function better as a unified whole, socially and politically. In this highly politicized reading of the Jacobite Rebellion from a later perspective Stevenson suggests that the division of the land is unproductive, destructive, and ultimately futile. **EMcCS**

The Mayor of Casterbridge

Thomas Hardy

Lifespan | *b*. 1840 (England), *d*. 1928
First Published | 1886, by Smith, Elder & Co. (London)
Full Title | *The Mayor of Casterbridge: The Life and Death of a Man of Character*

Michael Henchard, the most worldly and strong-willed of Hardy's heroes, begins and ends with nothing. Henchard rises to become the mayor and leading corn dealer of the provincial town of Casterbridge. He falls because of his impulsive, unreflecting nature. Desperate to secure the loyalty of those he needs, he alienates them by the demands he makes and the lies he tells. Donald Farfrae, a scientifically-minded young Scotsman who becomes his rival in love and commerce, arouses all the ill-judged excesses of Henchard's temperament: having passionately befriended him, the Mayor turns on him in near-murderous rage. The novel's psychological study, notable for this intense friendship between men, is set against its portrayal of provincial town life. In this intimate milieu, private indiscretion leads inexorably to public disgrace, as the melodramatic plot moves from concealment to revelation. Henchard attempts, in vain, to cover up his past. His former lover Lucetta, who arrives in town and takes up with Farfrae, has her fatal secret exposed when a mob parades crude effigies of her and Henchard through the streets.

The novel chronicles a pre-industrial world where conjurors were consulted about the weather and where the suburban streets of the county town were lined by "green-thatched barns, with doorways as high as the gates of Solomon's temple." Henchard's defeat by the rational, modernizing Farfrae marks the end of this world. **MR**

> *"One grievous failing of Elizabeth's was her occasional pretty and picturesque use of dialect words—those terrible marks of the beast to the truly genteel."*

⊙ Robert Barnes' illustration for *The Mayor of Casterbridge* was captioned: "'Don't cry, don't cry', said Henchard, 'I can't bear it ...'"

The Strange Case of Dr. Jeckyll and Mr. Hyde

Robert Louis Stevenson

Lifespan | *b.* 1850 (Scotland), *d.* 1894 (Samoa)
First Published | 1886
First Published by | Longmans, Green & Co. (Lon.)
Original Language | English

"All human beings, as we meet them, are commingled out of good and evil . . . "

An engraving from the book showing the moment of Dr. Jeckyll's transformation into the monster Mr. Hyde in Dr. Lanyon's office.

This novel was an immediate success on its first publication in January 1886, and has remained in print ever since. "It is indeed a dreadful book," commented the writer John Addington Symonds to the author in March 1886, "most dreadful because of a certain moral callousness, a want of sympathy, a shutting out of hope." This is a strong description of a tale that begins, quietly enough, with an urbane conversation between the lawyer, Mr. Utterson, and his friend, Mr. Enfield. The latter tells how, returning home in the early hours of the morning, he witnessed a "horrible" incident: a small girl, running across the street, is trampled by a man who leaves her screaming on the ground. "It sounds nothing to hear," Enfield concludes, "but it was hellish to see."

Such reticence is characteristic of Stevenson's retelling of this classic gothic story of "the double," the notion of a man pursued by himself, of a second personality inhabiting the true self. Embedding his tale in a very comfortable, and comfortably male, version of fin-de-siècle London—there is, as Vladimir Nabokov notes, a "delightful winey taste about this book"—Stevenson gradually discloses the identity of the "damned Juggernaut," Mr. Hyde, who disappears behind the door of the respectable, and well-liked, Dr. Jekyll. But identifying Hyde is not the same as knowing how to read the conflict, the double existence, unleashed by Jekyll's experiments with the "evil side of my nature." Notably, in 1888, the psychological phenomenon explored here was invoked to explain a new, and metropolitan, form of sexual savagery in the tabloid sensationalism surrounding the Ripper murders. This is an early example of the purchase of Stevenson's story, its ongoing role in public, and critical, reflection on the many discontents of modern cultural life. **VL**

She

H. Rider Haggard

As one of the many successors Rider Haggard wrote to *King Solomon's Mines*, *She* was an even greater hit at the time. The book is full of Haggard's usual traits of high adventure, highly exoticized African locations, fierce cohesive enemies and daring white heroes, but it is also a more fully realized book than *King Solomon's Mines*, perhaps because it was produced at the height of Haggard's foray into popular writing.

Most notable is of course the central figure of Queen Ayesha: "she-who-must-be-obeyed." It is this figure who dominates the text, indirectly luring the explorer, and narrator of the tale, Ludwig Horace Holly (a man, importantly, of "abnormal ugliness") to Africa in search of the secret of Eternal Life. She then plays him off against his ward and fellow adventurer, the vapid Leo Vincey, deliberately setting the two at loggerheads.

As Haggard noted, "Sexual passion is the most powerful lever with which to stir the mind of man, for it lies at the root of all things human." Ayesha is both intensely human, despite her ability to seemingly "blast" her rivals away, and flagrantly sexual in her behavior—seriously at odds with the apparently juvenile context of Haggard's writing. The figure of the matriarch-temptress is here revealed in a continually bold manner, eclipsing most of the rest of the text with her power; indeed, when the book was read by Carl Jung, he saw Ayesha's character as illustrative of the anima.

She is a potent example of how, early within the history of the genre, Haggard sets the trend by cleverly subverting the conventions of the adventure novel while playing it to its furthest potential, and it paved the way for later novels such as Conrad's *Heart of Darkness*. **EMcCS**

Lifespan | *b.* 1856 (England), *d.* 1925
First Published | 1887
First Published by | Longmans, Green & Co. (Lon.)
Full Title | *She: A History of Adventure*

DRAWN BY E. K. JOHNSON, R.W.S.

"Next instant I felt Leo seize me by the right wrist with both hands."

"It struck me that, on the whole, I had never seen a more evil-looking set of faces."

◉ E. K. Johnson provided illustrations for the first edition of *She*, including this typical Haggard moment of high adventure.

The Woodlanders

Thomas Hardy

Lifespan | *b.* 1840 (England), *d.* 1928
First Published | 1887
First Published by | Macmillan & Co. (London)
Original Language | English

At the opening of *The Woodlanders*, the village barber travels to the hamlet of Little Hintock, to make Marty South an offer. Felice Charmond, the lady of the manor, has offered two sovereigns for Marty's hair. Marty is working by firelight, making hazel spars for thatching; at eighteen pence per thousand, it will take her three weeks to earn two sovereigns. At first she refuses, but discovering that the man she loves is to be betrothed to another, she takes the scissors and cuts off her tresses.

The Woodlanders charts the defeat of the way of life personified by Marty, a poor laborer defenseless against power and money. The future lies with the restless, mobile, adventurous characters: Felice and Fitzpiers ("the young medical gentleman in league with the devil"), and Grace Melbury, the Hintock timber merchant's daughter who is sent to acquire accomplishments at a finishing school. Felice comes to a bad end, but Fitzpiers and Grace, whose marriage seems at first to be a disaster, recover their equilibrium—if not their happiness—and move away into the world beyond the Hintock woods.

The novel is a complex elegy for everything represented by Marty and the man she loves in vain, Giles Winterborne. When Grace, newly, fashionably, and unhappily married, meets Giles, who has taken to the road as an itinerant cider maker, the encounter with her former lover fills her with regret not only for the man she might have wed, but for the life she knows she can no longer live. **MR**

The People of Hemsö

August Strindberg

Lifespan | *b.* 1849 (Sweden), *d.* 1912
First Published | 1887
First Published by | A. Bonniers Förlag (Stockholm)
Original Title | *Hemsöborna*

A feat of straightforward folksy storytelling, *The People of Hemsö* is set on an island in Strindberg's beloved Stockholm archipelago. Written during a difficult period in exile from Sweden, the novel paradoxically has a strong sense of place, and is like a sunny, carefree summer holiday in comparison with some of his more psychologically intense work.

Mrs. Flod, a widow of some means, hires Carlsson to run the farm on the island. As a newcomer and a landlubber among sailors and fishermen Carlsson is implicitly distrusted by the locals. His main rival is Gusten, the son and heir, and a struggle for control of the farm develops between them. Although it may be possible to see traces of a Nietzschean power struggle in their confrontation, the novel is far too light and happy to carry any sustained philosophical weight. Nevertheless, this contest is a clever, page-turning device: is Carlson a slippery confidence trickster preying on the lonely widow, or an honest, hard-working man revitalizing the neglected farm? This question, also debated by the other characters in the novel, still exercises readers today. It explains, together with the magnificent passages describing the sea and the islands, the broad rustic comedy, and the dramatic final twists and turns of the plot, why *The People of Hemsö* has achieved its status as one of the most popular Swedish novels. **UD**

❯ Strindberg, portrayed here in 1899, endured three unhappy marriages and suffered long periods of mental instability.

AVG · STRINDBERG
SVRVSVND · JVLI · 1899 · RITADT AT HAN
GAMLE VÄN
C·L

Fortunata and Jacinta

Benito Pérez Galdós

Lifespan | *b.* 1843 (Spain), *d.* 1920
First Published | 1887, by Imprenta de La Guirnalda
Original Title | *Fortunata y Jacinta: dos historias de casadas*

Part of the series of fictional commentaries on the society and politics of Madrid in the 1870s that Galdós called his "contemporary novels," this is the most celebrated work of one of the masters of nineteenth-century European realism. Ostensibly, it focuses on the convergent histories of Jacinta, the virtuous but sterile wife of Juanito Santa Cruz, the adored playboy son of a wealthy merchant family, and Fortunata Rubín, his statuesque and fertile mistress from the traditional working class. Yet the complex interrelations of an enormous archive of characters from all strata of Madrid's burgeoning middle classes results in a colorful panorama of bourgeois Spanish society at a moment of economic modernization and turbulent political change.

Galdós developed an encyclopedic knowledge of his adopted city, and he provides a detailed depiction of Madrilenian life. The streets and squares of the Spanish capital, its churches, cafés, bars and markets, theaters and boutiques, slums and suburbs, turn the city into the novel's chief protagonist. Despite his fundamentally social-scientific rationale, Galdós was not indifferent to the minor tragedies, comedy and melodrama of human life, nor to the psychology of human consciousness, and his exploration of the internal world of dream, fantasy, and delusion produces some of the novel's most memorable and striking narrative sequences. **DP**

Pierre and Jean

Guy de Maupassant

Lifespan | *b.* 1850 (France), *d.* 1893
First Published | 1888
First Published by | V. Harvard (Paris)
Original Title | *Pierre et Jean*

Set in 1880s Le Havre, *Pierre and Jean* is a highly charged, gripping tale of a family breakdown. The title refers to two brothers, children of a respectable middle-class ex-jeweler and his wife, whose lives are torn apart by an unexpected inheritance. Jean, the younger son and an aspiring lawyer, discovers he is the sole beneficiary of a family friend's estate. All of the family except for Pierre are overjoyed at this sudden godsend. Pierre is at first plagued by simple feelings of jealousy, but his morose condition worsens when he begins to question his mother's honor and fears Jean may be the benefactor's illegitimate son. He is tormented by doubts and the jealousy turns to fear, guilt, and anger. He becomes deeply confused and his anguish forces him to probe deep within himself, thereby furthering his isolation from both his family and society at large. The port of Le Havre and the Normandy coastline form an integral, illustrative backdrop to Pierre's fear, agony, and ultimate yearning for escape.

Widely considered to be one of the masters of the short story, Guy de Maupassant was a highly prolific and successful writer. *Pierre and Jean*, his fourth novel, is illustrative of a shift in both Maupassant's own work and French literature generally; a shift away from the social realism typified by authors such as Balzac and Zola, toward a greater concern with the inner workings of human psychology. **AL**

The Master of Ballantrae

Robert Louis Stevenson

Lifespan | *b.* 1850 (Scotland), *d.* 1894 (Samoa)
First Published | 1889
First Published by | Cassell & Co. (London)
Full Title | *The Master of Ballantrae: A Winter's Tale*

In common with *Treasure Island* (1883) and *Kidnapped* (1886), the historical romances which brought Stevenson popularity, *The Master of Ballantrae* is a tale of adventure. It begins with the lost Jacobite cause at Culloden, and makes us experience the terror of piracy, the sweltering heat of India, and America's trackless wastes, as well as the decline of the Scottish aristocracy. The heart of the novel, however, lies in the conflict between James, the Master of Ballantrae, and his brother Henry over their ancestral seat of Durrisdeer. In their portrayal, Stevenson draws on an obsession with doubles and doppelgängers that has its defining instance in his own *Dr. Jekyll and Mr. Hyde* (1886). The earlier tale's splitting of moral impulses within the same personality is now enacted between the two central protagonists, as the satanic James returns to blackmail Henry, and destroy the family.

As in the tale of Jekyll and Hyde, evil is opposed to moral weakness or vacuity, rather than active goodness. This is personified not only in Henry's vacillations, but in the helplessness of the narrator, Mackellar, constantly struggling to keep up with events, and unable to act at crucial moments of decision. The Master, on the other hand, remains in constant control of the novel. He does this with debonair confidence and an intense consciousness of the literary structure of his significance. Drawing on readings of Milton, Richardson, and the Bible, *Ballantrae* becomes a study in literary as well as psychological and political mastery. **DT**

> *"Here is a tale which extends over many years and travels into many countries ... written by the loud shores of a subtropical island ... "*

⊙ Stevenson fought a lifelong struggle against respiratory illness, cultivating a wry optimism on the path to an early death.

Hunger

Knut Hamsun

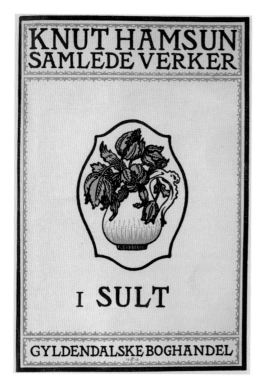

Lifespan | *b.* 1859 (Norway), *d.* 1952
First Published | 1890, by Philipsen (Copenhagen)
Original Title | *Sult*
Nobel Prize for Literature | 1920

Hamsun's reputation has suffered from his Nazi sympathies, but his early, semi-autobiographical portrait of the writer as a hungry young man is a seminal modernist classic. Influenced by Dostoevsky, Hamsun here develops a kind of Nietzschean individualism that rebelled against both naturalism and the progressive literary politics associated with Ibsen. The urban angst of *Hunger* prefigures the alienated cityscapes of Kakfa, but with an insistence on tensions between everyday economics and colloquial reverie worthy of James Kelman.

Told with the urgency of a starved present tense, the novel traces the various degradations of the narrator as he attempts to sustain himself through writing. Sometimes feverish from lack of food, other times merely contemptuous of humanity, the narrator has an overdeveloped sense of personal worth. The resulting encounters and misperceptions are both darkly existential and hilarious. Hunger gradually pulls apart the relation between need and dignity, inducing representations of madness that have an almost hallucinatory effect. Juxtaposing his fantasies and petty crimes with no less petty strategies of revenge and dreams of respect, the novel is carefully balanced between affirming this writer as exceptional and revealing him as a deluded soul, comically lost to spite and stupidity. In ways that prefigure the intellectual down and outs of Beckett's work, *Hunger* is an antidote for anyone planning a career as a starving writer. **DM**

"All of this happened while I was walking around starving in Christiania—that strange city no one escapes from until it has left its mark on him . . . "

The jacket of Hunger—*Sult* in Norwegian—published as the first volume of Knut Hamsun's *Collected Works* (*Samlede Werker*).

By the Open Sea

August Strindberg

Lifespan | *b.* 1849 (Sweden), *d.* 1912
First Published | 1890
First Published by | A. Bonniers Förlag (Stockholm)
Original Title | *I havsbandet*

When Strindberg wrote *By the Open Sea*, he had fallen under the influence of Nietzsche's "Superman" theories. He researched the fields of biology, geology, and geography to implement and authenticate the scientific method and to describe accurately a strong, intellectual man of science.

The novel has two main characters, Axel Borg, a fisheries inspector sent to investigate the dwindling supplies of herring, and the natural landscape of sea and islands, a constant source of fascination for the author. Snobbish and superior, Borg alienates the simple and down-to-earth fishermen, and assumes the stronger man's right to oppress the weak. Taught by his father to suppress the feminine within him, he dominates and conquers a young woman, Maria, but in his own unconscious she takes on the role of anima, exposing the dark recesses of his mind. When under pressure from the locals and the locality, cracks begin to appear in his ego and his confidence begins to look like insecurity. His ideas become increasingly grandiose, and he experiments on himself in an attempt to control and conquer nature.

Borg is clearly Strindberg's alter ego, a sensitive and lonely genius dragged down by the mediocrity of the common rabble. Pointing forward to his "Inferno" crisis of the 1890s, this psychological novel, which charts the frightening degeneration of a proud and intellectual man into a persecuted wreck, gives an interesting insight into Strindberg's own state of mind at the time. **UD**

La Bête Humaine

Émile Zola

Lifespan | *b.* 1840 (France), *d.* 1902
First Published | 1890
First Published by | Charpentier (Paris)
Original Language | French

La Bête Humaine was the seventeenth novel in Zola's twenty-novel series *Les Rougons-Macquart*, through which he sought to follow the effects of heredity and environment on a single family, using the "scientific" terms central to late nineteenth-century Naturalism and to contemporary theories of degeneration and "hereditary taint." *La Bête Humaine* was also a vehicle through which Zola explored the power and impact of the railway, bringing together his twin fascinations with criminality and railway life. The impersonal force of the train becomes inextricably linked in the novel with human violence and destructiveness, and in the character Jacques Lantier, a train driver tormented by his pathological desire to kill women, Zola depicted what a later generation would define as a serial killer. Murder is made inseparable from machine culture, and accident and psychopathology become indivisible. Lantier's violent desires are stimulated when he glimpses the murder, driven by sexual jealousy, of Grandmorin, one of the directors of the railway company. His "itch for murder intensified like a physical lust at the sight of this pathetic corpse." The effects of this murderous desire are played out in the rest of the novel.

Zola's meticulous observation of the physical world is shown in his depictions of the railways, which paint in words the qualities of light and shadow, fire and smoke, that also acted as a magnet to the Impressionist painters of his time. **LM**

The Kreutzer Sonata

Leo Tolstoy

Lifespan | *b.* 1828 (Russia), *d.* 1910
First Published | 1890 (Russia)
Original Title | *Kreitserova sonata*
Original Language | Russian

"In our day marriage is only a violence and falsehood."

⊙ Inspired by Tolstoy's novel, René Prinet painted this image of
a couple roused to passion by performing the Kreutzer Sonata.

The Kreutzer Sonata proffers a blistering attack on the "false importance attached to sexual love." It argues in favor of sexual abstinence (even within marriage), against contraception, and against sentimental ideas of romantic attachment. These morals are, in many respects, alien to the West today, but the novel cannot be simply dismissed as a reactionary rant. The idea that women will never enjoy equality with men while they are treated as sexual objects resonates with ongoing feminist debates. Here is the late Tolstoy at his most puritanical, following his famous late "conversion" to Christianity. If we were in any doubt that he shares the views advanced by the tormented protagonist, Pozdnyshev, he wrote a famous "Epilogue" the following year, an elaboration of his apologia for chastity and continence as befitting human dignity. The novel caused a scandal on its publication and attempts were made in Russia to ban it, though copies were widely circulated. Mere extracts were prohibited in the U.S., and Theodore Roosevelt called Tolstoy a "sexual moral pervert."

Set during a train journey, Pozdnyshev tells the narrator the story of how he came to kill his wife, blaming his actions on the sexual ethos of the times. Readers of *Anna Karenina* will know that the train in Tolstoy's world can often be seen as a symbol of degraded modernity. The most compelling aspect of this novella is the psychologically acute depiction of obsessive male jealousy. Like Shakespeare's Othello, Pozdnyshev's conviction that his wife is having an affair with her music partner finds confirmation in trifles. The barrier between his inner pain and his polished, scrupulously polite social exterior, between private passion and public decorum, ultimately breaks down in his final murderous outburst. **RMcD**

The Picture of Dorian Gray

Oscar Wilde

"There is no such thing as a moral or an immoral book. Books are well written, or badly written. That is all." The series of aphorisms that make up the "Preface" of Wilde's only novel was his response to those critics who had questioned the immorality and unhealthiness of the story after its scandalous first appearance in *Lippincott's Monthly Magazine*. However, for all its transgressive delights, *The Picture of Dorian Gray* could easily be read as a profoundly moral book, even a cautionary tale against the dangers of vice. Dorian's descent into moral squalor is neither admirable, as can be seen in his peremptory rejection of his fiancée, the actress Sybil Vain, nor enviable. Indeed the beautiful boy is the least interesting character in the book that bears his name.

After the artist Basil Hallward paints Dorian's picture, his subject's frivolous wish for immortality comes true. As the picture of him grows old and corrupt, Dorian himself continues to appear fresh and innocent for decades, despite the lusts and depravity of his private life. To be sure, it is the epigrammatic wit of Lord Henry Wotton that encourages Dorian on his quest for sensuality and sensation, but Dorian's values pervert the deeply serious Wildean ethic that they superficially resemble. Whereas Oscar Wilde's essays advocate individualism and self-realization as a route to a richer life and a more just society, Dorian follows a path of hedonism, self-indulgence, and the objectification of others. It is, nonetheless, a story that poignantly reflects Wilde's own double life and anticipates his own fall into ignominy and shame. The conceit on which it is based—the painting in the attic—seems immediately to mutate from fiction into the stuff of myth. **RMcD**

Lifespan | *b.* 1854 (Ireland), *d.* 1900
First Published | 1891
First Published by | Ward, Lock & Co. (London)
Given Name | Fingal O'Flahertie Wills

"How sad it is! I shall grow old, and horrid, and dreadful."

◉ A lounging Dorian Gray contemplates the portrait that is destined to grow old while its subject enjoys eternal youth.

Tess of the D'Urbervilles

Thomas Hardy

Lifespan | *b.* 1840 (England), *d.* 1928
First Published | 1891, by Osgood, McIlvaine & Co.
Full Title | *Tess of the D'Urbervilles: A Pure Woman Faithfully Presented by Thomas Hardy*

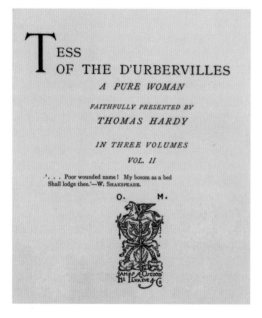

> *"'Justice' was done, and the President of the Immortals (in Aeschylean phrase) had ended his sport with Tess."*

⊙ The title page of *Tess'* first edition shows the subtitle *A Pure Woman*, a challenge to Victorian views of an unmarried mother.

Hardy's novel is as famous for its heroine as for its notoriously tragic plot, and *Tess* remains a moving and absorbing read today. Originally shunned by critics upon its publication in 1891 because of "immorality," the novel traces the difficult life of Tess Durbeyfield, whose victimization at the hands of men eventually leads to her horrific downfall. As with *Jude the Obscure*, *Tess* spares the reader none of the bitterness inherent in English country life, and Hardy's often romanticized love for the landscape of Wessex is balanced by the novel's grimly realistic depiction of social injustice.

When Tess' father discovers that his own family, the Durbeyfields, are related to a prominent local dynasty, he agrees that his daughter should contact the heir, Alec D'Urberville, with tragic results. He seduces her, and soon abandons her, leaving her an unmarried single mother. While she briefly finds happiness with another man, the seemingly upright Angel Clare, he too rejects her upon hearing of her sexual past, leaving her in poverty and misery. Forced back into the arms of Alec, Tess must sacrifice her personal happiness for economic survival, but when her feelings of injustice overwhelm her in a moment of passion, the consequences are tragic.

In *Tess*, Hardy presents a world in which the human spirit is battered down by the forces, not of fate, but of social hierarchy. Tess' eventual death, one of the most famous in literature, is a direct result of human cruelty and as such represents one of the most moving indictments of the lives of nineteenth-century English women in all of literature. Hardy's skill lies in presenting what might otherwise seem almost unbearable misfortune in a way that leaves the reader with a resounding sense of beauty and humanity even in the midst of arbitrary cruelty. **AB**

Gösta Berling's Saga

Selma Lagerlöf

In 1909, Selma Lagerlöf became the first woman to receive the Nobel Prize for Literature. *Gösta Berling's Saga*, her first great success as a novelist, went largely unnoticed until its Danish translation received widespread critical acclaim. It is now regarded as a masterpiece of Swedish literature. Although written at the dawn of the modern era, this novel, steeped in the local lore and legend of the mountainous and sparsely populated province of Värmland in the Swedish midwest, represents a return to traditional storytelling about glorious manor houses, beautiful women, gallant men, and extraordinary and romantic adventures.

In the bachelors' wing at Ekeby Manor, the generous and hospitable major's wife gives refuge to twelve homeless "cavaliers" led by Gösta Berling, a defrocked priest who is also a handsome and romantic Don Juan. These men represent old-fashioned, traditional values of chivalry and romance, but are also weak characters, dangerously devoted to bohemian living and reckless revelry. In a pact with the evil Sintram, the devil's local representative, the major's wife is evicted and the cavaliers take over Ekeby for a year, threatening to run it to rack and ruin. Fantastic events take place, and the Great Ball at Ekeby, in particular, is a classic episode of eventful drama.

The wish to recapture a golden age, when the local boom in iron-making created wealth and elegance, is offset by an interest in the nature of memory and reality. The novel is written in an old-fashioned, allegorical, and slightly mannered style, but the beginning, where the protagonist's state of mind and his dependence on the bottle is described, anticipates the modern novel in its intense focus on the psychology of the human mind. **UD**

Lifespan | *b.* 1858 (Sweden), *d.* 1940
First Published | 1891, by Hellberg (Stockholm)
Original Title | *Ur Gösta Berlings Saga: Berättelse från det gamla Värmland*

> *"He, to be a wayside beggar, to lie drunk in the ditches, to go clad in rags, and consort with vagabonds!"*

◆ Swedish novelist Selma Lagerlöf intertwined fairy tale and legend with realistic portrayal of rural life in a patriarchal society.

New Grub Street

George Gissing

Lifespan | *b.* 1857 (England), *d.* 1903 (France)
First Published | 1891
First Published by | Smith, Elder & Co. (London)
Original Language | English

Among the earliest and best novels about the business of authorship, *New Grub Street* draws a map of the late-Victorian publishing industry. Gissing highlights the split between literary writing and popular journalism, typified in magazines like the newly launched *Tit-Bits*, anticipating a hundred years of subsequent debate about art and mass culture. He gives a coolly realistic appraisal of the market, but still affirms that fiction can express its own kind of truth. Among a memorable, psychologically convincing cast of characters, the most fully drawn is Edwin Reardon, whose struggles to complete his novel *Margaret Home* are shown in detail. Desperate work gets the book finished, but it is feeble and full of padding, and Reardon, marked for failure, dreads seeing it reviewed. Jasper Milvain, by contrast, a shrewd, breezily assured literary operative with no aesthetic scruples, prospers. Harold Biffen is a garret-dwelling perfectionist who lives on bread and dripping. Biffen's novel *Mr. Bailey, Grocer*, a hyperrealist study of "ignobly decent" everyday life, is Gissing's intriguing guess at what twentieth-century avant-garde fiction might be like. Minor characters include, amongst others, the irascible Alfred Yule and his daughter Marian.

Gissing was a cannier author than Reardon or Biffen, and a more serious writer than Milvain. *New Grub Street*, commercially and artistically his most successful book, shows that good fiction sometimes thrives in the marketplace. **MR**

News from Nowhere

William Morris

Lifespan | *b.* 1834 (England), *d.* 1896
First Published | 1891, by Reeves & Turner (London)
Full Title | *News from Nowhere, or, an Epoch of Rest, being some chapters from a Utopian Romance*

As prophecy, William Morris' dream of a utopian future, in which there is no private property, no government, no legal system, no penal system, and no formal education, can seem comically unlikely. Morris imagines a future London which has been reforested, and in which the clothes, the crockery, the buildings, and the bridges have all been designed by William Morris. The ideal that Morris is imagining here belongs much less to the future than it does to a specifically nineteenth-century fantasy steeped in an agrarian past. But the value of this dream is not found in its representation of an imagined future, so much as in its characterization of the limits of contemporary political imagination. Morris' vision of a life that is not governed by an oppressive state-apparatus brings a sharp, satirical focus to bear on the irrationality and the contradictions of his own time, and indeed present-day political conditions. Morris leads us to see with a new clarity the rank injustices that are produced by an unequal distribution of wealth.

The novel's bright, witty prose makes it as much an entertaining tale as it is a socialist manifesto. It is also surprisingly sensual. An image of social justice is here entwined with an erotic delight in the possibilities of human beauty. **PB**

❯ The art nouveau cover of an issue of *Art Journal* magazine devoted to William Morris reflects his wide-ranging interests.

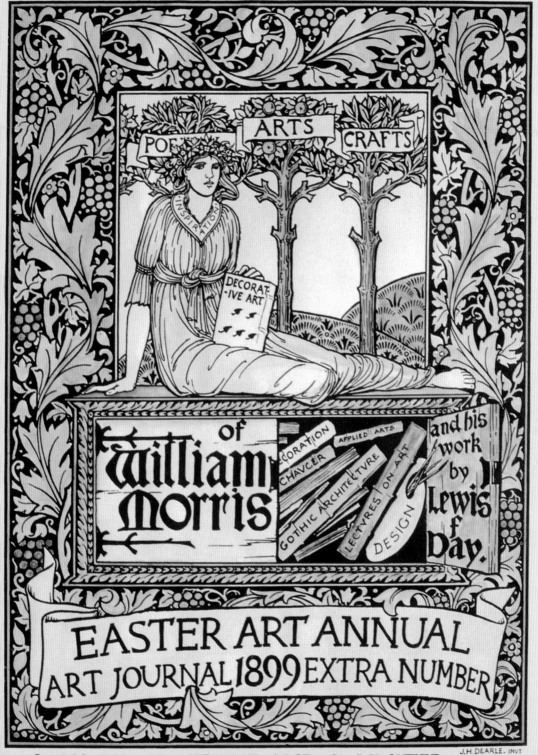

POETRY ARTS CRAFTS

INSPIRATION

DECORAT-IVE ART

of William Morris and his work by Lewis F. Day.

Decoration CHAUCER APPLIED ARTS GOTHIC ARCHITECTURE LECTURES ON ART DESIGN

EASTER ART ANNUAL
ART JOURNAL 1899 EXTRA NUMBER

LONDON: H VIRTUE AND Co LIMITED

J.H.DEARLE. INVT

Collier's

Household Number for November

Sherlock Holmes

In this Number Solves
The Mystery of

The
Norwood Builder

VOL XXXII NO 5   OCTOBER 31 1903   PRICE 10 CENTS

The Adventures of Sherlock Holmes

Sir Arthur Conan Doyle

Between 1891 and 1893 twenty-four Arthur Conan Doyle *Holmes* stories were published in *The Strand*, of which the first twelve were published in book form as *The Adventures of Sherlock Holmes*.

"To Sherlock Holmes she is always the woman." So begins "A Scandal in Bohemia," the first story in the collection. Irene Adler is "the" woman because she is the only person ever to have outwitted Holmes. The King of Bohemia fears that he will be blackmailed by Adler, his former lover, who has kept some compromising love letters and a photograph. However, she manages to turn the tables on the detective, retaining the photograph to ensure her own safety. Other highlights in the collection are the eerie "The Red-Headed League" where a red-headed man is offered employment by the League as a ruse to keep him occupied while criminals dig a tunnel from the cellar of his premises to a bank. In "The Man with the Twisted Lip" Holmes' help is enlisted to solve the mystery of the disappearance of Mr. Neville St. Clair. His wife has seen him at a window in a rougher part of town, but the police are unable to find anyone but a beggar. A number of enigmas follow before Holmes is able to reach a conclusion.

The first appearance of Sherlock Holmes in 1887 is particularly interesting in historical terms. For the first time, European cities had proliferated to the point where it was impossible to know more than a small percentage of their inhabitants. Yet the London that features in these stories manages to resist the idea that the city is sublime, that it is too large for any one person to be able to comprehend. Holmes and Watson represent Conan Doyle's bourgeois remedy to the terrifying and seemingly endless late nineteeenth-century expansion of urban and industrial civilization. **VC-R**

Lifespan | *b*. 1859 (Scotland), *d*. 1930 (England)
First Published | 1892
First Published by | G. Newnes (London)
Original Language | English

" HOLMES GAVE ME A SKETCH OF THE EVENTS."

◉ Illustrator Sydney Paget was responsible for establishing the original appearance of Sherlock Holmes and Dr. Watson.

◉ Frederick Door Steele created this image of Conan Doyle's great detective for the cover of *Collier's Weekly* magazine in 1903.

Diary of a Nobody

George & Weedon Grossmith

Lifespan (George) | *b.*1847 (England), *d.*1912
Lifespan (Weeden) | *b.*1852 (England), *d.*1919
First Serialized | 1892, by *Punch* magazine (London)
First Published | 1892, by J. W. Arrowsmith (Bristol)

One of the great English comic novels, *Diary of a Nobody* bridges the world of Dickens to that of Waugh and Wodehouse. Straitlaced London clerk Charles Pooter records his daily life, both in the office and at home in suburban Holloway: a life involving insolent junior employees, his long-suffering wife Carrie, and the serial amours of his son Lupin. The masterstroke of the novel is the ironic distance between Pooter's sense of himself and the world, and his dim recognition that matters might be otherwise; readers will enjoy tracing how events conspire to outwit Pooter's attempts at maintaining a certain kind of genteel English decorum.

Both Grossmith brothers had strong theatrical connections, and stage comedy certainly influences the *Diary's* best set pieces. The more neurotic Pooter becomes about the smallest matters of domestic order, the more life seems to fling banana skins in his path, as when the new boots he buys for a dance send him sliding over the dance floor. Like Dickens' Micawber, Pooter is a comic figure who transcends his immediate context, largely through the *Diary's* surreally funny style; a reader does not need to know much about the 1890s to luxuriate in Pooter's absurd obsession with red enamel paint, which even leads him to repaint the spines of the family Shakespeare. At the same time, he is a supreme example of anxious Englishness, and Helen Fielding's Bridget Jones and John Cleese's Basil Fawlty might not exist without his example. **BT**

Born in Exile

George Gissing

Lifespan | *b.*1857 (England), *d.*1903 (France)
First Published | 1892
First Published by | A. & C. Black (London)
Original Language | English

Born in Exile is George Gissing's fullest study of the figure which preoccupied him throughout his writing life: the alienated intellectual, who has the brains and talent to rise but is inexorably held back by poverty and the weight of established culture. Like Gissing, Godwin Peak, the novel's ambiguous hero, is a bright, ambitious child from a lower-middle-class family who gains a scholarship, but whose academic career is fatally cut short. However, whereas Gissing was expelled for stealing money from fellow students, Godwin leaves Whitelaw out of sheer social embarrassment when his cockney uncle sets up a restaurant close by the college gates. Fleeing the scorn of his privileged peers, Godwin starts work as an industrial chemist, but a chance meeting makes him determined to "knit himself into the social fabric" by retraining as a clergyman. The atheist Godwin performs the role of a practising Anglican while skeptically observing himself, and the novel brilliantly dissects the splits within his consciousness as he is inexorably driven toward further alienation. As a study of a man's existential struggle, *Born in Exile* belongs to the intellectual tradition of European literature and philosophy—it carries echoes of both Dostoevsky and Nietzsche. The figure of Godwin Peak, who paradoxically exposes the liberal myth of social mobility by colluding with the conservative hierarchy he attempts to scale, also highlights very English cultural conflicts. **JBT**

The Yellow Wallpaper

Charlotte Perkins Gilman

Lifespan | *b.*1860 (U.S.), *d.*1935
First Published | 1892 (in book form, 1899)
First Serialized by | *New England Magazine* (Boston)
Given Name | Charlotte Anna Perkins

This little slip of prose, a novella running to a mere twenty-nine pages, is a literary masterpiece, and one of the defining fictional studies of Victorian sexuality. It is a first-person account of a woman writer whose struggle to conform to the ideals of Victorian motherhood and wifeliness drives her to a nervous breakdown. Banished to an upstairs room by her husband, she is subjected to a version of the Weir Mitchell "rest cure" that Gilman herself underwent in 1885.

The novella is an immaculate depiction of descent into madness. The woman becomes increasingly obsessed with the floral yellow wallpaper that decorates her prison, as the story moves further into the realm of the surreal and the macabre. The convoluted pattern of the wallpaper becomes the bars of a cage, with the narrator convinced that behind the bars is a woman struggling to get out. Eventually she becomes a human animal, who tears and bites at the walls, desperate to free the image of herself that she can glimpse writhing behind the surface of the paper. To some extent, this uncanny and eerie story of gradual derangement belongs to a Gothic tradition, but it is also a deeply moving account of the narrator's yearning for sexual and intellectual freedom. Reduced to a bleeding, grotesque animal by the end of the story, the narrator has also freed herself from the constraints of Victorian propriety. She has let the woman behind the wallpaper out. **PB**

The Real Charlotte

Somerville & Ross

Lifespan (Somerville) | *b.*1858 (Greece), *d.*1949
Lifespan (Ross) | *b.*1862 (Ireland), *d.*1915
First Published | 1894
First Published by | Ward & Downey (London)

The Real Charlotte is a much darker text than the comic *"Irish R.M."* stories for which Edith Somerville and Violet Martin are best known. It is often acclaimed as Somerville and Ross' first full-length work of realist fiction, and their portrayal of the eponymous heroine, Charlotte Mullen, marks their full transition into a study of inner character to which they would return at different points in their joint career. It is set among the Anglo-Irish gentry in West Cork, and peopled with a host of eccentric characters who are evoked with a nostalgic and slightly satiric glow. Unlike the earlier works, however, this novel is suffused with darkness. This stems from the central depiction of a mind driven to destroy whatever relative, friend, or neighbor stands in her way. Charlotte is plain, ambitious, resentful, sexually frustrated, mocked, and despised. Hopelessly in love with the sponging land-agent Roderick Lambert, she knows she can only attract him by accumulating money and property. She is jealous of her naïve, pretty cousin Francie whom she cheats out of her inheritance. Her success in matters of business, due to a callous disregard for any kind of human frailty, is offset by her social humiliation at the hands of local aristocrats like Lady Dysart, and her sexual humiliation by Lambert. Charlotte becomes the focus of the text's interest in questions of gender and sexuality, especially as they relate to women without status, looks, or prospects, and her derangement provokes both fear and pity. **AM**

Jude the Obscure

Thomas Hardy

Lifespan | *b.* 1840 (England), *d.* 1928
First Published | 1895
First Published by | Osgood, McIlvaine & Co. (Lon)
Original Language | English

Jude the Obscure is the angriest and most experimental of Hardy's novels, preoccupied with themes of desire and displacement. When Jude Fawley leaves rural Marygreen and Alfredston behind him for the spires of Christminster City, a university town, he chooses to walk rather than ride the last four miles. He is physically pacing out the distance he is traveling, a distance only accurately measured in ambition and hope, or in the beautiful enthusiasm of one who knows not the obstacles on the path ahead.

When the stonemason Jude enters the city, he brings with him his class and its history. At first it enriches him; when he reads the monumental architectural pages of the college buildings, he does so through an artisan's eyes. Gradually, his class works to define limits for his ambition—the letter from the Master of "Biblioll College" warning Jude to remain "in your own sphere" provides one cruelly pragmatic moment of discovery. Jude's own broken marriage and his unconventional relationship with a free-spirited cousin ends in cruel tragedy, and the nature of Jude's response is telling.

Interwoven with despair, resentment, anger, and pride is a sense of exile all the more painful for being inarticulate. Forbidden access to the "world of learning," yet knowing such a world exists, Jude Fawley is doubly exiled, displaced by his desires from his social roots and hobbled by those roots in achieving his desires. **PMcM**

Effi Briest

Theodor Fontane

Lifespan | *b.* 1819 (Germany), *d.* 1898
First Published | 1895
First Published by | F. Fontane & Co. (Berlin)
Original Language | German

Thomas Mann declared *Effi Briest* among the six most significant novels ever written. Even more powerful testimony of its power comes from Krapp in Beckett's play *Krapp's Last Tape*: "Scalded the eyes out of me reading Effie again, a page day, with tears again." Effi Briest is indeed scalding and anyone worried about appearing red-eyed should take appropriate precautions.

Free of judgmental moralism, the novel—loosely based on a true story—nevertheless focuses its sympathies on the plight of the eponymous Effi, married too young to a much older man. In the framework of an otherwise conventional tale of love and adultery, Fontane weaves a beautiful and allusive sense of personal and social tragicomedy. Contrasting nature and culture, the naïvety of Effi shines through the troubling world she inhabits. Worthy of comparison with Eugénie Grandet, Emma Bovary, or Anna Karenina, Effi's character acts as a vehicle for exploration into the historical and social structure of society. The disruption of Effi's fragile humanity by the sexual and political undercurrents of the novel's social critique is particularly subtle. Sensitive to the risks of anything approaching melodrama, this novel, although told directly and with symbolic concentration, is built of oblique hints, acidic tangents, and dramatic ironies. **DM**

❯ Theodor Fontane was fifty-six when he first turned to writing novels and *Effi Briest* was produced in his seventies.

The Time Machine

H. G. Wells

Lifespan | *b.* 1866 (England), *d.* 1946
First Published | 1895
First Published by | W. Heinemann (London)
Full Title | *The Time Machine: An Invention*

The Time Machine, Wells' first novel, is a "scientific romance" which inverts the nineteenth-century belief in evolution as progress. The story follows a Victorian scientist, who claims that he has invented a device that allows him to travel through time, and has visited the future, arriving in the year 802,701 in what had once been London. There he finds the future race, or, more accurately, races, for the human species has "evolved" into two disparate forms. Above ground live the Eloi—gentle, fairy-like, childish creatures, whose existence appears to be free of struggle. However, another race of beings exists— the Morlocks, underground dwellers who, once subservient, now prey upon the feeble, defenseless Eloi. By setting the action nearly a million years in the future, Wells was illustrating the Darwinian model of evolution by natural selection, "fast-forwarding" through the slow process of changes to species, the physical world, and the solar system.

The novel is a class fable, as well as a scientific parable, in which the two societies of Wells' own period (the upper classes and the "lower orders") are recast as equally, though differently, "degenerate" beings. "Degeneration" is evolution in reverse, while Wells' dystopic vision in *The Time Machine* is a deliberate debunking of the Utopian fictions of the late nineteenth century, in particular William Morris' *News from Nowhere*. Where Morris depicts a pastoral, socialist utopia, Wells represents a world in which the human struggle is doomed to failure. **LM**

> *"There is no difference between Time and any of the three dimensions of Space except that our consciousness moves along it."*

⬤ The 1960 movie version of Wells' novel neglected the class war elements of the book in favor of melodrama and special effects.

The Island of Dr. Moreau

H. G. Wells

Lifespan | *b.* 1866 (England), *d.* 1946
First Published | 1896
First Published by | W. Heinemann (London)
Full Name | Herbert George Wells

A prophetic science fiction tale, *The Island of Doctor Moreau* takes on an even more sinister light given contemporary debates about cloning and genetic experimentation, as well as the contentious issues that still surround Moreau's modus operandi—vivisection.

As with *The Time Machine* and *The War of the Worlds*, *Moreau* confronts readers with a gruesome extrapolation of Darwinist theory, which embodies many of the concerns arising from the publication of *The Origin of Species* (1859). *Moreau* also represents a series of fundamental anxieties about the role of science and human responsibility. Here, the archetypal mad scientist who creates without due care or any apparent concern for the consequences of his work, is as vile as the beasts he manipulates. This orgiastic society of half-men, half-beasts, with their deliberately mutilated commandments—"Not to suck up Drink; that is the Law. Are we not Men?"—reflects contemporary society clearly enough, without needing the final sting. The barbarism of Moreau's methods is as horrific as the issues that lie beneath; developments in science mean that the text has as much capacity to shock now as on first publication, as Moreau flays his animals alive and slowly molds them into humans. This may be a far cry from the infinite delicacy of genetic manipulation, but it still succeeds in arousing all of the classic fears of "unknown" scientific methods. **EMcCS**

Quo Vadis

Henryk Sienkiewicz

Lifespan | *b.* 1846 (Poland), *d.* 1916 (Switzerland)
First Published | 1896, by Gebethner & Wolff
Original Title | *Quo vadis: Powieść z czasów Nerona*
Nobel Prize for Literature | 1905

An epic depiction of the cruelty and corruption of ancient Rome, *Quo Vadis* was an international bestseller in the decade after its publication. Its lurid scenes of decadent carousing at the court of Nero and of the persecution of early Christians made it highly suitable for screen adaptation.

The central plot traces the ill-starred love between Ligia, a Christian girl from the area that is now Poland, and a Roman officer, Marcus Vinicius, who is eventually converted to the new faith after meeting the apostles Peter and Paul. This somewhat hackneyed storyline is much enlivened by the presence of Vinicius' uncle, the Roman author Petronius, a cynical aesthete who provides a witty insider's view of life at Nero's court. Nero himself emerges as a complex villain, who deliberately sets fire to Rome to clear the way for his architectural ambitions. He then blames the fire on the Christians, unleashing a wave of persecution. Sienkiewicz's strong Catholic faith shines through, as the love and spirituality of the early Christians are pitted against the power and materialism of Rome. There is also a subtext of Polish nationalism—at the time the book was written, Polish citizens were under the oppressive rule of three neighboring empires.

A fellow Polish Nobel Prize winner, Czeslav Milosz, wrote that Sienkiewicz displayed "a rare narrative gift," and although this kind of novel has long been out of fashion, the author's superb craftsmanship ensures that it remains an excellent read. **RG**

Dracula

Bram Stoker

Lifespan | *b.* 1847 (Ireland), *d.* 1912 (England)
First Published | 1897
First Published by | A. Constable & Co. (London)
Original Language | English

"I trust . . . you will enjoy your stay in my beautiful land."

● Bram Stoker's was far from being the first vampire horror story, as is shown by this 1847 book illustration of the "feast of blood."

❯ A French poster for the 1958 film *Horror of Dracula*, one of the better movie exploitations of Dracula's potential to thrill.

Dracula is a true horror novel, as much rooted in the reality of the world where it takes place as it is in the forces of the supernatural that invade it. The blurring between these points is doubled in the story's telling, wherein the era's most cutting-edge modes of communication are corrupted, transmitting an ancient evil. Englishman Jonathan Harker travels to a remote castle in Transylvania to conduct a real estate deal with Count Dracula, whose fatal appetite for blood is unleashed. As the Count boards ship for England in search of fresh prey, Dr. Van Helsing embarks on a complex plan to thwart the vampire. The narrative progresses through a series of eyewitness reports, diary entries, and technical notes from doctors and scientists. Each of these narrative modes should represent a degree of accurate "truth," yet across them the figure of Dracula is a constant presence, lurking out of sight, contravening laws of physics. The fascination and prevailing horror of *Dracula* lie in the prospect that even the most advanced of technologies, developed in search of some ultimate rationality and truth, still cannot eradicate the forces of the irrational, regardless of the particular period in history or the advancement in question.

The bloodthirsty Count has become a popular icon, the figurehead of both Universal and Hammer Horror movies throughout the twentieth century. Critics have carried out extensive psychoanalytical and postcolonial readings of the text. As a result, the strengths of the work as a horror novel, let alone a revolutionary one, have been flattened, reduced to almost nothing throughout the century that lies between its creation and the present day. This must not be the case, regardless of what vast and repetitive mileage it has already generated. **SF**

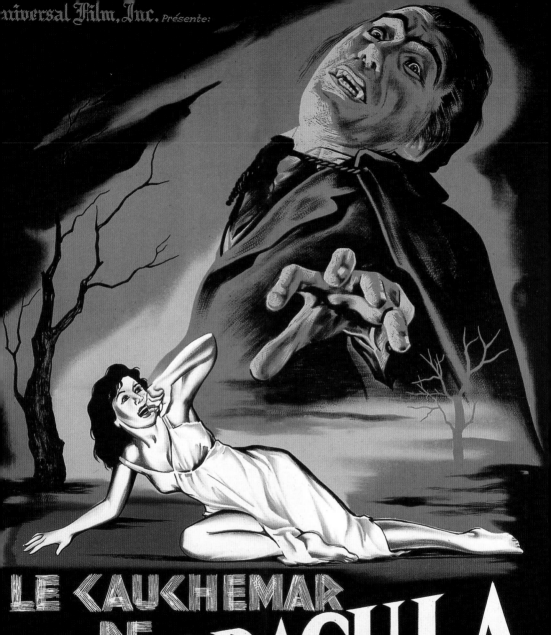

Fruits of the Earth
André Gide

> *"Old hands soil, it seems, whatever they caress, but they too have their beauty when they are joined in prayer."*
>
> *Gide,* Journals, *1929*

André Gide's espousal of paganism in *Fruits* was linked to a desire to give free expression to his own homosexuality.

Lifespan | *b.* 1869 (France), *d.* 1951
First Published | 1897, by Mecure de France (Paris)
Original Title | *Les Nourriture Terrestres*
Nobel Prize for Literature | 1947

André Gide wrote *Fruits of the Earth* while suffering from tuberculosis. It takes the form of a long letter or address written to an imagined correspondent—Nathaniel, a disciple and idealized companion—and is apparently a hymn to the heady pleasures that can be absolutely appreciated only by someone near to death to whom every breath is miraculous.

The book's mode—a combination of the didactic and the euphoric, incorporating verses and songs—caused it to be read as an alternative gospel, and it was for a long time Gide's most popular book, not least for its radical position on homosexuality. The new gods are sensation, desire, and instinct; the goals are adventure and excess. But an essential part of the book's doctrine is the necessity of renunciation. There is little pleasure in possession, and desire is dulled by consummation. Conventions are inimical because they are constraining, but also because they involve false consciousness.

This aspect of the book's message was taken up by Sartre and Camus, and explored more elaborately by Gide in *The Immoralist* (1902). It would be easy to argue that *Fruits of the Earth* is not itself a novel, but in it Gide discovered at their barest some of the most fundamental principles of novel writing, and in the relation between the narrator and his ideal reader—"I should like to speak to you more intimately than anyone has ever yet spoken to you"—he found a way of charging a work of fiction with a sense of urgency that few writers have matched. **DSoa**

What Maisie Knew

Henry James

Lifespan | *b.* 1843 (U.S.), *d.* 1916 (England)
First Published | 1897
First Published by | W. Heinemann (London)
Original Language | English

When Beale and Ida Farange get divorced, their daughter Maisie is "disposed of in a manner worthy of the judgment seat of Solomon ... They would take her, in rotation, for six months at a time." The actual arrangements are altogether messier, as Maisie is passed back and forth between parents, new spouses, and lovers. Yet because everything is refracted through Maisie's consciousness, she appears as the still center of the novel, while the monstrous adults loom in and out of view.

"Small children have many more perceptions than they have terms to translate them," James says in his "Preface" to the New York edition of the novel (1909). Maisie sees more than she understands. But she also knows more than she knows. At the root of her parents' tangled and unedifying relationships are sex and money, two subjects that Maisie, in a straightforward sense, knows nothing about. Yet she witnesses their effects in the behavior of the adults surrounding her, and in that way comes to know a very great deal about what sex and money mean.

Maisie's clarity of perception, uncluttered by the preoccupations of the grown-ups she is watching, and James' supple articulation of what she sees, provide a rich account of the fall out of an unhappy marriage. The activities of the adults are also thrown into sharp relief by the dignified figure of Maisie herself. And yet she is not unscathed by her experience: no one who knows as much as Maisie could be described as an innocent child. **TEJ**

The Invisible Man

H. G. Wells

Lifespan | *b.* 1866 (England), *d.* 1946
First Published | 1897
First Published by | A. Pearson (London)
Full Title | *The Invisible Man: a Grotesque Romance*

The antihero of *The Invisible Man*, Griffin, is a lowly scientific demonstrator who has found a way to make himself invisible, by which means he intends to make the world work for rather than against him: "An invisible man is a man of power." Griffin soon realizes, however, the disadvantages and dangers of invisibility. Even though he has no material self he is pursued by dogs, which pick up his scent; the food he eats has visible form inside his invisible body. Wells exploited the farcical possibilities of the situation he created, undoubtedly drawing on early cinema's exploitations of the new medium's abilities to animate inanimate objects and to move matter through space without visible agency. Griffin follows in the footsteps of other over-reachers—*Faust*, *Frankenstein*—becoming increasingly destructive as he pursues total power.

The black comedy of *The Invisible Man*, however, renders it no less of a moral fable. Invisibility becomes a metaphor for the ways in which Griffin places himself outside the norms of his society. One spur to the novel's creation was Wells' hostility to the widespread popularity of Nietzschean thought, and, in particular, of the model of the *Ubermensch* or "Superman." The novel is also a parable of the ways in which scientific discovery can be used to further evil ends as well as good. This was by no means a new theme, but Wells added to it a fascination with the details of scientific experimentation, bringing science and fiction together in new combinations. **LM**

The War of the Worlds

H.G. Wells

Lifespan | *b*. 1866 (England), *d*. 1946
First Published | 1898
First Published by | W. Heinemann (London)
Original Language | English

Like so many of H.G.Wells' pioneering science fiction texts, *The War of the Worlds* introduces a theme that was to find countless imitations. His work has been reproduced directly in film, comic book, and even progressive rock, but perhaps the most well-known exploration is Orson Welles' infamous radio broadcast of 1938. Interspersed with music from "Ramón Raquello and his orchestra," it reported a full scale Martian invasion. That the initial transmission provoked panic in America, though of course exaggerated by the media, is testament to the greatness of Wells' fiction.

The plot is simple: a strange disk lands on Horsell Common, Surrey, and eventually hatches. The alien inside is malevolent, destroying all with its "heat ray" and striking terror in the heart with the eerie battle-cry of "ulla." Humanity seems powerless in its wake and the Martians easily seize control.

The grandeur of Wells' vision is at once simple and deeply complex, suggesting humanity's inherent fallibility and lack of control. At the same time, Wells introduces a series of underlying motifs that question social and moral beliefs. Finally, the spectacle of the Martians is both awe- and fear-inspiring, and the nature of the aliens themselves has been continually reinterpreted since the novel's first publication. **EMcCS**

○ Orson Welles is photographed shortly after his broadcast of *The War of the Worlds* that panicked America.

The Turn of the Screw

Henry James

Lifespan | *b*. 1843 (U.S.), *d*. 1916 (England)
First Published | 1898
First Published by | W. Heinemann (London)
Original Language | English

The Turn of the Screw is a construction of ambiguities which build up to form a story, never ultimately resolved. The narrative itself, comprising the arrival of an unnamed governess at a remote country house and the subsequent suggestion of supernatural events surrounding the children in her charge, is today pure generic staple, but here all is in the telling. The continual blurring of reality and fevered imagination, of coolness and hysteria, takes the place of any ultimate revelation of the perceived threat. Fusing the paranoid imagination of the governess with that of the reader, the result is that the heightened sense of every detail, every creak, is potentially terrifying. This element of style is crucial to the ambiguity of the story; the book is constantly asking questions and producing effects in the reader, rather than attempting to set itself in stone.

It is significant, in terms of the contemporary importance of *The Turn of the Screw*, that the Spanish director Alejandro Amenábar, whose *The Others* is a quasi-adaptation of James' novella, made his name with *Abre Los Ojos*. In this movie, life and dream become indistinguishable and a sense of "reality" is chillingly undermined. More so than any actual apparition rattling windowpanes and clanking chains, it is the idea of the distinctions between inner and outer dimensions breaking down which provides the source of the sense of dread of all truly authentic ghost stories, which *The Turn of the Screw* undoubtedly is. **SF**

The Awakening

Kate Chopin

Lifespan | *b*. 1851 (U.S.), *d*. 1904
First Published | 1899
First Published by | H. S. Stone & Co. (Chicago)
Given Name | Katherine O'Flaherty

The Awakening was initially met with condemnation and outrage, forcing its author into financial crisis and literary obscurity. Coming back from this apparent literary death-at-birth, the effects of this novel live on, inveterate and relentless. Now widely read, *The Awakening* is critically acclaimed as an American version of *Madame Bovary*. When Edna Pontellier finds her position as young wife and mother in New Orleans unbearably stifling, her refusal to go by the laws and mores of society drives her up against a world at once disapproving and uncannily precognizant of her struggles, in a provoking and often progressive critique of marriage and motherhood in Creole society.

Chopin provides a startling account of what it might mean to "awaken" into a better understanding of one's position. The novel invites us to wonder if it might not be better to carry on "sleeping" through life, as well as dealing with the complicated ways in which different kinds of "production" and "destruction" merge with one another. Chopin's subject matter and observations are engrossing and, in many respects, ahead of their time. But what is most remarkable about *The Awakening* is the way in which it forces us to think about the very notion of time, of being ahead or outside of one's time, and of the time of reading. Reading, like awakening, is identified with a strange present; here the reader is left uncertain whether the awakening is still happening or, perhaps, has not yet begun. **JLSJ**

The Stechlin

Theodor Fontane

Lifespan | *b*. 1819 (Germany), *d*. 1898
First Published | 1899
First Published by | F. Fontane & Co. (Berlin)
Original Title | *Der Stechlin*

"In the end, an old person dies, and two young people get married; that's about all that happens over five hundred pages". This is Fontane's own laconic comment on the novel of his old age. In contrast to *Effi Briest's* intricate psychological motivation, there is a new type of realism, where a technique of extensive dialogue is used to characterize a society on the brink of profound changes.

The old person is Major Dubslav, called "the Stechlin", owner of a castle as well as lake Stechlin—the latter is, according to myth, said to boil whenever a major catastrophic event occurs anywhere in the world. The two young people are Woldemar, the Stechlin's son, and Armgard, the slightly colorless sister of the brilliant and lively Melusine. The Stechlin, warm, humane, and skeptical towards radicalism of any kind, is persuaded to stand as Conservative candidate for the Reichstag, though his phlegmatic approach to politics means that he is easily defeated by his Social Democrat rival. As the crumbling of the old elites, makes it necessary for the relationship between individual and society to be redefined, the Stechlin welcomes the changing times, even though the approach of democracy will do away with the privilege of those such as himself. It is left to Melusine, who shares the name of the seductive water fairy of legend, to point out the connection between the lake, so mysteriously linked to the rest of the world, and the importance of keeping in touch with a changing world. **MM**

Some Experiences of an Irish R.M.

Somerville and Ross

Lifespan (Somerville) | b.1858 (Greece), d.1949 (Ire)
Lifespan (Ross) | b.1862 (Ireland), d.1915
First Published | 1899
First Published by | Longmans & Co. (London)

A series of comic tales of late nineteenth-century Anglo-Irish life, dealing largely with hunting, shooting, and horse riding, might seem unlikely to have many attractions for readers today. The poor characters (servants, publicans, farmers' boys) play minor roles, while the foreground is occupied by the elite and their hangers-on. Only the faintest echoes are heard of the struggles against the landlord class, and for Irish self-government, that were convulsing the country. The authors were members of the landowning "Ascendancy," and the artifices and conventions of the storytelling reflect the angle, and the limits, of their vision. The fictitious narrator, Major Sinclair Yeates, is resident magistrate at Skebawn. Being "of Irish extraction," Yeates is not quite English—but he is certainly not Irish. We hear the wit and music of English as it was spoken in rural Ireland, and West Cork is pleasantly evoked in the descriptions of rivers, coasts, bogs, and fields that frame the many outdoor scenes.

One of the best stories among these witty, well-observed tales, "Lisheen Races, Second-hand," recounts the visit to Skebawn of Yeates' college friend Leigh Kelway, an Englishman and a well-intentioned bore. When Yeates takes him to some "typical country races," Kelway (much to the reader's delight) endures countless indignities and disasters, culminating in a collision with a mail coach. Yeates will always remain an outsider in Cork, but he knows and loves it as a foreigner in a way that Kelway never can. **MR**

"Nevertheless, the man who accepts a resident magistracy in the south-west of Ireland voluntarily retires into the prehistoric age; to institute a stable became inevitable."

◉ Edith Somerville wrote the Irish R. M. tales with her cousin and companion Violet Martin, who took the pseudonym Martin Ross.

//It was a cold, ~~blowy~~ day in early Ap

were ~~striking~~ thirteen, Winston Smith pushe

in an effort to escape the vile wind, slip

Victory Mansions, turned to the right down

doors of Victory Mansions, though not quickl

ed the button of the lift. Nothing happened

guilty dust from entering al

second time when a door at the end of the

The hallway smelt of b

a smell of boiled greens and old rag mats,

mats. At one end of it

acted as porter and caretaker thrust out a

large for indoor display had been tacked

for a moment sucking his teeth and watching

enormous face of a notice wi

about forty-five, with

"Lift ain't working," he announced at

heavy moustache & rugged, handsome featu

"Why isn't it working?"

Winston made for the stairs. If m

"No lifts ain't working. The currents

at the best of times it was seldom working, & at

The 'eat ain't working neither. All curren

was cut off during the daylight hours. It was f

daylight hours. Orders!" he barked in milit

preparation for Hate Week. The flat was seven

door again, leaving it uncertain whether t

was thirty-nine & had a varicose ulcer above h

felt was against Winston, or against the at

resting several times on the way. On each land

the current.

Winston remembered now. It was part o

the poster with the enormous face gazed from th

preparation for Hate Week. The 'eat was sev

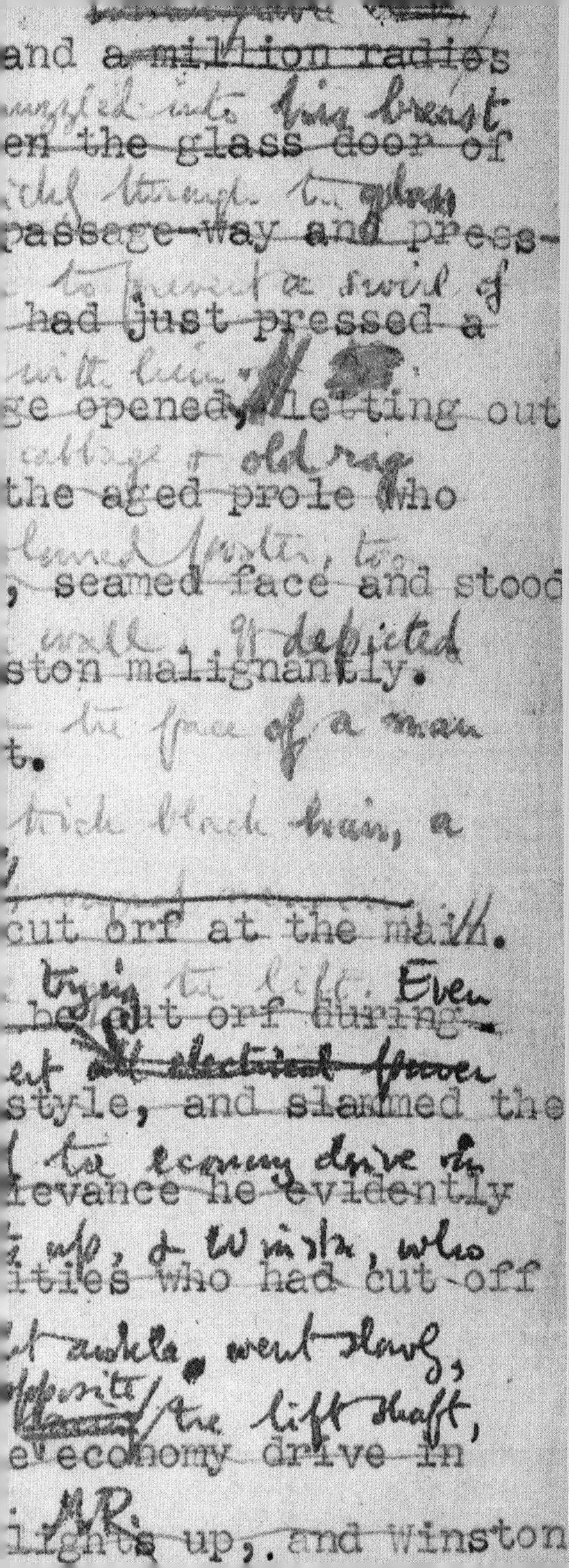

and a million radios
~~nuzzled into his breast~~
en the glass door of
~~self through the glass~~
passage-way and press-
to prevent a swirl of
~~had just pressed a~~
with him
ge opened, letting out
cabbage & old rag
the aged prole who
leaned poster, too
, seamed face and stood
wall. It depicted
ston malignantly.
the face of a man
t.
thick black hair, a
y
cut orf at the maih.
trying the lift. Even
~~been cut orf during~~
~~cut electrical power~~
style, and slammed the
the economy drive in
~~levance he evidently~~
up, & Winston, who
~~ities who had cut-off~~
awhile, went slowly,
~~opposite~~ the lift shaft,
e economy drive in
MR.
~~lights~~ up, and Winston

1900s

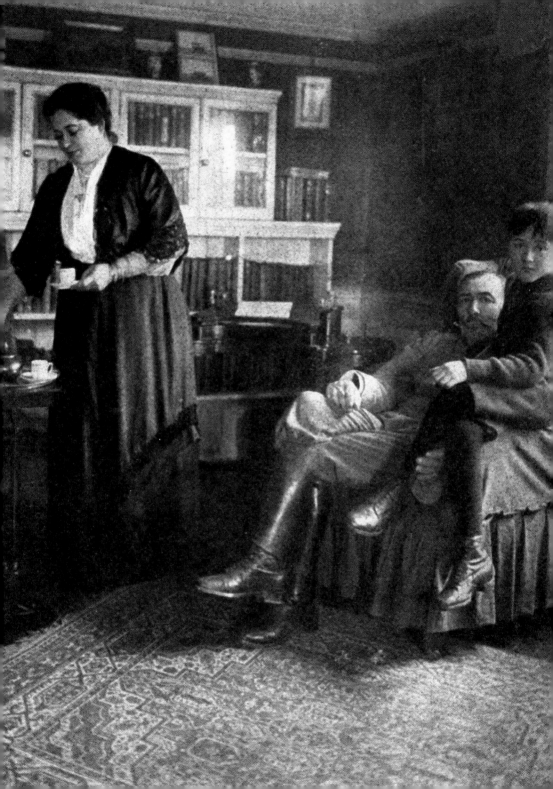

Lord Jim

Joseph Conrad

Lifespan | *b*. 1857 (Ukraine), *d*. 1924 (England)
First Published | 1900
First Published by | W. Blackwood & Sons (London)
Original Language | English

Based on an actual maritime scandal, *Lord Jim* tells how Jim himself, a handsome young mate in a steamship carrying pilgrims, is disgraced by deserting the vessel when he thinks that it is about to sink. Later, he endeavors to start a new life among a remote Malay community in Sumatra, and for a while enjoys well-earned glory as "Lord" Jim. Eventually, however, disaster ambushes both Jim and his community.

This novel resembles a boys' adventure story: a dashing British hero, perils at sea, exotic travels, leadership of a community in the tropics, a beautiful female companion, warfare, and (for a time) victory. Charles Marlow is the sophisticated intermediate narrator who offers philosophical and psychological reflections on Jim's nature as well as his general significance. Combining a sophisticated philosophical awareness with vivid descriptions, the novel is a probing assessment of the significance of human life. With the adventurous subject matter, Conrad recalled nineteenth-century master Stevenson, while his kaleidoscopic analytical techniques anticipated modernism and even postmodernism. Variously affirmative and skeptical, he was "ahead of his time" in his love of ambiguity and paradox. *Lord Jim* influenced Scott Fitzgerald, Orson Welles, and Albert Camus; it remains cogent today. **CW**

The Polish novelist and sailor Joseph Conrad photographed at home with his wife Jessie and his son Jack in the early 1900s.

Sister Carrie

Theodore Dreiser

Lifespan | *b*. 1871 (U.S.), *d*. 1945
First Published | 1900
First Published by | Doubleday, Page & Co.
Original Language | English

Sister Carrie is a gripping and grim novel which charts the fortunes of three main characters making their way at the turn of the nineteenth century. Carrie Meeber moves from the Midwest to Chicago to live with relatives who feel obliged to take her in. She takes a menial job and then moves in with the raffish salesman, Charles Drouet. However, she soon tires of him and attaches herself to the more socially elevated George Hurstwood. He leaves his wife and family for her, steals a large sum of money from his employers, and they run off to New York. There, Carrie rises while George falls. She becomes a celebrated actress and dancer, while he lapses into poverty after she leaves him.

Dreiser's novel is a landmark in American fiction which helped to establish a distinctly American literary identity. *Sister Carrie* is significant for a number of reasons. Deiser's sparse, journalistic style depicts the realities of everyday city life in a language that seems to hide nothing so that we feel we see characters as they really are. Equally important, the novel does not serve as a fable, and no serious judgments are offered on the protagonists' behavior. Carrie is a woman dealt a bad hand, who determines to make the most of what she has, seizing opportunity when it is offered. Charles is a pleasure-seeker, a mixture of the vulgar and the appealing. And George, a tormented and unhappy man, loses all he has in pursuit of a modest, but unobtainable, goal. **AH**

Kim

Rudyard Kipling

Lifespan | *b.* 1865 (India), *d.* 1936 (England)
First Published | 1901
First Published by | Macmillan (London)
Nobel Prize for Literature | 1907

◉ Rudyard Kipling, photographed here in 1890, was born
in Bombay and learned his craft as a journalist in Lahore.

◗ Printmaker William Nicholson made this portrait of Kipling in
his mid-thirties, by then Britain's acknowledged bard of empire.

In this imperialist bildungsroman the young hero, an Irish orphan, matures from a Lahore street-urchin into an invaluable member of the British Secret Service. Kipling equates Kim's personal maturity with a wider cultural maturity, linking the boy's journey into manliness with one from native childishness to an adult European civilization. These two ideas are deeply entwined in the novel as Kim must trade in the education of the street for that of a military boarding school, and the languages of India for his native tongue. Kipling's own language fully supports this hierarchy, so that the supposedly immature cultures of Asia are expressed through a deliberately archaic idiom.

Kipling has been rightly seen as an apologist for British imperialism; in *Kim* there is little doubt that British rule is the best thing for India. Moreover, as a Sahib who is a master of disguise, able to successfully appear as a Hindu, a Muslim, or a Buddhist-mendicant, Kim embodies the notion of western mastery over the Asiatic cultures.

Nevertheless, this view of Kipling's writing does not do justice to the complexity of his vision of India. Kipling frequently identifies similarities between the cultures of India and those of the Europeans-in-India. The Irish soldiers who discover Kim are just as superstitious and credulous as the Indian travelers on the Grand Trunk Road, and the Buddhist priest who shares responsibility for Kim's education with Creighton, the English surveyor and spy master, presents a perspective on India remarkably similar to Creighton's own. One of the charms of this novel is as a survey of India, and, though it repeatedly lumps together the "oriental" as an undifferentiated mass, its descriptions of individual Indians stresses the brightness and diversity of Indian public life. **LC**

Buddenbrooks

Thomas Mann

Lifespan | *b.* 1875 (Germany), *d.* 1955
First Published | 1901, by S. Fischer Verlag (Berlin)
Original Title | *Buddenbrooks: Verfall einer Familie*
Nobel Prize for Literature | 1929

The cover of an early twentieth-century German edition of Mann's family saga suggests a cosier vision than the book presents.

Buddenbrooks: The Decline of a Family is among the last and greatest achievements of the European realist novel. The book spans forty-odd years during the mid-nineteenth century.

Set in the Hanseatic city of Lübeck, it follows the fortunes of one of the leading families of the ruling merchant class. Its focus is on the growth of three siblings from childhood to mid-life. Christian Buddenbrook, lacking the self-discipline (or perhaps self-repression) required to become a businessman and solid citizen, performs instead the self-destructive role of half-licensed fool. His elder brother Thomas adapts himself fully, but at great physical and psychological cost, to his position as head of the firm, Consul and Senator. Their sister Tony passionately values the prestige of the family, but her infelicitous adventures in love and marriage show that she is incapable of playing the dutiful daughter and wife. The final chapters are devoted to Thomas' son, Hanno, who inherits from his Dutch mother an exceptional musical talent and an estrangement from the masculine, public shows of the Hanseatic state. With Hanno, we realize, the Buddenbrook line will take a new direction, or come to its end.

The novel's tapestry of closely observed scenes is seemingly inexhaustible—among them are family feasts and arguments, deathbeds and childbirth, weddings, seaside holidays, schoolrooms, and ship-launchings. Mann's detailed analysis of the interplay between public and private self, and between a declining ethic of civic and commercial propriety and a new spirit of aesthetic self-cultivation, is remarkable, not only for its subtlety and objectivity, but for the wider historical resonances evoked by his characters and their fates. **MR**

The Hound of the Baskervilles

Sir Arthur Conan Doyle

Arguably one of the best Sherlock Holmes stories and one of the all-time classical mysteries, the atmosphere of *The Hound of the Baskervilles* is ghoulish, full of suspense and fear, and Sherlock Holmes is at his most brilliant. When Sir Charles Baskerville dies suddenly, from heart failure, there are rumors that his death was caused by the gigantic ghostly hound of the title, said to have haunted his family for generations. When the estate's heir, Sir Henry Baskerville, arrives in London from Canada, Watson accompanies him to Baskerville Hall, and a skeptical Holmes is called in to investigate. Situated on the edge of Dartmoor, the Baskerville estate borders a vast, brooding, misty moor, containing features such as Grimpen Mire, a deadly quicksand-like bog. It is the descriptions of the moor and the oppressive Baskerville Hall, which provide much of the chilling atmosphere that pervades the novel. Into this setting Sir Conan Doyle weaves the sounds of a wailing woman, a mysterious butler, an escaped killer, and the specter of the ghostly, fire-breathing, murderous hound.

The Hound of the Baskervilles draws the reader in, not only to the world of the misty moor and strange goings-on, but also to the works of Conan Doyle. In this novel he displays his own interest in the occult, alongside Sherlock Holmes' talent for keen scientific detection, in a story that is full of atmosphere, suspense, and unexpected turns. It is a novel that keeps the reader fearful and guessing until the very last page, and then leaves them wanting more. Arguably the most popular of all the Sherlock Holmes mysteries, since its original serialization in 1901–1902, *The Hound of the Baskervilles* has been set to film no fewer than eighteen times, beginning with a German silent production of 1914. **LE**

Lifespan | *b.* 1859 (Scotland), *d.* 1930
First Published | 1902, by G. Newnes (London)
Original Title | *The Hound of the Baskervilles: Another Adventure of Sherlock Holmes*

Sydney Paget created this image of the ghostly hound for the original serialized version of the novel in *Strand* magazine.

Heart of Darkness

Joseph Conrad

Based on Joseph Conrad's own venture into Africa in 1890, *Heart of Darkness* is the best of his shorter novels and is the most brilliant of all his works. Eloquent, audacious, experimental, recessive, satiric, yet deeply humane, since its serialization in 1899 it has continued to provoke controversy and reward analysis. Charles Marlow, one of Conrad's "transtextual" characters (for he appears also in *Youth*, *Lord Jim*, and *Chance*), tells a group of British friends about his journey into a part of central Africa identifiable as the "Congo Free State," which was then the private property of Leopold II, King of the Belgians. Marlow recalls the absurdities and atrocities which he witnessed: a French warship shelling the continent, the cruel treatment of enslaved black laborers, and the remorseless rapacity of the white colonialists who are impelled by the desire for profits from ivory. He looks forward to meeting Mr. Kurtz, the greatly talented and idealistic European trader; but, when he reaches the dying adventurer, he finds that the idealist has become deranged and depraved. Virtually a savage god, Kurtz sums up his view of Africans in the phrase "Exterminate all the brutes!" The "heart of darkness," we learn, is not simply the jungle at the center of the "Dark Continent"; it is also the corrupt heart of Kurtz, and it may even be European imperialism itself. "All Europe contributed to the making of Kurtz," and London is depicted as the center of brooding gloom.

Written when imperialism was "politically correct", this brilliantly anti-imperialist and largely anti-racist work shows Conrad at the peak of his powers as a challenging innovator in ideas and techniques. *Heart of Darkness* has proved immensely influential, and numerous adaptations include the movie *Apocalypse Now*. **CW**

Lifespan | *b.* 1857 (Ukraine), *d.* 1924 (England)
First Published | 1902
First Published by | W. Blackwood & Sons (London)
Original Language | English

⬤ Conrad held a sternly pessimistic view of the world, suggesting no encouraging alternative to the corruption of imperialism.

◖ Marlon Brando's Colonel Kurtz embodies "the darkness" at the heart of the Vietnam war in the 1979 movie *Apocalypse Now*.

The Wings of the Dove

Henry James

Lifespan | *b.* 1843 (U.S.), *d.* 1916 (England)
First Published | 1902
First Published by | A. Constable & Co. (London)
Original Language | English

The Wings of the Dove is perhaps James' darkest moral drama, the story of a passionate love-triangle between the enigmatic Kate Croy, her secret fiancé Merton Densher, and Milly Theale, the young and fatally ill American heiress. All is played out against the symbolic backdrops of London materialism and Venetian beauty and decay. Milly's desperate desire to experience "the sense of having lived," provides both the sympathetic and self-serving motivations for Kate's scheme. She wants Densher to seduce Milly, filling her final days with happiness, in the knowledge that the fortune the girl will surely leave him after her death will enable him to marry Kate herself. James is a master of the complex moral situation, and combines the melodrama of his plot with nuanced values. Though elaborate and self-conscious, the narrative style lacks neither realism nor intensity. The sexual attraction between Kate and Densher, his developing feelings for Milly, her determined resistance of her fate, and Kate's jealousy, are vividly and powerfully portrayed.

When Milly finally learns the truth of her friends' deception but leaves them her fortune nevertheless, her own capacity for manipulation through moral victory becomes clear. For in renouncing the spoils of corruption, Densher also rejects Kate for Milly's idealized memory, with which she knows she cannot compete. In the very success of her plan Kate realizes that she has brought about her own downfall. "We shall never be again as we were," she declares. **DP**

> *"'Our dear dove then, as Kate calls her, has folded her wonderful wings' . . . 'Unless it's more true,' she accordingly added, 'that she has spread them the wider.'"*

🔘 Helena Bonham-Carter (right) plays Kate in the 1997 movie version of James' novel, a ruthlessly explicit popularization.

The Immoralist

André Gide

Lifespan | *b.* 1869 (France), *d.* 1951
First Published | 1902
First Published by | Mercure de France (Paris)
Original Title | *L'Immoraliste*

A thought-provoking work that still has the power to challenge complacent attitudes and unfounded cultural assumptions, *The Immoralist* recounts a young Parisian man's attempt to overcome social and sexual conformity.

Michel is a young, puritanical scholar, who has recently married solely to please his dying father. On his honeymoon in North Africa he becomes very ill and almost dies. His brush with death gives him an all-consuming desire to live, and his convalescence has the force of a religious awakening. Experiencing things with a heightened awareness, he is sexually drawn to the Arab boys he surrounds himself with. Sensually aroused, he realizes that conventional social morality and the trappings of bourgeois civilization—education, church, and culture—have alienated him from his true self. But the selfish pursuit of authenticity and pleasure he embarks upon causes him to neglect his wife as well as important practical matters. When she falls ill he persuades her they should go south, doing so merely in order to gratify his own desires, which he is incapable of resisting. His once radical freedom has turned to base enslavement. Michel's attempt to access a deeper truth by repudiating culture, decency, and morality results in confusion and loss. In being true to himself, Michel has harmed others. Yet the novel remains as much an indictment of the arbitrary constraints of a hypocritical society as it is of Michel's misguided behavior. **AL**

The Riddle of the Sands

Erskine Childers

Lifespan | *b.* 1870 (Ireland), *d.* 1922
First Published | 1903, by Smith, Elder & Co. (Lon.)
Full Title | *The Riddle of the Sands: a record of secret service…*

Erskine Childers wrote *The Riddle of the Sands* after returning home wounded from the Boer War, where he fought for the British. The narrator, Carruthers, who works for the Foreign Office, receives a mysterious invitation from an old friend, Davies, to join him on his yacht in the Baltic. The Dulcibella is not what Carruthers was expecting. There is no crew—or, rather, Carruthers is the crew—and Davies is not on a pleasure cruise. He is systematically mapping the shallows of the German North Sea coast, having realized that Germany could exploit the apparently unnavigable waters to launch a surprise large-scale invasion of Britain using shallow-draught troop-carriers.

Carruthers and Davies' activities attract the attention of the German authorities, and they soon face threats from more than just the treacherous seas. Matters are further complicated by Davies' having fallen in love with a German girl: perhaps Childers was able to dramatize Davies' conflict of loyalties as vividly as he does because it reflected his own divided sense of duty toward Ireland and Britain (which would eventually lead to his execution). This novel was intended to make a serious point about a potential threat to British national security. But just as Davies and Carruthers commit themselves to their adventure not only out of a sense of duty but also for its own sake, so *The Riddle of the Sands* easily transcends its role as propaganda. **TEJ**

The Ambassadors

Henry James

Lifespan | *b.* 1843 (U.S.), *d.* 1916 (England)
First Published | 1903
First Published by | Methuen & Co. (London)
Original Language | English

Henry James regarded *The Ambassadors* as his best novel, and it is certainly held to be his greatest artistic achievement. In the character of Lambert Strether, a middle-aged New Englander confronted with the social and aesthetic attractions of a beguiling Paris, he brought to perfection his style of first-person narrative.

Strether has been sent to Europe on behalf of his fiancée, the redoubtable Mrs. Newsome, charged with retrieving her son Chad from the clutches of a liaison which, it is assumed, is corrupting him with European moral laxness. But upon his arrival, Strether discovers a much more complicated affair, which leads him to re-evaluate both American and European cultures. Although he fails as an ambassador, he comes to a better understanding of both European and American strengths and weaknesses, and he quickly accedes to the suggestion that Chad's relationship with the beautiful Marie de Vionnet is actually a "virtuous attachment."

Overall, *The Ambassadors'* vision is tragic: its most sensitive characters are largely victims of a seemingly inescapable social regulation. Indeed, with *The Ambassadors*, James excels at representing figures who are aware of their loss of youth, and who seem increasingly out of pace with the world. In the figure of Strether, he has developed a character who proves capable of choosing his own destiny, though hardly a triumphant one. **DP, TH**

The Golden Bowl

Henry James

Lifespan | *b.* 1843 (U.S.), *d.* 1916 (England)
First Published | 1904
First Published by | C. Scribner's Sons (New York)
Original Language | English

Set in the appropriately financial world-capital of London, the novel opens with the marriage of wealthy American heiress Maggie Verver to the penniless yet aristocratic Prince Amerigo. Unbeknownst to his bride, he is the former lover of her impoverished best friend Charlotte Stant, who is still passionately in love with him. When he accompanies her on a shopping trip to buy a wedding present for Maggie, they discover the golden bowl of the novel's title, but Charlotte decides not to buy it because of a small, hidden imperfection. When Maggie's widowed father Adam Verver, with his daughter's blessing, later proposes to her, she accepts, but also resumes her relationship with Amerigo.

The flawed bowl stands as a symbol of their adultery and the means by which Maggie discovers their former liaison when she buys it for her father. Yet Maggie is far from the figure of duped naïvety she might seem, as her supposed innocence is mixed somewhat uncomfortably with dogmatic self-belief. Turning the tables of deception upon her friend, she reasserts her ownership of her husband at the same time as banishing Charlotte to middle America. The cost may be heavy—her close relationship with her father—but in a novel in which everything has a purchase value, it is a price she is willing to pay. **DP**

❯ Henry James based his novels upon the subtle psychological observation of characters in intense emotional situations.

Hadrian the Seventh

Frederick Rolfe

Lifespan | b. 1860 (England), d. 1913 (Italy)
First Published | 1904
First Published by | Chatto & Windus (London)
Original Title | Hadrian The Seventh: A Romance

Frederick Rolfe shortened his first name to "Fr" because he wished to be thought a priest; in this novel, he imagines himself appointed Pope. Hadrian is the first English Pope since Adrian IV, and he is also a version of Rolfe, an eccentric and penurious Catholic convert. As Pontiff, Hadrian sets Europe to rights, merging religious authority with political skill in a skewed but sometimes grimly prescient way. Pro-German in an anti-German period, the novel imagines a federal Europe under German hegemony. Hadrian is pursued by Jerry Sant, a member of a combined Liblab (Liberal and Labour) political group. Snubbed in his hope that the Pope will support Socialism, Sant shoots Hadrian: "The world sobbed, sighed, wiped its mouth; and experienced extreme relief ... He would have been an ideal ruler if He had not ruled."

These concluding ironies show that *Hadrian* is a peculiar but not a deluded fiction. A delightful, innocent, but unmistakeably male sensuality, mitigates the novel's puritan impulse to clean up the Catholic Church. In an episode of unexpected charm, he teaches one of his lithe young guards the key to color photography (then unknown). This hints at the novel's interest in new technologies, such as the Marconigraph. Above all, Hadrian is obsessed by the new journalism; he regularly consults thirty-seven newspapers, and organizes his political moves to satisfy them. For all its archaism, *Hadrian* identified significant components of modernity. **AMu**

Nostromo

Joseph Conrad

Lifespan | b. 1857 (Ukraine), d. 1924 (England)
First Serialized | 1904, by T. P.'s Weekly
First Published | 1904, by Harper & Bros. (Lon. & NY)
Full Title | Nostromo: a Tale of the Seaboard

Experimental in its shifting perspectives, *Nostromo* describes the turbulent history of a South American region as it evolves through the instability of predatory dictatorships to a modern era of democracy and flourishing capitalism. The fictional state of Sulaco fights to secure its secession from Costaguana, becoming an apparently independent state. This brilliantly prophetic novel shows how economic imperialism, led by the United States, proves a mixed blessing in Sulaco. New stability and civilized amenities replace the old insecurity, but colorful indigenous features are superseded, and the outlook for the new state is ominous.

Thanks partly to Conrad's friendship with R. B. Cunninghame Graham, well-traveled in those regions, and partly to his assiduous reading of memoirs and histories, he was able to confer vivid realism on his fictional Sulaco, despite having visited South America himself only briefly, and twenty years prior. Conrad interweaves large matters with small, political struggles with familial tensions, and the global with the intimate. As we follow the experiences of Nostromo, the foreman of the dockworkers, and of the diversity of people whose lives are connected with his deceptive character, we see the price exacted in human terms by historical evolution. Like Higuerota, the snow-capped mountain that dominates the region, this novel provides "the utmost delicacy of shaded expression and a stupendous magnificence of effect." **CW**

Where Angels Fear to Tread

E. M. Forster

Lifespan | *b.* 1879 (England), *d.* 1970
First Published | 1905
First Published by | W. Blackwood & Sons (London)
Original Language | English

In this, E. M. Forster's first novel, he examines middle class English values and the effects these values produce when placed out of context. Snobbishness and cultural insensitivity are at the heart of the narrative, and are themes that Forster continues to develop in his subsequent works. *Where Angels Fear to Tread* captures the social mores of the era alongside the beginnings of the British love affair with Tuscany.

When a young English widow, Lilia Herriton, sets off for an extended tour of Italy with her companion, Caroline Abbott, she embarks on a journey that will end in tragedy and provoke reactions from her relatives that are both unexpected and violent. Lilia becomes engaged to an Italian dentist, Gino Carella, twelve years her junior and completely unsuitable in the eyes of her in-laws. Her deceased husband's brother and sister are dispatched to put a stop to the match but arrive too late, finding the couple already married and expecting a child.

When Lilia dies in childbirth, the in-laws and Miss Abbott must rescue the baby from the imagined disaster of an Italian upbringing. However, their intentions waver as they fall under the spell of Italy and, in Miss Abbot's case, of Gino himself. The sequence of events that unfolds is grotesquely tragic and pathetic, ultimately caused by the English characters' adherence to conventions of respectability. While Forster rails against these conventions, he does so with a compelling sympathy and humor. **LE**

"I don't die—I don't fall in love. And if other people die or fall in love they always do it when I'm not there. You are quite right; life to me is just a spectacle . . . "

◉ A member of the Bloomsbury Circle, Forster criticized social convention from the safe vantage point of an intellectual elite.

Professor Unrat

Heinrich Mann

Lifespan | *b.* 1871 (Germany), *d.* 1955 (Switzerland)
First Published | 1905, by A. Langen (Munich)
Original Title | *Professor Unrat, oder das Ende eines Tyrannen*

◔ A socialist who believed in politically committed literature, Heinrich Mann was at one time Thomas' more famous brother.

◑ Based on *Professor Unra*t, von Sternberg's 1930 movie *The Blue Angel* made a star of Marlene Dietrich as the fatal seductress.

Elder brother of the great German writer Thomas Mann, Heinrich, an equally prolific novelist and essayist, differed from his brother in his commitment to political rather than aesthetic issues. Exiled by the Nazis for his attacks on their militarist-nationalist ideology he was also a passionate critic of imperial bourgeois capitalism and a staunch supporter of democracy and various forms of socialism. *Professor Unrat* is his best known novel, having been successfully adapted for screen, most famously as Josef von Sternberg's *The Blue Angel*, with Marlene Dietrich in the lead role, which launched her into international stardom.

The novel concerns an authoritarian, repressed, socially inept schoolteacher who falls in love with a young dancer named Rosa Frohlich. After an arbitrary meeting, Professor Unrat is soon enthralled by Rosa's compelling charm, and he determines that no one else shall have anything further to do with her. Unrat's close association with such a woman scandalizes the small-town community and he loses his job at the school. But he is unperturbed and with Rosa's help reinvents himself as a high society player. They establish a successful salon and he delights in watching the downfall of former pupils and enemies, as they lose their fortunes at the gambling table or their reputations in inappropriate liaisons. But the greatest downfall will be his own as he gradually learns the full extent of Rosa's suspect behavior, losing control of his all-consuming rage.

Professor Unrat is a fascinating examination of the social values of imperial Germany and the power of desire to transform and control even the most iron-willed of men. Unrat's slow demise at the hands of one of literature's great femme fatales is a captivating cautionary tale. **AL**

The House of Mirth

Edith Wharton

Lifespan | *b.* 1862 (U.S.), *d.* 1937 (France)
First Published | 1905
First Published by | Macmillan & Co. (London)
Original Language | English

🔼 A society hostess from a patrician American family, Edith
Wharton could write of upper-class life with insider knowledge.

▶️ Terence Davies' movie version of *The House of Mirth*, released
in 2000, made meticulous use of authentic costumes and settings.

Part love story, part social critique, *The House of Mirth*
begins hopefully with a flirtation. Lily Bart, while
settling her serious matrimonial sights on a more
lucrative target, allows herself the pleasure of
an infatuation with Lawrence Selden, a shabbily
genteel intellectual. With a lightness of touch and
arch wit reminiscent of Austen, Wharton creates
a heroine at the height of her sexual power:
beautiful, fashionable, and well-connected.

While retaining the external elements of a
traditional romance, however, Wharton has an
altogether less comforting vision to offer. The
feminine power that Lily represents is cast as
a barrier to intellectual freedom. Lily's perfection
as an object of desire, beautifully imagined in an
episode where she displays herself to an enraptured
audience as the tableau-vivant of a Reynolds
painting, is presented as a futile waste of female
creativity and becomes, rather than the triumph she
perceives, an emblem of women's commodified
status. As her relationship with Selden develops
Lily senses this but, in a tragic recognition of her
failure of imagination, is incapable of acting upon
it. Paralyzed by twin desires for spiritual fulfilment
and economic freedom, Lily vacillates, and is lost.

The novel's strength lies in Wharton's deft
control of the versions of Lily as, alternately, architect
of her own destiny and hapless pawn in a society
governed by capital, power, and sexual inequality.
Lily's only bargaining chip in society is the very thing
oppressing her. Her love of surface and luxury are
reflected in the fabric of a novel which delights in
producing one of fiction's most enthralling heroines,
whose potent mixture of power and powerlessness,
poise and vulnerability, breathes life into the very
myths it seeks to undermine. **HJ**

The Forsyte Saga

John Galsworthy

Lifespan | *b*. 1867 (England), *d*. 1933
First Novel of Saga Published | 1906
(*The Man of Property*)
Compiled as Saga | 1929, (entitled *A Modern Comedy*)

Keenly ironic, deeply engaged in the "state of England" from the 1880s to the 1920s (though tellingly withdrawn during the First World War), *The Forsyte Saga* is also Galsworthy's exploration of "the disturbance that Beauty effects in the lives of men." Beauty is a counter to, and incitement of, the urge to possession, to property, at the heart of the Forsyte family story. This tension is embodied by Soames Forsyte in whom the quest for beauty dovetails violently with the passion to possess (passion that culminates in the rape of his wife).

Chronicling three generations of Forsytes, the *Saga* is a monument to the Edwardians, and was received as a quintessentially English book by enraptured readers. Its vision of the "tribal instinct," of the "swarmings of savage hordes" embedded in the everyday lives of a respectable middle-class family, sustains the tension and dramatic conflict of Galsworthy's narrative: the Forsyte family is a spectacle of "almost repugnant prosperity," a "reproduction of society in miniature." As such, the Forsytes are also Galsworthy's means to pursue, in extraordinary and patient prose, the creative violence of family life: the "deprivation and killing of reality" at the heart of family intimacy, its imposition of a shared history, and a spirit of ruthlessly collective enterprise. **VL**

❮ John Galsworthy, here photographed in 1912, depicted with critical irony the affluent class to which he himself belonged.

Young Törless

Robert Musil

Lifespan | *b*. 1880 (Austria), *d*. 1942 (Switzerland)
First Published | 1906, by Wiener Verlag (Vienna)
Original Title | *Die Verwirrungen des Zöglings Törless*
(*The Confusions of Young Törless*)

Caught in an ominous spiral of introspection and experimentation, Törless and three of his fellow cadet pupils at a military academy move from pondering and playing with abstractions to the creation of situations in which they push the abstractions into a feverish life. A sense of power is already alive, but mute, in the structures of the academy and in the pupils' unquestioning assumption of their social destiny as rulers. The thoughtful sadism practiced by the boys turns power inside out, makes it feral and pungent and intoxicating. Their exploration of power in the ritualized humiliation of one of their peers spreads also to encompass an unfolding of the ideas of pity, honor, superiority, justice, will, and desire as the boys use each other to test out and shape their undefined identities. The coldness and clarity of cruelty becomes the raw material and the medium of their self-fashioning.

The beauty of Musil's writing is its capacity to infuse the novel with a duality that allows events their stark brutality while simultaneously existing as anxieties, possibilities, desires, precisely as perplexities (the "*Verwirrungen*" of Musil's original title) in Törless' mind. This is the power of *Young Törless*, and the mindset and world it so memorably describes. The reader comes away possessed not with the trite conclusion that we are all capable of terrible things, but with an enriched sense of how difficult it is to know what it is to be human. **PMcM**

The Jungle

Upton Sinclair

Lifespan | *b.* 1878 (U.S.), *d.* 1968
First Published | 1906
First Published by | Doubleday, Page (New York)
Original Language | English

The Jungle was not the first muckraking novel, although it is easily one of the most influential books of the twentieth century—Roosevelt used it to push through the stalled Pure Food and Drug Act and Meat Inspection Act. It is a raw and sometimes nauseating chronicle based on the real incidents of the 1904 stockyard workers' strike in Chicago. A manifesto for social change, it savagely reveals the American dream gone sour. Sinclair strips away the myth of America as a boon to the tired, the poor, the huddled masses yearning to breathe free. Instead, the golden land of manifest destiny is shown to be a Dickensian nightmare where wage slaves can barely survive, where powerless immigrants are chewed up by a capitalist machine oiled by corruption and bald greed.

But it is more than a polemic; it is a gripping and harrowing tale. Jurgis Rudkus, a recent immigrant from Lithuania, comes to a new and promising land in an attempt to build a family. His life is permeated by the stink of ordure and offal of a primitive meat industry and the struggle for daily bread. Systematically Jurgis' dreams, along with his family, are annihilated. Embittered by the brutal crimes wrought upon his family, Jurgis gradually descends into crime himself. But Jurgis does return from hell. The novel ends with a beacon of hope in the form of socialism; the last sentence, in upper case, is "CHICAGO WILL BE OURS!" A more socially important novel is hard to imagine. **GT**

The Secret Agent

Joseph Conrad

Lifespan | *b.* 1857 (Ukraine), *d.* 1924 (England)
First Published | 1907, by Methuen & Co. (London)
First Serialized | 1906, by *Ridgway's: A Militant Weekly for God and Country*

The Secret Agent tells of subversive politics, crime, and detection. The setting is late-Victorian London, depicted predominantly as a dank and murky metropolis. In the parlor of Adolf Verloc's seedy shop in Soho, a grotesque band of revolutionaries meets to pursue futile political arguments. Michaelis is grossly corpulent; Karl Yundt is totteringly decrepit; and Ossipon has the cranial features (including frizzy hair and Mongoloid eyes) which, according to his mentor Cesare Lombroso, signify the criminal degenerate. All these enemies of society are lazy, notes the slothful Verloc; and all, including Verloc himself, are dependent on women for support.

At an embassy that is clearly Russian, Mr. Vladimir, an elegant diplomat, urges Verloc to bomb Greenwich Observatory. Vladimir thinks that such an outrage will be blamed on foreigners in England, so that the British Government will be less hospitable in future to refugees, particularly enemies of czarist Russia. Verloc obtains a bomb from the diminutive "Professor" (a nihilistic anarchist) and directs his mentally immature brother-in-law, Stevie, to plant it. However, this ill-measured move sparks a series of cumulatively tragic events, as the story advances towards its conclusion.

This masterpiece of ruthlessly ironic narration looks back to such atmospheric Dickensian works as *Bleak House*, and forward to Greene's sleazy *It's a Battlefield*. Particularly relevant to present times is its anticipation of the era of the suicide bomber. **CW**

Mother

Maxim Gorky

Lifespan | *b.* 1868 (Russia), *d.* 1936
First Published | 1907
Original Title | *Mat*
Original Language | Russian

Tracing the life of a working-class woman in late nineteenth-century provincial Russia, *Mother* powerfully evokes the cruelty, absurdity, and bitterness of life under an increasingly oppressive czarist regime. In an anonymous factory town, a middle-aged mother, Pelagea Nilovna, is left to face what she assumes will be a life of loveless drudgery after the death of her abusive husband. She is slowly awakened, however, to the presence of her maturing son, Pavel, who, in an apparently sober and modest life, spends his evenings reading philosophy and economics. As Pavel and his mother become closer, he begins to let her into his secret world—one in which these apparently harmless texts represent radical new ideas, the spread of which ensures that Pavel is in almost constant mortal danger. Pelagea is gradually drawn into a revolutionary socialist group; and while she is radicalized by Pavel and his friends' conversation, at the same time she provides them with a valuable human perspective that stresses the value of kindness, mercy, and love.

Often described as socialist realism, such a term does not cover the breadth of Gorky's skill in a novel that, despite its ideological bent, resists becoming propaganda. Political goals are interwoven with passages of lyrical beauty, occasional humor and vivid and memorable characters. Moving and often painful to read, it remains an important perspective on the cultural and political extremes that existed in Russia at the time. **AB**

"The accumulated exhaustion of years had robbed them of their appetites, and to be able to eat they drank, long and deep, goading on their feeble stomachs with the biting, burning lash of vodka."

◉ Forced into exile because of his opposition to Czarist rule, Gorky is welcomed by Russian revolutionaries in London in 1907.

The House on the Borderland

William Hope Hodgson

Lifespan | *b.* 1877 (England), *d.* 1918
First Published | 1908
First Published by | Chapman & Hall (London)
Original Language | English

In this elusive novel, a recovered manuscript tells the broken tale of the Recluse and his sister who live in isolation, apparently under constant threat from glowing swine creatures. The Recluse has visions of incomprehensible cosmic landscapes, peopled by immobile ancient gods, menacing and indistinct. He tries to protect his home and his sister but she does not seem to see the creatures and fears him instead. He barricades the house against attacks. Here the manuscript stumbles. Left open to the elements, several pages are indecipherable. Finally, fragments concerning love and loss give way to a helpless trip into the future, a pre-psychedelic vision of souls in flight and the death of the universe. Then, under renewed attacks, the manuscript breaks off.

"The inner story must be uncovered, personally, by each reader," Hodgson suggests. This remains a work of vast imagination, unfettered by logic, plot, or traditional resolutions. In the position of the house, the character of the Recluse, even the recovery of the manuscript, there is an instinctive significance, but none of it is explained. The Recluse's visions of the future are imbued with a profound resonance that lurks just beneath the threshold of conscious comprehension. We feel he knows more than he will tell us or even admit to himself. Whatever is really going on, we can only try to imagine. There are many wonderful clues but no certainties. **JS**

The Old Wives' Tale

Arnold Bennett

Lifespan | *b.* 1867 (England), *d.* 1931
First Published | 1908
First Published by | Chapman & Hall (London)
Original Language | English

The Old Wives' Tale shares with many of Bennett's books its major setting in the Staffordshire potteries, the sleepy "Five Towns." At the same time it describes in vivid detail expatriate life in mid-nineteenth century Paris during a time of extraordinary political upheaval. This divided setting reflects the general scheme of the novel, which tells the story of the two "old wives," Constance and Sophia Baines, who grow up as the daughters of a modest tradesman. Their destinies, guided by their marriages, take them in vastly different directions. Demure Constance marries her father's assistant, outwardly leading the conventional life of a Victorian wife and mother. This is in sharp contrast to Sophia's disastrous elopement with a traveling salesman who leaves her abandoned and penniless in Paris. Neither sister's life is wholly positive or negative; the excitement of Paris under siege is balanced by Sophia's constant struggle for survival in a hostile foreign culture, while the domestic harmony of Constance's family life also suffers from smothering boredom.

Overall, *The Old Wives' Tale* is a compassionate novel, and the two sisters' touching reunion shows the importance of family love and loyalty in what might otherwise be seen as blighted lives. **AB**

◗ E. O. Hoppe depicts English author Arnold Bennett in a woodcutting done in 1900.

The Iron Heel

Jack London

Lifespan | *b.* 1876 (U.S.), *d.* 1916
First Published | 1908
First Published by | Macmillan & Co. (New York)
Original Language | English

The primary narrator of *The Iron Heel*, Avis Everhard, plays the role of political naïf to her husband's mastery of political knowledge, with her adoration for Ernest Everhard mediating the text's apocalyptic revelations about the nature and future of American and world capitalism. Everhard is a revolutionary hero possessed of a sublime physicality, an intellect worthy of a Nietzschean natural aristocrat, a chronic habit of speaking in speeches, and an addiction to "the facts." London seems to have gone out of his way to use conservative stereotypes about working-class demagogues.

The Iron Heel, one of the finest dystopian fictions of the twentieth century, is remarkable for the complexity of its narrative structure. The story is presented as a manuscript written by Avis Everhard between 1912 and 1932 but edited seven hundred years later by a historian, Anthony Meredith. It is this latter narrative frame that lends the book its historical depth and black humor. Meredith's footnotes position the Everhards, and the two revolutions that failed, as products of their era—drily termed "the Christian era"—and necessarily colored by the capitalism they existed to oppose.

The violence of Ernest Everhard's rhetoric, the biblical proportions of the world as seen by Avis Everhard, and the novel's sense of imminent total catastrophe, all shrink under the weight of Meredith's scholarly commentary, yet at the same time become oddly necessary. **PMcM**

A Room with a View

E. M. Forster

Lifespan | *b.* 1879 (England), *d.* 1970
First Published | 1908
First Published by | E. Arnold (London)
Original Language | English

A Room with a View is a classic coming-of-age novel. Forster introduces us to Lucy Honeychurch, who, accompanied by her anxious and over-protective guardian, Charlotte Bartlett, is touring Italy in her first introduction to a wider world far removed from the English countryside of her childhood. Lucy is a spirited piano player and her playing of Beethoven gives the reader the first hint of her real emotional depth. The great question of this novel is what will Lucy choose: a room with a view, or the closed walls of conventional society? This question is embodied by the two rivals for her affection. There is the thoughtful and passionate George Emerson, who understands and fully appreciates what he is seeing, whether it is the Italian people or Lucy herself. The sophisticated and arrogant Cecil Vyse, on the other hand, treats Lucy more as a work of art or a project than as a living, thinking individual. This novel is about the pains and crossroads of growing up—the temptation of self-deception, the pull between family and one's own desires.

Forster's novel offers a brilliant satire of early twentieth-century middle England and its rigorously upheld social conventions. The novel is also remarkably sensual—the scenery, both in the Italian and the English settings, is perfectly drawn with exquisite visual detail, and when Lucy plays the piano or the weather turns violent, the reader can almost hear the crescendo of the notes or the thunder. A simply delightful read. **EGG**

The Inferno

Henri Barbusse

Lifespan | *b.* 1873 (France), *d.* 1935 (Russia)
First Published | 1908, by Mondiale (Paris)
Alternate Title | *Hell*
Original Title | *L'Enfer*

Henri Barbusse began his writing career with *The Inferno*. This absorbing yet disquieting novel is an early modern example of the literature of alienated, disaffected manhood. Colin Wilson later used it in his introduction to *The Outsider* (1956), showing *The Inferno*'s direct influence on existentialist writers.

A nameless man checks into a hotel in Paris. He is thirty years old and without any ties. Other than this we only know that he is jaded, disillusioned, indifferent to and weary of life. He writes, "I don't know who I am, where I am going, what I am doing … I have nothing and deserve nothing," and yet he suffers from an obsessive, almost religious yearning for the unattainable. On his first night in the hotel his attention is drawn to noises emanating from next door. Finding a hole which grants him a view of the adjoining room, he remains transfixed for days, observing the changing occupants. His voyeurism becomes compulsive as he derives a strange feeling of omnipotence and psychosexual fervor from watching the many different aspects of private life that are on display: adulterous couples, single women undressing, homosexuality, childbirth, and death. However, he achieves little real satisfaction from this activity and the compulsion ultimately destroys him.

Scandalous at the time of publication, it still has the power to shock today; candid, explicit, and full of philosophical musings, *The Inferno* is a fascinating insight into one man's inner struggle. **AL**

Tono-Bungay

H. G. Wells

Lifespan | *b.* 1866 (England), *d.* 1946
First Published | 1908
First Published by | Macmillan & Co. (London)
Original Language | English

Wells' bildungsroman is told in the first person as an autobiography, though the fictional narrator, George Ponderevo, refers to it (oddly) as a novel. The work is loosely structured, replete with often suspect or woolly generalizations about the state of England around 1888–1908, and contains various anti-Semitic and racist features. Nevertheless, that new ways of thinking and creating are vigorously emerging from the muddle of history is an insistent theme.

The major storyline relates the rise and fall of the hero's uncle, Edward Ponderevo. By means of advertising campaigns for his quack medicines, notably the eponymous "Tono-Bungay", a supposedly vitalizing but "pretty intoxicating" concoction, Edward attains immense wealth. In return for a large salary, George is happy to cooperate in the "damned swindle," while Edward too readily rationalizes his own greed. Eventually, Edward's prodigality results in financial ruin, and it is only his death which conveniently saves him from prison. His accomplice, George, who seems to derive deeper satisfaction from his work on experimental aircrafts and a new destroyer than from love relationships with various women, advances from success to success with puzzling impunity.

Partly a satire on capitalism, advertising, and the gullibility of the public, *Tono-Bungay* nevertheless portrays George and Edward Ponderevo so sympathetically that Wells seems to be almost in love with the cynical greed that he depicts. **CW**

Strait is the Gate

André Gide

Lifespan | *b.* 1869 (France), *d.* 1951
First Published | 1909, by Mercure de France (Paris)
Original Title | *La Porte Étroite*
Nobel Prize for Literature | 1947

There is something irresistible, even seductively perfect about André Gide's *Strait is the Gate*. Technically the story is about love; as family comfort is withdrawn from them, two cousins find in each other resources of virtue and of beauty. Jerome loses his father before he is twelve years old. An only child, he watches his mother cherish her grief as he experiences his own in the too-early maturing of an already aged sensibility. His cousin Alyssa is despised by her adulterous mother because of her loyalty to her father, whose confidante she becomes. But to summarize thus puts undue emphasis on what is only a beginning; the facts of Jerome and Alyssa's existence—their high-bourgeois lives in a France that seems an endless round of luxuriantly flowered summers, but also scornful of the crudity of material change—have but a skeletal presence.

It is their doomed, delicate, intense and difficult love that fills the text, and which, establishing itself as the only reality, explains Jerome and Alyssa. As a love that remains unconsummated, indeed that remains devoid of any physical engagement, it therefore remains a yearning, a mutual and declared yet lonely striving for one another. It is the prolonged and seemingly pointless trajectory from youthful uncertainty and caution to considered postponement then denial, that fascinates. With exquisite control, Gide has created an exploration of love that manages to capture the absolute yet open-ended nature of yearning itself. **PMcM**

Martin Eden

Jack London

Lifespan | *b.* 1876 (U.S.), *d.* 1916
First Published | 1909
First Published by | Macmillan & Co. (New York)
Original Language | English

Like his eponymous protagonist, London struggled from obscurity to literary success and, when he found it, experienced intellectual disillusionment and spiritual destruction. London's style, like his subject matter, is sharp and often stark, so that one comes to feel the hardness of language.

Martin Eden charts a young seaman's double awakening, first to the allures of bourgeois cultural life, and then to its abhorrent emptiness. He sets out to shed his working-class manners and speech in order to marry Ruth Morse, the daughter of a well-to-do businessman. What starts as a quest to win a woman's heart through self-education becomes a blind and tenacious determination to write in spite of prolonged failure and brutal poverty. Eden believes in the myth of the self-made man, but his struggles expose the illusory and lethal character of the myth. Both London's novel and Eden's quest are as much about the absolute and self-destructive will to authorship, as a condemnation of a social structure that at once fosters and represses the figure of the author. Though his long and often arduous story of Eden's literary ambitions, London gives us one of the most concentrated accounts in American literature of what might by at stake in writing and authorship as labor in an industrial society. **JLSJ**

> London's best-selling novels earned him a fortune, but he clung to the attitudes and lessons of his roustabout background.

Three Lives

Gertrude Stein

Lifespan | *b*. 1874 (U.S.), *d*. 1946 (France)
First Published | 1909, by Grafton Press (New York)
Original Title | *Three Lives: Stories of the Good Anna, Melanctha, and the Gentle Lena*

Three Lives is a trilogy of stories: "The Good Anna," "Melanctha," and "The Gentle Lena." It was undoubtedly influenced by Stein's work translating Flaubert's short stories, *Trois Contes*: "The Good Anna," directly echoes Flaubert's "Un Coeur Simple." Stein's three female characters live at the margins: two (Lena and Anna) are German immigrant servants, while Melanctha, the most vibrant and rebellious of the three, is an African-American.

Stein composed the stories in front of a portrait of Madame Cézanne, and while sitting for her Picasso portrait. This suggests the extent to which she was connecting and comparing visual and verbal portraiture, and attempting to find a verbal equivalent to the "flatness" of Cézanne's painting and the fascination with the form and mass of Cubist art. *Three Lives* shows a focus on the linguistic rhythms and speech patterns of her characters, using a repetitive, unstructured dialogue to represent character types and conflicts. Repetition was, for Stein, an aspect of the "continuous present" that so fascinated her throughout her writing life: as a representation of the ways in which human consciousness functions; as a means to circumvent the demands of plot and linear chronology; as a way to discover the reality of objects by removing them from a temporal framework. Experimenting with literary and linguistic form, here Stein represents women's lives as concerned, if only indirectly, with sexuality, psychology, and culture. **LM**

Impressions of Africa

Raymond Roussel

Lifespan | *b*. 1877 (France), *d*. 1933 (Sicily)
First Published | 1910
First Published by | Librairie Alphonse Lemerre
Original Title | *Impressions d'Afrique*

The first nine chapters of *Impressions of Africa* describe a series of seemingly impossible feats against the backdrop of an imaginary African city. A marksman separates the yolk from the white of a soft-boiled egg with a single bullet; a statue made from corset stays tilts back and forth, its mechanism operated by a tame magpie. In the second half of the novel we learn that a group of shipwrecked passengers has been captured by an African king, and that to entertain him and ensure their freedom, the prisoners must perform elaborate theatrical tasks or build the fantastical machines that we have already seen in the first half.

In an essay published after his suicide in 1935, Roussel reveals that the starting point for his novel was not an impression of Africa at all, but a particular linguistic resource: the way in which a single word can have two or more different meanings. In one variation on his key writing technique, Roussel would start out with a homonym and then assign himself the task of writing a story, or inventing a scenario, which would get us from *baleines* (corset stays) to *baleines* (whales). This is a travelogue that takes us nowhere because, however far away from the initial term we go, the narrative only ever contrives to get us back to where started—from *baleines* to *baleines*. Language is no longer at the service of fiction. Rather, fiction is at the mercy of language; novels are generated in the dark space between a word and its repetition. **KB**

Howards End

E. M. Forster

Lifespan | *b.* 1879 (England), *d.* 1970
First Published | 1910
First Published by | E. Arnold (London)
Original Language | English

Reflecting on the social upheaval that characterized the Edwardian period, *Howards End* introduces the reader to two very different families, the Schlegels and the Wilcoxes. While the Schlegels are idealistic and intellectual, the Wilcoxes are materialistic and practical. The novel documents the connection that develops between these two families and the clashing of their very different worldviews.

The two Schlegel sisters, Margaret and Helen, respond to the Wilcoxes in contrasting ways. While Helen remains idealistic and passionately opposed to the materialism and pragmatism of the Wilcoxes, Margaret hopes to reconcile the two approaches to life and nurture an appreciation for both. In her writing she hopes to "only connect," in order to exalt both her prose and her passion. *Howards End* documents Margaret's attempt to connect, its successes and its failures—her marriage to Henry Wilcox, the vicissitudes of their relationship, and the driving conflict between her sister and her husband.

Truly a masterpiece, the novel has moments of real beauty and optimism. As with all of Forster's novels, the characters are brilliantly drawn, and the dialogue is superb—both realistic and moving. Although this novel deals with extreme emotions and actions, it never becomes melodramatic or absurd. Instead, it remains all too real a picture of human emotion, and the devastating consequences that can result from miscommunication, pride, anger, and hypocrisy. **EGG**

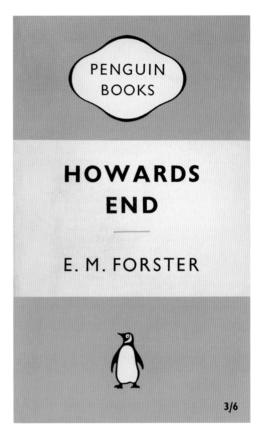

"To trust people is a luxury in which only the wealthy can indulge; the poor cannot afford it."

◉ Here published in the classic Penguin orange fiction format, *Howards End* bears as its motto the phrase: "Only connect ..."

Fantômas

Marcel Allain and Pierre Souvestre

Lifespan (Allain) | b. 1885 (France), d. 1970
Lifespan (Souvestre) | b. 1874 (France), d. 1914
First Published | 1911, by A. Fayard (Paris)
Original Language | French

First published in 1911, *Fantômas* was a sensation in the authors' native France and, although still relatively unknown to the English-speaking world, it continues to occupy a prominent place in the popular imagination across Europe and the globe. With the original *Fantômas* serving as inspiration for an extraordinary thirty-one sequels, various movie versions, and a successful comic book in Mexico, this mysterious creation lives on.

The eponymous "hero" of the novel is a masked arch-criminal, an amoral genius at war with bourgeois society. Fantômas is without history and without motive, a nightmare made flesh, an enigma whose physical existence is only confirmed by the trail of corpses he leaves in his wake, or the tantalizing swish of a cape at an open window. He is pursued by the brilliant but perpetually frustrated Inspector Juve. As Fantômas rapes, murders, and swindles his way through the Paris night, the very mention of his name comes to inspire fear in the hearts of all god-fearing citizens.

It is strange that this violent, crudely written tale should enjoy such staying power, as well as being a notable inspiration to both the Dada movement and the Surrealists. An uncanny work that reflects the paranoia, confusion, and thrill of the modern city, it communicates a feeling of Old World morals under threat, and exploits ongoing concerns. *Fantômas* casts a long shadow; it appeals to both the primal and the intellectual imagination. **SamT**

Ethan Frome

Edith Wharton

Lifespan | b. 1862 (U.S.), d. 1937 (France)
First Published | 1911
First Published by | Macmillan & Co. (London)
Original Language | English

Ethan Frome is a limpid account of mental isolation, sexual frustration, and moral despair in a turn-of-the-century New England farming community. The novel recounts the story of Frome's burgeoning desire for the mercurial Mattie Silver, a destitute relative of his wife Zeena, and traces the logic whereby the two lovers attempt to destroy themselves, with unexpected and harrowing consequences.

Frome stands at the heart of the story; his withered personality is the bitter fruit of a harsh environment and an inward-looking community. He is a man of hidden depths who intuits an abundant reality beneath the surface of prosaic life, and whose sociability is granted no outlet in an isolated community. An interplay between external environment and inner psyche is dramatized here; the inarticulacy of the characters is central to the novel, which is framed by the words of a narrator whose knowledge of the history he recounts is unreliable. We are left with disconcerting questions about moral choice and agency, the role of environment in determining behavior, and the conflict between social mores and individual passions. *Ethan Frome* focuses primarily on the suffering of its eponymous protagonist, but it also depicts the social conditions that enable the formation of so manipulative a figure as Zeena. **AG**

> This photograph of Edith Wharton was taken before she became a novelist, but already suggests a determined personality.

The Charwoman's Daughter

James Stephens

Lifespan | *b. c.* 1880 (Ireland), *d.* 1950 (England)
First Published | 1912
First Published by | Macmillan (London)
Original Language | English

The poet and novelist James Stephens was born and reared in a Dublin slum, and started his adult life as a clerk in a solicitor's office. All of his work carries with it an edge of claustrophobia, a haunting sense of loneliness amid overcrowding. But Stephens was in love with the idea of the imagination, and the Dublin of his work is at once a place of confines and of liberation, of small rooms and open streets, of the press of necessity and the beauty of a silk dress glimpsed in a shop window.

The Charwoman's Daughter is the strange, wistful story of sixteen-year-old Mary, the only child of her fiercely protective widowed mother. It is also a story about Dublin and about how we see that city. Usually depicted in Irish fiction as a man's town, a place trapped in its history, and home to big, busy conversations and random, unregulated encounters, this Dublin is both domestic and urban.

Mary and her mother live in a one-room tenement flat that is home to the rituals of their bitter love. By day her mother cleans the houses of the Dublin rich, while Mary makes observations as she walks through the city. The imaginative richness of her insights makes the city come alive as a place that is both strange and wonderful, remote yet friendly. It is this sense of discovery and the bittersweet richness it brings with it that makes this such an unusual but compelling Dublin novel. **PMcM**

Death in Venice

Thomas Mann

Lifespan | *b.* 1875 (Germany), *d.* 1955 (Switzerland)
First Published | 1912, by Hyperionverlag (Munich)
Original Title | *Der Tod in Venedig*
Nobel Prize for Literature | 1929

When renowned author Gustave von Aschenbach, with uncharacteristic spontaneity, travels to Venice, his attention is captivated by a young boy whose blond curls and exquisite proportions seem to embody the Greek ideal of beauty. Watching Tadzio soon becomes the focus of Aschenbach's days; and then, of his existence. On board the ship to Venice, Aschenbach looks on with horror as a simpering old man with a painted face mingles with a group of young men. But by the close of the story, Aschenbach has become that man, as, intoxicated, he pursues Tadzio through the passages and canals of an infected city. *Death in Venice*, as Mann maintained, is about the artist's loss of dignity, but Mann also examines the relationship between art and life. Aschenbach believes that with labor and discipline he can master life and even mold it into art. But Tadzio's Dionysus, inspiring unstructured emotion and unruly passion, forces him to recognize the fallacy of that conviction. The mythical elements of the novel offer a context for the portrayal of homosexuality. Written with subtlety and profound psychological insight, *Death in Venice* is a vivid account of what it is like to fall in love.

The novella was perhaps Mann's ideal artistic form (*Death in Venice* runs to a mere seventy pages): from the first hints of foreboding to the final pathetic climax, this is a masterwork of its genre. **KB**

Sons and Lovers

D. H. Lawrence

Lifespan | *b*. 1885 (England), *d*. 1930
First Published | 1913
First Published by | Duckworth & Co. (London)
Original Language | English

In *Sons and Lovers*, Lawrence compellingly describes the Nottinghamshire countryside and the mining community with which he felt such a deep connection. Bold in the honesty with which it tackles the subjects of family, domestic strife, class struggle, gender conflict, sexuality, industrialism, and poverty, *Sons and Lovers* is also alive to the natural world that it evokes with an intensity verging on mysticism.

The novel's key theme is the relationship between the boy Paul Morel and his mother, a ubiquitous maternal presence with great ambitions for her gifted son. Their powerful bond excludes the father, a poorly educated miner, who is treated with disdain by the mother, an attitude the boy internalizes as his own as he becomes a man. Urgent class issues thus overlap with volatile psychosexual questions. Paul lives out his mother's frustrated aspirations through education and art; but the almost incestuous relationship between mother and son threatens to prevent him from developing a separate adult identity and from forging mature sexual relationships with other women.

Sensitive to the social position of an intelligent woman such as Gertrude Morel, who is as trapped by the mining community as her embittered husband, it also captures the frustrations of adolescent love, the confusing allure of different kinds of sexual relationships, and the violence of male rivalries. **AG**

The Ragged Trousered Philanthropists

Robert Tressell

Lifespan | *b*. 1870 (Ireland), *d*. 1911
First Published | 1914
First Published by | G. Richards (London)
Original Language | English

This book remains perhaps the pre-eminent classic of English working-class literature, yet the first-time reader may well be surprised at its tone. Although at the heart of the novel there is an intelligent, passionate, and sustained attack on capitalism, there is also a violent bitterness directed at those workers who fail to see the necessity of socialism, and in this way, deliver their children into exploitation.

This is a strange kind of novel, where the reader's attention is held not by any trick of suspense or narrative flow but rather by the minute exploration of lives led under the heel of profit. The whole story is vividly fuelled by anger, directed mainly at those who are duped by their bosses; it is implied that the employers themselves can hardly behave in any other way. But the book is not only about the working class in a conventional sense, it is also about the nature of work itself, and how the possibility of pride in one's work is destroyed and ridiculed by the demands of greater "efficiency." Inevitably, the worker is forced to perform rapid, slapdash work, which removes all genuine satisfaction through labor, as with the protagonist who has much to give to his chosen "craft," but who is constantly denied by "the system." *The Ragged Trousered Philanthropists* is thus in tune with the broader socialist movements of Edwardian England which we now tend to associate with such figures as Ruskin and Morris. **DP**

Tarzan of the Apes

Edgar Rice Burroughs

Lifespan | *b.* 1875 (U.S.), *d.* 1950
First Published | 1914
First Published by | L. Burt Co. (New York)
Original Language | English

"Tarzan was appalled. It had been bad enough to be hairless, but to own such a countenance! He wondered that the other apes could look at him at all."

⊙ Burroughs was a goldminer, cavalryman, storekeeper, and cowboy before writing the popular novels that made his fortune.

Ideologically, the *Tarzan* series has so little to commend it that it is surprising the books have not been subject to a more severe pounding. It is also perhaps ironic that while factions are liable to ban or even burn more recent fictions, *Tarzan* still happily occupies a position in the popular canon, even becoming the subject of a Disney movie and subsequent ongoing cartoon series. Narratively, it is exciting, dynamic, often surprisingly well-written, and full of all the classic tropes one expects from good pulp fiction—survival against the odds, an unknown land, fierce adversaries, dramatic fights, and beautiful women. That said, the underlying subtexts of the book are racist, sexist, utterly formulaic, and overridingly imperialist, ultimately championing the figure of the white supremacist male. In *Tarzan of the Apes*, the eponymous hero conquers (in order) the apes, lions, and elephants, black tribesmen, degenerate sailors, professors of theology, women, and the British, before returning his ire to the tribesmen again.

Today *Tarzan*, like W. E. John's *Biggles* series, goes largely unread, with its considerable strengths largely forgotten—early discussions of ecology, the importance of Burroughs' writing on heroic texts, and the often piercing social commentary. Overall, the mythology of *Tarzan*, who first communicates with Jane Porter via written notes, and then in French, eschewing the sexually primal "Me Tarzan, you Jane," has superseded the real text. **EMcCS**

Rosshalde

Hermann Hesse

Lifespan | *b.* 1877 (Germany), *d.* 1962
First Published | 1914
First Published by | S. Fischer Verlag (Berlin)
Nobel Prize for Literature | 1946

Rosshalde is one of Hermann Hesse's early novels; he wrote it in his twenties, long before the cultish *Siddhartha*, read by many as a spiritual guidebook, or the involved dystopia *The Glass Bead Game*. The oddest of its features is its subtle presentation of artistic lateness and artistic compulsion.

Its central character, Johann Veraguth, is a very successful painter whose only interests are his work and his young son, Pierre, who competes for Veraguth's attention by being very interesting himself. The family, such as it is, lives at Rosshalde, a beautiful country estate. Veraguth's wife, Adele, lives in the house itself; he lives in the summerhouse he turned into a studio—sometimes they meet for lunch. Veraguth's hermit-like existence is interrupted when an old friend comes to visit. Otto Burkhardt thinks Johann's newest work is his best, but feels that the painter needs a change of scene. He suggests that Veraguth should leave Rosshalde for a while, and travel with him to India. Veraguth has nearly been persuaded when his beloved Pierre falls ill.

Hesse's great achievement in this quiet novel is to have collapsed a life and its memories—school, learning to paint, marriage, fatherhood—into a series of compressed and telling moments, without the details having to be laboriously related. Hesse does something in writing that ought to be possible only in painting: everything Veraguth looks at (the light, his son playing) is charged with the weight of feeling and experience. **DSoa**

Locus Solus

Raymond Roussel

Lifespan | *b.* 1877 (France), *d.* 1933 (Sicily)
First Published | 1914
First Published by | Librairie Alphonse Lemerre
Original Language | French

Strange and uncompromisingly difficult, Roussel's self-published novels and poems were ridiculed in his lifetime. Now, though, Roussel is enjoying fame for his solitary adventures into language, which have had a decisive impact on a number of key thinkers and writers of the twentieth century, from Michel Foucault to New York poet John Ashbery.

Locus Solus is marked by a macabre theatricality, and proceeds by unveiling a series of fantastical scenes: cats, teeth, diamonds, and dancing girls are showcased among a host of complex mechanisms. Our guide is the brilliant scientist and inventor Martial Canterel, who is taking a group of colleagues on a tour of his lonely estate—the solitary place of the title. The impressive central exhibit is a huge glass cage, in which eight elaborate tableaux vivants are on display. Only, the actors that we suppose are playing dead are, in fact, dead. Canterel has transformed corpses into automata by injecting them with a fluid of his own invention: revived by "resurrectine," the dead players are doomed to re-enact the key moments of their lives. Moments, of course, that were meaningful precisely because they were thought to be unique and unrepeatable. The kind of language machine that Roussel invented to write this and other novels operates at the switch-point where a word divides to mean two different things. His fiction is always dangerously close to mimicking the show of meaninglessness that is the central spectacle of his strikingly peculiar novel. **KB**

Kokoro

Natsume Soseki

Lifespan | *b.* 1867 (Japan), *d.* 1916
First Published | 1914
First Published by | Iwanami Shoten (Tokyo)
Original Language | Japanese

Although a writer on early British satire, Natsume Soseki was unimpressed by the work of his British contemporaries.

The building of a railway from Tokyo to Yokahama was typical of the modernization of Japan in the Meiji era observed by Natsume.

Kokoro is a novel that captures the changes in mentality that Japan experienced during a period of rapid modernization at the end of the nineteenth century. As Japanese society acclimatized to westernization and began to transform itself into a militaristic state it began to lose the hopeful spirit of the Meiji era's "civilization and enlightenment." The death of the Meiji emperor in 1913 and, in an assertion of traditional values, the ritual suicide of General Nogi the same year shocked contemporaries, who saw the two deaths as symbolizing the extinction of the Meiji spirit.

Kokoro, set in Tokyo in around 1910, is a three-part novel that traces the relationship between a young man, the narrator, and an old man, whom he calls *Sensei* (meaning "teacher," but suggesting the relationship of master and disciple). Sensei is haunted by a stigma in his past, which hangs over the entire novel. Parts one and two of the novel revolve around the deaths of the narrator's father and of Sensei's friend, and his frequent visits to the graveyard. The narrator becomes preoccupied by Sensei's secret, and his anxiety grows. One day a letter arrives, delivering Sensei's confession of his guilt in a tragic love triangle, and his sense of multiple self-contradictions. He is torn between morality and possessiveness, intellect and emotion, death and life. He suffers from the impossibility of understanding his and others' *kokoro* (the soul or the inner workings of the mind). In its delicate depiction of Sensei's malaise the novel is not only a testament to the rapid modernization of Japan, but also an examination of an individual's tortured sense of failure and responsibility. Natsume, who established the form of the first-person novel, is one of the greatest writers in modern Japanese literature. **KK**

Handcuffed TO THE GIRL WHO DOUBLE-CROSSED HIM

The "Monte Cristo" hero...
The MAN who put
the MAN in roMANce...

ROBERT MADELEINE
DONAT CARROLL
in
THE 39 STEPS

Directed by ALFRED HITCHCOCK

Director of The Man Who Knew Too Much

A GB PRODUCTION

A HUNDRED STEPS AHEAD OF ANY PICTURE THIS YEAR

The Thirty-Nine Steps

John Buchan

Lifespan | *b.* 1875 (Scotland), *d.* 1940 (Canada)
First Published | 1915
First Published by | W. Blackwood & Sons (London)
Original Language | English

A forerunner of the modern spy thriller, *The Thirty-Nine Steps* revolves around a German plot to declare war on an unprepared Britain through a secret invasion. Although this storyline was clearly topical and drew on the brutal conflict of the Great War, it also reflected Buchan's deep distaste for German culture. The narrative centers on Richard Hannay, an almost superhuman and ridiculously lucky South African engineer who rescues a hunted British spy, only to find himself the focus of a manhunt orchestrated by agents of the German state. Believing himself to be too visible in London, Hannay escapes to the Scottish Highlands in the hope of hiding out in what he takes to be an unpopulated wilderness. But Hannay is quickly disabused, when he finds that the "isolated" Highland landscape is overpopulated by motorcars and German agents posing as pillars of British society.

The novel is important in establishing a formula for the spy thriller: car chases, elaborate disguises, and an urgent quest to avert disaster. The dramatic turns of the plot rely upon a sense of paranoia where every potential ally is also a potential enemy. Buchan's own war work involved running the newly formed Department of Information, responsible for producing propaganda to support the war effort, and his novels clearly complement this work. **LC**

🄯 Alfred Hitchcock's movie version of Buchan's spy thriller, released in 1935, is now far more widely known than the original novel.

The Rainbow

D. H. Lawrence

Lifespan | *b.* 1885 (England), *d.* 1930
First Published | 1915
First Published by | Methuen & Co. (London)
Original Language | English

Central to Lawrence's break from well-established fictional conventions is his conviction that human subjectivity could no longer be described in terms of what he called "the old stable ego," and that a different way of presenting character was required. He considers the "realism" with which fictional characters had hitherto typically been presented as essentially unrealistic, and in *The Rainbow* he moves to a presentation of human individuals and their vexed relationships that draws on unconscious impulses.

Written under the shadow of the First World War, the novel contrasts the stretches of time in which the Brangwen family was rooted to the soil, against the far-reaching changes to human life (especially the inexorable destruction of communities) now occurring. Issues such as adolescent sexuality, marital relations, intergenerational conflict, exile, colonialism, national identity, education, upward social mobility, the New Woman, lesbianism, and psychological breakdown (the precursor of a necessary rebirth and regeneration) are woven together. Sexually explicit and brutally honest about relationships, *The Rainbow* delineates the breakdown of an established social order; focusing on the shifting balance of power in parent-child and male-female relations; at the same time it situates epochal transformations within a mythic frame of reference, which is indebted to Lawrence's rendering of biblical cadences and pantheistic traditions. **AG**

Of Human Bondage

William Somerset Maugham

Lifespan | *b.* 1874 (France), *d.* 1965
First Published | 1915
First Published by | W. Heinemann (London)
Original Language | English

Maugham's best known novel is based on his own experiences. It utilizes the technique of third-person narration, but filters everything through the presiding consciousness of its central character, Philip Carey. Characterized by a leisurely pace and an episodic structure, the novel traces Carey's story from childhood to young adulthood. It describes his difficult early years, the harsh conditions of his life at school (where he is tormented because of his clubfoot), the gradual loss of his religious faith, and his experiences as a young man hungry to encounter the world on his own terms.

The novel is preoccupied above all with the search for meaning in a human existence that appears to have none. Carey is convinced, through his glimpses into other people's lives, that they are mostly full of suffering, frequently sordid, and generally futile. His own experiences, in turn, seem only to confirm his cynical diagnosis. Yet he does not lose his desire to confront life's vicissitudes nor to search for a personal philosophy. The viewpoint he develops refuses the limiting categories of virtue and vice in favor of a Darwinian view of life. The terms "good" and "evil" are seen as labels deployed by society to make the individual conform— existence is in itself insignificant and futile. Carey's stoical conclusion, explored through loosely linked episodes in the novel, is that the thinking individual can only really find a measure of freedom in the aesthetics of life's random events. **AG**

The Voyage Out

Virginia Woolf

Lifespan | *b.* 1882 (England), *d.* 1941
First Published | 1915
First Published by | Duckworth & Co. (London)
Original Language | English

The Voyage Out, Woolf's first novel, sends its heroine, the motherless Rachel Vinrace, on a sea voyage out to South America, accompanied by her father, her aunt and uncle, and assorted travelers. Rachel's aunt, Helen Ambrose, takes on the task of "bringing out" her niece, whose sheltered upbringing has left her ignorant of sexual and emotional relationships between men and women. On their arrival in Santa Marina, Rachel meets a young man, Terence Hewet, an aspiring novelist, and they become engaged on a river trip into the interior of the country. They plan a future together, but Rachel is stricken by fever, and the last section of the novel charts her decline.

The novel both works within and subverts the genre of the bildungsroman, the novel of education or formation, struggling with the conventional narratives of "a woman's life." *The Voyage Out* has often been seen as an apprentice novel, bound by a narrative realism that Woolf was later to transcend, yet in many ways it laid the basis for her more experimental fiction. Woolf wished to explore the "perplexities of her sex," and these are reflected in the tone of the novel—which moves between visionary consciousness and social satire—and its shifting perspectives, which suggest the relativity of social and sexual values, as well as of time and space. Woolf spent nine years writing the novel: "What I wanted to do," she wrote, "was to give the feeling of a vast tumult of life, as various and disorderly as possible"—to render life as lived. **LM**

The Good Soldier

Ford Madox Ford

Lifespan | b. 1873 (England), d. 1939 (France)
First Published | 1915
First Published by | The Bodley Head (London)
Given Name | Ford Hermann Hueffer

Critical opinion on *The Good Soldier* is divided. Some regard it as a wholly improbable novel, in which substance is sacrificed to style, and others see it as one of the most finely crafted novels of the twentieth century, in which Ford examines whether it is possible to create a narrative of the modern world through aesthetic experimentalism. This book is the best example of the literary style known as impressionism, of which Ford was a chief exponent.

In *The Good Soldier*, Ford aims to demonstrate how thoroughly our experience of reality is shaped by the limits of our knowledge. Narrated solely from the point of view of an idle, rich American, John Dowell, *The Good Soldier* illustrates the extent to which Dowell's consciousness of reality alters as he acquires new knowledge and understanding of past events. Through the course of the novel, we realize that Florence, Dowell's wife, has been conducting a long affair with the "good soldier" of the title, Edward Ashburnham. Dowell is the ultimate unreliable narrator, unaware of his wife's true nature and the passionate coupling that has been taking place. He describes his idyllic friendship with the Ashburnhams, but following his realization of the affair, he must begin again, and attempt to retell the story of this friendship. Throughout the novel, Dowell tries and fails to conceive of a narrative method that can faithfully recount these contradictory perspectives: one of self-deluding innocence and one of tortured enlightenment. **LC**

"Six months ago I had never been to England, and, certainly, I had never sounded the depths of an English heart. I had known the shallows."

⬥ Madox Ford served in the Great War and is here photographed in uniform at about the time that *The Good Soldier* was published.

老婆鬼腕を
持去る図

Rashomon

Akutagawa Ryunosuke

Lifespan | *b.* 1892 (Japan), *d.* 1927
First Published | 1915 in *Teikoku Bungaku* magazine
Alternate Title | *The Rasho Gate*
Real Name | Chokodo Shujin

Rashomon and Other Stories comprises six short stories, written by Akutagawa in the early and middle period of his career between 1915 and 1921. "Remaking" or imitation is an important element in his work; in this collection he retells a number of historical fables. Akutagawa defends imitation against the ideology of the original, considering it not as a mere reproduction but as a subtle process of digestion and transformation.

Akutagawa applies a parabolic style and tone to these stories, which contrasts with their unexpected endings and creates curious emotional effects. Some of the stories are simply delightful, while others suspend our simplistic moral judgment and invite us to reflect further on the impulsive nature of human beings. Akutagawa is also a master of structure. "Dragon" and "Yam Gruel" effectively use the report form and create an amusing atmosphere by contrasting the narrow perspective of the characters with a broader perspective of the world as a whole. "Kesa and Morito" and "In a Grove" cleverly juxtapose multiple quasi-Dostoevskian monologues without background explanation, creating a faltering sense of reality. Akutagawa is one of the most widely read modernist writers in Japan. His timeless stories are perceptive and witty investigations into the very nature of literature itself. **KK**

❸ The demon of *Rashomon*, disguised as an old woman, carries off his arm that had been severed by the hero Watanabe no Tsuna.

Under Fire

Henri Barbusse

Lifespan | *b.* 1873 (France), *d.* 1935 (Russia)
First Published | 1916
First Published by | Flammarion (Paris)
Original Title | *Le Feu*

The members of the squad celebrated in Barbusse's story of front line fighting in the early years of the First World War, are the French army's *poilus* or "hairy ones," and there is not a liberal or an intellectual present among them. Yet Barbusse was a journalist with a purpose. His voluntary two years in the trenches led him to pacifism and Communism, and *Under Fire* is an early step on that road.

As the experience of war is primarily one of disintegration, it is difficult to construct the purposive narrative required for a pacifist polemic, and Barbusse doesn't try. Chapters describe life behind the lines or on leave, or express *poilu* anger at the "Rear," where soldier-administrators are able to avoid the bloodbath at the front. There are anecdotes within anecdotes, stories of crossing accidentally into enemy lines to return with a box of matches taken from a slaughtered German. Above all, there is the fighting, in which men die in so many appalling ways: crushed, shot, split open, rotting, buried, unburied. The stories are orchestrated by a participant narrator who directs the reader from above the struggle. In the final chapter, the squad—now much diminished—begins a discussion that disparages nationalism, exalts the soldiers' latent political power, and recognizes the need for equality and justice. This "dream of fumbling thought" is the beginning of a learning process for these ordinary working men, which is validated by the novel's unforgettable accounts of the front line. **AMu**

A Portrait of the Artist as a Young Man

James Joyce

Lifespan | *b.* 1882 (Ireland), *d.* 1941
First Published | 1916
First Published by | B. W. Huebsch (New York)
First Serialized | 1914–1915, in *The Egoist* (London)

First published in serial form between 1914 and 1915, *A Portrait of the Artist as a Young Man* is the novel that established Joyce as one of the most innovative literary talents of the twentieth century.

Portrait traces the development of Stephen Dedalus from childhood, through adolescence, to the first flushes of manhood. Over time, he gradually begins to rebel against his devout Catholic upbringing—questioning the values of his family, church, history, and homeland. At the same time, Stephen's interest in art and literature intensifies as he struggles to come to terms with his adult self. This, however, is no ordinary coming-of-age story. The language used at each stage of the narrative is skilfully manipulated in order to reflect Stephen's age and intellectual maturity. *Portrait* begins with "moocows" and ends with Stephen expressing his desire to "forge in the smithy of my soul the uncreated conscience of my race."

Portrait remains a work of startling invention and imaginative richness, in which Joyce began to hone his revolutionary "stream of consciousness" technique. It is the work in which the hallmarks of Joyce's writing are truly established: the broad sexual humor, the blasphemous fantasies, the erudite wordplay, the simultaneous eradication and exposure of authorial personality, the infinitely complex push/pull relationship with Ireland and Irishness. In *Portrait*, Joyce redefines both himself and the parameters of modern writing. **SamT**

"The artist, like the God of the creation, remains within or behind or beyond or above his handiwork, invisible, refined out of existence, indifferent, paring his fingernails."

This photographic portrait of Joyce as a penniless but confident young man was taken in 1904 by his friend Constantine Curran.

Bunner Sisters

Edith Wharton

Lifespan | *b.* 1862 (U.S.), *d.* 1937 (France)
First Published | 1916
First Published by | Macmillan (London & N.Y.)
First Published in | *Xingu and Other Stories*

Edith Wharton is best known for her novels, but she was also an accomplished writer of short stories. Indeed, Wharton worried that her novels were possibly weakened by her tendency to try to pack too much detail into them, whereas she considered that the more compact form of the short story enabled her to be concise and thus authoritative. She worked in the format of the short story throughout her life, and she often used the genre to try out new ideas and styles.

Bunner Sisters was written as early as 1892, but Wharton did not publish it until much later. Set in New York, it explores the complex relationship between two sisters, focusing on issues of choice and renunciation. But the story also describes the living conditions of the urban poor, depicting the misery and suffering of working-class characters who struggle to survive in desperately difficult circumstances. The plot of *Bunner Sisters* turns upon the moral dilemma that arises when the two sisters of the story's title both fall for the same man, Mr. Ramy. As in May Sinclair's chilling novella *The Life and Death of Harriett Frean*, one character chooses to sacrifice her own desires and hopes in order to give way to those of another, but this seemingly selfless action gives rise to unpredictable consequences. The story thus manages to confront the problem of renunciation head-on, suggesting that in certain circumstances sacrificial behavior may be not only pointless but also damaging in its effects. **AG**

Growth of the Soil

Knut Hamsun

Lifespan | *b.* 1859 (Norway), *d.* 1952
First Published | 1917 by Gyldendal (Oslo)
Given Name | Knut Pederson
Original Title | *Markens grøde*

Growth of the Soil, which led to Hamsun's Nobel Prize win in 1920, strives for a plain and uncomplicated prose suitable to the simplistic lifestyles of the farming community it describes. Beginning with one man's lone arrival in the Norwegian wilds, the narrative follows him as he clears the land, builds up his farm, marries, and has a family. This sense of the solitary hero forging his life gives an epic trajectory to a novel that seeks to explore the hardships facing those who live on the land, and to portray the isolation felt in small, rural communities. Although no paean to rural idylls, Hamsun's narrative gently prizes the qualities of hard-working, plain-thinking people whose lives follow the rhythm of nature's cycles. Repetition is indeed one of the keys to the novel, which is not without its dark underbelly of selfishness and even infanticide. In following two generations, it tracks the alterations wrought by man upon the land, and records the inevitable technological changes that slowly come to transform farming methods. As a family saga it also traces the troubles, tensions, and love within familial life, as the younger generation matures and the parents age. *Growth of the Soil* evinces an almost romantic nostalgia for the slow-changing earthy lives of the rural wilderness; this came at a time when the culture and celebrity of city living had come to make such communities seem archaic. In this winning, if strangely sad, novel, it is a now obsolete way of life that Hamsun portrays. **JC**

Summer

Edith Wharton

Lifespan | b. 1862 (U.S.), d. 1937 (France)
First Published | 1917
First Published by | Macmillan (London & N.Y.)
Original Language | English

The novella *Summer* emerged from Wharton's increasing knowledge of New England, and it focuses in a realistic manner on what the writer described as "a decaying rural existence." With an almost anthropological sensibility, Wharton traces the stages of decay through which the town of North Dormer has passed over a long period of time.

The character of Charity Royall is torn between two possible relationships and the conflicting claims of personal desire and socal obligation. The sexual interest shown in her by Lawyer Royall, her guardian, raises the specter of incest, while her love affair with Lucius Harney exists in a private realm of asocial passion, which cuts her off from the wider community. Charity feels alienated from the town society and, facing an impossible dilemma, she undertakes a voyage of self-discovery that leads her to reaffirm her loyalty to the "primitivism" of her forebears. Having rediscovered the source of natural passion and experienced its creative energy, she returns contented to so-called "civilized" society. The ending is ambiguous, and continues to mystify and divide readers: does it represent capitulation to the conformism of a small-minded and parochial community, or is it to be interpreted as a genuine resolution of the conflicts it has so convincingly dramatized? The novella as a whole witnesses the often harsh relationship between people and the natural world, and reveals the ease with which once vibrant societies can slide into desuetude. **AG**

The Shadow Line

Joseph Conrad

Lifespan | b. 1857 (Ukraine), d. 1924 (England)
First Published | 1917
First Published by | J. M. Dent & Sons (London)
Given Name | Józef Teodor Konrad Korzeniowski

Partly based on Conrad's experiences as captain of *The Otago*, this is one of Conrad's superb novels of sea-voyaging, combining descriptive virtuosity with acute psychological observation. The novel's anonymous hero is given the opportunity of a first command—after being almost deprived of the chance, he fortuitously becomes captain of a sailing-ship for its voyage from Bangkok to Sydney. Initially, he feels proudly confident; but, gradually, things go wrong. Crewmen are stricken by tropical disease, the quinine has been purloined, and the ship is becalmed. The young master learns that the previous captain had died at sea after cursing the ship, and the mate, Burns, claims that the curse is taking effect. Lonely and anxious, the captain struggles to maintain his self-possession. Eventually, with the aid of the steward, Ransom, he is able to bring the vessel to harbor.

This poetically evocative novel is both graphically realistic and richly symbolic. It extends the tradition of maritime works dealing with an accursed ship (to take one example, Coleridge's *Rime of the Ancient Mariner)*. Conrad, who admired Wagner's music, must have also known *Der fliegende Holländer*. Remarkably, given that in *The Shadow Line* a covert supernatural plot clearly accompanies the overt mundane plot, Conrad's "Author's Note" denied the presence of any supernatural element. This novel remains a memorable evocation of a man's initiation by ordeal into maturity. **CW**

The Return of the Soldier

Rebecca West

Lifespan | *b.* 1892 (England), *d.* 1983
First Published | 1918
First Published by | Nisbet & Co. (London)
Given Name | Cicily Isabel Fairfield

West's short novel, published when she was twenty-four, is one of the most compelling literary responses to the horrors of the First World War, told from the perspective of those left at home. At its opening, the narrator, Jenny, and her cousin Chris' decorative but vacuous wife Kitty, are living in a beautiful English house, Baldry Court, awaiting Chris' return from the Front. He comes back suffering from memory loss brought about by shell shock. Everything that has happened in the last fifteen years is erased from his mind, including his marriage and the death of his infant son, Baldry Court and its inhabitants have become meaningless to him. He is infatuated with a working-class woman, Margaret, whom he had known when she was a girl, and who becomes the only figure who can give him solace, as both a lover and mother figure. At the close of the novel, he is cruelly "cured" by being forcefully reminded of his dead child, a dead son in a society now full of dead sons. The "return" of memory will return him to the Front, and we must assume, to an almost certain death in the trenches, in "No Man's Land where bullets fall like rain on the rotting faces of the dead."

The novel is bitterly ironic and yet lyrical, particularly in its representation of the lost world in which Chris' amnesia, the "hysterical fugue" brought about by shell shock, has enabled him to take refuge. It is a love story of a kind, through which West explores some of the most complex and difficult questions arising out of the war experience. **LM**

Rebecca West

> *"She was not so much a person as an implication of dreary poverty, like an open door in a mean house that lets out the smell of cooking cabbage and the screams of children."*

◉ West made her name as a journalist campaigning in support of the suffragette movement before turning to the writing of fiction.

Tarr

Wyndham Lewis

"He must get his mouth on hers; he must revel in the laugh, where it grew. She was néfaste. She was in fact evidently 'the Devil.'"

🔹 Wyndham Lewis was a painter as well as a writer and founded the Vorticist art movement, an English version of Italian Futurism.

Lifespan | *b.* 1882 (Canada), *d.* 1957 (England)
First Published | 1918
First Published by | Alfred A. Knopf (New York)
First Serialized | 1916–1917, in *The Egoist* (London)

Like Joyce's *A Portrait of the Artist as a Young Man*, *Tarr* was originally serialized before its publication as a complete volume. Alongside Joyce's work, *Tarr* signaled a new era in English literary writing. Lewis stands a long way removed from the modernism of more "accepted" writers. Nevertheless, *Tarr* equals (if not exceeds) anything the period has to offer in terms of stylistic radicalism and imaginative scope. Although the novel was later rewritten, in 1928, the 1918 version remains definitive—retaining the experimental punctuation which gives the work such a distinctive appearance. Drawing heavily on Lewis' own experiences in Montparnasse between 1903 and 1908, *Tarr* is an account of expatriate bohemian life in Paris before the First World War. The novel dismantles the ideals of European art by tracking the decline of its central character, Otto Kreisler, whose pretentious gestures, frustrations, and sordid sexual conquests are the basis for an iconoclastic critique of the modern intellectual world.

What makes *Tarr* so striking is its emphasis on exteriority (as opposed to the interior life that so preoccupied the likes of Joyce and Woolf), on ways of seeing, and images of language. The novel is an exercise in "visual writing," an attempt to employ the principles of "Vorticist" painting in print. Lewis' characters are rendered as strange, abstracted forms —as gargoyles chiseled out of human matter. *Tarr* is a difficult, provocative, and extraordinarily crafted work, outside the familiar modernist canon. **SamT**

Night and Day

Virginia Woolf

Lifespan | *b.* 1882 (England), *d.* 1941
First Published | 1919
First Published by | Duckworth & Co. (London)
Original Language | English

In *Night and Day*, Woolf continued to explore the predicaments faced by a young upper-middle class woman whose passivity and obedience to social and familial norms and demands conceal a complex inner life. Her heroine, Katherine Hilbery, is a dutiful daughter who seeks escape from the world of letters, inextricably bound up with Victorian lives, which characterizes her own family. Woolf depicts the difficult search for solitude and contrasts Katherine's life with that of Mary Datchet, a young suffrage worker making her own way in London. She is a woman alone "working out her plans far into the night" who exists at a far remove from the marriage plot of which Katherine is ambivalently but inescapably a part.

The city is at the heart of *Night and Day*, its streets and spaces seemingly shaping, and shaped by, its characters' shifting moods. The novel offers a self-consciously comic resolution, in the tradition of a Shakespeare play or a Mozart opera, in which the curtains of drawing rooms part and close on scenes and in which courtship is played out in London parks. This narrative self-consciousness, and the invocation of a world of thought and experience underlying the busy texture of the everyday, indicate some of the ways in which Woolf sought to break with the "naturalism" of the early twentieth century. At the novel's close, Katherine stands on the threshold of her home, poised between past and future, her domain and the city, night and day. **LM**

Women in Love

D. H. Lawrence

Lifespan | *b.* 1885 (England), *d.* 1930 (France)
First Published | 1920 (private subscription only)
First Published by | M. Secker (London) in 1921
Full Name | David Herbert Lawrence

Women in Love, one of the greatest English twentieth-century novels, was written in a mood of rage and despair against an increasingly decadent, mechanical civilization. It offers an apocalyptic reading of English society in which a cleansing cataclysm is positively desired. A dream of annihilation animates this pessimistic text, which is very much a war novel, even though the war is not ostensibly its subject.

A profoundly unsettling work, *Women in Love* was refused publication for four years after it was completed. This was due to the candid appraisal of sexuality, the violence endemic to relationships, the instability of identity (portrayed as prey to unconscious drives and motives), and the seeming cynicism of several of the characters. In the novel, Lawrence continued to develop his modernist style, evolving an imagistic language to evoke the ineffable nature of human subjectivity, as well as a fragmented form to depict the chaos of contemporary social existence. The text is a heartfelt exploration of the struggle toward a new mode of being—one that would reject alike the dead hand of obsolete cultural traditions and the iron cage of modern rationality in favor of openness to what Lawrence called "the creative soul, the God-mystery within us." *Women in Love* is an unresolved text that nonetheless boldly avers the writer's conviction that "nothing that comes from the deep, passional soul is bad, or can be bad." **AG**

Main Street

Sinclair Lewis

Lifespan | b.1885 (U.S.), d.1951 (Italy)
First Published | 1920
First Published by | Harcourt, Brace & Howe (N.Y.)
Full Title | Main Street: the Story of Carol Kennicott

Sinclair Lewis' *Main Street* presents a searing portrait of small town America. The premier satirist of his day, Lewis delivers a scathing social commentary that also becomes, through the story of protagonist Carol Kennicott, an urgent humanist manifesto that cries out for change in the American way of life. Carol, a new bride, finds herself locked in a new relationship and trapped in the stifling world of Gopher Prairie, Minnesota. Confronted by suspicion and hostility, Carol at first tries to change the town through many of the "improvement" schemes typical of the era, including the Chautauqua (a summer adult education school). As she struggles, the town itself changes with the expansion of modern suburban culture and the coming of the First World War. *Main Street* is filled with incidents of exaggerated social hypocrisy and downright cruelty; however, despite Lewis' satiric tone, the human relations within the world of *Main Street* retain a dignity and pathos that are intensely moving. Carol's eventual defeat by the forces of small-minded convention urges the reader to contemplate the dangers of isolationist thinking, but at the same time acknowledge the strength of the flawed, human ties that bind her to Gopher Prairie.

Lewis' prose is by turns caustic and emotionally charged, making the novel at once very funny and extremely serious. *Main Street* demonstrates Lewis' power as an important chronicler of American society in the early twentieth century. **AB**

The Age of Innocence

Edith Wharton

Lifespan | b.1862 (U.S.), d.1937 (France)
First Published | 1920
First Published by | D. Appleton & Co. (N.Y.)
Pulitzer Prize | 1921

Winner of the 1921 Pulitzer Prize for fiction, *The Age of Innocence* was written in the fragmented aftermath of the First World War, which Wharton experienced first-hand in Paris. Newland Archer, the ambivalent protagonist, represents the apogee of good breeding. He is the ultimate insider in post-Civil War New York society. His upcoming marriage to young socialite May Welland will unite two of New York's oldest families. From the novel's opening pages, however, May's cousin, the Countess Ellen Olenska, imports a passionate intensity and mysterious Old World eccentricity that disrupt the conventional world of order-obsessed New York. Ellen's hopes of being set free from her past are dashed when she is forced to choose between conformity and exile, while Newland's appointment by the Welland family as Ellen's legal consultant begins an emotional entanglement the force of which he could never have imagined.

Drawing on the distinct observational style of anthropology, then a burgeoning science, Wharton narrates a romance doomed by duty in 1870s "Old New York." Though Wharton's is a critical eye, mindful of the suffering often inflicted by the unimaginative, oppressive enforcement of arbitrary mores, the equation of greater liberty with unqualified happiness does not go unquestioned. **AF**

⊙ Actress Katharine Cornell appears in a 1929 stage production of *The Age of Innocence*, which was also made into a movie in 1993.

Crome Yellow

Aldous Huxley

Lifespan | *b.* 1894 (England), *d.* 1963 (U.S.)
First Published | 1921
First Published by | Chatto & Windus (London)
Original Language | English

*"The proper study
of mankind is books."*

⏺ Aldous Huxley's father and brother were both biologists, but his
poor eyesight prevented him from following a scientific career.

Crome Yellow, Huxley's first and highly successful novel, would probably be better loved and more often read if it were not for the dystopian *Brave New World*. *Crome Yellow* is an altogether lighter, wittier, more amusing book, which takes up with the novel the country-house literary satire pioneered by Thomas Love Peacock's *Nightmare Abbey*. Huxley's thinly disguised satirical portraits of his contemporaries fall somewhere between D. H. Lawrence's romances of exploratory sincerity and the more acerbic asperity of Wyndham Lewis.

The plot is pleasingly perfunctory, but also functional, seeing the reader through the hopeless love muddle of one rather shy Dennis Stone, sensitive plant, aspirant poet and his clumsy amours for Anne Wimbush. Anne's uncle hosts a party on his country estate, Crome Yellow, and this theater allows Huxley to introduce a variety of more or less ridiculous characters, among them Priscilla Wimbush, the hostess with the mostest and occult leanings; the painters Gombauld and Tschuplitski, whose work verges on blank canvas; and the self-help guru Mr. Barbecue-Smith. A distinguishing feature of Huxley's early satire, a prototype for Evelyn Waugh's early novels, is its relaxed but verbally acute derision of the pretensions of Huxley's peers, not least their clumsy emotional entanglements and "modern" sensibilities. Where satire often tends to foster reactionary contempt, Huxley's stylized mockery allows a sense of social wit, existential exploration, and verbal play. This, then, is a novel of high spirits lightly deflated. *Crome Yellow* has the edge on Huxley's subsequent and similar novel *Antic Hay* (1923), perhaps because the comedy is rougher, and more deliberately absurd, but both are entertaining. **DM**

The Fox

D. H. Lawrence

In *The Fox*, Lawrence does not have anything to prove. The rich symbolism and mysticism that enlarges his other novels, making them essentially and unmistakably Lawrencian, is not here totally absent but is subordinate to a story too brief and too self-contained to act as a vehicle for any larger narrative. This is not a negative quality; Lawrence the writer is present here both as a craftsman with language and as a man intimate with the back-breaking and frustrating nature of labor. But the story—simple and clean in its minimalist yet evocative economy—is present here undisturbed; it tells of nothing but itself and is all the more powerful for being thus contained.

It is a short and violent story of a conflict generated by desire and compelled toward defeat. A soldier returns just after the end of the Great War to the farmhouse he once shared with his grandfather. His grandfather is now dead and the house is occupied by two young women, March and Banford. The soldier stays with them, and before long he determines to have March. Against the background threat of a fox who has been stealing the women's chickens, we see a human fox emerge in the form of the soldier, and a strange battle of endurance ensues as the solidarity of the two women is shaken. March's fascination with the fox is gradually transferred to the man. Ultimately female friendship is defeated: the soldier cannot be a man, cannot be free, until he possesses a woman; the woman cannot be herself, cannot be essentially a woman, until she submerges herself in the male. But the distance Lawrence keeps from his subjects in *The Fox* gives this text a freedom and a joyfulness hidden by any brief summary. The book may be brief, but it is beautiful. **PMcM**

Lifespan | *b.* 1885 (England), *d.* 1930 (France)
First Published | 1923
First Published by | M. Secker (London)
First Serialized | 1922, in *The Dial* (London)

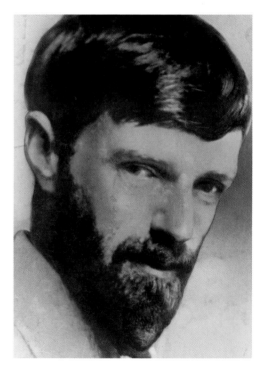

"She felt him invisibly master her spirit."

◉ In 1919, around the time this photograph was taken, Lawrence left England for good, subsequently living in Italy and Mexico.

Ulysses

James Joyce

Ulysses is one of the most extraordinary works of literature in English. At the literal level, it explores the adventures of two characters, Stephen Dedalus and Leopold Bloom, over the course of a single day in Dublin. But this is merely a peg onto which to hang all manner of streams-of-consciousness on topics ranging from such generalities as life, death, and sex through to the contemporary state of Ireland and Irish nationalism. Threaded through this work is a continuing set of allusions to the *Odyssey*—the original Homeric account of Ulysses' wanderings. Occasionally illuminating, at other times these allusions seem designed ironically to offset the often petty and sordid concerns which take up much of Stephen's and Bloom's time, and continually distract them from their ambitions and aims.

The book conjures up a densely realized Dublin, full of details, many of which are—presumably deliberately—either wrong or at least questionable. But all this merely forms a backdrop to an exploration of the inner workings of the mind, which refuses to acquiesce in the neatness and certainties of classical philosophy. Rather, Joyce seeks to replicate the ways in which thought is often seemingly random and there is no possibility of a clear and straight way through life.

Ulysses opened up a whole new way of writing fiction that recognized that the moral rules by which we might try to govern our lives are constantly at the mercy of accident, chance encounter, and by-roads of the mind. Whether this is a statement of a specifically Irish condition or of some more universal predicament is throughout held in a delicate balance, not least because Bloom is Jewish, and is thus an outsider even—or perhaps especially—in the city and country he regards as home. **DP**

Lifespan | *b.* 1882 (Ireland), *d.* 1941 (Switzerland)
First Published | 1922
First Published by | Shakespeare & Co. (Paris)
First Serialized | 1918–21, in *The Little Review* (N.Y.)

◔ Joyce had eye surgery to combat blindness; the world showed moral blindness in its response to his "immoral" book.

◔ The original manuscript of the *Circe* section of Ulysses shows the extensive revisions to which the author subjected his first draft.

Babbitt

Sinclair Lewis

Lifespan | *b.* 1885 (U.S.), *d.* 1951 (Italy)
First Published | 1922
First Published by | Harcourt, Brace & Co. (N.Y.)
Original Language | English

After the enormous success of his novel *Main Street*, Lewis turned to another icon of American life, this time the archetypal middle-class businessman, immortalized in the figure of George F. Babbitt. Babbitt is a real estate salesman who lives and works in the fictional Midwestern town of Zenith. His story is that of suburban life in a city which is filled with "neither citadels nor churches, but frankly and beautifully office-buildings." Lewis' novel satirically but lovingly details Babbitt's routines and rituals as he goes to and from work, socializes, plays golf, goes to the club, and becomes involved in local politics. In the midst of his contented and prosperous life, however, an event occurs that turns Babbitt's world upside down and forces him to examine his comfortable existence. Babbitt's resulting lurch from one uncertainty to another allows the reader to see beyond the shining office towers of Zenith to a grittier, more sobering but ultimately more human kind of American life.

Lewis' triumph here lies in taking a character that no one could possibly like—the self-important, conformist, and aggressively bigoted American businessman—and evoking not only barbed humor but vivid human feeling. *Babbitt* works as a political critique, piercing the smug veil worn by interwar American capitalism, but transcends mere amusing satire. Life in Zenith has a surprising depth; as such, it reminds us of the redemptive power of looking past ideology to the human relations beneath. **AB**

Aaron's Rod

D. H. Lawrence

Lifespan | *b.* 1885 (England), *d.* 1930 (France)
First Published | 1922
First Published by | M. Secker (London)
Full Name | David Herbert Lawrence

Although curiously neglected, *Aaron's Rod* is one of Lawrence's finest, most self-critical novels. Set amid the aftermath of the First World War and exhausted European sensibilities, the novel contrasts the mining community abandoned by Aaron with the pseudo-bohemian society of Bloomsbury London, before drifting into representations of the unstable, expatriot world of Milan and Florence.

Central to this comic structure is the cheekily implausible contrast implied between the biblical Aaron, brother of Moses, and Lawrence's latter-day Aaron, coal miner and amateur flautist. Aaron selfishly abandons the supposed slavery of domestic life, attempting to become a professional, itinerant musician. His flute doubles up as a modernist debunking of the power of biblical "rods," while also working as a hilarious deflation of Lawrencian phallic symbolism. Caught up in political riots, Aaron's flute is accidentally snapped, and the symbolic structure of the novel is broken apart with almost casual abandon. Working through acidic portraits of many of Lawrence's contemporaries, the novel offers a satirical self-portrait of Lawrence himself as Rawdon Lilly.

A very funny, sharp book, perhaps even more so than Lawrence intended, this novel's subtle dismantling of the paradigms associated with Lawrencian explorations into life, love, and sexuality may make awkward reading for particularly earnest Lawrence enthusiasts. **DM**

The Last Days of Humanity

Karl Kraus

Lifespan | *b.* 1874 (Czech Rep.), *d.* 1936 (Austria)
First Published | 1922
First Published in | *Die Fackel* (Leipzig)
Original Title | *Die Letzen Tage der Menscheit*

A play "to be performed on Mars," this immense work is sometimes put on by terrestrial theaters, but it is rather too long to be part of the regular repertoire. With its over 800 pages, it is more like a novel than a play in length, and it is certainly more often read than heard or seen in performance. Begun in 1915 and published in its final edition in 1922, this work is an overwhelming, incisive, and truthful indictment of the horrors and lies of the First World War, as seen from a Habsburg Empire living its "last days" without realizing it. Using collage techniques and combining quotes from every source imaginable (from Goethe to contemporary press reports to official bulletins to conversations overheard in the street), Kraus demonstrates that no invention can surpass the reality that is war, and that its fiercest opponent has no need to do anything but chronicle and repeat what he sees about him to show its inhumanity and absurdity. Kraus' great sensitivity to and love for language allows him to show just in how many ways and to what extent words, the means of beauty and of human interaction, can be desecrated and de-humanized. In *The Last Days of Humankind*, the intimate connection between a lack of respect for words and a lack of respect for mankind is traced. For Kraus, the empty, clichéd, manipulated language of press and politicians, generals, literati, and businessmen is directly linked to the horrors of a war in which countless men and women died for no good reason. **DG**

"The world has become uglier since it began to look into a mirror. . . so let us settle for the mirror image and do without an inspection of the original."

Kraus, In Praise, 1908

⊘ Austrian satirist Karl Kraus prophesied the approaching moral, aesthetic, and intellectual collapse of Western civilization.

Life and Death of Harriett Frean

May Sinclair

Lifespan | *b.* 1862 (England), *d.* 1946
First Published | 1922
First Published by | W. Collins & Sons (London)
Given Name | Mary Amelia St. Clair

Brief, bare, and cruelly ironic, this novel marked a turning point in Sinclair's career, reflecting her engagement with psychoanalysis as a (then new) theory of the unconscious mind, and the conflict between sexuality and social identity. On one level, it is a case history, inviting the reader to share the consciousness of Harriett Frean literally from cradle to grave. As the story opens, Harriett is in her cot, her parents amusing her with nursery rhymes, and wondering at her laughter: "Each kissed her in turn, and the Baby Harriett stopped laughing suddenly." It's a foreboding moment in a book that returns compulsively to the destruction written into parental love, to the demand for self-sacrifice embedded in their wish for their daughter to "behave beautifully."

Enraptured by the image of herself reflected by her parents, Harriett embarks on a life of renunciation. Its destructiveness is Sinclair's key theme, a critique of virtue that uncovers the fundamental attack on desire, on life itself, at work in the conventionally beautiful behavior of the Victorian middle classes. Sinclair's complex relation to modernity, and to literary modernism, is at the heart of this novel, which she uses to explore the "life" of a woman who cannot bring herself to destroy her parents' child. **VL**

🔾 Sinclair became a novelist after the First World War, in which she served as an ambulance driver, a formative experience in her life.

The Glimpses of the Moon

Edith Wharton

Lifespan | *b.* 1862 (U.S.), *d.* 1937 (France)
First Published | 1922
First Published by | Macmillan (London & N.Y.)
Original Language | English

In this novel Wharton continued to develop her interest in social satire, directing her comic eye to leisured society. *The Glimpses of the Moon* has been seen by some readers as a simplistic portrayal of the moral conflicts occasioned by love and marriage, eventually granted a comforting resolution. Two impoverished lovers, Nick Lansing and Susy Branch, decide to marry in spite of their lack of funds, somehow managing to survive by a variety of somewhat dubious means. The marriage all but collapses as a consequence of their morally questionable actions, and Nick is tempted by marriage to an heiress, while Susy looks set to make off with an English nobleman. But at the last minute both characters find themselves unable to go through with the divorce, since they feel that to marry solely for pecuniary gain would be morally corrupt. Ultimately, it is the institution of marriage that seems to be the mystical force which refuses to let these two chancers go their separate ways. It exerts an inexorable pressure on both protagonists, who are compelled to return to one another's arms and find themselves drawn "together again, in spite of reason, in spite of themselves almost."

The sentimental conclusion, of love triumphing over adversity, earned Wharton critical opprobrium. But the novel sold extremely well, thereby proving its popularity with the reading public. **AG**

Siddhartha

Hermann Hesse

Lifespan | *b.* 1877 (Germany), *d.* 1962 (Switzerland)
First Published | 1922
First Published by | S. Fischer Verlag (Berlin)
Nobel Prize | 1946

As the son of a Brahmin, Siddhartha enjoys both comfort and privilege while sequestered in his home village. However, as he grows older, his heart is moved by a burning desire to acquire wisdom and new experiences. Telling his father his intentions, Siddhartha and his childhood friend, Govinda, leave the safety of home to join the Samanas, a group of wandering ascetics. As Hesse's novel unfolds, we follow Siddhartha in his ongoing search for meaning and truth in a world of sorrow and suffering.

Drawing on both Hindu and Buddhist teachings, *Siddhartha* expertly explores the tension between the doctrinal dictates of organized religion and the inner promptings of the soul. As Siddhartha grows older, a fundamental truth gradually becomes apparent both to him and to us: there is no single path to self-growth, no one formula for how to live life. Hesse challenges our ideas of what it means to lead a spiritual life, to strive after and to achieve meaningful self-growth through blind adherence to a religion, philosophy, or indeed any system of belief. We should, rather, seek to seize hold of the reality of each moment, which is always new, alive, and forever changing. Hesse uses the potent symbol of a river to convey this sense of vibrancy and flux.

The particular brilliance of this novel is the way in which its profound message is delivered through a prose that flows as naturally and shimmeringly as the surface of the river beside which Siddhartha spends the final years of his life. **CG-G**

Jacob's Room

Virginia Woolf

Lifespan | *b.* 1882 (England), *d.* 1941
First Published | 1922
First Published by | Hogarth Press (London)
First U.S. Edition | Harcourt, Brace & Co. (N.Y.)

Jacob's Room, the first of Woolf's novels to be published by the press that she founded with Leonard Woolf, was also the work in which she broke with the fictional conventions that she felt had constrained her first two novels. *Jacob's Room* is an elegy for a lost brother and for the war-dead; one in which the narrative is structured around an absence—an empty room. It is a form of search or quest for a "character" who cannot be captured, not only because he himself is elusive but because other human beings are "utterly unknown" to us. The novel was in large part an ironic commentary on the over confident ways in which novelists had portrayed their characters as fully knowable and representable. While Jacob's experiences are typical of his privileged sex and class—public school, Cambridge, London life, travel abroad—he is given to the reader only in glimpses and through the limited perspectives of a narrator, and other, more fleeting figures. *Jacob's Room* works to deconstruct rather than to construct its central figure, and to expose the processes by which characters are composed in realist or naturalist novels.

Jacob's Room was, the novelist and critic Winifred Holtby wrote, Woolf's war book, though it "never mentions trenches, camps, recruiting officers, nor latrines." Rather, it asks what is lost when a young man is killed in war: "What was lost by him? What was lost by his friends? What exactly was it that had disappeared?" **LM**

The Enormous Room

E. E. Cummings

Lifespan | *b.* 1894 (U.S.), *d.* 1962
First Published | 1922
First Published by | Boni & Liveright (New York)
Full Name | Edward Estlin Cummings

This autobiography came about because Cummings and his friend B. (William Slater Brown) preferred, when in France in 1917, the company of French soldiers to that of their fellow Americans. They were working as volunteer drivers for the Norton-Harjes section of the American Red Cross when they were arrested and detained—in Cummings' case for nearly four months—in a holding prison in Normandy. B. had written home to his family in Massachusetts indiscreet letters concerning rumors of French mutinies that the authorities had intercepted, and Cummings was implicated. The eponymous room is where these interim prisoners live and sleep, their mattresses within inches of buckets of urine.

Cummings celebrates the oddity, and sheer peculiarity of his fellow detainees. They are given extraordinary names. He likes the Wanderer, Mexique, the Zulu, and above all Jean Le Nègre. He does not like The Sheeney With the Trick Raincoat or Bill the Hollander. Against these individuals, liked or not, stands (in irony) "the inexorable justice of *le gouvernement français.*" This classic anarchist structure sets individuals against all authority. Cummings asserts the values of a new, modernist art, which will require "that vast and painful process of Unthinking which may result in a minute bit of purely personal Feeling. Which minute bit is Art." For the rest of his life a more focused Cummings was to remain in his art an instinctive anarchist. **AMu**

"He is perhaps most curious of this pleasantly sounding thing which everyone around him, everyone who curses . . . and bullies him, desires with a terrible desire—Liberty."

Despite modernist techniques, Cummings belongs to the U.S. populist tradition, lauding love, individualism, and the underdog.

The Garden Party

Katherine Mansfield

Lifespan | *b.* 1888 (New Zealand), *d.* 1923 (France)
First Published | 1922
First Published by | Constable & Co. (London)
Given Name | Kathleen Mansfield Beauchamp

*"I'm a writer first
and a woman after."*

Mansfield, 1920

⊙ Mansfield's best stories are based on her memories of New
Zealand, where she grew up, although all were written in Europe.

The notoriously difficult-to-please Virginia Woolf famously cited Katherine Mansfield as the only writer whose work she had ever been jealous of, and Mansfield's high reputation as a modernist writer is borne out in *The Garden Party*, one of her finest stories. Set in an idyllic summer country house in New Zealand, it describes the seemingly innocuous plans of a large upper-middle class family as they prepare to host their annual outdoor picnic. The central consciousness is that of the family's idealistic daughter Laura, whose sensual response to the beauty of the summer day is combined with a heady sense of pleasure in her own growing-up. With the sudden, and violent, death of a laborer, Laura's happy self-confidence disappears, leaving her isolated from family and friends, unable to connect to the society in which she had felt so secure. Her resistance and conformity to her mother's ideas of appropriate class relations are painstakingly scrutinized.

Ambitious in scope but perfectly and minutely executed, in the space of just a few pages, *The Garden Party* takes its readers with fluid ease from a flower-filled summertime marquee to a sordid, death-filled cottage. As Laura confronts the world outside her own family for the first time, her certainties are eroded, but not to be definitely replaced; while for the reader, the subtlety of the conclusion and delicately shifting emotional landscape provide a much richer literary experience than most short stories. A premier modernist stylist, Mansfield's prose is spare and beautiful; no word in *The Garden Party* is superfluous or out of place, yet the resulting economy of style still allows for a readerly flexibility that was her hallmark. *The Garden Party* perfectly illustrates the ambiguity of love, and of family life; a masterpiece of short fiction. **AB**

Amok

Stefan Zweig

Stefan Zweig was a prolific novelist, biographer, translator, and world traveler. A notable pacifist, he fled his native Austria in 1934 to London and then Brazil where, disillusioned by the rise of fascism, he and his wife committed suicide. *Amok* is a short, intense story of a troubled doctor who loses his mind in the tropics. It is narrated by a worldly passenger who meets the mysterious doctor on board a ship returning to Europe from Calcutta. The doctor is in desperate need of human contact and has a chilling secret to confess. Written as reported speech that, like the colonial setting, recalls Joseph Conrad, it is a gripping tale of passion, moral duty, and uncontrollable unconscious forces.

The doctor has been forced to travel to Asia following a misdemeanor committed at a German hospital, where he was in thrall to a beautiful but domineering woman. Having set off full of romantic ideals of bringing civilization to the indigenous people, he finds himself isolated in a remote station, and his condition slowly deteriorates as the tropical torpor and solitude become too much for him. He becomes estranged from his European self and utterly dispirited. When an English lady arrives at his station requesting an abortion, he is provoked by her arrogance and domineering manner to such an extent that he loses control of his conscious will. At first he struggles to gain the upper hand in a veiled sado-masochistic scenario, but when she laughs in his face he can do nothing but pursue her in a manic attempt to appease his infatuation.

A Freudian exploration of the power of the unconscious and latent sexuality, *Amok* is a finely wrought story full of psychological insight. As such, it is an ideal introduction to Stefan Zweig's impressive body of work. **AL**

Lifespan | *b.* 1881 (Austria), *d.* 1942 (Brazil)
First Published | 1922
First Published by | S. Fischer Verlag (Berlin)
Original Language | German

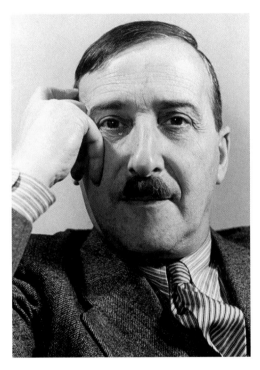

"We are all criminals if we remain silent . . . "

Zweig, 1918

◉ Zweig's work is notable for its psychological insight, which he applied in biographies of authors such as Stendhal and Tolstoy.

Antic Hay

Aldous Huxley

Lifespan | *b*. 1894 (England), *d*. 1963 (U.S.)
First Published | 1923
First Published by | Chatto & Windus (London)
Original Language | English

Antic Hay, Aldous Huxley's second novel, is an important book for two reasons: in its very structure and style, it captures the short-lived but profound cynicism of post-war English literary culture; in its arrogance and complacency, it reveals the blindness of that literary culture. Huxley came from an "intellectual aristocracy" that believed its values were universal. When the Great War threw into violent confusion precisely these values, Huxley and others of his class could see only the death of value. Because a belief in technological and joyless "progress" could no longer be adhered to, progress itself must be an illusion—because the educated classes of Europe, in a frenzy of nationalist pride, had slaughtered their sons in the names of Shakespeare and Goethe, education itself must be bankrupt. Because the civilizing power of "literature" had been unable to counter the uniformed credulity of "the masses," literature itself must be an illusion.

Antic Hay takes the values thrown into doubt by the war and subjects them to an effortlessly brilliant satire. With breathtaking insouciance and wit, Huxley shatters all the family crystal. Literature, in particular the novel, is also debunked: as the world is without meaning, the nineteenth-century novel's ambition to represent and explain that world was a pious piece of foolishness. Aldous Huxley's radicalism was limited—a nihilism bent on being amusing—but in producing *Antic Hay*, it created a wonderful record of the self-immolation of a culture. **PMcM**

Cane

Jean Toomer

Lifespan | *b*. 1894 (U.S.), *d*. 1967
First Published | 1923
First Published by | Boni & Liveright (New York)
First Reprint | 1967 (year of death)

Cane is a collection of poems, short stories, and what might today be called "flash fiction." *Cane's* tripartite structure suggests a striving after cultural synthesis. The first section gives life to a rural Georgia town. The second section looks to urban culture in Washington, D.C. with an interlude in Chicago. "Kabnis," the third section, is a short story hybridized with drama that details the vicissitudes of a Northern intellectual alienated from the spiritual underpinnings of American life in the South. Each section intertwines diverse forms and styles with elegant dexterity, exploring the structural integrity of the literary and social categories that define and divide. *Cane* navigates these classifications, among them race, class, and regionality, through the stories of characters marked as exceptional, whether by virtue of their beauty, their transgression of taboos, or their status as alien among naturalized populations. The artist figure as dramatized in "Kabnis" becomes the ultimate individual, struggling to harness the terrible intensity of his experience without being overtaken and destroyed by it.

This harbinger of the Harlem Renaissance appeared a decade after the regressive Wilson administration had turned the federal government into a segregationist institution. For Toomer, who was himself the child of an influential, mixed-race Washington family, this was above all an occasion to take stock of the complicated, multifarious experience of race in America. **AF**

Zeno's Conscience

Italo Svevo

Lifespan | b. 1861 (Italy), d. 1928
First Published | 1923, by Cappelli (Bologna)
Given Name | Ettore Schmitz
Original Title | La Coscienza di Zeno

In the life of Italo Svevo, the pen name of Ettore Schmitz, writing never took the place of a profession, but remained the secret passion he pursued when not involved in his office job or playing the violin. Two elements mark his life: his friendship with James Joyce, and his acquaintance with psychoanalysis through Freud, whose *Über der Traum* he translated.

This novel is Zeno's autobiography, written at the instigation of Doctor S. as part of his psychoanalysis. Zeno's account of his life is far from a tribute to Freud's science; rather, it is an opportunity to portray the transient and ephemeral character of people's desires. A typical anti-hero, Zeno has zero willpower and laughs at his incapacity to retain control of his existence. When he decides that marriage could cure his malaise, he proposes to the beautiful Ada, but accidentally ends up marrying Augusta, her unattractive sister. Zeno's neurosis becomes apparent in the account of his repeated and frustrated attempts to quit smoking. Helplessly dominated by the habit, Zeno fills his days with thousands of resolutions to ban cigarettes. Significant dates in his life are magical reminders of the possibility of a new smokeless life: "the ninth day of the ninth month of 1899," "the third day of the sixth month of 1912 at 12." Zeno needs to give himself prohibitions that he ritually infringes. His volatility and spinelessness always make his last cigarette the penultimate one, while he relishes the pleasure he derives from his own failure. **RPi**

The Devil in the Flesh

Raymond Radiguet

Lifespan | b. 1903 (France), d. 1923
First Published | 1923
First Published by | Grasset (Paris)
Original Title | Le Diable au Corps

Written only five years after the Great War, the story of a love affair between a sixteen-year-old boy and a young woman married to a soldier fighting on the front shocked public sensitivity. Radiguet himself added to the polemic by publishing an article on the novel just days after its appearance in which he calls his "false autobiography" all the more real for not being real. The youth of the author, his great promise, and the scandalous content of the story brought quick success to *The Devil in the Flesh*. Today it is regarded as a literary classic that has fascinated generations of readers and artists.

Because of his tempestuous life and early death Radiguet is often linked to Rimbaud. Radiguet denounced the label of "child prodigy" in his characteristically terse style, admitting, however, to an artistic affinity with both Rimbaud and Baudelaire. The anonymous protagonist of the story and his lover are thus initially brought together by their liking of *Les Fleurs du Mal*. Despite association with the surrealists and his love relationship with Jean Cocteau, Radiguet's influences can be traced back to French classicism. Consequently, *The Devil in the Flesh* is elegant and compact, often presenting psychological insight into the workings of ill-fated love in the form of short maxims. More importantly, however, the novel is a fiercely lucid indictment of the petit-bourgeois morals that left generations of young men and women tragically unprepared for the logic of both love and war. **IJ**

A Passage to India

E. M. Forster

Lifespan | b. 1879 (England), d. 1970
First Published | 1924
First Published by | E. Arnold & Co. (London)
Full Name | Edward Morgan Forster

Forster's last novel achieves a certain seriousness not evident in his earlier works. While he represents the British in India as stuffy caricatures of prejudice, Forster does not make them into the sustained parodies that we find in *Howard's End* or *A Room With A View*. At the heart of this liberal study of Anglo-Indian relations sits the vast emptiness of the booming Marabar caves, which Forster establishes as a site of ambiguity and uncertainty. Visitors to the caves are never sure what it is they have witnessed, if anything at all. Adele Quested, a British woman who is newly arrived in India, is accompanied to the caves by the Indian Dr. Aziz, and what happens between them there is never clearly established. Although the British assume that she was attacked by Aziz, Adele herself never confirms this. In fact, she spectacularly withdraws the allegation in court, and earns herself the opprobrium of her fellow countrymen. However, even this retraction fails to clarify the episode, which remains an example of the indeterminacy that characterizes Forster's modernist aesthetic.

If the rape trial is the center of the novel's plot, the friendship between Aziz and the sympathetic British humanists, Mrs. Moore and Cyril Fielding, represents the potential for connection across national lines (a central concept in Forster's writing). For some, the novel stands as a benevolent portrayal of the early nationalist campaign in India. Others, however, have pointed to Forster's inability to avoid exotic fantasy in his depiction of Indians. **LC**

We

Yevgeny Zamyatin

Lifespan | b. 1884 (Russia), d. 1937 (France)
First Published | 1924
First Published by | E. P. Dutton (New York)
Original Russian Title | *My*

The first novel to be banned by the Soviet censorship bureau in 1921, *We* is a prototypical dystopian novel, bearing similarities to later such fictions. The novel consists of a series of diary entries by D-503, a mathematician and a thoroughly orthodox citizen of the authoritarian, futuristic state to which he belongs. The diary sets out as a celebration of state doctrine, which dictates that happiness, order, and beauty can be found only in unfreedom, in the cast-iron tenets of mathematical logic and of absolute power. As the diary and novel continue, however, D-503 comes under the subversive influence of a beautiful dissident, named I-330. Enthralled by a wild desire for I, D loses his faith in the purity of mathematical logic, and in the capacity of a perfectly ordered collective to satisfy all human needs. Gradually, he finds himself drawn toward the poetic irrationality of $\sqrt{-1}$, and the anarchism of a private love. He no longer identifies with "we," and starts to think of himself, in an ironic reflection of the name of his guerrilla lover, as "I."

What sets Zamyatin's *We* apart is the intellectual subtlety of his understanding of authoritarianism. The novel is not a straightforward denunciation of communism, but a moving, blackly comic examination of the contradictions between freedom and happiness that state socialism produces. **PB**

❯ A poster from the early days of Bolshevik rule in Russia: Zamyatin's novel was later interpreted as an attack on Soviet totalitarianism.

The Magic Mountain

Thomas Mann

Lifespan | *b.* 1875 (Germany), *d.* 1967 (Switzerland)
First Published | 1924
First Published by | S. Fischer Verlag (Berlin)
Original Title | *Der Zauberberg*

The Magic Mountain opens with Hans Castorp making the journey from Hamburg to a tuberculosis sanatorium in the Swiss mountains. The first three weeks of what was supposed to be a temporary visit pass by achingly slowly. But Castorp is soon seduced by the repetitive, strangely enchanted existence of the patients. His imagination is caught by a series of vividly drawn characters who come to recuperate, and to die, on the mountain.

The novel belongs to the bildungsroman tradition, though Castorp's initiation is not into the world of action and events—the clamor of the approaching world war is consigned to somewhere below the quiet of the sanatorium—but into the world of ideas. Mann uses the debates between patients as a way of exploring the philosophical and political concerns of his time: humanism versus the very real threat of absolutism. Castorp must also struggle to understand what it means to fall in love in a place marked by illness and death—the troublingly intimate memento that Clavdia Chauchat confers upon her lover is an X-ray photograph of her clouded lungs.

The prospect of his return to the flatland is deferred, and as the weeks stretch into months and then into years, time seems not to pass by at all. We experience with Hans Castorp the intensity of the formative moments—tragic, erotic, mundane, absurd—of his seven years in the sanatorium, all suspended in a heightened present. **KB**

> *"Waiting we say is long. We might just as well — or more accurately — say it is short, since it consumes whole spaces of time without our living them or making any use of them as such."*

⊙ Thomas Mann drew material for *The Magic Mountain* from a period his wife Katia spent in a tuberculosis sanatorium in 1913.

The Green Hat

Michael Arlen

Lifespan | *b.* 1895 (Bulgaria), *d.* 1956 (U.S.)
First Published | 1924
First Published by | W. Collins & Sons (London)
Former Name | Dikran Kouyoumdjian

The Green Hat tells the story of the seductive Iris Storm—allegedly based on Nancy Cunard—whose forbidden love for her childhood sweetheart, Napier Harpenden, leads her through a series of tragic marriages and disastrous love affairs, culminating in her dramatic suicide. The novel made Arlen a celebrity, but this flamboyantly public figure also had close connections to some major figures of British modernism, such as D. H. Lawrence and Osbert Sitwell. Although *The Green Hat* remains a popular romance, its modernism is evident, for example in an affectionate parody of Sitwell's magazine, *The New Age*; the novel can also be read as a popular re-write of Ford's *The Good Soldier*, which Iris describes as an "amazing romance." Arlen's writing style, with its ambiguous, elliptical descriptions, is clearly influenced by modernism, while the imagery offers some particularly stark, oddly dislocated depictions resembling imagism.

These modernist elements combine with the conventional features of the romance, particularly where the novel comments on the pace of fashion and the modern age. For instance, Iris commits suicide by driving her car into the tree under which she and Napier declared their love. Clearly the grand romantic gesture is one of the clichés of the genre, but the use of the motor car, which figures as a symbol of high-speed modernity and is described through the image of a giant insect, seems an almost futurist diversion from convention. **LC**

Billy Budd, Foretopman

Herman Melville

Lifespan | *b.* 1819 (U.S.), *d.* 1891
First Published | 1924
First Published by | Constable & Co. (London)
Alternate Title | *Billy Budd, Sailor*

Billy Budd, Foretopman is Melville's last story, written late in his life and discovered among his papers posthumously. It is short enough to read in one sitting, but long enough to encompass a sense of life as tragedy. As with *Moby-Dick*, the main focus is on sailors and the ethical conflicts of naval life. This fable of human darkness and the fragile beauty of condemned youth somehow allows itself to be read from various perspectives, as a political morality play, as a metaphysical parable, or even as a tragedy of barely acknowledged male desires.

The tale, subtitled "an inside narration," tells how the youthful innocence and glamor of Billy Budd comes into conflict with the malign petty officer, Claggart. Goaded by Claggart, Billy strikes and accidentally kills him. In the subsequent trial, Captain Vere recognizes some of the moral complexity of Billy's "crime," but is nevertheless forced to convict him, and Billy is hanged, embracing his fate with beautiful resignation. The story is set historically, in the time before steamships, amid the shadows of the revolutionary spirit associated with the aftermath of the French Revolution, Paine's *Rights of Man*, and the Great Mutiny in the English navy. Providing ample material for diverse adaptations, such as Benjamin Britten's opera, it is nevertheless the unmatched, almost Shakespearean texture of Melville's narration that is most extraordinary, right through to the strange, concluding ballad. **DM**

The Professor's House

Willa Cather

Lifespan | *b.* 1873 (U.S.), *d.* 1947
First Published | 1925
First Published by | A. Knopf (New York)
Full Name | Willa Siebert Cather

*"He had never learned
to live without delight."*

⊙ Famous mostly for her portrayals of pioneer life in the American
West, Cather made it on to the cover of *Time* magazine in 1931.

The opening and closing sections of *The Professor's House* are chronologically sequential narratives of history professor Godfrey St. Peter's current domestic and professional lives. They flank an autobiographical confession made years before to St. Peter by his student Tom Outland. As Outland describes his discovery of an ancient civilization on New Mexico's Blue Mesa, a revelation of almost religious intensity, he imparts the dry, luminous clarity of his Southwestern origins. Tom Outland's seemingly boundless scientific and spiritual potential, and the paternal affection that St. Peter feels for him, sanctify him as a figure of lyrical perfection rendered complete by his early death in the First World War.

The professor's house is in fact two houses. On the one hand, there is the homely, perennially dilapidated house, now emptied and mostly uninhabited, where St. Peter raised his family and forged his career. On the other hand, there is the house that he had custom-built for his retirement, financed with a prestigious academic prize, which represents a comfortable future he has until recently resisted. When he first met Outland, St. Peter was an unorthodox young academic with financial and professional concerns, but by the time of the narrative he has achieved renown and even wealth by virtue of the same work that years ago was deemed unpublishable. St. Peter's daughter, who was engaged to Outland at the time of his death, capitalizes ruthlessly with her husband on Outland's tragic story and lucrative inventions. Though Outland has suffered, he has nevertheless been spared the petty indignities St. Peter endures as his sense of self is slowly usurped by institutional forces beyond his influence. **AF**

The Artamonov Business

Maxim Gorky

The Artamonov Business, one of Gorky's longest and most ambitious novels, tells the story of the merchant Artamonov family through three generations. Ilya Artamonov, a liberated serf, starts his own factory and tries to pass on what he sees as the bourgeois values of hard work and humility to his heirs, his son Pyotr and nephew Alexei. Ascending into the ranks of the middle classes brings only disaster for the Artamonovs, however, as Pyotr's weakness and Alexei's cold business sense lack the warmth and humanity that characterized Ilya's generation. In the third generation, the Artamonovs are visited by what seems to them to be disaster when their factory is taken over by the workers as part of the October Revolution. But as Gorky makes plain, the process of degeneration that has accompanied the family's rise to bourgeois status ensures the necessity of their downfall and paves the way for the possibility of a better world.

Here Gorky presents a sweeping family saga in the manner of *War and Peace*, but with Tolstoy's historical background replaced by a much more urgent and contemporary setting. The characters, both the damaged Artamonovs and the shifting cast of factory workers who co-exist with them, are vivid and lifelike. As in all of his novels, Gorky avoids the trap of political propaganda, treating all of the figures—workers and capitalists alike—with a sardonic yet ultimately sympathetic eye. Readers of the novel will find themselves catching a glimpse of the fervor of revolutionary Russia that allowed many, including Gorky, to be swept away on a wave of new hope for societal change. *The Artamonov Business* remains a valuable novel, both for its literary skill and for its value as the product of a poignant moment in Russian history. **AB**

Lifespan | *b.* 1868 (Russia), *d.* 1936
First Published | 1925, in *Russkaia Kniga* (Berlin)
Given Name | Aleksey Maksimovich Peshkov
Original Title | *Delo Artamonovic*

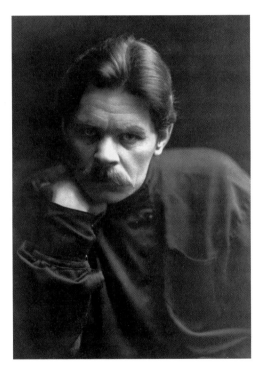

"When everything is easy one quickly gets stupid."

Gorky, 1926

◉ Gorky had an often difficult relationship with Russia's Bolshevik rulers; this novel was written during a period of self-exile in Italy.

The Trial

Franz Kafka

"Somebody must have made a false accusation against Josef K., for he was arrested one morning without having done anything wrong."

As in Kafka's long story *Metamorphosis*—which begins with the line "Gregor Samsa awoke one morning from uneasy dreams to find himself transformed in his bed into a gigantic insect"—the entire narrative of *The Trial* emerges from the condition that announces itself in the opening sentence. The protagonist, Josef K., never discovers what he is being charged with, and is never able to understand the principles governing the system of justice in which he finds himself ensnared. Instead, the narrative follows his exhausting determination to understand and to protest his innocence in the complete absence of any doctrine that would explain to him what it would mean to be guilty, or indeed, of what he actually stands accused. In following Josef K.'s struggle toward absolution, the novel presents us with an astonishingly moving account of what it is to be born naked and defenseless into a completely incomprehensible system, armed only with a devout conviction of innocence.

Intimacy with this novel has a peculiar effect. If the first response to K.'s grappling with the authorities is a sense of familiarity and recognition, there is soon a strange reversal. It begins to seem that our world merely resembles Kafka's; that our struggles are a faint likeness of the essential struggle that is revealed to us in K.'s endless plight. For this reason *The Trial*, in all its inconclusion, its impossibility, and its difficulty, is a wildly exhilarating book, which takes us to the very empty heart of what it is to be alive in a world of everyday trials pushed to the extreme. **PB**

Lifespan | *b.* 1883 (Czechoslovakia), *d.* 1924 (Austria)
First Published | 1925
First Published by | Die Schmiede (Berlin)
Original Title | *Der Prozeß*

Franz
Kafka
Der
Prozeß
Roman

◐ This "Man at Table" sketch forms part of a series taken from Kafka's 1905 lecture notes from the Kierling Sanatorium (Vienna).

◑ Anthony Perkins starred as the bewildered K. in Orson Welles' darkly expressionistic film version of *The Trial*, made in 1962.

The Counterfeiters

André Gide

Lifespan | *b.* 1869 (France), *d.* 1951
First Published | 1925
First Published by | Gallimard (Paris)
Original Title | *Les Faux-Monnayeurs*

Significantly, Gide's only novel worthy of the name is an investigation into the possibilities of the novel. Edouard, one of the many narrative voices in *The Counterfeiters*, is also a struggling novelist. He, like Gide, keeps a diary documenting the process of novel writing. He, too, is trying to write a novel called *The Counterfeiters*. In a vertiginous effect of mise-en-abyme, we are reading a novel about a novelist writing a novel about a novelist writing a novel . . . This is one of the many devices that Gide employs to wrongfoot the reader. Another is the deception of the title. Just as Gide flirts with recognized genres such as the romance and the bildungsroman, the possibility of a detective fiction with schoolboys passing off fake gold coins is hinted at but never followed through. Counterfeit coins serve as a metaphor for false values more generally—those put into circulation by the state, the family, the church, and the literary establishment.

The Counterfeiters does not make things easy for us: we are deprived of a reassuringly impersonal narrative voice, we are introduced to characters who turn out to have no role to play, and the threads of the novel's many different plots are left hanging. But this is also why it is so important. Reading *The Counterfeiters*, all of our certainties as readers of nineteenth-century novels are called in question. Which means that we are also uncertain of Gide: in the midst of all this inauthenticity, what actually guarantees the value of *The Counterfeiters*? **KB**

The Great Gatsby

F. Scott Fitzgerald

Lifespan | *b.* 1896 (U.S.), *d.* 1940
First Published | 1925
First Published by | C. Scribner's Sons (New York)
Full Name | Francis Scott Key Fitzgerald

The Great Gatsby is an American literary classic. Nick Carraway's enraptured account of the rise and fall of his charismatic neighbor during a single summer came to evoke the pleasurable excesses and false promises of a whole decade. The novel's extraordinary visual motifs—the brooding eyes of the billboard, the ashen wasteland between metropolitan New York and hedonistic Long Island, the blues and golds of Gatsby's nocturnal hospitality —combined the iconography of the "jazz age" and its accompanying anxieties about the changing social order characteristic of American modernism. Gatsby, infamously created out of a "platonic conception of himself," came to be synonymous with nothing less than the American Dream.

Gatsby's lavish and hedonistic lifestyle is a construct, we quickly learn, erected in order to seduce Daisy, the lost love of his youth who is now married to the millionaire Tom Buchanan. Fitzgerald's easy conjuring of Gatsby's shimmering fantasy world is matched by his presentation of its darker and more pugnacious realities. The novel frequently hints at the corruption that lies behind Gatsby's wealth, and Tom is shown to be a crude and adulterous husband. The novel's violent climax is a damning indictment of the careless excess of the very privileged, yet it concludes ambivalently. **NM**

❯ Fitzgerald and his wife Zelda during Christmas, 1925, belie the strains that soon brought their lives to breakdown point.

(Jan 3rd 1924)

100
80
80

at last

There was an age when the pavement was grass; another when it was swamp; an age of tusk & mammoth; an age of silent sunrise; & through them all the battered woman — for she wore a skirt — with her right hand exposed, her left clutching at her knees, stood singing of love; which love unconquerable in battle which she sang, after lasting for millions of years after a had lasted a million years. Yes, a million years so the sang, her lover, & which the sang was immortal through her lover, & millions of years ago her lover, in May, her lover, who had been dead three centuries, had walked, the crooned, with her in May; but in the course of ages, when long as summer days, & being flaming, so she remembered with nothing but red flowers, he had gone; death's enormous sickle had swept over those tremendous hills; & now, when she laid her hoarse immensely she laid her hoary & immensely aged head on the earth now become a mere cinder of ice. It would have outlived everything — her memory of happiness even — she implored that "Lay by my side a branch of purple heather"; there where on that high burial place what the last ray of the last sun caressed a prickle of purple heather; for the The pageant of the universe would be over.

Mrs. Dalloway

Virginia Woolf

Woolf's novel *Mrs. Dalloway* takes place over the course of a single day, and is one of the defining texts of modernist London. It traces the interlocking movements around Regent's Park of the two main protagonists: Clarissa Dalloway is a socialite, and wife of Richard Dalloway, a Conservative MP, while Septimus Warren Smith is a veteran and shell-shocked victim of the Great War. The passage of time in the novel, punctuated by the periodic striking of a giant, phallic Big Ben, ultimately takes us to a double climax; to the success of Mrs. Dalloway's illustrious party, and to the suicide of Septimus Warren Smith, who finds himself unable to live in the postwar city.

Much of the effect of this novel derives from the irreconcilability of its two halves, an irreconcilability which is reflected in the space of the city itself. Different people go about their different lives, preparing for suicide and preparing for dinner, and there is no way, the novel suggests, of building a bridge between them. Septimus and Clarissa are separated by class, by gender, and by geography, but at the same time, the novel's capacity to move from one consciousness to another suggests a kind of intimate, underground connection between them, which is borne out in Clarissa's response to the news of Septimus' death. A poetic space, which does not correspond to the clock time meted out by Big Ben, underlies the city, suggesting a new way of thinking about relations between men and women, between one person and another. *Mrs. Dalloway* is a novel of contradictions—between men and women, between rich and poor, between self and other, between life and death. But despite these contradictions, in the flimsy possibility of a poetic union between Septimus and Clarissa, the novel points toward a reconciliation we are still waiting to realize. **PB**

Lifespan | *b.* 1882 (England), *d.* 1941
First Published | 1925
First Published by | Hogarth Press (London)
First U.S. Edition | Harcourt, Brace & Co. (N.Y.)

Woolf was always dogged by bouts of depression, attempting suicide in her early thirties and finally drowning herself in 1941.

Woolf's draft notes for *Mrs. Dalloway* explore the experience of a reality she found "very erratic, very undependable."

Manhattan Transfer

John Dos Passos

Lifespan | *b.* 1896 (U.S.), *d.* 1970
First Published | 1925
First Published by | Harper & Bros. (New York)
Full Name | John Roderigo Dos Passos

Manhattan Transfer is a brilliant portrayal of the aesthetics and social dimensions of early twentieth century New York. In lieu of a conventional plot, Dos Passos stitches together numerous tableaux, quickly cutting from one visual frame to another, emulating a skillfully manned movie camera, as he records the bustling city's social inequalities and the potentially devastating effect of anonymity and alienation on the human psyche. Exemplifying the latter, a man who is severely injured by a falling object pathetically hopes that a girl he has been admiring from afar is among the crowd gathered to view the spectacle of his accident. Elsewhere, men entering and exiting a revolving door are compared to processed sausages—devoid of individuality and gradually consumed by the capitalist machine to which they are indentured. Headlines and billboards interpolate the plot, reflecting the extent to which desires and fears are shaped by capitalism. In the opening scene, Susie Thatcher complains to the nurse when she notices that her newborn daughter "hasn't any label on it," an overt commentary by the author on the extent to which market forces impinge upon the most intimate of human experiences. *Manhattan Transfer* deserves to be read for its unflinching depiction of both the visual intoxications and socio-economic deprivations that characterize modern urban life. **CG-G**

The Making of Americans

Gertrude Stein

Lifespan | *b.* 1874 (U.S.), *d.* 1946 (France)
First Published | 1925
First Published by | Contact Editions (Paris)
Original Language | English

Stein's innovative prose has a measured beauty that is best enjoyed with the rhythm and pace of the spoken word. This epic novel reinvents and simultaneously challenges the form of the traditional family saga, as it follows several generations of four families, but to summarize it in such a way fails to do it justice. Moving back and forth in time with fluidity, Stein traces the internal, emotional development of people as they mature, as they relate to their spouses and their community, and, ultimately, as they become American; this is done with an almost cubist desire to show the events in all their facets and from many angles. *The Making of Americans* also takes time to comment upon its own composition, and contains some of Stein's most comprehensive comments upon her conception of writing and her unique style.

Somewhat underrated as a modernist classic, the novel certainly has all the hallmarks of a text that forges a new and idiomatic use of language while challenging the previous Victorian concept of realism. It is also an epic interpretation of the Americans' psychological development, reaching back to the founding families and the generations they produce and nurture. Challenging, beautifully written, and rightfully a literary masterpiece, *The Making of Americans* deserves to be ranked among the forefront of modernist achievements. **JC**

The Murder of Roger Ackroyd

Agatha Christie

Lifespan | *b.* 1890 (England), *d.* 1976
First Published | 1926
First Published by | W. Collins & Sons (London)
Full Name| Agatha Mary Clarissa Christie, D. B. E

All detective novels have twists, but the masterpiece of Christie's extensive oeuvre trumps them all, reverting on some of the fundamental principles of the genre in its startling denouement. This novel contains many of the ingredients for which Christie became famous: a couple of bodies, a country house setting, a small group of suspects, and the moustache-twirling Belgian detective, Hercule Poirot. As narrated by the local doctor, Sheppard, there is a veritable profusion of possibilities as to who murdered Roger Ackroyd: is it the parlormaid, the retired major, Ackroyd's stepson, or a mysterious stranger seen lurking about the grounds? This (partial) list suggests some of the incidental interest of Christie's novel, which conveys social and class structures in rural 1920s England. Everyone, as Poirot says, has a secret, and the novel teasingly unveils an illegitimate son, a secret marriage, blackmail, and drug addiction as possible motives for the stabbing. Red-herrings and dubious alibis abound: the actual time of the murder has been ingeniously concealed, Ackroyd's voice being heard from beyond the grave, recorded on a dictaphone, the disappearance of which provides Poirot with a vital clue. For the reader, deducing the true criminal is almost impossible; this is one of the few detective novels which compels a second reading, to see how the murderer's tracks are so masterfully obscured. **CC**

One, None and a Hundred Thousand

Luigi Pirandello

Lifespan | *b.* 1867 (Italy), *d.* 1936
First Published | 1926
First Published by | R. Bemporad (Florence)
Original Title | *Uno, nessuno e centomila*

Being the object of a friend or relative's close scrutiny may at times come as a surprise, especially if the observer is cruelly right in highlighting some of our minor physical imperfections. But for Moscarda, the protagonist of Pirandello's novel, his wife's unexpected comment about his nose, slightly bent to the right, triggers a sensational change in his life. His wife sees Moscarda totally at variance with his self-image. Moscarda suddenly realizes that he lives with an inseparable stranger and that for others— his wife, his friends, and his acquaintances—he is not at all who he is for himself. Moscarda is forced to live with a thousand strangers, the thousand Moscardas that others see, who are inseparable from his own self and yet whom, dramatically, he will never know.

Pirandello's favorite theme of the relativity of perception and the fragmentation of reality into incomprehensible pieces is his philosophical core. Closely connected to it is the reflection on language and the impossibility of objective and satisfactory communication between speakers, due to the fact that we all charge words with our own meanings. As Moscarda obsesses over the painful realization that he is only what others make of him, he tries to subvert others' reality by reinventing himself as a new, different, Moscarda. But his attempt to own his own self is in vain, and his only way out is self-denial, starting with a refusal to look at mirrors. **RPi**

The Plumed Serpent

D. H. Lawrence

Lifespan | b. 1885 (England), d. 1930 (France)
First Published | 1926
First Published by | M. Secker (London)
Full Title | The Plumed Serpent: Quetzacoatl

By 1926 Lawrence's personal odyssey was well under way. The despair manifested in *Women in Love* had been displaced by the idea that the male self functions best alone, outside the constraints of marriage, but subordinated to powerful leaders, an idea developed further in *The Plumed Serpent*. Situated in Mexico, the novel traces the experiences of Kate Leslie, a woman who finds herself caught up in a revolution driven by the conscious manipulation of a primitivist religious cult. It is a perplexing novel, which has offended critics who see its obsession with strong, charismatic leaders as quasi-fascistic and its gender politics, which requires women to submit to "superior" men, as pernicious. Its concern with social and individual regeneration, however, makes it a characteristic Lawrencian work.

At its heart is an imagined opposition between two antithetical modes of life, one of which is seen as European, overly rational, and conscious, the other of which is depicted as pre-Columbian and associated with the instincts and a passionate relationship with the cosmos. In some of his critical writing, Lawrence insisted that his hostility to a mechanized European society did not mean that he wanted absolutely to reject conscious thought but rather that he wanted to radicalize it. But *The Plumed Serpent* almost exclusively emphasizes the positive value of a "blood-consciousness" that depends completely on disturbing racial stereotypes and objectionable phallocentric rhetoric. **AG**

The Good Soldier Švejk

Jaroslav Hašek

Lifespan | b. 1883 (Czechoslovakia), d. 1923
First Published | 1926, by A. Synek (Prague)
First Published in four volumes | 1921–1923
Original Title | Osudy dobrého vojáka Švejka

The Good Soldier Švejk is, in the original, a monumental and unfinished collection (Hašek died before he could complete the last two volumes) of comically epic adventures, involving an accidental soldier in the Austro-Hungarian army during the First World War. The brilliance of the novel depends on the hapless but well-meaning central figure Švejk—walking on the margins of history, yet somehow constantly altering its outcome. This he achieves by doggedly doing precisely what is required of him, while frustrating the system's expectations by being always and entirely himself.

In Švejk, Hašek—who had himself variously been a soldier, dog-stealer, drunkard, and cabaret performer—invented and perfected a fictional type. A prototypical Forrest Gump, Švejk was taken up in Czechoslovakia as a national hero, capable because of his (apparent) artlessness of exposing the assertive lies of power. The batman to a Czech lieutenant, Švejk was dragooned into service for idle remarks uttered in a tavern about the assassination of Archduke Ferdinand. Throughout his adventures, and perhaps because of their multiplicity, it is never clear how much of Švejk's character is calculation and how much wide-eyed innocence. Along the way he manages to attack propaganda, bureaucratic self-servingness, and an all-pervading secret state. **DSoa**

▶ Illustrator Josef Lada's original images of Švejk's misadventures have imposed his vision of the characters on readers ever since.

The Castle

Franz Kafka

FRANZ KAFKA

Das Schloss

ROMAN

KURT WOLFF VERLAG
MÜNCHEN

*"And must one have
a permit to sleep here?"*

The first edition of *The Castle* (*Das Schloss*) was published in
Munich in 1926, two years after Kafka's death from lung disease.

Lifespan | *b.* 1883 (Czech Rep.), *d.* 1924 (Austria)
First Published | 1926
First Published by | K. Wolff (Munich)
Original Title | *Das Schloss*

It stands as testament to the achievements of Franz Kafka that the unfinished state of *The Castle* is in no way detrimental to its effectiveness. Unlike *The Trial* and *The Metamorphosis*, the literal entirety of the story is not contained in the first line; whether this is due to the unfinished nature of the novel is impossible to know, but *The Castle* is certainly a more miasmic, elusive work than even these. In this respect it seems somehow right that there is no ending, that the events recounted seemingly form part of an infinite series of which a small segment has found its way onto the pages of a novel.

The arrival of the land surveyor K in the village that surrounds the castle, and the discovery that he is not wanted, and cannot stay, constitutes the total narrative, but the progression through the relatively straightforward points is typically nightmarish. Kafka's integration of absurdity and realism is at its most subtle here; events never veer from the apparently literal, but somehow remain totally alien. Despite the apparent fixedness of characters on a page, the feeling of detachment, that everyone is self-consciously playing a part, is inescapable. More than it tells a story, *The Castle* evokes an atmosphere, which is of perpetual unease. There is a suggestion of fear lurking just out of sight with all else obscured by the interminable obstacles of bureaucracy. The entirety of the novel is akin to that final moment in a dream when you try to speak and find no air to carry your voice, time slowed to a crawl. **SF**

Blindness

Henry Green

Lifespan | *b.* 1905 (England), *d.* 1973
First Published | 1926
First Published by | J. M. Dent & Sons (London)
Given Name | Henry Vincent Yorke

Green was to gain considerable renown as a writer's writer, and all of his novels are in some sense "experimental." His singular prose style inverts conventional word order, utilizes curious parenthetic constructions, deploys unnecessary demonstratives, and omits a whole range of words normally used to connect clauses. Green's first novel, *Blindness*, already reveals his fascination with language as a means of communication and his modernist desire to shape it anew.

The novel tells the story of John Haye, a young man who is accidentally blinded and must learn to live with the loss of visual perception. Haye gradually comes to realize that there are other ways of processing sensation, experiencing life and construing reality. Haye is preoccupied with the nature of language and with writers who are known as original literary stylists. His interest in the problem of expression marks him out as someone who is not content with the surface aspect of social life; phenomena observed from the outside and accepted as "reality" are shown to be products of a deeper blindness than that which afflicts the novel's protagonist. Narrated from a range of viewpoints, *Blindness* draws on the technique of stream of consciousness for its presentation of different perspectives. Here Green explored the inner world of the mind and suggested that the death of sight perhaps presaged the birth of a more profound form of experience and a deeper mode of knowledge. **AG**

"[A] kind of informal diary would be rather fun."

⊙ Cecil Beaton took this defiantly unrevealing photo of Green in 1949, perhaps hinting at the novelist's focus on inner experience.

The Sun Also Rises

Ernest Hemingway

The cynical irony of the title—an oblique reference to narrator Jake's mysterious First World War wound, and what no longer rises because of it—sets the tone for this "Lost Generation" novel. A band of cynical, hard-living expatriates swirls like a hurricane around a comparatively peaceful eye, Jake. In its depiction of the group's journey from *l'entre deux guerres* Paris to Pamplona for July's *fiesta*, *The Sun Also Rises* captures a war-shaken culture losing itself in drink and drama, and eschewing all but the occasionally comforting illusion of meaningful experience. Quixotically irascible, Robert Cohn dramatizes the romantic hero's final crash into absurdity, as he cultivates a disruptive infatuation with Jake's former lover, Brett, who shares neither Cohn's intense affection nor his fraught-with-significance worldview (though she does share his bed). Jake, by contrast, forms the spiritual center of the group, based on his stoic affability and capacity to withstand even the most intense emotional agitation, merely thinking to himself that he feels "damned bad." Condemned to be a perpetual outsider, he experiences a tortured admiration for the cultural values and aesthetics of Spain.

Hemingway's first major novel represented a stylistic breakthrough. Though its influence on later writing has slightly obscured its radical character, comparing the style of *The Sun Also Rises* with those more established contemporaries, such as Ford Madox Ford and Theodore Dreiser, gives a sense of Hemingway's innovation. The spare, journalistic prose—embodying the simple spirit of acceptance for which Jake is revered—creates a language seemingly devoid of histrionics, allowing characters and dynamics to come through cleanly and clearly, to a perhaps still unequalled degree. **AF**

Lifespan | *b.* 1899 (U.S.), *d.* 1961
First Published | 1926, by C. Scribner's Sons (N.Y.)
Alternate Title | *Fiesta*
Nobel Prize | 1954

The first edition cover was designed not to reflect the clipped prose style and modernist irony of Hemingway's innovative novel.

Hemingway stands with Sylvia Beech outside her bookshop, Shakespeare & Co., a focus for expatriate writers in Paris.

Amerika

Franz Kafka

Lifespan | *b.* 1883 (Czech Rep.), *d.* 1924 (Austria)
First Published | 1927, by K. Wolff (Munich)
Composed | 1912–1914
Original Language | German

At the tender age of sixteen, Karl Rossmann finds himself in exile, shipped to the New World after shaming his family by getting a serving girl pregnant. Despite being alone and vulnerable in a strange land, he has youthful optimism and irrepressible good humor on his side. Karl sets out to seek his fortune, and finds work as an elevator boy in a hotel. He gets fired and drifts on again, meeting a succession of bizarre characters, and in the final chapter joins a mysterious traveling theater.

This is an unsettling and disorienting vision of America. On arrival, Karl observes the Statue of Liberty holding a huge sword aloft. This and other puzzling details—a bridge across the Hudson conveniently connects New York with Boston—may simply reveal that Kafka never visited America, but they also create a paradoxical world that is fascinating and sinister, boundlessly open and broodingly claustrophobic. Here is a place where success can bring vast wealth and fine mansions, where failure can lead to misery and rootlessness.

Familiar Kafkaesque themes are already developing—the implied threat of nameless authority, the fear of being singled out, the sense of identity slipping away. *Amerika* was never finished, but there is enough to tantalize us into speculating about its conclusion. The final scene, in which Karl heads west on a train through spectacular scenery, is a paean to the American Dream. Was this intended as a Kafka novel with a happy ending? **TS**

Tarka the Otter

Henry Williamson

Lifespan | *b.* 1895 (England), *d.* 1977
First Published | 1927
First Published by | G. P. Putnam's Sons (London)
Original Language | English

An otter is born, grows up in the waterways of Devon, is hunted by men and dogs as well as facing a number of man-made hazards, and eventually, probably, dies by their hand. This is the essence of *Tarka the Otter*, but it is not its whole. *Tarka* is notable for its lack of anthropomorphic identification and its meticulous, sometimes pedantic depictions of pastoral life through the eyes of a wild animal.

This is not a comfortable tale of humanized creatures, and it avoids the rural idyll while skilfully exploiting it. Williamson's great strength in this book is the alienation of Tarka, who is, and always remains, feral. This refusal to succumb to personalization, a strong reflection of Williamson's sense of introversion following the First World War, makes *Tarka the Otter* stand apart from its successors. *Tarka* often shows disdain for both human and mechanized intervention; metal and guns are the enemy, providing rude interruptions in the steady life of the Devon waterways. This is not an easy or simple life—Williamson presents it as a neutral space of great pastoralism, yet this space is interrupted continually by man or his creations; traps, wires, and the great hunting dog "Deadlock," who pursues Tarka throughout the text. This disdain for metal and man is testimony to Williamson's post-war disgust with his fellow man, a disillusionment later echoed in his wartime novel, *The Patriot's Progress*, and the epic series *The Chronicles of Ancient Sunlight*, which saw him return to the subject of the human world. **EMcCS**

To The Lighthouse

Virginia Woolf

Lifespan | *b.* 1882 (England), *d.* 1941
First Published | 1927
First Published by | Hogarth Press (London)
Full Name | Virginia Adeline Woolf

To The Lighthouse was Virginia Woolf's most autobiographical novel, in which she represented her parents, Julia and Leslie Stephen, through the fictional characters of Mr. and Mrs. Ramsay. The novel's structure is that of two days separated by a passage of ten years. In the first part, "The Window," the Ramsay family and assorted guests are depicted during a day on the Hebridean island on which they have their summer home. The novel's central section, "Time Passes," is an experiment in modernist narration, as Woolf absorbed into her fiction the representational forms suggested to her by the new art of the cinema; Mrs. Ramsay dies and the world war intervenes to fracture history and experience. In the final section, "The Lighthouse," the artist figure Lily Briscoe finishes the painting of Mrs. Ramsay whose "vision" had formerly eluded her, and Mr. Ramsay and his two youngest children, James and Cam, reach the lighthouse, having made the journey planned with the first words of the novel.

The novel is a ghost story of a kind, in which Woolf explored the impact of death, representing it indirectly as it resonates throughout the narrative. She reversed the priorities of the novel, bracketing off death and marriage in the novel's central section, and focusing instead on the changes wrought by time on matter. It is a profound exploration of time and memory, of Victorian conventions of masculinity and femininity, and of the relationship between art and what it seeks to record. **LM**

TO THE LIGHTHOUSE

VIRGINIA WOOLF

PUBLISHED BY LEONARD & VIRGINIA WOOLF AT THE
HOGARTH PRESS, 52 TAVISTOCK SQUARE, LONDON. W.C.
1927

"So that is marriage, Lily thought, a man and a woman looking at a girl throwing a ball."

● *To The Lighthouse* was published by the Hogarth Press, which was set up by Virginia Woolf and her husband Leonard in 1917.

Remembrance of Things Past

Marcel Proust

It has often been said that the importance of Marcel Proust's monumental novel lies in its pervasive influence on twentieth-century literature, whether because writers have sought to emulate it, or attempted to parody and discredit some of its traits. However, it is equally important that readers have enjoyed the extent to which the novel itself unfolds as a dialogue with its literary predecessors.

Remembrance of Things Past, (or *In Search of Lost Time*) is the daunting and fashionable three-thousand-page "story of a literary vocation," on which Proust worked for fourteen years. In it, he explores the themes of time, space, and memory, but the novel is above all a condensation of innumerable literary, structural, stylistic, and thematic possibilities. The most striking one is the structural device whereby the fluctuating fortunes of the bourgeoisie and the aristocracy from the mid-1870s to the mid-1920s are narrated through the failing memories of an aspiring writer, Marcel, who succumbs to many distractions. This defect of memory entails misperceptions of all sorts, partly corrected, bringing rare moments of joy by the faculty of "involuntary" memory. These moments of connection with the past are brought about by contingent encounters in the present, which re-awaken long-lost sensations, perceptions, and recollections. It is these moments that give the novel its unique structure, which, no doubt more than any other novel, calls for careful reading. Appropriately, the publication of this epic novel in French is still evolving, as scholars continue to work on notes and sketches. The novel has also recently attracted new translators into English, long after the first translation into English between 1922 and 1930. Proust's "mass of writing," as it has sometimes been described, continues to expand. **CS**

Lifespan | *b.* 1871 (France), *d.* 1922
First Published | 1913-27 in seven volumes
First Published by | *Nouvelle Revue Française* (Paris)
Original Title | *À la recherche du temps perdu*

A hypersensitive, neurotic asthma sufferer, Proust had many characteristics in common with his novel's fictional narrator.

Proust handwrote his massive masterpiece in school exercise books, endlessly crossing out and rewriting as he went along.

Steppenwolf

Hermann Hesse

Lifespan | *b*. 1877 (Germany), *d*. 1962 (Switzerland)
First Published | 1927, by S. Fischer Verlag (Berlin)
Original Title | *Der Steppenwolf*
Nobel Prize for Literature | 1946

Harry Haller, the protagonist of *Steppenwolf*, feels himself painfully divided into two diametrically opposed personas. One is associated with his intellect and the noble ideals to which he aspires, while the other consists of the baser instincts and desires of the flesh. *Steppenwolf* chronicles this tension that dominates Haller's inner life from three distinct perspectives: his bourgeois landlady's nephew, a psychoanalytic tract, and Haller's own autobiographical account. With the help of some of the novel's other characters, Haller gradually learns that "every ego, so far from being a unity is in the highest degree a manifold world, a constellated heaven, a chaos of forms . . . " He determines to explore the multiple aspects of his being, experimenting with his sexuality, frequenting jazz clubs where he learns to dance the fox-trot, and socializing with groups of people whom he formerly regarded with condescension and derision. Thus he realizes that these pursuits are to be valued as much as the thrill of intellectual discovery. The highly experimental, perplexing nature of the conclusion goes some way to explaining why *Steppenwolf* is the most misunderstood of Hesse's works.

In addition to a brilliant and thought-provoking meditation on the tumultuous process of self-discovery, *Steppenwolf* is a scathing and prescient critique of the complacency of Germany's middle class amidst the escalating militarism that preceded and made possible Hitler's rise to power. **CG-G**

Nadja

André Breton

Lifespan | *b*. 1896 (France), *d*. 1966
First Published | 1928
First Published by | Gallimard (Paris)
Original Language | French

Breton's *Nadja* is the most well-known and most enduring example of the "surrealist novel." This semi-autobiographical work is an account of Breton's relationship with a strange and unconventional young woman in Paris. Nadja is an enigmatic, haunting presence; she is both material and immaterial, modern and ancient, artificial and carnal, sane and mad. She is a state of mind, a projection that disrupts the structures of everyday reality, a metaphor for "the soul in limbo." Using the figure of Nadja, perhaps rather questionably, Breton channels the key elements of surrealist thought: accident, shock, desire, eroticism, magic, and radical freedom. The narrative consists of a series of chance encounters around the city, jumping from point to point with its own unconscious logic. Notionally a "romance," *Nadja* is really a meditation on surrealism as a way of life, overturning the distinctions between art and world, dream and reality.

A literary collage, the prose is supplemented by images, including sketches by Nadja herself, prints of surrealist paintings, and numerous photographs. *Nadja* is a rich, textured surface of ideas, a repository of what the critic Walter Benjamin calls "profane illuminations." From the mainstream to the avant-garde, and from literature to advertising, *Nadja's* influence continues to be felt. **SamT**

⊙ Breton wearing a crown of thorns. Although not seen here, above is a quote from his Surrealist Manifesto headed "auto-prophecy."

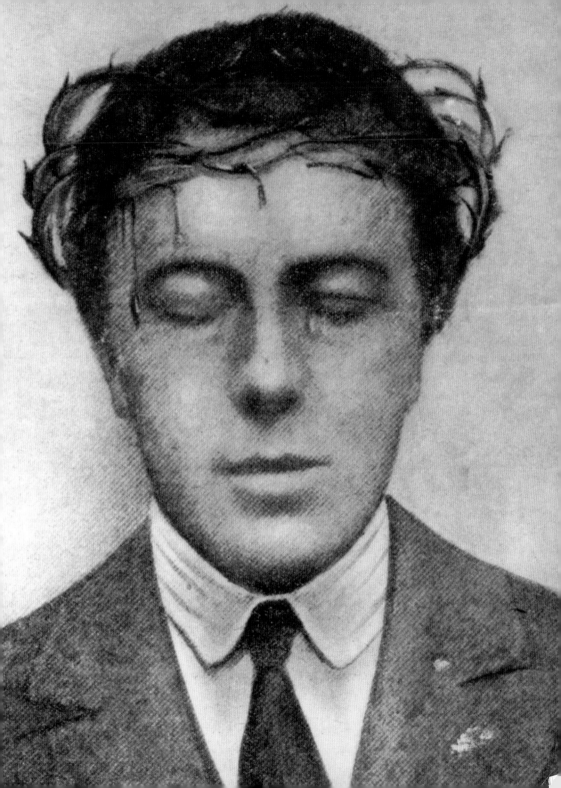

Parade's End

Ford Madox Ford

Lifespan | *b*. 1873 (England), *d*. 1939 (France)
Last Volume of Tetralogy Published | 1928
First Published by | Duckworth & Co. (London)
Tetralogy Published as Single Volume | 1950

Ford Madox Ford's gargantuan *Parade's End*, one of many First World War classics, is frequently hailed as the "best war book." This may be because it is both one of the most comprehensive, and yet most understated, of the war books, using Ford's characteristic modernism to subtly portray a world falling into deceit. Civilian concerns and activities are subtly investigated, as Ford charts the passage of Christopher Tietjen's wartime service and the breakdown of his marriage to the villainous Sylvia.

As with so many of the war books, it is often difficult to separate the author from their fictional counterpart, and Ford, who was blown up and partially deafened by a shell in the trenches whilst shaving, is no exception. The last of the *Parade's End* books were published slightly before the more aggressive diatribes against war formed a seemingly cohesive voice. As such Ford's is perhaps a more well-mannered war. Tietjen's shock and lack of comprehension of his circumstances is symptomatic of the confused responses of veterans, and the quartet's impressionist atmosphere adds to this inability to fully comprehend the impact of the war upon even one person. Yet Ford's work now stands as a rather dense investigation, and his indirect war message is less clearly received by the present generation, accustomed as it is to a more stereotypical vision of mud, guts, and poppies. "No more hope, no more glory, not for the nation, not for the world I dare say, no more parades." **EMcCS**

Quicksand

Nella Larsen

Lifespan | b. 1891 (U.S.), d. 1964
First Published | 1928
First Published by | A. Knopf (New York)
Original Language | English

Helga Crane is the protagonist in Nella Larsen's compelling and loosely autobiographical novel, *Quicksand*. Born of a white Danish mother and a West Indian father, Helga Crane is a restless and rootless figure in search of sexual and social acceptance. The novel begins in the claustrophobic atmosphere of "Naxos," a black college in the South, then moves north, first to Chicago and on to Harlem, where Helga is initially welcomed by the emerging intellectual class. Next she travels to Denmark, where her blackness is celebrated in problematically exotic and erotic ways. In each of these locations, Helga is forced to reject both the proposals of unsuitable lovers, and her own growing desire. In the end she marries a preacher and returns to the American South where she sinks into a "quagmire" of harsh reproductive and domestic labors.

The novel is an honest examination of the contradictory promises that twentieth-century America held out to women. Helga Crane is socially vulnerable, yet she is also able to hesitatingly articulate a desire for pleasure and self-fulfilment. The novel makes clear the particular tribulations faced by the "mulatto" woman who can claim no community. The promise of the future is suggested by depictions of the pleasures of urban anonymity and of the relations between gender and desire. But it is this future's utter failure to materialize, and Helga's acceptance of a blind sacrifice in its place, that makes the ending so bitterly damning. **NM**

Decline and Fall

Evelyn Waugh

Lifespan | b. 1903 (England), d. 1966
First Published | 1928
First Published by | Chapman & Hall (London)
Full Name | Evelyn Arthur St. John Waugh

Waugh's debut novel, *Decline and Fall,* introduced the world to the acerbic and hilarious style for which he became famous. The story is of the "mysterious disappearance" of Paul Pennyfeather, a young middle-class everyman, into "extraordinary adventures" that are as absurd as they are arresting. The appeal of the book, however, lies not in its plot, but in its relentless and caustic wit, and the biting satire it aims at swathes of British society.

Amongst the abysses that pepper Paul's "disappearance" are a ludicrous expulsion from Oxford, appointment as a master at a carnivalesque boarding school in North Wales, engagement to a wealthy socialite, and a spell in prison. Surrounding the roller-coaster rise and fall of this hapless protagonist are a cast of recurring characters that are intoxicating in their colorful absurdities. From a pedophilic lush with a peg leg, to a "modern churchman" destined to have his head hacked off by a crazed religious visionary, *Decline and Fall* teems with a host of unforgettable characters.

Underneath this incredible abundance lies a not-so-thinly veiled attack on a variety of targets. From the vicissitudes of modern architecture to the moral turpitude of the upper classes, Waugh casts satirical barbs with ruthless accuracy. Although a sense of hopelessness seems to underlie these critiques, it is impossible to criticize the direction of the moral compass of this novel, which remains unremittingly superb in its comic intensity. **DR**

Quartet

Jean Rhys

Lifespan | b. 1890 (Dominica), d. 1979 (England)
First Published | 1928, by Chatto & Windus (Lon.)
Given Name | Ella Gwendolen Rees William
Original Title | *Postures*

Quartet is a thinly veiled *roman à clef* resulting from Jean Rhys' lengthy and increasingly bitter affair with the novelist Ford Madox Ford. Its technical artistry owes much to the lessons of his literary mentorship. Marya Zelli is the first instance of a protagonist who is "reckless, lazy, a vagabond by nature," acquiescing in a cultural myth of vulnerable femininity with self-destructive passivity. Wandering aimlessly through Paris after the imprisonment of her husband, Marya is taken in by the expatriate art dealer H. J. Heidler and his wife Lois. The Heidlers are the villainous "good Samaritans" of the novel's epigraph, who offer comfort and support, yet who will ultimately manipulate her for their own ends.

Marya's seduction by Heidler, in which Lois is coldly complicit, her miserable acceptance of her role as a kept "petite femme," her eventual rejection and despair, and the final fight with her husband in which she is left for dead are portrayed with a mixture of stark realism and almost gothic metaphor. Ford's version of the same events present Rhys as delusional, pathologically dependent, and given to violent alcoholic rages, a reputation that has stuck despite the best efforts of her biographers. Through Marya, Rhys defends herself as a victim of psychological depression and the machinations of others, articulating, in her feverish interior monologue, a critical resistance to the hypocrisy of gendered power relations, even though this never manifests in self-recognition or outward action. **DPa**

The Childermass

Wyndham Lewis

Lifespan | *b*. 1882 (Canada), *d*. 1957 (England)
First Published | 1928
First Published by | Chatto & Windus (England)
The Human Age **Trilogy Published** | 1950

Lewis' hypnotic fiction of the afterlife is a forgotten masterpiece of high modernism. The first part of *The Human Age* trilogy, *The Childermass* is a critique of modernism itself, and a politically radical text that precedes and contradicts Lewis' later move to the right. The setting is "Outside Heaven," where Pullman (a version of James Joyce) meets Satters, who has the body of a man and the mind of a child. An odd couple, they wander through an ever-changing landscape near a river resembling the Styx, awaiting examination by the sinister Bailiff, who controls this world. Slowly it emerges that common-sense Satters, not the intellectual Pullman, accurately perceives the shifts in space and time that occur as they walk. Pullman wants to believe that all is stable, but is revealed as a deluded supporter of the Bailiff.

In the language given to Pullman, Lewis shows what it is like to be dominated by an idea—and therefore to be a victim of ideology. This is modernism's auto-critique, and is derived from Lewis' "An Analysis of the Mind of James Joyce" (in *Time and Western Man*), where Joyce is revealed to have absorbed ambient philosophical ideas, which reappear in *Ulysses*, to disintegrate the stable subject that Lewis valued. *Ulysses* is today the master-text of modernism, but Lewis saw it as a victim text. His objections to the cultural consequences of the dominance of "time-philosophies" over ideas valuing space make Lewis a founder of cultural studies. **AMu**

The Well of Loneliness

Radclyffe Hall

Lifespan | *b*. 1880 (England), *d*. 1943
First Published | 1928
First Published by | Jonathan Cape (London)
Given Name | Marguerite Radclyffe-Hall

On its publication in 1928, *The Well of Loneliness* prompted one of the most famous legal trials for obscenity in the history of British law, resulting in a twenty-year ban. At the same time, it brought the existence of lesbians to the attention of the public and each other in an unprecedented way.

The Well of Loneliness tells the story of the "invert" Stephen (named by a father desperate for a son) who is painfully aware of her "queerness" from an early age. Following her first love affair, Stephen is thrown out of her beloved family home in the secure and wealthy Midlands, and travels to London and then Paris, becoming a successful writer. Serving with the ambulance corps on the front line in the First World War, Stephen meets and falls in love with a young girl called Mary—the final part of the novel tells the story of their relationship.

For some modern readers, the novel is outdated with its almost gothic melodrama, its nineteenth-century theories of sexual orientation, and its deep pessimism with regard to the fate of those who choose lovers from their own sex. But there are others for whom the novel still strikes a painfully resonant chord. The book's power derives from its unerring and possibly unnerving perception of heterosexual society, and the devastating effects of both its prejudices and its norms. **SJD**

> Radclyffe Hall published poems and two other novels before *The Well of Loneliness* brought her notoriety.

Lady Chatterley's Lover

D. H. Lawrence

The publication history of *Lady Chatterly's Lover* provides a plot itself worthy of a novel. Published privately in 1928 and long available in foreign editions, the first unexpurgated edition did not appear in England until Penguin risked publishing it in 1960. Prosecuted under the Obscene Publications Act of 1959, Penguin was acquitted after a notorious trial, in which many eminent authors of the day appeared as witnesses for the defense.

Due to this infamous history, the novel is most widely known for its explicit descriptions of sexual intercourse. These occur in the context of a plot which centers on Lady Constance Chatterly and her unsatisfying marriage to Sir Clifford, a wealthy Midlands landowner, writer, and intellectual. Constance enters into a passionate love affair with her husband's educated gamekeeper, Oliver Mellors. Pregnant by him, she leaves her husband and the novel ends with Mellors and Constance temporarily separated in the hope of securing divorces in order to begin a new life together.

What remains so powerful and so unusual about this novel is not just its honesty about the power of the sexual bond between a man and a woman, but the fact that even in the early years of the twenty-first century it remains one of the few novels in English literary history that addresses female sexual desire. It depicts a woman's experience of the exquisite pleasure of good sex, her apocalyptic disappointment in bad sex, and her fulfilment in truly making love. As if all this were not enough to mark *Lady Chatterly's Lover* as one of the truly great English novels, it is also a sustained and profound reflection on the state of modern society and the threat to culture and humanity of the unceasing tide of industrialization and capitalism. **SJD**

Lifespan | *b.* 1885 (England), *d.* 1930 (France)
First Published | privately in 1928 (Florence)
First English-Language Publication | 1932
Published by | M. Secker (London)

Penguin's jacket for the first 1960 edition bears the emblem of the phoenix, which beckons to Lawrence's *Phoenix* Essays.

Eager purchasers of *Lady Chatterley* look for the dirty bits after the obscenity trial that cleared the book for sale in Britain in 1960.

Orlando

Virginia Woolf

Lifespan | *b.* 1882 (England), *d.* 1941
First Published | 1928
First Published by | Hogarth Press (London)
Original Language | English

For a demonstration of the sheer vitality of Woolf's writing, *Orlando* is unsurpassed. It is a provocative exploration of gender and history, as well as the very nature of biography; perhaps surprisingly, it was highly popular when first published.

Following the adventures of Orlando over a four-hundred-year life that encompasses wild adventure, love, and a shift in gender, the character was apparently based on Woolf's lover Vita Sackville-West. In the exuberant court of Elizabeth I, Orlando is a dazzlingly handsome sixteen-year-old nobleman. There follows a frost fair on the Thames at which a love affair with a Russian princess begins, only to end in heartache. Later he is sent by Charles II as ambassador to the Ottoman court in Constantinople, where he becomes a woman, before returning to England to reside in the company of Pope and Dryden. A marriage in the nineteenth century leads to a son and a career as a writer, and the story ends in 1928, as Woolf's text was published.

This extraordinary tale is augmented by a series of writerly flourishes, questioning our conception of history, of gender, and of biographical "truth." If these are constructs, then who constructs them? What do they mean for individuals living and telling their lives? Woolf uses a series of devices to facilitate this kind of speculation: clothes are prominent, as is their role in shaping perceptions of gender; the narrative voice too is brilliantly conscious of itself, and of us as readers. It is a remarkable text. **MD**

"The chief charges against her were (1) that she was dead, and therefore could not hold any property; (2) that she was a woman which amounts to much the same thing . . ."

⊙ Aristocratic bisexual novelist Vita Sackville-West was the model for the character of the androgynous Orlando in Woolf's novel.

Story of the Eye

Georges Bataille

Lifespan | *b.* 1897 (France), *d.* 1962
First Published | 1928
Original Title | *Histoire de l'oeil*
Pseudonym | Lord Auch

This classic of literary pornography also happens to be a significant surrealist novel. Bataille—French librarian, sometime Marxist thinker, and literary critic—also wrote a classic, non-fictional study of eroticism. *Story of the Eye* synthesizes traditions of French literary-pornographic writing, abandoning the complications of libertine plotting or the notorious encyclopedia of body parts and orifices associated with de Sade. Bataille instead offers a quicker, more associative kind of pornographic dream. There are sexual acts and various defilements, but Bataille's erotic novel is as much dominated by death, language, and literary analysis as it is by action. Here we have pornography, but pornography for intellectuals.

Told in the first person, this short novel's plot moves between fantasies and the subsequent acting out of various erotic obsessions involving an array of objects, ranging from a cat's saucer to an antique wardrobe. The story invests more meaning in objects than in characters, while narrative situations emerge as rhetorical conceits linking objects to contexts in a string of metaphorical displacements, characteristic of literary surrealism. Bataille's prose poetics, however, have a stringency and clarity very different from the arbitrary reverie characteristic of other surrealists. Overall, the novel is rounded off by Bataille's remarkable analysis of the book's confessional account of coincidences between memories and obscene images. **DM**

Look Homeward, Angel

Thomas Wolfe

Lifespan | *b.* 1900 (U.S.), *d.* 1938
First Published | 1929, by Grosset & Dunlap (N.Y.)
Full Title | *Look Homeward, Angel: A Story of the Buried Life*

On one level, *Look Homewood, Angel* is a portrait of the artist as a young man writ large, with the action transferred to a small but affluent hill town in North Carolina. Wolfe is no modernist, however, and lacks Joyce's subtle, ironic touch and Flaubertian control of his material. Yet in these shortfalls lie his distinct qualities, for instead he gives us sheer exuberant expression. Wolfe is an old-fashioned writer in the tradition of Whitman and Melville; he "tried the hardest to say the most," wrote Faulkner, who considered him the greatest writer of his generation, as well as the "best failure."

The narrator is budding artist Eugene Gant, an idealistic young man governed by an active imagination and a yearning for transcendence. Yet he is incapable of belief in the conventional idea of God, and equally unable to shake off a firmly held determinist view of the human condition. Eugene's growth from infancy to early manhood is a journey characterized by his quest for self-knowledge and his resultant loneliness and frustration. The real quality of the novel, however, lies not in the portrayal of Eugene's struggle to find a place in the world, but in the rich, vivid account of the life that surrounds him. At the heart of the family saga lies a compelling tension between Eugene's parents; his father is a heavy-drinking, womanizing, yet loveable man, while his mother is practical and hard-working, keeping their family of ten afloat despite her husband's hell-bent intention to destroy it. **AL**

GAUMONT DISTRIBUTION présente un Film de MELVILLE-PRODUCTIONS
Une Réalisation de **JEAN-PIERRE MELVILLE**
Les Enfants Terribles
d'après le Roman célèbre de
JEAN COCTEAU
avec **NICOLE STÉPHANE**, **EDOUARD DERMITHE**
RENÉE COSIMA, JACQUES BERNARD
MEL MARTIN, MARIA CYLIAKUS, JEAN-MARIE ROBAIN, MAURICE REVEL. ADELINE AUCOC, RACHEL DEVYRIS
et
ROGER GAILLARD

Les Enfants Terribles

Jean Cocteau

Lifespan | *b.* 1889 (France), *d.* 1963
First Published | 1929, by Grasset (Paris)
Alternate Title | *Children of the Game*
U.S. Title | *The Holy Terrors*

Les Enfants Terribles is a claustrophobic tale of love and attraction transformed into jealousy and malice, a comment on the destructive and unstable nature of human relationships, written in the wake of discoveries about the unconscious inaugurated by Freud and others. The book can also be read as a child's nightmare. Virtually all the story takes place within one room after the book's famous opening scene when Paul, a sensitive young man, is injured by a snowball thrown by the sexually charismatic bully, Dareglos, with whom he is infatuated. He is forced to take to his bed in the cluttered and oppressive room that he shares with his sister, Elisabeth. Here they play a series of games, alternately arguing and making up. When Elisabeth brings Agathe to stay with them, Paul develops a crush on her because of her resemblance to Dareglos, which inflames Elisabeth's jealousy.

Many find the novel's portrayal of damaged and obsessive adolescence prophetic of the roles played out by young Europeans and Americans after the Second World War. Paul and Elisabeth have few connections with life outside, retreating into a fantasy world in which they consume each other with their over-heated emotions and unrestrained needs. They are simultaneously tragic figures who stand for the fate of humanity and irritating, immature youths whose behavior is both comic and ridiculous. Cocteau also wrote the screenplay for Jean-Pierre Melville's celebrated film (1950). **AH**

> *"Wealth is an inborn attitude of mind, like poverty. The pauper who has made his pile may flaunt his spoils, but cannot wear them plausibly."*

○ This portrait of Cocteau is by Picasso, one of a galaxy of cultural superstars with whom he was associated in the course of his career.

○ In Melville's 1950 movie of Cocteau's novel, Nicole Stéphane and Edouard Dermithe played the over-intimate siblings.

The Sound and the Fury

William Faulkner

Lifespan | *b*.1897 (U.S.), *d*.1962
First Published | 1929
First Published by | J. Cape & Harrison Smith (N.Y.)
Full Name | William Cuthbert Faulkner

William Faulkner insisted that *The Sound and the Fury* "began with the mental picture" of a small girl's stained undergarment up a tree. Under the tree, two of her three brothers regard it. In post-publication interviews, Faulkner suggests that the four sections of the novel, three of them streams of consciousness belonging to the brothers, "grew" from his repeated attempt to explain that very "symbolical picture."

This begs two questions: why should the first viewpoint on this fictional account of a declining Southern middle-class family be that of an idiot incapable of drawing temporal distinctions? The idiot's section consists of fragmented scenes, drawn non-chronologically from between 1898 and 1928, which have no determinable pattern save concern for a sister. Since each brother is preoccupied with his sister's sexuality, the second question must be: why should a hymen elicit such sound and fury? In plantation Mississippi, in the 1920s, a sister's virginity signifies (the titular allusion to Macbeth not withstanding) "something." Where a regional economy depends on black agricultural labor held in place by debt, and black males are seen to pose a sexual threat, they are ever vulnerable to white violence in the preservation of the region's integrity. Sisters' drawers are therefore matters for surveillance. Where better to hide their wearer's integrity, and that of her region, than in the barely penetrable but fascinating consciousness of an idiot? **RG**

Harriet Hume

Rebecca West

Lifespan | *b*. 1892 (England), *d*. 1983
First Published | 1929
First Published by | Hutchinson & Co. (London)
Full Title | *Harriet Hume: a London Fantasy*

Harriet Hume is an enchantingly beautiful pianist, who lives alone in a flat with a magical, and inaccessible, London garden. One of her admirers is Arnold Condorex, a highly ambitious young man seeking to make his fortune and reputation in government. He and Harriet meet on occasion over the years, but his enthrallment to money and power prevents him from seeing her true worth and nearly leads to his ruination. Most disturbing to Arnold is Harriet's ability to read his mind, an uncanny power which leads him to view her as his malignant "opposite" until the novel's close, when they are united and the principles of femininity and masculinity are finally reconciled.

Harriet Hume is at once fantasy, allegory, satire, and wish fulfillment. Its style is mock-archaic, and it is one of a number of satires and historical fantasies to emerge in the first decades of the twentieth century. In West's novel, as in other works of the period, modernism is in dialogue with the eighteenth century, and the London of *Harriet Hume* is that of Nash's and Adam's architecture, its neo-classical figures and ornamentations taking on a vivid life of their own. Harriet is a fantasist, a teller of fairy-tales whose characters also come to life in Arnold's increasingly fevered and careworn imaginings. The city, with its squares, parks, and streets, is an enchanted place, and this "London Fantasy"—as the novel was subtitled—was written, West claimed, to find out why it was that she loved London. **LM**

The Last September

Elizabeth Bowen

Lifespan | *b.* 1899 (Ireland), *d.* 1973 (England)
First Published | 1929
First Published by | Constable & Co. (London)
Full Name | Elizabeth Dorothea Cole Bowen

Although *The Last September* is reminiscent in style of Virginia Woolf's early novels, Bowen's work remains more readable because it lacks the rather abrupt narrative discontinuities that characterize Woolf's orthodox modernism. The novel centers on the detached personality of Lois, the niece of an aristocratic Anglo-Irish family, and on the seemingly pointless socializing of her class. Danielstown, the Anglo-Irish "Big House," also serves throughout as a personification of this class, and its fading charms epitomize the dwindling significance of the Anglo-Irish ascendancy. In this milieu, the novel comes to resemble a sort of sterile updating of Jane Austen, with the search for a suitable marriage foundering on the double axes of an active snobbery based on family lineage, and a financial impoverishment born of the obsolete nature of Ireland's rural economy.

As the novel progresses, this haven of privilege is increasingly breached by the representatives of a new world in the form of English soldiers and Irish nationalists. Just as the Anglo-Irish are symbolized by Danielstown's deteriorating furnishings, these interlopers are seen as the scions of modernity, which is represented by their weaponry—whether a buried arms cache or an armored car. This clash of cultures is best realized through Bowen's depiction of an IRA gunman that Lois encounters in the grounds of Danielstown. The gunman is presented as indistinguishable from his pistol, suggesting a singleness of purpose that Lois realizes she lacks. **LC**

> *" . . . it appears to me that problems . . . loom unduly large when one looks ahead. Though nothing is easy, little is quite impossible."*
>
> Preface, The Last September, *1952 reprint*

⬤ Bowen, who wrote short stories as well as novels, is pictured here in the same year that *The Last September* was published.

Berlin Alexanderplatz

Alfred Döblin

Lifespan | *b.* 1878 (Poland), *d.* 1957 (Germany)
First Published | 1929
First Published by | S. Fischer Verlag (Berlin)
Original Language | German

"This awful thing which was his life acquires a meaning."

⬙ Phil Jutzi directed a successful movie version of the novel in 1932; it was made into a TV serial by Rainer Fassbinder in the 1980s.

Berlin Alexanderplatz ranks alongside the work of Joyce and Dos Passos both as one of the great urban epics of the 1920s, and as an attempt to innovate the novel. Utilizing a montage style that owes much to cinema, the novel is as much about a place as it is about a "story."

At one level, the novel can be thought of as a morality tale; its focus is ex-convict Franz Biberkopf, and his vain attempt to become a "decent" human being. He is an archetypally naïve "little man," around whom a playful narrator constructs a complex narrative of crime, temptation, and betrayal. Franz attempts a variety of jobs, loses his arm in a bungled robbery, becomes a pimp, falls in love, and is finally betrayed and framed for murder by his nemesis, Reinhold. Döblin populates working-class eastern Berlin with a memorable cast of shady underworld characters, and is sensitive both to the rhythms of their speech and the patterns of their lives.

However, the novel is chiefly remembered for its style. The narration incorporates and evokes the sensations of the city, and suggests a sense of the speed, contrasts, and bewildering simultaneity that define it. In a conscious rejection of traditional conceptions of the novel, the multi-layered narrative gives free rein to the competing discourses of the metropolis. The reader is greeted with newspaper reports, exchanges between random characters, advertising hoardings, street signs (literally, in the form of illustrations), and lines from popular songs. Additionally, biblical and classical allusions suggest, again in playful manner, Döblin's desire to create a modern epic. The effect is exhilarating, and what one initially assumes will simply form the setting—the city of Berlin—becomes the star of the show. **JH**

All Quiet on the Western Front

Erich Maria Remarque

The epigraph of *All Quiet on the Western Front* states that the intention of the book is to be neither an accusation nor a confession, but an account of a generation, including the survivors, "destroyed by the war." But rather than a warning, or even a statement of self-defense, this epigraph, marked by its simplicity and clarity, is a one-sentence declaration, however quiet, that what follows is a story of destruction.

In the polarized political debates of the Weimar Republic, the Great War was not a topic but a touchstone for all else. How you understood the war, its origins, its conduct, surrender, and defeat, was the index to your understanding of the past and to your understanding of how liveable or damaged the future could be. Given this interpretive context, the pacifism of the novel could satisfy neither left nor right ends of the critical spectrum in inter-war Germany. But Remarque's text does not assume or argue for pacifism; it simply enacts it as an appalled response to the daily efficiencies of organized slaughter. It is this quiet, certain, yet exploratory demonstration of the utter inhumanity of war that constitutes the magnificence of *All Quiet on the Western Front* as an anti-war novel.

Central to Remarque's achievement is the voice of Paul Bäumer, the novel's nineteen-year-old narrator. He is one of a band of front-line soldiers whose experience of war strips the mythology of heroism bare, leaving the tedium, the earth-shaking fear, the loneliness, and the anger of men whose bodies are neither protected nor honored by military uniforms. The novel ends with the disappearance of Bäumer's voice; it is replaced by the polite brevity of the report of his death on a day in which all was quiet on the western front. **PMcM**

Lifespan | *b.*1898 (Germany), *d.*1970 (Switzerland)
First Published | 1929, by Propyläen (Berlin)
Original Title | *Im Westen nichts Neues*
Given Name | Erich Paul Remark

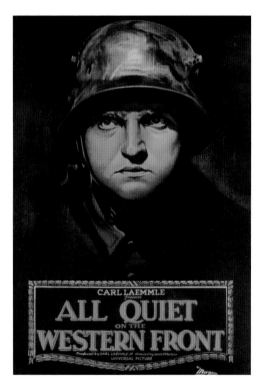

"One could sit like this forever . . . "

◉ Lew Ayres starred as Paul Bäumer in the 1930 movie version of Remarque's novel, regarded as one of the finest anti-war films.

The Time of Indifference

Alberto Moravia

Lifespan | *b.* 1907 (Italy), *d.* 1990
First Published | 1929, by Alpes (Milan)
Original Title | *Gli indifferenti*
Given Name | Alberto Pincherle

Moravia's early masterpiece, produced when he was eighteen, was written after the murder of Matteotti, who openly opposed Mussolini in parliament, when the Fascist regime enjoyed popular consensus. Although the work does not contain explicit references to the Italian political situation, the story of a middle class family, depicted as helpless victims of the corruption of their social entourage, clearly has a political message. The novel's central motif highlights the inadequacy and incapacity of the characters to deal with reality, marked by an indelible and congenital weakness. Mariagrazia, her son Michele, and daughter Carla, although afflicted by a serious financial crisis, keep up appearances and carry on a life of ostentatious bourgeois wealth. Slowly but inexorably they drift toward a miserable end. Michele, the central character, is oblivious to the dramas around him, indifferent to a reality that is disintegrating before his eyes. He is painfully unable to play by the social rules of his class or find the moral energy to react and rebel against them. He tries to eliminate Leo, his mother's—and later his sister's—loathsome lover, but (farcically) his gun is not loaded. With this novel, Moravia commenced his long-term investigation into the existential human condition. He went on to pursue the themes of conformism, contempt, and tedium as he portrayed the limitations of a social class at the end of its historical trajectory yet profoundly unable to renovate and transform itself. **RPi**

" . . . it also seemed to her, because of some fatalistic taste for moral symmetries, that this almost familial affair was the only epilogue her life deserved."

After his precocious debut in 1929, Alberto Moravia remained a prominent figure in Italian cultural life for over half a century.

Living

Henry Green

Lifespan | *b.* 1905 (England), *d.* 1973
First Published | 1929
First Published by | J. M. Dent & Sons (London)
Given Name | Henry Vincent Yorke

Green was a precocious writer. He began his first novel, *Blindness*, while at school, and completed it while still a student. His next novel, *Living*, was published in 1929, before his twenty-fifth birthday. It is the story of a working class community in Birmingham, or rather, a story about the self-expression of that community in the largest sense, with "expression" considered both as the inventiveness of colloquial and workplace speech, and as the optimistic social or antisocial behavior of working people.

Partly because it is a story about expression and not simply about people's lives, Green took on the challenge of finding a prose style through which the difficulties of expression could be expressed. As a result, this is Green's most linguistically adventurous novel, and readers may at first find themselves baffled by the omissions of definite articles and the strange disappearance of nouns. The prose reads jerkily, as though it had been composed under the duress of an artificial word limit and constrained to skip the decorum of grammar. However, Green did not intend to imitate the lives of workers; rather, he aimed to evoke—through the atmosphere of grammatical compression—the economy of expectations and desires characteristic of the working class community, and the dependence on simplicity of self-expression. Green conveys this effectively and movingly, allowing his narrative to carry the constrained language along with it. **KS**

Red Harvest

Dashiell Hammett

Lifespan | *b.* 1894 (U.S.), *d.* 1961
First Published | 1929
First Published by | A. Knopf (London & New York)
Full Name | Samuel Dashiell Hammett

Red Harvest is the first, and arguably the best, hard-boiled detective novel. At its most basic level, it remolds aspects of the western and classic detective novel into what has subsequently become a familiar formula. A lone investigator—as tough and violent as the world he inhabits—battles successfully and also in vain to stem the tide of endemic man-made corruption. Hammett's protagonist, the anonymous Continental Op, has no identity beyond his function as detective. This lack of identity, and an attendant social Darwinism, means that he cannot help but become immersed in the bloodletting when his task of ridding Personville—or Poisonville as it's called—of its criminal element results in an orgy of violence, as gang leaders turn on each other.

Hammett presents us with a squalid, ugly town despoiled by mining, where life, to quote Hobbes, is nasty, brutish, and short, and where self-interest inevitably prevails over communitarian instincts. But he doesn't gratuitously revel in the corruption. Rather, *Red Harvest* is a politically angry novel. Liberal reform has failed; rapacious capitalism goes unchecked; the unions have no power; democratic populism is dead; even individualism is irrelevant. The Op has little or no control over his actions. Later in his career, Hammett joined the Communist Party and his politics assumed a more identifiable form. Here, however, the Op's eventual success results not in revolution, but in the restoration of a decadent, morally bankrupt capitalist order. **AP**

A Farewell to Arms

Ernest Hemingway

Lifespan | *b.* 1899 (U.S.), *d.* 1961
First Published | 1929
First Published by | C. Scribner's Sons (New York)
Nobel Prize for Literature | 1954

A Farewell to Arms is set in Italy and Switzerland during the First World War. The very sparse and unadorned style of Hemingway's narrator Frederic Henry provides a realistic and unromanticized account of war on the Italian front and is typical of the writing style that was to become the hallmark of Hemingway's later writing. Henry's descriptions of war are in sharp relief to the sentimental language of his affair with Catherine, an English nurse he meets while recovering from an injury in Turin.

The novel has been particularly praised for its realistic depiction of war; this has often been attributed to personal experience. However, while there are strong autobiographical elements in the novel, the novelist's combat experience was more limited than that of his protagonist. Hemingway did work as an ambulance driver on the Italian front but for the Red Cross and only for a few weeks in 1918. Hemingway also fell in love with a nurse, Agnes von Kurowsky; but, unlike Frederic Henry, Hemingway's advances were subsequently rebuffed.

A Farewell to Arms established Hemingway as a successful writer and also as a spokesman of "The Lost Generation," a group of American intellectuals who lived in Paris in the 1920s and 30s and whose outlook—shaped by the experience of the First World War—was cynical and pessimistic. **BR**

⊙ Gary Cooper, star of the 1932 movie of *A Farewell to Arms*,
refreshes his knowledge of the book during a break in filming.

Passing

Nella Larsen

Lifespan | *b.* 1891 (U.S.), *d.* 1964
First Published | 1929
First Published by | A. Knopf (London & New York)
Original Language | English

Nella Larsen's novel explores the complexities of racial identity in early twentieth-century New York. Its central character, Irene Redfield, is a member of the African-American bourgeoisie that became increasingly fashionable and visible in New York during the Harlem Renaissance era of the 1920s. Irene is married to a doctor and dedicates her life to charitable and social causes. However, her accidental meeting with childhood friend Claire Kendry—who has concealed her mixed parentage in order to assume a white identity—serves to reveal the insecurities and anxieties that lie beneath this seemingly complacent and comfortable life.

At its most obvious, the novel offers a satire of the mores, pretensions, and ambitions of the Harlem Renaissance. The novel's main concern is with exploring the consequences of Claire Kendry's deliberate subversion of early twentieth-century America's stridently enforced desire for racial purity, which both confounds and demonstrates its power. Claire has married a wealthy, racist white American and many of her subsequent actions—from bearing his child to introducing him to Irene—involve the risk that her "true" identity will be revealed. Larsen explores this difficult territory, which is fraught with assumptions about authenticity, purity, and knowledge, by skillfully providing the reader with a silhouette of what can't be said. In the end, it seems that Irene's own deep ambivalence about Claire is the most dangerous and unstable force of all. **NM**

Hebdomeros

Giorgio de Chirico

Lifespan | *b.* 1888 (Greece), *d.* 1978 (Italy)
First Published | 1929
First Published by | Editions du Carrefour (Paris)
Original Language | French

Giorgio de Chirico is perhaps better known as the proto-surrealist painter of empty piazzas and arcades haunted by tailors' dummies and the impossible shadows of colonnades.

This recontextualization of elements from ancient history and modern life is key to de Chirico's "metaphysical" method of which *Hebdomeros* is both an exegesis and an example. The novel has no continuous narrative thread; we simply follow the mental and physical wanderings of Hebdomeros, a painter, athlete, and intellectual. Hebdomeros himself is a curious mixture of the Homeric hero and the modern depressive, plagued by restlessness and ennui. More "dreamlike" than most surrealist works, the novel proceeds via detour and digression; a location such as a hotel room will suddenly lose one of its walls and open up to another scene from memory, which in turn may give rise to another narrative episode. These spatio-temporal shifts happen without warning, sometimes in the middle of sentences, but, as in a dream, one senses an underlying logic at work. Hebdomeros is remarkably attuned to the "Stimmung" or "atmosphere" of the locations he finds himself in, often fleeing some perceived but undefined threat, propelling the images onward. With *Hebdomeros,* de Chirico invents a stylistic amalgam that manages to reorient vision. A largely overlooked masterpiece, one senses that its mysteries have yet to be explored; its time is still to come. **SS**

The Maltese Falcon

Dashiell Hammett

Lifespan | *b.* 1894 (U.S.), *d.* 1961
First Published | 1930, by A. Knopf (Lon. & N.Y.)
First Serialized | 1929
First Serialized in | *Black Mask* magazine

Along with Raymond Chandler, Hammett is more or less synonymous with the change in the detective story from the master detective versus impenetrable crime model to a more "everyday" approach. This change was evidently influenced by factors such as the rapid growth of urban space, big business, and corruption, all of which seem to characterize the era following the First World War in North America.

Taking a broad scope, Hammett introduces throughout his work a number of different protagonists, a series of locations both real and fictional, and very "open" descriptions. Hammett's style is convoluted in the plotting of its crimes, favoring an apparently endless series of twists and turns, in contrast to Chandler's all-enveloping miasma of corruption.

Hammett's character Sam Spade is quite clearly only one in a series of detective protagonists. Spade moves through a violent, sleazy world, where all the characters are selfish, dishonest, two-timing double-crossers. He is as prone to strokes of insight and masterfulness, in the vein of Sherlock Holmes or Dupin, as he is to brawling, cussing, and outbluffing thugs like a true pulp archetype. Above all else *The Maltese Falcon* mirrors this composite nature; it is at heart a fusion of detective stories, where elements from the reverential past of the genre meet scenes of action and adventure, played out in a world where reverence is only going to get you either robbed or killed. **SF**

Vile Bodies

Evelyn Waugh

Lifespan | *b*.1903 (England), *d*.1966
First Published | 1930
First Published by | Chapman & Hall (London)
Full Name | Evelyn Arthur St. John Waugh

In his preface to the 1965 uniform edition of *Vile Bodies*, Waugh said that it was distinguished only for being "the first English novel in which dialogue on the telephone plays a large part." A successor if not exactly a sequel to *Decline and Fall*, it was also the book with which Waugh secured his popularity.

The novel's protagonist is Adam Fenwick-Symes, one of the Bright Young People, though on the periphery of the set. Adam is engaged to Nina Blount, but has to call off his engagement when the manuscript of his memoirs, on which his "whole livelihood depends," is burned by a customs official whose "livelihood depends on stopping works like this coming into the country." In *Vile Bodies*, the very modern—the Bright Young People themselves, telephones, fast cars, zeppelins—coexists uneasily with the more traditional demands of Church and State.

In a whirl of parties, which take place endlessly, everywhere—in hotels, houses, a zeppelin, Number Ten Downing St. (though no one realizes that's where they are till the next morning)—Adam and Nina find their fortunes constantly in flux. Adam is given money then loses it, gets a job as a gossip columnist then loses it; and their engagement is on or off accordingly. The "transition from gaiety to bitterness," which Waugh notes in his preface—the result of his wife leaving him—is a more than apt epithet to a novel that brilliantly and hilariously reflects the volatile times in which it was written. **TEJ**

"All this fuss about sleeping together. For physical pleasure I'd sooner go to my dentist any day."

Diana Mitford, future wife of British Fascist leader Sir Oswald Mosley, is reputed to have been the model for Waugh's heroine.

Her Privates We

Frederic Manning

Lifespan | *b.* 1882 (England), *d.* 1935
First Published | 1930 by P. Davies (London)
Original Title | *The Middle Parts of Fortune*
Pseudonym | Private 19022

The uncensored (and original) version of this novel, called *The Middle Parts of Fortune,* is rumored to have come about when the publisher Peter Davies locked his recalcitrant and inebriated author in his study and demanded he write a war novel before he was released. During the War Books Controversy, a series of novels were published that irrevocably altered the way the war was depicted in literature; this is one of the most lucid of these graphic, uncompromising, and scandalous texts.

Manning's novel was published in two volumes under his army serial number: Private 19022 (his name did not appear on the spine until 1943). In contrast to the officer-experience theme that became popular through the writing of Graves, Sassoon, and Blunden, Manning's semi-autobiographical text follows the life of Private Bourne: drunk, freeloader, and raconteur. It is perhaps this emphasis on the lower ranks that has led to the continued success of the book, alongside concentration on the mundanities and discomforts of trench life. Unlike the more dynamic constructions of the other war books, ostensibly very little happens here, concerned as it is with the aftermath of battle and the gradual preparation for another attack, in which most of Bourne's companions are killed. In this way, *The Middle Parts of Fortune* is a far more accurate depiction of wartime life and one that still has the potential to subvert the war experience. **EMcS**

The Apes of God

Wyndham Lewis

Lifespan | *b.* 1882 (at sea, Canada), *d.* 1957 (London)
First Published | 1930
First Published by | Arthur Press (London)
Original Language | English

A monstrous, exhaustive, and sometimes exhausting work of English modernism, *The Apes of God* has an exuberant, excessive energy. A sustained satirical group portrait of the artistic pretensions of London upper-class society, the critique is aimed at the deluded idea of the "art world" and those who think they live in it. With hints of Pope and Swift, Lewis reworks eighteenth-century satire, deploying physical exaggeration, mock heroics, and reduction to absurdity. Lewis invents an unusual prose style, an almost cubist reinvention of fiction, as his own evidence of art as something more than a passive aping of existing powers.

The plot projects an impressionable young innocent, Dan, on a voyage round London, from his initial mentor, Horace Zagreus, through a gallery of grotesques. Once the reader becomes accustomed to Lewis' style, the plot gathers pace, as the various characters are assembled at Lord Osmund's Lenten party. Lewis' satire engages physical and ideological prejudices with a zest that is hard to condone, not least the continual racist, especially anti-Semitic, and sexist stereotyping. If it is often difficult to like Lewis' severity and the limited space it leaves for humans to distinguish themselves from apes of ideology; there is nevertheless plenty to relish in his style and his satirical provocations. **DM**

❯ A self-portrait by Wyndham Lewis, dating from 1920–21, conveys the satirical aggression that he brought to his writing.

Cakes and Ale

W. Somerset Maugham

Lifespan | *b.* 1874 (France), *d.* 1965
First Published | 1930, by W. Heinemann (London)
Alternate Title | *Cakes and Ale; or, The Skeleton in the Cupboard*

A lighthearted and readable work, *Cakes and Ale* is preoccupied with the vagaries of the literary life, which it treats with marked skepticism. The novelist Edward Driffield is lauded for the unsentimental realism with which he portrays working class and rural life. When he dies, a talentless but successful younger writer, Alroy Kear, is asked by Driffield's second wife to write a sanitized biography of his life. Kear is a relentless self-promoter whose ambition is drily mocked by William Ashenden, the first-person narrator. Ashenden refuses to countenance Kear's proposal to write a biography with all the objectionable details left out. At stake here are questions about literary value, the marketing of authors, modern advertising, the cult of the public personality, and the transient nature of literary reputations. *Cakes and Ale* includes all the salacious details that Kear is intent on excluding from his projected biography. The result is a warts-and-all account of Driffield's life.

The novel portrays the hypocrisy inherent in middle-class respectability and the candor of the lower-class Driffields. Ashenden satirizes a literary world that is characterized by such snobbery even as it is in thrall to the values of the market. In his account Driffield remains an unknowable enigma, "a wraith that went a silent way unseen between the writer of his books and the man who led his life, and smiled with ironical detachment at the two puppets that the world took for Edward Driffield." **AG**

The Glass Key

Dashiell Hammett

Lifespan | *b.* 1894 (U.S.), *d.* 1961
First Published | 1931
First Published by | A. Knopf (London & New York)
Original Language | English

The Glass Key paints a bleak picture of a society in which corruption and violence are routine, exploring the emotional and psychological cost of adhering to traditional values of loyalty, friendship, self-sacrifice, and independence in a world of rampant individualism. The narrative focuses on Ned Beaumont, right-hand man of Paul Madvig, dominant racketeer and unofficial boss of an unnamed American city. When Paul is suspected of murder, and gang warfare erupts, Ned executes a complex series of political maneuvers to find the real killer, protect Paul, and simply stay alive. Cynical, cruel, manipulative, and occasionally pathetic, Ned has a "constitutional weakness" (reminiscent of Hammett's own ill health), drinks heavily (again, much like Hammett), and is repeatedly beaten to within an inch of his life. At the heart of the novel is the strange bond between Ned and Paul, whose strengths and inadequacies complement Ned's own. Neither man can articulate the nature of a friendship that both attempt to sever, but which proves to be the strongest of the various dysfunctional relationships on display.

Hammett cultivated a sparse, economical prose style, wherein motives and intentions of characters remain obscure. With *The Glass Key*, among others, he helped to establish the genre of hard-boiled crime fiction, with its realistic representation of an urban American underworld, characterized by sex, violence, and the struggle for power. **RH**

The Waves

Virginia Woolf

Lifespan | *b.* 1882 (England), *d.* 1941
First Published | 1931
First Published by | Hogarth Press (London)
Given Name | Adeline Virginia Stephen

The Waves, though Woolf's most experimental piece of writing, is nevertheless endlessly rewarding. It shares many of the preoccupations of her other novels: experiments with time and narrative; the representation of lives in biographical writing; and the unfixing of identities. It also pushes the "stream of consciousness" in new directions: becoming an exploration of the relationship between inner life and the "impersonal" elements of waves and water, rather than a narrative technique.

Woolf uses the time-span of a day to explore the temporality of a life, or lives—the movement of the waves defines the passage from dawn to dusk and provides a structure for the novel. It was conceived as "prose yet poetry"—the six selves of the novel are represented by "dramatic soliloquies," and interspersed with "poetic interludes" that describe the passage of the sun across the sky and the rhythms of the tide.

The Waves traces the six lives from childhood to middle age, but seeks to show continuities rather than developments. "We are not single," as Bernard (the novel's chief chronicler) remarks. The characters speak their thoughts as separate entities, rarely in dialogue, yet the novel brings them together by listening in at synchronous moments in their lives and by regrouping them at various stages. The Waves is concerned with the experience and articulation of identity through a fascinating discourse that cannot be named either as speech or as thought. **LM**

"I have outlived certain desires; I have lost friends, some by death—Percival—others through sheer inability to cross the street."

⊙ The cover for the first edition of Woolf's poetic novel was designed by the novelist's elder sister, the painter Vanessa Bell.

The Radetzky March

Joseph Roth

Lifespan | *b.* 1894 (Ukraine), *d.* 1939 (France)
First Published | 1932
First Published by | G. Kiepenheuer Verlag (Berlin)
Original Title | *Radetzkymarsch*

The Radetzky March ranks as one of the finest European historical novels of the twentieth century and is the outstanding literary work produced by the prolific journalist and novelist Joseph Roth. In evoking a specific milieu—the provinces of the Habsburg Empire during its final years of ceremonial grandeur and political instability—the text draws in part on Roth's childhood at the Empire's periphery and on memories of a supranational pride in an almost abstract conception of "Austria." Strauss' prototypically Austrian march recurs as a leitmotif in the narrative, symbolizing tradition, order, and belonging—qualities that are gradually lost as the infrastructure of the Empire begins to crumble.

When Lieutenant Trotta saves the life of the Emperor at the battle of Solferino, he becomes the "Hero of Solferino." Neither he nor the generations that follow are able to live up to the expectations his legend creates. His grandson, Carl Joseph, is an undistinguished soldier who feels most at home in the borderlands of Galicia, in which parochial definitions of both nationality and identity seem irrelevant. Carl Joseph's death, serving on the Eastern Front during the First World War, represents not so much a personal tragedy as the end of an era. This novel movingly explores the complexities of family and friendship, translating a sense of nostalgia for a lost age into a historical narrative that is in no way sentimental. The atmosphere of imperial Austria has rarely been so convincingly and lovingly evoked. **JH**

The Thin Man

Dashiell Hammett

Lifespan | *b.* 1894 (U.S.), *d.* 1961
First Published | 1932
First Published by | A. Barker (London)
Movie Adaptation Released | 1934

At the center of what marks out *The Thin Man* from the mass of hard-boiled fiction is the detective, or in this case, detectives. The investigator of old, the Sam Spade or Marlowe, is defined solely in negative relief by the crimes he deals with; when there is no crime he is reduced to near invisibility, returned to the office, waiting for the phone to ring and bring the next case. In contrast to this, the investigators of *The Thin Man*, Nick and Nora Charles, are not only married, but to each other, with a beloved schnauzer in tow, and the vibrancy of their social life is clearly detailed. They are far removed from the mythical solitaries of conventional noir investigation, living it up in a luxury hotel room, and attending glittering parties as a backdrop to the case they are working on. What Hammett clearly realizes is that the corruption he sees as characterizing America is at work everywhere, in every space and strata of society, and must be represented as such. This is a novel where the deception, mistaken identity, and extreme narrative convolution of the genre do not form the entire world, but are moved beyond its parameters, juxtaposed with social and personal relationships. It must be seen as marking the culmination of Hammett's writing, where the world of the hard-boiled meets the vibrant American fantasy city of F. Scott Fitzgerald. **SF**

❯ A Pinkerton agency detective before he became a writer,
Dashiell Hammett looked like a character from his own novels.

To the North

Elizabeth Bowen

Lifespan | *b.* 1899 (Ireland), *d.* 1973 (England)
First Published | 1932
First Published by | Constable & Co. (London)
Original Language | English

With its manically driven characters, consumed by a new age of locomotion, and a plot that is hurled forth by car, bus, and plane, Elizabeth Bowen's mid-career novel offers startling insights into the effects of technological acceleration on the fabric of everyday lives. From the opening setting (in a house on the Abbey Road before a "funnel of traffic and buses"), to the narrative's apocalyptic climax, Emmeline Summers seems knowingly committed to the most destructive uses of travel, ever hurdling stability in favor of the unknown. This willing attraction to peril leads to her surrender to the sadistic Mark Linkwater—an escape from one form of domestic claustrophobia to a relationship at best glacial, at worst insufferably cruel. Her sister-in-law Cecilia finds herself suffocated with a similar inevitability, which only serves to highlight "how precious had been her solitude."

Bowen invites us into a denatured realm, conveying the most intimate consequences of mechanization upon her protagonists as they become gradually estranged from one another. *To the North* anticipates the fallout of modernity's love affair with the machine, evoking the sinister reification of transport as an inherently positive force. Stylistically, too, the novel's austere timbre complements this pattern of encroachment. The book's impersonal narrative voice seems to impersonate the harmful pressure of mechanical networks upon the basis of human will. **DJ**

Cold Comfort Farm

Stella Gibbons

Lifespan | *b.* 1902 (England), *d.* 1990
First Published | 1932
First Published by | Longmans & Co. (London)
Femina Vie Heureuse Prize | 1933

Cold Comfort Farm is a viciously funny novel and by far the most famous of Stella Gibbons' numerous works. Published in 1932, it is a parody of the rural novel and in particular the work of Mary Webb, but also of many writers now considered part of the canon of great "English literature."

It tells the story of Flora Poste, a young London socialite who finds herself confronted with a long-estranged branch of her family, the Starkadders, after her parents' death. The novel is peopled with a cornucopia of fantastic characters, from the brassiere-collecting Mrs. Smiling, to the tiresome Mr. Mybug, and the wonderful menagerie that is Cold Comfort Farm itself. The Starkadders are a truly remarkable creation, from Judith's obsession with her son, the smoldering Seth, to Elfine's wildness, and the sermons of Reuben, and of course, that something nasty in the woodshed. Far from being intimidated by the stern rusticity of her new location and family, Flora sets about transforming them, one by one, and the scenes that these various processes encompass are, without exception, delightful.

The targets of *Cold Comfort Farm*'s biting satire range from the social machinations of Austen to the melodramatic doom of Hardy and the overblown romanticism of Lawrence. The irreverence and sheer wit of the book are endlessly engaging. **DR**

❷ Gibbons, photographed a half-century after writing *Cold Comfort Farm*, was a prolific author who had no other major success.

Brave New World

Aldous Huxley

Huxley's futuristic dystopia depicts a world in which state power has grafted itself so thoroughly and so effectively to the psyche of its citizenry that the boundaries of exploitation and fulfillment seem irremediably blurred. The World State's professed ideal of social stability has been achieved through the proliferation of consumption and myriad sophisticated technologies. These include the State's monopolistic manufacture of human beings, enforced by making contraception mandatory and promiscuity a virtue. Each of five hierarchically arranged social castes undergoes its own complex pre- and post-natal conditioning to encourage self-satisfaction. The desire for unattainable social mobility within the lowest castes is eradicated, allowing the controlling upper class to maintain its power.

This hybridized philosophy of the World State draws on aspects of Plato's stratified Republic, and utilitarianism's focus on the concept of "happiness." The State facilitation of no-strings-attached pleasure may strike some readers as counterintuitive, given the vehemence with which sexuality is marketed today as the ultimate expression of individuality. Yet the uncoupling of sex from taboo and reproduction dismantles its emotional significance, which aids the World State in eliminating all private allegiances that do not contribute to tightening its stranglehold. In the end, the indiscriminate cultivation of what we might consider "adult" pursuits like drugs and sex renders them completely innocuous. For the childlike denizens of *Brave New World*, order is an end in itself, codified by the organized consumption of goods and services. But it is their conviction that they have been successful in achieving the fullest expression of human aspiration that should give contemporary readers everywhere the deepest shudder of recognition. **AF**

Lifespan | *b.* 1894 (England), *d.* 1963 (U.S.)
First Published | 1932
First Published by | Chatto & Windus (London)
Inspired by | *Men Like Gods* by H.G. Wells (1921)

The bold jacket design for the first edition of *Brave New World* reflects the author's dystopian vision of fractured futurity.

Huxley in 1935: his rejection of technological materialism led him later to embrace mysticism and consciousness-expanding drugs.

Journey to the End of the Night

Louis-Ferdinand Céline

Lifespan | *b*. 1894 (England), *d*. 1961 (U.S.)
First Published | 1932, by Denoël & Steele (Paris)
Original Title | *Voyage au bout de la nuit*
Given Name | Louis-Ferdinand Destouches

Journey to the End of the Night is a groundbreaking masterpiece that has lost none of its startling power and ability to shock. Loosely autobiographical, the first-person narrative traces the experience of the young narrator, Bardamu, from being a twenty-year-old volunteer in the army at the start of the First World War to becoming a qualified doctor at the beginning of the 1930s. During this period, he has a nervous breakdown, travels to Central Africa and the United States, then returns to France to complete his medical studies. The novel is characterized by a brash, vibrant, gritty prose, a deeply sardonic wit, and scathing cynicism. Still lyrical and eloquent throughout, it is full of slang, obscenities, and colloquialisms. Bardamu has an uncompromisingly bleak view of humanity—"mankind consists of two very different races, the rich and the poor," he claims—and although he is mostly concerned with the latter he has little but contempt for both. All we can be sure of is pain, old age, and death. From such an unpromising outlook, however, Céline extracts incredible humor which never ceases to entertain.

The influence of Céline's original, anarchic, and corrosive novel is inestimable; William Burroughs was a noted admirer. In Céline's mordant view of lowlifes we can see an obvious precursor to Beckett's pessimistic anti-heroes. This book is vital to our understanding of the development of the novel. **AL**

A Scot's Quair (Sunset Song)

Lewis Grassic Gibbon

Lifespan | *b*. 1901 (Scotland), *d. 1935* (England)
First Published | 1932
First Published by | Jarrold (Norwich)
Trilogy Published | 1932, 1933, 1934

Sunset Song was the first novel in the trilogy *A Scot's Quair*, which also included *Cloud Howe* (1933) and *Grey Granite* (1934). The trilogy charts the transition of Chris Guthrie and her son, Ewan, from tenant farmers in Aberdeenshire to working class militants during the Great War, the General Strike, and the Hunger Marches of the 1930s. While *Sunset Song* narrates the devastation of the traditional rhythms of rural Scotland, the trilogy concludes with narratives for a socialist revival of Scottish culture.

Sunset Song is the most successful of Gibbon's novels, although the characterization is typically brittle. The injured Chae Strachan, who returns diminished from the war, achieves a degree of pathos missing elsewhere in the novel, but neither he nor Chris, whose psychic conflict propels the novel, ever becomes a fully visceral attraction. However, this appears intentional because the most immediate and sympathetic episodes in the book occur in scenes of celebration, when the various characters are given a collective voice. This connects to the establishment of the culture's collectivity through use of a vernacular idiom, and to the addressing of the reader as "you," which seeks to include the reader within the community. Containing all of this is Gibbon's representation of the land as the constant that survives the cyclical pattern of human development and decline. **LC**

The Man Without Qualities

Robert Musil

Lifespan | *b.* 1880 (Aust.-Hungary), *d.* 1942 (Switz.)
Last Completed Volume Published | 1933
First Published by | Publikationsvermerk (Zurich)
Original Title | *Der Mann ohne Eigenschaften*

Unfinished at some two thousand pages, but written in short, digestible chapters, Musil's *The Man Without Qualities* is frequently ranked next to the masterpieces of Proust and Joyce. It is the definitive portrait of the fin de siècle and the end of the Austro-Hungarian empire.

Given the novel's length, the plot is strikingly insubstantial. Ulrich, the protagonist, is a trained mathematician who is experiencing a distinct lack of purpose in life. He is being pushed by his father—even a man without qualities has a father with qualities, Musil reminds us—to find a useful place in society. This Ulrich consistently fails to do, and instead he catches a succession of new lovers in the way that one catches successive colds. Through the intervention of his father, he does join the *Parallelaktion*, an attempt to find a suitable way of celebrating the sixtieth anniversary of the emperor's reign. The deliberations of the planning committee, in their utter vacuity, reflect the wider vacuity at large. Ulrich finally forms an incestuous relationship with his sister, Agathe, and enters into a different plane of existence, which has variously been labeled as opening the door to totalitarianism, or as an immoralist critique of totalitarian rationalism.

Whatever the judgement, Musil's style is unique and mesmerizing, and the "essayism" is nothing short of the embodiment of a philosophy. **DS**

> *"Ultimately a poem, and the mystery of it, cuts the meaning of the world clear, where it is bound fast by thousands of ordinary words . . ."*

⌃ Musil lived through the collapse of the Austrian Empire and the rise of Nazism, which forced him into exile after 1938.

A Day Off

Storm Jameson

Lifespan | b. 1891 (England), d. 1986
First Published | 1933
First Published by | Nicholson & Watson (London)
Full Name | Margaret Storm Jameson

Having "a day off" from work in the urban world of Jameson's interwar fiction scarcely affords any kind of lasting consolation or reprieve from everyday toil. Haunted by the "gaunt Yorkshire valley" from whose image she seeks distraction in the "coloured dusty circus of London," the pitiable heroine shifts about the streetscape clutching at chance re-encounters that rekindle the flame of past relationships. Over the course of one afternoon's wandering the commercial West End, events resolutely testify to all that this woman can't possess in her own domestic isolation—mean, cramped, and perpetually on the brink of psychological exhaustion. Jameson shadows her with a sense of crystalline immediacy, referring to this character anonymously with "she" and "her": abstracted pronouns complementing the alienation this woman feels unrelievedly at the bustling heart of that world-metropolis.

Jameson advocated a new role for the social novelist as silent witness for whom stylistic economy should always prevail over embellishment. In *A Day Off*, it is her depersonalized commentary that so pervasively implicates the reader, ever testing our capacity for empathic comprehension. Jameson makes us continually aware of our implied position as observers participating in her heroine's futile quest for belonging. **DJ**

❻ Jameson was at the peak of her popularity as a novelist in the 1930s: she was also well known as a left-wing political activist.

Testament of Youth

Vera Brittain

Lifespan | b. 1893 (England), d. 1990
First Published | 1933, by V. Gollancz (London)
Full Title | Testament of Youth: an autobiographical study of the years 1900–1925

Vera Brittain quickly became the spokesperson of her generation for this emotive account of her experiences in the First World War, during which all of her close male friends—brother, fiancé, and best friend—were killed in combat.

At first it might seem ironic that a female pacifist should produce the definitive literary account of the First World War, until Brittain's forward-thinking perspectives are carefully considered. During the reinvestigation of the First World War in the 1960s, Brittain's writing appeared to reflect perfectly the changing attitudes to war, which correlated more with the Peace Movement than the ideals of 1914–18. *Testament of Youth* collects all the ideas of the war "mythology," imaginatively presenting "the pity of war," the Lost Generation, and the idea that after 1918 nothing was ever the same again. Historical detail is then combined with these highly charged, emotive perceptions. Her intention was to inform a generation who still lacked the tools to describe war. But *Testament of Youth* has been instrumental in encouraging a negative perception of the war as unrelentingly grim, especially in the latter stages of the twentieth century, when the role of women during wartime was given greater attention. As an active participant who served in the Voluntary Aid Detachment, and as a woman, Vera Brittain brings a valid alternative perspective to the "horror of the trenches." Her evolution from naïve patriotism to disillusion is compelling. **EMcS**

The Autobiography of Alice B. Toklas

Gertrude Stein

Lifespan | *b.* 1874 (U.S.), *d.* 1946 (France)
First Published | 1933, by J. Lane (London)
First U.S. Publisher | Harcourt Brace & Co. (N.Y.)
Original Publication Source | *The Atlantic Monthly*

"I like a view but I like to sit with my back turned to it."

⬆ Gertrude Stein (left), her companion Alice B. Toklas, and dog Basket photographed at the author's French home in the 1940s.

▶ Stein's image is posthumously reinterpreted by Andy Warhol as part of his 1980 series *Ten Portraits of Jews of the 20th Century*.

This is Stein's best-selling and most accessible work. An "autobiography" written in the voice of her long-time companion, it is a work of sublime modernism, experimenting with voice and point-of-view, the nature of objectivity, and above all a superlative act of unabashedly unreliable narration.

Alice—or Gertrude—claims to have met only three geniuses in her life; the foremost, of course, is Gertrude herself. This is an astonishing claim, considering that the women's lives crossed with virtually every great and influential figure of the early twentieth century. Stein was at the forefront of modernism, arguably its midwife. Her atelier on the Rue de Fleurus in Paris was the centerpoint of art and ideas at a time when, in the mornings, you could choose between buying a new Gauguin or a pot of jam. Picasso and his varying wives are ever-present, as is the young Hemingway. Juan Gris also wanders in, puppy-dogging Picasso. Guillaume Apollinaire (who coined the term "surrealism") is an intimate, and Jean Cocteau, Lytton Strachey, Erik Satie, Ezra Pound, and Man Ray—to name a mere few—make appearances. It is a delirious time, and this ringside account by an unreliable witness, with all its various contradictions, paradoxes, and repetitions, is captivating. Gertrude was there as den mother to the birth of Cubism and the Fauves. She nurtured a renaissance of letters, was there for the birth of Dadaism, and when the Futurists came to town. She was also there when Nijinsky first danced *Le Sacre du Printemps* and created a scandal.

This is a mischievous act of ventriloquism, capturing the breathless, slightly dotty rambling of Alice, companion to the wives of geniuses. But, like the couple themselves, there's very little of Alice and a whole lot more of Gertrude. **GT**

Murder Must Advertise

Dorothy L. Sayers

Lifespan | *b.* 1893 (England), *d.* 1957
First Published | 1933
First Published by | V. Gollancz (London)
Adapted for Television | 1973

In Murder Must Advertise, Dorothy L. Sayers sends her private detective hero Lord Peter Wimsey into an advertising agency to investigate the death of one of its employees. Wimsey, working under the alias Death Bredon, adopts with gusto the role of a copywriter, as he uncovers a plot involving a cocaine-dealing ring. The chief pleasure of the novel is its vivid realization of the advertising world, for which Sayers drew upon her own years of experience as a copywriter. Sayers, like Joyce, was entranced by this language of persuasion, which allowed her fascination with word games full play, yet discomforted by a culture that had recourse to the easy slogan. "Advertise, or go under," are the last words of the novel.

Advertising, too, becomes the means through which the drug dealers operate, so that Sayers is able to intertwine her detailed depiction of the office world with her detective plot. Wimsey (the name fully intended to conjure up "whimsy") is a chameleon-figure in this as well as Sayers' other detective novels. He is a monocled and rather effete aristocrat with shades of P. G. Wodehouse's Bertie Wooster, a champion cricketer and athlete, and a detective whose involvement with crime and death is part of a moral universe. Sayers, for all her wit and whimsy, rarely lets her readers forget that the discovery of the murderer, at the heart of the detective novel's game, was at that time shadowed by the State-hangman's noose. **LM**

> *"'Part of the modern system of push and go' said Mr. Ingleby. 'All very distressing in an old-fashioned, gentle firm. Suppose I've got to put this blighter through his paces ...'"*

⊙ Dorothy Sayers was a committed Anglo-Catholic and in later life shifted from writing detective novels to theological dramas.

Miss Lonelyhearts

Nathanael West

Lifespan | *b.* 1903 (U.S.), *d.* 1940
First Published | 1933, by Liveright (New York)
First Translation | French, 1946
Given Name | Nathan Weinstein

Miss Lonelyhearts, the male protagonist of this novel, answers newspaper readers' despairing questions about how to handle their lives, which range from the mildly amusing to the genuinely grotesque. Known around town as a male "Dear Abby," Miss Lonelyhearts feels emasculated. The vast chasm between his ambivalent aspirations to Christianity, and the Depression-weary hedonism of 1930s New York precludes him from offering anything more than the feeblest clichés to inspire his readers. He would like to offer a vision of meaningful living through the redemptive power of Christ, but is silenced by his editor, Shrike, who mocks religious belief and sarcastically recommends alternatives such as art, sex, and drugs. Miss Lonelyhearts' own behavior throughout the novel swings between extremes. He makes halfhearted attempts to stabilize his life, for example through a marriage proposal to his dependable girlfriend, Betty (whom he then avoids for weeks), but also engages in ridiculously ill-advised escapades, including personal involvement with his readers.

The protagonist's lack of empathy for his readers exposes his failure to emulate Christ, while the extent to which suffering believers are able to confess their darkest secrets and fervent requests in the prayer of their letters is diminished to a function of the journalism market. *Miss Lonelyhearts* is an interesting examination of the problematic role of Christianity in the modern world. **AF**

Call it Sleep

Henry Roth

Lifespan | *b.* 1906 (Ukraine), *d.* 1995 (U.S.)
First Published | 1934
First Published by | R. O. Ballou (New York)
Original Language | English

Long overlooked until it was re-issued in the 1960s at a time when issues of cultural identity were highly prominent in American life, *Call it Sleep* is now widely recognized as one of the masterpieces of twentieth-century American fiction. The novel is an exuberant, visceral portrait of a slum childhood and the immigrant experience in New York's Lower East Side at the start of the century. It is written from the perspective of the developing consciousness of David Schearl, a young Jewish boy recently arrived from Austria-Hungry with his mother to join his previously settled father. The novel charts the early years of his childhood as he learns to live in a foreign culture and deal with his personal fears, troubling family relationships, and challenging social adjustments. A key element of the narrative is the drastic change between speaking Yiddish and English, the associated problems of assimilation, and being caught between two cultures. This is reflected in the combination of gritty urban realism and a modernist focus on consciousness. Roth's virtuoso prose brilliantly captures the child's confused but magical view of his strange surroundings and constant fear.

One of the most authentic, moving accounts of childhood terror in literature, *Call it Sleep* is a poignant, lyrical, and compelling tale of a child's rude awakening to a radically new world and an essential contribution to our understanding of American social history. **AL**

Thank You, Jeeves

P. G. Wodehouse

Lifespan | *b.* 1881 (England), *d.* 1975 (U.S.)
First Published | 1934
First Published by | H. Jenkins (London)
Full Name | Sir Pelham Grenville Wodehouse

"I just sit at a typewriter and curse a bit."

Wodehouse, 1956

⊙ The comic butler, a stock figure in fiction, reaches its supreme realization in Wodehouse's most famous creation, Jeeves.

People seem not to know how to read Wodehouse. Readers tend to see him as a comic writer and expect jokes—but there are none, just as there is little as regards an engaging plot or interesting characterization. P. G. Wodehouse is now somewhat unfashionable, as the world that he created, an everlasting midsummer England untouched by either of the world wars, peopled with characters endowed with the psychology of a prepubescent, has long gone—even in the realms of fantasy. The reactionary politics of his novels have not stood the test of time. However, to go to Wodehouse for politics, plot, characterization, or jokes is to miss the sheer wonder of his prose. He was a writer of fine and peerless talent whose literary creativity spoke to a popular audience in a way that no other novelist could. His ability to weave from nothing a supremely comic metaphor or simile is still unmatched in the novel form.

He is of course most famous for the *Jeeves and Wooster* series (of which *Thank You, Jeeves* is the first full-length novel). The condescending butler Jeeves had appeared in short stories since 1917. Wodehouse was to have great success with Jeeves in the novel form, but the plots of the novels are practically indistinguishable from one another. The stories seem to turn upon Jeeves' dislike of Wooster's clothing or music. Wooster always seems to get mistakenly engaged to someone frighteningly serious and intelligent, whereupon he is then victim to the violent suitor whose place he has usurped. All such events will be set in train by the unpleasant combination of purple socks and red cummerbund, or ownership of a stolen cow creamer. Floating serenely on the surface of all this silliness, though, is Wodehouse's utterly inimitable prose. **VC-R**

Tender is the Night

F. Scott Fitzgerald

F. Scott Fitzgerald is recognized as the ultimate chronicler of the American post-war boom and Jazz era, drawing on his own life to describe the extravagant nonstop, alcohol-fueled party of the pre-Depression years. *Tender is the Night* sold well and was generally well-received, attracting praise from Fitzgerald's peers, Ernest Hemingway among them. Set in the 1920s, the book tells the story of beautiful eighteen-year-old movie star Rosemary Hoyt, who is on holiday with her mother on the French Riviera when she meets Dick Diver, an American psychologist, and his wealthy wife Nicole. Nicole had been abused by her father, commited to a sanitarium, and subequently rescued by her doctor, who is now her husband. Entering their sophisticated, high society world, Rosemary falls in love with Dick, and he with her. They are blissfully happy for a while, but tragedy soon strikes when a friend of the Divers kills a man in a drunk-driving accident, and Nicole has a nervous breakdown. At this point in the novel, the Divers' idyll disintegrates as a series of unfortunate events begins to unfold.

This is Fitzgerald's most autobiographical work, drawing on his own experiences living with the expatriate fast set in the south of France. The Divers were based on Gerald and Sara Murphy, a glamorous American couple that he and his wife Zelda knew. The novel also features the same sort of psychological treatments that the schizophrenic Zelda sought in Switzerland; the high costs of the treatment drove Fitzgerald away from novel-writing and into the life of heavy drinking and Hollywood screenwriting that led to his early death. And unlike the novel, real life doesn't have a happy ending—in contrast to Nicole, Zelda never recovered, remaining institutionalized until her death in 1948. **EF**

Lifespan | *b*. 1896 (U.S.), *d*. 1940
First Published | 1934
First Published by | C. Scribner's Sons (New York)
Revised Edition Published | 1948

"If you're in love it ought to make you happy."

● The first edition jacket reflects the luxuriance of the novel's Riviera setting, with no suggestion of the book's darker themes.

A Handful of Dust

Evelyn Waugh

Lifespan | *b.* 1903 (England), *d.* 1966
First Published | 1934
First Published by | Chapman & Hall (London)
Abridged Edition Published | 2004, by Penguin

> *"I should say it was time she began to be bored."*

⊙ Of middle-class origins, Waugh aspired to belong to the British upper class whom he nonetheless satirized in his novels.

A Handful of Dust is an exhilarating and (blackly) comic attack on the decadence of 1930s English society. Tony Last, a likeable if complacent member of the decaying aristocracy, is shaken, first by the death of his young son, and then by the desertion of his wife Brenda, who has been having an affair with a callow and parasitic man-about-town, John Beaver. The novel wickedly sketches the sheer superficiality of London life, peopled with obscenely named characters such as Polly Cockpurse, whose glitteringly witty talk and faddish interest in bone-setting and foot-reading are a poor substitute for any more meaningful approach to life. Spiritual sustenance is no more authentic in Tony's neo-Gothic rural retreat, Hetton, where the local vicar, the Reverend Tendril, preaches absurdly inappropriate sermons, first delivered in an army garrison in India years before. Tony's response to the events that befall him is to depart for the Amazon, on a quest for a mysterious city. He is rescued from a near fatal fever by the sinister Mr. Todd, whose name recalls the German word for death. His fate—to read aloud forever the works of Dickens to his illiterate rescuer—is an example of Waugh's satire at its blackest: decency and the sentimental humanist pieties of Dickens are not, he thinks, enough.

Here Waugh demonstrates his fascination with the corrupt world he castigates; the repartee of his characters being very close to his own wit and irony. These divided allegiances are also manifest in the novel's style. Although it has a coherent narrative structure and a formally perfect story, it takes its title from T. S. Eliot's *The Waste Land*, and in its own mimicking of the fragmented telegraphese of its characters, as well as its nightmarish rendering of Tony's quest, recalls the work of the modernists. **CC**

Tropic of Cancer

Henry Miller

Henry Miller's infamous autobiographical novel was first published in the 1930s by the risqué Parisian press, Obelisk. Because of its sexually explicit themes and language the book was banned for the following thirty years in both America and Britain. When it was finally published, in America in 1961 and in the UK in 1963, the novel gained cult status. In the book, Miller explores the seedy underbelly of Paris, where he lived as an impoverished expatriate in the 1930s, with a unique sensuality and freedom. Unshackled by moral and social conventions, Miller peppers his book with philosophical musings, fantasies, and a series of explicitly described anecdotes about his sexual encounters with women.

The novel is, as Samuel Beckett remarked, "a momentous event in the history of modern writing," and undoubtedly did much to break down societal taboos about sex and the language used to talk about sex. The novel inspired the Beat generation, whose rejection of middle-class American values led to a search for truth through the extremes of experience. However, feminist critics, most notably Kate Millet, have identified the irrepressibly misogynistic character of the work. Women are frequently represented as passive and anonymous receptacles, whose only role is to satisfy men's physical desires. It is certainly true that the sheer violence of Miller's prose overshadows any putative eroticism or titillation that the novel's reputation may lead the reader to expect.

Although Miller's work has achieved great popularity, this is perhaps a result of his reputation as a writer of "dirty books" rather than as a writer of good literature, and indeed, there has been a good deal of critical disagreement about the "literary" quality of his work. **JW**

Lifespan | *b.* 1891 (U.S.), *d.* 1980
First Published | 1934, by Obelisk Press (Paris)
First Published in U.S. | 1961
Original Language | French

"A polite form of self-imposed torture, the concert."

◉ Miller's taboo-breaking novels made explicit aspects of life that were only obliquely handled in respectable literature.

The Postman Always Rings Twice

James M. Cain

Lifespan | *b.* 1892 (U.S.), *d.* 1977
First Published | 1934
First Published by | A. Knopf (New York)
First Adapted for Screen | 1946

This pulp masterpiece is a doomed Gothic romance, an account of the grim conditions of life in Depression-era California. Cain asks to what extent his protagonists, Frank and Cora, are able to act independently of the larger sexual, political, and economic forces that appear to determine their lives. Frank's self-knowledge is severely limited; although he would like to see himself as unattached and free, he quickly becomes embroiled in a passionate and destructive relationship. Cora's *petit-bourgeois* aspirations involve murdering her "dirty" Greek husband and thereby "inheriting" his roadside café. Bereft of all morality and even any sense of self, Frank readily agrees to assist Cora in her plans. On a cliff-top road they ply Cora's husband with alcohol, place him in his car, and dispatch him to his death.

As Frank and Cora turn on each other, both are placed at the mercy of the law, which is shown to be even more amoral and skewed than the two lovers. The novel's ending underlines the extent to which human existence, and indeed happiness, is both fleeting and arbitrary. Though *The Postman* was twice filmed, Cain's cinematic influence extends well beyond this, and it is hard to imagine the Coen brothers, for example, without James M. Cain. **AP**

◑ John Garfield carries bikini-clad actress Lana Turner off Laguna Beach in the 1946 movie adaptation of the novel.

Novel with Cocaine

M. Ageyev

Lifespan | *b.* 1898 (Russia), *d. c.* 1973
First Published | 1934
First Serialized in | *Illustrated Russia* (Paris)
Alternate Title | *Confessions of a Russian Opium-Eater*

The true identity of M. Ageyev is a mystery yet to be solved by literary historians; although rumored to be a pseudonym for the obscure Russian writer Marc Levi, nothing concrete is known about him. Causing a minor scandal at the time, the book was denounced as decadent and pornographic, but has now acquired something close to cult status. Set in Moscow during 1916 to 1919, it is an unsettling example of drug literature—curiously disengaged from the political realities of the Revolution, yet sensitive to the more subtle changes in man's inner life that accompany periods of massive upheaval.

The narrator is a young, glassy-eyed hedonist named Vadim Maslennikov. As his country plunges into war and unparalleled social transformation, Vadim turns to drugs, prostitutes, and narcotized inertia. Ageyev's prose recalls Proust (for its use of emotional memory), De Quincey (for its startling descriptions of the effects of drugs) and, more predictably, the tough-minded vision of Dostoevsky. While the Revolution is conspicuous in its absence, Ageyev's cold analysis of addiction and dependency resonates in unexpected ways with the events taking place just "offscreen." What separates the compulsion of the addict from that of the communist or capitalist? This book is a dark and brilliantly paced work that exists outside the ideological poles of the period it represents. **SamT**

Threepenny Novel

Bertolt Brecht

Lifespan | *b.* 1898 (Germany), *d.* 1956
First Published | 1934, by Verlag Allert de Lange
Original Title | *Der Dreigroschenroman*
First English Title | *A Penny for the Poor* (1937)

🔼 The cover of sheet music from *The Threepenny Opera* uses images from Pabst's 1931 movie of the Brecht-Weill musical.

▶️ Brecht (left) and Kurt Weill collaborated on the creation of *The Threepenny Opera*, the basis for Brecht's subsequent novel.

In the opening chapter of *Threepenny Novel*, the adult history of a soldier by the name of George Fewkoombey is created. In less than a dozen pages, the man returns from the Boer War, is cheated by the state out of compensation for the leg he "lost" in the war, fails as a publican, fails as a beggar, enters the employ of the beggar-manager Jonathan Peachum, and commits suicide. There is something legendary about the figure of Fewkoombey. An empty mute dignity is created as part of his history and this trickles into and colors the rest of the novel, pervading it with an edgy sadness that cannot be precisely located. But the chapter itself is a small masterpiece of realism, and while the chapters to come are more crowded, often surreally so, they continue and expand the magnificent precision and wit which the first chapter established as the core components of the narrative voice.

It is necessary to speak of the technical brilliance of this novel as a novel. Too often it is described as an adaptation of an adaptation, as the novelization of Brecht and Kurt Weil's adaptation of John Gay's 1728 *Beggar's Opera*. It then becomes an afterthought, a symptom of Brecht's habit of squeezing the most out of material, an expression of his polymorphous talents and of the political needs that exercised them. But *Threepenny Novel* remains outstanding as a novel. The nightmarish, tight-fisted, corroded London it uses as the arena for a story, which both understands and satirizes a decaying yet victorious capitalism, is meticulously detailed, as grimly vivid as any Dickensian depiction but devoid of the familiarity with which Dickens asks affection for his London. Polly Peachum, in particular, stands out as a rich model of endurance, a harassed anti-heroine who repels sympathy yet demands respect. **PMcM**

The Nine Tailors

Dorothy L. Sayers

Lifespan | *b.*1893 (England), *d.*1957
First Published | 1934
First Published by | V. Gollancz (London)
Full Name | Dorothy Leigh Sayers

The Nine Tailors reaches beyond Sayers' earlier work in its scope and ambition, creating a rich cast of characters in a vividly realized setting. The action takes place in a Fenland village and is centered on the parish church, Fenchurch St Paul. While the closed community setting is typical of the "Golden Age" detective fiction of the 1920s and 1930s, Sayers does not succumb to cozy and comfortable Englishness, instead depicting a rural world shadowed by secrecy and guilt, and a desolate landscape, whose flooding has deliberately Biblical overtones. The novel also uses campanology, or bell ringing, in highly ingenious ways, as regards both structure and content, interweaving with it the detective plot and its subsequent unravelling.

Unfortunately, Sayers never completed her biography of the nineteenth-century writer Wilkie Collins, author of *The Moonstone*, which has been described as the first English detective novel. A great admirer of Collins as a "plot-maker" who drew together romance and realism, Sayers was inspired by his example; *The Nine Tailors* has strong echoes of *The Moonstone*, not only in the details of the crime, which again revolves around a jewelry theft, but in the skillful orchestration of sub-plots. *The Nine Tailors* was the novel that secured Sayers' growing reputation as one of the finest twentieth-century detective novelists and as a writer who brought the "clue-puzzle" into the broader traditions of the English novel. **LM**

Burmese Days

George Orwell

Lifespan | *b.*1903 (India), *d.*1950 (England)
First Published | 1934
First Published by | Harper & Bros. (New York)
Given Name | Eric Arthur Blair

In his first novel, based in part on personal experiences, Orwell turned his sharp, unillusioned eye upon the myth of the British Empire. The very title, *Burmese Days*, whispers of the arid tracts of time endured by those engaged in colonial service. By turns grotesque and hilarious in its coruscating indictment of imperialism, Orwell's angry novel depicts the life of the English in Burma as an endless round of bridge, tennis, gossip, squabbling, nostalgia for a fantasized Raj, and alcoholic stupefaction. In this half-crazed microcosm driven by fear and corrupted by *amour-propre*, English self-esteem relies on a rigid enforcement of the color-bar and a visceral disgust at anything "native," while a precarious colonial order is upheld by violence.

Orwell's bold and prescient stroke is to challenge his English readers' assumptions by reversing the hierarchy of values upon which Empire depended. The English, with their racist reduction of different races to a single monolithic group simply labeled "niggers," are the savages, while the Burmese are associated with civilization. Much of this critique is articulated by Flory, the novel's flawed protagonist. But Flory's observation that all the English in Burma are corrupt because all are complicit in the crimes he identifies, is, of course, also true of himself. Able to condemn much of what he witnesses, but unable publicly to reject the ideological shackles of the "pukka sahib code," Flory is ultimately as doomed as the others. **AG**

England Made Me

Graham Greene

Lifespan | *b.* 1904 (England), *d.* 1991 (Switzerland)
First Published | 1935
First Published by | W. Heinemann (London)
Full Name | Henry Graham Greene

England Made Me ends with the words "a home from home." Leaving her job with the Swedish millionaire Krogh, Kate Farrant is not going back to England, to "home" in its misleadingly literal sense, but is "simply moving on," a reluctant wanderer in a world in which "home" is now so many familiar, mobile objects.

Krogh's is an international business; if he raises his interest rates he can bankrupt France; if he sells stock cheaply he can ruin investors in several countries, at once destabilizing fragile economic and political balances. International capital is fluid and rootless, cosmopolitan in its capacity to settle momentarily anywhere, destructively promiscuous in its compulsion to keep circulating, to settle finally nowhere. As a lender and an investor, as an employer and a producer, Krogh controls the purse strings of the countries, towns, and cities others call home. But if Greene here articulates the chaos of the 1930s, a decade in which speculation, credit, and slump came to be terms as newly familiar as mass unemployment, fascism, and communism, he also sets himself against the patriotism of nostalgia for "home." What will a human being not endure to realize the promise of "home"? How many small deceits and betrayals will be tolerated if they bear the look of familiarity and speak in native accents? For Kate and Anthony Farrant, a brother and sister who seduce each other with visions of belonging, the will to be at home somewhere is as destructive as it is inevitable. **PMcM**

The House in Paris

Elizabeth Bowen

Lifespan | *b.* 1899 (Ireland), *d.* 1973 (England)
First Published | 1935
First Published by | V. Gollancz (London)
Original Language | English

The House in Paris explores the disconcerting intelligence of children—and the complexities of their innocence—as they await the unfolding of the machinations of the adults around them. Part mystery, part melodrama, part modernist experiment with narrative time, the novel centers on two English children, Henrietta, age eleven, and Leopold, age nine, who meet in transit in the forbidding house of a dying, strangely sinister old French woman. Henrietta, whose mother is dead, is being shuttled to her grandmother's house; Leopold has traveled from Italy where he has been raised by adoptive parents. In the drawing room of a stranger's house in Paris, he is expecting to meet his mother for the first time. Despite the efforts of his chaperone to maintain secrecy, the mystery of Leopold's secret, illegitimate birth and the puzzle of his parents' identities unravel in the course of the single day. As the novel moves backward in time, Leopold's mother emerges as an upper-crust young Englishwoman, his father as penniless and Jewish. Throughout the novel, the complexities of adult interactions and motivations contrast sharply with the exquisitely rendered interactions between Henrietta and Leopold, whose journeys have become more internal and psychological than geographical. While the children await their fates, they gradually discover their own identities, a process through which they find one another unexpectedly, if only momentarily, indispensable. **LKF**

They Shoot Horses, Don't They?

Horace McCoy

Lifespan | *b.* 1897 (U.S.), *d.* 1955
First Published | 1935
First Published by | A. Barker (London)
Movie Adaptation Released | 1969

Overlooked at the time of its initial publication, *They Shoot Horses, Don't They?* was critically rehabilitated in the 1940s by the Parisian noirist Marcel Duhamel, who favorably compared McCoy to Hemingway. The novel's protagonists Robert and Gloria dream of Hollywood stardom, but in the bleak tawdriness of Depression-era Los Angeles they find only monotony, emptiness, and ultimately death. In the guise of the dance marathon, a form of spectacle in which contestants endlessly circulate around an arena over a period of days in the hope of being the last pair standing, McCoy found the perfect metaphor for life's randomness, absurdity, and meaninglessness. Battling exhaustion, Robert and Gloria fail in their pursuit of the cash prize when the event is ended by a bizarre accidental shooting. Set adrift, Gloria's insistence that life has no meaning persuades Robert to realize her morbid ambition.

The dance marathon is used to comment on the exploitative nature of popular forms of entertainment and on the ways in which human life has been organized and debased under capitalism. Unlike the sugarcoated banality of most Hollywood movies, the dance marathon is unpredictable, painful, violent, and nihilistic. The dance contestants are commodities—cattle, or rather horses, who can be shot once their value has been utilized. Here are the seeds of McCoy's social critique but, like the dance marathon itself, it is a critique that leads nowhere and yields nothing. **AP**

"'Your Honour,' Epstein said, 'we throw ourselves on the mercy of the court. This boy admits killing the girl, but he was only doing her a personal favor.'"

◉ McCoy's Depression-era novels earned him an enthusiastic
   following in Europe, but were little admired in the U.S.

The Last of Mr. Norris

Christopher Isherwood

Lifespan | *b.* 1904 (England), *d.* 1986 (U.S.)
First Published | 1935
First Published by | Hogarth Press (London)
Original Title | *Mr. Norris Changes Trains*

This intriguing novel portrays a series of encounters in 1930s Berlin between the narrator, William Bradshaw, and the mysterious and sinister Mr. Norris. When William first meets Arthur Norris on a train bound for Germany, he notes that his eyes were "the eyes of a schoolboy surprised in the act of breaking one of the rules." Always on the move, always involved in shady deals, Mr. Norris somehow manages to elude the scrutiny of the authorities but is finally undone by blackmailing secretary Schmidt.

The tone of the book is comical, at times farcical, but it is set in the final years of the Weimar Republic, and the rise of Nazi power provides an ominous counterpoint to the carefree café society that Isherwood depicts. This atmospheric evocation of a world on the very brink of ruin introduces us to a gallery of damned souls, prisoners in their own city, hounded by a ruthless new social order determined to expose and eradicate them. Their only hope resides in flight, but even this option is fraught with the risk of arrest. Posters appear on the streets of the capital urging Berliners to "Vote Hitler," and as the communists are driven underground, the rise in the tally of beatings and shootings fuels a feverish proliferation of gossip and rumor. Against the backdrop of Berlin's descent into civil war, Bradshaw's position remains one of detachment— he positions himself as a bemused observer, passively witnessing the collapse of civilization from the shadowy wings of a theater of the absurd. **TS**

Auto-da-Fé

Elias Canetti

Lifespan | *b.* 1905 (Bulgaria), *d.* 1994 (Switzerland)
First Published | 1935
First Published by | Herbert Reichner Verlag (Vienna)
Original Title | *Die Blendung*

This neglected masterpiece of German modernism offers a mysterious and indirect analysis of the perils of bookishness, and the darkness that ensues when the bookworm turns. Prophetically, this bonfire of the vanities attempts to dissect the social madness that was engulfing the German-speaking world. Echoing the dark comedy of Kafka, Canetti's "K"— Peter Kien—is a creature of the mind, determined to resist socialization in preference for a life of scholarship, but lacking worldly defenses. The novel details his series of encounters with creatures whose rapacious interests generate an extraordinary comedy of competing delusions.

Peter Kien, an obsessive scholar of sinology, has a large personal library. Beset by nightmares of his library going up in smoke, he stupidly marries Therese, the scheming and deluded housekeeper he has employed to look after the library. Descending into varieties of hallucinatory mania, Kien is ejected from his library by his "wife" and enters a nightmare underground world. After sundry misadventures at the hands of Fischerle, a crooked, hunchbacked dwarf with delusions of becoming the world chess champion, he becomes embroiled again with Therese and Bendikt Pfaff, proto-Nazi caretaker and retired policeman. Kien's brother, a Parisian psychologist, adds interpretative confusion to the dark brew before the book's violent logic of disintegration precipitates the final inferno. Dark, terrifying, disturbing, and funny. **DM**

Independent People

Halldór Laxness

Lifespan | *b.* 1902 (Iceland), *d.* 1998
First Published | 1935 (Reykjavík)
Original Title | *Sjálfstætt fólk*
Nobel Prize for Literature | 1955

Lost in a blizzard and close to death, Bjartur, the proud, stubborn, brutal, and often idiotic hero of this extraordinary novel, begins to hallucinate. As the snowstorm tears at him, its claws become those of Grimur, the mythical demon from Icelandic sagas. He fights his way, step by step, reciting all the poetry and ballads he can remember in a desperate attempt to stay awake. Finally, close to collapse, he reaches the safety of another crofter's hut, exhausted but victorious. In essence this novel is a reclamation of Iceland's mythical past, an attempt to redefine the sense of nation and history through those most often ignored. It gives voice to the ancient farming communities, their wit, their sufferings, and their conflicts. Full of tough realism, the novel's pages reek with the stink of sheep dung, of smoke and stone, and of deep, endless drifts of snow. It focuses on Bjartur and his fight to remain independent and free from debt during the early years of the twentieth century, through the prosperity of the war years to the economic crisis and growth of socialism after the war has ended. In hard, poetic, and often beautiful prose Laxness charts the struggles of Bjartur's growing family, the death of his first and second wives, and the longings and unfulfilled dreams of his three children.

Laxness, who spent much of his childhood on farms similar to those described, wrote over sixty literary works and is considered the undisputed master of Icelandic fiction. **JM**

Nightwood

Djuna Barnes

Lifespan | *b.* 1892 (U.S.), *d.* 1982
First Published | 1936
First Published by | Faber & Faber (London)
Introduction to the Original Edition by | T. S. Eliot

Nightwood has the reputation of a great novel written by a poet, a reputation partly fostered by T. S. Eliot's suggestion that the book will appeal primarily to readers of poetry. The prose style of the book is indeed remarkable, possessing varieties of urbane wit and a kind of modernist baroque seemingly schooled in Jacobean dramatic poetry. A pioneering representation of love between women, *Nightwood* makes uncomfortable reading for anyone looking for positive images of lesbian identity, but however troubling, this is a hilarious and stylish book.

Set mostly in Paris and New York, the novel suggests a cosmopolitan drift of bohemians and exiles in Europe. At the center of the novel is the dangerous figure of Robin Vote, who more or less ruins her husband, Felix Volkbein, their child Guido, and the two women who love her, Nora Flood and Jenny Petherbridge. Counterbalancing the destructive allure of Robin Vote, Doctor Matthew O'Connor administers the healing power of distractingly outlandish monologues. What at first seem like windy exercises in rhetoric for rhetoric's sake are gradually revealed as humane deflections of the suffering otherwise threatening to break out. The doctor's unorthodox efforts are finally reduced to drunken rubble by the wheels of this dark fable. A book to re-read many times. **DM**

❯ Barnes wrote about lesbian relationships, which she saw as narcissistic: "A man is another person—a woman is yourself."

At the Mountains of Madness

H.P. Lovecraft

Lovecraft's most effective novel begins as a tale of exploration at the cutting edge of science. Airplanes and drilling devices are shipped to Antarctica in 1930, just as the mapping of the continent begins in earnest. But this "awful place," more ancient than any other continent, is not so easily opened up to materialist exploitation. Soon enough, an entirely new history of the world is in evidence, one that undermines all previously held views of science and nature, a vision that contains vast alien cities buried beneath the ice and the awesome and awful survivors of its heyday.

The positive and efficient first person narrative of the geologist, Dyer, patiently and didactically explains the wonders of new technology. Only when the first survey group, isolated by a storm, begins to radio back of highly unusual finds in a cavern beneath the surface, do events begin to unravel. From then on Dyer and his companion, the student Danforth, are on a downward spiral of discovery that attacks every notion of time, space, and life until Danforth's speech is reduced to disconnected fragments, recalled only in dreams.

Deeply influenced by Poe, Lovecraft's horror tends to be implied and offstage, but this effectively deepens the abounding philosophical horror felt by the protagonists. This intriguing blend of gothic horror and lost world scenarios within a more modern genre framework can be rediscovered in many contemporary narratives, especially film. Lovecraft achieved little success in his lifetime but his work resonates with themes that consistently inspire later generations of writers, science fiction as much as horror. Largely due to his *Cthulhu* stories, called *Cthulhu Mythos* by August Derleth, Lovecraft is today the subject of a large cult following. **JS**

Lifespan | *b.* 1890 (U.S.), *d.* 1937
First Serialized | 1936
First Serialized in | *Astounding Stories* magazine
Full Name | Howard Phillips Lovecraft

Lovecraft, who was often ill as a child, claims that his work was often inspired by the experience of horror through nightmares.

Lovecraft's association with and influence on the genres of horror, occult, and the macabre continues to be perpetuated.

Absalom, Absalom!

William Faulkner

Lifespan | *b.* 1897 (U.S.), *d.* 1962
First Published | 1936
First Published by | Random House (New York)
Nobel Prize for Literature | 1949

Told five times between 1835 and 1910 (while Sutpen rests from hunting his absconded French architect with a pack of slaves), this is the peasant to planter story of Thomas Sutpen, his plantation (called "the Hundred"), and of Bon, his possible son who may be black and who, if black and acknowledged, will bring the house down.

The gaps and contradictions exposed by multiple narration beg epistemological questions concerning how we know what we know of historical matters. But given that, in *Absalom, Absalom!*, the questions arise from a regionally specific labor problem—that of the denied black body within the white, whose coerced work gives substance to the face, skin, sex, and land of the white owning class—those questions are recast. "Who knows what and how do they know it?" reforms as, "How, knowing that their face, skin, sex, and land are made by African-American labor (the good inside their goods), can they go on denying what they know?" Faulkner's answer would seem to be that to acknowledge their knowledge (or for Sutpen to face Bon as his son), would be to cease to be themselves. That William Faulkner should begin to think such unthinkable thoughts about his own ancestors in *Absalom, Absalom!*, even as his region continued to depend for its substance on bound black workers (bound by debt peonage rather than chattel slavery), may explain the structure of this, one of the greatest of modernist novels. **RG**

Wild Harbour

Ian Macpherson

Lifespan | *b.* 1905 (Scotland), *d.* 1944
First Published | 1936
First Published by | Methuen & Co. (London)
Original Language | English

Set in 1914, *Wild Harbour* takes the form of a diary written by Hugh who, with his wife Terry, attempts to escape becoming embroiled in the war by living in a cave in the remote Scottish hills. Much of the novel details the minutiae of Hugh and Terry's efforts to survive: Hugh's hunting, their attempts to preserve food, and, above all, their effort to remain hidden from the few stragglers that cross their path.

Wild Harbour offers a thoughtful meditation on different kinds of human violence. Hugh eschews pacifism, indicating his willingness to fight but a refusal to participate in the political folly of war. The novel dwells on the contrast between Hugh's necessary, but anguished, hunting of animals and the political bloodbath that forms the backdrop. Though the war itself remains largely undescribed, it retains a haunting presence. At various points, Hugh and Terry's wilderness is punctuated by suggestive but unintelligible noises—railway trains running to some mad wartime schedule or unexplained explosions. On their one trip home they are faced with the seemingly mindless, utter devastation of the social infrastructure; half-grown crops are ripped from the ground and shops and houses pointlessly vandalized. After witnessing the consequences of war in the form of the ragged and desperate refugees who haunt the Scottish Highlands, Hugh must ultimately decide whether to give up his life in order to preserve Terry's faith in the possibility of peaceful human interrelations. **LC**

Keep the Aspidistra Flying

George Orwell

Lifespan | *b.* 1903 (India), *d.* 1950 (England)
First Published | 1936
First Published by | V. Gollancz (London)
Given Name | Eric Arthur Blair

The changes Orwell was forced to make by his publisher, together with the weaknesses he himself saw in it, left him disappointed with this novel. But for all that, it is still a powerful and savagely satirical portrait of literary life. Very much a London novel, and perhaps even more a 1930s one, *Keep The Aspidistra Flying* describes the struggles of hapless Gordon Comstock. In Comstock's indictment of capitalism, access to culture is seen as inseparable from the possession of wealth and privilege, while the domination of contemporary life by advertising points to an all-embracing commodification of the everyday. These are the signs of a futile existence, a dying civilization; the threat of an impending cataclysm—a theme Orwell would develop further in *Coming Up for Air*—hangs over the action.

Comstock, however, appears to be trapped as much by his own weak character as by the system he deplores. He refuses to accept the respectability of middle-class life, represented by the potted plants of the novel's title, which in Comstock's eyes symbolize "mingy, lower-class decency." Yet he rejects revolutionary politics as a means of bringing about change, and his own attempt to embrace poverty by living like an anchorite among the destitute merely assuages his sense of guilt. Moreover, the novel nags away at Comstock's ambiguous character, asking whether his anger and despair should be read as a self-pitying drama or as a genuine rejection of capitalist exploitation. **AG**

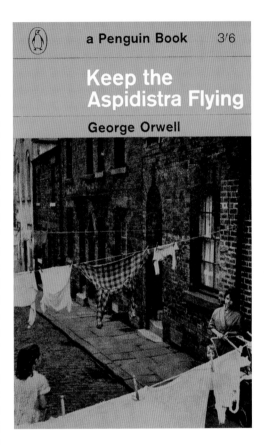

a Penguin Book   3/6

Keep the Aspidistra Flying

George Orwell

"Gordon eyed them with inert hatred. At this moment he hated all books, and novels most of all."

⊙ Orwell's novel on life in London in the 1930s, originally sharply contemporary, is now largely appreciated as a period piece.

Gone With the Wind

Margaret Mitchell

Lifespan | *b.* 1900 (U.S.), *d.* 1949
First Published | 1936
First Published by | Macmillan & Co. (London)
Pulitzer Prize | 1937

🔺 Margaret Mitchell was a shy and private individual who had great difficulty coping with the fame her novel brought her.

🔽 A poster advertising the novel in 1936 is surprising, as the iconography of *Gone With the Wind* is set by the 1939 movie.

Gone With the Wind's romanticized setting in Civil War and Reconstruction-era Georgia, as well as its central characters, the fiery Southern belle Scarlett O'Hara and her dashing husband Rhett Butler, have become the stuff of American mythology. Although David O. Selznick's 1939 film helped to immortalize Mitchell's novel, the book had already enjoyed phenomenal sales upon first publication and went on to win the Pulitzer Prize, a year later, in 1937.

A sweeping historical saga, it follows Scarlett and her friends and relatives through a period of major upheaval in American social and economic history. The novel traces the transition from the agricultural society of the early 1860s, represented by Tara, the family plantation, to the beginnings of Southern industrialization in the 1880s. While it is famously a tale about Scarlett, Rhett, and Ashley's love triangle, *Gone With the Wind* is also a love letter to a place, the city of Atlanta, Georgia. Mitchell was born in Atlanta and grew up hearing stories of the antebellum city and the battles fought by the Confederate army. She lovingly details Atlanta's expanding and changing society in passages that reveal the extent of her historical research. However, *Gone With the Wind* is not an uncontroversial novel, and Margaret Mitchell's own sympathies with Southern slave owners and idyllic portrayal of pre-war plantation society have exposed the book to an expansive cultural debate, producing critical analysis, protest, and even parody that continues today. Nevertheless, it remains an ambitious, gripping novel, and, far more importantly, an undisputed cultural phenomenon that not only helped to shape the direction of the American novel, but that has had a significant effect on America's popular conception of its own history. **AB**

GONE WITH THE WIND

The Thinking Reed

Rebecca West

Lifespan | b. 1892 (England), d. 1983
First Published | 1936
First Published by | Hutchinson & Co. (London)
Given Name | Cicily Isabel Fairfield

Rebecca West was well known throughout the twentieth century for her progressive and feminist politics, and her fifth novel *The Thinking Reed* sensitively examines the limitations of the life led by many middle-class women during the 1920s. It follows the fortunes of Isabelle Torrey, an intelligent young American widow who is prematurely thrust on to the European social scene. Disappointed in a love affair, she impulsively marries the immensely wealthy Marc Sallafranque, only to experience emotional swings from love to hate and back again over the course of their violent and passionate marriage. Charting an evolving relationship against the background of the decadent social scene of the very wealthy, *The Thinking Reed,* like Fitzgerald's *Tender is the Night,* highlights the disintegration of not only a class but an entire way of life. Strikes and industrial unrest grow daily more violent at Marc's automobile factory outside of Paris, while the stock market crash looms across the ocean. Marc and Isabelle's carefree lifestyle is clearly doomed, but in losing their fortune, the novel implies, they will gain the human dimension missing from their increasingly desperate and empty social maneuverings. Eventually Isabelle comes to feel only revulsion for the vapid and cruel social circle that she once embraced so enthusiastically.

The Thinking Reed remains an important and thoughtful exploration of relationships, class, and marriage for today's reader. **AB**

> *"Writing has nothing to do with communication between person and person, only . . . between different parts of a person's mind."*
>
> West, "The Art of Skepticism," 1952

◉ West appeared on the cover of *Time* magazine in 1947—her fame in America rested primarily on her work as a journalist.

Eyeless in Gaza

Aldous Huxley

Lifespan | *b.* 1894 (England), *d.* 1963 (U.S.)
First Published | 1936
First Published by | Chatto & WIndus (London)
Original Language | English

The title, which quotes Milton's Samson Agonistes ("Eyeless in Gaza at the Mill with slaves") inaugurates Aldous Huxley's partly autobiographical narrative of Anthony Beavis' quest for enlightenment. The novel traces his life from his English boyhood in 1902 to his risky commitment to pacifism in 1935. We encounter his predominantly upper-middle-class and highly articulate friends, relatives, and partners. The novel is chronologically experimental, moving to and fro in time, creating a range of ironic links between past and present. It is experimental, too, in the boldness with which customary plot development gives way to intellectual meditations, providing a range of witty or provocative reflections on topics such as sociology, democracy, and totalitarianism, particularly the problem of reconciling freedom with social harmony. In the most notorious passage, a live dog is dropped from an airplane and hits the flat rooftop where Anthony and his partner Helen are lying naked in the sun. It bursts, spraying them with its blood. Typically, the well-read Anthony says to Helen: "You look like Lady Macbeth." Ironies multiply: he feels tenderness, while she decides to leave him. Huxley's sense of the tragicomedy created by the entrapment of the human self is brilliantly encapsulated here.

Huxley's writing in *Eyeless in Gaza* may in places appear prolix and didactic. Nevertheless, in his lifetime, Huxley, like Lawrence and H. G. Wells, was for many readers an emancipatory influence. **CW**

Summer Will Show

Sylvia Townsend Warner

Lifespan | *b.* 1893 (England), *d.* 1978
First Published | 1936
First Published by | Chatto & WIndus (London)
Original Language | English

How does one tell the story of revolution, when writing in the early 1930s? The Soviet revolution is too close and too unmanageable, yet there has been no revolution in Western Europe since the nineteenth century. Sylvia Townsend Warner—not yet a communist—turns back to the year of revolutions, 1848, specifically to Paris, when a popular revolt removed the Orléanist Louis Philippe. Her heroine is Englishwoman Sophia Willoughby.

Personal tragedy prepares Sophia for revolution when she loses her children to smallpox, her home to legal trickery, and her husband to adultery. Following her husband, Frederick, to Paris, she falls in love with his mistress, Minna Lemuel. But in the violent summer of 1848, Minna is killed at the barricades by Caspar, whom Sophia has brought up in England. Sophia kills Caspar, yet refuses to believe Minna is dead. These melodramatic events are dissolved in a detached but involving prose.

Sophia is then employed by the revolutionary Ingelbrecht, a version of Engels, to distribute a mysterious pamphlet—*The Communist Manifesto*. The defeat of the summer of 1848 has shown that she will live on as a revolutionary. *Summer Will Show* tells three stories: Sophia as a *flâneuse* on the streets of radicalized Paris; Sophia in love with Minna, a subtle, almost impalpably sensitive lesbian romance; and Sophia's gradual discovery of what it means to be a revolutionary. Autobiographically speaking, the last two are Warner's own stories. **AMu**

To Have and Have Not

Ernest Hemingway

Lifespan | *b.* 1899 (U.S.), *d.* 1961
First Published | 1937
First Published by | J. Cape (London)
Nobel Prize for Literature | 1954

Charismatic Harry Morgan is a deeply memorable character, and behind his vivid presence are vignettes that are distinctively Hemingway and also deeply critical of a decaying American Dream. From the drunken and abandoned war veterans, to the morally degenerate and wealthy writing and yachting communities of Key West (Hemingway's home at the time of writing), the novel takes broad and barbed swipes at the state of 1930s America.

Tributes to the spare elegance of Hemingway's prose are as effusive and numerous as they are accurate. And it is tempting to say that there is no better example of Hemingway's characteristic style than the bleak tale of the "Spring," "Fall," and "Winter" of Harry Morgan. Certainly this ex-cop turned fisherman and sometime smuggler between the Florida Keys and Cuba seems to fit the stereotype of the Hemingway hero—a tough man of the world, who drinks, hunts, bullies, and kills. Yet in many ways, *To Have and Have Not* is unusual in Hemingway's oeuvre. Arguably his most socially committed novel, it is the product of his struggle for direction and inspiration in his writing during the 1930s. One of his few novels to be set in the United States, it was published in 1937 to a mixed reception. Criticism of the text's political naïveté in its representation of the upper classes and the social inequalities surrounding the Depression are to an extent fair, but the sheer, vital muscularity and the peculiar moral ambiguity of the book are not to be denied. **DR**

Out of Africa

Isak Dinesen (Karen Blixen)

Lifespan | *b.* 1885 (Denmark), *d.* 1962
First Published | 1937, by Putnam (London)
Given Name | Karen Christence Dinesen
Original Title | *Den afrikanske Farm*

Karen Blixen only narrowly missed out on the Nobel Prize for Literature, and *Out of Africa* is her most famous novel, both a memoir of her time on a coffee farm in Kenya and a vivid portrait of the beginning of the waning of European imperialism.

Dinesen recounts her struggles to make a success of the coffee plantation in the years before and after the First World War, fighting poverty and natural disasters to keep her farm, with the ghost of failure always a step behind her. Her reminiscences are peppered with references to God, lions (believed to be symbolic of nature's aristocracy), the violence of Africa, racism, and decency. Dinesen was in love with the African landscape and the descriptive passages in this book are at times exquisite, although some of her references to Africans will make modern readers uncomfortable. She hints at the differences between European and African culture—believing that men exist in a truer form in Africa—and recounts how she, as a woman, tried to bridge the chasm between them. In the end, she loses the farm and leaves for Europe, but she never stops loving the country she called home for twenty years. This is a novel about the death of imperialism and displacement, savagery, beauty, and the human struggle. Hailed as perhaps the greatest pastoral elegy of modernism, most of all it is a book about Africa. **EF**

❯ Karen Blixen is shot by photographer Carl van Vechten
   in a setting that suggests a loving remembrance of Africa.

The Revenge for Love

Wyndham Lewis

Lifespan | *b*. 1882 (at sea, Canada), *d*. 1957 (London)
First Published | 1937
First Published by | Cassell & Co. (London)
Full Name | Percy Wyndham Lewis

At the time of its publication, Wyndham Lewis considered *The Revenge for Love* to be the best work of fiction he had written. Yet over the years the novel has been bedevilled by various misconceptions about it, perhaps the most important being that it is about the Spanish Civil War. The novel is certainly concerned with the power-politics of the 1930s, and it offers a trenchant critique of the international communist movement at that time. It concentrates especially on issues of propaganda and political intrigue as symbolized above all by the agent provocateur Percy Hardcaster. But it is also preoccupied with what Lewis saw as the corruption of the art world by political values, and it mocks many of the intellectual currents of the day, including Lawrencian nature worship and Bloomsbury aestheticism.

Originally titled *False Bottoms*, this deeply ironic novel suggests that surface appearances—especially in the realm of politics—are never to be trusted because complex machinations always lurk beneath. The novel's characters are puppet-like dupes either of calculating figures who are pulling their strings offstage or of pernicious ideologies they barely comprehend. Picking up on arguments made in *The Art of Being Ruled* (1926), *The Revenge for Love* depicts a reality in which power is ubiquitous and unforgiving. The "love" of the novel's title cannot be redemptive in this harsh climate because power will always have its revenge. **AG**

In Parenthesis

David Jones

Lifespan | *b*. 1895 (England), *d*. 1974
First Published | 1937, by Faber & Faber (London)
Full Title | *In Parenthesis: Impressions, in a fictitious form, of life on the Western Front*

Often heralded as the unsung classic of the First World War, this lyrical tale is written from the point of view of an ordinary Welsh private. Jones' tale follows the journey of one man into a baffling, dangerous but often frighteningly beautiful world. Jones was also attempting to universalize the war experience; to portray his "truth" of the war in a new voice that gave it proper tongue and moved it away from the pretensions of modernism and the rhetoric of high diction. He did so within a form that has had a lasting impact on the understanding of the First World War: poetry. His work also encompasses long sections of lyric prose, and perhaps in these respects he was no different from writers such as Brooke, Sassoon, Brittain, and Graves, all of whom looked for new ways to describe the war they saw in a manner befitting their experiences.

However, what critics—from Stephen Spender, who erroneously thought the text was "probably the World War I monument most likely to survive," to Julian Mitchell in 2003, who extolled *In Parenthesis* as a classic waiting to be rediscovered—often forget is the sheer inaccessibility of the text. This is not a recent trend; Jones' work has always been marginalized because so few people are able to survive its depths. Yet it has always had its champions. Whether this makes it a good book that will endure as long as predicted remains to be seen, but it is certainly not, nor is it likely ever to be, a popular one. **EMcCS**

The Years

Virginia Woolf

Lifespan | *b*. 1882 (England), *d*. 1941
First Published | 1937
First Published by | Hogarth Press (London)
Given Name | Adeline Virginia Stephen

Covering a span of fifty years as it recounts the fortunes of the Pargiter family, this is the longest and most commercially successful of Woolf's novels. The Pargiters are headed by a retired military patriarch who, owing to his wife's disability, is also an occasional philanderer. The children (three sons and three daughters) variously flirt with nonconformity but ultimately spread themselves effortlessly among the middle-class professions. In many ways the Pargiter family is a remnant of the Victorianism that Woolf inveighed against throughout her career. This is not a chronicle in the conventional sense of the term. By the close of the novel, fortunes have been won and lost, loves forsaken, and lives have perished. Nevertheless, it is Woolf's characteristic attention to fragmentary moments of experience that produces the most intense writing. As the characters variously return to the past in a modern world that resists easy understanding, the poeticism of the writing focuses instead on unfinished vignettes and the particularity of sense impressions.

A perceptive critic and observer, Woolf reveals the plight of women in a world that denies them education and careers; she shows the tragic consequences of the Great War for its survivors and retains an unflinching eye for the mortifying effects of bourgeois social pretension. The reader will find that the extended lyricism and crystalline expressiveness of the writing lingers in the memory long after the final pages have been read. **VA**

The Hobbit

J. R. R. Tolkien

Lifespan | *b*. 1892 (South Africa), *d*. 1973 (England)
First Published | 1937
First Published by | G. Allen & Unwin (London)
Full Title | *The Hobbit: or, There and back again*

Although it stemmed from stories he had been writing about his fictional world, Middle Earth, for a decade, *The Hobbit* was Tolkien's first published work, which was to be followed over a decade later by its sequel, *The Lord of the Rings*. The plot and characters combined the ancient heroic Anglo-Saxon and Scandinavian epics Tolkien studied at Oxford with the middle-class rural England in which he lived and felt comfortable.

Bilbo Baggins, the hero of the story, is a hobbit—a race of small people about half the size of humans with hairy feet and a passion for food and drink. Encouraged by the wizard Gandalf, Bilbo leaves his village, the Shire, for the first time and sets off on an adventure with a group of dwarves seeking to reclaim their treasure from a dragon. When Bilbo meets Gollum, he finds himself the bearer of a magic ring that makes the wearer disappear. After a series of adventures, Bilbo and Gandalf return to the village, but Bilbo is no longer accepted, his adventurous behavior being deemed unhobbitlike. Bilbo is an unlikely hero, who achieves metamorphosis through pools of inner strength he didn't know he had. Some critics have tried to read metaphors for England's heroism during the war or the inherent evil in some nationalities. But Tolkien was known to dislike allegory, and it is more likely simply the heroic story of a small, charming person who has no idea how resourceful he is until his abilities are put to the test. **EF**

Their Eyes Were Watching God

Zora Neale Hurston

Lifespan | *b.* 1903 (U.S.), *d.* 1960
First Published | 1937
First Published by | J.B. Lippincott Co. (Philadelphia)
Movie Adaptation | 2005 (Harpo Studios)

"They sat in company with the others . . . They seemed to be staring at the dark, but their eyes were watching God."

⊙ Hurston trained as an anthropologist, developing a fine ear for speech patterns through the study of Afro-American oral culture.

Brutal experiences of slavery prompt sixteen-year-old Janie's maternal grandmother to marry her off to a respectable man. She hopes to insulate Janie from the potentially ruinous burdens she and other black women have had to bear. Yet Janie's fearless idealism leaves her feeling unfulfilled, and she abandons her emotionally stingy husband for Joe, an extravagant dreamer with whom she heads further south to build a thriving, all-black town out of little more than ambition and some roadside land. Joe elevates Janie's socio-economic status, but she becomes a trapping of his success rather than a respected partner. By the time of Joe's death, Janie is a middle-aged woman confident enough to withstand the town's persistent, speculative gossip and trust her instincts with Tea Cake, a mysterious younger man. By the novel's end, though she has lost everything, Janie has realized her vision of love like a blossoming pear tree in the intense, volatile bond she and Tea Cake shared.

Hurston was the mayor's daughter in America's first incorporated black town, where her social and political experience of African-American autonomy afforded a unique perspective on race. She eventually trained as an anthropologist, researching African-American folklore and oral culture in her native Florida. The dialogue in *Their Eyes Were Watching God* is written primarily in the strong Southern African-American dialect (framed by a standard English narrative), the pronunciation, rhythm, and playfulness of which Hurston renders in rich detail using almost phonetic spelling. This celebration of colloquial language and life was harshly criticized by contemporaries such as Richard Wright, but Hurston is now regarded as a highly significant figure in African-American literature. **AF**

Of Mice and Men

John Steinbeck

The title of quite possibly John Steinbeck's best known work refers to a line from a Robert Burns' poem *To a Mouse*, hinting simply at the tragedy of the tale. The novella tells the story of George and Lennie, two migrant workers who have been let off the bus miles from the California ranch where they work. George is a small, sharp man with dark features, and Lennie a mentally subnormal, shapeless giant who is deeply devoted to George and relies on him for protection and guidance. Camped out for the night, this unlikely couple share a dream of starting a farm together. Back on the ranch, the men meet Slim, the mule driver who admires their friendship. He gives Lennie one of his puppies and convinces the two men to include him in their dreams of buying a piece of land and setting up home. But the dream is shattered when Lennie accidentally kills the puppy and, without meaning to, breaks the neck of a woman on the ranch. Fleeing a terrible death at the hands of a lynch mob, Lennie encounters George, who gently reiterates the story of the idyllic life they will share together, before shooting his friend in the back of his head. When the mob arrives, Slim realizes that George has killed his friend out of mercy and leads him away.

This is a story about brotherhood and the harsh reality of a world that refuses to allow such idealized male bonds to be nurtured. George and Lennie's unique relationship approaches that ideal, but it is misunderstood by the rest of the world, who cannot comprehend true friendship, instead undermining one another and exploiting weakness wherever it can be found. But perhaps the real tragedy of the novel lies in the depiction of the death of the great American dream as a reality, exposing it as exactly what it purports to be: merely a dream. **EF**

Lifespan | *b.* 1902 (U.S.), *d.* 1968
First Published | 1937
First Published by | Covici Friede (New York)
Nobel Prize for Literature | 1962

"Might jus' as well spen' all my time tellin' you things and then you forget 'em, and I tell you again."

⊙ Steinbeck based most of his best writing on observation of life among the lower levels of rural society in his native California.

Murphy

Samuel Beckett

Lifespan | b. 1906 (Ireland), d. 1989 (France)
First Published | 1938
First Published by | G. Routledge & Sons (London)
Nobel Prize for Literature | 1969

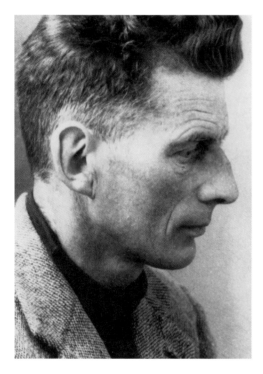

"Let our conversation now be without precedent in fact or literature ..."

◉ Largely ignored when first published, *Murphy* was relaunched on the back of the success of the play *Waiting for Godot* in the 1950s.

In a writing career that produced many masterpieces, *Murphy* is perhaps the most continuously delightful and engagingly disengaged Beckett wrote. Almost a conventional novel, lacking the rigorous austerity and reflexivity of Beckett's later novels, *Murphy* is closer in spirit to the play and pseudo-erudition of *Tristram Shandy,* with more than occasional hints of Joycean wit and Rabelaisian materialism. From the off, the novel takes lapidary strikes at the lazy pomp of the omniscient narrator. Dead phrases are turned over with amused scorn—"And life in his mind gave him pleasure, such pleasure that pleasure was not the word." Between arcane referentiality and lexical flicks, the jokes come thick and fast, so fast that thick is not the word.

The novel tells of the adventures of Murphy in London, with a particularity of specified urban geography unusual in Beckett's work. Aspiring to freedom and a quality of stillness in a rocking chair, Murphy variously attempts to avoid getting caught up in anything resembling a plot, but nevertheless finds himself propelled into misadventures with sundry implausible creations. Among other escapades, Murphy runs away from his betrothed, shacks up with a prostitute, and finds relatively gainful employment in a mental institution where he plays a peculiar brand of pacifist chess. Murphy dies in an accident, the revelation of which would only spoil what little suspense and final uplift the novel can offer. Notably buoyant among many bits of bravura narration is the description of Murphy's "mind," but perhaps the most lasting glow to emanate from this comic romance is the brio with which it resists the temptations and literary tedium of its darker leanings. A great way into Beckett, and a great way out. **DM**

U.S.A.

Dos Passos

The three novels collected as *U.S.A.* are the most successful of many twentieth-century attempts to write the inclusive story of American life. Dos Passos covers the years 1900 to 1930, describing the rise of the labor movement, the inner workings of capitalism, life at sea, the American experience of the First World War, the rise of Hollywood, and the decline into the great Depression. These events are skillfully evoked in the lives of the novels' twelve main characters, six men and six women. The centrality of violence to American life is firmly established, particularly in the accounts of attacks on the Wobblies (International Workers of the World) as they attempt to organize a union.

"But mostly *U.S.A.* is the speech of the people," Dos Passos writes, and his impeccable ear for the many voices of America puts these voices into conflict, or collusion, or concurrence, building up an overview that is also a socialist critique. Dos Passos is not a nineteenth-century naturalist but a modernist, and the speech of the people is embedded in a narrative that derives from Joyce, Gertrude Stein, and Hemingway. The autobiographical "Camera Eye" sections are in the style of Joyce's *A Portrait of the Artist*, and the "Newsreel" sections quoting actual newspaper headlines are a satirical documentary device. Stein's continuous present is here the model for the main text. This method works to convey equally the political hopes of working people, the social innocence of young women and men, and the inevitability of events when power intervenes. It also allows skips and jumps in consciousness that Dos Passos uses to push the narrative forward. The irruption of American voices into this process-language makes for a complex but unquestionably successful mix. **AMu**

Lifespan | *b.* 1896 (U.S.), *d.* 1970
First Published | 1938, by Constable & Co. (London)
Trilogy | *The 42nd Parallel* (1930); *1919* (1932); *The Big Money* (1936)

"non nein nicht englander amerikanisch americain Hoch Amerika Vive l'Amerique" [sic]

⬆ Like Hemingway and E. E. Cummings, Dos Passos served in the Ambulance Corps in the First World War.

Brighton Rock

Graham Greene

The two main characters in Greene's gripping reflection on the nature of evil are the amateur detective Ida and the murderous Pinkie, a Roman Catholic who chooses hell over heaven. Responsible for two murders, he is forced to marry the hapless Rose to prevent her from giving evidence. A good Catholic, Rose seems to represent Pinkie's lost innocence. Although Ida is ostensibly the heroine of the novel, her heroism belongs to the blank morality of the detective novel, where the measure of goodness is in the ability to solve the mystery. By contrast, through his contemplation of his own damnation Pinkie's evil achieves a sense of moral seriousness which Ida's agnosticism can never obtain. Rose is Pinkie's counterpart here, sharing his Catholic faith and prepared to corrupt herself in order to protect a man that she believes loves her. For Pinkie, the part he plays in Rose's corruption will ensure his damnation much more clearly than his role in the murders that punctuate the novel.

Brighton Rock began life as a detective novel, and the mark of that genre remains in Ida's pursuit of Pinkie. However, the structure of the detective novel merely contains the moral framework seen here. The contrast between Pinkie's theological morality and its insubstantial counterparts is reinforced using various narrative techniques. Principally, the language through which Pinkie's contemplation of hell is expressed contrasts vividly with the comparatively frivolous considerations of Ida and the other characters. What finally distinguishes Pinkie's tragic mode from the generic patterns of the detective story is a critique of commercialized popular culture in which, with the exception of Pinkie, almost every character is associated with the limited imaginative potential of mass culture. **LC**

Lifespan | *b.* 1904 (England), *d.* 1991 (Switzerland)
First Published | 1938
First Published by | W. Heinemann (London)
Movie Adaptation Released | 1947

Greene is photographed here in the late 1920s, shortly after the conversion to Catholicism that profoundly affected his fiction.

Richard Attenborough plays Pinkie in the 1947 movie *Brighton Rock*, which makes an excellent thriller out of Greene's drama.

Cause for Alarm

Eric Ambler

Lifespan | b. 1909 (England), d. 1998
First Published | 1938
First Published by | Hodder & Stoughton (London)
Postwar Pseudonym | Eliot Reed

In the late 1930s, Eric Ambler reinvented the British thriller, a genre that had been teeming with unconvincing villains pitted against, as he put it, heroes of "abysmal stupidity." His first novel, *The Dark Frontier* (1936), began as a parody. A scientist regains consciousness after a car crash believing himself to be a tough hero, and foils a charismatic Countess' dastardly plan for world domination. Five more followed in the next five years, of which the best is *Cause for Alarm*.

Nicholas Marlow—an engineer, as Ambler himself was—loses his job on the day he proposes to his girlfriend. Ten weeks later, still unemployed, he accepts a position in the Milan office of a British company that manufactures machines for making artillery shells. In Italy, he is approached by various spies of ambiguous affiliation, eager for information about how the Fascist government is arming itself. Caught up in a tangle of espionage and counter-espionage, Marlow eventually falls foul of the authorities. Trapped on the wrong side of a continent rolling toward war, with a price on his head, he has to flee. The last third of the novel is taken up by an impressively sustained and exhilarating chase across northern Italy. *Cause for Alarm* is the extremely exciting story of an innocent abroad who finds that his innocence is a kind of culpability, of a man who is forced to recalibrate his loyalties to his employers, to his country, to science, and to the world at large. **TEJ**

Rebecca

Daphne du Maurier

Lifespan | b. 1907 (England), d. 1989
First Published | 1938
First Published by | V. Gollancz (London)
Movie Adaptation Released | 1940

Rebecca still captivates readers today, nearly seventy years after its first publication when it became an immediate best-seller, spawning many adaptations and copycat narratives. The novel's resilience lies in du Maurier's combination of fairy-tale elements with aspects of gothic romance and thriller.

The shy narrator is chosen for marriage by a wealthy, mysterious, upper-class widower and thus saved from her life as the paid companion to an ill-mannered European woman. She moves to Manderley, an ancient English mansion filled with forbidden rooms, shrouded furniture, and labyrinthine passageways, only to find that both house and owner, the aristocratic Maximilian de Winter, are haunted and oppressed by the memory of the first Mrs. de Winter, Rebecca. Maxim himself bears a distinct resemblance to Mr. Rochester in *Jane Eyre*, and as with Rochester, Maxim's "secret self" masks the revelation around which the plot of the novel revolves. *Jane Eyre*'s madwoman in the attic is replaced here by the body of a murdered woman bobbing in the sea, refusing to be washed away. *Rebecca's* narrator breaks the Victorian mold of the novel with her neurotic fantasies, and she raises more questions than she answers. One of du Maurier's achievements is to secure readers' loyalty to this jealous, insecure narrator. **SN**

❯ Du Maurier's fascination with her initially abandoned and neglected house "Menabilly" inspired the house in *Rebecca*.

Nausea

Jean-Paul Sartre

Lifespan | *b.* 1905 (France), *d.* 1980
First Published | 1938, by Gallimard (Paris)
Original Title | *La Nausée*
Nobel Prize for Literature | 1964 (declined)

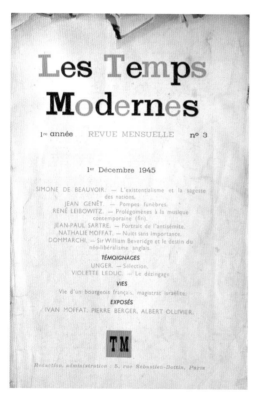

● Sartre was an editor for the journal *Les Temps Modernes*,
first published in 1945, which he used to develop his ideas.

❯ By 1946, when this photo of Sartre was taken, his existentialism
was being popularized as a hip attitude to life for young radicals.

Sartre's *Nausea* is that rare thing in literary history—
a "philosophical" novel that succeeds in both of its
endeavors. The novel is at once a manifesto for
existentialist philosophy and a convincing work of
art. In fact, it succeeds to such an extent that it blurs
the distinction between literature and philosophy
altogether. *Nausea* details the experiences of thirty-
year-old Antoine Roquentin, a researcher who has
settled in the French port of Bouville (a thinly
disguised Le Havre) after several years of travel.
Settling down, however, produces a series of
increasingly strange effects. As Roquentin engages
in simple, everyday activities, his understanding of
the world and his place in it is fundamentally altered.
He comes to perceive the rational solidity of
existence as no more than a fragile veneer. He
experiences the "nausea" of reality, a "sweetish
sickness," a ground-level vertigo. He is appalled
by the blank indifference of inanimate objects,
yet acutely conscious that each situation he finds
himself in bears the irrevocable stamp of his being.
He finds that he cannot escape from his own
overwhelming presence.

This is a delicately controlled examination of
freedom, responsibility, consciousness, and time.
Influenced by the philosophy of Edmund Husserl
and the literary stylings of Dostoevsky and Kafka,
Nausea is the novel that announced existentialism
to the world—a system of ideas that would go on to
become one of the most significant developments
in twentieth-century thought and culture. The
notion that "existence precedes essence" is writ large
for the first time here, several years before Sartre
"formalized" his ideas in *Being and Nothingness*
(1943) and before the horrors of the Second World
War had intensified their impact. **SamT**

Miss Pettigrew Lives for a Day

Winifred Watson

Lifespan | *b.* 1907 (England), *d.* 2002
First Published | 1938
First Published by | Methuen & Co. (London)
Radio Adaptation Released | 2000 (BBC Radio 4)

"Miss Pettigrew pushed open the door of the employment agency and went in as the clock struck a quarter past nine. She had, as usual, very little hope . . . " So begins Winifred Watson's recently rediscovered, enchanting tale. The story unfolds over twenty-four hours in the life of neglected spinster, Guinevere Pettigrew. Sent to the wrong address by her employment agency, Miss Pettigrew, a governess, is mistaken for the new housekeeper by the glamorous and rather amoral nightclub singer Miss La Fosse. Thrown into a world of cocktails before noon, cocaine that must be disposed of, and fistfights between dangerously handsome suitors, perhaps most shocking of all to Miss Pettigrew is the wicked thrill of makeup. As first-time readers, we worry for the frightened and sheltered Guinevere, but there is more to her than meets the eye. Over the course of the day, in a series of deft interventions, witty misunderstandings, brilliant repartee, and enough gin to sink a lesser woman, Guinevere is revealed not only to her newfound friends, but more importantly to herself, as a lifesaver, in more ways than one. A delightful, intelligent, and naughty novel, which reminds us that it is never too late to have a second chance; it is never too late to live. **MJ**

○ Winifred Watson, here pictured on her wedding day, October 26 1934, four years before writing *Miss Pettigrew Lives for a Day*.

After the Death of Don Juan

Sylvia Townsend Warner

Lifespan | *b.* 1893 (England), *d.* 1978
First Published | 1938
First Published by | Chatto & Windus (London)
Original Language | English

A revolution occurred in Republican Spain after Franco's forces rebelled in 1936. Sylvia Townsend Warner—a communist since 1935—allegorizes that revolution by turning back to the 1770s, the time of the Borbón king, Carlos III. She turns to rural Spain, to Don Juan's family village, Tenorio Viejo ("Old Ladykiller" or "Old Don Juan"). The characters from Mozart's opera and Molière's play are all present, but there is no main figure, for this is a novel with a collective subject.

To prepare for the revolution, a story of discovery must be told. The windswept journey from urbane Seville to the village of essential values and ineradicable conflicts tells of the power of priests and of the castle, and of the instinctive opposition of the pueblo. Narrative is limited. Leporello tells his story, that Don Juan is in hell; but Doña Ana is curiously insistent on visiting his father, Don Saturno, in Tenorio Viejo. When Don Juan reappears there, she denies that it is him. The Sevillians become bourgeois reactionaries, while the liberal Don Saturno is seduced to the side of "fascism" of Don Juan and the priests. Fulfilling allegory, they call soldiers to attack the village. Among the villagers is the subtle and complex Ramon who, dying, has a vision of the village as part of all Spain, with Madrid at its heart—for both village and city are necessary for successful revolution to take place. **AMu**

The Big Sleep

Raymond Chandler

Lifespan | *b.* 1888 (U.S.), *d.* 1959
First Published | 1939
First Published by | Hamish Hamilton (London)
Movie Adaptation Released | 1946

⊙ Chandler poses for the photographer while working on a movie
script in 1945—he hated Hollywood but needed the money.

⊙ Novelist William Faulkner was one of the screenwriters for
the impressively witty 1946 movie version of Chandler's novel.

The Big Sleep represents some major departures in the nature of the detective genre, changes that necessarily reflect the world in which it was written. Corrupt networks map out Chandler's post-prohibition era, be they explicitly criminal or nominally official, and it is the gray areas in between that allow the detective Philip Marlowe to exist. The gray, claustrophobic urban space is a major constituent; set in Southern California, the location could really be any major city given that exteriors are almost entirely absent. Rooms, cars and even phone booths represent a series of divided compartments in which the story develops, a series of points with no connections.

This is Chandler's first Marlowe story, but there is no introduction to the character; rather, we leap straight into the investigation as it gets underway. This is essential to the nature of the world and the character, a new kind of "hero" who seems only to become active when there is a crime to solve. We know nothing of his background and only ever see him return to his office, and this only when a trail is exhausted. Like Sergio Leone's *Man With No Name*, Marlowe combines a kind of shabby fallibility— a hard drinker who seems to be constantly beaten up by men and women alike—with an almost supernatural authority whereby he seems to serenely coast over the jumbled twists and turns of the case, observing and randomly following leads and providence, until a solution is finally reached. That this is in such contrast to the Sherlock Holmes school of detective work, where central to the plot is the immense intellectuality of the detective that allows him to simply consider at length the facts in order to succeed, is perhaps the most significant factor in the novel's literary importance. **SF**

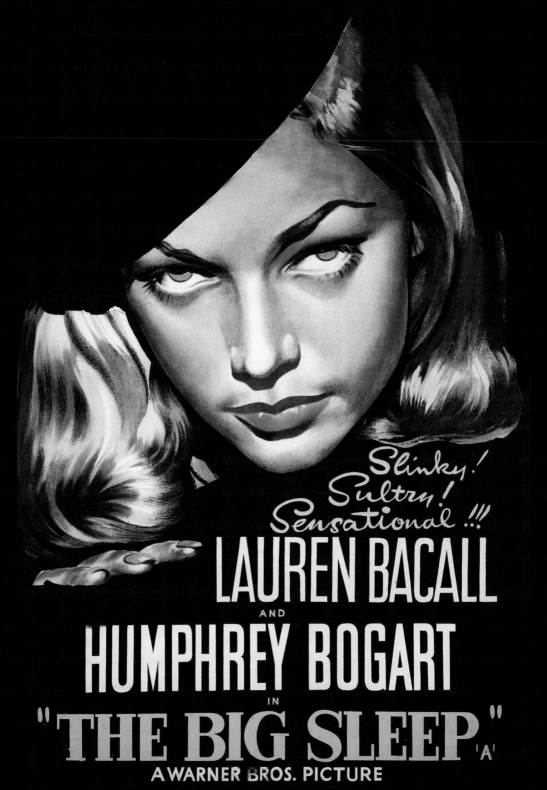

Good Morning, Midnight

Jean Rhys

Lifespan | *b.* 1890 (Dominica), *d.* 1979 (England)
First Published | 1939
First Published by | Constable & Co. (London)
Given Name | Ella Gwendolen Rees William

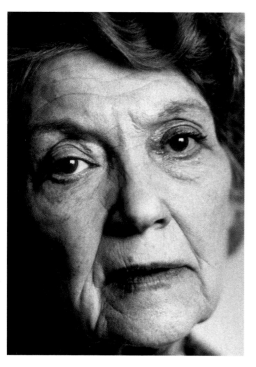

*"We can't all be happy,
we can't all be rich . . . "*

⬤ Rhys, born to a Welsh father and Creole mother in Dominica,
often wrote about the effects of women being uprooted.

The title of Jean Rhys' somber fifth novel is taken from an Emily Dickinson poem. *Good Morning, Midnight* is set between the wars and centers on Sasha, a middle-aged woman who has returned to the Paris of her youth. The fragmented and elliptical narrative slips between Sasha's past and present in exploring the paradoxical limitations of the life of a woman who has sought to free herself from convention.

As the novel opens, and Sasha attempts to locate herself among Paris' familiar landmarks, we are deluged with the bittersweet memories of her youth. We learn how she escaped from the strictures of a working-class London life by marrying the artistic Enno and moving with him to Europe. Sasha's pleasurable recollections of this marriage are frequently undercut, however, by her more anxious memories of the couple's poverty and fear of displacement. It is in these earliest memories that Sasha's awareness of her vulnerability starkly emerges. Enno's reluctance to protect his wife from degrading social and economic transactions makes her profoundly aware of how "cheap" she is to society. As we move further into the novel and further into Sasha's past we learn of the trauma—the death of her child in early infancy and her subsequent abandonment by her husband—that led to her rejection by even unconventional society. It is Sasha's rapid and poignant decline, her steady drinking and drifting between jobs that seem to value feminine youth and beauty above all, that offers a continuity between the novel's past and the present. As the novel ends, we see Sasha stumbling to accept how the inevitable and harsh combinations of poverty and age have rendered her only more vulnerable. **NM**

Tropic of Capricorn

Henry Miller

There is something monstrous about *Tropic of Capricorn*. As what Miller called a "fictional autobiography," it is hardly a novel at all but a proudly mongrel meeting place for diary, memoir, exposé, rant, and romance. It is Miller's egotism that makes the book addictive, the magnificent ambition of his fascination with himself. And it is Miller's egotism that similarly renders the book almost intolerable, his relentless fascination with a profoundly misogynistic self.

Written in a style that allows sentences to roll on for pages or spits them out in sharp brief sequences, *Tropic of Capricorn* is as enchanted with language and its madnesses as other texts of late modernism. But where Joyce and Beckett sculpt and order their texts with visible meticulousness, Miller's macho pioneer raids on his consciousness, sensibility, and sexuality have a chaotic artfulness.

Though begun in 1932 and not published until 1939, during which time Miller was in Paris, *Tropic of Capricorn* is a 1920s New York novel. It is a post-war novel in that it is simultaneously at ease with and appalled by the normalization of war and of the civilizations that spawn war. It is a New York novel in so far as only that city of innumerable voices could have given Miller the jumble of raw, damaged, and unfinished stories of exile, hope, and loss that he consumes with such appetite. At the loose heart of this novel is Miller's experience as an employment manager (and company spy) at Western Union. Appearing in the novel as the "Cosmodemonic Telegraph Company," it is a technologized network of miscommunication. There is therefore something appropriately and viciously ironic in Miller using his critique of the company to communicate so fiercely what *Tropic of Capricorn* is about: himself. **PMcM**

Lifespan | *b.* 1891 (U.S.), *d.* 1980
First Published | 1939
First Published by | Obelisk Press (Paris)
Original Language | English

"I was a philosopher when still in swaddling clothes. "

⊘ Miller asserted that possession of creative talent inevitably isolates the artist from less splendidly endowed mortals.

Goodbye to Berlin

Christopher Isherwood

'"I am a camera," Isherwood writes, "with its shutter open, quite passive, recording, not thinking." What he offers us are snapshots and newsreels of Berlin during the last days of the Weimar Republic. The city is caught in the eerie calm of an apocalyptic hurricane, the brief window wedged between the First World War and the distant thunder of the indomitable Third Reich.

Isherwood, the narrator and observer, is detached and numb as though shell-shocked—what he is witnessing hasn't been witnessed before. The demimonde he inhabits is a fatalistic free-for-all, fueled by a growing despair so great that the only recourse is a dance of abandon, the last and most memorable song of the dance band on the *Titanic* as the iceberg looms. It is a world of lost souls, where the great have fallen, where the good do what they can to make ends meet, where everything is for sale and virtue is an unaffordable luxury. Former socialites must take in lodgers, prostitutes mingle with opera singers, and Isherwood stumbles through opportunities with his fellow expatriate and co-lodger, the aspiring nightclub singer, Sally Bowles. Sally is a perfect emblem of the time: tragic and blind to consequences, capricious and predatory, and deadened by alcohol and sex. This is a melancholic though unsentimental novel about a world that will soon no longer exist. The hedonism of the Weimar is fading and soon will be eradicated. Sally grows distracted and disagreeable. The Jewish Landauers' tenuous safety will soon be destroyed. Rudi, the communist youth, will have his idealism prove fatal. Innocence will be lost.

With his understated and dispassionate prose, Isherwood throws the massive and terrifying events of 1930s Berlin into relief; his genius is chilling. **GT**

Lifespan | b. 1904 (England), d. 1986 (U.S.)
First Published | 1939
First Published by | Hogarth Press (London)
Compiled as | *The Berlin Stories* (1946)

The musical *Cabaret*, based on Isherwood's novel, was filmed in 1972 with Liza Minnelli cast as nightclub singer Sally Bowles.

When Isherwood moved to Berlin, the sexual freedom depicted here influenced both his personal life and his writing.

Coming Up for Air

George Orwell

Lifespan | *b.* 1903 (India), *d.* 1950 (England)
First Published | 1939
First Published by | V. Gollancz (London)
Given Name | Eric Arthur Blair

Coming Up for Air is a biting satire on post-war society in the 1930s, a singularly unpleasant tale about an equally unpleasant man, but also a prophetic anticipation on social development. George Bowling, the protagonist, seems to typify stereotypes of the lower middle class—it is better to complain than to act, everything was always better in the past, and society is going to the dogs. Yet the novel is far more complex than this and truly deserves the apocalyptic moniker of "Orwellian."

Bowling is an apparently mundane everyman who feels a bitter revulsion for his fellow man and continually harps back to the days before 1914. Tiring of his wife Hilda, Bowling returns to Lower Binfield, the heart of middle England, where the residents, who regard the past as a foreign country, are not only blithely indifferent, but utterly subservient to the status quo. Ultimately, the only thing that the self-aware Bowling has to look forward to is the same series of ideals presented through the looming specter of the coming war. Bowling's bitter resentment and Orwell's wry, dark, observational powers in a world that is increasingly turning away from the big questions show a dark undertone to British society, as well as highlighting the continual social unease of "dumbing down." Moments such as George's purchase of a hot dog that tastes like fish demonstrate not only the potency of observation, but also the disappointing reality of modern consumables. **EMcCS**

> *"Do you know the active, hearty kind of fat man, the athletic bouncing type that's nicknamed Fatty or Tubby and is always the life and soul of the party? I'm that type."*

🔵 Eric Blair, pictured here after having adopted his pseudonym, which he did in order not to embarrass his parents by his work.

At Swim-Two-Birds

Flann O'Brien

Lifespan | *b*. 1911 (Ireland), *d*. 1966
First Published | 1939
First Published by | Longmans & Co. (London)
Given Name | Brian O'Nuallain

Ireland in the 1930s, with its censorship and church domination, was hardly a hotbed for the avant-garde or experimental novel. But it was precisely the pieties and stifling atmosphere of Ireland at the time that impelled this delightfully transgressive, anti-authoritarian, and satirical experimental novel. Literary exuberance contrasted with the mundanity of social life is one of the anomalies within the novel that gives it such potent comic power.

This is a novel about a novelist writing a novel about the writing of novel. The frame story is narrated by a student living sullenly under his nagging uncle's roof, while engaged in writing a book about an author called Dermot Trellis. The student has firmly democratic and revolutionary ideas on the form: the novel should not be confined to one beginning and ending, nor should the characters be under any compulsion to be good or bad. They should, rather, be "allowed a private life, self-determination and a decent standard of living." Furthermore, the "entire corpus of existing literature" is simply a storehouse from which an author can draw whatever characters he wishes. The narrator and Trellis draw on cowboy stories, popular romances, folklore, and (mercilessly lampooned) figures from Irish mythology. Eager for revenge against his despotic creator, one character begins his own novel in which Trellis becomes trapped as a fictional creation. If ever a novel was before its time, undoubtedly this was it. **RMcD**

Finnegans Wake

James Joyce

Lifespan | *b*. 1882 (Ireland), *d*. 1941 (Switzerland)
First Published | 1939
First Published by | Faber & Faber (London)
Extracts Published | 1928–1939

Joyce's last book is perhaps the most daunting work of fiction ever written. Yet it is also one of the funniest, bringing pleasure to generations of readers willing to suspend the usual assumptions that govern the novel. Instead of a single plot, *Finnegans Wake* has a number of kernel stories, some of them occurring in hundreds of versions from a word or two long to several pages. The most ubiquitous is a story of a fall that turns out not to be entirely negative, including the Fall of Man; an indiscretion in Phoenix Park, Dublin, involving an older man and two girls; and Tim Finnegan's tumble from a ladder. In place of characters, the novel has figures who go by many different names, each figure consisting of a cluster of recognizable features. In place of settings, the novel merges place names from around the globe.

Joyce achieves this remarkable condensation through the "portmanteau": the fusing together of two or more words in the same or different languages. Thus "kissmiss" is both the festive season and something that might happen during it, with a further suggestion of the fatality of the event; the Holy Father becomes a "hoary frother"; and an old photo is a "fadograph." Reading *Finnegans Wake*—best done aloud and if possible in a group—means allowing these multiple suggestions to resonate, while accepting that many will remain obscure. The work's seventeen sections have their own styles and subjects, tracing a slow movement through nightfall and dawn, to the end that is not an end of … **DA**

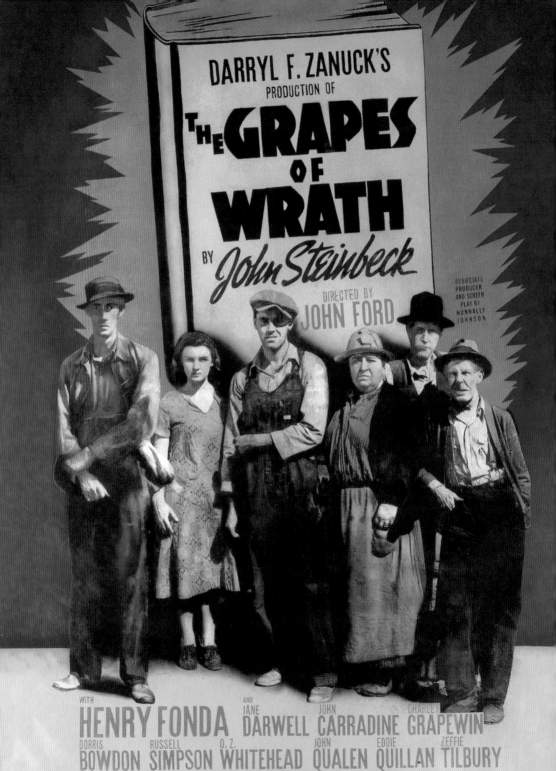

The Grapes of Wrath

John Steinbeck

It is something of a commonplace these days to talk of *The Grapes of Wrath* as a novel that has become profoundly ingrained in the consciousness of America, and yet no other writer chronicled the catastrophic period of the Great Depression in the 1930s with the same passion and political commitment. As Steinbeck's masterpiece, its place in the canon of great American literature is confirmed by the Pulitzer Prize it was awarded in 1940 (the same year it was adapted for film) and the Nobel Prize for Literature that the author received in 1962. It is concerned with the Joad family, who lose their Oklahoma farm and head west with dreams of a better life in California. As the journey unfolds, they and thousands of other "Okies" flocking westward converge along Highway 66, telling each other tales of injustice and relishing the plenty that lies ahead. What they find in California is exploitation, greed, low wages, hunger, and death. In a stunning indictment of the savage divisions that those with money seek to extend and exploit, Steinbeck represents the desperation of the family as the threat of violence, starvation, and death begin to eat away at them. It is only wrath, a defiant solidarity, and constant sacrifice that allow them to maintain their dignity.

Steinbeck has been criticized in the past for a perceived sentimentality in his characterization of the Joads, but while a reader is inevitably drawn into their plight, they are only ever actors in a tragedy that is bigger than they are. This is above all a political novel, and the defeats, the mud, the hunger, and the maltreatment all carry a political charge, a condemnation of injustice (and those in positions of power who create it), and a validation of the quiet anger and dignified stoicism of the common man in response. **MD**

Lifespan | *b.* 1902 (U.S.), *d.* 1968
First Published | 1939, by Viking (New York)
Pulitzer Prize | 1962
Nobel Prize for Literature | 1962

⬆ Californian photographer Peter Stackpole snapped this casual unposed image of Steinbeck for *Life* magazine in 1937.

◀ Steinbeck described Ford's 1940 movie version of his novel as "a hard, straight picture," although it ended with an optimistic twist.

Party Going

Henry Green

Lifespan | *b.* 1905 (England), *d.* 1973
First Published | 1939
First Published by | Hogarth Press (London)
Given Name | Henry Vincent Yorke

Written between 1931 and 1938, *Party Going* took Green longer to write than any other of his novels. Although it is not his most brilliant work, it does reveal, in a more concentrated performance than anywhere else in his oeuvre, the full force of his very sophisticated and perceptive contempt for the lifestyles of the pampered upper class and all their ruses of infantilism and self-importance.

Party Going takes place during a period of only four hours and is set in and around a London train station. A group of rich young friends intends to depart for a "party" (what we would now call a holiday); the story unfolds as they wait in a luxury suite of a railway hotel for their train, delayed by fog, to carry them away. The action of the book is all inert, confined to the psychological ornamentalism of the characters' various suspicions about, and designs on, each other. The fog outside is of course symbolic, to some degree, of the ignorance of the group with respect to the immense and chaotic organization of wage labor, both in the station and in the city of London in general. It is this same chaotic organization of wage labor that is obligated by economic reality to wait on them and which they find so oppressive and distasteful that they have demanded a haven from it for the indefinite duration of their wait. But Green is too good a novelist ever to allow the scenery of his novels to be fully symbolic, and so allows the meaning of the novel to emerge like a border trim. **KS**

The Tartar Steppe

Dino Buzzati

Lifespan | *b.* 1906 (Italy), *d.* 1972
First Published | 1940
First Published by | Rizzoli (Milan)
Original Title | *Il deserto dei Tartari*

In this mysterious and disquieting novel soldiers at a garrison await the attack of the enemy, the Tartars, due to arrive from the north any day. The fortress where the action takes place belongs to an undifferentiated past, and the atmosphere within the fortress, situated at the bottom of harsh and inaccessible mountains at the border of a stony desert, is suspended between reality and dream. The soldiers prepare continuously for that moment, although no one knows how and when the attack will take place. No one even knows who the enemy really is. Destiny is in charge of the lives of these men, especially Lieutenant Drogo, who finds himself at the fortress against his will, after an exhausting journey overshadowed by the enigmatic fortress and the threatening harshness of the landscape. In the surreal atmosphere within the garrison, life is disciplined by strict military routines. Sentries patrol nobody knows what to defend the fortress from nobody knows whom. Military maneuvers have no apparent meaning, while the soldiers' unreal life is dominated by an absurd wait.

Strongly existentialist in its themes, the novel remains elusive today, but it seems ironic that not long after publication the soldiers' long wait was ultimately met with a conflict far larger than they could ever have hoped for. **RPi**

⊙ *The Tartar Steppe* depicts the futility of military tactics such as that shown in this 1917 Italian poster: "Everyone must do his duty!"

Fate tutti il vostro dovere!

LE SOTTOSCRIZIONI AL PRESTITO SI RICEVONO PRESSO IL
CREDITO ITALIANO

The Power and the Glory

Graham Greene

Lifespan | b. 1904 (England), d. 1991 (Switzerland)
First Published | 1940
First Published by | W. Heinemann (London)
Movie Adaptation Released | 1962

The Power and the Glory, with its account of a priest's desperate flight from arrest and execution, is set against the bleak backdrop of the persecution of the Catholic Church in Mexico in the 1920s. The terrain Greene describes—whether physical, social, or psychological—is suitably desolate. The protagonist, described but never named, is a "whisky priest" and the father of an illegitimate child, whom he briefly and unhappily encounters on his journey. The psychological and spiritual avenues available to him for making sense of his fate seem as unpromising as his options for escaping from the secular authorities. He has a price on his head and his pursuers are liable to execute the villagers who come to his assistance. But through the despair, and despite Greene's resistance to various weightless forms of redemption (he is much exercised by the fraudulent, pride-sustaining qualities of piety), lies the hazily grasped apprehension of God's goodness. The priest comes to realize that conditions of suffering and sinfulness are, perhaps, the only means by which God's presence can be manifested in this world.

There are many triumphs in this novel: the priest's night-long incarceration in an overcrowded jail; his quest to buy wine for sacramental purposes; and the ideological and personal cat-and-mouse encounters between the priest and the zealous lieutenant. Greene succeeds in fashioning a fallen world marked, strikingly, by the twin poles of intense claustrophobia and unbounded emptiness. **RMcD**

Native Son

Richard Wright

Lifespan | b. 1908 (U.S.), d. 1960 (France)
First Published | 1940
First Published by | Harper & Row (New York)
Movie Adaptations Released | 1951, 1986

Richard Wright's novel leapt onto the American literary scene as a warning to white America of the violence that the country was harboring within it. The novel's opening presents its central protagonist, Bigger Thomas, beating a rat to death in front of his frightened sister, cowed mother, and admiring brother. Wright's identification of Bigger with the rat allows us to see him as both perpetrator and victim, and it is from this uneasy position that the reader views the ensuing, disturbing events.

This realist novel is divided into three parts. The first section describes Bigger's introduction into the middle-class world of the Daltons and his accidental killing of their daughter, Mary. The second sees a desperate Bigger pursued across the Chicago landscape and records the punitive effects of his crime on the wider African-American community. The final section focuses on Bigger's court case and Wright's attempt to defend his broken humanity.

The explicit and sexualized violence of the novel, in particular the decapitation and burning of the dead Mary Dalton, brought the book its initial notoriety. Wright was both celebrated for his fearless honesty and castigated for providing white America with the stereotype it most loved to fear. Seeking to avoid a sentimental view of black America, Wright was exploring the meaning of freedom. His commitments to black nationalism and communism are qualified finally by his commitment to the existential desire to truly know oneself. **NM**

For Whom the Bell Tolls

Ernest Hemingway

Lifespan | *b*. 1899 (U.S.), *d*. 1961
First Published | 1940
First Published by | C. Scribner's Sons (New York)
Nobel Prize for Literature | 1954

Set in 1937 at the height of the Spanish Civil War, *For Whom the Bell Tolls* follows the struggles of an American college instructor who has left his job to fight for the Republicans. Robert Jordan has been dispatched from Madrid to lead a band of *guerrilleros* that operates in a perpetual state of leadership crisis. Pablo, the ostensible head of the group, has lost his robust commitment to the hardships of war and wistfully dreams of living peacefully in the company of his horses. Pilar, Pablo's superstitious, half-gypsy companion, has kept the group cohesive with her darkly agitated care for both the guerrilleros themselves and the fight that has brought them together. Jordan finds an instant bond with Maria, a young woman who was raped by Fascist soldiers before being taken in by the Republican camp. Maria follows Pilar's counsel and explores her attraction to Jordan, hoping that it will also help to eradicate the memory of her trauma.

Jordan feels a creeping ambivalence toward the Republican cause and a more general self-alienation as he wrestles with his own abhorrence of violence. His inability to integrate his belief systems is dramatized through his relationship with Maria, for whom he bears a painfully intense love, although he shuns her while strategizing the risky bridge-blowing mission. Ultimately Jordan is forced to reassess his personal, political, and romantic values as his insistence on a coherent and orderly hierarchy of beliefs and experiences is shattered. **AF**

> *"You had to trust the people you worked with completely or not at all, and you had to make decisions about the trusting. He was not worried about any of that. But there were other things."*

⬥ Director Frank Capra, right, discusses the novel with Hemingway in 1941; the film version was eventually directed by Sam Wood.

Farewell My Lovely

Raymond Chandler

Lifespan | *b*. 1888 (U.S.), *d*. 1959
First Published | 1940
First Published by | Hamish Hamilton (London)
First Movie Adaptation | *Falcon Takes Over* (1942)

Chandler's second novel seems to exist as an extension of his first, an opening up of the tightly clenched Los Angeles, composed entirely of discrete interiors, that characterized *The Big Sleep*. Again it is the private detective Marlowe who guides the story, and again we know nothing of him beyond his uniquely positioned heroism, a combination of a superhuman ability to traverse the mangled twists and turns of the plot and a bruised fallibility that is an inescapable result of the size of the world he inhabits in relation to himself.

In *Farewell My Lovely*, however, the city is opened out further. While hardly returning to the green fields or open desert of the "great" American novel, *Farewell My Lovely* moves beyond centralized interiors of rooms, cars, and phone booths to take in a variety of distinct locations around L.A. Here the corruption extends along the same patterns as the modern city itself. As in *The Big Sleep*, the crime at the center of this novel is based in a world of overwhelming complexity, but always resolves to the actions of a single individual; not a gangster or crime lord, but a desperate woman who acts to protect her own possibility of escape from the realm of the underbelly. This juxtaposition of the macro scale, the compartmentalized universe of the city full of darkness and stories, with the micro scale of individual people with their own individual versions of the American Dream, gives Chandler's stories a mythical, almost folktale quality. **SF**

The Hamlet

William Faulkner

Lifespan | *b*. 1897 (U.S.), *d*. 1962
First Published | 1940
First Published by | Random House (New York)
Nobel Prize for Literature | 1949

The Hamlet is the first of the "Snopes" trilogy, completed by *The Town* (1957), and *The Mansion* (1959). For the idiot, Ike Snopes, to enter a cow would seem to be tantamount to making love to a hole in the ground. Ike, via his loving bestiality, is intimate with the earth. Faulkner gives the cow a human equivalent in Eula Varner, daughter to the chief landholder of Frenchman's Bend, and her courting is central to Faulkner's great comic novel. Eula, for the male inhabitants of the hamlet, is little more than a uterus decorated with mammaries and a ruminant "damp mouth." Her marital fate allows Faulkner to explore the inheritance of Southern land, even as that land was subject to a class war, fought over for control over the means of production. During the 1880s and early 1890s, enclosure of common land forced a tenantry, unable to graze stock on the newly enclosed commons, to commit to the cotton cash crop, and in so doing to maximize the profits of the landowning class and their own dependency on that class. Eula, impregnated and deserted, is given by her father to his commissary store clerk, the froglike Flem Snopes—a decision that indicates that the future belongs not to those who love the land, but to those who will capitalize it. Flem, named for what little he emits, is probably impotent and says virtually nothing during the entire novel, preferring to chew on nickels. *The Hamlet* records the early stages of his rise from cropper's cabin to banker's mansion. **RG**

Between the Acts

Virginia Woolf

Lifespan | *b.* 1882 (England), *d.* 1941
First Published | 1941
First Published by | Hogarth Press (London)
Original Language | English

Woolf's last novel, published posthumously, conveys a strong sense of finality, or more precisely, depicts a transitional moment, at the brink of something threatening and unknown. This was, of course, the war. Woolf set the novel in 1939 (all the action takes place at an English country house on one June day), but while she wrote it, London was under heavy bombardment. The day in question is that of the annual community pageant, to be staged (as always) in the grounds at Pointz Hall. The novel is concerned with everything that happens—not only between the acts, but before, after, and alongside—and with the interactions between the Oliver family and the outsiders and villagers attending the pageant. Even though the novel is comprised of fragments, the irrevocably separate bits of individual lives and experiences, it still conveys a profound sense of rhythm and interconnectedness.

Virginia Woolf's acute management of narrative perspective is both microscopic and macrocosmic—swinging in one moment between blades of grass to a consideration of the historical palimpsest that is the surface of the earth when viewed from above. The pageant itself—scenes and segments from English literature and history—mirrors the texture of the novel. Significantly, although the pageant mystifies its audience (like the novel, it is prone to disruption), a moment of fragile equipoise is caught, only to be dispersed, in turn, by military aircraft flying overhead. **ST**

Hangover Square

Patrick Hamilton

Lifespan | *b.* 1904 (England), *d.* 1962
First Published | 1941, by Constable & Co. (London)
Full Title | *Hangover Square: or, the Man with Two Minds: A story of darkest Earl's Court in 1939*

It is Christmas 1938, and when something goes "snap" in his head, George Harvey Bone knows he must kill Netta Longdon. Before that happens, Hamilton—in this "story of darkest Earl's Court"—narrates the definitive history of heavy drinking and (ill) public-house manners, recording the fine gradations of whiskey-drunkenness among a group of instinctive pre-war fascists. George is in love with Netta, who ruthlessly uses him, promising the "nice" time that never arrives. Meanwhile she entertains blond Peter, who has been imprisoned for "socking a certain left-winger" at a political meeting. George, "this enormous, ill, simple-minded man" drowns Netta in her bath and kills Peter with a golfclub as Chamberlain announces war with Germany on the morning of September 3, 1939. It is the symbolic elimination of the political right as war begins. George is a puzzled innocent, unhappy with the ambient politics, but unclear why. As he dies by gas poisoning after the murders, George remembers the hotel cat he had adopted. These simple recollections are the foundations of a complex fiction told almost entirely from George's point of view.

By telling the tale from "inside" the head of his protagonist, Hamilton successfully rescues a modernist technique. Here Hamilton's narrative permits him to resolve his difficult relations with literary modernism, at the same time working out with historical specificity the implications of his own self-taught 1930s Marxism. **AMu**

The Living and the Dead

Patrick White

Lifespan | b. 1912 (England), d. 1990 (Australia)
First Published | 1941
First Published by | Routledge & Kegan Paul
Nobel Prize for Literature | 1973

Set in London against the grim backdrop of the 1930s, the plot focuses on the fraught relationship between Catherine Standish and her two children, Elyot and Eden. Having been abandoned by her husband, Catherine is an emotionally distant mother. Elyot is a writer and critic who, while given to ruminating upon his lack of belonging in the world, willfully insulates himself from it through books. Eden, his sister, who at first appears to be a more expansive character, seeks fulfillment through her political activism and dalliances with men, only to meet with disappointment on both fronts.

While this summary may make the novel sound an unremittingly bleak affair, it is in those passages where White so penetratingly inhabits the minds of his characters that he deservedly earns his reputation as a writer of the very first rank. In these truthful yet compassionate glimpses into the self-doubts and self-delusions that motivate each life, White introduces some of the thematic concerns that came to dominate his later fiction: what is the value of self-sacrifice in a world increasingly indifferent to human suffering? What is the purpose of imagination in a universe vacated by God?

Some readers may find the frequent longueurs in the narrative a little cumbersome. Yet White's loftiness is never contrived in this moving account of how the socially inhibited struggle with, and are imprisoned by, an inability to give imaginative surrender to their own vision. **VA**

> *"During the early . . . months I hovered between London and New York writing too hurriedly a second novel, The Living and the Dead."*
>
> *White, 1973*

⊙ Patrick White, pictured here at age sixty-one, was the first Australian ever to win the Nobel Prize for Literature.

The Poor Mouth

Flann O'Brien

Lifespan | *b*. 1911 (Ireland), *d*. 1966
First Published | 1941, by Dolmen Press (Dublin)
Original Title | *An Beal Bocht*
Original Language | Gaelic

The Poor Mouth is presented as the first-person story of the hard life and unjust fate of Bonaparte O'Coonassa, from the imaginary district of Corkadoragha in the west of Ireland. It is a satire whose dark undertone—the all too real experience of starvation, poverty, and violence—predominates over the elements of comic exaggeration and parody (the endless rain, the endless boiled potatoes). Speakers of English, alternately patronizing and brutalizing the people, appear as an alien presence in a country whose language they do not understand. However, the cult of all things Gaelic is mocked too. A traveling ethnographer-linguist records the grunting of the O'Coonassas' pig Ambrose and later plays it to an admiring audience in Berlin as a "good, poetic, and obscure" sample of Irish speech. The speaker at the rain-drenched outdoor *feis* (festival) in Corkadoragha declares that "Every word I have ever uttered has been on the subject of Gaelic," while his audience is collapsing from cold, hunger, and boredom.

Foreign tourists and anthropologists, as well as the political establishment of the new Irish nation, venerated what they saw as the authentic traditions of the west. O'Brien suggests this was mere romantic fantasy and projection, with well-to-do outsiders oblivious to the material and cultural poverty of rural life. *The Poor Mouth*'s dismal closing image shows the realization of an ongoing cycle of injustice that shows little sign of ending. **MR**

Conversations in Sicily

Elio Vittorini

Lifespan | *b*. 1908 (Italy), *d*. 1966
First Published | 1941, by Bompiani (Milan)
Alternate Title | *Conversations in Sicily*
Original Title | *Conversazione in Sicilia*

The opening pages contain emblematic references to the events of 1936 that marked the beginning of the Spanish Civil War. Silvestro, the protagonist and narrator, has plunged into despondency and disillusionment at the realization of his powerlessness when confronted by the loss of humanity. He embarks on a metaphorical journey to his native Sicily. During a rediscovery of his origins and subsequent psychological transformation, Silvestro converses with numerous people. There is the orange picker who, unable to sell his produce, evokes southern poverty. There is the courageous man who feels he has a moral duty to humanity and would be ready to renounce all his possessions to fight in its defense. A knife sharpener laments the indolence of people who do not give him swords, daggers, or even cannons to sharpen. The abstract words of these conversations are a symbolic incitement to fight against the suppression of liberty and democracy. In the middle of the novel Silvestro converses with his mother, Concezione, and recalls his youth. A strong woman, unscathed by her husband's abandonment and unafraid of solitude, Concezione is a symbol of womanly and motherly strength. At the end of his three-day journey, which can be interpreted as a Christian metaphor for inner rediscovery, Silvestro has been "resurrected" to a higher human understanding. The author's antifascism, therefore, acquires a dimension that is not so much historical or political as it is moral. **RPi**

The Outsider

Albert Camus

Lifespan | *b.* 1913 (Algeria), *d.* 1960 (France)
First Published | 1942, by Gallimard (Paris)
U.S. Title | *The Stranger*
Original Title | *L'Étranger*

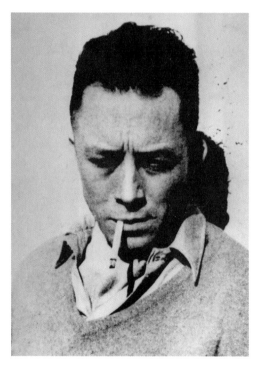

◔ Like his antihero Meursault in *The Outsider*, Albert Camus was
the son of European settlers in Algeria, then under French rule.

◑ Albert Camus' watercolor portrait, entitled "Alberic," is
detailed with a furrowed brow reminiscent of his own.

The Outsider is a novel of absolute flatness. The events of the story, despite taking in a murder and subsequent trial, seem to have no weight to them whatsoever, as if they simply float past on the page. This, it becomes clear, is absolutely essential to both the story's purpose, its much-discussed relationship with the philosophy of existentialism, and, oddly, to its readability. Camus' scrupulous simplicity roots the story at once in the everyday and in the fable, and it is left up to the reader to resolve this ambiguity.

This is a novel that displays an unwavering discipline in expounding a life where conventional self-conduct is undermined. There is no technical "cleverness" in the illustration of its themes; we are simply presented with a period of time in the life of a blank man named Meursault, a social outcast who chooses to live a private and solitary life. During this period, a number of significant events take place in his life—the death of his mother, the murder of a man, and a judgment that condemns Meursault to death—but each of these fails to rouse the expected emotional response from him.

On first impression, there appear to be certain parallels with Kafka, in the suggestion that vast complexities lurk behind a visibly spare style and in the general dreamy detachment that surrounds it. But there is nothing of the surreal and everything of the mundane in Meursault's world, over which he has little control. Dislocated from others as well as from his own life, Meursault's character demonstrates the meaninglessness of life, beyond the meaning one is willing to ascribe to it. It is the realization of and resignation to this essential meaninglessness that for Camus constitutes the absurd, a theme that he went on to develop more fully in his later work. **SF**

Celui-ci c'est Albéric, le "Jeune-homme-qui-croyait
que-c'était-arrivé-et-qui
-s'apercevait-que-ce
n'était-pas-ar
(Enteh chaleur

Go Down, Moses

William Faulkner

Lifespan | *b.* 1897 (U.S.), *d.* 1962
First Published | 1942
First Published by | Random House (New York)
Nobel Prize for Literature | 1949

Originally published as *Go Down, Moses and Other Stories*, the first edition's title met with Faulkner's disapproval; despite the short-story format, Faulkner considered the work a novel, and reference to the "other stories" was subsequently dropped. Seven stories, mainly but not exclusively, about the McCaslin family plantation, are here set side by side. Initially it is hard to see the common thread between them; for example, the link between "Pantaloon in Black," the story of the grief-unto-death of a giant African-American timber yard worker in 1941, and "Was," the first story, set in 1859, about a runaway slave, a game of poker, and the preservation of the celibate amity of Buck and Buddy McCaslin, twin inheritors of the McCaslin lands, seems tenuous indeed.

But by the end of the book, connections, such as the focus on black mobility, emerge. The social mobility of wage-earning non-agricultural workers and runaway slaves threatened white dominance by late 1941; U.S. entry into the Second World War had restarted the Great Migration of black workers from the South, with labor needs in the North stimulated by the war. As black workers took to the roads and rails, so the white landowning class suffered its own social death.

The disjunctions in the novel are evidence of the difficulty in recognizing that a revolution in the region's long-preserved archaic labor practices would mean that the South may cease to be Southern, at least outside the realm of elegy. **RG**

> *"To the sheriff Lucas was just another nigger and [they] both knew it, although only one of them knew that to Lucas the sheriff was a redneck without any... pride in his forbears nor hope... in his descendants."*

◉ Faulkner types on a balcony in Hollywood in the early 1940s, during one of several spells spent working as a screenwriter.

Embers

Sandor Marai

Lifespan | *b.* 1900 (Hungary), *d.* 1989 (U.S.)
First Published | 1942
First Published in | Budapest
Original Title | *A gyertyák csonkig égnek*

Embers is a rediscovered jewel of Central European literature—originally published in Budapest in 1942, but virtually unknown to a wider audience until its translation into English in 2001. Against the odds, the novel has gone on to become an international bestseller, although its author, who committed suicide while in exile in the U.S. in 1989, will never bear witness to its unexpected popularity.

Set in Hungary just after the outbreak of the Second World War, in a remote castle at the base of the Carpathian mountains, Henrik, a 75-year-old retired general dines with an old friend, Konrad, who he has not seen for over forty years. There are many unresolved issues between the pair, and what follows is a wonderfully controlled standoff—an unfolding series of anecdotes, reminiscences, silences, rebuttals, denials, and obfuscations. Márai paces his work with skill and precision, allowing each new revelation to emerge just as one feels some kind of reconciliation may be possible. Years of smoldering resentment are condensed into a single night.

Embers is a brief and remarkably intense work, a novel still steeped in the lore and atmosphere of the Austro-Hungarian empire. It is a novel of long shadows and vintage wine, of candlelight, ancient forests, and creaking mahogany. Márai maintains this atmosphere without ever resorting to cheap theatrics. For all its old-world charm, the novel remains an intricately observed study of class, friendship, betrayal, and masculine pride. **SamT**

The Glass Bead Game

Hermann Hesse

Lifespan | *b.* 1877 (Germany), *d.* 1962 (Switzerland)
First Published | 1943, by Fretz & Wasmuth (Zürich)
Alternate Title | *Magister Ludi*
Original Title | *Das Glasperlenspiel*

The Glass Bead Game purports to be the biography of Joseph Knecht, a member of an elite group of intellectuals in twenty-third-century Europe who live and carry out their work in isolation from the rest of society. The novel follows Knecht from his early schooling to his eventual attainment of the revered title of Magister Ludi, or "Master of the Game." This Glass Bead Game is the *raison d'être* of the intellectual community of which Knecht becomes the head. Although the game's exact nature is never fully explained, it becomes clear that it involves the synthesis of diverse branches of human knowledge; from philosophy, history, and mathematics, to music, literature, and logic. Despite the exquisite nature of the game, Knecht grows increasingly discontent with its players' complete detachment from worldly affairs.

Written amid the disastrous events of early 1940s Europe, *The Glass Bead Game* is an eloquent and powerful meditation on the relationship between the spheres of politics and the contemplative life. Hesse's novel is a passionate argument for a more symbiotic relationship between thought and action. Powerfully illustrating this very union, Knecht leaves the enclosed community in order to experience those aspects of life neglected by his studious existence. This novel is thus a continuation of one of Hesse's enduring themes: the importance of self-reflection as a means of discerning the ever-changing path toward self-growth and renewal. **CC-G**

Caught

Henry Green

Lifespan | *b.*1905 (England), *d.*1973 (Switzerland)
First Published | 1943
First Published by | Hogarth Press (London)
Given Name | Henry Vincent Yorke

Henry Green wrote *Caught*, his fourth novel, during the London Blitz of 1940–1942. As with all of Green's work, the story examines how people are kept apart by social and sexual differences and studies their attempts to affect and really to feel sympathy for each other. It is a realist novel, exposing social and class contradictions. The differences most coolly observed in *Caught*, however, are those between men's and women's experiences of London during the Blitz.

The novel is profoundly ambivalent. It describes the solidarity that develops between men of different classes working together in the Auxiliary Fire Service. In this environment, they are sharing for the first time a night and day routine that involves the gradual revelation of intimate habits and memories. War and the ensuing sense of vulnerability are shown to produce some tentative expectations of reconciliation between ordinarily separate or antagonistic social groups. The central character Richard Roe, modeled on Green himself and thus an affluent volunteer, gradually gets to know the working-class men in his fire station. But the shared traumas of wartime London leave Roe cursing women in general, and his sister-in-law in the seclusion of the countryside in particular. Green seems to be indicating that a true sense of solidarity, such as that found among wartime comrades, requires such an intensity of commitment that it impoverishes other types of human sympathy. This is an unpleasant idea, brilliantly evoked in *Caught*. **KS**

The Little Prince

Antoine de Saint-Exupéry

Lifespan | *b.*1900 (France), *d.*1944 (in the air)
First Published | 1943
First Published by | Reynal & Hitchcock (New York)
Original Title | *Le Petit Prince*

This charming fable tells the story of an adult's encounter with his inner child. Set in the heart of the Sahara, the tale unfolds after Saint-Exupéry's pilot-narrator finds himself stranded with a "broken" engine, facing the prospect of "life or death." The very largest question of all lies at the heart of the tale: one's life and how one spends it. The relationship between adult and child unfolds against a backdrop of human emergency, and its nature is one of acute questioning: the inimitable questioning of a child in the form of the "little prince," who asks his adult mentor so "many questions." The dialogue between narrator and child is a form of self-address: the adult engaging with his inner child through the unfettered imaginings and demands of a young child. The little prince and our narrator initially engage through the act of drawing, when the little prince first appears with his demand, "If you please, draw me a sheep."

Saint-Exupéry's tale is a surreal one, defying the conventions of reality and entering into the realm of dreamscape, where the imagination can run riot. The narrator is gently led into a rediscovery of his capacity for imagining. And so the role reversal begins, and the child tutors the adult in the sacred art of wondering. Written during the final year of his life, Saint-Exupéry's *The Little Prince* reads as a manifesto on how the adult life can and should be lived. **SB**

❯ Saint-Exupéry wrote the tale of *Le Petit Prince* at this desk at the home of French painter Bernard Lamotte in Connecticut, U.S.

Dangling Man

Saul Bellow

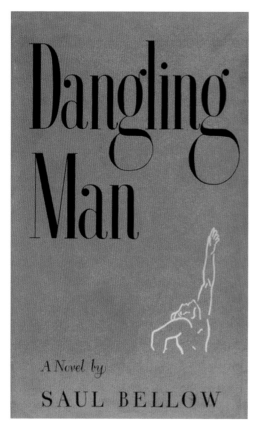

Lifespan | *b.* 1915 (Canada), *d.* 2005 (U.S.)
First Published | 1944
First Published by | Vanguard Press (New York)
Nobel Prize for Literature | 1976

Dangling Man was Bellow's first novel, and it established him as an important American writer. The novel is written in the form of the diary of its protagonist, Joseph. Having given up his job at the Inter-American Travel Bureau, Joseph, a "dangling man" is confined to a Chicago boarding house while awaiting the draft. He rarely leaves the confines of his room, immersing himself instead in the writing of the Enlightenment. His increasingly solipsistic lifestyle alienates both his wife, Iva, and his other intellectual friends.

In Joseph's search for the meaning of his "dangling" life, the novel testifies to the influence of French existentialism on the intellectual life of 1940s America. Sections of Joseph's diary are given over to a dialogue with an imaginary interlocutor, which he calls the Spirit of Alternatives or *Tu As Raison Aussi* ("You Are Also Right"). The existential concerns of *Dangling Man* can perhaps be thought of in the context of Sartre's *Nausea* and Camus' *L'Étranger*. It also prefigures Bellow's later writings in its juxtaposition of low life and high culture; Joseph's diary mixes the banality of everyday life with references to Goethe and Diderot. In Joseph's lonely wanderings through the city streets, we see Bellow beginning to combine the concerns of European literature with an authentically American urban experience. *Dangling Man* therefore bears witness to the birth of one the most important and influential voices of the modern American novel. **BR**

"He asked himself a question I still would like answered . . . 'How should a good man live; what ought he to do?'"

⊙ Published in 1944, *Dangling Man* reflected contemporary intellectual preoccupations with the nature of freedom.

Ficciones

Jorge Luis Borges

Lifespan | *b.* 1899 (Argentina), *d.* 1986 (Switzerland)
First Published | 1944
First Published by | Sur (Buenos Aires)
Original Language | Spanish

From an infinite Chinese labyrinth of books in "The Garden of Forking Paths" to the transformation of the universe into a giant game of chance in "The Babylonian Lottery," the seventeen short stories in Jorge Luis Borges' *Ficciones* are united by a common renunciation of traditional notions of space and time. This subversion of reality has seen the Argentine author and philosopher regarded as the father of magic realism, but Borges' writings bear little resemblance to the fantastical style usually associated with that genre. Rather, fact and fiction are juxtaposed in deliberate, authoritative prose to create alternative realities that simultaneously mirror and obscure our own. Drawing upon art, history, literature, myth, mathematics, and science, Borges renders his "fictions" truth through painstaking attention to detail, undermining the boundary between reality and fantasy.

Almost as engaging as the stories of *Ficciones* are the prologues that introduce the two different sections of the collection. Instead of analyzing or elucidating his often-difficult prose, Borges teases and tantalizes the reader with brief allusions to the places, writers, and sources that have influenced the text, as well to the stories themselves, providing the uninitiated with a jumping-off point. Perhaps more importantly, these prologues provide insight into the creative process of the man whom *Time* magazine once hailed as "the greatest living writer in the Spanish language," and his most important work. **BJ**

Transit

Anna Seghers

Lifespan | *b.* 1900 (Germany), *d.* 1983
First Published | 1944
First Published by | Nuevo Mundo (Mexico)
Given Name | Netti Reiling

Transit, one of the greatest treatments of flight and exile in modern German writing, is a powerful blending of documentary with fiction. Written on Seghers' own flight from the Nazis (she was Jewish, as well as a member of the Communist party), it was begun in France and finished in Mexico, where it was first published in Spanish (the German version was not published until 1948). This lived experience is mixed with a dramatized account of the fate of the Austrian writer and doctor Ernst Weiß. Weiß, unaware that a U.S. visa had been prepared for him, through Thomas Mann's intercession with President Roosevelt, killed himself in his hotel room, where Anna Seghers attempted to visit him just afterwards. Lines are blurred, and it is never clear how much of the real Weiß is present in his fictional counterpart.

The narrator of *Transit*, Seidler, flees a German concentration camp, only to be interned in France; he escapes again, this time to Marseille, outside the occupation. Joining the throng of those scrambling for passage to America, he attempts to get a message to an acquaintance, a writer named Weidel: on arrival at Weidel's hotel, Siedler learns that he has killed himself the night before. Among the dead man's effects is a transit visa to America; Seidler assumes his identity in order to make use of it. Complications arise when Weidel's wife arrives on the scene. At last Seidler comes to realize that his own identity is being eroded, and he turns down his chance of passage, opting instead to join the French Resistance. **MM**

The Razor's Edge

William Somerset Maugham

Lifespan | *b.* 1874 (France), *d.* 1965
First Published | 1944
First Published by | W. Heinemann (London)
Original Language | English

Social satire, philosophical novel, and saint's life, *The Razor's Edge* describes the spiritual quest of an extraordinary young American. After seeing his best friend die to save his life while serving as an airman during the First World War, Larry Darrell questions the meaning of his life. He returns to America with the need to find out more about the nature of good and evil and leaves behind his home, his fiancée, and his social set. After meeting a venerated maharishi high in the mountains of India, Larry experiences enlightenment. Maugham's narrator reports on his quest as observed from afar, "at long intervals," and sometimes secondhand. He also follows the lives of a number of characters connected to Larry.

The Razor's Edge should preferably be read not only before you die, but also before you turn twenty and while you are still capable of truly falling in love with a fictional character. As you get older, you may appreciate Maugham's art more: the subtle, sharp, yet kind irony with which he, or rather his narrator, treats his characters and their social setting—with the exception of Larry, who is simply described. You may better understand the cultural and philosophical background to the novel's discussions on the nature of God, the existence of good and evil, and the meaning of life. But you are less likely to feel actual yearning for the protagonist and his goodness. This work of fiction presupposes faith, or at least a longing for it, for its full appreciation—and there are certainly worse things that can be said of a novel. **DG**

" . . . If I call it a novel it is only because I don't know what else to call it. I have little story to tell and I end neither with a death nor a marriage."

⊙ Maugham was living in the United States when he wrote *The Razor's Edge*—here he is photographed bathing at Cape Cod.

Christ Stopped at Eboli

Carlo Levi

Lifespan | *b.* 1902 (Italy), *d.* 1975
First Published | 1945
First Published by | G. Einaudi (Turin)
Original Title | *Cristo si è fermato a Eboli*

Christ Stopped at Eboli has been variously described as a diary, a documentary novel, a sociological study, and a political essay. Its author is equally difficult to categorize. Carlo Levi trained as a doctor, but later devoted himself to politics, literature, and painting. Between 1935 and 1936, during the Abyssinian war, he was exiled to Gagliano, a remote hill town in the "foot" of Italy, because of his opposition to Mussolini and the Fascist regime. *Christ Stopped at Eboli*, Levi's account of the exile, refers to Eboli, the central town of the region, which he was occasionally allowed to visit.

The title of the book is a metaphor for the isolation of the people of this remote region, their poverty and deprivation of little concern to the middle-class Fascist party. Levi chronicles his life in the malaria-ridden village, while painting unsentimental portraits of the inhabitants, from the Fascist mayor to Giulia, a woman who had more than a dozen pregnancies with more than a dozen men. To the stoical peasant community, Levi is a figure of authority whom they turn to for help in their daily struggles against disease and poverty. But his attempts to help them with limited medical supplies is mostly in vain; in a world where a stethoscope has never been seen, the impact of his medical knowledge proves negligible. His novel, however, was an international sensation and, in a move toward social realism in postwar Italian literature, brought to the attention of the Italian public a long-neglected part of their own country. **LE**

Arcanum 17

André Breton

Lifespan | *b.* 1896 (France), *d.* 1966
First Published | 1945
First Published by | Brentano (New York)
Original Title | *Arcane 17*

The high point of the surrealist movement, which Breton had headed in France, was over by 1944, and Europe was in the midst of an exhausting war. Written from Québec in the months following D-Day, *Arcanum 17* has much to say about the role of the artist during war and the role of war in the work that will follow its aftermath. Yet Breton's text is neither gloomily pessimistic nor nostalgic; it has a quiet if cautionary optimism for the future of Europe and her artists. This is reflected in the title, which refers to the major Arcana tarot card, the Star which depicts a beautiful young woman emptying upon the earth two urns, labeled love, and intelligence.

Arcanum 17 is neither an essay nor a narrative, although it combines musings and opinions on art and war with a variety of literary themes. These include personalized accounts of Breton's life and his lover during this period, and evocative, poetic descriptions of the dramatic Canadian landscape. The main literary leitmotiv is the legend of Melusina, which A. S. Byatt was to draw upon later in her novel *Possession* (1990). Melusina keeps her fidelity to the man whose curiosity banishes her from the human realm; from this stems Breton's call for women to take the reins of power from the destructive hands of men. *Arcanum 17* is a poignant exploration of personal and European loss; it is also a testament to the fascinating maturation of a thinker whose youthful writings had been at the forefront of artistic change in France. **JC**

Loving

Henry Green

Lifespan | *b.*1905 (England), *d.*1973
First Published | 1945
First Published by | Hogarth Press (London)
Given Name | Henry Vincent Yorke

Henry Green's fifth novel, *Loving*, tells the uneventful story of an English aristocratic household in Ireland during the Second World War. The narrative of its little round of daily events is split between the servants of the house and their masters. Upstairs we follow the comedy of well-bred, largely hypocritical emotionalism played out by the lady of the house, Mrs. Tennant, and her daughter-in-law, Mrs. Jack. Downstairs the parallel comedy of restricted hopes and sensational fears is acted out by the star of the drama, the butler, Charley Raunce, and his staff. Raunce falls in love with a servant girl, Edith, and their daily round of flirtations and confessions of desire leads to a fairy-tale ending capped by the cliché "happily ever after."

What sets this book apart from other comedies of manners is the great sensitivity with which Green, the son of a rich Birmingham industrialist, reveals that the experience of loving is rooted in and cannot escape the experience of class relations. The novel exposes the contradictions of class society by tracing the limits imposed on even the most passionate longing by the accidents of birth and social status, and by the deep impression of emotional habits accumulated through physical labor or the freedom from it. To each social class, there belongs its own experience of love and its own manner of believing that love transcends class. Far from reducing the love story to sociology or historical analysis, Green's novel is suffused with a beautiful and implicit pathos. **KS**

The Pursuit of Love

Nancy Mitford

Lifespan | *b.*1904 (England), *d.*1973 (France)
First Published | 1945
First Published by | Hamish Hamilton (London)
Full Name | Nancy Freeman Mitford

Mitford's loosely autobiographical satire *The Pursuit of Love*, in the vein of witty novels about aristocratic manners, love, and decadence, is her best-loved and most-imitated work. Although comparisons could be made with Aldous Huxley, Evelyn Waugh, or Elizabeth Bowen, the pleasures of Mitford's work have been less widely recognized. Disguised as an elegant romantic fiction, *The Pursuit of Love* brims with *bons mots*, bathetic one-liners, and a preoccupation with the wit of narration and conversation. Indeed, it is as much about the fragile armor of wit as it is an engaging narrative of innocence, unrequited love, and marriage. The key to the novel's playful artifice is the tone adopted by its narrator. Abandoned by her mother—the so-called Bolter—Fanny is brought up by Aunt Emily, in the vicinity of various cousins, principally Linda, the central character. Linda dances her way through aesthetic education from Lord Merlin; love and unsuccessful marriage to Tony, the dull Tory MP; an affair and unsuccessful marriage to a communist; and successful, if tragically curtailed, love with Fabrice. Fanny, meanwhile, marries an Oxford don and lives happily enough to be able to tell Linda's story with poise and equanimity. Unlikely to win approval from earnest liberals, this often cutting novel nevertheless emerges from the Second World War's shadows with a curiously warm heart. **DM**

> The Mitford sisters, clockwise from bottom left, Nancy, Unity, Jessica, and Diana: Jessica became a communist, Unity a fascist.

Cannery Row

John Steinbeck

Lifespan | *b.*1902 (U.S.), *d.*1968
First Published | 1945
First Published by | Viking (New York)
Full Name | John Ernst Steinbeck

Much of Steinbeck's work is heavily political and infused with a large dose of sentimentality, but *Cannery Row* is remarkable for its ambiguity. In some ways, it is less of a story and more of an attempt to capture the singular essence of a people and place—the Cannery district of Monterey, California. This is a district populated by a mixture of those who avoid the more respectable "up town" areas because they have to, and those who do so because they choose to. The storyline follows Mack and his boys, a gang of resourceful but unemployed men who inhabit a fish shack and set about throwing a surprise party for Doc. On the night of the party, Doc is late getting back, and by the time he returns his place is trashed. A neighborhood influenza epidemic seems to mirror the bad feeling that follows the fateful party. Eventually, a successful party is thrown for Doc, and the district's run of bad luck turns. Although *Cannery Row* was published at a time when prosperity had returned to America after the end of the war, it depicts a population still trapped in the psychology of the Depression. Steinbeck takes a utopian view, seeing the poor as inherently good people whose noble intentions and feelings for one another get them through the bad times, but this is punctuated by a sense of realism, as violent incidents pepper the novel. The residents' surroundings become a metaphor for the evil that inevitably disrupts human life, as they struggle against circumstance, while their togetherness represents hope. **EF**

Animal Farm

George Orwell

Lifespan | *b.*1903 (India), *d.*1950 (England)
First Published |1945
First Published by | Secker & Warburg (London)
Given Name | Eric Arthur Blair

Orwell's fable of the animals who take over Manor Farm but are betrayed by their leaders has become a powerful myth of freedom for the post–Second World War generation. Its purpose was to destroy another myth, that the Soviet Union was a socialist state; the difficulties that Orwell faced in getting his book published confirmed his view that the British intelligentsia was in thrall to the Soviet system. *Animal Farm* was based on Orwell's own experience in the Spanish Civil War (1936–1939), when the left-wing militia in which he fought was ruthlessly eliminated for not being communist.

Animal Farm is a masterpiece of controlled irony, focused on essential developments in the rise of the Soviet state, but tied to Orwell's knowledge of rural life. Major, an elderly white boar representing Karl Marx, declares the animals' "duty of enmity towards Man and all his ways." When revolution comes all animals shall be equal. Unfortunately, the pig Napoleon (Stalin) and his fierce dogs (secret police) take over, working to death the carthorse Boxer (the Soviet people) and exiling Snowball (Trotsky). There is pathos in the carthorse Clover's realization that the seven founding commandments are now one: "All animals are equal but some animals are more equal than others." Such irony confirms the book's support of genuine revolution. **AMu**

> The cover of a 1954 Latvian translation of *Animal Farm*: the book was banned in Soviet bloc countries, but circulated clandestinely.

DŽ. ORVELS

DZĪVNIEKU FARMA

Brideshead Revisited

Evelyn Waugh

Lifespan | *b.* 1903 (England), *d.* 1966
First Published | 1945
First Published by | Chapman & Hall (London)
Full Name | Evelyn Arthur St. John Waugh

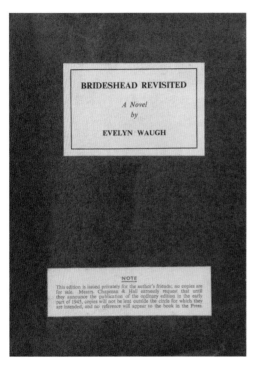

"[F]orgive him his sins, if there is such a thing as sin."

⊙ Written towards the end of the Second World War, *Brideshead* was partly a nostalgic tribute to an upper-class world.

Arguably Evelyn Waugh's best novel, and certainly his most famous, *Brideshead Revisited* follows the aristocratic Flyte family from the 1920s through to the Second World War. The novel is subtitled "The Sacred and Profane Memories of Captain Charles Ryder," and the narrator first meets Sebastian, an aesthete from the Catholic Flyte family, at Oxford University. The two form an intense friendship. Charles is a serious, earnest student, but there is a tension between the scholasticism of his under-graduate pursuits and his artistic ambitions. His friendship with Sebastian enables him to loosen his grip upon the conventional values that had until then structured his life, and the pair's decadent lifestyle encourages Charles' artistic development. During their breaks from Oxford they spend time together at Brideshead Castle, the home of the Flyte family, and Charles comes to realize that Sebastian's faith is one that he cannot always understand: to him it seems naïve and inconsistent.

Sebastian's continual heavy drinking increasingly drives a wedge between him and Charles; however, Charles' relationship with the Flyte family overall remains strong. Years later, after they have both married unhappily, Charles falls in love with Sebastian's sister, Julia. But Julia's strong Catholic beliefs eventually become insurmountable to a continuing relationship.

Waugh had himself converted to Catholicism in 1930, and in many ways *Brideshead Revisited* can be seen as an expression of his own belief, and an exposition of divine grace. Within the novel he explores a complex interdependency of relationships and in particular the overarching importance of religious faith, which, although not always prominent, ultimately prevails. **JW**

The Bridge on the Drina

Ivo Andrić

Ivo Andrić's work *The Bridge on the Drina* recounts the turbulent history of the famous Mehmed-pasha Sokolovich Bridge in Visegrad, Bosnia. In the novel Andrić chronicles the period from the building of the bridge in the sixteenth century to the start of the First World War in 1914 and the complete dissolution of the Austro-Hungarian Empire. (In 1993 the bridge was destroyed by Croatian armed forces, to be reopened after rebuilding in 2004.)

Strictly speaking, *The Bridge on the Drina* is more a chronicle than a novel, organized into a series of vignettes describing the life of the local population in Bosnia and Herzegovina and its transformations over the course of centuries. Given the recent Bosnian bloodshed, the novel provides a fascinating insight into the dynamics and the history of tensions between the local Christians, Muslims, and Jews. A beautiful piece of writing set in a rich local dialect, the book is also a story of language itself. The social and cultural changes brought on by successive rule of the Ottoman and Austro-Hungarian empires are reflected in the populace's vocabulary, their thoughts, bodies, and attitudes. Throughout, the bridge endures as a symbol of continuity.

Alongside the bridge persist age-old animosities. Even though the novel concludes in 1914 with the retreat of the Austro-Hungarian forces, foreshadowing the consequent fall of yet another empire, the bridge itself witnessed further historical strife during the 1990s. This, perhaps, is an incentive for a more cautious reading of Andrić, where the bridge emerges not so much as a metaphor of possible coexistence among nations but a stage for the relentless flow of history that— were it not for legends and stories—soon obliterates the many faces and voices caught in its pull. **IJ**

Lifespan | *b.* 1892 (Bosnia), *d.* 1975 (Yugoslavia)
First Published | 1945, by Prosveta (Belgrade)
Original Title | *Na Drini ćuprija*
Nobel Prize for Literature | 1961

"Here where the Drina flows with the whole force . . . "

◢ Ivo Andrić was the first Bosnian recipient of the Nobel Prize for Literature, which he was awarded in 1961.

Titus Groan

Mervyn Peake

Lifespan | *b.* 1911 (China), *d.* 1968 (England)
First Published | 1946, by Eyre & Spottiswoode (Lon.)
Titus Groan Novels | *Titus Groan* (1946),
Gormenghast (1950), *Titus Alone* (1959)

Packed with delicious grotesques and delirious prose, *Titus Groan* centers on the dark behemoth of Gormenghast, the walled ancestral home of the line of Groan. Crumbling, malignant, with corridors and towers and forgotten wings housing misplaced occupants, it is a living, seething universe. Its inhabitants—hostage to its mind-numbing routine, the original meaning of which is long forgotten— scurry to perform a ceaseless flow of rituals.

The players are a delightful menagerie of archetypes and caricatures. Lord Sepulchrave, 76th Earl of Groan, is morose, exhausted by endless duty; his career wife, Gertrude, is increasingly detached, comfortable only with the birds that nest in her hair and the sea of cats that surrounds her. Sourdust and Barquentine, the librarians, are keepers of the ritual, and Swelter, the demonic porcine cook, is despot in the steaming hell of the Great Kitchens. Mr. Flay is Sepulchrave's major-domo, willing to defend tradition to the death. Driving the narrative is Steerpike, low-born and opportunistic, who wheedles, flatters, and manipulates in his Machiavellian quest for power. He will stop at nothing in his relentless journey upward. To this house an heir is born, Titus, 77th Earl of Groan.

A novel of superb craft, full of intrigue and humor, it is a scathing allegory of British society, from blind deference to tradition to the merciless class system. There are no magic potions, no mythical beasts. The monsters are those we know: the boredom of routine, ruthless self-interest, and foolish vanity. **GT**

> *"Gormenghast . . . taken by itself would have displayed a certain ponderous architectural quality . . . "*

⊘ Before turning his hand to writing, Peake was known as an artist. Here he is pictured at work on a canvas in his London studio.

Back

Henry Green

Lifespan | b. 1905 (England), d. 1973
First Published | 1946
First Published by | Hogarth Press (London)
Given Name | Henry Vincent Yorke

Back is a fascinating war novel, which portrays the consequences of the war on a character who has returned home. Charley Summers is a lost individual, a benumbed and disorientated former soldier traumatized by recent experiences. He finds himself unable to connect with people around him and unable to relate his present to his past. *Back* depicts the perplexities and anguish of its central character with great subtlety. The loose narrative style adopted by Green cleverly approximates the meandering nature of Charley's confused thoughts. Rendered childlike by the psychological trauma of war, he is an innocent abroad, a hapless enigma who is incapable of either confronting or making sense of reality.

Back is, however, an optimistic, almost magical, work, which offers Charley a specific form of personal redemption when he hesitantly begins to fall in love with Nancy, the half-sister of his prewar lover, Rose. Through Nancy, Charley is able not only to relive the past, but also to work through the trauma that shattered it, although there is no naive resolution of the psychological ills that beset him. In fact, he remains an enigma to himself and to others, as Nancy frankly admits toward the end of the novel: "she did not know if he didn't, or just couldn't, tell about himself, tell even something of all that went on behind those marvellous brown eyes." The novel concludes with a tear-stained scene in which love, pain, and self-sacrifice are mingled together in a wonderfully lyrical epiphany. **AG**

The Plague

Albert Camus

Lifespan | b. 1913 (Algeria), d. 1960 (France)
First Published | 1947, by Gallimard (Paris)
Original Title | La Peste
Nobel Prize for Literature | 1957

This text has often been criticized for its "bleak existentialism," yet to do so is to miss the point of Camus' masterpiece altogether. What stands out in this text, despite its unflinching view of human suffering and despair, is an overriding sense of common humanity. This is far from evident as the narrative opens, however, with the death of thousands of rats in the streets of the Algerian city of Oran. When people begin to sicken and die, despite the disorganization and initial denial of the mercenary city authorities, it becomes apparent that it is the bubonic plague that is afflicting the city. Strict quarantine is imposed, and it is in the suffocating claustrophobia of this enforced isolation—brilliantly captured by Camus—that individuals are forced to confront the apparent inevitability of death, and the bonds that bind the community together begin to collapse. Yet even at the darkest point, all hope is not lost. After an initial retreat into their own reflective solitude that would seem to suggest the lonely and unique nature of human despair, the efforts of a number of prominent characters serve to bring the community together gradually in collective understanding of their plight.

The sensitivity and understanding with which a citywide cast of individuals is created is remarkably compelling and brings Oran to life. It is this that sets *The Plague* apart from Camus' other great work, *The Outsider*, and which makes it a timely and still relevant work today. **MD**

The Path to the Nest of Spiders

Italo Calvino

Lifespan | *b.* 1923 (Cuba), *d.* 1985 (Italy)
First Published | 1947
First Published by | Einaudi (Turin)
Original Title | *Il sentiero dei nidi di ragno*

"Your first book already defines you . . . "

Italian novelist and journalist Italo Calvino photographed in a cafe in 1981, the year he was awarded the Légion d'Honneur.

The fact that this is the first novel Calvino wrote, when he was just twenty-three and at the start of a prodigious literary career, should alone be enough to recommend it. Within are the stirrings of what was later to mature into a unique and inimitable style and sophistication; however, the story also represents the attempt of a young writer to come to terms with the aftermath of the partisan movement in Italy. The precocious Pin is the child whom we follow through the adult world of a rural Italy riven by civil discontent and confusion.

Pin is an orphan, lazy, foulmouthed, and worldly enough to use local gossip to his advantage; he is also a child who craves adult attention, but only crudely and imperfectly understands how to capture or retain it. The irony is that the two things Pin utterly fails to comprehend—politics and women—are those that equally mystify most of the other characters. When Pin's home village is occupied by the Germans, the locals join the partisans, although Calvino makes it clear that this is more about resistance to change than a committed political ideology.

Interestingly, although *The Path to the Nest of Spiders* won him a prize, Calvino refused to authorize a re-edition until nearly a decade later, a third and definitive edition being finally published in 1964, along with an invaluably revealing preface. This reluctance, Calvino admits, was to do with how he had used and caricatured the comrades with whom he had formerly fought alongside. *The Path to the Nest of Spiders*, while it lacks the obsession with symmetry and order of his later works, is beautifully written and represents the response from one of Italy's most famous twentieth-century writers to a singular moment in the country's history. **JC**

Under the Volcano

Malcolm Lowry

Lowry's masterpiece catapulted him to international literary fame after years as a struggling novelist. Lowry later claimed that the novel was the first volume of a trilogy based on Dante's *Divine Comedy*, *Under the Volcano* being a vision of hell. The story tells of the last day in the life of Geoffrey Firmin, the alcoholic British Consul in fictional Quauhnahuac (identifiable as Cuernavaca), Mexico; aptly enough, this day happens to fall on the macabre festival of the Day of the Dead. The novel is narrated in flashback by Firmin's former neighbor, Jacques Laruelle, who has had an affair with Firmin's wife, Yvonne. She returns to try to renew her troubled relationship with the consul, and together with her brother-in-law, Hugh, she visits the festival, which is haunted by an increasing threat of violence. When Geoffrey gets separated from Yvonne and Hugh by a terrible storm, the day ends with the deaths of the couple—Yvonne is killed by a runaway horse, and Geoffrey is murdered by fascist thugs, who throw him into a ditch beneath the volcano.

Lowry's work is more significant for its powerful symbolism and ornate prose style than for its characterization. The setting of the festival of the Day of the Dead under the volcano points to the inevitable death of the self-destructive protagonist, but it also suggests the wider eruptions of a culture in crisis—the novel is set in 1938 and was written during the Second World War. Firmin's death at the hands of the fascists anticipates a brutal world order that cannot be easily contained. Equally, like all Lowry's writing, *Under the Volcano* is autobiographical, and it charts the end of his relationship with former wife, Jan Gabrial, caused largely by his own excesses and obsessions, principally alcohol, which would ultimately lead to his "death by misadventure." **AH**

Lifespan | *b.* 1909 (England), *d.* 1957
First Published | 1947
First Published by | Jonathan Cape (London)
Full Name | Malcolm Clarence Lowry

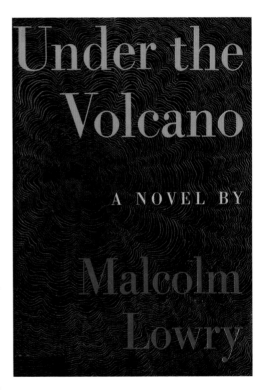

"I have no house, only a shadow."

The sober jacket of the first U.S. edition, published by Reynal & Hitchcock, carries no hint of the novel's macabre exuberance.

If This Is a Man

Primo Levi

"It was my good fortune," writes Primo Levi in his preface to *If This Is a Man*, "to be deported to Auschwitz only in 1944." It is a stark opening to this classic account of Levi's ten months in the German death camp, one that strikes the distinctive note of his writing on the Holocaust. Beginning with his capture by the Fascist Militia in December 1943, the chapters of *If This Is a Man* were written, Levi explains, "in order of urgency." He is acknowledging that this is an attempt both to explain to his readers what life was like in Auschwitz, and to work his way through the experience of life-in-death that emerges as the reality of the Lager ("The life of Ka-Be is a life of limbo").

What is a man in Auschwitz? What does an attrocity such as Auschwitz do to the idea of humanity? Levi delivers what has been described as a prose poem on this "exceptional human state"— thousands of individuals, enclosed together within barbed wire, yet "ferociously alone." In *If This Is a Man*, Levi introduces a number of important themes and categories that would return throughout his writing, notably those of *The Drowned and the Saved*. He reveals the pitiless division that holds sway in the world of the camp: the status of the "Organisator," "Kombinator," and "Prominent," and the lowly "musselman."

There is no third way—that is, no ordinary life—in the camp, and so Levi finds the image of evil that this book struggles to convey: "an emaciated man ... on whose face and in whose eyes not a trace of a thought is to be seen." No thought, and no story: Auschwitz was an attack on the life of the mind against which Levi writes in this book, an attack that generates what he describes as the elemental need to tell the "unlistened-to story." **VL**

Lifespan | b. 1919 (Italy), d. 1987
First Published | 1947, by De Silva (Turin)
U.S. Title | *Survival in Auschwitz*
Original Title | *Se questo è un uomo*

⊙ As a young man Levi joined the Italian anti-Fascist resistance, but he was soon arrested as a partisan and subsequently deported.

⊙ Railway tracks leading to the Auschwitz concentration camp; Levi was one of the few Italian Jews to survive imprisonment.

Exercises in Style

Raymond Queneau

Lifespan | *b.* 1903 (France), *d.* 1976
First Published | 1947, by Gallimard (Paris)
Revised Edition | 1963
Original Title | *Exercices de style*

When Queneau's *Exercises in Style* first appeared in France in 1947, it led at once to his election to the prestigious Académie Goncourt. Nothing quite like it had appeared in French or any other language before, nor has Queneau's feat been repeated successfully since. Queneau begins with a seemingly inconsequential anecdote. On a bus in rush hour, a man with a felt hat accuses another passenger of jostling him. Eventually, when a seat becomes vacant, the man sits down. Later, the man is encountered again in front of the Saint-Lazare station, in the company of a friend who is telling him to get an extra button put on his overcoat. Queneau spends the rest of the book retelling the story in ninety-nine different ways: as a dream, an ode, a sonnet, in the present, as an official letter, as a telegram, in reported speech, as blurb, in anagrams, slang, and so on.

We tend to take it for granted that style is somehow subservient to story, offering a window through which the reader is able to perceive a given and incontrovertible reality. Queneau reveals that style never can be transparent, that language itself shapes and defines the underlying reality that we perceive. Queneau's work forces us to come face to face with this perception in many amusing and dazzling ways. It is reminiscent of a whole tradition of the anti-novel, from Laurence Sterne to James Joyce to Alain Robbe-Grillet, a tradition that insists that what really matters is not the story, but the way in which you tell it. **PT**

The Victim

Saul Bellow

Lifespan | *b.* 1915 (Canada), *d.* 2005 (U.S.)
First Published | 1947
First Published by | Vanguard Press (New York)
Nobel Prize for Literature | 1976

Asa Leventhal is a moderately successful New York Jewish editor of a trade magazine. While his wife is away visiting her mother, he discovers that his nephew Micky has become the victim of a life-threatening disease, and he is confronted in his apartment by Kirby Allbee, a drunken former acquaintance. Allbee claims that Leventhal's aggression toward their former boss cost him his career and status and reduced him to the shambolic figure Leventhal now sees. Allbee moves into Leventhal's apartment, tries to force his host to help him find a new job, brings back a prostitute when he thinks that Leventhal is away, then attempts to commit suicide before disappearing, only to resurface at the end of the novel apparently having recovered his equilibrium.

The moral dilemma at the heart of *The Victim* is perhaps insoluble: when are we responsible for the misfortunes of others? Leventhal is forced to rethink his life and has to realize that what he saw as his finest moment has had dreadful consequences for someone else. The novel also asks the reader to think seriously about the problem of victimhood, and gives us no easy answers. The protagonist is Jewish, but has to ask himself whether he uses his status as a member of a victimized race to advance himself. His accuser is a WASP, prepared to use racist language when it suits him, but undeniably a man dealt a bad hand by life. *The Victim* is a bold work, and although it is not one of Bellow's most celebrated novels, it certainly ranks among his best works of fiction. **AH**

Doctor Faustus

Thomas Mann

Lifespan | *b.* 1875 (Germany), *d.* 1955 (Switzerland)
First Published | 1947
First Published by | Bermann Fischer (Stockholm)
Original Title | *Doktor Faustus*

Doctor Faustus tells the story of the rise and fall of the musician Adrian Leverkühn through the eyes of his friend Serenus Zeitbloom. In this novel, Thomas Mann adapts the Faust myth to suggest that Leverkühn achieves his musical greatness as a result of a pact with the devil. Interwoven with the narration of this bargain and its repercussions is an exploration of how and why Germany chose to ally itself with dark forces in its embracing of fascism through Hitler.

Doctor Faustus engages with the ideas of many European philosophers and thinkers, elaborating its own unique vision. Particularly brilliant are Mann's meditations on the evolution of musical theory over the course of the nineteenth and twentieth centuries, including the advent of the twelve-tone system of Arnold Schönberg, the composer on whom Leverkühn is partly based. Also in strong evidence is Mann's preoccupation with the ruthless demands of creative life. Leverkühn suffers excruciating periods of pain, punctuated by short bouts of breathtaking genius. Many of the finest passages are those that explore the relationship between illness and creativity.

The novel's major achievement is its eloquent synthesis of complex ideas on art, history, and politics, as well as its elaborate meditation on the relationship between the artist and society. The final description of Leverkühn's fate is tinged with the despair and isolation that Mann himself endured as he pondered the future of his native Germany from the vantage point of his exile in California. **CC-G**

DOCTOR FAUSTUS

THE LIFE OF THE GERMAN COMPOSER
ADRIAN LEVERKÜHN
AS TOLD BY A FRIEND

THOMAS MANN

Lo giorno se n'andava e l'aere bruno
toglieva gli animai che sono in terra
dalle fatiche loro, ed io sol uno
m'apparecchiava a sostener la guerra
sì del cammino e sì della pietate,
che ritrarrà la mente que non erra.
O Muse, o alto ingegno, or m'aiutate,
o mente che scrivesti ciò ch'io vidi,
qui si parrà la tua nobilitate.

Dante: *Inferno*, Canto II

LONDON
SECKER & WARBURG

" . . . a revered man sorely tried by fate, which both raised him up and cast him down."

◉ The cover of the first English edition carries lines from Dante, beginning: "Day was departing . . ." and calling on the Muses for aid.

Cry, the Beloved Country

Alan Paton

Lifespan | *b.* 1903 (South Africa), *d.* 1988
First Published |1948
First Published by | Scribner (New York)
Full Name | Alan Stewart Paton

One of the greatest South African novels, *Cry, the Beloved Country* was first published in the United States, bringing international attention to South Africa's tragic history. It tells the story of a father's journey from rural South Africa to and through the city of Johannesburg in search of his son. The reader cannot help but feel deeply for the central character, a Zulu pastor, Stephen Kumalo, and the tortuous discoveries he makes in Johannesburg. It is in a prison cell that Kumalo eventually finds his son, Absalom, who is facing trial for the murder of a white man—a man who ironically cared deeply about the plight of the native South African population and had been a voice for change until his untimely death. Here we meet another father, that of the victim, whose own journey to understand his son eventually leads to his life becoming strangely entwined with Kumalo's. The very different grievings of the men for their lost sons shape the latter half of the novel and offers us hope for redemptive change.

The novel captures the extremes of human emotion, and Paton's faith in human dignity in the worst of circumstances is both poignant and uplifting. The novel shows the brutality of apartheid, but despite its unflinching portrayal of darkness and despair in South Africa, it still offers hope for a better future. The novel itself is a cry for South Africa, which we learn is beloved in spite of everything; a cry for its people, its land, and the tentative hope for its freedom from hatred, poverty, and fear. **EG-G**

"There is a lovely road that runs from Ixopo into the hills. These hills are grass-covered and rolling, and they are lovely beyond any singing of it."

◉ Paton drew material for his writing from his experience as the principal of a South African reformatory for young offenders.

The Heart of the Matter

Graham Greene

Lifespan | *b.* 1904 (England), *d.* 1991 (Switzerland)
First Published | 1948
First Published by | Heinemann (London)
Full Name | Henry Graham Greene

Scobie is a senior policeman in an unnamed outpost in British West Africa during the Second World War. He is bound to his wife, Louise, by his Catholicism and "the pathos of her unattractiveness." In a colony where everyone is thought to be in the pay of the Syrian merchants, have a secret drinking problem, or be sleeping with the local black girls, Scobie is incorruptible and isolated. The drab horror of life in this community of British colonial administrators, based upon Greene's wartime experiences in Sierra Leone, is captured in coolly cinematic style. In the humidity, the slightest scratch turns septic and suppurates for weeks, refusing to heal. Rats and cockroaches are seen darting into the shadows. Life for the old-school-tie boys who run this colony is counted away in pink gins and gossip in the officers' mess. The novel is above all concerned with Scobie's faith and religious breakdown. His terrible pity for Louise and sense of duty toward her mean that he becomes indebted to one of the crooked Syrian traders, in order to arrange her passage out of the colony. While she is away he starts a miserable affair with a young widow—another shackling of pity and responsibility. Louise is aware of Scobie's adultery, and upon her return, exerts subtle pressure on him to attend Mass while not in a state of grace.

The ethical complexity at the center of this work, as well as Greene's understanding of worldly and spiritual corruption, makes *The Heart of the Matter* one of his finest novels. **RMcD**

Death Sentence

Maurice Blanchot

Lifespan | *b.* 1907 (France), *d.* 2003
First Published | 1948
First Published by | Gallimard (Paris)
Original Title | *L'Arrêt de mort*

The reclusive Maurice Blanchot exerted a profound influence on twentieth-century French thought while at the same time maintaining a scrupulous reserve, both in life and in writing. The original French title can be translated as both "death sentence" and "stay of execution"—both a final, definitive judgment and an indefinite reprieve. This short novel reverberates in the suspension of meaning generated by its title.

The first of two narrative sections details the struggle and treatment of a terminally ill woman known only as "J." She dies, and mysteriously comes to life only to be killed again by an overdose administered by the narrator. The second narrative documents the narrator's interactions with three other women against the background of the occupation and bombing of Paris in 1940. Between the two parts occur many parallels and repetitions, which multiply and complicate interpretations.

As the narrator struggles to recount the events he relates, he senses that words always double-back, consuming himself and the truth he is attempting to convey. For the narrator, this struggle is the condition of all writing; he feels the acute inability of words to capture adequately an event in all its complexity, and yet is overtaken by the insatiable desire to tell, condemned to explore the limits of what can be said by forever starting again. An astonishing text that transformed the understanding of what it is that novels do. **SS**

Disobedience

Alberto Moravia

Lifespan | *b.*1907 (Italy), *d.*1990
First Published | 1948
First Published by | Bompiani (Milan)
Original Title | *La disubbidienza*

One of Italy's most prominent literary figures of the past century, Alberto Moravia had a prolific and highly successful writing career. A great deal of his work concerns the obsessions and complexes of the Roman bourgeoisie, in particular the twinned themes of money and sex, seen as agents of power, rather than pleasure. It is characterized by an almost clinical clarity of expression, an open approach to sexuality, and a close attention to the psychological.

Disobedience is a highly original treatment of the coming-of-age theme. Luca is a disaffected only child of respectable middle-class parents who becomes increasingly dissatisfied with all that he previously cherished. He embarks upon a process of what he perceives to be logical, calculated disobedience, relinquishing all worldly goods and love. Eventually he falls ill and is bedridden for several months, during which time he experiences troubling hallucinations. When he recovers, his convalescence is accompanied by a sexual initiation with his nurse. The experience is heavily symbolic, and Luca sees it as a rebirth through which he overcomes his destructive self-denial and gains an almost mythic sense of oneness with reality. A heavily charged, complex work dealing with teenage rebellion, sexuality, and alienation, *Disobedience* is a fascinating psychological portrait of an oedipal awakening. **AL**

⊙ Alberto Moravia, far left, enjoys a relaxed convesation with other Italian writers, including Elsa Moranti and, on her left, Carlo Levi.

All About H. Hatterr

G. V. Desani

Lifespan | *b.*1909 (Kenya), *d.*2001 (U.S.)
First Published | 1948, by F. Aldor (London)
Revised Edition Published | 1972, by Penguin UK
Full Name | Govindas Vishnoodas Desani

All About H. Hatterr is a singular book, unmatched in its sustained comedy of rhetoric and language. Models might be perceived in the idiomatic style and formal play of Laurence Sterne, James Joyce, or Flann O'Brien, but nothing can quite prepare you for this book's inventive play of rhetoric, innocence, and wit. Part of the joke is that the central character-narrator, the eponymous H. Hatterr, continually reveals an acutely intelligent grasp of the English language, life, and literary artifice, but is perceived as a simple-minded dupe. Linguistic sophistication is blended with quixotic innocence, as if Joyce's Leopold Bloom, having acquired English as a second language, had learned to write like Rabelais or Laurence Sterne. Exhibit one, the book's much fuller title: *The Autobiographical of H. Hatterr, being also a mosaic-organon of Life: viz., a medico-philosophical grammar as to this contrast, this human horseplay, this design for diamond-cut-diamond … H. Hatterr by H. Hatterr.*

The novel relates how the orphaned Hatterr, of multicultural and multilingual background, is adopted into "the Christian lingo (English)" as his "second vernacular" and goes "completely Indian to an extent few pure non-Indian blood sahib fellers have done." Hatterr's adventures mostly focus on a variety of unlikely spiritual encounters with the society, sages, and anglo-grotesques of India and England. Rumor has it that this Indo-Anglian classic much influenced Salman Rushdie, but Desani more than has the edge. **DM**

Nineteen Eighty-Four

George Orwell

Lifespan | *b.* 1903 (India), *d.* 1950 (England)
First Published | 1949
First Published by | Secker & Warburg (London)
Given Name | Eric Arthur Blair

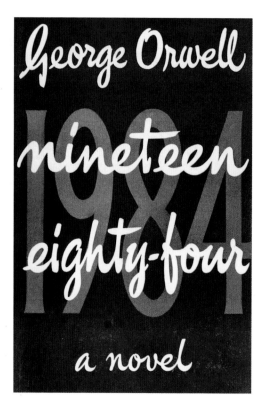

◉ Published in London in 1949, Orwell's novel reflected the drabness of postwar Britain, beset by austerity and shortages.

◉ The vibrant cover of the German translation of *Nineteen Eighty-Four* depicts the all-seeing eye of the sinister Big Brother.

Nineteen Eighty-Four is one of Orwell's most powerful politically charged novels, a beautifully crafted warning against the dangers of a totalitarian society, and one of the most famous novels in the dystopian genre. Winston Smith is a low-ranking member of the ruling party in London whose every move is monitored by telescreens. Everywhere Winston goes, the party's omniscient leader, Big Brother, watches him. The party is trying to eradicate the possibility of political rebellion by eliminating all words related to it from the language, creating sanitized "Newspeak." "Thoughtcrime" (thinking rebellious thoughts) is illegal. Winston, who works at the Ministry of Truth altering historical records for the party's benefit, is frustrated and oppressed by the prohibitions on free thought, sex, and individuality. He illegally purchases a diary to record his thoughts and spends his evenings wandering the poor areas where the "proles" live, relatively free from monitoring. Winston starts an illicit affair with Julia, a fellow party employee, but they are caught by a party spy, and in Room 101, Winston is forced to confront his worst fear. Giving up his love for Julia in terror, Winston is released, his spirit broken and his acceptance of the party complete.

In 1949, at the beginning of the nuclear age and before television was mainstream, Orwell's creation of a telescreen-monitored world just a single generation into the future was terrifying. This is an important novel not only for its stark warning against abusive authority (and its somewhat ironic contribution to modern television content), but also for its insights into the power of manipulating language, history, and the psychology of fear and control. These issues are perhaps even more pertinent today than when Orwell penned his novel. **EF**

GEORGE ORWELL

> 1984 <

ROMAN

The Man with the Golden Arm

Nelson Algren

Lifespan | *b.*1909 (U.S.), *d.*1981
First Published | 1949
First Published by | Doubleday & Co. (New York)
Movie Adaptation Released | 1955

Algren's best novel is perhaps first remembered through its cinematic adaptation in the movie starring Frank Sinatra as his hustling junkie anti-hero, Frankie Machine. This is as unjust a situation as the fact that Algren himself has, thanks to a biography of his lover, Simone de Beauvoir, come to be known principally as the man who helped the author of *The Second Sex* achieve her first orgasm.

The novel mingles the true-crime titillation of pulp fiction and low journalism with the crusading zeal of sociological investigation: a marketable blend of prurience and high-mindedness, lifted above its many rivals in the field by Algren's sustained poetic gift. His prose style, with its violently clashing registers, and the enduring resonance of its poetic voice, is indelibly marked by the influence of T. S. Eliot and James Joyce.

Chicago was the great subject of Algren's writing life and he dusted its dilapidated bars, damp flophouses, filthy holding tanks, and drenched sidewalks—all sites of the most harrowing indignity, with a dignified, perceptive language that he knew how to share with his central characters. If Algren's rhetorical style is very occasionally portentous, Frankie Machine, Sparrow Saltskin, Sophie, Molly, and the chorus of weary Chicago policemen survive with their expressive intensities intact, even as the bunch of petty criminals are sent into unsustainable downward spirals by addiction, violence, and inescapable poverty. **RP**

"I had a great big habit. One time I knocked out one of my own teet' to get the gold for a fix. You call that bein' hooked or not?"

The poster for Otto Preminger's 1955 movie adaptation of the book, initially banned because it showed drug addiction.

Kingdom of This World

Alejo Carpentier

Lifespan | *b.* 1904 (Cuba), *d.* 1980 (France)
First Published | 1949, by Publicaciones
Iberoamericana (Mexico)
Original Title | *El reino de este mundo*

With this book, Carpentier declared war on the exhausted inheritance of European surrealism and at the same time produced a defining text for the emergent magic realist movement. The novel is underpinned by a relatively straightforward historical narrative, which follows the major events of the only successful revolution in the Atlantic slave diaspora. Set in revolutionary Santo Domingo, the island that was to emerge in 1803 as Haiti, the first black ex-slave republic, the novel follows the fortunes of the central character, Ti Noël. Initially a servant to one of the *grand blanc* families before the revolution, Ti Noël forms an intense friendship with the charismatic Mandingo slave leader Macandal, then witnesses his execution and voodoo apotheosis. After the successful slave revolution, Ti Noël is re-enslaved as part of the immense labor force consigned by the black dictator Henri Christophe to erect his unearthly fortified mountaintop palace. The novel ends with a phantasmagoric account of the fall of Christophe, the sacking of Sans Souci, and Ti Noël's death.

Carpentier wrote the novel in a state of near despair at what he saw as the unrelenting formulaic nature of fantasy literature. However, in this short, delicately wrought masterpiece, Carpentier fuses a precisely researched external history with a series of anthropomorphic transformations and metaphoric juxtapositions, which constantly achieve his ideal of a "marvellous reality," a new fiction of the "marvellous in the real." **MW**

The Heat of the Day

Elizabeth Bowen

Lifespan | *b.* 1899 (Ireland), *d.* 1973 (England)
First Published | 1949
First Published by | A. Knopf (New York)
Full Name | Elizabeth Dorothy Cole Bowen

Elizabeth Bowen's *The Heat of the Day* is a beautiful novel: immersed in it, you do not want to leave it, but to stay encased in the symmetry and clarity of its vision. It is a love story set in wartime London. Stella discovers that her lover, Robert, is suspected of being a Nazi spy. He himself confesses to sympathy for the German vision of order and rule of law. Stella's delicately structured world slowly disintegrates.

This story and the strange hues of a summertime city at war give the novel its momentum and texture. There is, however, another level and another love story also at work, one that generates an intense and painful melancholy. This second love story is inarticulate, felt only as a sense of loss, a grieving for something loved and gone. What *The Heat of the Day* mourns would not have been mourned by many, nor will many today regret its passing. For it anticipates and lingers over the death of the cultural and social supremacy of the English property-owning class. Many of the sons of this class were slaughtered in the First World War, and in the interwar years the Great Depression had depleted their capital, while the existence of the Labour Party had drained their power and political prestige.

Bowen began writing *The Heat of the Day* in 1944, one year before the Labour landslide in the British general election of 1945. What enriches the text of this novel, enveloping and enlarging the individual stories of loss, is Bowen's elegy for an era even then already past. **PMcM**

The Case of Comrade Tulayev

Victor Serge

Lifespan | *b.* 1890 (Belgium), *d.* 1947 (Mexico)
First Published | 1949, by Editions du Seuil (Paris)
Given Name | Victor Lvovich Kibalchich
Original Title | *L'Affaire Toulaév*

The Case of Comrade Tulayev is about totalitarianism and hence is about defeat, enclosure, and the systematization of paranoia. It differs, however, from Orwell's *Nineteen Eighty-Four* or Koestler's *Darkness at Noon* in its determination to pay respect to the multiplicity and excesses of ordinary life. The novel takes the show trials and purges of Stalin's Russia as its core material. Serge himself had lived through the optimistic revolution of 1917 and the development of a total system of bureaucratic power in Stalinism. He had fought that development as part of Trotsky's Left opposition and had been deported to Central Asia between 1933 and 1936. It was at that time that Stalin's long waves of purges, the Great Terror, began.

There is a dense historical undercurrent in this novel, reaching back beyond Stalinism to incorporate, through memory, anecdote, and association, multiple varieties of Russian life. This is life as lived among the soldiers of the Great War, landless peasants, political activists in small exiled or underground parties, the life of scholars, clerks, travelers, and enthusiasts.

Serge's narrative is rich with voices, while the plot condenses with a shocking coolness and clarity. Yet Serge still manages to keep the narrative poised at a level where Russia is an arena pulsating with life. While terror, death, betrayal, and a painful confusion are pervasive, so, too, are the small rhythms of work, fraternity, conversation, and hope. **PMcM**

Love in a Cold Climate

Nancy Mitford

Lifespan | *b.* 1904 (England), *d.* 1973 (France)
First Published | 1949
First Published by | Hamish Hamilton (London)
Original Language | English

Love in a Cold Climate, set in roughly the same time and place as Nancy Mitford's earlier novel *The Pursuit of Love* (1945), delves into British aristocratic society between the wars with similarly hilarious results. Set against a background of privilege, wealth, and taste, it tells the story of Polly Montdore, an heiress whose unconventional choice of husband not only shocks her own family, but also provides scandal enough to occupy all of the country-house set to which she belongs. Told by her friend Fanny, the sensible narrator of many of Mitford's novels, Polly's story expands to become a larger commentary on the comic and tragic elements inherent within society life. Light and witty in tone, the novel describes what would usually appear to be an ordinary round of social engagements in a world in which the ordinary is a surprisingly rare phenomenon. Mitford's characters often verge on the bizarre; "Uncle Matthew," modeled on Mitford's father, typifies the eccentric aristocrat, while the insufferable Lady Montdore, who undergoes a hilariously drawn affair with Canadian nephew and arch-aesthete Cedric, remains a cutting portrait of the domineering but gullible matriarch. Mitford's novels, like those of Jane Austen, focus on the small social maneuverings of an exclusive family and their "set"; like Austen, she uses fond but mocking satire to gently send up the family, even while encouraging the reader to care about its fortunes. **AB**

The Garden Where the Brass Band Played

Simon Vestdijk

Lifespan | *b.* 1898 (Netherlands), *d.* 1971
First Published | 1950
First Published by | Gravenhage (Rotterdam)
Original Title | *De koperen tuin*

One of the giants among writers to come from the Netherlands, Vestdijk, who trained as a physician and published poetry as well as essays, was as prolific as he was versatile. His work had a major influence on the Dutch existentialists, and, if it were better known outside his own country, might be ranked with that of Joyce, Kafka, and Proust.

This novel, a moody study of the conflict between bourgeois society and the romantic ideal, is set in a fictional small town where Nol, a judge's son, first encounters enchantment. While still a child, he attends an outdoor concert with his mother and is seduced simultaneously by the music and dancing with the conductor's daughter. He subsequently takes piano lessons with the maestro, who opens his heart and mind to the mysteries of art. Nol's fascination and affinity for this way of knowing the world brings him into internal conflict with the milieu in which he has grown up and the class that claims him. His attachment to the musician Cuperus and especially to his daughter Trix, both of whom are quasi-outcasts in genteel society, is emblematic of the author's preoccupation with the unattainable beloved, and Nol's story is a sort of romantic quest that pits the ideal against social convention and the loss of innocence this entails. Vestdijk manages to combine rapture and suffering with comedy in a mix that is intensely realistic and completely engaging. **ES**

The Moon and the Bonfires

Cesare Pavese

Lifespan | *b.* 1908 (Italy), *d.* 1950
First Published | 1950
First Published by | Einaudi (Turin)
Original Title | *La luna e i falò*

Pavese's last novel has been acclaimed as his best, a lyrical walk through the Langhe region of Piedmont. The story is minimal, as the author did not want to create a complex plot or explore the psychology of the characters. After Italy is liberated from fascism, Anguilla, who has spent twenty years in America, returns to his native village. He has traveled enough to know that, ultimately, all countries in the world are similar and eventually one needs to settle somewhere. Consequently, he returns to the Langhe because "those villages were waiting for him." In a narrative that alternates between present and past, Anguilla—accompanied by his friend and guide, Nuto—rediscovers his homeland. Anguilla's desire is to find himself through the physical appropriation of Gaminella, the place where he spent his childhood, and Mora, where he worked during his adolescence. His idealized village has acquired the symbolic colors of an earthly paradise, but he soon finds that the trees have been cut down, and Santa, who was a young girl when he left, has been killed. Nuto shares with Anguilla the same faith in the value of the Resistance and the necessity of a social revolution and helps him to become aware of the deceptiveness of his search. He introduces Anguilla to the mythical essence of social revolution by affirming his belief in the peasants' traditions and superstitions and in the regenerative power of the bonfires. **RPi**

I, Robot

Isaac Asimov

Lifespan | *b.* 1920 (Russia), *d.* 1992 (U.S.)
First Published | 1950
First Published by | Gnome Press (New York)
Original Language | English

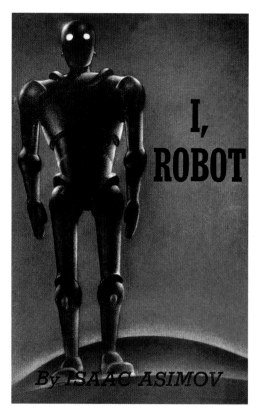

"Ninety-eight--ninety-nine . . ."

🔵 The classic image of the robot, as used on this jacket for *I Robot*, was influenced by 1920s movies such as Fritz Lang's *Metropolis*.

I, Robot is one of the great classics of science fiction. Ostensibly, it is a collection of short stories, but the fact that they are all linked together as they explore the twin subjects of robotics and philosophy warrants the book's inclusion in a list of great novels. In *I, Robot* Asimov coined the term "robotics" and set out the principles of robot behavior we know as the Three Laws of Robotics, followed by science-fiction writers ever since. The three rules read: 1) A robot may not injure a human being or through inaction allow a human being to come to harm; 2) A robot must obey orders given by human beings except where such orders would conflict with the First Law; 3) A robot must protect its own existence as long as such protection does not conflict with the First or Second Law.

The stories are connected by robo-psychologist Dr. Susan Calvin, who works for the corporation that manufactures intelligent robots, and her discussions with a reporter who is putting together a profile of her career. Dr. Calvin reflects on robot evolution and discusses how little humanity really understands about the artificial intelligence it has created. Each story illuminates a problem encountered when a robot interprets the three fundamental laws, and something goes awry. Although *I, Robot* was published in 1950 and includes stories from the 1940s, when computing was in its embryonic stage, Asimov's vision of the future of software is startlingly accurate and insightful. Asimov's writing is certainly not top-drawer, and the characterization is often weak, but the scientific style, the blend between fact and fiction, and the stunning insights into the world of robotics, from which so much else has developed, make this one of the most important works of science fiction in the history of the genre. **EF**

The Grass is Singing

Doris Lessing

Lessing's first novel, written in Africa, but not published until she was living in Europe, opens with the murder of the wife of a white Rhodesian farmer by her African servant. The novel's interest lies, however, in the story suppressed by the community of white farmers of the events that lead up to the tragedy. The retrospective narrative thus moves irrevocably toward an inevitable death. From the first pages it is clear that we are being asked to bear witness to a story of human relations that a colonial system of justice will not allow to be heard. Dick and Mary Turner are each possessed by need and a deluded idea of the other person. When they marry, city-girl Mary is brought to live on Turner's isolated and failing farm. As Mary is gradually disabused of her hopes about Dick and the future, she succumbs to torpor and hysteria in the sweltering heat of the veld. Only Moses, the latest in a series of native servants ill-treated by Mary, seems able to respond to her misery. But Moses' acts of kindness toward her violate the sacred colonial taboo—that separate races are not allowed to recognize one another as human beings. Desire and fear are inextricably intertwined as Mary feels herself surrendering to the authority of a man she associates with the surrounding bush, which threatens always to reconquer the land taken by the white farmers.

The portrait of lives destroyed is mitigated in its painful intensity only by the descriptions of the stark beauty of the African veld. *The Grass is Singing* is the first publication of a major literary figure, an angry denunciation of the hypocrisies of the colonial power known to Lessing from her youth in Southern Africa, and a dissection of colonial mentality and the deformations it performs on both the colonizer and the colonized. **VM**

Lifespan | *b*. 1919 (Iran)
First Published | 1950
First Published by | Michael Joseph (London)
First U.S. Edition | Crowell (New York)

"I'm not lonely."

⊙ This paperback edition of Lessing's novel was published by Heinemann in 1973 as one of their African Writers Series.

Gormenghast

Mervyn Peake

Lifespan | *b.* 1911 (China), *d.* 1968 (England)
First Published | 1950
First Published by | Eyre & Spottiswoode (London)
Full Name | Mervyn Lawrence Peake

"Oh, wonderful. He's behaving his damn self."

🔺 Mervyn Peake, an illustrator as well as a writer, peruses some sketches in a photo published in *Picture Post* magazine (1946).

This is the second volume of Peake's extraordinary *Gormenghast* trilogy and inarguably the apex of the series. It is also an outstanding feat of literature. *Gormenghast* takes up where *Titus Groan* left off. Lord Sepulchrave is dead, Swelter has been vanquished by Mr. Flay, and Steerpike, bald from his own arson—his disfiguring scars reflecting his progressive inner rot—continues his vicious ascent through the hierarchy. He has become a force to be reckoned with. Titus is approaching restless adolescence. As he closes in on manhood, he becomes a worthy adversary to the machinations of the increasingly powerful Steerpike. And Gormenghast itself, huge and malevolent, wheezes on.

The vast carnival of characters from *Titus Groan* returns with exhilarating vibrancy, coursing through the labyrinth of Great Halls and bedchambers, the dusty cellars and libraries. There are the lovelorn Fuschia, the nattering twin aunts having tea parties in the boughs outside their window, the toadying Dr. Prunesquallor, and his sister Irma, with her preening, unearned vanity. Peake takes his original scathing allegory of British life and expands it with new targets for his sublime wit: an excoriating and hilarious examination of Titus' education in a system that is eerily familiar. The novel culminates with an apocalyptic flood, as Steerpike and Titus do battle for the very heart of Gormenghast. With a fresh awareness of the outside world and the itch of adolescence, Titus finally decides to leave the craggy battlements of his home and sets out for the world beyond the crumbling walls.

Peake's prose is masterful; his characters so strange they become hyperreal. *Gormenghast* is as complex and dark as a Bosch triptych. It is a fairy tale without sugar, leaving only the skeletal nightmare. **GT**

The 13 Clocks

James Thurber

The 13 Clocks contains all the essential ingredients of a thrilling fairy tale. There are a prince disguised as a ragged minstrel, a tragic princess trapped in a castle by an evil duke, and the prospect of a daring task that must be completed within an impossible time frame. This constraint is a key element in the story because the duke claims to have "slain" time, and the thirteen clocks in the castle are frozen at ten minutes to five. The prince must find a priceless treasure and deliver it up as the clocks strike the hour. His only hope is the Golux, a tiny wizard possessed of a strange logic and an indescribable hat.

The castle is a dangerous place, noisily patrolled by huge metallic guards, silently controlled by the duke's velvet-hooded spies. Nightmarish creatures lurk in the darkest corners of the deepest dungeons. Playful counterpoints to these horrors are provided by touches of absurdity. Brightly colored balls come bouncing downstairs at unlikely moments—are there ghosts of murdered children playing above? Chimes of distant laughter hint at the possibility. There are also elements of parable: love conquers all, time is unfrozen, and evil meets inevitable nemesis. In the final pages the duke is pursued by "a blob of glup, that smells of old unopened rooms and makes a sound like rabbits screaming."

The language is dazzlingly inventive and the tone wickedly ironic—hallmarks of the most admired and controversial humorist of the first half of the twentieth century. At the time of writing *The 13 Clocks*, Thurber was rapidly losing his sight, and the descriptions of half-perceived figures moving in shadows, of shafts of sunlight piercing darkened rooms, and thickets of night lit by flashes of lightning create hallucinatory landscapes that suggest a great preoccupation with encroaching blindness. **TS**

Lifespan | *b.* 1894 (U.S.), *d.* 1961
First Published | 1950
First Published by | Simon & Schuster (New York)
Full Name | James Grover Thurber

"He called himself Xingu, which was not his name . . ."

James Thurber's cartoon drawings were as essential an expression of his comic vision as his ironic, inventive prose.

THE CAFE MOZART WALT

Based on Music Composed & Arrang

by

ANTON KARA

A LONDON FILM PRODUCTION Presented by
ALEXANDER KORDA & DAVID O. SELZNICK

JOSEPH COTTEN   VALLI
ORSON WELLES   TREVOR HOWARD

in Carol Reed's production

"The Third Man"

BASED ON A STORY BY GRAHAM GREENE

Produced and directed by CAROL REED

DISTRIBUTED BY BRITISH LION

5377

2/

CHAPPELL & CO., LTD

50, NEW BOND STREET, LONDON, W.I.

Made in Engl

The Third Man

Graham Greene

Greene's novella, written primarily to set the mood and plot of the screenplay he wrote for Carol Reed's film of the preceding year, initially seems a minor work—only 157 pages and never intended for publication. It is nonetheless a fascinating work in the way it creates a kind of European noir. Clearly the themes of the classic hard-boiled novels of Chandler and Hammett have universal significance in their depiction of a world where space is defined by urbanization, and where corruption springs up as a result of the modern city, but they are also very distinctly American. Greene's novella transfers these concepts to Vienna, evoking an urban space fractured by both war and development, but one that also has an immutable weight of history lacking in its American counterparts.

The demolished beauty of Vienna is at the center of *The Third Man*, and Greene sets up a recognizably convoluted noir mystery around it. The plot involves mistaken identities, mysterious women, and corrupt black-market networks, all further convoluted by the narrator, the British policeman Calloway, who is a third party to much of the information he recounts. This is a novel that seems impossible to read without reference to the film, because regardless of several key differences, they are so closely linked. But rather than this interlinking becoming a problem, it actually furthers the story's central feature, the idea of opposing things being forced together: the old and the new, the "serious" and the "entertaining," the novel and the film, Europe and America. The breaking down of boundaries between these concepts is a signal feature of twentieth century literature, and *The Third Man* remains a powerful example of how this can be made into something other than a disaster to lament. **SF**

Lifespan | *b.* 1904 (England), *d.* 1991 (Switzerland)
First Published | 1950
First Published by | Heinemann (London)
First U.S. Edition | Viking (New York)

Like many writers of his period, Greene was a heavy drinker —a characteristic with which he endows many of his heroes.

The shadow of Orson Welles as Harry Lime dominates the cover of the sheet music for Anton Karas' *The Third Man* zither score.

The Labyrinth of Solitude

Octavio Paz

> "*Modern man likes to pretend that his thinking is wide-awake.*"

◉ Paz, who was born during the Mexican Revolution in Mexcoac, is pictured here outside his native Mexico City home.

Lifespan | *b.* 1914 (Mexico), *d.* 1998
First Published | 1950, by Cuadernos Americanos
Original Title | *El laberinto de la soledad*
Nobel Prize for Literature | 1990

A book made up of nine individual essay-chapters on aspects of Mexican national character might seem an odd choice in a list of indispensable novels, but *The Labyrinth of Solitude* also marks an advance in prose fiction. It is an analytical and intensely poetic bildungsroman showing the formation not of an individual, but of a nation's identity.

Paz was already among the greatest Mexican poets of the twentieth century when he wrote *The Labyrinth of Solitude* in 1950. He was also a significant figure in public life: he traveled to Europe in the 1930s, fighting for the Republicans in the Spanish Civil War; he was an esteemed diplomat; and he went on to win the Nobel Prize for Literature in 1990. *Labyrinth* proved controversial with the Mexican establishment, as it held up a mirror to a nation that did not always like what it was shown. The book describes Mexico at a crucial moment of self-realization, but it is also often critical of aspects of Mexican identity: its machismo, dissimulation, harshness, and immovable gender roles.

In this work, Paz is part anthropologist and part semiologist, reading the signs through which Mexican culture was constructed, from the dress codes of disaffected Mexican-American youth gangs to the public rituals of the Day of the Dead. But he also brings all of his profound eloquence as a poet to bear on his subject, and the book resonates on every page with instinctive insights, connections, and verbal finesse. **MS**

The Abbot C

Georges Bataille

Lifespan | b. 1897 (France), d. 1962
First Published | 1950
First Published by | Les Editions de Minuit (Paris)
Original Title | L'Abbé C

George Bataille's short novel L'Abbé C follows the dangerously entangled relationship between twin brothers: Robert, a priest, who lives a life of such virtue that he has earned the sobriquet "the abbot," and his antipathetic brother Charles, who leads a dissolute life devoted to pleasure. The novel is comprised of various narrators and opens with the narrative of a mutual friend, who finds Robert in a state of anguish on account of his brother's grave ill health. As the story unfolds, the extent of the brothers' overlapping emotional lives becomes clear. Charles' involvement with Eponine, a woman who shares his decadent and licentious lifestyle, is complicated by her sexual desire for the abstemious Robert and, more sensationally, by Robert's uneasy physical desire for her. This painful triangulation puts unbearable strain upon the sibling relationship and causes the steady breakdown of Robert's sanity and simultaneous deterioration of Charles' physical health.

Fusing Bataille's familiar fascination with the relationship between eroticism, death, and sensuality, the novel explores the thin line between sexual desire and morbidity. In its concentration upon the fissure between the moral code demanded by religious observance and the truth of individual conscience, it explores an intriguing dimension of human experience. Readers may find the treatment of this issue somewhat excessive and the contrived intention to shock rather heavy-handed, but this is still an engaging and unusual piece of writing. **JW**

The End of the Affair

Graham Greene

Lifespan | b. 1904 (England), d. 1991 (Switzerland)
First Published | 1951
First Published by | Heinemann (London)
Full Name | Henry Graham Greene

Set in London during and after the Second World War, this is the tortured story of an affair between Maurice Bendrix, a novelist, and the married Sarah Miles. The lovers meet at a party thrown by Sarah's husband, who bores her, and proceed to liberate each other from the confines of duty and unhappiness. After several years, the affair is still continuing, against the backdrop of London during the Blitz. The building in which the lovers are enjoying an afternoon tryst is hit by a bomb, and Bendrix is knocked unconscious. Terrified that he is dead, Sarah makes a deal with God that if he lets him live she will give up her lover. Bendrix recovers, and Sarah—true to her promise—ends the affair with no explanation, leaving Bendrix unhappy and confused. Assuming she left him for another man, it is only years later when he hires a private detective that he finds out about her passionate vow to God.

Greene is known for his Catholicism, and also for questioning religious faith in the light of his own adulterous affairs. This is the most autobiographical of Greene's novels, probably based on his own wartime affair. It is a story of love, passion, and religious faith, and how love of self, love of another, and love of God collide. The tension that pervades The End of the Affair comes from the interplay of doubt and faith, and Greene's underlying message that human love and passion are inadequate for relieving suffering—for that, he believes, one must turn to the love of God. **EF**

Molloy

Samuel Beckett

Lifespan | *b.* 1906 (Ireland), *d.* 1989 (France)
First Published | 1951
First Published by | Les Editions de Minuit (Paris)
Nobel Prize for Literature | 1969

Beckett is better known for his plays than for his novels, but his novels are the greater achievement. They are the funniest prose alive. *Molloy*, written initially in French, then translated into English by Beckett and Patrick Bowles, is the first novel in the trilogy finished off by *Malone Dies* and *The Unnamable*. Although they complete the trilogy, these two later novels proved inadequate to the job of putting an end to the decline begun in *Molloy*, which extends into everything that Beckett would go on to write.

Beckett is the great master of every possible shade of decline and its unrivalled comedian. *Molloy* is probably the funniest of all his writing. It is made up of two stories, each the doppelgänger of the other. In the first, the wretched cripple Molloy stumbles through a lost thread of episodes peopled by his insensible mother, a litter of comic citizens, a policeman, and a grotesque feminine captor named Lousse, before ending up dumped by Beckett in a ditch. His place is then surrendered to Moran, whom Beckett dispatches, together with his son, on a quest to find his predecessor, a quest that Moran pursues with furious inertia only to find that Beckett has declined to contrive a meeting between them. He trudges home to find his bees turned to ash.

Beckett nails all the perks of fiction (all the events, sympathies, and glitter of fiction's "real life") into their smorgasbord and buries it. His stories are all the confessions of a syntax addict whose phantom fix is total disagreement with himself. **KS**

The Rebel

Albert Camus

Lifespan | *b.* 1913 (Algeria), *d.* 1960 (France)
First Published | 1951
First Published by | Gallimard (Paris)
Original Title | *L'Homme révolté*

The Rebel recalls the dispute between Camus and Sartre in 1952. It also represents the dispute between metaphysical freedom and actual revolution. In the aftermath of the Second World War, the French yearned for social change and activism. The verdict of the day favored Sartre. *The Rebel* was accused of supporting the vision of right-wing reactionaries. But does it really? In the cultural context of our time *The Rebel* appears to question the foundation of collectivist ideology and to present us with an acute insight into the preconditions of "being political." The thesis of the book can be summarized in the statement: "I revolt, therefore we are." However, in Camus, the absolute solitariness or freedom of the individual never allows the emergence of "we" to be the objective of individual revolt. Metaphysically speaking, we are already engaged with a political situation before the actual intended revolution. In the eyes of Camus, Sartrian left-wing existentialism dismisses the freedom of the individual. For Sartre, revolt means an actual engagement with politics so as to bring about changes, whilst for Camus it is a metaphysical condition of the inner life of the individual. Camus stands back from Sartrian activism, which promotes solidarity. How do we read *The Rebel* today? The way we read it will point to the political condition in which we live. **KK**

> Camus casts a mordant glance upon a Parisian street in 1957, the year in which he was awarded the Nobel Prize for Literature.

The Catcher in the Rye

J. D. Salinger

Lifespan | *b.* 1919 (U.S.)
First Published | 1951
First Published by | Little Brown & Co. (Boston)
Full Name | Jerome David Salinger

The Catcher in the Rye presents the dazzling mock-autobiographical story of an American teenager, Holden Caulfield, charting his rebellious encounters with the "phoney" world around him. Shadowed by apocalyptic anxieties ("I'm sort of glad they've got the atomic bomb invented. If there's another war, I'm going to sit right the hell on top of it."), it is also an extraordinary study of refused or impossible mourning, above all Holden's for his dead younger brother, Allie. Once asked "who was the best war poet, Rupert Brooke or Emily Dickinson," Allie said Dickinson. Salinger's novel is itself a kind of war poetry. It is at war with "phoney" adult (i.e., affluent, middle-class, white, patriarchal, U.S.) values, but also with itself: Holden brilliantly ridicules those around him, but in the process inevitably also makes himself ridiculous.

Hilarious and disturbing, satirical and strangely poignant by turns, *The Catcher in the Rye* is written in a deceptively simple and colloqiual style: "What really knocks me out is a book that, when you're all done reading it, you wish the author that wrote it was a terrific friend of yours and you could call him up on the phone whenever you felt like it." Novels to read before you die are novels like that. How phoney is *this* phone? Salinger's voice is enigmatically concealed in Holden's. There is the captivating ease and intimacy of someone directly speaking to us. At the same time the reader is left with the remarkable sense that the tone of the entire work is perhaps really audible only to the dead brother. **NWor**

> " . . . *I'm standing on the edge of some crazy cliff. What I have to do, I have to catch everybody if they start to go over the cliff . . .* "

⊙ To escape the unwanted fame that *The Catcher in the Rye* brought him, Salinger became a recluse, vigorously defending his privacy.

The Opposing Shore

Julien Gracq

Lifespan | b. 1910 (France)
First Published | 1951, by J. Corti (Paris)
Original Title | Le Rivage des Syrtes
Given Name | Louis Poirier

A strangely moody and distilled piece of writing, *The Opposing Shore* is set in decadent Orsenna, a fictional country long engaged in a phony war with Farghestan, the neighboring barbarian state. In a permanently suspended stalemate, all battles having ceased some 300 years earlier, neither side can afford either to concede or to continue, or is prepared to negotiate terms of peace. Yet legends of the war have stimulated the poets to an output far beyond what the situation might be expected to inspire.

Aldo, a young and dissipated man, scion of an aristocratic family, is disappointed in love and weary of the pleasures of the capital; he longs for exile and asceticism. So he takes on the position of Observer at the military post on the frontier, where the Admiralty, a long-disused fortress, maintains a purely symbolic presence. There Aldo, poet and loner, attempts to shake off his torpor and invigorate his fatherland by launching a naval maneuver that regenerates the hostilities to disastrous effect.

The novel follows a graceful path of sumptuous imagery that slows the action to a timelessness that reads like myth. Gracq's writing has a strong affinity to the surrealism of André Breton, although he was never part of this or any other literary movement.

Gracq, like his protagonist Aldo, disdained the effete cultural milieu of urban centers—in this case, Paris. Had he not categorically rejected the honor, *The Opposing Shore* would have been awarded the Prix Goncourt in 1951. **ES**

Foundation

Isaac Asimov

Lifespan | b. 1920 (Russia), d. 1992 (U.S.)
First Published | 1951, by Gnome Press (New York)
Trilogy | Foundation (1951), Foundation and Empire (1952), Second Foundation (1953)

Isaac Asimov's Foundation series, of which this is the first book, is one of his earliest and best known works, which he began when he was only twenty-one. It helped to redefine the science-fiction genre with its seamless interweaving of science fact with fiction. *Foundation* is set in the future, when the world is barely remembered, and humans have colonized the galaxy. The book introduces Hari Seldon, a brilliant visionary and psychohistorian whose job is to use mathematics and probability to predict the future. Seldon does not have the ability to prevent the decline of humanity that he predicts. Instead, he gathers together the galaxy's top scientists and scholars on a bleak outer planet and sets out to preserve the accumulated knowledge of humankind and begin a new civilization based on art, science, and technology. He calls his sanctuary the Foundation and designs it to withstand a dark age of ignorance, barbarism, and warfare he predicts will last for 30,000 years. But not even Hari has foreseen the intense barbarism lurking in space or the birth of an extraordinary creature whose mutant intelligence will destroy all he holds dear.

With his scientist-populated *Foundation*, Asimov became one of the first writers to theorize that atomic power would revolutionize society. In addressing the ways in which the Foundation responds to the problems Seldon has predicted, the author raises issues about traditional religion as the controlling drug of the masses, and the rise of science as the new faith for humankind. **EF**

BEWARE THE TRIFFIDS...they grow
...know...walk...talk...stalk...and KILL!

From the greatest
science-fiction novel
of all time!

THE DAY OF THE
TRIFFIDS

IN CINEMASCOPE
AND
EASTMANCOLOR

STARRING
HOWARD KEEL
NICOLE MAUREY

Executive Producer
PHILIP YORDAN · Produced by GEORGE PITCHER · Directed by STEVE SEKELY · Screenplay by From the Novel by JOHN WYNDHAM

A SECURITY PICTURES LTD. PRODUCTION

Day of the Triffids

John Wyndham

Lifespan | b.1903 (England), d.1969
First Published | 1951, by Michael Joseph (London)
Full Name | John Wyndham Parkes Lucas Beynon Harris

Published in 1951 to moderate acclaim, this novel was later to become a science-fiction classic and a defining novel of the post-disaster genre. The action opens with biologist Bill Masen, who has bandages over his eyes after a poisonous plant (triffid) sting, in hospital. Nurses describe to him the most spectacular meteorite shower England has ever seen, but when he awakes the next morning, the hospital routine he expects never starts. Overcoming his fear of damaging his eyes, he removes the bandages, finds thousands of sightless people wandering the streets and meets Josella, another sighted survivor. They leave the city together in an attempt to survive in a post-apocalyptic world. Triffids can grow to seven feet, walk on their roots, and kill a man with a sting. Having made their first attack, the Triffids are now poised to prey on humanity. Masen eventually convinces other survivors to band together to try to defeat these intelligent plants.

On the face of it, this is a straightforward survival adventure, but it was the first of its time to anticipate disaster on a global scale. Wyndham predicts the technologies of biowarfare and mass destruction, offering a sophisticated account of Cold War paranoia that was well before its time in terms of its exploration of the psyche of individuals in the face of social change. **EF**

◐ The movie poster for Steve Sekely's 1962 adaptation of this sci-fi classic, perfectly conveys Wyndham's apocalyptic vision.

Malone Dies

Samuel Beckett

Lifespan | b.1906 (Ireland), d.1989 (Paris)
First Published | 1951
First Published by | Les Editions de Minuit (Paris)
Original Title | Malone meurt

For those readers who easily tire of colorful fiction, *Malone Dies* will be as revitalizing as anything in the language. Following the departure of Molloy, *Malone Dies* is Beckett's attempt to winnow down still more violently the nib of his fiction. The stories are what the language uses to get away from itself, and they are all going nowhere. Early on in *Malone Dies* we are spoon-fed the story of the sorrows of young Sapo Saposcat, a fake and abortive bildungsroman in a suite of ludicrously colorless episodes so boring that even Beckett cannot bring himself to keep up his ventriloquism of it. Later he tries his hand at a love story, where the protagonists manage at great effort and discomfort to act out what are surely the most repulsive sex scenes in any comedy.

When the language of *Malone Dies* begins to resemble a novel, it is always faking it. As each consecutive excuse for a story is dumped, we are dragged back into the scene of syntax addiction and the parody of mystification over life and death, endlessly knocked on the head by casual remarks such as "ideas are so alike, when you get to know them," and endlessly restarted. So it goes until the brutal finish of the book, in which Beckett is perhaps more nearly terrified than anywhere else in his fiction by the corner he has crushed himself into and by his failure to lose control of language even in that corner. The fundamental horror and optimism of Beckett are that true claustrophobia is possible only in paradise. **KS**

Memoirs of Hadrian

Marguerite Yourcenar

Lifespan | *b.* 1903 (Belgium), *d.* 1987 (U.S.)
First Published | 1951, by Librarie Plon (Paris)
Original Title | *Mémoires d'Hadrien*
Given Name | Marguerite de Crayencour

Mme. Yourcenar will always be distinguished by becoming, in 1980, the first woman ever elected as a member of the Académie Française. And it is largely on the strength of work such as *Memoirs of Hadrian* that her literary reputation was built. The book is constructed as a long letter from the dying emperor to Marcus Aurelius, who was then an adolescent (and who succeeded as ruler of Rome following the intervening reign of his adoptive father, Antoninus Pius). The account relates the professional and historical aspects of Hadrian's two decades as Emperor, distilling from his worldly experience what he can transmit to the younger man of the judgment and insight he has attained. His reflections on the fundaments of life—the mysteries of love, the demands of the body, the question of human destiny—shared by all of us make this novel far more accessible to a contemporary reader than might be expected of the thoughts of a second-century titan.

Yourcenar's achievement is the thoroughness of her research; it is easy to forget that this is fiction written in a philosophical style, its tone that of a man of action examining and evaluating his existence. *Memoirs of Hadrian* has been admired equally by scholars of classical antiquity as by arbiters of literary art and secured the author's reputation internationally when it appeared. **ES**

○ Marguerite Yourcenar is pictured in a portrait taken in Bordeaux, France, some ten years after *Memoirs* was published.

The Killer Inside Me

Jim Thompson

Lifespan | *b.* 1906 (U.S.), *d.* 1977
First Published | 1952
First Published by | Lion Books (New York)
Full Name | James Myers Thompson

In the figure of Lou Ford, a West Texan sheriff full of both corny, small-town bonhomie and murderous psychosexual rage, Jim Thompson found the perfect embodiment of his own skewed, disquieting vision of 1950s American life. Ford's folksy manner and homespun charm quickly unravel to reveal something darker, baser, and more unfathomable within. In the process, Thompson suggests that the clichéd view of 1950s America as a land of communal benevolence and white picket fences requires considerable revision. Ford is a fascinating, reptilian creature whose sickeningly violent interventions cannot necessarily be explained or rationalized. It is a mark of Thompson's skill that our identification with Ford, encouraged by his first-person narration, is never quite frayed, even, for example, after he has cruelly beaten his fiancée to death with his bare hands. The scene in question is one of the most lurid, unsettling, and graphic accounts of male-on-female violence ever rendered in American writing. But Thompson never settles for easy explanations. Ford is not simply mad; the "sickness" inside him, which compels him to murderous rage, has a complex familial history. Ford's self-diagnosis borrows from the popularization of Freudian psychoanalysis in postwar America. Are Ford's "medical" explanations simply convenient excuses absolving him of responsibility for his horrific actions? More disturbingly, Thompson proposes Ford's sickness as a manifestation not of individual dysfunction, but rather of the ills of postwar American society. **AP**

Wise Blood

Flannery O'Connor

Lifespan | *b.* 1925 (U.S.), *d.* 1964
First Published | 1952
First Published by | Harcourt, Brace & Co. (N.Y.)
Full Name | Mary Flannery O'Connor

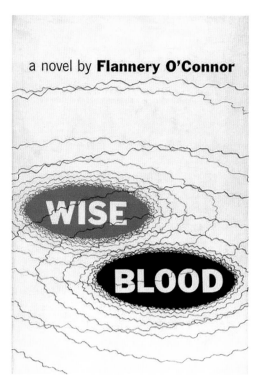

a novel by **Flannery O'Connor**

WISE

BLOOD

"Nothing matters but that Jesus was a liar."

⊙ *Wise Blood* was O'Connor's first novel—on the jacket of the first edition, the unknown author's name is given little prominence.

Since its publication in 1952, Flannery O'Connor's *Wise Blood* has become one of several American novels that have gone on to define the so-called "Southern Gothic" genre. It is a work deeply embroiled in the intense humidity and religious fervor of the old South. The story revolves around a young man named Hazel Motes. Raised by an uncompromisingly conservative family, Hazel returns home after a spell in the military with his faith destroyed by the experience of war. As a way of coming to terms with his newfound sense of loss, Hazel creates his own church: the Church without Christ. It is a church where "the deaf don't hear, the blind don't see, the lame don't walk, the dumb don't talk, and the dead stay that way." Hazel becomes a kind of heretical anti-priest, a renegade street preacher driven by an urge to save those around him from Christian salvation. The further away he tries to push himself from faith, however, the deeper his need for redemption becomes.

Wise Blood is populated by an eccentric collection of misfits, thieves, con artists, scumbags, and false prophets. It is partly a theological allegory, a meditation on the place of God in modern culture, and partly a grotesque, madcap comedy. It is a novel of miracles and murder, of lustful flesh and pure spirit, of blindness and vision, of violence and healing. O'Connor presents a complex vision of the rural South in which she was raised. The novel unravels many of the South's myths and prejudices, yet at the same time pays homage to its traditions, heritage, and defiance. The spare, economical prose finds insight and wonder in the smallest detail, acutely sensitive to the transformative power of both faith and doubt. The world of *Wise Blood* is tough, tarnished, and visceral, but it is also brushed with grace. **ST**

The Old Man and the Sea

Ernest Hemingway

Critical opinion tends to differ over *The Old Man and the Sea,* which moves away from the style of Hemingway's earlier works. Within the frame of this perfectly constructed miniature are to be found many of the themes that preoccupied Hemingway as a writer and as a man. The routines of life in a Cuban fishing village are evoked in the opening pages with a characteristic economy of language. The stripped-down existence of the fisherman Santiago is crafted in a spare, elemental style that is as eloquently dismissive as a shrug of the old man's powerful shoulders. With age and luck now against him, Santiago knows he must row out "beyond other men," away from land and into the deep waters of the Gulf Stream. There is one last drama to be played out, in an empty arena of sea and sky.

Hemingway was famously fascinated with ideas of men proving their worth by facing and overcoming the challenges of nature. When the old man hooks a marlin longer than his boat, he is tested to the limits as he works the line with bleeding hands in an effort to bring it close enough to harpoon. Through his struggle he demonstrates the ability of the human spirit to endure hardship and suffering in order to win. It is also his deep love and knowledge of the sea, in her impassive cruelty and beneficence, that allows him to prevail.

The essential physicality of the story—the smells of tar and salt and fish blood, the cramp and nausea and blind exhaustion of the old man, the terrifying death spasms of the great fish—is set against the ethereal qualities of dazzling light and water, isolation, and the swelling motion of the sea. And the narrative is constantly tugging, unreeling a little more, pulling again. It is a book that demands to be read in a single sitting. **TS**

Lifespan | *b.* 1899 (U.S.), *d.* 1961
First Published | 1952
First Published by | C. Scribner's Sons (New York)
Pulitzer Prize for Literature | 1953

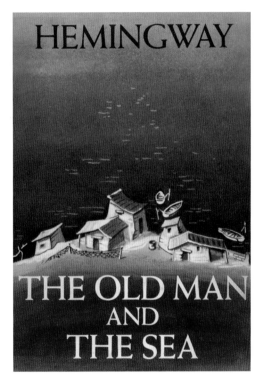

"A man can be destroyed but not defeated."

◉ The cover illustration of the British first edition, published by Jonathan Cape, depicts the novel's Cuban fishing village.

Invisible Man

Ralph Ellison

Lifespan | *b.* 1914 (U.S.), *d.* 1994
First Published | 1952
First Published by | Random House (New York)
National Book Award | 1952

"I am an invisible man."

⊙ This is one of a series of photographs staged by Gordon Parks,
a friend of Ellison, as a visual interpretation of *The Invisible Man*.

⊙ Another of Parks' photographs illustrates Ellison's invisible hero
rising from underground: "I must come out, I must emerge ..."

Invisible Man is Ralph Ellison's only novel and is widely acknowledged as one of the great novels of African-American literature. The invisibility of Ellison's protagonist is about the invisibility of identity—above all, what it means to be a black man—and its various masks, confronting both personal experience and the force of social illusions.

The novel's special quality is its deft combination of existential enquiry into identity as such—what it means to be socially or racially invisible—with a more sociopolitical allegory of the history of the African-American experience in the U.S. The first-person narrator remains nameless, retrospectively recounting his shifts through the surreal reality of surroundings and people from the racist South to the no less inhospitable world of New York City. While *Invisible Man* bears comparison with the existentialist novels of Sartre and Camus, it also maps out the story of one man's identity against the struggles of collective self-definition. This takes the narrator-protagonist through the circumscribed social possibilities afforded to African-Americans, from enslaved grandparents through southern education, to models associated with Booker T. Washington, through to the full range of Harlem politics. Ellison's almost sociological clarity in the way he shows his central character working through these possibilities is skillfully worked into a novel about particular people, events, and situations, from the nightmare world of the ironically named Liberty Paints to the Marxist-Leninist machinations of the Brotherhood. In the process, Ellison offers sympathetic but severe critiques of the ideological resources of black culture, such as religion and music. Fierce, defiant, and utterly funny, Ellison's tone mixes various idioms and registers to produce an impassioned inquiry into the politics of being. **DM**

The Judge and His Hangman

Friedrich Dürrenmatt

Lifespan | *b*. 1921 (Switzerland), *d*. 1990
First Published | 1952
First Published by | Benziger (Einsiedeln)
Original Title | *Der Richter und sein Henker*

"Truth is always a delusion."

Dürrenmatt, Marriage of Mr. Mississippi, *1952*

⊙ Friedrich Dürrenmatt was famous not only for his crime
novels, but also for his avant-garde plays and satires.

Written while he was flourishing in postwar Germany as a playwright, novelist, essayist, theater director, and painter, Friedrich Dürrenmatt's *The Judge and His Hangman* weaves a suspenseful tale of murder in a remote part of Switzerland. The stark minimalism of the author's Brechtian theatrical work is counteracted in this atmospheric novel, in which words paint foreboding and thrilling backdrops to the tale of Police Commissioner Bärlach, who is investigating the murder of a fellow police officer, Schmied. Bärlach, an ageing and dying man whose investigative faculties have not yet taken a backseat to his physical frailties, hands over the bulk of the detective work to his colleague Tschanz. The two of them launch into a harrowing investigation (Bärlach is brain; Tschanz is brawn), but there are very few clues: a bullet on the side of the road, beside the car in which Schmied, dressed in evening clothes, was murdered, and an entry—a single "G"—in the victim's diary on the night he was killed. This last clue leads Bärlach and Tschanz to the home of the cold and brilliant Gastmann. This mysterious man is involved in clandestine international relations—and his associations serve to heighten the novel's intrigue.

Although Dürrenmatt set aside his distinctly Brechtian style in his non-dramatic prose, he did not turn away from using art as a springboard for political criticism, and *The Judge and His Hangman*, the first of his books to be published in America, addresses the theme of modern detective work in a way that is far from secondary to its mysterious plot. Critiquing policing methods is bound up inextricably both with the plot and with an equally important study of human imperfection. It is this last aspect in particular that causes this piece of crime fiction to stand apart from the hundreds of novels written in the genre. **JuS**

Casino Royale

Ian Fleming

We have been let down, badly, by Cubby Broccoli's James Bond films. Sean Connery may occasionally have caught something of the thin-lipped coldness of Ian Fleming's creation, but there was, from the first film on, a refusal to take things too seriously, and Connery's arch one-liners found their camp culmination in Roger Moore's arched eyebrow. If the producers had any sense, they would make *Casino Royale*—Fleming's first Bond story and so far filmed only as a spoof with David Niven as the secret agent—as a period piece. Everything in the novel— from the now-antiquated black-and-white of Cold War ideology, to Bond's then impossibly exotic choice of avocado and vinaigrette as a starter in the faded casino towns of northern France—is redolent of the early 1950s in which it was written.

The plot is simple, even elemental. The villain is Le Chiffre, a Russian spy operating in France, who has misappropriated KGB funds and turned to gambling to make good the loss. Bond, as the Secret Service's most accomplished gambler, is sent to Royale-les-Eaux to defeat Le Chiffre at the tables, thereby ruining him and his French network. There is an attempt on Bond's life, a game of baccarat over twenty-five pages, a car chase, a lovingly described scene of grotesque torture, and a rescue. The final chapters are a curiously distended account of Bond's convalescence with Vesper Lynd, the first "Bond girl"; the novel ends in a gratuitous burst of betrayal and misogyny. The prose is hard and unsparing, the detail minutely fetishistic (along the way we learn how—exactly—to make Bond's signature martini). Only in the descriptions of gambling and flagellation—two of Fleming's most treasured pursuits—does the writing run away with itself. Otherwise, the book takes on the same aspect as its hero's face: "taciturn, brutal, ironical and cold." **PMy**

Lifespan | *b.* 1908 (England), *d.* 1964
First Published | 1953
First Published by | Jonathan Cape (London)
Full Name | Ian Lancaster Fleming

"Vodka dry Martini . . . "

Fleming's James Bond in Dr. No, *1958*

◉ Ian Fleming used his experience of working for British naval intelligence to provide background for his espionage fantasies.

Go Tell It on the Mountain

James Baldwin

Lifespan | *b.* 1924 (U.S.), *d.* 1987 (France)
First Published | 1953
First Published by | Knopf (New York)
Full Name | James Arthur Baldwin

" . . . I ain't going to have that boy's blood on my hands."

⊙ This undated photograph publicized Baldwin's election
to the National Institute of Arts and Letters in the 1950s.

This semi-autobiographical bildungsroman focuses on the complex and often fragile social bonds surrounding protagonist John as he celebrates his fourteenth birthday and, that night, falls to the "threshing-floor" of his stepfather Gabriel's Harlem church in a climactic adult initiation. Gabriel, whom John believes to be his biological father, is a volatile, domineering force who ran wild as a very young man before experiencing an early religious epiphany that prompted him to preach the wrath of God. Gabriel married John's mother to rescue her from the trials of single motherhood, but condemns her loving acceptance of John, which to Gabriel shows an unconscionable shamelessness over John's illegitimacy and her relationship with his father, her first love. Gabriel himself fathered an illegitimate child during his first marriage—a fact that he has continually guarded under the guise of repentance. He holds his silence regarding his orphaned son, who grew up hard and died violently and young.

While most of this history is not known to John, he is an intuitive boy who senses exactly the sorts of hazard that Harlem presents to black adolescents, especially those unprotected by an institution, usually the church. The loving support that John receives from Elisha, one of the church's young leaders, vibrates with an intensely joyful homoeroticism on which John can imagine building a fulfilling future in the church. Insofar as his stepfather is the figure responsible for doctrinal exegesis and enforcement, however, there is only a cruel vindictiveness that works to frighten and shame its believers into unquestioning obedience. The physical and emotional exhaustion of John's hallucinatory conversion allows him an early morning moment of triumphant respite, however brief. **AF**

The Adventures of Augie March

Saul Bellow

This lavish, bustling narrative written in the picaresque tradition reinvents the hero as a modern-day Jewish Huck Finn. Augie is a handsome and contemplative character who becomes embroiled in a series of increasingly exotic escapades. In an odyssey that takes him from Chicago to Mexico, from Europe to an open boat in the mid-Atlantic, the footloose hero is recruited to a series of crackpot scams that include book stealing, arms trading, and being appointed the task of guarding Trotsky.

The episodic structure of the narrative means that Augie is less a fully formed character than an observer of the colorful array of manipulators and opportunists who seek to fashion his identity to their own ends. While this structure dilutes narrative suspense, it does permit some exquisitely rendered descriptive passages, particularly in the novel's evocation of post-depression Chicago.

What ultimately rescues the reader's sympathy for Augie is his capacity for genuine and spontaneous human feeling. He loves his family and his idiot brother without reservation. The fact that he escapes the cast of would-be destiny-molders serves as a reaffirmation of Bellow's conviction that human nature will triumph over contingent social structures. Throughout the novel, Augie's concern with the need to maintain a sense of his own "distinctness" champions human agency in a postwar America that increasingly came to fall out of step with Bellow's essentially conservative vision.

The novel begins with the conviction that "Man's character is his fate" and it ends with the syllogism that "Man's fate is his character." There are few writers capable of capturing in a way as penetrating as Bellow the seductions, sufferings, and chaotic gaiety of twentieth-century America. **VA**

Lifespan | *b.* 1915 (Canada), *d.* 2005 (U.S.)
First Published | 1953
First Published by | Viking Press (New York)
National Book Award | 1953

" . . . first to knock, first admitted . . ."

◉ Saul Bellow, photographed here in 1958, yokes the European intellectual tradition to the bustling energy of modern America.

Junkie

William Burroughs

Lifespan | *b.*1914 (U.S.), *d.*1997
First Published |1953, by Ace Books (New York)
Original Title | *Junkie: Confessions of an Unredeemed Drug Addict*

" . . . he kept it for himself."

⬥ A 1959 photo of Burroughs captures the harrowed look of the addict but gives no hint of the dry humor revealed in his writing.

William Burroughs is well remembered for a variety of reasons: the literary iconoclast, revered for the perceived experimentalism of his writing and art; his "coolness" in influencing a generation of artists, filmmakers, and musicians; and his legendary drug use. As a result, he has become reduced to a two-dimensional image. In today's environment, his legacy has inevitably been boiled down to so much aimless psychedelia and pottering "experimentation"; the actual breadth of his writing becomes almost irrelevant. Burroughs remains a writer who, far from simply employing surface-level gimmicks, writes about his life using whatever seems to be the most appropriate technique. Where *The Naked Lunch* employs a high degree of abstraction to describe both the polyglot, paranoid environment of middle-of-the-century Tangier and the process of opiate withdrawal, other works, notably *Junkie* and the later *Queer*, use far more simplistic narrative methods.

What *Junkie* seems to do is present the interior world of *The Naked Lunch* as a contemporary, exterior reality. A semi-autobiographical work, it outlines the author's relationship with opiates from early experiences to full-blown long-term addiction. In fact, Burroughs found the discipline required to write the novel with the help of a daily morphine injection. The Burroughs of *Junkie* is inescapably a man rather than the cartoon outlaw of hipster folklore. He openly describes addiction's vicious circle, while highlighting the way in which society holds addicts up as scapegoats to conceal its chronic failings and addictions. The book's real importance is in this candor; the way in which it props up the Burroughs canon with a truthful simplicity that stubbornly undermines attempts to position its author as the Mickey Mouse of a marketable "counterculture." **SF**

Lucky Jim

Kingsley Amis

Amis had already published several collections of poetry when he achieved popular success with his first novel, *Lucky Jim*, which was influential in defining the direction of English postwar fiction. *Lucky Jim* is iconoclastic, satirical, and disrespectful of the norms of conservative society, and very funny. It tells the story of Jim Dixon, a mediocre but sharp-witted assistant lecturer at an uninspiring provincial university who realizes that he has made a terrible career choice. He decides that what he studies—medieval history—is dull and pedantic and he cannot stand the awful pretensions he encounters at his institution and in the grim town where he is forced to live. Jim pushes his luck more and more, barely disguising his contempt for his colleagues, especially the absurd Professor Welch, until he manages to lose his job when he delivers a lecture on "Merrie England," unprepared, blind drunk, and keen to parody the university authorities. Despite this he leaves academia for a better job, and he gets the girl.

Lucky Jim has usually been seen as a very English novel. Jim Dixon has intellect, but, unwilling to fit in with the expectations of his social superiors, he is quite prepared to misuse it. The novel is really a story of frustrated ambition and talent, which exposes England as a drab wilderness that is ruled and run by colorless charlatans. *Lucky Jim* is written with considerable verve and a keen satirical eye. It contains numerous magnificent comic descriptions and sequences, especially at the start of the novel when Jim reflects on the value of his utterly worthless research. The most celebrated passage is an account of a cultural weekend at Professor Welch's house, which ends with what is probably the best description of a hangover in English fiction. **AH**

Lifespan | *b*. 1922 (England), *d*. 1995
First Published | 1953
First Published by | V. Gollancz (London)
Somerset Maugham Award | 1953

"Doing what you wanted . . . "

⬥ C. P. Snow, who gave this ringing endorsement to Amis' novel, had published his own campus novel, *The Masters*, two years earlier.

Watt

Samuel Beckett

Lifespan | *b*. 1906 (Ireland), *d*. 1989 (France)
First Published | 1953
First Published by | Olympia Press (Paris)
Nobel Prize for Literature | 1969

This novel represents an essential stage in the development of Beckett's fiction. As *Watt* progresses, it literally unravels and collapses. The recognizably linear comic opening is easily identifiable with the Joycean style that characterized the preceding *Murphy*. It becomes increasingly fragmented, however, as the formal, temporal, and syntactical structures break down; the "Beckettian" world of his later work begins to take hold.

In the opening chapter, we encounter the titular character, who meets a number of misfortunes in the shape of a porter pushing a milk can and an irate lady who pelts him with a stone. Watt rests in a ditch before continuing his journey to the house of Mr. Knott, his subsequent employer and the center of the novel's impending collapse. Upon reaching his destination, Watt takes his position as the first-floor servant, gradually progressing up the floors, and closer to Mr. Knott. Knott himself is a mystery, less a character than a presence, a singularity, and it is under his service that Watt's obsession with exhaustive logic, the source of the novel's formal fragmentation, increasingly takes control. The role of multiple unreliable narrators assumes a central importance here for the first time in Beckett's work, as do the great formal innovations, particularly in terms of temporal structure. *Watt* is essential reading for the spectacle of a writer developing his style on the page and for a demonstration of the strict order and intent that underpin Beckett's chaos. **SF**

The Unnamable

Samuel Beckett

Lifespan | *b*. 1906 (Ireland), *d*. 1989 (France)
First Published | 1953
First Published by | Les Editions de Minuit (Paris)
Original Title | *L'Innommable*

The Unnamable marks the conclusion of Beckett's drive toward the reduction of the novel form begun in *Watt*, and it is only logical that a move away from prose writing into drama immediately follows. This is the third part of the trilogy that begins with Molloy's haunted detective story and progresses through the deathbed hallucinations of *Malone Dies*. In *The Unnamable*, Beckett attempts formally to address a question he has been skirting around in his previous work: what is left of a novel once the story, characters, fictional space, and narrator have been removed?

The first notable quality of *The Unnamable* is the way it makes such indispensable use of its status as the third part of a trilogy. The end of the preceding novel, *Malone Dies*, begins to falter and die along with its narrator, spluttering and collapsing in a series of logical and syntactical breakdowns. Finally it is silent, and a turn of the page leads to all that is left of the novel—the disembodied voice in the darkness, "where now, who now." This voice is the voice of the unnamable, the "voice" of the novel, a ghost of sorts, exposed with no world to inhabit, no characters to speak through, and no events to describe, so speaking only of itself. In *The Unnamable* Beckett seems at last to have reached the core, speaking of the succession of previous Beckett characters as one and the same. **SF**

◗ A portrait of Beckett by fellow author J. P. Donleavy brings out
   the intense blank gaze and tight lips of a death-haunted man.

Samuel Beckett

by

The Long Good-Bye

Raymond Chandler

Lifespan | *b.* 1888 (U.S.), *d.* 1959
First Published | 1953
First Published by | Hamish Hamilton (London)
Movie Adaptation Released | 1973

A work of Chandler's maturity, written a good decade after Philip Marlowe first became a household name, *The Long Good-Bye* has a good claim to being his finest achievement. With *The Big Sleep* (1939), he began to graft mainstream literary sophistication onto the generic templates of pulp gumshoe fiction, and *The Long Good-Bye* can equally be read as a significant work of American fiction.

After helping Terry Lennox to escape to Mexico, private detective Philip Marlowe finds that he may have unknowingly abetted the flight of a murderer; not only that, Terry apparently kills himself as well, leaving Marlowe with a bewildering knot of unsolved problems and posthumous responsibilities. The puzzle aspect in Chandler's novels is often a pretext for a larger and more world-weary social observation, and this is particularly true here; as Marlowe's quest for solutions leads him into the corrupt, leisured world of Idle Valley, the novel's larger satirical purposes come into focus. Away from the downtown "mean streets," Chandler can indulge Marlowe's cultured side more (referencing Flaubert is not common in 1950s crime novels). And it is right that the initial detective premise somewhat recedes into the background: in Chandler's world, the solving of a crime cannot return us to innocence. If the detective genre is often turned to more serious and resonant literary purposes nowadays, this was a possibility opened up by the laconic, deadpan example of *The Long Good-Bye*. **BT**

"No way has yet been invented to say goodbye to them."

⬤ The British first edition jacket plays up the thriller's traditional appeal to voyeurism, rather than more sophisticated literary aims.

The Go-Between

L. P. Hartley

Lifespan | *b.* 1895 (England), *d.* 1972
First Published | 1953
First Published by | Hamish Hamilton (London)
Movie Adaptation Released | 1971

Hartley's semi-autobiographical novel is constructed around the retrospective narrative of Leo Colston. Now an elderly man, Colston thinks back to his boyhood and the summer he spent at the affluent family home of his school friend. During his stay with the Maudsley family, Leo becomes embroiled in the socially unacceptable relationship between his friend's older sister Marian and Ted, a local farmer.

Leo becomes the "go-between" of the book's title, facilitating an illicit sexual relationship that defies the restrictive class conventions of Edwardian England. Made aware of sexual desires, he views them with a mixture of fascination and horror. His role in enabling this relationship is a catalyst for Leo's coming-of-age, precipitating a loss of childish innocence. In his adult revisitation of these events, Colston's disapproval of Marian and Ted is clear. But the sense of nostalgia is not limited to a loss of sexual naïveté: the novel is heavily inflected with the class dynamics of Edwardian society, and inherent in Colston's reflections is a longing for a way of life permeated by class differences that function to his advantage. In this quintessentially English novel, Leo's epiphany occurs during a cricket match, which for him represents the "struggle between order and lawlessness, between obedience to tradition and defiance of it, between social stability and revolution."

This novel is of interest for its unusual take on the familiar theme of love divided by social barriers, but also for the studied honesty of Leo's narrative. **JW**

Under the Net

Iris Murdoch

Lifespan | *b.* 1919 (Ireland), *d.* 1999 (England)
First Published | 1954
First Published by | Chatto & Windus (London)
Full Name | Dame Jean Iris Murdoch

Iris Murdoch's first published novel, *Under the Net*, captures the exuberant spirit of freedom in postwar Europe. Jake Donaghue, the novel's swashbuckling first-person narrator, is a rootless, impoverished young writer who relishes this freedom. He has no home, no commitments, and no permanent job and conducts relationships based only on a woman's ability to provide sex and shelter. But chance, misfortune, and a series of hilarious misunderstandings startle Jake into an awareness that others have existence outside his perception of them, and that the world holds mysteries that he can barely imagine. A stark period of depression and a candid renegotiation of his love life follows. Jake finally becomes an aspiring novelist committed to producing work that engages with the world that he has begun, at last, to see.

Beneath the surface of the fast-moving narrative lies a wealth of philosophical questioning: Murdoch contests existential ideas of freedom; she asks what it means to be in love; and she rigorously questions what makes a good writer and what constitutes good art. Underlying these ideas are the questions of how accurately thought can be translated into language (language is the "net" of the title) and how far art distances us from reality, rather than bringing us closer to it. But Jake's visits to *The Laughing Cavalier* at the Wallace Collection in London, and to the Fontaine de Médicis in Paris, illustrate Murdoch's belief that art is not divorced from the real world and that, in particular, "art and morality are one." **AR**

Lord of the Flies

William Golding

Lifespan | *b.* 1911 (England), *d.* 1993
First Published | 1954, by Faber & Faber (London)
First Movie Adaption Released | 1963
Nobel Prize for Literature | 1983

◉ The first edition of Golding's novel appeared at a time of public concern about the destructive nature of human beings.

◉ Peter Brook's 1963 movie version of the novel was filmed in an unsparing documentary style that suited the apocalyptic theme.

A staple of many a schoolroom, *Lord of the Flies* is a gripping examination of the conflict between the two competing impulses that exist within all human beings. On the one hand, there is the instinct to live peacefully, abide by rules, and value the moral good over the instinct for immediate gratification of desires. On the other, there is the impulse to seize supremacy through violence, sacrificing the individual at the expense of the group.

This is the story of a group of young schoolboys marooned on a tropical island after their plane is shot down during the war. Alone, without adult supervision, the boys begin by electing a leader, Ralph, who narrowly defeats Jack in the vote (Jack is elected head of the hunt). The moral conflict at the novel's heart—between good and evil, order and chaos, civilization and savagery, the rule of law and anarchy—is represented by the differing characters of sensible, levelheaded Ralph and savage, charismatic Jack. As the boys split into two different factions, their island society is plunged into chaos. While some behave peacefully, working together to maintain order and achieve common goals, others rebel, generating terror and violence. Frightened, the boys become convinced there is a monster on the island, and when one of them, Simon, realizes the beast is not an external figure, but exists within each and every one of them, he is murdered.

This thought-provoking exploration of human evil and original sin reflects the society of the time and is steeped in Golding's experiences of the Second World War, when he witnessed the isolated savagery of desperate men unconfined by the rules of civilized society. Although the gripping story is confined to a small group of boys on a small island, it explores issues central to the wider human experience. **EF**

A Ghost at Noon

Alberto Moravia

"During the first two years of our married life my relations with my wife were, I can now assert, perfect."

 Moravia's vision of the boredom and isolation at the heart of modern life is both the strength and limitation of his work.

Lifespan | *b.* 1907 (Italy), *d.* 1990
First Published | 1954
First Published by | Bompiani (Milan)
Original Title | *Il Disprezzo*

Like most of Moravia's work, this novel is a political accusation: capitalist culture reduces the intellectual to a mere producer of goods. Riccardo Molteni, the protagonist, is a failed intellectual who betrays his ambition to become a playwright and sells his soul to consumerism to make money by writing screenplays. He convinces himself that he does this to pay for the apartment he bought to make his wife, Emilia, happy. Molteni increasingly loses sight of reality and becomes incapable of noticing what is happening around him, unable to see that his wife no longer loves him. In a nostalgic and regretful way, he carries on loving a semblance, or a "ghost," of what Emilia once was (hence the English translation of the novel's title).

Molteni takes refuge in Greek myths, with their protagonists who lived in a world where the relationship with reality was straightforward and unmediated. When faced with the challenging task of transforming the *Odyssey* into a movie, Molteni discovers that a text such as Homer's holds the key to his existence. Odysseus and Molteni are united by a similar destiny. Their wives, Penelope and Emilia, despise their passivity and self-assurance. Molteni is excessively confident that Emilia is faithful and disregards the producer's courtship of her. She is hurt, and feels she is being sold cheaply to secure her husband's occupation. Her contempt for him grows and is finally shouted into his face before she abandons him on the island of Capri. **RPi**

The Story of O

Pauline Réage

Lifespan | b. 1907 (France), d. 1998
First Published | 1954
First Published by | Pauvert (Sceaux)
Original Title | Histoire d'O

Pauline Réage is a complex mask. It is the pen name of Dominique Aury, itself the pen name of Anne Desclos, a French journalist and translator who became one of the most infamous pornographers of all time when she published *The Story of O* in Paris in 1954. "Réage"—a name invented specifically for *The Story of O*—was apparently told by her lover, Jean Paulhan, that no woman could ever write an erotic novel. *The Story of O* is her response. The novel is one of the most thorough and challenging ripostes ever made in a lovers' quarrel.

The novel is distinguished less by its plot than by the manner of its prose, in particular the control exercised by Réage in her depiction of O's private musings and reflections during and after her submission to acts of torture and humiliation. The intense erotic effect is achieved by a kind of mismatch between language and psychological content. If the language were made to imitate the full violence of O's mental and physical suffering, it would often be shattered and reduced to an incoherent scream. Instead, the prose is constrained by Réage and proceeds unruffled and at an unvarying pace through a series of degraded sexual episodes, leading eventually to the disappearance of O behind yet another mask, that of an owl. The most tightly fitted mask is style itself. *The Story of O* is a shocking novel and at the same time a masterfully boring one. The deep erotic joy of suffering, it tells us, is rooted in the terror of boredom. **KS**

Self Condemned

Wyndham Lewis

Lifespan | b. 1882 (Canada), d. 1957 (England)
First Published | 1954
First Published by | Methuen (London)
Full Name | Percy Wyndham Lewis

The mood of this searingly candid novel draws on Wyndham Lewis' experiences in Canada, where he lived during the Second World War, although it should not be seen as "autobiographical" in any straightforward sense. *Self Condemned* both satirizes the provinciality of Canada and participates in a debate with his earlier writing, particularly with regard to the conflict between intellect and emotion.

The novel's protagonist, René Harding, is an intensely cerebral and self-obsessed figure. He resigns as a professor of history because his unorthodox views on the subject no longer permit him to teach it in good conscience. Harding's pessimism inclines him to view history as a narrative of decline in which destructive forces predominate over creative ones. Convinced that war is about to break out, but contemptuous of English political hypocrisy, Harding departs with his wife, Hester, for Canada, where they endure years of neglect and poverty. The Hardings' isolation breeds a harsh, even bitter, intimacy. The novel turns on the contradiction between Harding's idealistic conception of what human history should be, which encourages him to look forward to a new enlightenment, and his egotistical personality, which leads him to mock humanity, and stops him from sustaining a relationship with Hester. The novel's devastating conclusion shows Harding deflecting tragedy by denying his partial responsibility for it and leaves him as a a chill parody of his former self, "a glacial shell of a man." **AG**

I'm Not Stiller

Max Frisch

Lifespan | *b*. 1911 (Switzerland), *d*. 1991
First Published | 1954, by Suhrkamp (Frankfurt)
Original Title | *Stiller*
Original Language | German

Widely considered Switzerland's greatest literary figure of the last century, Max Frisch was a novelist, playwright, diarist, and journalist. The popular and critically acclaimed *I'm Not Stiller* is a remarkably sustained narrative, which combines anguish and humor to explore issues of identity, self-loathing, and humanity's intense longing for freedom.

The novel begins with the arrest at the Swiss border of a man traveling under a false identity. He claims to be Mr. White from America, but the Swiss authorities believe him to be Anatol Stiller, a famous sculptor from Zürich, who has been missing for six years. In prison, the man is asked to write down his life story in order to prove his identity. In the process he tells not only stories of the past few years of his life, but also of his meetings in the present with Stiller's wife, Julika, and other important people from his past. Through these accounts we learn about his life before the disappearance and are able to piece together a picture of this deeply troubled character. Stiller writes about himself as if he is another person—a self he has attempted to escape from, but which he now has to confront anew as he is slowly compelled to accept both his past and his real identity.

An ironic exploration of an extreme existential crisis, this is also a touching portrayal of a failed marriage and a social critique of Swiss conformity. Complex, psychologically profound, and intellectually challenging, it still manages to be entertaining, funny, and poignant at the same time. **AL**

Bonjour Tristesse

Françoise Sagan

Lifespan | *b*. 1935 (France), *d*. 2004
First Published | 1954
First Published by | Julliard (Paris)
Given Name | Françoise Quoirez

When Cécile, a precocious fifteen-year-old, leaves boarding school to live with her widowed libertine father, Raymond, she enters into a world of decadence that is a far cry from her strict convent-school days. Gallivanting between Paris and the French Riviera, the golden-skinned duo embraces a hedonistic existence, consisting of short-lived affairs, glittering characters, and every luxury imaginable. But their life of gay frivolity is threatened two years later when Raymond believes he has fallen in love with Anne Larsen, a former friend of Cécile's mother who moves within more staid, intellectual circles. Fearing for her freedom, Cécile, the quintessential *enfant terrible*, invokes the help of her lover, Cyril, and her father's former paramour Elsa, to intervene. But her cunning plot proves to have tragic consequences, forever coloring her future happiness with *tristesse*.

Written when she was just eighteen years old, Françoise Sagan's first novel was an instant international best-seller. With its description of overt sexuality, celebration of wealth and opulence, and intimation of same-sex desire, the novel shocked and titillated its first readers, paving the way for a permissive French society. Simmering beneath the façade of the jaded ingénue is the unsettling portrait of a child who will do anything to maintain the life outlined for her by the only parent she knows. **BJ**

> ❷ The teenage Sagan shocked contemporary readers with her cool, non-judgmental approach to sex and relationships.

The Ragazzi

Pier Paolo Pasolini

Lifespan | b. 1922 (Italy), d. 1975
First Published | 1955
First Published by | Garzanti (Milan)
Original Title | *Ragazzi di Vita*

Ragazzi di vita, translated literally into English as *Boys of Life*, is the story of a group of boys who live in the slums of Rome during the years immediately following the Second World War. One of the notable aspects of the Italian edition is that it contains a glossary of words in the "Romano" dialect for the Italian reader unfamiliar with it. Those acquainted with the Italian cinematographic neorealism of the period will know that the use of regional dialects and of non-professional actors was common in the films of Rossellini, De Sica, Fellini, and other directors. Pasolini was an unorthodox Marxist who thought that the emphasis on exploitation, alienation, and marginalization needed to be supplemented by an analysis of the mechanism of integration in modern, liberal democracies. Hence the ambiguity of the socio-political condition of the sub-proletariat in Pasolini's novels of the later 1950s; the class occupies the unique position of running the simultaneous risk of complete integration or complete marginalization. But Pasolini's achievement here is his non-sentimental portrayal of the choice between joining a banal, all-encompassing mainstream, or accepting life on a hopelessly bleak periphery. Today better known as a director, Pasolini's literary status was established by *Ragazzi di vita*, and it is more than worthy of the best aspirations of the Italian neorealist movement. **DS**

Pasolini's homosexuality, central to the writing of *The Ragazzi*, led to his expulsion from the Italian Communist Party in the 1940s.

The Recognitions

William Gaddis

Lifespan | b.1922 (U.S.), d. 1998
First Published | 1955
First Published by | Harcourt Brace (New York)
Original Language | English

It is in pursuit of the real that this immense novel explores every imaginable way that cultural products can be forged, or counterfeited. Paintings are faked, ideas for novels are stolen, plays are plagiarized, book reviews are paid for, and somebody in a Paris café has "a fake concentration camp number tattooed on her left arm." The main character, Wyatt Gwyon, is an artist whose skills are appropriated by an unscrupulous art dealer and a gallery owner to produce work by the nonexistent Flemish painter van der Goes. Feeling himself to be unreal, Wyatt insists to his wife, Esther, that being moral "is the only way we can know ourselves to be real." She asks him pointedly if women can afford to be moral. In this novel, no thought is effective, no discussion concludes, and no narrator intervenes on behalf of truth.

Almost every character here is an American, but the context is European high culture. You need to know Latin, French, Spanish, and Italian to get the many jokes. The same scenes recur at the end as at the beginning, so this novel resembles a snake swallowing its tail. Based on confused conversations—often at parties or in cafés—the word predominates, but the physical evidence of corruption is that the characters keep tripping up and falling down. Bodily incompetence eventually extends to the built environment when a hotel collapses and an organ-player brings down upon himself an entire church. *The Recognitions* was an influential "sleeper" novel: Thomas Pynchon is Gaddis Americanized. **AMu**

The Last Temptation of Christ

Nikos Kazantzákis

Lifespan | *b.*1883 (Greece), *d.*1957 (Germany)
First Published | 1955, by Diphros (Athens)
Movie Adaptation Released | 1988
Original Title | *Ho teleutaíos peirasmós*

This novel is a retelling of the life of Jesus Christ. Although Kazantzákis was himself a Christian, he was also a Nietzschean and a worshipper of nature, and his Jesus is intensely alive to his physical surroundings in Palestine and fully a man of flesh and blood. He is as much tormented by the divine call to become the Messiah as by his desire for Mary Magdalene. He is surrounded by a group of very fallible disciples, and one of the strengths of the novel is its presentation of these larger-than-life creations.

The descriptions of Jesus' life are largely based on the New Testament. The full-blown prose of the narrative spills over into a sort of magic realism at times as, for example, when flowers blossom around the feet of the Messiah. At the climactic moment of the crucifixion, Jesus is rescued, as he thinks, by an angel who leads him to an earthly contentment in which he marries both Martha and Mary, has children, and lives a good human life. Years later he realizes that the angel is in fact Satan and that this earthly paradise is a dream. Waking up, he finds himself back on the cross and dies. This seems to be where the author finds Jesus' value: in a spiritual not a natural dimension. In spite of this, the Vatican condemned the novel, finding its Jesus too carnal and self-doubting, placing it on the index of forbidden books, while in Greece, Orthodox authorities sought Kazantzákis' prosecution, delaying the book's publication. **PM**

The Quiet American

Graham Greene

Lifespan | *b.*1904 (England), *d.*1991 (Switzerland)
First Published | 1955
First Published by | Heinemann (London)
Movie Adaptations Released | 1958, 2002

This novel is in some sense an allegory for the end of paternalistic European colonialism in Indochina and the beginning of zealous American imperialism. Set in Vietnam during the early 1950s, it recounts the conflict between Fowler, the jaded English journalist, and Pyle, the idealistic American spy, for the affections of Phuong, a young Vietnamese woman anxious for a Western husband to provide shelter from poverty and prostitution. Phuong is constantly associated with the Vietnamese landscape and flora, but also with the intoxicating opium and an aura of unintelligibility. Pyle is young and wealthy and offers the promise of financial security, whereas Fowler is old and jaded, offering only the prospects of a continuing and unsatisfactory informal union. For these reasons, the book has most frequently been read as prophetic and critical of America's role in the Vietnam War.

Typically, however, Greene's novel is not contained by the limitations of its genre and expands from this central allegory to offer a study of masculinity and responsibility. The novel is infested with references to what is manly. It seeks to puncture the mock heroics of soldiers and, by extension, journalists, in an attempt to undermine the reverence for physical action usually found in thrillers. Finally, it questions Fowler's desire for disengagement in the face of conflict, suggesting that to be a man requires him to take a moral responsibility for events. **LC**

The Trusting
and the Maimed

James Plunkett

A World
of Love

Elizabeth Bowen

Lifespan | *b.* 1920 (Ireland), *d.* 2003
First Published | 1955
First Published by | The Devin-Adair Co. (New York)
Given Name | James Plunkett Kelly

Lifespan | *b.* 1899 (Ireland), *d.* 1973 (England)
First Published | 1955
First Published by | Jonathan Cape (London)
Full Name | Elizabeth Dorothea Cole Bowen

The stories that make up *The Trusting and the Maimed*, originally published in the Dublin magazines *The Bell* and *Irish Writing*, share characters and locales to create an elegiac yet satirical portrayal of post-independence Ireland. Dublin is prominent, but it is a Dublin of dilapidated suburbs and of longed-for trips to the country, as much as it is a city of streets, offices, and pubs. A combination of evocative lyrical moments and precisely defined vignettes of everyday life build up a memorable account of a stagnating, crippled country. It is the harshness of the novel's conclusion and the gentleness of its method that constitute Plunkett's achievement.

Ireland in the 1940s and the 1950s was a depressed, inward-looking, wounded place, and Plunkett captures this melancholy beautifully. While the stories' episodic structure needs no center, there is a dominant tone set by the recurrence of the lives of city clerks. Young, frustrated, and restless, they rot in their safe jobs from nine to five. They could be white-collar workers in any city. They save for "sin," for the weekends of liquor, sex, and bawdy humor they use to endure the working week. The book is steeped in an atmosphere of palpable decay, a religion reduced to self-parodying remnants, and a patriotism shrunk to disciplinary fetishes and pub songs. It eloquently expresses the pity and resentment that were the cultural hallmarks of post-colonial Ireland. **PMcM**

Arguably Bowen's most beautifully written, lyrical, and haunting work, *A World of Love* is also perhaps her funniest. Focused around Montefort, a large dilapidated country house in Ireland, the novel presents the reader with the interwoven lives of its disparate inhabitants: Fred Dandby; his wife, Lilia; their daughters, Jane and Maud; and Montefort's owner, Antonia. These characters are held together by the house and its grounds, and by the continued presence of Antonia's beloved cousin Guy—also Lilia's former fiancé—who died in the First World War.

Written soon after the death of Bowen's husband in 1952, and after the loss of generations of young men in two world wars, *A World of Love* is a profound reflection on the incomprehensibility of death. Through descriptions of the house—which remains physically haunted by its past—and the people who live in it—who remain spiritually and emotionally so—the novel evokes the uncanny way in which the past continually inhabits the present. Bowen's unusual prose style shares a quirkiness with her modernist contemporaries such as Lawrence and Woolf; in its acute social observations it harks back to the comedy of manners perfected by Jane Austen. While the older characters are cripplingly haunted, Jane, on the cusp of adulthood and romantic love, represents the possibility of a future free from the constraints of a persisting past. **SD**

Lolita

Vladimir Nabokov

Lifespan | *b.* 1899 (Russia), *d.* 1977 (Switzerland)
First Published | 1955
First Published by | Olympia Press (Paris)
Original Language | English

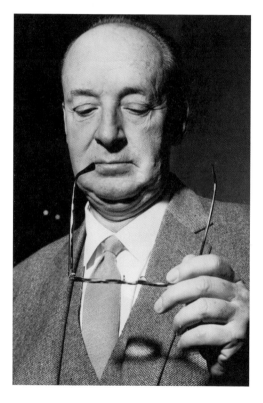

Nabokov produced a whole body of work in Russian before transforming himself into an American novelist in the 1940s.

Dominique Swain, playing Lolita in the 1998 movie version, was older than Nabokov's prepubescent nymphet.

The first publication of *Lolita*, by risqué Parisian press Olympia, caused widespread outrage. The violent erotic passion of the novel's protagonist and narrator, Humbert Humbert, for the twelve-year-old Lolita, and the intensity and extent of Humbert's abuse of her, remain genuinely shocking, particularly in a culture preoccupied with child abuse and the sexualization of children.

Written in Nabokov's characteristic immaculate style, this violent and brutal novel poses fascinating questions about the role of fiction. Is it possible for us to find beauty, pleasure, and comedy in a narrative that is ethically repugnant? Can we suspend moral judgment in favor of aesthetic appreciation of a finely tuned sentence or a perfectly balanced phrase? The answers to these questions remain unclear, but in pitting substance against style, in balancing the ethical so delicately against the aesthetic, Nabokov invents a new kind of literary fiction. Humbert's abduction of Lolita and his fleeing with her across the U.S. in a crazed attempt to outrun the authorities make this novel an inaugural work of postmodern fiction, as well as a kind of proto–road movie. Humbert is an old-world European, a lover of Rimbaud and Balzac, who finds himself displaced in the shiny world of corporate 1950s America and entranced by the lurid charms of gum-sucking, soda-drinking Lolita. The story of this encounter between venerable age and crass youth, between Europe and America, between high art and popular culture, is the story upon which many of the novels and films that come in the wake of *Lolita* are based. Without *Lolita*, it is difficult to imagine Pynchon's *The Crying of Lot 49* or Tarantino's *Pulp Fiction*. It is a mark of its originality and power that, after so many imitations, it remains so troubling, so fresh, and so moving. **PB**

The Talented Mr. Ripley

Patricia Highsmith

Lifespan | *b.* 1921 (U.S.), *d.* 1995 (Switzerland)
First Published | 1955
First Published by | Coward-McCann (New York)
Given Name | Mary Patricia Plangman

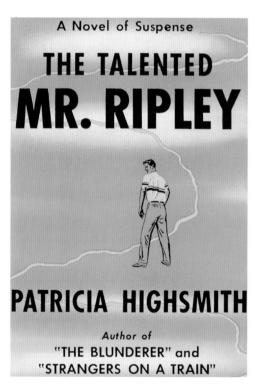

A Novel of Suspense

THE TALENTED

MR. RIPLEY

PATRICIA HIGHSMITH

Author of
"THE BLUNDERER" and
"STRANGERS ON A TRAIN"

"There was no doubt the man was after him."

◉ As indicated on this 1955 first edition jacket, Patricia Highsmith's preferred term for her genre of writing was "suspense fiction."

Tom Ripley is the one of the great creations of twentieth-century pulp writing, a schizophrenic figure at once charming, ambitious, unknowable, utterly devoid of morality, and prone to outbursts of extreme violence. Indeed, the line that Highsmith draws between psychosis on the one hand, and class envy and sexual yearning on the other, means that it is possible to read his deviant behavior both in relatively straightforward terms as a symptom of mental illness and as a complex manifestation of bourgeois ambitions and repressed homosexual desire. At the story's center is the relationship between Tom and Dickie Greenleaf, a wealthy socialite who has taken up residence in the quiet Italian coastal village Mongibello with his girlfriend, Marge. Tom is at once appalled by Dickie's clumsy attempts to paint and by his "inexplicable" attachment to Marge, whom he clearly does not love, and attracted by his style, affluence, and good looks. This uneasy mixture of sentiments is brought into explosive conflagration when Tom murders Dickie and assumes his identity in a calculated bid to benefit financially.

In the hands of a lesser writer, *The Talented Mr. Ripley* might simply have been an enjoyable tale of "cat-and-mouse," as Tom is hunted down by the Italian police, Marge, and Dickie's father across a series of attractively rendered Italian settings. But Highsmith infuses her story with all kinds of moral, psychological, and philosophical complexities. How can we distinguish between different categories of desire—sexual and material? How can we talk about identity as something fixed or essential, if Tom can "become" Dickie with such effortlessness and success? How is sexual desire related to sexual disgust? And, for readers, is it morally aberrant to cheer quietly for a cold-blooded murderer? **AP**

The Lord of the Rings

J. R. R. Tolkien

The Lord of the Rings is actually three books—The Fellowship of the Ring, The Two Towers, and The Return of the King. It follows on from the story of The Hobbit, which Tolkien had published well over a decade earlier, further exploring the world of Middle Earth and war that would determine the fate of all men. Like The Hobbit, it is the story of an unlikely hero—a childlike, unassuming hobbit, Frodo—whom fate has destined for greater things. At the beginning, elves, dwarves, hobbits, and men come together under the wizard Gandalf's watchful eye to set off on a journey to destroy the magic ring, which Bilbo Baggins had found in The Hobbit. The ring holds inside it the essence of evil and therefore must be destroyed before Lord Sauron can find it and plunge Middle Earth into darkness. Through a series of misadventures, the fellowship either die or become separated. Only Frodo, his loyal friend Sam, and the wasted creature Gollum—who had fallen for many years under the ring's power and is now its slave—are left to return the ring to the fires of Mount Doom, which is the only way to destroy it.

The book is about power and greed, innocence, and enlightenment. Ultimately, it describes an old-fashioned battle of good against evil, of kindness and trust against suspicion, and of fellowship against the desire for individual power. Tolkien's evil is an internal force—most evident in the "good" and "bad" sides of the character Gollum, who epitomizes the struggle to be good. This is also a story about war, no doubt drawn from Tolkien's own experience, and how enemies in life are united in death, the one great equalizer. If there is a message, it is that there is little point to war and that the search for ultimate power is futile in a world where togetherness will always (justly) win out. **EF**

Lifespan | b. 1892 (South Africa), d. 1973 (England)
First Published | 1954-1956, by G. Allen & Unwin (Lon.)
Trilogy | The Fellowship of the Ring (1954), The Two Towers (1955), The Return of the King (1955)

"Even the wise cannot see all ends."

◉ Tolkien's academic grounding in Anglo-Saxon, Celtic, and Norse mythology helped shape his personal imaginative world.

The Floating Opera

John Barth

Lifespan | *b.* 1930 (U.S.)
First Published | 1956
First Published by | Appleton Century Crofts (N.Y.)
Full Name | John Simmons Barth Jr

At the age of fifty-four, narrator and protagonist Todd Andrews, a successful small-town lawyer with a heart condition, a grumbling prostate, and an increasing penchant for "Sherbrook rye and ginger ale," reflects on the events seventeen years earlier that led him to contemplate suicide and works through the reasons why he subsequently decided not to carry out the act. He also recalls the protracted love affair that he pursued with the wife of his best friend and his unsuccessful attempts to discover why his father mysteriously hanged himself.

Such a simple plot outline of *The Floating Opera* cannot do it justice, however, because everything else that happens in John Barth's extraordinary debut novel is unpredictable, subversive, and riotous. The constantly shifting, unraveling, and reconfiguring narrative generates an unstoppable energy, unfolds a sequence of spectacles, calamities, and melodramas, and introduces a cast of characters drawn from a tidewater Maryland setting. When entertainment for the townspeople aboard the glittering showboat *Floating Opera* rapidly descends into chaos and disorder, we are provided with an appropriate metaphor for this postmodern "nihilistic comedy."

Underlying the perfectly sustained pitch of absurdity and ambiguity, and the sliding scale of humor from ribaldry and slapstick to dark chuckling cynicism, there is an inquiry into the arbitrary nature of existence and Barth's "tragic view" that its ultimate boundary is fragmentation and death. **TS**

Seize the Day

Saul Bellow

Lifespan | *b.* 1915 (Canada), *d.* 2005 (U.S.)
First Published | 1956
First Published by | Viking Press (New York)
Nobel Prize for Literature | 1976

Bellow's brilliant novella follows one day in the life of Tommy Wilhelm, a frustrated, anxious, and middle-aged failure. His inability to sell children's toys has forced him to appeal to his distant and unpleasant father, Dr. Adler, for financial help. Adler refuses to help his son because of his burning anger at the mess that Tommy has made of his life, which he feels reflects badly on him. We learn that Tommy changed his name as part of an attempt to become a Hollywood actor when he dropped out of college, something Dr. Adler bitterly resents. But his fury is also directed at his son's failure to disguise his desperate state of mind. Tommy is hounded by his ex-wife's demands for money and, in a last effort to save himself, becomes involved in a desperate venture to raise money on the stock market. His partner proves to be a con man, and the novella ends with Tommy sinking to new depths of despair.

Seize the Day is an American tragedy about the fear of failure and an inability to take any action to prevent it. Bellow's use of the Latin aphorism *carpe diem* suggests that for those who cannot manage to act in the modern world, a terrifying void awaits. On one level this is a tale of the misery of an unimpressive, ordinary man; on another it is an odyssey into hell. The last sentence suggests that Tommy, a drowning man, has joined the ranks of the damned: "He heard it ['the heavy sea-like music'] and sank deeper than sorrow, through torn sobs and cries toward the consummation of his heart's ultimate need." **AH**

The Roots of Heaven

Romain Gary

Lifespan | b. 1914 (Lithuania), d. 1980 (France)
First Published | 1956
First Published by | Gallimard (Paris)
Original Title | *Les Racines du ciel*

This fifth novel by Gary, which brought him his first Prix Goncourt (he won the second under a different name to confound the prize's restrictions), conveys the author's ardent support of dignity and compassion with wry humor and brilliant insight.

Curiously contemporary, almost prescient, the story is set in French Equatorial Africa. Morally complex and compromised characters—doubting priests, aspiring revolutionaries, big game hunters, colonial administrators, arms dealers—all revolve around the mysterious figure of Morel, who launches a campaign to save the elephant herds, the only free creatures on earth, from total destruction. The elephants represent the companionship that Morel craves in the absence of God, when a dog is simply no longer adequate to satisfy the need for friendship and comfort. His fight to conquer the despair of the human condition, his "Jewish idealism"—as the Nazi commander of his war camp had termed the belief in noble conventions and the primacy of spirituality—attracts pragmatists, eccentrics, men of good will and understanding, as well as schemers of all descriptions, who try to exploit Morel's defense of nature to further their own causes, projecting onto him the reflection of what is essential in themselves.

Richly deserving its great distinction, *The Roots of Heaven* pays tribute to an ancient, imperishable, and desperate gaiety that is itself a form of subversion and means of survival. The movie adaptation of the book was released in 1958. **ES**

> *"Reality is not an inspiration for literature. At its best, literature is an inspiration for reality."*
>
> Gary, 1956

⊙ Romain Gary later also wrote novels under the name Emil Ajar; the true identity of Ajar was kept secret until after Gary's death.

The Lonely Londoners

Sam Selvon

Lifespan | *b.* 1923 (Trinidad), *d.* 1994 (Canada)
First Published | 1956
First Published by | Allan Wingate (London)
Original Language | English

Often identified as part of Sam Selvon's Moses cycle of novels, *The Lonely Londoners* was one of the first attempts to narrate the life of black Caribbean men in London during the wave of mass migration to Britain during the 1950s. The novel takes the form of a modern picaresque, with an episodic structure where blackness is normalized and where the few peripheral white characters that we encounter are seen as exotic or strange. This is achieved primarily through the novel's innovative use of language—the book is written almost wholly in a version of Trinidadian Creole. Selvon never attempts to translate the language into standard English, and in this sense it can be felt to anticipate later novels such as Irvine Welsh's *Trainspotting*. The novel also centers on black experience through its construction of monumental London as a fantasy, projected through the colonial imaginings of Britain's imperial subjects. The novel offers a stark contrast between the actual, lived-in locations of Bayswater or Marble Arch, and imagined landmarks such as Charing Cross.

While the central characters are overwhelmingly male and lower class, the book does attempt to raise challenging questions about gender politics. Issues of domestic violence and of women's roles within Caribbean family structures are vital to the way that Selvon seeks to represent the dizzying effects of migration, and the relative absence of black women in the novel is intimately connected to a pervasive sense of loss and longing for home. **LC**

Giovanni's Room

James Baldwin

Lifespan | *b.* 1924 (U.S.), *d.* 1987 (France)
First Published | 1956
First Published by | Dial Press (New York)
Full Name | James Arthur Baldwin

Giovanni's Room explores a struggle with the need for social approbation, in which the protagonist must ultimately abandon his dependence on conventional norms of success and worth. The white, middle-class narrator, David, quietly flees his home environment to live aimlessly in Paris, far from his father's wordless pressure to settle down. Facing financial difficulties, however, he proposes to another traveling American, Hella, who leaves Paris to think it over. While she is gone, David accompanies a friend to a gay bar, where he forms an instant, ecstatic connection with Giovanni, the mysterious Italian bartender. David immediately takes up residence in Giovanni's tiny room, but secretly longs for Hella's return, which he thinks will free him from his desperate love for Giovanni. When David leaves their room to continue his heterosexual charade, the consequences are tragic for all three points in his surreptitious love triangle.

Baldwin's spare prose unsentimentally exposes the cruelty and cynicism animating David's abject terror in the face of desire. Giovanni locates David's self-aversion in the American cult of cleanliness and distaste for the body. In the end, David's willingness to shield himself using the overwhelming authority of white American maleness, no matter how forged and self-destructive his claim to it may be, isolates him as much as the empty room in which he writes. **AF**

⊙ Photographed by Carl Mydans for *Time* magazine in 1962, Baldwin's steady ironic gaze makes no bid for public approbation.

Justine

Lawrence Durrell

Lifespan | *b.*1912 (India), *d.*1980 (France)
First Published | 1957
First Published by | Faber & Faber (London)
U.S. Edition Published by | E. P. Dutton (New York)

Durrell's novel, the opening gambit of his Alexandria Quartet, should be highly regarded for its extended passages of remarkable prose poetry. The author's impressionist or imagist treatments describe parts of a city that refuses to become a whole for its protagonist. The narrative appears to assume a suspect but romantic theory of physical causes, detecting a symbiosis between the landscape, the weather, and the city's women: sultry, enigmatic, and perhaps ultimately disappointing. Its first-person account of the dissatisfaction of an indolent déclassé English intellectual trying to make sense of a Mediterranean city and its citizens has him attributing their readable histories and personalities to the influence of the place they inhabit. The natives of the Egyptian city are seen as a set of intrinsic predispositions determined by racial inheritances, whereas his actions and emotions are put down to his mostly dire economic situation and a shameful lack of motivation. Sexual promiscuity, the smoking of hashish, constant reference to Cafavy, and nods to decadent French novels of the fin de siècle make this a very different book from most English novels of its time. Essentially it is a superior kind of travel writing, constructed in often extraordinarily vivid and painterly language, but hobbled every once in a while by its dated sexual and racial politics. **RP**

⊘ Durrell indulges his amateur interest in painting: much of his best writing consists of descriptions of places seen with an artist's eye.

The Wonderful "O"

James Thurber

Lifespan | *b.*1894 (U.S.), *d.*1961
First Published | 1957
First Published by | Simon & Schuster (New York)
Full Name | James Grover Thurber

This is the story of a deal struck between two men with a lust for treasure—the roaring pirate Littlejack, who has a map, and the mysterious Black, who has a ship. Black also has a hatred of the letter O, ever since the night his mother became wedged in a porthole: "We couldn't pull her in so we had to push her out." They set sail with a villainous crew. The map leads to the island of Ooroo, where they find no sign of treasure, and receive no cooperation from the gentle islanders. By way of punishment, Black issues an edict banning the letter O from the language. Although evil is not allowed to triumph ultimately, there is mayhem and destruction as the pirates terrorize the inhabitants.

This is a parody of brutal occupation and passive resistance, carrying with it chilling themes of looting, cleansing, and language death. Yet the story also resonates with sparkling humor and complex wordplay. Thurber delights in lists, and on every page he spins trails of language without the forbidden vowel, then creates alternative clusters of "O words." There is fun at the expense of individual islanders. A man named Otto Ott found that he could only stutter his name, while the unfortunate Ophelia Oliver repeated hers and "vanished from the haunts of men."

For all its disturbing undertones, this is primarily a fairy tale, and it is fitting that magic, rather than a protracted bloody struggle, should succeed in bringing down the regime. The barbarians are driven out empty-handed, and freedom returns. **TS**

Doctor Zhivago

Boris Pasternak

Pasternak's epic story of the love affair between Lara and Yuri, set against the historical and geographical vastness of revolutionary Russia, was banned in the USSR from its first publication in Italy until 1988. While Pasternak was silenced by the Soviets, he won extravagant plaudits in the West, receiving the Nobel Prize for Literature in 1958.

It is a bitter irony that this divergence between Soviet and Western responses to *Doctor Zhivago* has had such a profound influence on the way that the novel has been read. Pasternak has been caricatured by both the West and the East as a writer who prioritizes a romantic Western concept of individual freedom over the iron cruelties of the socialist state. In fact, rather than being in any simple sense counter-revolutionary, the book is a subtle examination of the ways in which revolutionary ideals can be compromised by the realities of political power. The relationship between Lara and Yuri, one of the most compelling in postwar fiction, grows out of a fascination with the possibilities of revolutionary justice and is closely interwoven with it. The novel is driven by the struggle to achieve a kind of perfect truth, in both personal and political terms, but its drama and pathos are found in the failure of this striving toward the ideal and in the extraordinary difficulty of remaining faithful to a personal, political, or poetic principle.

One of the most striking things about the novel is the Russian landscape itself, which emerges with a wonderful spaciousness and an extraordinary beauty. It is from its elegiac encounter with the vast landscape upon which this drama is played out that *Doctor Zhivago* produces an extraordinary sense of happiness and a sense of the boundlessness of historical and human possibility. **PB**

Lifespan | *b.* 1890 (Russia), *d.* 1960
First Published | 1957, by Feltrinelli (Milan)
Nobel Prize for Literature | 1958 (declined)
Original Language | Russian

BORIS PASTERNAK

Doctor Zhivago

When this English paperback edition appeared in 1960, Pasternak's novel was hailed in the West as an attack on the Soviet system.

David Lean's 1965 film version, a huge box office hit, made *Doctor Zhivago* into a scenic epic of doomed romantic love.

Pnin

Vladimir Nabokov

Lifespan | *b.* 1899 (Russia), *d.* 1977 (Switzerland)
First Published | 1957
First Published by | Doubleday (New York)
Original Language | English

This short comic novel brought Vladimir Nabokov his first National Book Award nomination, widespread popularity, and first commercial success. An early example of the 1950s campus novel, it follows the experiences of the hapless Russian émigré Professor Timofey Pnin. As a teacher of Russian at Waindell College, he inhabits the rather strange and detached world of academia, and he struggles to adapt to American university life. Physically awkward and an implacable pedant, Pnin's greatest misfortune is his inability to marshal English idiom, and much of the comedy of the book arises from his idiosyncratic use of the language. However, his ultimately dignified conduct ensures that his character cannot be reduced to the pared-down stereotype offered by the somewhat uncharitable narrator, and in comparison with his other non-American colleagues he is an undeniably decent man.

Evolving out of a series of short stories originally published in the *New Yorker* between 1953 and 1955, the book has been criticized for appearing more as a series of discrete sketches than a novel. This criticism is unfair, however, as—in keeping with Nabokov's concern for thematic rather than plot-driven cohesion—the novel returns to Pnin's inability to feel physically or linguistically "at home" in North American culture. Above all, the unmistakably deft Nabokovian style, with its extended linguistic digressions and offbeat humor, make this novel a comic masterpiece and a real joy. **JW**

On the Road

Jack Kerouac

Lifespan | *b.* 1922 (U.S.), *d.* 1969
First Published | 1957
First Published by | Viking Press (New York)
Screenplay by | Russell Banks

Jack Kerouac's novel has become a classic text in American literary counterculture. Set in the aftermath of the Second World War, Sal Paradise's account of his travels across America has become emblematic of the struggle to retain the freedom of the American dream in a more sober historical moment. Paradise's journey with the free and reckless Dean Moriarty (based on fellow Beat adventurer Neal Cassady) from the East to the West coast of America is a celebration of the abundance, vitality, and spirit of American youth. The pair's rejection of domestic and economic conformity in favor of a search for free and inclusive communities and for heightened individual experiences were key constituents of the emerging Beat culture, of which Kerouac—along with literary figures such as Ginsberg and Burroughs—was to soon to become a charismatic representative.

Reputedly written by Kerouac in a three-week burst of Benzedrine and caffeine-fueled creativity on a single scroll of paper, the production of this loosely autobiographical novel became a legend of the sort that occurred within it. Yet the novel also holds within it an acknowledgement of the limitations of its vision, and Dean's gradual decline slowly reveals him to be something of an absurd and unlikely hero for Sal to follow into maturity. **NM**

⊙ Jack Kerouac, left, glances away from his friend Neal Cassady, a folk hero of the Beats depicted in *On the Road* as Dean Moriarty.

Homo Faber

Max Frisch

Lifespan | *b.*1911 (Switzerland), *d.*1991
First Published | 1957
First Published by | Suhrkamp (Frankfurt)
Original Language | German

Homo Faber is a tragicomic tale of the alienation of modern man and the dangers of rationalism. Walter Faber is a fifty-year-old Swiss émigré working as an engineer for UNESCO. He is a punctilious creature of habit with a strongly held view that science and reason can account for all things. The novel begins when, on a flight to Venezuela, his plane is forced to land in the Mexican desert. This disruption to his ordered life and a chance meeting with the brother of his erstwhile best friend are the beginnings of a series of events that force him to confront his past.

Before the war Faber was in a relationship with a German Jew, Hanna, who became pregnant. He offered to marry her, she refused, and he went away, understanding that she would terminate the pregnancy. But in Mexico he learns that Hanna in fact married another. This shock discovery creates a fissure in his rationalist armor that will crack completely by the time he is united with Hanna and the daughter he never knew he had. Walter's failure to address his emotional side, and his dogmatic belief that he can control his environment through logic make this reunion anything but happy. Frisch is a master of irony, used here to full effect to produce a troubling, ambivalent work that leaves you torn between feelings of sympathy and contempt for his perfectly realized but deeply flawed creation. **AL**

◐ Frisch contemplates a typewriter in Zurich,1967, where he is now considered one of Switzerland's most influential writers.

Blue of Noon

Georges Bataille

Lifespan | *b.*1897 (France), *d.*1962
First Published | 1957
First Published by | Pauvert (Paris)
Original Title | *Le Bleu du ciel*

Despite having met his ideal woman in the wealthy, beautiful, and debauched "Dirty," Troppmann, the narrator of *Blue of Noon*, is impotent, forcing him to explore his insatiable appetites by other means. His sexual impotence reflects a wider sense of powerlessness that pervades this novel, written in 1935, but unpublished until 1957. Moving around Europe in 1934, Troppmann witnesses the first signs of the rise of Nazism, seemingly resigned to its eventual triumph. Convinced of the failure of politics in general, he remains resolutely disengaged from any political revolutionary activity. Instead, accompanied by Dirty, he embarks on a project of willful self-destruction. Bataille wrote elsewhere about the state of "sovereignty" that is achieved precisely when the self is lost in a moment that exceeds any potential use, any recuperative "experience." Troppmann tries to attain this state through repeated acts of transgression, by negating values and violating taboos. Mirroring the descent of Europe into fascism in the drunk, sick, and decaying bodies of its protagonists, Bataille points to the fascination with an abject, deathly sexuality that Nazism taps into. The novel is attuned to the allure of the ecstatic violence of fascism while finally suggesting that it might be possible to turn these forces against themselves. Very few can match Bataille's willingness to search for a degree zero, the headlong pursuit of absolute nullity coupled with the acute knowledge of its ultimate unattainability. **SS**

The Midwich Cuckoos

John Wyndham

Lifespan | *b.* 1903 (England), *d.* 1969
First Published | 1957
First Published by | Michael Joseph (London)
First Movie Adaptation | *Village of the Damned* (1960)

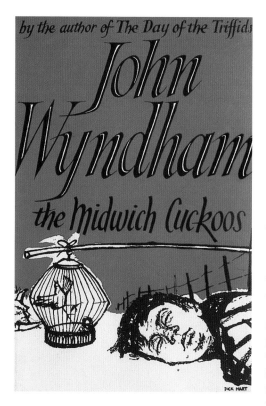

"Cuckoos lay eggs . . . "

⊙ *The Midwich Cuckoos* sets a science fiction story of hostile alien invasion in the apparently tranquil setting of an English village.

Midwich is a tiny and unexceptional rural village where very little ever happens until a mysterious force envelops it, and everyone falls unconscious. Soon after, the inhabitants wake to find that everything remains normal, and most have no ill effects. However, it becomes clear that every woman of childbearing age is simultaneously pregnant. The resulting children are extraordinary: uncannily alike, remarkably well-developed, and endowed with a telepathic sense that allows all to know exactly what one has learned. Unsurprisingly, they prompt a great deal of unease in the village and, in classic sci-fi style, a professor arrives to investigate the phenomenon. What follows is a compelling struggle between the children, the villagers, and the authorities around them that quickly takes on global proportions.

This synopsis may seem familiar, since although it was initially popular as a novel, the story is probably better known as a result of the two filmed versions (the first considerably superior), both rather unnecessarily titled *Village of the Damned*. This novel has also had an enduring influence upon successive generations of science fiction writers. Although *The Midwich Cuckoos* has undeniably dated, as with many of Wyndham's novels—the most popular being *The Day of the Triffids*—it nevertheless powerfully epitomizes the concerns and questions that preoccupied writers following the end of the Second World War and during the Cold War that followed. The fear that is engendered in Midwich by the possibility of invasion, infiltration, and pollution is masterfully manipulated by Wyndham in terms of the domestic, the personal, and the body. He also brilliantly captures the uncomprehending intrusion of Cold War propaganda and politics into the most unlikely setting—little England. **MD**

Voss

Patrick White

The novel with which Patrick White first achieved international fame is both a love story and an adventure story, and yet it is neither. Set in Australia in the mid-nineteenth century, the novel dramatizes an expedition, led by Johann Ulrich Voss, into the center of the vast Australian continent. At the same time, it follows the growing relationship between Voss and Laura Trevelyan, wealthy daughter of one of the sponsors of Voss's voyage. Laura, like the colonial society to which she belongs, never leaves the fringes of the continent. But as Voss penetrates deeper and deeper into the dark heart of the country, Laura travels with him, telepathically or in spirit, so that a relationship which begins somewhat frigidly in the drawing rooms of colonial Australia reaches a passionate, feverish intensity in the harsh, otherworldly conditions of the interior.

This tale of love and exploration has many antecedents. Voss' dogged, driven attempt to penetrate the land resembles Marlow's journey in Conrad's *Heart of Darkness*. The precise attention to nineteenth-century sensibility lends the drawing-room scenes an unmistakable quality of Jane Austen; and the intensity of the personal relations sometimes reads like Lawrence transposed to the outback. But while Voss' journey and his difficult relationship with Laura have all these overtones, the most striking feature of this novel is its discordance, its unnavigable strangeness. The land itself is the most imposing presence, and the deadly vastness of the unmapped interior exerts an extraordinary influence on the European culture that the colonists bring to it. This culture is remade by the silent land that Voss seeks to penetrate, just as the novel form is refashioned from this confrontation with the hidden depths of the desert. **PB**

Lifespan | *b.* 1912 (England), *d.* 1961 (Australia)
First Published | 1957
First Published by | Eyre & Spottiswoode (London)
Nobel Prize for Literature | 1973

"His legend will be written ... "

An artist's impression of White's dogged hero appears on the striking cover of the first edition, which made the novelist's name.

Jealousy

Alain Robbe-Grillet

Lifespan | *b*. 1922 (France)
First Published | 1957
First Published by | Les Editions de Minuit (Paris)
Original Title | *La Jalousie*

Robbe-Grillet's *Jealousy* is one of the most famous examples of the *nouveau roman*, or "new novel," which tried to extend the limits of the realist approach to novelistic plotting, setting, and characterization. The style is one of rigorous objectivity that is restricted to the visual description of the planes and surfaces of the observable world and the stances and gestures of human figures. The reader is denied any direct access to the thoughts of either the nameless narrator or the people he observes. Looking through a venetian blind ("jalousie" in French), he watches his wife engaging in what looks like an affair with his neighbor Franck. He makes no attempt to comment or reflect upon what he is seeing—in fact he never uses the pronoun "I" at all.

The true originality of the novel lies in its ability to communicate the force of jealousy despite the self-imposed limitations of its objective style. The reader gradually becomes attuned to the repetitions and minute variations of the text and eventually forms the impression of a consciousness constituted and consumed by jealousy. The narrative style brilliantly captures the behavior of the jealous lover whose obsessive attention to detail manages to see in every stray glance and unconscious gesture evidence of a hidden betrayal. The flat, filmic mode of narration perfected here has been tremendously influential for later postmodern writers attempting to describe the curious depthlessness of a world seen primarily through the lens of the camera. **SS**

The Bell

Iris Murdoch

Lifespan | *b*. 1919 (Ireland), *d*. 1999 (England)
First Published | 1958
First Published by | Chatto & Windus (London)
Original Language | English

The Bell is generally agreed to be Iris Murdoch's best early novel. The plot, which clearly belongs to the Anglo-Irish literary genre of the "big house" novel, involves the tense, unhappy relationships between a group of characters on a retreat at a Benedictine monastery, Imber Court. Here they hope to resolve the issues that trouble them in the world outside. They represent a cross section of weak and confused humanity whose spiritual needs prevent them from integrating properly with their fellow men and women, but whose lust for life precludes them from being able to accept a contemplative life cut off from the world. The main figure is Michael Meade, an ex-priest and schoolteacher struggling to suppress his homosexuality and who is racked with a mixture of guilt and frustration. The plot revolves around the plan to restore the cracked bell of the community, a labor that proves endless and futile. The unstable community starts to disintegrate after the arrival of two outsiders. Dora Greenfield is the unhappy wife of Paul, a scholar studying documents at the Abbey, who is unsure whether to end their marriage. Toby Gashe is a young man who finds himself attracted to both Dora and Michael.

The Bell established Iris Murdoch as a major figure in British fiction. It poignantly explores the tragic interaction of a group of people who need to balance their own needs and desires against those of others, as well as understand how far life can or should be lived in terms of spiritual ideals. **AH**

The Once and Future King

T. H. White

Lifespan | b. 1915 (India), d. 1964 (Greece)
First Published | 1958
First Published by | Collins (London)
Full Name | Terence Hanbury White

White's complex and often brilliant retelling of the Arthurian legends was written over a twenty-year period as a sequence of four novels and first published as a single volume in 1958. It is best known for the rather saccharine Disney cartoon of the first book, *The Sword in the Stone* (published in 1939; movie released in 1963). *The Once and Future King* was based on Thomas Malory's ambitious prose romance of the Arthurian court, *Le Morte d'Arthur*, written in the fifteenth century. White does not update the story, but he is always conscious of the parallels that can be made between the brutality of the dying Middle Ages and the rise of fascism in his lifetime. In the course of the four published novels, Arthur grows from a gangly, nervous youth ("the Wart") into a vigorous military leader. He is eventually forced to emulate the actions of the Nazi-esque Celtic forces assembled by his nemesis, Mordred, in an attempt to try to preserve the innocence of England. The result is disastrous and, as he rides out to meet his death, Arthur concludes that only without nations can humankind be happy. There are some magnificent set pieces, notably when the Wart, transformed into a perch by Merlin, is nearly eaten by the pike, Mr. P., who warns him that the only reality is that of power. *The Once and Future King* is a messy sequence of novels that is not always properly integrated, as the author acknowledged. Still, it is a powerful, disturbing work about the evil that men can do and the desperate struggle for values in a hostile world. **AH**

EXCALIBVR RETVRNS TO THE MERE

"Whoso pulleth Out This Sword of This Stone and Anvil, is Rightwise King Born of All England."

◉ The return of the magic sword to the Lady of the Lake as visualized by British illustrator Henry Justice Ford in 1902.

The End of the Road

John Barth

Lifespan | b. 1930 (U.S.)
First Published | 1958
First Published by | Doubleday (New York)
First UK Edition | 1962, by Secker & Warburg

An example of postwar academic seduction fiction, *The End of the Road* has a lengthy critical history. Read at first as a philosophical novella with a shocking ending, it was later regarded as an early example of American postmodernism.

Joe Morgan is an extreme relativist playing the game of discussing everything with his wife, Rennie, in order to remake her for himself. When she acts apologetically, he socks her on the jaw. She must become real for him. Joe welcomes newly appointed lecturer Jake Horner into this apparently stable relationship, offering every opportunity for Jake and Rennie to be together. Rennie becomes pregnant, and a sinister unnamed Doctor botches the abortion. This fiction explores what would happen if certain philosophical positions were worked out in reality. The Doctor, a behaviorist, forces Jake to teach grammar to counter his inertia, or catatonia. Joe's post-Sartre relativism, together with the Sartre–de Beauvoir "open relationship" attitude, seals Rennie's fate. Jake, who narrates, is fully aware that he has no settled identity. The Doctor, jeering at "the vacuum you have for a self," urges a parodic existentialist engagement: "Remember, keep moving all the time. Be *engagé*. Join things." Jake acts, and Rennie dies, the responsive victim of Jake and Joe, who are bad philosophers of daily life. It was the radically unstable moral situation generated by these philosophical considerations that was later identified as a nascent postmodernism. **AMu**

Borstal Boy

Brendan Behan

Lifespan | b. 1923 (Ireland), d. 1964
First Published | 1958
First Published by | Hutchinson (London)
Full Name | Brendan Francis Behan

Borstal Boy is Brendan Behan's angry, generous, and bawdy account of life for a "paddy" in an English borstal. From a working-class Republican family in Dublin, Behan himself had been arrested in Liverpool in 1939 in possession of IRA explosives. Sentenced to three years' borstal detention, he served two and was then expelled from England at the age of eighteen.

Part of the beauty of *Borstal Boy*, a novel he was to write seventeen years later, is the skill with which it recaptures the contradictions that make up the "young offender." Behan himself appears in the text as a riddle of pride, fear, loneliness, and aggression. He is at once a cynically knowing critic of the pieties of both Irish nationalism and English imperialism and a homesick boy; aggressively at home with his fists in the macho culture of his institution and tempted to gentleness and desire by the bodies and strengths of his borstal comrades.

Magistrates, screws, detainees, friends, foes, priests—all are drawn with a respect for both the differences that separate and those that unite. The result is a fine social history of interwar England, as well as a classic of prison literature. What sets *Borstal Boy* apart from other such classics is the generosity of Behan's anger and his skill as a writer in exposing the many ways in which prison dehumanizes all who come into contact with it. **PMcM**

❯ Behan poses in front of a poster for the French version of his 1956 play *The Quare Fellow*, which first established his reputation.

Mrs. 'Arris Goes to Paris

Paul Gallico

Lifespan | *b.*1897 (U.S.), *d.*1976 (France)
First Published | 1958
First Published by | Doubleday (New York)
UK Title | *Flowers for Mrs. Harris*

> *"I'm a rotten novelist.*
> *I'm not even literary."*
>
> *Gallico*, New York Magazine, *1969*

Paul Gallico was a well-known sports correspondent for the *New York Daily News* before turning his hand to fiction in the 1930s.

This short novel is a happy, heartwarming, and cheerful book which, when first published, reinforced the author's reputation as a writer of unapologetic sentimental fiction. Having initially achieved fame as a sport's journalist, Gallico began writing fiction in the 1930s, mainly in the form of short stories, and in 1941 he was catapulted into international consciousness when he attained critical acclaim with the publication of *The Snow Goose*.

This book was the first in the Mrs. Harris series, which would later include *Mrs. Harris Goes to New York*, *Mrs. Harris, M.P.*, and *Mrs. Harris Goes to Moscow*. Here we follow the simple but captivating story of a London charlady, Mrs. Harris, who falls in love with a Dior dress she spots in a magazine discarded by one of the wealthy women she "does" for. This marks the beginning of a dream—to own a Dior dress of her own—and Mrs. Harris begins scrimping and saving so that she may one day buy one. In her desire to own a Dior dress, the honest, dowdy but determined cleaning lady represents anyone who has ever hoped to realize a seemingly impossible dream. "What would you do with it when you got it?" asks her sensible friend Mrs. Butterfield, to which she replies, with the logic of every aspiring shopper throughout the ages: "'Ave it! Just 'ave it!" As Mrs. Harris struggles to save up enough money for the dress, a small miracle occurs. When she wins one hundred pounds on the football pools she finds she now has the money required to go off to Paris to buy her dress. There she encounters adventure and a cast of characters who are captivated by her simple charms and moved to help her in her quest. Using the conventions of fairy tales, Gallico makes the story appear logical and convincing, as well as enchanting and delightful. **LE**

Saturday Night and Sunday Morning

Alan Sillitoe

From the outset of his writing career, English author Alan Sillitoe found a vibrant catalyst for his imagination in Nottingham, the region he had grown to know intimately since birth. Yet his debut novel, *Saturday Night and Sunday Morning*, was more than an exercise in regional realism. In a narrative that makes nimble transitions between the naturalistic and the mythical, Sillitoe shadows Arthur Seaton from factory floor to fractious love life, offering an unsentimental, pseudo-autobiographical picaresque. Arthur's riotous enjoyment of the "best and bingiest glad-time of the week," as he drinks in pubs and chases girls, is a "violent preamble to prostrate Sabbath." In his evocations of Arthur's everyday detailed perception of Nottingham's once resilient environment under change, Sillitoe does perfect justice to the local people and regional place, scrupulously mapping a townscape that is barely resisting the parasitic "empires" of suburbia, which are encroaching upon it. Sillitoe returned to this "Seaton saga" in *Birthday*, published in 2001, aligning himself with Balzac in conducting across the decades what he described recently as a "Nottingham *comédie humaine*."

Central to this ongoing project, Sillitoe's imaginative geography has contributed richly to the postwar regional novel's stylistic and thematic scope. By using his personal acquaintance with Nottinghamshire's cartography, he articulates with formidable precision a prospective map of what the county could potentially become. Sillitoe's fiction is never straightforwardly realist: it often blends urban verisimilitude with visionary speculation in order to demonstrate how an author can allow factual experiences of indigenous place to inform a fable of social possibilities alive in its midst. **DJ**

Lifespan | *b*.1928 (England)
First Published | 1958, by W. H. Allen (London)
Movie Adaptation Released | 1960
Author's Club First Novel Award | 1958

"For it was Saturday night, the best and bingiest glad-time of the week . . . "

◆ In 1960, when this photo was taken, Sillitoe's gritty regional realism appealed to a public eager for working-class heroes.

Things Fall Apart

Chinua Achebe

Lifespan | *b.*1930 (Nigeria)
First Published | 1958
First Published by | Heinemann (London)
Full Name | Albert Chinualumogu Achebe

Things Fall Apart is Chinua Achebe's first and most famous novel, written in response to the negative ways that Africans are represented in canonical English texts such as Joseph Conrad's *Heart of Darkness* and Joyce Cary's *Mister Johnson*. It has sold over eight million copies and been translated into more than thirty languages. The novel describes the historical tragedy caused by the arrival of the British in Igboland, in eastern Nigeria. In the first part of the novel the local culture is shown to be complex and dynamic, pristine and untouched by Europe. The second section reveals the social transformations brought about by early imperialists and Christian missionaries. The final part dwells upon the theme of African silence as a direct consequence of British colonial rule. The story of the protagonist, Okonkwo, is caught up in these broader historical currents.

Things Fall Apart is an anti-colonial novel. It contains numerous scenes of African silence, or absence, in the face of Europe's speech, or presence. Over and against these acts of silencing, the novel as a whole works in the opposite direction, pulling against colonialism and celebrating the noisiness of an uncolonized Igbo world. It is shown to be filled with oral genres, including ceremonies, proverbs, folktales, debates, gossip, and conversations, overseen by the ubiquitous West African "talking drum." **SN**

◀ Achebe's powerful critique of imperialism appeared just as African countries, including Nigeria, were winning independence.

The Bitter Glass

Eilís Dillon

Lifespan | *b.*1920 (Ireland), *d.*1994
First Published | 1958
First Published by | Faber & Faber (London)
Original Language | English

The Irish Civil War of 1922–23 pitted "free staters" against Republicans, those who accepted the partition of Ireland drawn out in the Treaty of 1921 against those who held out for a united Ireland. The war was as bitter and as personal as only a civil war can be, as the first Irish Free State Government authorized the execution of Republicans committed to a cause they had shared but two years before.

Eilís Dillon's *The Bitter Glass* is set in the west of Ireland in the hot summer of 1922 and uses the conflict to pinpoint the redundancy of the war to those in whose name it was being fought. A party of wealthy young Dubliners makes the journey to a remote summer house in Connemara, rich with memories of childhood alliances, hopes, and betrayals. Dillon uses the opening sections of the novel to build up a vivid sense of the ambiguous conflicts pulsing under the surface of the Dubliners' personal relationships. When the house, as much as its inhabitants, are taken prisoner by a flying column of IRA men on the run from Free State forces, the idyllic holiday home is turned into an arena of rage that explodes with an emancipatory shock.

Dillon crafts a poetic and sardonic narrative that identifies women as those who resent most strongly the lack of, and hope most keenly for, freedom. The freedom they yearn for, however, exceeds the political liberties being fought for around them, as it embraces liberation from both material want and emotional shame. **PMcM**

A Town Like Alice

Nevil Shute

Lifespan | b. 1899 (England), d. 1960 (Australia)
First Published | 1950
First Published by | Heinemann (London)
Given Name | Nevil Shute Norway

Nevil Shute's *A Town Like Alice* received international acclaim and became an Australian classic. A love story set against the backdrop of the Second World War in the Far East and the postwar Australian outback, it is a tale of shifting societies and changing times, brought about by the impact of war. The novel is based on a real event, when the Japanese invaded Sumatra and captured eighty Dutch women and children, who were then forced to trek around the island for the next two and a half years. The narrator tells the story of Jean Pagett, an English secretary in Malaysia. Captured along with other English women and children, she spends the next three years on a grueling "death march" around the Malay Peninsula. While on this forced march, Jean strikes up a close friendship with an Australian prisoner of war, Joe Harman, but later believes he has been killed. After the war Jean revisits Malaysia and discovers Joe is not dead. She travels to Australia, their romance is rekindled, and they turn the one-horse town in which Joe lives into a thriving community, based on Alice Springs. *A Town Like Alice* has all the elements of a great love story and was written when the British-born author had just embarked upon a love affair of his own—with his new country, Australia. **LE**

🔵 Nevil Shute, an aeronautical engineer as well as a novelist, satisfied popular taste for moral dilemmas and happy endings.

Pluck the Bud and Destroy the Offspring

Kenzaburo Oe

Lifespan | b. 1935 (Japan)
First Published | 1958 by Kodansha (Tokyo)
Original Title | *Memushiri kouchi*
Nobel Prize for Literature | 1994

Pluck the Bud and Destroy the Offspring vividly captures the devastating conditions that war can inflict on even the most innocent of victims. The novel is told from the view of a vulnerable boy determined to live, and presents us with a personal experience of Japan toward the end of the Second World War. As bombs rain down daily on the cities of Japan, the coming end is foreshadowed. A group of boys abandoned by their parents and incarcerated in a rehabilitation center are about to take refuge in a country village. As outsiders, they are treated inhumanely by the villagers, but unity among them remains tight. Through the voice of the narrative "I" they are determined to become the "we," and to survive. When a deadly plague arrives, the villagers abandon the boys and flee, closing all the gates to the village. Although the boys find themselves locked in, they gain a transitory freedom. In the most devastating conditions, they set up a kind of paradise, occupying the villagers' houses and managing to create a life for themselves. Their happiness is short-lived, however, as their fear of the plague develops into conflict and disputes. The villagers' return brings the final blow. "Listen, someone like you should be throttled while they're still a kid. We squash vermin while it's small. We're peasants: we nip the buds early." Paradise is about to disappear. **KK**

The Leopard

Giuseppe Tomasi di Lampedusa

Lifespan | *b.* 1896 (Italy), *d.* 1957
First Published | 1958
First Published by | Feltrinelli (Milan)
Original Title | *Il gattopardo*

Appearing posthumously in 1958, one year after the author's death, *The Leopard* received unexpected international success. Translated into many languages, it became the subject of cinematographic epic by Visconti in 1963. *The Leopard* struck a new chord, as it deliberately ignored the Italian neorealist narrative tradition, both stylistically and thematically. While neorealism centered on low-class characters and unveiled the crude reality of fascist Italy, *The Leopard* is the saga of the aristocratic Sicilian family of the Salinas (whose coat of arms bears a leopard). From 1860 to 1910, a series of events affects the microcosm of the protagonist, Prince Fabrizio, and his relatives, as well as the macrocosm of the Italian nation. In Italy's south, the Bourbon kingdom is crumbling under the impetus of Garibaldi, and the Kingdom of the Two Sicilies is being joined with the rest of the country; however, the end of Spanish colonization coincides with the death of the aristocracy, which had long been supported by the feudal system and which is being supplanted by the bourgeoisie. *The Leopard* portrays the melancholy of that loss. The most poignant pages are those in which Prince Fabrizio bemoans the harsh landscape of Sicily and the Sicilians, who have developed an irredeemable sense of indifference and vanity in the attempt to survive numberless foreign colonizations. The new course of history will not touch Sicily, Don Fabrizio predicts, as the national Unification that is underway is for the Sicilians nothing but a new form of domination. **RPi**

Breakfast at Tiffany's

Truman Capote

Lifespan | *b.* 1924 (U.S.), *d.* 1984
First Published | 1958
First Published by | Random House (New York)
Given Name | Truman Streckfus Persons

Breakfast at Tiffany's is a charmingly naughty fable, capturing in crystal a glorious moment of New York during the last gasp of American innocence. The story is the reminiscence of a writer in New York during the Second World War. With Holly Golightly, Capote has given us one of the most indelible heroines in fiction. Pushing the boundaries and paving the way for the revolution to come, Holly is a gamine—sexually free, hedonistic, a prostitute. She lives for the moment, damns the consequences, and makes up her morality as she goes along. Like her cat without a name, she is unfettered, untameable. The novel's unnamed narrator meets Holly when she climbs through the writer's window, to escape an overzealous and unmuzzled john. They become fast friends, and the narrator is swept up in Holly's thrill-seeking subsistence living. At the core they want "happiness" and connection, dreams that seem like fate to those young enough to hope. But hints of darkness cloud their lives. The novel was a turning point for Capote. Gone is the lyrical Southern gothic of his early writing. Here he takes his place among New York's glitterati. Daring in its day—promiscuity and homosexuality are discussed openly—it may have lost its ability to shock, but its charm does not diminish. A fresh breeze off the East River—from a time when such a thing was still possible. **GT**

⊙ Blake Edwards' 1961 movie version of the story was toned down and sweetened up to meet Hollywood requirements of the time.

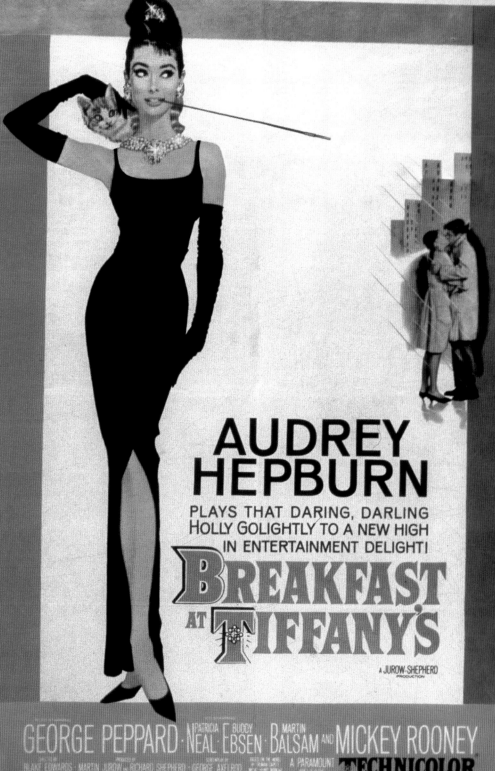

Billiards at Half-Past Nine

Heinrich Böll

Lifespan | *b.*1917 (Germany), *d.*1985
First Published | 1959, by Kiepenheuer & Witsch
Original Title | *Billard um Halbzehn*
Nobel Prize for Literature | 1972

This family saga about three generations of architects living and working in a town in Catholic West Germany unfolds in conversations and inner monologues, all set during the course of one day, September 6, 1958. Over sixty years of German history are revealed through the lives of the family—from the Kaiser era through the Third Reich and into the West German economic miracle of the 1950s.

Billiards at Half-Past Nine is about the refusal to forgive and forget the failure of civilization and the Catholic Church's complicity in war, persecution, and torture. When the monastery that was the first great project of successful architect Heinrich Fähmel in 1907 is blown up at the end of the Second World War by his son Robert, an explosions expert for the Wehrmacht, it is really in an act of protest against the civilization it represents. The grandson Joseph, who is involved in the restoration of the monastery after the war, is deeply confused when he finds out about this. Family tensions, as well as the contradiction of living in a society to which one cannot be reconciled, find a strangely redemptive resolution in a symbolic act of violence against a new supporter of "the buffalo." The novel is remarkable for its depth and humanism, and its call to readers to share the characters' moral revulsion and their refusal to forget. **DG**

Memento Mori

Muriel Spark

Lifespan | *b.* 1918 (Scotland), *d.* 2006 (Italy)
First Published | 1959
First Published by | Macmillan & Co. (London)
Given Name | Muriel Sarah Camberg

Comedy of the very blackest kind, Spark's novel dwells on old age and the imminence of death, with a steely gaze. Despite its macabre subject matter, it is a grimly funny work, reveling in the indignities and absurdities of the aging process. From the selfish seventy-nine-year-old Dame Lettie Colson, her irascible miserly octogenarian brother, and her intermittently senile sister-in-law, to their black-mailing housekeeper, Mrs. Pettigrew, the cast of the eccentric elderly is both grotesque and fascinating.

The premise of the plot is simple. Each character in turn receives a series of phone calls, with the stark and chilling message: "Remember you must die." The source of the messages is never identified, although the wiser among Spark's elderly characters think it is Death him- or herself. What *Memento Mori* is more interested in unveiling is the range of psychological and personal responses that the reminder of death's imminence prompts. Many of the characters merely become baser versions of themselves, driven by fear or denial into frenzies of egotism, obsession, or cruelty. Others achieve a new clarity and generosity. Surveying the action from her hospital bed, the Catholic Jean Taylor displays a stoical serenity. While its promotion of a Catholic moral might not be to all readers' tastes, the ironic and dispassionate narrative voice allows for little easy consolation, and is one of the chief delights of this unique novel. **CC**

Henderson the Rain King

Saul Bellow

Lifespan | *b.* 1915 (Canada), *d.* 2005 (U.S.)
First Published | 1959
First Published by | Viking Press (New York)
Nobel Prize for Literature | 1976

A rare move away from Bellow's characteristic Chicago-Jewish milieu, *Henderson the Rain King* sees Bellow crossing hard-edged realism with satirical fable, in a comedy of quixotic and unfulfilled want. An atypical Bellow hero, Eugene Henderson (as fittingly suggested by his initials) has something of Ernest Hemingway about him, being a rich, larger-than-life adventurer. His life, however, has been perpetually unsatisfactory, never living up to his grand expectations, and so he ends up, via a bizarre chain of circumstances, in Africa: "there are displaced persons everywhere," and Henderson becomes another. When King Dahfu and his people adopt him as their rainmaker, he finds himself reassessing his ideas of belonging, rootedness, and responsibility.

The novel forms part of Bellow's larger existential comedy about people's need for shapes and stories, and experience's habit of slipping out of people's grasp. It has a freewheeling, improvisatory quality, but from today's distance it does pose problems. Much in Bellow's treatment of Africa and African English feels disturbingly prehistoric, belonging in the same imaginative world as Evelyn Waugh's African-set satires *Scoop* and *Black Mischief*. But as a staging of the classic Bellovian themes ("the repetition of a man's bad self, that's the worst suffering") in an unusual location, *Henderson the Rain King* will remain an intriguing companion to his larger novels. **BT**

Absolute Beginners

Colin MacInnes

Lifespan | *b.* 1914 (England), *d.* 1976
First Published | 1959
First Published by | MacGibbon & Kee (London)
UK Musical Movie Adaptation Released | 1986

The best known of Colin MacInnes' London trilogy, which includes *City of Spades* (1957) and *Mr. Love and Justice* (1960), *Absolute Beginners* has had a curious afterlife, thanks to the David Bowie–featured 1980s movie musical, which culled large sections of the text. Frequently appearing on top-ten "hip lists" alongside Jack Kerouac's superficially similar *On the Road* (1957), the novel has as its star not its central character, a bohemian photographer "out for kicks and fantasy," but London in all its frenetic glory. It is narrated in a language replete with "spades," "daddy-os," "reefers," "oldies," and "oafos," yet behind the coming-of-age tale lies a society in the throes of radical transformation.

This is postwar London in the aftermath of the Suez crisis, in the year of the Notting Hill riots: previously ironclad certainties concerning the God-given destiny of the British Empire and the racial homogeneity of its metropolitan center are archaic irrelevancies. This is an emerging London entirely incomprehensible to the pre-war "oldies" in positions of authority. It is also a city fizzing with excitement and tension—racial, generational, sexual. When it finally breaks down in riots, it is not just law and order, nor the social bonds of community, but also the city itself that begins to disintegrate. Fresh, vital, and relevant, *Absolute Beginners* offers extraordinary insight into the origins of contemporary society and the one that was left behind. **MD**

The Tin Drum

Günter Grass

Oskar Matzerath is detained in a mental hospital for a murder he did not commit. His keeper watches him. His keeper also brings him the paper on which Oskar writes his autobiography. Oskar considers the keeper a friend, rather than an enemy, for the simple reason that the keeper has eyes that are the right shade of brown. Oskar Matzerath is a dwarf: he claims to have willed himself to stop growing at the age of four. He has a singing voice that can cut holes in glass at fifty paces. During the Second World War, Oskar was part of a traveling band of dwarves that entertained the troops. He also uses his tin drum to beat out the story of his life. That life story is also the story of pre-war Poland and Germany, of the rise of Hitler, the defeat of Poland, the Nazi onslaught on Europe, then the defeat and partition of Germany.

An important book in the exploration of postwar German identity, Grass' novel is heartbreakingly beautiful. Oskar Matzerath's voice continues to haunt long after the novel itself is finished. It is the voice of an "asocial," those the Nazis considered to belong (along with criminals, gay men, and vagabonds) to "life unworthy of life." Grass draws on the picaresque tradition to map out his dwarf drummer's journey through a brutal and brutalizing era in European history, but he also reinvents the traditions of a popular culture despised by the Nazis as "degenerate art." Fairy tales, the carnivalesque, the harlequin, the mythological trickster—all jostle and combine in *The Tin Drum* to reveal the deathlike inhumanity of the rationalization of racial hygiene. The result is not a fetishization of the irrational, but rather an expansion and transformation of the normal, until the life Oskar inhabits ultimately becomes swollen to grotesque, yet all the more painfully human, proportions. **PMcM**

Lifespan | *b*. 1927 (Poland)
First Published | 1959, by Luchterhand (Neuwied)
Original Title | *Die Blechtrommel*
Nobel Prize for Literature | 1999

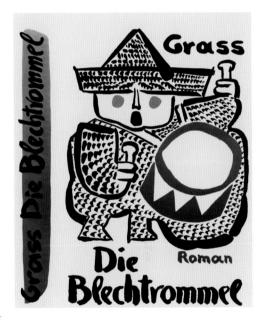

"How blind, how nervous and ill-bred they are!"

⌃ A striking representation of "little Oskar," Grass' compulsive drummer, illustrates the jacket of the German first edition.

◔ Oskar was played by twelve-year-old David Bennent in Schlondorff's 1979 movie, which won an Oscar for Best Foreign Language Film.

The Naked Lunch

William Burroughs

Lifespan | *b.* 1914 (U.S.), *d.* 1997
First Published | 1959
First Published by | Olympia Press (Paris)
Full Name | William Seward Burroughs

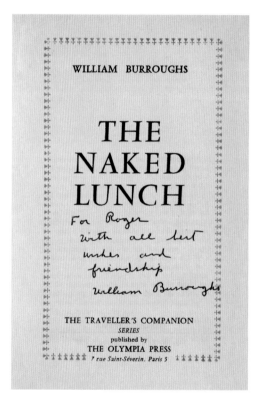

The Parisian Olympia Press issued the first edition of this and other novels thought too obscene for UK or U.S. publication.

Burroughs called hard drugs "…the ultimate merchandise. No sales talk necessary. The client will crawl through a sewer and beg to buy."

William Burroughs has often been hailed as a celebrator of drug indulgence and (homo)sexual excess, but his best works, among which *The Naked Lunch* is preeminent, provide a far deeper and more complex account of Western culture. The novel's central argument is that drugs are not an accidental problem; the whole notion of addiction is deeply engrained in a society which fetishizes commodity and consumption. Furthermore, the line between so-called "prescription" drugs and illegal drugs is a narrow one, which can be manipulated by those in power to serve their need for ever-increasing profits.

But these arguments alone would not make *The Naked Lunch* a great book. What is more important is the tremendous energy and vividness that Burroughs brings to his scenes of violence and mayhem. He presents us with a cast of characters who are constantly tearing at the walls of the prisons their lives have become; they see something of the truth of "the system," but are too paralyzed by dependence to escape. Further, Burroughs invents his own style, here and in other novels, based on what he called the "cut-up technique," which serves to render the reader equally unable to make full sense of the surroundings. Narratives begin, interweave, become lost, and are found again; scenarios are glimpsed then vanish from sight.

There are plenty of postmodern texts that use unreliable narrators. Burroughs goes farther than this, producing a world that seems to have no recognizable coordinates at all. Lost in the world of the junkie, we are sometimes painfully aware that the paranoid visions of the drug world may be more accurate about the systems of corporate and state power than the consoling fictions we tell ourselves in asserting the freedom of the individual will. **DP**

Billy Liar

Keith Waterhouse

Lifespan | *b.* 1929 (England)
First Published | 1959
First Published by | Michael Joseph (London)
Stage Adaptation | 1960

When people refer to the "angry young men" of 1950s British fiction and drama, they will usually have in mind Kingsley Amis' Jim Dixon; perhaps John Braine's Joe Lampton and William Cooper's Joe Lunn; certainly John Osborne's Jimmy Porter. Billy Fisher, Keith Waterhouse's feckless antihero, gets less of a look-in. He would be the first to feel the injustice: Billy is every bit as thwarted and furious as his peers, and this novel is just as telling a document of the postwar crises of class and masculinity as *Lucky Jim* or *Room at the Top*. Billy, maybe twenty-years-old, still lives with his parents in the middling Yorkshire town of Stradhoughton, where he works as an undertaker's clerk and dreams of escape. A compulsive fantasist, Billy has invented Ambrosia, an imaginary world where he can be prime minister, lover, revolutionary, and writer all at once. His life has become a tangle of increasingly elaborate lies, and *Billy Liar* is the story of the day when it all goes wrong. Much of the unraveling is hysterical, but only some of it is funny, reflecting as it does the impotence of a generation of British men born too late to have had their lives defined by the war, but too soon to enjoy the class mobility afforded by the postwar settlement. Billy's anxiety pierces every line, and at the end, the reader is left with the queasy sense that for him, finally, there can be no escape. **PMy**

Tom Courtney played the lovable fantasy-prone undertaker's clerk Billy in John Schlesinger's 1963 movie version of the novel.

Cider With Rosie

Laurie Lee

Lifespan | *b.* 1914 (England), *d.* 1997
First Published | 1959
First Published by | Hogarth Press (London)
Original Language | English

An extremely vivid semi-autobiographical description of life in a small Cotswold village in the early part of the twentieth century, *Cider With Rosie* depicts a world that was soon to vanish: a world where transport was restricted to the horse and cart, and where, in any case, there were few reasons to travel away from one's home. What is perhaps most remarkable about it, and has kept it a firm readers' favorite since it was first published, is the rich lushness of the description. The cottage garden, for example, as seen through the eyes and other senses of a young child, becomes a world of its own, and the adult characters have the grandeur and grotesquerie, which only a child's eye can fully see. Many of the episodes are richly comic, yet there is also a sense of tragedy, a sense that the certainty and routine that once controlled village life have now vanished with the spread of travel and other mechanized comforts. The protagonist's mother, abandoned by her husband with two families to cope with, leads a life of extraordinary drudgery, yet her longing for, and recognition of, the greater things in life rarely falters. Most of all, perhaps, Lee makes no attempt to prettify country life; although there are marvelous things to be found in the fields and hedgerows, there is also a commonplace brutality to country living, including incest, violent sexual relations, and even murder. The counterbalance to this is the sense of tradition, of belonging, which has disappeared as the distant places of England have been opened up by the advent of modernity. **DP**

Promise at Dawn

Romain Gary

Lifespan | *b.* 1914 (Lithuania), *d.* 1980 (France)
First Published | 1960
First Published by | Gallimard (Paris)
Original Title | *La Promesse de l'aube*

"Then she began to cry . . . "

⬤ Gary with his wife, American actress Jean Seberg: she committed suicide in 1979, and he shot himself the following year.

A tribute to the woman who single-handedly, and single-mindedly, raised him to become the great artist that she believed to be her own destiny, *Promise at Dawn* is Romain Gary's memoir of his youth in Vilna and Nice. It reads as a self-portrait in double, reflecting the mix of East European and French cultures that shaped him.

Written with contagious humor and profound affection, it recounts his formative experiences with a mother who, if she had not existed, would have certainly required being invented, and to some degree probably was. But this is only fair, as she herself went to such lengths to create her son's fate, her years of struggle and hard work recounted with a restraint that gives them poignant if often comic immediacy. Her unshakable desire that her son grow up as a Frenchman and not a Russian was one of many goals that she set—and he met.

Every facet of Gary's mother's life, every effort she made, was dedicated to the child she adored and to his future triumphs. This was the promise at the dawn of his life. She foresaw and directed him toward his accomplishments as author, officer, and diplomat, and he did his utmost to fulfill and reward her faith in him. Her unremitting devotion sustained him through law school, military training, and wartime service, as well as his early attempts at getting his fiction published. Hers was a love that would leave him forever hungry and longing to find its perfection again, but also one that served as inspiration for his courage and conviction in justice.

The story closes at the end of the Second World War, with Gary's formidable, indefatigable, and sometimes embarrassing mother, with her romantic and noble soul, demonstrating yet another surprising facet of the artistic genius she truly was. **ES**

Rabbit, Run

John Updike

In *Rabbit, Run*, his second novel, John Updike introduced one of the towering characters of postwar American fiction. Harry "Rabbit" Angstrom was a basketball star at school, famous throughout his hometown of Brewer, Pennsylvania. Now in his late twenties, he lives in a small apartment in one of the poorer parts of town with his pregnant wife, Janice, and young son, Nelson. He has a dead-end job selling vegetable peelers door to door. Alienated and estranged, desperate to escape, he drives away one night without telling anyone he is leaving. But he soon loses heart and turns back toward Brewer. His old basketball coach, one of the few who has not forgotten Harry's glory days, introduces him to a girl called Ruth, with whom he begins an affair.

Updike tells the story in the present tense: if it has become commonplace since, the technique was fairly innovative at the time, and Updike's use of it has rarely been bettered. The novel is also in the third person: although the bulk of the narrative takes place inside Harry's head, it is not Harry's voice that we hear, or not exactly. In sensuous, elegant, hyper-articulate prose, Updike represents Harry's consciousness in the language that Harry would use if only his mind moved as gracefully as his body once did on the basketball court.

Harry is not so much an everyman as a nobody and a far from admirable one: his impulsive and thoughtless behavior has appalling consequences. Yet our sympathy is secured by the quality of careful attentiveness that Updike brings to describing the intricacies of Harry's character. With its sequels— *Rabbit, Redux* (1971), *Rabbit Is Rich* (1981), and *Rabbit at Rest* (1990)—*Rabbit, Run* presents a detailed and extraordinary portrait of an ordinary American man in the second half of the twentieth century. **TEJ**

Lifespan | *b.* 1932 (U.S.)
First Published | 1960
First Published by | A. Knopf (New York)
National Medal for Humanities | 2003

"Love makes the air light."

⊘ The young John Updike, photographed here in 1960, published books of poetry and short stories before turning to novels.

To Kill a Mockingbird

Harper Lee

Lifespan | *b.* 1926 (U.S.)
First Published | 1960
First Published by | Lippincott (Philadelphia)
Pulitzer Prize | 1961

🔺 The jacket of the novel's first edition: it was an immediate success and was made into a movie within two years of publication.

🔻 Harper Lee was thirty-four-years-old when *Mockingbird*, her first book, was published; she has not written another novel.

Set in Depression-era Alabama, Harper Lee's Pulitzer-winning novel weaves together a young girl's coming-of-age story and a darker drama about the roots and consequences of racism, probing how good and evil can coexist within a single community or individual. Scout, the novel's protagonist, is raised with her brother, Jem, by their widowed father, Atticus Finch. He is a prominent lawyer who speaks to them as competent interlocutors and encourages them to be empathetic and philosophical, rather than swept away by the superstition bred of ignorance. Atticus lives his convictions when a spurious rape charge is brought against Tom Robinson, one of the town's black residents. Atticus agrees to defend him, puts together a case that gives a more plausible interpretation of the evidence, then prepares for the town's attempts to intimidate him into abandoning his client to their lynch mob. As the furor escalates, Tom is convicted and Bob Ewell, the Robinson plaintiff, tries to punish Atticus with an unimaginably brutal act.

The children, meanwhile, play out their own miniaturized drama of prejudice and superstition centering on Boo Radley, a local legend who remains shut inside his brother's house. They have their own ideas about him and cannot resist the allure of trespassing on the Radley property. Their speculations thrive on the dehumanization perpetuated by their elders; Atticus reprimands them, however, and tries to encourage a more sensitive attitude. Boo then makes his presence felt indirectly through a series of benevolent acts, finally intervening in a dangerous situation to protect Jem and Scout. Scout's continuing moral education is twofold: to resist abusing others with unfounded negativity, but also the necessity of perseverance when these values are inevitably, and sometimes violently, subverted. **AF**

The Country Girls

Edna O'Brien

Lifespan | *b.* 1932 (Ireland)
First Published |1960, by Hutchinson (London)
Trilogy Published | *Country Girls Trilogy and Epilogue* (1986)

Sick of the privations and oppressions of the convent school where they have been sent to board, Caithleen, the narrator of *The Country Girls*, and her best friend, Baba, compose an obscene letter about one of the nuns and leave it where they know it will be found. Duly expelled and sent home, they are met by Caithleen's furious father, who strikes his daughter's face. Edna O'Brien's first novel shows girls growing up in the shadow of the patriarchal family and the Church, the twin powers that dominate gossip-ridden small town east Clare, where it is largely set. The heroines' irreverent, pleasure-seeking temperament is irreconcilably at odds with the claustrophobic limitations of that world, vividly depicted in the novel, and their eventual departure for Dublin is inevitable.

In *The Country Girls* the author subtly conceals her own more complex understanding and brings her narrator's artless impulsiveness to the foreground. Caithleen's narrative is impressionistic rather than reflective, focused on the pains and pleasures of the everyday: the nastiness of the convent soup, her enjoyment of *Tender Is the Night*, dressing up to go out on the town. Unlike Baba, Caithleen nurses romantic illusions, not least about the clammy-handed "Mr. Gentleman" who pursues her in Clare and tries to seduce her after her flight to the capital. She has yet to discover that to seek happiness through love, sex, and men is not necessarily to find it, as the two succeeding novels in O'Brien's trilogy were to show. **MR**

Our Ancestors

Italo Calvino

Lifespan | *b.* 1923 (Cuba), *d.* 1985 (Italy)
First Published | 1960
First Published by | G. Einaudi (Turin)
Original Title | *I nostri antenati*

Calvino's *Our Ancestors* is a trilogy of three romances, beginning with *The Cloven Viscount* (1951), the story of Viscount Medardo of Terralba who, hit by a Turkish cannon ball, returns home split into two halves, one good and one bad. The subsequent two books were no less strange. In *The Baron in the Trees*, Baron Cosimo, at the age of twelve, takes to the trees following a family quarrel, never to set foot on earth again. *The Nonexistent Knight* tells the story of a soldier in Charlemagne's army, Agilulf, who turns out to be nothing but an empty suit of armor. In all these tales, Calvino links up to quite different traditions than his Italian contemporaries: the stories of Stevenson, Voltaire's *Candide*, medieval romance, and Sicilian puppet theater. In doing so, he offers his readers breathtaking parables of modern humanity. Baron Cosimo's life, as he embarks on a series of adventures with thieves and outsiders, corresponding from his aerial perch with Denis Diderot, can be seen as a parable of the Enlightenment's questioning of values. Similarly, Viscount Medardo's story can be read as a metaphor for the Cold War. Agilulf's tale has much in common with science fiction's soulless androids that address our fears of turning into heartless company bureaucrats. Calvino discovered in this trilogy a central truth of fiction writing: that only by approaching a subject indirectly can the artist give it life. As Calvino puts it: "through all these literary filters I may have managed to express myself far better than if I had started from my own experience." **PT**

How It Is

Samuel Beckett

Lifespan | *b.* 1906 (Ireland), *d.* 1989 (Paris)
First Published | 1960, by Les Editions de Minuit
Original Title | *Comment c'est*
Nobel Prize for Literature | 1969

Following the Second World War, nothing occupied Beckett so much as the idea that his writing should be as difficult to imagine and to desire as it possibly could be. There is nothing in the English language comparable with *How It Is*, a novel that both ends and cannot ever end itself with every sentence. It ends not only itself, but also the whole tradition of the novel conceived from the nineteenth century onward, as a grand historical effort to bring literature up to date with the infinite detail of social and moral existence. Detail is erased and replaced by an exhausting round of repetitions and automatic verbal reflexes, uttered by a body barely crawling through mud, listing the contents of a sack, straining to contrive even the outline of a story or remembrance as if empty and straining to defecate.

Beckett ejects from his last full-length novel even the caricature of linear narration that sustained him through *The Unnamable*, sinking instead into a prose so unsustainable and so much like pathological or obsessive utterance that it barely allows the composition of a paragraph. We now receive only the poltergeist of grammar, only the leveled succession of clauses without punctuation, none and all of which are subordinate clauses. There is the shadow, or recollection, of a plot, flickering through the language. But read this book for what it does to how language is and to how we are in consequence. In its most suspended animation, Beckett's prose turns into poetry. **KS**

The Violent Bear It Away

Flannery O'Connor

Lifespan | *b.* 1925 (U.S.), *d.* 1964
First Published | 1960, by Farrar, Straus & Giroux (N.Y.)
First Chapter Published as Short Story | *You Can't be Any Poorer Than Dead* (*New World Writing*, 1955)

Flannery O'Connor's second novel is one of fervor and religious ecstasy, with a violent, distinctly Southern God of penance and vengeance. Francis Tarwater is a fourteen-year-old orphan stolen by his great-uncle Mason (a backwoods preacher of apocalypse) to be raised as a prophet. Tarwater prefers the fire of moonshine to that of prophesy, and when Mason dies in his shack Tarwater burns it down to deny him Resurrection. He goes to his uncle Rayber, who had also been abducted by Mason, but had rebelled. Yet Tarwater cannot escape his vocation when he is compelled to baptize Rayber's retarded son, Bishop. Rayber eventually consents to the baptism while on a fishing trip. He watches as Tarwater drowns his son to prove to himself that he is not a prophet. Tarwater returns to the woods— after being drugged and raped and setting fire to a forest. Once there he finally answers God.

Like her God, O'Connor does not indulge in subtlety. The battle for the soul is not for the meek. Brilliantly capturing the voice and religious extravagance of the South, she paints it big. Characters fall hard; sins are cardinal sins. There is seismic violence—and grace—around every corner. Devoutly Catholic, O'Connor was diagnosed early with lupus, which she had seen kill her father. She knew God was merciless and did not doubt in her own suffering. Why should she spare her characters? Her God worked in mysterious ways; "what's left after everything else has been explained." **GT**

Catch-22

Joseph Heller

First published in 1961, Joseph Heller's frenetic satire on the madness of war and the excesses of bureaucracy has now been canonized as a cult classic. The novel tells the story of Captain Joseph Yossarian, a member of a U.S. bomber crew stationed on the Mediterranean island of Pianosa during the Second World War. Unmoved by patriotic ideals or abstract notions of duty, Yossarian interprets the entire war as a personal attack and becomes convinced that the military is deliberately trying to send him to an untimely death. He therefore spends much of the book concocting evermore inventive ways of escaping his missions—faking various medical conditions, oscillating between sanity and insanity, trapped in the circular logic of his "Catch-22" situation (the phrase that has become Heller's gift to the English language). Heller inserts a cast of manic, cartoonish characters into the island's hothouse environment—from demented disciplinarian Colonel Scheisskopf to Milo Minderbinder, a ruthless profiteer.

Heller presents war as a form of institutional insanity, a psychosis that overtakes the machinery of public and private life. *Catch-22* turns its back on conventional notions of heroism and "fighting the good fight," in order to place war in a much broader psychological, sociological, and economic context. Hilariously funny, the novel's insights are also deadly serious, stretching far beyond the limits of peacenik propaganda. It marks a major departure from the austere, realist approach that had dominated U.S. war fiction until the sweeping changes of the 1960s. Alongside works by Roth, Vonnegut, and Pynchon, *Catch-22* opened the floodgates for a wave of U.S. fiction in which war was represented with a new, countercultural sensibility in a language every bit as wild, grotesque, and bizarre as the real thing. **SamT**

Lifespan | *b.* 1923 (U.S.), *d.* 1999
First Published | 1961
First Published by | Simon & Schuster (New York)
Sequel | *Closing Time* (1994)

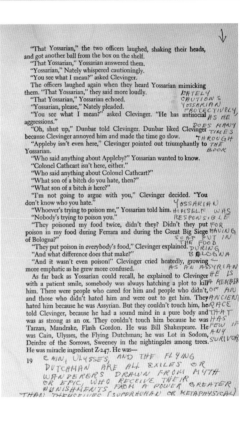

The writing of *Catch-22* was a lengthy process: Heller wrote the first section in 1953 while working as an advertising copywriter.

Heller is shown here in 1974, when his second novel was published, thirteen years after *Catch-22*, a hard act to follow.

The Prime of Miss Jean Brodie

Muriel Spark

Lifespan | *b.* 1918 (Scotland), *d.* 2006 (Italy)
First Published | 1961
First Published by | Macmillan & Co. (London)
Stage Adaptation | 1966

Out of one
Jean Brodie
would come
a whole
generation of
Jean Brodies
experimenting
with sex, society
and everything
else.

20th Century-Fox presents

THE PRIME OF
MISS JEAN BRODIE

MAGGIE SMITH
ROBERT STEPHENS · PAMELA FRANKLIN · GORDON JACKSON · CELIA JOHNSON
Produced by ROBERT FRYER · Directed by RONALD NEAME · Adapted from the Novel by MURIEL SPARK · Based on the Play by JAY PRESSON ALLEN
Screenplay by JAY PRESSON ALLEN · Music by ROD McKUEN · Colour by DE LUXE

"'You will end up as a Girl Guide leader in a suburb like Corstorphine,' she said warningly to Eunice, who was in fact secretly attracted to this idea . . . "

◉ Maggie Smith won a Best Actress Oscar for her portrayal of Muriel Spark's quirky fascist-leaning teacher in the 1969 movie.

◉ Spark, photographed here in 1960, was educated at an Edinburgh girl's school not unlike the one at which Miss Brodie is employed.

The qualities of Spark's best-known work *The Prime of Miss Jean Brodie* as a novel, have been obscured by the popularity of the stage show and movie versions. Phrases such as the "crème de la crème" have entered popular consciousness, without the sophistication of Spark's overlapping purposes receiving the same recognition. From Miss Brodie's chilling Jesuitical assertion—"Give me a girl at an impressionable age, and she is mine for life"—through to the novel's dark conclusions, Spark poses a series of difficult questions about education, femininity, and authoritarianism. The very allure and asperity of Miss Brodie cut back into the elegant severity of Muriel Spark's own style and artifice. For all the minor trappings of glamour, Miss Brodie's deluded romanticizing is matter for this novel's inquiry into the authority of Spark's omniscient narrator. While maintaining an eminently readable narrative form, the novel is also as self-critical about its construction as any formalist could wish.

The story overlaps a number of time frames and alternative perspectives, notably the retrospective judgements of different members of the Brodie set that pepper the novel. This provides hints as to the ultimate unfolding of the modest rise and nasty downfall of an inspiring but dangerous teacher, the eponymous Jean Brodie. Miss Brodie teaches her charges with a reductive but inspiring severity that verges on criminal propaganda for authoritarianism, molding them as her *fascisti*. Tapping into the strange sadomasochistic fantasies of pedagogical crushes and schoolroom sexual tensions, the novel works through the curiously ineffective consequences of this "education" on the Brodie set, seen darkly through pupil Sandy Stranger's eyes. Satirical comedy as political diagnosis, it brings the morality of teaching and storytelling into stark relief: a delight. **DM**

Cat and Mouse

Günter Grass

> "Still practicing, the cat came closer. Mahlke's Adam's apple attracted attention because it was large, always in motion, and threw a shadow. Between me and Mahlke the caretaker's black cat tensed for a leap."

⊙ An outspoken participant in German politics, Grass wrote his Danzig novels partly as a critique of amnesia about the Nazi past.

Lifespan | *b.* 1927 (Poland)
First Published | 1961, by Luchterhand (Neuwied)
Original Title | *Katz und Maus: eine Novelle*
Nobel Prize for Literature | 1999

Grass was born in Danzig in 1927 and with *Cat and Mouse*, the central work in the Danzig Trilogy (the others being *The Tin Drum* and *Dog Years*), he attempts to recapture the past of that city and understand the impact of Naziism upon it. The novel presents wider historical events through the eyes of a small group of children, allowing the author to ground the narrative in his memory of the city and its people. Its central and elusive figure, Joachim Mahlke, dreams of becoming a clown and becomes instead a war hero. He is an outsider and possibly a Pole who refuses to bow to the pressure the regime places upon him to conform and to believe. His mysterious life satirizes Nazi preoccupation with heroism and hero worship; the other children hold him in awe and reverence, while he holds the regime in something approaching contempt. His desire to be a clown stems from his desire to perform for others, to be watched and admired, and it enables Grass to explore the contradictions at the heart of many of those raised to the rank of hero within the Nazi era.

The story, told by his friend Pilenz, is written as a confessional, a format that deliberately mirrors and engages with the postwar attempts to "confess" the Nazi past and thereby receive absolution. The novel moves between comic fantasy, brutality, realism, and myth; between moments of almost lyrical beauty and horrific violence. It is also in constant dialogue with its own storytelling, the distorting power of memory, and the impossibility of reconciliation. **JM**

Solaris

Stanislaw Lem

Lifespan | *b.* 1921 (Poland), *d.* 2006
First Published | 1961, by Wydawnictwo (Warsaw)
Original Language | Polish
Movie Adaptation Released | 1972, 2002

Science fiction has always been an obsessively debated literary category. For outspoken Polish writer Stanislaw Lem, who spent much of his career dismissing American science fiction as kitsch commercial fodder, its shortcomings were all too plain. It is no small irony then that his 1961 novel *Solaris* has become one of the undisputed classics of the genre, spawning two cinema adaptations (Andrei Tarkovsky's in 1972 and Steven Soderbergh's in 2002). Predictably, Lem poured scorn on them both.

The initial premise of *Solaris* is almost textbook: human scientists try and fail to make contact with aliens from the eponymous planet. Solaris is covered by an oceanlike organism whose intelligence outwits them continually. Their attempts to understand it are thrown back on themselves; their experiments reveal only their own psychological weaknesses. Kris Kelvin, the protagonist, is gradually destroyed by memories of his suicidal lover, whose image, regenerated by Solaris, haunts him. The other characters are in turn plagued by unspecified traumas. Perhaps what the movies could never capture is the book's distinctive tone: dispassionate academic language describes inexplicable phenomena on the planet that our protagonists can never hope to comprehend. By revealing the absolute alienness of that oft-imagined fantasy world beyond our blue planet, Lem suggests a new literary hybrid. Part Kafka, part Huxley, here is an unmapped mutation of sci-fi that is compelling precisely because of its refusal to be explained. **ABl**

Faces in the Water

Janet Frame

Lifespan | *b.* 1924 (New Zealand), *d.* 2004
First Published | 1961
First Published by | Pegasus Press (Christchurch)
Order of New Zealand Awarded | 1990

This novel is one of the most powerful descriptions of mental illness ever written. Although a work of fiction, *Faces in the Water* is informed by Frame's own experience as a patient (wrongfully diagnosed with schizophrenia) in a New Zealand mental asylum.

Istina Mavet, the novel's main character, relates her experiences on the wards of Cliffhaven and Treecroft hospitals in a highly lyrical but disjointed fashion. Through her gaze, we see the deplorable conditions of these institutions, the horrible side effects of electroconvulsive shock therapy, insulin-induced comas, and lobotomies, as well as the occasional kindnesses and more frequent cruelties of the on-site psychiatric nurses.

The book is a biting critique of the mistreatment of the mentally ill and the gross power differential between medical "professional" and patient. While the skillful way in which the novel makes this point is enough to make it memorable, the prose's striking quality elevates it to a truly great novel. Istina's thoughts and narrative descriptions combine an accomplished lyricism with the fractured digressions and associations symptomatic of psychological trauma. Istina's psychological disturbance is unmistakable at times, but her ability to narrate these experiences is what sets her apart from her mostly inarticulate fellow patients. Frame herself won release from the mental institution in which she was a patient after eight years, an escape she attributed to publication of her book *The Lagoon and Other Stories* in 1951. **CG-G**

A Severed Head

Iris Murdoch

Lifespan | *b.* 1919 (Ireland), *d.* 1999
First Published | 1961
First Published by | Chatto & Windus (London)
Married Name | Mrs. J. O. Bayley

As Martin Lynch-Gibbon enjoys a lazy afternoon in his mistress' apartment he ponders his life. He has no intention of leaving his slightly older wife, Antonia, but nonetheless he relishes his liaisons with Georgie. Only blithely aware of Georgie's emotional needs, Martin is obtuse and complacent, despite his self-conscious civility and middle-class propriety—and ripe for moral education. This education comes in the form of the compelling, demonic Honor Klein, an anthropologist with something of the primitive about her, but who stands for truth and unmasking. Martin is shocked when he learns that his wife wishes to leave him for Klein's half brother, Palmer, but can readjust himself as a sort of a child to their surrogate parenting. Honor cuts through the cant and fake civility of this arrangement. When Martin learns that Antonia has also been having an affair with his brother, and when Honor exposes the truth about his relationship with Georgie, Martin's world comes undone.

A Severed Head has all the antic sexuality of a restoration comedy, yet chimes resonantly with the 1960s revolution in values and sexual mores. It uses surprise and suspense, incorporates farce and melodrama, balances its unlikely plot elements, integrates symbolism and imagery into its realist structure, and manages to comment wisely on the stupidities of human relationships. **RMcD**

❸ Murdoch combined a flair for plot and character with an interest in currents of thought such as psychoanalysis and existentialism.

Franny and Zooey

J. D. Salinger

Lifespan | *b.* 1919 (U.S.)
First Published | 1961, by Little, Brown & Co. (Bost.)
Published as Short Stories | *Franny* (1955), *Zooey* (1957) in *New Yorker* magazine

The notoriety of *The Catcher in the Rye* has had the effect of deflecting attention both from J.D. Salinger's other writings and from what remains the essential quality of his writing in general: it is all about the details, rather than the broad strokes of disaffection and alienation. *Franny and Zooey* is almost entirely composed of details. A lopsided pair of stories about two children of the Glass family, the "novel" almost has the air of a minor work or sketch because of its deformed structure and apparently unfocused story-telling. Yet it deals throughout with ideas that are to be found at the edges of Salinger's other books, in particular the egotism and "phoniness" of people who, particularly as a result of intellectualism or religion, believe they can provide absolutes and remove the need to keep addressing daily the events of their lives.

Salinger's interest in Eastern religion—especially the rejection of absolutes and the refusal to provide anything as guaranteed—is at its clearest at the center of *Franny and Zooey*. The Glass family's youngest children are tormented by an idea that they move toward grasping as the novel progresses, the idea that learning, religion, and even happiness have been reduced to commodities. As such, each and every choice, irrespective of what it concerns, has the potential to be negative or positive. In the modern world, where all that many people desire is a lifestyle that removes the need to think constantly about their lives, the parallels with Salinger's apparently minor work are all too clear. **SF**

Stranger in a Strange Land

Robert Heinlein

Lifespan | *b.* 1907 (U.S.), *d.* 1998
First Published |1961
First Published by | Putnam (New York)
Hugo Award | 1961

A strange and disturbing book, which won the 1962 Hugo Prize and rocked the science fiction world, Heinlein's *Stranger in a Strange Land* not only gave science fiction books a place on mainstream bookshelves, but also became an emblem of the 1960s counterculture movement toward free love and unconstrained living. It tells the story of Valentine Michael Smith, the orphaned son of the first Mars explorers, who has been raised by Martians and returned to Earth by a second human mission. Although by the time he comes back to Earth Smith is in his twenties, he looks on the world with the eyes of a child, as he faces the arduous task of learning to be human. He has never seen a woman and has no knowledge of human culture or religions. Smith preaches his message of spirituality and free love and disseminates the psychic powers he learned on Mars. As time goes on, he converts many people to his way of thinking and becomes a messiah-like figure, with explosive results. The story is a reflection on the conceits of its time, a sprawling satire of the human condition that takes in love, politics, sex, and, above all, organized religion, which is seen as a sham. The fact that in reality several religious movements emerged as a result of people reading the novel must have been alarming to an author whose message seems to reveal a frustration at people's desire to follow prophets and causes. **EF**

The Garden of the Finzi-Continis

Giorgio Bassani

Lifespan | *b.* 1916 (Italy), *d.* 2000
First Published | 1962, by G. Einaudi (Turin)
Movie Adaptation Released | 1970
Original Title | *Il giardino dei Finzi-Contini*

Bassani's novel is a moving story of Italy in the 1920s and 1930s, as Fascism starts to take hold and seep into every aspect of ordinary life. The narrator is a frequent visitor to the splendid walled garden of the Finzi-Continis, a wealthy, cosmopolitan, and popular Jewish family in the prosperous Ferrara. This town was also one of the key Fascist strongholds, but this dramatic irony escapes the narrator. He loves and admires the graceful, eccentric family and becomes increasingly absorbed in the garden's pleasures as events make the world outside more threatening; soon his world has shrunk to this small space. He falls in love with the beautiful, mysterious Micòl, but they both have to watch her brother, Alberto, waste away and die from a mysterious illness. Micòl, who grasps that she has no future, is forced to withdraw from all forms of public life, abandoning hopes of a brilliant career. Eventually even the myopic narrator starts to understand what is happening, and the novel reaches its sad, inevitable conclusion. This novel of corrupted innocence and blighted talent and opportunity is also an indictment of ordinary citizens too blind to see the threat of creeping authoritarianism and prejudice. While affirming ordinary human values of friendship and kindness, it shows what happened to Italy when it made the fatal error of uniting with Nazi Germany— a moral vacuum rendered the beauty and intelligence of Italian culture vulnerable and delusive. **AH**

Girl with Green Eyes

Edna O'Brien

Lifespan | b. 1932 (Ireland)
First Published | 1962
First Published by | Jonathan Cape (London)
Kingsley Amis Award | 1962

Originally published as *The Lonely Girl*, this is the second novel of *The Country Girls* trilogy narrated by naïve convent girl Caithleen Brady. After moving to Dublin with her childhood friend Baba, Caithleen (the shier and less streetwise of the two) becomes involved with Eugene, a filmmaker several years her senior, who is married but estranged from his wife. Perhaps inevitably, it is a fundamentally imbalanced romance, and Eugene exerts disproportionate control over their relationship. Caithleen's family's vehement disapproval forces a confrontation between the Catholic values of her upbringing and the changing cultural attitudes of the 1960s. Her desire to pursue a sexual relationship puts her at odds with strict Irish religious mores at the time, but Caithleen's moral conflict contrasts starkly with Eugene's inability to understand religious observance of any kind.

Upon its publication in 1962, the novel won critical acclaim for its frank, fresh, unpretentious portrayal of a young woman's experiences. Both the subject matter and O'Brien's explicit treatment of it were to prove contentious in her native Ireland, however, and the Irish Censorship Board banned all three novels of the trilogy. O'Brien's willingness to engage with the culturally sensitive issues of the period makes her writing of the first importance. Her sensitivity to the realities of individual experience within a defined social milieu makes this novel unmissable. **JW**

"They used to ban my books, but now when I go there, [Irish] people are courteous to my face, though rather slanderous behind my back."

O'Brien, Writers at Work, 1986

◉ O'Brien was born in County Clare and educated in a convent school—one of the Irish "country girls" that people her novels.

Labyrinths

Jorge Luis Borges

Lifespan | *b.* 1899 (Argentina), *d.* 1986 (Switzerland)
First Published | 1962
First Published by | New Directions (New York)
Original Language | English

Borges never wrote a novel. A novel would be either unnecessary or unfinished. Instead there are these "episodes," brought together in *Labyrinths*, a collection of his major works, comprising some of his most important short stories and most challenging essays. Here the reader can see the impact of vast ideas on tiny spots of history and individuals; the perspective of one person seeing the infinite for the first and only time. Borges' lucid prose, at once melancholy and scientific, is the ideal vehicle for tales of unending libraries, dreamers who are dreamt in turn, and men paralyzed by the inability to forget anything at all.

Fictions, essays, and parables—the range of his reading and inspiration is evident. Pascal, Kafka, Judas, and Bernard Shaw all put in appearances. As André Maurois says: "Borges has read everything and especially what no one reads anymore." From Old Norse sagas to Arab philosophy, Borges favors the trick of reading between the lines, making the unseen connections and realizing the immense, sometimes terrible implications. Despite separation into the three genres, all the pieces operate on similar levels. There is a constant wonder at the potential of both mankind and the universe, a certain irony about the actions of individuals and an elusive sadness at the ending of things. Magical realism, intertextuality, and postmodernist trickery are all here, fresh and absorbing, before the burden of such descriptions. Somewhere in Borges all the reading and writing in the world has already been done. **JS**

The Golden Notebook

Doris Lessing

Lifespan | *b.* 1919 (Iran)
First Published | 1962
First Published by | Michael Joseph (London)
Prix Medicis | 1976

When, in 1972, Margaret Drabble characterized Doris Lessing as a "Cassandra in a world under siege," she brought into focus what has become a truism in the reception of Lessing's writing: namely, that we read her to find out "what's going on," for an independent "diagnosis" of the dilemmas of our individual and collective lives. First published in 1962, *The Golden Notebook* was immediately taken up—or, in Lessing's terms, "belittled"—as a crucial intervention in the so-called sex war. It was seen as a literary plea for psychic and political change in the lives of the "free women" at the book's heart. It is a complex novel, narrated through the four notebooks that divide, and contain, the life of the protagonist, Anna Wulf. As a struggling writer and single mother closely associated with the Communist Party through the 1950s, Wulf is the figure through whom Lessing writes about the conflicts of sexuality and sexual difference, politics and creativity—and, in particular, the theme of breakdown—that is omnipresent throughout the book. The crisis of political belief that shadowed the British Communist Party through the 1950s, the paranoia of the Cold War, is refracted through both the crisis of imagination that afflicts Anna Wulf as a writer and the disturbance in the relationship between the sexes that so preoccupies her as a "modern" woman. **VL**

> Lessing grew up in Southern Rhodesia—now Zimbabwe—where she learned the political activism that infuses her writing.

The Drowned World

J. G. Ballard

Lifespan | *b.* 1910 (China)
First Published | 1962
First Published by | V. Gollancz (London)
Full Name | James Graham Ballard

In 2145, climate change has caused the polar ice caps to melt, turning cities into steaming tropical swamps. Increased radiation has triggered mutations in the Earth's ecological systems, causing them to revert to more primitive evolutionary stages. This scenario allows Ballard's considerable descriptive powers full rein to generate haunting surrealistic imagery of a transfigured London where colossal Triassic vegetation is juxtaposed with the rotting detritus of human civilization. The characters feel compelled by ambiguous motives to remain in this inhospitable landscape of primeval lagoons and jungle flora, abandoned hotels, rusting cars, and dead neon signs.

The novel is not interested in showing humanity's triumph in the face of impossible odds, but is more concerned with the mind's capacity for change. The protagonist, Kerans, comes to understand that the landscape is causing human consciousness to devolve along with it. Many of the characters experience "deepdreams" that erode the borders of fantasy and reality, self and other, and reset their body clocks to "archeopsychic" temporality, as they edge toward mental states before and beyond ego identity. Kerans accepts and ultimately welcomes the emergence of atavistic mind states and the collapse of civilization. By mapping the processes of psychic adaptation in response to changes in the exterior environment, Ballard's novel suggests that we will eventually be led beyond ourselves, necessitating a redefinition of consciousness and what it means to be human. **SS**

Pale Fire

Vladimir Nabokov

Lifespan | *b.* 1899 (Russia), *d.* 1977 (Switzerland)
First Published | 1962
First Published by | Putnam (New York)
Original Language | English

Entering a web of reflections, imputations, madness, neighborliness, gayness, exiled royalty, murder, and literary criticism, it is hard to discern any stable world outside the text of Nabokov's novel. With astonishing literary dexterity, Nabokov takes to considerable lengths here the notion that writing need be about nothing but itself. The novel is divided into two parts: the four cantos of the poem "Pale Fire," attributed to invented author John Shade, and their annotated exegesis written, after Shade's death, by his friend, neighbor, and editor, Charles Kinbote. The poem and its notes, along with Kinbote's explanatory preface and index, form the novel's entire substance. Shade's poem is an apparently uncomplicated reflection upon his life, his daughter's suicide, and his Christian thoughts on the nature of divine order. Kinbote's notes suggest that he believes himself to be Charles the Beloved, king of an obscure European country called Zembla. Escaping to the United States from revolution, Charles pseudonymously took up a post at Wordsmith University alongside his favorite poet, John Shade, whom he befriended and whose work he claims to understand. In his opinion, "Pale Fire" is really a coded history of Zembla. Is Kinbote an editor, a stalker, a madman, or an academic? Or is he a fiction supplied by a Shade writing his own annotations? Welcome to the funhouse. **DH**

◗ Nabokov is photographed in 1958 on a butterfly hunt—he was a distinguished lepidopterist as well as an elusive novelist.

A Clockwork Orange

Anthony Burgess

A Clockwork Orange, Burgess' best-known work, shot to fame following Stanley Kubrick's controversial 1971 movie adaptation. The novel was inspired by a group of Russian teddy-boy ruffians Burgess encountered in St. Petersburg. It is narrated by teenage hooligan Alex and dotted with Russian-derived slang. Alex, along with his friends and followers Dim, Pete, and Georgie, leads a life of violence—beating up an old man and raping his wife as part of a normal night out. When Alex is set up, arrested, and sent to prison, he is chosen for a new, Pavlovian style anti-violence treatment called "Ludovico's technique." Soon, if so much as a violent thought passes through Alex's mind he feels ill, and his treatment is hailed as a great success. When Alex is released from prison, unable to fight back, he is beaten and left for dead in a field before being rescued by the very man he attacked at the beginning of the novel. Following his failed suicide attempt, while Alex is still unconscious, government psychologists reverse Ludovico's technique. For a time he reverts to his old violent ways, but by the end of the book he is thinking about settling down. In the U.S. edition of *A Clockwork Orange*, the last chapter was removed—against Burgess' will—because it was thought to be too sentimental.

The novel is a comment on what the author saw as society's will to swallow up individual freedom and the rise of mass popular culture in the early 1960s, which brought a new rebellious conformism. Burgess rails against the psychological conditioning techniques of the time, which he thought were abhorrent. Alex's free choice of leaving the violence behind brings him to a final moral level infinitely higher than the forced harmlessness of his conditioning—a complete freedom. **EF**

Lifespan | *b.* 1917 (England), *d.* 1993
First Published | 1962
First Published by | W. Heinemann (London)
Movie Adaptation Released | 1971

⌃ Penguin's Pop Art-influenced cover for the novel offers a faceless, dehumanized image of Alex, the violent leader of the Droogs.

◁ Burgess was an exceptionally prolific writer—*A Clockwork Orange* was one of five novels he published between 1960 and 1962.

One Flew Over the Cuckoo's Nest

Ken Kesey

Lifespan | *b.* 1935 (U.S.), *d.* 2001
First Published | 1962
First Published by | Viking Press (New York)
Movie Adaptation Released | 1975

"'I been silent so long now it's gonna roar out of me . . .'"

Kesey become a hero of the 1960s hippie counterculture, leading the hallucinogen-inspired Pranksters in trips on the Magic Bus.

Kesey's novel depicts a mental asylum in which repeated attempts to diagnose the patients as insane are conceived as part of a larger scheme to produce pliant, docile subjects across the United States. A key text for the antipsychiatry movement of the 1960s, it addresses the relationship between sanity and madness, conformity and rebellion. The novel remains finely balanced throughout. It is never clear, for example, whether the so-called "Combine" is, in actuality, a boundless authority designed to ensure social control across the whole population, or a projection of the narrator Chief Bromden's paranoid imagination. Also, the question of whether insanity, to quote R. D. Laing, "might very well be a state of health in a mad world," or at least an appropriate form of social rebellion, is raised but never quite answered.

Into the sterile, hermetically sealed world of the asylum wanders Randall P. McMurphy, a modern day "cowboy" with a "sideshow swagger" who disrupts the ward's smooth running and challenges the near-total authority of the steely Nurse Ratched. Insofar as McMurphy's acts of rebellion assume mostly self-interested forms, the novel's efforts at political mobilization fall short, and there remains something uneasy about its racial and gender politics. It takes the "cowboy" McMurphy to save the "Indian" Bromden and, in the era of civil rights and feminism, the white male patients are painted as "victims of a matriarchy," ably supported by a cabal of black orderlies. But Kesey's impressive attempts to come to grips with the amorphous nature of modern power—a power not necessarily tied to leaders or even institutions—make this a prescient, foreboding work. If McMurphy's fate is what awaits those who push too hard against the system, then Bromden's sanity depends upon not turning a blind eye to injustice and exploitation. **AP**

The Collector

John Fowles

The Collector was John Fowles' first published novel, a precocious and original text that points toward the later innovations of *The Magus* (1965) and *The French Lieutenant's Woman* (1969). Yet unlike the radical experimentation with narrative and generic expectations that characterize his later texts, the virtue of *The Collector* lies in its simplicity.

Frederick Clegg is an orphan: neglected, ill-educated, and a collector of butterflies. He admires from afar a local art student, Miranda, who appears to offer the prospect of a better life, a life with beauty. When he miraculously wins a substantial amount of money, he takes events into his own hands and kidnaps her, keeping her locked in his basement, but attending to her every whim. She can have anything she wants, except her freedom. Fowles' masterstroke is to shift fundamentally the narrative perspective a third of the way into the text; it is so powerful because it suddenly demonstrates to us as readers how fully we have inhabited Clegg's mind—the mind of a kidnapper. We are then given access to the secret diaries Miranda keeps during her captivity, and it is through them that we see her character develop and her awareness of that development. Imperceptibly, the bond between kidnapper and prisoner also becomes apparent. The prevailing allusions to *The Tempest* are instructive, too—Clegg fashions himself as Ferdinand, the lover of Miranda, yet in her diaries Miranda characterizes him as her Caliban. Just as in Shakespeare's play, Fowles asks us to think about who is representing whom. Fowles has described *The Collector* as a "parable," and it has a spartan logic that suits the term. In this, as in the desperate circumstances of the climax, Fowles' skills as a novelist are abundantly apparent. The nightmare is only truly recognized when it is over. **MD**

Lifespan | *b.* 1926 (England), *d.* 2005
First Published | 1963
First Published by | Jonathan Cape (London)
Movie Adaptation Released | 1968

". . . first time I saw her, I knew she was the only one."

Fowles is photographed in 1970 at Lyme Regis, Dorset, the setting for his later novel *The French Lieutenant's Woman*.

One Day in the Life of Ivan Denisovich

Aleksandr Isayevich Solzhenitsyn

Lifespan | *b.* 1918 (Russia)
First Published | 1963, by Sovetskii pisatel (Moscow)
Original Title | *Odin den Ivana Denisovicha*
Exiled from Soviet Union | 1974

"Better to . . . submit. If you were stubborn they broke you."

⬆ In the early 1960s the Soviet authorities allowed Solzhenitsyn to address foreign journalists, but he soon fell out of favor again.

⬇ A rare photograph of Solzhenitsyn as an anonymous convict during the eight years that he spent in Soviet labor camps.

This contemporary literary classic is quite literally what it says it is: a single day in the life of a prisoner in a Stalinist labor camp in 1951. Ivan Denisovich Shukov is punished with three days in solitary confinement for not getting out of bed, but the threat is idle, and he only has to wash a floor before being taken back to breakfast. As the day goes on, the reader gains insight into the workers' suffering and companionship, and the uneasy coexistence between the prisoners and guards. At the end of the day, Ivan is lucky to be rewarded with a few extra mouthfuls of food from another inmate and thanks God for getting him through another day. This day, we find out at the end, is just one out of 3,653 of Ivan's prison existence. Ivan is an unlikely protagonist for Russian literature of this time, being a peasant, a normal man, and possibly illiterate. He represents the uneducated and persecuted mainstream of Soviet society. Despite his background, however, Ivan develops an inner dignity as he builds some meaning out of his mundane and degrading camp existence, transcending his surroundings with a spiritual intensity. Throughout, the story reverberates with the desperate dehumanization of the prisoners; the unjust punishments and arbitrary rules that reduce men to mere numbers. Yet despite the degradation a hope rings out as the twin strengths of camaraderie and faith help the men to survive.

Solzhenitsyn was arrested in 1945 for criticizing Stalin in a private letter, spending eight years of his life in labor camps similar to the one he describes here. In 1962, he became famous with this novel's publication, a landmark event in the history of Soviet literature. This memorable work was the first public recognition of the existence of the labor camps and the hideous conditions endured by their inmates. **EF**

The Bell Jar

Sylvia Plath

Lifespan | *b.* 1932 (U.S.), *d.* 1963 (England)
First Published | 1963
First Published by | W. Heinemann (London)
Pseudonym | Victoria Lucas

Casually described by Sylvia Plath in a letter to her mother as a "pot boiler," *The Bell Jar* has become one of the most notorious depictions of a mental breakdown in American literature. First published in 1963 under the pseudonym Victoria Lucas, the novel provides a thinly disguised autobiographical account of Plath's teenage years. It covers the life of Esther, from her spell as a guest editor of a teen magazine to her failed suicide attempt and the crude care of mid twentieth-century American psychiatry. Initially celebrated for its dry self-deprecation and ruthless honesty, it has been subsequently read as a damning critique of 1950s social politics. Plath makes clear connections between Esther's dawning awareness of the limited female roles available to her and her increasing sense of isolation and paranoia. Esther's eventual recovery relies upon her ability to dismiss the dominant versions of femininity represented by the false role models that populate the novel. Yet concern with the stifling atmosphere of 1950s America is not limited to examination of gender. The opening sentence—"It was a queer sultry summer, the summer they electrocuted the Rosenbergs"—very precisely locates the novel in Cold War McCarthyism and makes implicit connections between Esther's experiences and the other paranoias and betrayals that characterized the decade. **NM**

◉ Plath types in the backyard of her family home in Massachusetts in 1954, the year after the breakdown described in *The Bell Jar*.

Inside Mr. Enderby

Anthony Burgess

Lifespan | *b.* 1917 (England), *d.* 1993
First Published | 1963
First Published by | W. Heinemann (London)
Pseudonym | Joseph Kell

This novel, the first in a trilogy, makes the case for Burgess as the preeminent comic novelist of the 1960s and 1970s, succeeding Waugh and surpassing Kingsley Amis. Burgess' substance and staying power derive from an intense interest in language, both literary and spoken, and from inspired technical ingenuity. Burgess' ear for pub speech, for example, permits verbal misunderstandings to develop into startling outcomes, always to the disadvantage of the baffled, too-talkative but tough-minded poet Enderby. Inside Mr. Enderby are his guts. He farts and belches incessantly, the exact sounds carefully transcribed by Burgess, a connoisseur of wind. The body's disgustingness is evoked in Rabelaisian mode, as is the domestic filth in which Enderby lives. His other "inside" is his poetry, written with trousers down on the toilet. A series of accidents leads from poetry to marriage to a mental hospital. An epigraph from Jules Laforgue ("Tout le monde est dehors") indicates he should get out more, so *Enderby Outside* appeared in 1968. The trilogy was completed in *A Clockwork Testament* (1974). Burgess writes as a contemporary Catholic, and guilt about sex and masturbation are pervasive, as is a refreshingly innocent prefeminist satire of women. Near death, Enderby's bodily eructations return in language of astonished disgust: "Enderby was suffocated by smells: sulphuretted hydrogen, unwashed armpits, halitosis, feces, standing urine, putrefying meat—all thrust into his mouth and nostrils in squelchy balls." **AMu**

The Girls of Slender Means

Muriel Spark

Lifespan | *b.* 1918 (Scotland), *d.* 2006 (Italy)
First Published | 1963
First Published by | Macmillan & Co. (London)
Shortened Version | *Saturday Evening Post* (1963)

"Long ago in 1945 all the nice people of England were poor."

⬥ Spark is photographed here carrying out research for her 1965 novel *The Mandelbaum Gate*, which involved traveling to Palestine.

Brilliantly constructed, this slender novel combines multiple ironies of tone with a series of allegorical levels of storytelling that develop the different narrative possibilities suggested by the title. Out of the adventures of several more or less slender young ladies coping with postwar austerity, Spark spins a remarkable reworking of Gerard Manley Hopkins' *The Wreck of the Deutschland*. That this unlikely model for an amusing short novel should figure so unobtrusively and effectively indicates some of the underlying seriousness with which Spark blends comic and religious levels of meaning. Apparently trivial details show up fundamentals, without any loss to the seductive surface of plotting and social wit.

Set in the ruins of London toward the end of the Second World War, the novel appears at first to engage a delightfully carefree world of girls living in a residential club for unmarried women and variously on the make. This circumscribed context provides an optic through which to view the wider historical context. Spark's satirical eye is quick to deflate the romantic purposes of youth, male and female, along with withering passages of brief literary pastiche. More than one girl becomes involved with a certain Nicholas Farringdon, and there is plenty of pith and verbal rapacity to amuse and delight. Amid rivalries and the development of peacetime corruption, the plot heads toward an apocalyptic conclusion. The way circumstances bring death suggests the virtues of staying slender, while reminding us that even in the midst of life we are in death, with all that this implies for reflections on mortality. Less decisive readers might care to reflect on Spark's formal ingenuity in offering a metaphysical parable as rigorously well made as it is light and entertaining. A treat for the jaded literary palette. **DM**

The Spy Who Came in From the Cold

John Le Carré

Before Le Carré, the British espionage novel was dominated by the dashing spy, a man of action, either amateur or professional, who reflects a confident civilization—a Richard Hannay or James Bond. With *The Spy Who Came in From the Cold*, Le Carré introduces a much grimmer, antiheroic perspective, a world where there is no clear sense of the democratic West's moral superiority over the communist East.

Set largely in Cold War Germany, the novel is a story of deception at all levels. Dismayed by the East German intelligence service's success in capturing his agents, Lamas, who runs a British operation from Berlin, agrees to become a double agent so that he can sow confusion in East German intelligence by proposing that its head is in the pay of the British. According to plan, Lamas becomes dissolute, leaves "the Service"—Britain's overseas intelligence agency, MI6—and is eventually recruited by the East Germans in the hope of obtaining information about British operations. Part of the book's quality is Le Carré's ability to convey the shabby, unglamorous world of the spy while maintaining a wonderful sense of tension and intrigue. Spying here is an elaborate game, a complex operation of trying to outwit the opposition. What is reality and what constructed fantasy remains unclear. In fact, Lamas, too, discovers that he is actually a pawn in a larger game.

What elevates this book beyond the superior thriller is its critique of the intelligence services' cynical manipulation of their own citizens in playing espionage games, questioning what they are supposed to be protecting. The human cost is high, and it is never obvious that there is any real intelligence to be obtained. Lamas' ultimate recognition of this, and his refusal to abandon an innocent girl, leads to his death. **TH**

Lifespan | *b*. 1931 (England)
First Published | 1963
First Published by | V. Gollancz (London)
Given Name | David John Moore Cornwell

"What do you think spies are: priests, saints, and martyrs?"

David Cornwell, better known as spy novelist John Le Carré, gives the camera a suitably stern and suspicious look in 1967.

Manon des Sources

Marcel Pagnol

Originally published as a two-part novel, *Jean de Florette* and *Manon des Sources* present an epic tragedy involving three generations of Provençal peasants. Cesar Soubeyran and his nephew Ugolin are all that is left of a family cursed with a history of misfortune. To Cesar, known as Papet, the rather simple Ugolin is the last supreme hope of the Soubeyran race. When a hunchback from the city inherits a nearby farm, Papet's exceptional talent for connivance and deception is mobilized. Conscious that acquiring the farm would be a means of restoring wealth and distinction to the Souberyan name, the uncle and nephew patiently plot to bring about the interloper's downfall. The hunchback's daughter, Manon, grows up in the time between the novel's two parts. Ugolin falls desperately in love with her, but far from returning his love her heart is set passionately on avenging the ill treatment of her father. The repercussions of unrequited love ensue, but it is not only Ugolin who suffers this fate.

Marcel Pagnol was born in the hills near Marseille where the novel is set. He spent long summer holidays in the region as a child, among the people who were to inspire his novel's characters. His story is interspersed with entertaining detours, offering vignettes of lives long steeped in the peasant tradition. Best known, in France at least, as a filmmaker and playwright, it was perhaps Pagnol's awareness of the visual that allowed his simple prose style in *Jean de Florette* and *Manon des Sources* to be translated so beautifully into two successful movies by Claude Berri. Starring Daniel Auteuil, Emmanuelle Béart, Gérard Depardieu, and Yves Montand, these movies provide great accompaniments to the novel, but when it comes to a picture of rural French life it is Pagnol's text that provides the richness of detail. **PM**

Lifespan | *b.* 1895 (France), *d.* 1974
First Published | 1963
First Published by | Editions de Provence (Paris)
Sequel to | *Jean de Florette*

"The spring no longer flowed"

↟ Famous in France primarily as a playwright and movie director, Pagnol is shown here with his wife, actress Jacqueline Bouvier.

◁ The bewitching Emmanuelle Béart plays Manon in Claude Berri's highly successful 1986 movie version of Pagnol's epic novel.

The Graduate

Charles Webb

Lifespan | *b.* 1939 (U.S.)
First Published | 1963
First Published by | New American Library (N.Y.)
Movie Adaptation Released | 1967

This 1963 novel is so much eclipsed by the 1967 movie with Anne Bancroft and Dustin Hoffman that we should recall that most of its iconic moments already exist in Webb's text. The advice to go into "plastics" does not, but the underwater diving-suit scene, Benjamin's embarrassment at booking a hotel room for sex, the un-naming of "Mrs. Robinson" (no first name), and Benjamin fighting off Elaine's parents and friends with a crucifix are all in the original. A mild attack on the values of the white American professional middle class, *The Graduate*, in both forms, has become a much admired populist satire.

Mrs. Robinson's alcoholism and silence might signal psychosis, but do not; Benjamin's post-university distress is short of existential dread; the malice of his parents and their friends is harmless in the face of true love. Written in the early 1960s, Webb's satire provided that necessary medium of social criticism on which the harder attitudes of the late 1960s were founded. As fiction, *The Graduate* is notable for its flat and understated but expressive prose. Much hinges on the difference between "What?" and "What." The question mark signals anguish or outrage and warns of imminent distress in personal relationships. "What" without the expected query makes a genuine inquiry of the other person and predicts positive consequences. At the iconic moment when Benjamin and Elaine escape from her wedding on the bus, she says "Benjamin?" and he replies "What." As the bus moves off no more is said. **AMu**

Cat's Cradle

Kurt Vonnegut, Jr

Lifespan | *b.* 1922 (U.S.)
First Published | 1963
First Published by | Holt, Rinehart & Winston (N.Y.)
Alternate Title | *Ice 9*

Felix Hoenikker, father of the A-bomb, is without sin. Rationality abjures abstracts such as morality; he is a man of hard science. Be it nuclear weapons or turtles, Hoenikker is a whirring brain needing occupation. Take away his turtles, and he can blow up Hiroshima. It is when hard science falls to soft humans that things get messy. But Hoenikker's "greatest" creation is Ice-nine, an isotope of water that freezes at room temperature, creating a chain reaction—like the A-bomb or the children's game of cat's cradle—elegant, never ending, and ultimately pointless. Whereas the A-bomb fell short of total annihilation, Ice-nine will do the trick. John, the narrator, while researching a book on the day the bomb was dropped on Hiroshima, stumbles across the Books of Bokonon. Bokonism baldly declares itself a bunch of "shameless lies"; Truth plays no part in religion. The least it can do is offer some comfort. Vonnegut creates a religion in order to mock religion. He also targets technology, the big, destructive twentieth-century lie, which supplants it. The end of the world comes as a roaring whimper, the result of carelessness and laziness—technology and stupidity are a very dangerous alchemy indeed. In *Cat's Cradle* Vonnegut reveals the meaning of life: there is none. But he is a master and can make even the end of the world funny. The serious implications come to us later, after we have our breath back. **GT**

Kurt Vonnegut at home in 1969: a writer obsessed by memories of the destructiveness of war recollected in ironic tranquillity.

V.

Thomas Pynchon

Lifespan | *b.* 1937 (U.S.)
First Published | 1963
First Published by | Lippincott (Philadelphia)
William Faulkner Foundation Award | 1963

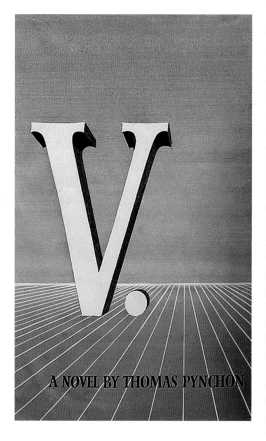

◉ The jacket of the first edition of *V.*, the novel that established
Pynchon as an enigmatic cult hero of American literature.

V. marks the arrival of one of North America's most imaginative and challenging literary talents. The novel is constructed around two separate but interconnected narratives. The first of these concerns the ex-sailor Benny Profane, who bums his way around the eastern seaboard during the mid-1950s in search of odd jobs, kicks, and a sense of identity. In the course of his wanderings, Profane encounters a strange character named Herbert Stencil. Stencil is obsessed with the mysterious figure of V., a woman who manifests herself in different forms at violent flashpoints in twentieth-century history. Stencil's paranoid quest to decode the incarnations and abstractions of V.—who becomes less and less corporeal as the novel progresses—sets up an elaborate second narrative spanning the decades from 1880 to 1943. This wild, panoramic sweep takes in Egypt during the Fashoda crisis, rioting Venezuelan expatriates in Florence, the German occupation of South-West Africa, and much more. Stencil is searching for a unifying order amid the violence and strife, what Pynchon calls "the century's master cabal," the "Plot Which Has No Name." But perhaps the real danger is to be found in the novel's "present"—a modern America profoundly transformed by the Second World War, about to hit boiling point through the social and cultural revolutions of the 1960s. V. establishes many of the themes that continue to occupy Pynchon: the use and abuse of power, the patterns of historiography, the status of marginalized communities, and altered states of perception. It is grandiose, architectural writing, yet also intimate and humane. V. recalls Joyce, Beckett, Kafka, and European surrealism, but ultimately coheres into a remarkable, entirely new kind of contemporary American writing. **SamT**

Herzog

Saul Bellow

The novel that made Saul Bellow's name as a literary best-seller is a comedy of manners and ideas, loss and partial redemption. The cuckolded academic Moses Herzog is neurotically restless, a pathological condition that notably manifests itself in his habit of composing unsent letters to the great and good of past and present times ("Dear Doktor Professor Heidegger, I should like to know what you mean by the expression 'the fall into the quotidian.' When did this fall occur?"). We follow Herzog's musings on the events that have brought him to this state, most notably his amatory betrayal at the hands of his former friend Valentine Gersbach, and we follow him physically as he heads into Chicago for an abortive attempt at bloody revenge. Typically, he ends up arrested for possessing a firearm instead; however, in the process, we find, something may have begun to fall back into place in his life ("At this time he had no messages for anyone").

Indeed, the phrase "no messages" could well provide the epigraph for Moses Herzog because, for all its overt intellectualizing, this is not a novel that offers formulaic meanings. Rather, *Herzog* works as a whole; we need to take in both Herzog the character's fretful inner life and his comic wanderings, as part of a larger exploration of the boundaries of human choice ("There is someone inside me. I am in his grip."). The power of Bellow's novel comes not only from his famously imaginative prose, but also from what such exercises of the mind can reveal; it is a testimony to *Herzog* that readers may find themselves thinking more in terms of what its characters are and do than what they "represent." Herzog comes to recognize how life is always bigger than the shapes we impose on it, and, in following him, we may have a parallel experience. **BT**

Lifespan | *b.* 1915 (Canada), *d.* 2005 (U.S.)
First Published | 1964
First Published by | Viking Press (New York)
National Book Award | 1965

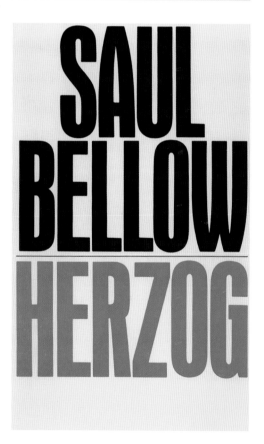

An U.S. edition of Bellow's novel—the name of the eponymous protagonist means "prince" in German.

The Ravishing of Lol V. Stein

Marguerite Duras

Lifespan | *b.* 1914 (Vietnam), *d.* 1996 (France)
First Published | 1964
First Published by | Gallimard (Paris)
Original Title | *Le Ravissement de Lol V. Stein*

"Lol was funny, an inveterate wit, and very bright . . ."

⬤ A prominent figure in Parisian intellectual circles, Duras wrote the script for Alain Resnais' classic 1959 movie *Hiroshima, Mon Amour*.

Lol Stein is nineteen-years-old, and the stuff of local legend. She is engaged to Michael Richardson, we are told by an anonymous narrator, when into the ballroom step two strikingly beautiful women, Anne-Marie Stretter and her daughter. Richardson is transfixed, abandons Lol, and spends the rest of the night dancing in the arms of Anne-Marie Stretter, while Lol looks on. At dawn, the couple leave the ballroom, and Lol lets out a cry. One question that haunts the remainder of the novel is whether the events at the ball constituted a moment of rapture for Lol, or whether in fact it was rupture.

The action starts long after Lol's recovery from her supposed trauma, when she is married with three children and has recently returned to her home. She starts to run over the ball in her mind, then begins to orchestrate a repetition of the night's events: this time she is the outsider, and the unwitting couple are her old friend Tatiana and her lover, Jack Hold (who only now reveals himself as the narrator). Jack falls hopelessly in love with Lol, but, rather than urge him to leave Tatiana, she persuades him to keep on loving her, pushing all three beyond the usual economies of desire.

For psychoanalysts, the love triangle always contains rivals and can be resolved only by the elimination of one of them. Interestingly, Duras herself was involved in a ménage à trois with her husband, the poet Robert Antelme, and Dionys Mascolo; when Duras had Mascolo's child, Antelme (who also had a lover or two) eventually left, but that relationship was not to last either. Duras' novel explores the possibility of moving beyond this: the possibility of maintaining desire without rivalry. In doing so, it offers its readers one of the most powerful antioedipal myths of recent times. **PT**

Arrow of God
Chinua Achebe

Set in Nigeria in 1921, this novel tells how the elderly Ezeulu, an Ibo community's polygamous high priest, endeavors to adapt to the power of the white colonial officials (whose black messenger terms him "witch-doctor"). In a bitter comedy of errors, an attempt by a well-meaning English District Officer to declare him an accredited chieftain results in his humiliation by a white deputy and his black emissary. Thereafter, Ezeulu seeks to humiliate his community by post-poning an impending harvest day; the people then turn away from him to the Christian mission, which encourages timely harvesting. Ezeulu withdraws into "the haughty splendor of a demented high priest."

The interest of *Arrow of God* lies partly in the novel's subtle plotting and largely in the vivid rendering of the complexities of the evolving indigenous society. We see how diversely the people respond to the challenges of colonialism. Ezeulu's community maintains traditional celebrations and intimate rituals, but also sanctions the ubiquitous exploitation of women by men; lepers are scorned; its religion veers between the profoundly intuitive and the superstitiously silly. Achebe's intelligent objectivity extends to the British community, too. If one official is naïvely arrogant, another tries to be fair-minded. If the English colonialists cause cultural disruption, they also terminate tribal warfare and build schools, roads, and hospitals. Achebe reminds us that British imperialism, however culpable, was far more constructive than the African imperialism of the nineteenth-century Benin dynasty.

Achebe writes with wit, humor, sharp realism, and imaginative empathy. His prose is refreshingly original, pungently spiced with translated idioms ("Unless the penis dies young it will surely eat bearded meat."), and coolly ironic. **CW**

Lifespan | *b.* 1930 (Nigeria)
First Published | 1964
First Published by | W. Heinemann (London)
Peace Prize of the German Book Trade | 2002

"What kind of power was it if it was never to be used?"

◔ Achebe addresses the complexities of the situation created when a traditional society comes into contact with colonial power.

Albert Angelo

B. S. Johnson

Lifespan | *b.* 1933 (England), *d.* 1973
First Published | 1964
First Published by | Constable (London)
Full Name | Bryan Stanley Johnson

Johnson wrote in 1973, "To the extent that a reader can impose his imagination on my words, then that piece of writing is a failure ... what I am really doing is challenging the reader to prove his existence as palpably as I am proving mine by the act of writing." This call for a more interactive relationship between reader and the material book is central to *Albert Angelo*. It is perhaps Johnson's most self-referential work, relentlessly experimenting with typography and authorial voice to question the distinction between truth and fiction. *Albert Angelo* shadows the progress of an aspiring architect struggling to make ends meet in London and obliged to teach in a local high school. The action is divided into four sections resembling the arc and decline of a Chekhovian tragedy: "Prologue," "Exposition," "Development," and "Disintegration." A memorial "Coda" sparely records Albert's fate one night when a callous gang recognizes and confronts him. Speaking about his later novel, *Trawl* (1966), Johnson said: "I explored my sense of isolation, my failure to make lasting relationships. I wanted to define this isolation and thereby understand and erase it, in the classic way." Arguably, he had already achieved this in *Albert Angelo*, without compromising the plot's dramatic verve. The book is an absorbing challenge to reflect upon the ways in which we customarily read. **DJ**

◀ A portrait of Bryan Stanley Johnson in 1969. He wrote many of his works between writing football reports for *The Observer*.

Come Back, Dr. Caligari

Donald Barthelme

Lifespan | *b.* 1931 (U.S.), *d.* 1989
First Published | 1964
First Published by | Little, Brown, & Co. (Boston)
Original Publication of Select Stories | *New Yorker*

Barthelme approaches language with surprise and delight, savoring it, testing it, toying with it, like an extremely inquisitive foreigner or a new visitor to Earth. He incorporates headlines from movie gossip magazines about Liz Taylor, scientific trivia, and lessons from a teacher's manual on how to make teaching fractions fun. It is verbal chinoiserie—bizarre, elaborate, and surreal. Welcome to his world.

In "Florence Green Is 81" a man tries to ingratiate himself with old Florence Green to see if he can get some of her money. He competes with Onward Christian to make the best remarks and win her largesse. Florence just wants to go someplace different. In "A Shower of Gold" an artist named Peterson, answering an ad to appear on television, struggles with the question: "Who am I?" His work is interrupted when the president, whom he admires, enters with a sledgehammer and smashes his art while secret service men hold Peterson down and bite him. "Me and Miss Mandible" deals with a thirty-five-year-old former insurance adjuster who inexplicably finds himself back in sixth grade. He suspects a conspiracy. He has a crush on the teacher, as well as Sue Ann, who sits across the aisle. "The classroom is a furnace of love, love, love."

Barthelme's stories are elemental, transcendental, something felt rather than understood. The flow and rhythm of absurd logic starts to make sense, like a pleasant dream. It is masterful, uncommon fiction—or at least we hope it is fiction. **GT**

Sometimes a Great Notion

Ken Kesey

Lifespan | *b.* 1935 (U.S.), *d.* 2001
First Published | 1964
First Published by | Viking Press (New York)
Movie Adaptation Released | 1971

Ken Kesey's second novel is a text that defines a period of twentieth-century U.S. history with originality, passion, and skill. Set in and around an Oregon logging camp, it explores the dynamics of one family, the Stampers, at odds with their town, at odds with their union, and—most of the time—at odds with each other. The tale revolves around the conflict between two brothers, Hank and Leland, two competing versions of manhood, played out in an environment redolent of the American frontier. Hank is big, brash, committed, and used to running the place, and the narrative begins with a conflict with the trade union. His younger half-brother Leland then arrives, an East Coast college-educated dope smoker. Leland is unwilling to conform to Hank's straightforward rough-and-ready notion of manhood, or to his family's expectations. Kesey skillfully explores the dynamics of their relationship—their similarities, respect, and loyalty, and their destructive differences, particularly when competing in love. This is made all the more powerful as he switches between narrators, countering initial sympathies for Leland by showing the depths of Hank's struggle for the family and his own peace of mind. A raw exploration of the survival of the American dream and a near-mythic fable of man pitted against nature, community, and big business, the novel is an important and unjustly neglected classic of American literature. **MD**

The Passion According to G. H.

Clarice Lispector

Lifespan | *b.* 1920 (Ukraine), *d.* 1977 (Brazil)
First Published | 1964
First Published by | Editôra do Autor (Rio)
Original Title | *A paixão segundo G. H.*

Ukranian-born Lispector lived in Brazil and wrote in Portuguese, but this work took more than twenty years to be translated into English. *The Passion According to G. H.* could hardly be considered a conventional novel. To describe it using the familiar literary language of plot and characterization would make little sense; in fact, it reads more like an existential enquiry than a narrative. For this reason it is also a text that calls for careful, thoughtful reading, one that challenges and invites its reader, posing and exploring some of the fundamental questions that more normally appear in the often dry prose of philosophers. The protagonist, known to us only as G. H. from the initials on her luggage, is propelled into a whirlpool of thoughts and emotions when she enters the room of her former maid, who has left a curious drawing on the wall. Further to the feelings that this evokes for G. H., there is an encounter with a dying cockroach, which becomes a central symbolic image around which the narrative sweepingly circles. Each chapter is beautifully linked through the repetition at the start of the previous section's final line, and the writing has the feel of a deeply personal internal monologue, encompassing questions and disquisitions on love and living, on the role of the past, and that of the future. Addressed to a personalized and also mysteriously undefined "you," this is a very intimate reading experience. **JC**

Everything That Rises Must Converge

Flannery O'Connor

Lifespan | *b.* 1925 (U.S.), *d.* 1964
First Published | 1965
First Published by | Farrar, Straus & Giroux (N.Y.)
Full Name | Mary Flannery O'Connor

Like the sweet rot of fallen magnolia blooms, volatile notions of class and color, generational schisms, and convictions of belief permeate these stories from a time when the genteel South still tenuously hung onto outdated conventions and prejudices. This is a Manichean world full of grotesques and eruptions of unexpected cruelty. Characters rise and converge, through civil rights and through religious clarity. With the rising comes knowledge, but with the convergence comes collision—with old ideas, unexamined self-images, and the harsh light of truth. These are stories of dangerous epiphanies; sometimes finding grace is not a pleasant thing. And sometimes to find God you have to take a bullet in the chest, get thrashed with a broom, or get gored through the heart by a bull. In one story, on a newly integrated bus, Julian, educated and stricken with class guilt, takes his mother to her slimming class at the "Y." She is mired in tradition and prejudice, and tension mounts when a black woman, with her own son, boards wearing the same new hat. Julian is so blinded by rage when his mother gives the black boy a penny that he cannot see her tragic chastening. O'Connor is funny, trenchant, and brutal. The ignorant are punished; the well-intentioned even more so because of their insufficient strength to act. Her genius lies in writing profoundly moral stories where it is up to the reader to decide between right and wrong. **GT**

"The door closed and he turned to find the dumpy figure, surmounted by the atrocious hat, coming towards him."

◉ *Everything That Rises Must Converge* was O'Connor's last work, pulling together many religious and social themes from her earlier fiction.

God Bless You, Mr. Rosewater

Kurt Vonnegut, Jr

Lifespan | *b.* 1922 (U.S.)
First Published | 1965
First Published by | Holt, Rinehart & Winston (N.Y.)
Alternate Title | *Pearls Before Swine*

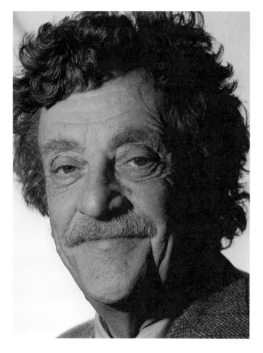

"'You're the only ones with guts enough to really care about the future'"

⬤ Vonnegut, photographed here in his sixties, has always been modest about the scope of his literary achievements.

"A sum of money," Kurt Vonnegut tells us in the first sentence of what is his fifth novel, "is a leading character in this tale about people . . . " The sum of money in question is vast, constituting as it does the core of the Rosewater Foundation, a charitable organization set up as a tax shelter by Senator Lister Ames Rosewater of Indiana. It is a sum that can inspire hatred, ruin lives, and create and destroy dreams. Eliot Rosewater, who inherited the directorship of the foundation, is perhaps the man most affected by the money. His avaricious opponents claim it has driven him mad and has destroyed his wife and marriage; however, his loose coterie of whores, drunkards, arsonists, and various volunteer fire departments see it as the cause of his saintliness. For Eliot Rosewater has committed what can be considered a cardinal sin in capitalist America: he wants to share.

Privilege, however, is a sacred trust, and one of the mandates of the lawyers in charge is "the prevention of saintliness on the part of our clients." So the battle between good and greed ensues, with opportunistic young lawyer Norman Mushari, assisted by Fred Rosewater—the "filthy-minded insurance bastard" and atrophied knot at the end of the poor branch of the Rosewater family tree—attempting to have Eliot declared insane.

God Bless You, Mr. Rosewater is a merciless satire on wealth and entitlement, a brilliant and biting diatribe against capitalist America that is hilarious and written without charity. It is also vintage early Vonnegut and marks a move away from the science fiction of his previous books, for which he is so well-known. Here we have a tale of holy innocents just trying to get by and make sense of a modern world. **GT**

August Is a Wicked Month

Edna O'Brien

Ellen, divorced, worried that she loves her young son too much, is old at twenty-eight. Hers is the struggle of the average; nothing is wrong, but then again nothing is perfect. She goes through life in a stream of unconsciousness: the false starts, the tiny victories, niggling anxieties, a slow suffocation until old age and death. O'Brien expertly captures the isolation in small details—Ellen's ex-husband drinking out of the guests' china, while she drinks out of a mug; being the last person on the beach on the first day save for the lesbian with lorgnette. These insights are like the phrases of poetry evolving into a portrait of a life of ordinary desperation.

She is suddenly made aware of her need to connect—to touch somebody other than herself—after an unexpected one night stand awakens her atrophied desire. Her numb sense of resignation is melted, and the reawakening of the senses means that she can again feel pain. She realizes, with a passionate hunger, that she wants something more. She goes to the south of France to quench her lusts—more spiritual than carnal—and finally allows herself to wear trousers, to show some midriff, and to not think obsessively about her son. But all does not go as a romantic fantasy should. Ellen cannot blind herself to the seediness of holiday Lotharios or the vacuousness of the idle rich. Seduction becomes attempted rape; hedonism becomes pathetic delusion. And there is no escape from tragedy. Even the dignity of grief is cruelly snatched away as Ellen's isolation is accentuated by hope and affection, which prove fleeting and make the subsequent pain even greater. This is a novel of sublime devastation, written with the quiet force of Hemingway. *August Is a Wicked Month* is extraordinary and powerful, and its effect is not soon forgotten. **GT**

Lifespan | *b.* 1932 (Ireland)
First Published | 1965
First Published by | Jonathan Cape (London)
Original Language | English

"They used to ban my books, but now . . ."

O'Brien, **Writers at Work**, *1986*

◉ Distinguished portrait photographer Mark Gerson took this picture of Edna O'Brien aging very gracefully in the mid-1970s.

The River Between

Ngugi wa Thiong'o

Lifespan | *b.* 1938 (Kenya)
First Published | 1965
First Published by | Heinemann Education (Lon.)
Original Language | English

The River Between, Ngugi's second novel, established his reputation as a major African writer. At one level, this is a simple love story set in the mid-colonial period, an African *Romeo and Juliet* in which two young people from opposing Gikuyu villages fall in love and attempt to transcend the ancient rift between their communities, with tragic results. On a more complex level, the novel engages with Kenya's precolonial and colonial history. It depicts the slow but steady infiltration of the country by the British; the alienation of local people from their land; the negative effects of Christian mission on local power structures, rituals, and relationships; and the deep disunity between different African factions that preceded the anticolonial struggle of the 1950s.

Centrally, the novel engages in the debate about female circumcision and reconciling this practice with Christian and European ones. Circumcision comes to symbolize Gikuyu cultural purity and anticolonial resistance to such an extent that the "unclean" status of the young heroine, Nyambura, seals the lovers' fate. In spite of its tragic consequences, circumcision is shown to be an important element of Kenyan national identity, a vital ritual in the face of colonial incursions and an increasingly absolute Christian education system. In describing the mythological origins of the Gikuyu people, and in setting his story in Kenyan hills as yet untouched by colonialism, Ngugi works to preserve African cultural differences within the English-language novel. **SN**

Things

Georges Perec

Lifespan | *b.* 1936 (France), *d.* 1982
First Published | 1965, by Julliard (Paris)
Original Title | *Les Choses: Une Histoire des années soixante* (*Things: A Story of the Sixties*)

Already the author of four unfinished and rejected novels when he erupted onto the literary scene in 1965, George Perec won the Renaudot prize for *Things: A Story of the Sixties*, his first published novel. The book recounts the intellectual decline of a young and likable couple of sociologists, Jerôme and Sylvie. Their search for happiness, promoted and stimulated by an affluent society, imperceptibly transforms them into a frustrated and resigned middle-class couple. The story shocked the public, who saw in the novel a purely sociological representation of the so-called "consumer" society—not an appropriate subject for a work of literature. By his own admission, Perec wanted to describe the evolution of his own social milieu—that of the students who fiercely opposed France's war with Algeria and became disillusioned and indifferent to politics by the war's end. He also wanted to bring Roland Barthes' *Mythologies* (1957), in which Barthes used semiological concepts in the analysis of myths and signs in contemporary culture, to bear on his writing. The unusual character of *Things* is due in great part to the coldness of the narrator-witness, who refuses to criticize, to judge, and to interpret the attitude of the protagonists. He merely records the things that they covet and accumulate in their apartment, describing them like "signs" or "images," by means of advertising formulas. **JD**

> Perec appears suitably amused that his critique of the consumer society has become a mass-produced object of consumption.

The Crying of Lot 49

Thomas Pynchon

Lifespan | *b.* 1937 (U.S.)
First Published | 1966
First Published by | Lippincott (Philadelphia)
Rosenthal Foundation Award | 1966

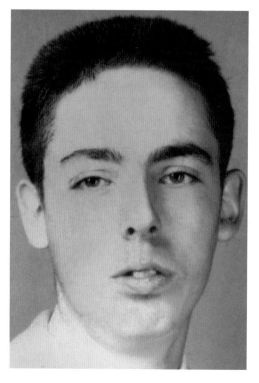

"The reality is in this head. Mine."

⌾ Thomas Pynchon in 1955: his determined refusal of all publicity
means that only a few photos of the author are known to exist.

Joyously brief compared with the rather too-drawn-out literary pyrotechnics of Pynchon's longer novels, this is the postmodernist's perfect thriller, guaranteed to fox the literal-minded sleuth, while deliciously deft with its play of possible interpretations. Where many sophisticated novels resist plot summary because plot is an entirely secondary concern, this confection weaves a rich tapestry of narrative threads. As befits a novel with a protagonist called Oedipa, this box of puzzles wears its enigmas with the smile of a sphinx. Set somewhere approximating California, the book's names work both as clues and as a comedy of connotations. From bands called Sick Dick and the Volkswagens to a cast of characters that includes Mike Fallopian, Dr. Hilarius, Genghis Cohen, and Professor Emory Bortz, Pynchon strains the limits of literary invention. The play of names mirrors the larger structure of narrative gaming, interweaving conspiracy theories, more structural social critique, and doses of slapstick, including spoof mop-top popsters, The Paranoids, and a pastiche Jacobean revenge tragedy. Pynchon's spoofs are researched to within an inch of plausibility. The Paranoids' lyrics, for example, are sufficiently convincing that the group begins to take on an imaginary existence as lifelike as that of their nonfictional prototypes. Oscillations between ideological absurdity and mediated superficiality sketch out a wasteland of seemingly empty but wildly proliferating signs, and the story careers from thought experiments to anarchist miracles. As well as providing the idle dullness of stamp collectors with a most intriguing rationale, there is an almost Borgesian history of the modern world. The blueprint for a generation of clever-clever novels that combine highbrow and pop cultural sensibilities, this is the one with which to start. **DM**

Giles Goat-Boy

John Barth

Giles Goat-Boy opens with various publishers' written qualms (charting their various deteriorating mental states) and a faux cover letter that was attached to this orphan—if not feral—manuscript. Publishing is just one of the many targets for Barth's vitriolic comic genius; others are technology, sexual mores, jingoism, and the idea of the noble savage. It is giddy and profane, a ribald tilt-a-whirl packed tight with wit as dry as the academic density that it mocks. The story concerns the journey of Billy Bockfuss, saved as a baby from the belly of a super-computer and raised at the teat of a goat. With the turbulence of adolescence Billy grows ambivalent, not wanting to leave his beautiful goathood to become an uncertain, hairy-in-all-the-wrong-places human being. But the ewes are unresponsive, and his needs are as relentless as spring. He adopts life as a human, first as George the Undergraduate and finally as the messianic George the Heroic Grand Tutor, savior of New Tammany College. In a retelling, rife with odd usages and neologisms, of the myths and legends of humanity—from the New Testament to Cold War internecine politics—the entire language is corrupted, transmuted, a patois of academic terminology becoming the lingua franca. The campus becomes a microcosm of the world: the East Campus is the Soviet Union, the Great Founder is God Almighty, copulation is commencement exercise, and Enos Enoch is Jesus Christ. Academic verbiage is used as everyday colloquialisms; "flunk" is a multipurpose vulgarity (as in "flunk it" or "this flunking gate"). In Barth's hands the story becomes a living thing, like electricity. It is both a satire and a celebration of language, with phrases like succulent nuggets of hard candy: rich, delicious, to be savored. It is doubtful that it is like anything you have read before. **GT**

Lifespan | *b.* 1930 (U.S.)
First Published | 1966, by Doubleday (New York)
Full Title | *Giles Goat-Boy; or, The Revised New Syllabus*

"George is my name; my deeds have been heard of . . ."

John Barth's conservative appearance gives no hint at the anarchic invention and ribald wit manifested in his novels.

Wide Sargasso Sea

Jean Rhys

Lifespan | *b.* 1890 (Dominica) *d.* 1979 (England)
First Published | 1966
First Published by | Andre Deutsche (London)
WH Smith Literary Award | 1967

Wide Sargasso Sea is Jean Rhys' literary response to Charlotte Brontë's 1847 novel, *Jane Eyre*. Rhys takes as her starting point Brontë's animalistic, sexualized depiction of Bertha Mason, Edward Rochester's dangerously insane first wife. In rewriting this literary classic, Rhys allows Antoinette to speak (Bertha is revealed as Rochester's imposed name for his wife) and also explores the uneven desires and fears that have dominated relationships between the Caribbean and Europe. The novel is divided into three parts: in the first, Antoinette gives an account of her unhappy childhood, in the second, Rochester describes his uneasy first marriage, and in the third, we are witness to the confused dreams and thoughts of Antoinette after she has been imprisoned in England. This structure allows Rhys to make explicit connections between the story of *Jane Eyre* and the violent colonial history underpinning it. Rhys sets the events in *Wide Sargasso Sea* against slavery's ending in the Caribbean and positions Antoinette—whose mother was from Martinique—between the black and European communities. Her social vulnerability is used by Rhys to explore the colonial relations of desire and identity that Brontë could only imply. The doomed arranged marriage between Antoinette and Rochester is sexually charged and yet profoundly precarious because of the incomprehension and mistrust that both bring to it. In this parallel narrative, Antoinette is no longer merely an insanely vengeful wife, but a tragic victim of a complex historical moment. **NM**

> " . . . I don't know what I am like now. I remember watching myself brush my hair and how my eyes looked back at me. The girl I saw was myself yet not quite myself."

◉ When Rhys wrote *Wide Sargasso Sea* she was an elderly woman existing in alcohol-soaked poverty in a primitive Devon cottage.

The Vice-Consul

Marguerite Duras

Lifespan | *b.* 1914 (Vietnam), *d.* 1996 (France)
First Published | 1966
First Published by | Gallimard (Paris)
Original Title | *Le Vice-Consul*

The Vice-Consul might be categorized as a *nouveau roman*, in that it rejects traditional conventions of realist fiction, such as morality and psychology, in favor of the visual, even cinematic, description of action. Two stories emerge. The first depicts the solitary journey of a young Vietnamese peasant girl who is turned out of her home by her mother when she becomes pregnant. The second revolves around several figures associated with the French Embassy in Calcutta, most notably the Vice-Consul of Lahore. The Vice-Consul creates a scandal that preoccupies the French diplomatic community when he fires gunshots indiscriminately at lepers and dogs living in the Shalimar gardens. He also falls in love with Anne-Marie Stretter, the Ambassador's enigmatic, promiscuous wife. Duras' minimalist style handles issues of love, sexual desire, jealousy, motherhood, hunger, violence, waiting, and boredom with beautiful and exceptional subtlety. Through the story of the Vice-Consul's scandalous shooting, she explores the effects of confronting human suffering, illness, and poverty in a way that exposes rational reaction as highly suspect and even fraudulent. One of the most fascinating aspects of this novel is the texture and layering of its narrative voice. The novel's structure places the reader in a disturbing position, inspiring consideration of questions such as "Who is writing?" and "Whose story are we reading?" Duras ensures that we do not forget that we are experiencing a literary construct and not a representation of reality. **PM**

The Magus

John Fowles

Lifespan | *b.* 1926 (England), *d.* 2005
First Published | 1966
First Published by | Little, Brown & Co. (Boston)
Revised Edition | 1977

The Magus, although not Fowles' first published work, was in fact his first novel, begun in the 1950s. An absorbing book, redolent with the atmosphere of a gray, decaying London and a resplendent Greece, it charts the stage-managed masque both endured and enjoyed by the novel's protagonist, Nicholas Urfe. Nicholas is in many ways a fundamentally unlikable character. A middle-class English everyman of the postwar period, he is self-absorbed, naïve, and a sexual predator. Yet it is impossible not to empathize with both his humanity and the extraordinary ordeal he undergoes. Indeed, the events surrounding his encounters with Conchis and the beautiful twins are as compelling and intoxicating for the reader as they are for Nicholas himself. The novel is steeped in Jungian ideas about the psychological. The overall effect is powerful, but ambiguous, interrogating ideas of freedom, absolute power, and knowledge, as well as the concept and experience of love. It does not seek to provide an answer to the questions it raises, and as such it is both exhilarating and disturbing, as well as frustrating at times. Yet the book's engagement with humanity's longing for transcendence in both life and art is fascinating. Fowles' foreword to the revised edition (1977) speaks of his uncomfortable relationship with the text, which he feels to be deeply flawed. In this debate it is impossible not to side with the readers who have given *The Magus* its lasting popularity. This is a novel difficult to put down and difficult to forget. **DR**

In Cold Blood

Truman Capote

Lifespan | b. 1924 (U.S.), d. 1984
First Published | 1966
First Published by | Random House (New York)
Full Name | Truman Streckfus Persons

Capote's most famous work is a pioneering example of both the "nonfiction novel" and the modern "true crime" story. It retells the story of the 1959 murders of the Clutter family in Kansas by a pair of drifting misfits, Dick Hickock and Perry Smith, and of the subsequent trial and execution of the killers. Capote also uses the polarities of this particular case as the starting point for a larger examination of the values of late 1950s and early 1960s America; the respectable Clutters are so wholesomely all-American that they could almost have been invented, while Smith and Hickock come over as brutal real life versions of the James Dean "rebel" culture. The world of the victims is painstakingly and sympathetically reconstructed, but Capote's real interest is in the emotional lives of Perry and Dick, and what might have led them into such murderous excess. Indeed, some argue that Capote was so fascinated by Perry Smith because he saw in him a possible alternative version of himself. Given that Capote wrote about the crime throughout the trial, it has even been suggested that the final verdicts were conditioned by the way in which his journalism had portrayed the killers. In this light, *In Cold Blood* offers a larger, more disturbing insight. Like Mailer's *The Executioner's Song* (1979), it embodies a debate about fact, fiction, and the overlaps and differences between their ethical responsibilities. **BT**

🔇 Truman Capote poses as a self-consciously sophisticated and hedonistic observer of life in this photograph dating from 1955.

Trawl

B. S. Johnson

Lifespan | b. 1933 (England), d. 1973
First Published | 1966
First Published by | Secker & Warburg (London)
Full Name | Bryan Stanley Johnson

Trawl invokes the nemesis of the genre of maritime fiction: traveling across the sea is reciprocated by the self; a trawler's quest through the waves both invites and causes a solitary inquest into private memories. The narrator's journey is shaped by the practical exigencies of his enclosed surroundings. Workaday routines aboard the trawler, geared toward the demands of processing each catch, punctuate his retrospection; every withdrawing of the nets also provokes him to enmesh and retrieve memories previously unexamined under the critical light of hindsight. Johnson's seascape is thus for the narrator a realm whose vacancy and indistinctness are all the more appropriate for giving definition to the past. The setting evokes a medium for self-understanding gained through involuntary remembrance: "There, something to start me, from nowhere." Events returning by chance collide and coincide in their associations, spelling the possibility of redemption from regret. Johnson insisted throughout his short but prolific career that the novel as a form should always be pursued as a truth-purveying medium for expressing lived experience over make-believe. Johnson's solipsistic narrator is all too aware that personal history can shape itself into false completion. That is why he has consigned himself to this grueling voyage. In *Trawl*, Johnson reminds us that cherished memories can offer ambiguous forms of self-consolation—cautioning us to query what we selectively choose to forget. **DJ**

The Birds Fall Down

Rebecca West

Lifespan | *b.* 1892 (England), *d.* 1983
First Published | 1966
First Published by | Macmillan (London)
Given Name | Cicely Isabel Fairfield

The story of the unwitting involvement of eighteen-year-old Laura Rowan in the events leading up to the Russian Revolution, *The Birds Fall Down* is part historical novel, part political thriller, and part acute psychological character study. Taking place over only a few days, the novel focuses on Laura's sudden emergence from innocent childhood into the middle of a political conspiracy. West follows with forensic care the delicate modulations in Laura's response to the discovery that her exiled Russian grandfather is surrounded by spies and double agents who are intent on killing them both. Despite this intense and narrow focus on Laura's psychological response to trauma, the novel has a vast historical range. West places Laura's plight at the very fulcrum of the balance of power in the early twentieth century. The shadowy political forces that gather around her are intimately bound up with the decline of the British Empire at the end of the Boer War, the beginning of revolutionary unrest in Europe, and the first stirrings of Leninist Marxism in Russia. One of the remarkable achievements of West's prose is that it can survive this contradiction between the vast historical sweep and the intimate psychological study. She writes with such elegance and precision that the faultlines between the micro and the macro are never allowed to open up. Rather, the novel exploits the tension at its heart between the personal and the political to produce a new kind of historical writing. **PB**

A Man Asleep

Georges Perec

Lifespan | *b.* 1936 (France), *d.* 1982
First Published | 1967
First Published by | Éditions Denoël (Paris)
Original Title | *Un Homme qui dort*

In *A Man Asleep*, Perec recounts the experience, partly autobiographical, of a student who, just as he is about to take his last exam, decides to hibernate, ceases to speak and to see his friends, and reduces his life to an entirely vegetative set of activities. The inner narration alternates between descriptions of Paris streets, where the hero wanders about as mechanically as a rat in a cage, and passages where the hero, half asleep in his room, experiences the mingling of reality and hallucinations. This recalls Proust's famous sentence, from which the title of the book derives: "A man who is asleep gathers round him the flow of time."

In an interview, Perec stated how he wanted to rewrite Melville's *Bartleby*, to attain a degree of neutrality that would not be the matter of any ideology or mythology, and that would deny his character the chance to embody saving or redemptive forms of heroism. Indeed, the amazing feat of this "journey to the limit of indifference" is that it does not conclude with suicide, martyrdom, madness, or an escape elsewhere, but with a "mere banal return to normal life." Eventually the hero, having logically reached a horrible state of anxiety, understands that he cannot live isolated from the world. *A Man Asleep* is written entirely in the second person singular, and the novel's narrative voice, which is addressed both to the character and to the reader, acquires an incantatory neutrality and monotony. **JD**

The Third Policeman

Flann O'Brien

Lifespan | *b.* 1911 (Ireland) *d.* 1966
First Published | 1967
First Published by | MacGibbon & Kee (London)
Given Name | Brian O'Nolan

There is a fascination with the bicycle in the Irish experimental novel. Flann O'Brien's comic masterpiece *The Third Policeman*, written in 1940 but unpublished until 1967, treats the bicycle with an obsessive philosophical interest, at once absurd and hilariously plausible. The story starts off in a humdrum world of Irish pubs, farms, and petty ambitions. Following a brutal murder, this realist beginning unravels, and the first-person narrator wanders into a two-dimensional, perplexing, and incomprehensible world. He shows up at a bizarre police barracks where he finds the two policemen, MacCruiskeen and Pluck and is introduced to "Atomic Theory" and its relation to bicycles. The title's third policeman, Sergeant Fox, bears a striking similarity to the man the narrator has killed and operates the machinery that generates "eternity" which, it turns out, is just down the road. The narrator's obsession throughout is with fictitious philosopher De Selby, who is a skeptic about all known laws of physics. His eccentric ideas on the delusory nature of time and space are repeatedly footnoted in a wonderful parody of academic scholarship and intellectual pretension. It places the novel in a distinctly Irish strain of comic writing associated with the likes of Jonathan Swift, in which po-faced scholasticism and internally plausible reasoning lead to bizarre conclusions. For first-time readers, the surprise ending casts events in this delightfully weird but deeply intelligent novel in a wholly new light. **RMcD**

No Laughing Matter

Angus Wilson

Lifespan | *b.* 1913 (England), *d.* 1991
First Published | 1967
First Published by | Secker & Warburg (London)
Original Language | English

When Angus Wilson submitted *No Laughing Matter* to his publishers they were sufficiently bemused for him to send a thematic synopsis to guide them through a second reading. At first, the outline's territory would have been familiar even to Jane Austen: according to Wilson, the book is the story of "three brothers and three sisters" from a "shabby genteel … middle-class family." By its end, however, Wilson's summary has name-checked Guernica, Hitler, Stalin, the Suez crisis, *Look Back in Anger*, Kandinsky, Ben Hur, and the challenges of providing honorably for an extended household of same-sex Moroccan lovers. Clearly, this is not a conventional family saga. The book's scale can be inferred from the list of "Principal Players," "Supporting Roles," and "Additional Cast" with which it is prefaced. Yet one of its joys is its evocation of the ties and rivalries of the Matthews family; Wilson's command of domestic interiors enables him to dramatize a century of change without sacrificing the fine observations of class, gender, and sexuality that characterize his earlier fiction. More than that, the Matthews family *becomes* the twentieth century, as experienced by middle-class Britons adjusting to the loss of empire. In retrospect, the book can be seen as both the high point of the traditional family-based English novel and the beginning of magic realism. Mixing naturalism, hyperrealism, and fantasy, the book is a missing link in British fiction, connecting Alan Hollinghurst to Jane Austen and E. M. Forster. **VQ**

The Joke

Milan Kundera

Lifespan | *b.* 1929 (Czechoslovakia)
First Published | 1967
First Published by | Ceskoslovensk spisovatel (Pr.)
Original Title | *Žert*

Milan Kundera's first novel is set in Czechoslovakia in the 1950s and 1960s. The original joke of the title refers to the spurned principal narrator Ludvik's decision to send his adolescent sweetheart a postcard bearing the inscription "Optimism is the opium of the people! The healthy atmosphere stinks! Long live Trotsky!" Although his original motivation for writing this provocative card is little more than a petulant reproof, the implications of his actions prove far-reaching. Ludvik is expelled from the Communist Party, and his compulsory national service is spent in a virtual no-man's land of paid but inconsequential manual work. His bitterness at his expulsion from the party, his anger at those responsible for his concomitant removal from university, and the difficulties he has forming intimate relationships with others inform the novel's events. Ludvik attempts revenge against the man who had him expelled from school by seducing his wife. He soon discovers that his adversary has been given a welcome excuse to get rid of his wife, and the woman has, unpredictably, fallen in love with Ludvik—he again finds himself at the wrong end of a joke. As Ludvik himself asks, "What if history plays jokes?" This vexed question is a preoccupation of the novel, which offers a closer political focus and a narrative more directly plot driven than Kundera's later work. **JW**

🔾 Kundera strolls the Paris boulevards in 1975 after quitting communist Czechoslovakia, where his writings were banned.

Pilgrimage

Dorothy Richardson

Lifespan | *b.* 1873 (England), *d.* 1957
First Published | 1967
First Published by | J. M. Dent & Sons (London)
Published Separately | 1915–1938

Pilgrimage was Richardson's life work, in many senses of the term. Its thirteen volumes recount the experiences of the years between 1891 and 1912 through the consciousness of her autobiographical/fictional persona, Miriam Henderson. It opens with the seventeen-year-old Miriam on the eve of her departure to Germany, where she will work as a pupil-teacher; her middle-class family's financial losses, like those of her creator, plunge her into the world of work. In the central volumes of the series, Miriam is in London, living on a pound a week, a "New Woman" embracing the intellectual and personal freedoms of the city and the new century. The later volumes take Miriam out of London and into rural existence, as she pursues her journey and the "adventure" of the questing, and writing, self.

When she began to write *Pilgrimage* in 1913, at the age of forty, Richardson understood that, at the center of her novel, her heroine must be alone in her narration. Miriam's consciousness is all we have, though the narrative moves between third- and first-person narration, and as readers we are fully immersed in the world she touches, feels, hears, and sees. The publication of the collected volumes by Dent did not persuade Richardson that *Pilgrimage* was complete. It was a project, perhaps, that could not be brought to a conclusion. As she was to write of the work: "To go ahead investigating, rather than describing, was what seemed to me from the first minute must be done." **LM**

The Master and Margarita

Mikhail Bulgakov

Lifespan | *b.* 1891 (Ukraine), *d.* 1940 (Russia)
First Published | 1966, in *Moskva* journal
First Published (Book) by | YMCA Press (Paris)
Original Title | *Master i Margarita*

🔵 Bulgakov's Margarita, as represented in this painting by Serbian artist Gordana Jerosimic, is hauntingly mysterious and erotic.

🔵 A poster for a performance based on Bulgakov's masterpiece, staged in Moscow in 2000 on the sixtieth anniversary of his death.

In 1966, almost thirty years after the author's death, the monthly magazine *Moskva* published the first part of *The Master and Margarita* in its November issue. The book had circulated underground for many years before surfacing into the public arena. Had it been discovered during Bulgakov's lifetime, there is little doubt that the author would have "disappeared" like so many others—despite the dubious honor of being named as Stalin's favorite playwright for a short period. *The Master and Margarita* has survived against the odds and is now recognized as one of the finest achievements in twentieth-century Russian fiction. Sentences from the novel have become proverbs in Russian: "Manuscripts don't burn" and "Cowardice is the most terrible of vices" are words with a special resonance for the generations who endured Soviet totalitarianism's worst excesses. Its influence can be detected further afield—from Latin American magic realism to Rushdie, Pynchon, and even the Rolling Stones ("Sympathy for the Devil" is said to be inspired by Bulgakov). The novel is composed of two distinct but interconnected narratives. One is set in modern Moscow; the other in ancient Jerusalem. Into these Bulgakov inserts a cast of strange and otherworldly characters that includes Woland (Satan) and his demonic entourage, an unnamed writer known as "the master," and his adulterous lover, Margarita. Each is a complex, morally ambiguous figure whose motivations fluctuate as the tale twists and turns in unexpected directions. The novel pulsates with mischievous energy and invention. By turns a searing satire of Soviet life, a religious allegory to rival Goethe's *Faust*, and an untamed burlesque fantasy, this is a novel of laughter and terror, of freedom and bondage—a novel that blasts open "official truths" with the force of a carnival out of control. **SamT**

One Hundred Years of Solitude

Gabriel García Márquez

Widely acknowledged as García Márquez's finest work, *One Hundred Years of Solitude* tells the story of the fictional Colombian town Macondo and the rise and fall of its founders, the Buendía family. Revealed through intriguing temporal folds, characters inherit the names and dispositions of their family, unfolding patterns that double and recur. The mighty José Arcadio Buendía goes from intrepid, charismatic founder of Macondo to a madman on its fringes. Macondo fights off plagues of insomnia, war, and rain. Mysteries are spun out of almost nothing. This beguilingly colorful saga also works out a wider social and political allegory—sometimes too surreal to be plausible, at times more real than any conventional realism could afford. An exemplification of so-called magic realism, this allegorical texture incorporates a sense of the strange, fantastic, or incredible. Perhaps the key sociopolitical example is the apparent massacre by the army of several thousand striking workers whose dead bodies seem to have been loaded into freight trains before being dumped in the sea. Against the smoke screen of the official version, the massacre becomes a nightmare lost in the fog of martial law. The disappeared's true history takes on a reality stranger than any conventional fiction, demanding fiction for the truth to be told. While the novel can be read as an alternative, unofficial history, the inventive storytelling brings to the foreground sensuality, love, intimacy, and different varieties of privation. Imagine the wit and mystery of the *Arabian Nights* and *Don Quixote* told by a narrator capable of metamorphosing from Hardy into Kafka and back in the course of a paragraph. García Márquez may have spawned clumsy imitations whose too clever inventions merely tire, but this is a strange and moving account of solitude. **DM**

Lifespan | *b.* 1928 (Colombia)
First Published | 1967, by Sudamericana
Original Title | *Cien años de soledad*
Nobel Prize for Literature | 1982

"'The farce is over, old friend'"

◔ This rare hardcover edition evokes the galleon found in the forest, a beguiling moment from the novel's early pages.

◔ In this photograph by Isabel Steva Hernandez, García Márquez appears physically oppressed by a copy of his famous novel.

The Cubs and Other Stories

Mario Vargas Llosa

Lifespan | *b.* 1936 (Peru)
First Published | 1967
First Published by | Editorial Lumen (Barcelona)
Original Title | *Los Cachorros*

Mario Vargas Llosa's *The Cubs and Other Stories* is not, in fact, a novel. A sweeping depiction of one boy's tough coming-of-age in an affluent neighborhood in Peru, the story reminds us that the very genre of the novel is characterized, not by the plot of a story, but how that story is told. It is thus that the narrative style of *Cubs*, renders it novel indeed.

The oscillating voices that narrate *Cubs* form the conglomerate voice of the barrio; *Cubs* therefore seems to be told from the point of view of the streets, schools, soccer fields, cars, and bars that nurture the boys around which the tale unfolds. One can't help but think that it is Llosa's own Peruvian childhood he is evoking; far from the politics and honed narrative style of his later works, the story suggests the faithful eagerness of its pre-academic author with as much naïvité as it depicts the tender rituals that beckon the boys of the barrio into manhood. And yet there is nothing innocent about the protagonist's shunted development: raised with the expectation of success, Cuellar's castration as a boy full of potential turns the story of youthful innocence into the sinister tale of a dysfunctional adult; itself, a criticism of machismo and the complacency of affluence in Latin American culture. This latent criticism suggests other ways in which Vargas Llosa will come to appropriate the novel form, both in terms of writing and the ways in which his style will be used to invoke political criticism. **JSD**

The Electric Kool-Aid Acid Test

Tom Wolfe

Lifespan | *b.* 1931 (U.S.)
First Published | 1968
First Published by | Farrar, Straus & Giroux (N.Y.)
Full Name | Thomas Kennerly Wolfe, Jr.

The Electric Kool-Aid Acid Test is one of the most notable works of the American "New Journalism"—which, in the writing of Wolfe, Hunter S. Thompson, Norman Mailer, and Joan Didion, creatively blurs the boundaries between the techniques of fiction and those of journalistic reporting. In his account of novelist Ken Kesey and his roving band of political performance artists, the Merry Pranksters, Wolfe tries, as he claims, "to re-create the mental atmosphere or subjective reality" of the experience. As the Pranksters' bus travels around, leaving a trail of LSD trips and improvised "happenings" in its wake, Wolfe's book unfolds like a verbal pop art painting. It offers an extraordinary verbal collage of the Pranksters' world, taking in hippie slang, comic book impressionism, and cinematic jump cuts. Wolfe's style bends and skews to fit itself to the contours of how it might have felt to "be there" with them, making it a necessary document of the rise and eventual fall of a particular era and mentality. *The Electric Kool-Aid Acid Test* hangs together so well stylistically that one cannot always tell where history ends and Wolfe's journalistic riffs begin. It is an exhilarating and exhausting experience, but, like the movie of Woodstock, it cannot define its times, only respond to them. **BT**

> Fashionable 1960s photographer Jack Robinson captured Wolfe in suit, tie, and waistcoat in the decade of jeans, beads, and kaftans.

Chocky

John Wyndham

Lifespan | *b.* 1903 (England), *d.* 1969
First Published | 1968, by Michael Joseph (London)
Given Name | John Wyndham Parkes Lucas
Beynon Harris

*"Babies, in a world that
already has far too many"*

⬤ Wyndham embedded most of his fantasy tales in an English
middle-class setting with which he was personally familiar.

In this overlooked classic, Wyndham explores two recurrent preoccupations—the alienation between adult and child perception and the otherness of suburban life. The story involves an eleven-year-old boy, Matthew Gore, who begins to talk to an imaginary friend and asks bizarre, precocious questions. Soon Matthew is able to comprehend binary mathematics and asexual reproduction, while at the same time producing a series of extraordinary watercolors, drawn with an oddly skewed perspective. David Gore, Matthew's father, has initially overlooked his children for the sake of a career. He clearly lacks the tools to comprehend his son, and when the imaginary friend theory becomes increasingly untenable, Gore reaches out to psychologists and scientists. It is only when he observes Matthew for himself that he begins to grasp what is actually happening. The entity that has been both guiding and eavesdropping through Matthew is revealed as Chocky, a benign and youthful alien explorer. Ultimately, human intervention makes Chocky's position untenable, and she departs to find another subject. While this is an apparent resolution, the book's conclusion is pessimistic; malign curiosity, incomprehension, and fear are shown to prevent human development. At the novel's end, Chocky encourages Matthew to become an artist, rather than the brilliant physician she had envisaged through her guidance. Scientifically, then, the ultimate conclusion of the book is reductive. *Chocky* was made into a memorable children's television series by Anthony Read in 1984, which excellently preserved the eeriness and tone of Wyndham's writing. The series encouraged the potential in children's drama for science fiction on a relatively low budget throughout the late 1980s. **EMcS**

The Quest for Christa T.

Christa Wolf

Christa Wolf is undoubtedly the most significant author to have lived and worked in the German Democratic Republic (the former East Germany). She was a convinced socialist and a member of the ruling party, yet her work nevertheless demonstrated a sensitivity to some contradictions of the system. She frequently investigated the difficulty of maintaining a sense of personal identity and integrity in a society in which the emphasis was always on the collective.

The novel presents a dense, nonlinear narrative in which the organizing principle is the narrator's "quest" to reconstruct the life of a friend, Christa T., who has recently died of leukemia. The focus is upon Christa T.'s struggle to balance her eccentric character with the political conformism expected of her and her intense desire for a private, personal existence with a willingness to serve the community. The narrator, who evidently functions as an alter ego for Wolf, combines her own fragmentary memories of her friend with extracts from diaries, letters, and other sources. From the beginning she concedes that the project can never be complete, that one can never wholly "know" another person, and that in a sense it is as much about getting to know herself as it is about her dead friend. The narrator's highly self-conscious investigation becomes a meditation upon Wolf's characteristic themes: politics and morality, memory and identity, and the purpose of writing. Unsurprisingly, the novel prompted a good deal of controversy in East Germany, and authorities went so far as to instruct bookshops to sell it only to well-known literary professionals. Despite this, or perhaps because of it, the novel established her as an important figure in the cultural life of the eastern bloc. **JH**

Lifespan | *b.* 1929 (Germany)
First Published | 1968
First Published by | Mitteldeutscher Verlag (Saale)
Original Title | *Nachdenken über Christa T.*

"It was I who ended up knowing most about her."

A critical but committed supporter of East German communism, Christa Wolf opposed the reunification of Germany in 1990.

A Kestrel for a Knave

Barry Hines

Lifespan | *b.* 1939 (England)
First Published | 1968
First Published by | Michael Joseph (London)
Movie Adaptation Released | *Kes* (1969)

More lyrical than deadpan social reportage, more impressionistic than might be presumed, with opening scenes of a Yorkshire town under the grip of mining pit monotony, Barry Hines' portrait of one teenager's survival with the companionship of his kestrel singularly defies generic categorization. Ambitiously, Hines divides the novel's timescale between the hardship of the present and the pull of sudden remembrance. His uncompromising journey thus shadows Billy Casper's routine paper round and his subsequent day at school. These successive events are interspersed with flashback episodes, rewinding to Billy's first discovery of the hawk to whom he will become devoted, against the meanness and futility of the mundane. Hines becomes our guide to Billy's austere mining community, evoking the tenderness the boy develops by training his hawk. From chick, to leash, to exercising her with a lure as an adult raptor freely off the glove, falconry itself opens up an ultimately fragile space of resistance to Barnsley's everyday necessities.

The novella subsequently appeared as the remarkable movie *Kes* (1969), directed by Ken Loach. Loach's working methods at that time chime with a kind of Italian neorealism, and the movie refuses to embellish the rhetorical economy that for Hines had remained so crucial. **DJ**

◉ David Bradley played teenage falconer Billy Casper in Ken Loach's hard-hitting 1969 movie *Kes*, based on Hines' novella.

In Watermelon Sugar

Richard Brautigan

Lifespan | *b.* 1935 (U.S.), *d.* 1984
First Published | 1968
First Published by | Four Seasons Foundation
Full Name | Richard Gary Brautigan

To be in watermelon sugar is a state of mind. Or a state of grace. Or a hallucination. Most people in watermelon sugar live in iDEATH, a village that is constantly reshaping itself. It is a place full of statues (there is one of a potato, another of grass), where the sun shines a different color every day, and where everyone has a job (whether it be writing a book about clouds, tending the watermelon fields, or simply planting flowers). And everything in iDEATH is made out of watermelon sugar, pine, and stones. Or trout. There were once tigers in iDEATH, who spoke beautifully, but had to eat people or die. They were very pleasant about it. They even helped the young narrator with his arithmetic as they ate his parents. But there is a disturbance in watermelon sugar. Margaret, her heart broken by the narrator, has fallen under the influence of inBOIL, a disgruntled alcoholic who left iDEATH and started making whiskey. He and his band of like-minded drunkards mean to prove to those in watermelon sugar that they do not know what iDEATH really means. They arrive at the Trout Hatchery and dismember themselves with jackknives, bleeding to death, having made their point. What may have seemed nonsensical begins to make perfect sense. Brautigan's language casts a spell. Repetitive and hypnotic, his guileless prose is a transcendental mantra. Gradually, painlessly, the reader soon finds himself in watermelon sugar. More than just a document of the 1960s, it is a passport to revisiting that time. **GT**

The German Lesson

Siegfried Lenz

Lifespan | *b.* 1926 (Germany)
First Published | 1968
First Published by | Hoffman & Campe (Hamburg)
Original Title | *Deutschstunde*

"It was all simply too much. I was swamped."

⬤ Like Günter Grass and Heinrich Böll, Lenz was concerned with the impact of Germany's totalitarian past on the postwar era.

Siggi Jepsen, an inmate in a juvenile offenders' institution, has to write an essay on "The Joys of Duty". He writes about his father, Jepsen, who, during the Second World War, held the post of police chief in a village in the north of Germany. In Siggi's account, his father is charged with implementing the Nazi policy against "degenerate art"; in this role, he is required to enact a prohibition against the local painter Nansen (a character based on the expressionist painter Emil Nolde, 1867–1956), who has been his friend since their youth. Jepsen carries out his orders, even going so far as to destroy some of Nansen's work. Siggi refuses to help his father, and instead becomes the painter's ally, hiding his pictures and warning him when danger threatens.

When the war is over, matters acquire a strange dynamic of their own. Although Jepsen no longer holds the authority of his post, he is unable to stop persecuting the painter, and Siggi is equally unable to give up the role of protector. When some of Nansen's paintings are destroyed in a fire, and Siggi suspects his father, his frustration leads him to steal other pictures from an exhibition—the action that has landed him in the juvenile offenders' institution.

What Siggi achieves in his own private "German lesson"—the examination of his private history—is also applicable, on a broader scale, to what Lenz regards as the task of German literature as a whole: to work through the past in order to understand the present. In *The German Lesson*, Lenz is particularly interested in the concept of duty: as it affects the father, who must do what he is told; as it affects Nansen, who is commanded by his conscience and vocation; and as it affects Siggi, who is caught between the two. *The German Lesson* is a plea for the questioning of authority. **MM**

Dark as the Grave Wherein My Friend Is Laid

Malcolm Lowry

In December 1945, Malcolm Lowry, accompanied by his second wife, flew from Vancouver to Mexico City. From there they set out on a journey by bus through Mexico, retracing the steps of a disastrous earlier visit, and instigating a series of comic catastrophes that culminated in his deportation from the country. This fragmentary, unfinished novel grew from the detailed notes that Lowry had made during the fateful trip.

The protagonist of *Dark as the Grave Wherein My Friend Is Laid*, Sigbjorn Wilderness, is Lowry's alter ego, a writer unable to write, a drunk of "gargantuan proportions" who is on a voyage of breathless self-destruction. Sigbjorn's voyage is also a pilgrimage to the dreaded city of Oaxaca, and a search there for the man who has come to serve as a complex metaphor not only for life and vitality, but also for drunkenness and despair. It turns out that his friend Juan Fernando is dead, murdered years before in a barroom brawl and long laid in his dark grave. In an extraordinary moment of epiphany, having fought drunkenly with his wife and slashed his wrists, Sigbjorn realizes that he has been set free from the ghosts of the past and discovers the courage to drag himself away from the brink of his personal destruction.

There is little discernible plot or movement in *Dark as the Grave Wherein My Friend Is Laid* because so much of the writing is preoccupied with the internal roiling of Wilderness–Lowry's brilliant mind. Other characters appear simply as sketches, or as memories. Even the Mexican landscape, by turns hauntingly beautiful and unspeakably horrific, unfolds as a surreal imaginary landscape pieced together from hallucinatory flashbacks. The novel was eventually completed by Lowry's widow. **TS**

Lifespan | *b.* 1909 (England), *d.* 1957
First Published | 1968
First Published by | New American Library (N.Y.)
First UK Edition | 1969, by Jonathan Cape (London)

"'Bad luck always waits you in the barranca . . . '"

Dark as the Grave ... was one of several works resurrected from Lowry's unpublished material after his death in 1957.

Do Androids Dream of Electronic Sheep?

Philip K. Dick

Lifespan | *b.* 1918 (U.S.), *d.* 1982
First Published | 1968
First Published by | Doubleday (New York)
Movie Adaptation | *Blade Runner* (1982)

The novels of Philip K. Dick are a continual and often surprising source of inspiration for the mundane fantasies of Hollywood. *Total Recall* (1990) (from the short story of 1966 "We Can Remember It for You Wholesale," *Minority Report* (2002), *Paycheck* (2003), and *A Scanner Darkly* (2006) have all graced blockbuster screens. The complexities of *Do Androids Dream of Electric Sheep?* inspired Ridley Scott's groundbreaking *Blade Runner* (1982), but the movie is still a pale shade of the text. Ultimately, the book questions the nature of humanity through the figure of Rick Deckard, a man who hunts "replicants"— androids designed to be "more human than human." The nominal "sheep" of the title is an artificial creation that dies through Deckard's neglect, a source of intense shame to him. This lack of empathy, fundamental to Dick's distinction between human and replicant, suggests the interminably argued point that Deckard himself may be one of the replicants he hunts. Deckard's growing ethical confusion about "retiring" the replicants is highlighted by the book's extension into the quasi-religious undertones of persuasion and vicarious empathy. The religion of Mercerism—from which replicants are prohibited—is a typical Dick invention. Ultimately Mercer is proven a false idol, and the text not only asks what it means to be human, but also, in an expression of Dick's philosophy, questions the viability of reality itself. **SS**

2001: A Space Odyssey

Arthur C. Clarke

Lifespan | *b.* 1917 (England)
First Published | 1968
First Published by | Hutchinson (London)
Original Movie Released | 1968

A "book-of-the-movie" every bit as superbly crafted as the Stanley Kubrick movie of the same name, *2001: A Space Odyssey* was not written after the movie was made, but rather in tandem with it. The fabric of both movie and text were woven simultaneously, with Clarke and Kubrick collaborating to create one of the most enduring and influential science fiction works ever envisioned. Clarke's novel does sometimes seem overly specific in its technical detail, especially in instances where the passage of time has made his projected futuristic developments date badly. It is important (and remarkable) to remember, however, how many of Clarke's fictional predictions have become fact, and how respected he is not simply as an author, but also as one of the foremost celebrators and visionaries of the space age. It is in the final part of *2001* . . . that his vision truly bursts forth. The all-powerful computer HAL 9000, which controls the exploratory spacecraft *Discovery*, turns the human emotions of its creators back on themselves, becoming a terrifying psychotic. The magnificent climax of Clarke's *2001* . . . leaves the reader in little doubt as to why it is considered one of the best novels of its type, and shows why it has garnered such a central place in our imaginings of the future. **DR**

❯ Stanley Kubrick's enigmatic movie version of Clarke's science fiction work has tended to overshadow the author's novel.

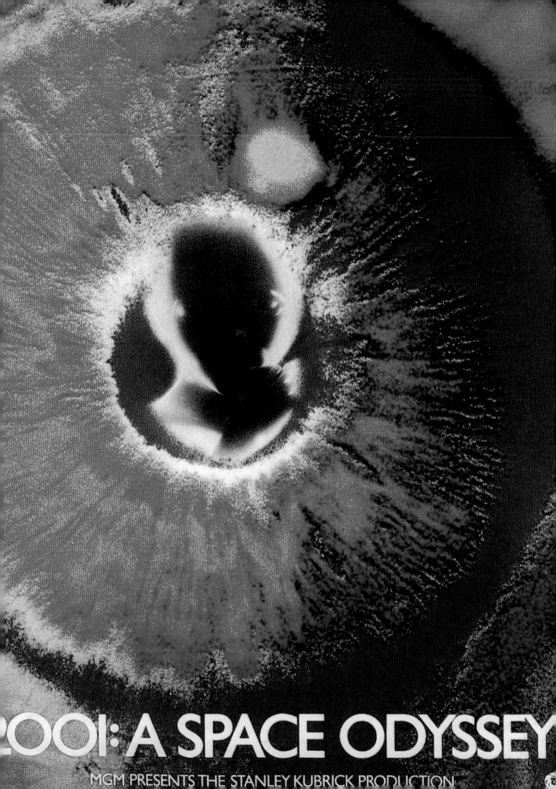

2001: A SPACE ODYSSEY

MGM PRESENTS THE STANLEY KUBRICK PRODUCTION

The First Circle

Aleksandr Isayevich Solzhenitsyn

Lifespan | *b.* 1918 (Russia)
First Published | 1968
First Published by | Harper & Row (New York)
Original Title | *V kruge pervom*

Solzhenitsyn's novel, initially published in a shorter version in the hope of passing Soviet censorhip, was revised into a "final" version, first published in Russian ten years later, in 1978. His novel is at the same time a portrait of late Stalinist society and a philosophical inquiry into the nature of patriotism. The book is set mainly in a special privileged prison for engineers, scientists, and technicians forced to work on inventing gadgets for Stalin's police apparatus. It describes Soviet society not only from the point of view of the prison inmates, but also from that of their families, their non-inmate colleagues, and their jailers. It is Solzhenitsyn's special talent to speak convincingly in many different voices, immersing us in each character's inner world.

The First Circle of the title refers mainly to the privileged nature of the special prison, which forms a Dantean first circle in the hell of the gulag. In the final version the phrase is also used in a different sense, when one of the characters speaks of his own people or nation as "the first circle" and the outside world as "the next one." The relationship between inner and outer in this sense, and the loyalties owed to each one, is an important element in the plot of the book. Yet it is the great merit of *The First Circle* that the characters discussing these questions never become pure mouthpieces, but are given to the reader as full and complex human beings inhabiting their own interconnected worlds. **DG**

Cancer Ward

Aleksandr Isayevich Solzhenitsyn

Lifespan | *b.* 1918 (Russia)
First Published | 1968
First Published by | Il Saggiatore (Milan)
Original Title | *Rakovy korpus*

Strongly autobiographical, like most of Solzhenitsyn's work, *Cancer Ward* takes place in the post-Stalinist 1960s in a provincial hospital in Central Asia. It was published abroad in 1968, after prolonged and unsuccessful efforts to place it in the Soviet literary journal *Novyi Mir.* It constructs a whole social world by unmediated shifts of perspective and of narrative focus from one character to the next. However, it seems less interested in the overtly political and philosophical questions raised by the Soviet system of camps and oppression than in focusing on the way a distorted society affects the lives of individuals. The main character, Kostoglotov, is—like Solzhenitsyn —a former political prisoner, who is faced with a life-threatening cancer for which he needs radiotherapy, with potentially devastating consequences for his sexual life. Not long released from the camps into internal exile, this represents a brutal shattering of his hopes for what remains of his life after the gulag has robbed him of his youth and early manhood. Kostoglotov develops an unlikely relationship with a lonely middle-aged female doctor, and the main plot of the novel explores their tentative and ultimately unrealized emotional intimacy. It is the enmeshing of their personal stories into a whole tableau of other characters and their voices, however, that makes the novel's impact so striking. It tells of self-deception and careerism; of youthful desire and innocence; of anger, faith, and resignation. Most of all it tells of broken lives in a society still shaped by the gulag. **DG**

Belle du Seigneur

Albert Cohen

Lifespan | *b.* 1895 (Greece), *d.* 1981 (Switzerland)
First Published | 1968
First Published by | Gallimard (Paris)
Original Language | French

Comic and tragic in almost equal measure, *Belle du Seigneur* is many things, but remains essentially a love story. The tone is set from the beginning, as the opening scene finds protagonist Solal, posturing in the guise of Don Juan, fresh but firm in his resolve to seduce another man's wife: the incorrigibly vain Ariane d'Auble. The other man in question is Adrien Deume, an ingratiating social climber under Solal's employ, whom Solal smoothly outmaneuvers by exploiting his position as Under-Secretary-General of the League of Nations. He does succeed in his endeavor, though not without consequence, and a passionate if rather contrived love affair unfurls as he and Ariane elope. However, their initial happiness soon subsides as the threat of boredom, coupled with their respective sacrifices, reveals the fragility of their love, and they hobble toward an unhappy finale. Within the predominantly third-person narrative, different characters' perspectives are given in first-person stream of consciousness style passages, adding texture, and often humor, to the novel. The incorporation of certain autobiographical elements means that beneath the blithe veneer of sprawling text are sharp observations on society mores, as well as psychological comment on Jewishness and associated themes, such as messianism and exile.

Despite being highly rated in France and recognized as a significant contributor to French Jewish fiction, it is fair to say that Albert Cohen has been largely forgotten, perhaps unfairly. **TW**

The Nice and the Good

Iris Murdoch

Lifespan | *b.* 1919 (England), *d.* 1999
First Published | 1968
First Published by | Chatto & Windus (London)
Original Language | English

The Nice and the Good evokes the heady atmosphere of sexual permissiveness that characterized the Swinging Sixties, as Iris Murdoch questions how far the "dark force that is sex makes us do things we don't understand and often don't want to do." The "nice" and the "good" of the title relate to the contest in us all between the desire for sex, power, and possession (the "nice") and for love, beauty, and knowledge (the "good"). Ducane, the moral pilgrim at the center of the story, wants to lead a moral life amid the temptation of immediate, unthinking sexual gratification offered by almost every woman he meets. The most demanding is his former girlfriend Jessica, who is the symbol of a rootless generation fixated on momentary pleasures that substitute for spiritual needs. The novel is structured around moments where characters confront intense sexual temptation, but offers no facile moral platitudes. Ducane comes to perceive his own moral hubris, "the great evil, the real evil is inside myself," and he learns not to judge. Murdoch demands sharp discriminatory moral perception to accompany the new sexual freedoms, yet views frailty with compassion. The novel suggests that ultimately it is impossible to understand sexuality and spirituality as separate. While Murdoch does not condemn sexual freedom, she does question its indulgence by those without the moral vision to use it wisely: we can encourage or discourage certain ways of perceiving that affect actions, even in moments of intense desire. **AR**

Myra Breckinridge

Gore Vidal

Lifespan | *b.* 1925 (U.S.)
First Published | 1968
First Published by | Little, Brown & Co. (Boston)
Full Name | Eugene Luther Gore Vidal

⊙ Gore Vidal devoted much of his literary career to attacks on sexual hypocrisy and the corruption of American political life.

⊙ Raquel Welch as Myra reveals the nub of the plot in a saucy scene from the disastrous 1970 Hollywood version of Vidal's novel.

Myra Breckinridge is a reeling tour de force, a bawdy full-frontal attack on decency and polite behavior. Shocking in its time—not least for its content and rude prose—it is even more so considering Vidal had run for Congress eight years before. This is not the kind of book one expects from a politician. Myra is a sublime creation. She is a voracious dominatrix, a brazen superhero, a big slut, a voluptuous omnivore: "Myra Breckinridge is a dish, and never forget it, you motherfuckers, as the children say nowadays." Myra used to be Myron, a meek film critic, but after a radical act of self-creation—a sex change in Copenhagen— Myra comes to Hollywood to take on the forces of male domination and become "woman triumphant." More feminine than a proper woman, more masculine than an intact man, she is a woman so liberated she may be a mockery of feminism. She certainly calls into question sexual stereotypes and reflexive morality. The focus of Myra's gleeful battle is Uncle Buck Loner. Buck is a he-man who runs an academy for burgeoning Hollywood stars and starlets. Myra tries to fool him into thinking she is Myron's widow—which in a way is true—so that she can claim Buck's estate as her inheritance. She is convincing, knowing things only Myron could. Buck does not believe her, insisting that Myron was a "fruit." He does not part with his money easily and staves off her lawsuit by hiring her to teach Empathy and Posture. She wreaks havoc, an Amazon let loose in a china shop of American innocents. Sadly, there is a problem. Something goes wrong with her sex change, and she reverts to being Myron. She may not have succeeded in becoming woman triumphant, but she—and Vidal—have indisputably triumphed in bringing American hypocrisy and self-obsession forever to its knees. **GT**

Eva Trout

Elizabeth Bowen

Lifespan | *b.* 1899 (Ireland), *d.* 1973
First Published | 1968
First Published by | A. Knopf (New York)
First UK Edition | 1969, by Jonathan Cape (London)

Eva Trout is Bowen's final and in some ways most demanding masterpiece. It shares with her earlier great works the brilliantly funny and disquieting incisiveness of her descriptions of people and places, feelings and ideas, love and loss, but it moves out to weird new depths. It is a marvelously fishy book. In some ways apparently still inhabiting the social ambience and language of earlier decades, it is also one of the most remarkable, elusive, and yet strangely representative literary works of the 1960s. *Eva Trout* tells the story of an improbably large or "outsize" young woman who inherits enough money to do virtually anything. The protagonist somehow acquires a child in the United States, a deaf and mute boy called Jeremy, and back in England falls in love with Henry, a Cambridge undergraduate a good deal younger than herself. In a surreal, compelling finale at Victoria Station, about to depart for a fake wedding and honeymoon with Henry, she is shot dead by Jeremy. A sense of anarchic possibility affects everything, including Bowen's syntax: you often can hardly guess where or how a sentence is going to land. There is a profound impression of diffusion and seeking new, multiple channels of feeling and communication. As the narrator puts it, "What a slippery fish is identity … What is a person? Is it true, there is not more than one of each?" Adrift from the shores of fictional realism, Bowen's novel casts bizarre, fascinating, and comical reflections on the sense that, as a character remarks, "Life is an anti-novel." **NWor**

A Void / Avoid

Georges Perec

Lifespan | *b.* 1936 (France), *d.* 1982
First Published | 1969
First Published by | Editions Denoël (Paris)
Original Title | *La Disparition* ("The Disappearance")

A Void / Avoid, Gilbert Adair's remarkable translation of the title of Georges Perec's extended lipogram—a literary exercise that involves writing without a given letter of the alphabet—adds a further layer of self-reflexivity to a novel that does nothing but point (obliquely) to what is missing. Writing without the letter "e" requires mastering avoidance techniques, and here Perec proves himself a virtuoso, mobilizing the often forgotten resources of the French language so as to inscribe within it a new "e"-less idiom. But Perec's novel is far more than an elaborate linguistic game. It is proof that it is possible to do without the letter "e," a demonstration that affirms the expressive possibilities of (even a deficient) language that—as the second sense of Adair's title suggests—is deeply troubling. In *A Void / Avoid* there is something missing, a hole or vacuum that threatens to suck in all the other letters. An indispensable vowel, what Perec calls "a basic prop," turns out to be dispensable. What then cannot be removed? The question takes on added urgency when the experiment in the removal of a vowel is repeated in the obliteration of a people. The missing letter is the clue not only to the genesis of the novel, but also to the series of disappearances punctuating the plot. The forbidden "e" turns out to be a kind of malediction, an invisible bodily mark that condemns the characters, one by one, to death. An exercise in style brilliantly executed, this is a ludic detective fiction in which the key to the mystery is visible everywhere and nowhere. **KB**

them

Joyce Carol Oates

Lifespan | *b.* 1938 (U.S.)
First Published | 1969
First Published by | Vanguard Press (New York)
National Book Award | 1970

Deliberately labeled with a lowercase "t", *them* was written early on in Joyce Carol Oates' prolific career, and remains one of her most original and best executed works. It focuses on the working-class lives of Loretta Wendall and her children, Maureen and Jules, in inner-city Detroit between 1937 and 1967. One of the novel's most challenging features is the way it takes the representation of the naturalistic novel to the limits. It opens with a famous author's note claiming that the text was based on the life of one of Oates' students at the University of Detroit. This note gives way to a naturalistic narrative about the lives of the Wendalls, juxtaposing a forceful psychological portrayal of each of the characters with the violent realities of their everyday life. Halfway through the novel, however, the main narrative is unexpectedly interrupted—with several letters from Maureen to "Miss Oates." Maureen questions her teacher about the role of literature and Miss Oates' suggestion that literature gives form to life. Maureen, who has prostituted herself and been beaten by one of her mother's lovers, asks contemptuously if literary form can really give order and coherence to a life such as hers. Maureen's impassioned letters voice an irrepressible anger toward the type of literature that can only be understood and savored in the safe middle-class world inhabited by Miss Oates and her kind. Through the very process of writing, Miss Oates is no longer part of the working-class experience she describes—she is no longer one of them. **SA**

Ada

Vladimir Nabokov

Lifespan | *b.* 1899 (Russia), *d.* 1977 (Switzerland)
First Published | 1969
First Published by | McGraw-Hill (New York)
Alternate Title | *Ardor*

Ada or *Ardor* is Nabokov's irrepressively inventive novel, which can, for want of a better description, be called a family chronicle. Using Tolstoy as a cultural touchstone and point of departure, Nabokov embarks upon an extraordinary epic prose adventure involving, invoking, and expanding upon a diffuse intertextual network. In common with *Lolita*, *Ada* is the story of an intense but taboo sexual relationship. The incestuous union between Ada and Van, raised as cousins but biologically brother and sister, is presented in such a way that the reader is not encouraged to feel the sense of moral condemnation that might be expected.

Ada is undoubtedly one of Nabokov's most challenging novels, which above and beyond its subject matter, confuses, bewilders, and delights the reader in turn. Quite apart from the sheer intricacy and ingenuity of his writing, the novel confounds expectations of time and place. The events of the novel unfold not on Earth but within the alternative geography of Antiterra, playing with our perceptions of what is real and what is realistic, and as the elderly Ada and Van reflect upon their relationship the narrative is complicated by the continued but unsignaled temporal shifts.

In its treatment of a forbidden romance, the novel follows the couple over eighty years. The unique combination of myth and fairy tale, eroticism and romance is matched only by the singularity of Nabokov's writing style. **JW**

The Godfather

Mario Puzo

Lifespan | *b.* 1920 (U.S.), *d.* 1999
First Published | 1969
First Published by | Putnam (New York)
Movie Trilogy Released | 1972, 1974, 1990

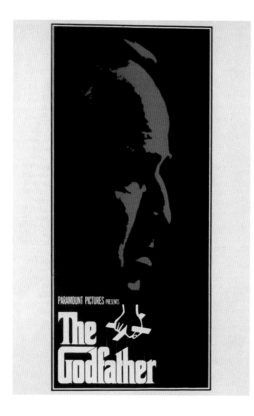

⊙ Coppola's *Godfather* movies retained the strengths of the novel, sustaining moral weight and a somber atmosphere.

⊙ Author Mario Puzo is given something of the arrogant, menacing look of a Mafia godfather in this 1969 photo by Bernard Gotfryd.

Few novels have forced themselves into the cultural imagination as brutally as Mario Puzo's *The Godfather*. Arriving on the bestseller list at a highly contentious moment in U.S. history, when political institutions and social practices were being scrutinized and questioned as never before (or, arguably, since), *The Godfather* raised the stakes. The novel poses questions about the origins and legitimacy of power by interrogating the notion that, as the epigraph from Balzac puts it, "Behind every great fortune there is a crime." Here is a novel that purports to show you how things "really" work, while also playing games with the reader. Making the bad guys seem good, the novel redefined the gangster genre. Puzo's strategy of rhetorical inversion, overturning conventional moral presuppositions of right and wrong, enforces a new understanding of the manipulative and treacherous capacities of language. Twisting distinctions between hero and villain, Puzo's enthralling story of the Corleone's "family business" and Italian American immigrant culture serves also to affirm the "outlaw" character of the United States in general. Although *The Godfather* has filtered into the culture mostly through the movie trilogy and other derivations, the novel remains the driving force behind the mobster culture industry. It is the novel that gives us such legendary sayings as "I'll make him an offer he can't refuse" and "a lawyer with his briefcase can steal more than a hundred men with guns." Above all, in spite and perhaps because of the clear, accessible prose, the novel testifies to the myth-making potential of contemporary writing. Puzo's depictions of Italian Americans have been seen as both celebratory and defamatory: either way, Puzo's *The Godfather* remains remarkably influential, compelling, and readable. **JLSJ**

Portnoy's Complaint

Philip Roth

Lifespan | *b.* 1933 (U.S.)
First Published | 1969
First Published by | Random House (New York)
Full Name | Philip Milton Roth

When *Portnoy's Complaint* first appeared in 1969, it was immediately hailed as scandalous. This was partly because of its explicit sexual content, which is considerable and inventive, but it was also because this content was linked to a kind of diagnosis of the American male of the times. Portnoy's situation—his fixation on his mother; his difficulties with members of the opposite sex; his occasionally maudlin self-pity—described and defined a syndrome with which all too many of Roth's (male) readers were familiar. Into this mix also goes Portnoy's Jewishness, here seen as a kind of exaggeration of the repressive orthodoxies against which the book and Portnoy himself impotently rail. In a sense it is not a book with a story to tell, but rather one with a condition to portray. Portnoy is trapped in a world that cannot fulfill his bizarre and extreme fantasies. Yet the reader does not blame Portnoy; if nothing else, he at least has occasional flashes of insight into his condition, and Roth writes with a great deal of wit and panache. Perhaps in light of the further increase in sexual explicitness since the 1960s, *Portnoy's Complaint* now looks less extreme than it did at the time; despite this, its capacity if not to shock, then at least to deeply embarrass, is undiminished. In the end the book's real strength lies in the figure of Portnoy himself and the universality of his complexes and humiliations. **DP**

🔵 Roth is posed in front of a photo of Franz Kafka, a fellow Jewish writer whom he regards as a major inspiration for his work.

The Green Man

Kingsley Amis

Lifespan | *b.* 1922 (England), *d.* 1995
First Published | 1969
First Published by | Jonathan Cape (London)
Full Name | Sir Kingsley Amis

This experimental novel is a combination of a ghost story that looks back to M. R. James and the more familiar Amis fare of an exploration of moral and spiritual crisis in dull middle England, seen through the eyes of an overeducated protagonist. Maurice Allington owns a smart pub and restaurant, The Green Man. Despite a relatively recent marriage he is unhappy and ill at ease, lacking direction and obsessed with petty detail. He amuses himself by drinking far too much and by having a series of affairs, one of which is with the wife of a friend and neighbor. Allington's life changes in predictable ways as a result of his selfish behavior, but he also has to deal with the problems caused by the fact that The Green Man is haunted by the ghost of Dr. Thomas Underhill, a seventeenth-century scholar rumored to have murdered his wife and conjured up the spirit of the devil. The plot concludes with a metaphysical climax, as Maurice realizes that Underhill had actually conjured up the spirit of God, who is far more malign than traditional Christianity imagines. Like many of Amis' novels, *The Green Man* attempts to link different types of writing and opposed ways of explaining how the world works. On one level, it seems that Maurice is simply having a breakdown and that his problems stem from his poor behavior and self-obsession. On another, however, Amis is clearly keen to wrestle with the fundamental problems of human existence and show that they are more relevant than ever in an age that has lost touch with the possibility of faith. **AH**

The French Lieutenant's Woman

John Fowles

Lifespan | *b.* 1926 (England), *d.* 2005
First Published | 1969
First Published by | Jonathan Cape (London)
WH Smith Award | 1969

🔼 John Fowles and his wife clamber up the Cobb at Lyme Regis, a central setting for the action of *The French Lieutenant's Woman*.

▶️ Meryl Streep plays the eponymous heroine in Karel Reisz' 1981 film version of the novel, which was scripted by Harold Pinter.

In *The French Lieutenant's Woman,* John Fowles set out to do what should have been an impossibility: to reconcile the scope and enthusiasm of Victorian realism with the cynicism and uncertainties of a self-reflective experimental narrative. That Fowles realized his purpose in a novel that is a magnificent blend of story, history, and literary critique is testament both to his skill as a writer, and to the ambition of his humanism. The novel is a pastiche of Victorian realism—undermining the latter's formal claim to comprehensiveness and truth by drawing attention to what was rendered unspeakable by a complacent sense of narrative propriety. Yet it is also full of respect and almost envy for the fundamental premise of nineteenth-century realism: that human reality is representable, and that the novel has an explanatory function with a moral duty to be as truthful as possible. In this tale of a nineteenth-century gentleman, Charles Smithson, who falls in love with the enigmatic, jilted Sarah Woodruff, the twentieth-century narrator plays with his reader's expectations. He scorns especially the illusion of narrative omniscience and omnipotence and flirts with the endless possibilities of interpretation. He also utilizes an essentially Dickensian narrative license to address the reader as familiar and intimate. The "dear reader" addressed here is expected to tolerate—and welcome—a range of devices. Footnotes give information on sources in the style of a scholar and a gentleman. There are long historical digressions, copious quotations from Victorian classics, and digs at the twentieth century's own complacencies. Still, just as the reader addressed by Dickens or George Eliot was credited both with an interest in knowing and a capacity to understand others, so, too, Fowles works to make us see the ties that bind us all. **PMcM**

Slaughterhouse Five

Kurt Vonnegut, Jr

"All time is all time. It does not change. It does not lend itself to warnings or explanations. It simply is. Take it moment by moment, and you will find that we are all . . . bugs in amber."

⊙ Like his novel's hero Billy Pilgrim, in 1969 Vonnegut was "living in easy circumstances on Cape Cod," where this photo was taken.

Lifespan | *b.* 1922 (U.S.)
First Published | 1969, by Delacourte Press (N.Y.)
Alternate Title | *The Children's Crusade: A Duty-Dance with Death*

Vonnegut's *Slaughterhouse Five* is an indispensable achievement in twentieth-century writing, juggling broad thematic and structural complexities alongside a narrative that combines autobiography with a story of time-traveling aliens taken straight from some particularly imaginative science fiction, and with an apparent ease that makes the joins impossible to spot.

In this absurdist classic, Billy Pilgrim, a German American and a former infantry scout in the Second World War, is a man "unstuck in time" after he is abducted by aliens. Who is this single man to make decisions upon universal solutions, let alone trouble us with his workings? Time, memory, and the literary combination of invention and experience are at the book's center, but Vonnegut rejects any undue artifice in his language. The absurdities of war and those of time-traveling aliens appear to Billy Pilgrim on an even footing, as we follow him through all the many phases of his life in a novel that refuses to subscribe to any incarnation of rigid authority. Having fought in the Second World War, been imprisoned, seen thousands dead, and witnessed the devastating fire-bombing of Dresden, the author has produced from his experiences a representation of the literal result of all such authority being simultaneously let go. **SF**

Blind Man with a Pistol

Chester Himes

Lifespan | b. 1909 (U.S.), d. 1984 (Spain)
First Published | 1969
First Published by | Morrow (New York)
Alternate Title | Hot Day, Hot Night

The final, completed novel of a series featuring two black Harlem police detectives, Coffin Ed Johnson and Grave Digger Jones, *Blind Man with a Pistol* takes the detective fiction genre as far as, and beyond, its breaking point. In previous novels, Himes found a way of reconciling his coruscating anger at the open-ended nature of racial discrimination and injustice in the United States with the genre's demands for explanations and closure. Writing from Paris about New York, the results were an often beguiling mix of surreal violence, political protest, and police procedural. In *Blind Man with a Pistol*, Himes is no longer interested in performing such a convoluted juggling act. Rather, the debilitating effects of living in a racist, white-controlled world finally mean that Coffin Ed and Grave Digger, already set against the black community they police and the white justice system they reluctantly serve, can no longer fulfil their function as detectives.

Entering the novel invisible and nameless, they leave it, frustrated and impotent, while a blind, black man fires his pistol indiscriminately into a crowded subway car. Marginalized within the white-controlled police department they served for their whole careers, they end up shooting rats on a derelict Harlem construction site. *Blind Man with a Pistol* is a bleak antidote to the hopeful yearnings of the Civil Rights movement. **AP**

Pricksongs and Descants

Robert Coover

Lifespan | b. 1932 (U.S.)
First Published | 1969
First Published by | E. P. Dutton (New York)
Original Language | English

Coover takes as his source the fables and myths of our collective psyche, the folk tales and television programs and nameless anxieties that keep us awake at night. A master of legerdemain, he plays with the familiar, contorting it into something more complexly sinister than even the grimmest of fairy tales. There are Disneyland woods and breadcrumb trails where birds join in on children's songs about God's love. Why are the children singing? Childish imbecility? To comfort the old man? What is the old man gazing at with such sadness? Distant regrets? His destination? Small details burn with inchoate sexual energy. A carnival sideshow is a riotous self-contained universe where the fat lady becomes thin and the thin man beefs up, through vanity, for each other's love, creating a chaos of multiple voices and absurdist anarchy. The language is refracted through a prism; phrases seem familiar or new, depending on the facet Coover shows us. Meanings, chronologies, become fundamental elements that coalesce like quick fades in a movie— sometimes a montage of color; sometimes a sound cue in an empty frame. Each chapter is a fantasy of modern alienation. Coover makes the archetypal real and the mundane archetypal. Bedtime stories teem with real shadows, deep phobias are made manifest, and biblical characters are confused. He is the ringleader of a universe that operates with the dark and heavy logic of delta-wavelength sleep. **GT**

Tent of Miracles

Jorge Amado

Lifespan | *b.* 1912 (Brazil), *d.* 2001
First Published | 1969
First Published by | Livaria Martins Editora (Rio de J.)
Original Title | *Tenda dos milagres*

With this novel, Amado, Brazil's greatest twentieth-century novelist, wrote his most ambitious political satire and also his richest articulation of the complexity of Afro-Brazilian culture. Mainly set in the crumbling colonial labyrinths of Pelhourinho, a black district in the heart of Salvador Bahia, the novel confronts the legacy of Pedro Archanjo, Amado's most seductive, yet ambiguous, fictional creation. He is a mestizo—an autodidact, author of cookbooks, poet, part-time ethnographer, carnival king, black rights activist, worshipper, and lover of women. Archanjo is also, in the eyes of the Brazilian white cultural elite, a drunk, a seducer, a libertine, a scoundrel, and an intellectual charlatan.

The novel opens as Arachanjo dies drunk and alone in a gutter in the small hours of the morning while the Second World War rages. Some fifty years later James D. Levenson, Nobel Laureate from East Coast American academe, discovers the now-forgotten Archanjo's publications, and goes to Bahia to cash in on the cultural gold mine he has unearthed. An exploration of why Black Brazil matters follows, and of the ways in which North America and Europe only see it through stereotypes, parody, and patronization. Amado's approach is tolerant and celebratory of cultural and sexual miscegenation. Black and white people are "gonna go on being born and growing up and mixing and making more babies, and no son-of-a-bitch is gonna stop 'em!" You can't argue with that. **MW**

"Lídio gave up and signed the painting. On the red border around the picture he wrote his name and address in white ink: Mestre Lídio Corró, Tent of Miracles, Rua Tabuão, 60."

In Brazil, Jorge Amado is a massively popular novelist, some of whose books have been turned into television soap operas.

The Atrocity Exhibition

J. G. Ballard

Lifespan | *b.* 1930 (China)
First Published | 1970
First Published by | Jonathan Cape (London)
Revised Edition Published | 1984

First published in 1970, *The Atrocity Exhibition* remains one of the most provocative and disturbing works in contemporary fiction. The book has caused outrage on both sides of the Atlantic. Indeed, a chapter entitled "Why I Want to Fuck Ronald Reagan" was the subject of an obscenity trial in England when it was published as a separate booklet in 1968, and the U.S. release of the novel was delayed by some years after being dropped by nervous distributors. *The Atrocity Exhibition* is made up of fifteen fragmentary chapters (or "condensed novels" as Ballard likes to describe them). The effect is like walking through a jumbled gallery of the grotesque. Malpractice, car crashes, sexual perversion, newsreel overload, and celebrity are all incorporated into Ballard's penetrating vision. Magnified portions of Marilyn Monroe's body are projected across concrete underpasses, mental patients watch endless footage of hardcore porn in underground research facilities, and middle-aged housewives are aroused by executions.

It is testament to Ballard's skill and insight that the novel continues to be as disquieting as it ever was. In fact, many of his outlandish imaginings now seem much closer to reality than they may have done in the past. Ballard dissects modern culture in a way that few have dared to attempt. Strange, uncompromising, yet often witty and stylish, *The Atrocity Exhibition* perhaps tells us more about ourselves than we would like to know. **SamT**

Jahrestage

Uwe Johnson

Lifespan | *b.* 1934 (Germany), *d.* 1984 (England)
First Published | 1970, by Suhrkamp (Frankfurt)
Full Title | *Jahrestage: Aus dem Leben von Gesine Cresspahl* (*Anniversaries: From the Life of Gesine Cresspahl*)

Jahrestage is Uwe Johnson's masterpiece, a magisterial sweep through German history from the days of the Kaiser and ending in 1960s New York. Born in a part of eastern Germany that became Polish territory, Johnson left the DDR for West Germany, before eventually settling in Kent, England. There, while recovering from a breakdown, caused by the discovery that his wife was spying on him for GDR secret services, he finished *Jahrestage*.

Published in four volumes, *Jahrestage* tells of three hundred and sixty-five days in the life of Gesine Cresspahl. Gesine lives in New York with Marie, her daughter from a past relationship with Jakob Abs, the protagonist of Johnson's earlier novel *Mutmaßungen über Jakob*. The ten-year-old Marie makes Gesine talk about the past: in the narrative that follows, one year in New York becomes the lens through which German history is filtered. Gesine moves back in time, to her family in a small village in Mecklenburg. The story is interwoven with that of the rise and fall of the Third Reich, and links back to the time of Wilhelm II and the Weimar Republic, before returning to the present in a divided Germany. Marie takes the information in her stride; Gesine realizes that she will always be a stranger in the U.S., but prefers exile to a return to Germany. While the formidable length of *Jahrestage* has put off many readers, a recent film version by Margarethe von Trotta (2000) is helping to restore Johnson to his place among the most important writers of postwar Germany. **MM**

Troubles

J.G. Farrell

Lifespan | b. 1935 (England), d. 1979 (Ireland)
First Published | 1970, by Jonathan Cape (London)
Empire Trilogy | Troubles (1970), The Siege of
Krishnapur (1973), The Singapore Grip (1978)

Set in Ireland during the nationalist struggles of 1919–1920, *Troubles* is a tragicomic exploration of British imperialism. The seeming civilizing certainties of British rule, which the Protestant Anglo-Irish imagine will be re-established in Ireland following the First World War, are confronted with the actuality of the majority Catholic nationalist community's struggle for self-determination. Against a backdrop of increasing sectarian violence, Major Brendan Archer arrives in Ireland to claim his bride, the consequence of a brief encounter in wartime England. She dies, but the Major lingers, exemplifying an English amused incomprehension of the apparent comic absurdities of Irish colonial life. However, his Anglo-Irish host's excesses strain the Major's sense of decency and fair play.

Farrell's brilliance is to place The Majestic, the decaying grand hotel in which the characters reside, at the center of the book. The deteriorating hotel takes on a life of its own, mirroring the decline of the Anglo-Irish. Inhabited by those who cannot afford to leave, or who refuse to do so, the hotel comes to represent a civilization that is shell-shocked, no longer secure of itself, and which is being eroded as much from within as by assault from without. Farrell is both critical of, and affectionate toward, the Anglo-Irish world he investigates. *Troubles* is both an entertaining gothic farce and a serious exploration of the social and individual traumas that accompany the end of empire. **TH**

Mercier et Camier

Samuel Beckett

Lifespan | b. 1906 (Ireland), d.1989 (France)
First Published | 1970
First Published by | Éditions de Minuit (Paris)
Nobel Prize for Literature | 1969

The first of Beckett's novels to be written in French, he refused to publish it (on the grounds that it was merely an experiment or draft) for twenty-four years following its completion in 1946. Its story is quite as preposterous and evacuated as that of *Molloy*; it consists of episodes hitched together more by the opportunities they present for derangement of the phantom traditional narrative of bourgeois fiction than by any logic or order that could amount to the portrait of a life or two.

Mercier and Camier, a Beckettian duo deserving of our attempts at contempt and exasperation, often want to leave each other, but do not. Their speech to each other is reported by Beckett with a merciless, and monotonous, repudiation of variety: everything they say is followed by "said Mercier" or "said Camier." The atmosphere throughout is a kind of abstract vaudeville, hilarious and intensely violent by turns and at the same time, as in, for example, an episode in which a fat woman is run over and killed in the street while the duo sigh with relief.

Beckett was here on the cusp of his mature fiction, the novels from *Molloy* onward, in which he switched from the faked narrator's voice to the multiple faked and unfaked voice of the first person chronicling his own nonadventures in the void. It is worth reading for the chapter summaries alone. **KS**

❯ Beckett's presence was dignified and infused with humor, although the skull-like head hinted at his obsession with mortality.

I Know Why the Caged Bird Sings

Maya Angelou

Lifespan | *b.* 1928 (U.S.)
First Published | 1970
First Published by | Random House (New York)
Given Name | Marguerite Ann Johnson

I Know Why the Caged Bird Sings is the first of five volumes of Maya Angelou's autobiography and is a milestone for African American writing. In her distinctive lyrical prose, Angelou recounts her unsettled childhood in America in the 1930s and her changing relationships. When her parents separate, Maya and her brother Bailey, three- and four-years-old respectively, are sent from their parental home in California back to the segregated south, to live with their grandmother (Momma) in rural Arkansas. Momma provides a strict moral center to their lives. At the age of eight, Maya goes to stay with her mother in St. Louis where she is molested and raped by her mother's partner. With her brother she later returns to stay with Momma before returning again to live with her mother and her mother's husband in California. The book ends with the birth of Maya's first child, Guy.

Against the backdrop of racial tensions, Maya Angelou confronts the traumatic events of her own childhood, and explores the evolution of her own strong identity as an African American woman. Her individual and cultural feelings of displacement are mediated through her passion for literature, which proves both healing and empowering. **JW**

⬦ An exuberant Maya Angelou, self-discovered through her passion for literature, radiates joy and life on a San Francisco beach.

Goalie's Anxiety at the Penalty Kick

Peter Handke

Lifespan | *b.* 1942 (Austria)
First Published |1970
First Published by | Suhrkamp (Frankfurt)
Original Title | *Die Angst des Tormanns beim Elfmeter*

Handke's novella is a surrealist or hyperrealist tale of the absurd, which bears obvious resemblances to Camus' *The Outsider*. Joseph Bloch is a football referee who suddenly, and without explanation, murders a prostitute. The narrative follows his thoughts as he wanders provincial, working-class Austria. Bloch makes little effort to explain his actions or to come to terms with them. Rather, he experiences his life becoming increasingly absurd and pointless. Handke does not lead the reader in any direction and we are never encouraged to believe anything about Bloch. Is he a psychopath and are we seeing inside the mind of a killer? Or are his actions a response, albeit an extreme one, to the alienation that many working-class people experience in modern society? Is his journey through a desolate urban landscape a version of the great voyages of classical literature?

Handke's novella ends with a magnificent set piece that uses the banality of football clichés to represent the absurd nature that life can assume. Bloch watches a football match and engages another spectator in conversation. A penalty is awarded and they discuss the options open to the kicker—a metaphor for the possibilities of human action. The novella ends with an outcome not envisaged, when the kicker shoots the ball straight into the arms of the immobile goalkeeper. **AH**

The Bluest Eye

Toni Morrison

Lifespan | b. 1931 (U.S.)
First Published | 1970
First Published by | Holt, Rinehart & Winston (N.Y.)
Nobel Prize for Literature | 1993

This is Morrison's first novel and recounts the life of the Breedlove family after they move from the country to set up home in Lorain, Ohio (also the author's birthplace). The Breedloves' dislocation, and the descent into madness of their daughter, Pecola, becomes a powerful metaphor for the difficulties of trying to inhabit a space of black identity that is not already part of a racist mythology.

The novel suggests that the categories of gender, race, and economics are enmeshed in determining the fate of the eleven-year-old tragic heroine. Pecola's obsessive desire to have the bluest eyes is a symptom of the way that the black female body has become dominated by white masculine culture. Morrison offers a typically powerful critique of the way that black subjectivity continues to be repressed in a commodity culture. The complex temporal structure of the novel and the restless changes in point of view are in part an attempt to imagine a fluid model of subjectivity that can offer some kind of resistance to a dominant white culture. The adolescent black sisters who relate the narrative, Claudia and Freda MacTeer, offer a contrast to the oppressed Breedlove family in that here they exercise both agency and authority.

In this early novel, Morrison's writing not only captures the hidden cadences of speech; she writes with a keen sensitivity to the protean quality of words. She offers a poetry infused with the promise of alternative modes of being in the world. **VA**

The Ogre

Michel Tournier

Lifespan | b. 1924 (France)
First Published | 1970, by Gallimard (Paris)
Original Title | Le Roi des aulnes
Alternate Title | The Erl-King

The flamboyant baroque novels of Michel Tournier came as a breath of fresh air to a French literary scene dominated by the austere nouveau roman. The Ogre, a heady mix of war story, reworked myth, and sexual perversion, was Tournier's second novel.

The central character, Abel Tiffauges, is introduced to us through his diary, which makes up the first third of the novel. A garage mechanic in 1930s Paris, Tiffauges sees himself as a monster with obscure supernatural powers, although he is aware this may simply mean that he is insane. In conflict with a society he despises, he is only saved from a trial for rape by the outbreak of the Second World War. The rest of the book describes his often bizarre wartime experiences. As a prisoner in Germany, he becomes a ranger on the estate of Hermann Goering, one of the "ogres" of the title. In the last section of the book, he joins the SS, stealing children for the Nazis. He finally dies saving a Jewish child's life. This narrative is at times almost submerged in reflections on Tiffauges', obsessive pedophilia and on the contrast between the Germanic myth of the evil Erl King, stealing children from their parents, and the legend of St. Christopher, carrying a child to safety on his back. Tournier powerfully deploys style and imagination to evoke magic, myth, and reality. **RG**

❯ Michel Tournier is photographed in 1970 by Sophie Bassouls, a French photographer specializing in portraits of literary figures.

The Driver's Seat

Muriel Spark

Lifespan | *b.* 1918 (Scotland), *d.* 2006 (Italy)
First Published | 1970
First Published by | Macmillan (London)
Given Name | Muriel Sarah Camberg

In this short novel, the narrative is told in terse present-tense sentences with minimal adjectival intrusion, as if deliberately foregoing the novelist's traditional powers. Yet, Spark brings her own characteristic sense of anticipation when, very early on, she lets us know that her heroine, Lise, an office worker on vacation somewhere in southern Europe, is going to die. It would be easy to conclude that Lise plans her own destruction from the outset—at the climax of the novel she is the one in the driver's seat, telling her reluctant murderer to tie her hands then stab her. Yet nothing could be further from the truth. Lise, as Spark says at one point, has "no definite plans." However, she is certainly looking for something from the outset, whether we call it satisfaction, control, or a voice. It only gradually becomes apparent to her that what she is looking for amounts to her own death. For only in death do we truly attain our own voice, only here are we free from the claims and demands of others, only here, as we cease to be, can we experience a paradoxical fullness of being.

Interviewed about the novel, Spark once said that the book had given her a terrific shock. The shock was perhaps the same that Freud felt when he discovered the death drive, but for the novelist, whose work ultimately relies on finding a voice, there is a cruel irony in the realization that this might only be discovered at the moment of final loss, in death. **PT**

The Sea of Fertility

Yukio Mishima

Lifespan | *b.* 1925 (Japan), *d.* 1970
First Published | 1965–1970
First Published by | Shinchosha (Tokyo)
Original Title | *Hōjō no umi*

Published in four volumes, *The Sea of Fertility* is Mishima's final work. It first appeared in serial form in the Japanese literary magazine *Shincho*. Volume One, *Spring Snow*, is set in the sequestered world of Tokyo's imperial court in around 1910 and depicts the hopeless love between the young aristocrat Kiyoaki Matsugae and his lover Satoko. Kiyoaki keeps a distance from Satoko, until her engagement to a son of the Emperor makes the impossibility of their love all too real. At this point, their desperate but passionate affair begins, witnessed by Shigekuni Honda, Kiyoaki's closest friend. When Kiyoaki dies, Honda embarks on a search for his reincarnation.

The protagonists in the later volumes (*Runaway Horses* and *The Temple at Dawn*) bear the shade of Kiyoaki—as a political fanatic in the 1930s, as a Thai princess before and after the Second World War, and, in the final volume (*The Decay of the Angel*), as an evil orphan in the 1960s. The idea of this reincarnation nourishes Honda until the final volume. The ending suggests that human life is irretrievable and its end inevitable. In a stunning finale, Honda finally realizes the impossibility of reliving the past and reviving the dead. The novel, which some consider to be the Japanese version of Proust's *In Search of Lost Time*, provides us with a fabulous insight into life and the experience of memory. **KK**

⊙ Yukio Mishima poses as a samurai ready to commit ritual suicide
  by disembowelling—which he eventually did, in November 1970.

Rabbit Redux

John Updike

Lifespan | *b.* 1932 (U.S.)
First Published | 1971
First Published by | Knopf (New York)
Pulitzer Prizes | 1982, 1991

Rabbit Redux, Updike's second novel in his four-volume "Rabbit" series, takes place in 1969, ten years after the end of *Rabbit, Run*. Set in the small town of Brewer, Pennsylvania, the Rabbit books trace the story of Harry Angstrom, nicknamed "Rabbit," as he goes from high school basketball star to young husband and father, and finally through middle age and into retirement.

Updike's Everyman, now in his thirties, is uncomfortably aware of being on the verge of middle age. Set against the surreal background of the *Apollo 11* moon landing, *Rabbit Redux* charts, through Rabbit's own chaotic personal life, the positive and damaging changes to small town America, brought about by the collision of traditional values and hierarchies and the irresistible rise of 1960s counterculture. When his apparently conformist marriage begins to crumble, Rabbit must acknowledge the wider events that are occurring in the lives of those around him, pitting him against his working-class Midwestern roots. Rabbit's certainties about life begin to crumble, threatening his relationships with his family and colleagues. However, Rabbit is granted unexpected spiritual growth that changes his life.

Rabbit Redux not only describes but captures the feeling of the 1960s, plunging the reader into a world characterized by confused sensuality and political chaos, but also a touching and expansive hope for the future. **AB**

The Wild Boys

William Burroughs

Lifespan | *b.* 1914 (U.S.), *d.* 1997
First Published | 1971
First Published by | Grove Press (New York)
Full Name | William Seward Burroughs

William Burroughs famously described his writing as an attempt to say the most repulsive things he could imagine. His success, in the form of cult status and a notoriety probably unmatched by any other twentieth-century author is in large measure due to the hunger among western consumers for whatever will most sharply repel them.

Following the public uproar surrounding the appearance of *Naked Lunch* in 1959, Burroughs would never again manage to publish anything that played the American morality complex so fiercely at its own game. *The Wild Boys* is still a pretty wild ride, even for readers familiar with the superficial moral onslaught of *American Psycho* or other "shocking" books whose violence is vacuum-packed in an implicit homily on "our society." Burroughs was never really a pusher of allegories, despite the nonsense about his religious or "deeply moral" mission spouted by Ballard, Mailer, and other middle class authors. These writers were unprepared to believe that fiction could truly set out to smash up the morality of its readers altogether, and without remorse or justification. *The Wild Boys* at least aims to do that. The heroes are involved in a kind of violent, homosexual terrorist cell, haters of the state and particularly of women, physically beautiful and possessed of magical powers. The novel wades through the detail of their brutal sex acts. This work is paranoid, often nonsensical, and no good at all for the weak stomach. **KS**

Group Portrait With Lady

Heinrich Böll

Lifespan | b. 1917 (Germany), d. 1985
First Published | 1971
First Published by | Kiepenheuer & Witsch (Cologne)
Original Title | Gruppenbild mit Dame

What Böll creates in his Nobel Prize-winning novel is an ensemble of transitory identities. The novel leads into the German past between 1890 and 1970. Psychological insights from the perspectives of various characters are heterogeneous and convincing. We encounter young intellectuals, a Jewish nun, a female freedom fighter, a notorious upstart, a political opportunist, and stupefied Nazis. Yet, one person remains a matter of pure conjecture: Leni Pfeiffer. She is the lady in the center of the portrait around whom the series of interviews, letters and personal stories revolve. Leni is seen through the eyes of the narrator, who tends to mystify his blond and allegedly naïve protagonist. Nevertheless, her character resists cliché; her insistence on overcoming racial and social limits points to a subversive, intelligent character.

Böll's writing is bound up with the aims of Gruppe 47 (Group 47)—a literary association founded by Alfred Andersch and Walter Richter in West Germany in 1947. These authors responded to the gulf that had been opened between them and those German intellectuals who had fled Nazi rule. Initially, the authors of the Gruppe 47 felt the need to cleanse their language of Nazi propaganda by advocating a sparse realism. In *Group Portrait With Lady*, the naturalistic narrative indicates the complexity of real life, particularly toward the end of the novel when the narrator reveals his partiality by actively participating in the events. **MC**

> *"The Author is far from having insight into all aspects of Leni's ... life, yet everything ... has been done to obtain the kind of information on Leni that is known to be factual."*

⊙ Böll's writing is dominated by memories of the Second World War and by a critique of the moral vacuum of postwar Germany.

Fear and Loathing in Las Vegas

Hunter S. Thompson

"We were somewhere around Barstow on the edge of the desert when the drugs began to take hold." Thompson's novel has one of the most recognizable first lines in modern fiction. It tells the story of the narrator's chemical-fueled sojourn in and around Las Vegas in the manic company of his Samoan attorney, on an assignment to cover an off-road dune-buggy-and-motorbike race called the Mint 400 for a New York sporting magazine. Having spent his advance on a trunkload of illegal drugs, the pair begin their adventure at a crazed pitch, abandoning any sense of personal responsibility. This frenzy intensifies when they hit the city and, among other questionable decisions, decide to hole up in a hotel which is hosting the National District Attorneys' Conference on Narcotics and Dangerous Drugs.

The heroes' self-indulgence is simply American over-consumption turned up many notches in a parodic take-off of thoughtless consumerism. At the same time, the journey is an extreme but somehow admirable celebration of traditional American freedoms, in Nixon's first term as president, while the war in Vietnam is being waged, and scandalously punitive jail sentences are being handed out at home for draftcard burners and marijuana smokers. *Fear and Loathing* . . . is experienced through doors of perception, which are set so fantastically awry that no-one can be said to know for sure what just happened, what is happening, and what might happen. The book provides an invigorating and hilarious demolition job on the ultimate postmodern city, suggesting that the best way to resist Vegas's rapacious demands is to screw yourself up so entirely beforehand that you are altogether unable to respond in the way which the city commands that you do. **RP**

Lifespan | *b.* 1939 (U.S.), *d.* 2005
First Published | 1971, by Random House (N.Y.)
Full Title | *Fear and Loathing in Las Vegas: A Savage Journey to the Heart of the American Dream*

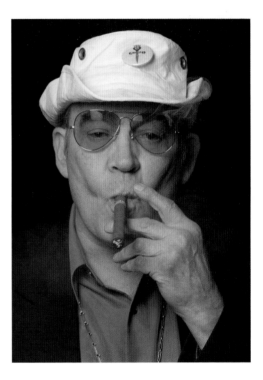

"'How about some ether?'"

⬆ Thompson enjoys a cigar in 2003, two years before his death by suicide; at his funeral, his ashes were fired from a cannon.

◀ A caricature of Thompson's friend Johnny Depp playing the author in Terry Gilliam's 1998 movie version of *Fear and Loathing*.

The Book of Daniel

E. L. Doctorow

"'Few books of the Old Testament have been so full of enigmas as The Book of Daniel.'"

Lifespan | *b.* 1931 (U.S.)
First Published | 1971
First Published by | Random House (New York)
Full Name | Edgar Lawrence Doctorow

The Book of Daniel examines the nature and effectiveness of different forms of political protest in the United States, and the passage from the Old Left of the1940s and 1950s to the New Left of the 1960s. For the narrator, Daniel Isaacson, it is about the difficulties of coming to terms with the political and familial legacy of his parents—Ethel and Julius Rosenberg in all but name—who were executed by the state for allegedly passing nuclear secrets to the Soviet Union in 1953. Doctorow's novel asks how political power manifests itself in the hands of individuals and institutions, and what can be done to oppose the concentration and abuse of power by government and corporations. In a choice between the "gutsy and pathetic" radicalism of his father, and the flaccid, hubristic counter-cultural pronounce-ments of Artie Sternlicht, who promises to "overthrow the United States with images," Daniel finds only disillusionment and dead-ends. The former is naïve and easily crushed by the state. The latter finds its fullest realization in Disneyland, a theme park world that proposes "a technique of abbreviated shorthand culture for the masses." Daniel must put together the different fragments of his life in order to reconcile the political legacy of his parents' activism with his own disenchanted view of the world. This moving account of protest and family succumbs neither to the optimistic belief that personal struggle conquers all nor the pessimistic belief that all political struggle is futile. **AP**

In a Free State

V. S. Naipaul

Lifespan | *b*. 1932 (Trinidad)
First Published | 1971, by Deutsch (London)
Full Name | Vidiadhar Surajprasad Naipaul
Booker Prize | 1971

Winner of the 1971 Booker Prize, *In a Free State* contains two short stories and a novella enveloped by a diary-form prologue and epilogue. One of Naipaul's best-known novels, it is a profound examination of dislocation and the meaning and limitations of freedom in a context of displacement.

In the first story, an Indian servant finds himself in Washington after his boss is posted there as a diplomat. He ends up as an illegal immigrant and marries to become naturalized. In the second narrative, an Indian from the West Indies follows his brother to England and is left fending for himself. In both cases, freedom arrives only with the loss of those anchors that once provided meaning and security in their home countries.

The longest narrative, "In a Free State," is set in an unnamed, newly independent country in Africa. Bobby, a homosexual colonial civil servant with a penchant for seducing young black men, and Linda, a colonial radio host's wife, who harbors a disgust for Africans, travel by car to the Southern Collectorate, an autonomous region still controlled by the king. During the journey, a series of antagonistic encounters take place with local inhabitants that progress from insults and vandalism to physical violence. The old colonial confidence that surrounds the start of the journey is gradually eroded and the brutal reality of what the new free state implies for the expatriate community begins to appear. **ABi**

House Mother Normal

B. S. Johnson

Lifespan | *b*. 1933 (England), *d*. 1973
First Published | 1971
First Published by | Collins (London)
Full Title | *House Mother Normal: A Geriatric Comedy*

Johnson's "comedy" is a razor sharp parody of the world of geriatric state-care. Cruelty between proprietor and patient is normalized as an accepted routine for nursing the elderly under meager sponsorship. *House Mother Normal* is structured by descent, both psychological and moral. It unfolds as a series of monologues from the most able-minded resident, Sarah Lamson, whose disabilities are largely rheumatic, and climaxes with the ninety-four-year-old Rosetta Stanton, whose physical and cognitive ailments are too numerous to list. Rosetta has been addressed by the authorities as a case unworthy even of pity simply because "she has everything everyone else has," and her utterances scatter the page as though indiscriminately placed, evacuated of all intention or reference.

This is a challenging, if uncomfortable, position in which to be placed as reader. Johnson offers us a privileged, almost forensic access to the mind of each of his speakers. Little is inevitable in this anarchic care home as we move, in the case of each occupant, through the vicissitudes of their recollections, interrupted only by the House Mother's grim party game of pass-the-parcel, organized solely for her sadistic gratification. Johnson compels us to acknowledge our freedom as observers who can go on thinking and speculating—the freedom, potentially, to choose not to be at the mercy of institutional abuse—while the narrators lapse between pain and slumber. **DJ**

Surfacing

Margaret Atwood

Lifespan | *b.*1939 (Canada)
First Published | 1972
First Published by | McClelland & Stewart (Toronto)
Movie Adaptation Released | 1981

Surfacing, Atwood's second novel, draws on elements of the thriller, the ghost story, the travelogue, and the pioneer narrative. It strikes a perfect balance between around-the-campfire suspense and intellectual insight. *Surfacing* is the story of an unnamed narrator who returns to her birthplace on a remote island in Québec after her father mysteriously disappears. She is accompanied by three lifelong city-dwellers: her partner Joe and an obnoxious married couple, Anna and David. After arriving on the island, dark secrets "surface" like sunken objects from the lake that surrounds it. The weaknesses, vanities, and prejudices of each character are slowly squeezed out by the experience of isolation. As the pressures of both past and present intensify, the narrator regresses into a paranoid, animalistic state, and eventually imagines herself in a shamanic union with nature after discovering an underwater cave painted with Native American glyphs.

Surfacing is a novel preoccupied by the question of boundaries: of language, of national identity, of "home," of gender, and of the body. One of its most engaging features, however, is the depiction of a rural Canada transformed by commercialization and tourism. The novel shows that it is not only refugees or armies who cross borders but the whole gigantic machinery of capital and the mass media. This is a novel of belonging and displacement told with remarkable precision and economy. **SamT**

"Now we're on my home ground, foreign territory. My throat constricts, as it learned to do when I discovered people could say words that would go into my ears meaning nothing."

⏏ Margaret Atwood is photographed in rural Ontario in 1972, when she was beginning to make her mark as a novelist.

G

John Berger

Lifespan | *b.* 1926 (England)
First Published | 1972
First Published by | Weidenfeld & Nicolson (London)
Booker Prize | 1972

G is a chronicle of the sexual exploits of a nameless protagonist (helpfully identified in the novel as "the protagonist") at the turn of the century. Set against the backdrop of Garibaldi and the failed revolution of Milanese workers in 1898, the novel provides an intimate portrait of the numerous dalliances of this aspiring Don Juan, who is seemingly impervious to the calamities that are occurring outside the bedroom. *G* is an exploration of how the domain of private experience can ultimately also translate into a recognition of broader social belonging.

What is most immediately striking about the novel is the experimental narrative style. As the story is recounted largely from the perspective of the narrator and the women who yield to his seductions, "the protagonist" largely becomes the layered accumulation of these perceptions rather than a fully defined character from the outset. The novel is notable for its attention not merely to what occurs during sexual intimacy, but also how this is structured through a perception of intersubjectivity. Eroticism arises from the way the characters fashion their experience of consciousness through an awareness they have of the experience while actually performing it. This narrative absorption in the realm of the senses, rather than insulating the reluctant hero further from a world of contact with others, becomes the mainspring for an aroused consciousness of the oppression and injustice that is taking place around him. **VA**

The Summer Book

Tove Jansson

Lifespan | *b.* 1914 (Finland), *d.* 2001
First Published | 1972, by A. Bonnier (Stockholm)
Original Language | Swedish
Original Title | *Sommarboken*

The writer and artist Tove Jansson is best known as the creator of the much-loved Moomin children's stories. *The Summer Book* was one of ten novels she wrote for adults and is regarded as a modern classic in Scandinavia, where it has never been out of print.

Based loosely on the author's own experiences, *The Summer Book* spans a season during which an elderly artist and her six-year-old granddaughter, Sophia, while away the long days together on a tiny island in the Gulf of Finland. It is a magical, elegiac, quietly humorous book that slowly draws the reader into the lives of Sophia (whose mother has recently died), her grandmother, and her largely absent "Papa." The color and depth of the characterization moves the narrative forward, despite the fact that very little actually happens. The old woman and the young girl spend their days pottering around their tiny, idyllic island summer home, collecting driftwood, discussing death, putting down new turf, and infuriating each other. Descriptions, such as that of the texture of moss that has been trodden on three times, are written in minute, leisurely detail and through these descriptions the reader comes to understand the special relationship between the grandmother and granddaughter. Jansson's style is unsentimental and, as the book meanders through summer, the two learn to adjust to each other's fears and idiosyncrasies, allowing a deep, understated love to unfold that extends beyond the family to both the island and the season. **LE**

The Breast

Philip Roth

Lifespan | *b.* 1933 (U.S.)
First Published | 1972
First Published by | Holt, Rinehart & Winston (N.Y.)
Number of Awards (1960–2005) | 12

This surreal novella (the first of a trilogy) concerns the bizarre fate of David Kepesh, a Professor of Literature, who as a result of some mysterious hormonal malfunction has been transformed into a one-hundred-and-fifty-five-pound female breast. Kepesh attempts to convince himself and others that he has merely gone insane. Not surprisingly, Kepesh's misfortune allows Roth to indulge in gleeful and unrestrained lampoonery of some of the more earnest preoccupations of the literary firmament: he sends up the pomposity of a modish Freudianism, pokes fun at existentialist navel-gazing, and cannot resist the occasional swipe at feminist dogma. This grotesque fable of male fantasy gone horribly wrong also allows Roth to indulge in a forthright contemplation of the grubby interface between subjectivity and sexuality.

However, Roth is also questioning the role of the non-realist novel in contemporary America. Kepesh, in fact, finally finds some kind of peace through abandoning existential angst in favor of accepting the ordinariness of his situation. This is a culture, Roth suggests, that has become much too flimsy to bear the weight of the kind of metaphysical questions that Kepesh's strange predicament initially provokes.

In many ways *The Breast* is a distillation of Roth's irreverent style and sardonic wit: and for readers inclined toward such literary wheezes, this boisterous and ribald fable will not disappoint. **VA**

Invisible Cities

Italo Calvino

Lifespan | *b.* 1923 (Cuba), *d.* 1985 (Italy)
First Published | 1972
First Published by | G. Einaudi (Turin)
Original Title | *Le città invisibili*

Invisible Cities is constructed as a series of imaginary travel anecdotes told to the Tartar emperor Kublai Khan by the Venetian explorer Marco Polo. Fifty-five prose pieces each describe a different fabulous city and each contains a conceptual or philosophical puzzle or enigma. Zemrude, for example, is a city that changes according to the mood of the beholder. It is divided into upper and lower parts, windowsills and fountains above, gutters and wastepaper below. The upper world is known chiefly through the memory of those whose eyes now dwell on the lower. In Diomira, one feels envious toward those other visitors for whom the city instils melancholy. Zoe, a city of "indivisible existence," where every activity is possible everywhere, becomes indistinct: "Why, then, does the city exist? What line separates the inside from the outside, the rumble of wheels from the howl of wolves?"

Tucked between some of the descriptions are brief but telling episodes in which the relationship between the interlocutors is developed. Kublai Khan finds in the Venetian's stories something to transcend his earthly, temporal empire. In their art he discerns, "through the walls and towers destined to crumble, the tracery of a pattern so subtle it could escape the termites' gnawing." For his part, Polo invents cities on a redemptive principle. He says, "I am collecting the ashes of the other possible cities that vanish to make room for it, cities that can never be rebuilt or remembered." **DH**

Sula

Toni Morrison

Lifespan | *b.* 1931 (U.S.)
First Published | 1973
First Published by | Knopf (New York)
Nobel Prize for Literature | 1993

Written during the Vietnam War, *Sula* has been described as an anti-war novel, as well as a black woman's epic, a story of female friendship, an exploration of the feminine psyche, and a prime postmodern text. It is, in fact, all of these and more. A disconcerting parable of female selfhood, the novel explores the nature of good and evil, questioning the dualism that structures our lives.

The black community, the subject of *Sula*, lives in the Bottom, a hillside neighborhood overlooking a valley. Soldiers returning from the First World War, sent mad by that conflict, are further discomposed by the enduring racism of the American south. The community defends its right to exist by defining its own limits and singling out its own pariahs. Sula herself is a marked woman. Her return from exile is greeted with suspicion, not least because she is a self-made woman. She flouts convention, her sexual profligacy eventually estranging her from the whole community. But where does evil reside in this narrative, when the social order relies on scapegoats to preserve its morality? Is Sula an evil presence responsible for the community's ills, or is she an anarchic savior, exposing the inherent moral confusion at the community's heart? The novel records how women's suspicion of other women prevents a feminine revision of communal values and highlights how female solidarity is sacrificed to the pursuit of narrow material gains and an atrophied freedom offered by men and white society. **CJ**

The Black Prince

Iris Murdoch

Lifespan | *b.* 1919 (Ireland), *d.* 1999 (England)
First Published | 1973
First Published by | Chatto & Windus (London)
Full Name | Dame Jean Iris Murdoch

The title of Iris Murdoch's literary thriller refers to Shakespeare's dithering anti-hero and reflects an ongoing concern of the novel. Bradley Pearson, a writer with writer's block, is the awkward and self-conscious narrator of Murdoch's metafictional novel. Crafted around the process of writing a work of fiction, the novel ostensibly arises out of the events that overtake Bradley's attempts to write his long-overdue masterpiece. Arnold Baffin, his literary nemesis, whose novels are numerous and all commercially successful, is a long-standing friend but their relationship has always been fraught with tensions. Bradley's relationship with Arnold and his family has nonetheless been an important one, which throughout the course of the novel reaches new levels of intensity and interdependency.

Bradley's fascination with *Hamlet* is bound up with the repeated frustration of his desire to write, and with his ultimate success. As a fifty-eight-year-old retired tax inspector he cuts an unlikely hero, but in ways which have frequently been conflated with Murdoch herself, Bradley interrogates the role of the artist in the exploration of the relationship between morality and truth. The structure of the novel as the plumbing of a truth uncovered in the process of writing creates a multilayered effect. In *The Black Prince* Murdoch rehearses themes that are familiar to readers of her other work, but the tight structure and her typically dry humor make this an engaging novel with a pleasing twist in the tale. **JW**

Gravity's Rainbow

Thomas Pynchon

Lifespan | *b.*1937 (U.S.)
First Published | 1973
First Published by | Viking Press (New York)
National Book Award | 1974 (joint)

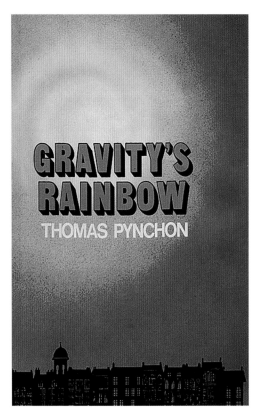

Pynchon's massive work opens with London under attack from V-2 rockets during the closing stages of the Second World War.

It would be as futile to attempt a plot summary of *Gravity's Rainbow* here as it would be to say that *Ulysses* is about two men and their day in Dublin. Indeed, Pynchon's extraordinary novel is already famous (or perhaps infamous) for its linguistic experimentation, its esoteric knowledge systems, and the way in which it so visibly dismantles its own sense of space and time. Nevertheless, much of the novel can be located in Europe during the years just preceding the end of the Second World War and the years of fragile peace just after. The central motif that binds the work together is the German V-2 rocket bomb, a weapon one hears only after it has already hit its target (the rocket travels faster than the speed of sound). The V-2 becomes a mystic object, a Kabbalistic text, an apocalyptic phallus, an emblem of "the World's suicide." Behind the scenes, shadowy (but very real) companies such as IG Farben and Shell Oil form another order of power—as if the whole war had been staged in order to find uses for their technologies and to expand their markets.

It is almost impossible to convey the scope of Pynchon's writing in a few words. *Gravity's Rainbow* is a proliferating, encyclopedic work with multiple points of entry and exit. There are literally thousands of allusions and enigmas in which to lose oneself: references to comics, B-movies, popular and classical music, drugs, magic and the occult, engineering, physics, Pavlovian psychology, economic theory—the list goes on. It remains a milestone in American fiction; a massively ambitious, carnivalesque epic that tracks the realignment of global power through the theater of war. For all the novel's complexity and darkness, it is Pynchon's commitment to oppressed and unrecorded voices, to justice, to partnership, and to community that shines through. **SamT**

The Honorary Consul

Graham Greene

Charley Fortnum, the alcoholic British Honorary Consul in a remote region of northern Argentina, has been kidnapped by mistake. Rebels from over the border in Paraguay intended to capture the American Ambassador. Fortnum may not have been the target, but he is now the hostage, and will be killed in four days' time unless a number of political prisoners are released in Paraguay. The General—Alfredo Stroessner, who ruled Paraguay from 1954 until 1989—holds power only by virtue of American patronage. But Fortnum is more of a nuisance than an asset to the British authorities, and British influence is anyway negligible.

Fortnum's only friend is Dr. Eduardo Plarr, who arrived in Argentina twenty years previously as a teenage refugee with his Paraguayan mother, leaving his English father behind. As a child in Paraguay, Plarr went to school with two of the kidnappers, and when the sedatives they've given their hostage react badly with the alcohol in his system, they call on the doctor for help. But Plarr's motives are suspect, even to himself: his father is one of the prisoners the rebels want released; he's also sleeping with Fortnum's wife.

Like many of Greene's novels, *The Honorary Consul* is concerned with the intersections of politics, religion, and sex. But the burden of Catholic guilt is carried not, as in previous books, by the protagonist, but by the leader of the kidnappers, a defrocked priest. And if Plarr seems unusually world-weary for a man in his thirties, his cynicism can be traced not only to the age of the author (Greene was nearly seventy when he wrote the novel) but to the age in which he lived. *The Honorary Consul* was published the year that Allende was overthrown in Chile by General Pinochet and the CIA. **TEJ**

Lifespan | *b.*1904 (England), *d.* 1991 (Switzerland)
First Published | 1973
First Published by | Bodley Head (London)
Full Name | Henry Graham Greene

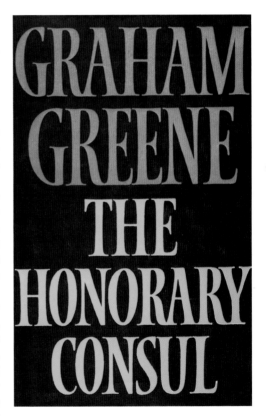

The title of Greene's novel is of course ironic, with its suggestion of "honor" in a world that seems quite devoid of that quality.

Crash

J.G. Ballard

Lifespan | *b.* 1930 (China)
First Published | 1973
First Published by | Jonathan Cape (London)
Movie Adaptation Released | 1996

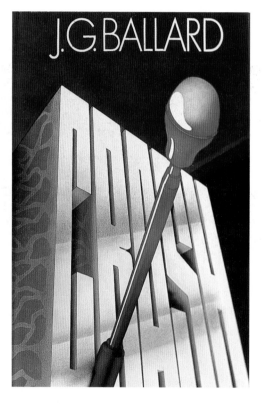

The striking jacket of the first edition of Ballard's novel gives eye-catching prominence to an undisguisedly phallic gearstick.

This wrecked Pontiac was one of the exhibits at the "Atrocity Exhibition" which was staged by Ballard in London in 1970.

J.G. Ballard's *Crash* is the story of the narrator's relationship with Vaughan and of Vaughan's obsession with the actress, Elizabeth Taylor. Contemporary desire, the violence of the look, has a new vehicle, the car. There are bodies everywhere; sex and chassis, metal and skin. Photographs, radio transmissions, cameras, motor shows—all these are the new manifest content of our waking dreams. Disturbingly, the characters appear to have no internal life in any traditional novelistic sense, as every excess is exposed on film or, finally, by actions. Gestures of apparent intimacy become a search for new wounds, barriers are smashed, and damage is hallowed.

Ballard's novel, "the first pornographic book dominated by twentieth-century technology" (Maxim Jakubowski), is an exception within an exceptional body of work. It contains none of the more explicit, worldwide catastrophes of his earlier works. This breakdown is something we can all identify with; it has already happened, inside us. Given that the narrator is named Jim Ballard, the novel jumps other barriers, providing a link with his later, lightly fictionalized, autobiographies, especially *The Kindness of Women*, where it is unnervingly possible to identify certain characters from *Crash*.

Nevertheless, this is still classic Ballard; the shocking insights are unerring, the perversions intensely sane and personal. Frighteningly, it all makes sense. Not everyone appreciates such sentiments. "The author of this book has gone beyond psychiatric help," a publisher's reader stated. This inadvertently perceptive comment begs the question—where is that place? Ballard considered the assessment"…the greatest compliment you can be paid." **JS**

The Castle of Crossed Destinies

Italo Calvino

Lifespan | b. 1923 (Cuba), d. 1985 (Italy)
First Published | 1973
First Published by | G. Einaudi (Turin)
Original Title | Il castello dei destini incrociati

In his essay collection, *Six Memos for the Next Millennium*, Calvino argued passionately for the qualities in literature that future generations should cherish: lightness, quickness, exactitude, visibility, and multiplicity. *The Castle of Crossed Destinies* exemplifies all of these qualities, though perhaps, above all, visibility. As Calvino has said: "This book is made first of pictures—from tarot cards—and secondly of written words." The two short books that make up *The Castle of Crossed Destinies* both follow the same pattern: a traveler arrives at his destination (a castle in one book, a tavern in the next), to discover that everyone there, including himself, has been struck dumb. The guests communicate their stories to each other by means of tarot cards. The resulting tales are like a distillation of all the stories ever told. They include tales of the alchemist who sold his soul, of Roland crazed with love, tales of St. George and St. Jerome, of Faust, Oedipus, and Hamlet. Calvino's own invention, *The Waverer's Tale*, tells the story of a man unable to choose in a world that continues to inflict the torment of choice upon him. In the tarot decks of Bonifacio Bembo and of Marseille, Calvino discovers, or rediscovers, the oldest story generating machine of them all. **PT**

◐ This confident portrait photo of Italo Calvino was taken in the author's home by French photographer Sophie Bassouls in 1974.

The Siege of Krishnapur

J. G. Farrell

Lifespan | b. 1935 (England), d. 1979 (Ireland)
First Published | 1973
First Published by | Weidenfeld & Nicolson (London)
Booker Prize | 1973

Set during the Indian Mutiny of 1857, *The Siege of Krishnapur* is concerned with a large group of characters. It might even be viewed as a kind of nineteenth-century pastiche, but it is odder and funnier than that. Beyond the siege, the novel's point of reference is the Great Exhibition of 1851, when all the new technology of the Victorian world was brought together and displayed in London. Krishnapur's taxman, Mr. Hopkins, is an enthusiast who brings examples of the new technology to India, although most of it is eventually fired at the attacking sepoys.

The fighting is an opportunity for debates between the padre, who stresses God's existence even as he helps fire a cannon, the rationalist magistrate who believes in phrenology, and competing views of medical research. Dr. McNab correctly understands how to treat cholera, but his rival refuses treatment and dies. The novel is a mosaic of mid-Victorian languages in dispute. The languages of belief, of rationalist skepticism, and quite bad poetry embody new (and old) perceptions. Women are modernized and liberated by the siege; Lucy, trapped in Krishnapur, becomes expert in making cartridges and when the siege is raised and they are no longer needed, she weeps. The anti-imperialist rising provokes debates about occupation of countries that are as relevant now as then. **AMu**

A Question of Power

Bessie Head

Lifespan | *b.* 1937 (South Africa), *d.* 1986 (Botswana)
First Published | 1973
First Published by | Davis-Poynter (London)
Paperback | Heinemann African Writers Series (1973)

A Question of Power raises fascinating questions about the relationship of fiction to autobiography. Like Head herself, the novel's protagonist Elizabeth has fled apartheid South Africa for Botswana; the daughter of a black father and a white mother imprisoned for insanity, she was brought up by a foster-mother she believed to be her birth mother until adolescence. Elizabeth, like Head, undergoes an experience in Botswana that could be variously described as spiritual journey or mental breakdown.

The novel shifts continually between two narratives. One concerns Elizabeth's life in a Botswanan village. The other strand tells the story of Elizabeth's debilitating visions of the monk-like figure Sello and the sadistic seducer Dan. Head never allows her reader to know whether these figures are supernatural apparitions of ancient souls or the figments of a disordered mind. Not least of the haunting presences in the novel is South Africa itself. *A Question of Power* is perhaps most profoundly concerned with what Head calls "the problem of evil." Elizabeth's wrestling with the visions comprises a meditation upon the nature of evil. The final outcome of her journey is the realization that life must be sacred. Perhaps the greatest triumph of this fine novel is that to read it is to feel oneself go just a little mad—to have thrown into disarray one's certainties about the boundaries between fiction and autobiography, reality and unreality, madness and cure. **VM**

Fear of Flying

Erica Jong

Lifespan | *b.* 1942 (U.S.)
First Published | 1973
First Published by | Holt, Rinehart & Winston (N.Y.)
Full Name | Erica Mann Jong

An uninhibited tale of sexual liberation and self-discovery, as well as being a self-consciously feminist text, *Fear of Flying* tells the story of a twice-married, over-psychoanalyzed woman writer named Isadora Wing, who models herself on predecessors such as Mary Wollstonecraft and Virginia Woolf, and leaves her psychiatrist husband at an international conference in order to take up with an inappropriate lover. They travel around Europe in a drunken daze, making love and feeling guilty in equal measures, before the lover leaves Isadora. Isadora returns to her husband, having learned, in the space of twenty-four hours of solitude, to stand on her own two feet.

A flawed, articulate heroine, Isadora is unable to incorporate feminism fully in her life. Escape fantasies loom large in her imagination, and are intimately bound up, for her, in being a woman. The novel is peppered with both graphically sexual flashbacks and didactic statements of feminism; the combination doesn't always work. While Jong attempts to portray sexual infidelity as liberating, Isadora's emotional dependence on the men in her life undercuts this message. *Fear of Flying* breaks many taboos, but the novel ultimately leaves the status of the institution of marriage intact. It is this ambivalence toward feminism that makes this a key text in the feminist canon. **HM**

❯ Young and vivacious, Erica Jong interpreted feminism as a woman's right to the pursuit of unbridled heterosexual pleasure.

Breakfast of Champions

Kurt Vonnegut, Jr

Lifespan | *b.* 1922 (U.S.)
First Published | 1973
First Published by | Delacorte Press (New York)
Alternate Title | *Goodbye Blue Monday*

This is the story of two "lonesome, skinny, fairly old white men on a planet that was dying fast." Kilgore Trout is a misanthropic science fiction writer whose stories are used as filler for pornographic magazines. They have, however, attracted a tiny if passionate fan base, notably among the insane. Trout is invited to appear at an arts festival in Midland City. He thinks there must be some mistake. Dwayne Hoover is a lunatic soon to find the locus of his insanity in the writings of Trout. He runs the Exit Eleven Pontiac Village and has lately seen a huge duck directing traffic. He believes that all humans are robots except himself: Trout's writing will turn Dwayne into a "homocidal maniac."

Vonnegut wants to set his characters free. Fictions have made us unhappy; they are why America is such a mess and people keep shooting each other. "Breakfast of Champions" is a slogan used to hawk wheat-flakes to children, a fiction allowing slothful Americans to think themselves superheroes. "Goodbye Blue Monday" adorns Hoover's Pontiac dealership. It is also what Hoover, during the war, painted on the side of a five-hundred-pound bomb dropped on Hamburg. The text is peppered with infantile drawings and written with simplicity. Vonnegut's supreme ironic detachment allows the inanity of living in an idiot country on a damaged planet to shine brightly of its own accord. **GT**

Tinker Tailor Soldier Spy

John Le Carré

Lifespan | *b.* 1931 (England)
First Published | 1974, by Hodder & Stoughton (Lon.)
Trilogy | *Tinker Tailor Soldier Spy* (1974), *The Honourable Schoolboy* (1977), *Smiley's People* (1980)

During the 1960s, the British intelligence service was demoralized by finding that a number of its highly placed agents, notably Kim Philby, were Soviet spies. In a number of respects, Le Carré's novel addresses many of the issues raised by these revelations: the role of the intelligence services in the Cold War, the social disguises people adopt, the decay of post-imperial Britain, and most fundamentally the questions of loyalty and treachery—to self, to friends, to the nation.

The book follows the endeavors of George Smiley, called from retirement, to discover a "mole" (a Soviet agent working in the highest levels of British Intelligence with the code name of "Gerald"). Through the character of Smiley, Le Carré deftly proposes searching questions about the state of Britain. In many ways, Smiley is the logical successor to Sherlock Holmes. He has a wonderful forensic capacity and lacks a zealous conviction of a firm difference between the criminal and the upright, the loyal and the treacherous. Smiley is aware of how both he and "Gerald" are remnants of an imperial era. They are out of place in a post-Second World War Britain, a country now relatively unimportant between the superpowers of the United States and Russia. The novel wonderfully captures a dark, brooding environment where human warmth appears a rare commodity. **TH**

The Lost Honor of Katharina Blum

Heinrich Böll

Lifespan | *b.* 1917 (Germany), *d.* 1985
First Published | 1974
First Published by | Kiepenheuer & Witsch (Cologne)
Original Title | *Die Verlorene Ehre der Katharina Blum*

The Lost Honor of Katharina Blum is possibly best known now as the basis for Volker Schlöndorff's and Margarethe von Trotta's acclaimed film by the same name (1975). On the surface the novel appears as a moral tale with a lesson about the evil of the unscrupulous sensationalism of the mass media. This is born out by the fact that it was written after Heinrich Böll himself was made the subject of a virulent hate campaign by the populist right-wing tabloid *Bild* after he criticized the newspaper in the liberal weekly *Der Spiegel*.

Katharina Blum is a normal young woman who lives a reclusive life, working as a housekeeper. At a party she meets and falls in love with Ludwig Gotten, wanted by the police for an undefined crime. The pair spend the night together at her flat, but when the police storm the building in the morning, Ludwig has gone. Over the next four days, Katharina's life is taken apart by the police and her name is dragged through the mud by a mass tabloid clearly modeled on *Bild*. She gives an interview to the tabloid reporter responsible, and when he makes a sexual pass at her, she shoots him dead. Böll's text is more than simply an outraged response to the excesses of a specific tabloid. It contains an awareness of the power of language, and a warning about the violence that words can do if respect for facts is not accompanied by respect for people. **DG**

"... she rings the front door bell at the home of Walter Moeding, Crime Commissioner, who is at that moment engaged, for professional rather than private reasons, in disguising himself as a sheikh, and she declares to the startled Moeding that at about 12:15 noon that day she shot and killed Werner Tötges ..."

◉ A poster for the original German version of Schlöndorff and Von Trotta's highly acclaimed 1975 movie adaptation of Böll's novel.

Dusklands

J.M. Coetzee

Lifespan | *b.* 1940 (South Africa)
First Published | 1974
First Published by | Ravan Press (Johannesburg)
Full Name | John Maxwell Coetzee

Dusklands is composed of two short narratives. The first deals with Eugene Dawn's work on "The Vietnam Project," devising and analyzing mythographies that will both allow America to justify its own position in that war, and undermine the Viet Cong's resistance. The second is the self-told, brutal tale of Jacobus Coetzee, one of the "heroes who first ventured into the interior of Southern Africa, and brought back news of what we had inherited."

The parallels and crossovers of these two narratives make for unsettling, stark juxtapositions. The lines between the physical, mental, and cultural methods of colonial domination are blurred, and the psychology of the imperialist is laid disturbingly bare. Underneath this tantalizing exploration, never quite on the surface, lies a strong interrogation of the way in which history is itself constructed. Yet despite this density of theoretical allusion and exploration, the text is never sterile. Coetzee's prose is characteristically direct and vivid. Conjured from the spare passages are visions of horror and empathy, falsehood, and truth. From the twenty-four pictures of the Vietnam War that Dawn carries round in a lunch pail, to the horrific "vengeance" meted out by Jacobus Coetzee, *Dusklands* is viscerally gripping. It is a novel that manages to be a breathtakingly direct attack on its targets, but also an unnerving reminder of the spreading tentacles of complicity, and of the presence in all our stories of the things that we would rather were not told. **DR**

The Fan Man

William Kotzwinkle

Lifespan | *b.* 1938 (U.S.)
First Published | 1974
First Published by | Avon (New York)
First UK Edition | A. Ellis (Henley-on-Thames)

Books take us to many exotic and strange places, but few are stranger than the sublime depths of the mind of Horse Badorties, the Fan Man. Kotzwinkle plants us into the psychedelic rollercoaster of Horse's dirt and drug-addled brain. We wander with Horse through the "abominated filthiness" of his Lower East Side apartment, a "pad" stacked so high with garbage and cockroach nests that he needs to get another pad on the same floor. "The rent will be high but it's not so bad if you don't pay it."

Not a paragraph passes without Horse's focus abruptly shifting onto a new plan. Swept along on this exuberant torrent, we are left exhausted and not a little disoriented. We travel with Horse in his cardboard Ukrainian slippers and his Commander Schmuck Imperial Red Chinese Army hat as he embarks on his greatest scheme: recruiting teenage runaway "chicks" for his apocalyptic Love Chorus. He is constantly waylaid by his frenzied craving for a Times Square hotdog, the procurement of an air-raid siren from a junkyard, or, startlingly, Dorky Day (a ritualistic mind-cleaning where Horse utters "Dorky" 1,382 times in a single chapter). This marijuana-fuelled rhapsody, combined with a grab-bag of eastern philosophy, is a hippie celebration of all things hippie, at a time when hippies were regarded, without nostalgia, as dirty, lazy, and deluded (all of which Horse gleefully is). A week in the head of Horse Badorties is exhilarating. And your mind will never be the same, man. At least not legally. **GT**

Ragtime

E. L. Doctorow

Lifespan | *b.* 1931 (U.S.)
First Published | 1975
First Published by | Random House (New York)
Musical Adaptation | 1998

The first paragraph of *Ragtime* extends over nearly two pages. Remember to breathe. The sentences tumble after one another in a torrent. Look at the passage again and you'll find that it consists of a series of short, declarative statements, almost all of them based on past tenses of the verb "to be": "It was ...," "There were ...," "He was ...," "She had been ..." The effect is to consign the things described to an irretrievable past: the sentences gather, like the fragments of a mosaic, to form a picture of American life in the early 1900s—an era whose sensibilities, Doctorow seems to suggest, belong now to history. As the novel develops out of the threads begun in this opening passage, the stories of real historical figures—Henry Ford, Theodore Roosevelt, Emma Goldman, Freud, Houdini, and countless others—intersect with the fictional destinies of a white bourgeois American family, called simply Mother, Father, Mother's Younger Brother, and so on, and an equally emblematic immigrant Jewish family, Mameh, Tateh, and The Little Girl. Among the stories that stand out against the panorama is that of Coalhouse Walker, a successful ragtime pianist, who has his new Model T Ford vandalized by racist firemen. He leaves the car to rot in the road where it stands, but his protest escalates, finally ending in a hail of bullets outside the home of Pierpont Morgan, the weathiest man in America. The stories are rich, vivid, and involving; but what will stay with you is the writing, the eddying jazz in Doctorow's prose. **PMy**

> *"She happened once to meet Emma Goldman, the revolutionary. Goldman lashed her with her tongue. Apparently there were Negroes. There were immigrants."*

⊙ Doctorow photographed in 1971: his novel *Ragtime* inextricably weaves historical and fictional characters together.

Correction

Thomas Bernhard

Lifespan | *b.* 1931 (Netherlands), *d.* 1989 (Austria)
First Published | 1975
First Published by | Suhrkamp (Frankfurt)
Original Title | *Korrektur*

In this demanding masterpiece, Bernhard recounts the self-destruction of an eccentric and brilliant scientist, Roithamer, who is fanatically obsessed with achieving perfection in his design and building of a giant cone-shaped home for his sister. The novel consists of two parts. The first part is narrated by Roithamer's friend, a mathematician, who has returned to Austria from England following Roithamer's suicide in order to sort out his papers. The second part is a selection from Roithamer's papers. It traces the development of Roithamer's work and explores his solipsistic nihilism, cultural exile, and passionate love and hatred of Austria.

Correction is Bernhard's most sustained expression of his fascination with Wittgenstein. Roithamer shares many biographical details with Wittgenstein, but more important is the latter's rejection of his social and cultural background and inheritance, his ascetic genius, and the purity and rigor of his thought and philosophical method. Roithamer's compulsive pursuit results in his sister's death, a death he has brought about despite his great love for her. In killing his sister he kills himself. She represents a more complete emotional and artistic self than the hyper-intellectual Roithamer.

The novel's strength lies largely in the energy of the tormented prose. It is a perfectly paced, complex study of the dangers of intellectual obsession and Bernhard's most serious working of the issues that he dealt with throughout his writing career. **AL**

Dead Babies

Martin Amis

Lifespan | *b.* 1949 (England)
First Published | 1975
First Published by | Jonathan Cape (London)
First U.S. Edition | 1976, by Knopf (New York)

In an atmosphere thick with sex, drugs, rock-and-roll, and pornographic recreation, a houseful of ill-matched characters pursue their pleasures, only to find their neuroses are pursuing them. Giles Coldstream is haunted by the fear of losing his teeth, Keith Whitehead ("an almost preposterously unattractive young man") is tormented by the "beautiful people" around him. So far, this could just be an updating of earlier comic modes, but the reader comes to sense that matters are not quite as they seem. Mysterious, obscene hate-mail from "Johnny" begins to appear, and Amis' narrator unveils a shocking twist. By suggesting that the events of the main plot might not yet have taken place, Amis opens up larger questions about the inevitability of consequences, about whether the characters are condemned from birth to their excessive futures—the repeated slang phrase "dead babies" takes on a set of nastily ironic resonances.

Dead Babies is very much a novel of the 1970s, and some of its social satire may seem time-locked; but the grotesque philosophical wit transcends the immediate context. Here, amidst the literal and metaphorical filth of the 1970s, Amis begins to grow his characterstic voice, grafting on to his comic sensibility that zest for Nabokov-like game-playing for which he is now famed. **BT**

❯ Martin Amis in 1977: despite his good looks, he was obsessed with the bad state of his teeth, a trait lent to a character in *Dead Babies*.

Humboldt's Gift

Saul Bellow

Lifespan | *b.* 1915 (Canada), *d.* 2005 (U.S.)
First Published | 1975
First Published by | Viking Press (New York)
Pulitzer Prize | 1976

The Pulitzer prize-winner in 1976, this novel is narrated in the first person. It is essentially a portrait of the artist, Charlie Citrine, a successful writer who is prompted by the death of his friend, Humboldt, into reflecting upon his own meager talents. The novel provides an episodic rather than sequential account of Citrine's travails: not only is he in thrall to a Chicago mobster, Citrine is crushed by divorce and is ultimately even abandoned by his mistress.

However, it is in Citrine's admiration for Humboldt that the novel becomes an extended lament for men of feeling who are annihilated by the testosterone-fuelled credo of greed and self-aggrandizement that characterizes American society. As an increasingly disillusioned Citrine begins to fathom how his own character has been shaped by these forces, the novel is not coy in identifying the decadents: sexual guru Kinsey, corporate capitalism, an intellectually bankrupt philosophical discourse, and the rise of feminism all make for some rather unlikely bedfellows.

Bellow hoped that this novel would "hold up a mirror to our urban society and to show its noise, its incertitudes, its sense of crisis and despair, its standardization of pleasures." Armed with his dazzling prose style and gift for social satire, Bellow achieves this task with conviction and intelligence. **VA**

⊙ Bellow, aged sixty-one, cheerfully engages in one of the routine tasks of a writer's life with a book signing in his native Chicago.

High Rise

J. G. Ballard

Lifespan | *b.* 1930 (China)
First Published | 1975
First Published by | Jonathan Cape (London)
Movie Adaptation Scheduled Release | 2006

Urban tower blocks are architecturally mediocre, and emblematic of how much the uninhabitable becomes normalized in the fabric of the city. In *High Rise*, Richard Wilder attempts to make a documentary in which he proposes that the tower block's internal partitioning is an architectural microcosm of society's crippling individuation, offering Ballard a prism for refracting a prophetic account of London condemned. No longer inanimate, the "high-rise had a second life of its own," enveloping Wilder, the supposedly detached observer. And for the medical academic Robert Laing, likewise, the block feeds a "powerful phobia" that Wilder rapidly develops.

The growing anarchy within this novel's eponymous building reveals Ballard's wider, more allegorical concerns. Spiralling events represent how the city's core mechanisms fail when conventional social divisions begin to atrophy, exposing the sense that the British "class system," as Ballard has himself asserted to Will Self, "has always served a political function as an instrument or expression of political control." No mending of this malaise is forecast; as *High Rise* reflects, Ballard remains the unapologetic antagonist of reparation, whether public or psychic. As readers we stray into Ballard's narrative of urban degeneration less in fear of a definitive reflection of the capital's social conditions as they persist today, than of an ominous prediction of just how degraded a space "the social" may imminently become. **DJ**

Willard and His Bowling Trophies

Richard Brautigan

Lifespan | b. 1935 (U.S.), d. 1984
First Published | 1975, by Simon & Schuster (N.Y.)
Full Title | Willard and His Bowling Trophies:
A Perverse Mystery

"'Does the gag hurt?'"

Photographed here in 1970, Brautigan expressed the anxieties, aspirations and humor of the American West Coast counterculture.

Roger Ressmeyer snapped Brautigan in his office in North Beach, San Francisco in 1981, hitting the wastebasket with rejected words .

In *Willard and His Bowling Trophies*—subtitled "A Perverse Mystery"—Richard Brautigan, San Francisco's Haight-Ashbury muse, ventures into genre fiction. As a mystery it is marginal, but it is definitely perverse.

Bob, his very existence and psyche devastated by a persistent case of venereal warts (it is San Francisco; it is the 1970s), has taken up amateur sadism in order to preserve his relationship with Constance. Constance, who gave him the warts, mourns for the loss of her old Bob, and is frustrated by this mere shell of her former husband. Willard is a large, exotically painted papier maché bird. The bowling trophies (which are, in fact, stolen) that he presides over are located in Pat and John's apartment downstairs. Their sex life is fine. Unknown to either couple is the ever-widening, ever more violent swath of crime scarring America as the Logan brothers ruthlessly search for their stolen bowling trophies. Formerly clean-cut exemplars of middle-American masculinity—healthy, law-abiding, good at bowling—they are driven by rage and an obsession that leads from petty theft to armed robbery to, eventually, murder. It takes them three years—"America was a very large place and the bowling trophies were very small in comparison"—before they wind up at the house on Chestnut Street.

A novel about the arbitrary devastation wrought by fate, about the disintegration of meaning and purpose in the nadir of 1970s America, *Willard and His Bowling Trophies* is made hypnotic by Brautigan's unique style. His short, expository, sterile sentences—simple language like an explanation to a child—act like a rhythmic metronome leaving the reader breathless, mesmerized. And laughing. **GT**

Fateless

Imre Kertész

Lifespan | b. 1929 (Hungary)
First Published | 1975
First Published by | Szépirodalmi Könyvkiadó
Original Title | Sorstalanság

Initially rejected for publication, *Fateless* (*Sorstalanság*) was eventually published in 1975 in Communist Hungary. At its publication, the novel, singled out for the Nobel Prize in 2002, was met with complete silence. No doubt this is due to the main concern of Kertész' writing, which explores the struggle of an individual confronted with the faceless brutality of history. György Köves, a fifteen-year-old Jewish boy, is sent first to Auschwitz and then to Buchenwald. On arrival at the camp Köves lies about his age and thus unknowingly avoids the gas chamber. Written in the first person, the novel describes the mechanisms of survival.

Kertész, himself a Holocaust survivor, described the novel as being autobiographical in form, yet not an autobiography. The linearity of narration, and the frequent use of the present tense draw the reader into concentration camp life as it unfolds, including the tediousness, the physical pain, and, as Köves shockingly asserts on his return to Hungary after the end of war, the "happiness." *Fateless* thus avoids objectivity and any simple moral judgment.

Fateless asks questions in the wake of Auschwitz that need to be answered in the present, since, as Kertész insists, the Holocaust cannot be written about in the past tense. What does it mean to be Jewish? How do we become free? Auschwitz is the zero point of European culture—it marks the death of God, the beginning of solitude, and, surprisingly, the potential to fulfill a promise of liberty. **IJ**

> *"Still, even the imagination is not completely unbounded, or at least is unbounded only within limits, I have found."*

Holocaust survivor Kertész is photographed in 2005 on a visit to Berlin, a city where the death camps are now memorialized.

The Dead Father

Donald Barthelme

Lifespan | *b.* 1931 (U.S.), *d.* 1989
First Published | 1975
First Published by | Farrar, Straus & Giroux (N.Y.)
Jesse H. Jones Award | 1976

A seminal work of postmodernist fiction, *The Dead Father* ostensibly tells the tale of the journey of a Dead Father (who "is only dead in a sense") across the countryside in search of an object called The Golden Fleece. This monolithic father (an imposing and ridiculous 3,200 cubits long) is towed by a crew of nineteen men. The Golden Fleece will rejuvenate the Dead Father and, he is assured, restore him to his former position of authority as the father of all culture. Erratic and tyrannical, the Dead Father spends his time seducing women, lamenting his lost youth, and, whenever he is so inclined, slaughtering indiscriminately those unfortunate enough to be within striking distance. It soon transpires, however, that he is being conducted not toward a place of rejuvenation but toward his burial.

In this merciless assault upon "authority", Barthelme systematically slays the sacred cows of western culture: Freudiansim is lampooned, high priests of modernism such as Eliot and Joyce are parodied, and any notion of an objective "truth" discarded. His freewheeling narrative is comprised of seemingly inconsequential digressions that only provisionally coalesce around a meaningful plot. With its wholesale departure from reason, its flight from naturalism, and its emphasis on the textuality of text, this novel serves up a heady concoction. Readers curious as to why postmodern fiction has proved to be so contentious need look no further than this exuberant and challenging novel. **VA**

Grimus

Salman Rushdie

Lifespan | *b.* 1947 (India)
First Published | 1975
First Published by | V. Gollancz (London)
Full Name | Ahmed Salman Rushdie

Grimus, unlike Rushdie's later novels, is a work of fantasy/science fiction, and on publication was not greeted with either critical acclaim or successful sales. Yet *Grimus* does not deserve such continuing disdain. The tale of the "Born-from-Dead" Native American Flapping Eagle, it is a fascinating and compelling novel, shot through with a fairy-tale exuberance and teeming with ideas. Like his later work, it is a book centrally concerned with the place of the exile, the problems of both rootedness and rootlessness, and arguably centers on the problems of community and nationhood. Even the notion that Calf Island, where much of the novel takes place, is located "not quite" in the Mediterranean foreshadows Rushdie's fascination with using fiction to refract the realities he seeks to present.

Grimus is also involved in a typically playful use and misuse of mythology and stories. It draws on a variety of sources, from the twelfth-century Sufi poem *The Conference of Birds*, to Dante's *Divine Comedy*. The eponymous villain of the piece takes his name from a reordering of "Simurg", the all-knowing bird of Persian fables. This superb novel is interesting for its reflections and hints on Rushdie's preoccupations. It also draws the reader into a carnivalesque world a little removed from our own, and uses its fantastic plot devices to create something unique and sparkling. Whether coming to Rushdie for the first time, or as an existing fan, it would be a crime to overlook this novel. **DR**

A Dance to the Music of Time

Anthony Powell

This series of twelve novels, each short enough to read in a day and comprehensible if read in isolation, is an English response to Proust's *À la recherche du temps perdu*. Nick Jenkins, the mild hero of Powell's magnum opus, like Proust's narrator, observes the comic and amazing antics of his contemporaries from his schooldays at Eton in the 1920s to old age in the 1970s. The first three volumes (sometimes published together as "Spring") deal with school, university, and early life in London. The next three ("Summer") take us up to the war and through, among other things, love. The third set ("Autumn") deals with the farcical and fascinating events of 1939–1945 as seen from the entirely personal, worm's-eye view of a junior officer. The final three volumes ("Winter") find Jenkins involved in the mixed scenarios of his middle and later age: a literary conference in Venice, and English country life.

However, as with Proust, the joy of these addictive novels does not lie in their plots or in the portrait they give, such as it is, of half a century of largely upper-class English life. Powell's success comes from his comedy, his characterizations, and his style—the first two of these being indivisible from the third. Beautifully written, his assessments of the private experiences of his hero comfort us and steady our view of the world. Everything, in his quiet but elegant prose, becomes matter for comedy and puzzlement. Prime among his triumphs of character is the monstrous egoist, Kenneth Widmerpool, who features in each of the novels, appearing always in a new and more repellent incarnation until his final comeuppance in the last volume. Widmerpool might be taken as the perfect symbol of a century gone mad; Nick Jenkins, who soldiers quietly on, goes some way toward restoring the balance. **PM**

Lifespan | *b.* 1905 (England), *d.* 2000
First Published | 1951–1975
First Published by | Heinemann (London)
Full Series Includes | Twelve volumes

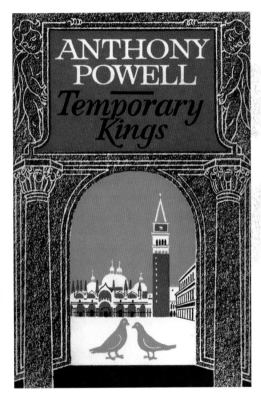

The eleventh novel in the *A Dance to the Music of Time* series, here pictured with its original UK hardback jacket.

Powell, pictured here in the 1930s, was influenced by interwar modernism as well as by the traditon of English social comedy.

W, or the Memory of Childhood

Georges Perec

Lifespan | *b.* 1936 (France), *d.* 1982
First Published | 1975
First Published by | Éditions Denoël (Paris)
Original Title | *W, ou le souvenir d'enfance*

Georges Perec's compelling fictional autobiography alternates between two very different, apparently unrelated narratives. In the first, the narrator is told a curious story about a boy lost at sea and an island called W, where a fictional society is organized around sport. The second is autobiographical: still in the first person, Perec, who was born into a family of Polish Jews in 1936, narrates episodes from his childhood and boarding school years in the south of France. The customs and organization of the imagined olympian society are presented with the accuracy and precision of a factual account. The facts of Perec's life, however, appear as mutable and as open to revision as fiction. Perec claims not to have any childhood memories and false memory, doubt, and uncertainty beset his memoir. Dates, measurements, statistics, certificates and so on, however accurate, do nothing to describe the inexpressible horror of Auschwitz, where Perec's mother was sent in 1943. The imaginary account of life on W, where the athletes are identified by a sign stitched to their shirts, where failure to achieve is punished by food deprivation, where a kind of utopia is slowly assimilated to a Nazi death camp—goes some way toward filling in the blanks. With *W or the Memory of Childhood* Perec effectively re-invents the autobiographical form for the twentieth century. **KB**

Autumn of the Patriarch

Gabriel García Márquez

Lifespan | *b.* 1928 (Colombia)
First Published | 1975
First Published by | Plaza & Janés (Barcelona)
Original Title | *El otoño del patriarca*

Autumn of the Patriarch is García Márquez' most demanding and most experimental novel. It is also the most underrated—a novel all too often eclipsed by his more commercially successful work, and the cause of much confusion among critics. The novel is described by Márquez as "a poem on the solitude of power." At its center is a nameless South American dictator whose political genius is offset by his profound sense of loneliness and paranoia. The "Patriarch" is a synthesis of the various autocrats and lunatics who have held office during the twentieth century. He is a creature of pure cruelty and pure despair, holding sway over a long-suffering population through the mythic aura he has created for himself. After revolutionaries discover the Patriarch's decomposing body in his palace, a fantastical space of unimaginable riches, Márquez unleashes a great torrent of words, rebuilding the public and private life of the deceased tyrant from the fragments he has left.

The novel unfolds through six sections of almost entirely unpunctuated prose, often recalling Molly Bloom's soliloquy in the final chapter of Joyce's *Ulysses*. Space and time are consistently disrupted, with the narrative taking unexpected detours into real historical events and wild flights of fancy. The novel is a remarkable study in charisma, corruption, violence, and the apparatus of political power. **SamT**

Patterns of Childhood

Christa Wolf

Lifespan | *b.* 1929 (Germany)
First Published | 1976
First Published by | Aufbau Verlag (Berlin)
Original Title | *Kindheitsmuster*

At the heart of *Patterns of Childhood* is the question of the relationship between the adult and the child she once was. Can the one really leave the other behind? And will a child who has received all her earliest impressions in Nazi Germany ever be free from its influence?

Nelly Jordan, the autobiographical narrator of *Patterns of Childhood*, sets out to reflect on these questions when she revisits her home town, L, now the Polish G. The last time Nelly saw L was as a child, at the climax of the Second World War, as she fled from the Russian advance. The visit is a catalyst for painful memories: images she has suppressed rise again as she looks at a childhood under the Nazis with the eyes of a grown-up citizen of East Germany. Nelly's shocking conclusion is that the casual fascism in the day-to-day existence of her family and those they knew then is not so far removed from the cowardice and hypocrisy of the socialist GDR of the time at which she was writing. A country of Nazis cannot overnight be turned into one populated by socialist heroes. Change, if it happens at all, will happen incrementally. *Patterns* is remarkable for its recognition that it is necessary to look at Germany's past with total honesty, notwithstanding the discomfort this entails. Wolf's resolution in challenging the ideology of the GDR earned her admiration and respect in Germany and beyond. **MM**

"You imagine a nation of sleepers, a people whose dreaming brains are complying with the given command: Cancel cancel cancel."

◈ Christa Wolf, who is renown for openly criticizing the leadership of East Germany during the GDR era, now lives in Berlin.

Amateurs

Donald Barthelme

Lifespan | *b.* 1931 (U.S.), *d.* 1989
First Published | 1976
First Published by | Farrar, Straus & Giroux (N.Y.)
First UK Edition | 1977, by Routledge & Kegan Paul

Where other authors play with character and setting, Barthelme plays with language. These are simple stories, absurdist morality tales from an alternate universe. Precise, succinct, their simplicity is surprised by bursts of erudition and parody of high style. The incredible occurs in the most mundane circumstances and goes unremarked. In "The School," all manner of flora and fauna, from orange trees to Korean orphans, are raised as class projects. All come to untimely ends—"It's been a strange year." At last, to offer the students an "assertion of value," the teacher agrees to make love to Helen, the new teaching assistant. But just then a new gerbil comes in. In "Porcupines at the University," thousands of porcupines are spotted three miles down the road. The first response is anxiety over whether they'll enroll. People on the expressway stare in awe. "Are those porcupines wonderful? Are they significant? Are they what I need?" In "Some of Us Had Been Threatening Our Friend Colby," Colby's friends decide to hang him. They dismiss legalities because they are within their rights: he is their friend, he belongs to them, and he has gone too far. They generously involve Colby in the planning, from the choice of music to be played to the discussions of the gibbet versus the tree.

Amateurs is like looking into mirrors in a side-show funhouse—we see ourselves distorted, and we laugh, but the recognition is even more acute through the exaggeration. **GT**

Cutter and Bone

Newton Thornburg

Lifespan | *b.* 1929 (U.S.)
First Published | 1976
First Published by | Little, Brown & Co. (Boston)
Full Name | Newton Kendall Thornburg

A lost masterpiece of the Vietnam era, Thornburg's novel traces the domestic fallout of a period of protest that promised social and political revolution but ultimately produced little or no change. At its center is the relationship between Alex Cutter, an alcoholic, disillusioned, crippled Vietnam veteran, and Bone, a self-interested gigolo. When Bone witnesses someone dumping a woman's corpse in a trashcan, and provisionally identifies the killer as conglomerate tycoon J. J. Wolfe, the two men decide to pursue Wolfe for profit and justice.

Throughout, Thornburg's impeccable control of his narrative means that we are never certain about anything. Is Cutter really as self-interested as he pretends to be or does his antipathy for Wolfe conceal a deeper political motive? Is the fire that kills his wife and baby the result of Cutter's own negligence or his pursuit of Wolfe? Grieving for himself and for his country, which has sold its soul to corporations and has lost its way in the quagmire of Southeast Asia, Cutter's mission to bring down Wolfe is either the last, desperate act of an heroic man with nothing to lose or the product of a deranged mind. *Cutter and Bone* constitutes an extended suicide note in which Cutter's nihilistic disillusionment is mitigated only by an acknowledgement that the world is as lost as he imagines it to be. **AP**

❯ John Heard played the mutilated Vietnam veteran Alex Cutter in *Cutter's Way*, Ivan Passer's 1981 movie version of Thornburg's novel.

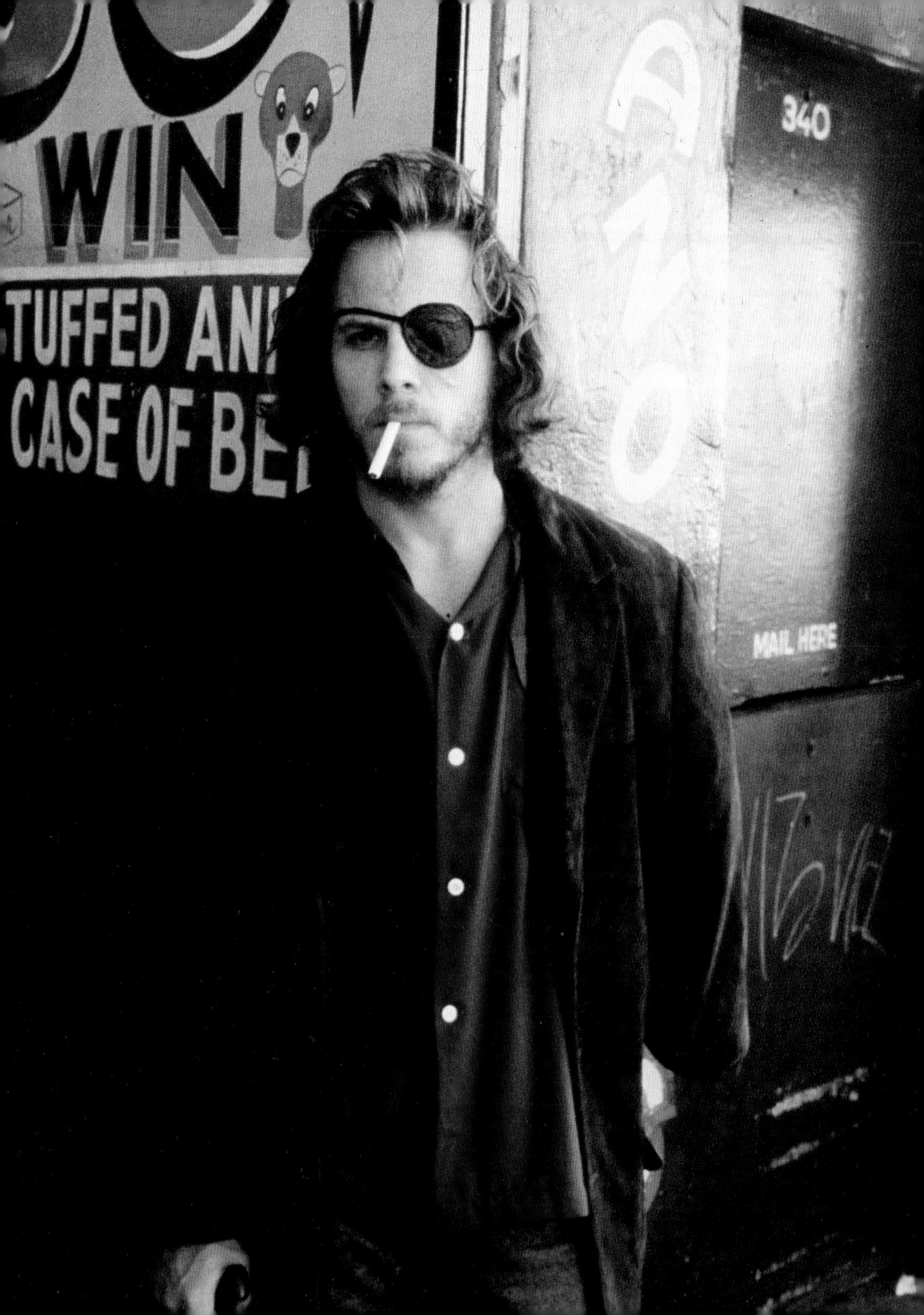
WIN
TUFFED AN
CASE OF BE
340
MAIL HERE

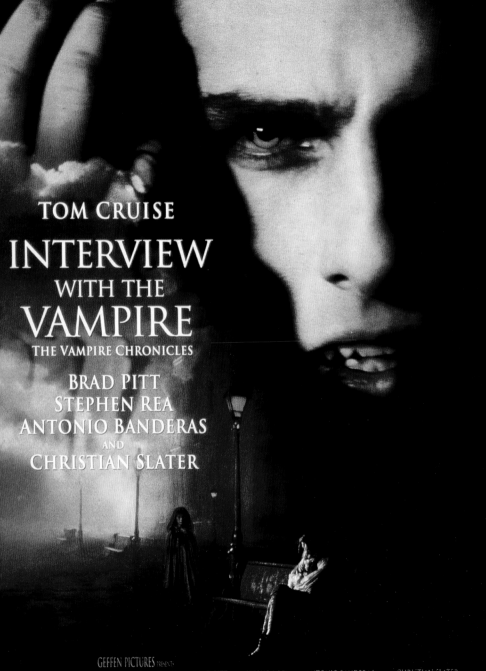

DRINK FROM ME AND LIVE FOREVER

TOM CRUISE

INTERVIEW WITH THE VAMPIRE
THE VAMPIRE CHRONICLES

BRAD PITT
STEPHEN REA
ANTONIO BANDERAS
AND
CHRISTIAN SLATER

GEFFEN PICTURES PRESENTS
A FILM BY NEIL JORDAN • TOM CRUISE • BRAD PITT • STEPHEN REA • ANTONIO BANDERAS AND CHRISTIAN SLATER
'INTERVIEW WITH THE VAMPIRE' KIRSTEN DUNST VAMPIRE MAKEUP AND EFFECTS BY STAN WINSTON EDITOR MICK AUDSLEY PRODUCTION DESIGNER DANTE FERRETTI
DIRECTOR OF PHOTOGRAPHY PHILIPPE ROUSSELOT MUSIC COMPOSED BY ELLIOT GOLDENTHAL CO-PRODUCER REDMOND MORRIS SCREENPLAY BY ANNE RICE BASED ON HER NOVEL
PRODUCED BY STEPHEN WOOLLEY AND DAVID GEFFEN DIRECTED BY NEIL JORDAN

Interview With the Vampire

Anne Rice

Across a long series of books, Anne Rice has substantially reworked the ancient legends of the vampire into a more modern mold. Her vampires take on many of the qualities of Dracula, but she portrays a more eroticized and more violent world than Bram Stoker, one that is brought up to date and resituated in her home town of New Orleans.

The central figure of *Interview With the Vampire* is Louis, who has been a vampire for two hundred years and is gifted, or cursed, with immortal life. As he tells his story, we begin to understand what such a life might be like. Vampires see the world through different senses—their world is at once more brutal and yet more startlingly vivid than it can ever be to mere human perception. Louis himself, however, is plagued by doubt: doubt as to how he has come into this condition, doubt as to what combination of gods and devils are actually responsible for his plight. Furthermore, he is a vampire with a conscience. Unwilling to feed off humans, he tries to assuage his uncontrollable appetite in other ways. It is a measure of the strength of the book that this improbable situation never veers into being mawkish or sentimental; the reader is brought to understand both the terrors and the attractions of being an outcast, not only from humankind but also to a large extent from the other vampires who are, perforce, his only kind.

Permeating this dilemma are the bright lights and shadows of New Orleans, a city at once ancient and modern, broodingly pagan and showily contemporary. In *Interview With the Vampire,* a novel of brilliant chiaroscuro, we find ourselves immersed in a nighttime world that sometimes seems to be the negative image of the world we perceive through our limited human senses. **DP**

Lifespan | *b.* 1941 (U.S.)
First Published | 1976
First Published by | Knopf (New York)
Given Name | Howard Allen O'Brien

"The vampire smiled."

◈ Photographed here in 1986, Anne Rice is a popular writer of erotic fantasy fiction, mostly set in her native New Orleans.

◈ Rice herself wrote the screenplay for the 1994 movie version of her novel, directed with lush, decadent style by Neil Jordan.

The Public Burning

Robert Coover

Lifespan | *b.* 1932 (U.S.)
First Published | 1976
First Published by | Viking Press (New York)
First UK Edition | 1978, by Allen Lane (London)

This fantasia of the McCarthy-era is America at its most enamel shiny: infallible, a land of motherhood, morality, homogeneity, heterosexuality. The novel centers on the execution of the "atomic spies" the Rosenbergs, as told by Richard M. Nixon. Its sprawling cast includes Dwight Eisenhower, Betty Crocker, and the great and demonic specter of Uncle Sam himself. In a pitiless portrayal of Nixon, Coover subjects him to humiliations that reach breathtaking heights, climaxing in his rape by Uncle Sam, who claims it is a rite of passage to which all future presidents must submit. He embodies all that is great and flawed in America—energetic and relentlessly optimistic, indomitable, and racist.

This is satire as shotgun blast. Coover takes American history and runs amok—nothing is sacred. The deadly serious is hybridized with the luridly surreal as Coover gives us his own pyrotechnical floorshow. The tragedy of the Rosenbergs is morphed into a televised super-spectacle taking place in Times Square. Walt Disney and Cecil B. DeMille fight for the broadcast rights. *Time* magazine covers the court case in blank verse. This is fiction at its most wickedly irreverent and downright vulgar. Exhaustively researched and vigorously drawn, it was written during America's crises of faith in the 1970s. As satire it could have been cautionary; oddly, it has become prophetic. Times Square really is now a super-spectacle orchestrated by Disney, and American hubris has not yet led to a fall. **GT**

Ratner's Star

Don DeLillo

Lifespan | *b.* 1936 (U.S.)
First Published | 1976
First Published by | Knopf (New York)
Original Language | English

Don DeLillo is a master of contemporary fiction and *Ratner's Star* is an example of his experimentation with language, as form and function intertwine to reveal concealed layers of complexity. It is the story of Billy Twillig, a teenage number theory genius who is flown to a secret scientific think-tank to decode a message received from a distant star. In structure, DeLillo borrows and twists Lewis Carroll's work, sending Twillig down the scientific rabbit hole and through the modern cultural looking glass. The headings of the two parts—"Adventures" and "Reflections"—refer to *Alice's Adventures in Wonderland* and *Through the Looking Glass*, and reflect the fear of uncertainty in Carroll's work. As in Carroll's works, the characters in DeLillo's satirical novel are reduced to the theories in which they believe. Above all, though, this book is about structure. As Billy Twillig encounters a range of intentionally flattened characters, each reflecting in demeanor their scientific principles, DeLillo's familiar dark humor emerges. The storyline, too, is about form and structure, so that in the end the feeling about Billy Twillig's quest, and indeed the whole book, is that it is not only about mathematics, it is itself a piece of mathematics. It not only embodies but actually becomes the pattern, order, and harmony that have been the holy grail of traditional pure mathematicians for centuries. Like the red dwarves the scientists are investigating, this book is best viewed obliquely. **EF**

The Left-Handed Woman

Peter Handke

Lifespan | *b.* 1942 (Austria)
First Published | 1976
First Published by | Suhrkamp (Frankfurt)
Original Title | *Die linkshändige Frau*

Peter Handke was very much the *enfant terrible* of Austrian literature in the late 1960s and 1970s, whose wide-ranging output explores political, aesthetic, psychological, and philosophical issues unflinchingly, even aggressively. This novella, a story of existential crisis narrated in spare, icy prose, is a fine example of his rigorous modernism. Disaffected housewife Marianne, in a moment of spontaneous self-assertion, decides to split up with her husband, the father of her eight-year-old son. Over the course of several days of self-imposed near-isolation, she attempts to rediscover a sense of independence and identity beyond marriage and motherhood.

Handke discourages subjective identification with characters. Marianne, for example, is referred to by the narrator simply as "the woman," her son Stefan for the most part as "the child." The narrator avoids descriptive detail and interior monologues, and translates the characters' inner confusion into a narrative of disjointed dialogue and awkward silences. The message, reinforced by moments in which Marianne contemplates her image in the mirror, is that personal identity is fragile and difficult to maintain; it is threatened even by everyday acts of naming and description. The symbolic idea of "left-handedness" evokes this desire for individuality, for the right to be different, and the text concludes with a note of reserved optimism when Marianne asserts: "You haven't betrayed yourself. And no one will humiliate you any more." **JH**

". . . you should learn how to run properly and scream properly, with your mouth wide open . . . even when you yawn you're afraid to open your mouth all the way."

◉ Handke sits firmly in the European tradition of intellectual writers who make serious demands upon their readers.

The Hour of the Star

Clarice Lispector

Lifespan | *b.* 1920 (Ukraine), *d.* 1977 (Brazil)
First Published | 1977
First Published by | Livraria José Olympio Editora
Original Title | *A Hora da estrela*

Lispector is known internationally as one of the great exponents of the short story, and the delicacy, evanescence, and unremitting intensity of her work do not translate easily into more extended narrative modes of fiction. In her final novel, *The Hour of the Star*, she is stretched to her formal limits. This novel operates in familiar territory for Lispector and traces the tragic life and sudden death of a poor young black Brazilian woman, Macabéa, who travels from the backwoods of Alagoas to Rio, where she ekes out a precarious existence as a barely functioning secretary. Lispector's peculiar abilities to evoke the inner lives of oppressed, uneducated, and inarticulate women are triumphantly displayed here. Her strategies for giving a voice to the voiceless include a constant humor, sometimes laconic, sometimes shot through with a wild despair. Lispector's tremulous narrative evokes a game of life and death, in which it is the author's sacred duty to redeem her characters from oblivion. Lispector as narrator talks of her relationship with Macabéa, and gives some sense of the passionate fragility with which she negotiates her sacred task as author: "As the author I alone love her. I suffer on her account. And I alone may say to her: 'What do you ask of me weeping that I would not give to you singing?'" Lispector dedicated this book to a series of great composers, clearly aware that her work is as untranslatable as beautiful music. Lispector must be read, not written about. **MW**

Song of Solomon

Toni Morrison

Lifespan | *b.* 1931 (U.S.)
First Published | 1977
First Published by | Knopf (New York)
Given Name | Chloë Anthony Wofford

Song of Solomon opens with a desperate and lonely man attempting to fly, watched by a woman who is in the early stages of labor. The novel goes on to tell us the story of this baby, the first black child to be born inside the Mercy Hospital on Not Doctor Street. His laboring mother was allowed into the hospital because of the commotion following the failed flight from its roof and because his father had been the town's first doctor. The circumstances of this child's birth—the desires, disappointments, and dispossessions that infuse it—are the questions that he grows up to eventually resolve.

The child, Macon Dead Jr., is the son of the richest black family in a Midwestern town, and has a privileged if largely loveless childhood. His parents are long estranged. It is only when Macon becomes familiar with his paternal aunt's family that he learns of a family history rich in secrets and stories that he needs to gain access to. His desire for manhood takes him on a quest and he returns to the South and to the folklore from which he has been estranged. Macon finds a family history that explains him to himself and lets him, finally, possess his name. It is not until he returns home, however, and realizes the damage that his former privileged casualness has wreaked, that he learns the responsibilities that come with this knowledge. **NM**

▶ Toni Morrison has always been a politically committed author; she once stated that no "real artists have ever been non-political".

Petals of Blood

Ngugi Wa Thiong'o

Lifespan | b. 1938 (Kenya)
First Published | 1977
First Published by | Heinemann Educational (Lon.)
Original Language | English

Selling out repeatedly in Nairobi on its release, *Petals of Blood* offers a searing attack on the Kenyan neo-colonial order. Its publication in 1977 led to the author's incarceration for a year.

On the surface, the novel revolves around the murder of three corrupt directors of a foreign-owned brewing company. But its political heart lies in a series of flashbacks and oral narratives that recount the past of the rural town of Ilmorog and the histories of the four main characters. In differing ways they embody the difficulties of resisting the decadence, corruption, and self-aggrandizement at the core of the new political regime. Munira acts out of a sense of religion and sexual jealousy and this blunts his political efficacy. Abdulla is an ex-revolutionary fighter maimed in the 1950s rebellion and able in the end to transform only his own circumstances. Wanja, a prostitute, fails to overcome the creed of "eat or be eaten" that is the moral law in the new Kenya. Finally, Karega, a revolutionary figure, is the character seemingly favored by Ngugi as the only possible salvation for the hopes of the Kenyan people.

Ngugi employs a number of narrative methods including the use of a collective voice common in traditional Gikuyu songs, a complex temporal scheme, and various competing viewpoints to produce a fiery and impassioned epic that is an outstanding modern example of politically committed fiction. **ABi**

Dispatches

Michael Herr

Lifespan | b. 1940 (U.S.)
First Published | 1977
First Published by | Knopf (New York)
First UK Edition | 1978, by Pan Books (London)

Ostensibly journalism, *Dispatches* is above all great literature. The book charts the year Herr spent in Vietnam (1967–1968), where he witnessed some of the most brutal fighting and significant events of the war, including the Tet offensive and Khe Sanh siege. It is a carefully structured, finely wrought work that reads at times like a memoir, but with the impact and intensity of live action reporting. There is little by way of conventional journalism, but only a frank, raw account of what it felt like to be there.

Herr is unsentimental yet sympathetic in his treatment of the "grunts," the regular soldiers. He brilliantly captures the verve and wit of their slang as well as the fear, boredom, and drug-fueled insanity of the Vietnam experience. His astonishing prose ranges from a soldier's crude cynicism, "that's just a load, man. We're here to kill gooks. Period," to lyrical evocations of the jungle where "your cigarettes taste like swollen insects rolled up and smoked alive, crackling and wet." The book is an exploration of man's seemingly intractable need for thrill-seeking and the terrible fact that war is the ultimate hit. It doesn't shy away from the absolute horror of the war and yet it also shows how nothing can possibly match the feeling of being so alive. This is all too clearly illustrated to the reader by the disquieting fact that the book is utterly compelling to read. **AL**

◉ Michael Herr, accompanied by photographer Larry Burrows, covers the Vietnam War as a journalist in Saigon in May 1968.

The Shining

Stephen King

Stanley Kubrick's adaptation of *The Shining*, starring Jack Nicholson, is well established as classic cinema. The immense popularity of the film, however, has perhaps eclipsed the achievement of King's novel as an exceptional and thrilling piece of storytelling. When Jack Torrance takes the job as caretaker of the remote Overlook Hotel for the winter he thinks it will provide the perfect setting in which to soothe damaged bonds between himself, his wife Wendy, and his son Danny, and to put an end to his long-lingering unfinished play. Nothing could be further from the truth. Marital tension, alcoholism, the destructiveness of feelings of guilt, writer's block, telepathy—not to mention wasps' nests—all converge in King's Jack Torrance more subtly and even more disturbingly than Kubrick manages to depict on screen. Perhaps one of the most impressive aspects of this novel, however, is the way that King handles and narrates the experience of a psychic/telepathic five-year-old boy who has a direct link to his father's growing insanity. As a character, Danny is neither clichéd nor overblown.

What is fascinating about this book is the balance it provokes between internal and external worlds, and the questions it raises about whether madness comes from the inside out or vice versa. It is also a novel about voices, the telepathic voices received and transmitted by Danny, but also voices as they come in the shape of histories: the history of Wendy and Jack's marriage; their private histories; the sinister history of the Overlook that Jack discovers in a scrapbook in the basement. Histories in *The Shining* become dangerous and destructive. It is without a doubt among the most sophisticated of King's novels and is filled with some of the most disturbing and intriguing of all King's characters. **PM**

Lifespan | *b.* 1947 (U.S.)
First Published | 1977
First Published by | Doubleday (New York)
Movie Adaptation Released | 1980

A MASTERPIECE OF MODERN HORROR

"'I don't believe you care much for me, Mr. Torrance. I don't care. Certainly your feelings toward me play no part in my own belief that you are not right for the job.'"

Kubrick's adaptation of *The Shining* was not well received on its first release in 1980, but is now revered as a classic horror movie.

Photographed by Alex Gotfryd in the 1970s, Stephen King looks more like an academic than a writer of horror stories.

Delta of Venus

Anaïs Nin

Lifespan | *b.* 1903 (France), *d.* 1977 (U.S.)
First Published | 1977
First Published by | Harcourt Brace Jovanovich (N.Y.)
Original Language | English

○ Anaïs Nin is best known for her diaries, which include a record of her relationships with many lovers, including author Henry Miller.

◑ Audie England starred in Zalman King's 1995 movie *Delta of Venus*, a steamy if aesthetically dubious piece of cinematic erotica.

Nin's *Delta of Venus* is a collection of strikingly Freudian erotica written for the titillation of an aged but wealthy collector at the rate of a dollar a page. Each story is a self-contained erotic episode or series of episodes, but the whole has the mark of a novel since some characters, notably the prostitute, Bijou, recur in several places. The action occurs throughout in a stylized urban and suburban Paris as distinctive and amorphous as that in Baudelaire's *Le Spleen de Paris*. The evocation of evenings in the cold studios of failing artists, the fumes of drugs, the sound of cheap music, and the rain in the gutters make Nin's tales of sexual encounter her own most impressive prose-poem: a kind of *Le Cul de Paris*.

Unlike the formulae of mainstream pornography, Nin's work touches upon homosexuality, hermaphroditism, interracial affairs, fetishism, incest, and pedophilia, and its depiction of heterosexual love-making is remarkable for the genre. Everyone who takes part in the erotic cycle of tension and release, and the class of prudes who attempt to remove themselves from it, is on the road to or from a personal pathology. The characters are in thrall to infatuations, repressions, and deep-seated hatreds that can only be allayed in their brief obliteration by orgasm. Bijou, however, is Nin's most remarkable creation, a voluptuous cipher, part-owner of a body placed permanently on display, endlessly enticing to men and women alike. Her total immersion in the performance of sex scarcely allows for an inner life worth having, but the unavailability of a "real" Bijou, set against the descriptions of her total sexual availability, proves much more intriguing than the recklessly conventional introspection and motivations of the other protagonists. **RP**

The Passion of New Eve

Angela Carter

Lifespan | *b.* 1940 (England), *d.* 1992
First Published | 1977
First Published by | V. Gollancz (London)
Given Name | Angela Olive Stalker

"'And now you yourself become what you've made!'"

Angela Carter's concern with gender identity and sexual politics was combined with a fascination with myths and fairy tales.

Evelyn, the English narrator of *The Passion of New Eve*, arrives in a futuristic America as a casually misogynist young man completely unprepared for the violence on the ground. The country has exploded into absolute war, a rapacious conflict in which myriad incompatible bands of allegiance struggle for sovereignty based on identity politics alone. He is abducted by women who live underground in a medico-scientific colony. They are led by Mother, the enormous embodiment of multiple myths hyperbolizing (especially black) female fertility, sexuality, and maternity. Evelyn learns to his horror that Mother and the colony plan to recreate him as "New Eve." After remodeling him biologically, they proceed to indoctrinate him/her with the norms of femininity through forced viewings of a hilarious mélange of audiovisual stimuli including Hollywood films, footage of frolicking baby animals, and Western art depicting virgins and children. Eve(lyn) seems condemned to experience herself simultaneously as subject and object of her own gaze. Any salvageable semblance of wholeness comes only when Eve stumbles upon her psychological mirror image in Tristessa, the actress Evelyn most admired before becoming Eve: she discovers that Tristessa is biologically a man.

This is a dystopic narrative using and parodying various narrative conventions of science fiction, gothic, grotesque, and western, among others. In this searing interrogation of cultural mythology, snippets of Oedipus, Lacan, Freud, and popular notions regarding gender and sexuality are put through the chopper and reassembled as if by Dr. Frankenstein. The result is a challenging text that is by turns mocking, shocking, and sympathetic, and which always pushes the boundaries. **AF**

In the Heart of the Country

J. M. Coetzee

In the Heart of the Country, Coetzee's second novel, is a tale of madness, lust, and fantasy in the heart of the South African veld. Magda is the spinster daughter of a widowed white farmer on an isolated farm. When her father seduces the young bride of their African servant Hendrik, Magda collapses into jealousy, alienation, and an ambivalent desire for the love and sexuality she has never known. Feeling herself to be dried-up, barren, sexless, and unused, Magda believes that she has been spoiled for all others by her lifetime of isolation with her distant and oppressive father—a "spoiling" that in her fantasies becomes an act of paternal rape. As her stream-of-consciousness narration about past and present spirals further into fantasy the line between fact and fiction becomes blurred, and the reader is unsure as to the reality of the shocking and violent "events" that unfold.

Coetzee's stark, dense prose achieves a kind of dark poetry as Magda struggles to fill in the void of her life with words. In enforced seclusion from history, time stretches before and behind Magda without meaning or event, and through her incessant weaving of stories she strives to pull this life into some kind of significance. But the very proliferation of words takes on a nightmarish quality. Stories multiply, language fails, and her mind begins to consume itself.

In the Heart of the Country is the story of a woman that history has abandoned, but the book does not itself abandon history in its journey into the inner psyche. Shocking, challenging, and disturbing, this is one of the earliest of Coetzee's fictional explorations of the webs of sexual and racial oppression bequeathed to South Africa by its history of colonial rule. **VM**

Lifespan | b. 1940 (South Africa)
First Published | 1977
First Published by | Secker & Warburg (London)
Nobel Prize for Literature | 2003

> *"To my father I have been an absence all my life."*

◉ Coetzee has often set his novels in rural South Africa, a place he loves despite the cruel conflicts of race and culture it reveals.

The Virgin in the Garden

A. S. Byatt

Lifespan | *b.* 1936 (England)
First Published | 1978
First Published by | Chatto & Windus (London)
Given Name | Antonia Susan Drabble

The Virgin in the Garden is the first part of a tetralogy (latterly known as the *Frederica Quartet*) that was completed in 2002. The four novels, set between the 1950s and 1970s, take as their anchor point the life of Frederica Potter, her family and friends. Beginning in Yorkshire in 1953, the year of Elizabeth II's coronation, *The Virgin in the Garden* recounts Frederica's coming of age. The novel's center is the staging of a verse drama, *Astraea,* written by Alexander Wedderburn, about the Virgin Queen, to celebrate the coronation. Frederica's competitive nature drives her to desire only the title role in Wedderburn's play. Stephanie, Frederica's sister, although as intellectually capable as Frederica, instead chooses domesticity by marrying the local vicar. The comedy of Frederica's attempts to lose her virginity is adept and amusing, as is the sense of both time and place that Byatt conjures. The lightness of the social comedy of Frederica's story is offset by a rather dark subplot involving the mental deterioration of Frederica's younger brother, Marcus.

Many critics have noted parallels between the relationship of Frederica and Stephanie and Byatt's own relationship with her sister, the writer Margaret Drabble. As the tetralogy developed, Byatt played down the novels' historicity and their comedy (the third novel, *Babel Tower*, reads more like a thriller than a social comedy). She also went on to develop a more sophisticated model of what the historical novel ought to be in *Possession* (1990). **VC-R**

Yes

Thomas Bernhard

Lifespan | *b.* 1931 (Netherlands), *d.* 1989 (Austria)
First Published | 1978
First Published by | Suhrkamp (Frankfurt)
Original Title | *Ja*

Yes, a novella consisting of a single paragraph monologue, is an intense, haunting story of failure and self-destruction. The narrator is reclusive, and suicidal. He has shut himself off from the outside world in order to concentrate better on his studies, but this extreme solitude results only in a vicious cycle of obsessive self-observation and paralyzing apathy. His emotional and mental state worsens until he feels compelled to unburden himself to his only friend, Moritz, a real estate agent. While at his friend's house, however, he meets a couple, a Swiss man and a Persian woman, who are there to buy some land. He befriends the woman and they begin to go for walks together, during which they discover shared intellectual interests. The friendship is short-lived though, as she soon confides her own misery, her overwhelming sense of failure, and he is incapable of helping her. Ruthlessly abandoned by her uncaring partner, whom she has never loved, she falls into the same desperate state the narrator was in prior to meeting her.

Despite its bleak, pessimistic view of the human condition, the narrative is compelling, dynamic, and even amusing. Told with almost breathless intensity, mirroring the narrator's compulsive state, the novella is full of irony and moments of self-parody. *Yes* marks the beginning of a change of mood and style in Bernhard's fiction, and is a fascinating fusion of the relentless gravity and gloom of his early work with the lighter, funnier irony of his later novels. **AL**

The Singapore Grip

J. G. Farrell

Lifespan | *b.* 1935 (England), *d.* 1979 (Ireland)
First Published | 1978
First Published by | Weidenfeld & Nicolson (London)
Full Name | James Gordon Farrell

Set in Singapore just before the Japanese invasion in the Second World War, *The Singapore Grip* is the final book in Farrell's *Empire Trilogy* that began with *Troubles* and the *Siege of Krishnapur*. In each book Farrell takes a critical view of the British Empire, representing its demise through a cast of characters, both fictional and historical, whose lives are irrevocably changed by events beyond their control.

The money that Farrell received from the Booker Prize for the *Siege of Krishnapur* helped him fund a trip to Singapore in 1975, where he began the meticulous research into the history and people of the era about which he was to write. For the Blackett Family, Singapore in 1939 was a world of tennis and cocktail parties. But as Walter Blackett, the head of Singapore's oldest and most powerful rubber firm, Blackett and Webb, struggles to contain strikes by his workers, there are signs of a change in the air.

As Blackett struggles to break the strikes and fend off his daughter's unsuitable beaux, the fixed boundaries between classes and nations begin to crumble. In Farrell's account of Singapore's fall to the Japanese and the end to British superiority in the region, he creates a vivid portrait of Singapore at a historical watershed. The novel is lengthy and leisurely, but full of suspense and humor. Quietly and humorously critical of the conventions and ideologies of empire, Farrell anticipates a style of postcolonial writing that came to be embodied by authors such as Timothy Mo and Salman Rushdie. **LE**

"The city of Singapore was not built up gradually, the way most cities are ... It was simply invented one morning early in the nineteenth century by a man looking at a map."

◉ Farrel died only a year after this 1978 photo was taken; he had been weakend by polio contracted while a student in the 1960s.

The Sea, The Sea

Iris Murdoch

Lifespan | *b.* 1919 (Ireland), *d.* 1999 (England)
First Published | 1978
First Published by | Chatto & Windus (London)
Booker Prize | 1978

Charles Arrowby is a washed-up thespian who retires to a dilapidated house by the sea to write his memoirs. Former colleagues and lovers descend upon his coastal retreat and stir up some unhappy memories, but it is with the appearance on the scene of Mary Hartley, with whom Charles has enjoyed an unconsummated fling many years previously, that the story threatens to take a more tragic turn. Alternately pathetic and absurd, Arrowby's self-absorption is ridiculed by the narrator in a number of comic set-pieces. But his efforts to evade the past are doomed to failure and Arrowby's development into a character worthy of our sympathy must be accompanied by a painful self-understanding.

The sea of the novel's title is not only the source of the dominant strain of imagery, it is itself a major protagonist. As a force of indeterminacy and flux, it is a counterpoint in the narrative to the deluded and narcissistic efforts of Arrowby to freeze the past into an image of his own myth-making. In a way that bears closest affinity to *The Tempest*, Arrowby's Prospero-like pretensions to orchestrate the lives of those who trespass upon his island is an egotistical tyranny that also must be surrendered in time for the denouement.

Murdoch's gift for elevating even the most seemingly banal of events into the focus of enduring philosophical and ethical questions is nowhere more convincingly wrought than in this novel by a writer at the peak of her powers. **VA**

Life: A User's Manual

Georges Perec

Lifespan | *b.* 1936 (France), *d.* 1982
First Published | 1978
First Published by | Hachette (Paris)
Original Title | *La Vie, mode d'emploi*

Dwarfing its contemporaries like "a Pompidou Center amongst bus shelters," as one reviewer put it, Perec's gargantuan work won the prestigious Médicis Prize in 1978. The novel seeks to write the teeming minutiae of everyday life as well as provide engaging narrative. It is also an astonishing exercise in form. The book is a portrait of a Parisian apartment block. We move around the building, each room allocated a chapter. Ever a fan of puzzles and games, Perec uses mathematical formulae to generate prepared lists of objects each of the ninety-nine chapters should contain, while a tortuous chess problem determines the route of the narrative.

The central conceit is equally labyrinthine. A rich Englishman named Percival Bartlebooth sets out to organize his life around a fifty-year project: "an arbitrarily constrained program with no purpose outside its own completion." His aesthetic endeavor entails the production and destruction of a number of paintings, resulting in nothing. Lest this nullity seems to reflect Perec's own aesthetic gesture, we must be aware that his writing is experimental, not existential. A member of the Oulipo ("Workshop for Potential Literature") group since 1967, Perec keeps to Oulipian maxims, seeking to reunite literature with the disciplines from which it has been separated, like mathematics or game theory. **DH**

> ❯ Georges Perec, genial as well as a genius, had the gift of making experimental writing an entertaining experience for the reader.

The World According to Garp

John Irving

Lifespan | *b.* 1942 (U.S.)
First Published | 1978
First Published by | E. F. Dutton (New York)
Movie Adaptation Released | 1982

> *"In the world according to Garp, we are all terminal cases."*

French photographer Sophie Bassouls has John Irving pose with obvious symbols of American identity on a visit to Paris in 1989.

The World According to Garp is Irving's most commercial novel and is widely recognized as a modern classic. The novel is based around the central character of Garp, a novelist and born storyteller whose bizarre and imaginative fictions are interspersed through an account of his life, the stories echoing off his character and providing humor and tragedy in equal measure.

The book begins with Jenny Field, a 1940s nurse, impregnating herself with the seed of a hapless sergeant, wounded during the war and reduced to the mentality of a baby. It is the first and last time she ever has sex and she names her child after the sergeant, T. S. Garp. The young Garp attends the Steering School, an academy for boys where Jenny is employed as head nurse. Garp meets his first love, Helen, and begins to write short stories to impress her. Jenny becomes a revered icon for feminist extremists and a hate figure for sexist extremists, and Garp becomes mixed up in all the politics. Garp is delighted by the little things in life, and takes rare joy in being attentive to the world around him. He marries Helen and takes care of their two sons, but the specter of tragedy always seems to be lurking in the background of their happiness.

Although many parts of the book are funny, filled with Irving's quirky, characteristic black humor, there is an underlying current of sadness as Garp realizes that the family, although the greatest thing in creation, is not impenetrable but violated by an exterior world that is terrifying both in its familiarity and its strangeness. By the end, despite their attempts to be different, both strands of the Garp family are hit by tragedy, and Irving's haunting message is that there is simply no way to make the world safe for those we love. **EF**

The Cement Garden

Ian McEwan

As is the case for many of McEwan's novels, *The Cement Garden* elaborates upon short stories published in his two inaugural collections: *First Love, Last Rites* (1975) and *In Between the Sheets* (1978). Both stories and novel are preoccupied with sexual maturation and initiation, incest, and violation, yet these surface continuities are ultimately less significant than their deeper proximities of form and structure. *The Cement Garden* shares the economy of the short story, with its calibrated presuppositions, pressure-cooker plot, and claustrophobic prose.

Set during a hot, indeterminate post-war summer, the novel describes the inexplicable yet inevitable actions of four children following the deaths of their parents. In an atmosphere of disturbing intimacy, the children begin to explore their adolescent sexuality, both alone and with each other. The novel becomes at once an epitome of domestic fiction, and the cold suffocation of such family narratives. A horrifying theme is rendered bizarrely seductive by the lure of form. McEwan proceeds by juxtaposition rather than justification or discursive explanation. Events are simply placed alongside their responses, with a disconcerting gap where the reassurance of explanation might otherwise reside. In this world, morality is not merely forestalled: it is a dialect with which the story's language does not quite coincide. Instead, events follow their own logic, which we, as outsiders, can only translate. As a result, the final, incestuous sexual coupling of its climax becomes a perverse celebration, provoking the regeneration not only of the children's shared memories, but also their family. Whatever has been concealed in the course of the book—human remains, sexual desire, family history—refuses to stay "buried." **DT**

Lifespan | *b.* 1948 (England)
First Published | 1978
First Published by | Jonathan Cape (London)
First U.S. Edition | Simon & Schuster (New York)

"I did not kill my father, but I sometimes felt I had helped him on his way."

⊚ McEwan was one of the first graduates of Malcolm Bradbury's creative writing course at the University of East Anglia.

Hitchhikers' Guide to the Galaxy

Douglas Adams

Lifespan | *b.* 1952 (England), *d.* 2001 (U.S.)
First Published | 1979
First Published by | Pan (London)
Series Published | 1980–1992

Adams' "trilogy in four parts" began life as a BBC radio series in 1978. This, the first book, combines the science fiction genre with pithy, tongue-in-cheek humor and some underhand satire directed at everything from bureaucracy and politics to bad poetry and the fate of all those biros . . . When the Earth is destroyed to make way for an intergalactic motorway, hapless everyman Arthur Dent finds himself journeying through the galaxy with his friend Ford Prefect, who turns out to be from not Guildford but Betelgeuse Five. Ford's job is as a writer for the eponymous *Hitchhiker's Guide to the Galaxy*, a brilliant fusion of travel book and electronic guide. Insights from the guide punctuate the narrative, providing hilarious explanations of the workings of the universe. The well-observed and eccentric characters, and a suitably bewildered Arthur, provide a rare kind of chemistry in a work of fiction that is well plotted, well paced, and surprisingly sophisticated.

Adams combines extraordinary inventiveness with an understanding of science shamelessly flouted in the name of chuckle-out-loud wit. He affectionately mocks the planet while putting it firmly back in the center of the universe. **AC**

⬅ Adams (left) and comic book publisher Nick Landau hold a copy of Adams' book and an LP recording of the radio series.

If on a Winter's Night a Traveler

Italo Calvino

Lifespan | *b.* 1923 (Cuba), *d.* 1985 (Italy)
First Published | 1979
First Published by | G. Einaudi (Turin)
Original Title | *Se una notte d'inverno un viaggiatore*

If on a Winter's Night a Traveler is a novel about the urgency, desire, and frustration bound up in the practice of reading novels. Calvino devises a narrative containing a library-shelf of incomplete novels—enticing fragments from imagined books that are brutally interrupted by the contingencies of faulty binding or missing pages. For this novel is also about all that can go wrong on that hazardous journey between a writer and a reader who sits down to read a novel. That reader is me—potentially you. But it is also a character called the Reader, whose initial desire to get hold of an undamaged copy of Italo Calvino's latest novel (which happens to be titled *If on a Winter's Night a Traveler*) is soon confused with his desire for Ludmilla, another reader. Theirs is the framing narrative, interspliced with the fragments of the other novels they read— each passing itself off as the sequel to the fragment they (and we) have just read. This complex organization allows Calvino to write ten brilliant extracts from ten very different novels, the tour of reading taking us across genres, periods, languages, and cultures.

Above all, this novel is a manifesto for the pleasures and the adventures of reading alone as well as a celebration of the thrill of mutual recognition experienced when two readers discover that they have read and loved the same book. **KB**

The Safety Net

Heinrich Böll

Lifespan | *b.* 1917 (Germany), *d.* 1985
First Published | 1979
First Published by | Kiepenheuer & Witsch (Cologne)
Original Title | *Fürsorgliche Belagerung*

In the cast-list that prefaces Heinrich Böll's *The Safety Net*, Fritz Tolm is described as "president of the Association; a newspaper owner." Occupying the claustrophobic center of this claustrophobic narrative, he both holds and is held by power. A powerful newspaper magnate, as the text opens, he is appointed caretaker president of an industrial association. A scion of wealth and influence, he is a target for left-wing revolutionary terrorist organizations. He is also the grandfather of the son of a woman involved in one such organization; she is in hiding with her son, and Tolm and other members of his family are placed under police surveillance. Already under police protection because of the prestige and vulnerability of his position, Tolm is locked into his public role. He does not have the freedom to walk or talk openly, to light his own cigarette, or to choose to be on his own.

From this core, Böll builds up a sense of the neuroses of West Germany in the early 1970s, a time when press coverage of the Baader-Meinhof terrorist group created a net of fear and suspicion. Exploring the paradox that the paraphernalia of security destroys what it seeks to protect, Böll uses his novel to define and question a historical period and the illogicality of the social rules that governed it. The prose is dense and detailed but the web of names, events, places, and memories is necessary to show how the promised safety net can only ever be a thing of flimsy but implacable limits. **PMcM**

Burger's Daughter

Nadine Gordimer

Lifespan | *b.* 1923 (South Africa)
First Published | 1979
First Published by | Jonathan Cape (London)
Nobel Prize for Literature | 1991

Burger's Daughter is a novel that explores the impossibility and the necessity of a private life. In South Africa in the late 1960s and 1970s, private life is a luxury, belonging only to those whites who can blind themselves to the fact that their "normality" is underpinned by other peoples' suffering. For Rosa Burger, a private life comes also to be a necessity, a strategy for survival after the death of her father in prison, a means whereby she can resist the absorption of herself into his reputation and his South Africa.

Both of Rosa's parents were Afrikaner Marxists, freedom fighters, figures for whom politics was no respecter of the thin line demarcating the supposed sanctity of the private domain. By the novel's end, Rosa Burger is also in prison. But in the defeat of her painful attempt to carve out a life of her own there is a strange liberation.

Gordimer articulates a critique of what passes for "freedom" through the anguish of a white woman trapped in a past not of her making. The untold histories interlaced with the story of her struggle are the stories of migrant miners, factory workers, homeless servants, and landless peasants. This corrodes sympathy, leaving the reader no choice but to read on, to be glad this novel was written, and to regret the need for it to be written. **PMcM**

❯ Gordimer, here at her Johannesburg home in 1981, expresses the dilemmas of a white woman in a racially divided country.

A Bend in the River

V. S. Naipaul

Lifespan | *b.* 1932 (Trinidad)
First Published | 1979
First Published by | Deutsch (London)
Nobel Prize for Literature | 2001

A Bend in the River is set in an unnamed central African state, closely modeled on Mobutu's Zaire, and is narrated by Salim, a Muslim of Indian descent who travels from his family's home on the East African coast to run a sundries shop in a crumbling town "on the bend in the great river." The Europeans have largely departed; this is a dangerous new land.

Salim is surrounded by people of all sorts: a tribal woman who visits his shop and deals in charms and potions; an old Belgian priest who collects African masks and carvings; and upwardly mobile entrepreneurs, including a fellow Indian who sets up a Bigburger joint in town. Salim has a protégé, a young African called Ferdinand; he sends him to school and watches him transform himself from a rural nobody into a politically engaged government administrator. Always felt but never foregrounded in the narrative are the turbulent events—guerrilla uprisings, corruption, killings—of a nation that is seeking an identity. The president, always referred to as the Big Man, creates his own darkly Africanized myth of himself, aided by a white historian with whose wife Salim has a violent affair.

Everyone's lives are interconnected, and their complications are driven by larger forces: the clash of cultures, the weight of history. *A Bend in the River* shares with Naipaul's other novels a deep skepticism about the direction of non-European civilization, but what really resonate are the individual stories and the human calamities they involve. **DSoa**

> *"The river and the forest were like presences, and much more powerful than you. You felt unprotected, an intruder."*

⊙ Based in England for the whole of his adult life, Naipaul has adopted much of the air of the traditional English gentleman.

Shikasta

Doris Lessing

Lifespan | *b.* 1919 (Iran)
First Published | 1979
First Published by | Jonathan Cape (London)
Full Name | Doris May Lessing

This is Doris Lessing's most ambitious and startling novel, a complete work of science fiction that tells the story of life on Earth and the alien interventions that formed it. A number of reports and documents make up the novel, recording the views of God and his angels, who are actually aliens, about Earth's degeneration. The development of humanity has faltered, the current suffering on Earth is due to a longstanding disruption in spirituality, caused when conditions in space disconnected Earth from its parent culture. Because of this, human life has become dangerously unbalanced. Lessing depicts a utopian golden age, where peace and longevity are the norm, but she subverts this utopia with stories of genocide and genetic engineering that form the "truth" behind bible stories. The novel addresses the importance of individual freedom and the possibility of morality and spirituality, and is obliquely critical of an arrogant Western world that fails to admit its weaknesses. Ultimately, the novel is a story of the fight between good and evil, of light and dark, and of how in a world where everything is created with an inherent will to prosper and succeed at the expense of everything else, expecting the opposite is the ultimate fiction. At a time when the gaps between genres were more pronounced, this work did much to meld the science fiction genre into mainstream literature. With its grand themes and adept characterization, this is Lessing's most memorable work. **EF**

Smiley's People

John Le Carré

Lifespan | *b.* 1931 (England)
First Published | 1979
First Published by | Knopf (New York)
Given Name | David John Moore Cornwell

Smiley's People captures the dark, unglamorous world of espionage in the last days of the Cold War. Le Carré maintains his fine sense of plotting and pace that is the hallmark of the accomplished thriller. George Smiley, a British intelligence agent, is called from retirement to discover why a former Soviet defector has been murdered. The novel portrays the hunt to destroy Carla, the ruthless and formidable grand master of Soviet espionage who featured in *Tinker, Tailor, Soldier, Spy*. Smiley gradually uncovers an intricate web that leads him to realize that Carla has a weak link: a parental concern for a daughter who is mentally ill. In many respects, this novel is Le Carré's bleakest depiction of a world that has seemingly lost its ideals. There is no longer even a vestige of ideological struggle between East and West; espionage here is conducted for private purposes. At the same time, he depicts politically displaced figures who have suffered enormous indignity seeking justice. The book powerfully articulates that individuals of integrity can make a difference in a morally anarchic world.

It is the human cost of the Cold War that fascinates Le Carré; both sides have generated an environment that seems to lead to psychological instability. Smiley emerges with credit because he almost wishes not to succeed: he recognizes that there is something repugnant about blackmailing Carla, that he must stoop to using methods Western values are supposed to oppose. **TH**

The Book of Laughter and Forgetting

Milan Kundera

Lifespan | *b.* 1929 (Czechoslovakia)
First Published | 1979
First Published by | Gallimard (Paris)
Original Czech Title | *Kniha smíchu a zapomnění*

Kundera
Le livre du rire et de l'oubli

folio

● Following the blacklisting of his works in his native Czechoslovakia, Kundera fled to France in 1975, where this novel was published.

◗ After Kundera became a French citizen in 1981, his work slowly drew away from concern with his politically troubled Czech past.

Kundera compares the structure of this novel to variations upon a musical theme. This is an apposite analogy because the novel profoundly challenges our expectations of the form. It is separated into seven sections that cannot be assimilated within the conventions of a linear or cohesive narrative, and it is interspersed with historical information and Kundera's own autobiographical recollections.

Tamina, the novel's principal character, leaves Czechoslovakia with her husband to escape the realities of the communist regime. When he dies soon afterward, she struggles with an overwhelming anxiety that she will forget him. The importance of remembering is a preoccupation of the novel and of Kundera's wider work. It is his conviction that erasure and forgetting are political tools that are exploited by the communist state, sometimes literally, as when dissenting party members are airbrushed out of propaganda photographs. The events of the novel take place against the backdrop of Czechoslovakia in the post-war period. Under the leadership of Alexander Dubcek, the country was working to make socialism more "human." The 1968 Soviet invasion put paid to that ambition, however, and led to disillusionment with the political process.

The Book of Laughter and Forgetting is recognizably the work of Kundera but, perhaps more than any of his other works, it is suffused with an ineffable strangeness that is at once provocative and forbidding. As with his other writing, this novel raises questions about the representation of female characters, and invites accusations of latent misogyny. These are valid objections that may engender fruitful considerations of this novel as an historical document as much as a work of experimental fiction. **JW**

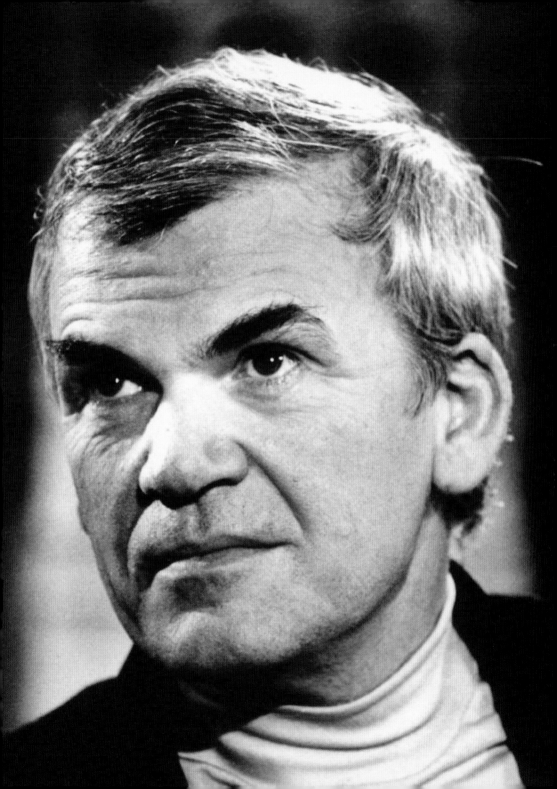

The Name of the Rose

Umberto Eco

Lifespan | *b.* 1932 (Italy)
First Published | 1980, by Bompiani (Milan)
Movie Adaptation Released | 1986
Orginal Title | *Il nome della rosa*

With a narrative apparatus as complex as it is beautiful, Umberto Eco's *The Name of the Rose* gives the reader both a clear defense of the study of signs and an intricate detective story. Both facets are framed by the unfinished story, a pre-narrative, of a scholar who finds in a number of manuscripts a story worth telling. Perhaps because the space this pre-narrative is given is so slight compared to the density of what is to follow or perhaps because of the tone of the scholar, these first few pages remain with the reader as the text goes back to the source of the manuscripts in the early fourteenth century.

A young Benedictine novice, Adso of Melk, tells of his travels with a learned Franciscan, William of Baskerville, to a troubled Benedictine monastery. This monastery, a cruel enclosed arena of conflicts and secrets, is ruled by books. The Benedictines who inhabit it live for books. As, one by one, six of them are murdered, William of Baskerville searches for the truth of their internal mute warfare by finding and reading the signs of jealousy, desire, and fear.

The Name of the Rose asks its readers to share Baskerville's task of interpretation, to respect the polyphony of signs, to slow down before deciding upon meaning, and to doubt anything that promises an end to the pursuit of meaning. In this way, Eco opens up the wonder of interpretation itself. **PMcM**

◉ Eco tries hard not to look ridiculous posed by photographer David Lees with the rose of his novel's title in a medieval setting.

City Primeval

Elmore Leonard

Lifespan | *b.* 1925 (U.S.)
First Published | 1980
First Published by | Arbor House (New York)
Full Title | *City Primeval: High Noon in Detroit*

Elmore Leonard began his career writing westerns, and his crime novels carried explicit and implicit traces of the western genre. *City Primeval* constitutes the fullest and most successful realization of Leonard's fusion of these American popular forms. Detroit's grimy post-industrial landscape might seem a long way from America's Wild West, but the novel's protagonist-antagonist coupling is lifted straight from the pages of the pulp western. Police detective Raymond Cruz is the "no-bullshit Old West lawman," while Clement Mansell, the self-styled "Oklahoma wildman," is the conscienceless killer, who must be brought to justice. Further Wild West allusions are created by the presence of a clan of Albanians, whose old world customs and blood ties take them outside the rule of law.

As in the rest of Leonard's writing, contingency and moral ambiguity replace straightforward moral posturing. Essentially, Cruz is good—the decent man who is pushed too far—while Mansell is an amoral psychopath. But just as Cruz must contemplate extra-legal means for dealing with his adversary, Leonard's darkly humorous portrayal of Mansell means that he becomes hard to dislike, in spite of his murderous ways. Further blurring these distinctions is Mansell's lawyer, Carolyn Wilder, whose claim that even killers have rights under the law is eroded by her burgeoning relationship with Cruz. In the end, Wild West justice prevails, but Leonard's grinning psychopath lingers longest in the memory. **AP**

Confederacy of Dunces

John Kennedy Toole

Lifespan | *b.* 1937 (U.S.), *d.* 1969
First Published | 1980
First Published by | Louisiana State University Press
Pulitzer Prize | 1981 (posthumous)

"When a true genius appears in the world, you may know him by this sign, that the dunces are all in confederacy against him." The quote is by the satirist Jonathan Swift, and the unlikely genius at the center of John Kennedy Toole's grotesquely comic novel is the corpulent Ignatius J. Reilly, a man of huge appetites and extraordinary erudition. Intent on spending his time in his bedroom, binge-eating, ranting, and recording his musings on a jumbled pile of writing-pads, he is forced through an unfortunate turn in circumstances to venture out into the world of work. He is drawn into a series of misunderstandings and misadventures as he struggles to deal with the horrors of modern life. Orbiting around him are the dunces, the eccentric inhabitants of a splendidly described low-life New Orleans. The atmosphere of decay adds a discordant undertone to the comedy, and there are disquieting insights into the hypocrisy and discrimination lurking behind the city's grinning carnival mask.

John Kennedy Toole struggled for years to find a publisher for the novel. It was only years after his suicide that his mother convinced the novelist Walker Percy to read the manuscript, and it was his enthusiasm for the book that led to its publication. It went on to become a bestseller. This is a timelessly funny and fast-moving novel, spiralling through a uniquely unhinged world in which, according to Ignatius J. Reilly, "the gods of Chaos, Lunacy and Bad Taste" have gained ascendancy over humankind. **TS**

Rituals

Cees Nooteboom

Lifespan | *b.* 1933 (Netherlands)
First Published | 1980
First Published by | Arbeiderspers (Amsterdam)
Original Title | *Rituelen*

Nooteboom has been described as the Netherlands' answer to Nabokov or Borges. *Rituals* is neither outspokenly postmodern nor especially magic realist, but it is certainly not linear or predictable.

Concerning Inni Wintrop, a thinker privileged with a prosperous life and too much time on his hands, the novel conjures an impressionistic literary landscape where events and people mirror each other but are never fully explained. Perhaps Wintrop's self-confessed dilettantism cannot allow for answers, only endless and restless questioning, yet it is not his life that lies at the heart of the novel as much as the story of two men by the name of Taads; father Arnold and son Philip. Both end up committing suicide. Nooteboom uses the divergent circumstances of their lives and deaths to explore how different generations face similar crises of intellectual and spiritual faith.

Cees Nooteboom is neither burdensomely philosophical nor anthropological in his approach; ramblings on the nature of God and existence are leavened by the macabre whimsy of a circumcision or satirical soundings on the art world. Much of the language, too, is crisply and poetically precise, whether conveying existential doubt or paying homage to Amsterdam's engrossing cityscape. *Rituals* became Nooteboom's first major success in the English-speaking world; in the case of such an idiosyncratically "European" novel, perhaps this is telling of its assured greatness. **ABI**

Rites of Passage

William Golding

Lifespan | *b.* 1911 (England), *d.* 1993
First Published | 1980
First Published by | Faber & Faber (London)
Booker Prize | 1980

This sea-novel, set in the early nineteenth century, is the first volume in a trilogy which describes events during a voyage from England to Australia. The second and third volumes were *Close Quarters* (1987) and *Fire Down Below* (1989). The three novels were eventually combined in one volume entitled *To the Ends of the Earth* (1991).

Golding employs his remarkable descriptive powers to evoke in detail the conditions of the voyage, the sights, sounds, and smells of the vessel as she proceeds through the lonely seas, bearing her microcosm of fallible human beings. Golding constructs a plot-sequence that is so elliptically or obliquely presented that the reader may not perceive it as a coherent sequence until a second or subsequent reading of the work. In *Rites of Passage*, the main narrator, Talbot, describes incidents aboard the massive but aging sailing-ship. As he keeps the journal that his godfather is intended to read, we come to realize that he lacks self-knowledge: he betrays his own arrogance, snobbery, and lack of perception. He gets to know Colley, a callow clergyman, and becomes involved in the mystery of his death. A dramatic contrast in perspective occurs when the narrative is continued by means of a long letter from Colley to his sister. As Talbot reads this, he gains some measure of penitent self-knowledge. The reader, in turn, is shown ironic and even fatal disparities between the ways in which different observers interpret the same events. **CW**

"'The stink,' said I, my hand over my nose and mouth as I gagged, 'the fetor, the stench, call it what you will!' . . . 'Lord, sir!' said he. 'You'll soon get used to that!'"

William Golding, photographed here in 1983, was still a highly productive, original and innovative novelist in his seventies.

Midnight's Children

Salman Rushdie

Midnight's Children is narrated by Saleem Sinai, who was born at midnight on August 15, 1947: the moment of the creation of India. Saleem's life comes to embody that of the young nation. Yet rather than allowing the novel or this protagonist to stand as representative of the country, Rushdie explores the complex fantasies and failures that the myth of nationalism offers.

All of the children born during the hour of midnight are uniquely gifted, the closer to midnight the more powerful the gift. This cohort of the fantastic and the surreal—children who can move through time, multiply fishes, become invisible—is an imaginary expression of India's rich potential. Of the group two are born on the stroke of midnight, and are its potential leaders: Saleem, who can see into the hearts and minds of others, and Shiva, who is given the converse gift, the gift of war, and becomes a brutish killer. The adversarial relationship between the two is crucial to this huge and sprawling narrative, which is set against the backdrop of the first years of independence. Saleem comes from a privileged and well-connected family, whereas Shiva, a motherless street child, has nothing. Midway through the novel, however, we discover that these two children were swapped at birth and that neither is who they are assumed to be. The anxieties around paternity, dispossession, authenticity, and trust that this knowledge raises come to reverberate throughout the novel and are constantly read back against the partitioned history of India itself. This masterly novel, which transfixes the reader with its imaginative scope, humor, dizzying wordplay, and heartbreaking pathos is an exciting blend of magic realism and political reality, Rushdie's heartfelt tribute to his native land. **NM**

Lifespan | *b.* 1947 (India)
First Published | 1980
First Published by | Jonathan Cape (London)
Booker Prize | 1981

Salman Rushdie, shown here in 1988, became an internationally famous writer as a result of the success of *Midnight's Children*.

Indians celebrate independence from Britain in Calcutta on August 15, 1947, the day of the birth of Rushdie's narrator Saleem.

Waiting for the Barbarians

J. M. Coetzee

Lifespan | *b.* 1940 (South Africa)
First Published | 1980
First Published by | Secker & Warburg (London)
Nobel Prize for Literature | 2003

Critics frequently attempt to read into Coetzee's dense, elliptical narratives allegories of the South African state during and after the period of apartheid. *Waiting for the Barbarians* is certainly open to such an interpretation.

Set in an unnamed empire, in an unspecified location, at an unnamed time, the novel relates the tale of a magistrate. He comes up against the machinery of a brutal state by attempting, in some small way, to recompense a "barbarian" girl for the torture inflicted upon her by the inscrutable Colonel Joll. The magistrate collects wooden slips retrieved from the desert containing an ancient and unreadable script. He concludes that these fragments of writing form an allegory that arises not from the slips themselves but from the order and manner in which they are read. In this way, *Waiting for the Barbarians* is a more general meditation on the act of writing and on the potential failures of writing to communicate meaning. Here the "barbarians" seem to represent a testimony of suffering that cannot be articulated. The woman that the magistrate rescues says little and he largely infers her consciousness, seeking to read a narrative of the Empire from her wounds. Similarly, through the magistrate's abasement, Coetzee offers a portrait of political commitment as something that is simultaneously total and also empty of ideology. **LC**

Broken April

Ismail Kadare

Lifespan | *b.* 1936 (Albania)
First Published | 1980, in *Gjakftohtësia*
First Published by | Naim Frashëri (Tirana)
Original Title | *Prilli i Thyer*

Set in Albania between the world wars, in a nation on the brink of European modernity, the novel focuses on the story of Gjorg Berisha's embroilment in a blood feud whose rules are strictly governed by the Kanun, an ancient code of honor that has dominated Albanian culture for generations. Gjorg's family have been involved in a seventy-year-old feud with a neighboring family, the Kryeqyqes. The novel begins when Gjorg assassinates a member of the Kryeqyqe family, in revenge for the earlier murder of his own brother. The murder makes Gjorg himself the next victim in the cycle of recrimination.

The Kanun decrees that there is a thirty-day period of truce after a murder occurs, and before it can be avenged. It is this period that the novel covers, from the moment that Gjorg murders his victim, in mid March, to the moment that Gjorg will be delivered to the implacable justice of the Kanun, in mid April. During this period, Gjorg is neither alive nor dead, but suspended in empty time.

Written with an extraordinary simplicity and elegance, this is a haunting and haunted tale. The space between life and death that the novel maps out is given a dreamlike articulation that is infused with the spirit of Homer, Dante, and Kafka. Kadare is also stunningly original, inventing a newly ancient language in which to express the contradictions of contemporary life in eastern Europe. **PB**

Summer in Baden-Baden

Leonid Tsypkin

Lifespan | *b.* 1926 (Belarus), *d.* 1982 (Russia)
First Published | 1981, in *Novyy Amerikanets* (N.Y.)
Original Title | *Leto v Badene*
First UK Edition | 1987, by Quartet (London)

This extraordinary novel, first published in 1981 just before the author died, was recently brought to the attention of the reading public by the critic Susan Sontag just before her own death.

The novel dramatizes Fyodor and Anna Dostoevsky's tempestuous relationship, focusing on a summer trip the couple took to Baden-Baden in 1867. The story of Anna and Fyodor is folded into an autobiographical account of Tsypkin's own travels, and folded again into scenes and moments from Dostoevsky's writing, and from the wider Russian literary heritage.

As the reader becomes lost between the real and the imagined, the beautiful and the ugly, Tsypkin's wild, uncontainable prose starts to take over, to produce its own crazed reality. Tsypkin's prose is unlike any other, an entirely new and vivid invention. In the rhythms of his writing, as he imagines his way toward the insanity of Dostoevsky's love for Anna, he catches the very movement of Dostoevsky's thought, of his paranoia, his desperation, and his brilliance.

Summer in Baden-Baden gives Dostoevsky to us in a new way, and in doing so it promises to redraw the map of contemporary fiction. That it should be rescued from the dark by a woman at the end of her life, in an act that is itself a testament to the love of literary fiction, is almost uncannily fitting. **PB**

July's People

Nadine Gordimer

Lifespan | *b.* 1923 (South Africa)
First Published | 1981
First Published by | Jonathan Cape (London)
Nobel Prize for Literature | 1991

This apocalyptic novel is set during the imaginary civil war that follows upon an invasion of South Africa from Mozambique in 1980. The cities are alight, the houses burning, as Maureen and Bam Smales and their children set out in a pickup truck, "the yellow bakkie," with their servant July to escape to safety in his distant village.

Confronted with the gritty realities of village life, Maureen prospers, and Bam, lost without his rifle, is defeated. In their new dependence, the relationship with July becomes increasingly difficult as the white couple lose their culture day by day: Maureen poses like a model across the bakkie, and July fails to recognize the moment or the meaning. Desire and duty are now shaped by economics, and the white liberal assumption of a shared human nature is brought into question. Gordimer's complex prose performs extraordinary feats of allusion and implication to relate past certainties to present doubt, and scarcely a paragraph is set in an undisturbed present. These profound questions are hardly capable of resolution. When a helicopter lands, Maureen rushes out to it, not knowing if it is army or revolutionary, and there the novel ends, itself unresolved. Untrue to history and the actual moment of change in South Africa, *July's People* nevertheless provides a truthful dissection of white liberal vulnerability. **AMu**

The Comfort of Strangers

Ian McEwan

Lifespan | *b*. 1948 (England)
First Published | 1981
First Published by | Jonathan Cape (London)
First U.S. Edition | Simon & Schuster (New York)

The setting for this atmospheric story of sexual predation and entrapment is recognizably Venice, but the city is never named. Instead, Ian McEwan uses the anonymous alleys, bridges, and piazzas to create a labyrinth of seedy decadence and foreboding in which Colin and Mary, the beautiful young couple at the center of the novel, are wandering tourists without a map. Late at night, hungry and disoriented and unable to find a restaurant, they meet Robert. This is no chance encounter. Robert has kept Colin and Mary under surveillance since they arrived. He persuades them to accompany him, first to a bar—where he describes a childhood in which he was humiliated by his powerful, bullying father—and subsequently to his home, where they meet his wife Caroline, a housebound invalid. It later becomes apparent that Caroline's disability is the result of Robert's sadistic sexual violence.

The theme of male dominance and brutality toward women is explored and then re-examined when it is revealed that the object of Robert's desire is Colin. The ease with which he is drawn into the trap poses fascinating and troubling questions about victims' behavior. As the narrative moves toward its hypnotic climax, McEwan maintains the pace and suspense with a precision and detachment that is so characteristic of his early short stories. **TS**

Lanark: A Life in Four Books

Alasdair Gray

Lifespan | *b*. 1934 (Scotland)
First Published | 1981
First Published by | Canongate (Edinburgh)
Saltire Society Book of the Year | 1981

When Alasdair Gray made his debut with *Lanark*, he seemed to reset the benchmarks for invention in Scottish fiction. Gray continued a twofold legacy, inheriting the impulse for typographic innovation from Jonathan Swift and Joyce, while sustaining a Blakean vision of radical social possibilities latent within the texture of everyday Glaswegian life. Traversing between Unthank and Glasgow, the narrative spans two urban underworlds as it traces the attempts by Lanark and Duncan Thaw to resist the drudgery of workaday routine.

Throughout *Lanark*, the reader's attention is drawn to the value of the physical book by its material layout. From chapter to chapter, Gray's iridescent etchings of imaginary topographies offset his written documentary of cynicism as an affliction of Scotland's youth. The portrayal in words of urban disaffection provokes illustrations that prospect Scotland's regeneration. With both cities portrayed as perpetual transit zones, shifting between stagnation and restitution, the reader is encouraged to interact with Gray's typographical designs (just as his protagonists mature on their journeys of self-discovery). It is this state of interactivity that testifies to the indispensability of the printed page. **DJ**

❯ Drawn by the author himself, this rare illustration typifies Gray's clever use of fantasy and typography in his work.

PROPERTY OF
ALASDAIR
GRAY 30"7"59
II FINDHORN ST
GLASGOW E.3

POEMS

By

Robert
Walker

Rabbit is Rich

John Updike

Lifespan | *b.* 1932 (U.S.)
First Published | 1981
First Published by | Knopf (New York)
Pulitzer Prize | 1982

Rabbit is Rich, the third novel in John Updike's acclaimed four-part "Rabbit" series, jumps forward another ten years to 1979. Set in the fictional small town of Brewer, Pennsylvania, it again takes up the story of Harry Angstrom, nicknamed "Rabbit," who, now in his forties, is enjoying a prosperous career as a used-car salesman. Happily settled with his wife, and renegotiating difficult relationships as his son grows older and marries, Rabbit has seemingly grown into the role of "solid citizen" mocked by Sinclair Lewis' *Babbitt*, which serves as an epigraph to the book. Set against the background of the worldwide oil crisis of the late 1970s, the novel's action turns on the ironies implied by Rabbit's change of occupation from a working-class linotyper to an upwardly mobile dealer in used cars. Selling Toyotas to newly gas-conscious middle-class drivers has become Rabbit's own ticket into the middle-class world of country clubs and cocktails. His pleasure in achieving the riches implied by the title is balanced by the book's sensitive portrayal of the loss of American working-class jobs.

Rabbit is Rich charts the emotional upheavals of Rabbit's personal life against the background of an America that was just on the cusp of what would become the grim anxieties of the 1980s. Updike's lyric prose and thoughtful characterizations are as strong as ever. As Rabbit ages, the sensitive portrayal of the emotional connections that underpin everyday life achieves a new poignancy. **AB**

The Names

Don DeLillo

Lifespan | *b.* 1936 (U.S.)
First Published | 1982
First Published by | Knopf (New York)
Original Language | English

Don DeLillo's prose is always instantly recognizable through his characteristic style and mastery of the sentence. Yet within this consistency of language and his recurrent themes—death, consumer culture, and Americanism—a wide-ranging play and many different approaches are to be found.

Set among an ex-pat American community in Greece and beyond, this peculiar novel is part murder-mystery, part thriller, and part exploration of one man's broken marriage and persistent neuroses. The strange magic inherent in language and all its permutations—from the rituals of a hidden cult to the broken syntax of a child's storywriting—is brought to the foreground and set against the odd otherworldliness of the narrative.

The Names is very much about being American and an American living abroad. The novel encompasses a wide-reaching notion of distance and exile, weaving together many of the threads present in the novels that DeLillo penned both before and after it. This is not a mark of ubiquity of theme but rather serves to highlight the extraordinary breadth of exploration in DeLillo's effortlessly sharp writing. Underneath the novel's welter of strands, the emotional focus remains the poignant relationship between James Axton, the protagonist, and his fractured family. A beautiful, hypnotic novel, *The Names* is both an excellent first novel for the DeLillo initiate and superb as a deeper exploration of his work for the existing devotee. **DR**

Concrete

Thomas Bernhard

Lifespan | *b.* 1931 (Netherlands), *d.* 1989 (Austria)
First Published | 1982
First Published by | Suhrkamp (Frankfurt)
Original Title | *Beton*

Concrete is perhaps Bernhard's most accessible novel and his best example of self-parody. It is an ironic treatment of many of the themes that dominate his work: failure, isolation, obsession with perfection, and the dangers of idealizing the intellectual way of life. The novel's almost slapstick humor rebuts the temptation to equate Bernhard's outlook with that of the self-obsessed, misanthropic failures that feature in all his novels.

In *Concrete* the failure and narrator is Rudolf, an ailing music scholar, who is incapable of writing the first line of a book on Mendelssohn that he has been planning for ten years. In the novel, Rudolf rails against all the factors preventing him from getting started. In addition to many amusing excuses, and tirades on the stifling philistinism of Austrian society, he mostly blames his sister. The sister, a recurring figure in Bernhard's fiction, represents in *Concrete* the need for a more grounded approach to things. She shows him that his book is merely a pretense to justify his failure to interact with everyday reality. She is also Rudolf's salvation and encourages him to go to Majorca to prevent his self-destruction. On arriving in Majorca, he is reminded of a prior visit when he experienced the concrete reality of human tragedy. The tragedy haunts him and is in stark contrast to his intellectual aspirations and his ridiculous self-importance. *Concrete* is a very funny novel. It is also a highly original account of loneliness and the need for others. **AL**

On the Black Hill

Bruce Chatwin

Lifespan | *b.* 1940 (England), *d.* 1989 (France)
First Published | 1982
First Published by | Jonathan Cape (London)
Whitbread Literary Award | 1982

For an author who spent much of his short life traveling and writing about traveling, *On the Black Hill* is a curious book to have written. It concerns eighty years in the lives of Benjamin and Lewis, identical twins from the Welsh border country, who remain for that entire period either within or near an isolated farm on which they live and subsequently work. Apart from a very brief period in the Army, from which Benjamin is dishonorably discharged, they avoid the draft for the First World War, they never marry, and after the death of their parents, they sleep in their parents' bed for over forty years.

The novel looks back over the lives of the twins, recounted in a distinctive realist prose. Chatwin favors the short single clause summary sentence over more complex, longer structures. He also relegates complexity of plot in favor of detailed character portrayal without crude simplification or sentimental excess.

On one level the novel contains all the appeal of a traditional rural drama: a hot-headed father who mistreats his educated wife and disrupts her attempts at schooling the twins, rural family feuds involving violence, a suicide, army brutality, the demise of a noble family due to corruption. But the book is also a study in the local and sedentary, and the tensions created within traditional lifestyles by motion and flight, as created by Lewis's interest in aviation and the opposite sex, and the brief and difficult moments where the twins are parted. **ABi**

The Newton Letter

John Banville

Lifespan | *b.* 1945 (Ireland)
First Published | 1982
First Published by | Secker & Warburg (London)
Full Title | *The Newton Letter: An Interlude*

The Newton Letter is the third installment in a tetralogy exploring the limits of, and relationship between, language and the significatory capacity of the "real world," explored through narratives of revolutionary scientists' personal and scientific worlds. The novella immediately departs from its predecessors, *Doctor Copernicus* (1976) and *Kepler* (1981), in treating not Newton himself but a twentieth-century Newton biographer, the book's unnamed narrator. As the narrator prepares to complete what he predicts will be the final stages of the biography, he rents a small cottage in rural Ireland. Here he becomes an ambivalent participant-observer in the lives of proprietors Edward and Charlotte, their niece Ottilie, and young Michael.

This dense meditation on the process of narrating history is by turns maddening and darkly funny. The narrator constructs myriad salacious stories to explain his observations of the family, as he embarks on an uncaring sexual relationship with Ottilie, develops a "spiritual" obsession with otherworldly Charlotte, and therefore casts Edward as the alcoholic, wastrel husband. What remains most troubling—what makes this infinitely more than the tale of a bad historian—is the realization that, although we may laugh at or be shocked by the outlandish, unjust stories the narrator constructs, the facts on which they are based still remain unchanged, ever silent and pliable, powerless to resist even the grossest (mis)interpretation. **AF**

The House of the Spirits

Isabel Allende

Lifespan | *b.* 1942 (Peru)
First Published | 1982
First Published by | Plaza & Janés (Barcelona)
Original Title | *La casa de los espíritus*

The vivacity of the imagination that shines through the fantastic tale of *The House of the Spirits* is difficult to describe in any way other than magical. The novel playfully traverses the boundary between the real and the incredible, while never losing its grounding in the history and political reality of Chile.

The House of the Spirits is a deeply personal novel. Begun as a letter to Allende's dying grandfather, it tells the story of the Trueba family, with the rise to power of Isabel's own uncle, Salvador Allende ("The Candidate" in the text), and his subsequent death in the coup of 1973 as its tragic backdrop. The atrocities that surround this bloody moment of Chilean history are strikingly evoked, and what has seemed an enchanting fairy tale becomes a dark and powerful narrative. The chronicle of these events may be the most striking element of the book, and has much to do with its (deserved) acclaim, but it is the exuberant presentation of the Trueba clan that is its emotional heart. Allende's tender and sentimental, caustic and biting assessments of thinly-veiled figures from her own life are brilliantly evocative. The empathy inspired by the tale of this extraordinary family is gripping, and the deep involvement engendered by Allende's writing makes the tragic and horrifying end personally moving. **DR**

> ❱ Isabel Allende is the niece of Chilean president Salvador Allende, killed in the coup that brought General Pinochet to power in 1973.

Lfd. Nr.	H.Art u.Nam.	H.Nr.	Name und Vorname	Geburts- datum	Beruf
361	Ju.Po.	6920 8	Hahn Dawid	20.10.97	Werkzeugschlosse
362	" "	9	Immerglück Zygmunt	13.6. 24	Stanzer
363	" "	10	Katz Isaak Josef	3.12.08	Klempnergehilfe
364	" "	1	Wiener Samuel	11. 5.07	Tischlergehilfe
365	" "	2	Rosner Leopold	26. 6.08	Maler
366	" "	3	Gewelbe Jakob	22. 9.97	Photografmeister
367	" "	4	Korn Edmund	7. 4.12	Metallarbeiter
368	" "	5	Penner Jonas	2. 2.15	Stanzer
369	" "	6	Wachtel Roman	5.11.05	Industriediamant
370	" "	7	Immerglück Mendel	24.9.03	Eisendrehergesel
371	" "	8	Wichter Feiwel	25. 7.26	ang. Metallverarb
372	" "	9	Landschaft Aron	7. 7.09	" "
373	" "	6922 0	Wandersmann Markus	14. 9.06	Stanzer
374	" "	1	Rosenthal Izrael	24.10.09	Schreibkraft
375	" "	2	Silberschlag Hersch	7. 4.12	Ang. Metallverarb
376	" "	3	Liban Jan	29. 4.24	Wasserinst.Gehil
377	" "	4	Kohane Chiel	15. 9. 25	Zimmerer
378	" "	5	Senftmann Dawid	6. 9.09	Ang. Metallverarb
379	" "	6	Kupferberg Izrael	4. 9.98	Schlossermeister
380	" "	7	Buchführer Norbert	12. 6.22	Lackierer Gesell
381	" "	8	Horowitz Schachne	3.1288	Schriftsetzermei
382	" "	9	Segal Richard	9.11.23	Steinbruchmineur
383	" "	6923 0	Jakubowicz Dawid	15. 4.26	"
384	" "	1	Sommer Josef	21.12.14	ang.Metallverarb.
385	" "	2	Smolarz Szymon	15. 4.04	"
386	" "	3	Rechem Ryszard	30. 5.21	Automechank.Gs.
387	" "	4	Szlamowicz Chaim	16. 5.24	Stanzer
388	" "	5	Kleinberg Szaija	1. 4.20	Steinbruchmineur
389	" "	6	Miedziuch Michael	3.11.16	Fleischergeselle
390	+ "	7	Millmann Bernhard	24.12.15	Stanzer
391	" "	8	Königl Marek	2.11.11.	Ang.Mettallverar
392	" "	9	Jakubowicz Chaim	10. 1.19	Steinbruchmineur
393	" "	6924 0	Domb Izrael	23. 1.08	Schreibkraft
394	" "	1	Klimburt Abram	1.11.13	Koch
395	" "	2	Wisniak Abram	30	Lehrling
396	" "	3	Schreiber Leopold	15.10.25	Schlossergeselle
397	" "	4	Silberstein Kacob	1. 1.00	Galvaniseurmeiste
398	" "	5	Eidner Pinkus	20.12.14	Dampfkesselheizer
399	" "	6	Goldberg Berisch	17. 5.13	ang.Metallverarb.
400	" "	7	Feiner Josef	16. 5.15	Automechanikcer
401	" "	8	Feiner Wilhelm	21.10.17	Stanzer
402	" "	9	Löw Zcycze	28. 6.97	Kesselschmied Mei
403	" "	6925 0	Löw Jacob	3. 3.00	" "
404	" "	1	Pozniak Szloma	15. 9.16	Bäcker
405	" "	2	Ratz Wolf	20. 6.09	Metallverarb.
406	" "	3	Lewkowicz Ferdinand	12. 3.09	Arzt Chrirug
407	" "	4	Lax Ryszard	9. 7.24	Automechaniker G.
408	" "	5	Semmel Berek	5. 1.05	Tischler Gehilfe
409	" "	6	Horowitz Isidor	25. 9.95	ang.Installateur
410	" "	7	Meisels Szlama	2.2.16	Fleischergeselle
411	" "	8	Kormann Abraham	15. 1. 09	Buchhalter
412	" "	9	Joachimsmann Abraham	19.12.95	Stanzer
413	" "	6926 0	Sawicki Samuel	9. 4.17	Koch
414	" "	1	Rosner Wilhelm	14. 9.25	Schlossergehilfe
415	" "	2	Hirschberg Symon	23. 7.08	Stanzer
416	" "	3	Goldberg Bernhard	10.10.16	Koch

Schindler's Ark

Thomas Keneally

Schindler's Ark begins with a "note" from Thomas Keneally describing the chance encounter with Leopold Pfefferberg, a "Schindler survivor," that prompted him to write the story of Oskar Schindler, "bon vivant, speculator, charmer." An industrialist and member of the Nazi Party, Schindler risked his life to protect Jews in Nazi-occupied Poland.

Winning the Booker Prize on its publication in 1982, *Schindler's Ark* is a "novel" deeply embedded in the trauma of modern European history, a story that, Keneally insists, attempts to avoid all fiction. Driven to understand Schindler's "impulse towards rescue," to explore the enigma that, on this telling, still haunts "Schindler's Jews", the book combines historical research with imaginative reconstruction to portray the complex and provocative character of Oskar Schindler. In the process, Keneally draws his readers into the world of those condemned by the Nazis as a form of "life unworthy of life." He examines the volatile mix of political violence and sexual sadism that prompts one of the most unsettling questions in the book: "What could embarrass the SS?" At the same time, in taking the decision to represent the Holocaust, Keneally writes his way into the controversy that surrounds that project: not only how "true" is this portrayal of Schindler, but who is licensed to bear witness to the Holocaust? What literary form can memorialize the reality of those events? In 1993, the release of Steven Spielberg's award-winning *Schindler's List* (the U.S. title of Keneally's book) reinforced that controversy. In particular, as part of the so-called "Holocaust boom," Spielberg's film refracts what remains, in one critical view, the untroubled, but profoundly troubling, sentimentality of Keneally's narrative: its novelistic depiction of history through the life of one man. **VL**

Lifespan | *b.* 1935 (Australia)
First Published | 1982, by Hodder & Stoughton (Lon.)
Alternate Title | *Schindler's List*
Booker Prize | 1982

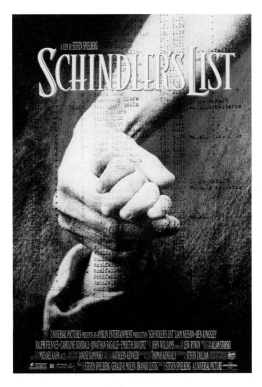

⊙ Spielberg's epic movie version of the Schindler story has inevitably tended to overshadow Thomas Keneally's book.

◁ A copy of Oskar Schindler's original list of twelve hundred Polish Jews to be saved from death in the Holocaust.

A Pale View of Hills

Kazuo Ishiguro

Lifespan | *b.* 1954 (Japan)
First Published | 1982
First Published by | Faber & Faber (London)
Original Language | English

A Pale View of Hills is narrated by Etsuko, a war-ravaged widow from Nagasaki, who is living in England. Her memories of the past and of her daughter Keiko, who committed suicide, are prompted by the arrival in England of her second child, Niki. Not only does Etsuko try unsuccessfully to articulate a meaningful response to her daughter's death, the reader is also never fully certain about the events that took place in the hot summer in Nagasaki to which her narrative returns time and again. Ishiguro is less interested in offering an account of the central trauma that defines a character's identity than in demonstrating how the very act of storytelling is never straightforward.

As past and present interweave in increasingly enigmatic ways, the novel raises as many questions as it answers. Ishiguro's narrative style urges the reader to consider the ways that subjectivity is both provisional and improvised, and how identity, rather than the pre-existing stories we come to tell about ourselves, may be something that is perhaps always in process. Just as the horror of Nagasaki broods over the narrative without ever being mentioned directly, so too the interplay between memory, identity, and trauma in this haunting debut novel challenges any naive conception of language as a clear window onto a world of objective truth. **VA**

🔇 Born in Nagasaki, Ishiguro was brought to England aged five; as a child he was the only one of his family who spoke fluent English.

Wittgenstein's Nephew

Thomas Bernhard

Lifespan | *b.* 1931 (Netherlands), *d.* 1989 (Austria)
First Published | 1982
First Published by | Suhrkamp (Frankfurt)
Original Title | *Wittgensteins Neffe: eine Freundschaft*

In *Wittgenstein's Nephew*, an intellectual, sick, and obsessive narrator reflects on the tragic life and unfortunate death of a close friend, who is also an intellectual and sick and obsessive. The narrator is Bernhard himself and in this, his most personal novel, he reveals a compassionate humanity that is so glaringly absent from his work in general.

The novel is written in the form of a tribute to Bernhard's friendship with Paul Wittgenstein, nephew of the famous Austrian philosopher. It opens with Paul and Bernhard staying in the same Viennese hospital, though in separate wards. Paul suffers from a recurring mental illness and Bernhard from a recurring pulmonary condition. From this starting point Bernhard creates a brutally honest and uncharacteristically touching account of Paul's life, his gradual demise, and Bernhard's reaction to it. He reflects on illness, intellectual and artistic passion, and the two men's hatred for the complacency of Austrian society. Bernhard sees Paul as a victim of his patrician family's suffocating conformity and Austrian society's blinkered provincialism. He considers Paul to be an intellectual equal to his uncle, who he believes would have shared a similar fate had he not escaped to England.

Wittgenstein's Nephew is an affectionate account of the value of friendship and a meditation on the perilous link between intellectual energy and insanity, which addresses issues of isolation, illness, and death without being sentimental or morose. **AL**

The Color Purple

Alice Walker

Lifespan | *b.* 1944 (U.S.)
First Published | 1982
First Published by | Harcourt Brace Jovanovich (N.Y.)
Pulitzer Prize | 1983

"You better not never tell . . . "

◐ A feminist as well as a civil rights activist, Walker has been criticized for an allegedly negative portrayal of African-American men.

◑ A scene from Spielberg's 1985 movie version of *The Color Purple*, a film adaptation that failed to match the impact of the book.

The Color Purple documents the traumas and gradual triumph of Celie, a young African American woman raised in rural isolation in Georgia, as she comes to resist the paralyzing self-concept forced on her by those who have power over her. Celie is repeatedly raped by her father, and gives birth twice as a result of the abuse, but assumes the children have been killed when her father secretively disposes of them. When a man proposes marriage to Celie's sister, Nettie, their father pushes him to take Celie instead, forcing her into a marriage as abusive as her early home. Nettie soon flees that home, first to Celie and her husband and then out into the wide world. By the time of her reunion with Celie almost thirty years later, Nettie has met and traveled to Africa with an African American missionary couple, whom she discovers to be the adoptive parents of Celie's children. In Africa, Nettie lives among the Olinka, whose patriarchal society and indifference toward the role of Africans in the slave trade underline the prevalence of exploitation.

Celie narrates her life through letters to God. These are prompted by her father's warning to tell "nobody but God" when he makes her pregnant for a second time at the age of fourteen, and she writes to God with the unselfconscious honesty of someone who thinks nobody is listening. As she builds relationships with other black women, and especially with those women engaging forcefully with oppression, however, Celie draws strength and insight from their perspectives and develops a sense of her own right to interpret herself and her world. Her independence develops symbiotically through her expanded first and secondhand experience of the world until she is able to construct her relations to others according to her own values. **AF**

A Boy's Own Story

Edmund White

Lifespan | *b.* 1940 (U.S.)
First Published | 1982, by E. P. Dutton (N.Y.)
Trilogy | *A Boy's Own Story* (1982), *The Beautiful Room is Empty* (1988), *A Farewell Symphony* (1998)

A Boy's Own Story is a coming out novel significant not only for its timing, being one of the first, but also for its frank portrayal of a young teenager's anxious self-conception, growing up gay in 1950s America. Based to some extent on White's own story, the narrator is eccentric and slightly creepy. However, the boy's precociousness, combined with his physical self-disgust and ambivalent sexual shame, make the novel a quintessential narrative of teenage angst and self-discovery.

The veneer of seedy sexual exploration defines the boy's journey toward young adulthood in a social climate that pathologized homosexuality. Though never in doubt of his orientation, the boy undergoes psychoanalysis in an attempt to cure his "impossible desire to love a man but not to be a homosexual." This impossible desire is fulfilled in the final pages of the novel by his shocking betrayal of a teacher he lures into a sexual liaison. This event dramatically marks the boy's entry into an adult world of sex and power.

White lyrically evokes a poignant longing for love and highlights the disorientating lack of romantic narratives for gay people. In stubbornly creating, articulating, and undermining its own fantasies, the novel is effectively a postmodern fairytale of a brutally repressed desire. At the time of its publication, it affirmed a history and a material and psychic presence for the gay community at a moment of crisis with the emergence of AIDS. **CJ**

If Not Now, When?

Primo Levi

Lifespan | *b.* 1919 (Italy), *d.* 1987
First Published | 1982
First Published by | G. Einaudi (Turin)
Original Title | *Se non ora, quando?*

By the time of his death in 1987, Primo Levi had established his reputation as a writer of the Holocaust, a survivor who bore witness to the horrors of Auschwitz. Perhaps inevitably, the broader range of his writing has been relatively neglected (science fiction, poetry, drama).

Described as Levi's most conventional novel, *If Not Now, When?* tells the story of a band of Jewish partisans, and their acts of resistance against the Germans as they journey through Eastern Europe toward Italy from 1943 to 1945. "For the most part," Levi notes, "the events I depict really did take place ... It is true that Jewish partisans fought the Germans." Levi continues to bear witness, but this time in the shape of a novel: imaginary characters, omniscient narrator, period reconstruction, description of landscape. Levi views it as "a story of hope," even if set against the backdrop of massacre. In fact, at key moments, Levi refuses to tell that story of death and extermination: characters disappear ("Immediately hidden from sight by the curtain of snow, they vanish from this story"), and events are not depicted ("But what happened in the courtyard of the Novoselki monastery will not be told here"). Described by Philip Roth as less imaginative in technique than Levi's other books, *If Not Now, When?* was defended by Levi as an account of Ashkenazi civilization: "I cherished the ambition," he once acknowledged, "to be the first (perhaps the only) Italian writer to describe the Yiddish world." **VL**

The Sorrow of Belgium

Hugo Claus

Lifespan | *b.* 1929 (Belgium)
First Published | 1983
First Published by | De Bezige Bij (Amsterdam)
Original Title | *Het Verdriet van België*

Covering the years 1939 to 1947, this intense and vivid novel is set in anti-Semitic West Flanders, where young Louis Seynaeve emerges from childhood and adolescence amid the deprivations and moral conflicts of World War II.

The story begins in the convent school where Louis and his friends form a secret society in resistance to the stern rule of the Sisters, and where his imagination vies with his ignorance to satisfy a hunger to know and understand the world—a complex of fragmented loyalties, rumors of war, and impending invasion by the Germans. This first part, "The Sorrow," has a child's confused perspective, with its unintentional comedy uncannily rendered. In the second section, "Of Belgium," the saga of the Seynaeve family continues under Nazi occupation. Friends and relatives become complicit with the new regime, Louis's parents actively participating—his father as publisher of propaganda, his mother as secretary and mistress to an officer. As a wartime chronicle, this rich and dense novel is unusual for its eccentric characters and lively dialogue, and for being a portrait of the artist at the same time—Louis's brilliant tendency toward invention results in his developing into a novelist by the book's end.

Claus is one of only a handful of Belgian writers to live solely by his creative output, which includes works of poetry, drama, movie scenarios, and short stories, as well as longer fiction, essays, and translations, and an opera libretto. **ES**

The Piano Teacher

Elfriede Jelinek

Lifespan | *b.* 1946 (Austria)
First Published | 1983, by Rowohlt (Berlin)
Original Title | *Die Klavierspielerin*
Nobel Prize for Literature | 2004

Jelinek's oeuvre is embroiled in her critique of capitalist and patriarchal society, and her construction of human intimacy. The prose is relentless in its exploration of the unlived sexuality of voyeurism, addressing as it does the woman's appropriation of the male rights to sexual looking.

In this unnerving, painful portrayal of a woman's sexuality, the protagonist, Erika Kohut, is a woman given over to the uncertain pleasures of looking—from peepshow to porn film, to the couple on whom she spies in the meadows of the Vienna Prater. But Jelinek also binds the looking to the experience of heterosexual sadomasochism at its most violent edge: "Erika seeks a pain that will end in death." As Erika attempts to contract the terms of her own torture with her student lover, Walter Klemmer, Jelinek embeds her sexuality in her unsettling tie to her mother, to a form of maternal love that demands, above all, the daughter's submission: "never could she [Erika] submit to a man after having submitted to her mother for so many years."

Contributing to a literature committed to the exploration of sexual dissidence, Jelinek also brings her readers up against the anxiety that has haunted feminist responses to women's sadomasochism. Refusing either to condemn or to celebrate Erika's desires, Jelinek sustains her critical gaze, even against the usual pleasures of reading and writing: "I strike hard," she has commented, "so nothing can grow where my characters have been." **VL**

The Diary of Jane Somers

Doris Lessing

Lifespan | *b.* 1919 (Persia)
First Published | 1983
First Published by | Michael Joseph (London)
Pseudonym | Jane Somers

Doris Lessing published this novel, originally written as two books, *The Diary of a Good Neighbor* and *If the Old Could*, under a pseudonym. Already well known and well respected, she wanted to test what she perceived to be the hardened attitudes of publishers and reviewers of the time.

Writing in the first person, Lessing introduces us to Jane (Janna) Somers, an intelligent, beautiful, successful glossy-magazine editor. When her husband and then her mother die from cancer, she comes to realize that, despite her worldly success, she is incapable of forming deep attachments. Into this emotional void comes 90-something Maudie, who is living in poverty and squalor. Janna forms her first truly intimate relationship with this unlikely character, describing their developing intimacy in extraordinary and minute detail in her diaries. As their friendship grows, Janna allows herself to fall in love for the first time in her life. In the second book of the diaries, Janna is forced to care for her 19-year-old niece Kate, who is struggling with an emotional breakdown. Janna realizes that she understands young people as little as she recently did the old.

With the benefit of knowing the author's true identity, the books reveal themselves in many ways as classic Lessing, resonant with social, political, and feminist themes and written with great imagination, sensitivity, and feeling. **LE**

The Life and Times of Michael K

J. M. Coetzee

Lifespan | *b.* 1940 (South Africa)
First Published | 1983
First Published by | Secker & Warburg (London)
Booker Prize | 1983

This novel uses the enduring South African pastoral ideal to challenge the myths that sustained the apartheid regime. Michael K, a hare-lipped non-white in apartheid-era South Africa, becomes a gardener in the Sea Point district of Cape Town where his mother works as domestic help. When she begins to die, he tries to return her to the farm in the Karoo where she was born, but she dies in transit. Michael continues his journey alone to scatter her ashes on the abandoned farm. He stays on, growing pumpkins and living off the land. Meanwhile a civil war is raging. Accused of aiding the insurgency, Michael is arrested and interned in a labour camp where he refuses to eat. He escapes and returns to Sea Point where he lives as a vagrant.

The second part of the novel is a diary, written by the medical officer of the internment camp, in which the officer recounts his attempts to get Michael to yield something of significance. But very little passes Michael's misshapen lips: food is rarely consumed and speech rarely emanates. Michael's refusal to be part of any system undermines all the officer's own certainties, and the richness of the novel lies in the enigma and resistance that Michael poses both to the authorities and to the reader. **ABi**

◗ Coetzee once described himself as an author who represents "people slipping their chains and turning their faces to the light."

Waterland

Graham Swift

Lifespan | *b.* 1949 (England)
First Published | 1983
First Published by | Heinemann (London)
Guardian Fiction Award | 1983

When narrator Tom Crick's wife, Mary, kidnaps a child from a local supermarket, it creates a firestorm of publicity. In the lead-up to his final days as a secondary school history teacher, Crick examines his own history and childhood to consider just where things went so wrong. He recalls the silent, inscrutable, mentally disabled brother who eventually committed suicide; his own feeling of guilty implication in the early death of a neighborhood boy; and the frights he and Mary faced when trying to procure an abortion after their teenaged sexual experimentation. The procedure, alluded to as a fearful quasi-religious rite presided over by high priestess Martha Clay, widely supposed to be a witch, renders Mary sterile and permanently traumatized. Even the lyrical story of Crick's parents' romance does not escape the sinister shadow of a silent crime and its tragic fallout.

The metaphor of land reclamation plays a significant role in Crick's assessment of the consolations of storytelling and historical narrative. Crick sees history not as the march of progress, but something more like the constant, cyclic battle against the encroaching waters of the Fens. As Crick debates the value of history with one particularly insistent student, he advances the idea that narrative cannot be argued for by appealing to its beneficial consequences, but inevitably exercises its own endemic power to fend off nothingness— the only resource people have against despair. **AF**

LaBrava

Elmore Leonard

Lifespan | *b.* 1925 (U.S.)
First Published | 1983
First Published by | Arbor House (New York)
Full Name | Elmore John Leonard, Jr.

Elmore Leonard's razor-sharp portrayals of the ordinary underbelly of American urban life have consolidated his reputation as one of the sharpest, funniest, toughest, and most insightful contemporary American writers. *LaBrava* is certainly the best example of Leonard's effortless mastery of a form he would make his own: part mystery, part suspense, part crime, part thriller, part urban treatise.

Enter Joe LaBrava, an ex-Secret Service agent and photographer whose style, like Leonard himself, "is the absence of style" or rather whose work is without artistic pretensions. LaBrava befriends Jean Shaw, an aging movie actress famous for her femme fatale roles in the fifties, who is herself plotting with Richie Nobles, a grinning redneck psychopath, to defraud a friend of hers, Maurice, of $600,000. Nobles, in turn, has fallen in with Cundo Rey, a Cuban go-go dancer whose preference for leopard jockstraps barely conceals his own pecuniary ambitions. What delights about *LaBrava* is Leonard's ear for dialogue and the skillful way in which he brings these characters into collision with each other, shifting points of view in order to generate suspense. As the characters strive to twist circumstances to suit their own ambitions, they take on a life of their own, but in spite of the novel's self-referential nods (whereby Jean Shaw's movies bleed into the "reality" of the plot), Leonard resolutely avoids postmodern trickery. In the end, this is not a dissertation on literary artifice but a cracking good read. **AP**

Fools of Fortune

William Trevor

Lifespan | *b.* 1928 (Ireland)
First Published | 1983
First Published by | Bodley Head (London)
Whitbread Novel Award | 1983

Trevor's poignant novel explores the legacy of Ireland's decolonization. The Quintons are an Anglo-Irish family with nationalist sympathies in the period leading up to Irish independence following the First World War. They become victims of the Black and Tans, the violent British irregular troops sent to Ireland ostensibly to keep order; their ancestral home at Kilneagh is burned and the father killed. From the perspective of different characters, the novel traces the consequences of this event through the decades until the 1980s.

Fools of Fortune poses a world of love and devotion against their destructive opposites. Willie, the surviving Quinton son, falls in love with his English cousin, Marianne, a pattern of familial interrelation that has been played out across the centuries. Though they have a daughter, they are doomed to live apart. Trevor's view combines both Yeats' intense vision of tragic cycles with a more benevolent Chekovian sense of a rural world in which a futile human tragicomedy is played out. Despite the momentous events of the twentieth century, it can seem as though fundamentally nothing has altered in this vision of Ireland.

Trevor is a writer of wonderful economy and precise observation, whose focus is distinctly on the intimacy of his characters' relations and the local world they inhabit. Through the different voices, Trevor builds an intricate portrait of a fragile Anglo-Irish society that seems doomed to extinction. **TH**

Worstward Ho

Samuel Beckett

Lifespan | *b.* 1906 (Ireland), *d.* 1989 (France)
First Published | 1983
First Published by | John Calder (London)
Original Language | English

Early in his career, Nobel Prize winner Samuel Beckett professed an interest in works of art that avoided the need to be ever more powerful, more resourceful, and more expressive. Instead, he indicated a desire to work with impotence and failure, to say less rather than more. In this novella, one of Beckett's very last works, his project of non-expression is most fully realized.

But even to say this much is to do a great injustice to the novella, for it lends an aura of success and positivity to the work, values that the work itself is at great pains to undermine. From its opening words, "On, Say on," what is remarkable about this deceptively short and concentrated novella, no more than forty pages printed in large type, is its painstaking determination to continually reduce what has already been said, to not leave a mark, and to stall progression in its tracks. As such it is a novel that traverses an impossible tension, wanting to preserve an immaculate silence that has already been disturbed and can never be restored. Moving by a characteristic process of statement and denial, *Worstward Ho* is by any standards a challenging read. Words are redefined, objects and spaces are diminished, narrative duration is destabilized, and anything said is "missaid." By the end of the novella, if anything like a progression has occurred, then it is only in a sense conveyed by the title of the trilogy, of which this work forms the final part, *Nohow On*. **ABi**

Shame

Salman Rushdie

Lifespan | *b.* 1947 (India)
First Published | 1983
First Published by | Jonathan Cape (London)
Full Name | Ahmed Salman Rushdie

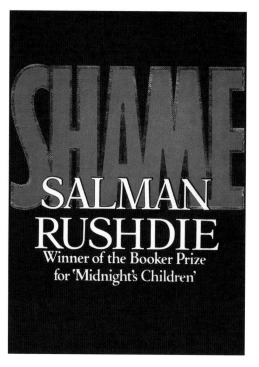

"'Come quickly, your fatherji is sending himself to the devil.'"

◆ The red lettering on the jacket of the first edition symbolizes the central theme of the novel—that violence is born out of shame.

Taking its cue from the partition of India that established Pakistan, *Shame* is a novel of borders. It has a "peripheral" hero who watches from the wings, the disreputable Omar Shakil. He is the child of three sequestered sisters who all consider themselves the boy's mother. The novel is set in the remote border town of Q in a country that is not quite Pakistan but a place "at a slight angle to reality." The narrative is frequently disrupted with asides and newspaper reports, violating the frontier between fiction and history, and creating a satire of the Pakistan of Zulfikar Ali Bhutto and Zia al Haq, in their fictional equivalents, Iskander Harappa and Raza Hyder.

The narrative follows the feud between Iskander Harappa, the Prime Minister, who is a gambler and womanizer, and Raza Hyder, who usurps his power in a coup. Across this political struggle, the Hyder and Harappa families are inextricably bound up in a series of sexual and marital intrigues, which largely center on the female characters, particularly Sufiya Zinobia, the daughter of Harappa who eventually marries Omar Shakil. Zinobia is the embodiment of the barely translatable Urdu noun "sharam," rendered in English as "shame." As the brainsick daughter who should have been a son, she also symbolizes Pakistan, the miracle that went wrong. It is the beast of shame hidden deep inside Zinobia that finally surfaces to exact retribution on the whole cast of characters.

A daring blend of historical commentary, political allegory, and a fantastical fictional style that owes a stylistic debt to Gabriel García Márquez, *Shame* is a fitting successor to the enormously successful *Midnight's Children*, displaying the same capacity for comic excess, complex narrative, and biting political critique. **ABi**

Money: A Suicide Note

Martin Amis

John Self, the empty everyman of *Money*, is one of Amis' more powerful and memorable creations. Set in the summer of 1981, the opening sees Self escape the nationalist romance of the Royal Wedding and his own failing and violent love affair by flying to New York. There he embarks on a corporately financed yet profoundly pleasureless binge of drugs, alcohol, pornography, violence, and sex.

The novel offers a darkly satirical celebration of the insatiable but righteous greed of Reaganite America and Thatcherite Britain. *Money* also invites us to identify with John Self, who makes a thoroughly unpleasant but oddly likeable hero. Self has been lured from Britain and his successful career in advertising—that most archetypal of Eighties industries—by the promise of Hollywood fame, and it is the money pressed upon him by the movie's financiers that he so recklessly spends throughout the novel. However, we soon become aware that Self's profound loss of control is leading him to a moment of humiliating hubris. As the novel unravels we realize that Self has been the victim of a hugely elaborate corporate hoax that will leave him financially destitute. By the novel's end we see that he has lost not only his ambition, his livelihood, his father, and friends but also, more poignantly, the salvation offered by his unlikely and redemptive lover. The final irony of the novel, although it offers little solace to Self, is that he inadvertently thwarts the hoax that ruins him. His limited participation in the movie that was destined never to be made involves hiring a lowly British novelist—Martin Amis— whose rewriting of the ludicrously unfilmable screenplay began the chain of events that led to the plot's unraveling. **NM**

Lifespan | *b.* 1949 (England)
First Published | 1984
First Published by | Jonathan Cape (London)
First U.S. Edition | 1985, by Viking (New York)

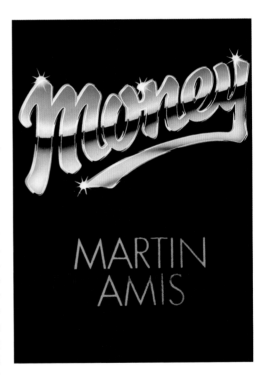

"I'm drinking tax-exempt whisky from a toothmug . . ."

◉ Designed by Mon Mohan and Dick Jones, the jacket of the first edition of the book evokes Eighties-style material wealth.

Flaubert's Parrot

Julian Barnes

Lifespan | *b.* 1946 (England)
First Published | 1984
First Published by | Jonathan Cape (London)
Pseudonym | Dan Kavanagh

FLAUBERT'S PARROT

Julian Barnes

🔺 Shortlisted for the Booker Prize in 1984, the novel began three
years earlier on the sighting of two stuffed parrots in Normandy.

🔻 Photographed here in 1990, Julian Barnes became an admirer
of Flaubert's work at age 15 when he first read *Madame Bovary*.

Funny and erudite, this is a novel about quiet
passion and the delusion of academic celebrity. It is
a love story, spectacularly unrequited, between a
lonely amateur scholar and the object of his
affection, Gustave Flaubert. And it is a detective
story—though less Chandler than Borges.

Geoffrey Braithewaite stumbles onto what
seems to him a great unsolved literary mystery:
which of two stuffed parrots is the one that sat on
Flaubert's desk—the parrot featured in *Un Coeur
Simple*? Ultimately pointless, it is a parody of
the ineffectuality of academe and the hermetic
viciousness of overspecialization. It explores the
nature of creativity, of criticism, and of creating
heroes. Beauty can be fragile: do we risk destroying it
through intimate dissection or is part of the magic in
the mystery? The novel is less about Flaubert (and
even less about the parrot) than about Braithewaite
and the danger that, in getting too close to one's
heroes, one is getting uncomfortably close to
oneself. "All art is autobiographical," claims Lucien
Freud, and that includes the art of biography.
Braithewaite is a tragic figure: numb to life, his own
memories and feelings go unregarded, so empty he
must devote himself not to another human being
but to something far safer.

A dusty retired doctor consumed by a dead
French writer seems unlikely to be fertile ground for
humor—but the novel is full of wit and insight. It
brims with detail, including three biographies of
Flaubert (one unctious, one critical, one objective),
the appearance of real-life Flaubert expert Enid
Starkie, and even a mock university exam. It also
contains whimsical material like Braithewaite's
Dictionary of Accepted Ideas. This is a fascinating
jigsaw puzzle of a book. **GT**

Neuromancer

William Gibson

Lifespan | b. 1948 (U.S.)
First Published | 1984
First Published by | Ace Books (New York)
Video Game Adaptation | 1988

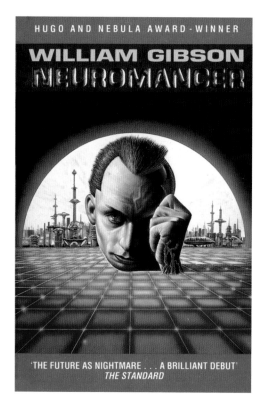

HUGO AND NEBULA AWARD - WINNER

WILLIAM GIBSON

NEUROMANCER

'THE FUTURE AS NIGHTMARE . . . A BRILLIANT DEBUT'
THE STANDARD

◉ The first cyberpunk novel has sold more than 6.5 million
copies worldwide and won three major science fiction awards.

◉ William Gibson, seen here walking through New York's Chinatown
in 1991, has never had any special affinity with computers.

Neuromancer is a landmark novel, not only in the science fiction genre, but also in the contemporary imagination as a whole. With extraordinary prescience, William Gibson invented the concept of "cyberspace" (a three-dimensional representation of computer data through which users communicate and do business, alongside a whole host of more dubious activities) long before the Internet and other virtual technologies were integrated into everyday life. It is a book that has inspired a generation of technophiles.

The plot revolves around a "computer cowboy" known as Case—a data thief who "jacks in" to the virtual world until his nervous system is badly maimed by a client he has double-crossed. Unable to interface with a "deck," he ekes out a precarious living in the lawless zones of Chiba City, Japan. However, Case is offered the chance of regaining his old powers by the mysterious Armitage—a businessman whose motives remain unclear until the final, exhilarating denouement. Gibson creates a world of televisual twilight and fiber optic shocks, all realized in lavish detail with a rich, sometimes disorienting vocabulary of jargon and slang. It is a world of techno-hustlers, strung-out junkies, bizarre subcultures, surgically enhanced assassins, and sinister "megacorps"—a world that increasingly resembles parts of our own.

Neuromancer is an enduring work because it combines the pace and urgency of the best thrillers with the scope, invention, and intellectual rigor of Orwell or Huxley. Perhaps its most compelling and disquieting feature, however, is Gibson's refusal to make any clear-cut moral distinctions between virtual and organic life—between human and cyborg, between program and reality. **SamT**

Blood and Guts in High School

Kathy Acker

Lifespan | *b.* 1947 (U.S.), *d.* 1997 (Mexico)
First Published | 1984
First Published by | Grove Press (New York)
First UK Edition | Pan Books (London)

Kathy Acker's *Blood and Guts in High School* re-interprets the familiar rite-of-passage novel. The result is a narrative that combines the troubled life of Janey (an American teenager who hates school, is bored by her part-time job, and gets into trouble with the police) with the profane, the shocking, and the surreal. Its opening tone is that of the familiarly banal daytime talk show as it depicts Janey and her father as adults wrangling with the guilt and responsibility attendant upon a failed sexual relationship. The reader's inability to determine Janey's age, or to distinguish between what is either a metaphorical comment on gender politics or a literal and disturbingly normalized representation of incest, characterizes the profoundly disquieting experience that the book as a whole imparts.

As the novel progresses, the depiction of Janey's life becomes increasingly preposterous, frightening, and comic. The narrative of her sexual liberation and subsequent enslavement is interpolated with hand-drawn images of her dreams, pieces of her homework, and childish translations of rudimentary Arabic. This unruly and challenging text is an affront to the assumption that literary texts should be neat, complete, and somehow true. In the face of this, Acker places the sexual and anarchic energy of a young woman firmly at odds with the stifling patriarchal order she so literally caricatures. **NM**

" ... Janey ... regarded her father as boyfriend, brother, sister, money, amusement, and father."

A sex-positive feminist writer, Kathy Acker supported herself as a stripper before she became a literary force in the mid-1970s.

The Unbearable Lightness of Being

Milan Kundera

Lifespan | *b.* 1929 (Czech Republic)
First Published | 1984
First Published by | Gallimard (Paris)
Original Czech Title | *Nesnesitelná lehkost bytí*

This is a novel about exile and persecution in Czechoslovakia, written by a man who knew a great deal about both. It is about lightness, where nothing means anything, and the heaviness that is Nietzsche's philosophy of eternal return.

It is the dangerous year of 1968 in Prague. Tomas is a surgeon who embraces lightness. He is willfully free of all heaviness, shunning labels and ideals. Sabina is the epitome of lightness, an artist who, like Tomas, believes in unfettered individualism. Tereza is heaviness. Escaping from provincial life, she believes in the romantic ideal of Tomas. Her love is a binding thing—not bad, just heavy. She also has fervent political ideals; Tomas is held by none. As their three lives collide, the viability of lightness is questioned. What is our responsibility to ourselves, to others?

When the Soviet tanks roll in to crush the Prague Spring, Tomas and Tereza flee to Switzerland. But Tereza decides to return, leaving Tomas to make a choice. He accepts heaviness and follows her to certain persecution, unwilling to be a pawn of either the Communists or the insurgents. It is unbearable that each choice can only be made once with one possible result, and that we can never know what other choices would have wrought. A novel that is not as much political as about the primacy of personal freedom, it is a bittersweet celebration of the individual; urgent and necessary. **GT**

Nights at the Circus

Angela Carter

Lifespan | *b.* 1940 (England), *d.* 1992
First Published | 1984
First Published by | Chatto & Windus (London)
Given Name | Angela Olive Stalker

Angela Carter's dazzling aerialist, the tough and beguiling Fevvers, a winged-woman who defies gravity and sexual ideology, takes center stage of a novel that explores the eccentric limits of gender and geography. With the narrative's three-part excursion from London to St. Petersburg, finally reaching the vast expanses of Siberia, we journey with reporter Jack Walser, assigned to shadow the fortunes of Fevver's carnivalesque circus community. In his position as commentator, he is at once convivial and satirical.

The novel is filled with burlesque ebullience, a carnival riot of voices, dialects, and stories, through which Carter explores the reality of the perpetual masquerade with shrewd discretion. Performers from the circus emerge each night disheveled, wearied by the outward selves that they are compelled to assume. Carter brings a degree of rationality, of subtle reticence, to her narrative, enabling her to exploit the self-parodic energies of magic realism. But she does not compromise pragmatism in her depiction of self-transformation, charting Fevvers' uneven journey, "turning, willy-nilly, from a woman into an idea." Tirelessly defying generic consistency, Carter's work invites us to assume a pleasurable if disarming repose, which swings between complicity and detachment, while at the same time thwarting our preconceptions. **DJ**

The Wasp Factory

Iain Banks

Lifespan | *b.* 1954 (Scotland)
First Published | 1984
First Published by | Macmillan (London)
Full Name | Iain Menzies Banks

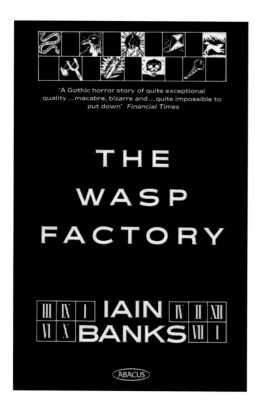

'A Gothic horror story of quite exceptional quality...macabre, bizarre and...quite impossible to put down' *Financial Times*

THE WASP FACTORY

III IX I IAIN IV II XII
VI X BANKS VII I

ABACUS

🔺 The destructive impact of Thatcherite policies on British society resonate throughout this highly political novel.

🔻 When asked to express himself for an exhibition in Aberdeen, Scotland, in 2001, Iain Banks submitted this self-portrait.

Like many of Iain Banks' novels, much of the impact of *The Wasp Factory* comes from its surprise ending and from the hyperbolic qualities of its content. It is a story of exceptional cruelties inflicted upon animals and humans alike. The narrator, Frank Cauldhames ("cold homes"—a name with appropriate metaphoric content), spends his time carrying out idiosyncratic rituals: inventively killing animals and capriciously murdering siblings and cousins. Haunted by his apparent castration by the family dog, Frank's life is formed around a bizarre exaggeration of masculinity. Frank imagines himself, unmutilated, as a tall, dark, lean hunter; he despises women, eschews sex, but childishly revels in the adolescent drinking and the pissing games invented by his friend Jamie. Frank's father is an eccentric libertarian who, having failed to register Frank at birth, allows Frank's behavior to continue almost unchecked. It is only at the end of the novel that we realize that both Frank and his half-brother Eric are the products of their father's experimentation and impersonal cruelty. A surprising revelation comes during the cataclysmic conclusion to the novel when the insane Eric returns home driving a herd of burning sheep.

As a whole, the novel develops a deeply layered mythology based upon a series of masculine clichés: the potency of bodily fluids; the cosmic superiority of men over creation, which is manifested as violence toward animals; and the totemic effectiveness of their corpses. However, despite its occasionally exaggerated fantasies, the true value of *The Wasp Factory* is in the quality and style of Banks' writing, which is both beautiful and arresting. His skill is in characterization and his depiction of Frank as both psychotic and believably mundane. **LC**

Iain Banks

Empire of the Sun

J. G. Ballard

Lifespan | *b.* 1930 (China)
First Published | 1984
First Published by | V. Gollancz (London)
Movie Adaptation | 1987

In a career spanning over forty years, J. G. Ballard has published a long series of science fiction and futuristic novels. With *Empire of the Sun*, however, he approaches what seems at first glance a very different topic, namely his own incarceration as a child in a Japanese concentration camp in Shanghai during the Second World War. The story charts the fall of Shanghai to Japanese occupying troops, the capture of the protagonist, Jim, and his various complicated means of managing his survival in the Lunghua camp. Though predominantly from Jim's perspective, there are terrifying moments when we see Jim as the other camp inmates do and realize the madness within him. The book culminates when the world lights up as the first atom bomb is dropped on Japan, after which Jim escapes.

A major strength of the book lies in the way we as readers are drawn into a frightening closeness to Jim, a boy who is obviously being forced to mature beyond his years under circumstances of chronic degradation. Because of his youth, he is perhaps more resilient than the others, but we are left in no doubt as to the trauma of his imprisonment. Interestingly, many of the motifs of the book—the sudden atomic explosion, the lonely lives and deaths of airmen, the presence of torn and mangled bodies—occur throughout Ballard's work. *Empire of the Sun*, a fully and remarkably achieved work in its own right, also serves as a key to the preoccupations of the rest of Ballard's fiction. **DP**

The Lover

Marguerite Duras

Lifespan | *b.* 1914 (Indochina), *d.* 1996 (France)
First Published | 1984, by Éditions de Minuit (Paris)
Original Title | *L'Amant*
Prix Goncourt | 1984

Set in Sa Dec, French Indochina, in the 1930s, this ostensibly autobiographical novel details fifteen-year-old French girl Hélène Lagonelle's relationship with a wealthy Chinese man twelve years her senior. This taboo sexual relationship unfolds against the backdrop of her unstable and largely unhappy family life. Living with her depressive mother and two older brothers, Hélène and her family exist in a poverty induced by her eldest brother's drug and gambling addictions. His sadistic treatment of her, and the disturbing pleasure he derives from her mother's abuse of her, lend the novel an unsettling dimension that is perhaps underplayed by the adult voice of the narrator. While her family disapprove of the interracial relationship, they benefit financially from it, and their awkward meetings with her lover throw into relief the tensions generated by the French colonial regime and the differences in their status and cultural backgrounds. Challenging sexual stereotypes, Hélène instigates the relationship, she is the partner able to detach the physical from the emotional, and despite being a child and financially insecure, she is ultimately the one with the upper hand in the relationship.

With its shifts between the first and third person, the use of flashbacks, and its impressionistic, disrupted style, Duras' writing is very cinematic, influenced as she was by the French nouveau roman of the 1950s. The novel was turned into a movie in 1993, directed by Jean-Jacques Annaud. **JW**

The Year of the Death of Ricardo Reis

José Saramago

Lifespan | *b.* 1922 (Portugal)
First Published | 1984
First Published by | Editorial Caminho (Lisbon)
Original Title | *O ano da morte de Ricardo Reis*

Ricardo Reis was one of the pseudonyms used by the celebrated Portuguese poet Fernando Pessoa (1888–1935), for example, in his poetry collection, *Odes de Ricardo Reis* (1946). In Saramago's novel, Reis, a doctor and unpublished poet, returns to Lisbon after many years abroad in Brazil. This is the year following Pessoa's death, and Reis meets the ghost of Pessoa, with whom he holds a number of dialogues on matters great and small.

Against the backdrop of the rise of fascism in Europe and Salazar's oppressive regime in Portugal, Saramago skillfully employs a panoply of literary methods to bring issues under scrutiny. Most important among these are questions of identity: who precisely is Ricardo Reis and what is his relationship to Pessoa? There is also the gently implied but finally irresistible suggestion that there is a thin line between the monarchism, social conservatism, and stoicism of Reis, and the successful rise of Salazar.

Notwithstanding its weighty concerns, it remains an eminently readable novel. The narrative is intimate, almost conversational. The plot has conventional elements: Reis has an affair with a hotel chambermaid and falls in love with an aristocratic woman from Coimbra. Large parts of the novel are taken up with walks though the streets of Lisbon, giving the book a flavor of a Portuguese *Ulysses*. And like Joyce's masterpiece, the more one brings to this erudite novel, the richer it becomes. **ABi**

"Lisboa, Lisbon, Lisbonne, Lissabon, there are four different ways of saying it . . . And so the children come to know what they did not know before, and that is what they knew already, nothing . . . "

◉ This photograph of Saramago was taken by Horst Tappe in 1998, the year the novelist won the Noble Prize for Literature.

The Busconductor Hines

James Kelman

Lifespan | *b.* 1946 (Scotland)
First Published | 1984
First Published by | Polygon (Edinburgh)
Original Language | English

🔵 Kelman's distinctive use of vernacular Glaswegian speech patterns influenced successive generations of Scottish writers.

With his first novel, *The Busconductor Hines*, Kelman extends the short story mode, which initially earned him recognition, into what is his funniest and most likable book. Robert Hines, the eponymous hero, is a bus conductor on the verge of an existential collapse. The episodic events of the novel develop through an innovatively woven mix of idiomatic and colloquial registers, which offers an acute representation of spoken Glaswegian, moving fluidly between a first-person narration centered on Hines and third-person description. One signature stylization is the introduction of emphasis in the middle of words, as in "malnufuckingtrition," "exploifuckingtation," or "C.B. bastarn I."

The world of Hines is one of domestic incidents, family life on limited resources, the trials of work, and occasional reveries that reveal an intellectual imagination attuned to the reality of his situation without the trappings of populist ideology. Hines is quick to reject the typical strategies of capitalist common sense, instead offering an amusingly skeptical take on the lives available. Indeed, the novel is notably free of the world of media and what passes for popular culture. Time spent watching television is mentioned, but as if it were a piece of furniture, the inspection of which constitutes a kind of emptying loss of consciousness.

Although focussed on everyday life, the novel moves toward larger class confrontations through the politics of the workplace. Kelman reinvigorates the naturalism of Joyce with occasional nods toward the more estranged and oblique worlds of Kafka and Beckett, but he remains more firmly rooted in the project of working-class realism. *The Busconductor Hines* is recommended reading for public transport workers. **DM**

Dictionary of the Khazars

Milorad Pavić

Part encyclopedia, part intellectual puzzle, part deconstruction (or spoof of same), part myth, part hodgepodge, and many other elements besides, one thing *Dictionary of the Khazars* is not, is a traditional novel that respects the conventions of beginning/middle/end. In addition to its other oddities, the book was published in male and female editions, with seventeen lines of differing text that distinguish them from each other. The author himself encourages readers to make of it what they please, without regard to chronology.

It is almost impossible to relate the teeming abundance of such a non-narrative, although there is a plot of sorts. This concerns the attempt of three modern day scholars to locate the last remaining copies of a lexicon otherwise destroyed during the Inquisition. The dictionary is composed of three distinct, but intertwined and cross-referenced versions—one each for the Christian, Muslim, and Jewish interpretations—of the fate of the long-lost Khazars, a Turkish people who once lived in the Balkan region, and the biographies of those involved in the so-called Polemic, which involved an effort to interpret a medieval dream. But it is the dictionary entries in themselves, by their repetition, that provide whatever structure there may be. And, more to the point, they supply the pleasure too.

What is important is to take this book in the spirit of erudite playfulness in which it is offered. Enjoy the whimsy, the inventive imagery, the surrealistic complexity, and the delights afforded by the imaginative application of language itself. These devices are employed for their own sake and also to skewer organized religion, anthropology, literary theory, psychoanalysis, and so on and so on. No one could charge Pavić with a lack of generosity. **ES**

Lifespan | *b.* 1929 (Yugoslavia)
First Published | 1984
First Published by | Prosveta (Belgrade)
Original Title | *Hazarski Recnik*

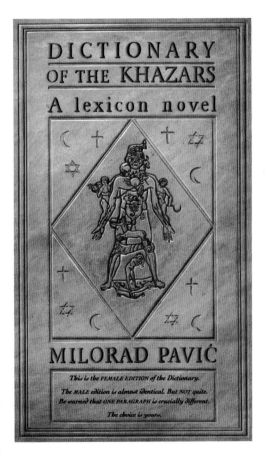

DICTIONARY
OF THE KHAZARS
A lexicon novel

MILORAD PAVIĆ

This is the FEMALE EDITION of the Dictionary.
The MALE edition is almost identical. But NOT quite.
Be warned that ONE PARAGRAPH is crucially different.
The choice is yours.

⊙ The cover of the Hamish Hamilton edition of the book, shown here, is based on the original Rita Muhlbauer jacket design.

Legend

David Gemmell

Lifespan | *b.* 1948 (England)
First Published | 1984
First Published by | Century (London)
Original U.S. Title | *Against the Horde*

David Gemmell's aging Druss the Legend represents one of the definitive characters in fantasy literature. With a man at the end of his life as a central protagonist, Gemmell's book is as much a meditation on a warrior long past his prime, as it is a rip-roaring fantasy. While its story may appear linear, it is the recourse to alternative perspectives and the complex split narrative—in which Druss is largely defined by the people who choose to follow him into his last battle—that sets it apart as a classic of fantasy literature.

Legend, the first book in Gemmell's "Drenai" series, is always aware of its predecessors, with clear undertones of Robert E. Howard and Edgar Wallace, but it is also very much a novel of the 1980s, seeking always to present events in a more realist tone. The text is a classic example of a simplistic narrative rendered in a novel manner. Druss is at times an unsympathetic figure, yet he is always heroic, and his humanism renders him powerfully empathic. Druss demonstrates the complexities of a man who has become a warrior through circumstance rather than straight volition. At the same time, the unspoken code that he follows throughout his life makes him a powerful, and often fatherly figure, fulfilling the traditional role of reluctant hero by default rather than intent. Overall, *Legend* provides a fresh perspective in the genre by emphasizing the ordinariness of heroes, rather than resorting to inexplicable heroics. **EMcS**

Hawksmoor

Peter Ackroyd

Lifespan | *b.* 1949 (England)
First Published | 1985
First Published by | Hamish Hamilton (London)
Whitbread Award | 1985

Hawksmoor, Peter Ackroyd's breakthrough as a novelist, is set in London in two different time frames —the early eighteenth and late twentieth centuries. It is a detective novel that deliberately subverts any coherent concepts one might have either of detection or history. In the twentieth-century narrative, detective Nicholas Hawksmoor is assigned to investigate a series of murders when the bodies of tramps and boys are discovered at seven churches in the city. There are six real London churches designed by the architect Nicholas Hawksmoor; in the world of the novel however, the eighteenth-century architect of the London churches is given the name of Nicholas Dyer. One of Ackroyd's main achievements in the novel is the ventriloquism that he performs in recreating the earlier period. He narrates the design and erection of the buildings as well as the similar murders committed by Dyer, who, it is revealed, has designed churches that covertly represent the occult.

History, rather than being represented as purely linear, is shown here to have a distinctly spatial aspect. Time and history are drawn together in the voices of the two characters in the novel; each chapter united by a repetition of the closing words of the previous chapter. Indeed, the novel turns upon the notion of repetition, which, in turn, leads to one of the most spectacular and peculiar endings to any novel. **VC-R**

❯ Peter Ackroyd is here photographed in 1990 in Paris on the release of his detective thriller *First Light*.

Queer

William Burroughs

Lifespan | *b.* 1914 (U.S.), *d.* 1997
First Published | 1985
First Published by | Viking Press (New York)
Full Name | William Seward Burroughs

Written in 1952, the year after Burroughs' accidental killing of his wife in a drunken misadventure, *Queer* was not published until 1985. Based on his own experiences, the book depicts the aimless excesses of the expatriate population in Mexico City and an unprepossessing but fascinating main character, Burroughs' alter ego, William Lee. He suffers from a humiliating attachment to Eugene Allerton, a young, attractive American student on the G. I. Bill. Lee's needy attempts at seduction are complicated by his simultaneous withdrawal from heroin. When Lee and Allerton embark together on an expedition to Ecuador in search of a hallucinogenic plant known as yage, they first agree that Lee will pay Allerton's expenses in return for rationed sexual favors, a contract that proves difficult to enforce. The trip ends in frustration and estrangement; the yage proves elusive, and relations with Allerton peter out in the face of the young man's sullen resentment.

In the "Introduction" Burroughs comes to the "appalling" conclusion that, since the novel arose from his wife's death, that event is the act of founding violence that made him an author. Lee's comic monologues in front of audiences, intended to keep emotional and physical contact alive, uncannily dramatize the process of "becoming literary," when Lee continues to perform after the bar's patrons have departed. He remains captive to the unfolding narrative that originates with him but which he finds he cannot control. **RP**

White Noise

Don DeLillo

Lifespan | *b.* 1936 (U.S.)
First Published | 1985
First Published by | Viking Press (New York)
American Book Award | 1985

(Post)modern American consumer culture streams through DeLillo's landmark novel like a fatal sugar rush. The book presents a highly detailed yet utterly mass-mediated world wherein human skin is "a color that I want to call flesh-toned," television is a member of the family, and one can prayerfully murmur "Toyota Celica" in one's sleep. But the characters here are not the dupes of the system; they are its professional analysts. Set in a Midwestern college town, the central protagonists are Jack Gladney, professor of Hitler Studies at the College-on-the-Hill, his faculty wife Babette, and their children from Brady Bunch-style previous marriages. Children, as DeLillo points out, are savvier, more adapted, and yet more disillusioned about modern culture than adults; fourteen-year-old Heinrich, for example, plays chess by mail with an imprisoned mass murderer.

Much of the novel, told from Jack's perspective, is domestic in orientation, detailing fragments of information and conversation in a way that is both alienating and comforting. It is unclear whether DeLillo affirms a human ability to create meaningful and intimate relationships from the most unpromising of materials or whether he laments a wholesale loss of "authenticity." *White Noise* inhabits the hyperreal with wit and warmth, but deals too with a more sinister reality that crashes into the later part of the book, a shadow that no amount of shopping and chattering will obviate. **DH**

Old Masters

Thomas Bernhard

Lifespan | b. 1931 (Netherlands), d. 1989 (Austria)
First Published | 1985, by Suhrkamp (Frankfurt)
Full Title | *Old Masters: A Comedy*
Original Title | *Alte Meister*

Old Masters covers typical Bernhard territory: grief, failure, solitude, and the dangers of using art as an escape from life. It is set in Vienna's History of Art Museum where the narrator, Atzbacher, is observing his friend, Reger, as he in turn contemplates Tintoretto's *White-Bearded Man*, a painting he has been examining every other day for over thirty years. While waiting for their arranged meeting time, Atzbacher recalls his friend's acerbic reflections on the arts, society, and the moral and cultural decrepitude of Austrian people and history. Interwoven with the outbursts are personal recollections of Reger's recently deceased wife, who he believes saved him from certain demise.

In the latter part of the novel Atzbacher records what Reger says during the two friends' meeting, and we get a fuller picture of his need for companionship and the source of his anger. As always with Bernhard the emotional is enmeshed with the intellectual, and there is no attempt to make Reger's opinions seem anything other than the idiosyncratic outpourings of a highly gifted but disenchanted and grieving misanthropist. The novel's subtitle, a comedy, may seem like a Beckettian joke, yet it is genuinely a very funny piece of work. As with Nietzsche, Bernhard's most obvious forebear, the exaggerated scorn and posturing are there to provoke, and the writing itself is utterly compelling from beginning to end: impassioned, moving, beautiful, and ultimately life-affirming. **AL**

Perfume

Patrick Süskind

Lifespan | b. 1949 (Germany)
First Published | 1985, by Diogenes (Zürich)
Full Title | *Perfume: The Story of a Murderer*
Original Title | *Das Parfum*

Set in eighteenth-century France, Süskind's novel tells the story of Jean-Baptiste Grenouille, born with a supernatural sense of smell and the complete absence of any odor of his own. The narrative style of *Perfume* is distinguished by its emphasis on smell, in which every scene is recounted, via Grenouille's nose, through the layered complexity of its olfactory detail. Süskind paints a series of beautifully elaborate pictures of the smells of everyday objects (such as the depth and variety of aromas emitted by wood) and of the manipulation of smell by eighteenth-century perfumery. What could become just a literary gimmick is prevented from being such by a focus on the psychology of the characters. A veritable psychopath, Grenouille is convinced that his acute sense of smell elevates him above ordinary humanity. He conceives a fantasy of himself as the capricious ruler of men, bestowing upon the masses the most delicate of fragrances, before surrendering to his own gratification. However, in a world constructed of scents, Grenouille becomes obsessed with his own lack of odor, since this effectively renders him a cipher, able to discern the substance of everything but lacking a substance of his own. Intent on creating a scent for himself, Grenouille embarks on the murderous process of capturing the most beautiful human scents: those of 'ripe' young women. But even the most exquisite aroma can only mask his essential odorlessness and his consequent insignificance within a fragrant universe. **LC**

The Handmaid's Tale

Margaret Atwood

Atwood creates a dystopic future in which the population has become threateningly infertile and women are reduced to their reproductive capabilities. Patriarchy takes on a new, extreme aspect; one that oppresses in the name of preservation and protection, one in which violence is perpetrated by the language of ownership and physical delineation. In this nightmare society women are unable to have jobs or money, and are assigned to various classes: the chaste, childless Wives; the housekeeping Marthas; and the reproductive Handmaids, who turn their offspring over to the Wives. The tale's protagonist, Offred—so named to denote the master to whom she belongs—recounts her present situation with a clinical attention to her body, now only an instrument of reproduction. A counterpoint is provided through moving glimpses into her past life: memories of a sensual love for her lost family. Set in a future Cambridge, Massachusetts and partly inspired by New England's puritan American society, Atwood transforms the institutions and buildings of a familiar landscape into a republic called Gilead. Atwood's prose is chillingly graphic, achieving the sense that all of life's past physical pleasures have been reduced to mechanical actions, throwing the value of desire into sharp relief. Through her imagined world she shows sexual oppression not so much taken to its extreme conclusion, as sexuality obliterated from the desiring body; an act every bit as violent as sexual violation. Atwood expertly handles the different forms that power manages to take within the handmaids' emotional dilemmas, as she describes the timeless tensions evoked by the body's immediate needs and our ability to look beyond desire to greater political ends. **AC**

Lifespan | *b.* 1939 (Canada)
First Published | 1985
First Published by | McClelland & Stewart (Toronto)
Governor General's Award for Fiction| 1986

◉ The cover illustration shows women wearing the uniform imposed on handmaids in Atwood's fictional totalitarian society.

◉ Stephanie Marshall plays Offred in Poul Ruder's operatic adaptation staged by the English National Opera in 2003.

Contact

Carl Sagan

Lifespan | *b.* 1934 (U.S.), *d.* 1996
First Published | 1985
First Published by | Simon & Schuster (New York)
Locus Award | 1986

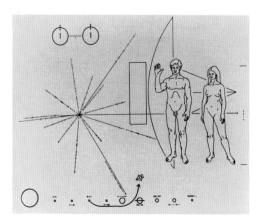

"Science fiction, You're right, it's crazy . . . You wanna hear something really nutty? I heard of a couple guys who wanna build something called an airplane . . . "

⬆ The plaque Carl Sagan designed for the Pioneer space probe was meant to be comprehensible to any extraterrestrial intelligence.

⬇ Sagan in 1972 displays his space probe plaque, which failed to escape the sexism of its day—the man active, the female passive.

Carl Sagan, an astronomer who was inextricably tied to the search for extraterrestrial intelligence, was one of the most famous popular scientists of the last century, as respected by his fellow professionals as he was by the public. A major proponent of the search for extraterrestrial life, Sagan designed a special plaque for the exterior of NASA spacecraft. It bore a universal message for spacecraft bound outside the solar system, which could be understood by any extraterrestrial intelligence that might find it. He was also one of the first scientists, along with Frank Drake, to use a radio telescope to search for deliberate signals from nearby galaxies, estimating that our galaxy was home to over a million civilizations.

The highly successful novel *Contact*, which was adapted for screen a year after Sagan died, was Sagan's best-known foray into the world of fiction, bringing scientific principles to mainstream entertainment. Unsurprisingly, its overriding theme is that of extraterrestrial contact. The main character, astronomer Ellie Arroway, detects a signal from a nearby star, a repeating sequence of the first two hundred and sixty-one prime numbers, which she deduces could only be sent from an intelligent civilization. It turns out that the message is more complex than initially realized; it actually contains a blueprint for an advanced space traveling machine. Religious fundamentalists, scientists, and governments argue over whether to build it and, in the end, a multinational team is chosen to make the trip. Throughout the story, Sagan intertwines complex mathematics with fiction, and through the knots in his story come hints of deep questions about the meaning of religion and spirituality, humanity, and social consciousness. **EF**

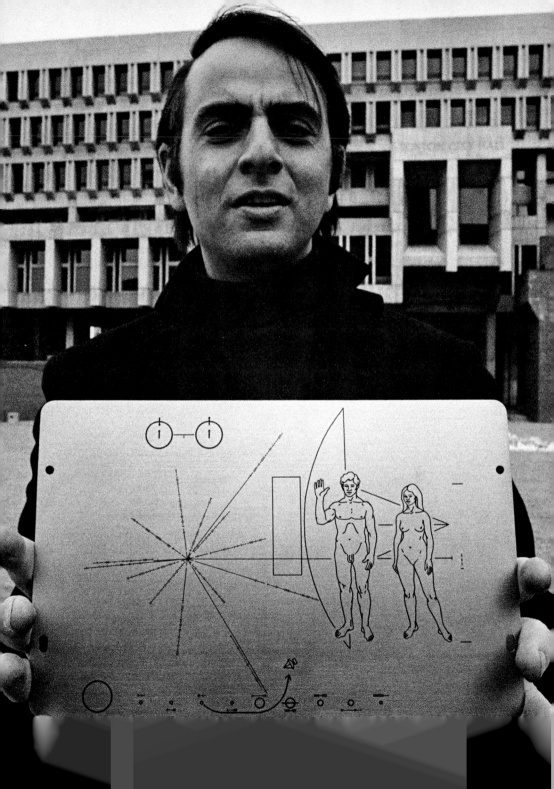

Less than Zero

Bret Easton Ellis

Lifespan | *b.* 1964 (U.S.)
First Published | 1985
First Published by | Simon & Schuster (New York)
First UK Edition | 1986, by Pan Books (London)

Bret Easton Ellis is a writer who specializes in creating a kind of blur. His novels are so packed with events and details that it quickly becomes difficult to keep track of specific characters, where they are going and why. Ellis' style reflects the experience of the late twentieth century; being influenced by magazine and advertising copy much more than any of his obvious literary forebears. This is why his work remains so important, regardless of subjective arguments about "taste" in which it is often ensnared.

Less Than Zero is Ellis' first novel, written aged just twenty while a student—it is full of monotonous partying, sex, and drugs. It documents a single Christmas break spent floating around Los Angeles by the narrator, Clay. In its generalized disaffection the novel recalls, at least thematically, *The Outsider* or *The Catcher in the Rye*, but here any suggestion of an underlying morality or ethics is bleached out. All that remains are the events, piled upon each other in a way that, true to the content, manages to be at once full of detail and completely colorless. In many respects this is the "purest" of Ellis' novels, free of gruesome murders, corrupt agencies, and urban vampires. All that is left are the bare bones—the city and the generation that grew up knowing nothing else, rendered incapable of understanding anything about themselves or those that surround them. **SF**

❶ Ellis, photographed here in 1991, is seen as a spokesman for Generation X—the blank consumerized Americans born after 1960.

A Maggot

John Fowles

Lifespan | *b.* 1926 (England), *d.* 2005
First Published | 1985
First Published by | Jonathan Cape (London)
First U.S. Edition | Little, Brown & Co. (Boston)

At a glance, this book is a historical murder mystery returning to the layered pastiche style of Fowles' earlier work, *The Magus*. In the spring of 1736 four men and one woman, all traveling under assumed names, are crossing the Devonshire countryside en route to a mysterious rendezvous. When one is found dead and the others disappear, it falls to a lawyer called Ayscough to find out what really happened. Gradually the lawyer extracts the story in a series of verbatim interviews. Rebecca Hocknell, a London prostitute, is led astray by her employer, Mr. Bartholomew; he takes her to a cave where mysterious events occur, after which she discovers she is pregnant and he disappears, possibly abducted by aliens or time travelers. Rebecca gives birth to Ann Lee (the woman who in reality founded the feminist religious movement the Shakers). Although Fowles' atheism is evident, there is room for a religious reading of these mystical events.

A Maggot incorporates historical documents, and works as a meditation on the modern emergence and recent disappearance of the sense of self, the changing modern ego, and how this relates to the future of humanity. Fowles distances himself from his earlier existentialism and returns to his original beliefs in literature as a personal, mysterious voyage and the importance of preserving the autonomy of the individual as creator, demonstrating his debt to high modernism and romanticism. **EF**

The Cider House Rules

John Irving

Lifespan | *b.* 1942 (U.S.)
First Published | 1985
First Published by | W. Morrow (New York)
Movie Adaptation | 1999

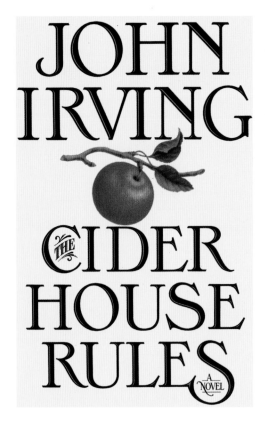

⬀ Jonathan Cape was the first to publish the novel in the UK.
Their jacket, shown here, was designed by Honi Werner.

One of Irving's most political novels, *The Cider House Rules* explores the contentious issue of abortion, as well as those of addiction, racism, and rejection. Dr. Wilbur Larch is the ether-addicted and childless, proprietor of the St. Clouds Orphanage in 1920s Maine. After many years witnessing unwanted children and deaths from backstreet abortions, Dr. Larch starts an illegal, and safe, abortion clinic at the orphanage. Homer Wells is one of the orphans, a bright and enterprising boy who appears to be inexplicably unadoptable, being returned again and again to the orphanage from would-be families. In this way, the fatherless son and childless father are brought together, as Larch realizes Homer will probably spend his life in the orphanage and decides to train him to take over his profession as St. Clouds' illegal abortionist. When Homer sees a dead fetus he decides he doesn't agree with abortion, and decides instead to take a trip with a young couple whom he met at the orphanage to an apple farm on the coast, from which he never returns. Dr. Larch must come to terms with Homer's reluctance both to follow his professional footsteps and to return to St. Clouds, while Homer's life develops complications of its own as love, and the Second World War, intervene. In dealing with the racism of the time, the novel's title derives from a list of rules Homer posts in the Cider House. These are supposed to keep order and safety among the black migrant workers who come to pick apples, but Homer is unaware that these rules are resented by the workers. Along with Homer, we come to realize that the real rules of the Cider House, and of life, aren't written down, itemized, or ordered. When the book was made into a movie in 1999, Irving won an Academy Award for his screenplay adaptation. **EF**

An Artist of the Floating World

Kazuo Ishiguro

Lifespan | *b.* 1954 (Japan)
First Published | 1986
First Published by | Faber & Faber (London)
Whitbread Award | 1986

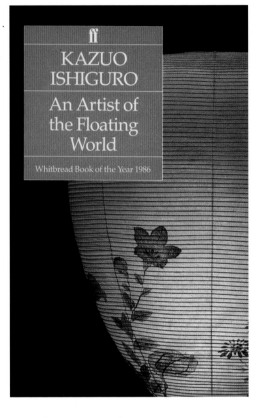

In his second novel, Ishiguro examines the "floating world" of postwar Japan, as it struggles to come to terms with social upheaval and changing cultural values. Told through the personal tale of Masuji Ono, an artist and propagandist for Japanese imperialism during the Second World War, the novel examines the country's prewar history and the difficulties it faces in coming to terms with the mistakes of the past.

The story begins three years after Japan's defeat. Ono's wife and son have been killed, leaving him to examine his role in the imperialist movement that led the country to disaster. He is involved in negotiations over his younger daughter's proposed marriage. The groom's family had abruptly canceled his other daughter's wedding, a year previously. Ono begins to question whether his artistic support of Imperial Japan has put his daughters' futures at risk. Yet while he attempts to keep his personal history under wraps, he is reluctant to exchange his prewar values for dubious modern ones.

Ishiguro, who left Nagasaki aged five and moved to Britain, vividly evokes the time and place of postwar Japan. His style mimics that of classical Japanese literature, the rigid prose reflecting the inflexibility of the aging artist. As in his subsequent novel, *The Remains of the Day,* Ishiguro creates an essentially expressive individual, who is forced by circumstance to repress his feelings. He writes like the painter of the title, creating a canvas on which his characters are set amid a wealth of intricate details. **LE**

"'Of course, circumstances oblige us to consider the financial aspect, but this is strictly secondary.'"

⊘ *An Artist of the Floating World* is set in Ishiguro's birthplace, Nagasaki, following the detonation of the atomic bomb.

Foe

J. M. Coetzee

Lifespan | *b.* 1940 (South Africa)
First Published | 1986
First Published by | Secker & Warburg (London)
Full Name | John Maxwell Coetzee

J. M. Coetzee's *Foe* revisits the eighteenth century in order to provide new perspectives on the classic tale of Robinson Crusoe, inhabiting and disrupting its fictional world. *Foe*, unlike its "master" text, tells a woman's story. Susan Barton finds herself stranded on an isolated island after she travels to Brazil in search of her abducted daughter. She shares her exile with Cruso, the lazy, cruel tyrant of his small empire, and Friday, who is unable to utter a word after losing his tongue. After a year on the island, the trio are rescued by an English ship. Safely back in London, she starts to write letters detailing her experiences to Daniel Foe, a writer under pressure to produce a successful story after incurring huge debts. "I was not intended to be the mother of my story," she writes, "but to beget it. It is not I who am the intended, but you."

This reimagining of the classic tale is a profound and delicately constructed examination of the politics of narrative, playing with the silences, missing links, and hidden violence behind our most well-known stories. It is a sensitive study in mastery and submission, in the hierarchies of race and gender, and in the fragility of history. Like Jean Rhys' *Wide Sargasso Sea*, *Foe* is a novel that forces us to reappraise our relationship (and our complicity) with the past. Its subtle but penetrating insights come through long immersion in what can be imagined of another century seen through new and modern eyes. **SamT**

Extinction

Thomas Bernhard

Lifespan | *b.* 1931 (Netherlands), *d.* 1989 (Austria)
First Published | 1986
First Published by | Suhrkamp (Frankfurt)
Original Title | *Auslöschung: ein Zerfall*

Thomas Bernhard's final novel, *Extinction*, is a powerfully sustained monologue on the subject of family, Austria, the scars of Nazism, and the impossibility of escaping cultural inheritance. It is a final reckoning of the formal and thematic concerns Bernhard worked on throughout his career.

Franz-Joseph Murau is an Austrian intellectual living in Rome, where he has taken refuge from Austria and his family in the "infinite paradise" of literature and the arts. The novel begins when Murau receives a telegram informing him that his parents and older brother have been killed in a car accident, leaving him heir to the family estate, Wolfsegg. As he prepares to leave for the funeral he reflects on his family, his hatred for them, and the lack of remorse he feels for their untimely deaths. The second half of the novel takes place at Wolfsegg, where he is forced to confront the burden of individual and collective history. Murau charges both his family and a large part of Austrian society with complicity in Nazi crimes and berates them for their complacent and hypocritical treatment of the past. Declamatory but never self-righteous, Murau is constantly aware of his own failings and the bitter tirades never descend into facile moralizing. Such insistent diatribes form part of a provocative attempt to awaken Austria from its historical amnesia. Far from a parochial concern, his savage indictment of Austria is directed at all forms of repressive dogma, and is an incitement for cultures to remain open to continuous reevaluation. **AL**

Reasons to Live

Amy Hempel

Lifespan | *b*. 1951 (U.S.)
First Published | 1985
First Published by | Knopf (New York)
Original Language | English

In these stories the tragedies happen offstage. As in life, tragedies are seldom terminal and life goes on. These are stories about just getting on—they are stories about grace. In "Nashville Gone to Ashes" a widow tends to an ark of pets when her veterinarian husband dies. This includes the ashes of her husband's beloved saluki—the Egyptian temple dog—who ought to have an Egyptian name. The pick of the litter was named Memphis. They misunderstood and named theirs Nashville. Embedded in the daily details, the narrator takes her husband's bed, so that when she looks over, the empty bed she sees is her own.

In "Tonight is a Favor to Holly" the narrator waits for a blind date. The story ends before the date because it is actually about the tenuous bond between the narrator and her friend Holly, adrift in the sunshiny limbo of L.A.'s beach communities, where "just because you have stopped sinking doesn't mean you're not still underwater."

These are stories of people who cope in the little ways they know how, keeping occupied with the tender and absurd details of living. They illustrate the intricate smokescreens of minutiae hiding the current of grief that might swallow us up if it were acknowledged. Fragile as the surface tension on water, so enthralling and so funny, one almost overlooks the exquisite sadness. Almost. **GT**

The Drowned and the Saved

Primo Levi

Lifespan | *b*. 1919 (Italy), *d*. 1987
First Published | 1986
First Published by | G. Einaudi (Turin)
Original Title | *I Sommersi a i salvati*

Published a year before his death, *The Drowned and the Saved* is Levi's final return to the tormenting question of how to write about the experience of Auschwitz, the "abyss of viciousness" we are so tempted to forget. In particular, he returns to the question explored in *If this is a Man* (1947); how to bear witness to the death camps when the "true witnesses"—those put to death—have been obliterated. Survivors, Levi reflects in his chapter on "Shame" are an "anomalous minority": "we are those who by their prevarications or abilities or good luck did not touch bottom."

Throughout the book, Levi brings to bear the resources of memory, anecdote, and reflection on the questions of survival, communication, and judgement that are part of the legacy of the death camps. "Almost everybody," Levi insists, "feels guilty of having omitted to offer help," a statement that pulls his readers into the drama of accusation, and self-accusation, that prolongs the suffering of the camps throughout a lifetime. It is a burden of guilt that, Levi suggests, is vital to the totalitarian system; its most extreme example the Sonderkommandos of the extermination camps, the squads of prisoners selected to run the crematoria. Levi's work is to bring readers toward the paralysis of judgement that results from trying to hear the message of the horrific atrocities perpetrated in the camps. **VL**

Love in the Time of Cholera

Gabriel García Márquez

Lifespan | *b.* 1928 (Columbia)
First Published | 1985, by Bruquera (Barcelona)
Original Title | *El amor en los tiempos del cólera*
Nobel Prize for Literature | 1982

On the day of her husband's funeral, Florentino Ariza—poet, prodigious lover, and president of the River Company of the Caribbean—reiterates his undying love and fidelity to the fiancée of his youth, Fermina Daza. Appalled, Fermina rejects him, fifty-one years, nine months, and four days after his first unceremonious rejection by her, ordering him never to show his face again. The body of the novel catapults the reader back more than fifty years to the beginning of Florentino and Fermina's courtship, as well as their subsequent lives, and a multitude of other characters' stories are interwoven. The final chapter returns to the present, recounting Florentino's infinitely more successful second wooing of his beloved.

Love in the Time of Cholera is an epic love story. At the same time, it is utterly unsentimental, leaving its reader with a profound sense of the astonishing power of patience and determination to overcome all obstacles, more than some romantic eternal power of love. Peopled by ghostly apparitions, cursed dolls, and sinister parrots, the book contains enough delightful moments of everyday unreality to confirm Márquez's place among the most outstanding of magic realist writers. More aware of the weight of history and the scourges of urban living, this is darker but no less captivating than *One Hundred Years of Solitude*, its great predecessor. **SJD**

The Parable of the Blind

Gert Hofmann

Lifespan | *b.* 1931 (Germany), *d.* 1993
First Published | 1985
First Published by | Luchterhand (Darmstadt)
Original Title | *Der Blindensturz*

Pieter Breughel's painting *The Parable of the Blind* depicts six blind men walking in line, one following the other; disturbingly, the leader has stumbled into a pond and lies sprawled on his back as the others approach. Narrated in the first-person plural, the collective "we" in which these blind men think, Hofmann's novel retells the big day on which they have come to visit the famous artist, so that he can paint them. On the way they lose their bearings several times, before eventually finding their way, bruised and confused, to the pond beside which the famous artist lives. In these frail, exposed, and vulnerable blind men, the reader is brought face to face with bare life. Part of the poignancy of the narrative is that while the blind men pin their hopes on the meeting with the painter, they never in fact encounter him face-to-face. To make matters worse, they are forced to walk into the pond again and again, so that they can be painted in a situation that exaggerates the helplessness of their predicament. In Hofmann's masterful hands, Breughel's painting becomes a parable of not just the blind—who here stand for everyman—but of the ambiguous power relationship between the artist and his models. By imagining how these unfortunates came to be painted, Hofmann fixes permanently on the strange, shifting world of those who cannot see in a world where sight is all that matters. **PT**

Oranges are Not the Only Fruit

Jeanette Winterson

Jeannette Winterson's largely autobiographical first novel was published to immediate critical acclaim. The novel's dryly ironical depiction of a child growing up in a fundamentalist Christian community in the North of England became one of the Eighties' most surprisingly popular novels and gave Jeanette Winterson's prolific and controversial literary career a powerful launch.

The beguilingly innocent narrative voice of the central protagonist Jess allows Winterson to question the lines that are drawn between the exceptional and the unexceptional, the real and the fantastic, the normal and the abnormal. For Jess, the dour realities and commonplace assumptions of a working-class northern mill town are seen as contradictory and confusing compared to the fervent certainties of her mother and her church. Her early anxieties about the differences between her own childhood and that of her peers are easily offset against the particularly childish pleasures of a literal life: she enacts scripture, she plays tambourine in a church band, she proselytizes, and saves lost souls. Her imaginative life is as nourishing and protective as the community within which she lives. The novel's crisis comes when these two worlds break apart, when Jess' emerging lesbian identity is seen as not only threatening and immoral but a direct consequence of her active and vocal role in the church. At the end of the novel Jess emerges from this imposed sense of madness (ironically represented by her false acquiescence to an exorcism) able to participate in new opportunities in a new world. Her richly imaginative life, represented by a fairy tale parable that shadows this realist narrative, interprets this story as a quest that she has succeeded in winning. **NM**

Lifespan | *b.* 1959 (England)
First Published | 1985
First Published by | Pandora Press (London)
Whitbread First Novel Award | 1985

⊙ Charlotte Coleman stars as Jess in the 1989 BBC TV miniseries, directed by Beeban Kidron, which won a BAFTA for Best Drama.

The Cider House Rules

John Irving

Lifespan | *b.* 1942 (U.S.)
First Published | 1985
First Published by | W. Morrow (New York)
Movie Adaptation | 1999

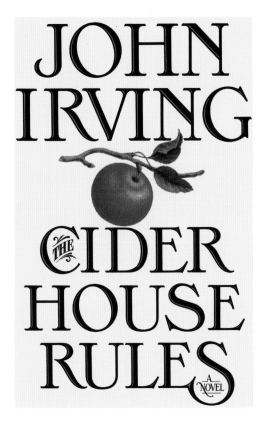

🔵 Jonathan Cape was the first to publish the novel in the UK.
Their jacket, shown here, was designed by Honi Werner.

One of Irving's most political novels, *The Cider House Rules* explores the contentious issue of abortion, as well as those of addiction, racism, and rejection. Dr. Wilbur Larch is the ether-addicted and childless, proprietor of the St. Clouds Orphanage in 1920s Maine. After many years witnessing unwanted children and deaths from backstreet abortions, Dr. Larch starts an illegal, and safe, abortion clinic at the orphanage. Homer Wells is one of the orphans, a bright and enterprising boy who appears to be inexplicably unadoptable, being returned again and again to the orphanage from would-be families. In this way, the fatherless son and childless father are brought together, as Larch realizes Homer will probably spend his life in the orphanage and decides to train him to take over his profession as St. Clouds' illegal abortionist. When Homer sees a dead fetus he decides he doesn't agree with abortion, and decides instead to take a trip with a young couple whom he met at the orphanage to an apple farm on the coast, from which he never returns. Dr. Larch must come to terms with Homer's reluctance both to follow his professional footsteps and to return to St. Clouds, while Homer's life develops complications of its own as love, and the Second World War, intervene. In dealing with the racism of the time, the novel's title derives from a list of rules Homer posts in the Cider House. These are supposed to keep order and safety among the black migrant workers who come to pick apples, but Homer is unaware that these rules are resented by the workers. Along with Homer, we come to realize that the real rules of the Cider House, and of life, aren't written down, itemized, or ordered. When the book was made into a movie in 1999, Irving won an Academy Award for his screenplay adaptation. **EF**

Less than Zero

Bret Easton Ellis

Lifespan | *b.* 1964 (U.S.)
First Published | 1985
First Published by | Simon & Schuster (New York)
First UK Edition | 1986, by Pan Books (London)

Bret Easton Ellis is a writer who specializes in creating a kind of blur. His novels are so packed with events and details that it quickly becomes difficult to keep track of specific characters, where they are going and why. Ellis' style reflects the experience of the late twentieth century; being influenced by magazine and advertising copy much more than any of his obvious literary forebears. This is why his work remains so important, regardless of subjective arguments about "taste" in which it is often ensnared.

Less Than Zero is Ellis' first novel, written aged just twenty while a student—it is full of monotonous partying, sex, and drugs. It documents a single Christmas break spent floating around Los Angeles by the narrator, Clay. In its generalized disaffection the novel recalls, at least thematically, *The Outsider* or *The Catcher in the Rye*, but here any suggestion of an underlying morality or ethics is bleached out. All that remains are the events, piled upon each other in a way that, true to the content, manages to be at once full of detail and completely colorless. In many respects this is the "purest" of Ellis' novels, free of gruesome murders, corrupt agencies, and urban vampires. All that is left are the bare bones—the city and the generation that grew up knowing nothing else, rendered incapable of understanding anything about themselves or those that surround them. **SF**

A Maggot

John Fowles

Lifespan | *b.* 1926 (England), *d.* 2005
First Published | 1985
First Published by | Jonathan Cape (London)
First U.S. Edition | Little, Brown & Co. (Boston)

At a glance, this book is a historical murder mystery returning to the layered pastiche style of Fowles' earlier work, *The Magus*. In the spring of 1736 four men and one woman, all traveling under assumed names, are crossing the Devonshire countryside en route to a mysterious rendezvous. When one is found dead and the others disappear, it falls to a lawyer called Ayscough to find out what really happened. Gradually the lawyer extracts the story in a series of verbatim interviews. Rebecca Hocknell, a London prostitute, is led astray by her employer, Mr. Bartholomew; he takes her to a cave where mysterious events occur, after which she discovers she is pregnant and he disappears, possibly abducted by aliens or time travelers. Rebecca gives birth to Ann Lee (the woman who in reality founded the feminist religious movement the Shakers). Although Fowles' atheism is evident, there is room for a religious reading of these mystical events.

A Maggot incorporates historical documents, and works as a meditation on the modern emergence and recent disappearance of the sense of self, the changing modern ego, and how this relates to the future of humanity. Fowles distances himself from his earlier existentialism and returns to his original beliefs in literature as a personal, mysterious voyage and the importance of preserving the autonomy of the individual as creator, demonstrating his debt to high modernism and romanticism. **EF**

Lost Language of Cranes

David Leavitt

Lifespan | *b.*1961 (U.S.)
First Published | 1986
First Published by | Knopf (New York)
First UK Edition | 1987, by Viking (London)

David Leavitt's first novel, an impressive debut, explores the terrible secrets that families keep from one another. Set in New York against the terrifying backdrop of the AIDS epidemic, the novel recounts the coming out of Philip Benjamin to his parents, Owen and Rose. His disclosure has an immediate impact on their comfortable, settled lives. His mother feels a kind of shocked "grief," driven by the sense of sexual danger that her son is to negotiate as a homosexual. For his father "it is the end of the world." Confronted by Philip's "news," Owen is utterly inconsolable, overwhelmed by his inability to cope with his own undisclosed homosexuality, realized only in clandestine Sunday afternoon visits to gay porn theaters. The novel progresses through Philip's sexual and emotional development in his relationship with his lover, Eliot, who feels thwarted by the effeminacy of Philip's desire. By far the most adept aspect of the novel is the way in which Owen and Rose's marriage changes once she realizes that they have been living a lie for the last three decades. Without slipping into cliché where other writers might, Leavitt's assiduous, scrupulous style here conveys the fissures that all too easily appear between generations and within families. **VC-R**

⊙ A graduate of Yale University, David Leavitt is English professor at Florida University where he heads the creative writing program.

The Old Devils

Kingsley Amis

Lifespan | *b.* 1922 (England), *d.* 1995
First Published | 1986
First Published by | Hutchinson (London)
Booker Prize | 1986

The Old Devils is regarded as one of Kingsely Amis' finest novels, the only one to rival 1954's *Lucky Jim* in popularity. The targets of his satire this time are Peter, Charlie, and Malcolm, the "Old Devils," a group of aging Welshmen who, along with their wives, spend life gossiping and drinking.

When Alun Weaver, a "professional Welshman" and his seductive wife Rhiannon appear on the scene, the "Old Devils" must re-evaluate their way of life and face hard truths about their own standing in the community. As always, Amis' understated realism and keen eye for the ridiculous minutiae of middle-class life produces a novel that occasionally makes for uncomfortable reading, where any sort of pomposity or pretence is immediately exposed to mockery. Despite this, the reader is also encouraged to feel a grudging sympathy with the curmudgeonly antics of the Old Devils, and it is in this combination that Amis' talent really lies. This savage comic novel nevertheless contains a strong strain of human sympathy, as the buffoonish characters can't help but win the reader's admiration. Amis in the late period of his career has often been derided for his famous misanthropy and often offensive conservatism. In *The Old Devils* he exposes the fallacy of this charge, combining the poise and control of his early satires with a gentleness and humanity that makes this novel a pleasure to read. **AB**

Watchmen

Alan Moore & Dave Gibbons

Lifespan | b. 1953 (England), b. 1949 (England)
First Published | 1986
First Published by | DC Comics/Titan Books (N.Y./Lon.)
Hugo Award | 1987

A meditation on the Nietzschean Superman. A murder mystery. An alternate world sci-fi epic. A psychological study of power and corruption. A comic.

The year 1986 marked a significant turning point for the graphic novel. Alongside Frank Miller's reinvention of Batman came Alan Moore's twelve-part saga of superheroes and their troubles. Set in America in 1985, Nixon is president for a third term, and costumed adventurers have been outlawed by the 1977 Keene Act. Two are still operational: the Comedian, a tough, vicious soldier with a dark past, and Dr. Manhattan, the victim of an atomic accident, whose extraordinary powers give America the decisive edge in the Cold War. The other superheroes are arguably happier in their enforced retirement. Except for Rorschach, the sociopath, whose response to the Keene Act was to deliver the dead body of a multiple rapist to New York's police along with a note saying "Never." But then the Comedian is killed. Someone has a plan. The Cold War is not over but escalating. Who can rise above it? And at what cost?

With a broad cast of characters, *Watchmen* maintains a human heart in the face of Armageddon. Moore knows comics, their attractions and their pitfalls, and there is no place here for a simple tale of heroes and villains. In addition to Moore's multiple narratives, Dave Gibbons' lucid artwork can bring a tear to the eye. These days, the term "graphic novel" is both overused and ill-defined. *Watchmen* remains the standard and the challenge. **JS**

Marya: A Life

Joyce Carol Oates

Lifespan | b. 1938 (U.S.)
First Published | 1986
First Published by | E. P. Dutton (New York)
Pseudonyms | Rosamond Smith; Lauren Kelly

Marya Knauer is a girl from a working-class background who enters the privileged, patriarchal world of language and culture, represented by an Ivy League university. Innisfail, where the first part of the novel is set, resembles the rural area around Lockport (New York) where Oates grew up and where so many of her works are set. The narrative opens with death of Marya's father and the desperate plight of her alcoholic mother, who abandons her daughter to a paternal aunt. Marya nevertheless excels as a student. She gets a job at a small New England liberal arts college but finally gives it up to become a political journalist. The novel is marked by Marya's journey of self-definition, guided by a sequence of male mentors. Her cousin Lee abuses her as a child, while her high school teacher introduces her to the world of writing. Father Shearing exposes Marya to religious beliefs. Her lovers, the academic Maximilian Fein and the editor Eric Nichols, initiate her into their respective worlds. The beautifully elliptical ending shows us Marya holding a photograph and trying to understand part of herself in the unfocused image of her mother's face. While the photo speaks of her mother's mysterious influence on Marya, the blurred quality of the print also highlights how identity is never absolutely fixed, but always in motion. **SA**

❯ Joyce Carol Oates referred to this novel as one of the most difficult to write because it was both "personal" and "fictional."

Matigari

Ngugi Wa Thiong'o

Lifespan | *b.* 1938 (Kenya)
First Published | 1986
First Published by | Heinemann (Nairobi)
Original Language | Kikuyu

Matigari returns from the mountains after years of struggle against colonial settlers to find his country and home bequeathed to the heirs of the opponents he has defeated. But in place of a victorious and proud homecoming he finds an oppressive and corrupt neocolonial order and an acquiescent population. The struggle for justice must begin again, and Matigari becomes the instigator of events that, in their re-telling, take on the power of myth. Matigari awakens a taste for rumor that loosens the tongues of the poor. Truth and reality have become difficult to distinguish between, and the president's "voice of truth," which blurts incessantly over the radio, is no longer immune from questioning.

Set "once upon a time, in a country with no name," Ngugi avoids determinacy of time or place. But in weaving together allusions to recent Kenyan history with pre-independence ideals from the Gikuyu oral traditions, the novel creates a sense of loss and historical obligation alongside a characteristically sharp critique of post-independence Kenya. Some months after the novel's first publication, intelligence reports in Kenya stated that a figure known as Matigari was traveling across the country preaching about peace and justice. Orders were given for his immediate arrest. The situation uncannily mirrors the last part of the novel where it is the inability to pin down any meaning to Matigari that prohibits his capture and assimilation. **ABi**

Anagrams

Lorrie Moore

Lifespan | *b.* 1957 (U.S.)
First Published | 1986
First Published by | Knopf (New York)
Given Name | Marie Lorena Moore

This debut novel from one of America's foremost short story writers displays all the brilliance of her early stories, only delightfully longer. This is a commonplace fable of ordinary lives confused by the fact that they are not extraordinary. It opens with a mischievous literary anagram. We are given successive versions of the first chapter, each slightly different, shuffled. Details fluctuate and merge until Moore comes up with the right one. Not just a self-reflexive trick, the gambit captures the theme of the narrative: the attempts of the characters to rearrange details of their lives, their outlooks, and their partners to create something that makes sense. Benna, alternately, is a nightclub singer, an unemployed aerobics instructor, and an art history professor. In one incarnation she wonders, "perhaps there are really only a few hundred people in the whole world and they all have jobs as other people." Gerard is her friend, her neighbor, her ex-lover, her student. How do the characters fit their lives and how do they fit their lives best? How do we create ourselves, our lives, to be successful?

In elaborate yet casual prose, *Anagrams* is about friendship, connection, barely missed connections, love, and loneliness. The characters try to be a part of things but can't find the courage to try hard enough. There are no grand evils here, only the careless indignities of everyday life; simple pathos, more of a shrug than a scream. At its heart is Moore's incisive humor coupled with compassion. **GT**

The Taebek Mountains

Jo Jung-rae

Lifespan | *b.* 1943 (Korea)
First Published | 1986
First Published by | Hangilsa (Seoul)
Original Title | *Taebaek sanmaek*

The Taebek Mountains is a ten-volume epic novel by one of South Korea's most respected and bestselling writers. It spans a period of Korean history that saw intense ideological conflicts between the political right and left following the establishment of the South Korean government in 1948—these conflicts continued until the end of the Korean War.

The novel focuses on the fate of Beolgyo, a small town in southwest Korea, from 1948–1950. This proves to be a tumultuous time for ordinary civilians, as control of the town shifts from faction to faction. The struggles are frequently violent: each time the balance of power shifts, it is the townspeople who suffer.

Within a cast of almost five hundred characters, the saga follows a number of protagonists, including Yeom Sang-ku, a violent inspector general who takes the lead in ferreting out the leftists; his brother, Yeom San-jin, a leftist military party chairman; Kim Beom Woo, a middle-of-the road anti-communist; Seo Min-young, a landowner who decides to share his land with his tenants; and So-hwa, a Korean shaman who represents traditional Korean values. The novel skillfully conveys intimate personal dramas played out in a climate of suspicion and terror.

The Taebek Mountains has sold more than six million copies. Jo has revealed that people often ask him which part of his novels are fiction and which are fact, "I answer with a grin that in a good novel there is no distinction between them." **HO**

Beloved

Toni Morrison

Lifespan | *b.* 1931 (U.S.)
First Published | 1987
First Published by | Knopf (New York)
Pulitzer Prize | 1988

Beloved has become an influential force in articulating the profound horror of slavery's legacy in American culture. At the novel's absent center are the consequences of the actions of Sethe, a mother who commits infanticide rather than allow her child to be taken back into the slavery from which she has just escaped. In the narrative's opening, Sethe and her one remaining child live on in the house in which the crime occurred, now haunted by the hungry sadness of the dead child. The appearance of Paul D., who had shared Sethe's traumatic experience of slavery on the ironically named "Sweet Home" Farm, appears to banish the ghost, only for her to reappear as the woman she would have been if allowed to live. Her now malevolent physical presence forces Paul D. away from the family and begins to punish Sethe. By the novel's end, the community, which had been presented as complicit with the murder, regroups around the family and allows Sethe to be free and, finally, her lover to return.

The novel was critically acclaimed for finding an appropriate form for remembering the inhumane violence of slavery. Sethe's slow and partial recollection of the debased treatment she endured during slavery, the emotional and physical hurts that carried her to a defensive act of infanticide, are central to the recovery the novel allows her. Morrison's lack of recourse to either sentiment or identification make it one of the most startlingly powerful books in twentieth-century American literature. **NM**

Enigma of Arrival

V. S. Naipaul

Lifespan | *b.* 1932 (Trinidad)
First Published | 1987
First Published by | Viking (London)
Nobel Prize for Literature | 2001

The setting of a Wiltshire valley near Stonehenge in the heart of Hardy's "Wessex," is typical of a landscape deeply inscribed in the English literary imagination. At the start of the novel, this rural idyll is obscured by incessant rain and the narrator's romantic image of England that he has gleaned from from his literary studies in Trinidad. Through five sections that interweave time and space, a picture of England slowly emerges, which seriously disrupts the narrator's original vision of an undisturbed culture. At every juncture, the appearance of England's ancient purity is contaminated by change, and the lasting impression is one of incongruity. Even Jack, the landlord who is the subject of the first part of the novel, turns out not to be rooted in the apparent antiquity of the location but is, like the narrator, a later arrival.

Situated on the border between autobiography and fiction, *The Enigma of Arrival* belongs to a tradition of novels including Proust's *In Search of Lost Time* and Joyce's *Portrait of the Artist*. It tells the story of the narrator's settling in England, his arrival at an understanding of England filtered necessarily through his colonial heritage, and his eventual writing of this very novel. Here we see the realization that the changes wrought on the English landscape and lifestyles by the newcomers are in essence no different to the narrator's restyling of England for his own literary purposes: the colonies have already taken root in the colonizer. **ABi**

World's End

T. Coraghessan Boyle

Lifespan | *b.* 1948 (U.S.)
First Published | 1987
First Published by | Viking Press (New York)
PEN/Faulkner Award | 1988

World's End is Boyle's great novel, a grand symphony of themes, motifs, and variations. He roots it in the Hudson Valley where the ancestral bond to the land —and actual ancestors—still suffocates the present. It is the story of the Van Brunts, a family abused by fate, and begins with a distant ancestor, Harmanus Van Brunt, the victim of the illusion of a better life who sails for New Amsterdam. Far from finding the promised land he is beset by hardships and blights that could make the God of the Old Testament cringe. And so begins the curse, the bad luck, and loss of limbs. But these Van Brunts are not inculpable. They betray their own sons, their own fathers, wives, cousins, and in-laws. They succumb to passion and caprice. They are human; they are Americans. The future is adumbrated by the past, the past plays off the future. There can't be losers without winners, however, and the winners are the Van Warts. Seventeenth-century patroons and tormenters of the Van Brunts, their ancestries are symbiotically entwined. They rule, and always will. But it does all end hopefully—or at least with the possibility of an end to the damage.

In *World's End* Boyle tackles three hundred years of history and myth in America, and does it with verbal sleight of hand and wickedly subversive wit. It is a breathtaking feat of prose. **GT**

❯ T. Coraghessan Boyle sits on the steps of his house in Santa Barbara, CA, which was designed by Frank Lloyd Wright.

The New York Trilogy

Paul Auster

Lifespan | *b.* 1947 (U.S.)
First Published | 1987, by Faber & Faber (London)
Trilogy | *City of Glass* (1985), *Ghosts* (1986),
The Locked Room (1986)

City of Glass
Paul Auster

The New York Trilogy, volume 1

◉ The first novella in the New York trilogy, *City of Glass* was first
published in 1985, when it was presented as detective fiction.

◐ Paul Auster, photographed here in Paris, France, in 1990, lived in
France for four years after graduating from Columbia University.

Auster's three novellas explore the possibility of meaningful coincidence, necessity, and accident through the conventions of detective fiction and ordinary people's investigations of their mysterious worlds. *City of Glass* features a mystery writer, Daniel Quinn, with an insatiable love for the genre and its artificiality who, after answering two wrong number calls for the Paul Auster Detective Agency, decides to impersonate Auster and take the case. However, he is soon plunged into homeless ruin through his monomaniacal pursuit of a man who tried to beat his infant son into abandoning derivative, "human" language and letting a divine language pour forth. Yet along with his inevitable desperation and hardship, Quinn seems to develop a Zen-like, uncluttered awareness as his world shrinks drastically. The characters of *Ghosts*, caught up in a highly stylized, surrealistic game of who's watching who, are named after colors, lending a quasi-allegorical air to the action. Black's inaction pushes Blue, the man hired to spy on him, both to read voraciously and nearly lose his mind. *The Locked Room*, itself named after a subgenre of detective fiction, watches an unnamed first-person narrator slowly take over the life of a disappeared childhood friend. He marries his wife and shepherds the publication of his previously unknown literary masterpiece, only to be contacted by said friend and informed that the whole scenario has been intricately orchestrated.

The New York Trilogy is full of terrifying brushes with the zero point that is both complete potentiality and the collapse of identity. The effect of deprivation forms an intriguing subtext to all three stories, not least with respect to their own sparse language and brevity, as the worlds of the novellas gradually drift or lurch toward nothingness. **AF**

The Bonfire of the Vanities

Tom Wolfe

An ambitious brick of a book, Tom Wolfe's first excursion out of the realm of journalism and into novel writing is a savage indictment of the excrescences of 1980s Wall Street capitalism. Sherman McCoy, a wealthy, upwardly mobile bondtrader at a prestigious city firm is involved in a car accident in the South Bronx, in which his mistress, Maria Ruskin, runs over and fatally injures a young black man, Henry Lamb. The novel charts the fall of the once-mighty Sherman, and the range of vested interests that contribute to his public disgrace, arraignment, and trial. While some people emerge triumphantly from the events the novel charts, morally there are no winners. Wolfe cynically suggests—and his own right-wing viewpoint is in evidence here—that the city's political and legal systems, as well as its media, are all complicit in the complicated structures of class and race warfare he describes. The posthumous conversion of Lamb into an idealized "honors student," for example, happens as a result of the career ambitions of the louche journalist Peter Fallow, who wins fame, fortune, and a Pulitzer from his reporting of the accident.

Whatever one's view of Wolfe's politics, it is hard not to admire his prose. His minutely detailed accounts of Park Avenue apartments, the maze of Bronx streets in which a panicked Sherman finds himself lost, the Southern drawl of Maria, and the impassioned accents of the Harlem-based black rights activist, the Reverend Bacon, render the sheer variety of New York with relish. This is a city seething with ethnic hostilities and class envy, driven by the desire to get rich quick; here sex, money, and power rule almost everyone. Wolfe makes good on his claim to offer a twentieth-century rival to the Victorian blockbusters of Dickens and Thackeray. **CC**

Lifespan | *b.* 1931 (U.S.)
First Published | 1987
First Published by | Farrar, Straus & Giroux (N.Y.)
First UK Edition | 1988, by Jonathan Cape (London)

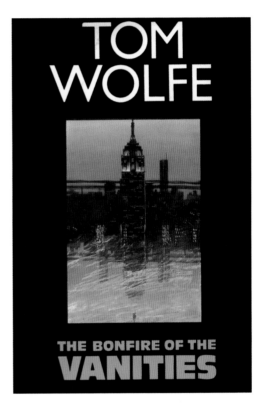

Shown here is the UK edition with jacket design by Mark Holmes. The novel was first serialized in *Rolling Stone* magazine.

Tom Wolfe is pictured here in his trademark white suit at his New York home, a year after the publication of *The Bonfire of the Vanities.*

Cigarettes

Harry Mathews

Lifespan | *b.* 1930 (U.S.)
First Published | 1987
First Published by | Weidenfeld & Nicolson (N.Y.)
First UK Edition | 1988, by Carcanet (Manchester)

Harry Mathews is the only American member of the Oulipo, the Paris-based group of writers who experimented with inventions in literary combinatorics, mathematically derived rules imposed upon sentences, poems, and whole novels. Mathews' best-known contribution to the forum is the Mathews Algorithm, a way of recombining arbitrary elements of plot in order to discover unthought-of sequences. This may or may not be the organizing principle behind *Cigarettes*, which is set over a period of thirty years among New York's generally idle rich—the kind of people Mathews grew up among. Each chapter is a subtle transformation of those surrounding it, where similar events are seen from a different point of view, and each is devoted to the power-play between a particular pairing of characters—Owen, who is blackmailing Allen, whose daughter Priscilla has an affair with Walter, who is the mentor of Phoebe, who forges a portrait of Elizabeth, who everyone loves. There are multiple miscommunications and deceptions—between lovers, business partners, parents, and children—and talismanic objects move through the text, from one person to another, connecting them all. It is impossible to avoid the feeling—typical of Mathews—that something intricate is going on beneath the surface. But even that surface is phenomenally rich, and it displays a great range of forms and registers, all engineered with faultless precision. **DSoa**

The Child in Time

Ian McEwan

Lifespan | *b.* 1948 (England)
First Published | 1987
First Published by | Jonathan Cape (London)
First U.S. Edition | Houghton Mifflin (Boston)

The Child in Time marked a turning-point novel in Ian McEwan's career. The novel retains something of the linguistic concision of McEwan's early stories, while allowing it a thematic scope unprecedented hitherto in his career. The whole novel pivots on a singularly terrifying event. Stephen Lewis, a writer of children's fiction, faces the nightmare of his daughter's abduction when his back is fleetingly turned in a supermarket checkout line. The event unfolds with horrifying immediacy, its description all the more incisive for being so understated and spare. We then proceed to make satirical excursions into Thatcherism's quango-ridden infrastructure, whose tendentiousness contrasts with the many more iridescent moments of involuntary recollection in which Stephen returns to his childhood past.

After being reluctantly conscripted to an advisory committee for a Childcare Handbook, Stephen daydreams through the quango's bureaucratic meetings; these mental wanderings provide a structural conceit for long voyages of retrospection. In one episode, Stephen passes through a wormhole to a pub where his parents sit as a young couple. But the adult Stephen "was a dreamer who knows his dream for what it is and, though fearful, lets it unfold out of curiosity." By inducing that very same unnerving "curiosity" throughout, McEwan solicits the attention of even the most skeptical reader, sustaining it with a hallmark style that quivers in anticipation of what has yet to "unfold." **DJ**

The Pigeon

Patrick Süskind

Lifespan | *b.* 1949 (Germany)
First Published | 1987
First Published by | Diogenes (Zürich)
Original Title | *Die Taube*

This short, tightly written novella is pervaded by a dark intensity. Süskind has been admired for his exploration of psychological themes and possesses a skill for closely drawing society's outsider individuals and their peculiarities. Jonathan Noel, a somewhat eccentric everyman, is a bank guard in his fifties who leads an almost automated existence of monotonous uniformity. He has withdrawn from all but the most perfunctory necessities of social interaction. Instead of depending upon people, who in his youth had consistently let him down or disappeared, Noel relies for stability on the simplicity of uneventfulness and the security of familiar surroundings and routines. The novella takes place over twenty-four hours, beginning with an early morning encounter with a pigeon outside the studio apartment Noel has occupied for over thirty years. Looking into the bird's eye, which seems devoid of life, Noel is precipitated into what is commonly and crudely known as a midlife crisis. The event is to disrupt and deeply disturb not only his regimen but also his carefully maintained internal equilibrium. For the first time in his life he finds himself inattentive at work and unable to return home; for the first time he questions the meaningfulness of the existence he has built for himself. Powerful for its potential universality, this short tale is also a persuasive examination of how an apparently trivial if unusual occurrence can force the self into new perspectives. **JC**

The Passion

Jeanette Winterson

Lifespan | *b.* 1959 (England)
First Published | 1987
First Published by | Jonathan Cape (London)
John Llewellyn Rhys Prize | 1987

The Passion is set in Napoleonic France and tells the tale of the young naïve Henri (a soldier who cooks for the insatiable Napoleon) and the more worldly Villanelle (a prostitute who has been sold to his insatiable army). The two meet while deserting during the cruel "zero winter" of the Russian campaign and together make the dangerous trek to Villanelle's Venetian home. In entwining their narratives, Winterson conjures a world in which the historical facts of Napoleon's march across Europe can be set beside the magical realm of stolen hearts, webbed feet, and women who can walk across water.

The novel contrasts the paternal imperialism of Napoleonic France with the shifting and unmappable landscape of Venice, a place of chance and paradox in which rules, even those of identity and sexuality, can be easily flouted. Henri's obsession with the inevitable passage of time is contrasted against Villanelle's more sensuous association with the mutability of space. This also evokes two models of love: Henri's deifying adoration of his Emperor is contrasted against Villanelle's passion for her female lover which forces her to—quite literally—risk her beating heart. Although Villanelle and Henri eventually become lovers, and even have a child, the two can never really be reconciled. Which of the two characters is really free is not obvious in this novel of reversals and contradictions. Still, as Winterson reminds us throughout the novel: "Trust Me, I'm Telling You Stories." **NM**

The Black Dahlia

James Ellroy

James Ellroy's *The Black Dahlia*, the first of a quartet of novels to pick the scab off L.A.'s dark underbelly between the late 1940s and mid-1950s, is both a straightforward police procedural and a complex, disquieting meditation on voyeurism and sexual obsession. At its heart is the horrific murder of Elizabeth Short, a.k.a. the Black Dahlia, a young woman who arrives in Hollywood looking for stardom and romance and finds only prostitution, pornography, and death. To track down her killer, police detective Bucky Bleichert must piece together the final days of her life, an act of recovery that brings him to confront not just powerful figures from the law enforcement and business communities, but also his own barely suppressed demons.

Later, Bleichert's discovery of the murder "scene" in a building that, quite literally, supports part of the famous Hollywood sign brings together the novel's primary areas of concern: pornography, spectacle, and the construction industry. Just as the rebuilding of Los Angeles in the post-Second World War era involves physically scarring the landscape for profit, the spectacular cutting of Elizabeth Short is linked to the commercial ambitions of a sexually deviant property developer. In all of this, unlike Raymond Chandler's archetypal detective, Bleichert cannot remain emotionally and sexually detached: his own obsession with the murdered woman ruins both his marriage and his promising career. The scene where he lures a prostitute back to a motel room littered with photographs of Elizabeth Short's horribly mutilated corpse and forces the terrified woman to dress up as the Black Dahlia is as disturbing as it is effective. Though the killer is eventually revealed, it is the supersaturation of violence, sexual depravity, and corruption that endures. **AP**

Lifespan | *b.* 1948 (U.S.)
First Published | 1987
First Published by | Mysterious Press (New York)
Given Name | Lee Earle Ellroy

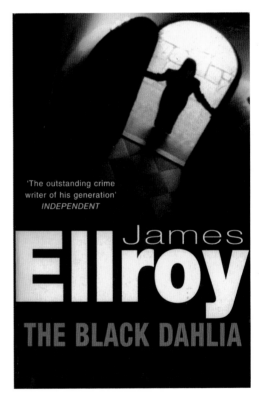

'The outstanding crime writer of his generation'
INDEPENDENT

James **Ellroy**

THE BLACK DAHLIA

⊙ The unsolved murder of Ellroy's mother, Geneva, in Los Angeles in 1958, shaped Ellroy's life and led him to write crime novels.

⊙ Elizabeth Short was twenty-two-years-old when her mutilated dead body was found in a Los Angeles parking lot in 1947.

The Afternoon of a Writer

Peter Handke

Lifespan | *b.* 1942 (Austria)
First Published | 1987
First Published by | Residenz Verlag (Salzburg)
Original Title | *Nachmittag eines Schriftstellers*

"If a nation loses its story-tellers, it loses its childhood."

◉ Both a novelist and a playwright, Handke co-wrote the Wim Wenders movie, *Wings of Desire*, also released in 1987.

"Afternoon" in *The Afternoon of a Writer* is, on the one hand, a definite temporal category. The writer finishes his day's work in a house saturated with the dull, melancholy sunlight of a winter's afternoon. But on the other hand, "Afternoon" is also a spatial and sensual arena, a matter of the body's movements in habitual spaces, when the body itself is impelled by its own needs rather than by the purposeful structures of work. "Afternoon" in this sense is the aftermath of labor, a period and a sensibility marked by a certain freedom yet also by a fatigue which transmutes that freedom into something semiconscious, a precious yet barely endurable return to a self stripped of external purpose or motivation.

Handke's writer in *The Afternoon of a Writer* is a man who lives, works, eats, and walks on his own, but this physical isolation only barely protects the privacy he nourishes and cherishes. Seduced, yet at the same time repelled, by the abstract chatter of words and images that engulf a city street, the writer embarks on a walk, hesitates, plunges in, and is lost.

Uneasily self-conscious about calling himself a writer, he is a man for whom art is a daily, sweaty activity and an overarching proud goal. Confronted with the depth of the writer's solitude and the consequent richness of his relations to language and to observation, the world "outside" cannot but pale a little. Handke indeed encourages such an opposition by refusing to name the city the writer walks in; its streets are anonymous and the language or languages spoken on them are unspecified. An opposition is not an unbridgeable chasm, however, and it is the beauty of this small book to make the writer—and the reader—hunger for the things of the world. **PMcM**

The Radiant Way

Margaret Drabble

Margaret Drabble's acclaimed novel is the first book in a sweeping trilogy that follows the lives of three women who, like Drabble herself, found themselves at Cambridge in the 1950s. Opening at a party on New Years' Eve, 1979, *The Radiant Way* begins by examining the life of Liz Headland, whose apparent success in family, career, and London social life have resulted in twenty years of settled contentment. However, as the 1980s begin, Liz's certainties about life begin to crumble in a dramatic fashion, and she finds herself again thinking of her childhood and adolescence in the provincial north of England, before Cambridge provided her with a passport to the welcome sophistication of London. Interwoven with Liz's story are those of her two Cambridge friends: Alix, whose naïve political convictions and cheerful romanticism make her frighteningly vulnerable to the emotional and financial vagaries of adult life, and Esther, whose mysterious reserve, amusing at Cambridge, has grown to extreme lengths that worry her friends. All three are confident, happy women, but the life-changing events of the 1980s, culminating in a suggestion of violence previously unimaginable within their comfortable lives, force them to reconsider their success in life and to find value once again in their long friendship.

Here, as usual, Drabble explores the issues of freedom, ambition, and love that face working women in a subtle and often ironically funny way. The otherwise mundane details of characters' lives are interwoven with the surreal background of London during exciting cultural change and political uncertainty. Both an ironic feminist bildungsroman and a magnificent state-of-England novel, this remains one of Drabble's finest and most absorbing books. **AB**

Lifespan | *b.*1939 (England)
First Published | 1987
First Published by | Weidenfeld & Nicolson (London)
First U.S. Edition | Knopf (New York)

"...knowledge must always be omnipresent in all things ..."

◉ This photograph of Margaret Drabble was taken by Sophie Bassouls in 1981, a year after the author received a CBE.

Dirk Gently's Holistic Detective Agency

Douglas Adams

Lifespan | b. 1952 (England), d. 2001 (U.S.)
First Published | 1987
First Published by | Heinemann (London)
First U.S. Edition | Simon & Schuster (New York)

Dirk Gently's Holistic Detective Agency deals with all the big questions that informed the author's earlier work in the *Hitch Hiker's Guide to the Galaxy* series. But a playful and comic interweaving of the science fiction, ghost story, whodunit genres serves to mask a darker and altogether more haunting set of themes.

Private detective Dirk Gently undertakes to track down the murderer of the millionaire founder of a computer empire, by employing his trademark holistic method. His belief in the underlying interconnectedness of all things yields results. The conventions of the detective genre are inverted: the clues follow Dirk and reveal themselves to him one after another. But there is plenty left for him to do, for the central mystery that Dirk Gently is trying to solve is none other than the origins of life on earth and the forces behind the course of history. Although Gently is painted as an absurd and slightly tragic figure, it is through him that Adams accesses some of the more profound currents of thought of the 1980s. This is one of few novels to investigate chaos or complexity theory. In rescaling his canvas from the intergalactic *Hitch Hiker's Guide* to the terrestrial, Adams reflects an emerging popular awareness of the interconnectedness of a globalizing world. As his characters grapple with a malevolent enemy, they become conscious that their choices have an unintended but far-reaching impact. **AC**

The Long Dark Teatime of the Soul

Douglas Adams

Lifespan | b. 1952 (England), d. 2001 (U.S.)
First Published | 1988
First Published by | Heinemann (London)
Full Name | Douglas Noël Adams

The unusual sleuth Dirk Gently returns. When Dirk's long-suffering ex-secretary disappears in a mysterious explosion at Heathrow Airport, and his latest client is decapitated in a room locked from the inside, it is only a matter of time before the interconnectedness of the two events becomes clear. Sherlock Holmes, ruling out the impossible, liked to think that the improbable must point toward the solution. Dirk Gently sees no good reason to rule out the impossible, and he is soon proved right. This is a novel where gods walk among men, where the gothic spires and turrets of St. Pancras Station reflect a shadow Valhalla. Humanity has forgotten the immortal deities it once worshiped, but those deities, called into being by humanity's need for faith, still linger.

Although Adam's light touch is very much present, the book seems more melancholic than his previous works. At the same time, the influence of Swift and Lewis Carroll are at their most apparent. The mundane and absurd form a poignant contrast with the grander themes of science and faith, while Adams again reveals his keen interest in contemporary physics, as Dirk finds himself forced to slip behind molecules and adventure across the frontier of his own universe. **AC**

❯ Douglas Adams is here photographed in 1984 by Roger Ressmeyer, surrounded by psychedelic halos of white light.

Nervous Conditions

Tsitsi Dangarembga

Lifespan | *b.* 1959 (Zimbabwe)
First Published | 1988
First Published by | Women's Press (London)
Commonwealth Writer's Prize (Africa) | 1988

Nervous Conditions is a colorful personal memoir, but also a clear-eyed snapshot of colonial Rhodesia in the 1960s. Tambu's branch of the family are subsistence farmers, and her early life on the homestead is marked by hard work and a deep sense of injustice. She is a canny observer of the Shona patriarchy in operation, but will not, like her mother, resign herself to the "poverty of blackness on the one side and the weight of womanhood on the other." Her father deems that there is no point sending Tambu to school, as she can't "cook books" to feed a husband. But she realizes early that education will be her escape; though clearly a gifted student, she succeeds through chance and sheer determination.

The novel's title is taken from its epigraph, itself a quotation from Sartre's introduction to Fanon's *The Wretched of the Earth*: "The condition of native is a nervous condition." Once at the mission school, Tambu enters a different world: the world of her successful uncle and his family, each member of whom has been marked by time spent in England. Tambu sees firsthand, in her cousin Nyasha's eating disorder, in her uncle's nervousness and excessive control, the tensions produced by the colonial condition, by being caught between two worlds. This is the minefield Tambu must negotiate in her formal education, but it is exacerbated by larger questions about black female identity articulated through the unique experience of the four women of her utterly engaging story. **ST**

The Player of Games

Iain M. Banks

Lifespan | *b.* 1954 (Scotland)
First Published | 1988
First Published by | Macmillan (London)
Full Name | Iain Menzies Banks

In *The Player of Games*, Banks presents a far distant future that could almost be called the end of history. Humanity has expanded to fill the galaxy, evolving into the Culture, a society where humans and machines live symbiotically, and thanks to technological advancement, everyone has everything they want—no one suffers ill health and no one dies. Life (the Culture) has become a playground society of sports, extended parties, stellar cruises, and festivals. A new breed of elite has emerged—game players—and one of the most famous of all is Jernau Morat Gurgeh. Bored with success and searching for a more substantial challenge, Gurgeh is sent by the Culture to the alien, cruel, and incredibly wealthy Empire of Azad, to try his hand at a game so complex, so like life itself, that the winner becomes emperor. Mocked, blackmailed, and almost murdered, Gurgeh accepts the game, and with it the challenge of his life—and very possibly his death. While the Culture's society appears rich from the outside, not all is as it seems. In the Empire of Azad, unspeakable acts occur in secret.

As with much of Banks' fiction, the protagonist is an outsider and the story is one of realization as Gurgeh understands how nasty the real world is compared to games, and how the lust for power threatens the future of everything. As Gurgeh is manipulated and maligned, Banks subverts the author-reader relationship, forcing the reader to repeatedly consider the meaning of truth and trust. **EF**

Libra

Don DeLillo

Lifespan | *b.* 1936 (U.S.)
First Published | 1988
First Published by | Viking (New York)
First UK Edition | 1989, by Penguin (London)

It is one of the many achievements of DeLillo's brilliant historical novel that events and names so closely bound up with "the seven seconds that broke the back of the American century," the Kennedy assassination, are so freshly and powerfully reimagined. At one level, *Libra's* plot is a simple one: we follow the series of events that turned the disaffected Lee Oswald into the more historically resonant "Lee Harvey Oswald," paralleled with the investigations of Nicholas Branch, an FBI deskman charged with cataloging it all afterward. But out of this material, DeLillo draws the finest demonstration of his characteristic skill—of shaking events so hard that the secret history of America suddenly falls out. Oswald's story expands into a lyrical and ideological meditation on power, control, and how we see ourselves as belonging to history; the novel's epigraph quotes a letter from Oswald on the point where "there is no borderline between one's own personal world, and the world in general."

In this postmodern thriller, Branch often operates as a reader-surrogate, keen to make connections, yet frequently frustrated by the sheer excess of data. As Oswald comes to realize that the plot runs much deeper that he thought, so a reader feels the layers of conspiracy and double-bluff spiralling beyond what can safely be contained. With the assassination, and Jack Ruby's murder of Oswald, we return, inevitably, to the official history, but we return there disoriented and creatively suspicious. **BT**

"Never again in his short life, never in the world, would he feel this inner power, rising to a shriek, this secret force of the soul of the tunnels of New York."

◉ Born in New York to Italian parents, DeLillo believes that the writer's true position lies "on the margins of culture."

Oscar and Lucinda

Peter Carey

Lifespan | *b.* 1943 (Australia)
First Published | 1988
First Published by | University of Queenstown Press
Booker Prize | 1988

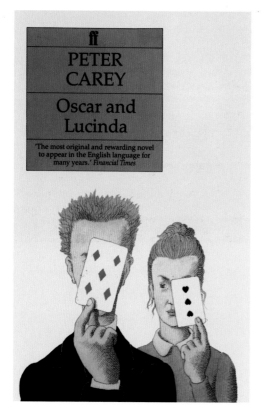

🔾 *Oscar and Lucinda*, here shown with its UK cover, won the Booker Prize in 1988. A movie version was made in 1997.

Peter Carey is probably Australia's best-known postcolonial writer. *Oscar and Lucinda* is set in mid-nineteenth-century England and Australia. Oscar Hopkins is the son of a preacher, an effeminate Englishman with hydrophobia. Lucinda Leplastrier is an Australian heiress who, fighting against society's expectations of the confinement of her gender, buys a glass factory with her inheritance. Both suffer childhood traumas, Oscar's the result of his relationship with his controlling, religious father, and Lucinda's centered around a doll, a present from her mother. In adulthood, both protagonists develop a passion for gambling and it is this love of risk that unites them when they finally meet, on a boat bound for New South Wales. Between the two there develops an uneasy and unspoken affection. Finally, they set out to transport a glass church across godforsaken terrain and the love developing between them, instead of blossoming, becomes isolated inside their skins.

Several important themes run through the book—not least the idea of love as the ultimate gamble, the high risk play to which Oscar and Lucinda ironically cannot commit themselves. Carey explores the idea of gender confinement at a time and place in history where society was happiest with strictly defined roles. Lucinda discovers again and again that if she manages to step outside the boundaries placed upon her by society, she will be excluded. Finally, the novel is an acerbic comment on colonialism as the couple attempt to transport a glass church unharmed across native land. In the end it is glass (so similar to his feared water) which, although providing Lucinda with her fortune, plays a hand in Oscar's ultimate death and in the eventual destruction of the Australian outback. **EF**

The Swimming-Pool Library

Alan Hollinghurst

When Hollinghurst published *The Swimming-Pool Library*, he was already well engaged in the literary scene, having published two collections of poetry and being on the staff of the *Times Literary Supplement*. This, his first novel, is an exuberant narrative of gay life set in 1983, which portrays the hedonism of "the last summer of its kind there was ever to be," before the AIDS crisis had really taken hold. By turns enraptured with the present and nostalgic for the past, the novel revels in the company of men and ubiquitous gay sex, while conducting the reader to a finely pitched denouement.

Two lives are contrasted here, that of Lord Nantwich, an ex-colonial administrator in Africa, and William Beckwith, a young gay man of independent means. After saving the aging peer's life, William is subsequently persuaded to write his biography and takes possession of his diaries. These provide a parallel narrative, and it becomes apparent that, though the two men are generations apart, their lives contain disquieting similarities. Racism and queer-bashing endure—even fifteen years after the legalization of homosexuality, the harassment of gay men persists as the arrest of William's best friend by an undercover policeman, himself gay, echoes the circumstances in which Nantwich served a prison sentence in the 1950s. For all the licentious liberty, the machinery of oppression is never far away in this novel, and further, the whiff of nostalgia for the alluring eroticism of the outlaw highlights the complexity of desire. The shadowing of contemporary gay liberation with the dangers of the illicit homosexual life is a reminder, lest we become complacent, of our connection and debt to past defeats as well as present victories. **CJ**

Lifespan | *b.* 1954 (England*)*
First Published | 1988
First Published by | Chatto & Windus (London)
Somerset Maugham Award | 1989

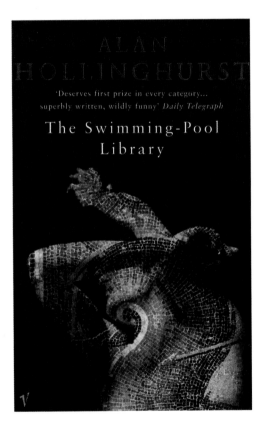

'Deserves first prize in every category... superbly written, wildly funny' *Daily Telegraph*

The Swimming-Pool Library

◉ On its publication, Edmund White hailed the novel as "the best book about gay life yet written by an English author."

The Satanic Verses

Salman Rushdie

Lifespan | *b.* 1947 (India)
First Published | 1988
First Published by | Viking (London)
Fatwa Issued | 1989

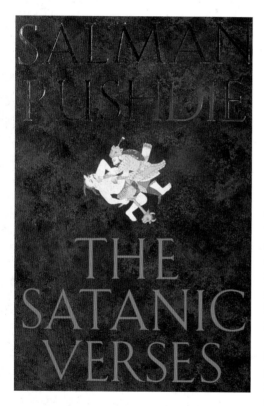

This is the book that triggered riots around the world in 1988 and 1989, brought a fatwa (death sentence) upon its author from Ayatollah Khomeini of Iran, and forced Rushdie into hiding for over a decade. The "Rushdie Affair" represents a seminal moment in literary history in which a host of religious and political tensions crystallized explosively around one novel and its Indian-born, British-educated author.

Written in a playful, magic realist style, *The Satanic Verses* is a transcultural view of the world as perceived by two Indian migrants, Saladin Chamcha and Gibreel Farishta. In the moment of genesis that opens the novel, both men fall into Britain, angel-like from the sky, when their plane is bombed by terrorists. British racism and the colonial legacy affect these characters in different ways, driving Gibreel into delusional, psychotic dream-sequences in which he appears as the Angel Gabriel, bringing divine revelations to the Islamic Prophet. Meanwhile, the sycophantic Anglophile, Saladin, becomes more devilish by the minute in a physical mutation he cannot control. A multitude of Black and Asian British characters probes postcolonial migrant experience in the novel. Mixing words, worlds, histories, fictions, dreams, delusions, and prophesies, Rushdie's style is an exercise in cosmopolitanism.

In Gibreel's dream-sequences, set in and around Mecca, Rushdie asks what makes a "new idea," Islam, stick fast, while a multitude of other ideas fail to take hold of the imagination. The answer to this question lies in the Prophet's "ramrod-backed" conviction that his idea is absolute and pure. In fictionalizing the Prophet's life, however, and by inserting a psychotic character into the role of angel, Rushdie offended millions of Muslims worldwide and provoked a sense of outrage that persists today. **SN**

The fatwa declared by Ayatollah Khomeini on Rushdie extended to his translators and publishers, several of whom were attacked.

In a pro-Iranian rally in southern Beirut in 1989, a girl stands ready to kill Rushdie before a poster of Ayatollah Khomeini.

Wittgenstein's Mistress

David Markson

Lifespan | *b.* 1927 (U.S.)
First Published | 1988
First Published by | Dalkey Archive Press (Illinois)
First UK Edition | 1989, by Jonathan Cape (London)

It must be a fantasy most, if not all, of us had at some point in our lives: you are the last person left alive on earth. This is what happens to Kate, the protagonist of David Markson's novel *Wittgenstein's Mistress*. Or does it? "In the beginning, sometimes I left messages in the street," the work begins, but the reader never learns anything about what precedes this beginning other than through Kate's interior monologue. The story which unfolds leaves open two basic possibilities: Kate can be trusted, in which case she lost a son in a fire she probably caused, and now is, for some unknown reason, the last representative of humankind. Or she cannot be trusted, in which case she lost a son in a fire she probably caused, and subsequently went mad, now imagining she is the last representative of humankind.

This theme of trust, in others and oneself, and its relationship with language is what fully justifies the book's title. It is, in fact, a fictional interpretation of Wittgenstein's thought, and the turmoil and torment of Kate's voice reads like an uncanny echo of what lies behind Wittgenstein's philosophical texts. As her knowledge of the past and her personal memory becomes ever more unreliable, we realize that there can be no knowledge of the present and no sense of self without it. The brilliance of this underrated author lies in the subtlety with which doubt creeps in and finally engulfs the reader as well. **DS**

The Beautiful Room is Empty

Edmund White

Lifespan | *b.* 1940 (U.S.)
First Published | 1988, by Knopf (New York)
Trilogy | *A Boy's Own Story* (1982), *The Beautiful Room is Empty* (1988), *The Farewell Symphony* (1998)

The second in White's series of autobiographical novels is at once a coming-of-age and a coming out story. The unnamed narrator takes us through the 1950s and 1960s, from the Midwest to New York, from adolescence to young adulthood, and from guilt about his sexuality to acceptance and the politicized defiance of Stonewall. Its cast of characters—friends, family, and lovers—is large, and each is elegantly drawn, while their introduction into the novel has the haphazard, episodic, and unplotted quality of life. Most memorable are the bohemian Maria, a painter and political activist who encourages the narrator in his journey of self-discovery, and Lou, an advertising copywriter and addict, who is also a guru figure. The narrative cruises, like the narrator himself, through a variety of locales, lyrically recalling lust, love, anguish, and excitement, and sketching both the ingrained homophobia of many institutions and the movements toward gay liberation. The book ends with the momentous Stonewall protests, which are not recorded in any newspapers, despite being, as White writes, "the turning point" in the lives of those who participated in them.

While there is much in this book about bodies, it is about the mind too: intellectual as well as sensual excitements, the pleasure of discovering new books, and the coincidences between life and art. **CC**

Foucault's Pendulum

Umberto Eco

Lifespan | *b.* 1932 (Italy)
First Published | 1988
First Published by | Bompiani (Milan)
Original Title | *Il pendolo di Foucault*

Everything is open to interpretation in this novel, which is why we should not overlook the fact that the narrator is the namesake of Dorothea's scholarly husband in *Middlemarch*. Eco's Causabon also wants to rewrite the messy confusion of world history as a single, coherent narrative, but unlike Eliot's Causabon, who is convinced of the truth of his project, Eco's character is well aware that his story is just one version.

Foucault's Pendulum is a vast, sprawling novel all about the desire for meaning. Causabon, Belbo, and Diotallevi work together at Garamond Press, researching a book on the histories of secret societies. In what starts out as an elaborate joke, they feed all the explanations and interpretations they can find into Belbo's computer, and end up recreating the Plan of the Knights Templar. The Plan is the ultimate conspiracy theory: each apparently unconnected historical event takes on new significance in the context of a synthesized story in which everything accounts for everything else. This is a dangerous game, and one that will eventually catch up with its players. Foucault's Pendulum is a novel that has all the elements of a detective fiction apart from the final (dis)closure; an alternately compelling and frustrating narrative in which everything points to a greater truth outside of itself—only that truth is, precisely, the fiction. **KB**

"Above her head was the only stable place in the cosmos . . . and she guessed it was the Pendulum's business, not hers."

◉ The novel was translated into English by William Weaver and published the following year in the U.S. and the UK.

Cat's Eye

Margaret Atwood

Lifespan | *b.* 1939 (Canada)
First Published | 1988
First Published by | McClelland & Stewart (Toronto)
First UK Edition | 1989, by Bloomsbury (London)

Though Margaret Atwood is very well-known for her dystopic *The Handmaid's Tale*, and more recently, the Booker Prize-winning *The Blind Assassin*, *Cat's Eye* is the most celebrated of her books, not only for its vivid descriptions of childhood but because it is accepted as being her most autobiographical work.

The story is of a successful middle-aged painter, Elaine Risley, who is thrust into a reconstruction of her past while attending a retrospective show of her work in Toronto, a city she had fled years earlier to escape painful memories of childhood. At the center of Risley's recollections are the cruelties she suffered from three childhood friends. As a result, Risley developed neurotic habits and depressive impulses, as well as a sharp understanding of the nature of destruction and its relationship to love. Through eloquent portrayals of friendship, the novel explores feminine betrayal and touches on the coercive, conformist society of female acquaintance. Despite her vivid recollections, Risley is aware of how unreliable memory can be, as well as how experience of the present is colored by past events. The story also charts Risley's growing creativity, and in doing so raises a favorite Atwood theme; creativity as a pathway and the way in which creativity is inextricably linked to memory. Emerging stronger for her final adult understanding of herself, Risley rises above the ties that bind her to her past, with the hope of being able to see new light where hitherto there has been only emptiness. **EF**

The Book of Evidence

John Banville

Lifespan | *b.* 1945 (Ireland)
First Published | 1989
First Published by | Secker & Warburg (London)
Guiness Peat Aviation Award | 1989

Freddie Montgomery narrates *The Book of Evidence* from his jail cell as he awaits trial for a murder he committed during a burglary so inexplicable it brings into question his declining mental state. Freddie appears to be a family man, living on a Mediterranean island with his wife and their young son; he steps into a dangerous world, however, when he blackmails a local criminal into loaning him a large sum of money. Inexperienced as a criminal, he returns to Ireland ostensibly to raise the money he owes, leaving his wife and son as human collateral, but shortly into his voyage he "realizes" that really he is fleeing the irretrievable mess he has made. Thus begins his downward spiral.

Freddie's narrative is mesmerizing not least for its mysterious ability to unravel itself. He insistently denies his own agency, which is reflected in his corresponding ghostlike levitation across continents, which ultimately leaves him unable to resist his "drift" into calamity. This inner vacuity engenders a failure to imagine others' inner lives. Insofar as Freddie has no discernible identity, he generalizes his own case to that of others, acting as though they are similarly adrift and external. As he recounts the exasperated and forlorn reactions of his mother and wife to his latest horror, he sees perhaps for the first time that all around him people take seriously the bonds they share with others. The eerie sensation for Freddie—and for readers—is that he may simply be a different sort of beast. **AF**

London Fields

Martin Amis

Lifespan | *b.* 1949 (England)
First Published | 1989
First Published by | Jonathan Cape (London)
First U.S. Edition | 1990, by Harmony (New York)

London Fields is a darkly ironic inversion of the whodunit plot in which the central protagonist, Nicola Six, conspires with the narrator to create two potential "murderees," in an exploration of the possibility of the end of time.

Nicola Six uses the weaknesses of her failed suitors—the vicious, criminally-minded working-class Keith and the gentle, guileless upper-class Guy—to associate herself with a crudely feminized version of nuclear holocaust. The narrative takes place in the final weeks of the twentieth century where ominous yellow clouds threaten an environmental catastrophe and "Faith," the American President's wife, fights for her life. These literal evocations of the end of the world are set within an ambivalent fear of the death of culture. The deeply self-conscious form of the novel itself only reinforces this fear. Keith's slavish dependence upon an impoverishing mass culture is contrasted against mocking references to high literary culture, including a lengthy parody of a passage from Lawrence's *The Rainbow*. Samson Young, the narrator, is slowly dying throughout the novel and by its end he is dead. The novel's closing anxious reference to Samson's more successful doppel-ganger (Mark Asprey or "M.A.") renders the novel's author uncertain. Indeed this uncertainty seems generally characteristic of the novel, as it delves unflinchingly into the darker side of urban life without ever quite reconciling itself to anything as obvious as critique. **NM**

MARTIN AMIS
LONDON FIELDS

"Keith Talent was a very bad guy. You might even say that he was the worst guy. But . . . not the very worst ever."

⊙ This novel is the second in a loose trilogy that begins in 1984 with *Money* and ends in 1995 with *The Information*.

A Prayer for Owen Meany

John Irving

Lifespan | *b.* 1942 (U.S.)
First Published | 1989
First Published by | W. Morrow (New York)
Full Name | John Winslow Irving

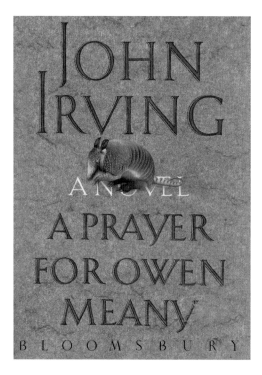

"I am doomed to remember a boy with a wrecked voice . . ."

Just like the narrator in the novel, John Irving's mother always refused to reveal the identity of his father.

Irving's novels characteristically revolve around intricate plots and memorable comic characters, leaving his work balanced somewhere between literary and popular fiction. *A Prayer for Owen Meany* is widely considered to be his finest work.

A rich and deeply comic account of faith, doubt, and memories, the novel also reflects on American culture, and is probably Irving's most autobiographical. In Toronto in 1987, a troubled and past-obsessed John Wheelwright narrates the story of his early life, remembering the time he spent during the 1960s and 70s with his friend Owen Meany. He remembers Owen as a weird, luminous-skinned dwarf, whose underdeveloped vocal chords shaped the sound of his bizarre, nasal voice (which is represented in the text in capital letters) and led him to bear the brunt of many cruel pranks. He also remembers Owen as the person who accidentally killed his mother.

John writes on the first page that Owen Meany is the reason he's a Christian; the rest of the book serves to narrate the story of how and why this happened, of how John discovers his own spiritual faith. The main theme of the book is the relationship between faith and doubt in a world—or at least in the world according to John—in which there is no obvious evidence for the existence of God. The most important symbol is Owen himself, who embodies the relationship between the natural and the supernatural that is at the heart of the novel. For all his strangeness, Owen represents the spiritual condition of humankind; the difference between Owen and most other people is that he knows he is the instrument of God. Owen's fatalistic faith centers on his prophetic knowledge of his own heroic death, for which he prepares all his life. **EF**

Like Water for Chocolate

Laura Esquivel

Each of the twelve chapters of this delightful love story set in Mexico bears the name of a month and opens with a recipe. The combination of ingredients results in a book as earthy and full of flavor as the cuisine it describes. Thus the recipes become as integral a part of *Like Water for Chocolate* as food is to our daily lives. It is the story of Tita, the youngest daughter of the all-female De La Garza family who is forbidden, by the matriarch Mama Elena, to marry because of a Mexican tradition that dictates that the youngest daughter must care for her mother until her death.

Inevitably, Tita falls in love with Pedro, who then decides to marry Tita's ugly older sister, Rosaura, in order to at least stay close to his true love. The marriage marks the start of a twenty-two-year-long conflict, filled with passion, deceit, anger, and love, during which the two lovers are forced to circle one another, their passion unconsummated. In her position as head cook on the family ranch, Tita produces food that is imbued with her own feelings of love and longing—food that affects both everyone who eats it and ultimately the outcome of the story.

The culinary backdrop to the lovers' tale features mouthwatering recipes for Wedding Cake, Quail in Rose Petal Sauce, and Chilies in Walnut Sauce, which, as well as whetting the appetite, provide a metaphorical commentary on the characters. The blending of these recipes with the tale of romance produces a novel with an unusual and distinct flavor, at once vibrant and sensual, funny and passionate, bittersweet and delicious. Like Tita's Chocolate and Three King's Day Bread, this original and compelling tale is hard to resist. **LE**

Lifespan | *b.* 1950 (Mexico)
First Published | 1989
First Published by | Editorial Planeta Mexicana
Original Title | *Como agua para chocolate*

"From that day on, Tita's domain was the kitchen . . ."

⊙ Pictured here in 2001 in her home in New York, Laura Esquivel's first novel was made into a movie, which was released in 1993.

The History of the Siege of Lisbon

José Saramago

Lifespan | *b.* 1922 (Portugal)
First Published | 1989, by Editorial Caminho (Lisbon)
Original Title | *História do Cerco de Lisboa*
Nobel Prize | 1998

As in all his extraordinary novels, here Saramago writes with the absolute minimum of punctuation. The result, something akin to the serial music of Schoenberg, is a reinvention of the historical novel as we know it, which makes most efforts in this direction look clumsy and heavy-handed. By a conjurer's sleight of hand, Saramago transports his reader straight to the heart of another world.

Raimundo Silva, proofreader for a Lisbon publisher, decides on a whim to put a negative into a history text, effectively recasting Portugal's past: during the siege of Lisbon in the twelfth century the Crusaders did *not* come to the help of the king of Portugal against the Saracens. Rather than causing Silva to lose his job, his act of insubordination grabs the attention of his new superior, Dr. Maria Sara, who is fifteen years his junior. She persuades him to actually write this new history, and as he begins to create his revisionist tale the two fall in love. Characteristically, Saramago lets us into their love affair via glimpsed moments of awkwardness, humor, and tenderness.

In the whole of twentieth-century writing, there is no purer example, and certainly no funnier one, of what novelist Christine Brooke-Rose has referred to as "palimpsest history," that is the novel that offers us a rewriting of history and, in so doing, a reinvention of our world. **PT**

The Trick is to Keep Breathing

Janice Galloway

Lifespan | *b.* 1956 (Scotland)
First Published | 1989
First Published by | Polygon (Edinburgh)
MIND/Allen Lane Book of the Year | 1990

A frank account of female psychological crisis, *The Trick is to Keep Breathing* is by turns soul-destroying and bleakly comic. When the lover of the ironically named Joy Stones dies in an accident, she senses his spirit in an omnipresent aromatic cloud, until she finds the overturned, leaking aftershave bottle under the bed. This scene of self-delusion provides a quintessential model of a stereotypical femininity that, in a desperate quest for love and intimacy, is complicit in its own oppression. It is not only Michael who dies, but Joy herself experiences a kind of living death along with him when she becomes socially invisible as the mistress of a still-married man, excluded from the rituals of mourning. In her subsequent anguish, Joy becomes anorexic and literally almost disappears. Her body feels remote and fragmented in an experience of psychic fracture only intensified by her time in a psychiatric unit.

Embodying Joy's breakdown, the novel fragments, dissolves, and reconstitutes itself in myriad of different forms: extracts from magazines, recipes, horoscopes, letters, and self-help books—all the accessories of insecure femininity. In navigating this haphazard textual landscape, we appreciate the destructiveness of Joy's predicament and the absurdly precarious nature of woman's position in the world. Eventually Joy regains a coherent sense of self when she realizes that life, like swimming, is a trick to be learned. **CJ**

The Temple of My Familiar

Alice Walker

Lifespan | *b.* 1944 (U.S.)
First Published | 1989
First Published by | Harcourt Brace (San Diego)
Full Name | Alice Malsenior Walker

A story about remembering and forgetting, this is a novel that seeks to excavate and reclaim the diverse cultural memory of the U.S., a country that is founded upon the ability to forget.

At the heart of the novel is the character Lissie, "the one who remembers everything." Walker's vast epic—a history of the world that sprawls through time—is drawn from Lissie's supernatural capacity to remember. The novel contains a dizzying array of characters and stories, but the novel's cacophony is tuned into a kind of harmony through the work of Lissie's telepathic memory and through the access she grants us to a universal, Jungian unconscious. In redeeming this diversity of memory and experience, the novel points toward a new way of telling the past that does not involve the silencing of marginal voices, but that recognizes instead that being one and whole involves also being many and varied.

Walker might be speaking as Lissie when she says in the acknowledgements to *The Temple* that "it is a pleasure to have always been present." Whatever one makes of this spiritualist bent to the novel, the power of Walker's act of remembrance here—her extraordinary ability to conjure the richness of black diasporic experience—is astonishing. Even if it doesn't bring you into contact with your past lives, reading *The Temple* can change forever the way you hear the singularity of your own voice. **PB**

The Melancholy of Resistance

László Krasznahorkai

Lifespan | *b.* 1954 (Hungary)
First Published | 1989
First Published by | Magveto Kiadó (Budapest)
Original Title | *Az ellenállás menaкóliája*

The Melancholy of Resistance is the first work by the reclusive Hungarian novelist László Krasznahorkai to be translated into English. A small, anonymous, and impoverished Hungarian town is utterly transformed when a traveling circus arrives on a winter's night carrying the desiccated corpse of an enormous whale. After the exhibit is parked in the central square, a wave of suspicious rumors and paranoia sweeps the town, eventually descending into rioting and violence. But the whale is only a Trojan horse. Behind the scenes, a horribly deformed dwarf known as the Prince has ordered the town to be destroyed, and he expertly manipulates the townspeople into a state of fear and nihilism. Struggling against this tide of senseless aggression are Valuska, a naïve young man treated as a kind of village idiot by the locals, and his mentor Mr. Eszter, a strange figure who is obsessed by the idea of retuning a piano to its "original" harmonies using mathematically pure intervals.

This is a deeply strange, unsettling, intensely detailed, and richly atmospheric work. It is a novel of long shadows, bitter cold, and sinister whispers—all rendered in treaclelike prose. Perhaps the novel can be read as an allegory for the upheavals of Eastern Europe; perhaps it is a meditation on folk culture and the formation of social consciousness; perhaps it is an attempt to reclaim the gothic from the clutches of kitsch; perhaps it is all this and more. **SamT**

Remains of the Day

Kazuo Ishiguro

Lifespan | *b.* 1954 (Japan)
First Published | 1989
First Published by | Faber & Faber (London)
Booker Prize | 1989

"What a terrible mistake . . ."

⊙ Time is running out for both Stevens and the British
Empire on the jacket of the first edition, shown here.

Stevens is the butler of thirty-four years at Darlington Hall, right in the dying heart of the British class system. He is precise, rigid, and will broach no effusion. His father, also a butler, taught him that to be great, dignity is key. He staves off any inchoate passions and thwarts any slackening of the cold precision with which he runs the house. Four years after Darlington's death, Stevens travels to persuade the former housekeeper, Miss Kenton, to return to work for a new master, a wealthy American named Farraday. Farraday is as brash and casual as Stevens is staid and frigid. Stevens is not comfortable with "banter." Miss Kenton had been as conscientious as Stevens, but her warmth ran counter to his severity. Their squabbles were petty and endearing, surges sublimating affection. When she reveals her life may have turned out better had she married Stevens, he is deeply shaken, though reticent. This lost possibility goes not only unacted upon but undiscussed.

Stevens' journey to visit Miss Kenton gives him an opportunity to reminisce. He longs for times of pomp and decency and grows melancholic about a world that is gone, a world in which he knew his place. He has become an anachronism, an outdated tradition. Finally he confronts the truth that Lord Darlington, though a perfect gentleman, was a Nazi supporter. Stevens had always been loyal to the point of blindness, but his long overdue lucidity leaves him bereft. He recognizes that his life has been one of misplaced trust and unplaced affection. He finally locates dignity—too late—where he previously ignored it, in Miss Kenton's honesty. This is a breathtaking feat of voice, by turns hilarious and poignant. Ishiguro casts a merciless eye on British society, but never with cruelty, always with affection. **GT**

Billy Bathgate

E. L. Doctorow

Billy's real surname is not Bathgate at all, but then most of Doctorow's characters have at least one pseudonym to hide behind in this evocative romp through 1940s gangland New York. The fifteen-year-old Billy is a Bronx kid who falls in with a gang he has long admired in their shady local operations. His story begins with the account of a grisly murder by the gang of one of their own, to which Billy is a scared and rather green witness. His position is precarious: too young to be a fully fledged gang member but inexplicably favored by the boss, his knowledge is as potentially dangerous as it is intoxicating, but it secures him the alien insider perspective, which ensures that the unfolding events do not feel overfamiliar.

Billy Bathgate is a surprisingly well-handled combination of fresh style and jaded content. All the usual gangland suspects are present: the unpredictable boss and his wise moneyman; the silent hitmen; the beautiful woman shimmering in evening dress; the seedy bars and the shootouts. But what keeps these clichés from becoming oppressive is the youthful wide-eyed naïveté of the narrative voice. Essentially, *Billy Bathgate* is a piece of New York nostalgic mythmaking: a retelling of an idealized rags-to-riches American dream. Despite the references to contemporary cultural items and New York's infrastructure of the period, the dreamlike landscape still feels like a prettily painted façade, which in reality would never have been as safe and easy to negotiate as Billy finds it. Above all, it is for the prose that this novel should be appreciated, as it manages to give Billy's voice the perceptive edge of an uneducated but sharp youngster on the make, a child striving to understand and master the adult world which he admires yet fears. **JC**

Lifespan | *b.* 1931 (U.S.)
First Published | 1989
First Published by | Random House (New York)
PEN/Faulkner Award | 1989

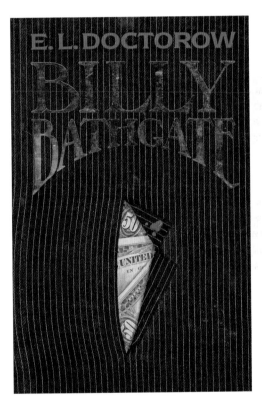

"I was capable, I knew it . . ."

The jacket of the UK edition, published by Macmillan in the same year, was designed by Robert Updegraff.

Moon Palace

Paul Auster

Lifespan | *b.* 1947 (U.S.)
First Published | 1989
First Published by | Viking Press (New York)
Full Name | Paul Benjamin Auster

Moon Palace is a meditation on the obstacles that can frustrate and derail fatherhood: the novel is littered with men ignorant of, overeager for, or ambivalent toward their prospective or actual paternity. The protagonist, Marco Stanley Fogg, has never known his father and was raised by his mother until her death when he was eleven-years-old. He went on to live with his Uncle Victor in a congenial but emotionally casual household. On Victor's death, Fogg inherits his massive book collection, which he sells piece by piece to fend off eviction, homelessness, and ruin. Kitty Wu, the child of an elderly, polygamist father, rescues Fogg, and they fall in love. He finds work recording the life story of Thomas Effing, a bizarre, reclusive painter, but this period of stability is short-lived. Fogg forms a crochety bond with Effing, who becomes an adopted spiritual mentor, and Fogg later discovers that Effing is in fact his paternal grandfather. Through Effing's will, Fogg is finally reunited with his biological father, with whom he shares an intense but brief connection. Kitty's pregnancy takes on symbolic dimensions for Fogg, who sees an opportunity to redeem his own disheartening experiences, but their love cannot survive the mutual sense of betrayal generated by his controlling behavior. Ultimately Fogg is left alone, yet perhaps with a newfound clarity. **AF**

⊙ Paul Auster has lived in Brooklyn, New York since 1980, preferring this district to Manhattan. Here he is at home with his typewriter.

Sexing the Cherry

Jeanette Winterson

Lifespan | *b.* 1959 (England)
First Published | 1989
First Published by | Jonathan Cape (London)
First U.S. Edition | Atlantic (New York)

Set in seventeenth-century London, *Sexing the Cherry* brings to life a tumultuous time of exploration, revolution, and the discovery of a perversely shaped tropical fruit. The Dog Woman, a living mountain of flesh, camps with an assortment of raucously disturbing neighbors, scores of home-bred dogs, and her adopted son Jordan, the child she found in the Thames whom she raises as her own. She is of superhuman scale: by virtue of her extreme size and deeply held ethical convictions, the Dog Woman is a sovereign avenging force in the lawless bustle of her world, achieving by might anything she cannot achieve by argument or persuasion. She comes to lament having named young Jordan after a body of moving water when he falls in love with discovery on seeing the explorer Tradescant's exhibition of bananas. Jordan eventually sets off on an expedition that is as much metaphysical as it is geographical. The final section of the novel, identified as taking place "some years later," reincarnates Jordan and the Dog Woman as a Royal Navy sailor and an environmental scientist-turned-activist, who recapture their primal bond.

Winterson's trademark style is here at its most glittering. With stories of twelve dancing princesses, or "word cleaners," dispatched to cleanse cities' atmospheres of their logomaniacal citizens' pollution, the narrative complicates notions of reality and fantasy until they dissolve. Myth, fable, fairy tale, and history are cannibalized until a new genre is achieved. **AF**

A Disaffection

James Kelman

Lifespan | *b.* 1946 (Scotland)
First Published | 1989
First Published by | Secker & Warburg (London)
James Tait Black Memorial Prize | 1989

In *A Disaffection*, Kelman sets out to liberate a working-class man from the dehumanizing stereotypes of brute ignorance he sees perpetuated in English literature. He reclaims a European intellectual tradition, employing Goethe, Goya, and Hölderlin as symbolic reference points to explore the psychic complexity of an ordinary life. Patrick Doyle is a Glasgow schoolteacher deep in existential crisis. He is a man of great sentiment in a callously unsentimental society, which repudiates sensitivity in men. Feeling subject to an inscrutable authority, Pat's despair is profound and overwhelming.

Pat is alienated from his family by his education, and from his colleagues by his working-class roots. Socially, psychologically, and spiritually dispossessed, Pat's unhappiness is compounded by his love for a married colleague, a relationship doomed by his own pessimism and ineffectuality. For Kelman, tradition is only another vehicle of constraint, and Pat's confinement in this alienating environment pushes him to the verge of paranoid insanity. Whether the policemen at the close of the novel really are threatening to arrest him is beside the point; they also are symbolic of Pat's self-oppression. Kelman invests his working-class subject with the sensibility of a high-brow metaphysical tradition, a subversive union forged in the vernacular of a Scottish city. Without this insurrection, Irvine Welsh could not have given such sensational life to an underclass that challenges a stubbornly class-biased English fiction. **CJ**

The Midnight Examiner

William Kotzwinkle

Lifespan | *b.* 1938 (U.S.)
First Published | 1990
First Published by | Houghton Mifflin (Boston)
First UK Edition | 1990, Black Swan (London)

Howard Halliday is an editor at Chameleon Publications, publisher of *Bottoms, Knockers, Brides Tell All*, and *The Midnight Examiner*. Fuelled by peppermint caffeine tablets and his love for Amber Adams, the beauty editor, he leads his staff on a manic ride through the sleaziest tidepool of publishing.

Howard longs for a proper job. As do his eccentric staff. There is Fernando, the layout artist prone to catatonic seizures and obsessed with drawing his masterpiece, "Big Womans," on Howard's kitchen wall. Nathan Feingold shoots pigeons—and staff—with hot-sauce-tipped darts from his blow-gun. Forrest Crumpacker is hired against his will to head the new religious magazine and forcibly ordained as a mail-order bishop. Hattie Flyer is disfigured by the beauty products their papers sell. Hip O'Hopp, alcohol-sodden, was once a reporter on real newspapers; now he wants to find some Chinese woman to marry so he won't wind up alone on the sidewalk with a bottle. They spend their days turning everything into a lurid headline ("UFO Found in Girl's Uterus"; "I Was A Hooker Until I Met Jesus"). They spend their nights drinking. When erstwhile model Mitzi Mouse "accidentally" shoots a crime lord while filming a porno movie, the forces of Chameleon come to her rescue. Armed with boomerangs, Nathan's blowgun, and a fishing pole—with invaluable assistance from Madame Veronique's hoodoo magic—they go to battle. This is an affectionate slapstick farce, wicked, and impossible to put down. **GT**

The Buddha of Suburbia

Hanif Kureishi

Lifespan | *b.* 1954 (England)
First Published | 1990
First Published by | Faber & Faber (London)
Whitbread First Novel Award | 1990

The Buddha of Suburbia's irreverent comedy often takes political correctness as its target as it follows its seventeen-year-old narrator, Karim Amir, growing up in the suburbs of London in the 1970s. His father Haroon, a civil servant, is encouraged to pursue his less conventional interests by his mistress Eva, and he assumes the status of a New Age guru, a "Buddha" of suburbia. The affair has a devastating effect upon Haroon's English wife, Karim's mother Margaret, who becomes increasingly marginalized and depressed. The support Margaret receives from her sister proves invaluable, and the attention from her brother-in-law quite unhelpful, but their attitudes throw into relief their latently patronizing views. Throughout the disintegration of his parents' marriage, Karim is bolstered by the support of his friends. Jamilla, a strong-willed and confident young woman, challenges many of the traditions of her Asian upbringing and her experimental sexual relationship with Karim continues after her engagement to another man. Eva's son Charlie is also a significant figure. Their sexual relationship opens Karim's eyes to the uninhibited zeitgeist but does not ultimately lead beyond friendship. The novel engages with many of the nebulous aspects of identity that are negotiated during the transition into adulthood. Karim experiments with drugs, explores his bisexuality and considers the interrelationship of the two histories that have contributed to his sense of Englishness. The novel was adapted into a successful BBC drama. **JW**

"And you'd get point A followed by points B and C, and on the one hand F, and on the other foot G, until you could see the whole alphabet ..."

◉ Hanif Kureishi has often courted controversy, spurning both traditional moral stances and the pieties of political correctness.

Possession

A. S. Byatt

Lifespan | *b.* 1936 (England)
First Published | 1990
First Published by | Chatto & Windus (London)
Booker Prize | 1990

"The librarian tiptoed away…"

◉ The use of a Pre-Raphaelite painting on the cover of Byatt's
novel refers to the historical period of its "story-within-a-story."

Possession, Byatt's fifth novel, received international critical and public acclaim. It is a literary mystery novel, a pastiche that mixes the genres of the campus novel, the romance, biography, the detective novel, the historical novel, and the fairy tale. Like many other contemporary works of fiction, the novel tells a story set in the present day that discovers a historical mystery. Roland Michell is a struggling and barely employed academic who specializes in the study of the fictional nineteenth-century poet, Randolph Henry Ash (a Robert Browning figure). Michell discovers a secret correspondence between Ash and a less successful poetess, Christabel LaMotte. Keeping it secret from the Ash aficionados that he works with (who he fears would take credit for his discovery), he cautiously persuades a LaMotte expert, Maud Bailey, to assist him. Together, they discover that an intense relationship existed between Ash and LaMotte, and as they make these discoveries their own relationship also develops.

Byatt reproduces not only the correspondence of the two poets, but also substantial examples of Ash's and LaMotte's nineteenth-century poetry. The novel is committed to the forensic fictionalization of history. Moreover, it also attacks the integrity of biography and historiography. The novel's "Epilogue" presents an emotionally powerful if brief exchange between Ash and his illegitimate daughter who believes her father is dead. The exchange is important, not only in its content, but because Michell, Bailey, and all the other biographers, scholars, and historians that follow will never have access to this unrecorded piece of history. The novel suggests that biography and historiography are but shadows on a cave wall in comparison to "real" history's shining light. **VC-R**

Like Life

Lorrie Moore

Like Life met with excellent reviews on its publication, and it is no secret that Moore crafts stories like a gem cutter wields a chisel. In this collection of eight short stories, most take place in the Midwest, a noticeably innocent swath of America less prone to self-examination than, say, to snowmobiling and deer hunting. "There were gyms but no irony . . . people took things literally, without drugs." These are stories about people who watch, baffled, as life seems to go easily for others. "Sometimes she thought she was just trying to have fun in life, and other times she realized she must be terribly confused."

Mary is dating two men. It all seems daring and utterly modern. And of course that's the impression she gives in postcards to envious friends. But she is slowly unraveling, wearing only white and sitting in public parks reading "bible poetry." Harry is a playwright who, through naïve enthusiasm and hunger for success, gives his life story, his life's work, to a predatory television producer over drinks. Zoe is a teacher at a small university in rural Illinois, a land so blond that just because she has dark hair she is presumed to be from Spain. She tries to make a home, like others do, and buys an oriental rug. The salesgirl tells her the pictograms mean "Peace" and "Eternal Life." But how can she be sure? How can she ever know that they don't in fact say, for instance, "Bruce Springsteen"? Plagued with uncertainty, she has no choice but to return the rug.

These are characters who are fragile, hilarious, and heartbreaking in their familiarity. The title of Moore's second collection of stories—*Like Life*—could hardly be more apt. We laugh until it catches in our throats, out of recognition, but never mockery. **GT**

Lifespan | *b.* 1957 (U.S.)
First Published | 1990
First Published by | Knopf (New York)
Given Name | Marie Lorena Moore

"'Is this a TV show?'"

Moore's stories are set in the Midwest, a part of the U.S. where in the author's words, "there were gyms but no irony."

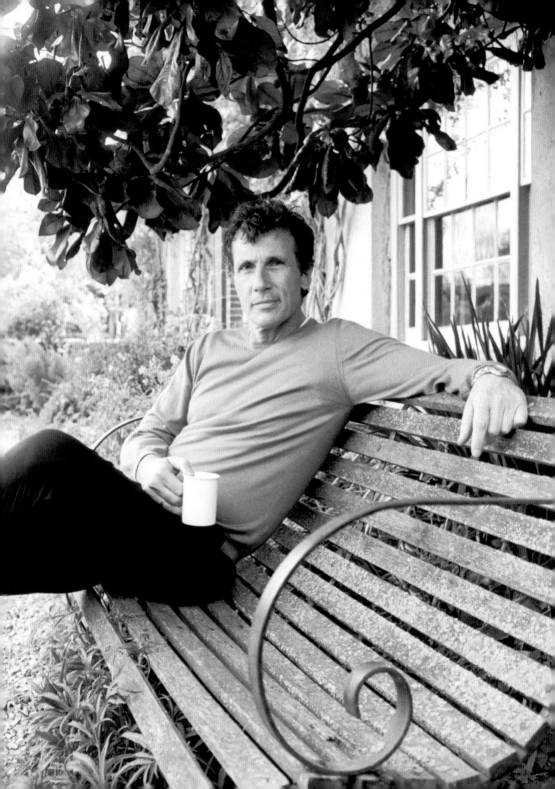

A Home at the End of the World

Michael Cunningham

Lifespan | b. 1952 (U.S.)
First Published | 1990
First Published by | Farrar, Straus & Giroux (New York)
First UK Edition | 1991, by Hamish Hamilton

This is a contemporary fairy tale that examines the fallout when a trio of urbanites try to reinvent the nuclear family without succumbing to the propriety or volatility that dominated their childhood homes. The triangle brings together a pair of boyhood best friends (Jonathan, who is gay, and the bewildered, malleable Bobby) with Jonathan's straight best friend, Clare, who initially adopts Bobby as a cultural charity case when he's freshly arrived in New York and eventually winds up carrying his child. On their way home from burying Jonathan's father, the three have a scorching argument that uncovers Clare's pregnancy and catalyzes a wild-eyed, occasionally jealous but unifying desire to form a family. At the young age of nine, Bobby had seen his older brother, Carlton, die in a shocking accident. The irrepressible energy of the party planned for that evening, the sense of endless possibility shared between the brothers, renders Carlton's death heavily significant of a vast spectrum of failed promise. Bobby's enduring allegiance to Carlton gives him the feeling that he is living for two and, along with Jonathan (who also lost a sibling, albeit unborn) and Clare, he aims to create a haven from suffering, but is unsurprised when he ultimately loses his grasp. **AF**

◐ *A Home at the End of the World* was Cunningham's first novel; he is here photographed at Charleston in Sussex in 2001.

The Things They Carried

Tim O'Brien

Lifespan | b. 1946 (U.S.)
First Published | 1990
First Published by | Houghton Mifflin (Boston)
First UK Edition | Collins (London)

Though this Vietnam War text is purportedly a work of fiction, O'Brien, and his first-person narrator "Tim O'Brien," never stop playing with readers' assumptions about the possibility of achieving truth through careful description. O'Brien earlier wrote a Vietnam memoir (*If I Die in a Combat Zone*, 1973), but here he self-consciously probes the conventions that we typically rely on to distinguish fiction from memoir and fact from interpretation. The copyright page states that the book's "…incidents, names, and characters are imaginary," but it faces O'Brien's (or is it "O'Brien"'s?) "loving" dedication to "the men of Alpha Company," a striking juxtaposition once we realize these "men" are the book's primary characters. This tension permeates the text as "Tim O'Brien" wrestles with how best to convey his experience of Vietnam: must a war story literally be true in order to be a "true war story"? O'Brien's narrative goes from profound sorrow to self-mockery to dark humor and back again. This sense of narrative uncertainty creates for readers a feeling of anxiety and mistrust that O'Brien indicates was the existential condition of American soldiers fighting in Vietnam. O'Brien uses various mismatches between experience and description against his readers, who may find themselves longing for the deceptive luxury and easy comfort of uncritical narrative the way "O'Brien" and his fellow soldiers long for home. **AF**

The Music of Chance

Paul Auster

Lifespan | *b.* 1947 (U.S.)
First Published | 1990
First Published by | Viking Press (New York)
Movie Adaptation | 1993

A sizable inheritance from his absentee father allows Jim Nashe to do his own disappearing act, leaving his daughter in his sister's care when he abruptly quits his job as a firefighter to drive aimlessly about the country in a brand-new Saab. Though he envisions liberation in living unfettered by any meaningful relation to others, Nashe's experience of this life leaves him in a curious state of numbness. When Nashe sees a badly beaten kid wandering along the side of a road, he goes against his instincts and offers him a ride. Jack Pozzi is a poker hustler trying to make his way to the mansion of an odd couple of millionaires he's hoping to take for all they are willing to put up. When the unthinkable happens—through study, luck, or cheating, the millionaires emerge victorious—Nashe and Pozzi surrender their freedom to pay back their debts. Through Nashe and Pozzi's opposite reactions to their shared fate, Auster explores the concept of freedom itself and whether self-determination is necessary or sufficient to achieve it. Despite Nashe's sense of emptiness while he had the luxury of being completely non-responsible, his captivity and forced labor reacquaints him with the value of deliberate action. Physical labor brings him not despair but a new self-possession; rather than deludedly chasing self-realization down the interstate, Nashe creates it himself. Pozzi, however, bristles with resentful rage until he sets off a chain reaction of retribution that eventually destroys both of their worlds. **AF**

Stone Junction

Jim Dodge

Lifespan | *b.* 1945 (U.S.)
First Published | 1990
First Published by | Atlantic Monthly Press (N.Y.)
Full Title | *Stone Junction: An Alchemical Potboiler*

Stone Junction chronicles the life and times of one Daniel Pearce, born in 1966 to Analee, a sixteen-year-old runaway. Dodge's novel is a vibrant, anti-authoritarian romp that combines page-turning urgency with a serious examination of the margins of American society. From a remote shack in the wilderness, Daniel and Analee fall in with an organization known as AMO (an Alliance of Magicians and Outlaws). As Daniel grows up, he is placed into the custody of a series of wonderfully eccentric teachers who provide an unorthodox education. He is taught meditation, outdoor survival, sex, drugs, safe-cracking, impersonation, and poker. However, a second plotline interrupts Daniel's learning curve in the form of a whodunit. His mother is suspiciously killed on a mission for AMO when he is aged just fourteen. The two narratives combine when Daniel learns the art of invisibility from the Great Volta (one of the prime suspects in Analee's death). At the novel's climax, Daniel is sent to steal a mysterious, six-pound diamond from a maximum security compound. But like all the best mysteries, things are not as they seem. In Dodge's own words, *Stone Junction* is an "alchemical potboiler"—a defiant celebration of magic and the outlaw tradition in an age where living and communicating in the margins becomes increasingly difficult. **SamT**

◉ Dodge in a suitably zany pose in 1984—his novel *Stone Junction* was described by author Thomas Pynchon as "a nonstop party."

Vertigo

W. G. Sebald

Lifespan | *b.* 1944 (Germany), *d.* 2001 (England)
First Published | 1990
First Published by | Eichborn (Frankfurt)
Original Title | *Schwindel, Gefühle*

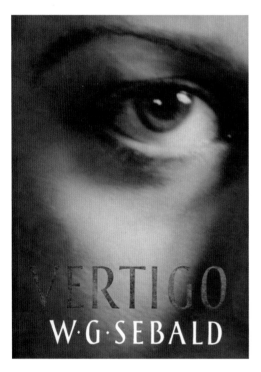

"... he tried to persuade Mme. Gherardi to believe in love ..."

◉ An image by Czech photographer Josef Sudek makes a seductive and mysterious cover for Sebald's subtly vertiginous narrative.

This was the first novel published by the now highly acclaimed author, W. G. Sebald. Similar to his other works, *Vertigo* defies generic conventions, combining elements of fiction, reportage, travel writing, autobiography, and the photographic essay to create a distinctive literary form that is without precedent. Divided into four parts, the novel follows the narrator's perambulations through Italy and southern Germany. We accompany the narrator on a spiritual pilgrimage whose purpose is to raise the dead so that the living might interrogate them on the meaning of life.

Although highly discursive and meandering, several key themes emerge over the course of the narrator's descriptions of the lives, loves, and losses of Marie Henri Beyle (Stendhal), Giacomo Casanova, and Franz Kafka, among many others. Chief among these themes is the chimerical and unreliable nature of memory, its tendency to invent and even obscure the past as much as it recalls it. The mastery of *Vertigo* is in its skillful interbraiding of multiple narrative strands, its breathtaking revelations of the mysterious coincidences and points of crossover that bind together disparate lives, times, and places. While there is a decidedly sinister ambience evoked by the hallucinatory journeys of the narrator, there are also moments of unmistakable playfulness and humor, an underappreciated facet of Sebald's prose.

Vertigo is enhanced and made more enigmatic by the numerous photographs of paintings, diagrams, drawings, and documents that are interspersed throughout. Despite their obvious differences, one cannot shake the sense that these images are joined together by an invisible thread of meaning. *Vertigo* offers the impression of a finely woven pattern that connects seemingly random experiences. **CG-G**

Vineland

Thomas Pynchon

Finally emerging seventeen years after the dark complexities of *Gravity's Rainbow*, Pynchon's *Vineland* was a disappointment to many critics, and it remains Pynchon's most misunderstood and underrated novel. However it is also Pynchon's most accessible and rigorously focused work—a dazzling political examination of two generations of American life.

The novel is set in 1984 (a date that is surely no accident) in the fictional town of Vineland, California —a place of contradictions where the natural beauty of the redwoods is set against the neon glare of the mall. Pynchon traces out a complex family triangle involving Zoyd, an aging hippie who survives on fraudulently obtained mental disability checks, his estranged wife Frenesi, a former member of a radical film collective, and their free-spirited teenage daughter, Prairie. The story chronicles the hard, techno-political realities of Reagan's America during the 1980s and the legacy of a revolutionary generation that has now grown old—its losses, its betrayals, its complicity with power. In many respects, the novel functions as kind of companion piece to *The Crying of Lot 49*, revisiting a generation that had promised so much until its innocence was spoiled.

Vineland bears many of the hallmarks of Pynchon's earlier, more acclaimed work—unexpected detours to fantastical, faraway places, and an oddball cast of punks, martial artists, TV addicts, and ghosts. It is densely packed with improbable erudition and linguistic inventiveness (including some wonderful contemporary Californian slang). What is unique about *Vineland* though is its sense of clarity and precision. It is a sustained, cohesive, and penetrating study of the relationship between the individual and the state, between those who wield power and those who choose to resist it. **SamT**

Lifespan | *b.* 1937 (U.S.)
First Published | 1990
First Published by | Little, Brown & Co. (Boston)
Full Name | Thomas Ruggles Pynchon

"He groaned out of bed . . . Zoyd was out of smokes."

⊙ In *Vineland* Pynchon returns to a modern American setting, after the historical European excursions of *V.* and *Gravity's Rainbow*.

Amongst Women

John McGahern

Lifespan | *b.* 1934 (Ireland)
First Published | 1990
First Published by | Faber & Faber (London)
Irish Times Literary Award | 1991

John McGahern's lyrical, resonant, and subtle meditations on rural Irish life have a long and loving gestation, appearing every ten or twelve years. *Amongst Women* tells the story of power relations within a rural Irish family, set within the history and the thwarted promise of the independent Irish state.

Michael Moran, an old IRA man who fought in the Anglo-Irish War, feels utterly alienated and detached from the independent Ireland that he helped to create. Disdaining a part in the new political or social order, he sits in patriarchal dominance at the center of his big farmhouse, Great Meadow. Luke, the oldest son, flees to England, away from Moran's overbearing authority. His other children, three daughters and another son, regularly return to Great Meadow. Moran is deeply loved by his daughters and his second wife, Rose, but his mood swings and desperately fragile pride have long impeded them and deflated their aspirations. He holds down his daughters in order to protect the suffocating unity of the family. The struggle between wife, daughters, and patriarch is compellingly recreated, as Moran's grip on power weakens alongside his grip on life. For all his authoritarianism and implacable surliness, Moran is a tormented, complex, vulnerable man in existential crisis. The story is laced with poetic language and generously humane depictions of frailty. It is at once an expression of a postcolonial condition, generational change, and shifting gender relations in rural Catholic Ireland. **RMcD**

Get Shorty

Elmore Leonard

Lifespan | *b.* 1925 (U.S.)
First Published | 1990
First Published by | Delacorte Press (New York)
Movie Adaptation | 1995

Hollywood has been a significant influence on Leonard's writing, not simply because he began his career as a writer of westerns and many of his subsequent novels have been turned into mostly unsuccessful motion pictures. Nor can this influence be measured in terms of the cinematic references that pepper his novels; long before Tarantino, Leonard's characters discussed movies with passion and humor. Movies pervade Leonard's novels insofar as his characters see themselves as performing roles—killer, lover, robber, cop—and their relationship to these roles has been shaped by their interaction with the movies.

When Chili Palmer, a debt collector and one in a long line of "no-bullshit" Leonard heroes, follows a dry cleaner who has "scammed" an airline and absconded to Hollywood, he agrees to chase up another bad debt, this time owed by a Hollywood producer. Quickly realizing that everyone is playing a role, Chili reinvents himself as a producer, pitching a version of what has occurred so far in the novel. Above all, the resulting scam, which involves drug dealers, limousine drivers, and movie players, is handled with a comic but assured touch. In an irony worthy of Leonard himself, the movie version of *Get Shorty*, a story about the stupidity and vacuity of Hollywood filmmakers, became the best and most successful of all Leonard adaptations. **AP**

⊙ John Travolta plays phony producer Chili Palmer in Barry Sonnenfeld's acclaimed movie version of Leonard's scam novel.

Wise Children

Angela Carter

Lifespan | *b.* 1940 (England), *d.* 1992
First Published | 1991
First Published by | Chatto & Windus (London)
Given Name | Angela Olive Stalker

🔾 Illegitimate twins, Dora and Nora, convey "What a joy it
is to dance and sing" on the cover of Carter's last novel.

This joyously exuberant unraveling of purity, legitimacy, and other cultural fantasies almost leaps off the page. *Wise Children* gives a sweeping account of the intermingled Chance and Hazard families, bursting at the seams with twins, secret identities, and performers at every cultural "level" from Shakespeare to strip shows. Narrator Dora Chance and her twin Nora form the families' link, though they are members simultaneously of both and neither. They were born from an affair between the starving young actor Melchior Hazard, who would go on to become a celebrated emblem of Shakespearean performance, and the maid who worked at the south London boarding house he then called home. The young woman died during childbirth and Hazard had long since disappeared, so the proprietress of the boarding house, Mrs. Chance, raised the girls as Chances while picking up various other "family members" along the way. After a lifetime spent performing together with Nora in innumerable vaudeville acts, Dora attempts to assemble the highlights of the years they spent within fluctuating proximity of their father's life, always somehow still on the wrong side of the river.

Wise Children celebrates the joys and vicissitudes of existence, from the pleasure of song and dance to the libidinous cravings that can attack family loyalties, creating a carnivalesque atmosphere. Hazard stands for all dominant cultural groups insofar as he must maintain at least the appearance of pure breeding. The world of vaudeville, however, is not the opposite of this dynamic so much as the cacophonous enormity of everything banished from its realm where relations are endlessly building and destroying themselves. *Wise Children* gleefully documents the comic hybridizing force of worlds colliding. **AF**

Señor Vivo and the Coca Lord

Louis de Bernières

Perhaps better known for the cult success of *Captain Corelli's Mandolin*, de Bernières had already produced a vivid trilogy set in a mythical South American country, a composite of reality and the author's fertile imagination. This is the second book, preceded by *The War of Don Emmanuel's Nether Parts* and followed by the third, *The Troublesome Offspring of Cardinal Guzman*. Each novel is self-contained, while at the same time including characters and settings from the others. The charm of this novel in particular lies in its protagonist, the innately heroic Dionisio Vivo, an idealistic university lecturer who writes impassioned letters to a paper in protest against the corrupt coca trade and the disintegrating effect it is having on his society. The result, described with more than a dash of macabre humor, is that several corpses are deposited on his front lawn as warnings. A cast of characters, which includes a president with a cat for a daughter, Dionisio's quirky girlfriend, and a senile angel, will charm you with their inventiveness. The shocking, funny, moving, and horrific moments of the characters' lives are all recorded with a kind of matter-of-fact gentleness.

While de Bernières employs elements of magic realism, his characters are grounded in the earthy realities of their situations and they are handled with a cinematic intensity. Dionisio's idealism has consequences, which allow de Bernières to deepen his character with an unusual blend of vitality and melancholy and to create an impressively three-dimensional literary hero. Though dark subject matter often makes de Bernières an unforgiving writer, the sheer panache and color of his people, and his black comedy, make the upsetting moments both forceful and fair—an apt counterpoint to the injustices that lie at the core of this novel. **AC**

Lifespan | *b.*1954 (England)
First Published | 1991
First Published by | Secker & Warburg (London)
Original Language | English

De Bernières' experiences in Colombia while teaching English strongly influenced this and the other two novels in the trilogy.

Downriver

Iain Sinclair

Lifespan | *b.* 1943 (Wales)
First Published | 1991
First Published by | Paladin (London)
James Tait Black Memorial Prize | 1991

With its alternative subtitle *The Vessels of Wrath*, Sinclair's ferocious second novel leads us back from the banks of the Thames across the remnant scars of Conservative under-investment amid central London. Sinclair dramatizes the efforts of a posse of documentary filmmakers struggling to piece together a visual archive of Thatcher's legacy. In the process, his typical self-consciousness as a surveyor of urban decline peels forth in a series of demotic confessions and paranoiac concessions—all angled toward the task of developing a satire on the deprivation he so despises. In *Downriver* London emerges as an uncanny, almost human presence: a terrain radically uncoordinated with its publicized image. Sinclair's account of a peculiarly conspiratorial metropolis influences the very style by which he conveys the city's overlapping realities. Stark images are rapidly superimposed; shock impressions predominate, as his inquests face a terrain where the "occult logic of 'market forces' dictated a new geography."

Stalking through inner-London's world of workaday routine, Sinclair remains a compulsive fabulist of factual events—one ever concerned about his own ability to scrutinize the improbable behind the seemingly unremarkable. Sinclair's visionary rhetoric of frenzied distrust serves to tear open the capital's "urban texture," fixing on East End zones of social discrimination, alienation, and decline as part of a relentless examination of local community environments. **DJ**

Regeneration

Pat Barker

Lifespan | *b.* 1943 (England)
First Published | 1991
First Published by | Viking (London)
First U.S. Edition | 1992, by E. P. Dutton (New York)

With the "Regeneration Trilogy" Pat Barker extended the formal and thematic frontiers of contemporary historical fiction. This first book is a psychologically penetrating novel which revises the account of events at Craiglockhart War Hospital, Edinburgh, in 1917, involving the neurologist Dr. Rivers and traumatized soldier and poet Siegfried Sassoon.

In her "Author's Note" Barker warns, "Fact and Fiction are so interwoven in this book that it may help the reader to know what is historical and what is not." Yet it is precisely her braiding together of actuality and dramatization that sustains arresting insights for the reader. She uses the novel to trace the progression of Sassoon's complicated commitment to pacifism, and to investigate the cruelty of institutional psychiatry epitomized by Dr. Lewis Yealland's horrific techniques for treating so-called hysterical disorders. When evoking the scenes of that brutality, Barker's style remains impersonal and taut. The navigation between pared-down dialogue and interior reflection invites an uneasy sympathy for Rivers. The reader is enticed to collude with his struggle to reform the clinical approach to "shell-shock." But the fluctuating affects of this disorder are everywhere inscribed upon the inhospitable social landscape that unfolds for sufferers like Sassoon on their return. *Regeneration* reveals the Great War's indelible and manifold legacy and compels us to reexamine the relationship between public authority and personal memory. **DJ**

Typical

Padgett Powell

Lifespan | *b.* 1952 (U.S.)
First Published | 1991
First Published by | Farrar, Straus & Giroux (New York)
Original Language | English

One of the most inventive writers to emerge in New Southern Writing—hailed by his peers, from Donald Barthleme to Saul Bellow—Padgett Powell takes the reader on a stylistic tour de force in *Typical*. The voice of America is the true subject of these stories, in particular the language of the South. It is a South of long-neck Buds and shotguns in the back windows of pickup trucks; of the peculiar joy in defeat of backwater trailer parks. Powell captures the music in the language, colorful to the point of poetry.

From the stream of self-excoriation of the narrator in "Typical," who has come to terms with being "a piece of crud ... an asshole" to Aunt Humpy in "Letter from a Dogfighter's Aunt, Deceased," who corrects the grammar of her trash family from beyond the grave, Powell explores the soul of a South too complacent to rise again. In "Florida" and "Texas" he paints entire emotional landscapes with lists. In "Mr. Irony" the writer searches for his voice under the tutelage of Mr. Irony, "a therapist of self-deprecation." "Limn with humility," Mr. Irony extols. The narrator—the writer—ultimately fails to master irony and absents himself from the story. "Dr. Ordinary" where every sentence begins with "He found ..." and "General Rancidity" where each sentence begins with "He ran ..." are bravura performances. That such technical acrobatics rise above mere novelty to create sublime explorations of self knowledge without regret is a testament to Powell's genius. **GT**

Mao II

Don DeLillo

Lifespan | *b.* 1936 (U.S.)
First Published | 1991
First Published by | Viking (New York)
PEN/Faulkner Award | 1992

Mao II adopts the title of a Warhol portrait and brings to the foreground the role of images in the interdependence of individualism, social traditions, and terrorism. This story of reclusive writer Bill Gray's progressively deeper political involvement opens with a mass wedding conducted by Reverend Sun Myung Moon. The narrative perspective continually vacillates between the soon-to-be-spouses and invited, or interloping, observers in the stands. Bill has spent many years in virtual hiding, holed up in a compound with his affairs managed by a disconcertingly insistent fan-turned-executor. When Bill agrees to meet portrait photographer Brita, and later to act in support of a poet kidnapped in Beirut, he stops interminably writing, reworking, and unwriting the same narrative. His emergence ultimately leads to direct involvement with the poet's struggle.

Mao II is preoccupied with the figure of the terrorist, particularly in relation to the isolated writer, and the dynamics of crowds. In the wake of Salman Rushdie's metaphorical abduction by Ayatollah Khomeini's 1989 fatwa, the writer is no longer the artistic counterpart of the terrorist, but also his potential adversary or victim. Bill's fiercely guarded isolation, in part an act of resistance against the culture of consent in late capitalist America, becomes more like a terrorist abduction of the self. In the process the writer's and the terrorist's shared but unrealizable dream of complete autonomy is exposed. **AF**

Time's Arrow

Martin Amis

Lifespan | *b.* 1949 (England)
First Published | 1991
First Published by | Jonathan Cape (London)
First U.S. Edition | Harmony (New York)

MARTIN AMIS

TIME'S ARROW

"'Dug,' I join in. 'Oo y'rrah?'"

⬤ Time runs backward in this novel, allowing a doctor to
bring Holocaust victims back to life and restore their health.

Here Martin Amis attempts the impossible twice. Not only is this novel written backwards, with events unfolding against the chronological sequence without explanation, it also includes, centrally, a comic treatment of the Holocaust. If this is an allegory of twentieth-century history, it has the same shock value as works such as Swift's *Modest Proposal* or Orwell's *Animal Farm*.

Amis is brilliant and original in his language. The intriguing prose tantalizes and amuses, describing the astonishing events of a life that goes from modern America back to birth in the Germany of 1916. The "hero," who has many names, starts as a boy who takes everything, including Hitler, in his stride. He is so naïve that he cheerfully goes about frontline action as a doctor in Auschwitz, and accepts, with only mild surprise, relationships that begin with a terminal row and end with the woman retreating into girlhood. The madness of reversed time is somehow a symbol of his numbed inability to become morally or emotionally involved in anything. And it's all confusingly funny.

For instance: whenever the "hero" buys anything he seems to come out richer (because the money travels the wrong way) and people begin meals by "dirtying the plates." In a reversal of the Holocaust, he sees himself as rescuing the Jews in the camps because he takes the gas-pills out of the chambers and supervises the exit of the prisoners, their re-clothing, fattening up, and journey on the trains that will take them homeward. This Final Solution in reverse ends up with happy communities of unpersecuted European Jews. This inversion has a bizarre effect on the reader: everything appears normal as well as mad, but above all, our relationship to our own pasts and responsibilities is seen under a strange new light. **PM**

American Psycho

Bret Easton Ellis

American Psycho is, above all, an ugly book. It is an extraordinarily graphic description of obscene violence, which is spliced with reviews of music by Phil Collins and Whitney Houston, and with endless, repetitive descriptions of Eighties main street fashion. The novel's protagonist, Patrick Bateman—brother of Sean Bateman who was featured in Ellis' previous novel, *The Rules of Attraction*—is a psychopath who also works on Wall Street. He conducts business meetings, goes to upmarket restaurants, and commits rape and murder. The novel registers no difference between these activities. Depravity, it suggests, is so finely woven into the fabric of contemporary life that it is no longer possible to see it or depict it, to know when capitalism stops and brutalization begins. Descriptions of nouvelle cuisine and Armani jackets are as pornographic, here, as descriptions of anal rape. Pop music, movies, and fashion—these are so complicit in a murderous culture that they become part of the murder.

There is no attempt to take a moral stance on Bateman, or the culture to which he belongs. But the extremity of the violence, coupled with the uninflected way in which it is described, produces a strange, ethereal dimension to the writing, which is as close as the novel can come to an ethics, or to an aesthetic. As Bateman struggles to understand why he has been summoned to this particular damnation, he is unable to formulate to himself his own misery, or his own confusion. As a result, the novel produces a longing for ethical certainty, for some kind of clear perspective on a culture that has become unreadable, and unthinkable. This is a longing that speaks of a kind of innocence, even in the midst of depravity, and for this reason alone, *American Psycho* must continue to be read. **PB**

Lifespan | *b.* 1964 (U.S.)
First Published | 1991
First Published by | Vintage (New York)
First UK Edition | Picador (London)

"'She's essentially daring me.'"

⊙ The inhumane face attached to the Wall Street suit on the jacket of the novel epitomizes the character of the novel's serial killer.

Wild Swans

Jung Chang

Lifespan | *b.* 1952 (China)
First Published | 1991
First Published by | HarperCollins (London)
Full Title | *Wild Swans: Three Daughters of China*

"With luck, one could fall in love after getting married."

⊙ The author at home in London in 2005. *Wild Swans* is still banned in mainland China and has sold over 10 million copies elsewhere.

In *Wild Swans*, Jung Chang recounts how three generations of her family's women fared through the political storms of China in the twentieth century. Her grandmother, whose feet were bound according to ancient Chinese custom, was the concubine of an Emperor. Her mother struggled during Mao's revolution before rising, like Chang's father, to a prominent position in the Communist Party, only to be denounced during the Cultural Revolution. Chang herself was brought into the world a Communist and also followed Mao enthusiastically, before the harsh excesses of his policies and the destructive purges that crushed millions of innocent Chinese, including her parents, created the shadow of doubt. Working as a "barefoot doctor," Chang saw the worst effects of Mao's rule and eventually fled to the United Kingdom in 1978.

This personal memoir is written in strong yet delicate prose. An important work in terms of its examination of the effects of grand historical movements on the human soul, as well as a vivid depiction of life in twentieth-century China, it covers a particularly eventful period of Chinese history. It traces the demise of Imperial China, the Japanese wartime occupation, the rise of the nationalist movement, the civil war between the nationalist Kuomintang and the Communists, the Communist takeover, Mao's Great Leap Forward (starving tens of millions to death), and finally the Cultural Revolution, which uprooted the nation's identity and broke its collective spirit. This is a revelatory book, and readers must constantly remind themselves that they are reading a work of fact rather than one of fiction—which at some points is a terrible thought. **EF**

Arcadia

Jim Crace

Visions of a garden-city, of a pastoral idyll preserved at the core of a modern commercial center, hold Jim Crace's aging millionaire in thrall. Alone with his fortune on his eightieth birthday, Victor resolves to pay tribute to the vibrant yet rugged fruit market at the city's heart by building a vaulted glass enclosure as an epitaph in place of its current traders. The quest to realize this architectural ambition is overseen by a reporter who with sympathy recounts the way Victor's idyllic monument is eventually overturned by the trading community it romanticizes, and with disastrous consequences. Crace offers a shrewd yet sensitive commentary on a wishful effort to resuscitate an urban environment simply by refurbishing its visible topography within the confines of nostalgia.

If Crace can be seen as ironically appropriating certain pastoral conventions, he does so to evoke a time-honored contest between landscape and redevelopment, rurality and commercial modernity. *Arcadia's* voyage unfolds in a pristine style that remains as sensuous as it is polemical; drawing us into that "amiable and congested tension of the streets which kept the traffic and pedestrians apart," Crace's evanescent descriptions immerse the reader in a bustling marketplace whose aestheticization he then later interrogates. As elsewhere in his oeuvre, Crace furnishes an anonymous setting in such a way that personifies its physical terrain: it is as though this fictional place itself is auditioned from the outset as a fellow protagonist among the novel's events, events whose volatile succession the marketplace does ultimately survive, but scarcely unscathed. **DJ**

Lifespan | *b.* 1946 (England)
First Published | 1992
First Published by | Jonathan Cape (London)
E. M. Forster Award | 1992

"'The tallest buildings throw the longest shadows . . .'"

⬥ In the year of *Arcadia's* publication, Crace was awarded the E. M. Forster Award by the American Academy of Arts and Letters.

Hideous Kinky

Esther Freud

This novel is semi-autobiographical and based on the author's own experience of traveling with her mother Bernadine Coverley, in North Africa, between the ages of four and six. Weaving between the vivid descriptions of life on the move, the desert, and its cast of exotic characters, is a deeply moving and poignant tale of what it's like, as a child, to be part of an unconventional family. For Freud herself, daughter of the artist Lucien, and great-granddaughter of the famed Sigmund, childhood was unlikely ever to be normal. The novel beautifully evokes the bohemian life that she and her sister, the fashion designer Bella Freud, unwittingly witnessed as children, while all the while craving a more stable upbringing.

Hideous Kinky is the story of Julia, a hippie mother, and her daughters Lucia and Bea, who travel to Morocco. Early on in the trip the girls decide that many of the sights they witness are best described in the words of the title. Events are narrated through the voice of five-year-old Lucia, who observes their exotic foreign surroundings with mixed emotions. One moment she is seduced by the vast desert skies and the magic of colorful street markets, but the next she is craving a normal, English upbringing, complete with childhood staples such as regular school and set bedtimes. As their mother immerses herself in Sufism, in her quest for personal fulfillment and spiritual enlightenment, the girls' longing for stability amidst the shifting desert sands intensifies. In this, her first novel, Freud not only paints a vivid and compelling picture of a country that was the Mecca of the hippie movement of the 1970s, but also tells a touching story about childhood, with a simplicity and lightness, which both moves and enchants. **LE**

Lifespan | *b.* 1963 (England)
First Published | 1992
First Published by | Hamish Hamilton (London)
Movie Adaptation | 1998

'Fresh and clear, funny and sharp'
– Margaret Forster in the *Spectator*

HIDEOUS KINKY

The image on the cover of the Penguin edition, shown here, was drawn by the author's father, Lucien Freud.

Esther Freud, pictured here in 2004, was named as one of the Best of Young British Novelists by *Granta* magazine in 1993.

Black Dogs

Ian McEwan

Lifespan | *b.* 1948 (England)
First Published | 1992
First Published by | Jonathan Cape (London)
First U.S. Edition | Nan A. Talese (New York)

Orphaned at the age of eight after a car accident, the narrator of *Black Dogs* is fascinated by other people's parents. In his in-laws, Bernard and June Tremaine, he finds a complex and remarkable story of love, war, and the everlasting conflict between heart and head, intellect and feeling. This novel is their story, but it is also the story of their son-in-law's attempts to understand them through writing.

Ian McEwan's trademark is the catalytic event, and the Tremaines' occurs on their honeymoon in 1946, when June has a life-changing experience, renounces the Communist Party of which they are both members, and embraces religion. Five years later, they separate, and Bernard remains a party member until his belief wanes in 1956. Set as the Berlin Wall is falling, the novel travels back in time to show how the demons of the Second World War changed the characters forever. When we later discover that June's experience was an encounter with two huge, ferocious black dogs, it is difficult not to read them as a representation of the evil of mankind, the wars and suffering that emerge throughout history. This is a story not only about love, belief, and idealism, but about the fragility of civilization which is threatened by our capacity for cruelty and evil. At its heart is the perennial question of whether it is civilization that causes the suffering of humanity, or whether the evil stems from individuals. Finally, it is a rumination on the question of belief—where does it come from, and what purpose does it serve? **EF**

Asphodel

H.D.

Lifespan | *b.* 1886 (U.S.), *d.* 1961 (Switzerland)
First Published | 1992
First Published by | Duke University Press
Given Name | Hilda Doolittle

Asphodel is a remarkably complex, innovative, and hugely underrated work of modernist fiction. The story follows the European travels of Hermione Gart, a young American who experiences artistic and sexual awakenings in the years leading up to the First World War. Themes of marriage, infidelity, and illegitimacy all connect the novel with the Jamesian literary tradition. More radically, however, the novel also explores one failed and one hopeful lesbian relationship. H. D. attempted to deter publication of this autobiographical novel—written in 1922 and unpublished for seventy years—by pencilling "DESTROY" across the title page of the manuscript; it has been presumed that this was due to *Asphodel's* lesbian theme. Perhaps also psychological trauma and the stillbirth of Hermione's first child were themes that were just too close to home.

As a feminist novel, this is the story of female expatriation, an experience that is immeasurably different from that of young expatriate men. As a novel that reinscribes the psychological experience of war, it presents a landscape where both interior and exterior spaces are violated. If for the modernists, the world of the mind was the only safe space to retreat to, then where does one go when even interior space has been violated by the public trauma of war, or the private trauma of stillbirth? **VC-R**

❯ Hilda Doolittle, photographed here in the 1910s, was prominently known simply by her initials, H. D.

The Heather Blazing

Colm Tóibín

Lifespan | *b.* 1955 (Ireland)
First Published | 1992
First Published by | Picador (London)
Encore Prize for Best Second Novel | 1992

Widely praised for its restrained, rhythmically fluent prose, *The Heather Blazing* is remarkable also for its imaginative sympathy. It is a critical but ungrudging tribute to the generation that created Tóibín's Ireland.

Eamon Redmond, the main character, is a judge in the Four Courts and an acquaintance of Charles Haughey's. The son of a Republican school teacher from County Wexford, he has made good thanks to his talents and energy and his active membership of Fianna Fáil. His politics invoke inward-looking national-Catholic conservatism, suspicious of "foreign influences" and conservative on questions of gender and sexuality. As his children become adults, their beliefs, and their lives, directly contradict his own. His wife, Carmel, finds him sometimes inflexible and ungenerous in his personal demeanor as well as his public judgements. Alternating scenes from the 1980s with remembered episodes of childhood and youth, and weaving together aspects of intimate, professional and public life, Tóibín charts the forces that have made Redmond what he is.

This was a generation of public men, Tóibín suggests, that might be characterized as narrow, patriarchal, and repressed. But their ultimate historical achievement in sustaining and developing a democratic, law-governed state, against much adversity, is to be given its full due. **MR**

◐ Colm Tóibín, photographed here by Sophie Bassouls at St. Malo, France, in 1996, also works as a journalist in Ireland and abroad.

Black Water

Joyce Carol Oates

Lifespan | *b.* 1938 (U.S.)
First Published | 1992
First Published by | E. P. Dutton (New York)
Pseudonyms | Rosamond Smith; Lauren Kelly

In the voice of a female narrator the story evokes the event that later became known as the Chappaquiddick incident, involving Senator Edward Kennedy and Mary Jo Kopechne, a young woman who drowned when Kennedy's car accidentally plunged into Poucha Pond. *Black Water* transforms the 1969 incident into a plot set in the early 1990s, and converts the story of Kopechne into the fictional narrative of Kelly Kelleher. While Kelly's experiences before and during the accident are vigorously portrayed, the senator remains anonymous and allegorical, an amalgam of several American politicians who used their power and status for sexual exploits. The narrative comments ironically on the politics of compromise and the vacuity of liberalism epitomized by the Kennedy brothers. The performance of political power in America is conveyed throughout as a theater of empty gestures and tired rhetoric. The novel is also about the limits of female roles and desires. Despite her political perceptiveness, Kelly is denied value and the ability to exert power. She clings to the hope that the senator will swim back for her but as the black water rises it becomes clear that she will not be saved. And as she realizes her lonely end, Kelly travels back to her childhood revisiting a time of absolute dependence.

This critique of the exploitation of power by American male politicians, initially written as a prose-poem, was a finalist for both the Pulitzer and National Book Critics Circle Award. **SA**

The Butcher Boy

Patrick McCabe

Lifespan | *b.* 1955 (Ireland)
First Published | 1992
First Published by | Picador (London)
Irish Literature Prize for Fiction | 1992

"I was thinking about Mrs. Nugent standing there crying."

◉ Patrick McCabe, pictured here in 1999, also writes radio plays and children's books. He has published five novels.

The Butcher Boy is as exciting as it is horrific, as comic as it is disturbing. The story is told in tightly controlled flashback from Francie Brady's wooded hideout, where we learn the whole town is after him "on account of what I done on Mrs. Nugent." Set in the Irish Republic in the early 1960s, Francie is the neglected only child of an alcoholic father and a suicidal mother. His troubled family is very unlike that of the well-to-do, Mrs. Nugent and her namby-pamby son Phillip. Francie's imagination is saturated with comic books, American movies, television, and the mischief he gets up to with his only friend Joe Purcell. The stifling town in which Francie lives, and his twisted family life, makes him love-starved, emotionally stunted, and ultimately unhinged. While Joe can grow into adolescence, Francie remains undeveloped and childlike, despite leaving school early and getting a job in an abattoir, an appropriate occupation for one obsessed by Mrs. Nugent's comparison of his family to "pigs." Exploiting the tendency of the childish voice to imitate what it overhears, the narrative recycles adult cliché through the mind of a disturbed boy. Francie absorbs and invigorates the banal conversational idiom of life in a small Irish town, infusing it with energy and menace. The first-person narrative here races along in colloquial fluency, for despite the utter dysfunctionality of Francie's family life, his inner, fantasy life is explosive and dynamic. The more the world outside rejects him and fails to meet his needs, the more recourse he has to this fantasy world, so that the descent into madness and murder, however genuinely shocking, comes with its own childish logic. It is a powerfully original voice, deftly crafted into a compelling, shocking, and entertaining novel about damaged childhood. **RMcD**

Smilla's Sense of Snow

Peter Høeg

Six-year-old Isaiah is found lying facedown in the snow at the foot of an apartment complex in Copenhagen, Denmark. The authorities record the death as an accident, but Smilla Jasperson, Isaiah's neighbor and surrogate mother, feels convinced that something more sinister lies behind the tragedy. An expert reader of snow and ice, Smilla is able to deduce from Isaiah's footprints that he jumped on purpose, something he only would have done had he been pursued. Her subsequent research leads her to the Arctic ice cap, as a stowaway on a cruise liner, as she slowly uncovers a conspiracy involving numerous members of Denmark's scientific elite intent on safeguarding their secret at any cost.

Smilla's Sense of Snow is narrated in the first person: we inhabit the perspective of a highly intelligent woman whose pluckiness and abrasive sense of humor at first belie the tremendous grief she feels as a result of Isaiah's death. As the story progresses, we learn more about Smilla's relationship with Isaiah, particularly the bond they shared as displaced Greenlanders forced to make a life for themselves in homogenous Denmark. The novel is a bracing critique of Denmark's colonization of Greenland as well as of the continuing prejudices harbored by many Danish toward Greenland's indigenous people.

What elevates this to the status of a great novel is the eloquence with which Høeg deftly interweaves a detective plot with striking character portraitures and philosophical musings. "Ice and life are related in many ways," Smilla tells us at the beginning of her story, and the rest of the novel ingeniously expounds on this relationship, juxtaposing adventure on the high seas with finely crafted meditations on love and loss. **CG-G**

Lifespan | *b.* 1957 (Denmark)
First Published | 1992, by Rosinante (Copenhagen)
Alternate Title | *Miss Smilla's Feeling for Snow*
Original Title | *Frøken Smillas fornemmelse for sne*

"This winter I've been able to watch the ice forming. "

⬤ Peter Høeg has written six novels, all published in Denmark by Rosinante. This novel was made into a movie by Bille August.

The English Patient

Michael Ondaatje

Michael Ondaatje writes the most remarkable prose. Beautifully crafted sentences flow effortlessly through his work, hypnotic in their perfection. *The English Patient* is a spellbinding novel, both because of this endlessly rich language, and for the story itself, filled as it is with sadness and tragedy.

Set in the closing days of the Second World War, the novel moves between war-ravaged Italy, and the pre-War African desert of Ladislaus de Almásy's memory, the terribly burned "English Patient" of the title. Scarred beyond recognition, and dying, he is cared for by a young nurse, Hana, in a partially ruined and deserted villa. Into the lives of this strange couple come Kip, a young Indian "sapper" in the British Army, and Caravaggio, a charming Italian-Canadian thief, who has been broken by his experiences of war. The tale of Almásy's doomed affair with a married woman, and its tragic end, weaves around the lives of Hana, Caravaggio, and Kip, pouring forth from the strange living corpse that the English Patient has become. The horror of war is distant, but central, as Hana and Kip begin a tentative love affair. The characters are warm, human, likable, yet morally flawed, ambiguous, and damaged.

In one of the finest scenes in the novel, the uneasy peace of the villa is shattered when Kip hears the news of the bombing of Hiroshima and, shocked and outraged, abandons the villa. It presents the damage and the terrible strain on each character in a way that manages to be both a microcosm of the novel as a whole, and its perfect conclusion. Division and unity, ally and enemy, the boundaries become confused and indistinguishable, running into each other like the sands of the English Patient's memories. This novel is a virtuoso performance from Ondaatje and an endlessly pleasurable read. **DR**

Lifespan | *b.* 1943 (Sri Lanka)
First Published | 1992
First Published by | McClelland & Stewart
Booker Prize | 1993 (joint)

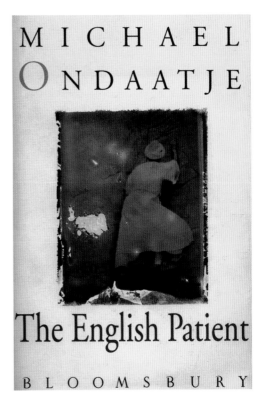

The cover picture of Indian sapper Kip on the UK edition is strongly reminiscent of Kipling's Kim.

Ralph Fiennes plays disciple of Herodotus, Count Ladislaus de Almásy, in the 1996 movie adaptation by Anthony Minghella.

Jazz

Toni Morrison

Lifespan | b. 1931 (U.S.)
First Published | 1992
First Published by | Knopf (New York)
Nobel Prize | 1993

Published the year before Morrison won the Nobel Prize for Literature, the subtly experimental *Jazz* tells the story of Joe, a cosmetics salesman, and his wife, Violet, a hairdresser. They have settled in Harlem during the Harlem Renaissance of the 1930s, after participating in the African American mass exodus from the South. At first intoxicated by the seemingly endless possibilities of the glittering, urban north, Violet and Joe, like many fellow migrants, in time settle into a life that brings its own uniquely urban harshness. At the thematic core of the novel, filial and parental relationships intertwine with romantic love and notions of beauty. Joe has an affair with Dorcas, a girl who is young enough to be his daughter, which leaves Violet to fantasize about the comfort of a large family, although she and Joe have remained childless. Joe's mother, Wild, was a Southern gothic figure, living mad and alone in the depths of the forest. Joe feels her absence sharply all through his life; by the time he shoots Dorcas because she's seeing another man, he has conflated her so thoroughly with Wild that this act is seems a desperate attempt to connect with the mother he never knew.

The narrative works linearly in time and laterally across geography, race, and politics, with the tone mutating from local gossip, to sweeping history, to wise observer. This expressive reworking of a common narrative thread connects *Jazz* with jazz, the rich instrumental and vocal narrative of urban Black experience contemporaneously finding its voice. **AF**

Written on the Body

Jeanette Winterson

Lifespan | b. 1959 (England)
First Published | 1992
First Published by | Jonathan Cape (London)
First U.S. Edition | 1993, Knopf (New York)

Set against the comic relation of the narrator's previous sexual liaisons, *Written on the Body* tells the story of the narrator's deeply serious love affair with a married woman called Louise. Although in this book Winterson eschews the explicit engagement with sexual and gender politics that characterized her infamous first novel, *Oranges are Not the Only Fruit* (1985), her decision to make the gender of the narrator in *Written on the Body* ambiguous has prompted much debate. Various textual clues—including the evidently easy bisexuality of the narrator, and the ease with which Louise's husband allows them to carry on their affair under the eaves of the marital home—suggest that the narrator is female. While the novel might therefore be read as an acutely observed reflection on female sexuality, the mystery of the narrator's gender might also indicate a more radical undermining of assumptions about gender and sexuality.

The novel begins and ends with more abstract poetic reflections on love, testifying to Winterson's skill as one of the few contemporary prose writers who can both write a compelling narrative about the vicissitudes of love and sex and construct sentences with the precision and beauty of the poetic. Sharing the magic realism of contemporary novels such as Angela Carter's *The Passion of New Eve* and Salman Rushdie's *Midnight's Children*, the story is a poetic and philosophical reflection on the body—a complex, interwoven palimpsest of who we are. **SJD**

The Crow Road

Iain Banks

Lifespan | *b.* 1954 (Scotland)
First Published | 1992
First Published by | Scribner (London)
Adapted for Radio (BBC) | 1996

Iain Banks' *The Crow Road* begins with one of the most memorable paragraphs in modern literature: "It was the day my grandmother exploded. I sat in the crematorium listening to my Uncle Hamish quietly snoring in harmony to Bach's Mass in B Minor, and I reflected that it always seemed to be death that drew me back to Gallanach." This is the voice of Prentice McHoan, the middle son of an affluent Scottish family whose narrative forms the greater part of the book, while the rest is told in the third person, a kind of saga of the McHoan, Watt, and Urvill families. Away at university, Prentice finds himself returning to his family home (or rather, after a falling-out with his father over religious belief, to the home of his Uncle Hamish). Another uncle, Rory, hasn't been seen in eight years. As the mystery of Uncle Rory's fate takes greater and greater hold on the text, Prentice takes on the role of fallible detective, charged with making sense of all that happened to the generations before him and piecing together fragments to form a single truth. *The Crow Road* is a novel about death: desire in relation to death, the body in life and death, and the exhuming of buried secrets. By the end of the book, despite the concentration on a bleak and stark Scottish landscape, the real map is created within Prentice's mind, as he reaches inside himself to discover the lost truths of a generation and the fragility of memory. **EF**

Indigo

Marina Warner

Lifespan | *b.* 1946 (England)
First Published | 1992
First Published by | Chatto & Windus (London)
First U.S. Edition | Simon & Schuster (New York)

Novelist, literary critic, and historian, Warner is a chameleon of the pen, and *Indigo* derives from all these aspects of her interest. Skipping between the fifteenth-century British appropriation of an imaginary Caribbean island, with many references to Shakespeare's *The Tempest*, and the story of the founding family's heirs in the twentieth century, *Indigo* draws upon several facets of English history. Warner draws out all the more sinister colonial implications of Prospero's enslavement of Ariel and Caliban, and revives the witch Sycorax, mentioned fleetingly in *The Tempest* as Caliban's mother. She is the island wise woman and herbalist, learned in the art of extracting indigo and dying cloths. As the British misunderstand and all but destroy the local population, Sycorax's daughter escapes death, if not the ravages of the community established by the conquerors. Alongside this narrative of colonial tyranny, is the tale of London-born Miranda, a descendant of the island's colonial governor, who eventually finds her way to the Caribbean island that her family helped to alter dramatically. Warner also manages to poignantly portray the struggle of Miranda to understand and come to terms with her relatives. However, while the tale is played out within a single family, the message is clearly wider: the legacy of colonialism and its crimes do not disappear but are part of the fabric and history of our culture and those they have impacted in a way that is extremely real and present. **JC**

Possessing the Secret of Joy

Alice Walker

Lifespan | *b.* 1944 (U.S.)
First Published | 1992
First Published by | Harcourt Brace Jovanovich (N.Y.)
First UK Edition | Jonathan Cape (London)

Possessing the Secret of Joy is an angry, impassioned defence of femininity, and of the female body, against the horrific violence of female genital mutilation. The novel focuses on the story of Tashi, an Americanized member of Walker's fictional African people, the Olinka. Tashi opts in adult life to have herself circumcised, or, as she calls it, "bathed." For Olinkans, "bathing" involves not only the excision of the clitoris, but also the removal of the labia, and the stitching closed of the vagina.

Tashi is demonstrating her allegiance to Olinkan tradition and her fierce devotion to a culture that is under threat. As the novel progresses, however, she comes to believe that her genital mutilation is a symptom of a more general, transcultural oppression of women by men. In dramatizing Tashi's choice between her nation and her sexuality, Walker sets up an extremely difficult and troubling set of oppositions; the powerful claims of allegiance to African nationalism cannot be reconciled with equally powerful demands of feminism. The novel seeks a universal understanding of female suffering at the hands of a violent patriarchal culture and a universal horror at the form that such suffering has taken. It is the possibility of a universal resistance to patriarchal oppression that turns out, here, to be the real secret of joy. Whatever its difficulties, as a poem of resistance to the violence of misogynist cultures in both Africa and the West, this novel is unforgettable. **PB**

A Heart So White

Javier Marías

Lifespan | *b.* 1951 (Spain)
First Published | 1992
First Published by | Editorial Anagrama (Barcelona)
Original Title | *Corazón tan blanco*

The novel opens with an almost documentary account of a suicide and ends with a meditation on the untranslatable mysteries of the gender divide. Javier Marías is no stranger to the implications of bilingualism. As a former Oxford Spanish lecturer, his career has seen him in constant dialogue with his two selves, one Anglophilic and English-speaking, the other Madrid-born and Mediterranean in temperament. Juan, who narrates *A Heart So White*, is a translator by trade; his storytelling, whilst direct, also acknowledges that much of his life has been subject to imperfect or incomplete interpretation; as readers, we are a further step removed. As if to dramatize our predicament, Marías allows Juan to overhear important conversations through walls and doors, piecing together his narrative from conjecture and emphasizing his own interpretative shortcomings. It nevertheless avoids more well-trodden postmodernist routes, opting instead for an urbane realism which makes its observations on the literal and metaphorical acts of translation we must perform in our everyday lives all the more recognizable.

Ultimately, it is the human need for language to be a comfort that wins through. Marías shows that even in the most private of domestic setups, there are enough narratives for a whole world of divergent experience. **ABI**

⊙ Novelist, translator, and columnist Javier Marías won the 1997 International IMPAC Dublin Literary Award for *A Heart So White*.

The Discovery of Heaven

Harry Mulisch

Lifespan | *b.* 1927 (Netherlands)
First Published | 1992, by De Bezige Bij (Amsterdam)
Movie Adaptation | 2001
Original Title | *De Ontdekking van de Hemel*

"'This has nothing to do with the toasters. It has begun!'"

⬤ Harry Mulisch, photographed here in 1993, received
the once-in-a-lifetime Award for Dutch Literature in 1995.

Although Harry Mulisch is less well-known in the English-speaking world, he is a prolific writer and a prominent figure in twentieth-century Dutch literature. On the basis of its physical heft alone, *The Discovery of Heaven* is a book to be reckoned with. It may also be the work of fiction that brings its author closer than any other Dutch writer before him to the Nobel Prize for Literature. And this is even before a consideration of the theme, which entails nothing less than the failure of humanity's covenant with God. One premise of the novel is that the scientific method is a trick of Lucifer's, one that has succeeded incredibly well. As the narrative unfolds, two supremely talented men, Max Delius, an astronomer, and Onno Quist, a linguist, meet by chance one dark night and become friends. Later, on a trip to Cuba, they jointly and repeatedly impregnate a young cellist named Ada Brons, who had earlier been involved with each of them in turn. Though she suffers a serious accident and dies, her baby survives. Named Quinten Quist, his mission is to retrieve the Ten Commandments and return them to heaven because of mankind's utter inability to fulfill God's will on earth. Delius, meanwhile, makes a stupendous astronomical discovery, before being killed by a meteorite. If the plot sounds contrived and more fraught with coincidence than even an artist's imagination might warrant, that's the result of the intervention of angels or, more precisely, demiurges. It is they who concoct the plan to create a human being to accomplish their objective of reclaiming the Biblical tablets.

This monumental and controversial effort, cosmic in scope and comic in tone, has been heralded internationally and may be considered a contemporary instance of myth creation. **ES**

Life is a Caravanserai

Emine Özdamar

The book with the unconventional title (*Life is a Caravanserai Has Two Doors I Came in One I Went Out the Other*) breaks conventions throughout. That unpunctuated running together of phrases starts us off as we will go on. The first sentence continues: "First I saw the soldiers, I was standing there in my mother's belly between the bars of ice . . ." Clearly, *Caravanserai* is not your usual memoir: in the process of describing childhood in the Turkey of the turbulent 1950s and 60s, we can switch between the protagonist in her mother's womb and the train carriage in which the mother stands surrounded by soldiers just as easily as the book continuously shifts its diction, register, and perspective.

The marriage of stylistic and thematic concerns is absolute: while the narrative is about the way in which female identity can be newly constructed in a laden political and social context, the stylistic experiments at first seem disorienting, but come to create a poetic and challenging sort of logic of their own. The boundaries of linguistic categories are fluidly reinvented as subjective, national, and gender roles are rethought. The book is wonderfully anarchic: both in the verbal marvels that disrupt its own narrative texture (from the Arabic prayer for protection and forgiveness that runs throughout to Joycean renderings of the sounds of a crunching apple), and also in its physical openness and pungency, replete with dozens of farts, all kinds of bodily fluid, and deliciously vivid catalog of smells.

Özdamar emigrated to Berlin and writes in a hybridized German, which has made a dramatic impact. *Caravanserai* was the first book by a "non-originary" German to receive the high-powered Ingeborg-Bachmann Prize, and its force of originality justifies the hype. **MS**

Lifespan | *b.* 1946 (Turkey)
First Published | 1992, by Kiepenheuer & Witsch
Original Title | *Leben ist eine Karawanserai hat zwei Türen aus einer kam ich rein aus der anderen ging ich raus*

"Then I lost sight of my grandfather in the carpet . . ."

◉ This portrait of the author and actress was taken by Eric Fougere in 2001 at the Paris Book Fair.

The Secret History

Donna Tartt

Lifespan | *b.* 1963 (U.S.)
First Published | 1992
First Published by | Knopf (New York)
First UK Edition | Viking (London)

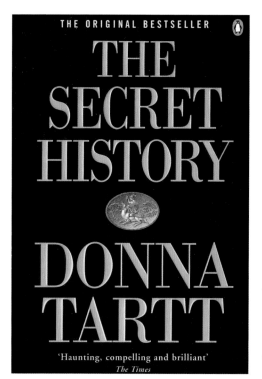

"... how I longed to be an orphan when I was a child!"

🔵 After the sensational success of *The Secret History*, her first novel, Tartt was determined to remain "a writer, not a TV personality."

Good publicity can give a book a bad name. Donna Tartt's first novel, begun when she was still at college and bought for $450,000 by Knopf after a bidding war, quickly became a bestseller and made its author a reluctant star. The critics were not impressed: they thought the book leaden, pretentious, and thinly characterized. In some ways, they were taking it too seriously; in others, perhaps, not seriously enough.

The novel is a page-turner, certainly, but there is more to *The Secret History* than plot alone. Telling his story as if it were still unfolding, though in fact he is recalling events long since past, the narrator, Richard Papen, leaves behind his unsatisfying teenage years in Plano, California, to enroll at Hampden, a small, exclusive college in Vermont. He is soon captivated by a group of five rich, otherworldly classics students and their mercurial tutor, Julian Morrow, and gradually becomes enmeshed in the clique. He learns that the group—Henry, Francis, Bunny, and the twins Charles and Camilla—have been attempting to stage a bacchanal, the consequences of which culminate in Bunny's death. The remainder of the novel charts the slow splintering of the group's friendships under the pressures of fear, remorse, and sickened self-knowledge.

The Secret History is a study of ruin, of lives blighted forever by adolescent hubris. It is also about charisma: the reader is seduced, along with Richard, by the charming and dissolute Francis, by Julian's sublime sensibility, and the twins' ethereal self-containment, and above any of these by Henry, who is by turns benevolent and warm, aloof and forbidding, but always, in the end, opaque. A strange confection, Tartt's melancholy murder mystery is quality trash for highbrows: the storytelling retains its grip to the final page and beyond. **PMy**

The Emigrants

W. G. Sebald

Lifespan | *b.* 1944 (Germany), *d.* 2001 (England)
First Published | 1992
First Published by | Eichborn (Frankfurt)
Original Title | *Die Ausgewanderten*

Through four different accounts, *The Emigrants* vividly portrays aspects of twentieth-century European anti-Semitism. The narrator shares aspects of Sebald's own environment (his arrival in England in the 1960s, his residency in East Anglia), and the book records his encounters with characters who gradually reveal their sense of displacement and trauma. Sebald publishes period photos within his text to support the accounts' apparent authenticity. However, it would be misleading to view this writing as other than carefully prepared fictions. His narrator's investigations of the stories of his former landlord, his old school teacher, an uncle, and finally the family of a painter he encounters often have a quality of serendipity: he appears to stumble accidentally as he recounts a piece of information.

Sebald's technique creates a most effective and unsettling exploration of the effects of anti-Semitism. He peers into areas that he proposes modern Germany is still trying to repress. Yet Sebald does not propose an overarching theory to explain what has taken place. By making the stories the narrator discovers seem to be almost accidental encounters, he proposes a wider sense of hidden histories that shape the world. *The Emigrants* succeeds in capturing the way ordinary, educated people who believed themselves integrated into their communities are suddenly excluded because of race and religion. The terrifying irrationality of anti-Semitism is vividly exposed. **TH**

The Robber Bride

Margaret Atwood

Lifespan | *b.* 1939 (Canada)
First Published | 1993
First Published by | McClelland & Stewart (To.)
First UK Edition | Bloomsbury (London)

Set in Canada in the 1970s, *The Robber Bride* explores several of Atwood's favorite topics—sex, the empowerment of women, the nature of violence, and the inescapable binding of women's fates to the men they know. Loosely based on *The Robber Bridegroom* by the Brothers Grimm, where an evil groom lures three unsuspecting women into his lair and devours them, the story follows the lives of three women who have been injured by a mutual friend, Zenia, a sociopath whose only joy is hurting people. In Atwood's characteristic style, each of them—Tony, Roz, and Charis—is in some way weak and vulnerable. Beautiful and arrogant, Zenia befriends each woman long enough to determine what would hurt her most deeply, then steals, seduces, and casts aside the man each woman loves. The course of the novel spans less than a week, beginning at a moment of revelation for each woman, when she finds out Zenia is not, as she had believed, dead. Each is forced to deal with the threat Zenia poses to her sanity and relive her defeat at her hands. Driven to act, the three women each arrive on their own at Zenia's hotel to seek retribution but they each, independently, reach the decision not to kill her.

On the surface, this is a bleak tale that wallows in the destructive side of human emotions—envy, hatred, and retribution—but by the end, a warmer message emerges: the consolation offered by shared companionship and affection. **EF**

The House of Doctor Dee

Peter Ackroyd

Lifespan | *b.* 1949 (England)
First Published | 1993
First Published by | Hamish Hamilton (London)
Commander of the British Empire (CBE) | 2003

Peter Ackroyd has said that "London has always provided the landscape for my imagination. It becomes a character—a living being—within each of my books," and in *The House of Doctor Dee*, London is again at the very center of his novel. In this unusual work of historical fiction, Matthew Palmer, the twenty-nine-year-old principal narrator, inherits his father's house in the Clerkenwell district of central London. He later discovers that Doctor John Dee, mathematician, alchemist, and astrologer to Queen Elizabeth I, a man embedded in Renaissance thought, previously inhabited the property. The novel traces the complex interweaving of the two men's stories, and, in an intriguing cross-temporal twist, suggests that their lives are profoundly linked—indeed Matthew's job as a historical researcher has ensured that the realities of his present are always bound up with those of the past.

For those familiar with Ackroyd's fiction, this novel fuses his preoccupation with London with his desire to blur the distinction between fact and fiction. The rich historical detail has produced an absorbing evocation of sixteenth-century London. But more than this, it explores the relationship between the spatial and temporal dimensions of our lives and demonstrates that our experience of both is culturally determined. Part ghost story, part detective novel, this book defies adequate categorization, and for those who enjoy a stimulating read, it will not disappoint. **JW**

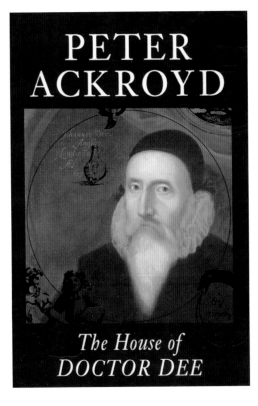

PETER
ACKROYD

The House of
DOCTOR DEE

"I had grown up in a world without love—a world of magic, of money, of possession —and so I had none for myself or for others."

⌃ Peter Ackroyd's fiction is infused with a sense of history, often including passages written in a pastiche of past literary styles.

The Virgin Suicides

Jeffrey Eugenides

Lifespan | *b.* 1960 (U.S.)
First Published | 1993
First Published by | Farrar, Straus & Giroux (New York)
Movie Adaptation | 1999

"Cecilia, the youngest, only thirteen, had gone first, slitting her wrists like a Stoic . . ."

⊙ Jeffrey Eugenides, here photographed by Robert Maas in 1993, was born in Detroit, Michigan, of mixed Greek and Irish descent.

Part detective story, part bildungsroman, part tragedy, *The Virgin Suicides* starts from a premise so shocking it is almost inconceivable (though supposedly drawing its basic facts from a real-life case). Eugenides' adult narrator recalls the "year of the suicides," in which all five of the Lisbon family's daughters ultimately succeed in committing suicide. The novel brings together "evidence" such as the girls' journals and notes, the collected memories of the narrator and his clique, and interviews conducted around the time of the narrative—yet the atmosphere is thick with confusion.

Several aspects of the Lisbon girls' lives seem to collude in the air of mystification. Neighborhood boys have always romanticized them into a monolithic blond fantasy of unreachability, while neighbors create a whispering backdrop for familial eccentricities. After the first suicide, the remaining four girls become isolated at school by the awkward pity of their peers and teachers. For all the persistence with which the narrator pursues the "truth" behind the suicides, he is never able to illuminate the mystery that enshrouds the girls and their self-inflicted, eternal silence. Never having attempted to look beyond his own interpretation of the girls' mental state, the narrator can only allude to his contributing role in their deaths. The sense that the suicides are simply physical enactments of their complete effacement by their environment is reinforced by the paranoia of their mother, Mrs. Lisbon, about spiritual propriety and pollution. Dutch elm disease hysteria provides a metaphor for the hypochondriacal fear of pandemic at the heart of suburban American culture, where killing something healthy is the preferred resolution to fear of the possibility of contamination. **AF**

The Stone Diaries
Carol Shields

The Stone Diaries is a panoramic novel, a masterful odyssey through the trials, minor joys, and ennui of the nearly century-long life of Daisy Goodwill. Starting with her tragic birth in rural Manitoba in 1905 and ending with her death in Florida, the story is told in chapters, spaced a decade apart, that visit childhood, marriage, remarriage, motherhood, independence, grief, and finally old age and death. We glimpse in the distance, from these windows into Daisy's life, the changing face of the twentieth century. We also see the evolution of women's position in society.

But is this purely a women's book? It is about a woman, and the mundane crises of being a woman, but more fundamentally it is about being human. It is a complex narrative—made more complex in that it is ostensibly a first-person "autobiography," but one that alerts us to its unreliability at every step of the way. It offers us multiple versions of Daisy's life— some from before she was born, some after she has died—from a variety of characters. But through all of the different subjective viewpoints, through entire sections made up of letters and newspaper columns on gardening, oddly the one point of view most often absent is that of Daisy. This is a novel about the difficulty of finding an identity, and—considering the position of women—the complication that we are most often defined by others.

Throughout the decades, two motifs reflect minor triumphs and ordinary devastation: the resolute rigidity of stone and the irrational growth of plants. But plants win. Where loss, ossifying grief, or age would be a dead end to other heroines, Carol Shields repeatedly gives us renewal. She shows that life—in surprising ways—finds a way to bloom. There is dignity in the ordinary. There is hope. **GT**

Lifespan | *b.* 1935 (U.S.), *d.* 2003 (Canada)
First Published | 1993
First Published by | Random House (New York)
Pulitzer Prize | 1995

"It is frightening, and also exhilarating, her ability to deceive those around her . . ."

◉ Carol Shields, who did not publish her first novel until she was forty-years-old, died of cancer at the age of sixty-eight.

A Suitable Boy

Vikram Seth

"You too will marry a boy I choose," announces Mrs. Rupa Mehra to her younger daughter, Lata, at the start of Seth's colossal novel. Lata, however, is unconvinced, and at the heart of the story is the decision she has to make. Will she comply with her mother's wishes and marry Haresh Khanna, the most "suitable" of the three men who are courting her, a shoe factory manager with great enthusiasm for his work who was introduced by a family friend? Will she marry the poet Amit, her brother's brother-in-law, who proposes after they become friends during Lata's university holidays? Or will she defy her mother and marry the most unsuitable boy of them all, Kabir, a Muslim fellow university student, with whom she has fallen in love? The story of the search for a husband follows the fortunes of four families during one year, 1951, four years after Indian independence. It is set against the background of the passage of land reform legislation, religious festivals such as the Pul Mela, and the considerable Hindu-Muslim tensions that lurk beneath the surface and occasionally erupt into violence.

Why read such a long book, shorter than *War and Peace* by only some fifty pages? In Seth's novel there are none of the weighty meditations of Tolstoy, nor is the intention behind the novel one of a grand epic. Instead, there is a lightness of touch in his prose that moves effortlessly through his vast cast of characters, spanning the frivolous world of the anglicized elite, the tensions of academia and politics, and the grinding poverty of the villages and slums. Surprisingly, the novel is a remarkably accomplished example of restraint and temperance in narrative. It avoids excess despite its enormous scope, and there is a respect for character and detail that is now rare among modern writers. **ABi**

Lifespan | *b.* 1952 (India)
First Published | 1993
First Published by | Phoenix House (London)
Commonwealth Writers Prize | 1994

Seth's epic novel is set in India, the country of his birth, although the author has lived primarily in the UK and U.S. since his teens.

Seth, jauntily posed above copies of his novel, looks a thoroughly suitable boy—a writer of serious but never heavyweight fiction.

What a Carve Up!

Jonathan Coe

Lifespan | *b.* 1961 (England)
First Published | 1993
First Published by | Viking (London)
John Llewellyn Rhys Prize | 1994

In this, Jonathan Coe's fourth and overwhelmingly most successful novel, Michael Owen is the hapless biographer of the Winshaw family, a gallery of monsters whose greed and unscrupulousness have enabled them to profit from, and indeed to have made possible, the Thatcherite climate of 1980s Britain. As we move from formative episodes of Michael's life to his account of the Winshaws' rise to positions of power and influence, we discover, along with him, that the family has determined the course of his life in unimaginably far-reaching ways. In the end, a traumatized Michael is transported to the Winshaws' family home, where he and they live out a Carry On movie spoof called *What a Carve Up!*, in which Michael's dreams are fulfilled and the Winshaws, in turn, receive their just deserts.

Critics, in calling Coe's dazzling novel "postmodern," presumably have in mind its metatextual playfulness—its unreliable narrator, its mingling of literary forms, and the apparently arbitrary interconnectedness of its characters and plots. However, it sits just as happily in the tradition of Victorian social realism, in which personal destinies and sociopolitical contexts are entwined in ways revealed by the story. Many of Coe's novels are detective stories in disguise, beginning with loose ends and gradually tying them into elegant knots. Here, the story's resolution is as satisfying as its literary tricks are delightful, but do not be deceived: at heart this novel is a furious social satire. **PMy**

On Love

Alain de Botton

Lifespan | *b.* 1969 (Switzerland)
First Published | 1993
First Published by | Macmillan (London)
Alternate Title | *Essays in Love*

As its title suggests, Alain de Botton's *On Love* is in the same genre of philosophical essay that received its fullest expression in the work of Michel de Montaigne. But it is also a thoroughly modern love story. This skillful combination of the intellectual and the emotional, the philosophical and the novelistic, makes *On Love* a delightful and original work. With references to Wilde, Heidegger, Hegel, Marx, Nietzsche, Kant, Wittgenstein, Plato, Mill, Heraclitus, Freud, and Flaubert, among others, *On Love* is unashamedly intellectual. But its narrator uses erudition in order to reflect with wit and insight upon the universal experiences of falling in and out of love: that feeling when we first fall in love that we were meant to be together; the way we idealize the beloved; the subtext of seduction; the lack of authenticity involved in wanting to be whoever you think your beloved wants you to be; the disjunction between mind and body when making love; the insecurity of the lover when the beloved eventually returns their affection; and the way in which being a lover reaffirms everything about oneself and is in fact the mirror in which one sees oneself. The novel's philosophical reflections are interwoven with the story of the narrator's love affair with a woman called Chloë, who he meets on a Paris-London flight. This is not a novel for the incurably romantic, but it is a sharp and sustained philosophical dissection of love that also achieves the irresistible seductiveness of a well-told love story. **SJD**

Complicity

Iain Banks

Lifespan | *b.* 1954 (Scotland)
First Published | 1993
First Published by | Little, Brown & Co. (Boston)
Movie Adaptation | *Retribution* (2000)

Iain Banks is widely acclaimed as one of modern Britain's most compelling writers of fiction. *Complicity* is both a gripping crime whodunit and a piercing comment on social morality. The protagonist, Cameron Colley, is a loathsome hack working on a local news rag, a self-proclaimed gonzo journalist who lives his life in the fast lane—alcohol, drugs, adulterous sex, video games, and chasing the next big headline. Banks is well-known not only for his vivid characterization but also for the dark, treacly humor he injects into his writing, and Colley is one of his most celebrated creations. Colley has been receiving tip-offs from a mysterious Mr. Archer, who claims to be a government intelligence agent, suggesting he look into a series of gruesome and bizarre deaths occurring in London. Colley's research suggests the three victims were linked by an arms scandal, but police inspector McDunn believes there could be a connection between the murders and a story Colley wrote suggesting that certain public figures who betray the trust of the public might be better off dead. As the plot thickens, the two independent streams begin to merge into a clever conclusion. The novel is written in the present tense and switches between first (where we find out more about the character Colley) and second (where the violent attacks are described) person narratives. *Complicity* is a vivid, disturbing, and at times uncomfortable exploration of human greed, corruption, violence, and retribution. **EF**

Operation Shylock

Philip Roth

Lifespan | *b.* 1933 (U.S.)
First Published | 1993
First Published by | Simon & Schuster (New York)
Full Title | *Operation Shylock: A Confession*

Written in his own idiosyncratic, confessional style, Philip Roth, the narrator, gets entangled in a battle of wits with a double who is also called Philip Roth. This "impostor" is stirring up controversy in Israel by his passionate advocacy of "Diasporism," a policy that urges Jews to forsake Israel as their homeland and resettle in Eastern Europe. Roth's attempt to rescue his reputation by exposing his *doppelganger* and tormentor as a fake has to contend with the problem that the borders between fact and fiction, as well as truth and falsehood, become increasingly nebulous.

Paranoid fantasies are generated by a succession of plots and counterplots initiated by the Israeli and Palestinian intelligence agencies, and the beleaguered narrator also becomes involved in the trial of an American auto worker accused of being a former Nazi torturer. The Arab-Israeli dispute, and the competing claims to moral authority made by both sides, rests on whether the accused is really a monster being brought to justice or merely a convenient stooge in a show trial.

It is the labyrinthine plot that absorbs most of Roth's energies, rather than development of the dilemma posed by the novel—how to reconcile Jewishness and identity in a world that has fallen out of love with grand narratives and moral certainties. All the hallmarks of Roth's style are here: the sly irreverence, absurdist plot twists, and daring comic asides, and Roth demonstrates once again that he is incapable of writing a lame sentence. **VA**

Looking for the Possible Dance

A. L. Kennedy

Lifespan | *b.* 1965 (Scotland)
First Published | 1993
First Published by | Secker & Warburg (London)
Somerset Maugham Award | 1993

" . . . a compliment directed to one's teeth."

⊘ A. L. Kennedy is a Christian and has expressed her faith politically through an involvement in anti-war and anti-nuclear protests.

Looking for the Possible Dance is an almost everyday story of life, love, and sacrifice in the fraught world of male-female relations. In charting Margaret's resistance to the limited womanly roles of daughter, wife, and mistress, the novel demonstrates the fragility of men and their desperate and resented dependence on the women in their lives, a dependence that must breed hate alongside love.

During a train journey from Glasgow to London, Margaret recounts the events that have brought her to this moment. Her beloved but possessive father has died, and she has lost her job at a community center because her boss, who indulged himself in an imaginary and unreciprocated affair with her, has engineered false accusations against her. Her lover Colin has been severely disabled by a gangland attack in which he was nailed to a warehouse floor in a gruesome crucifixion, a punishment for exposing loan sharks in the community. Having earlier refused to marry him, Margaret now has to decide whether to return to that relationship on his terms, reciprocating his public sacrifice with her own private one. In a typically ambiguous conclusion, Kennedy sends her heroine home, completing the journey of discovery that takes her back where she started. Anxious love and uneasy fear coexist in Margaret, suspending her in this finely balanced narrative of duty and desire. Only dancing offers a glimpse of social harmony, but even this affirmation of the possibility of new relations is finally denied. The present soulless reality is sustained by violence: the public brutality of men's relationships with men and the private coercion of men's relationships with women. In this novel, the dance of life provides little opportunity to escape a routine that creates love and resentment in equal measure. **CJ**

Birdsong

Sebastian Faulks

Birdsong is "a story of love and war." A mixture of fact and fiction, the book was born of the fear that the First World War was passing out of collective consciousness. At one level, it upholds the promise: "We Shall Remember Them," and Faulks' fictional soldiers give an identity to the "lost" of the war—both the dead and "the ones they did not find." By means of an unashamed emotional manipulation, Faulks solicits a heartrending sympathy. He redefines heroism by presenting valor, not as gung-ho bravado, but as fear and the numbing endurance of pointless suffering.

Stephen Wraysford's notebooks, containing his war diaries, are found by his granddaughter, Elizabeth, in 1978. In reading Wraysford's history, Elizabeth relives his past and finds her own identity —a way "of understanding more about herself." The explicit intensity of Stephen's sexual passion for his mistress, Isabelle, stands as vicarious sexual experience for those, like Stephen's friend, Weir, who lost their lives without experiencing sex. And the graphic horror of the trenches is seared into the reader's consciousness to provide a vicarious national identity for a generation that has never experienced combat. By glimpsing how we might respond in extreme situations that arise only in national crises, *Birdsong* enables readers to learn, as Elizabeth learns, more about themselves. But the novel is not nationalistic, for Stephen is saved by a German soldier, and they weep together "at the bitter strangeness of human lives." Ultimately, the novel acknowledges that any attempt to tell the truth about war lies beyond language, for that truth is too awful both to tell and to comprehend. The "birdsong" of the title is the voice of a lost generation and also the voice of art, which attempts, and necessarily fails, to capture it. **AR**

Lifespan | *b.* 1953 (England)
First Published | 1993
First Published by | Hutchinson (London)
First U.S. Edition | 1994, by Vintage (New York)

"Madame Azaire had not fully engaged Stephen's eye."

⊙ Sebastian Faulks is a popular writer who seeks to engage the emotions of contemporary readers with historical subjects.

Trainspotting

Irvine Welsh

Lifespan | *b.* 1958 (Scotland)
First Published | 1993
First Published by | Secker & Warburg (London)
Movie Adaptation | 1996

"Johnny wis a junky as well as a dealer. Ye hud tae go a wee bit further up the ladder before ye found a dealer whae didnae use. We called Johnny 'Mother Superior' because ay the length ay time he'd had his habit."

⊙ The cast of Danny Boyle's 1996 movie version of Welsh's novel included Robert Carlyle as the unpredictably violent Begbie.

⊙ Welsh has a superb ear for Scottish vernacular, a sharp sense of humor, and an indulgent sympathy for his junkie characters.

Welsh's first novel was filmed by Danny Boyle in 1996, coinciding with a renaissance in British pop culture. The novel's portrayal of a group of Leith junkies helped represent modern Britain as a cool, edgy place that was somehow both hedonistic and headily creative. Welsh's book, however, is a considerably denser affair than Boyle's showy and self-conscious film. Firstly, this is because the narrative is written almost entirely in a transcribed Edinburgh dialect. Initially difficult for a non-Scottish reader—"Yiv goat tae huv fuckin brains to be a fuckin judge"—the intimacy this generates with the colloquial wit of the novel's narrators more than compensates for the effort it demands. Secondly, the story is less linear narrative than a series of stream-of-consciousness vignettes. In an uncertain chronology, scenes are delivered from different characters' perspectives, sharply exposing their often hostile relationships, both to one another and to the world at large.

It is, though, the tone of *Trainspotting* that really catches the reader's attention. The lack of any authorial, moralizing voice naturalizes the internal universe of the text so that the protagonists' immediate needs, for heroin, sex, or money, become the sole logic driving events. Sometimes harrowing—the HIV/AIDS death toll in the book is high—there is still much to find amusing here. Forced to score a couple of opium suppositories in lieu of proper smack, the main character, Renton, complains to his dealer that "For aw the good they've done ah might as well huv stuck them up ma erse." This black humor, combined with an implicit critique of the anomie of Scottish youth in post-Thatcher Britain, ensures Welsh's novel the status of both popular and cult success. **DH**

The Shipping News

E. Annie Proulx

Lifespan | *b.* 1935 (U.S.)
First Published | 1993
First Published by | Scribner (New York)
Awards | Pulitzer Prize; National Book Award

Quoyle is a thirty-six-year-old reporter from New York with a traumatic and stressful life—his parents have committed suicide, and his wife died in a car accident. His aunt has always wanted to return to the land of her history and she convinces Quoyle to move with her to Newfoundland. He overcomes his fear of water to become the shipping correspondent on a local paper. A series of strange events soon beset Quoyle. In the town, he notices a graceful woman whose child has Down's syndrome, and they form a bond that nearly leads to intimacy. Quoyle's ancestors, who lived nearby, were reputedly pirates and murderers. He visits their burial ground and on his way home finds a suitcase with a head in it.

In the end, there is the triumph of life over death as Quoyle survives a boat wreck, and his friend Jack cheats drowning. *The Shipping News* was reputed to have been an experiment in writing a novel with a happy ending, after Proulx had received feedback that her first novel seemed dark. But this happy ending is neither euphoric or easy—it seems that the only form of happiness Proulx can bestow on her characters is an absence of trauma and pain, and the resolution of this strange and unsettling novel is filled with unease. **EF**

◔ Annie Proulx, photographed here at her home at Arvada, WY, did not begin writing fiction until she was in her fifties.

The Invention of Curried Sausage

Uwe Timm

Lifespan | *b.* 1940 (Germany)
First Published | 1993
First Published by | Kiepenheuer & Witsch (Cologne)
Original Title | *Die Entdeckung der Currywurst*

In *The Invention of Curried Sausage,* successful and prolifc author Uwe Timm packs in enough material for a work four times its length. It distills challenging subject matter—the end of the Second World War, adultery, Nazism—to its emotional essence, the seemingly inconsequential, yet potent symbol of postwar German cultural integration—the ubiquitous Currywurst.

Timm's investigation of the invention of this delicacy is sparked off by childhood memories of eating the sausage at Lena Brücker's fast-food stand. Brücker claims to be the genuine inventor, but before revealing the details of her culinary discovery, she must excavate her past for the events that led to it. Timm, the narrator, pretends that his sole motivation for interviewing Brücker is to solve the riddle of the sausage, when in reality it is more a device for untangling the riddles of war, duty, and love. Our encounter with the accidental recipe is preceded by Brücker's affair with Bremer, a fugitive soldier hiding from the Nazi authorities. She betrays the unwritten rules of love by lying to him in order to keep their relationship afloat.

The curried sausage becomes a twentieth-century analogy to the stone in the soup of folklore. The deftly handled big issues give the novella its overriding flavor, while the sausage provides the spicy seasoning. **ABI**

Disappearance

David Dabydeen

Lifespan | *b.* 1956 (Guyana)
First Published | 1993
First Published by | Secker & Warburg (London)
Original Language | English

'David Dabydeen's poetry has already demonstrated that he has an original and idiosyncratic voice. His fiction now shows him to be the best of the younger generation of Caribbean novelists, writing powerfully of the immigrant experience.'   **Penelope Lively**

Disappearance

⊙ Chris Shamwana designed the jacket for Dabydeen's novel, which reflects his experience as a Guyanese living in Britain.

The narrator, a young Guyanese engineer, is sent to Dunsmere Cliff on the Kent coast to oversee the building of a containing wall to save the village from collapse into the sea. A serious and contemplative man, he boards in the home of a fiery old Englishwoman who is fascinated by Africa, where she had spent many years of her life. As the old woman probes into the narrator's African ancestry, the question at the heart of the novel, whether one can ever "get rid of the past," begins to trouble the narrator. He begins to understand the nature of the village, discovering that under its apparent Englishness is a latent violence that connects it to its imperial past. What results is a powerful meditation on the condition of England, seen as a land of monuments and national narratives that serve finally to mark what has disappeared, or what was never really properly acknowledged: the imperial encounters, the violence that created great civic works, and the deaths of slaves. As the narrator sets off to leave the village, having completed the sea-defense, he wonders how his contribution too will be erased in the national memory. The building and architectural references serve also to highlight how the narrator's own sense of selfhood is built upon a denial of the traces of his African heritage.

A novel employing epigraphs from both the philosopher Jacques Derrida and former prime minister Margaret Thatcher ought perhaps to demand one's attention for this reason alone. But it is the way in which Dabydeen incorporates the theoretical idea that absences articulate more than presences into the fabric of recent British national sentiments that gives this short novel a seriousness and resonance that transcends its lightness of touch. **ABi**

Felicia's Journey

William Trevor

In *Felicia's Journey*, William Trevor grafted a new literary form onto one of the most insistent themes of his fiction; the fraught historical relationship between his native Ireland and his adopted England. In a psychological thriller set in the English Midlands, Trevor exposes Felicia, an innocent Irish girl, to the clutches of Mr. Hilditch, a middle-aged English bachelor with a tenuous hold on reality. The pregnant Felicia has escaped her paternalistic Catholic and Republican family in provincial Ireland to search for the baby's father in the heavily industrialized area around Birmingham. Unable to find him, Felicia is offered help and refuge by Mr. Hilditch in his large Victorian house, an edifice full of pseudo-artistic reminders of Britain's imperial past, where time seems to have stopped somewhere in the 1950s. Hildich's motives seem uncertain, and the exact nature of his relationship with a string of other women, and their final fate, is equally unclear.

The contrast between the perverse, evil, and manipulative Englishman and his intended victim, the young and naïve Irish girl, has clear political and historical overtones, but these aspects of the novel were largely ignored in Atom Egoyan's 1999 feature film version. As the reader's sense of foreboding increases, a cat and mouse game develops between the two protagonists, and Felicia is unwittingly assisted in escaping Mr. Hilditch by the persistent attention of Miss Calligary, a zealous West Indian missionary. As the focus of the novel changes to the disintegration of Hilditch's mind, Felicia is subsumed into society as an anonymous vagrant dependent on the generosity of humankind. She assumes an aura like that of a nun, a personification of unselfish sacrifice, whose mysterious gift of goodness has always fascinated Trevor. **UD**

Lifespan | b. 1928 (Ireland)
First Published | 1994
First Published by | Viking (London)
Whitbread Book of the Year | 1994

● The cover image selected for William Trevor's novel reflects its setting in the English Midlands, while hinting at sexual menace.

Captain Corelli's Mandolin

Louis de Bernières

Lifespan | *b.* 1954 (England)
First Published | 1994
First Published by | Secker & Warburg (London)
Commonwealth Writers Prize | 1995

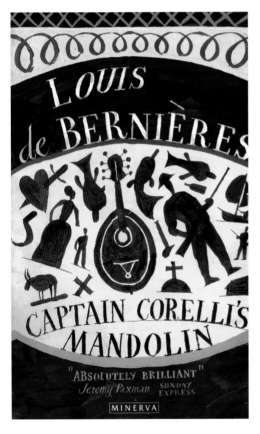

⊙ *Captain Corelli's Mandolin* achieved major bestseller status only gradually, as news of its readability spread by word of mouth.

Louis de Bernières writes in the great tradition of Gabriel García Márquez—vast, sprawling narratives that take in a whole world, that evoke and depict a community and the interrelatedness of its inhabitants from the birth to the death of its most long-lived members. Such a technique creates novels of remarkable depth, breadth, and humor.

The primary narrative of *Captain Corelli's Mandolin* focuses around Pelagia and her father Dr. Iannis, two inhabitants of the beautiful Greek island of Cephallonia. Against the backdrop of the horrific events of the Second World War and the Italian and German occupation of the island, the novel traces the love that develops between Pelagia and a musically gifted Italian, Captain Corelli. The novel is inhabited by a multiplicity of other characters and its seventy-three sections are narrated from multiple perspectives, ranging from omniscient narrative to secret letters, from the historical writings of Iannis to the imagined megalomaniacal ravings of Mussolini. With its combination of all these narratives—at once beautiful, funny, sad, horrific, and, above all, human—the novel can, at first, seem a little disjunctive and alienating. However, as its momentum builds, the reader is caught up in a multifaceted narrative that testifies with sagacity and humor to the way in which the lives of disparate individuals are at the same time infinitely separate and yet intimately interwoven. Despite a wealth of historical description, this novel is not intended to be a textbook of world events against which personal stories are set. Rather, the novel eschews the pretence to objectivity of official history and, more effectively than any textbook, evokes the horror, pain, and strange small miracles that happen during war to "the little people who are caught up in it." **SJD**

How Late It Was, How Late

James Kelman

How Late It Was, How Late is a novel of existential alienation. Awarded the 1994 Booker Prize for fiction, the resulting public consternation culminated in the charge of "literary vandalism" by the editor of *The Times*. Consequently the novel became more famous for its "bad" language than its remarkable innovations in form and style.

Told from the viewpoint of an unemployed Glasgow man, this is the story of Sammy Samuels, who wakes up blind after a police beating. Thereafter he struggles to navigate the labyrinthine city and welfare state as he attempts to claim benefit for his "dysfunction," all the while meditating on his predicament. The Kafkaesque sensibility of the book conjures up a shadowy establishment arbitrarily wielding an oppressive authority. However, for Kelman the instrument of this horror is language itself, and he rids his novel of a traditional English narrative framework to let Sammy speak for himself in the Glaswegian vernacular. In a further liberating move, the text slips back and forth between the first- and third-person narrative voice, effacing the boundary between narrator and character and eliminating this traditional linguistic hierarchy. Sammy becomes narrator and narrated, subject and object, an unstable identity that signals a crisis in Sammy's sense of self, a sense of alienation that is amplified by the repetition of words, actions, and events. Sammy is thus trapped in the present moment, devoid of meaning, direction, and opportunity for action. In the postindustrial Scottish context this predicament points to a particularly masculine crisis. However, the dehumanizing forces of society are resisted here with enormous emotional complexity, intellectual insight, and disarming humor. **CJ**

Lifespan | *b.* 1946 (Scotland)
First Published | 1994
First Published by | Secker & Warburg (London)
Booker Prize | 1994

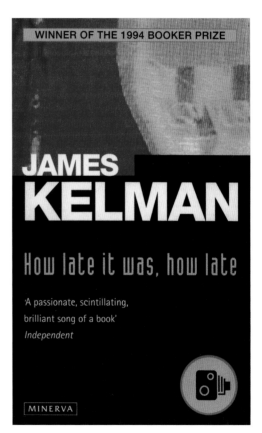

WINNER OF THE 1994 BOOKER PRIZE

JAMES KELMAN

How late it was, how late

'A passionate, scintillating, brilliant song of a book'
Independent

MINERVA

◉ Despite his humor and imaginative verve, Kelman alienated mainstream readers with an insistent use of "bad" language.

City Sister Silver

Jáchym Topol

Lifespan | *b.* 1962 (Czechoslovakia)
First Published | 1994
First Published by | Atlantis (Brno)
Original Title | *Sestra (Sister)*

"We were the People of the Secret. And we were waiting."

⬥ A subversive poet and songwriter in the last years of communist rule, Topol is now seen as an intriguing young Czech novelist.

Jáchym Topol is one of the bravest and most vibrant Czech voices to emerge since the Velvet Revolution in 1989. Son of the playwright Josef Topol and brother of Filip (the frontman for the rock band Psí vojáci), Topol was the youngest signatory of the dissident initiative Charter 77 and has been involved in the artistic and political underground for his entire adult life. *City Sister Silver* is perhaps the only literary work to give the postrevolutionary period a sustained treatment. It is also one of the first works to experiment fully with the use of colloquial Czech—reveling in the slang and profanities of a language often suppressed by decades of occupation. *City Sister Silver* can be read as a declaration of independence for the modern Czech imagination.

The novel begins at the early stages of the Revolution with an account of the flight of East German refugees from Prague and establishes its primary narrator—an alienated, poetic soul named Potok who falls in with a crew of semi-criminals who are looking for business opportunities amid the chaotic energy of the new era. From this point on, however, time "explodes." *City Sister Silver* is a fantastical trip through European history, veering drunkenly between passages of clipped social realism, news events, madcap dream sequences, and esoteric mythology. It is a difficult experience for a reader unfamiliar with Czech culture, but one that reflects the acute uncertainties—moral, social, political, economic, linguistic, religious—of the postrevolutionary moment. Running parallel to the drift and flux, however, is a moving love story as Potok searches for, and eventually finds, his "sister," or soul mate. This is a beautiful, bewildering, and consistently inventive work. **SamT**

Pereira Declares: A Testimony

Antonio Tabucchi

The story is recounted to the narrator—as we are reminded by the phrase "declares Pereira" ritually introducing each chapter—by Pereira, the editor of the cultural page of the *Lisboa* newspaper. Tabucchi's love for Portugal is tangible in the novel's descriptions of Lisbon glittering under the sun or shivering under the ocean breeze. It is the summer of 1938 and, while dictatorships in the rest of Europe are already strongly established, Portugal is still witnessing the early manifestations of Salazar's regime. *Pereira Declares* is a story about the power of words and how they can make people politically and ethically responsible. At the opening, Pereira is a rather heavy, inward looking widower who converses depressingly with a photograph of his dead wife. Untouched by the erosion of democracy and the violent silencing of protest under Salazar's dictatorship, Pereira is divided between his worries about his heart condition and his intellectual concerns about death. From the beginning, the smell of death permeates the novel. When Pereira discovers a philosophical essay on the topic by the young revolutionary Monteiro Rossi, Pereira is awakened to echoes of the collective extermination of Jews and the beating of workers. The violent murder of Monteiro at the hands of Salazar's police convinces Pereira to take a political stance.

Death is a political metaphor for the absence of freedom. Symbolically, out of death comes life and Pereira's decision to fight for it. The novel closes on a transformed Pereira, feeling younger and lighter and committed to fight political repression with the use of words. Before fleeing Portugal, his last piece in *Lisboa* is not just another timid book review but a fearless accusation of government responsibility for the death of his friend Monteiro. **RPi**

Lifespan | *b.* 1943 (Italy)
First Published | 1994, by Feltrinelli (Milan)
Awards | Super Campiello
Original Title | *Sostiene Pereira: una testimonianza*

> *"But he, Pereira, was meditating on death."*

⊘ Italian author Tabucchi is a professor of Portuguese literature and has spent much of his life in Lisbon, the setting of this novel.

The Wind-Up Bird Chronicle

Haruki Murakami

The Master of Petersburg

J. M. Coetzee

Lifespan | b. 1949 (Japan)
First Published | 1994
First Published by | Shinchosa (Tokyo)
Original Title | Nejimaki-dori kuronikuru

Lifespan | b. 1940 (South Africa)
First Published | 1994
First Published by | Secker & Warburg (London)
Nobel Prize for Literature | 2003

The narrator of *The Wind-Up Bird Chronicle*, Haruki Murakami's heftiest novel, has recently quit his job. Toru Okada spends his days at home in a Tokyo suburb while his wife goes out to work. Then a series of strange events disrupts his life: the cat goes missing, he receives sinister erotic phone calls from a woman he doesn't know, he inherits an empty box from an old fortune-teller. Then one day his wife doesn't come home.

The novel takes on the form of an ambiguous quest, with many intriguing clues. Okada meets a teenage girl who, like him, doesn't have much to do all day. A platonic friendship develops. She points him in the direction of a garden with a dried-up well in it. An old soldier tells him a story of how during the war he spent several days at the bottom of a well in Mongolia. Okada takes to meditating in the well in the garden, where the borders between alternative realities become porous.

"Most Japanese novelists," Murakami has said, "are addicted to the beauty of the language. I'd like to change that . . . Language is . . . an instrument to communicate." His flat style is more remarkable in Japanese, because the flatness itself is more striking, but it lends itself well to translation. **TEJ**

🔾 Murakami's Japan is the everyday contemporary urban world, but strangely penetrated by mysteries and historical reflections.

The Master of Petersburg deals with the events leading to the authorship of Dostoevsky's most political novel, *The Devils*. Coetzee's Dostoevsky returns covertly from Dresden to St. Petersburg in 1869 after the mysterious death of his stepson, Pavel. Either the Tsar's secret police have murdered Pavel, a follower of the revolutionary Nechaev, or else Nechaev himself has orchestrated the death in the hope of drumming up support for his burgeoning movement. Dostoevsky remains in St. Petersburg and he becomes increasingly embroiled in Nechaev's circle. He imagines that some event might occur, such as an appearance from Pavel in a form that he cannot predict, which would require him to respond.

It is the knife-edge quality of Coetzee's writing that sustains the sense of precarious balance that characterizes Dostoevsky's protracted stay in the city, and evokes the dark mood of the Russian master's novels. Dostoevsky is at once drawn to the revolutionary urge in Nechaev that reminds him of his own politically engaged past, but he is also disgusted by him. As the novel progresses, the reader is drawn into the mind of Dostoevsky as he sits down to compose *The Devils*. The ethical question that torments him, where his responsibility to Pavel ends and whether it can ever be faithfully discharged, is left finally to trouble the reader. **ABi**

Land

Park Kyong-ni

Lifespan | b. 1926 (South Korea)
First Published | 1969–1994
First UK Edition | 2002, by Kegan Paul (London)
Original Title | Toji

This five-part saga relates the tragic story of four generations of the Choi family of rich landowners—from 1897 to Korea's liberation from Japan in 1945—revealing in the process many little-understood aspects of Korean life and history.

In Part 1 (1897–1908), Park describes the collapse of the Choi family and the seizing of their property by Cho Joon-ku, a remote relative. Also covered is the childhood of Seo-hee, a daughter of the family, who eventually travels to Jendao in Jilin Province, China, with some villagers who hate Cho Joon-ku. Part 2 (1911–1917) is concerned with Seo-hee's life and success in Jendao. Seo-hee marries Gilsang, a former servant of the Choi family, before returning home. The reader is introduced to the Korean independence movement, and conflicts in the expatriate Korean community are exposed. In Part 3 (1919–1929), Seo-hee succeeds in driving out Cho Joon-ku. Meanwhile, the narrative touches on the predominant issues and difficulties of Korean intellectuals under Japanese colonial rule.

In Part 4 (1930–1939), as Seo-hee's sons, Hwan-kuk and Yoon-kuk, grow up, Park delves deeper into Korean history, culture, and art. She explores how Korea evolved greater self-knowledge as Japanese oppression resulted in growing disorder in Korean society. Part 5 (1940–1945) is focused on the Koreans who sought liberation. It climaxes with the news of Japan's surrender, when Seo-hee feels as if a heavy iron chain on herself has finally been removed. **Hoy**

Whatever

Michel Houellebecq

Lifespan | b. 1958 (Réunion)
First Published | 1994, by M. Nadeau (Paris)
Given Name | Michel Thomas
Original Title | Extension du domaine de la lutte

Whatever is a study in contemporary alienation. In straightforward, almost journalistic prose, the first-person narration documents the lonely life of a computer engineer. He is well-off, but finds no satisfaction in his job or any of the products that it allows him to buy. He manages to do a passable imitation of a functioning individual, but is unable to form attachments to either things or people.

The original French title, which translates as "Extension of the Domain of the Struggle," provides an insight into the novel's main theme. The insidious advance of capitalist values has infiltrated every aspect of our lives. Even the realms of love and sex are subject to the same forces of competition and exchange as the marketplace. This creates a sexual underclass, represented in the novel by the narrator and his ugly colleague Tisserand, still a virgin at age twenty-eight, although not through want of trying. Drunk, bored, and on the verge of a breakdown, the narrator tries halfheartedly to talk Tisserand into murdering the latest in a long line of women who have turned him down, as if to redress the imbalance he perceives in the sexual economy.

Houellebecq's is a highly deterministic outlook, where one is merely the sum of the quality of one's genetic inheritance and the strength of one's socio-economic position. This view of contemporary European society may be what makes Houellebecq one of the most popular and influential novelists currently writing. **SS**

The Folding Star

Alan Hollinghurst

Lifespan | *b.* 1954 (England)
First Published | 1994
First Published by | Chatto & Windus (London)
James Tait Black Memorial Prize | 1994

Hollinghurst's second novel is a dark, though often funny, tale of obsessive love, art, mourning, fetishism, and death. Its narrator, Edward Manners, is a teacher who has come to a Belgian town to teach English to two schoolboys, with one of whom, Luc Altidore, he is infatuated. The story charts the progress of his fascination, from his first longings, to their sexual consummation, and beyond into the desolation of Luc's disappearance. Hollinghurst writes perhaps the best sex scenes of any modern novelist: there are beautiful, erotic encomia to the male body, lusty accounts of passion and its aftermath, and acute renderings of the self-conscious thought processes of Manners as he takes his pleasure with a range of men.

The novel is highly, although never obtrusively, allusive and is crammed with anagrams, puns, and puzzles—for example, the surname Altidore unscrambles, aptly, as "idolater," while the book's title refers to Milton's *Comus* as well as a poem by William Collins. These encryptions place the novel within a tradition of gay literature, in which homosexual love could only speak its name in riddles. This is not, however, simply a book for an initiated cognoscenti. Manners is enamored of the Georgian and Romantic poets—the sense that human love is shot through with loss and death informs the whole novel, making it into a profound and melancholy meditation on the transience of pleasure and passion. **CC**

Mr. Vertigo

Paul Auster

Lifespan | *b.* 1947 (U.S.)
First Published | 1994
First Published by | Faber & Faber (London)
First U.S. Edition | Viking (New York)

Mr. Vertigo is the story of Walter Rawley, a wisecracking street urchin from St. Louis who is rescued by Master Yehudi, a quasi-religious master who hails from Budapest via Brooklyn. The story is told through Walt's eyes as he looks back, now an old man, and reminisces about his time with Master Yehudi. The teenage Walt has a hard head, a sharp tongue, and a gift Master Yehudi has been searching for in strange young men for years—he can fly. Once his gift is honed, Master Yehudi and Walt the Wonder Boy take their act on the roads of the Midwest. In seeking to defy the laws of nature, as he proposes to do with Walt, Master Yehudi places himself in a precarious position in relation to God, the universe, and his fellow man. In the end, Walt is forced to choose between continuing to work with his gift and his developing manhood, a powerful dilemma.

In part, this is a classic tale of master and disciple, the young man having to give in to the older man's will to discover his true potential. The story asks how the mythical and the mundane can meld together in the everyday world, where nothing is certain. This ambiguity establishes the tone of the book and is reflected in the characters themselves—Walt is a smart-ass as well as a spiritual vessel, and Master Yehudi is a charlatan with a deep-rooted spirituality. Walt's story can be read as a childhood parable, but it is also a comment on American history, on interior and exterior spaces, myth and magic, show business, money, and, finally, success and failure. **EF**

The End of the Story

Lydia Davis

Lifespan | *b.* 1947 (U.S.)
First Published | 1995
First Published by | Farrar, Straus & Giroux (New York)
First UK Edition | 1996, by High Risk (London)

True to its title, *The End of the Story* begins at the end of the love affair at its heart. Flashing forward a year, the nameless narrator, a writer and university teacher, goes on to tell us of her failed attempts to find "him" (also nameless) in a strange city. Tracing him to his last known address, she finds unfamiliar names above the doorbell. With more than a nod to Proust (of whom Davis is a distinguished translator), the narrator spends the novel ringing the doorbell of the past in the vain hope of finding truth on the other side. The hope is all the more urgent in that she is writing a novel about the affair, the very novel we are reading (or is it?).

Like many contemporary novels, *The End of the Story* is in large part about itself, about the painful process of its own making. Yet it is not a novel seeking to subvert conventional modes of storytelling from some self-conscious and superior ironic perspective. Rather, it is about the strange paradox under which all writers (and indeed non-writers) labor, namely that the very attempt to clarify our experience can end up obscuring it. Thus, the narrator starts to doubt the apparent solidity of her memory—did she really fall in love by candlelight? Indeed, was that really what she was feeling?

The crystalline simplicity and precision of Davis' prose only intensifies this sense of the profound elusiveness of life and love. We can tell our stories, her novel painstakingly shows us, only after they happen—that is, after they are lost to us. **JC**

Love's Work

Gillian Rose

Lifespan | *b.* 1947 (England), *d.* 1995
First Published | 1995
First Published by | Chatto & Windus (London)
Full Title | *Love's Work: A Reckoning With Life*

Sigmund Freud described love and work as the foundations of human happiness. The philosopher and social theorist Gillian Rose's autobiographical text, *Love's Work*, intertwines them in order to explore the love of work (the work of thought, of philosophy) and the work, and workings, of love. The book opens with Rose's first meeting with Edna, a New Yorker in her nineties, who has lived with cancer since the age of sixteen. *Love's Work* thus begins with an exploration of the meanings of survival and the necessity of living "skeptically." Contradiction, difference, and the ways in which we negotiate them are at the heart of the book and are strongly figured for Rose in the relationship between Protestantism and Judaism (her family's religion), the appeal to "inwardness" or to a law that compels obedience but not belief. This is a story about "education," but one in which the meanings of this term are continually tested.

It is not until several chapters into the book that Rose reveals to the reader that, as she writes, she has advanced cancer. She has already described the destruction wrought by an unhappy love affair, which has to be embraced in order that "I may have a chance of surviving . . . I hear the roaring and the roasting and know that it is I." The reader, confronted with his or her own preconceptions of the disease, is challenged to think in new ways about living and dying, the comedy of life and the tragedy of philosophy, and their ultimate inseparability. **LM**

A Fine Balance

Rohinton Mistry

Lifespan | *b.* 1952 (India)
First Published | 1995
First Published by | McClelland & Stewart (Toronto)
Commonwealth Writers Prize | 1996

Rohinton Mistry's *A Fine Balance* is set in India in the mid-1970s. Two tailors, Ishvar and his nephew Omprakash, leave their small village under tragic circumstances to work in the city. Their employer is the widowed Dina Dalal, who is also supplying accommodation for her friends' student son, Manek. These four lives become intertwined and tremulous friendships are made amid the chaos of Indian life under the State of Emergency, declared in 1975.

The epic scale of the novel confronts the ruthless brutality of class and caste as the protagonists are left vulnerable to the vagaries of poverty and discrimination. This is a historical novel, which meticulously recreates Indira Gandhi's India, and the author uses this context to present a paradoxically humane vision of inhumanity.

Rigorously unsentimental and full of black humor, *A Fine Balance* takes the reader through a vicious and sometimes carnivalesque world of poverty and utter powerlessness. The novel's harrowing denouement is as shocking and as distressing as anything in twentieth-century literature. Perhaps Mistry's greatest achievement is his clear-sighted depiction of relentless, impersonal brutality. What we are given is a heartbreaking story of lives torn apart not by individual weakness but by institutional inequity and the horrors of corrupt power. This is a beautiful and devastating novel whose genius lies in its refusal to allow the reader to escape to either pathos or cynicism. **PMcM**

"Dina pretended to be upset, saying he had never praised her meals with superlatives. He tried to wriggle out of it."

⊙ Rohinton Mistry has lived in Canada since 1975, but his novels and short stories have been set in India, the country of his birth.

The Reader

Bernhard Schlink

Lifespan | *b.* 1944 (Germany)
First Published | 1995
First Published by | Diogenes (Zürich)
Original Title | *Der Vorleser*

"When rescue came, it was almost an assault. The woman seized my arm and pulled me through the dark entryway into the courtyard."

⬙ Photographed here in 1995, Schlink was well known in Germany as a writer of popular crime fiction before publishing *The Reader*.

Falling ill on his way home from school, fifteen-year-old Michael Berg is rescued by Hanna Schmitz, a streetcar conductor twice his age. When he returns later to thank her, a passionate and volatile relationship ensues between the two. Torn between his youth and his desire for Hanna, Michael is nonetheless devastated when she mysteriously disappears. While the affair is short-lived, the experience fundamentally affects the way in which he shapes his own identity. Subsequently, Michael's sense of self is shattered when he encounters Hanna years later on trial for Nazi war crimes. As he watches her refuse to defend herself, he slowly realizes that she is hiding a secret she considers more humiliating than murder. Simultaneously a student of law and her former lover, Michael must attempt to reconcile the horrendous crimes of which she is accused with the memory of the woman he loved.

Schlink, himself a professor of law and a practicing judge, grapples with the complex ethical questions that inevitably emerge after the trauma of mass genocide. But instead of concentrating on its victims, Schlink shifts his focus to the inheritors of the Nazi legacy. *The Reader* asks its readers to consider to what extent we can hold the postwar generation responsible for the sins of its fathers and mothers, if such atrocities can even be redressed. Does the demonization of the Nazis serve to chastise their behavior, or is it a selfish measure to create a false division between them and us? **BJ**

The Rings of Saturn

W. G. Sebald

Lifespan | *b.* 1944 (Germany), *d.* 2001 (England)
First Published | 1995, by Eichborn (Frankfurt)
Original Title | *Die Ringe des Saturn: eine englische Wallfahrt*

The Rings of Saturn is ostensibly the record of a walking holiday Sebald takes through Suffolk in 1992. It considers past and present, discovering strange, usually overlooked, aspects of places. This is not, however, simply a memoir or historical reflection. *The Rings of Saturn* is principally a book of mourning: for two colleagues who suddenly die, for the world before the two World Wars, for the author's realization that, as Walter Benjamin puts it, each act of civilization is also one of barbarism. An aura of melancholy and trauma pervades his account. Many of the figures he encounters have withdrawn from the world, seemingly unable to bear the burdens of modern life. The landscape, too, more regularly bears witness to decline than to prosperity. Yet Sebald's precise and economical style resists a collapse into overt despondency. His unexpected encounters absorb the reader, not least to wonder at how apparently random meetings generate such fascinating hidden histories.

A figure in the book who notably commands Sebald's attention is the seventeenth-century East Anglian writer Sir Thomas Browne, whose treatise on human mortality, *Urn Burial*, is in many respects a model for *The Rings of Saturn*. Sebald has a wonderful capacity to combine natural history, antiquarian findings, and observations on contemporary northern European life into an intriguing if sober reflection on "the long account of calamities" that compose history. **TH**

Sabbath's Theater

Philip Roth

Lifespan | *b.* 1933 (U.S.)
First Published | 1995
First Published by | Houghton Mifflin (Boston)
National Book Award | 1995

The central character of the novel, Mickey Sabbath, is a sixty-four-year-old forced into retirement because of arthritis. Most of the narrative is a gleeful recounting of Mickey's many infidelities, and even his grief at the death of his latest mistress is motivated more by anxieties about his failing powers of seduction than by any romantic longing. The unsuspecting reader should be aware that the theater of the novel's title refers to Mickey's pioneering puppet act from the 1960s that was performed by his middle finger—while his other fingers deftly set about disrobing female members of the audience.

Roth offers a series of vignettes that are occasionally too knowingly calculated to test the reader's sympathy to the limit. There is no profanity, it seems, that is too awful for Mickey Sabbath to contemplate: he plunders the underwear drawer of his best friend's daughter in search of an aid to masturbation, he sneers at his wife's attempts to combat alcoholism, and he urinates upon the grave of a former mistress.

Lechery, it seems, is Mickey's vocation in life, and Roth is blithely indifferent to the agenda of political correctness. The novel is often darkly comic, and the carnivalesque energies that it unleashes do sometimes make Mickey uncomfortably engaging. For those in search of the vicarious thrills of cocking a snook at bourgeois morality, this novel will certainly not disappoint. **VA**

The Moor's Last Sigh

Salman Rushdie

Lifespan | *b.* 1947 (India)
First Published | 1995
First Published by | Jonathan Cape (London)
Whitbread Novel Award | 1995

"No more secrets any more."

⬥ Rushdie's novel indulges a magic realism that leans
  more towards magic than the depiction of reality.

The Moor's Last Sigh is big. It is a carnival of magic realism—complex, comic, and political. It is religious, profane, idealistic, a gadfly. It is a novel like India itself. And India, indeed, is like Moraes Zogoiby.

Moraes, known as "the Moor," is a mishmash of disparate identities. His mother, Aurora, "the outlaw bandit queen" of Bombay, descends from the Portuguese; his father, from a tribe of Cochin Jews; and he is, perhaps, the descendant of Boabdil, the last Moorish Sultan of Granada. His life is a metaphor for the divisiveness of India, its intolerance, instability, and bounty, moving perhaps too fast for its own good, too fast to secure an identity. Moraes lives life at "double speed." At age thirty-six, he has the body of a seventy-two-year-old. Moraes is exiled by Aurora, who is beautiful, turbulent, both loving and hateful: a mother like Mother India. He narrates not only his family's history, and where it went wrong, but India's as well. He wants to set the record straight and to counter the history proffered by what he calls "Hindufundamentalist triumphalism." His is a story of schisms and passion, revenge and prejudice. It is about democracy that soured and secularism that proved untenable.

The novel is fecund with characters and events, constantly multiplying, crowding into the narrative, and demanding to be heard. Starting generations before his own birth, it is about the fall of a great family and the ambivalent and seismic soul of a beloved country. This is perhaps Rushdie's most masterful performance. His language is rich in puns and allusions, and the hilarious patois of Aurora is exhilarating. He creates a vibrant tapestry as perhaps only a polyglot can. India inspires greatness and nourishes the soul; it is this hope of India, hope for India, that Moraes, like Rushdie, will not let die. **GT**

The Information

Martin Amis

Self-delusion, bitterness, paranoia, hypochondria—just a few of the traits that Martin Amis bestows upon protagonist Richard Tull in this sprawling comic novel about the rivalry between two writers. Richard is not merely an unsuccessful writer, he is a writer who has achieved literary failure on an epic scale. His latest novel, the unpublishable *Untitled*, is so excruciatingly complex and unreadable as to induce a blinding migraine in anyone determined enough to get to page four. The other writer, Gwyn Barry, is the author of a bestseller. What makes his success so unbearable for Richard is the fact that the two have been close friends since their days as striving novelists dreaming of publication. Richard always regarded himself as the more talented, and never imagined that his plodding rival might one day produce a work of genius. Now Gwyn has not only achieved recognition with *Amelior*, a bland Utopian novel that Richard contemptuously dismisses as "trex," but it is being acclaimed as a masterpiece. In a jealous rage, Richard searches for ways to ruin Gwyn—first trying to destroy his literary reputation, then attempting to break up his marriage to a wealthy aristocrat, and finally in desperation arranging to have him attacked by a vicious psychopath.

London, a city poised uneasily on the cusp of the millennium, with anonymous menace stalking its pubs and parks, is familiar Amis territory. A shifting cast of high-life and low-life characters—agents and moneymen, reprobates, and fools—are caught up in the mayhem, celebrated in Amis' cool and exquisitely controlled prose. The novel is pervaded by dark obsession, explored by Amis' wonderful sense of the absurd. And there is the information, "which comes at night." **TS**

Lifespan | *b.* 1949 (England)
First Published | 1995
First Published by | Flamingo (London)
First U.S. Edition | Harmony (New York)

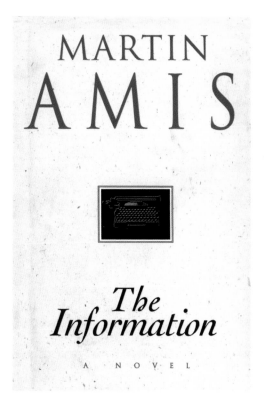

"He was in a terrible state..."

⊘ *The Information*'s plot of a rivalry between two authors is said to be partly based on Amis' rift with his contemporary Julian Barnes.

Morvern Callar

Alan Warner

Lifespan | *b.* 1964 (Scotland)
First Published | 1995
First Published by | Jonathan Cape (London)
First U.S. Edition | 1997, by Anchor (New York)

It is just before Christmas, and there is something on the kitchen floor that Morvern Callar is putting off dealing with—the dead body of her boyfriend. Her first reaction is, understandably, to consider ringing for an ambulance, but she smokes a Silk Cut (the first of many), turns away from "His" body, and leaves for a night of untroubled alcoholic, narcotic, and sexual excess. This, it turns out, is typical of our heroine. As Warner draws the reader into the fallout from this suicide and Morvern's complex reactions to it, we encounter a brilliantly eccentric succession of West Highland misfits debauched in their apathy, and "the Port," a dreamlike town on the coast where they are all marooned.

Yet this is definitively Morvern's novel, and—just as in Lynne Ramsay's recent film adaptation—it is her dispassionate voice and her eclectic music tastes that dominate. Warner does not pretend to offer insights into Morvern's soul, but she is governed by her own sense of morality: it is this, in fact, that raises her above the druggies, townies, and no-hopers she encounters on her travels. She simply and genuinely adapts to situations as they arise; she takes advantage of circumstances; ultimately she gains a different perspective upon her life and those around her as a result. Taking in the unrepentant hedonism of rave culture of the early nineties, Club Med holidays, and British tourism, this was a defining text for a generation. This powerful and original voice remains unsurprisingly vital. **MD**

The Unconsoled

Kazuo Ishiguro

Lifespan | *b.* 1954 (Japan)
First Published | 1995
First Published by | Faber & Faber (London)
Original Language | English

Few readers will know a book as mesmerizing as Kazuo Ishiguro's unique *The Unconsoled*. The text is oriented around (if it can be said to be oriented at all) the uncanny sense that we as readers, and Ryder the narrator, have somehow been here before. The novel opens with Ryder entering a hotel in an unnamed Central European city for a performance at the Civic Concert Hall, probably the most important concert of his life. Ryder is confident in the knowledge that he is the greatest pianist of his generation, but he suffers from severe and disorienting bouts of amnesia.

The music-obsessed city in which he finds himself is as much a city of the mind as a physical space: as he wanders the streets, he encounters people he knows intimately, and people similarly seem to know him. His past continually intrudes on the present, and with deft surrealist touches Ishiguro allows the fictional world of the novel to overflow its bounds. Space becomes compressed and expanded, time loses meaning, and Ryder finds himself entangled in a situation where he only knows that he has the solution, although what that answer is, he has no idea. The narrative plays tricks with Ryder and with the reader, combining his limited sense of his own past and events around him with a prescient third-person narrative that allows him apparently impossible insights. A virtuoso performance, this thrillingly original text demands engagement from its readers and is a richly rewarding experience. **MD**

Alias Grace

Margaret Atwood

Lifespan | *b.* 1939 (Canada)
First Published | 1996
First Published by | McClelland & Stewart (Toronto)
Giller Prize | 1996

Alias Grace is a lyrical work of historical fiction based around the story of servant girl, Grace Marks, who is one of Canada's most notorious female criminals. Grace tells her story in a vivid, bitter voice, from her childhood in Ireland through life as part of the underclass in colonial Victorian Canada to her conviction for murdering her employer in 1843 at the age of sixteen. The novel is told through Dr. Simon Jordan, a mental illness specialist who is engaged by a group of reformers and spiritualists seeking a pardon for the young woman. As he brings Grace closer and closer to the day she cannot remember, he comes to learn about the strained relationship between her employer, James Kinnear, and his housekeeper and mistress, Nancy, and of the alarming behavior of Grace's fellow servant, James McDermott.

As always, Atwood includes elements of social and feminist comment in her work, exploring the relationships between sex and violence in a historically repressed society. The author also reflects, in people's reactions to Grace, the period's ambiguity about the nature of woman. Some factions of society felt that women were weak and therefore that Grace must have been a victim who was forced into a desperate act. Others believed that women were intrinsically more evil than men. This dichotomy between the demonic and pathetic woman is subtly reflected in the character of Grace who, having spent time in a lunatic asylum, claims to have no memory at all of the murders. **EF**

"It's 1851. I'll be twenty-four years old next birthday. I've been shut up in here since the age of sixteen. I am a model prisoner, and give no trouble."

The design for the jacket of Atwood's novel aptly reflects the themes of imprisonment and the mystery of human motivation.

The Clay Machine-Gun

Victor Pelevin

Lifespan | *b.* 1962 (Russia)
First Published | 1996
First Published by | Vagrius (Moscow)
Original Title | *Chapaev i Pustota*

The main character of this novel is Petr, a comrade of Chapayev, a Soviet civil war hero made famous by a 1930s propaganda movie that spawned a whole series of irreverent "Chapayev jokes." Hard drinking and hard living in the turbulent early 1920s, Petr has recurrent alcohol and cocaine-induced dreams, which, in a reversal of ordinary flashback techniques, take him and the plot to a post-Soviet insane asylum, where the tales of three inmates are revealed during their therapy. Overarching all this is a Buddhist vision centered on Chapayev turned spiritual teacher, which explores the meaning and dissolution of reality.

The Clay Machine-Gun weaves together its various strands and characters in a way that is nothing less than random. Its language and motives, taken variously from post-Soviet daily life, outdated ideology, history, literature, Zen philosophy, and pop culture may seem incongruent. Yet they all form part of a plot constructed with the absurd stringency of a children's play, where there can be no loose ends left untied, and every element must be connected into a tapestry of the strange, the exaggerated, and the delusional, asserting a sense of an overall meaning. The charm of the book is the playful way in which it denies yet enjoys meaning, and the sheer joy of invention it exudes. It is a bit like one very long, very complex, and, above all, very good joke, and like all good jokes it has a great deal to say about the "real world." **DG**

Infinite Jest

David Foster Wallace

Lifespan | *b.* 1962 (U.S.)
First Published | 1996
First Published by | Little, Brown & Co. (Boston)
First UK Edition | 1997, by Abacus (London)

Where does one begin with a book of over a thousand pages, of which the last ninety-six feature three hundred and eighty-eight detailed (but also wildly funny) footnotes? A plot synopsis is sadly doomed to inadequacy. Set in the near future, *Infinite Jest* is the title of a film made by the maverick avant-garde filmmaker James O. Incandenza, which is apparently so funny that the viewer ultimately expires in a state of uncontrollable hilarity. When both film and filmmaker disappear, all manner of sinister individuals, government agencies, and foreign governments attempt to track them down, and the ensuing chaos incorporates the recovering addicts of Ennet House (a Boston dependency clinic), and the Enfield Tennis Academy. These last two locations provide two opposing points of focus for the text. One allows Wallace to explore the centrality of addiction to consumer culture and the place of narcotics within that culture. The other is an extraordinary vision of a hothouse sporting school, which produces children for an industry that will disregard most of them.

Infinite Jest satirically attacks the vacuous predilections of contemporary American culture mercilessly, while shamelessly revelling in them. Wildly inventive, linguistically original, extravagantly detailed, and playful, this text is the one you would take with you to a desert island. **MD**

> Wallace's zany satire and fascination with conspiracy places him in the same modern American tradition as DeLillo and Pynchon.

Forever a Stranger

Hella Haasse

Lifespan | *b.* 1918 (Java)
First Published | 1996, by Oxford University Press
First Published as *Oeroeg* | 1948
Full Title | *Forever a Stranger and Other Stories*

Hella Haasse is one of the Netherlands' most esteemed, venerable, and prolific authors, although English-language translations of her works have been mysteriously slow to arrive. *Forever a Stranger* was her first prose work, written at the age of thirty, and it made her name. Written as the deeply controversial Dutch military operations against the Indonesian struggle for independence were beginning, this spare and incisive ninety-page story of friendship between a Dutch boy and an Indonesian boy is at once a moving and engaging narrative, a telling historical fable, and a treatise on "irrevocable, incomprehensible differentness."

The original Dutch title was *Oeroeg*, after the Indonesian boy with whom the (unnamed) Dutch narrator is friends. The story covers their inseparable childhood, through to an adolescence of increasing alienation and displacement governed by the immovable judgement: "Some day you'll have to live without Oeroeg ...You're European!" The implications of this difference are followed through to the final confrontation: "Am I forever to be a stranger in the land of my birth?"

Forever a Stranger and Other Stories is tellingly aware of the ways that language, personal identities, and national destinies intersect and are at odds. Although the finer points of these qualities were lost in *Oeroeg's* translation to the big screen (*Going Home*, 1993), the continuing power Haasse's tale has over Dutch culture is evident. **MS**

The Ghost Road

Pat Barker

Lifespan | *b.* 1943 (England)
First Published | 1996
First Published by | Viking (London)
Booker Prize | 1995

Ghost Road is the final part of Barker's World War trilogy that began with *Regeneration* (1991) and *The Eye in the Door* (1993), and which started to change the face of war writing by depicting alternative perspectives on the war, including its investigation of trauma patients and the roles of working-class women, homosexuals, protest organizations, and government officials on the home front.

Her introduction of fictional characters among established figures, such as the war poets Siegfried Sassoon and Wilfred Owen, and military psychologist W. H. R. Rivers, has led to criticism and historical confusion. But Barker's trilogy attempts to portray the complexities that are inherent in our attitude to *all* combat. In *The Ghost Road*, she sends her protagonists back to the arena of the Western Front and enables the familiar device of a wartime diary to discuss the responses to direct combat. At the same time she chronicles the doubts and declining health of W. H. R. Rivers, whose job is to rehabilitate men in order to return them to the field of war. The text is a clear example of later social values being imposed on wartime circumstances, especially in the liberal responses to trauma and homosexuality, but Barker recognizes this and draws a complex, if modern, picture of men at war. This may not be historically accurate, but Barker's trilogy firmly expands the staid vision of mud, blood, and poppies into a version that suggests both complexity and the potential for later war literature to develop further. **EMcCS**

Fugitive Pieces

Anne Michaels

Lifespan | *b.* 1958 (Canada)
First Published | 1996
First Published by | McClelland & Stewart (Toronto)
Orange Prize | 1997

Winner of several prestigious awards and critically acclaimed, *Fugitive Pieces* recounts the life of a Jewish boy, Jakob, rescued from a Polish city during the Holocaust and taken by Athos, a Greek scholar, to the island of Zakynthos. In a hilltop refuge, surrounded by botany, geological artifacts, and classic poetry, Jakob soaks up knowledge while he grieves for his murdered parents and lost sister.

From the start, this is a novel with a difference. Written by an already successful poet, the prose is richly textured, resonant, and rhythmic. Michaels employs the vocabularies of archaeology, geology, and literature to build a unique sense of personal and political history, as we witness the developing relationship between Jakob and his savior. We follow the journey of Athos and Jakob to a Canada imbued with a new sense of its immigrant population. Still haunted by the death of his family, Jakob continues the literary career encouraged in him by Athos. The key to Jakob's redemption comes through his poetry and the late awakening of the sensual possibilities of his own body. In the last section of the novel, the repercussions of the emotional traumas that Jakob has absorbed throughout his life are shown by their redemptive effects on a reader of his poetry. Michaels presents the interlocking of lives across cultures through the passing on of a written knowledge that has the power to heal. She does not balk from the complex notion that beauty applies equally to devastation and to love. **AC**

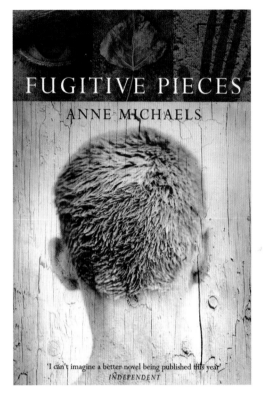

"Grief requires time. If a chip of stone radiates its self, its breath, so long, how stubborn might be the soul."

The cover of the Bloomsbury edition of *Fugitive Pieces* underlines the imaginative quality of the book, a poet's first novel.

Hallucinating Foucault

Patricia Duncker

Lifespan | *b.* 1951 (Jamaica)
First Published | 1996
First Published by | Serpent's Tail (London)
First U.S. Edition | Ecco Press (Hopewell)

Hallucinating Foucault is a dark and tragic novel. It is also beautiful, romantic, and funny. Like its characters, it is a deeply idiosyncratic work that is both disturbing and seductive. While negotiating themes of death, sexuality, crime, and madness, this novel is in fact primarily about love—for both books and people. It is about the surreal disjunction between an author and his work, and the madness of the reader, who loves both of these at once and yet distinctly.

In a first-person retrospective narrative, the novel tells the story of a young student writing his doctoral thesis on the works of a (fictional) gay French novelist, Paul Michel. Early in his research, the narrator is drawn into a love affair with a captivating Germanist, who compels the narrator to travel to France to seek out Michel; the novelist has been incarcerated in psychiatric institutions since his violent bout of madness following Michel Foucault's death in June 1984. In doing so, the narrator embarks on a love affair that will change his life, if not his work, forever.

A masterfully told story, *Hallucinating Foucault* leaves its own readers with that profound sense of loss felt when the final lines of a book signal ejection from a world that has both captivated and contained them. Reading Duncker's first novel, a tale of the kind of love that can exist between reader and author, cannot but be the beginning of a personal love affair with her work. **SJD**

Cocaine Nights

J. G. Ballard

Lifespan | *b.* 1930 (China)
First Published | 1996
First Published by | Flamingo (London)
Full Name | James Graham Ballard

In *Cocaine Nights*, Ballard explodes one of the modern myths of utopian paradise—early retirement, a place in the sun, a vibrant community, and plentiful leisure. The narrator Charles Prentice has traveled to the retirement resort of Estrella del Mar on the Costa del Sol, Spain, to try and clear his brother Frank, who has confessed to an arson attack that left five people dead. Neither he nor many of the residents believe that Frank is guilty. Prentice discovers that until recently the expatriate community was adrift in a haze of tranquilizers and alcohol but then seemed to undergo a kind of cultural renaissance. Investigating further, he finds that the catalyst for this explosion of creative activity is a series of petty crimes and an underground trade in drugs and pornography orchestrated by the local tennis coach.

Ballard uses the conventions of the detective thriller genre to probe the links between creativity and transgression, the paralyzing boredom of achieving what we are told we should want, and the role of "sacrificial" deaths, all with a persistent background hum of ambient fear. Written in Ballard's trademark deadpan prose, the novel unnerves in its ability to manipulate the reader into accepting the "deviant logic" that it demonstrates lies at the heart of the consumerist dream. **SS**

> Ballard has specialized in various forms of dystopia—disturbing visions of dreams fulfilled that logically evolve into nightmares.

Silk

Alessandro Baricco

Lifespan | b. 1958 (Italy)
First Published | 1996
First Published by | Rizzoli (Milan)
Original Title | Seta

One day, Hervé Joncour leaves his small town of Lavilledieu and starts regular journeys to Japan in search of silkworm eggs to bring back to Europe, where the silk industry is beginning to thrive. It is 1861, the year, as the author informs us, when Flaubert was writing Salammbô, electricity was still only a future project, and on the other side of the ocean, Lincoln was engaged in a civil war.

Hervé's journeys to Japan are ritualized in their repetitiveness and in the appointments with the unknown characters who provide the Frenchman with eggs in return for gold chips. No dialogue accompanies the repeated gestures, in the same places on the same days of the year. Hervé grows increasingly used to the long silences of the people he meets, witnesses the wars that European countries wage against Japan in the attempt to open the borders of the silk trade, and describes the ensuing consequences of the war with simplicity. But, as impalpable as silk, love embraces Hervé, who exchanges furtive glances with a mysterious Asian woman with Western features, who gives him a secret love message that he will take back to Lavilledieu with his precious load, always on the same day of the same month. Love becomes dream and an urge to explore when Hervé's journeys to Japan end. The memory of his ethereal love and the desire to interpret the message, the only precious token left of the Orient, are a caress for Hervé even when his wife dies. **RPi**

The Untouchable

John Banville

Lifespan | b. 1945 (Ireland)
First Published | 1997
First Published by | Picador (London)
Sir Anthony Frederick Blunt | b. 1907, d. 1983

On November 15, 1979, Margaret Thatcher, the British Prime Minister, announced to the House of Commons that Anthony Blunt was a confessed spy. A deluge of abuse descended upon Sir Anthony, who had been Surveyor of the Queen's Pictures, a leading Poussin scholar, and head of the Courtauld Institute of Art. Banville fictionalizes Blunt as Victor Maskell, who tells his own story in a witty narrative that catches exactly the manner of this stylish deceiver: "The K [knighthood] is to be revoked. I mind. I am surprised how much I mind." The novel realizes with consummate skill a host of worlds: Cambridge in the 1930s, wartime London, France before the Nazi occupation, Germany in 1945, and "the Institute" in the 1950s and 1960s. We encounter "Mrs. W." (Queen Elizabeth II), and above all explore the uneasy and eventually betraying friendships of Maskell's Marxist group. The protagonist's discovery of his essential homosexuality as bombs fall on London is dramatic and persuasive.

This is a novel about forgery, about the faking of multiple identities that have only an eloquent but icy sense of style to hold together scholar, lover, and spy: " . . . have I double dealt for so long that my true self has been forfeit?" He resembles his beloved painting by Nicolas Poussin, The Death of Seneca, which may itself be a forgery. Contrasted with Maskell's reserve is the outrageous character of Boy Bannister (spy Guy Burgess); but that too conceals a void. This is a vivid history of the inauthentic. **AMu**

American Pastoral

Philip Roth

Lifespan | *b.* 1933 (U.S.)
First Published | 1997
First Published by | Houghton Mifflin (New York)
Pulitzer Prize | 1998

At a high school reunion, Philip Roth's alter ego narrator, Nathan Zuckerman, meets up with Jerry Levov, little brother of the school's golden boy. Tall, blond, and beautiful, a sporting hero and all-round nice guy, Jerry's brother was nicknamed "the Swede." His was the postwar success story that everyone loved to tell: the blank, blue-eyed screen onto which the Jewish community of Newark would project all their hopes and aspirations.

American Pastoral is a tragedy of classical proportions, charting in three acts the downfall of an all-American king betrayed by his daughter. In the late 1960s, the sixteen-year-old Merry plants a bomb in the local post office in a protest against Vietnam. Her bomb kills a man instantly. Merry—fat, silly, and spoiled—is now a murderer. What went wrong? Was it too much love? Too much indulgence? Too little discipline? But there are no answers or explanations, and that is the point.

In acute, angry prose, *American Pastoral* describes the impotence of the Swede's complete incomprehension, his frustration, grief, and rage standing in for the bewilderment of a generation faced with a changing America. The questions the novel asks are being asked again today: Why would anyone want to bring the events of outside within the walls of our safe, suburban kingdoms? How could anyone not want what we have here? How could it go so wrong when we did everything so right ... didn't we? **KB**

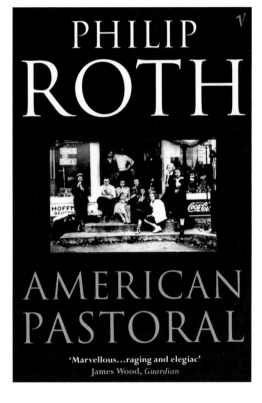

" . . . girls he passed on the street would ostentatiously swoon, and the bravest would holler after him, 'Come back, come back, Levov of my life!'"

◉ Roth evokes an illusory image of the 1950s as an American age of innocence and optimism in order to question and destroy it.

The Life of Insects

Victor Pelevin

Lifespan | *b.* 1962 (Russia)
First Published | 1997, by Vagrius (Moscow)
First Serialized | 1994, in *Znamya* (Moscow)
Original Title | *Zhizn' Nasekomyk*

This is a bizarre collection of interconnected vignettes about life in a shabby Crimean Black Sea resort, where people change from insects into humans and back in seemingly random mutations. In fact, the oscillation between human and insect does not form part of the narrative, but rather a change of optical apparatus on the part of the narrator. It sometimes takes the reader a while to understand which lens he is looking through at any given moment, and this produces an effect that is both unsettling and amusing.

In using and subverting the fable genre, Pelevin gives us a picture of contemporary Russian society. This ranges from straightforward satire, as in the joint venture negotiations between Russian and American mosquitoes out to make money, to the invention of an entire mythology and world view for dung beetles, to a surprisingly poignant portrayal of an ordinary swarming female ant's inner life. There are plenty of intriguing allusions, double entendres, and incongruous, yet carefully constructed, allegories and metaphors. But there is more to the novel than pure intellectual playfulness, and a concrete and wistful account of the human condition emerges. Somehow, and unaccountably, one puts down this novel convinced of having learned something true about life in post-Soviet Russia. The absurd acquires verisimilitude perhaps because it takes absurdity to break through the opacity of language in describing the world. **DG**

Jack Maggs

Peter Carey

Lifespan | *b.* 1943 (Australia)
First Published | 1997
First Published by | University of Queenstown Press
Miles Franklin Literary Award | 1998

Jack Maggs is a complex historical novel that addresses issues of literary, financial, and emotional indebtedness. In the London of 1837—importantly, the year of both Queen Victoria's accession and Charles Dickens' move from journalism to fiction writing—the transported criminal Jack Maggs has come back from Australia, risking execution. He adopts the disguise of a servant in order to track down the young man whose fortune he has made from afar. Meanwhile, he catches the eye of Tobias Oates, a young, Dickens-like journalist on the make, who finds out Maggs' secrets and eventually cannibalizes them for his own fictional creations.

Jack Maggs is in fact a creative reworking of the central motifs of Dickens' *Great Expectations*. Carey's novel is like a musical variation on Dickens' material. But it is no simple act of Victorian literary "karaoke"; Carey sounds out the distance between reworking and original text in order to pose questions about the sources of art, and the determinism of literary plotting—if things happened one way in the original, we might ask, are they doomed to turn out the same way again? As Oates' writing draws parasitically on Maggs' life, so Carey draws parasitically on Dickens, challenging his readers to feel, even as they take pleasure in his fiction, what the cost of that pleasure might be. **BT**

⊙ The most successful contemporary Australian novelist, Peter Carey lives in New York, where this photograph was taken in 2001.

Underworld

Don DeLillo

Lifespan | *b.* 1936 (U.S.)
First Published | 1997
First Published by | Scribner (New York)
First UK Edition | 1998, by Picador (London)

Underworld is a vast, encyclopedic novel, which reaches back from the brink of the twenty-first century to the early 1950s, and to the beginnings of the Cold War. Told as the private story of the central character, Nick Shay, as well as the public story of the Cold War, the narrative offers to bring the hidden connections that have driven the second half of the twentieth century into the light. In a liquid, versatile, and immaculate prose the narrative burrows back through the decades, both toward the shrouded space of Nick's personal secret, and toward the unconscious, abject places from which postwar history itself emerges. One of the most remarkable things about this revelatory novel is that its search for a universal voice with which to reveal the secrets of history leads it, repeatedly, to those historical, political, and personal moments that cannot be spoken of, to those secrets that cannot be given away.

Written at the end of a century, and at the end of a millennium, *Underworld* offers a way of understanding our collective past. It excavates the arcane workings of our culture, articulating connections between the overt and the hidden mechanisms of state power. At the same time, its awed intuition of the unseen forces that continue to drive history toward redemption or annihilation looks forward to a new millennium. **PB**

🔇 DeLillo is fascinated by the underside of events—he wrote that "history is the sum total of all the things they aren't telling us."

Enduring Love

Ian McEwan

Lifespan | *b.* 1948 (England)
First Published | 1997
First Published by | Jonathan Cape (London)
Movie Adaptation | 2004

Scientific journalist Joe Rose has planned an idyllic picnic with his wife Clarissa in the English countryside. Above them a hot-air balloon gets into trouble, and they watch as the pilot catches his leg in the anchor rope and the other passenger, a boy, is too scared to jump to safety. With this characteristic catalytic event, McEwan's story begins. As Joe and four other men rush to help secure the basket, a gust of wind whips four of them skyward. Joe and two of the other men let go and drop safely to the ground while the fourth hangs on, falling to his death in a nearby field.

All of the men's lives are affected by the incident, and we follow Joe as he tries to make sense of the memory and his guilt over the stranger's death (the boy lands safely). His feelings are complicated when Jed Parry, a fellow would-be rescuer, develops an obsession with Joe and begins to stalk him with a series of letters, phone calls, and confrontations. Joe's scientific mind is driven to distraction by the conditionals of the balloon experience, the what-ifs and the if-onlys, bringing frustration and chaos to his previously ordered life and threatening his relationship with Clarissa as well as his own self-confidence. The central theme is obsession, not only Jed's obsession with Joe but also Joe's obsession with rooting out meaning from chaos. Trust and doubt are also central; as Clarissa's belief in Joe's version of events begins to falter, the reader is never quite sure of what exactly happened. **EF**

Great Apes

Will Self

Lifespan | *b.* 1961 (England)
First Published | 1997
First Published by | Bloomsbury (London)
First U.S. Edition | Grove Press (New York)

Simon Dykes is a celebrated artist embroiled in a simmering crisis of debauchery, an intermittent loss of perspective, and an acute sense of disassociation with his own corporeality. After a particularly heavy night of excess, Dykes wakes up in a recognizably contemporary world inhabited by chimpanzees, exactly alike but subtly different from the human world. *Great Apes* is the story of this dysfunctional chimp's attempts to come to terms with his "chimpunity." Self's chimps—led by the irrepressible Dr. Zack Busner, Dykes' psychiatrist and confidant—are extraordinary creations. Their uncannily familiar London world allows Self to revel in the satirical potential of inversion with a Swiftian eye for detail. His celebration of the physicality of the body and appetites of the flesh are reminiscent of the Earl of Rochester at his dissipated best. The chimps communicate in a vivid combination of noises and sign language, pay homage to each other's anal scrags, fight, have sex with a series of available females, and are preoccupied with what distinguished them from the evolutionary dead end represented by humankind.

All of Will Self's familiar touches are here, but paradoxically with a degree of humanity that is not always present in his fiction. The full range of human–ape contact is exploited, from Jane Goodall to animal testing, from the *Planet of the Apes* films to HIV/AIDS and the Rwandan massacres. All human life is here—it just takes a chimp to see it. **MD**

Memoirs of a Geisha

Arthur Golden

Lifespan | *b.* 1957 (U.S.)
First Published | 1997
First Published by | Knopf (New York)
Movie Adaptation | 2005

Written in the first person, this novel traces the story of Nitta Sayuri and how she overcomes her Japanese fishing village roots to become one of Japan's most celebrated geishas. Chiyo is the stunningly pretty child of impoverished parents who is taken away at the age of nine and sold into the slavery of a geisha house in the Gion district of Kyoto. Renamed Sayuri, she undergoes cruel treatment as she transforms herself into a desirable geisha, skilled in the arts of pouring sake, dancing, singing, and pleasing men. Through her eyes, a vicious, competitive world is revealed where women are measured by the attention of men, where virginity is auctioned off to the highest bidder, and where there is no such thing as trust or love. But with the Second World War comes the realization that the old ways are disappearing. By then a well-known geisha, Sayuri is forced to reinvent herself in order to survive.

The book is important for its glimpses into a way of life that has all but disappeared. It also provides a disturbing view of the place of women in Japan. Sayuri was respected as a geisha but not as a woman, and it was only through resourcefulness and beauty that she managed to transcend the bounds of her position. This is also a story about a young girl's survival at the expense of her dreams, and how society's expectations smother love. **EF**

▶ Mineko Iwesaki, the Japanese woman on whose story Golden's novel is partly based, holds a photo of herself as a young geisha.

The God of Small Things

Arundhati Roy

Lifespan | *b.* 1961 (India)
First Published | 1997
First Published by | India Ink (New Delhi)
Booker Prize | 1997

Set in Kerala in the 1960s, this Booker Prize winner follows Ammu's family through both ordinary and tragic events, focusing most memorably on her "two-egg twins," Estha and Rahel. The accidental death by drowning of a visiting English cousin is to have a pivotal effect on their young lives. The novel is told in nonlinear time through a jigsaw of vivid encounters and descriptions, recounted in exquisite prose. The reader pieces together a childhood world, interrupted by adult tragedies and the effect these have on Velutha, the twins' boatman friend who belongs to India's "untouchable" caste. Roy's prose is distinctly rhythmic and poetic, and the overall effect is unique in its sensuality.

The novel's political concerns revolve around the notion of who decides "who should be loved and how much," with Roy's imaginative transgressions designed not so much to shock as to move the reader. A champion of the cause of the oppressed, Roy's politics are concerned with the small powers of the human, powers that are shocking in their ability to redeem and destroy. She sacrifices neither structure, complexity, nor beautiful prose to convey her beliefs. This book is a challenge to others who have attempted to tell us what love means. **AC**

⊙ Photographed here in Delhi in 1997, Arundhati Roy has now abandoned writing fiction to devote herself to political activism.

Mason & Dixon

Thomas Pynchon

Lifespan | *b.* 1937 (U.S.)
First Published | 1997
First Published by | H. Holt & Co. (New York)
Full Name | Thomas Ruggles Pynchon

Pynchon's *Mason & Dixon* is, loosely speaking, a kind of "updated" eighteenth-century novel that re-animates the lives, loves, and adventures of the two astronomer/surveyors who drew the boundary line across America that would eventually be used to distinguish the slaveholding states from the free states and is still used to distinguish the South from the North to this day. The tale is narrated retrospectively by the Reverend Wicks Cherrycoke in 1786—visiting Philadelphia for the funeral of Charles Mason. Cherrycoke becomes a Boswell-like figure, chronicling the experiences of these two Englishmen in a foreign land. This, however, is no ordinary Age of Reason. Pynchon combines years of painstaking historical research with outrageous comical imaginings and supernatural flights of fancy. Frontiersmen turn into beavers on full moons, the Jesuits invent the modern coffee machine, and Benjamin Franklin gives demonstrations of electricity while dressed as the grim reaper.

For all the jokes, songs, riddles, whimsies, and anachronisms, *Mason & Dixon* is ultimately a poignant and profound meditation on the origins and cost of modernity. A sustained exploration of the relationships between technology, capital, myth, magic, violence, and folk culture, this is an epic, sprawling work. In *Mason & Dixon*, Pynchon creates an old world for our uncertain times. **SamT**

Veronika Decides to Die

Paulo Coelho

Lifespan | *b.* 1947 (Brazil)
First Published | 1998
First Published by | Objetiva (Rio de Janeiro)
Original Title | *Veronika decide morrer*

○ Much of Paulo Coehlo's work has been based on his personal
struggle to discover a religious path in an oppressive world.

◑ Coelho has sold some 70 million copies of his spiritually uplifting
books, which have been translated into every major language.

With a steady stream of boyfriends, a secure job in a library, a room to call her home, caring friends and family, Veronika is a normal young woman leading a normal life. Yet she decides to kill herself, leaving behind a note that deplores global ignorance as to the whereabouts of Slovenia. As she regains consciousness in Ljubljana's psychiatric hospital, Villete, she learns that she has one week to live as her heart is now apparently damaged. The novel follows Veronika's shift from seeking death to her awareness that there are facets of her world that make life worthwhile. In Villete, she blossoms. Since the insane have no behavioral norms, she embraces the freedom to behave in any way she wants. This new-found autonomy prompts her to hit a man who annoys her, to masturbate in front of a stoic schizophrenic, to reconnect with her passion for playing the piano, and ultimately to discover love with Eduard, a man hospitalized by his parents because he wants to be an artist.

The character Eduard is one of several elements that link Coelho himself with the fictional world of the novel. He actually enters the narrative in the third chapter, where he reveals his own stays in Brazilian asylums, committed by his parents because of his artistic inclinations. It is this direct personal knowledge that makes the novel so stark in its simplicity. Details of electroconvulsive therapy, insulin shock, and other treatments imposed on the insane lead us to reconsider the meaning of sanity.

In a world of increasing uniformity, conformity, and isolation, the novel reflects its late twentieth-century provenance with its blend of world religious sentiment, its self-help angle, and its advocacy that life can have meaning if we do not heed the social mores that stifle the human spirit. **CK**

The Hours

Michael Cunningham

> *"'I begin to hear voices, and can't concentrate. So I am doing what seems the best thing to do. You have given me the greatest possible happiness.'"*

◉ Cunningham won the Pulitzer Prize, PEN/Faulkner award, and
Gay, Lesbian, Bisexual and Transgendered Book Award, all in 1999.

Lifespan | *b.* 1952 (U.S.)
First Published | 1998
First Published by | Farrar, Straus & Giroux (New York)
Pulitzer Prize | 1999

An intricate reworking of Virginia Woolf's *Mrs. Dalloway* (1925), *The Hours* splits Clarissa Dalloway's internal monologue into third-person narratives of three women. Clarissa Vaughan is a middle-aged lesbian living in contemporary New York. She is even nicknamed "Mrs. Dalloway" by Richard, a prominent gay poet with whom she has shared a sexually ambiguous friendship. Los Angeles housewife Laura Brown reads *Mrs. Dalloway* and other novels to fight the emptiness of suburban motherhood in the late 1940s and finds herself deeply shocked by her own moment of lesbian desire. Meanwhile a fictionalized Virginia Woolf frets over her novel *Mrs. Dalloway*. As Clarissa prepares a party to celebrate Richard's receiving a prestigious literary award, Laura tries to invest herself in her young son, and Woolf struggles to navigate illness in order to complete her work.

Cunningham reproduces Woolf's anatomy of the mourning of lost possibility—her heroine Clarissa Dalloway remains haunted by the unexplored lesbian connection. Clarissa Vaughan's successful long-term relationship and urban social freedom become the mundane background against which her youthful relationship with Richard and a single, ecstatic kiss shine all the more intensely. The uncertain way in which the eventful (suicide, kiss) complements ongoing ordinariness permeates the novel, as it meditates on the alchemical process through which temperament and experience act on each other to create our worlds. **AF**

Another World

Pat Barker

Lifespan | *b.* 1943 (England)
First Published | 1998
First Published by | Viking (London)
First U.S. Edition | 1999, by Farrar, Straus & Giroux

Another World investigates the traumas experienced during the First World War through the survivor figure of veteran Geordie Lucas, whose age and failing memory are the primary subjects of the text. Barker questions both the viability of recollection after so long a period has elapsed and the potential for false memory, especially of a war almost continuously reinvestigated from the moment it ended. George's fading reminiscences are unreliable and often incoherent, and the process by which his grandson Nick goes about recovering them can be read as intrusive and sometimes even manipulative. At the same time, *Another World* counterpoises the world of Geordie with that of the Lucas family: their failing marriage, disaffected children, and the upheaval of moving into a new house that appears to be haunted. The standard conventions of the ghost story, including the suggested possession of one child and the uncovering of a lurid, sexualized Edwardian painting in the living room, are all used in counterpoise to Nick's attempts to document Geordie's memories and recover the past. The "other worlds" of the text become increasingly ephemeral.

In *Another World* Pat Barker prepares to leave behind the horror of the First World War, and move toward a preoccupation with later, particularly Irish, conflicts. The novel questions whether or not a modern observer can ever recover knowledge of the past without the distorting effect of later social values upon the process of remembering. **EMcS**

Glamorama

Bret Easton Ellis

Lifespan | *b.* 1964 (U.S.)
First Published | 1998
First Published by | Knopf (New York)
First UK Edition | 1999, by Picador (London)

Glamorama begins with beauty and ends with terror, illustrating Rilke's idea that far from being opposites, they are more like opposite ends of a continuum. The protagonist-narrator Victor Ward is a model on the verge of becoming very famous. He is involved in opening a nightclub in New York and is dating the world's top supermodel while also sleeping with his boss's fiancée. Ellis is superb at rendering the vacuity of the high fashion celebrity milieu with its litany of brand names and incessant name-dropping, and has a fine ear for the strange literalism and unintended insights of pleonastic media-speak. As the novel progresses, the tone darkens as Victor becomes involved with an organization of terrorists who also happen to be famous models, killing hundreds with bombs hidden in their Louis Vuitton handbags. Victor, and thus the narrative, becomes increasingly dissociated, sliding unanchored across the surface of images slick with blood.

This disturbing novel addresses the ability of the media to reshape our perception of reality, showing the obsession with celebrity and the tyranny of beauty to be some of its most potent weapons. The novel is so unremittingly flat that there is no height from which the reader can look down and judge, and no moral framework to refer to. That is not to say there is nothing at work here, just that this world of branded products, celebrity name-checks, and terrorism is too uncomfortably close to our own. **SS**

The Poisonwood Bible

Barbara Kingsolver

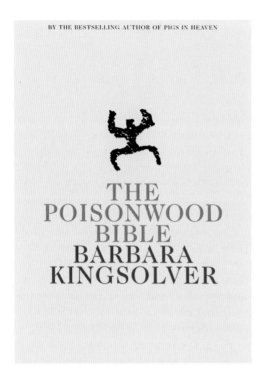

BY THE BESTSELLING AUTHOR OF PIGS IN HEAVEN

THE
POISONWOOD
BIBLE
BARBARA
KINGSOLVER

"Ants. *We were walking on, surrounded, enclosed, enveloped, being eaten by* ants. *Every surface was covered and boiling, and the path like black flowing lava in the moonlight.*"

The anti-colonial subject matter of *The Poisonwood Bible* reflects the author's overriding concern with promoting social change.

Lifespan | *b.* 1955 (U.S.)
First Published | 1998
First Published by | HarperFlamingo (New York)
Establishes Bellwether Prize | 1997

Set in the Congo, this novel is narrated by Orelanna Price and her four daughters and tells the story of her husband, the overzealous Baptist preacher Nathan Price. As a child, Kingsolver lived in the Congo, but it was only in adulthood that she learned of the political situation that had seized the Congo while she lived there, when the United States had sabotaged the country's independence. She wrote this novel to address and publicize these issues.

The missionary's four children—Rachel, Ruth May, Leah, and the crippled mute Adah—react differently to their father's work, but when poisonous snakes appear in their house, planted by the village's religious leader, they try to convince their father to let them leave. He refuses, and Ruth May is killed, prompting her mother to leave the village with the other three daughters. Rachel goes on to marry three men and inherit a hotel in the Congo; Leah marries the village schoolteacher and dedicates herself to African independence; and Adah becomes an epidemiologist. The mother lives her life wracked with guilt. Each of the narrators struggles to deal with their guilt over Ruth May's death, but also the guilt of their role in the ruin of a country and, on a wider scale, Western guilt over its colonial past. The novel's title comes from the poisonwood, a African tree that Nathan Price is warned not to touch; he ignores the warning and suffers painful swelling. Kingsolver's message about Price's missionary zeal is clear. **EF**

Tipping the Velvet

Sarah Waters

Lifespan | *b.* 1966 (Wales)
First Published | 1998
First Published by | Virago (London)
Adapted for Television | 2002

Tipping the Velvet is a story of cross-dressed sexual adventurism that reconstitutes a repressed history of lesbian eroticism in the style, structure, and length of a Victorian novel. Set mainly in 1890s London, it reclaims the period's famed Wildean exuberance and sexual excess. Funny and romantic, Waters' beautifully crafted pastiche seduces its readers into a journey of cultural discovery.

The novel chronicles Whitstable oyster girl Nancy Astley's education in lesbian lifestyles as she becomes a male-impersonating music hall performer, rent "boy," plaything of upper-class Sapphists, and finally lesbian partner of feminist, socialist "New Woman" Florence. The preoccupations of the mainstream fiction of the period, such as social class, femininity, the development of the individual, and transgression, are fully explored. However, the novel also pays homage to those other Victorian fantasies, the erotica and pornography prolifically produced in this era of mass production and mass circulation of literature. Though wickedly bawdy in its double entendres, proficiency in Victorian slang (the term "tipping the velvet" refers to cunnilingus), and knowledge of sex toys, the narrative is ultimately a love story.

In *Tipping the Velvet*, Waters stimulates the ongoing reassessment of our stereotypical views of a morally pious Victorian age, and the novel's account of the sexual duplicity of the period only encourages us to examine our own. **CJ**

The Talk of the Town

Ardal O'Hanlon

Lifespan | *b.* 1965 (Ireland)
First Published | 1998
First Published by | Sceptre (London)
U.S. Title | *Knick Knack Paddy Whack*

Based on this novel, Ardal O'Hanlon, the stand-up comic famous for playing stupid, sweet-natured Father Dougal in the TV comedy *Father Ted*, could not be accused of writing opportunistic fluff or seeking manufactured gravitas. His brilliantly observed tale captures the atmosphere and rituals of small-town Irish life in the early 1980s through the experiences of its narrator, nineteen-year-old Patrick Scully. At the start of the novel, he is going home on the bus for the weekend from his dead-end job as security man at a Dublin jeweler's. Through the winningly cynical meanderings of Scully's mind, we start to discover the discontents of his life. There are some virtuoso comic moments, such as when, in the process of losing his virginity against a wall outside Mirage nightclub, Scully carries on a conversation with a mate peeing on the other side of the wall who cannot see what is going on. But the humor is layered with bleak desperation. The flow of language is fast-paced and colloquial, and the plot holds some dark surprises. The narrative skillfully deploys a double perspective. Interspersed with Scully's first-person narrative are pages from his girlfriend Francesca's diary that undercut his understanding of events and tell, in particular, about her feelings for Scully's more successful friend, Xavier "Balls" O'Reilly. The claustrophobia of Scully's life creates disturbances in him that he cannot confront directly, bringing his tale to an inexorable conclusion of madness and violence. **RMcD**

All Souls Day

Cees Nooteboom

Lifespan | *b.* 1933 (The Netherlands)
First Published | 1998
First Published by | Atlas (Amsterdam)
Original Title | *Allerzielen*

The novel's central character Arthur Daane is a man with time on his hands; he has arranged it that way. He spends his days wandering through post-Wall Berlin, ruminating and reflecting as he negotiates his way through a city's past, and his own.

Ten years earlier, his wife and young son were killed in a plane crash, and since then he has tried to live with the burden of his freedom. As a documentary filmmaker, he is accustomed to being an observer; when he meets a young woman who bears the scars of trauma on her face, he is called upon to engage in life more directly. Love—and, ultimately, another random act of violence—shock him out of his anonymity and propel him forward. The story is told at a rambling, walking pace, with scenes that read like verbal snapshots interposed with long discussions among a handful of Arthur's friends, who are as inclined to intellectual discourse as he is.

As much a romance as a kind of dialogue with the dying twentieth century, this novel of ideas contemplates the catalog of horrors, losses, and destruction wrought in recent history—a contemporary reader will be chastened by considering all that has transpired since it was written. With occasional, more far-reaching, narration offered by some of the souls already above and beyond the scope of time, *All Souls Day* is a sober inquiry into the meaning of life, art, and historical events, both personal and public. **ES**

Cloudsplitter

Russell Banks

Lifespan | *b.* 1940 (U.S.)
First Published | 1998
First Published by | HarperFlamingo (New York)
First UK Edition | Secker & Warburg (London)

Narrated by Owen Brown, the novel retrospectively relates the story of his father, the complex and charismatic John Brown, who from uncertain beginnings becomes a radical abolitionist, a terrorist fighter, and ultimately a martyr for the cause. The reflective, elegiac voice of the son relates the triumphs and failures of the father, detailing his extraordinary plan to free the slaves and the increasing radicalism of his politics. Yet in the background is the knowledge of what was inevitably to follow from such divisions—the terrible slaughter and division of the Civil War itself. Denying a recent tendency to airbrush this crucial period in American history, Owen's fragile voice offers the reader an idiosyncratic and truthful vision of events.

Banks' great achievement is the way in which he builds an extraordinarily compelling narrative from the interaction of relatively obscure historical characters with recognizably human frailties. This is coupled with an eye for detail and a sense of the profound divisions of the society in which the Brown family live, all animated by a pervasive sense of injustice, individual right, and the intense aura of religious devotion. For *Cloudsplitter* is not simply a novel about grand ideas; it moves seamlessly between lyrical evocations of rural life and the landscape, domestic intimacy, violent conflict, and familial strife. It shows us modern America in the process of formation. **MD**

Amsterdam

Ian McEwan

Lifespan | *b.* 1948 (England)
First Published | 1998
First Published by | Jonathan Cape (London)
Booker Prize | 1998

For many, *Amsterdam* continues a shift in McEwan's concerns from individual evasions of morality to an awareness of politics and responsibility. Like the city of its title, it is open and empty, a stage for conflicting possibilities rather than a place at which we will arrive.

The novel's plot is geometrical in its clarity: the story of three men—Clive, Vernon, and Julian—and their pursuit of substitute satisfactions for a dead woman, the alluring Molly Lane. What is most striking, however, is the book's persistent wrongness of tone. Clive's complacent communing with nature is a missed high point, a failure to connect with his own artistic ambitions, just as Vernon's fantasies of editorial command reflect a similar pattern of delusion. Their bombastic monologues thus cause us to wince, but no more so than the judgments they render upon one another. Vernon's prim declaration that "people" are "more important than symphonies" thus struggles to convince us as much as his professional opinion of himself. What we are left with is not so much badness as a most peculiar compulsion. In its counterpoint of false tone with uncompromising plot, *Amsterdam* provides us with a study of the addictive qualities of the unpleasant, and a fascination with its moral emptiness. This has more in common with the clarity of early McEwan than the occasional pretensions of his later career, but for those prepared to make it, the return journey occurs by a most interesting route. **DT**

> *"There was something seriously wrong with the world for which neither God nor his absence could be blamed."*

⊘ Despite the impression created by this jacket image, *Amsterdam* is set in contemporary times and does not include a duel.

Intimacy

Hanif Kureishi

Lifespan | b. 1954 (England)
First Published | 1998
First Published by | Faber & Faber (London)
First U.S. Edition | 1999, by Scribner (New York)

Intimacy is a leaner, more reserved novel than Kureishi's autobiographical debut, The Buddha of Suburbia. Here, the narrative of maturation and self-scrutiny assumes a more painful trajectory. The narrator, Jay, is contemplating his determination to leave his wife and their almost "complete, ideal family." Intimacy is set in Jay's final evening in that household from which he has hidden his decision.

We are invited into a claustrophobic zone where self-persecution provokes Jay into retrospection, yet denies him the comforts of mawkish reminiscence. The novel's manner of telling is digressive rather than linear. By using the historic present tense, Kureishi braids remembrance and self-examination together for a night on which Jay "will set the record crooked." The reader soon becomes absorbed in Jay's remembering. His confessions of incompetence raise questions concerning the cultural constitution of masculinity itself. Without reducing character to cipher, Kureishi enlists Jay's acute introspection with great tact. He is never simply a mouthpiece for gender polemic, though his tale certainly highlights the very real penalties of remaining so accountable to "habit, convention and morality, as well as the fear of who you might become." Intimacy explores the inability to survive within a rigid family unit because of the role it prescribes. The narrator's cumulative flashbacks help him to understand his own identity, and Kureishi unleashes his most perceptive interrogation yet of manhood's defining terms. **DJ**

Elementary Particles

Michel Houellebecq

Lifespan | b. 1958 (Réunion)
First Published | 1998, by Flammarion (Paris)
Alternate Title | Atomized
Original Title | Les Particules élémentaires

This was the novel that first brought Michel Houellebecq's bleak worldview to an international audience. Western civilization has failed on a grand scale and human beings are miserable and lonely, barely capable of communication or emotion. Houellebecq charts the ascent of the modern leisure society with persuasive cultural analysis, concluding that the injunction to pursue personal pleasure and happiness is itself repressive and painful.

The book's central characters, Michel and Bruno, are brothers separated until middle age. Michel is a brilliant yet emotionally isolated scientist, Bruno a hopeless libertine. Sex is the arena in which the novel's argument is played out. Michel cannot form sexual relationships—he declines the affection of his beautiful childhood sweetheart Annabelle—while Bruno's escapades in New Age holiday camps, swingers' clubs, and as an occasional flasher provide a comic stage for Houellebecq's dissertation on the momentary utopias and abjections of the sexual act. The supremacy of the biological imperative leads to a series of conclusions about men and women. Women are self-sacrificing signifiers of mortality, men condemned to the destiny of their glandular promptings. This is no elegy to humanity—Houellebecq can't wait to see the back of us. The question, though, is, does he really mean it? **DH**

⊙ Houellebecq has been accused of misogyny and racism, but the main thrust of his books is a much broader distaste for human life.

Sputnik Sweetheart

Haruki Murakami

Lifespan | *b.* 1949 (Japan)
First Published | 1999
First Published by | Kodansha (Tokyo)
Original Title | *Supuutoniku no koibito*

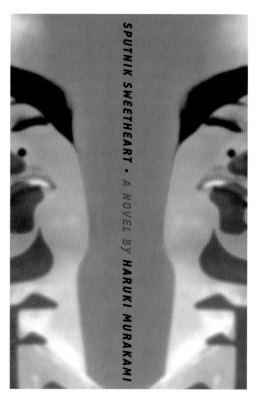

"I was in love with Sumire."

● Chip Kidd designed the jacket for the first U.S. edition of
Murakami's novel of unrequited desire and unresolved enigmas.

Sputnik Sweetheart tells the story of a very peculiar love triangle. Sumire is an aspiring and frustrated writer, whose attempts at writing are fragmentary and unresolved. Her best friend, the narrator, is a schoolteacher known only as K: he is constantly aroused by Sumire, but she appears totally unaware of his interest, and professes to be unaware of any sexual feelings at all until she meets a sophisticated older woman, Miu.

Sumire's feelings for Miu are puzzling. While there is a simple possibility that Sumire might be a lesbian, that would be far too simple an explanation for her feelings, which might have more to do with at last finding somebody who represents everything for which she constantly, but fruitlessly, strives. At all events, Miu takes Sumire on as an assistant in her wine business, and they travel together to a Greek island. From there, K is telephoned to say that Sumire has vanished without trace, and he flies out to Greece to find her. Once there, he finds some tantalizing clues, including a diary entry that speaks of "entering the world of dreams and never coming out. Living in dreams for the rest of time." He also discovers the secret of a traumatic event in Miu's past, that turned her hair snow-white overnight.

To tell the "story" of *Sputnik Sweetheart*, however, will not convey the tone of the book, which is delicate, wistful, and full of loss and longing. Murakami is a remarkable, poetic stylist; every sentence echoes in our heads as we follow K's unrequited desires and try, with him, to penetrate mysteries of which we will never be a part. The enigma endures to the very end of the book when we become aware that nothing will ever truly be resolved—everything hangs on a thread of doubt and uncertainty. **DP**

Disgrace

J. M. Coetzee

South Africa after the end of apartheid is a country in which structures that had seemed immutable have crumbled, and many among the once-dominant white population are forced to make difficult adjustments. David Lurie, a fifty-two-year-old professor at a fictional university in Cape Town, is less troubled by the demise of institutionally sanctioned racism than by the entry of the country into a global culture that devalues his lifelong devotion to literature, to Romantic literature in particular. When an ill-judged seduction of a student results in a disciplinary hearing, he cannot bring himself to go through with the required public breast-beating and gives up his job, plunging into an unknown future.

Coetzee's novel, which had begun in the vein of campus satire, turns darker with Lurie's visit to his daughter Lucy on her small farm in the Eastern Cape. In an attack by three black men, Lucy is raped and Lurie burned; Lurie's appalled sense of a changed world is exacerbated by his daughter's refusal to make her violation public or to abort the child that has resulted. His response is to dedicate his time to an animal shelter where the region's excess dogs are put down and to work on an opera that becomes less performable as it develops. Distanced from his daughter, he nevertheless hopes for a new relationship of "visitorship."

Disgrace caused fierce debates in South Africa over its portrayal of the new social and political order. Yet the novel's ethical stance is more challenging than its painful realism about some of the country's problems. Does Lurie's dedication to animals and to musical creation represent some kind of redemption after a life of self-centered sexual predation? **DA**

Lifespan | *b.* 1940 (South Africa)
First Published | 1999
First Published by | Secker & Warburg (London)
Booker Prize | 1999

WINNER OF THE 1999 BOOKER PRIZE

J. M. Coetzee

DISGRACE

'Exhilarating…One of the best novelists alive'
SUNDAY TIMES

"Follow your temperament."

◉ Coetzee stirred up controversy with his apparently bleak and pessimistic vision of the condition of post-apartheid South Africa.

The Ground Beneath Her Feet

Salman Rushdie

Lifespan | *b.* 1947 (India)
First Published | 1999
First Published by | Jonathan Cape (London)
Full Name | Ahmed Salman Rushdie

The Ground Beneath Her Feet tells the story of a series of love affairs gone awry. The novel focuses on the love affair between singers and childhood sweethearts, the rootless and hungry, American-reared Vina Apsara and the volatile genius Ormus Cama, who grew up in a grand, and grandly dysfunctional, Bombay family. Vina and Ormus grow from gifted children to superstars, and much of the novel is concerned with exploring the fascinations and dangers of the contemporary pop world. The significance of the unions between Vina and Ormus (and hence between Indian and American popular cultures) is managed in Rushdie's typically epic style: it crosses continents, it moves mountains, it acquires alternative dimensions in time and in space.

The story of Vina and Ormus is narrated by their childhood friend Rai, a photographer, and the ability that his profession requires to be both inside and outside of an image characterizes both his narrative style and his relationship to the hedonistic lives of the friends he describes. The alternative love stories that Rai tells us are not simply of thwarted love but also of familial and civic love. Rai's story, including his collection of images of Bombay, and the faltering of his architect parents' shared vision of one another gives the novel's attention to the "ground" an emotional and historic resonance that complements its more obvious and stellar concerns. **NM**

Fear and Trembling

Amélie Nothomb

Lifespan | *b.* 1967 (Japan)
First Published | 1999, by A. Michel (Paris)
Original Language | French
Original Title | *Stupeur et tremblements*

No one ever said that bridging the gap between East and West would happen peacefully. In this French novel about a Belgian employee of a Japanese corporation dealing in everything from Canadian optical fibers to Singaporean soda, the problems of adjusting to the global village are conveyed with satiric delight.

Fear and Trembling relates the experience of Amélie as she begins a one-year contract on the bottom rung of a massive Japanese corporation. Having been partly raised in Japan, she is simultaneously native and foreigner, but her nativeness serves to ostracise her as much as her foreignness (she is punished for understanding Japanese). She finds herself facing one degrading demotion after another, moving from mindless photocopying to the full-time cleaning of a restroom used only by herself and her immediate superior, Fubuki Mori, an exquisitely beautiful and dangerously proud woman for whom Amélie develops a self-destructive infatuation.

Nothomb's attack on what is presented as crazed labor relations in a massive Japanese corporation is not entirely vituperative—she exhibits a sympathy to people obedient to their sense of honor and tradition. In this satiric and thoughtful novel, East and West are both ridiculed with a certain fondness for the foibles of every individual. **JuS**

Everything You Need

A. L. Kennedy

Lifespan | b. 1965 (Scotland)
First Published | 1999
First Published by | Jonathan Cape (London)
Full Name | Alison Louise Kennedy

If you ever wanted to experience a consciousness that is not your own, one that you could almost taste, then Kennedy, in her most intense moments, is the writer for you. Perhaps more of a natural master of short fiction, she brings her unflinching gaze to this lengthy novel. A succession of distinct episodes, themselves very much like short stories, are linked by the two main characters. *Everything You Need* draws the reader in with a compelling description of a suicide. Kennedy combines descriptive capabilities with earthy emotional details and the momentum of plot. Her likable but carefully flawed protagonist, Nathan Staples, lives in a remote writer's colony and contrives to have his estranged daughter, also a writer, brought there so that he might build a relationship with her. The emotional developments of the characters over the next seven years are explored through Kennedy's brave and tender prose. This is a book of slow suspense that creates an emotional involvement you don't realize you have until the end. Kennedy cleverly conveys the protagonist's struggles through passages of his own writing, dispersed throughout the narrative to build a picture of his past. This short-fiction framework brought to bear on an epic narrative is an unusual attempt at combining genres. In this genuinely moving work, Kennedy pulls off the often-failed-feat: a great novel about being a writer. **AC**

As If I Am Not There

Slavenka Drakulić

Lifespan | b. 1949 (Yugoslavia)
First Published | 1999
First Published in | *Feral Tribune* (Split)
Original Title | *Kao da me nema*

The Croatian journalist Slavenka Drakulić is one of the most insightful and evenhanded observers of recent Balkan history. Her novel *As If I Am Not There* is set in Bosnia in the years 1992 and 1993. The narrative tells of the horrifying experiences endured by S.—a schoolteacher of mixed Serbian and Bosnian heredity—when Serbian forces enter her village. S. spends months in an all female compound of a Serbian concentration camp where she is subjected to continual sexual violence and beatings. The novel culminates with her arrival in Scandinavia as a refugee—pregnant, homeless, and ambivalent about her unborn son, conceived during a gang rape in the camp. What is more, S. is unable to find an individual or a community who will listen to her story without judgment.

Told in sparse, unflinching detail, devoid of literary tricks, this is a haunting novel. Simply told but morally complex, it draws powerful links between warfare, masculinity, sexual violence, and the female body, but offers no simplistic conclusions. Most strikingly, the novel refuses to demonize Serbia in its depiction of the war, and the use of initials to identify characters means that questions of nationality and religion are handled with great subtlety. We are asked to see each character in his or her own light, as an agent and an actor, as flexibly rational, as well as terrifyingly irrational. **SamT**

Cryptonomicon

Neal Stephenson

Lifespan | *b.* 1959 (U.S.)
First Published | 1999
First Published by | Avon Press (New York)
First UK Edition | 2000, by Arrow (London)

Cryptonomicon is a masterpiece of cyberfiction, although it has been remarked that it should more properly be referred to as "cypher-fiction," since its main concerns are with codes and code-breaking. The plotlines sprawl across history, beginning with the origins of computer culture in the information battles that accompanied the Second World War.

We see these battles, both technical and physical, through the eyes of two main characters, Lawrence Waterhouse, a mathematician deeply involved in code-breaking and the concealment of that code-breaking, and Bobby Shaftoe, a U.S. marine who is at the sharp end of planting misinformation in physical settings. We also explore the story of Waterhouse's grandson Randy as he uses computer skills in an attempt to set up an offshore data haven in Southeast Asia. At its heart the novel reads like a set of fast-paced, relentless adventure stories. The reader is left feeling an immense sense of pity for those operating in a war zone where the possible outcomes of their actions are prearranged for them by controllers who are willing, or perhaps forced, to expend human life for larger ends.

Although this may indeed be cyberfiction, it is also deeply humane, setting the fragility of the human body in stark contrast to the conspiracies and mind games of the military powers. It opens up to us a vision of a world that operates according to an entirely different geography from the one we commonly think we inhabit. **DP**

The Romantics

Pankaj Mishra

Lifespan | *b.* 1969 (India)
First Published | 1999
First Published by | Picador (London)
First U.S. Edition | 2000, by Random House (N.Y.)

Mishra's debut novel is a beautifully constructed account of a young Indian man, his intellectual vision garnered from Western culture, and his attempts to understand modern India. Samar, a young Brahmin student, goes to live amid English and French expatriates in Benares, India's holiest Hindu city. With a knowledge of his own country that is almost as meager as that of the Western "seekers" that he lives among, he steeps himself in Schopenhauer, Flaubert, Turgenev, and Proust, and this inclines him toward an outsider's vision of India.

Samar's immersion in the expatriate community in Benares engages him in a kind of romantic education. But the education is limited. Samar's world is fashioned from books, and Mishra captures with precision and humor the incongruity between this ideal vision and the reality around him. There are fine moments of comedy in Samar's attempts at understanding the world through his reading, such as his suprised confession when Catherine, a young French woman he falls in love with, tells him that she had come to Benares to move as far as possible from "bourgeois" parents: "this deployment of a word I had previously encountered only in Marxist texts was new to me." His sexual innocence is disrupted by an abortive affair with Catherine, and his worldly naïveté is overturned by Rajesh, a secretive campus agitator. On leaving Benares to become a schoolteacher, Samar is left feeling calm and, if not more worldly-wise, certainly more India-wise. **ABi**

Timbuktu

Paul Auster

Lifespan | *b.* 1947 (U.S.)
First Published | 1999
First Published by | H. Holt & Co. (New York)
Full Name | Paul Benjamin Auster

It was no great surprise when Paul Auster, long hailed as master of the modern American fable, published this short novel in the tradition of the beast fable. Here we have the Auster novel in a distilled form. Auster has always been fascinated by different ways of being and different worlds, so to describe the world from a dog's eye-view is a logical step. Mr. Bones, the canine hero of *Timbuktu*, cannot speak like the animals in Aesop, but he is a highly intelligent mutt and can more or less follow the ramblings of his half-crazed, burned-out owner, the poet Willy G. Christmas. As Willy approaches death, man and dog go on a pilgrimage in search of Willy's inspirational high school teacher, Bea Swanson. But before they find her, Willy collapses by the roadside, and Mr. Bones has to leg it or face getting caught by the police. As Mr. Bones moves from one owner to the next, he has a series of picaresque adventures. After spending some time with the son of a Chinese restaurant owner, in constant fear of being served up for dinner, he eventually ends up in a suburban home, though even here, all is not as it seems.

Just as one adventure is taking shape, we move off into another world, yet curiously, in this constant movement, we see each place we pass through as if for the first time. The novel ends on a knife edge between two such worlds, with Mr. Bones dodging trucks on a road: will he reach the other side or will he be knocked down and taken to the next world, Timbuktu, to rejoin his former master? **PT**

"He knew the difference between reality and make-believe, and if Santa Claus was talking to him from his mother's television set . . . he was a lot drunker than he supposed."

⌃ Auster uses genre conventions to explore existential concerns on the nature of memory and identity.

Two days later Richard ^Brinsley^ Sheridan entered the ~~little~~ books[

Ireland, having been alerted by a scrawled message an h[

him. "My dear sir. An honour." Sheridan bowed. "We[

"Where is the young man of the ~~day~~ ^hour^?" Sherida[

found it difficult to turn as William descended the stairc[

"I am William Ireland, sir."

"May I shake your hand, sir? You have done t[^sen^

^announced^
~~pronounced~~ each word as if he were addressing others u[

believe, who recommended Vortigern as a great subject

in Holborn Passage. Samuel

before, was waiting to greet

'_immensely_

all ~~very~~ proud.”

ıs a large figure, and he

“Is it you?”

a great purpose ”

~~a great service~~.’ Sheridan

ı. “It was Mr Dryden, I

ı drama.”

Peter Ackroyd, _The Lambs of London_, 2004

2000S

Pastoralia

George Saunders

Lifespan | *b.* 1958 (U.S.)
First Published | 2000
First Published by | Riverhead Books (New York)
First UK Edition | 2001, by Bloomsbury (London)

Saunders' characters are adrift in a soulless, corporate America, the America of slogans and winning, success, and smiles. But they are somehow lost. They don't feel what they think they should, what they believe the rest of America feels. They know they should be happy, must achieve, but somehow they can't and it must be their own fault.

Saunders describes a world that is familiar but that is not our own; we recognize the mundanity of modern life, the outlet malls and downsizing, the foolish love. But it is also an unfamiliar world where characters live as cavemen in a theme park, thankful for the daily goat that comes through "The Big Slot" and who become panicked when their partners insist on smoking cigarettes and doing crosswords (both strictly forbidden by the caveman behavioral guidelines). It is a world where an ordinary man, dressed in a G-string and wearing a Penile Simulator, serves food to drunken secretaries while his sister stays at home with her fatherless baby watching "How My Child Died Violently" on daytime TV. It is a world where Neil Yaniky tries to stay "stoked" at a seminar where he hopes to develop self-esteem by learning "not to let anyone crap in your oatmeal."

Saunders is a modern-day Borges, a magical surrealist, creating immaculately constructed pseudo-realities, X-rays of modern American vapidity in extremis. Saunders takes our world to nightmarish extremes; that is, if nightmares were funny. **GT**

Blonde

Joyce Carol Oates

Lifespan | *b.* 1938 (U.S.)
First Published | 2000
First Published by | Echo Press (New York)
Pseudonyms | Rosamond Smith; Lauren Kelly

Blonde is an exploration of the transformation of Norma Jean Baker into the greatest sexual icon of the twentieth century, Marilyn Monroe. Despite all the rituals that Norma Jean has to endure—she has to bleach her hair, undergo plastic surgery, wear excessively tight and provocative clothes—there are always bodily reminders of lack and excess (sweat stains, menstruation, vomit) which Norma Jean anxiously associates with her mother's madness. Norma Jean's need to perform, to embody other roles, is presented as a necessary escape from this difficult background. Oates depicts Norma Jean's childhood in an orphanage and her lackluster youth in working-class peripheries of Los Angeles with striking detail, typical of her early naturalistic fiction.

Blonde also offers a vivid portrayal of America from the 1930s to the 1950s, emphasizing the effects of the red scare of the 1950s in Hollywood. Norma Jean's husbands and lovers are portrayed as allegorical figures (the Ex-Athlete, the Playwright, the President, and the Dark Prince), highlighting the staged quality of these various romantic bonds, each of them adding their own symbolic twist to the myth of Marilyn Monroe. *Blonde* forces us to experience the suffocating weight of a myth carved in flesh, but made to endure long beyond that flesh, abstracted into iconography. **SA**

◗ Joyce Carol Oates' self-description as "a serious writer, as distinct from entertainers or propagandists" has never deterred her fans.

House of Leaves

Mark Z. Danielewski

Lifespan | *b.* 1966 (U.S.)
First Published | 2000
First Published by | Pantheon (New York)
First UK Edition | Anchor (London)

House of Leaves is an essay about a documentary, itself shot in various formats—hi-8, camcorder, digital video, tape—with a second, later story told in the footnotes, and with each part assembled by an unseen third party. The novel's concerns are essentially those of three distinct and inquisitive individuals, who approach from differing angles a single point where reason breaks down—a house occupied by the documentary maker is revealed to be bigger inside than out—and their attempts to inscribe and therefore make sense of this through varying forms of recorded media.

Alongside the mixed-media element of the novel, it attempts to forge together a variety of separate registers. Immaculately constructed horror sits alongside passages from mythology, with the history of literature and philosophy in the footnotes. The main body of the text consists of a lengthy critical discourse, complete with various real and made-up citations. Like an end-of-the-century partner to *Dracula*, a progress report if you like, *House of Leaves* presents its mixed-media technologies as having become corrupted with a perpetual gothic dread. It is a heavily metaphorical reminder; even hyperspace, digital video, and the reduction of every type of story into currency remain incapable, no matter how far they are developed, of isolating the human being from the force of the irrational that takes root in both interior and exterior landscapes. **SF**

Super-Cannes

J. G. Ballard

Lifespan | *b.* 1930 (China)
First Published | 2000
First Published by | Flamingo (London)
Full Name | James Graham Ballard

In *Super-Cannes,* J.G. Ballard turns his forensic gaze on the one-way glass and steel of globalized postindustrial capital, here represented by the pristine high-tech business park "Eden-Olympia" on the French Riviera. For the inhabitants of this self-sufficient complex, work is everything—so fulfilling that there is apparently no need for outmoded diversions such as rest or recreation. Arriving at the park with his young wife Jane, the narrator Paul Sinclair sets about trying to discover why her predecessor David Greenwood had recently embarked on an apparently motiveless shooting spree, killing several of the park's most influential inhabitants before turning the gun on himself. He quickly becomes fascinated with Wilder Penrose, the resident park psychiatrist who has some unorthodox methods of increasing productivity levels among the executive elite, prescribing violence and sexual perversion as cures for stress and insomnia.

Super-Cannes suggests that the nearer societies get to total stability and security the more they will throw up a wide range of aberrant mental states and psychotic behavior. While the novel can be read on one level as a satirical attack on the culture of overwork and corporate amorality, it is also deeply concerned with modern notions of community—how our morality and sense of civic duty are affected in the age of "immaterial labour," the gated estate, the private police force, and the CCTV camera. **SS**

Small Remedies

Shashi Deshpande

Lifespan | *b.* 1938 (India)
First Published | 2000
First Published by | Viking (New Delhi)
Original Language | English

Madhu, a writer, travels to a small town to write a biography of the now elderly Savitribai, an accomplished classical vocalist who dared to "reach beyond her grasp" and leave the comfortable world of Brahmin respectability to follow her passion for music and live with her Muslim lover. Savitribai explains how in singing a raga, you confidently "find the right pitch and begin" but that the result invariably takes on a life of its own. So it is with Madhu's biography, the words never quite capturing the truth of the life they are describing but leading out in innumerable directions. Yet they always culminate in the central trauma of the novel, the recent death of Madhu's young son in a bus bombing, which acts like the "sam" point in a raga to which the musicians continually return.

Written in careful sparse prose without ornate description, Deshpande's novel skillfully blends episodes from Madhu's past and present to offer a complex portrayal of the few central characters. Among these is Leela, Madhu's aunt, a political activist and trade unionist whose life, like Savitribai's, seems impossible to capture in words. It is in her attempts to make sense of the lives of these two women that Madhu finds she is unable to suppress her own tragic memories, not least because Savitribai's own daughter, like Madhu's son, was also killed in a bus bombing. But in the encounter, Madhu learns the healing power of memories and how the dead clamor for release through them. **ABi**

After the Quake

Haruki Murakami

Lifespan | *b.* 1949 (Japan)
First Published | 2000
First Published by | Shinchosha (Tokyo)
Original Title | *Kami no kodomo-tachi wa mina odoru*

After the Quake is a collection of six short stories written in 1999, five of which were first serially published in the Japanese magazine *Shincho*. The original title in Japanese is *All God's Children Dance*, which is the title of one of the stories in the book. All six stories revolve around the catastrophic Hanshin earthquake that killed more than 6,000 people in the Hanshin area, southwest Japan, in January 1995, although the stories are actually set in Tokyo or its surrounding areas.

None of the characters directly experienced the earthquake, but most of them are directly or indirectly related to the Hanshin area, and find that the crisis of the earthquake suddenly retrieves their relationship with the area, people, and the past. The nameless character Komura's wife in "UFO in Kushiro" is exposed, like millions of other Japanese at the time, to the television reports that mercilessly keep reckoning the number of nameless dead. "Landscape in Flatiron" evokes the image of fire devouring the houses soon after the earthquake. The figure of Frog ("Kaeru-kun" humanized by the addition of "-kun" in the original Japanese version) may represent the suffering of the dead.

The writer's simple, pared-down style effectively depicts the ambiguous feelings of the characters and grasps the subtlety of their inner lives and actions. With its arresting mixture of realism and fantasy, the collection presents us with a serious yet enjoyable read. **KK**

The Blind Assassin

Margaret Atwood

Lifespan | *b.* 1939 (Canada)
First Published | 2000
First Published by | McClelland & Stewart (Toronto)
Booker Prize | 2000

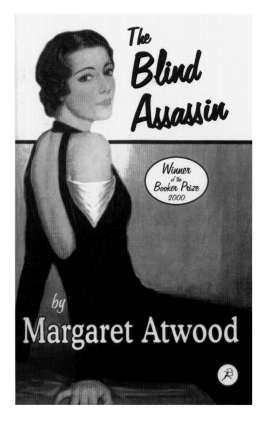

🔺 Atwood's receipt of the Booker Prize in 2000 came as little surprise as three earlier novels had already reached the shortlist.

Margaret Atwood has always sought to collapse the boundaries of different genres, and it is no surprise that in this family epic she employs pulp sci-fi, classic detective novel, newspaper reportage, and tragic confessional romance, as well as the "novel within a novel" format. Beginning in the 1940s, the novel seems to be the fictional autobiography of a woman, Iris, whose life spans the last century. After her sister Laura's suicide, Iris published Laura's novel, *Blind Assassin*, to critical acclaim, projecting the author to posthumous fame. Only weeks later, Iris was widowed when her husband drowned, and many years later, Iris' daughter dies from the ravages of drug and alcohol abuse. Iris' story includes excerpts from Laura's novel, which tell the story of the love affair between a young Marxist and a wealthy young woman, both unnamed. Inside this novel, the young Marxist invents a science fiction novel about a country in which children are blinded and then trained as assassins. This fantastical story centers on a young assassin who falls in love with his intended victim, a temple girl who has had her tongue cut out for the glory of God.

Atwood has achieved here not so much a novel but a kind of Russian doll, with layer upon layer of narrative. In this compelling novel, mid-twentieth-century America emerges as that very same strangely cruel society in which child labor, ritualistic rape, and human sacrifice are routine and where killers are blinded by such social constructs as love, duty, family loyalty, and vengeance. Through Iris' story, and her intricately captured reminiscences, the novel pivots on themes of authorship and confession, the empowerment and impotence of secret storytelling, and the powerless women whose destinies are tied to men. **EF**

The Human Stain

Philip Roth

In *The Human Stain*, Roth brings together two common preoccupations—a hero with a secret, and an affair between an older man and a younger woman—in the character of Coleman Silk, the undefeated boxer-turned-professor whose life story is narrated by a neighbor, Nathan Zuckerman. Coleman Silk is vilified by his university department following false allegations of racism and retires to his home, discovering Viagra and beginning an affair with Faunia, an illiterate maid who is grieving over the death of her children and being pursued by a violent Vietnam veteran ex-husband.

Through flashbacks to his childhood in the Bronx, we discover that Silk has been covering up an enormous secret—he is a black man who has rejected the racism he has experienced from both blacks and whites. Silk's liberation—both personal and sexual—after his involvement with Faunia is startling, and Nathan Zuckerman, at first simply a curious observer, begins to develop a relationship with Silk himself.

The book is worth noting among Roth's repertoire for its strongly sketched female character. While the investigation of the role of the writer and interpreter of events is cunning, raising questions about objectivity in a world of emotions, on a more simple level this book is about guilty secrets, assumptions, and perceptions. Coleman Silk may appear to be the archetypal man fallen from grace, but there is far more at work here than simple parables. It is a sly glance at American social politics, replete with judgment, shame, and hypocrisy, and at the stain left on life by humanity itself. And at the end it is a book that, although ostensibly about the black and white of things, is inherently a thousand shades of gray. **EF**

Lifespan | *b.* 1933 (U.S.)
First Published | 2000
First Published by | Houghton Mifflin (New York)
PEN/Faulkner Award | 2000

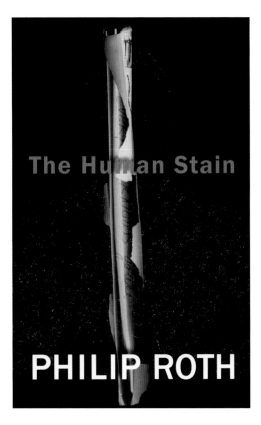

In this tale of a light-skinned black man, Philip Roth goes behind political correctness to grapple with problems of racial identity.

How the Dead Live

Will Self

Lifespan | *b.* 1961 (England)
First Published | 2000
First Published by | Bloomsbury (London)
First U.S. Edition | Grove (New York)

"There, pirouetting between my knees, is a tiny gray manikin."

⊙ Dressing in black often suggests a desire to appear sinister, antisocial, and dangerous; Will Self carries it off better than most.

How the Dead Live is the story of the life, death, and afterlife of Lily Bloom, a cantankerous Londoner whose life is blighted by cancer and the trauma of having a drug-addicted daughter.

Through Lily, the author deals with the issue of death, of how it is both ordinary and extraordinary at the same time, as well as the perennial question of what happens to us when we die. The story begins when sixty-five-year-old Lily succumbs to cancer in a London hospital and is met by her afterworld guide, an Aborigine by the name of Phar Lap Jones. Soon after her arrival in the afterworld, Lily discovers that the real world and the afterworld are strikingly similar, as the pair are transported by a Greek Cypriot minicab driver to the dead neighborhood of North London's Dulston.

In death, Lily is joined by those in her family who have died before her and she meets not only her dead son Rudeboy but a lithopedion she didn't know existed. In a dark comedic fashion, Lily is introduced to the twelve-step Personally Dead Meetings as Self explores the similarities between death and addiction. From the other side, Lily watches over her two daughters—Charlotte, who is cold and ambitious, and the favored Natasha, a heroin addict.

Through Lily's remembrances and the detailed descriptions of life on the other side of death, the author examines not only the meaning of death but the gulf between contemporary Western life—illustrated by the dramatic inclusion of several modern catastrophes that resulted in the gross loss of human life, as well as Lily's ascerbic observations of modern culture—and a non-Western spirituality, which is epitomized by the Aboriginal character Phar Lap Jones. **EF**

City of God

E. L. Doctorow

E. L. Doctorow, an author well-known for fusing history with social criticsm in his fiction, once commented that "history is the present. That's why every generation writes it anew." *City of God*, like much of Doctorow's work, explores universal themes on a grand scale within the small, very real world of contemporary New York City. The novel opens with a description of the Big Bang, thrusting the reader into a bewildering barrage of interlocking stories, letters, and events.

The novel centers on an appropriately religious crime—the stealing of a cross from St. Timothy's Episcopal Church, an event that leads to a startling array of unconnected consequences. For the doubting Reverend Tom Pemberton, the crime serves as a catalyst for a religious, but also very human, experience as his attempt to get to the bottom of it leads him into an uneasy, then eventually loving relationship with a female rabbi, Sarah Blumenthal. The resulting clash of religion and sex is only one in a collage of divergent events and points of view as the novel speeds toward its thrilling conclusion.

Doctorow plays with the idea of the text as both literary and sacred, linear and disjointed, and as the characters try to find their way through a mystery that increasingly appears unsolvable, the city itself comes more and more to the forefront, mirroring the disjointed text of the narrative. *City of God* is an ambitious and sweeping book from a confident author at the height of his literary powers. The novel remains both a sensitive inquiry into the elusive meaning of the religious life in modern times, as well as a metafictional commentary on the dangerously textual nature of our own contemporary lives. **AB**

Lifespan | *b.* 1931 (U.S.)
First Published | 2000
First Published by | Random House (New York)
Full Name | Edgar Lawrence Doctorow

"All history has contrived to pour this beer into my glass."

◈ E. L. Doctorow was born in New York City, and the sights, sounds, and teeming life of that metropolis are never far from his novels.

Celestial Harmonies

Péter Esterházy

Lifespan | *b.* 1950 (Hungary)
First Published | 2000
First Published by | Magveto (Budapest)
Original Title | *Harmonia caelestis*

Recognize the name? Esterházy is a scion of Hungary's most prominent aristocrat clan. And boy, he doesn't let us forget it. A decade after the end of Central European Communism, under which the Esterházys lived in diminished circumstances, *Celestial Harmonies* is a massive attempt to reinscribe the family chronicles. It is literally massive: even the 900-page paperback weighs in at a pound-and-a-half. But it is massive too in the reach of its anecdotes, judgements, and apercus: Even when the book is being deliberately footling and evasive, the reader feels a shock of recognition at the extent to which private and public significances are entwined here, as Esterházy rolls out cameos for figures like Haydn, Béla Bartók, Winston Churchill, and Napoleon III.

Celestial Harmonies is divided into two very different halves. While "Book Two" gives us "Confessions of an Esterházy Family" in a narrative of the author's immediate ancestors, "Book One" is a playful, capricious, and somewhat insane catalog of "Numbered Sentences from the Lives of the Esterházy Family," in which a singular protagonist takes on a myriad of historical identities, stretched across several hundred years and many forms. No mistaking, this is a deeply odd book; possible English-language counterparts might be the more hallucinatory parts of *Ulysses*. If *Celestial Harmonies* seems sometimes oppressively Old World, Alpha-Male, hierarchical, and willful, it makes up for it with the anarchic brilliance of its imagination. **MS**

"When my father . . . turned his attention to the duke's mistress into the bargain, the doubly cuckolded husband cried for blood, which, via a duel, he got . . ."

Péter Esterházy, a descendent of one of Hungary's most aristocratic families, has transformed Hungarian fiction writing.

Nineteen Seventy Seven

David Peace

Lifespan | b. 1967 (England)
First Published | 2000
First Published by | Serpent's Tail (London)
Original Language | English

Nineteen Seventy Seven is the second novel in Peace's so-called "Red Riding" quartet, which also comprises of *Nineteen Seventy Four*, *Nineteen Eighty*, and *Nineteen Eighty Three*. All are part of the same grotesquely compelling story of corrupt police officers, bent lawyers, and property developers, of perversion and pornography, of child murders and sexual abuse, and of the Yorkshire Ripper, a figure who hovers, gargoyle-like, at the margins of all of the novels. Peace isn't interested in writing an objectively true history. The "real" hunt for the Yorkshire Ripper is interwoven into a fictionalized history.

This, the most harrowing installment of the quartet, is a furious hymn to failure and despair. It opens with the "Ripper" investigation moving into full swing and another slain prostitute to identify and mourn. For unhappily married police detective Bob Fraser and alcoholic journalist Jack Whitehead, the anxiety elicited by the attacks is heightened by their own involvement with Chapeltown's whores. Haunted by personal loss and sexual frustration, and chasing demons inside and outside their heads, neither man is finally able to expose guilt and apportion blame. Knowing too much to ensure their safety and too little to satisfy their dark curiosities, their failure to catch or even identify the various murderers foreshadows their own demise and contributes to the unstated ambition of the quartet as a whole: an all-out assault on the foundations and conventions of the crime fiction genre. **AP**

Ignorance

Milan Kundera

Lifespan | b. 1929 (Czechoslovakia)
First Published | 2000
First Published by | Tusquets (Barcelona)
Original Title | *L'ignorance*

Focusing on Czech émigrés' experiences of returning to Prague after the 1989 fall of communism, this novel powerfully contrasts expectations with realities. Irena and Josef, who have spent decades in exile, return to Czechoslovakia. Both have found that during their absence their status as émigrés and their memories of their homeland have been central to their identity and sense of self. Their divergent experiences lead them to an awareness of the unreliability of memory and the influence it exerts upon their lives.

Kundera has a particular fascination with the nature of memory and teases out the etymological and emotional implications of nostalgia. Indeed, the title plays with the roots of the word "nostalgia" and draws attention to the pain of ignorance. His extended digressions and reflective meditations often circle around the story of Ulysses and in particular his love for Penelope and Calypso. He asks why Penelope retains such a hold over Ulysses' heart when so much more of his life has been spent with Calypso, and why we seem unquestioningly to have sympathy for Penelope rather than Calypso.

This is a beautifully written novel, and its gentle pace belies the sophistication of Kundera's prose. He provides a nuanced representation of the dynamics of human relationships and, although less overtly political than his earlier work, this is nonetheless a powerful examination of the profound personal implications of a country's political life. **JW**

Under the Skin

Michel Faber

Lifespan | *b.* 1960 (The Netherlands)
First Published | 2000
First Published by | Canongate Press (Edinburgh)
First U.S. Edition | Harcourt (New York)

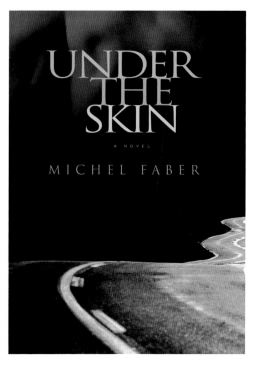

"She was looking for big muscles: a hunk on legs."

⊙ The jacket design of *Under the Skin*, by Claudine Guerguerian, evokes the novel's strange and seductive atmosphere.

Michel Faber's first novel focuses on the life and work of its main female character, Isserley, who trawls the Scottish Highlands in an old Corolla searching for well-built and muscular male hitchhikers. To reveal her purpose in doing so would be to ruin a novel whose shocking power is derived primarily from its perfect orchestration of beautiful description, cunning deception, suspense, and macabre revelation. Suffice to say that reading this novel will force you to confront the arbitrariness of divisions between the human and the animal, as well as the often overlooked ethics of our culture's industrial-scale slaughter and consumption of meat. This novel cannot but force even the most hardened and unreflecting meat-eater to consider such complex and often unpalatable issues as animality, humanity, capitalism, and animal ethics. But it does so within the context of a compelling and original story that defies any simple generic classification— it is a thriller, a science fiction novel, and a lyrical portrayal of one individual's struggle to make sense of the world in which she lives.

The novel is saturated with powerful and evocative descriptions of the landscape. For Isserley, the breathtaking beauty of nature is compensation for the hardships of her life and work, but she has undergone immense personal sacrifice and pain to gain the freedom to appreciate it. Herein lies Faber's elegiac yearning for delight in the natural world and a recognition of our privilege to be living in it, attitudes that the reader senses he feels might be irretrievable or unachievable in the face of the urbanization, consumption, waste, and destruction of contemporary global capitalism. *Under the Skin* is deeply moving, beautifully ethical, and utterly original. It will haunt you for the rest of your life. **SJD**

The Heart of Redness

Zakes Mda

Set in the hinterland of the Eastern Cape, Mda's novel interweaves the astonishing events of the Xhosa people's nineteenth-century independence revolts with an ambivalent perspective on the new South Africa. In the mid-1850s during the devastation of the British "scorched earth" policies, the prophetess Nongqawuse claimed to have been visited by her ancestors who promised that if the Xhosa killed their cattle and burned their crops, the British would be defeated. Thus began an extraordinary episode in which the Xhosa were split between the Believers, those who were determined to follow the prophesies and destroy their means of survival, and those that would not.

Mda brings this story together with a modern tale of a return to contemporary South Africa, where the promises of deliverance are now through tourism and development and the destruction of heritage rather than cattle and crops. Camagu returns to South Africa after years abroad in the U.S. When he visits the village of Qolorha he is drawn into the dispute between the traditionalists, who are fighting to preserve their way of life, and the modernizers, who support the development of a new giant casino on their land. "Redness" is a term for the values symbolically represented by the red ocher with which the Xhosa women dye their clothes. If in the end Camagu is drawn more to the traditionalist Believers, this victory is seen as provisional and the threat of the casino development remains. This enigmatic ending places this novel in that tradition of early post-apartheid novels such as Coetzee's *Disgrace*, which address the painful move toward an uncertain future from the past that nevertheless must be made without erasing it from the collective consciousness. **ABi**

Lifespan | *b.* 1948 (South Africa)
First Published | 2000
First Published by | OUP (Cape Town)
Original Language | English

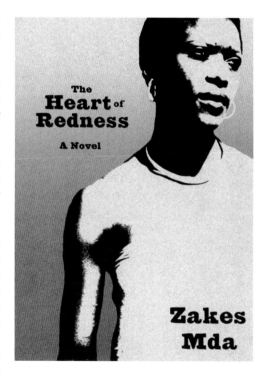

"Beautiful things are celebrated not only with tears."

◉ The difficulty of coping with fundamental change and an uncertain future is the theme of the jacket design, by Kwasi Osei.

White Teeth

Zadie Smith

Lifespan | *b.* 1975 (London)
First Published | 2000
First Published by | Hamish Hamilton (London)
Whitbread First Novel Award | 2000

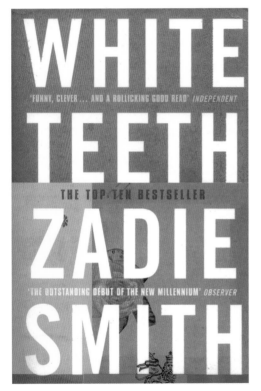

"We're not licenced for suicides."

⬥ Zadie Smith's English father and Jamaican mother met at a party, just as Archie Jones and Clara were made to do in her novel.

White Teeth opens with the attempted suicide and rebirth of Archie Jones. Archie is a war veteran, a career paper-folder, and basically irrelevant. He is an affectionate archetype, unable to make a decision without the toss of a coin. His suicide foiled, he wanders—drunk on carbon monoxide—into the aftermath of a New Year's party. He meets a toothless angel, a Jamaican goddess named Clara. She is a Jehovah's Witness and Archie's fresh start. They beget Irie, a hybrid, put-upon, and quintessential Brit of the new sort; multiethnic, rootless, and disenchanted. "Irie" is Jamaican for "no problem." It is used ironically.

Samad Iqbal is a Bengali waiter at an Indian restaurant. He too was in the war, where he met Archie. He too has a fresh young wife. A traditionalist, he too is trying to come to terms with postwar England. His twin sons do not make it easy. He has to kidnap one and take him to Bangladesh to prevent him from becoming too English. Anchored in the twin histories of Archie and Samad, *White Teeth* is an epic diorama spanning decades of postcolonial England. A narrative that is suffused with accident, fate, and disappointment, it is about immigration, assimilation, and hybridity. It is about religion, tradition, politics, and the end of the world as we know it. It is about rethinking what it is to be English in an increasingly impersonal landscape.

White Teeth, a virtuoso debut from a twenty-four-year-old writer, is crawling with vibrant characters, each with a distinct voice that sings with authenticity. Smith writes with equal facility about teenage love or the trenches of the Second World War; she knows the hearts of her characters and treats them with humor and compassion. The maturity and scope of her talent seems preternatural. **GT**

Spring Flowers, Spring Frost

Ismail Kadare

Lifespan | *b.* 1936 (Albania)
First Published | 2000
First Published by | Onufri (Tiranë)
Original Title | *Lulet e ftohta të marsit*

Spring Flowers, Spring Frost is set in contemporary Albania and tells the story of Mark Gurabardhi, an artist who is struggling to live and work after the fall of the communist regime. Kadare's novel is structured by balanced opposites, between movement and stasis, between sleep and wakefulness. Everywhere in the novel there are signs of rebirth, and everywhere these signs are balanced against omens of talismanic death, betokened most powerfully in the resurrected "book of blood," or Kanun, that has regulated ritual murder in Albania since medieval times.

These oppositions create an extraordinarily jarring effect. Elements from contemporary Europe sit side-by-side with stories and rituals that are derived from deep in the Albanian cultural memory. These oppositions suggest a deadlock, an impasse between a bankrupt mythical history and an equally bankrupt present. Mark cannot feel at home, either in the Albanian past, or in the present dominated by global capital. The novel vividly depicts this nightmarish impasse. But in the quietly poetic movement of Kadare's prose we can glimpse a new set of possibilities: a new art, and a new Albania, for which there is not yet a language. **PB**

⊙ Ismail Kadare won his international reputation as an outspoken and talented critic of the dictatorship of Enver Hoxha.

The Devil and Miss Prym

Paulo Coelho

Lifespan | *b.* 1947 (Brazil)
First Published | 2000
First Published by | Objetiva (Rio de Janeiro)
Original Title | *O demônio e a Senhorita Prym*

The Devil and Miss Prym concludes Coelho's trilogy "And on the Seventh Day." Each of the three books is concerned with a week in the life of ordinary people, who find themselves suddenly confronted by love, death, and power and are forced to face their own inner conflicts and make choices that will affect their very futures.

In *The Devil and Miss Prym*, a stranger descends on Viscos, a small town in France, depicted both as paradise on earth and a dead-end, lifeless place. This contradiction illustrates the author's belief that we choose our own attitudes to life; either affecting reality by making it better for ourselves or failing to find happiness in even the most perfect conditions. Into the village comes a stranger, the Devil of the title, with a mission to discover within a week the answer to the question: are humans essentially good or evil? He finds his Eve in the local barmaid, Chantal Prym, and tempts her to commit evil. In welcoming the mysterious foreigner, the whole village becomes an accomplice to his sophisticated plot. The novel illustrates how the actions of a moment can affect the entire course of our lives and makes us question how we respond to those moments of no return. In a world where we are quick to condemn murderous regimes and "axes of evil," this is a book that reminds us that all humans are fallible and that each and every one of us has the capacity for good or evil. **LE**

An Obedient Father

Akhil Sharma

Lifespan | *b*. 1971 (India)
First Published | 2000
First Published by | Farrar, Straus & Giroux (New York)
PEN/Hemingway Foundation Award | 2000

Ostensibly a low-ranking official of the Delhi Education Department, Ram Karan in reality gathers bribes from schools for aspiring local politician Mr. Gupta. His involvement in the murky, violent world of city politics has served him well: he lives in comfortable surroundings with his daughter Anita, recently widowed, and granddaughter Asha. But a darker secret lurks behind the façade of this neat domestic scene. Anita was repeatedly raped as a young girl by Ram, who has absolved himself of guilt by convincing himself that no physical harm was done to her and that any mental harm is of her own making. Seeing her father alone with Asha reignites Anita's hatred, and she exacts her revenge. Guilt and fear make Ram Karan accede to her demands for money. She also demands that he stay in his room, and he makes little protest when she throws away his medicine and cooks food that she hopes will induce a heart attack.

Set in 1992, on the eve of the assassination of Rajiv Gandhi, *An Obedient Father* is a novel of corruption and moral transgression. Sharma's focus is on the voracious and mercenary social and political context of modern India, within which Ram's deplorable deeds appear both plausible and indicative of a much wider malaise. This bold debut novel makes for uncomfortable reading in part because by skillfully intermingling the personal and the public realms, it continually gestures toward the unsavory that lies hidden beneath the everyday. **ABi**

The Feast of the Goat

Mario Vargas Llosa

Lifespan | *b*. 1936 (Peru)
First Published | 2000
First Published by | Alfaguara (Madrid)
Original Title | *La Fiesta del Chivo*

The dictator novel is not new to Latin America. Yet while established authors of the genre—most notably Marquez' *Autumn of the Patriarch*—typify their writing by drawing on myth and allegory, in *The Feast of the Goat*, Mario Vargas Illosa draws readers down to the street-level of conspirators, the dinner table of victims, and into the stained-trousers of Rafael Trujillo to explore the last day of the dictator's thirty-one year tyrannical rule of the Dominican Republic.

The novel unravels three interweaving storylines. Urania's story represents the Dominican Republic's political relationship to the rest of the post Cold-War world, but also depicts the collective memory of Dominican citizens, of their suffering, and also of their blind faith and complicity in the regime that compromised them so. The second plotline is that of the consipirators, the once-upon-a-time Trujillo loyalists. Finally there is the Trujillo himself. Obsessed with cleanliness as much as the bladder problem that challenges the discipline of his public persona, even Trujillo is a character that suffers from compromise.

Llosa once claimed that in writing about one dictator he writes about all dictators. But painstaking research spent on Dominican streets interviewing real people for this novel make it a tense and unnerving read; bringing human psychology into the genre of the dictator. **JSD**

❯ Mario Vargas Llosa was a conservative candidate for the Peruvian presidency in 1990—an unusually ambitious aim for a novelist.

Life of Pi

Yann Martel

This book, which won the Man Booker Prize in 2002, is the story of Pi Patel, the sixteen-year-old son of a zookeeper from Pondicherry, India. Pi is a religious zealot, he's just not sure which religion he's zealous about, attracting different beliefs "like flies" to become a practicing Christian, Muslim, and Hindu all at the same time. Planning a move to start a new life in Canada, Pi's father packs up the belongings and the menagerie, and the family set off aboard a freighter. After a terrifying shipwreck, Pi finds himself adrift in the Pacific Ocean, trapped on a twenty-six-foot lifeboat with a wounded zebra, a spotted hyena, a seasick orangutan, and a Bengal tiger named Richard Parker. After Richard Parker dispatches the others, Pi must use all his zoological knowledge, wits, and faith to stay alive. The two remain the boat's sole passengers, drifting hungry and exposed for 227 days. Pi recounts the harrowing journey but hidden in his account is an examination of the strengths and weaknesses of religion and writing, and the difference between truth and fiction. Pi realizes he must learn to become the tiger's master, with the interaction between the two forming rich metaphors for spirituality and belief—to some extent, each of the (possibly imaginary) animals could represent a different facet of the hallucinating Pi. The underlying current of the book is that Pi must master his own dark side, his fear, despair, and desperation at his condition and the loss of his family. In a philosophical twist at the end after Richard Parker disappears and Pi is rescued, Pi placates doubting officials with a more credible version of his survival story. This is the version he is convinced they want to hear, and the reader is reminded yet again of how hard it is to tell whether a story is true. **EF**

Lifespan | *b.* 1963 (Spain)
First Published | 2001
First Published by | Knopf Canada (Toronto)
Hugh MacLennan Prize for Fiction | 2001

◉ *Life of Pi*'s dust jacket clearly demonstrates Pi's stark options: keeping a tiger under control or facing the animals overboard.

◉ Yann Martel has said that "God is a shorthand for anything that is beyond the material—any greater pattern of meaning."

Choke

Chuck Palahniuk

Lifespan | *b.* 1961 (U.S.)
First Published | 2001
First Published by | Doubleday (New York)
Full Name | Charles Michael Palahniuk

Victor Mancini spent his childhood in foster care, and relatively mundane periods were occasionally interrupted by his mother kidnapping him and going on the run. In one incident, she whisks him off in a stolen school bus and paints his headlight-projected shadow onto an isolated cliffside in order to demonstrate what an impressive figure he will cut if he works hard. As an adult, Victor—medical school dropout, sex addict, scam artist, colonial theme park employee—is filled with disgusted scorn at his childhood credulity. Now that his mother needs expensive institutional care for dementia, Victor has begun to capitalize on an unlikely source of magnanimity: by simulating choking episodes in restaurants, he attracts myriad of "saviors" who revel in their supposed heroism. Their innocent self-satisfaction, rendered nauseating by narrative repetition, generates in them concern for Victor's well-being and makes some of them eager to rescue him financially from whatever subsequent distresses he invents. Only Victor's complete unmasking precipitates the slim possibility of redemption.

Palahniuk aggressively imports pathological corporeality into his spiritually probing narratives—being persistently presented with such intercontamination of bodily function and cultural understanding might just expand our worldview. It is disturbing that the revolting image of zoo animals' listless masturbation might hold some clues toward understanding late capitalist civilization. **AF**

"What you're getting here is a stupid story about a stupid little boy. A stupid true life story about nobody you'd ever want to meet."

⊙ Chuck Palahniuk's expression says it all. At the start of *Choke*, he even warns the unwary: "Get out while you're still in one piece."

At Swim, Two Boys

Jamie O'Neill

Lifespan | *b.* 1962 (Ireland)
First Published | 2001
First Published by | Scribner (London)
First U.S. Edition | Scribner (New York)

At Swim, Two Boys follows the lives of four characters in 1916, one of the most turbulent years in Ireland's history. There is Jim, self-flagellating, living in fear of a Catholic God. Doyler, a dark and cocky ruffian, is free with his passions. Aunt Eveline is a fierce patriot aware of the twilight of her own aristocracy. MacMurrough, bitter and disgraced, is the victim of a love that didn't yet have a name, except perversion.

Meeting daily at the Forty Foot, where gentlemen swim, scandalously, in the nude, fifteen-year-old Jim and Doyler form a pact: to teach Jim to swim to Muglins rock, where they will claim it for Ireland, and for themselves. But more than just a youthful prank, their bond steadily grows into something more noble and profane, and they fall in love. It is year of great change. Doyler finds within him the seeds that will germinate into open rebellion against Britain. Jim comes to terms with the brutal strictures of the Catholic Church. And MacMurrough, the jaded victim of the same passions as Jim and Doyler, finds hope and dignity in the bond between the boys.

Culminating in the brutally truncated Easter Rising of 1916, this is a panegyric about the purity of love and the vanquishing of the ghosts of the past: the crimes of MacMurrough, the cowardice of Jim's father, and the life denied to Doyler when he is forced out of school. It is also about the dawning of an uncertain future, about pride, and about identity. It is beautifully told in the rich, sensual, and passionate poetry of O'Neill's prose. **GT**

Fury

Salman Rushdie

Lifespan | *b.* 1947 (India)
First Published | 2001
First Published by | Jonathan Cape (London)
Full Name | Ahmed Salman Rushdie

Malik Solanka is the figure at the center of Salman Rushdie's novel *Fury*. Solanka has abandoned his British wife and child and has settled in a fast-moving and equally furious New York in an attempt to retrieve himself from the thick uncomprehending anger that has engulfed him.

The life that he has left behind was seemingly a contented and rich one. Solanka had left the frustrations of a provincial academic life for the more glamorous attractions of show business. There he created "philosophical dolls," charismatic characters ironically able to impart more knowledge than a life spent teaching, which make him rich and famous. Yet his blind furies threaten this life, and he leaves his family because he is terrified of the harm that his rage may inflict upon them. The New York that replaces them for him is itself in the grip of an appropriately violent fear. One of the novel's subplots revolves around the activities of a midnight murderer that Malik secretly fears may be himself, and he cannot find peace until the perpetrator—an overindulged American college boy involved in a fantasy gone awry—is found. But the primary concern of the novel, in common with so much of Rushdie's later fiction, is the search for a perfect and redemptive love. By the end of the novel, Malik finds this love in the figure of Neela, an Indian woman whose beauty is described in hyperbolic loving detail. Yet in the novel's closing images, Malik returns for his child, and it is in this that he finds peace. **NM**

The Body Artist

Don DeLillo

Lifespan | b. 1936 (U.S.)
First Published | 2001
First Published by | Scribner (New York)
First UK Edition | Picador (London)

Despite her regime of physical self-perfection as a body artist, Lauren has discovered that "the world was lost inside her." When her husband Rey dies in the presence of his first wife, Lauren withdraws into her home. As DeLillo evokes her perceptions of apparently mundane routines, the reader becomes immersed in the sense that the insularity of mourning can intensify to a crippling extreme.

Facing this volatile dissociation of inference and full comprehension, Lauren enters a new arena of supernatural engagement. Discovering in an upstairs sideroom a child living "outside the easy sway of either/or," Lauren finds his presence strangely familiar, somehow wholly to be expected—the cause of many anomalous sounds in previous weeks. Defenseless yet unconcerned for his own peril, the boy advises and assuages rather than answers to Lauren's bewilderment. His ineffable spoken language appeases Lauren in ways she can't immediately understand, compelling her to rethink the supposed threat of all things spectral. Forced to allay her own terror, she comes to value "the breathless shock of his being here." DeLillo's free indirect style entices us to peer into Lauren's mind. Beyond the narrative's seemingly unruffled surface, states of heightened sensation succeed one another in perpetual irresolution. Therein resides the novel's peculiarity—and its radiance. Like the perimeters of measurable time it renders so specious, *The Body Artist* "passes through you, making and shaping." **DJ**

Don't Move

Margaret Mazzantini

Lifespan | b. 1961 (Ireland)
First Published | 2001
First Published by | Mondadori (Milan)
Original Title | *Non ti muovere*

A motorbike accident, a hospital, a nurse, a discovery, a doctor, a revelation, a parent's explosive grief. Thus begins *Don't Move*: a multilayered drama of love, loss, and desperation, set upon the affluent backdrop of Northern Italy. Our protagonist Timoteo, a life-weary surgeon, is performing a routine operation, when his fifteen-year-old daughter Angela is rushed into the hospital with serious head injuries from a motorbike accident. The nurse on duty, Ada, breaks the news to Timoteo, bringing the intimate world of fatherly grief crashing in upon the professional, sterile, medical world.

Timoteo waits outside the operating theater while major surgery takes place, and in fear of his daughter's life, he begins his emotionally purgatorial address to her, opening up the structure of the book. What follows is Timoteo's account, his confession to a secular idol, of a bleak period in his life fifteen years ago, of the tumultuous and twisted relationships with his beautiful, materialistic, and slightly false wife, and his emaciated, trashy, but ultimately compelling former lover.

In *Don't Move*, nothing is clear cut: relationships with wives, daughters, lovers, parents, even ourselves; nothing is easily resolved or resolvable. A superbly executed psychological love story for the anti-Austen post-postmodern reader. **RLP**

> The actress Penelope Cruz at the Spanish premiere of the movie *Don't Move* (2004), directed by Italian Sergio Castellitto.

The Corrections

Jonathan Franzen

Lifespan | *b.* 1959 (U.S.)
First Published | 2001
First Published by | Farrar, Straus & Giroux (New York)
National Book Award for Fiction | 2001

'Jonathan Franzen has built a powerful novel out of the swarming consciousness of a marriage, a family, a whole culture.' **Don DeLillo**

JONATHAN FRANZEN

THE CORRECTIONS

WINNER OF THE NATIONAL BOOK AWARD 2001

"You could feel it: something terrible was going to happen."

⊙ The understated dust jacket of the original edition has nothing in common with the book's attention-grabbing paperback cover.

It is ambition that makes Jonathan Franzen's third novel, *The Corrections*, an important novel. It sets out to be important, to declare unapologetically and often ferociously that the novel itself, literature in all its tenuous glory, is important.

The novel's significance for Franzen lies not with the stories it can tell but with the fact that it can tell any story at all, that the novel as a form enables the making visible of that stream of connections and unities that constitute a life whereas life itself, pummelled with distractions and weak with forgetting, hides nine-tenths or more of the work that creates and sustains it.

The Corrections asks as much of its readers as it asks of itself. The ambition that drives it to melt down and merge the interlocking relations, careers and madnesses of a mid-Western, middle-class, middle-aged American family, is an ambition the reader must take on herself if she is to make it through pages that simultaneously have the cognitive shape of a hangover and a high.

The pace of *The Corrections* is frenetic because it has to be: it is encyclopedic, meticulously detailed about the areas of American life it brings under its gaze. These are so many, their significances are so varied yet so irrefutable that the novel creates something of the multi-colored polyphony of history itself.

Published in America a week before the atrocity of 9/11—when terrorists crashed two planes into the World Trade Center causing huge loss of life—there is plenty in this novel to support the view that America is bent on dancing with death. The scope and exuberance of *The Corrections*' appetite for the world, however, makes it an oddly affirmative and even joyful novel. **PMcM**

Atonement

Ian McEwan

The first part of the novel begins in the summer of 1935 as thirteen-year-old Briony Tallis attempts to direct her three cousins in a self-penned play to celebrate the homecoming of her adored older brother, Leon. The children's lives should be idyllic in their upper-middle-class, interwar setting, but real-life events soon enrapture Briony more than her play. She witnesses a moment of sexual tension between her older sister Cecilia and Robbie Turner, the housekeeper's son, whom her father has been helping through medical school. Assuming he is forcing Cecilia into something, and later intercepting a letter Robbie sends to Cecilia declaring his lust, Briony decides that Robbie is an evil beast. When her cousin Lola is mysteriously attacked, Briony wrongly points the finger at Robbie, who is arrested and jailed. Cecilia, heartbroken at her lover's confinement and never ceasing to believe in him, leaves to become a nurse in London and refuses to speak to Briony.

The second part of the novel follows Robbie five years later, now in the army, as he undergoes the horrors and suffering of the Dunkirk evacuations. In the third, and final, part, Briony becomes a war nurse in London and begins to come to terms with her guilt over what she did to Robbie and Cecilia, now finally together.

In the epilogue, McEwan paints Briony as an aging novelist, revisiting her past in fact and fiction and casting doubt over the truthfulness of her stories, which brings into question the author's struggle to relinquish control over the reaction of his readers. This novel is not only about love, trust, and the war. It is also about the pleasures, pains, and challenges of writing, the burden of guilt, and, above all, the danger of interpretation. **EF**

Lifespan | b. 1948 (England)
First Published | 2001
First Published by | Jonathan Cape (London)
National Book Critics Circle Award | 2001

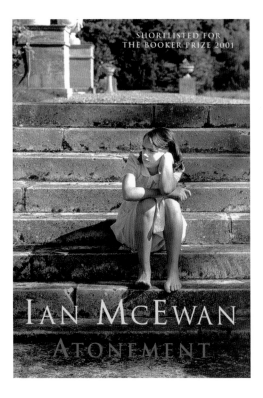

"How much growing up do you need to do?"

Atonement's cover photograph by Chris Fraser Smith captures the feverish cerebral activity of McEwan's protagonist, Briony.

Schooling

Heather McGowan

Lifespan | *b.* 1964 (U.S.)
First Published | 2001
First Published by | Doubleday (New York)
First UK Edition | Faber & Faber (London)

"Upper lip up to no good."

⬤ Patti Ratchford's provocative jacket design continues around
the book to reveal the face of "Catrine" on the back cover.

Heather McGowan's first novel is set in an English boarding school and told from the point of view of Catrine Evans, a thirteen-year-old American girl who has been deposited there by her widower father. Homesick, dislocated from her home, friends, and culture, she is determined to fit in and to be herself.

The setting is a familiar one for a novelist, allowing her to write from the perspective of a person newly learning to see and understand. The language is stream-of-consciousness—apparently influenced by Virginia Woolf—and, as such, seems difficult to read. It isn't always clear what is dialogue, what is invented, and what (if anything) has actually happened. The combination of hackneyed setting and apparently impenetrable language doesn't sound promising, but McGowan has made an important discovery. She knows that a novelist doesn't have to make excuses about borrowed plot elements: the burned-down cricket pavilion, the abortive seduction of a student by a teacher. All these are incorporated into Catrine's sweeping consciousness, and the language reflects the deliberate role-playing of her contemporaries. When someone is determined to make a dramatic entrance, the text resolves into playscript, complete with stage directions; when a once-admired teacher makes insincere apologies, they come accompanied by a musical score, with glissandos and crescendos underlining its artificiality.

McGowan revives a form that had seemed empty since the passing of literary modernism, and she does this by writing against the pretence that stream-of-consciousness is transcribed thinking. Events from the past and the future insinuate themselves into her present tense, making the book a rewarding network of allusions and echoes. **DSoa**

Platform

Michel Houellebecq

This Swiftian analysis of Western decadence and its global impact interweaves narrative with the thought of Baudrillard, Comte, and a trademark essay style voiced through the central protagonist, Michel. Houellebecq offers an argument justifying Third World prostitution through market forces. Prefaced by a citation from Balzac that states, "The more contemptible his life, the more a man clings to it," the book also concerns Michel's quest for redemption through love.

At the novel's outset, middle-aged bachelor Michel discovers his father has been murdered, a fact that, far from forming a psychological angle to the plot, simply allows him to resign his dull job at the Ministry of Culture and indulge in foreign travel. Once abroad, his taste for Thai prostitutes, nurtured already by peep shows and prostitutes in Paris, is only offset by his distaste for more worthy, conventional tourists. He meets Valérie, with whom, back in Paris, he begins an affair. Valérie, it transpires, is an executive for a large travel agency and, with her boss, Jean-Yves, she and Michel develop the "platform" of the novel's title: a travel agency dealing specifically with sex tourism.

Houellebecq's thesis is that, no longer empire builders or "civilizers," modern Europeans barely deserve to survive: their only use is to redistribute the wealth of their industrious forebears. In the absence of more concrete principles, the exchange of sex, rationally, should follow the exchange of money: "a concept in which neither race, physical appearance, age, intelligence, nor distinction plays any part." Magisterially ironic, scurrilous, and dangerous, the novel is a timely provocation for both liberal orthodoxies and Islamic morality, as the novel's devastating conclusion demonstrates. **DH**

Lifespan | *b.* 1947 (Réunion)
First Published | 2001
First Published by | Flammarion (Paris)
Original Title | *Plateforme*

"In fact, nothing disturbs me."

⊙ Chip Kidd is the designer credited for the dust jacket of the hardback edition, with its oblique allusion to Thai prostitution.

Austerlitz

W. G. Sebald

Lifespan | *b.* 1944 (Germany), *d.* 2001 (England)
First Published | 2001
First Published by | C. Hanser (Munich)
Original Language | German

This novel begins with a chance encounter between its unnamed narrator and the eponymous Austerlitz in a railway station in Antwerp. Their ensuing discussion, focusing on the relationship between architecture and historical time, lasts for several hours, and then is rejoined as the two men meet up repeatedly, and always by chance, over a number of years. Their relationship remains cold and distant, until Austerlitz decides to tell the narrator his life story, a story which he is still in the process of remembering. Austerlitz has been brought up as Daffyd Elias by an austere Welsh minister and his wife, and kept in total ignorance of his real name and early childhood living with his biological family in Prague. He was evacuated to Wales before the Second World War, where his amnesiac, dislocated life as Daffyd Elias began.

The novel follows Austerlitz's attempt to penetrate the depths of his memory, seeking, like Austerlitz himself, to reclaim a time lost in the shadows of the Second World War—a time made inaccessible by the unspeakable horrors of Nazism. The narrative style performs with an uncanny fidelity the process of remembering, of delving into the darkness of repressed personal and cultural memory. It is written in long sentences that act like delicate word bridges reaching into the gloom, offering a magical insight into the dark heart of the twentieth century, bringing hidden historical material into the light. To read the novel is to experience the regaining of time. **PB**

Gabriel's Gift

Hanif Kureishi

Lifespan | *b.* 1954 (England)
First Published | 2001
First Published by | Faber & Faber (London)
First U.S. Edition | Simon & Schuster (New York)

Gabriel, son of separated, aging hippie parents, grows up in north London under the amateur care of Hannah, an Eastern European nanny. Gabriel spends his life avoiding Hannah and his mother's drunken friends, visiting his father—a musician whose career ended after he broke his ankle falling off platform heels—in a squalid studio, and escaping into schooling and art. Throughout it all, he holds imaginary conversations with his dead twin brother, Archie, the memory of whom helps him to grow up and take on the challenges his life throws at him. Gabriel has a strong visual imagination, an artist's desire to turn the gray streets of his surroundings into vivid color and an ability to create objects simply by drawing them. He has a chance meeting with 1970s rock star Lester Jones, who his father once performed with. Lester gives Gabriel one of his drawings, which proves to be a turning point for the whole family. In the end, his parents reunite and Gabriel embraces Lester's message, that life and work must be the same thing. Kureishi's story about love and expectation between father and son turns a grim setting into a modern fairy tale. It meditates on failure, talent, and the power of imagination, but it is the family that is central to the book's theme, as first it threatens to destroy its youngest member, and then is brought together by him. **EF**

> Hanif Kureishi is perhaps best known for his screenplay *My Beautiful Laundrette*, which premiered as a movie in 1985.

The Book of Illusions

Paul Auster

Lifespan | *b.* 1947 (U.S.)
First Published | 2002
First Published by | H. Holt & Co. (New York)
Full Name | Paul Benjamin Auster

"Hector Mann had vanished..."

"Everyone thought he was dead." Death is hard to avoid in Paul Auster's work—he may be one of the best living writers about the textures of mourning—and *The Book of Illusions* portrays the various forms nostalgia can take and the gaps it might fill. After academic David Zimmer loses his wife and children in a plane crash, he himself goes into a tailspin of alcohol and television, until a chance encounter with the work of silent movie star Hector Mann offers him a route back. Silent movies, in particular Mann's comedies, shift Zimmer's energies from grief to imaginative revival, and after becoming the world authority on Mann's movies, he discovers that the actor is in fact alive, and in possession of a lost, unreleased masterpiece.

Data, research, and acts of historical recovery have become major fictional subjects in their own right since the 1980s, and Auster's novel can be seen as feeding off such concerns. However, *The Book of Illusions* engages with cinema's intertwinings of presence and absence at a depth that goes beyond nerdy information-mania. Cinematic images can rescue lives from time, but only by fixing them in another medium ("because they were dead, they probably spoke more deeply to us now than they had to the audiences of their time"). In portraying Zimmer's quest for the lost Mann movie, and his flittings round the end of the forgotten genius' life, Auster finely suggests the possible overlaps between what cinema does to time, and the needs it can fulfil in its viewers and critics. Indeed, when Zimmer finally reveals that his whole story is itself a dead man's posthumous request, we too suddenly realize that, like him, we have been alive to the power of ghostly voices. Auster's writing proves that "metafiction" and sentiment can coexist. **BT**

Nowhere Man

Aleksandar Hemon

Aleksandar Hemon arrived in the United States from Sarajevo in 1992, and started writing in his adoptive language three years later. The most striking feature of his writing is his wonderfully innovative use of the English language. Like his postcolonial antecedents, Hemon's work expands the limits of English and challenges the cultural authority of the standard forms of the language.

Nowhere Man, Hemon's first novel, comprises of six interrelated narratives, each with its own narrative style. These different narrative voices recount moments in Josef Pronek's life in Sarajevo prior to the outbreak of the Yugoslav war, in the Ukraine, and in Chicago. They range from the self-consciously scholarly idiom of the graduate student, littered with Shakespearean quotations, to imperfect English as Josef struggles to express himself in his adopted language. Salman Rushdie has commented that translation is a physical movement from one cultural space to another. Hemon vividly represents the exertion that this physical movement requires by depicting the effort that Josef must expend in order to make himself understood. Words strain out of him like the imperfect distillation of ideas. The novel is most striking in those passages where he forces the reader to contemplate the English language afresh by stretching the literal meaning of English words into contexts in which they are not usually applied. For instance, he talks of a light switch "pending in the darkness" which, although consistent with the literal meaning of pending (in the sense of hanging or waiting), is so idiomatically unusual and fresh that it estranges speakers of standard English from their own language. By compelling us to reflect upon his word choices, Hemon's writing forces us to reconsider the very contours of language itself. **LC**

Lifespan | *b.* 1964 (Yugoslavia)
First Published | 2002
First Published by | Nan A. Talese (New York)
Original Language | English

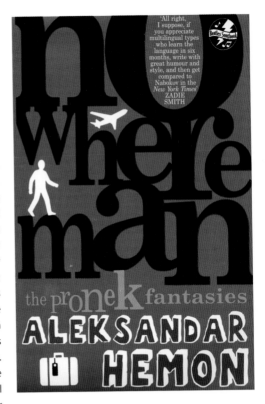

'All right, I suppose, if you appreciate multilingual types who learn the language in six months, write with great humour and style, and then get compared to Nabokov in the *New York Times*'
ZADIE SMITH

"The blinds gibbered . . . "

⬆ Josef Pronek's journey from Sarajevo to the United States is referred to in the novel's quirky hardback dust jacket artwork.

Dead Air

Iain Banks

Lifespan | *b.* 1954 (Scotland)
First Published | 2002
First Published by | Little, Brown & Co. (London)
Full Name | Iain Menzies Bank

"Dead air," the term for the absence of sound when a radio broadcast is in progress, permeates this book. Ironically, most of it is made by "shock-jock" Ken Nott, as he pontificates on his own particular brand of noncompromising leftism throughout the novel.

Dead Air is a deliberate parody of the cynicism of political and social self-awareness. Nott's politics, while palatable to most contemporary readers, are also presented through such a morally bankrupt man that they are rendered as unpalatable as the Holocaust-refuter whom Nott attempts to thwart by punching in the face (and then denying it ever happened). Banks focuses on a series of set piece hypotheses about the state of the world in the new century, in which he highlights the preoccupation of the middle classes with their own beliefs, while at the same time exposing the individual to the reader's scrutiny.

There is little to endear Ken Nott to the reader, and his promiscuous, expensive lifestyle has all of the hallmarks of 1980s callousness, spread with a veneer of pseudo-socialism that indeed makes it the perfect reflection of the downmarket world of "bright young things" in the early 2000s. In *Dead Air*, Banks is once again engaged by the recurring subtexts of the new millennium—avarice, cynicism, and pretensions to libertarianism. **EMcCS**

◀ In *Dead Air*, Iain Banks pillories innumerable woeful shortcomings of early twenty-first-century British thinking.

Youth

J. M. Coetzee

Lifespan | *b.* 1940 (South Africa)
First Published | 2002
First Published by | Secker & Warburg (London)
Nobel Prize for Literature | 2003

Youth is the second of Coetzee's autobiographical works (the first being *Boyhood*), although the similarities to Coetzee's personal history are heavily fictionalized through the perspective of his anti-hero John, a South African migrant who comes to London searching for culture at the start of the 1960s. Hoping to make his way as a writer, John is constantly frustrated by the provinciality of South Africa and the failure of his own artistic work to meet the standards of impersonality and detachment that he draws from high modernism. He only wins literary recognition when he attempts to incorporate Pablo Neruda's work into his own poetry.

Many of Coetzee's repeated themes are present here—notably in the failure of John to communicate meaningfully with his peers and in his inability to articulate the depth of his consciousness. However, *Youth* is also a humorous novel, and John is portrayed with a sense of irony that undercuts his pretensions. John's self-aggrandizement is evident when, appalled by the Cold-War hostilities toward the Soviet Union and China, he writes to the Chinese embassy offering to serve the Revolution and then fears that his letter has been intercepted by the British Secret Services. Such an episode is easy to read ironically, but it should perhaps be considered in the context of the post-Sharpeville South African state, where such surveillance was commonplace. Indeed, it is possible to read *Youth* as a reflection on the nature of committed writing. **LC**

Middlesex

Jeffrey Eugenides

Lifespan | *b.* 1960 (U.S.)
First Published | 2002
First Published by | Farrar, Straus & Giroux (New York)
Pulitzer Prize | 2003

Jeffrey Eugenides' novel tells the story of three generations of a Greek American family. Cal, the narrator, is a forty-one-year-old man who was born a hermaphrodite and brought up as a girl for fourteen years. He recounts the story of the love affair between his grandmother and her brother, who escape the Turkish massacre of Greeks in Smyrna in 1922. On board a ship bound for America, they marry and spend their remaining time at sea attempting to divest themselves of the familiarity of their sibling relationship, the first of many identity reinventions that structure this narrative.

In this novel the "I" of the narrator is both grandchild, grandniece, and grandnephew. Cal is both a son and daughter whose mother and father are cousins. Through this sparsely branched family tree the narrator follows the DNA trail of the Stephanides clan, which determines his own complex gender identity. Through recording the migratory experiences of his grandparents, Cal also richly details key events of twentieth-century America—Prohibition, the Great Depression, the Second World War, and the Detroit race riots. The confusion of identity that Cal wrestles with is mirrored in the culturally stratified neighborhoods of Detroit. The barriers between Greek/Turk, sibling/lover, male/ female, black/white, and immigrant/native are questioned with sharp, compassionate humor. This novel asks profound questions about identity, but it does so with wit in a strikingly original story. **PMcM**

Shroud

John Banville

Lifespan | *b.* 1945 (Ireland)
First Published | 2002
First Published by | Picador (London)
First U.S. Edition | 2003, by Knopf (New York)

Summoned to Turin by a letter disclosing his impending disgrace, Axel Vander, the narrator, senses his arrival will expose a cherished secret. Threatening to secure his exposure, Cass Cleave awaits him, seductive yet inscrutable. Reliability soon becomes an issue of the veracity with which events are relayed as well as the deeds they reveal. To this extent, Banville often places the integrity of his narrator's self-inspection in jeopardy. "What do I know?" wonders Vander, early in the novel "Less now than yesterday. Time and age have brought not wisdom, but confusion, and a broadening incomprehension, each year laying down another ring of nescience." Even the name "Vander" betrays an uncertain provenance: We get the sense that it is merely a temporary label under which the narrator addresses his own diasporic memories.

This kind of existential self-commentary frequently bisects with a certain self-parody; it is as though Vander knows all too well that Turin's cityscape will petition against his protecting the past from scrutiny. Turin becomes a mausoleum for memories yet to be readdressed. We are given the disarming illusion of privileged access to another's mind under duress, within a labyrinthine built environment that coerces its inhabitants into states of recessive self-delusion. **DJ**

⊙ John Banville's magical evocation of Turin in *Shroud* recalls *Prague Pictures*, his 2003 collection of travel memoirs.

In the Forest

Edna O'Brien

Lifespan | *b.* 1932 (Ireland)
First Published | 2002
First Published by | Weidenfeld & Nicolson (London)
First U.S. Edition | Houghton Mifflin (Boston)

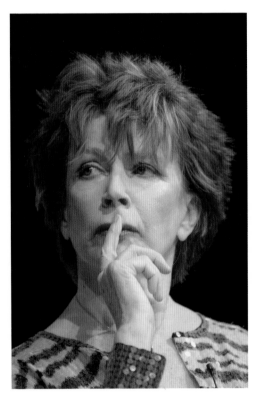

"God hates me . . . I am hated."

⬈ *In the Forest* is an unusual departure for Edna O'Brien in
that the novel is an imaginative foray based on real-life events.

The question of murder is at the heart of this controversial book, which is a response to the true story of the abduction and murder of Imelda Riney, her son, Liam, and Father Joseph Walshe in County Clare in April, 1994. The young man convicted of the murders, Brendan O'Donnell, was confined to the Central Mental Hospital in Dublin, where he was found dead in 1997. O'Brien delves into the psychiatrist reports and court records in order to extrapolate and recreate the story of what happend in Country Clare, and in doing so fictionalizes real-life events, a trademark also shared by *Down By the River* (1997). "I believe," O'Brien comments, "that the novelist is the psychic and moral historian of his or her society." *In the Forest* takes on that task by revisiting (some would say exploiting) the shock of these murders to weave a telling fable of modern Irish life.

The narrative recounts the fatal encounter between a mother and child, Eily Ryan and Maddy, the "blow-ins" to the West of Ireland, and a local man, Michael O'Kane, who, on the death of his mother, appears to lose any protection against the violence of Church and State.

Insistently understated, splicing together the events of past and present, *In the Forest* broaches the maddening effects of both loss and violence, exploring the urge to self-destruction with which O'Kane lives and murders. An enigma lies at the heart of this novel; in the words of a priest, "What is it that warps a child . . . what is it that changes a child from being a child?" This disturbing novel struggles to represent the hatred that afflicts O'Kane, a hatred that is especially acute in the face of hope, when he is confronted by the "sacred bond" (O'Kane's words) between mother and child. **VL**

That They May Face the Rising Sun

John McGahern

That They May Face the Rising Sun traces the fortunes of a couple who have moved from London to rural Ireland in the hope of finding a new way of life. Joe and Kate Ruttledge's project to build their dream home arouses more than neighborly curiosity, finding each stage of construction "carefully observed," betraying a "resentment fuelled by an innate intolerance of anything strange or foreign." That the couple remain oblivious to this thinly veiled hostility occasions McGahern's own commentary. In relative detachment from all the to-ings and fro-ings of the building work, our narrator questions the motivations for their emigration through the expectations they harbor: "Would the move succeed or fail? If it failed they would return to London?" Indeed, the handling of this calm voice-over epitomizes McGahern's poise as a prose stylist who stands before a provincial setting where emerging prosperity tremors portentously beneath the serene community.

McGahern achieves a tempered, cumulative narrative style, as passage by passage requires patience and diligence from the reader. He never romanticizes the countryside as an edifying resource for those, like Joe and Kate, who strive to become versed in its traditions. This level of reserve is characteristic, as he reveals the complexities of a regional community maintaining its integrity before the uncertain prospect of outside investment and redevelopment. Just as his recent *Memoir* focuses on the idiosyncratic and "delicate social shadings of the place," so McGahern's latest novel sustains its poignant account of a couple acclimatizing to rural Ireland by unfolding through the everyday demands and rewards of pursuing family life among established native customs. **DJ**

Lifespan | *b.* 1934 (Ireland)
First Published | 2002
First Published by | Faber & Faber (London)
U.S. Title | *By the Lake*

"None of us believes . . ."

⊙ In describing an Irish rural community both resisting and surrendering to change, John McGahern has lessons for us all.

The Story of Lucy Gault

William Trevor

Lifespan | b.1928 (Ireland)
First Published | 2002
First Published by | Viking (London)
First U.S. Edition | Viking (New York)

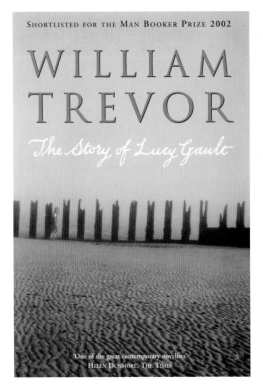

SHORTLISTED FOR THE MAN BOOKER PRIZE 2002

WILLIAM TREVOR

The Story of Lucy Gault

'One of the great contemporary novelists'
HELEN DUNMORE, THE TIMES

"The past was the enemy."

◉ William Trevor is widely admired, not least by his fellow novelists, for the beauty, lucidity, and perfection of his writing style.

The Story of Lucy Gault has the same sense of historical sweep as many of Trevor's other novels and short stories about the Protestant Anglo-Irish landowner class in Ireland. It is set at a time when political events in the early twentieth century begin to threaten their domination over the native Catholic population. When Captain Everard Gault, owner of the Big House Lahardane in County Cork, wounds a nighttime intruder intent on firebombing the property, he sets in motion a familiar cycle of intimidation and violence. The position of the Gaults in the local community becomes impossible, and they prepare to leave Ireland. But Lucy, their eight-year-old daughter, refuses to give up her beloved Lahardane and runs away. Chance plays some cruel tricks, and the child is presumed drowned. The painful loss of their daughter and the destruction of their social and political identity make Captain Gault and his wife Heloise shadows of their own past, and they travel aimlessly around Europe. At Lahardane their young daughter is miraculously found alive, and frantic efforts are made to contact the parents. As time passes, Lucy remains stuck in an ideal and unreal past, and the final reunion between father and daughter is a tragic reminder of wasted lives.

The innocent happiness of childhood being cruelly destroyed by extremes of adult behavior often lies at the heart of Trevor's writing, but here this familiar theme is also intriguingly reversed. The peace and quiet of Lucy's Irish Big House suggests both a longing for an ideal and uncomplicated existence free from conflict and violence, and, at the same time, a façade masking an unequal and unfair historical relationship. Trevor's characters, and his readers, are asked to navigate between these polemical positions. **UD**

Kafka on the Shore

Haruki Murakami

Lifespan | *b.* 1949 (Japan)
First Published | 2002
First Published by | Shinchosha (Tokyo)
Original Title | *Umibe no Kafuka*

"Being able to converse with cats was Nakata's little secret."

⊙ The fantastical imaginings of Haruki Murakami's later work are, for some readers, less satisfying than his earlier realistic style.

Murakami, born in Kyoto to a Buddhist father and merchant mother, spent much of his childhood absorbing the Japanese literature that his parents both taught. His interest, however, is in American literature, a tension between East and West that he reconciles in much of his work.

Kafka on the Shore could perhaps be described as a piece of psychoanalytic magic realism. Kafka Tamura is a fifteen-year-old boy whose father has told him, in an Oedipal prophecy, that he will kill his father and sleep with his mother and sister. Kafka runs away from his father to escape this prediction but also, ironically, to go in search of his mother, who took his sister and abandoned him when he was a child. A second parallel story about an elderly simpleton called Nakata haunts Kafka's world. Kafka and Nakata never meet, but their journeys through life are inextricably bound together.

The novel explores the relationship between life events and the folds of time, connections between ghosts and music, the healing effects of forgiveness, dream-realities, violence, love, memory, and loss. We are presented with a world of inexplicable events where humans communicate with cats and dogs, and fish fall from the sky. Larger-than-life characters such as Johnny Walker and Colonel Sanders have an effect on the fate of everyone.

Through his finely tuned prose style and attention to detail, Murakami pulls the tones of a chaotic, surrealist universe into harmony with a Zen-like meditation. *Kafka on the Shore* is a piece of writing that attempts to come to terms with the modern world by weaving together Eastern and Western thinking in a way that explores and enhances our attitudes toward the mysteries of time, life, and death. **PM**

Unless

Carol Shields

Unless broaches a terrifying prospect for any parent. Against the relatively comfortable background of a stable marriage and buoyant career writing popular fiction, Reta Winters' eldest daughter, Norah, disappears from her university life to join the outcasts on Toronto's streets. In her destitution, Norah takes up a position against the world's inhumanity, crouching on a street-corner with a necklace sign on which the word "GOODNESS" appears. The novel traces Reta's twofold quest to retain some form of coherence amid the everyday as she negotiates between the shattering aftermath of her daughter's withdrawal and her commitments as wife, mother, writer, friend—personal roles that are rapidly subsumed by grief. Reta struggles to bring her novel, *Thyme in Bloom*, to fruition in spite of the prescriptions of her imperious publisher. Reta's resistance to his chauvinistic revision suggestions ignites *Unless'* satirical commentary on the status of women novelists.

Throughout this duel-pronged narrative, Shields exemplifies her singular ability to ambush the most ordinary experiences with verbal economy and suppleness, caressing without sentimentalizing that everyday event of personal introspection. It is this attentiveness to the beguiling and epiphanic contortions of self-knowledge, sprung amid the commonplace, that Shields achieved in *Happenstance* (1980) and recaptures again in *Unless*. In so doing, she exhibits in her final novel how verbal discretion can hold the reader in thrall. For Shields, it is a discretion that supersedes the need for florid diction. Instead, she unleashes a mercurial syntax in which crippling recognitions and domestic routines are juxtaposed to forge a grammar attuned to the everyday world. **DJ**

Lifespan | *b.* 1935 (U.S.), *d.* 2003 (Canada)
First Published | 2002
First Published by | Fourth Estate (New York)
First UK Edition | Fourth Estate (London)

"They published my 'text,' such a cold, jellied word . . . "

◈ Carol Shields is noted for her meticulous attention to the ordinary but highly significant detail of her characters' lives.

Everything is Illuminated

Jonathan Safran Foer

Lifespan | *b.* 1977 (U.S.)
First Published | 2002
First Published by | Houghton Mifflin (Boston)
Guardian First Book Award | 2002

"I am unequivocally tall."

⊙ *Everything is Illuminated* was inspired by Jonathan Safran Foer's own visit to the Ukraine in 1999 to research his grandfather's life.

Jonathan Safran Foer's *Everything is Illuminated* is a strikingly ambitious first novel that has enjoyed a rare combination of commercial success and critical acclaim. The story revolves around a young Jewish American author (also named Jonathan) who, with little more than a faded photograph, travels to the Ukraine in search of Augustine—a woman who may have saved his grandfather from the Nazi occupation. Much of the novel is built around a series of retrospective letters to Jonathan from Alex Perchov, a Ukrainian in his late teens who he hires as his guide and translator. Alex's limited grasp of English ("my second tongue is not so premium," he admits) and misconceived use of a Thesaurus are rendered in a dazzling feat of linguistic invention. However, although his mistakes and malapropisms are often wildly comical, Alex is no simpleton and he grows in dignity and insight as the novel progresses. These letters are broken up by strange, magic-realist style episodes, which recount the history of Jonathan's ancestral village (or "shtetl") from the day of its founding at the beginning of the nineteenth century to the tragedy of the Final Solution.

Everything is Illuminated is a willful conflation of fact and fantasy—an audacious vision of the Holocaust and its legacy presented through skewed translations, twists of fate, half-remembered conversations, fragile friendships, and competing narrative voices. It is a novel deeply concerned with the politics of memory, with how our relationship to the past is negotiated by the needs of the present. It is a novel about ancient secrets, about ignorance and knowledge, innocence and experience, atonement and guilt. It is both riotously funny and quietly devastating and may well signal the arrival of a major new voice in contemporary fiction. **SamT**

The Double

José Saramago

Tertuliano Máximo Afonso, the central character of Saramago's fable, is a modest history teacher who watches a movie one evening and discovers a bit-part actor who is identical to him in every way, right down to the last freckle. The premise, the possibility that someone else exists that is yourself in "every respect" is a classic literary device, but unlike Robert Louis Stevenson's *The Strange Tale of Dr. Jekyll and Mr. Hyde* or Fyodor Dostoevsky's *The Double*, Saramago explores his theme in a downbeat, ponderous manner, shot through with an unsettling insidious anxiety.

On the surface, this appears to be a narrative that both questions and satirizes individuality as a concept. The "double" is himself an actor, conversations are presented as unindividuated tides of prose, Tertuliano struggles to distinguish himself within his emotional life and profession. The novel's action is contained within simple, everyday acts that are recontextualized in ways that make them deeply disturbing. Though Saramago never enters the realms of the surreal, an ordinary, if not dull life is rendered increasingly strange. An ineffectual man, threatened with a loss of identity, gains a sense of purpose as the narrative brings the character into relief.

Undoubtedly *The Double* demands a certain commitment from its reader to be fully appreciated. Its style is characteristically digressive, with dialogue where it is sometimes impossible to distinguish between voices, but these elements are also at the core of the novel's achievements. Though requiring hard work at times, the novel's ending is a payoff well worth the effort—it will leave you quietly astounded, with your sense of what constitutes "self" unsettled. **AC**

Lifespan | *b.* 1922 (Portugal)
First Published | 2002, by Editorial Caminho (Lisbon)
Original Title | *O homem duplicado*
Nobel Prize for Literature | 1998

WINNER OF THE NOBEL PRIZE FOR LITERATURE

JOSÉ SARAMAGO

THE DOUBLE

"He lives alone and gets bored."

⊘ The jacket illustration by Tom Gauld encapsulates the withdrawn and depressed existence of José Saramago's protagonist.

Fingersmith

Sarah Waters

This captivating, beautifully crafted book has rightly earned Waters the title of "the modern Charles Dickens" or Wilkie Collins. Its gripping, multilayered plot transports us feelingly around the dark back alleys, gloomy mansions, pornographic libraries, lunatic asylums, and prisons and scaffolds of Victorian England. As in Dickens, the sights and sounds of the Victorian underworld are brought to life in this vast, seductive novel.

The story begins in 1862 in London's Lant Street, where a teenage Sue Trinder lives under the care and tutelage of Mrs. Sucksby and her family of farmed babies and thieves; but there is a great deal of warmth in this vibrant city womb. By contrast, many miles away another orphan, shy and lonely Maud Lilly, lives captive to her seedy uncle in a cavernous bleak house. Hers might be described as a privileged, wealthy upbringing, but it is isolated, devoid of love, and exploitative—she is even forced to read pornographic books. As the twists, turns, and shocks of this disturbing tale unravel from the viewpoints of both Sue and Maud, we discover that the lives of these two young women are intertwined and that they are both enmeshed in a painful web of lies, deceit, and fraud outside their control. Murder is the only escape.

Waters paints a moving picture of the evolving relationship between Sue and Maud as it passes from one of mistress-servant, to one of kindness and comfort, to one incorporating charged scenes of mutual desire and love. At one level then, this is a fine gothic tale incorporating lesbian romance, at another it is Dickensian conspiracy at its best. Water's ability to craft an original plot is stunning. This amazing story of secrets, lies, pain, and desire demands to be read again and again. **MH**

Lifespan | *b.* 1966 (Wales)
First Published | 2002
First Published by | Virago (London)
First U.S. Edition | Riverhead (New York)

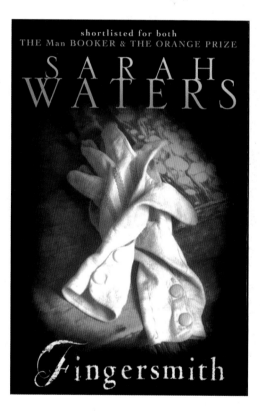

Clasped ladies' gloves imply Sarah Waters' theme of lesbian love set nineteenth-century London.

Part of Waters' tale takes place in the poverty and squalor depicted by Gustave Doré's engraving *Blue Gate Fields* (1872).

Family Matters

Rohinton Mistry

Lifespan | *b.* 1952 (India)
First Published | 2002
First Published by | Faber & Faber (London)
Kiriyama Pacific Rim Book Prize | 2002 (joint)

Family Matters charts the effects of religous fanaticism and traditionalism working through a Parsi family in Mumbai. Resembling King Lear, Nariman Vakeel, an elderly widower, is forced to live with his daughter and her husband, Yezad, after breaking his ankle. The strains of this arrangement are played over Nariman's reminiscences of how he had given up the woman he loved, a Catholic, to satisfy the religious and familial constraints imposed by his parents. The religious imperative that Nariman recounts has its more sinister parallel in the rise of the right wing Shiv Sena movement in Mumbai.

Meanwhile, Yezad hatches a plan for promotion that involves actors impersonating Shiv Sena thugs and intimidating his boss. In a central irony of the book, Yezad loses his job when real Shiv Sena thugs kill his employer. Unable to find a new job, Yezad turns toward Parsi religious purity. As the novel ends, despite a change of heart and a new tenderness toward his father-in-law, Yezad is apparently unable to learn from Nariman's unhappy life or from the growing tensions in the city.

One of the notable features of Mistry's novels is his passion for imbuing characters and events with metaphorical meanings. For many readers this places him more comfortably in the tradition of nineteenth-century English writers than alongside his Indian contemporaries. *Family Matters* combines a grand scope with meticulous detail, and with the focus squarely on the characters. **ABi**

London Orbital

Iain Sinclair

Lifespan | *b.* 1943 (Wales)
First Published | 2002
First Published by | Granta (London)
Movie Adaptation | 2002 (Iain Sinclair & Chris Petit)

Voted number one on a BBC Radio Four poll of "The Seven Horrors of Britain," the M25—the 120-mile freeway that encircles London like a giant concrete artery—might at first seem an unlikely setting for an epic journey on foot. However, this is precisely the path that author Iain Sinclair chooses to tread "in the belief that this nowhere, this edge, is the place that will offer fresh narratives." *London Orbital* proves that even the unsightly and prosaic landscape of one of the world's busiest highways can be transformed by a unique poetic vision.

Like the automobiles that zoom around the M25 in the fast lane, Sinclair's inventive prose accelerates across the page with energy and precision, rapidly leading the eye from personal anecdotes and literary allusions to commentaries on the politics of urban planning. *London Orbital* criticizes the way in which the architecture of cities and roads reinforces the inequalities between socio-economic groups, rigidly monitoring the movements of the populace through the ubiquitous eyes of surveillance cameras. Once the dumping ground for the mentally ill and industrial waste, the land through which the M25 passes is now peppered with apartment complexes, golf courses, warehouses, shopping malls, and well-guarded corporate headquarters. Sinclair savagely attacks the mismanagement of the landscape. *London Orbital* turns an otherwise dull and uneventful nowhereland into a highly charged and contested geopolitical site. **CC-G**

Elizabeth Costello

J. M. Coetzee

Lifespan | *b.* 1940 (South Africa)
First Published | 2003
First Published by | Secker & Warburg (London)
Nobel Prize for Literature | 2003

Subtitled "Eight Lessons," *Elizabeth Costello* is an innovative book, concerned with writing as a work of sympathetic imagination. Two of the "lessons"— "The Philosophers and the Animals" and "The Poets and the Animals"—appeared earlier in *The Lives of Animals* (1999), which offers a disturbing perspective on the (in)human capacity to disregard the lives of those who fall outside the claims of sympathy and imagination. The controversial point of comparison here is the Holocaust and the death camps that bear witness to the fact that "the killers refused to think themselves into the place of their victims, as did everyone else." This theme pervades the lectures, which blur the boundary between fiction and criticsm, delivered by Elizabeth Costello, an acclaimed novelist obliged to respond to the critical industry that surrounds her work by offering up her consciousness to her readers. Elizabeth is a reluctant celebrity, never quite giving her audiences what they want on the issues apparently close to their hearts: the African novel, the woman writer, the question of censorship, and the representation of evil.

Her son, John, recalls Costello as a woman who "stormed around the house in Melbourne . . . screaming at her children, 'You are killing me! You are tearing the flesh from my body!'" Secreted within her lectures is a "life"—elliptic, tantalizing—that fractures the domain of public speech, of public reason, already in question throughout Costello's provocative "Lessons." **VL**

Islands

Dan Sleigh

Lifespan | *b.* 1935 (South Africa)
First Published | 2003
First Published by | Tafelberg (Cape Town)
Original Title | *Eilande*

Islands is a vastly ambitious novel of origins and empire, written originally in Afrikaans, by a researcher at the National Archives of South Africa. Set against the first half-century of the Dutch settlement of the Cape of Good Hope, Sleigh ranges across continents and oceans to explore the clash between colonizers and indigenous populations. At the center of the interlocking tales of seven different men is the product of the colony's first "mixed marriage," Pieternella. Her life is inextricably linked with the developing Dutch presence at the Cape and the mechanics of the Dutch East India Company, the VOC. Her hybrid experience in the emerging colony, neither entirely African nor Dutch, offers a series of perspectives, and her ultimate fate becomes a powerful metaphor for the fate of the colony itself.

The many characters, all superbly realized, are dwarfed by forces beyond their comprehension or control, taking place across the early modern world. This is Sleigh's great achievement: the lives of his characters throw into sharp relief the inexorable and brutal process of Dutch colonial expansion. Casting a long shadow over proceedings is the developing fort, which from humble beginnings gradually becomes an intimidating fortress, the base from which territorial control is expanded further and further into the interior. This was a novel that the new South Africa badly needed, and as such the scale of the accomplishment is immense, and its importance cannot be overstated. **MD**

The Curious Incident of the Dog in the Night-Time

Mark Haddon

Lifespan | *b.* 1962 (England)
First Published | 2003
First Published by | Jonathan Cape (London)
Whitbread Award | 2003

WINNER OF THE WHITBREAD
BOOK OF THE YEAR
MARK HADDON
The CURIOUS INCIDENT of THE DOG IN THE NIGHT-TIME
'OUTSTANDING...A stunningly good read' *INDEPENDENT*

◉ The innocence of Mark Haddon's young narrator is hinted at in the children's book styling of this paperback edition's cover.

◉ Mark Haddon was praised for his empathy and sureness of touch in describing a young mind affected by Asperger's syndrome.

This strange and captivating novel took the public by storm when it was first published, appealing to adults and children alike. The central character of the book is Christopher Boone, who is fifteen-years-old and suffers from Asperger's syndrome, a mild form of autism, a condition that limits his emotional understanding of the world around him, but not his innate intelligence.

We are introduced to a strange world where food colors must not be mixed on a plate, everything is taken literally, red things are good but yellow and brown things are bad, and where people should never tell lies. Christopher, who lives with his widowed father in Swindon, a provincial English town, sets about trying to solve the mystery of who killed his neighbor's pet dog with a garden fork. Along the way he introduces us to his father, his teacher, his pet rat, his neighbors, and a host of the bizarre and unusual facts he keeps locked away in his brain—the book is filled with mathematical explanations. Haddon gives us a startling insight into Christopher's world, where noise is frightening, physical contact with people difficult, and reading people's faces and emotions impossible.

Christopher encounters adult resistance to his quest to investigate the dog's death, which—by a fluke—leads him to begin investigating the story of his dead mother. The beauty of the book isn't the detective story, although that is bittersweet enough, it is the dazzling portrayal of a boy living in a world offset from normality, confounded by different rules, and where modern society, with all its foibles and idiosyncracies, is subverted by honesty and innocence. **EF**

What I Loved

Siri Hustvedt

> "*Violet was smiling. She lowered her arm to her side, and I thought of Ovid's Pygmalion kissing, embracing, and dressing the girl he had carved out of ivory.*"

🔎 In *What I Loved*, Siri Hustvedt returns to the theme of how events can shape our lives and determine who we become.

Lifespan | *b.* 1955 (U.S.)
First Published | 2003
First Published by | H. Holt & Co. (New York)
First UK Edition | Sceptre (London)

A sense of loss already seeps into the past-tense title of *What I Loved*, in which aging art historian Leo Hertzberg examines familial bonds he and his closest friend Bill Wechsler created and lost throughout their twenty-five-year relationship.

Bill's early *Self-Portrait*, an enormous painting of a young woman, captivated Leo, prompting him to seek out the unknown artist. An intellectually charged discussion in Bill's Bowery studio culminates in Bill giving Leo "permission" to see the shadow in the painting as his own, a gesture of intimacy that launches their fraternal affection. Throughout the intervening years, the men share improbable but evocative parallels. Bill and his wife, Lucille, move into the loft above Leo and his wife, Erica, and later Bill's model and second wife, Violet, comes to stay. The families welcome baby boys within weeks of each other. Both suffer the loss of their sons—precocious Matt Hertzberg in a childhood boating accident and Mark Wechsler in a perplexing yet persistent drift into mental disorder, the thrall of "horror art," and chaos. By the time of the narrative, Leo is the lone remnant of a once robust world of personal and creative engagement.

Hustvedt's novel bristles with an experimental energy against which the characters' domestic tragedies unfold. Bill's art stakes its claim at the periphery of the intelligible. Leo's patient readings of Bill's work ease it into articulateness, while testing the boundaries of interpretation. **AF**

The Light of Day

Graham Swift

Lifespan | *b.* 1949 (England)
First Published | 2003
First Published by | Hamish Hamilton (London)
First U.S. Edition | Knopf (New York)

The Light of Day recounts a day in the life of private detective George Webb. It is November 20, 1997, and the second anniversary of the day that Sarah Nash, the woman George loves, murdered her husband. George's journey to visit Sarah in prison begins and ends in his office on Wimbledon Broadway. During the course of the day, George visits Putney Vale Cemetery, puts roses on Bob's grave for Sarah, and visits her in prison. While this chronological journey forms the structural framework of the novel, another journey, which spans the fifty years of George's life, forms the internal monologue that disrupts chronological time. George relives traumas from his childhood, analyzes his marriage, wonders at his relationship with his daughter, and relives the humiliation of his dismissal from the police force for fabricating evidence.

Meticulous attention to the detail of the suburbia where George travels provides the backdrop for a meditation on the relationship between past and present, the motives for violence, the need for salvation and redemption, and the nature of love. Swift exposes the fragility of the veneer of civilization and the ease with which anyone can slip over the boundaries of civilized behavior. It is not by means of CCTV, policing, or even justice, that civilization is sustained in this novel, but simply by the ability to keep secrets. Love, though, offers a possibility, though not a certainty, of redemption. **AR**

Thursbitch

Alan Garner

Lifespan | *b.* 1934 (England)
First Published | 2003
First Published by | Harvill Press (London)
Original Language | English

Alan Garner is probably best known as the author of a series of books, including *The Owl Service* and *The Weirdstone of Brisingamen*, written in the 1960s and usually regarded as aimed at a young audience. The much more recent *Thursbitch* is a very different proposition. Set in the Peak District, on the borders of Cheshire and Derbyshire, it interlocks two stories from very different times.

One is the story of Jack Turner, a "jagger" or salt trader of the mid-eighteenth century; he is found frozen to death amid various strange signs and symbols. It emerges that he was a kind of shaman in a pagan cult fuelled by hallucinogenics and about to be defeated by Christianity. In the other story a contemporary geologist, Sal, who is dying of a degenerative disorder, is lost on the moors with her partner Ian, and they discover ruins that figure on no maps. Fragments of these vastly disparate lives are interleaved, but exactly what the hidden connections are between past and present is never fully revealed. The setting, a valley called Thursbitch, is a prime mover in the book—it is a place of cruelty and redemption, violence and passion. There is a visionary quality to the writing, but this never degenerates into becoming merely fanciful. In some ways the modern world is made to seem flimsy beside the ancient certainties of the older narrative. At the same time we are aware that this older world has now largely passed away, even if it still haunts the perceptions of the living. **DP**

The Colour

Rose Tremain

Lifespan | *b.* 1943 (England)
First Published | 2003
First Published by | Chatto & Windus (London)
Given Name | Rosemary Jane Thomson

"Cob House had been built in the pathway of the winds."

⊙ Impossible dreams, and the costs and consequences of going after them, animate this novel by Rose Tremain.

From the seclusion of rural Norfolk, Harriet and Joseph Blackstone have journeyed with Joseph's mother Lilian to nineteenth-century Christchurch, New Zealand, in the quest for wealth and solitude. Sparsely populated, the land initially seems to fortify their hopes of self-made prosperity; its territory, however, so "vast outside," is scarcely benign. Little by little this relatively unmapped terrain works divisively upon the couple. Harriet, "a woman who longed for the familiar and the strange," and who, in spite of the landscape's agricultural aridity, "wanted to go still further, into a wilderness," soon feels alienated from Joseph. He, in turn, is consumed by the frenzy of Canterbury's great gold rush.

Gold ("the color"), ephemeral until found and handled in actuality, yet addictive nevertheless in holding the mind captive—becomes a moral axis for the novel. Joseph goes willfully in search of it at the expense of his own wife and sanity, possessed by the idea of "the color waiting in miraculous quantities." New Zealand's merciless West Coast is littered with wrecks, as an imminent destination for gold seekers who, by "their solitude and in their determination," were surviving as "people who had nothing to lose." Seduced by gold, Joseph journeys across the Southern Alpine wilderness; Tremain uses the contrasting hostility and luminescence of the landscape as a spiritual cipher for his destitution and Harriet's independence. Yet the novel also retains its focus on the distinctiveness of the secluded hamlets dotted amid the countryside's wild expanses—which Harriet, the newcomer, is reassured will "re-create, if not the past exactly, then something very like it, something homely." With *The Colour* Tremain sets new horizons, both geographic and imaginary, for the contemporary historical novel. **DJ**

Drop City

T. Coraghessan Boyle

This mammoth tale of dropping out alternates between a Californian commune and a new generation of subsistence trappers and bushmen in the Alaskan interior. Set in 1970, the novel traces the rise, fall, and transforming migration of Drop City, populated by mostly young, mostly white, and mostly middle-class dropouts living off the social services of a government they claim to abhor. Their willful espousal of the redemptive value of "ideals" like free love, mind-expanding drug use, and equality through historical ignorance makes conflict especially painful, since it gestures beyond itself to the general inadequacy of a "Can't we all just get along?" mentality. Boyle cuts between Drop City and the wilds beyond Boynton, Alaska, where Pamela and Sess Harder have also dropped out of "straight" society, but achieve their existence through intricately planned management of the fruits of hard labor, in order to participate in mass production economy as infrequently and independently as possible. These two worlds come together when Norm, Drop City's founder and patron, avoids a court date with "the Man" by moving everyone to the Alaskan cabin formerly inhabited by his uncle, Sess' early mentor.

Boyle masterfully depicts the hypocritical sincerity at the heart of the hippie movement, and the mutual mistrust between the suspicious, xenophobic few making their living in the wild and the busload of freaks who turn up on their doorstep. The hedonism of the Californian commune is based on a flabby dependence on the consumer society it disdains. Yet the compensatory emphasis on caring for the soul of life gives rise to moments of lyrical beauty, especially as the freaks and the bushmen come to exert a mutual, humanizing influence. **AF**

Lifespan | *b.* 1948 (U.S.)
First Published | 2004
First Published by | Viking (New York)
Given Name | Thomas John Boyle

"Her smile came back, blissed-out, drenched with sun."

◈ Few novelists have bothered to revisit the unfashionable hippie era, but Boyle finds in it a rich source of dramatic material.

Cloud Atlas

David Mitchell

Lifespan | *b.* 1969 (England)
First Published | 2004
First Published by | Sceptre (London)
First U.S. Edition | Random House (New York)

Shortlisted for the Man Booker Prize
Winner of the Richard and Judy Best Read of the Year

'Superbly entertaining' *Daily Telegraph*
'A masterful feast' *Evening Standard*
'Shamelessly exciting' *Spectator*
'Remarkable' *Guardian*
'Stunning' *Daily Mail*

◉ The psychedelically styled cover, by Kal and Sunny, suggests an unfamiliar world after the downfall of science and civilization.

◗ David Mitchell was inspired by the Moriori people of the Chatham Islands, who forgot that any other world existed.

Cloud Atlas is a glittering compendium of interlacing parables. Sectionalized into six different accounts that span several centuries, Mitchell leads us from the journal of a nineteenth-century Pacific explorer to a postapocalyptic memoir of a herdsman, Zachry. Each testament breaches time and space. Thus, in the second story, the financially destitute musician Robert Frobisher happens upon the pacific journal and includes it in a letter to his lover Rufus Sixsmith; in the novel's third epoch, Sixsmith enters as a scientific advisor committed to blowing the whistle on a nuclear conglomerate's reactor; the hard-boiled report of the young journalist accompanying him then enters the custody of Timothy Cavendish, a broke publisher fleeing his underworld creditors. As Cavendish hides in a nursing home, Mitchell propels his readers forward through the ages. There we bear witness to the plangent lasttestament of genetic fabricant Somni-451, detailing for the archives prior to execution her life as an automaton under state control. Finally, Somni is posthumously elevated into a deity for the novel's central, most futuristic section.

Mitchell has recalled that "lurking in *Cloud Atlas'* primordial soup was an idea for a novel with a Russian-doll structure. What if narrative A was interrupted halfway by narrative B which mentioned narrative A as an artifact . . .? How many narratives deep could I go?" He notes how Italo Calvino accumulated twelve plot layers with this device, yet "never 'came back' to recontinue his interruptions." Mitchell does make the return journey, allowing *Cloud Atlas* to "boomerang back through the sequence." And if the novel's sprawling structure boomerangs chronologically, so linguistically it is equally dynamic. Mitchell has secured his infectious originality with this rhapsody of contrasting dialects. **DJ**

Dining on Stones

Iain Sinclair

Lifespan | b. 1943 (Wales)
First Published | 2004
First Published by | Hamish Hamilton (London)
Original Language | English

At the end of the long first section of this novel of London, a small-time East End crook is hit by an HGV lorry as he runs across the M25 carrying the severed head of the book's narrator. The protagonist, Andrew (or A. M., or Andy) Norton, a writer, is less a "character" than an opportunity for narrative inventiveness. New narratives cluster around such story threads as a journey to Peru (documented with photographs but eventually revealed to be a fiction), a plan to kidnap the singer Max Bygraves, and the search for the room from which a landscape was painted.

At first sight committed to place and space, particularly the towns along the A13 road from Stepney to Southend, *Dining on Stones* is interested more in the idea of London than in its physical appearance. Place is significant because Conrad wrote there, the Krays killed there, or Max Beckmann (the expressionist painter) can be infiltrated into an episode set in a Travelodge. Place becomes culture to such an extent that the novel is populated by crowds of real people, living and dead: Patrick Hamilton, Wyndham Lewis, George Orwell, Tracey Emin, Howard Marks, J. G. Ballard.

The clue to Sinclair's activities lies in the book's subtitle: "(*or, The Middle Ground*)." That tempting space may be eliminated, as in an expressionist painting, or exploited, as in the space between reality and fiction. Sinclair works these possibilities, moving between them with sinuous skill, renewing narrative for the twenty-first century as he goes. **AMu**

The Lambs of London

Peter Ackroyd

Lifespan | b. 1949 (England)
First Published | 2004
First Published by | Chatto & Windus (London)
Tales from Shakespeare First Published | 1807

The "Lambs" of the title are Charles and Mary Lamb, the brother and sister writing team whose *Tales from Shakespeare* was obligatory reading for children in the nineteenth century. Ackroyd's story is set in the period before their literary fame. Charles is a drunken clerk and Mary a domestic slave to her strict mother and senile father. Their lives are rendered tolerable by devotion to the works of Shakespeare, quotes from whose plays pepper their conversation. The plot is set in motion by their encounter with William Ireland, an attractive rogue who convinces them that he has discovered manuscripts of lost Shakespearean dramas.

As a literary biographer and historian of London, Ackroyd is playing to his strongest suits in this novel. The pastiche of literary styles of the time is faultless, and the research into the Lambs and Ireland (also a real-life figure) has unearthed much that is fascinating and bizarre. But the book inevitably —and deliberately—raises the issues of authorial responsibility to historical fact, and of the relationship fictionalization creates between writer and reader. Readers insufficiently well informed to distinguish the truth from the invention in *The Lambs of London* are likely to feel uneasy—surely it makes a difference whether the real-life Mary Lamb murdered her mother, as occurs in the book (she did!). But the uncertain line between reality and imagination is itself a key theme of a book much concerned with literary and personal fraudulence. **RG**

Vanishing Point

David Markson

Lifespan | b. 1927 (U.S.)
First Published | 2004
First Published by | Shoemaker & Hoard (N.Y.)
Original Language | English

This work, like all Markson's novels, eschews decisively traditional forms of narration, characterization, and description. "Author," the opening of the novel tells us, "has finally started to put his notes into manuscript form." And yet what we go on to read seems closer to the formlessness of his notes, "scribbled … on three-by-five-inch index cards," than to a fully formed novel. As Author intimates, the experience is "Non-linear. Discontinuous. Collage-like. An assemblage."

Nonetheless, this apparent incoherence is deceiving. Allusions to artworks, quirky philosophical observations, and anecdotes of the creative life are subtly interwoven with references to Author's mental and physical exhaustion. *Vanishing Point* is peculiarly compulsive. Its fragments of insight into the life and work of artists, intriguing in their own right, inspire new and creative forms of reading when read cumulatively. Myriad lines of connection emerge between these apparently disordered fragments. One such line is the constant reference to erasure (from Quintillian: "Erasure is as important as writing") and suicide (from Virginia Woolf: "The one experience I shall never describe"). These allusions slowly cohere with Author's sense of his own disappearance ("Where can the book possibly wind up without him?"), such that the book becomes a vivid enactment of its own "suicide." Simultaneously challenging and accessible, *Vanishing Point* demonstrates that radical innovation in fiction need not preclude readability. **JC**

The Master

Colm Tóibín

Lifespan | b. 1955 (Ireland)
First Published | 2004
First Published by | Picador (London)
Novel of the Year | 2004

In *The Master,* Tóibín recreates the period in Henry James' life between 1895, the year in which James endured the humiliating failure of his play *Guy Domville*, and 1899, closing with the visit of his brother William and his family to James' beloved Lamb House in Rye. Time in the novel is for the most part subordinated to space, and, more particularly, to the spaces of rooms and of houses. The novel creates a "Jamesian" world of consciousness without falling into pastiche.

The Master is episodic, depicting in vivid detail a number of scenes and events; James' visit to Ireland, his painful negotiations with incompetent servants, the surreal aftermath of his friend Constance Woolson's suicide. Tóibín imagines his way into James' consciousness through the representation of dreams and memories, which take the novel back into his boyhood and youth, and a series of deaths and losses throughout his life. He also seeks to show how experience, or the turning away from experience, transmuted itself into the stuff of James' fiction. The novel opens up, in ways both subtle and powerful, the question of authorial revelation and secrecy, and of the nature of James' desire, which is neither separable from the question of homosexuality, nor fully explicable by it. Published at a time when many novelists are turning to biographical sources, *The Master* finds a new way for biography and fiction to meet, and to transform each other. **LM**

The Plot Against America

Philip Roth

Lifespan | *b.* 1933 (U.S.)
First Published | 2004
First Published by | Houghton Mifflin (Boston)
Sidewise Award for Alternate History | 2004

"Our homeland was America."

A Nazi overprinting of a U.S. stamp offers a potent symbol of the alternative history created by Philip Roth in his fact-based novel.

This remarkable piece of "faction" seems to be the true story of part of the author's childhood—another of those loving evocations of Jewish American life in the mid-twentieth century—with a hero named Philip Roth, along with the political story of the U.S. in the 1940s. The shock comes when the story swerves into "What if?" mode. The anti-Semitic, isolationist air-ace Charles Lindbergh unexpectedly wins the 1940 presidential election and, for the two years before his mysterious disappearance, gradually unleashes quasi-Nazi forces in the U.S. He negotiates a cordial "understanding" with Adolf Hitler, and accepts his anti-Semitic policies. His temporary successor begins to establish a fascist regime complete with pogroms, but in the subsequent election F. D.R. wins and history as we know it is restored.

The strength of the book lies in its weaving of remembered personal detail with equally credible public events. Roth takes care not to exaggerate—this novel is no *1984*—and he manages to make the incredible just about plausible. He draws on known facts to strengthen the impact of the unknown: the lynchings of Jews clearly echo the 1930s lynchings of blacks, for instance, and some of the real phenomena of European anti-Semitism such as the collaboration of certain Jews with fascist regimes are reproduced here quite subtly. The picture of the melting pot of urban American immigration is entirely convincing. And, of course, being written by Philip Roth, this is a funny novel in spite of its subject. It has a delightful take on American-ness, on Jewishness, and on the times in which the author grew up. It is neither fully indignant nor fully patriotic, but, behind the entertainment, the reader can feel a mind and a heart at work. **PM**

The Red Queen

Margaret Drabble

The title of Margaret Drabble's novel *The Red Queen* refers to the Queen of Korea, a position that one of the novel's two heroines, the Crown Princess Lady Hyegyong, never attains. *The Red Queen* mixes the story of the Crown Princess—a real-life figure whose nonfiction memoirs, written between 1795 and 1805, are widely available in both Korea and the West—with the fictional Dr. Babs Halliwell, a lecturer who finds herself in Seoul to attend an academic conference. The Crown Princess' memoirs tell the story of the execution of her husband Prince Sado by his father, the king, in 1762. After reading them on the airplane, Dr. Halliwell is gripped by the Crown Princess' story. As she attends conference sessions, interacts with her fellow delegates, and tours historical monuments, her own journey begins to take on a narrative significance that points back to the dignified tragedy of the Crown Princess' life. Haunted as she is by the ghost of this powerful woman, the tragedy inherent within Dr. Halliwell's past returns to confront the reader's easy assumptions about the limitations of cultural continuity and human universality.

This is an academic novel, family saga, and ghost story all at once, and Drabble's evocative prose and deliberately elusive tone combine to create a haunting and lyrical atmosphere. *The Red Queen* painstakingly exposes the human passions inherent within the most mundane of domestic situations. But the addition of the parallel story of the Crown Princess allows the novel to explore the cultural and political issues that inform women's lives within a much broader arena. *The Red Queen* is an ambitious and risk-taking book whose departures from convention place it in the forefront of Margaret Drabble's fiction. **AB**

Lifespan | b. 1939 (England)
First Published | 2004
First Published by | Viking (London)
First U.S. Edition | Harcourt (New York)

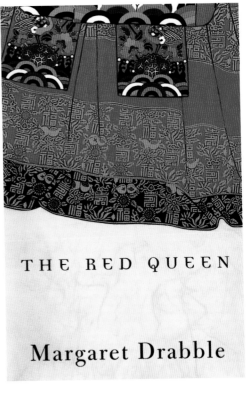

THE RED QUEEN

Margaret Drabble

"I could not abandon them."

◐ *The Memoirs of Lady Hyegyong*, translated by Ja Hyun Kim Haboush (1995), inspired Drabble to write *The Red Queen*.

The Sea

John Banville

Lifespan | *b.* 1945 (Ireland)
First Published | 2005
First Published by | Picador (London)
Man Booker Prize | 2005

"Memory dislikes motion, preferring to hold things still." This perception lies at the heart of Banville's latest novel. *The Sea* tells the story of Max Morden's bereavement and his subsequent journey to the scene of a childhood romance. This trip is an attempt by Morden, an art historian with an acute visual sense, to reclaim the past as a work of art. His grieving for his wife compels him to search for some original scene of love and loss, some original drama that remains proof against the tidal, erosive work of time.

Banville's prose often has something of the miraculous to it, and the miracle here is its capacity to use words to produce images, to find beneath the constant movement of the everyday, an attitude, or glance, or shape that seems suddenly, magically present. The novel depicts the ugliness of death and of bodily decrepitude, as it conjures the experience of loss with an uncanny intensity. But if this novel is about death and the steady humiliation of dying, it is more than anything about the power of memory, and of art, to catch at something that doesn't die, something that is as immune to death as innocence. This novel is soaked in images and phrases drawn from works of art—from Bonnard, Whistler, and Vermeer; from Shakespeare, Proust, and Beckett. Morden's journey to early childhood is woven into this homage to art, seamlessly and exquisitely. Reading the novel is at once to feel what it is to die, and to find oneself lifted from the choppy motion of time, into the quiet midst of an unmoving image. **PB**

Adjunct: An Undigest

Peter Manson

Lifespan | *b.* 1969 (Scotland)
First Published | 2005
First Published by | Edinburgh Review (Edinburgh)
Original Language | English

This is assuredly not a novel, but it unquestionably is one of 1001 books you must read before you die. Peter Manson did not write it, if by "write it" we understand the routines and maneuvers in finding-the-right-word commonly associated with that phrase. He did build it, however, and was discerning enough in his choice of materials to include every scrap of advertising robot-talk, talk-show drivel, SPAM, and poetic utterance to float by over the final years of the twentieth century in a council flat in Glasgow.

Adjunct is a monstrous work of completely unnecessary restitution, saving from the creep of oblivion only those bits of language positively designed to comprise oblivion. In other words it is full of shit, perhaps more hilariously and movingly so than any British writing since Beckett. Language is pieced together, unclogged by logic or narrative, and the language is only rarely "Peter Manson's." The great majority of it is torn out of its context and made simply to accumulate in an unremitting paragraph governed only by the duration it took to be generated. The bits of language all point outward to the mess of social relations that produce and rely on them. For example: "Caron Keating finds that juggling motherhood with a successful television show doesn't leave much time for eating. A quick hot snack with soft cheese is the answer. Non-self-identity card. juDGemening. Insecurity = teeth. Why do we travel to work like little baps?" **KS**

Slow Man

J. M. Coetzee

Lifespan | *b.*1940 (South Africa)
First Published | 2005
First Published by | Secker & Warburg (London)
Nobel Prize for Literature | 2005

With his reputation established as "one of the best novelists alive," the publication of J. M. Coetzee's *Slow Man* sustained a predictably conflicted discussion of its literary merit. Not shortlisted for the Booker Prize in 2005, *Slow Man* begins with an accident: "The blow catches him from the right, sharp and surprising and painful, like a bolt of electricity, lifting him up off the bicycle." In a characteristically spartan prose—Coetzee has been described as an author of omission—*Slow Man* introduces its first protagonist, Paul Rayment, as a man of sixty-odd who, surviving the accident, now has to live with the loss of his leg.

Through Rayment, Coetzee can reflect on what it means to be lonely, and infirm, in a laissez-faire world. When Paul falls in love with his married Croatian nurse, Marijana, and disrupts her marriage, the novel underlines its psychological, and affective, terrain. But then, unexpectedly, Elizabeth Costello appears to accompany Rayment for the foreseeable future. What she wants is a proposal about where his story—the story of exile and passion she prompts him to elaborate—is going.

At this point, *Slow Man* becomes a metafiction: Elizabeth Costello is the celebrated Australian writer in Coetzee's novel of the same name, frequently read as her author's alter ego. Her appearance in this novel divided critical opinion: is Coetzee trying to write arid literary theory under the guise of fiction, or does *Slow Man* reflect anew on the elusive ties between a novelist, his characters, and readers? **VL**

On Beauty

Zadie Smith

Lifespan | *b.*1975 (England)
First Published | 2005
First Published by | Hamish Hamilton (London)
Given Name | Sadie Smith

This is a novel about art, love, race, class, family, England and America, and the beautiful and the ugly. The plot turns around the relations between the Kippses and the Belseys, two families who have directly opposing views on art, politics, and religion. The Belseys are a secular ramshackle of a family, anti-war, anti-state religion, anti the idealization of art. The Kippses are right-wing Christians, impassioned by traditional family values, devout in their belief that art is a gift from God. The tension between these two families crystallizes around a disagreement about Rembrandt, as both Howard Belsey and Monty Kipps are academics writing books about the painter.

The beauty of this novel is that, whilst it is organized around a set of apparently stable oppositions, Smith's prose is subtle and nuanced enough to seek out those places where such oppositions are unsettled. At the heart of the novel is a moving relationship between two women, the wives of the egotistical academics Howard and Monty. Their relationship stretches across all of the divides that the novel charts, but they find, to their own constant surprise, that they are able to find some common ground. This novel is a virtual rewriting of Forster's *Howards End*, a work in which Forster urges us to "only connect." In rewriting Forster for the new millennium, Zadie Smith has given us some new ways to connect, some new ways to reconcile the differences that separate and define us. **PB**

Saturday

Ian McEwan

Lifespan | *b.* 1948 (England)
First Published | 2005
First Published by | Jonathan Cape (London)
First U.S. Edition | Nan A. Talese (New York)

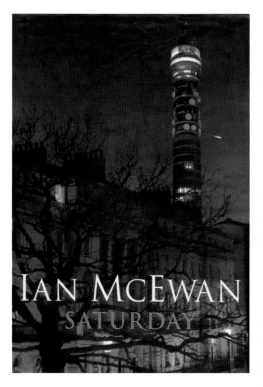

"The noise of the engine's distress is fading."

⊙ In *Saturday*, the vulnerability of human lives to cataclysmic events is explored against a backdrop of international terrorism.

Saturday, February 15, 2003. Henry Perowne, famous neurosurgeon (he's rubbed shoulders with Prime Minister Tony Blair) and contented family man, wakes abruptly in the early hours of the morning and makes his way to the bedroom window of his perfect London home. Through an accretion of meticulously realized images (the ease of "cool fresh water coursing down pipes," and "sewage borne away in an instant of forgetting") we experience his wideawake euphoria and are pivoted into a day in the life and mind of a middle-aged, successful man.

Perowne's anticipation of a well-earned day off is shaped ominously, however, by a cometlike portent—actually a plane on fire—that crosses his line of vision, reminding him of 9/11 and terror in the skies. In previous novels, McEwan has tackled huge political and social topics such as the Holocaust, the Cold War, and Thatcherism, and in *Saturday* it is global terrorism and the prospect of carnage in Iraq that cast a darkening shadow of "real life" over his fictional landscape.

The flaming cargo plane lands safely, but Perowne's day is soon dominated by terror of a more personal kind, an unsettling confrontation with a knife-wielding street thug named Baxter. On his way to play squash and shop for the planned family dinner party, his car clips the side mirror of a passing BMW, and his life collides with that of its driver—a thug with a brain disease that only a neurosurgeon could recognize. Baxter and his sinister friend then return to inject terror into the Perowne family's evening. The anticipated grand correspondence between the political backdrop and the Baxter plot never quite materializes, but perhaps that's a good thing. *Saturday* is the work of a novelist at the height of his powers. **MH**

Never Let Me Go

Kazuo Ishiguro

Never Let Me Go begins from a startling premise. In the English countryside, a number of special institutions have been secretly set up in the later twentieth century to raise and educate young people whose destiny, unsuspected during the innocent years of childhood, is to be sacrificed for the collective good. As in his two previous novels, Ishiguro disorients the reader by combining realism of psychology and setting with growing implausibility of event. It seems at first that this is a clumsy science fiction story, meant perhaps to promote debate about the ethics of cloning. The matter-of-fact prose offers few immediate stylistic pleasures, and the novel has no dramatic twists, no tales of escape, recapture, or redemption. By the time we finish it, however, it has cast an unsettling and unforgettable illumination on the world we thought we knew. This is a dreamlike parable, rather than a schematic allegory. Its compelling narrative metaphors make us think in new ways about mortality, individuality, and social democracy. As ever with Ishiguro, the elements of the puzzles refer not inward, to the riddles of a closed text, but outward. The book's questions are about the life we lead. What is the purpose of fostering the creative imagination of beings whose fate is to live for a while and then die? What kind of world is it in which not even the evidence of lifelong love can defer what awaits the lovers?

Against the resurgent politics of individualism, and in reaction to anticollectivist fictions like Huxley's *Brave New World* (to which this is a subtle and imaginative reply), Ishiguro suggests that educating the children of an interdependent society has been infinitely worthwhile. In the face of death everyone can make the art that shows they have a soul. **MR**

Lifespan | *b.* 1954 (Japan)
First Published | 2005
First Published by | Faber & Faber (London)
Original Language | English

"'You poor creatures,' she repeated, almost in a whisper."

⬤ Sinister secrets overshadow the lives of innocents in *Never Let Me Go*, as suggested by Carol Devine Carson's jacket design.

Author Index

General Index

Acknowledgments

Quintet Publishing would like to thank the following people for their help in the preparation of this book:

Mark Abley, Bianca Jackson, and Simon Doubt for researching contributors; Martha Magor for researching quotes; Reg Grant for writing picture captions; Sonia Land at Sheil Land Associates for liaison with Peter Ackroyd; Liz Wyse, Cathy Meeus, and Siobhan O'Connor for copyediting; Victoria Wiggins for editorial assistance; Elaine Shatenstein for proofreading; Ann Barrett for the index; Maria Gibbs for picture research and for compiling the picture credits; Simon Goggins for layout assistance; Phil Wilkins and Robert Gillam for additional photography; Irene Scheimberg, Marcus Deyes, Lucy Holliday, and Elisabeth de Lancey for the loan of books.

Quintet Publishing would also like to thank the following people and picture libraries:

Elbie Lebrecht at Lebrecht, Teresa Riley at Getty, Tessa Ademolu at Corbis, Jenny Page at Bridgeman, Lucy Brock at AKG, Angela Minshull at Christie's, and Anna Barrett at Art Archive/Kobal.

Picture Credits

Every effort has been made to credit the copyright holders of the images used in this book. We apologise in advance for any unintentional omissions or errors and will be pleased to insert the appropriate acknowledgment to any companies or individuals in any subsequent edition of the work.

2 Vanitas, 1543 (oil on panel), Holbein, Hans the Younger (1497/8–1543)/Private Collection, Lauros/Giraudon/Bridgeman **22** Corbis **23** Bettmann/Corbis **24** Bettmann/Corbis **27** TopFoto.co.uk **28** TopFoto.co.uk **29** Lebrecht **30** Lebrecht **31** TopFoto.co.uk **32** Getty Images **33** Archivo Iconografico/Corbis **34** Lebrecht **35** Lebrecht **36** Roger-Viollet/TopFoto.co.uk **37** Getty Images **41** Bodleian Library Oxford/The Art Archive **43** Getty Images **44** Getty Images **45** Lebrecht **47** TopFoto.co.uk **48** Bettmann/Corbis **50** Lebrecht **51** Victoria and Albert Museum London/Eileen Tweedy/The Art Archive **52** Sheryl Straight/www.eroticabibliophile.com **53** Bettmann/Corbis **55** Lebrecht **59** Lebrecht **60** Getty Images **61** Getty Images **63** TopFoto.co.uk **64** Museo di Goethe Rome/Dagli Orti/The Art Archive **65** Private Collection Paris/Dagli Orti/The Art Archive **66** Getty Images **67** Lebrecht **70** AKG Images **72** Lebrecht **73** The British Library/TopFoto.co.uk **75** Lebrecht **76** Lebrecht **78** Gianni Dagli Orti/Corbis **82** Getty Images **84** The Art Archive **86** Time Life Pictures/Getty Images **87** MGM/The Kobal Collection **89** Getty Images **90** Lebrecht **92** Lebrecht **93** Lebrecht **94** FIA RA/Lebrecht **95** Getty Images **96** Musée du Louvre Paris/Dagli Orti/The Art Archive **99** Lebrecht **100** Burstein Collection/Corbis **102** Lebrecht **103** Getty Images **104** Lebrecht **105** Victor Hugo House Paris/Dagli Orti/The Art Archive **106** Leonard de Selva/Corbis **108** Lebrecht **109** British Museum/Eileen Tweedy/The Art Archive **110** Bettmann/Corbis **113** The Art Archive **114** Maison Balzac Paris/ Dagli Orti/The Art Archive **115** Bibliothèque de l'Institut de France, Paris, France/Archives Charmet/Bridgeman **116** Getty Images **118** Stefano Bianchetti/Corbis **120** Lebrecht **121** Getty Images **122** David Lyons/Alamy **123** Getty Images **124** Brian Seed/Lebrecht **126** Getty Images **128** Getty Images **130** Bettmann/Corbis **131** The Art Archive **133** Culver Pictures/The Art Archive **134** The Art Archive**136** TopFoto.co.uk **137** Culver Pictures/The Art Archive **139** TopFoto.co.uk **140** Bibliothèque des Arts Décoratifs Paris/Dagli Orti/The Art Archive **141** Lebrecht **142** TopFoto.co.uk **145** Lebrecht **146** Getty Images **148** Getty Images **150** Getty Images **151** Bibliothèque des Arts Décoratifs Paris/Dagli Orti/The Art Archive **152** Lebrecht **153** TopFoto.co.uk **155** Bettmann/Corbis **156** Lebrecht **157** Lebrecht **158** Rex Features **159** Getty Images **160** Time Life Pictures/Getty Images **161** Roger-Viollet/TopFoto.co.uk **162** TopFoto.co.uk **163** Private Collection, Archives Charmet/Bridgeman **164** Bettmann/Corbis **167** Popperfoto/Alamy **168** Lebrecht **169** The Art Archive **171** Lebrecht **172** Getty Images **173** Lebrecht **174** Getty Images **176** The Art Archive **178** Getty Images **181** Musée Carnavalet Paris/Dagli Orti/The Art Archive **182** Rex Features **185** Lebrecht **189** The Art Archive **190** Lebrecht **191** Lebrecht **193** Roger-Viollet/TopFoto.co.uk **194** Stapleton Collection/Corbis **195** Lebrecht **196** Archivo Iconografico/Corbis **197** Roger-Viollet/TopFoto.co.uk **199** Getty Images **200** Getty Images **201** Getty Images **202** Getty Images **205** Lebrecht **206** Lebrecht **208** Lebrecht **209** Corbis **210** TopFoto.co.uk **211** Bettmann/Corbis **213** Chris Hellier/Corbis **214** Eileen Tweedy/The Art Archive **215** Historical Picture Archive/Corbis **219** Lebrecht **220** MGM/The Kobal Collection **222** The Art Archive **223** RA/Lebrecht **224** Lebrecht **226** Getty Images **229** Getty Images **232** Time Life Pictures/Getty Images **234** Private Collection/MD/The Art Archive **235** © Elizabeth Banks/The Art Archive **236** Private Collection/Marc Charmet/The Art Archive **237** Getty Images **237** Getty Images **238** Zoetrope/United Artists/The Kobal Collection **240** Tillie, Mark/Miramax/Renaissance Films/The Kobal Collection **243** Getty Images **245** Getty Images **246** Getty Images **247** Getty Images **248** Bettmann/Corbis **249** Buitendijk, Jaap/Granada/Arts Council/Film Four/The Kobal Collection **250** E.O. Hoppé/Corbis **253** Domenica del Corriere/Dagli Orti (A)/The Art Archive **255** Getty Images **259** Getty Images **261** Lebrecht **263** Bettmann/Corbis **266** Condé Nast Archive/ Corbis **268** TopFoto.co.uk **269** Asian Art & Archaeology/Corbis **270** Rex Features **273** E.O. Hoppé/Corbis **274** Asian Art & Archaeology/Corbis **276** British Library/The Art Archive **279** TopFoto.co.uk **280** Getty Images **283** Condé Nast Archive/Corbis **284** Getty Images **285** Getty Images **286** Lorenzo Ciniglio/Corbis **287** Bettmann/Corbis **289** AKG Images **290** Condé Nast Archive/Corbis **293** Getty Images **294** Bettmann/Corbis **295** Time Life Pictures/Getty Images **299** Corbis **300** Lebrecht **302** Time Life Pictures/Getty Images **303** TopFoto.co.uk **304** Paris Europa/FICIT/HISA/The Kobal Collection **307** Getty Images **308** The British Library/HIP/TopFoto.co.uk **309** HIP/Ann Ronan Picture Library/TopFoto.co.uk **313** Lebrecht **314** Lebrecht **315** Condé Nast Archive/Corbis **316** Getty Images **317** Time Life Pictures/Getty Images **319** Lebrecht **320** Harlingue/Roger-Viollet/TopFoto.co.uk **321** Getty Images **323** Getty Images **328** Getty Images **329** Getty Images; Penguin **330** E.O. Hoppé/Corbis **332** Bettmann/Corbis **333** Jean-Pierre Muller/AFP/Getty Images **335** TopFoto.co.uk **336** Allianz/Capital/The Kobal Collection **337** Universal/The Kobal Collection **338** Condé Nast Archive/Corbis **340** Bettmann/Corbis **343** Getty Images **345** Ferens Art Gallery, Hull City Museums and Art Galleries/Bridgeman **347** © 1961 Estate of Vanessa Bell, courtesy Henrietta Garnett/The Stapleton Collection/Bridgeman **349** John Springer Collection/Corbis **351** Hulton-Deutsch Collection/Corbis **352** Getty Images **353** Christie's Images **355** Getty Images **356** Bettmann/ Corbis **358** Bettmann/Corbis **359** Andy Warhol Foundation for the Visual Arts/Corbis **360** Getty Images **362** Images.com/Corbis **363** Christie's Images **364** Getty Images **365** Corbis **366** Time Life Pictures/Getty Images **368** Kurt Weill Foundation/Lebrecht **369** Kurt Weill Foundation/Lebrecht **372** Condé Nast Archive/Corbis **375** Oscar White/Corbis **376** TopFoto.co.uk **377** TopFoto.co.uk **379** Penguin/Lebrecht **380** MGM/Album/ AKG Images **381** Getty Images **382** Time Life Pictures/Getty Images **385** Corbis **388** Corbis **389** Getty Images **390** AGIP RA/Lebrecht **391** Topfoto.co.uk **392** Associated British/The Kobal Collection **393** Bettmann/Corbis **395** Rex Features **396** Private Collection/Archives Charmet/Bridgeman **397** Condé Nast Archive/Corbis **398** TopFoto.co.uk **400** Rex Features **401** Warner Bros/The Kobal Collection **402** TopFoto.co.uk **403** Corbis **404** Viola Roehr v. Alvensleben, München/AKG Images **405** ABC/Allied Artists/The Kobal Collection **406** Rex Features **408** AKG Images **409** Time Life Pictures/Getty Images **411** AKG Images **413** Bettmann/Corbis **416** TopFoto.co.uk **418** Roger-Viollet **419** Collection Albert Camus/Archives Charmet/Bridgeman **420** Time Life Pictures/Getty Images **423** Condé Nast Archive/Corbis **424** Penguin/Christie's Images **426** Time Life Pictures/Getty Images **429** The Illustrated London News Picture Library/Bridgeman **431** Random House/The British Library/HIP/TopFoto.co.uk **432** Penguin/ Christie's Images **433** TopFoto.co.uk **434** Getty Images **436** Sophie Bassouls/Corbis **437** Harper Collins/Christie's Images **438** Getty Images **439** AGIP RA/Lebrecht **441** Random House/Lebrecht **442** FIA RA/Lebrecht **444** Time Life Pictures/Getty Images **446** Random House/Christie's Images **447** Random House/AKG Images **448** Rex Features **452** Random House; Christie's Images **453** Random House/Lebrecht **454** Getty Images **455** Time Life Pictures/Getty Images **456** Random House/Lebrecht **457** Getty Images **458** Time Life Pictures/Getty Images **462** TAL RA/Lebrecht **464** Rex Features **466** Worldimage RA/Lebrecht **468** Harcourt/Christie's Images **469** Random House/Lebrecht **470** Time Life Pictures/Getty Images **471** Time Life Pictures/Getty Images **472** Lipnitzki/Roger-Viollet/TopFoto.co.uk **473** Horst Tappe/Lebrecht **474** Bettmann/Corbis **475** Bettmann/ Corbis**476** Time Life Pictures/Getty Images **477** Orion Publishing Group/Christie's Images **479** Private Collection/ Bridgeman **480** Penguin/Christie's Images **482** Faber & Faber/Christie's Images **483** Two Arts/CD/The Kobal Collection **484** Roger-Viollet/ TopFoto.co.uk **487** Time Life Pictures/Getty Images **488** Getty Images **492** Hulton-Deutsch Collection/Corbis **493** MGM/The Kobal Collection **494** Random House/Christie's Images **495** Harper Collins/TopFoto.co.uk **497** J. Cuinières/Roger-Viollet/TopFoto.co.uk **499** Time Life Pictures/Getty Images **500** Time Life Pictures/Getty Images **502** MGM/The Kobal Collection **503** Harper Collins/ Lebrecht **505** Rex Features **506** Barnabas Bosshart/Corbis **508** Penguin/ Christie's Images **509** Penguin/Lebrecht **511** TopFoto.co.uk **513** Getty Images **514** Getty Images **515** Getty Images **516** Time Life Pictures/Getty Images **518** Picture Post/Hulton Archive/Getty Images **521** Paramount/The Kobal Collection **524** Seitz/Bioskop/ Hallelujah/The Kobal Collection **525** Random House/AKG Images **526** Harper Collins/Christie's Images **527** Loomis Dean/Time Life Pictures/Getty Images **528** VIC/Waterhall/The Kobal Collection **530** Darlene Hammond/Hulton Archive/Getty Images **531** Hulton Archive/Getty Images **532** Harper Collins/Christie's Images **533** Donald Uhrbrock/Time Life Pictures/Getty Images **536** Condé Nast Archive/Corbis **537** Christie's Images **538** 20th Century Fox/The Kobal Collection **539** Hulton-Deutsch Collection/Corbis **540** Bettmann/Corbis **542** Time Life Pictures/Getty Images **545** TopFoto.co.uk **547** AGIP RA/Lebrecht **549** Time Life Pictures/Getty Images **550** Time Life Pictures/Getty Images **551** Penguin **552** Getty Images **553** Time Life Pictures/Getty Images **554** Getty Images **555** TopFoto.co.uk **556** Everett Collection/Rex Features **558** Time Life Pictures/Getty Images **559** Time Life Pictures/Getty Images **560** RENN/A2/RAI-2/The Kobal Collection **561** TopFoto.co.uk **563** Time Life Pictures/Getty Images **564** Harper Collins/Christie's Images **565** Random House/Lebrecht **566** Roger Viollet/ Getty Images **567** Interfoto/Lebrecht **568** Time Life Picture/Getty Images **571** Getty Images **572** ArenaPAL Picture Library/TopFoto.co.uk **573** Hulton- Deutsch Collection/Corbis **575** KIPA/Corbis **576** Bettmann/Corbis **577** Oscar White/Corbis **578** TopFoto.co.uk **580** Getty Images **584** AFP/Getty Images **586** Margarita from Bulgakov's "Master and Margarita." Jerosimic, Gordana (Contemporary Artist)/Private Collection/Bridgeman **587** Novosti/TopFoto.co.uk **588** Colita/Corbis **589** Christie's Images **591** Getty Images **592** TopFoto.co.uk **593** Interfoto/Lebrecht **594** Woodfall/Kestrel/ Barnett, Michael/The Kobal Collection **596** Interfoto/Lebrecht **597** Rex Features **599** MGM/The Kobal Collection **602** TopFoto.co.uk **603** 20th Century Fox/The Kobal Collection **606** Paramount/The Kobal Collection **607** Getty Images **608** Time Life Pictures/Getty Images **610** Time Life Pictures/Getty Images **611** United Artists/The Kobal Collection **612** Getty Images **614** Biblioteca National do Rio de Janiero Brazil/Dagli Orti/The Art Archive **617** Rex Features **618** Bettmann/Corbis **621** Sophie Bassouls/Corbis **623** TopFoto.co.uk **625** Sophie Bassouls/Corbis **626** Louis Monier/RA/ Lebrecht **627** Lynn Goldsmith/Corbis **628** Pan Macmillan/Lebrecht **630** Rex Features **634** Penguin/Christie's Images **635** Random House/Lebrecht **636** Random House/Christie's Images **637** Getty Images **638** Sophie Bassouls/Corbis **641** Bettmann/Corbis **643** Bioskop/Paramount-Orion/WDR/The Kobal Collection **645** Getty Images **647** Getty Images **648** Bettmann/ Corbis **650** Time Life Pictures/Getty Images **651** Roger Ressmeyer/Corbis **652** Micheline Pelletier/Corbis **654** TopFoto.co.uk **655** Random House **657** Interfoto/Lebrecht **659** United Artists/The Kobal Collection **660** Warner Bros/Everett/Rex Features **661** Bettmann/Corbis **663** AGIP/RA/Lebrecht **665** Rex Features **667** Christian Simonpietri/Corbis **668** Alex Gotfryd/Corbis **669** Everett Collection/Rex Features **670** Bettmann/Corbis **671** Corbis **672** TopFoto.co.uk **673** Topfoto.co.uk **675** TopFoto.co.uk **677** Michel Clement/AFP/Getty Images **678** Sophie Bassouls/Corbis **679** Getty Images **680** Getty Images **683** William Campbell/Corbis **684** Sophie Bassouls/Corbis **686** Gallimard/Lebrecht **687** Louis Monier RA/Lebrecht **688** Time Life Pictures/Getty Images **691** TopFoto.co.uk **692** Getty Images **693** Horst Tappe/Lebrecht **697** © 1981 Alisdair Gray. Reproduced by permission of the author c/o Rogers, Coleridge & White Ltd., 20 Powis Mews, London W11 1JN/Special Collections Dept, University of Glasgow **701** Rex Features **702** Reuters/Corbis **703** Amblin/Universal/The Kobal Collection **704** Sophie Bassouls/Corbis **706** Getty Images **707** Warner Bros/The Kobal Collection **711** Paul Hackett/Reuters/Corbis **714** Random House/Lebrecht **715** Random House/Lebrecht **716** Random House **717** L. Birnbaum/ Lebrecht **718** Harper Collins **719** Time Life Pictures/Getty Images **720** Allen Ginsberg/Corbis **722** Time Warner Book Group UK **723** Rex Features **725** Horst Tappe/Lebrecht **726** Rex Features **727** Penguin/ Lebrecht **729** Sophie Bassouls/Corbis **732** TopFoto.co.uk **733** Virago **734** Getty Images **735** Jeff Albertson/Corbis **736** Corbis **738** Random House/Lebrecht **739** River's Oram Press **743** Faber & Faber **744** Maria L Antonelli/Rex Features **747** Christopher Felver/Corbis **751** Macduff Everton/Corbis **752** Faber & Faber/Christie's Images **753** Sophie Bassouls/Corbis **754** Roger Ressmeyer/Corbis **755** Random House/Lebrecht **758** Bettmann/ Corbis **759** Random House **760** Arici Graziano/Corbis **761** Sophie Bassouls/Corbis **763** Roger Ressmeyer/Corbis **765** William Coupon/Corbis **766** Faber & Faber **767** Random House **768** Penguin/ Corbis **769** Reuters/Corbis **771** AGIP/RA/Lebrecht **773** Random House/Lebrecht **774** Bloomsbury **775** James Leynse/Corbis **778** Faber & Faber **779** Pan Macmillan/Lebrecht **780** Arnold Newman/ Getty Images **783** Faber & Faber **784** Random House **785** Faber & Faber **786** Tony Trée/Lebrecht **789** Roger Ressmeyer/Corbis **790** Random House **791** Random House **793** MGM/Jersey Films/The Kobal Collection **794** Random House **795** Random House **798** Random House **799** Pan Macmillan **800** Barry Lewis/Corbis **801** Sophie Bassouls/Corbis **802** Rex Features **803** Penguin/Lebrecht **805** Bettmann/Corbis **806** Sophie Bassouls/Corbis **808** Rex Features **809** TopFoto.co.uk **810** Fotos International/Rex Features **811** Bloomsbury **815** Sophie Bassouls/Corbis **816** Sophie Bassouls/ Corbis **817** Eric Fougere/Corbis **818** Penguin **819** Polfoto/Miriam Dalsgaard/TopFoto.co.uk **821** Penguin **822** Robert Maass/Corbis **823** Christopher J. Morris/Corbis **824** Times Newspapers/Rex Features **825** Orion Publishing Group **828** Rex Features **829** Rex Features **830** Figment/Noel Gay/Channel 4/The Kobal Collection **831** Rex Features **832** Eamonn McCabe/Lebrecht **834** Random House/Lebrecht **835** Penguin/Lebrecht **836** Random House **837** Random House **838** Getty Images **839** Sophie Bassouls/Corbis **840** Rex Features **845** McClelland & Stewart **846** Najlah Feanny/ Corbis **848** Random House **849** Harper Collins **851** Random House/Lebrecht **853** Steve Liss/Time Life Pictures/Getty Images **855** Bloomsbury **857** Rex Features **859** Random House/ Lebrecht **861** Marc Asnin/Corbis **862** Arnold Newman/Getty Images **865** Tom Wagner/Corbis **866** Karan Kapoor/Corbis **868** AFP/Getty Images **869** Paulo Fridman/Corbis **870** Rex Features **872** Faber & Faber **875** Random House **877** Ted Soqui/Corbis **878** Random House/Lebrecht **879** Random House/Lebrecht **883** Robert Eric/Corbis **887** Getty Images **890** Bloomsbury **891** Random House/ Lebrecht **892** Lebrecht **893** Michael Brennan/Corbis **894** AFP/Getty Images **896** Harcourt/Lebrecht **897** Farrar, Straus & Giroux/Lebrecht **898** Penguin **899** Colin McPherson/Corbis **00** Christopher Furlong/Getty Images **903** Ruben Cacho/AFP/Getty Images **904** TopFoto.co.uk **905** Canongate **906** Rune Hellestad/Corbis **909** Paul Hanna/Reuters/Corbis **910** Harper Collins **911** Random House **912** Random House/Lebrecht **913** Random House/ Lebrecht **915** Rune Hellestad/Corbis **916** Henry Holt/Lebrecht **917** Pan Macmillan/ Lebrecht **918** TopFoto.co.uk **921** Sophie Bassouls/Corbis **922** Rex Features **923** Sophie Bassouls/Corbis **924** Penguin/Lebrecht **925** Getty Images **926** Eamonn McCabe/Lebrecht **927** Getty Images **928** Penguin **929** Random House/ Lebrecht **930** Museum of London/HIP/Héliodore Joseph Pisan/TopFoto.co.uk **931** Virago **934** Random House **935** Rex Features **936** Rune Hellestad/ Corbis **938** Getty Images **939** Norbert Millauer/AFP/Getty Images **940** Hodder Headline **941** Tom Wagner/Corbis **944** Random House **945** Harcourt/Lebrecht **948** Random House **949** Random House/Lebrecht